The Complete Record of Chicago White Sox Baseball

Historical Text by
Richard Lindberg

White Sox Graphics by
John Warner Davenport

MACMILLAN PUBLISHING COMPANY
New York
COLLIER MACMILLAN PUBLISHERS
London

Copyright © 1984 by Macmillan Publishing Company,
a division of Macmillan, Inc.

All rights reserved. No part of this book may be reproduced or transmitted in any form or by any means, electronic or mechanical, including photocopying, recording or by any information storage and retrieval system, without permission in writing from the Publisher.

Macmillan Publishing Company
866 Third Avenue, New York, N.Y. 10022
Collier Macmillan Canada, Inc.

Library of Congress Cataloging in Publication Data
Lindberg, Richard, 1953-
Sox: the complete record of Chicago White Sox baseball.
1. Chicago White Sox (Baseball team)—Statistics.
2. Chicago White Sox (Baseball team)—History.
I. Davenport, John Warner, 1931-   . II. Title.
GV875.C58L53   1984   796.357'64'0977311   84-3954
ISBN 0-02-029430-1

Macmillan books are available at special discounts for bulk purchases for sales promotions, premiums, fund-raising, or educational use. Special editions or book excerpts can also be created to specification. For details, contact:

Special Sales Director
Macmillan Publishing Company
866 Third Avenue
New York, New York 10022

10 9 8 7 6 5 4 3 2 1

Printed in the United States of America

Contents

The All-Time White Sox Leaders	3
The White Sox and Their Players, Year-by-Year	19
White Sox Graphics	193
Player Register	211
Pitcher Register	339
Manager Register	417
White Sox World Series Highlights and Summaries	423

The All-Time White Sox Leaders

This section provides information on individual all-time single season and lifetime White Sox leaders. Included for all the various categories are leaders in batting, base running, fielding, and pitching. All the information is self-explanatory with the possible exception of Home Run Percentage, which is the number of home runs per 100 times at bat.

LIFETIME LEADERS

Batting. The top ten men are shown in batting and base-running categories. For averages, a minimum of 1500 at bats is necessary to qualify, except for pinch-hit batting average where 45 pinch-hit at bats is the minimum necessary to qualify. If required by ties, 11 players are shown. If ties would require more than 11 men to be shown, none of the last tied group is included.

Pitching. The top ten pitchers are shown in various categories. For averages, a minimum of 750 innings pitched is necessary to qualify. If required by ties, 11 players are shown. If ties would require more than 11 men to be shown, none of the last tied group is included. For relief pitching categories, the top five are shown.

Fielding. The top five in each fielding category are shown for each position. For averages, the minimum for qualification at each position except pitcher is 350 games played. For pitchers, 750 innings pitched are necessary. If required by ties, six players are shown. If ties would require more than six men to be shown, none of the last tied group is shown.

ALL-TIME SINGLE SEASON LEADERS

Batting. The top ten men are shown in batting and base-running categories. For averages, a player must have a total of at least 3.1 plate appearances for every scheduled game to qualify, except for pinch-hit batting average where 30 pinch-hit at bats are the minimum necessary to qualify. If required by ties, 11 players are shown. If ties would require more than 11 men to be shown, none of the last tied group is included.

Pitching. The top ten pitchers are shown in various categories. For averages, innings pitched must equal or exceed the number of scheduled games in order for a pitcher to qualify. If required by ties, 11 players are shown. If ties would require more than 11 men to be shown, none of the last tied group is included.

Fielding. The top five in each fielding category are shown for each position. For averages, the minimum for qualification at first base, second base, shortstop, third base, and catcher is 100 games played. For outfield, games played must equal or exceed two-thirds of the number of scheduled games. For pitchers, innings pitched must equal or exceed the number of scheduled games. If required by ties, 6 players are shown. If ties would require more than 6 men to be shown, none of the last tied group is shown.

All-Time Single Season Leaders - Individual Batting

BATTING AVERAGE
1. Luke Appling, 1936 .388
2. Joe Jackson, 1920 .382
3. Eddie Collins, 1920 .369
4. Eddie Collins, 1923 .360
5. Carl Reynolds, 1930 .359
6. Bibb Falk, 1924 .352
7. Joe Jackson, 1919 .351
8. Eddie Collins, 1924 .349
9. Luke Appling, 1940 .348
10. Eddie Collins, 1925 .346

SLUGGING AVERAGE
1. Richie Allen, 1972 .603
2. Joe Jackson, 1920 .589
3. Carl Reynolds, 1930 .584
4. Zeke Bonura, 1937 .573
5. Richie Allen, 1974 .563
6. Zeke Bonura, 1934 .545
7. Happy Felsch, 1920 .540
8. Roy Sievers, 1961 .537
9. Minnie Minoso, 1954 .535
10. Roy Sievers, 1960 .534

HITS
1. Eddie Collins, 1920 222
2. Joe Jackson, 1920 218
3. Buck Weaver, 1920 210
4. Rip Radcliff, 1936 207
5. Luke Appling, 1936 204
6. Carl Reynolds, 1930 202
6. Joe Jackson, 1916 202
8. Nellie Fox, 1954 201
9. Al Simmons, 1933 200
10. Nellie Fox, 1955 198

DOUBLES
1. Floyd Robinson, 1962 45
2. Chet Lemon, 1979 44
3. Bibb Falk, 1926 43
3. Earl Sheely, 1925 43
5. Red Kress, 1932 42
5. Joe Jackson, 1920 42
5. Luke Appling, 1937 42
5. Zeke Bonura, 1937 41
8. Johnny Mostil, 1926 41

TRIPLES
1. Joe Jackson, 1916 21
2. Joe Jackson, 1920 20
3. Jack Fournier, 1915 18
3. Harry Lord, 1911 18
3. Carl Reynolds, 1930 18
3. Minnie Minoso, 1954 18
7. Joe Jackson, 1917 17
7. Eddie Collins, 1916 17
7. Sam Mertes, 1901 17
7. Shano Collins, 1915 17

HOME RUNS
1. Richie Allen, 1972 37
2. Ron Kittle, 1983 35
3. Bill Melton, 1970 33
3. Bill Melton, 1971 33
5. Richie Allen, 1974 32
5. Greg Luzinski, 1983 32
7. Oscar Gamble, 1977 31
8. Richie Zisk, 1977 30
9. Gus Zernial, 1950 29
9. Eddie Robinson, 1951 29

RUNS
1. Johnny Mostil, 1925 135
2. Fielder Jones, 1901 120
2. Zeke Bonura, 1936 120
2. Johnny Mostil, 1926 120
2. Rip Radcliff, 1936 120
6. Minnie Minoso, 1954 119
6. Lu Blue, 1931 119
8. Eddie Collins, 1915 118
9. Eddie Collins, 1920 115
10. Dummy Hoy, 1901 112

RUNS BATTED IN
1. Zeke Bonura, 1936 138
2. Luke Appling, 1936 128
3. Joe Jackson, 1920 121
4. Al Simmons, 1933 119
5. Eddie Robinson, 1951 117
6. Minnie Minoso, 1954 116
7. Happy Felsch, 1920 115
8. Smead Jolley, 1930 114
9. Richie Allen, 1972 113
10. Gee Walker, 1939 111
10. Earl Sheely, 1925 111

STOLEN BASES
1. Rudy Law, 1983 77
2. Wally Moses, 1943 56
2. Luis Aparicio, 1959 56
4. Eddie Collins, 1917 53
4. Luis Aparicio, 1961 53
6. Frank Isbell, 1901 52
7. Luis Aparicio, 1960 51
7. Don Buford, 1966 51
9. Rollie Zeider, 1910 49

RUNS PER GAME
1. Fielder Jones, 1901 .90
2. Johnny Mostil, 1925 .88
3. Rip Radcliff, 1936 .87
4. Dummy Hoy, 1901 .85
5. Harry Hooper, 1924 .82
6. Johnny Mostil, 1926 .81
7. Zeke Bonura, 1936 .81
8. Luke Appling, 1936 .80
9. Minnie Minoso, 1951 .79
10. Sammy Strang, 1902 .79

RUNS BATTED IN PER GAME
1. Zeke Bonura, 1936 .93
2. Luke Appling, 1936 .93
3. Zeke Bonura, 1934 .87
4. Zeke Bonura, 1936 .86
5. Joe Jackson, 1920 .83
6. Al Simmons, 1933 .82
7. Happy Felsch, 1920 .81
8. Jackie Hayes, 1936 .78
9. Eddie Robinson, 1951 .77
10. Richie Allen, 1972 .76

HOME RUN PERCENTAGE
1. Richie Allen, 1972 7.3
2. Richie Allen, 1974 6.9
3. Ron Kittle, 1983 6.7
4. Bill Melton, 1970 6.4
5. Greg Luzinski, 1983 6.4
6. Roy Sievers, 1960 6.3
7. Bill Melton, 1971 6.1
8. Richie Zisk, 1977 5.6
9. Greg Luzinski, 1981 5.6
10. Roy Sievers, 1961 5.5

All-Time Single Season Leaders - Individual Batting

AT BATS
1. Nellie Fox, 1956 — 649
2. Nellie Fox, 1952 — 648
3. Nellie Fox, 1955 — 636
3. Jorge Orta, 1976 — 636
5. Nellie Fox, 1954 — 631
6. Buck Weaver, 1920 — 630
7. Tommie Agee, 1966 — 629
8. Luis Aparicio, 1961 — 625
9. Nellie Fox, 1953 — 624
9. Nellie Fox, 1959 — 624

EXTRA BASE HITS
1. Joe Jackson, 1920 — 74
2. Richie Allen, 1972 — 70
3. Happy Felsch, 1920 — 69
4. Zeke Bonura, 1934 — 66
4. Minnie Minoso, 1954 — 66
4. Floyd Robinson, 1962 — 66
4. Smead Jolley, 1930 — 66
8. Carl Reynolds, 1930 — 65
9. Joe Jackson, 1916 — 64
10. Chet Lemon, 1979 — 63
10. Joe Kuhel, 1940 — 63

TOTAL BASES
1. Joe Jackson, 1920 — 336
2. Carl Reynolds, 1930 — 329
3. Richie Allen, 1972 — 305
4. Minnie Minoso, 1954 — 304
5. Smead Jolley, 1930 — 303
6. Happy Felsch, 1920 — 300
7. Al Simmons, 1934 — 296
8. Eddie Collins, 1920 — 294
8. Joe Kuhel, 1940 — 294
10. Joe Jackson, 1916 — 293

BASES ON BALLS
1. Lu Blue, 1931 — 127
2. Luke Appling, 1935 — 122
3. Luke Appling, 1949 — 121
4. Eddie Collins, 1915 — 119
5. Ferris Fain, 1953 — 108
6. Luke Appling, 1939 — 105
7. Larry Doby, 1956 — 102
8. Joe Cunningham, 1962 — 101
8. Cass Michaels, 1949 — 101
10. Richie Allen, 1972 — 99

STRIKEOUTS
1. Dave Nicholson, 1963 — 175
2. Ron Kittle, 1983 — 150
3. Tommie Agee, 1967 — 129
4. Tommie Agee, 1966 — 127
5. Dave Nicholson, 1964 — 126
5. Richie Allen, 1972 — 126
7. Greg Luzinski, 1982 — 120
8. Greg Luzinski, 1983 — 117
8. Deron Johnson, 1975 — 117
10. Ken Henderson, 1974 — 112

HIGHEST STRIKEOUT AVERAGE
1. Dave Nicholson, 1963 — .390
2. Ron Kittle, 1983 — .288
3. Richie Allen, 1972 — .249
4. Tommie Agee, 1967 — .244
5. Pete Ward, 1967 — .233
6. Greg Luzinski, 1983 — .233
7. Greg Luzinski, 1981 — .212
8. Deron Johnson, 1975 — .211
9. Larry Doby, 1956 — .208
10. Bill Melton, 1970 — .208

BB AVERAGE
1. Luke Appling, 1949 — .197
2. Ferris Fain, 1953 — .195
3. Luke Appling, 1935 — .189
4. Larry Rosenthal, 1940 — .188
5. Eddie Collins, 1915 — .186
6. Eddie Collins, 1918 — .181
7. Lu Blue, 1931 — .177
8. Eddie Collins, 1925 — .170
9. Luke Appling, 1939 — .169
10. Larry Doby, 1956 — .168

PINCH HITS
1. Smoky Burgess, 1966 — 21
2. Smoky Burgess, 1965 — 20
3. Pete Ward, 1969 — 17
3. Jerry Hairston, 1983 — 17
5. Ron Northey, 1956 — 15
6. Smead Jolley, 1931 — 14
7. Eddie Murphy, 1920 — 13
7. Greg Walker, 1983 — 13
7. Tom Wright, 1953 — 13

PINCH HIT AT BATS
1. Smoky Burgess, 1966 — 66
2. Smoky Burgess, 1965 — 65
3. Jerry Hairston, 1983 — 62
4. Smoky Burgess, 1967 — 60
5. Jerry Hairston, 1982 — 47
6. Pete Ward, 1969 — 46
7. Bob Sadowski, 1962 — 44
8. Tom Wright, 1953 — 42
9. Earl Torgeson, 1960 — 41

PINCH HIT BATTING AVERAGE
1. Smead Jolley, 1931 — .467
2. Eddie Murphy, 1920 — .394
3. Ron Northey, 1956 — .385
4. Eddie Murphy, 1917 — .375
5. Greg Walker, 1983 — .371
6. Pete Ward, 1969 — .370
7. Walt Dropo, 1957 — .355
8. Smoky Burgess, 1966 — .318
9. Tom Wright, 1953 — .310

All-Time Single Season Leaders - Relief Pitching

GAMES
1. Wilbur Wood, 1968 88
2. Eddie Fisher, 1965 82
3. Bob Locker, 1967 77
3. Wilbur Wood, 1970 77
5. Wilbur Wood, 1969 76
6. Hoyt Wilhelm, 1964 73
7. Hoyt Wilhelm, 1968 72
8. Bob Locker, 1968 70
9. Gerry Staley, 1959 67

WINS
1. Ed Walsh, 1908 40
2. Eddie Cicotte, 1919 29
3. Eddie Cicotte, 1917 28
4. Doc White, 1907 27
4. Ed Walsh, 1912 27
4. Ed Walsh, 1911 27
7. Red Faber, 1921 25

LOSSES
1. Patsy Flaherty, 1903 25
2. Pat Caraway, 1931 24
3. Ted Lyons, 1933 21
3. Stan Bahnsen, 1973 21
3. Jim Scott, 1913 21

COMPLETE GAMES
1. Ed Walsh, 1908 42
2. Frank Smith, 1909 37
2. Ed Walsh, 1907 37
4. Frank Owen, 1904 34
5. Ed Walsh, 1910 33
5. Ed Walsh, 1911 33
7. Frank Owen, 1905 32
7. Red Faber, 1921 32
7. Ed Walsh, 1912 32

WINNING PERCENTAGE
1. Sandy Consuegra, 1954 ..... .842
2. Eddie Cicotte, 1919 ..... .806
3. Clark Griffith, 1901 ..... .774
4. Rich Dotson, 1983 ..... .759
5. Bob Shaw, 1959 ..... .750
5. Doc White, 1906 ..... .750
5. Monty Stratton, 1937 ..... .750
8. Joe Horlen, 1967 ..... .731
9. Ed Walsh, 1908 ..... .727
9. Dick Donovan, 1957 ..... .727

EARNED RUN AVERAGE
1. Ed Walsh, 1910 ..... 1.27
2. Ed Walsh, 1909 ..... 1.41
3. Ed Walsh, 1908 ..... 1.42
4. Doc White, 1906 ..... 1.52
5. Eddie Cicotte, 1917 ..... 1.53
6. Eddie Cicotte, 1913 ..... 1.58
7. Ed Walsh, 1907 ..... 1.60
8. Doc White, 1904 ..... 1.71
9. Doc White, 1909 ..... 1.72
10. Doc White, 1905 ..... 1.76

INNINGS PITCHED
1. Ed Walsh, 1908 464
2. Ed Walsh, 1907 422
3. Ed Walsh, 1912 393
4. Wilbur Wood, 1972 377
5. Ed Walsh, 1910 370
6. Ed Walsh, 1911 369
7. Frank Smith, 1909 365
8. Wilbur Wood, 1973 359
9. Red Faber, 1922 353
10. Eddie Cicotte, 1917 347

STRIKEOUTS
1. Ed Walsh, 1908 269
2. Ed Walsh, 1910 258
3. Ed Walsh, 1911 255
4. Ed Walsh, 1912 254
5. Gary Peters, 1967 215
6. Wilbur Wood, 1971 210
7. Tom Bradley, 1972 209
8. Tom Bradley, 1971 206
8. Ed Walsh, 1907 206
10. Gary Peters, 1964 205

BASES ON BALLS
1. Vern Kennedy, 1936 147
2. Billy Pierce, 1950 137
3. Bill Wight, 1948 135
4. Vic Frazier, 1931 127
5. Vern Kennedy, 1937 124
6. Early Wynn, 1959 119
7. Stan Bahnsen, 1973 117
8. Eddie Smith, 1941 114
9. Billy Pierce, 1949 112
9. Early Wynn, 1960 112

All-Time Single Season Leaders - Individual Pitching

HITS PER 9 INNINGS
1. Ed Walsh, 1910 ..... 5.89
2. Joe Horlen, 1964 ..... 6.07
3. Eddie Cicotte, 1917 ..... 6.39
4. Eddie Fisher, 1965 ..... 6.42
5. Frank Smith, 1908 ..... 6.44
6. Gary Peters, 1967 ..... 6.47
7. Ed Walsh, 1909 ..... 6.49
8. Joe Horlen, 1967 ..... 6.56
9. Doc White, 1906 ..... 6.57
10. Frank Smith, 1905 ..... 6.63

STRIKEOUTS PER 9 INNINGS
1. Juan Pizarro, 1961 ..... 8.69
2. Floyd Bannister, 1983 ..... 7.99
3. Bart Johnson, 1971 ..... 7.74
4. Juan Pizarro, 1962 ..... 7.66
5. Gary Peters, 1967 ..... 7.44
6. Tom Bradley, 1972 ..... 7.23
7. Billy Pierce, 1954 ..... 7.06
8. Steve Stone, 1973 ..... 7.04
9. Gary Peters, 1963 ..... 7.00
10. Billy Pierce, 1955 ..... 6.87

BASES ON BALLS PER 9 INNINGS
1. LaMarr Hoyt, 1983 ..... 1.07
2. Roy Patterson, 1906 ..... 1.08
3. Ed Walsh, 1908 ..... 1.09
4. Doc White, 1907 ..... 1.18
5. Ted Lyons, 1942 ..... 1.30
6. Nick Altrock, 1907 ..... 1.31
7. Roy Patterson, 1904 ..... 1.31
8. Nick Altrock, 1906 ..... 1.31
9. Eddie Cicotte, 1918 ..... 1.35
10. Ted Lyons, 1939 ..... 1.36

SHUTOUTS
1. Ed Walsh, 1908 12
2. Ed Walsh, 1906 10
3. Ed Walsh, 1909 8
3. Reb Russell, 1913 8
3. Wilbur Wood, 1972 8

RELIEF GAMES
1. Wilbur Wood, 1968 86
2. Eddie Fisher, 1965 82
3. Bob Locker, 1967 77
3. Wilbur Wood, 1970 77
5. Wilbur Wood, 1969 76

RELIEF WINS
1. Eddie Fisher, 1965 15
2. Earl Caldwell, 1946 13
2. Gerry Staley, 1960 13
4. Hoyt Wilhelm, 1964 12
4. Wilbur Wood, 1968 12

SAVES
1. Ed Farmer, 1980 30
2. Terry Forster, 1972 29
3. Hoyt Wilhelm, 1964 27
4. Goose Gossage, 1975 26
5. Lerrin LaGrow, 1977 25

RELIEF WINS PLUS SAVES
1. Eddie Fisher, 1965 39
1. Hoyt Wilhelm, 1964 39
3. Ed Farmer, 1980 37
4. Goose Gossage, 1975 35
4. Terry Forster, 1972 35

RELIEF WINNING PERCENTAGE
1. Sandy Consuegra, 1954 ..... 1.000
2. Turk Lown, 1959 ..... .818
3. Earl Caldwell, 1946 ..... .765
4. Dave Danforth, 1917 ..... .750
4. LaMarr Hoyt, 1981 ..... .750

All-Time Single Season Leaders - Individual Fielding

1B

PUTOUTS
1. Jiggs Donahue, 1907 1846
2. Jiggs Donahue, 1906 1697
3. Jiggs Donahue, 1905 1645
4. Earl Sheely, 1921 1637
5. Earl Sheely, 1925 1565

ASSISTS
1. Jiggs Donahue, 1907 140
2. Earl Sheely, 1921 119
3. Jiggs Donahue, 1906 118
4. Jiggs Donahue, 1905 114
5. Jim Spencer, 1976 112

FIELDING AVERAGE
1. Jim Spencer, 1976 .... .998
2. Chick Gandil, 1919 .... .997
3. Mike Squires, 1983 .... .996
4. Zeke Bonura, 1934 .... .996
5. Zeke Bonura, 1936 .... .996

2B

PUTOUTS
1. Nellie Fox, 1956 478
2. Nellie Fox, 1957 453
3. Nellie Fox, 1953 451
4. Eddie Collins, 1920 449
5. Nellie Fox, 1958 444

ASSISTS
1. Jackie Hayes, 1933 497
2. Jackie Hayes, 1937 490
3. Eddie Collins, 1915 487
4. Cass Michaels, 1949 484
5. Nellie Fox, 1955 483

FIELDING AVERAGE
1. Nellie Fox, 1962 .... .990
2. Nellie Fox, 1954 .... .989
3. Nellie Fox, 1959 .... .988
4. Nellie Fox, 1963 .... .988
5. Tony Bernazard, 1981 .... .987

3B

PUTOUTS
1. Willie Kamm, 1928 243
2. Willie Kamm, 1927 236
3. Willie Kamm, 1929 221
4. Willie Kamm, 1924 190
5. Willie Kamm, 1925 182

ASSISTS
1. Bill Melton, 1971 371
2. Lee Tannehill, 1904 369
3. Lee Tannehill, 1905 358
4. Willie Kamm, 1923 352
5. Bill Melton, 1973 347

FIELDING AVERAGE
1. Floyd Baker, 1947 .... .980
2. Willie Kamm, 1926 .... .978
3. Willie Kamm, 1929 .... .978
4. Eric Soderholm, 1977 .... .978
5. Willie Kamm, 1928 .... .977

SS

PUTOUTS
1. Buck Weaver, 1913 392
2. Buck Weaver, 1914 367
3. Bill Cissell, 1929 357
4. George Davis, 1904 347
5. Buck Weaver, 1912 342

ASSISTS
1. Luis Aparicio, 1969 563
2. Luke Appling, 1935 556
3. Luis Aparicio, 1960 551
4. Bucky Dent, 1975 543
5. Luke Appling, 1937 541

FIELDING AVERAGE
1. Ron Hansen, 1963 .... .983
2. Bucky Dent, 1975 .... .981
3. Luis Aparicio, 1960 .... .979
4. Luis Aparicio, 1968 .... .977
5. Bucky Dent, 1976 .... .976

OF

PUTOUTS
1. Chet Lemon, 1977 512
2. Ken Henderson, 1974 462
3. Johnny Mostil, 1925 446
4. Johnny Mostil, 1926 440
4. Happy Felsch, 1917 440

ASSISTS
1. Happy Felsch, 1919 32
2. Sam Mertes, 1902 26
2. Nemo Leibold, 1919 26
2. Bibb Falk, 1924 26
5. Fielder Jones, 1902 25
5. Happy Felsch, 1920 25

FIELDING AVERAGE
1. Ken Berry, 1969 .... 1.000
1. Sam Mele, 1952 .... 1.000
3. Sam Mele, 1953 .... .996
4. Jim Landis, 1962 .... .995
5. Mike Kreevich, 1941 .... .994

C

PUTOUTS
1. Brian Downing, 1975 730
2. Carlton Fisk, 1983 709
3. Sherm Lollar, 1956 679
4. Sherm Lollar, 1955 664
5. Ray Schalk, 1915 655

ASSISTS
1. Ray Schalk, 1914 183
2. Ray Schalk, 1916 166
3. Ray Schalk, 1915 159
4. Billy Sullivan, 1908 156
5. Ray Schalk, 1913 154

FIELDING AVERAGE
1. Sherm Lollar, 1961 .... .998
2. Sherm Lollar, 1957 .... .998
3. Phil Masi, 1950 .... .996
4. Ed Herrmann, 1971 .... .995
5. Sherm Lollar, 1960 .... .995

P

PUTOUTS
1. Nick Altrock, 1904 43
2. Ed Walsh, 1908 41
3. Ed Walsh, 1907 35
4. Doc White, 1907 33
5. Nick Altrock, 1905 32

ASSISTS
1. Ed Walsh, 1907 227
2. Ed Walsh, 1908 190
3. Ed Walsh, 1911 159
4. Ed Walsh, 1910 154
4. Frank Smith, 1909 154

All-Time Single Season Leaders - Individual Fielding

TOTAL CHANCES | TOTAL CHANCES PER GAME | DOUBLE PLAYS

1B

TOTAL CHANCES		TOTAL CHANCES PER GAME		DOUBLE PLAYS	
1. Jiggs Donahue, 1907	1998	1. Jiggs Donahue, 1907	12.7	1. Tony Lupien, 1948	155
2. Jiggs Donahue, 1906	1837	2. Frank Isbell, 1909	12.7	2. Zeke Bonura, 1936	150
3. Jiggs Donahue, 1905	1780	3. Jiggs Donahue, 1905	11.9	3. Eddie Robinson, 1952	145
4. Earl Sheely, 1921	1778	4. Jiggs Donahue, 1906	11.9	4. Eddie Robinson, 1951	143
5. Earl Sheely, 1925	1680	5. Jiggs Donahue, 1904	11.7	4. Joe Kuhel, 1943	143

2B

TOTAL CHANCES		TOTAL CHANCES PER GAME		DOUBLE PLAYS	
1. Eddie Collins, 1920	943	1. John Kerr, 1929	6.5	1. Nellie Fox, 1957	141
2. Jim Morrison, 1980	932	2. Eddie Collins, 1921	6.3	2. Cass Michaels, 1949	135
3. Nellie Fox, 1957	919	3. Jackie Hayes, 1933	6.2	3. Nellie Fox, 1960	126
4. Nellie Fox, 1955	906	4. Eddie Collins, 1920	6.2	4. Nellie Fox, 1956	124
5. Cass Michaels, 1949	898	5. Jackie Hayes, 1937	6.0	5. Nellie Fox, 1958	117
				5. Jim Morrison, 1980	117

3B

TOTAL CHANCES		TOTAL CHANCES PER GAME		DOUBLE PLAYS	
1. Lee Tannehill, 1904	580	1. Lee Tannehill, 1906	4.3	1. Bill Melton, 1969	36
2. Sammy Strang, 1902	566	2. Sammy Strang, 1902	4.1	2. Willie Kamm, 1928	33
3. Lee Tannehill, 1905	565	3. Lee Tannehill, 1905	4.0	3. Willie Kamm, 1925	32
4. Willie Kamm, 1923	547	4. Fred Hartman, 1901	3.9		
5. Bob Kennedy, 1940	533	5. Lee Tannehill, 1904	3.8		
5. Willie Kamm, 1928	533				

SS

TOTAL CHANCES		TOTAL CHANCES PER GAME		DOUBLE PLAYS	
1. Buck Weaver, 1913	982	1. Lee Tannehill, 1911	6.6	1. Luke Appling, 1936	119
2. Luke Appling, 1935	930	2. Buck Weaver, 1913	6.5	2. Luis Aparicio, 1960	117
3. George Davis, 1904	919	3. Buck Weaver, 1914	6.1	3. Luke Appling, 1943	115
4. Luke Appling, 1933	903	4. Luke Appling, 1935	6.1	4. Chico Carrasquel, 1950	113
5. George Davis, 1905	877	5. Luke Appling, 1936	6.1	5. Luke Appling, 1937	111

OF

TOTAL CHANCES		TOTAL CHANCES PER GAME		DOUBLE PLAYS	
1. Chet Lemon, 1977	536	1. Chet Lemon, 1977	3.6	1. Happy Felsch, 1919	15
2. Ken Henderson, 1974	475	2. Thurman Tucker, 1944	3.6	2. Fielder Jones, 1902	11
3. Happy Felsch, 1917	471	3. Mike Kreevich, 1939	3.2	3. Happy Felsch, 1920	10
4. Johnny Mostil, 1926	470	4. Johnny Mostil, 1928	3.2	4. Ping Bodie, 1911	9
5. Johnny Mostil, 1925	464	5. Dave Philley, 1948	3.2	4. Bibb Falk, 1927	9

C

TOTAL CHANCES		TOTAL CHANCES PER GAME		DOUBLE PLAYS	
1. Ray Schalk, 1916	829	1. Fred Payne, 1910	6.8	1. Ray Schalk, 1916	25
2. Ray Schalk, 1915	827	2. Ray Schalk, 1916	6.7	2. Ray Schalk, 1923	20
3. Brian Downing, 1975	822	3. Ray Schalk, 1914	6.6	2. Ray Schalk, 1914	20
4. Ray Schalk, 1914	817	4. Johnny Romano, 1966	6.6	4. Ray Schalk, 1921	19
5. Ray Schalk, 1917	787	5. Ed Herrmann, 1972	6.4	4. Ray Schalk, 1920	19

P

TOTAL CHANCES		TOTAL CHANCES PER GAME		DOUBLE PLAYS	
1. Ed Walsh, 1907	266	1. Ed Walsh, 1907	4.8	1. Nick Altrock, 1905	10
2. Ed Walsh, 1908	237	2. Nick Altrock, 1905	4.4	2. Eddie Cicotte, 1913	9
3. Ed Walsh, 1911	194	3. Nick Altrock, 1904	4.3	2. Ed Walsh, 1908	9
4. Ed Walsh, 1910	184	4. Ed Walsh, 1910	4.1		
4. Frank Smith, 1909	184	5. Frank Owen, 1904	4.1		

10

All-Time Single Season Leaders - Individual Fielding

PUTOUTS PER GAME		ASSISTS PER GAME	

1B
1. Frank Isbell, 1909 .... 11.9
2. Jiggs Donahue, 1907 .... 11.8
3. Jiggs Donahue, 1905 .... 11.0
4. Jiggs Donahue, 1906 .... 11.0
5. Earl Sheely, 1921 .... 10.6

1. Tom McCraw, 1967 9
2. Jiggs Donahue, 1907 9
3. Jiggs Donahue, 1904 8
4. Lu Blue, 1932 8
5. Ferris Fain, 1953 8

2B
1. Nellie Fox, 1956 .... 3.1
2. Eddie Collins, 1920 .... 2.9
3. Nellie Fox, 1953 .... 2.9
4. Nellie Fox, 1957 .... 2.9
5. Nellie Fox, 1958 .... 2.9

1. John Kerr, 1929 .... 3.8
2. Jackie Hayes, 1933 .... 3.6
3. Jackie Hayes, 1937 .... 3.4
4. Eddie Collins, 1921 .... 3.4
5. George Davis, 1908 .... 3.3

3B
1. Willie Kamm, 1927 .... 1.6
2. Willie Kamm, 1928 .... 1.6
3. Willie Kamm, 1929 .... 1.5
4. Buck Weaver, 1917 .... 1.4
5. Willie Kamm, 1930 .... 1.4

1. Lee Tannehill, 1906 .... 2.8
2. Lee Tannehill, 1905 .... 2.5
3. Lee Tannehill, 1908 .... 2.5
4. Bill Melton, 1971 .... 2.5
5. Floyd Baker, 1947 .... 2.5

SS
1. Buck Weaver, 1914 .... 2.7
2. Buck Weaver, 1913 .... 2.6
3. Lee Tannehill, 1911 .... 2.6
4. Bill Cissell, 1929 .... 2.3
5. Luke Appling, 1936 .... 2.3

1. Freddy Parent, 1908 .... 3.7
2. Lee Tannehill, 1911 .... 3.7
3. George Davis, 1907 .... 3.7
4. George Davis, 1906 .... 3.7
5. Luis Aparicio, 1969 .... 3.7

OF
1. Thurman Tucker, 1944 .... 3.5
2. Chet Lemon, 1977 .... 3.4
3. Thurman Tucker, 1943 .... 3.0
4. Mike Kreevich, 1939 .... 3.0
5. Johnny Mostil, 1928 .... 3.0

1. Happy Felsch, 1919 2
2. Sam Mertes, 1902 2
3. Nemo Leibold, 1919 2
4. Bibb Falk, 1924 2
5. Ping Bodie, 1911 2

C
1. Johnny Romano, 1966 .... 6.1
2. Ed Herrmann, 1971 .... 5.7
3. Ed Herrmann, 1972 .... 5.7
4. Cam Carreon, 1962 .... 5.6
5. Ed Herrmann, 1973 .... 5.4

1. Ray Schalk, 1914 .... 1.5
2. Fred Payne, 1910 .... 1.4
3. Ray Schalk, 1916 .... 1.3
4. Billy Sullivan, 1911 .... 1.3
5. Ray Schalk, 1913 .... 1.2

P
1. Nick Altrock, 1904 .... 1.1
2. Doc White, 1904 .... 1.0
3. Doc White, 1910 9
4. Nick Altrock, 1907 9
5. Nick Altrock, 1905 8

1. Ed Walsh, 1907 .... 4.1
2. Frank Owen, 1904 .... 3.5
3. Nick Altrock, 1905 .... 3.5
4. Ed Walsh, 1910 .... 3.4
5. Nixey Callahan, 1901 .... 3.1

Lifetime Batting Leaders

GAMES
1. Luke Appling 2422
2. Nellie Fox 2115
3. Ray Schalk 1755
4. Eddie Collins 1670
5. Luis Aparicio 1511
6. Minnie Minoso 1379
7. Sherm Lollar 1358
8. Shano Collins 1335
9. Buck Weaver 1254
10. Willie Kamm 1170

AT BATS
1. Luke Appling 8857
2. Nellie Fox 8486
3. Eddie Collins 6064
4. Luis Aparicio 5856
5. Ray Schalk 5304
6. Minnie Minoso 5011
7. Buck Weaver 4810
8. Shano Collins 4787
9. Fielder Jones 4299
10. Sherm Lollar 4229

HITS
1. Luke Appling 2749
2. Nellie Fox 2470
3. Eddie Collins 2005
4. Luis Aparicio 1576
5. Minnie Minoso 1523
6. Ray Schalk 1345
7. Buck Weaver 1310
8. Shano Collins 1254
9. Bibb Falk 1219
10. Fielder Jones 1170

DOUBLES
1. Luke Appling 440
2. Nellie Fox 335
3. Eddie Collins 265
4. Minnie Minoso 260
5. Bibb Falk 245
6. Willie Kamm 242
7. Shano Collins 230
8. Luis Aparicio 223
9. Johnny Mostil 209
10. Earl Sheely 207

TRIPLES
1. Shano Collins 104
1. Nellie Fox 104
3. Eddie Collins 102
3. Luke Appling 102
5. Johnny Mostil 82
6. Joe Jackson 79
6. Minnie Minoso 79
8. Buck Weaver 69
9. Willie Kamm 66
10. Mike Kreevich 65

HOME RUNS
1. Bill Melton 154
2. Minnie Minoso 135
3. Sherm Lollar 124
4. Pete Ward 97
5. Richie Allen 85
5. Al Smith 85
5. Carlos May 85
8. Jim Landis 83
9. Zeke Bonura 79
9. Jorge Orta 79

BATTING AVERAGE
1. Joe Jackson .... .339
2. Eddie Collins .... .331
3. Carl Reynolds .... .322
4. Zeke Bonura .... .317
5. Al Simmons .... .315
6. Bibb Falk .... .315
7. Taffy Wright .... .312
8. Luke Appling .... .310
9. Rip Radcliff .... .310
10. Earl Sheely .... .305

SLUGGING AVERAGE
1. Zeke Bonura .... .518
2. Carl Reynolds .... .499
3. Joe Jackson .... .498
4. Eddie Robinson .... .482
5. Al Simmons .... .480
6. Minnie Minoso .... .468
7. Chet Lemon .... .451
8. Harold Baines .... .447
9. Al Smith .... .444
10. Bibb Falk .... .442

TOTAL BASES
1. Luke Appling 3528
2. Nellie Fox 3118
3. Eddie Collins 2567
4. Minnie Minoso 2346
5. Luis Aparicio 2036
6. Shano Collins 1740
7. Bibb Falk 1714
8. Buck Weaver 1710
9. Sherm Lollar 1698
10. Ray Schalk 1676

HOME RUN PERCENTAGE
1. Eddie Robinson 4.5
2. Bill Melton 4.4
3. Zeke Bonura 3.8
4. Harold Baines 3.4
5. Ed Herrmann 3.4
6. Al Smith 3.4
7. Pete Ward 3.3
8. Sherm Lollar 2.9
9. Al Simmons 2.8
10. Minnie Minoso 2.7

EXTRA BASE HITS
1. Luke Appling 587
2. Minnie Minoso 474
2. Nellie Fox 474
4. Eddie Collins 398
5. Shano Collins 350
6. Bibb Falk 345
7. Willie Kamm 333
8. Luis Aparicio 320
9. Sherm Lollar 319
10. Johnny Mostil 314

RUNS BATTED IN
1. Luke Appling 1116
2. Minnie Minoso 808
3. Eddie Collins 803
4. Nellie Fox 740
5. Sherm Lollar 631
6. Bibb Falk 627
7. Ray Schalk 594
8. Willie Kamm 587
9. Earl Sheely 582
10. Shano Collins 541

Lifetime Batting Leaders

RUNS BATTED IN PER GAME
1. Zeke Bonura .... .83
2. Joe Jackson .... .66
3. Earl Sheely .... .61
4. Happy Felsch .... .60
5. Bibb Falk .... .59
6. Minnie Minoso .... .59
7. Bill Melton .... .55
8. Harold Baines .... .54
9. Taffy Wright .... .54
10. Rip Radcliff .... .54

RUNS
1. Luke Appling 1319
2. Nellie Fox 1187
3. Eddie Collins 1063
4. Minnie Minoso 893
5. Luis Aparicio 791
6. Fielder Jones 695
7. Buck Weaver 625
8. Johnny Mostil 618
9. Ray Schalk 579
10. Shano Collins 572

RUNS PER GAME
1. Zeke Bonura .... .74
2. Harry Hooper .... .67
3. Minnie Minoso .... .65
4. Rip Radcliff .... .64
5. Eddie Collins .... .64
6. Johnny Mostil .... .64
7. Joe Jackson .... .61
8. Fielder Jones .... .60
9. Mike Kreevich .... .59
10. Joe Kuhel .... .58

BASES ON BALLS
1. Luke Appling 1302
2. Eddie Collins 965
3. Minnie Minoso 658
4. Nellie Fox 658
5. Ray Schalk 638
6. Willie Kamm 569
7. Fielder Jones 551
8. Sherm Lollar 525
9. Jim Landis 483
10. Carlos May 456

BB AVERAGE
1. Floyd Baker .... .156
2. Eddie Collins .... .137
3. Nemo Leibold .... .133
4. Luke Appling .... .128
5. Willie Kamm .... .123
6. Alex Metzler .... .122
7. Jim Landis .... .119
8. Thurman Tucker .... .119
9. Jimmy Dykes .... .119
9. Joe Kuhel .... .119

STOLEN BASES
1. Eddie Collins 366
2. Luis Aparicio 318
3. Frank Isbell 250
4. Fielder Jones 206
5. Shano Collins 192
6. Luke Appling 179
7. Johnny Mostil 176
7. Ray Schalk 176
9. Buck Weaver 172
10. Minnie Minoso 171

PINCH HITS
1. Smoky Burgess 50
2. Eddie Murphy 42
3. Walt Williams 37
4. Earl Torgeson 32
5. Jerry Hairston 32
6. Sherm Lollar 30
7. Ralph Hodgin 27
8. Bud Stewart 26
9. Ron Northey 24
9. Pete Ward 24

PH BATTING AVERAGE
1. Eddie Murphy .... .326
2. Ron Northey .... .316
3. Pete Ward .... .300
4. Bob Fothergill .... .278
5. Wayne Causey .... .273
6. Earl Torgeson .... .267
7. Sherm Lollar .... .263
8. Gail Hopkins .... .260
9. Ralph Hodgin .... .260
10. Smoky Burgess .... .255

STRIKEOUTS
1. Jim Landis 608
2. Bill Melton 595
3. Luke Appling 528
4. Pete Ward 517
5. Carlos May 508
6. Red Faber 477
6. Jorge Orta 477
8. Jim Rivera 450
9. Minnie Minoso 427
10. Luis Aparicio 410

HIGHEST STRIKEOUTS PER AT BAT
1. Pete Ward .... .175
2. Jim Landis .... .170
3. Bill Melton .... .170
4. Pat Kelly .... .152
5. Ken Berry .... .150
6. Jim Rivera .... .146
7. Harold Baines .... .145
8. Carlos May .... .140
9. Tom McCraw .... .137

LOWEST STRIKEOUTS PER AT BAT
1. Nellie Fox .... .023
2. Eddie Collins .... .034
3. Rip Radcliff .... .035
4. Joe Jackson .... .036
5. Ralph Hodgin .... .036
6. Taffy Wright .... .042
7. Earl Sheely .... .046
8. Harry Hooper .... .049
9. Chick Gandil .... .052
10. Zeke Bonura .... .053

Lifetime Pitching Leaders

GAMES
1. Red Faber 669
2. Ted Lyons 594
3. Wilbur Wood 578
4. Billy Pierce 456
5. Ed Walsh 426
6. Doc White 361
6. Hoyt Wilhelm 361
8. Eddie Cicotte 353
9. Joe Horlen 329
10. Jim Scott 317

COMPLETE GAMES
1. Ted Lyons 356
2. Red Faber 275
3. Ed Walsh 249
4. Doc White 206
5. Billy Pierce 183
6. Eddie Cicotte 182
7. Frank Smith 156
8. Thornton Lee 142
9. Jim Scott 125
10. Roy Patterson 119

INNINGS PITCHED
1. Ted Lyons 4161
2. Red Faber 4088
3. Ed Walsh 2946
4. Billy Pierce 2931
5. Wilbur Wood 2524
6. Doc White 2516
7. Eddie Cicotte 2322
8. Joe Horlen 1917
9. Thornton Lee 1888
10. Jim Scott 1872

WINS
1. Ted Lyons 260
2. Red Faber 254
3. Ed Walsh 195
4. Billy Pierce 186
5. Wilbur Wood 163
6. Doc White 159
7. Eddie Cicotte 158
8. Joe Horlen 113
9. Jim Scott 111
10. Frank Smith 107

WINNING PERCENTAGE
1. Lefty Williams .... .648
2. Juan Pizarro .... .615
3. Ed Walsh .... .609
4. Dickie Kerr .... .609
5. Eddie Cicotte .... .608
6. Dick Donovan .... .593
7. Rich Dotson .... .583
8. Eddie Fisher .... .575
9. Frank Smith .... .569
10. Britt Burns .... .565

EARNED RUN AVERAGE
1. Ed Walsh 1.81
2. Frank Smith 2.18
3. Eddie Cicotte 2.24
4. Doc White 2.28
5. Jim Scott 2.32
6. Reb Russell 2.34
7. Nick Altrock 2.40
8. Joe Benz 2.42
9. Frank Owen 2.48
10. Roy Patterson 2.75

STRIKEOUTS
1. Billy Pierce 1796
2. Ed Walsh 1732
3. Red Faber 1471
4. Wilbur Wood 1332
5. Gary Peters 1098
6. Doc White 1095
7. Ted Lyons 1073
8. Joe Horlen 1007
9. Eddie Cicotte 961
10. Jim Scott 945

STRIKEOUTS PER 9 INNINGS
1. Juan Pizarro 6.88
2. Gary Peters 6.33
3. Early Wynn 5.98
4. Ken Kravec 5.80
5. Bart Johnson 5.78
6. Britt Burns 5.72
7. Billy Pierce 5.51
8. Tommy John 5.35
9. Ed Walsh 5.29
10. Rich Dotson 4.96

SHUTOUTS
1. Ed Walsh 58
2. Doc White 43
3. Billy Pierce 35
4. Red Faber 30
5. Eddie Cicotte 28
6. Ted Lyons 27
7. Jim Scott 26
8. Frank Smith 25
9. Reb Russell 24
9. Wilbur Wood 24

Lifetime Pitching Leaders

HITS PER 9 INNINGS
1. Ed Walsh 7.10
2. Frank Smith 7.12
3. Gary Peters 7.74
4. Jim Scott 7.81
5. Juan Pizarro 7.83
6. Reb Russell 7.86
7. Eddie Cicotte 7.94
8. Doc White 7.96
9. Early Wynn 7.97
10. Eddie Fisher 8.03

BASES ON BALLS
1. Red Faber 1213
2. Ted Lyons 1121
3. Billy Pierce 1052
4. Wilbur Wood 671
5. Thornton Lee 633
6. Jim Scott 609
7. Ed Walsh 608
8. Bill Dietrich 561
9. Eddie Smith 545
10. Doc White 542

BASES ON BALLS PER 9 INNINGS
1. Nick Altrock 1.49
2. Roy Patterson 1.80
3. Frank Owen 1.84
4. Ed Walsh 1.86
5. Reb Russell 1.86
6. Doc White 1.94
7. Sloppy Thurston ... 2.03
8. Eddie Cicotte 2.07
9. Joe Benz 2.21
10. Dick Donovan 2.26

LOSSES
1. Ted Lyons 230
2. Red Faber 212
3. Billy Pierce 152
4. Wilbur Wood 148
5. Ed Walsh 125
6. Doc White 123
7. Jim Scott 113
7. Joe Horlen 113
9. Thornton Lee 104
10. Eddie Cicotte 102

RELIEF WINS
1. Hoyt Wilhelm 41
2. Wilbur Wood 32
3. Gerry Staley 31
4. Clint Brown 29
5. Bob Locker 28

RELIEF WINNING PERCENTAGE
1. Luis Aloma .... .850
2. Joe Haynes .... .760
3. Eddie Cicotte ..... .708
4. Dave Danforth ..... .640
5. Turk Lown .... .625

SAVES
1. Hoyt Wilhelm 98
2. Terry Forster 75
3. Wilbur Wood 57
4. Ed Farmer 54
5. Clint Brown 53

WINS PLUS SAVES
1. Hoyt Wilhelm 139
2. Terry Forster 96
3. Wilbur Wood 89
4. Clint Brown 82
5. Bob Locker 76

RELIEF GAMES
1. Hoyt Wilhelm 358
2. Wilbur Wood 292
3. Bob Locker 271
4. Gerry Staley 260
5. Eddie Fisher 237

Lifetime Fielding Leaders

GAMES	CHANCES PER GAME	FIELDING AVERAGE

1B

1. Earl Sheely 938	1. Jiggs Donahue 12.1	1. Mike Squires .... .995
2. Joe Kuhel 880	2. Frank Isbell 11.7	2. Zeke Bonura .... .994
3. Tom McCraw 735	3. Earl Sheely 10.7	3. Chick Gandil .... .994
4. Lamar Johnson 659	4. Zeke Bonura 10.7	4. Joe Kuhel .... .992
5. Jiggs Donahue 646	5. Chick Gandil 10.6	

2B

1. Nellie Fox 2098	1. Jackie Hayes 5.9	1. Nellie Fox .... .984
2. Eddie Collins 1654	2. Don Kolloway 5.9	2. Jackie Hayes .... .977
3. Jackie Hayes 758	3. Cass Michaels 5.8	3. Al Weis .... .977
4. Jorge Orta 688	4. Eddie Collins 5.6	4. Jorge Orta .... .974
5. Don Kolloway 545	5. Nellie Fox 5.6	5. Eddie Collins .... .973

3B

1. Willie Kamm 1157	1. Lee Tannehill 3.8	1. Floyd Baker .... .972
2. Bill Melton 867	2. Buck Weaver 3.6	2. Willie Kamm .... .967
3. Lee Tannehill 669	3. Willie Kamm 3.5	3. Jimmy Dykes .... .952
4. Pete Ward 562	4. Bill Melton 3.3	4. Bill Melton .... .949
5. Jimmy Dykes 462	5. Bob Kennedy 3.2	5. Buck Weaver .... .946

SS

1. Luke Appling 2218	1. Lee Tannehill 6.1	1. Bucky Dent .... .975
2. Luis Aparicio 1506	2. George Davis 5.8	2. Luis Aparicio .... .971
3. Chico Carrasquel 835	3. Buck Weaver 5.8	3. Chico Carrasquel ...... .971
4. Buck Weaver 822	4. Luke Appling 5.5	4. Ron Hansen .... .971
5. George Davis 721	5. Bill Cissell 5.4	5. Luke Appling .... .948

OF

1. Minnie Minoso 1262	1. Thurman Tucker 3.1	1. Jim Landis .... .990
2. Fielder Jones 1158	2. Johnny Mostil 3.0	2. Thurman Tucker ...... .987
3. Jim Landis 1035	3. Chet Lemon 3.0	3. Ken Berry .... .987
4. Bibb Falk 1030	4. Mike Kreevich 3.0	4. Mule Haas .... .986
5. Shano Collins 937	5. Happy Felsch 2.8	5. Al Simmons .... .986

C

1. Ray Schalk 1721	1. Ed Herrmann 5.9	1. Sherm Lollar .... .993
2. Sherm Lollar 1241	2. Billy Sullivan 5.6	2. Carlton Fisk .... .992
3. Billy Sullivan 1032	3. Brian Downing 5.6	3. Brian Downing .... .989
4. Mike Tresh 981	4. Carlton Fisk 5.5	4. Ed Herrmann .... .988
5. Ed Herrmann 612	5. Ray Schalk 5.3	5. Luke Sewell .... .985

P

1. Red Faber 669	1. Nick Altrock 4.0	
2. Ted Lyons 594	2. Nixey Callahan 4.0	
3. Wilbur Wood 578	3. Patsy Flaherty 3.7	
4. Billy Pierce 456	4. Ed Walsh 3.5	
5. Ed Walsh 426	5. Frank Owen 3.2	

Lifetime Fielding Leaders

PUTOUTS	PUTOUTS PER GAME	ASSISTS

1B

1. Earl Sheely 9395	1. Jiggs Donahue 11.2	1. Earl Sheely 591
2. Joe Kuhel 8383	2. Frank Isbell 10.8	2. Joe Kuhel 544
3. Jiggs Donahue 7234	3. Zeke Bonura 10.0	3. Jiggs Donahue 514
4. Frank Isbell 6663	4. Earl Sheely 10.0	4. Frank Isbell 455
5. Tom McCraw 5431	5. Chick Gandil 10.0	5. Tom McCraw 423

2B

1. Nellie Fox 5654	1. Nellie Fox 2.7	1. Nellie Fox 5852
2. Eddie Collins 4113	2. Cass Michaels 2.6	2. Eddie Collins 4885
3. Jackie Hayes 1842	3. Don Kolloway 2.6	3. Jackie Hayes 2546
4. Jorge Orta 1544	4. Eddie Collins 2.5	4. Jorge Orta 1693
5. Don Kolloway 1441	5. Jackie Hayes 2.4	5. Don Kolloway 1657

3B

1. Willie Kamm 1593	1. Willie Kamm 1.4	1. Willie Kamm 2365
2. Lee Tannehill 753	2. Buck Weaver 1.3	2. Bill Melton 2004
3. Bill Melton 685	3. Lee Tannehill 1.1	3. Lee Tannehill 1624
4. Buck Weaver 554	4. Harry Lord 1.1	4. Pete Ward 1182
5. Harry Lord 498	5. Bob Kennedy 1.0	5. Floyd Baker 954

SS

1. Luke Appling 4398	1. Buck Weaver 2.3	1. Luke Appling 7218
2. Luis Aparicio 2684	2. Bill Cissell 2.2	2. Luis Aparicio 4917
3. Buck Weaver 1878	3. Lee Tannehill 2.1	3. Buck Weaver 2570
4. George Davis 1503	4. George Davis 2.1	4. Chico Carrasquel 2561
5. Chico Carrasquel 1496	5. Luke Appling 2.0	5. George Davis 2467

OF

1. Johnny Mostil 2561	1. Thurman Tucker 2.9	1. Fielder Jones 150
2. Minnie Minoso 2514	2. Chet Lemon 2.8	2. Shano Collins 128
3. Jim Landis 2511	3. Mike Kreevich 2.8	3. Happy Felsch 116
4. Fielder Jones 2432	4. Johnny Mostil 2.8	3. Bibb Falk 116
5. Mike Kreevich 2229	5. Happy Felsch 2.6	5. Minnie Minoso 106

C

1. Ray Schalk 7164	1. Ed Herrmann 5.3	1. Ray Schalk 1811
2. Sherm Lollar 5883	2. Carlton Fisk 5.0	2. Billy Sullivan 1217
3. Billy Sullivan 4455	3. Brian Downing 5.0	3. Mike Tresh 567
4. Mike Tresh 3890	4. Sherm Lollar 4.7	4. Sherm Lollar 537
5. Ed Herrmann 3240	5. Billy Sullivan 4.3	5. Buck Crouse 385

P

1. Ed Walsh 232	1. Nick Altrock 8	1. Ed Walsh 1203
2. Ted Lyons 219	2. Nixey Callahan 7	2. Red Faber 1108
3. Doc White 214	3. Doc White 6	3. Ted Lyons 945
4. Joe Horlen 154	4. Patsy Flaherty 6	4. Doc White 807
5. Nick Altrock 152	5. Frank Smith 5	5. Eddie Cicotte 706

Lifetime Fielding Leaders

ASSISTS PER GAME		DOUBLE PLAYS		CHANCES	
1B					
1. Jiggs Donahue	.8	1. Joe Kuhel	737	1. Earl Sheely	10082
2. Frank Isbell	.7	2. Earl Sheely	680	2. Joe Kuhel	9003
3. Shano Collins	.6	3. Zeke Bonura	476	3. Jiggs Donahue	7834
4. Bud Clancy	.6	4. Tom McCraw	446	4. Frank Isbell	7217
5. Earl Sheely	.6	5. Eddie Robinson	393	5. Tom McCraw	5914
2B					
1. Jackie Hayes	3.4	1. Nellie Fox	1499	1. Nellie Fox	11694
2. Don Kolloway	3.0	2. Eddie Collins	836	2. Eddie Collins	9244
3. Cass Michaels	3.0	3. Jackie Hayes	545	3. Jackie Hayes	4493
4. Eddie Collins	3.0	4. Jorge Orta	414	4. Jorge Orta	3322
5. Nellie Fox	2.8	5. Don Kolloway	393	5. Don Kolloway	3211
3B					
1. Lee Tannehill	2.4	1. Willie Kamm	210	1. Willie Kamm	4093
2. Bill Melton	2.3	2. Bill Melton	181	2. Bill Melton	2833
3. Buck Weaver	2.1	3. Floyd Baker	94	3. Lee Tannehill	2533
4. Pete Ward	2.1	4. Pete Ward	87	4. Pete Ward	1749
5. Floyd Baker	2.1	5. Lee Tannehill	84	5. Buck Weaver	1543
SS					
1. Lee Tannehill	3.5	1. Luke Appling	1424	1. Luke Appling	12259
2. George Davis	3.4	2. Luis Aparicio	943	2. Luis Aparicio	7825
3. Luis Aparicio	3.3	3. Chico Carrasquel	540	3. Buck Weaver	4759
4. Luke Appling	3.3	4. Ron Hansen	408	4. George Davis	4202
5. Bucky Dent	3.3	5. Buck Weaver	348	5. Chico Carrasquel	4177
OF					
1. Nemo Leibold	.2	1. Fielder Jones	44	1. Johnny Mostil	2741
2. Happy Felsch	.2	2. Happy Felsch	41	2. Minnie Minoso	2692
3. Shano Collins	.1	3. Shano Collins	32	3. Fielder Jones	2655
4. Ping Bodie	.1	4. Bibb Falk	31	4. Jim Landis	2599
5. Harry Hooper	.1	5. Harry Hooper	25	5. Bibb Falk	2354
C					
1. Billy Sullivan	1.2	1. Ray Schalk	221	1. Ray Schalk	9150
2. Ray Schalk	1.1	2. Billy Sullivan	98	2. Sherm Lollar	6466
3. Buck Crouse	.9	3. Sherm Lollar	79	3. Billy Sullivan	5806
4. Luke Sewell	.7	4. Mike Tresh	69	4. Mike Tresh	4535
5. Mike Tresh	.6	5. Ed Herrmann	51	5. Ed Herrmann	3627
P					
1. Nixey Callahan	3.1	1. Ted Lyons	57	1. Ed Walsh	1490
2. Nick Altrock	3.0	2. Red Faber	33	2. Red Faber	1309
3. Ned Garvin	2.9	3. Ed Walsh	32	3. Ted Lyons	1215
4. Ed Walsh	2.8	4. Eddie Cicotte	29	4. Doc White	1060
5. Patsy Flaherty	2.8	5. Billy Pierce	27	5. Eddie Cicotte	833

The White Sox and Their Players Year-by-Year

This section is a chronological listing of every White Sox season through 1983. All format information and abbreviations are explained below.

ROSTER INFORMATION

POS	Fielding Position	R	Runs
B	Bats B(oth), L(eft), or R(ight)	RBI	Runs Batted In
		BB	Bases on Balls
G	Games	SO	Strikeouts
AB	At Bats	SB	Stolen Bases
H	Hits		
2B	Doubles	*Pinch-Hit*	
3B	Triples	AB	Pinch-Hit At Bats
HR	Home Runs	H	Pinch Hits
HR%	Home Run Percentage (the number of home runs per 100 times at bat)	BA	Batting Average
		SA	Slugging Average

Regulars. The men who appear first on the team roster are considered the regulars for that team at the positions indicated. There are several factors for determining regulars of which "most games played at a position" and "most fielding chances at a position," are the two prime considerations.

Substitutes. Appearing directly beneath the regulars are the substitutes for the team. Substitutes are listed by position: first infielders, then outfielders, then catchers. Within these areas, substitutes are listed in order of most at bats, and can be someone who played most of the team's games as a regular, but not at one position. The rules for determining the listed positions of substitutes are as follows:

One Position Substitutes. If a man played at least 70% of his games in the field at one position, then he is listed only at that position, except for outfielders, where all three outfield positions are included under one category.

Two Position Substitutes. If a man did not play at least 70% of his games in the field at one position, but did play more than 90% of his total games at two positions, then he is shown with a combination fielding position. For example, if a player has an "S2" shown in his position column, it would mean that he played at least 90% of his games at shortstop and second base. These combinations are always indicated by the first letter or number of the position. The position listed first is where the most games were played.

Utility Players. If a player has a "UT" shown in his position column, it means that he did not meet the above 70% or 90% requirement and is listed as a utility player.

Pinch Hitters. Men who played no games in the field are considered pinch hitters and are listed as "PH."

Individual League Leaders. (Applies to batting, fielding, and pitching.) Statistics that appear in bold-faced print indicate the player led or tied for the league lead in the particular statistical category.

Traded League Leaders. (Applies to batting, fielding, and pitching.) An asterisk (*) next to a particular figure indicates that the player led the league that year in the particular statistical category, but since he played for more than one team, the figure does not necessarily represent his league-leading total or average.

Meaningless Averages. Indicated by use of a dash (-). In batting, the dash may appear in averages. This means that the player had no official at bats even though he played in at least one game. A batting average of .000 would mean he had at least one at bat with no hits. In pitching, the dash may appear in winning percentage. This means that the pitcher never had a decision even though he pitched in at least one game. A percentage of .000 would mean that he had at least one loss.

Anytime the symbol "infinity" (∞) is shown for a pitching average, it means that the pitcher allowed at least one earned run, hit, or base on balls without retiring a batter.

INDIVIDUAL FIELDING INFORMATION

T	Throws L(eft) or R(ight)	E	Errors
	(blank if not available)	DP	Double Plays
G	Games	TC/G	Total Chances per
PO	Putouts		Game
A	Assists	FA	Fielding Average

Each man's fielding record is shown for each position he played during the year. Fielding information for pitchers is not included.

TEAM AND LEAGUE INFORMATION

W	Wins	*Fielding*	
L	Losses	E	Errors
PCT	Winning Percentage	DP	Double Plays
GB	Games Behind the League Leader	FA	Fielding Average
R	Runs Scored		
OR	Opponents' Runs (Runs Scored Against)	*Pitching*	
		CG	Complete Games
		BB	Bases on Balls
Batting		SO	Strikeouts
2B	Doubles	ShO	Shutouts
3B	Triples	SV	Saves
HR	Home Runs	ERA	Earned Run Average
BA	Batting Average		
SA	Slugging Average		
SB	Stolen Bases		

Team League Leaders. Statistics that appear in bold-faced print indicate the team led or tied for the league lead in the particular statistical category. When teams are tied for league lead, the figures for all teams who tied are shown in boldface.

INDIVIDUAL PITCHING INFORMATION

T	Throws R(ight) or L(eft)	BB	Bases on Balls Allowed
W	Wins	SO	Strikeouts
L	Losses	R	Runs Allowed
PCT	Winning Percentage	ER	Earned Runs Allowed
ERA	Earned Run Average	ShO	Shutouts
SV	Saves	H/9	Hits Allowed Per 9 Innings Pitched
G	Games Pitched		
GS	Games Started	BB/9	Bases on Balls Allowed Per 9 Innings Pitched
CG	Complete Games		
IP	Innings Pitched	SO/9	Strikeouts Per 9 Innings Pitched
H	Hits Allowed		

The abbreviations for the teams appear as listed below.

BAL	Baltimore	MIN	Minnesota
BOS	Boston	NY	New York
CAL	California	OAK	Oakland
CHI	Chicago	PHI	Philadelphia
CLE	Cleveland	SEA	Seattle
DET	Detroit	STL	St. Louis
KC	Kansas City	TEX	Texas
LA	Los Angeles	TOR	Toronto
MIL	Milwaukee	WAS	Washington

BEFORE THE BEGINNING

Two singular, strong-willed men of principle founded the American League in 1899. Convinced that the National League could finally be challenged, Byron Bancroft Johnson and Charles Albert Comiskey renamed their obscure little Western League the "American League" on October 11, 1899. It was a grandiose gesture that must have caused some chuckles among the National League power bloc. The new American League was not seen as a serious threat; Cap Anson, Chris Von Der Ahe, and brewer Adolph Busch were attempting to revive the corpse of the American Association. With big money and some big names backing them up, this rival group of St. Louis sportsmen seemed the better bet to start a second league.

When Ban Johnson called his league together for a meeting at the Great Northern Hotel in Chicago, the National League was ready to placate him. In Johnson, they saw a man they thought they could control. His three requests were modest: the right to relocate the St. Paul team to Chicago under the aegis of Charles Comiskey, the right to retain players in the Western League two full seasons before they became subject to the National League draft, and an increase in payment to the Western League from $500 to $1,000. Since Johnson agreed to abide by the terms of the National Agreement, the older league was receptive.

Johnson was content to wait, because he suspected that Anson's group was mere bluster. Passing through Chicago, Milwaukee Brewer manager Connie Mack gave his views on the second-league rumors. "I'm not interested in the scheme in any way," he said of Anson and his colleagues. "But the time is ripe for a second strong organization. Properly managed, it ought to prove a success."

By 1899, the National League was weak and corrupt. Frank Robison and Harry Vonderhorst owned four teams between them. The aging and ineffectual Nicholas Young was a president in name only. He was powerless as Robison stripped the Cleveland Spiders of their best players simply because he thought his St. Louis Cardinals were in a better market. The Spiders lost 134 games in 1899 and then disappeared altogether.

The National League believed that Anson's St. Louis group posed a legitimate threat to its monopoly. With the memory of the costly American Association war of the 1880s in mind, John T. Brush summoned Ban Johnson to Indianapolis for a high-level meeting. For years Brush had been a Johnson detractor. At the National League meeting in 1897, Brush had flatly refused to consider Johnson's request for the two-year draft freeze and the $1,000 payment to Western League clubs. But things were different in 1899. Brush told Johnson that the National League would allow him to buy up the vacated Cleveland property for $10,000. At their meeting of October 11, W.F. Golt of Indianapolis resolved that the name of the league should be the American League. It was rapidly adopted.

Anson's dream of a second American Association fizzled. Johnson meanwhile pushed ahead his plan to help Comiskey move his financially strapped St. Paul club to Chicago. Whether another baseball war would result from the move was entirely up to James Hart, owner of the west side Chicago White Stockings of the National League.

Hart declared that it would violate the spirit of the National Agreement and erode his profit base if there were a second Chicago team. This was quite a reversal of form, since Hart himself had petitioned for a Western League team in 1894. In his letter to Johnson that year, he argued that a Western League franchise in Chicago would afford South Siders the chance to see baseball at popular prices. He was turned down by Johnson, who didn't want to see any of his teams used as a "farm" by the National League.

A series of conferences was held between Hart, Comiskey, and Johnson during the week of March 13, 1900. Hart's arguments against Johnson and his league didn't wash, and he knew it. Since Johnson didn't make any indication of his larger plans, Hart signed the agreement that landed the White Sox in Chicago on March 21, 1900. Hart had only one timid request: Please don't use the name Chicago in any club dealings. Comiskey agreed, but nothing was said about the nickname, so they too became the White Stockings (until 1902, when headline writers shortened it to the White Sox). By contrast, Hart's nameless aggregation was dubbed the "Orphans" by the Chicago press.

Comiskey secured loans from the First National Bank and sold stock to raise enough capital to purchase a tract of land at 39th and Wentworth on the city's South Side. The grounds once belonged to the Chicago Wanderers, a cricket team that had long since abandoned the property. The wooden grandstand featured an overhanging roof along the baselines, with a total seating capacity of 5,000. Despite being a minor-league attraction, the White Stockings drew well. Comiskey charged just twenty-five cents admission, and sponsored such blue collar promotions as Railway Workers Day. He understood his clientele, something that his crosstown rivals never did. The sweat, the stench, the grit of the South Side produced a singular character that separated White Sox fans from all others.

Encouraged by the 1900 success, Johnson pressed forward his secret plan for war on the National League. When the National League players presented a list of grievances against management, the owners locked them out. Their demands were tame: they merely wanted a moratorium on suspensions, a review of the reserve system, and the right to a release if the owners breached their contracts. But Charles Ebbets and his cronies took a hard line. Delegations of unhappy players turned to Ban Johnson and his new league.

Johnson induced them to jump their contracts with the promise that the American League would be square with them and grant concessions that the Nationals refused to even discuss. With the backing of Cleveland coal magnate Charles Somers, Johnson pushed into Boston and Philadelphia. The terms of the National Agreement expired in 1901, and the war was officially on.

By offering generous pay raises and modifications in the reserve clause, Johnson was able to induce 74 rostered players from the National League to jump contract. Their drafting policy called for an allotment of four players to each AL club, and Comiskey seized the moment. He signed three of Hart's Orphans: pitchers Clark Griffith and Jimmy Callahan, and outfielder Sam Mertes. Griffith tried to induce Honus Wagner to jump, but settled for Boston catcher Billy Sullivan. Johnson had outflanked the National League, and Comiskey had outflanked Johnson. Other AL magnates grumbled about an emerging Chicago dynasty and the cronyism that seemed to exist between league president and Chicago owner. Both men enjoyed the pleasures of Mercer, Wisconsin, and Comiskey's palatial estate there. Both men had offices in the same building, and both men kept one ear to the ground. But Johnson was sensitive to the charge that he had gone soft on wayfaring Chicago players. The legendary Johnson-Comiskey feud began sometime during the 1901–1902 war.

Comiskey's views on the battle with the National League were radical. Where Johnson favored peaceful coexistence and healthy competition, the "Old Roman" believed that the American League should use the opportunity to stamp out the Nationals. Torn by the shenanigans of New York Giants' owner Andrew Freedman and the exodus of their top stars, the National League teetered on the brink of extinction. We will never know how close to that it came, but it is known that John T. Brush came to Chicago after the 1901 season, registering at the Great Northern under an assumed name.

Brush met with Johnson secretly to discuss a "peace plan" that was more of a sellout than anything else. The Cincinnati magnate was allied with Andrew Freedman and Arthur Soden in what was known as the anti-Spalding faction of the National League. Under their plan, Brush was authorized to arrange a consolidation of the American League with the New York and Cincinnati clubs. Brush further proposed that the rival teams in St. Louis and Boston merge under the American League banner, thus dealing a final, telling blow to the National League. If all this was unacceptable to Johnson, Freedman and Brush stood ready to purchase the Cleveland and Baltimore teams. It was an amazing reversal of form for the one-time National League hardliners.

Stung by his memory of the results of the 1890 "Brotherhood War" and the capitulation of the American Association in 1891, Comiskey harbored some old grudges. He pushed for immediate adoption of the Soden-Freedman-Brush plan. But Johnson saw major problems. Allowing Freedman and his Tammany Hall connections into the American League would bring the same problems into the new league as had existed in the old one. Johnson also realized that consolidation in St. Louis and Boston would open up the territory for future interlopers. (This very thing happened in 1914 when James Gilmore began the Federal League.)

Johnson's answer to Brush was no. It was not his intention to wipe out the National League, just to gain equal footing with them. Comiskey could not be placated. This was the first rift in their friendship, one that intensified in 1901, when Johnson blacklisted Fred Shugart for slugging umpire Jack Sheridan. In 1905 he suspended outfielder Ducky Holmes for threatening umpire Silk O'Laughlin, and a host of other petty squabbles followed, culminating in the John Picus Quinn case of 1918.

Hindsight tells us that Johnson acted with good sense. Peace with the National League was finally reached on January 10, 1903. Johnson agreed to stay out of existing National League territory in return for recognition of his New York Highlander team, which had just moved from Baltimore. The young American League had flexed some muscle and had won the power struggle that seemed like a hopeless fight in 1899. In Chicago, Comiskey went to work on his White Sox team. With a group of influential friends known as the White Sox Rooter Association, he established some important political, social, and economic connections in Chicago. In return for their civic support, he wined and dined them at his Mercer resort. Player, manager, and mogul, the Chicago White Sox story is really Charles Comiskey's. Who could foresee in 1901 that the baseball empire he was building would tumble down in twenty years due to his own avarice and greed?

Chicago 1901   Won 83 Lost 53 Pct. .610 1st

MANAGER	W	L	PCT
Clark Griffith	83	53	.610

POS	Player	B	G	AB	H	2B	3B	HR	HR%	R	RBI	BB	SO	SB	Pinch Hit AB	Pinch Hit H	BA	SA
REGULARS																		
1B	Frank Isbell	L	137	556	143	15	8	3	0.5	93	70	36		52	0	0	.257	.329
2B	Sam Mertes	R	137	545	151	16	17	5	0.9	94	98	52		46	0	0	.277	.396
SS	Frank Shugart	L	107	415	104	9	12	2	0.5	62	47	28		12	0	0	.251	.345
3B	Fred Hartman		120	473	146	23	13	3	0.6	77	89	25		31	1	1	.309	.431
RF	Fielder Jones	L	133	521	177	16	3	2	0.4	120	65	84		38	0	0	.340	.393
CF	Dummy Hoy	L	132	527	155	28	11	2	0.4	112	60	86		27	0	0	.294	.400
LF	Herm McFarland	L	132	473	130	21	9	4	0.8	83	59	75		33	0	0	.275	.383
C	Billy Sullivan	R	98	367	90	15	6	4	1.1	54	56	10		12	0	0	.245	.351
SUBSTITUTES																		
S3	Jimmy Burke	R	42	148	39	5	0	0	0.0	20	21	12		11	0	0	.264	.297
P3	Nixey Callahan	R	45	118	39	7	3	1	0.8	15	19	10		10	10	3	.331	.466
2B	Dave Brain	R	5	20	7	1	0	0	0.0	2	5	1		0	0	0	.350	.400
OF	Pop Foster	B	12	35	10	2	2	1	2.9	4	6	4		0	3	1	.286	.543
C	Joe Sugden	B	48	153	42	7	1	0	0.0	21	19	13		4	2	0	.275	.333
PITCHERS																		
P	Roy Patterson	R	41	117	26	1	0	1	0.9	17	12	7		0	0	0	.222	.256
P	Clark Griffith	R	35	89	27	3	1	2	2.2	21	14	23		0	0	0	.303	.427
P	John Katoll	R	27	80	10	1	1	1	1.3	7	8	4		2	0	0	.125	.200
P	Erwin Harvey		17	40	10	3	1	0	0.0	11	3	2		1	1	0	.250	.375
P	John Skopec	L	9	30	10	0	1	1	3.3	4	4	1		1	0	0	.333	.500
P	Wiley Piatt	L	7	17	2	0	0	0	0.0	2	1	2		0	0	0	.118	.118
P	John McAleese	R	1	1	0	0	0	0	0.0	0	0	0		0	0	0	.000	.000
P	Frank Dupee		1	0	0	0	0	0	—	0	0	0		0	0	0	—	—
TEAM TOTAL				4725	1318	173	89	32	0.7	819	656	475		280	17	5	.279	.374

INDIVIDUAL FIELDING

POS	Player	T	G	PO	A	E	DP	TCG	FA	POS	Player	T	G	PO	A	E	DP	TCG	FA
1B	F. Isbell	R	137	**1387**	101	31	79	11.1	.980	OF	H. McFarland	R	132	283	14	17	3	2.4	.946
	J. Sugden	R	5	21	2	0	0	4.6	1.000		D. Hoy	R	132	278	16	13	6	2.3	.958
2B	S. Mertes	R	132	337	396	47	54	5.9	.940		F. Jones	R	133	216	20	16	5	1.9	.937
	D. Brain	R	5	14	16	3	4	6.6	.909		S. Mertes	R	5	20	0	0	0	4.0	1.000
	F. Isbell	R	2	1	2	0	0	1.5	1.000		P. Foster	R	9	9	1	1	0	1.2	.909
	N. Callahan	R	2	1	0	1	0	1.0	.500	C	B. Sullivan	R	97	396	104	17	13	5.3	**.967**
SS	F. Shugart	R	107	223	338	73	32	5.9	.885		J. Sugden	R	42	179	47	7	4	5.5	.970
	J. Burke	R	31	56	94	23	10	5.6	.867										
	F. Isbell	R	1	1	1	0	0	2.0	1.000										
3B	F. Hartman	R	119	151	263	49	15	3.9	.894										
	J. Burke	R	11	17	31	8	0	5.1	.857										
	N. Callahan	R	6	7	10	3	2	3.3	.850										
	F. Isbell	R	1	0	2	1	0	3.0	.667										
	B. Sullivan	R	1	0	0	2	0	2.0	.000										

Chicago 1901

In the year the American League became officially "major," the White Sox won their second pennant in a row. Clark Griffith was given shares of the White Sox stock as an added inducement to pitch for and manage the 1901 edition. He won 24 that year, the first coming on April 28, when he beat Cleveland 13–1. More American League firsts for the Sox: they lost the first forfeited game on May 2, when they stalled for darkness during a game with Detroit; the first official no-hitter was recorded against them by Cleveland pitcher Earl Moore on May 9, in Cleveland. Unfortunately for Moore, the Sox won a 4–2, ten-inning decision.

Violence against umpires continued in 1901. In the heat of the pennant race, pitcher Jack Katoll threw a ball at umpire Haskell's shins during a loss to the Senators. Frank Shugart then punched Haskell in the mouth, and a police escort was required to keep the Washington fans away from the belligerent Sox. These incidents were the fallout of years of National League tolerance of threats against the umpires.

No matter, though, the Sox clinched their second pennant on September 21, despite going winless in second-place Boston's ballpark. The year was a financial success for Comiskey; his upstarts drew 354,350 fans, over 150,000 more than Hart's National League Chicago "Orphans."

TEAM STATISTICS

	W	L	PCT	GB	R	OR	2B	3B	HR	BA	SA	SB	E	DP	FA	CG	BB	SO	ShO	SV	ERA
CHI	83	53	.610		819	632	173	89	32	.276	.370	280	345	100	.941	110	312	394	11	2	2.98
BOS	79	57	.581	4	759	608	183	104	37	.278	.381	157	337	104	.943	123	294	396	7	1	3.04
DET	74	61	.548	8.5	742	696	180	80	29	.279	.370	204	410	127	.930	118	313	307	8	2	3.30
PHI	74	62	.544	9	805	760	239	87	35	.289	.395	173	337	93	.942	124	374	350	6	1	4.00
BAL	68	65	.511	13.5	761	750	179	111	24	.294	.397	207	401	76	.926	115	344	271	4	5	3.73
WAS	61	73	.455	21	683	771	191	83	34	.269	.365	127	323	97	.943	118	284	308	8	1	4.09
CLE	55	82	.401	28.5	666	831	197	68	12	.271	.348	125	329	99	.942	122	464	334	7	3	4.12
MIL	48	89	.350	35.5	641	828	192	66	26	.261	.345	176	393	106	.934	107	395	376	3	4	4.06
LEAGUE TOTAL					5876	5876	1534	688	229	.277	.371	1449	2875	802	.938	937	2780	2736	54	19	3.66

INDIVIDUAL PITCHING

PITCHER	T	W	L	PCT	ERA	SV	G	GS	CG	IP	H	BB	SO	R	ER	ShO	H9	BB9	SO9
Roy Patterson	R	20	16	.556	3.37	0	41	35	30	312.1	345	62	127	164	117	4	9.94	1.79	3.66
Clark Griffith	R	24	7	.774	2.67	1	35	30	26	266.2	275	50	67	114	79	5	9.28	1.69	2.26
Nixey Callahan	R	15	8	.652	2.42	0	27	22	20	215.1	195	50	70	94	58	1	8.15	2.09	2.93
John Katoll	R	11	11	.500	2.81	0	27	25	19	208	231	53	59	126	65	0	10.00	2.29	2.55
Erwin Harvey	L	3	6	.333	3.62	1	16	9	5	92	91	34	27	59	37	0	8.90	3.33	2.64
John Skopec	L	6	3	.667	3.16	0	9	9	6	68.1	62	45	24	39	24	0	8.17	5.93	3.16
Wiley Piatt	L	4	2	.667	2.79	0	7	6	4	51.2	42	14	19	29	16	1	7.32	2.44	3.31
John McAleese	R	0	0	–	9.00	0	1	0	0	3	7	1	1	3	3	0	21.00	3.00	3.00
Frank Isbell	R	0	0	–	9.00	0	1	0	0	1	2	0	0	1	1	0	18.00	0.00	0.00
TEAM TOTAL		83	53	.610	2.95	2	164	136	110	1218.1	1250	309	394	629	400	11	9.23	2.28	2.91

Chicago 1902   Won 74 Lost 60 Pct. .552 4th

MANAGER	W	L	PCT
Clark Griffith	74	60	.552

POS	Player	B	G	AB	H	2B	3B	HR	HR%	R	RBI	BB	SO	SB	Pinch Hit AB	Pinch Hit H	BA	SA
REGULARS																		
1B	Frank Isbell	L	137	520	133	14	4	4	0.8	65	59	14		38	0	0	.256	.321
2B	Tom Daly	B	137	489	110	22	3	1	0.2	57	54	55		19	0	0	.225	.288
SS	George Davis	B	132	485	145	27	7	3	0.6	76	93	65		31	1	1	.299	.402
3B	Sammy Strang	B	137	536	158	18	5	3	0.6	108	46	76		38	0	0	.295	.364
RF	Danny Green	L	129	481	150	16	11	0	0.0	77	62	53		35	0	0	.312	.391
CF	Fielder Jones	L	135	532	171	16	5	0	0.0	98	54	57		33	0	0	.321	.370
LF	Sam Mertes	R	129	497	140	23	7	1	0.2	60	79	37		46	0	0	.282	.362
C	Billy Sullivan	R	76	263	64	12	3	1	0.4	36	26	6		11	2	0	.243	.323
SUBSTITUTES																		
PO	Nixey Callahan	R	70	218	51	7	2	0	0.0	27	13	6		4	12	2	.234	.284
OF	Herm McFarland	L	9	29	5	0	0	0	0.0	5	4	2		1	2	0	.172	.172
PO	Jimmy Durham	R	5	15	1	0	0	0	0.0	3	0	2		0	0	0	.067	.067
C	Ed McFarland	R	73	244	56	9	2	1	0.4	29	25	19		8	2	0	.230	.295
C	Ed Hughes		1	4	1	0	0	0	0.0	0	0	0		0	0	0	.250	.250
PITCHERS																		
P	Roy Patterson	R	34	105	20	1	0	0	0.0	11	6	3		0	0	0	.190	.200
P	Clark Griffith	R	35	92	20	3	0	0	0.0	11	8	7		0	4	0	.217	.250
P	Wiley Piatt	L	32	85	17	2	1	0	0.0	12	6	6		1	0	0	.200	.247
P	Ned Garvin		23	59	9	0	0	0	0.0	3	2	2		0	0	0	.153	.153
P	Dummy Leitner	L	1	3	0	0	0	0	0.0	0	0	1		0	0	0	.000	.000
P	John Katoll	R	1	1	0	0	0	0	0.0	0	0	0		0	0	0	.000	.000
P	Sam McMackin		1	1	0	0	0	0	0.0	0	0	0		0	0	0	.000	.000
TEAM TOTAL				4659	1251	170	50	14	0.3	678	537	411		265	23	3	.269	.335

INDIVIDUAL FIELDING

POS	Player	T	G	PO	A	E	DP	TCG	FA	POS	Player	T	G	PO	A	E	DP	TCG	FA
1B	F. Isbell	R	133	1401	93	21	97	11.4	.986	OF	F. Jones	R	135	323	25	10	11	2.7	.972
	G. Davis	R	3	13	1	0	2	4.7	1.000		S. Mertes	R	120	223	26	21	5	2.3	.922
	S. Mertes	R	1	10	1	0	1	11.0	1.000		D. Green		129	217	11	14	4	1.9	.942
	B. Sullivan	R	2	11	0	0	2	5.5	1.000		N. Callahan	R	23	33	1	1	0	1.5	.971
	E. McFarland	R	1	9	0	0	0	9.0	1.000		H. McFarland	R	7	13	0	0	0	1.9	1.000
2B	T. Daly	R	137	312	370	31	70	5.2	.957		J. Durham	R	2	2	0	1	0	1.5	.667
	S. Mertes	R	1	6	2	0	1	8.0	1.000		C. Griffith	R	3	3	0	0	0	1.0	1.000
SS	G. Davis	R	129	289	427	37	72	5.8	.951		B. Sullivan	R	2	1	0	0	0	0.5	1.000
	S. Mertes	R	5	17	15	0	2	6.4	1.000	C	E. McFarland	R	69	282	71	12	7	5.3	.967
	F. Isbell	R	4	4	7	1	3	3.0	.917		B. Sullivan	R	70	242	81	11	8	4.8	.967
	N. Callahan	R	1	3	1	0	0	4.0	1.000		E. Hughes	R	1	5	2	2	0	9.0	.778
3B	S. Strang	R	137	170	334	62	21	4.1	.890		S. Mertes	R	2	3	0	1	0	2.0	.750
	S. Mertes	R	1	4	1	1	0	6.0	.833		F. Isbell	R	1	0	2	0	0	2.0	1.000

Chicago 1902

Comiskey continued his raids on the National League. The Old Roman landed slick-fielding shortstop George Davis, as well as Sammy Strang, Danny Green, Ed McFarland, and Tom Daly. On paper, this team appeared stronger than the 1901 champs, but after building up a comfortable five-game lead on July 13, they suffered a sharp decline that dropped them to fourth place on August 29.

In a bold move designed to regain top stars for the National League, Orioles manger John McGraw sold his interest in the team to John Brush, who promptly released seven players, including Iron Man McGinnity and Joe Kelley. The Orioles were restocked with fourteen players, including Jack Katoll and Herm McFarland of the Sox. When the O's appeared at the 39th Street Grounds on August 2, Sox fans held a banner aloft that said, "Kelley and McGraw? Haw! Haw! They're gone you say? God bless the day!"

Baseball was still in its rough and tumble days, and ballplayers could be a bit uncivilized at times. Sox pitcher Jimmy Callahan was arrested in a Cleveland hotel after he slugged a bellhop in the mouth for slow service. Fielder Jones kicked umpire Bob Caruthers in the shins on September 21 after being called out on strikes. The ump pulled out a stopwatch and said, "Mr. Jones, you have exactly one minute to leave the field!" Jones scowled and walked away. Was it any coincidence that these two men were to be the next two Sox managers?

TEAM STATISTICS

	W	L	PCT	GB	R	OR	2B	3B	HR	BA	SA	SB	E	DP	FA	CG	BB	SO	ShO	SV	ERA
PHI	83	53	.610		775	636	235	67	38	.287	.389	201	270	75	.953	114	368	455	5	2	3.29
STL	78	58	.574	5	619	607	208	61	29	.265	.353	137	274	122	.953	120	343	348	7	3	3.34
BOS	77	60	.562	6.5	664	600	195	95	42	.278	.383	132	263	101	.955	123	326	431	6	1	3.02
CHI	74	60	.552	8	675	602	170	50	14	.268	.335	265	257	125	.955	116	331	346	11	0	3.41
CLE	69	67	.507	14	686	667	248	68	33	.289	.389	140	287	96	.950	116	411	361	16	3	3.28
WAS	61	75	.449	22	709	790	261	66	48	.283	.396	121	316	70	.945	130	312	300	2	1	4.36
DET	52	83	.385	30.5	566	657	141	55	22	.251	.320	130	332	111	.943	116	370	245	9	4	3.56
BAL	50	88	.362	34	715	850	202	107	33	.277	.385	189	357	109	.938	119	354	258	3	0	4.33
LEAGUE TOTAL					5409	5409	1660	569	259	.275	.369	1315	2356	809	.949	954	2815	2744	59	14	3.57

INDIVIDUAL PITCHING

PITCHER	T	W	L	PCT	ERA	SV	G	GS	CG	IP	H	BB	SO	R	ER	ShO	H9	BB9	SO9
Nixey Callahan	R	16	14	.533	3.60	0	35	31	29	282.1	287	89	75	150	113	2	9.15	2.84	2.39
Roy Patterson	R	20	12	.625	3.06	0	34	30	26	268	262	67	61	111	91	2	8.80	2.25	2.05
Wiley Piatt	L	12	13	.480	3.51	0	32	30	22	246	263	66	96	129	96	2	9.62	2.41	3.51
Clark Griffith	R	15	9	.625	4.19	0	28	24	20	212.2	247	47	51	117	99	3	10.45	1.99	2.16
Ned Garvin	R	9	10	.474	2.21	0	23	19	16	175.1	169	43	55	68	43	2	8.67	2.21	2.82
Jimmy Durham	R	1	1	.500	5.85	0	3	3	3	20	21	16	3	15	13	0	9.45	7.20	1.35
Sam Mertes	R	1	0	1.000	1.17	0	1	0	0	7.2	6	0	0	2	1	0	7.04	0.00	0.00
Dummy Leitner	R	0	0	–	13.50	0	1	0	0	4	9	2	0	7	6	0	20.25	4.50	0.00
Sam McMackin		0	0	–	0.00	0	1	0	0	3	1	0	2	1	0	0	3.00	0.00	6.00
Frank Isbell	R	0	1	.000	9.00	0	1	1	0	1	3	1	1	2	1	0	27.00	9.00	9.00
John Katoll	R	0	0	–	0.00	0	1	0	0	1	1	0	2	0	0	0	9.00	0.00	18.00
TEAM TOTAL		74	60	.552	3.41	0	160	138	116	1221	1269	331	346	602	463	11	9.35	2.44	2.55

Chicago 1903   Won 60 Lost 77 Pct. .438 7th

MANAGER	W	L	PCT
Nixey Callahan	60	77	.438

POS	Player	B	G	AB	H	2B	3B	HR	HR%	R	RBI	BB	SO	SB	Pinch Hit AB	H	BA	SA
REGULARS																		
1B	Frank Isbell	L	138	546	139	25	9	2	0.4	52	59	12		26	0	0	.255	.344
2B	George Magoon	R	94	334	76	11	3	0	0.0	32	25	30		4	0	0	.228	.278
SS	Lee Tannehill	R	138	503	113	14	3	2	0.4	48	50	25		10	0	0	.225	.276
3B	Nixey Callahan	R	118	439	128	26	5	2	0.5	47	56	20		24	5	3	.292	.387
RF	Danny Green	L	135	499	154	26	7	6	1.2	75	62	47		29	2	1	.309	.425
CF	Fielder Jones	L	136	530	152	18	5	0	0.0	71	45	47		21	0	0	.287	.340
LF	Ducky Holmes	L	86	344	96	7	5	0	0.0	53	18	25		25	2	0	.279	.328
C	Ed McFarland	R	61	201	42	7	2	1	0.5	15	19	14		3	4	1	.209	.279
SUBSTITUTES																		
2B	Tom Daly	B	43	150	31	11	0	0	0.0	20	19	20		6	0	0	.207	.280
1B	Cozy Dolan	L	27	104	27	5	1	0	0.0	16	7	6		5	4	0	.260	.327
3B	Pep Clark	R	15	65	20	4	2	0	0.0	7	9	2		5	0	0	.308	.431
OF	Bill Hallman		63	207	43	7	4	0	0.0	29	18	31		11	6	0	.208	.280
C	Jack Slattery	R	63	211	46	3	2	0	0.0	8	20	2		2	2	0	.218	.251
C	Billy Sullivan	R	32	111	21	4	0	1	0.9	10	7	5		3	1	0	.189	.252
PITCHERS																		
P	Roy Patterson	R	34	105	11	1	1	0	0.0	6	2	4		0	0	0	.105	.133
P	Patsy Flaherty	L	40	102	14	4	0	0	0.0	7	5	5		4	0	0	.137	.176
P	Doc White	L	38	99	20	3	0	0	0.0	10	5	19		1	0	0	.202	.232
P	Frank Owen		26	57	7	0	0	0	0.0	3	3	7		0	0	0	.123	.123
P	Davey Dunkle	B	12	33	10	0	0	0	0.0	1	4	1		0	0	0	.303	.303
P	Nick Altrock	B	13	30	9	0	0	0	0.0	6	3	3		1	1	0	.300	.300
	TEAM TOTAL			4670	1159	176	49	14	0.3	516	436	325		180	27	5	.248	.316

INDIVIDUAL FIELDING

POS	Player	T	G	PO	A	E	DP	TCG	FA	POS	Player	T	G	PO	A	E	DP	TCG	FA
1B	F. Isbell	R	117	1180	87	20	57	11.0	.984	OF	F. Jones	R	136	**324**	11	5	3	2.5	**.985**
	C. Dolan	L	19	218	16	7	7	12.7	.971		D. Green		133	219	16	17	**8**	1.9	.933
	J. Slattery	R	5	33	7	2	3	8.4	.952		D. Holmes	R	82	151	14*	6	0	2.1	.965
	E. McFarland	R	1	4	0	0	0	4.0	1.000		B. Hallman		57	114	7	6	0	2.2	.953
2B	G. Magoon	R	94	198	253	31	28	5.1	.936		C. Dolan	L	4	16	0	1	0	4.3	.941
	T. Daly	R	43	96	103	11	12	4.9	.948		N. Callahan	R	8	15	1	0	0	2.0	1.000
	F. Isbell	R	2	17	0	0	0	8.5	1.000		F. Isbell	R	1	3	0	0	0	3.0	1.000
SS	L. Tannehill	R	138	291	457	76	**58**	6.0	.908		D. White	L	1	2	0	0	0	2.0	1.000
	F. Isbell	R	1	0	0	0	0	0.0	.000	C	E. McFarland	R	56	240	65	10	7	5.6	.968
3B	N. Callahan	R	102	113	203	**37**	5	3.5	.895		J. Slattery	R	56	215	44	7	0	4.8	.974
	F. Isbell	R	19	25	49	15	1	4.7	.831		B. Sullivan	R	31	123	35	2	1	5.2	.988
	P. Clark	R	15	14	36	7	1	3.8	.877										
	D. Holmes	R	3	3	5	2	0	3.3	.800										

30

Chicago 1903

Jimmy Callahan was named the second White Sox manager on March 16 with a vote of confidence from Charles Comiskey: "He has the ability, and all it needs is development the right way." What a shame Callahan's on-the-job training came with the 1903 edition, a team bereft of talent following Griffith's defection to become manager of the new New York AL franchise, and George Davis's season-long holdout. Davis had jumped back to the National League following the 1902 season but was awarded to Comiskey as one of the terms of the peace agreement. John Brush swiped at Johnson again, allowing Davis to play in a game for the Giants. An injunction was filed against Davis and a countersuit was filed by Brush. The case was thrown out in District Court on July 15, and Davis spent the season at the Brighton Beach Racetrack.

The season wasn't a total washout, though. Contract jumper Guy Harris "Doc" White won his first game for the Sox on May 2. An off-season dentist, songwriter and evangelist, the soft-spoken White was a real bargain. Then, on June 30, the Sox batted about a gnome-like Boston pitcher named Nick Altrock. This one outing left the Boston club unimpressed. Altrock was claimed by the Sox a week later, and their "almost perfect" pitching staff was almost complete.

TEAM STATISTICS

	W	L	PCT	GB	R	OR	2B	3B	HR	BA	SA	SB	E	DP	FA	CG	BB	SO	ShO	SV	ERA
BOS	91	47	.659		707	505	222	113	48	.272	.392	141	239	86	.959	123	269	579	20	3	2.57
PHI	75	60	.556	14.5	597	519	228	68	31	.264	.362	157	217	66	.960	112	315	728	10	1	2.97
CLE	77	63	.550	15	639	578	231	95	31	.265	.373	175	322	99	.946	125	271	521	20	1	2.66
NY	72	62	.537	17	579	573	193	62	18	.249	.330	160	264	87	.953	111	245	463	7	1	3.08
DET	65	71	.478	25	567	539	162	91	12	.268	.351	128	281	82	.950	123	336	554	15	3	2.75
STL	65	74	.468	26.5	500	525	166	68	12	.244	.317	101	268	94	.953	124	237	511	12	4	2.77
CHI	60	77	.438	30.5	516	613	176	49	14	.247	.314	180	297	85	.949	114	287	391	9	2	3.02
WAS	43	94	.314	47.5	438	691	172	72	18	.231	.311	131	260	86	.954	122	306	452	6	2	3.82
LEAGUE TOTAL					4543	4543	1550	618	184	.255	.344	1173	2148	685	.953	954	2266	4199	99	17	2.95

INDIVIDUAL PITCHING

PITCHER	T	W	L	PCT	ERA	SV	G	GS	CG	IP	H	BB	SO	R	ER	ShO	H9	BB9	SO9
Doc White	L	17	16	.515	2.13	0	37	36	29	300	258	69	135	119	71	3	7.74	2.07	4.05
Patsy Flaherty	L	11	25	.306	3.74	0	40	34	29	293.2	338	50	65	173	122	2	10.36	1.53	1.99
Roy Patterson	R	14	15	.483	2.70	0	34	30	26	293	275	69	89	119	88	2	8.45	2.12	2.73
Frank Owen	R	8	12	.400	3.50	1	26	20	15	167.1	167	44	66	85	65	1	8.98	2.37	3.55
Davey Dunkle	R	5	4	.556	4.06	1	12	7	6	82	96	31	26	58	37	0	10.54	3.40	2.85
Nick Altrock	L	4	3	.571	2.15	0	12	8	6	71	59	19	19	35	17	1	7.48	2.41	2.41
Nixey Callahan	R	1	2	.333	4.50	0	3	3	3	28	40	5	12	24	14	0	12.86	1.61	3.86
TEAM TOTAL		60	77	.438	3.02	2	164	138	114	1235	1233	287	412	613	414	9	8.99	2.09	3.00

Chicago 1904   Won 89   Lost 65   Pct .578   3rd

MANAGER	W	L	PCT
Nixey Callahan	22	18	.550
Fielder Jones	67	47	.588

POS	Player	B	G	AB	H	2B	3B	HR	HR%	R	RBI	BB	SO	SB	Pinch Hit AB	Pinch Hit H	BA	SA
REGULARS																		
1B	Jiggs Donahue	L	102	367	91	9	7	1	0.3	46	48	25		18	1	1	.248	.319
2B	Gus Dundon		108	373	85	9	3	0	0.0	40	36	30		19	0	0	.228	.268
SS	George Davis	B	152	563	142	27	15	1	0.2	75	69	43		32	0	0	.252	.359
3B	Lee Tannehill	R	153	547	125	31	5	0	0.0	50	61	20		14	0	0	.229	.303
RF	Danny Green	L	147	536	142	16	10	2	0.4	83	62	63		28	1	0	.265	.343
CF	Fielder Jones	L	154	564	137	14	6	3	0.5	74	43	54		25	0	0	.243	.305
LF	Nixey Callahan	R	132	482	126	23	2	0	0.0	66	54	39		29	1	0	.261	.317
C	Billy Sullivan	R	108	371	85	18	4	1	0.3	29	44	12		11	1	0	.229	.307
SUBSTITUTES																		
12	Frank Isbell	L	96	314	66	10	3	1	0.3	27	34	16		19	3	0	.210	.271
OF	Ducky Holmes	L	68	251	78	11	9	1	0.4	42	19	14		13	5	2	.311	.438
OF	Frank Huelsman	R	4	7	1	1	0	0	0.0	0	0	0		0	3	0	.143	.286
C	Ed McFarland	R	50	160	44	11	3	0	0.0	22	20	17		2	1	1	.275	.381
C	Mike Heydon		4	10	1	1	0	0	0.0	0	1	1		0	0	0	.100	.200
C	Claude Berry	R	3	1	0	0	0	0	0.0	1	0	1		0	0	0	.000	.000
PITCHERS																		
P	Nick Altrock	B	38	111	22	1	0	1	0.9	13	8	4		0	0	0	.198	.234
P	Frank Owen		37	107	23	2	0	2	1.9	10	7	10		2	0	0	.215	.290
P	Doc White	L	33	76	12	2	0	0	0.0	7	2	10		3	0	0	.158	.184
P	Frank Smith	R	26	72	18	5	0	0	0.0	8	6	4		0	0	0	.250	.319
P	Roy Patterson	R	22	58	6	0	0	0	0.0	1	1	3		0	0	0	.103	.103
P	Ed Walsh	R	18	41	9	1	1	1	2.4	5	4	3		1	0	0	.220	.366
P	Patsy Flaherty	L	5	12	4	1	0	0	0.0	1	0	4		0	0	0	.333	.417
P	Elmer Stricklett	R	1	3	0	0	0	0	0.0	0	0	0		0	0	0	.000	.000
P	Tom Dougherty	L	1	1	0	0	0	0	0.0	0	0	0		0	0	0	.000	.000
TEAM TOTAL				5027	1217	193	68	14	0.3	600	519	373		216	16	4	.242	.316

INDIVIDUAL FIELDING

POS	Player	T	G	PO	A	E	DP	TCG	FA
1B	J. Donahue	L	101	1067	85	25	49	11.7	.979
	F. Isbell	R	57	599	48	9	22	11.5	.986
2B	G. Dundon	R	103	186	282	13	25	4.7	**.973**
	F. Isbell	R	27	53	80	11	6	5.3	.924
	N. Callahan	R	28	49	70	10	5	4.6	.922
SS	G. Davis	R	152	**347**	**514**	58	**62**	6.0	.937
	F. Isbell	R	4	6	17	5	1	7.0	.821
	G. Dundon	R	2	4	6	0	1	5.0	1.000
3B	L. Tannehill	R	153	180	**369**	31	**22**	3.8	.947
	G. Dundon	R	3	4	1	0	0	1.7	1.000

POS	Player	T	G	PO	A	E	DP	TCG	FA
OF	F. Jones	R	154	325	15	8	4	2.3	.977
	D. Green		146	231	13	9	5	1.7	.964
	N. Callahan	R	104	158	9	4	0	1.6	.977
	D. Holmes	R	63	111	8	3	3	1.9	.975
	F. Isbell	R	5	5	0	0	0	1.0	1.000
	D. White	L	2	4	0	0	0	2.0	1.000
	F. Huelsman	R	1	0	0	1	0	1.0	.000
C	B. Sullivan	R	107	463	**130**	22	10	5.7	.964
	E. McFarland	R	49	195	39	6	2	4.9	.975
	M. Heydon	R	4	16	5	0	1	5.3	1.000
	C. Berry	R	3	5	1	0	0	2.0	1.000

Chicago 1904

The White Sox' stay in the second division was short-lived. By adding two new players a year, Comiskey had altered the complexion of the team since the 1901 season. The team batting average dropped from a 1901 high of .276 to .242 in 1904. This was the first of the scrappy "Hitless Wonder" teams that etched their names into baseball history.

Two unproven pitchers turned up in spring training. One was piano mover Frank Smith, the other was a former "coal breaker" from Plains, Pennsylvania, Ed Walsh. What made Walsh so great was his total mastery of the spitball. He learned the pitch from a spring training prospect named Elmer Stricklett, who lost a game on April 22 and was never seen again. Walsh lasted considerably longer.

Callahan quit unexpectedly on June 5, deciding that the rigors of management distracted from his everyday play. Consistent with his policy of promotion from within the ranks, Comiskey named the little firebrand Fielder Jones as his next skipper. Under Jones the Sox played .588 ball the rest of the way.

The Sox' rise coincided with the maturity of Doc White. Thanks to his five consecutive shutouts in September, the team battled down to the wire with New York and Boston. The largest crowd in three years, some 30,004, watched Willie Keeler end White's scoreless streak on October 2 when he raced home in the first inning. The good Doctor then pitched shutout ball the next eight innings.

TEAM STATISTICS

	W	L	PCT	GB	R	OR	2B	3B	Batting HR	BA	SA	SB	E	Fielding DP	FA	CG	BB	Pitching SO	ShO	SV	ERA
BOS	95	59	.617		608	466	194	105	26	.247	.340	101	242	83	.962	148	233	612	21	0	2.12
NY	92	59	.609	1.5	598	526	195	91	26	.259	.347	163	275	90	.958	123	311	684	15	1	2.57
CHI	89	65	.578	6	600	482	193	68	14	.242	.316	216	238	95	.964	134	303	550	26	2	2.30
CLE	86	65	.570	7.5	647	482	225	90	27	.260	.354	178	255	86	.959	141	285	627	20	0	2.22
PHI	81	70	.536	12.5	557	503	197	77	31	.249	.336	137	250	67	.959	137	366	887	26	0	2.35
STL	65	87	.428	29	481	604	153	53	10	.239	.294	150	267	78	.960	135	333	577	13	1	2.83
DET	62	90	.408	32	505	627	154	69	11	.231	.292	112	273	92	.959	143	433	556	15	2	2.77
WAS	38	113	.252	55.5	437	743	171	57	10	.227	.288	150	314	97	.951	137	347	533	7	3	3.62
LEAGUE TOTAL					4433	4433	1482	610	155	.244	.321	1207	2114	688	.959	1098	2611	5026	143	9	2.60

INDIVIDUAL PITCHING

PITCHER	T	W	L	PCT	ERA	SV	G	GS	CG	IP	H	BB	SO	R	ER	ShO	H9	BB9	SO9
Frank Owen	R	21	15	.583	1.94	1	37	36	34	315	243	61	103	95	68	4	6.94	1.74	2.94
Nick Altrock	L	21	13	.618	2.96	0	38	36	31	307	274	48	87	117	101	6	8.03	1.41	2.55
Doc White	L	16	10	.615	1.71	0	30	30	23	237	201	68	115	82	45	7	7.63	2.58	4.37
Frank Smith	R	16	10	.615	2.09	0	26	23	22	202.1	157	58	107	62	47	4	6.98	2.58	4.76
Roy Patterson	R	9	9	.500	2.29	0	22	17	14	165	148	24	64	52	42	4	8.07	1.31	3.49
Ed Walsh	R	5	5	.500	2.60	1	18	8	6	110.2	90	32	57	45	32	1	7.32	2.60	4.64
Patsy Flaherty	L	1	2	.333	2.09	0	5	5	4	43	36	10	14	19	10	0	7.53	2.09	2.93
Elmer Stricklett	R	0	1	.000	10.29	0	1	1	0	7	12	2	3	10	8	0	15.43	2.57	3.86
Tom Dougherty	R	0	0	—	0.00	0	1	0	0	2	0	0	0	0	0	0	0.00	0.00	0.00
TEAM TOTAL		89	65	.578	2.29	2	178	156	134	1389	1161	303	550	482	353	26	7.52	1.96	3.56

Chicago 1905   Won 92 Lost 60 Pct. .605 2nd   34

MANAGER	W	L	PCT
Fielder Jones	92	60	.605

POS	Player	B	G	AB	H	2B	3B	HR	HR%	R	RBI	BB	SO	SB	Pinch Hit AB	Pinch Hit H	BA	SA
REGULARS																		
1B	Jiggs Donahue	L	149	533	153	22	4	1	0.2	71	76	44		32	0	0	.287	.349
2B	Gus Dundon		106	364	70	7	3	0	0.0	30	22	23		14	0	0	.192	.228
SS	George Davis	B	157	550	153	29	1	1	0.2	74	55	60		31	0	0	.278	.340
3B	Lee Tannehill	R	142	480	96	17	2	0	0.0	38	39	45		8	0	0	.200	.244
RF	Danny Green	L	112	379	92	13	6	0	0.0	56	44	53		11	5	0	.243	.309
CF	Fielder Jones	L	153	568	139	17	12	2	0.4	91	38	73		20	0	0	.245	.327
LF	Ducky Holmes	L	92	328	66	15	2	0	0.0	42	22	19		11	3	2	.201	.259
C	Billy Sullivan	R	99	323	65	10	3	2	0.6	25	26	13		14	3	0	.201	.269
SUBSTITUTES																		
UT	Frank Isbell	L	94	341	101	21	11	2	0.6	55	45	15		15	0	0	.296	.440
32	George Rohe	R	34	113	24	1	0	1	0.9	14	12	12		2	1	0	.212	.248
OF	Nixey Callahan	R	96	345	94	18	6	1	0.3	50	43	29		26	3	1	.272	.368
C	Ed McFarland	R	80	250	70	13	4	0	0.0	24	31	23		5	9	4	.280	.364
C	Hub Hart	L	10	17	2	0	0	0	0.0	2	4	3		0	4	1	.118	.118
PITCHERS																		
P	Frank Owen		42	124	18	2	0	0	0.0	8	4	5		2	0	0	.145	.161
P	Nick Altrock	B	41	114	14	1	0	0	0.0	8	5	6		0	1	0	.123	.132
P	Frank Smith	R	41	106	24	6	0	1	0.9	11	11	7		0	2	0	.226	.311
P	Doc White	L	37	86	14	4	1	0	0.0	7	7	4		3	0	0	.163	.233
P	Ed Walsh	R	29	58	9	2	0	0	0.0	5	2	4		0	2	0	.155	.190
P	Roy Patterson	R	13	30	8	2	0	0	0.0	2	1	1		0	0	0	.267	.333
	TEAM TOTAL			5109	1212	200	55	11	0.2	613	487	439		194	33	8	.237	.304

INDIVIDUAL FIELDING

POS	Player	T	G	PO	A	E	DP	TCG	FA		POS	Player	T	G	PO	A	E	DP	TCG	FA
1B	J. Donahue	L	149	1645	114	21	77	11.9	.988	OF		F. Jones	R	153	337	21	11	5	2.4	.970
	F. Isbell	R	9	68	14	1	4	9.2	.988			D. Holmes	R	89	150	11	11	1	1.9	.936
	B. Sullivan	R	2	15	0	0	2	7.5	1.000			D. Green		107	119	9	12	3	1.3	.914
	N. Altrock	L	1	4	0	0	0	4.0	1.000			N. Callahan	R	93	120	10	6	0	1.5	.956
2B	G. Dundon	R	104	218	321	12	23	5.3	.978			F. Isbell	R	40	65	5	4	1	1.9	.946
	F. Isbell	R	42	76	112	7	11	4.6	.964			E. Walsh	R	5	4	1	1	0	1.2	.833
	G. Rohe	R	16	31	40	5	7	4.8	.934			D. White	L	1	0	2	0	0	2.0	1.000
SS	G. Davis	R	157	330	501	46	56	5.6	.948	C		B. Sullivan	R	93	389	104	13	8	5.4	.974
	F. Isbell	R	2	10	5	1	2	8.0	.938			E. McFarland	R	70	343	88	12	8	6.3	.973
	G. Dundon	R	2	5	7	0	2	6.0	1.000			H. Hart	R	6	21	2	0	0	3.8	1.000
3B	L. Tannehill	R	142	168	358	39	17	4.0	.931											
	G. Rohe	R	17	16	32	1	3	2.9	.980											
	B. Sullivan	R	1	0	0	0	0	0.0	.000											

It was a winter of discord for Comiskey. James Hart refused to play the 1904 City Series with the White Sox because he believed that one of his pitchers, Jack Taylor, had thrown games to the Sox in the 1903 series. In a message to the National Commission, Comiskey said, "There must be no dishonest club owners or players. Our national game must be free from the slightest breath of suspicion. If one player in question is guilty, his expulsion is imperative."

The dark thoughts were pushed away as the Sox embroiled themselves in a torrid three-team pennant race with Philadelphia and Detroit. The lead changed hands on a daily basis that summer, as the big four of Frank Owen, Doc White, Nick Altrock, and Frank Smith (with a little help from apprentice Ed Walsh) carried the Sox hopes. There seemed no limit to the endurance of this pitching staff. In one six-day span in August, they played five doubleheaders against Philadelphia and Boston and came away with eight wins. On September 26 Ed Walsh duplicated an earlier feat of Frank Owen's by winning both ends of a doubleheader. He was, however, unable to match Owen's performance of giving up only two runs in the eighteen innings.

But the pennant champagne would have to wait another year. The Sox went into Philadelphia on September 28 tied for first, but they dropped two out of three to hand Philly the pennant. There was always next year.

TEAM STATISTICS

	W	L	PCT	GB	R	OR	2B	3B	HR	BA	SA	SB	E	DP	FA	CG	BB	SO	ShO	SV	ERA
PHI	92	56	.622		617	486	256	51	24	.255	.339	189	264	64	.958	117	409	895	20	7	2.19
CHI	92	60	.605	2	613	443	200	55	11	.237	.304	194	217	95	.968	131	329	613	17	1	1.99
DET	79	74	.516	15.5	511	608	190	54	14	.243	.312	129	265	80	.957	124	474	578	16	2	2.83
BOS	78	74	.513	16	583	557	165	69	29	.234	.311	131	294	75	.953	125	292	652	15	3	2.84
CLE	76	78	.494	19	559	582	211	72	18	.255	.335	188	229	84	.963	139	334	555	16	0	2.85
NY	71	78	.477	21.5	587	644	163	61	21	.248	.318	200	293	88	.952	88	396	642	10	7	2.93
WAS	64	87	.424	29.5	560	613	193	68	22	.223	.302	169	318	76	.951	118	385	539	11	3	2.87
STL	54	99	.353	40.5	509	606	153	49	16	.232	.289	130	295	78	.955	133	389	633	10	2	2.74
LEAGUE TOTAL					4539	4539	1531	479	155	.241	.314	1330	2175	640	.957	975	3008	5107	115	25	2.65

INDIVIDUAL PITCHING

PITCHER	T	W	L	PCT	ERA	SV	G	GS	CG	IP	H	BB	SO	R	ER	ShO	H9	BB9	SO9
Frank Owen	R	21	13	.618	2.10	0	42	38	32	334	276	56	125	109	78	3	7.44	1.51	3.37
Nick Altrock	L	22	12	.647	1.88	1	38	34	31	315.2	274	63	97	89	66	3	7.81	1.80	2.77
Frank Smith	R	19	13	.594	2.13	0	39	31	27	291.2	215	107	171	97	69	4	6.63	3.30	5.28
Doc White	L	18	14	.563	1.76	0	36	33	25	260.1	204	58	120	67	51	4	7.05	2.01	4.15
Ed Walsh	R	8	3	.727	2.17	1	22	13	9	136.2	121	29	71	52	33	1	7.97	1.91	4.68
Roy Patterson	R	4	5	.444	1.83	0	13	9	7	88.2	73	16	29	29	18	1	7.41	1.62	2.94
TEAM TOTAL		92	60	.605	1.99	2	190	158	131	1427	1163	329	613	443	315	16	7.33	2.07	3.87

Chicago 1906   Won 93   Lost 58   Pct. .616   1st

MANAGER	W	L	PCT
Fielder Jones	93	58	.616

POS	Player	B	G	AB	H	2B	3B	HR	HR%	R	RBI	BB	SO	SB	Pinch Hit AB	H	BA	SA
REGULARS																		
1B	Jiggs Donahue	L	154	556	143	17	7	1	0.2	70	57	48		36	0	0	.257	.318
2B	Frank Isbell	L	143	549	153	21	11	0	0.0	71	57	30		37	0	0	.279	.357
SS	George Davis	B	133	484	134	26	6	0	0.0	63	80	41		27	3	1	.277	.355
3B	Lee Tannehill	R	116	378	69	8	3	0	0.0	26	33	31		7	0	0	.183	.220
RF	Bill O'Neill	B	94	330	82	4	1	1	0.3	37	21	22		19	1	0	.248	.276
CF	Fielder Jones	L	144	496	114	22	4	2	0.4	77	34	83		26	0	0	.230	.302
LF	Ed Hahn	L	130	484	110	7	5	0	0.0	80	27	69		19	0	0	.227	.262
C	Billy Sullivan	R	118	387	83	18	4	1	0.3	37	33	22		10	0	0	.214	.289
SUBSTITUTES																		
3B	George Rohe	R	75	225	58	5	1	0	0.0	14	25	16		8	12	2	.258	.289
2S	Gus Dundon		33	96	13	1	0	0	0.0	7	4	11		4	1	0	.135	.146
SS	Lee Quillin		4	9	3	0	0	0	0.0	1	0	0		1	1	0	.333	.333
OF	Patsy Dougherty	L	75	253	59	9	4	1	0.4	30	27	19		11	0	0	.233	.312
OF	Frank Hemphill	R	13	40	3	0	0	0	0.0	0	2	9		1	0	0	.075	.075
OF	Rube Vinson		7	24	6	0	0	0	0.0	2	3	2		1	1	1	.250	.250
C	Frank Roth	R	16	51	10	1	1	0	0.0	4	7	3		1	1	0	.196	.255
C	Hub Hart	L	17	37	6	0	0	0	0.0	1	0	2		0	2	0	.162	.162
C	Babe Towne	L	13	36	10	0	0	0	0.0	3	6	7		0	1	0	.278	.278
C	Ed McFarland	R	7	22	3	1	0	0	0.0	0	3	3		0	3	1	.136	.182
PITCHERS																		
P	Frank Owen		42	103	14	4	0	0	0.0	7	7	8		0	0	0	.136	.175
P	Nick Altrock	B	38	100	16	2	0	0	0.0	4	3	8		2	0	0	.160	.180
P	Ed Walsh	R	42	99	14	3	2	0	0.0	12	4	3		0	1	0	.141	.212
P	Doc White	L	28	65	12	1	1	0	0.0	11	3	13		3	0	0	.185	.231
P	Roy Patterson	R	21	49	3	2	0	0	0.0	4	1	0		1	0	0	.061	.102
P	Frank Smith	R	20	41	12	2	2	0	0.0	6	6	3		0	2	1	.293	.439
P	Lou Fiene	R	6	10	2	1	0	0	0.0	0	1	0		0	0	0	.200	.300
TEAM TOTAL				4924	1132	155	52	6	0.1	567	444	453		214	29	6	.230	.286

INDIVIDUAL FIELDING

POS	Player	T	G	PO	A	E	DP	TCG	FA	POS	Player	T	G	PO	A	E	DP	TCG	FA
1B	J. Donahue	L	154	1697	118	22	62	11.9	.988	OF	F. Jones	R	144	312	23	4	5	2.4	.988
	N. Altrock	L	1	3	0	0	0	3.0	1.000		E. Hahn	R	130	164	21	10	3	1.5	.949
2B	F. Isbell	R	132	292	363	35	36	5.2	.949		B. O'Neill		93	118	12	7	1	1.5	.949
	G. Dundon	R	18	53	52	9	5	6.3	.921		P. Dougherty	R	74	118	10	2	1	1.8	.985
	G. Rohe	R	5	9	15	1	2	5.0	.960		F. Hemphill	R	13	31	1	1	0	2.5	.970
	G. Davis	R	1	3	0	0	1	3.0	1.000		F. Isbell	R	14	17	0	1	0	1.3	.944
SS	G. Davis	R	129	263	475	42	44	6.0	.946		R. Vinson		4	6	0	4	0	2.5	.600
	L. Tannehill	R	17	42	54	6	1	6.0	.941		G. Rohe	R	1	1	0	1	0	2.0	.500
	G. Dundon	R	14	28	39	5	3	5.1	.931		D. White	L	1	1	0	0	0	1.0	1.000
	L. Quillin	R	3	4	5	6	1	5.0	.600	C	B. Sullivan	R	118	475	134	16	7	5.3	.974
3B	L. Tannehill	R	99	131	278	21	12	4.3	.951		F. Roth	R	15	76	19	1	1	6.4	.990
	G. Rohe	R	57	66	122	15	6	3.6	.926		H. Hart	R	15	36	7	3	1	3.1	.935
											B. Towne	R	12	39	9	4	0	4.3	.923
											E. McFarland	R	3	32	4	1	0	12.3	.973
											F. Isbell	R	1	4	0	0	0	4.0	1.000

Chicago 1906

How Hitless were they? The team batting average of .230 was good for last in the league, and their home run leader was the manager, with two. And they weren't exactly Wonders during the long dry stretch that began in April and ended in July. Indeed, the 1906 champs had a Jekyll-and-Hyde character. As late as July 29, they were ten games out of first. Frank Smith feuded with Fielder Jones. Billy Sullivan was sidelined with yet another in a long series of injuries, and Charles Comiskey threatened to return to his Camp Jerome retreat in Wisconsin unless the Sox improved.

Then magic happened. Doc White shut out Boston on August 2, 3–0. Ed Walsh and "Boy Wonder" Roy Patterson followed with two more whitewashes, Walsh's a one-hitter. In the next eleven days, the ten-game deficit became a one-game lead. On August 23, after their nineteenth straight win, the lead stood at five and a half games, and with the crosstown Cubs in first, Chicago's baseball "cranks" were fired up.

The World Series pitted the Sox "Davids" against the Cub "Goliaths," and the underdog Sox won a surprise victory in a six-game set. Pitching and more pitching did it. Doc White and Ed Walsh, who had pitched four one-hitters between them that season, won three of four decisions. As a team, the powerhouse Cubs hit only .196. It didn't matter that the Sox hit .198. In 1906, next year came early.

TEAM STATISTICS

	W	L	PCT	GB	R	OR	2B	3B	Batting HR	BA	SA	SB	E	Fielding DP	FA	CG	BB	Pitching SO	ShO	SV	ERA
CHI	93	58	.616		570	460	152	52	6	.230	.286	214	243	80	.963	117	255	543	32	6	2.13
NY	90	61	.596	3	643	544	166	77	17	.266	.339	192	272	69	.957	99	351	605	18	4	2.78
CLE	89	64	.582	5	663	482	240	73	11	.279	.356	203	216	111	.967	133	365	530	27	5	2.09
PHI	78	67	.538	12	561	536	213	49	31	.247	.330	166	267	86	.956	107	425	749	19	6	2.60
STL	76	73	.510	16	565	501	145	60	20	.247	.312	221	290	80	.954	133	314	558	17	3	2.23
DET	71	78	.477	21	518	596	154	64	10	.242	.306	205	260	86	.959	128	389	469	7	4	3.06
WAS	55	95	.367	37.5	518	670	144	65	26	.238	.309	233	279	78	.955	115	451	558	12	1	3.25
BOS	49	105	.318	45.5	462	711	160	75	13	.239	.306	99	334	84	.949	124	285	549	6	4	3.41
LEAGUE TOTAL					4500	4500	1374	515	134	.249	.318	1533	2161	674	.958	956	2835	4561	138	33	2.69

INDIVIDUAL PITCHING

PITCHER	T	W	L	PCT	ERA	SV	G	GS	CG	IP	H	BB	SO	R	ER	ShO	H9	BB9	SO9
Frank Owen	R	22	13	.629	2.33	2	42	36	27	293	289	54	66	114	76	7	8.88	1.66	2.03
Nick Altrock	L	20	13	.606	2.06	0	38	30	25	287.2	269	42	99	95	66	4	8.42	1.31	3.10
Ed Walsh	R	17	13	.567	1.88	3	41	31	24	278.1	215	58	171	83	58	10	6.95	1.88	5.53
Doc White	L	18	6	.750	1.52	0	28	24	20	219.1	160	38	102	47	37	7	6.57	1.56	4.19
Roy Patterson	R	10	7	.588	2.09	1	21	18	12	142	119	17	45	46	33	3	7.54	1.08	2.85
Frank Smith	R	5	5	.500	3.39	2	20	13	8	122	124	37	53	58	46	1	9.15	2.73	3.91
Lou Fiene	R	1	1	.500	2.90	0	6	2	1	31	35	9	12	17	10	0	10.16	2.61	3.48
Frank Isbell	R	0	0	–	0.00	0	1	0	0	2	1	0	2	0	0	0	4.50	0.00	9.00
TEAM TOTAL		93	58	.616	2.13	8	197	154	117	1375.1	1212	255	550	460	326	32	7.93	1.67	3.60

Chicago 1907   Won 87 Lost 64 Pct. .576 3rd

MANAGER	W	L	PCT
Fielder Jones	87	64	.576

POS	Player	B	G	AB	H	2B	3B	HR	HR%	R	RBI	BB	SO	SB	Pinch Hit AB	Pinch Hit H	BA	SA
REGULARS																		
1B	Jiggs Donahue	L	157	609	158	16	4	0	0.0	75	68	28		27	0	0	.259	.299
2B	Frank Isbell	L	125	486	118	22	8	0	0.0	60	55	22		22	1	0	.243	.321
SS	George Davis	B	132	466	111	16	2	1	0.2	59	52	47		15	0	0	.238	.288
3B	George Rohe	R	144	494	105	11	2	2	0.4	46	51	39		16	2	0	.213	.255
RF	Ed Hahn	L	156	592	151	9	7	0	0.0	87	45	84		17	0	0	.255	.294
CF	Fielder Jones	L	154	559	146	18	1	0	0.0	72	47	67		17	0	0	.261	.297
LF	Patsy Dougherty	L	148	533	144	17	2	2	0.4	69	59	36		33	0	0	.270	.321
C	Billy Sullivan	R	112	339	59	8	4	0	0.0	30	36	21		6	3	0	.174	.221
SUBSTITUTES																		
3B	Lee Quillin		49	151	29	5	0	0	0.0	17	14	10		8	0	0	.192	.225
3B	Lee Tannehill	R	33	108	26	2	0	0	0.0	9	11	8		3	0	0	.241	.259
3B	Jake Atz	R	3	7	1	0	0	0	0.0	0	0	0		0	1	0	.143	.143
OF	Mike Welday	L	24	35	8	1	1	0	0.0	2	0	6		0	6	1	.229	.314
OF	Piano Legs Hickman	R	21	23	6	2	0	0	0.0	1	1	4		0	16*	4	.261	.348
C	Ed McFarland	R	52	138	39	9	1	0	0.0	11	8	12		3	7	2	.283	.362
C	Hub Hart	L	29	70	19	1	0	0	0.0	6	7	5		1	4	0	.271	.286
C	Charlie Armbruster	R	1	3	0	0	0	0	0.0	0	0	1		0	0	0	.000	.000
PITCHERS																		
P	Ed Walsh	R	57	154	25	6	3	1	0.6	7	10	0		2	1	0	.162	.260
P	Frank Smith	R	42	92	18	3	0	0	0.0	11	11	16		2	1	0	.196	.228
P	Doc White	L	48	90	20	1	0	0	0.0	12	2	12		2	0	0	.222	.233
P	Nick Altrock	B	30	72	13	3	0	0	0.0	7	2	3		0	0	0	.181	.222
P	Roy Patterson	R	19	31	3	0	0	0	0.0	3	6	0		0	0	0	.097	.097
P	Frank Owen		11	16	4	0	0	0	0.0	0	0	0		0	0	0	.250	.250
P	Lou Fiene	R	7	11	2	0	0	0	0.0	0	3	0		1	1	0	.182	.182
TEAM TOTAL				5079	1205	150	35	6	0.1	584	488	421		175	43	7	.237	.284

INDIVIDUAL FIELDING

POS	Player	T	G	PO	A	E	DP	TCG	FA
1B	J. Donahue	L	157	1846	140	12	78	12.7	.994
2B	F. Isbell	R	119	276	384	30	41	5.8	.957
	G. Rohe	R	39	87	115	20	16	5.7	.910
	B. Sullivan	R	1	2	2	0	1	4.0	1.000
SS	G. Davis	R	131	223	485	38	53	5.7	.949
	G. Rohe	R	30	38	96	11	8	4.8	.924
	F. Isbell	R	1	0	0	0	0	0.0	.000
	L. Tannehill	R	2	4	9	1	1	7.0	.929
3B	G. Rohe	R	76	58	161	25	14	3.2	.898
	L. Quillin	R	48	45	103	22	4	3.5	.871
	L. Tannehill	R	31	21	82	10	3	3.6	.912
	J. Atz	R	2	0	8	0	1	4.0	1.000

POS	Player	T	G	PO	A	E	DP	TCG	FA
OF	F. Jones	R	154	307	18	9	6	2.2	.973
	P. Dougherty	R	148	209	19	13	4	1.6	.946
	E. Hahn	R	156	182	24	2	6	1.3	.990
	M. Welday	L	15	13	2	1	0	1.1	.938
	D. White	L	2	0	0	0	0	0.0	.000
	F. Isbell	R	5	9	1	0	0	2.0	1.000
	P. Hickman	R	3	2	0	1	0	1.0	.667
C	B. Sullivan	R	108	477	117	10	12	5.6	.983
	E. McFarland	R	43	192	47	7	4	5.7	.972
	H. Hart	R	25	85	23	5	2	4.5	.956
	C. Armbruster	R	1	9	1	0	0	10.0	1.000

Perhaps it was too much too soon. Following the championship season, disillusionment set in. It began in the spring, when George Davis was a lengthy holdout. Salary grumbling was widespread as the Sox became the first team to conduct spring training outside the U.S. borders. They played well in Mexico City, and even better once the season started. They were 29-12 and comfortably in first place on June 4. But the injury list soon resembled a hospital emergency room. Billy Sullivan split his thumb. Frank Isbell was spiked during horseplay with teammate Patsy Dougherty, and Lee Tannehill nearly lost his leg due to blood poisoning.

Nick Altrock, a one-time mainstay, didn't win a game from May 21 to September 4. All this adversity made Fielder Jones testy. His usual run-ins with umpires took an ugly turn, and by season's end, he wasn't talking to reporters. The Sox were in the thick of the race, but it was a hard climb. There were only seven days out of the year when Jones was able to field a healthy lineup. They watched unhappily as the hated Cubs went to the World Series for the second year in a row. On October 4 Jones announced he wouldn't be back in 1908. Comiskey reluctantly opened up the checkbook, offering a then unheard of $10,000 a year. Fielder decided he could delay retirement for one more year.

TEAM STATISTICS

	W	L	PCT	GB	R	OR	2B	3B	Batting HR	BA	SA	SB	E	Fielding DP	FA	CG	BB	Pitching SO	ShO	SV	ERA
DET	92	58	.613		696	519	179	75	11	.266	.335	192	260	79	.959	120	380	512	15	4	2.33
PHI	88	57	.607	1.5	582	509	220	45	22	.255	.330	138	263	67	.958	106	378	789	27	7	2.35
CHI	87	64	.576	5.5	584	475	147	34	6	.237	.283	175	233	101	.966	112	305	604	17	6	2.22
CLE	85	67	.559	8	528	523	182	68	11	.241	.310	193	264	137	.960	127	362	513	20	4	2.26
NY	70	78	.473	21	604	671	150	67	14	.249	.314	206	334	79	.947	93	428	511	9	5	3.03
STL	69	83	.454	24	538	560	154	63	9	.253	.312	144	266	97	.959	129	352	463	15	8	2.61
BOS	59	90	.396	32.5	466	556	155	48	18	.234	.292	124	274	103	.959	100	337	517	17	6	2.45
WAS	49	102	.325	43.5	505	690	137	57	12	.243	.300	223	311	69	.952	106	341	567	11	2	3.11
LEAGUE TOTAL					4503	4503	1324	457	103	.247	.310	1395	2205	732	.958	893	2883	4476	131	42	2.54

INDIVIDUAL PITCHING

PITCHER	T	W	L	PCT	ERA	SV	G	GS	CG	IP	H	BB	SO	R	ER	ShO	H9	BB9	SO9
Ed Walsh	R	24	18	.571	1.60	2	56	46	37	422.1	341	87	206	120	75	5	7.27	1.85	4.39
Frank Smith	R	22	11	.667	2.47	0	41	37	29	310	280	111	139	105	85	3	8.13	3.22	4.04
Doc White	L	27	13	.675	2.26	2	47	35	24	291	270	38	141	93	73	7	8.35	1.18	4.36
Nick Altrock	L	8	12	.400	2.57	1	30	21	15	213.2	210	31	61	76	61	1	8.85	1.31	2.57
Roy Patterson	R	4	6	.400	2.63	0	19	13	4	96	105	18	27	42	28	1	9.84	1.69	2.53
Frank Owen	R	2	3	.400	2.49	0	11	4	2	47	43	13	15	22	13	0	8.23	2.49	2.87
Lou Fiene	R	0	1	.000	4.15	1	6	1	1	26	30	7	15	17	12	0	10.38	2.42	5.19
Frank Isbell	R	0	0	–	0.00	1	1	0	0	.1	0	0	0	0	0	0	0.00	0.00	0.00
TEAM TOTAL		87	64	.576	2.22	7	211	157	112	1406.1	1279	305	604	475	347	17	8.19	1.95	3.87

Chicago 1908   Won 88 Lost 64 Pct .579 3rd

MANAGER	W	L	PCT
Fielder Jones	88	64	.579

POS	Player	B	G	AB	H	2B	3B	HR	HR%	R	RBI	BB	SO	SB	Pinch Hit AB	H	BA	SA
REGULARS																		
1B	Jiggs Donahue	L	93	304	62	8	2	0	0.0	22	22	25		14	10	1	.204	.243
2B	George Davis	B	128	419	91	14	1	0	0.0	41	26	41		22	5	1	.217	.255
SS	Freddy Parent	R	119	391	81	7	5	0	0.0	28	35	50		9	0	0	.207	.251
3B	Lee Tannehill	R	141	482	104	15	3	0	0.0	44	35	25		6	0	0	.216	.259
RF	Ed Hahn	L	122	447	112	12	8	0	0.0	58	21	39		11	3	1	.251	.313
CF	Fielder Jones	L	149	529	134	11	7	1	0.2	92	50	86		26	0	0	.253	.306
LF	Patsy Dougherty	L	138	482	134	11	6	0	0.0	68	45	58		47	9	2	.278	.326
C	Billy Sullivan	R	137	430	82	8	4	0	0.0	40	29	22		15	1	0	.191	.228
SUBSTITUTES																		
12	Frank Isbell	L	84	320	79	15	3	1	0.3	31	49	19		18	1	0	.247	.322
2S	Jake Atz	R	83	206	40	3	0	0	0.0	24	27	31		9	17	4	.194	.209
3B	Billy Purtell	R	26	69	9	2	0	0	0.0	3	3	2		2	1	0	.130	.159
OF	John Anderson	B	123	355	93	17	1	0	0.0	36	47	30		21	25	5	.262	.315
C	Al Shaw	R	32	49	4	1	0	0	0.0	0	2	2		0	3	0	.082	.102
C	Art Weaver		15	35	7	1	0	0	0.0	1	1	1		0	0	0	.200	.229
C	Ossee Schreckengost	R	6	16	3	0	0	0	0.0	1	0	1		0	0	0	.188	.188
PITCHERS																		
P	Ed Walsh	R	66	157	27	7	1	1	0.6	10	10	7		2	0	0	.172	.248
P	Doc White	L	51	109	25	1	0	0	0.0	12	10	12		4	6	1	.229	.239
P	Frank Smith	R	43	106	20	7	0	0	0.0	15	10	5		1	2	0	.189	.255
P	Frank Owen		25	50	9	3	0	0	0.0	3	4	3		1	0	0	.180	.240
P	Nick Altrock	B	23	49	10	2	0	0	0.0	6	3	0		1	0	0	.204	.245
P	Moxie Manuel		18	16	1	0	0	0	0.0	0	1	1		0	0	0	.063	.063
P	Lou Fiene	R	1	3	0	0	0	0	0.0	0	0	0		0	0	0	.000	.000
P	Andy Nelson		2	2	0	0	0	0	0.0	0	0	1		0	0	0	.000	.000
P	Fred Olmstead		1	1	0	0	0	0	0.0	0	0	2		0	0	0	.000	.000
TEAM TOTAL				5027	1127	145	41	3	0.1	535	430	463		209	83	15	.224	.271

INDIVIDUAL FIELDING

POS	Player	T	G	PO	A	E	DP	TCG	FA
1B	J. Donahue	L	83	968	57	6	30	12.4	.994
	F. Isbell	R	65	824	46	9	30	13.5	.990
	J. Anderson	R	9	80	4	1	4	9.4	.988
	G. Davis	R	4	49	5	0	0	13.5	1.000
2B	G. Davis	R	95	191	314	21	25	5.5	.960
	J. Atz	R	46	82	137	15	12	5.1	.936
	F. Isbell	R	18	40	58	9	0	5.9	.916
SS	F. Parent	R	118	212	442	49	33	6.0	.930
	G. Davis	R	23	51	65	11	6	5.5	.913
	J. Atz	R	18	18	50	2	3	3.9	.971
	L. Tannehill	R	5	7	13	2	6	4.4	.909
3B	L. Tannehill	R	136	135	**341**	33	15	3.7	.935
	B. Purtell	R	25	18	60	5	5	3.3	.940
	J. Atz	R	1	0	1	0	0	1.0	1.000
OF	F. Jones	R	149	288	17	10	5	2.1	.968
	P. Dougherty	R	138	173	7	10	1	1.4	.947
	E. Hahn	R	118	160	4	6	2	1.4	.965
	J. Anderson	R	90	96	9	4	7	1.2	.963
	D. White	L	3	2	0	0	0	0.7	1.000
C	B. Sullivan	R	137	553	156	11	11	5.3	**.985**
	A. Shaw	R	29	87	15	5	1	3.7	.953
	A. Weaver	R	15	32	9	2	2	2.9	.953
	Schreckengost	R	6	50	5	1	1	9.3	.982

40

Fred Merkle's bonehead play in the last week of the 1908 season made this year unlike any other. His one moment of infamy largely overshadowed an equally exciting pennant race in the American League that saw the Sox' hopes dashed on the last day of the season.

The dissension of 1907 grew in scope as the season began. Jimmy Callahan sued the Sox for his release, the White Sox Rooter Association was accused of harboring a slush fund for aldermanic candidate James Considine, and pitcher Frank Smith deserted the Sox in July after repeated altercations with Fielder Jones.

All the glory in 1908 belonged to Ed Walsh. The "Big Reel" was credited with 40 victories in 66 games, a staggering number of appearances even during that "iron man" era. One hard-luck win that got away from Walsh resulted from Addie Joss's perfect game on October 2. In that game, Walsh fanned fifteen batters, and the only run scored on a passed ball. Frank Smith returned to the Sox in time to pitch a near-perfect game himself, but had to settle for a no-hitter when Frank Isbell booted a routine grounder.

In the end Smith figured indirectly in the Sox downfall. On the last day of the season, the Sox trailed Detroit by just one half game. The arm-weary Walsh had pitched and won the day before, and Doc White had had just one day's rest. But Jones harbored a grudge against Smith, whom he considered to be less than a "gamer." He went with White, who was blown out, 7–0. That was Fielder Jones's last game as Sox manager. He retired to Portland, Oregon, and some lucrative investments. The greatest of all Sox managers went out on a sour note.

TEAM STATISTICS

	W	L	PCT	GB	R	OR	2B	3B	HR	BA	SA	SB	E	DP	FA	CG	BB	SO	ShO	SV	ERA
DET	90	63	.588		645	552	199	86	19	.264	.347	165	305	95	.953	120	318	553	14	6	2.40
CLE	90	64	.584	0.5	570	471	188	58	18	.239	.309	169	257	95	.962	108	328	548	18	5	2.02
CHI	88	64	.579	1.5	535	480	145	41	3	.224	.271	209	232	82	.966	107	284	623	21	11	2.22
STL	83	69	.546	6.5	543	478	173	56	21	.245	.312	126	237	97	.964	107	387	607	16	3	2.15
BOS	75	79	.487	15.5	563	515	116	88	14	.246	.312	168	297	71	.955	102	366	624	12	7	2.27
PHI	68	85	.444	22	487	554	183	49	21	.225	.293	116	272	68	.957	102	409	740	23	6	2.57
WAS	67	85	.441	22.5	479	530	131	74	8	.235	.295	170	275	89	.958	105	348	649	13	7	2.34
NY	51	103	.331	39.5	458	700	142	51	12	.236	.291	230	337	78	.947	91	457	584	11	5	3.16
LEAGUE TOTAL					4280	4280	1277	503	116	.239	.304	1353	2212	675	.958	842	2897	4928	128	50	2.39

INDIVIDUAL PITCHING

PITCHER	T	W	L	PCT	ERA	SV	G	GS	CG	IP	H	BB	SO	R	ER	ShO	H9	BB9	SO9
Ed Walsh	R	40	15	.727	1.42	7	66	49	42	464	343	56	269	112	73	12	6.65	1.09	5.22
Frank Smith	R	17	16	.515	2.03	1	41	35	24	297.2	213	73	129	96	67	3	6.44	2.21	3.90
Doc White	L	19	13	.594	2.55	0	41	37	24	296	267	69	126	95	84	5	8.12	2.10	3.83
Frank Owen	R	6	9	.400	3.41	0	25	14	5	140	142	37	48	79	53	1	9.13	2.38	3.09
Nick Altrock	L	3	7	.300	2.71	2	23	13	8	136	127	18	21	59	41	1	8.40	1.19	1.39
Moxie Manuel		3	3	.500	3.28	1	18	6	3	60.1	52	25	25	25	22	0	7.76	3.73	3.73
Lou Fiene	R	0	1	.000	4.00	0	1	1	1	9	9	1	3	7	4	0	9.00	1.00	3.00
Andy Nelson		0	0	–	2.00	0	2	1	0	9	11	4	1	4	2	0	11.00	4.00	1.00
Fred Olmstead		0	0	–	13.50	0	1	0	0	2	6	1	1	3	3	0	27.00	4.50	4.50
TEAM TOTAL		88	64	.579	2.22	11	218	156	107	1414	1170	284	623	480	349	22	7.45	1.81	3.97

Chicago 1909   Won 78 Lost 74 Pct. .513 4th   42

MANAGER	W	L	PCT
Billy Sullivan	78	74	.513

POS	Player	B	G	AB	H	2B	3B	HR	HR%	R	RBI	BB	SO	SB	Pinch Hit AB	H	BA	SA
REGULARS																		
1B	Frank Isbell	L	120	433	97	17	6	0	0.0	33	39	23		23	5	2	.224	.291
2B	Jake Atz	R	119	381	90	18	3	0	0.0	39	22	38		14	1	0	.236	.299
SS	Freddy Parent	R	136	472	123	10	5	0	0.0	61	30	46		32	0	0	.261	.303
3B	Lee Tannehill	R	155	531	118	21	5	0	0.0	39	47	31		12	0	0	.222	.281
RF	Ed Hahn	L	76	287	52	6	0	1	0.3	30	16	31		9	0	0	.181	.213
CF	Dave Altizer	L	116	382	89	6	7	1	0.3	47	20	39		27	7	1	.233	.293
LF	Patsy Dougherty	L	139	491	140	23	13	1	0.2	71	55	51		36	1	0	.285	.391
C	Billy Sullivan	R	97	265	43	3	0	0	0.0	11	16	17		9	0	0	.162	.174
SUBSTITUTES																		
32	Billy Purtell	R	103	361	93	9	3	0	0.0	34	40	19		14	0	0	.258	.299
1B	George Davis	B	28	68	9	1	0	0	0.0	5	2	10		4	14	1	.132	.147
2B	Barney Reilly	R	12	25	5	0	0	0	0.0	3	3	3		2	0	0	.200	.200
1B	Jiggs Donahue	L	2	4	0	0	0	0	0.0	0	2	1		0	0	0	.000	.000
1B	Ham Patterson		1	3	0	0	0	0	0.0	2	0	1		0	0	0	.000	.000
OP	Doc White	L	72	192	45	1	5	0	0.0	24	7	33		7	8	1	.234	.292
OF	Willis Cole	R	46	165	39	7	3	0	0.0	17	16	16		3	0	0	.236	.315
OF	Bobby Messenger	L	31	112	19	1	1	0	0.0	18	0	13		7	0	0	.170	.196
OF	Mike Welday	L	29	74	14	0	0	0	0.0	3	5	4		2	8	2	.189	.189
OF	Gavvy Cravath	R	19	50	9	0	0	1	2.0	7	8	19		3	0	0	.180	.240
OF	Cuke Barrows	R	5	20	3	0	0	0	0.0	1	2	0		0	0	0	.150	.150
C	Frank Owens	R	64	174	35	4	1	0	0.0	12	17	8		3	6	1	.201	.236
C	Fred Payne	R	32	82	20	2	0	0	0.0	8	12	5		0	2	1	.244	.268
PITCHERS																		
P	Frank Smith	R	53	127	22	6	3	0	0.0	11	20	10		0	1	0	.173	.268
P	Jim Scott	R	36	85	9	2	0	0	0.0	7	5	9		0	0	0	.106	.129
P	Ed Walsh	R	32	84	18	5	0	0	0.0	5	11	6		4	0	0	.214	.274
P	Bill Burns	B	22	58	10	3	0	0	0.0	3	3	5		0	0	0	.172	.224
P	Rube Suter		18	32	3	0	0	0	0.0	1	0	2		0	0	0	.094	.094
P	Lou Fiene	R	15	29	2	0	1	0	0.0	1	1	0		0	2	0	.069	.138
P	Fred Olmstead		8	21	2	0	0	0	0.0	0	0	1		0	0	0	.095	.095
P	Frank Owen		3	6	1	0	0	0	0.0	1	0	0		0	0	0	.167	.167
P	Nick Altrock	B	1	3	0	0	0	0	0.0	0	0	0		0	0	0	.000	.000
	TEAM TOTAL			5017	1110	145	56	4	0.1	494	399	441		211	55	9	.221	.275

INDIVIDUAL FIELDING

POS	Player	T	G	PO	A	E	DP	TCG	FA	POS	Player	T	G	PO	A	E	DP	TCG	FA
1B	F. Isbell	R	101	1204	66	8	48	12.7	.994	OF	P. Dougherty	R	138	184	10	12	0	1.5	.942
	D. Altizer	R	45	441	33	4	24	10.6	.992		D. Altizer	R	62	99	12	6	1	1.9	.949
	G. Davis	R	17	189	15	3	7	12.2	.986		W. Cole	R	46	83	5	11	1	2.2	.889
	J. Donahue	L	2	11	0	0	0	5.5	1.000		E. Hahn	R	76	93	3	1	1	1.3	.990
	H. Patterson	R	1	3	2	0	0	5.0	1.000		F. Parent	R	37	73	6	0	0	2.1	1.000
2B	J. Atz	R	118	202	311	25	40	4.6	.954		D. White	L	40	56	7	5	1	1.7	.926
	B. Purtell	R	32	72	90	5	13	5.2	.970		M. Welday	L	20	35	4	5	1	2.2	.886
	F. Parent	R	1	0	0	0	0	0.0	.000		B. Messenger	R	31	34	4	2	1	1.3	.950
	B. Reilly	R	11	18	33	2	0	4.8	.962		G. Cravath	R	18	34	0	2	0	2.0	.944
	F. Isbell	R	5	15	13	2	3	6.0	.933		B. Reilly	R	1	0	0	0	0	0.0	.000
	G. Davis	R	2	1	3	2	0	3.0	.667		E. Walsh	R	1	0	0	0	0	0.0	.000
SS	F. Parent	R	98	182	357	41	34	5.9	.929		C. Barrows	L	5	10	2	1	0	2.6	.923
	L. Tannehill	R	64	126	251	24	21	6.3	.940		F. Isbell	R	9	7	1	2	0	1.1	.800
	J. Atz	R	1	2	1	0	0	3.0	1.000		J. Atz	R	3	4	3	0	1	2.3	1.000
											F. Payne	R	3	1	0	0	0	0.3	1.000
3B	L. Tannehill	R	91	103	168	17	11	3.2	.941	C	B. Sullivan	R	97	452	119	10	6	6.0	.983
	B. Purtell	R	71	90	158	19	11	3.8	.929		F. Owens	R	57	266	62	14	2	6.0	.959
											F. Payne	R	27	110	38	2	5	5.6	.987

Chicago 1909

The White Sox entered the third phase of their history in 1909, year one of a five-year transition period. This was a time of growth and rebuilding. The Hitless Wonder era died in the October sun of 1908. The Sox were now committed to youth, and in the process were assembling one of the greatest baseball forces in history — and one of the most tragic.

Frank Isbell was released after the season ended. Jiggs Donahue and George Davis played sparingly, and Nick Altrock was traded to Washington for Sleepy Bill Burns, the pitcher who ultimately served as the go-between during the Black Sox Scandal.

Billy Sullivan's loyalty was rewarded the day before the season began. Like a jilted lover, Comiskey waited all winter in the hope that Fielder Jones would return to the Sox. When he didn't, Sullivan was named manager. It was quite a year for Sully, who secured a patent on January 31 for the first chest protector known to baseball. It featured a ribbed cushion with compressed air. Sportswriters joked that it resembled a snowplow.

All this didn't help Sullivan. Ed Walsh held out for $7,500 and didn't report to the Sox until the season was a month old. The Sox were still hitless, but not the wonders they once were. Newcomer Freddy Parent paced the hitters with a robust .261. Comiskey blamed the fourth-place finish on Sullivan, and went out and hired an old baseball crony, Hugh Duffy, to manage in 1910.

TEAM STATISTICS

	W	L	PCT	GB	R	OR	2B	3B	HR	BA	SA	SB	E	DP	FA	CG	BB	SO	ShO	SV	ERA
DET	98	54	.645		666	493	209	58	19	.267	.342	280	276	87	.959	117	359	528	16	12	2.26
PHI	95	58	.621	3.5	600	414	186	89	20	.257	.343	205	245	92	.961	111	386	728	27	5	1.92
BOS	88	63	.583	9.5	590	561	151	69	20	.263	.333	215	292	95	.955	75	384	555	10	15	2.60
CHI	78	74	.513	20	494	465	145	56	4	.221	.275	211	246	101	.964	112	341	671	26	4	2.04
NY	74	77	.490	23.5	591	580	143	61	16	.248	.311	187	329	94	.948	94	422	597	16	12	2.68
CLE	71	82	.464	27.5	519	543	179	84	11	.242	.314	183	275	110	.957	110	349	569	15	2	2.39
STL	61	89	.407	36	443	574	116	45	11	.232	.280	136	267	107	.958	105	383	620	21	4	2.88
WAS	42	110	.276	56	382	655	148	41	9	.223	.275	136	280	100	.957	99	424	653	10	1	3.04
LEAGUE TOTAL					4285	4285	1277	503	110	.244	.309	1553	2210	786	.957	823	3048	4921	141	55	2.47

INDIVIDUAL PITCHING

PITCHER	T	W	L	PCT	ERA	SV	G	GS	CG	IP	H	BB	SO	R	ER	ShO	H9	BB9	SO9
Frank Smith	R	25	17	.595	1.80	1	51	41	37	365	278	70	177	104	73	7	6.85	1.73	4.36
Jim Scott	R	12	12	.500	2.30	0	36	29	19	250.1	194	93	135	86	64	4	6.97	3.34	4.85
Ed Walsh	R	15	11	.577	1.41	2	31	28	20	230.1	166	50	127	52	36	8	6.49	1.95	4.96
Doc White	L	10	9	.526	1.72	0	24	21	14	177.2	149	31	77	56	34	3	7.55	1.57	3.90
Bill Burns	L	8	13	.381	1.96	0	22	19	8	174.1	169	35	52	65	38	3	8.72	1.81	2.68
Rube Suter	L	2	3	.400	2.47	1	18	6	3	87.1	72	28	53	34	24	1	7.42	2.89	5.46
Lou Fiene	R	2	5	.286	4.13	0	13	6	4	72	75	18	24	37	33	0	9.38	2.25	3.00
Fred Olmstead		3	2	.600	1.81	0	8	6	5	54.2	52	12	21	17	11	0	8.56	1.98	3.46
Frank Owen	R	1	1	.500	4.50	0	3	2	1	16	19	3	3	8	8	0	10.69	1.69	1.69
Nick Altrock	L	0	1	.000	5.00	0	1	1	1	9	16	1	2	6	5	0	16.00	1.00	2.00
TEAM TOTAL		78	74	.513	2.04	4	207	159	112	1436.2	1190	341	671	465	326	26	7.45	2.14	4.20

Chicago 1910   Won 68 Lost 85 Pct .444 6th   44

MANAGER	W	L	PCT
Hugh Duffy	68	85	.444

POS	Player	B	G	AB	H	2B	3B	HR	HR%	R	RBI	BB	SO	SB	Pinch Hit AB	H	BA	SA
REGULARS																		
1B	Chick Gandil	R	77	275	53	7	3	2	0.7	21	21	24		12	0	0	.193	.262
2B	Rollie Zeider	R	136	498	108	9	2	0	0.0	57	31	62		49	0	0	.217	.243
SS	Lena Blackburne	R	75	242	42	3	1	0	0.0	16	10	19		4	0	0	.174	.194
3B	Billy Purtell	R	102	368	86	5	3	1	0.3	21	36	21		5	0	0	.234	.272
RF	Shano Collins	R	97	315	62	10	8	1	0.3	29	24	25		10	4	1	.197	.289
CF	Paul Meloan	L	65	222	54	6	6	0	0.0	23	23	17		4	0	0	.243	.324
LF	Patsy Dougherty	L	127	443	110	8	6	1	0.2	45	43	41		22	3	1	.248	.300
C	Fred Payne	R	91	257	56	5	4	0	0.0	17	19	11		6	9	2	.218	.268
SUBSTITUTES																		
S1	Lee Tannehill	R	67	230	51	10	0	1	0.4	17	21	11		3	0	0	.222	.278
2O	Charlie French	L	45	170	28	1	1	0	0.0	17	4	10		5	0	0	.165	.182
3B	Harry Lord	L	44	165	49	6	3	0	0.0	26	10	14		17	0	0	.297	.370
1B	Charlie Mullen	R	41	123	24	2	1	0	0.0	15	13	4		4	1	1	.195	.228
2B	Amby McConnell	L	32	119	33	2	3	0	0.0	13	5	7		4	1	0	.277	.345
O2	Freddy Parent	R	81	258	46	6	1	1	0.4	23	16	29		14	0	0	.178	.221
PO	Doc White	L	56	126	25	1	2	0	0.0	14	8	14		2	8	0	.198	.238
OF	George Browne	L	30	112	27	4	1	0	0.0	17	4	12		5	1	0	.241	.295
OF	Dutch Zwilling	L	27	87	16	5	0	0	0.0	7	5	11		1	0	0	.184	.241
OF	Felix Chouinard	B	24	82	16	3	2	0	0.0	6	9	8		4	0	0	.195	.280
OF	Willis Cole	R	22	80	14	2	1	0	0.0	6	2	4		0	0	0	.175	.225
OF	Ed Hahn	L	15	53	6	2	0	0	0.0	2	1	7		0	0	0	.113	.151
OF	Red Kelly	R	14	45	7	0	1	0	0.0	6	1	7		0	0	0	.156	.200
OF	Bobby Messenger	L	9	26	6	0	1	0	0.0	7	4	4		3	1	0	.231	.308
OF	Cuke Barrows	R	6	20	4	0	0	0	0.0	0	1	3		0	0	0	.200	.200
OF	Red Bowser		1	2	0	0	0	0	0.0	0	0	0		0	0	0	.000	.000
C	Bruno Block	R	55	152	32	1	1	0	0.0	12	9	13		3	6	0	.211	.230
C	Billy Sullivan	R	45	142	26	4	1	0	0.0	10	6	7		0	0	0	.183	.225
PITCHERS																		
P	Ed Walsh	R	52	138	30	3	3	0	0.0	12	4	5		5	7	1	.217	.283
P	Jim Scott	R	41	74	15	3	1	0	0.0	6	6	3		0	0	0	.203	.270
P	Fred Olmstead		32	65	10	0	1	0	0.0	1	1	1		0	0	0	.154	.185
P	Frank Lange	R	23	51	13	4	0	0	0.0	3	8	2		0	0	0	.255	.333
P	Irv Young	L	27	44	5	0	1	0	0.0	3	1	1		1	0	0	.114	.159
P	Frank Smith	R	24	43	8	3	0	0	0.0	4	5	5		0	5	0	.186	.256
P	Chief Chouneau	R	1	1	0	0	0	0	0.0	0	0	1		0	0	0	.000	.000
P	Bill Burns	B	1	0	0	0	0	0	—	0	0	0		0	0	0	—	—
TEAM TOTAL				5028	1062	115	58	7	0.1	456	351	403		183	46	6	.211	.261

INDIVIDUAL FIELDING

POS	Player	T	G	PO	A	E	DP	TCG	FA	POS	Player	T	G	PO	A	E	DP	TCG	FA
1B	C. Gandil	R	74	854	57	10	34	12.4	.989	OF	P. Dougherty	R	121	158	9	14	2	1.5	.923
	C. Mullen	R	37	364	23	7	21	10.6	.982		S. Collins	R	65	101	11	6	6	1.8	.949
	S. Collins	R	27	255	19	13	11	10.6	.955		F. Parent	R	62	92	5	3	1	1.6	.970
	L. Tannehill	R	23	206	18	2	6	9.8	.991		P. Meloan	R	65	76	16	5	1	1.5	.948
2B	R. Zeider	R	87	205	242	33	31	5.5	.931		F. Chouinard	R	23	44	7	2	2	2.3	.962
	A. McConnell	R	32	61	78	7	10	4.6	.952		D. Zwilling	L	27	45	2	3	1	1.9	.940
	C. French	R	28	53	54	8	6	4.1	.930		G. Browne	R	29	38	2	2	1	1.4	.952
	F. Parent	R	11	24	35	3	3	5.6	.952		W. Cole	R	22	31	6	1	0	1.7	.974
	F. Chouinard		1	2	3	0	0	5.0	1.000		C. French	R	16	16	0	2	0	1.1	.889
SS	L. Blackburne	R	74	173	265	43	29	6.5	.911		E. Hahn	R	15	14	0	1	0	1.0	.933
	R. Zeider	R	45	100	117	24	15	5.4	.900		R. Bowser		1	0	0	0	0		.000
	L. Tannehill	R	38	52	126	10	15	4.9	.947		R. Kelly	R	14	18	1	0	0	1.4	1.000
	F. Parent	R	4	3	14	1	1	4.5	.944		D. White	L	14	14	3	0	0	1.2	1.000
3B	B. Purtell	R	102	117	233*	36*	16	3.8	.907		B. Messenger	R	9	9	2	2	0	1.4	.846
	H. Lord	R	44	44	75	6	4	2.8	.952		C. Barrows	L	6	7	0	1	0	1.3	.875
	R. Zeider	R	4	7	13	3	1	5.8	.870		C. Gandil	R	2	3	0	0	0	1.5	1.000
	L. Tannehill	R	6	9	12	1	0	3.7	.955		C. Mullen	R	2	1	0	0	0	0.5	1.000
	F. Parent	R	1	0	1	0	0	1.0	1.000		F. Payne	R	2	1	0	0	0	0.5	1.000
										C	F. Payne	R	78	409	106	14	11	6.8	.974
											B. Sullivan	R	45	290	71	9	5	8.2	.976
											B. Block	R	47	244	77	12	8	7.1	.964

The game on the field took a back seat to the opening of "The Baseball Capitol of the World." Spacious Comiskey Park was erected over the winter despite a steelworker's strike, Halley's Comet, and the meddlesome Charles Comiskey. The owner battled architect Zachary Taylor Davis every step of the way as he insisted on his own functional style. The architect wanted a cantilevered grandstand and a Roman facade, much like Shibe Park. The owner wanted to save money.

The Sox concluded their stay at the 39th Street Grounds on June 27 with a depressing 7–2 loss to Cleveland. The old park was then turned over to Frank Leland's "Black American Giants." Comiskey Park opened to rave reviews on July 1, though Ed Walsh dropped a 2–0 decision to the Browns in the inaugural contest. Lena Blackburne made the first hit; Ed Walsh's first pitch was a ball.

A bumper crop of rookies dotted the 1910 roster. The rebellious Frank Smith was traded to Boston for Harry Lord and Amby McConnell, as Comiskey continued to search for the right combination. Chick Gandil joined the Sox but was too green to make a lasting impression. The 1910 Sox never rose above fifth place and finished last in hitting during a season when batting averages were on the rise. The dead ball era was disappearing from the baseball scene.

TEAM STATISTICS

	W	L	PCT	GB	R	OR	2B	3B	HR	BA	SA	SB	E	DP	FA	CG	BB	SO	ShO	SV	ERA
PHI	102	48	.680		672	439	194	106	19	.266	.356	207	230	117	.965	123	450	789	24	7	1.79
NY	88	63	.583	14.5	629	502	163	75	20	.248	.322	288	284	95	.956	110	364	654	14	8	2.59
DET	86	68	.558	18	679	580	192	73	26	.261	.344	249	288	79	.956	108	460	532	17	5	3.00
BOS	81	72	.529	22.5	637	564	175	87	43	.259	.351	194	309	80	.954	100	414	670	11	8	2.46
CLE	71	81	.467	32	539	654	185	63	9	.244	.308	189	247	112	.964	92	487	614	13	10	2.89
CHI	68	85	.444	35.5	456	495	115	58	7	.211	.261	183	314	100	.954	103	381	785	23	8	2.01
WAS	66	85	.437	36.5	498	552	145	46	9	.236	.289	192	264	99	.959	119	374	675	19	3	2.46
STL	47	107	.305	57	454	778	131	60	12	.220	.276	169	377	113	.944	100	532	557	9	4	3.09
LEAGUE TOTAL					4564	4564	1300	568	145	.243	.314	1671	2313	795	.956	855	3462	5276	130	53	2.53

INDIVIDUAL PITCHING

PITCHER	T	W	L	PCT	ERA	SV	G	GS	CG	IP	H	BB	SO	R	ER	ShO	H9	BB9	SO9
Ed Walsh	R	18	20	.474	1.27	6	45	36	33	369.2	242	61	258	90	52	7	5.89	1.49	6.28
Doc White	L	15	13	.536	2.56	1	33	29	20	245.2	219	50	111	84	70	2	8.02	1.83	4.07
Jim Scott	R	8	18	.308	2.43	1	41	23	14	229.2	182	86	135	99	62	2	7.13	3.37	5.29
Fred Olmstead		10	12	.455	1.95	0	32	20	14	184.1	174	50	68	74	40	4	8.50	2.44	3.32
Irv Young	L	4	8	.333	2.72	0	27	17	7	135.2	122	39	64	54	41	4	8.09	2.59	4.25
Frank Lange	R	9	4	.692	1.65	0	23	15	6	130.2	93	54	98	49	24	1	6.41	3.72	6.75
Frank Smith	R	4	9	.308	2.03	0	19	15	9	128.2	91	40	50	43	29	3	6.37	2.80	3.50
Chief Chouneau	R	0	1	.000	3.38	0	1	1	0	5.1	7	0	1	2	2	0	11.81	0.00	1.69
Bill Burns	L	0	0	—	0.00	0	1	0	0	.1	0	1	0	0	0	0	0.00	27.00	0.00
TEAM TOTAL		68	85	.444	2.01	8	222	156	103	1430	1130	381	785	495	320	23	7.11	2.40	4.94

Chicago 1911　　　Won 77　Lost 74　Pct .510　4th

MANAGER	W	L	PCT
Hugh Duffy	77	74	.510

POS	Player	B	G	AB	H	2B	3B	HR	HR%	R	RBI	BB	SO	SB	Pinch Hit AB	Pinch Hit H	BA	SA
REGULARS																		
1B	Shano Collins	R	106	370	97	16	12	3	0.8	48	48	20		14	3	0	.262	.395
2B	Amby McConnell	L	104	396	111	11	5	1	0.3	45	34	23		7	1	0	.280	.341
SS	Lee Tannehill	R	141	516	131	17	6	0	0.0	60	49	32		0	0	0	.254	.310
3B	Harry Lord	L	141	561	180	18	18	3	0.5	103	61	32		43	2	0	.321	.433
RF	Matty McIntyre	L	146	569	184	19	11	1	0.2	102	52	64		17	0	0	.323	.401
CF	Ping Bodie	R	145	551	159	27	13	4	0.7	75	97	49		14	1	0	.289	.407
LF	Nixey Callahan	R	120	466	131	13	5	3	0.6	64	60	15		45	5	1	.281	.350
C	Billy Sullivan	R	89	256	55	9	3	0	0.0	26	31	16		1	0	0	.215	.273
SUBSTITUTES																		
UT	Rollie Zeider	R	73	217	55	3	0	2	0.9	39	21	29		28	8	4	.253	.295
SS	Roy Corhan	R	43	131	28	6	2	0	0.0	14	8	15		2	0	0	.214	.290
1B	Charlie Mullen	R	20	59	12	2	1	0	0.0	7	5	5		1	0	0	.203	.271
1B	Tex Jones	R	9	31	6	1	0	0	0.0	4	4	3		1	0	0	.194	.226
2B	Freddy Parent	R	3	9	4	1	0	0	0.0	2	3	2		0	0	0	.444	.556
2B	Marty Berghammer	L	2	5	0	0	0	0	0.0	0	0	0		0	0	0	.000	.000
OF	Patsy Dougherty	L	76	211	61	10	9	0	0.0	39	32	26		19	19	3	.289	.422
OF	Cuke Barrows	R	13	46	9	2	0	0	0.0	5	4	7		2	0	0	.196	.239
O2	Felix Chouinard	B	14	17	3	0	0	0	0.0	3	0	0		0	0	0	.176	.176
OF	Bobby Messenger	L	13	17	2	0	1	0	0.0	4	0	3		0	9	2	.118	.235
OF	Paul Meloan	L	1	3	1	0	0	0	0.0	0	1	0		0	0	0	.333	.333
OF	Jimmy Johnston	R	1	2	0	0	0	0	0.0	0	2	0		0	0	0	.000	.000
C	Fred Payne	R	66	133	27	2	1	1	0.8	14	19	8		6	9	3	.203	.256
C	Bruno Block	R	39	115	35	6	1	1	0.9	11	18	6		0	1	0	.304	.400
C	Ralph Kreitz	R	7	17	4	1	0	0	0.0	0	0	2		0	0	0	.235	.294
C	Wally Mayer	R	1	3	0	0	0	0	0.0	0	0	2		0	0	0	.000	.000
PITCHERS																		
P	Ed Walsh	R	62	155	32	3	0	0	0.0	22	9	1		0	7	2	.206	.226
P	Doc White	L	39	78	20	1	1	0	0.0	12	6	7		1	0	0	.256	.295
P	Frank Lange	R	54	76	22	6	2	0	0.0	7	16	7		0	19	8	.289	.421
P	Jim Scott	R	39	71	11	2	0	0	0.0	5	4	4		0	0	0	.155	.183
P	Fred Olmstead		25	37	7	1	1	0	0.0	3	4	1		0	0	0	.189	.270
P	Jesse Baker	L	22	29	3	0	0	0	0.0	0	3	2		0	0	0	.103	.103
P	Irv Young	L	24	28	5	2	0	0	0.0	0	2	1		0	0	0	.179	.250
P	Joe Benz	R	12	17	1	0	0	0	0.0	1	0	0		0	0	0	.059	.059
P	Joe Hovlik	R	11	13	1	0	0	0	0.0	1	0	3		0	0	0	.077	.077
P	George Mogridge	L	4	5	2	0	0	0	0.0	1	0	0		0	0	0	.400	.400
TEAM TOTAL				5210	1399	179	92	19	0.4	717	593	385		201	84	23	.269	.349

INDIVIDUAL FIELDING

POS	Player	T	G	PO	A	E	DP	TCG	FA
1B	S. Collins	R	97	878	67	19	46	9.9	.980
	R. Zeider	R	29	294	24	1	10	11.0	.997
	C. Mullen	R	20	176	12	6	2	9.7	.969
	T. Jones	R	9	96	12	0	6	12.0	1.000
	L. Tannehill	R	5	52	3	0	1	11.0	1.000
	D. White	L	2	7	0	0	0	3.5	1.000
2B	A. McConnell	R	103	189	280	13	31	4.7	**.973**
	L. Tannehill	R	27	67	96	7	12	6.3	.959
	P. Bodie	R	16	31	40	7	4	4.9	.910
	R. Zeider	R	9	20	12	5	0	4.1	.865
	F. Parent	R	3	5	10	0	0	5.0	1.000
	S. Collins	R	3	3	6	2	0	3.7	.818
	M. Berghammer	R	2	5	2	0	0	3.5	1.000
	F. Chouinard	R	4	3	3	1	1	1.8	.857
SS	L. Tannehill	R	102	262	380	29	37	6.6	**.957**
	R. Corhan	R	43	98	146	20	18	6.1	.924
	R. Zeider	R	17	34	44	8	5	5.1	.907
3B	H. Lord	R	138	175	226	25	21	3.1	.941
	R. Zeider	R	10	10	12	1	1	2.3	.957
	L. Tannehill	R	8	4	14	2	3	2.5	.900

POS	Player	T	G	PO	A	E	DP	TCG	FA
OF	P. Bodie	R	128	256	24	9	9	2.3	.969
	M. McIntyre	L	146	235	18	14	5	1.8	.948
	N. Callahan	R	114	173	10	7	2	1.7	.963
	P. Dougherty	R	56	78	6	6	1	1.6	.933
	C. Barrows	L	13	17	0	1	0	1.4	.944
	F. Chouinard	R	4	8	1	1	0	2.5	.900
	B. Messenger	R	4	7	0	1	0	2.0	.875
	S. Collins	R	3	3	0	0	0	1.0	1.000
	D. White	L	1	2	0	0	0	2.0	1.000
	J. Johnston	R	1	1	0	0	0	1.0	1.000
	P. Meloan	R	1	0	0	1	0	1.0	.000
C	B. Sullivan	R	89	447	114	8	13	6.4	**.986**
	F. Payne	R	56	213	48	10	10	4.8	.963
	B. Block	R	38	201	40	7	2	6.5	.972
	R. Kreitz	R	7	24	4	0	1	4.0	1.000
	W. Mayer	R	1	7	2	1	0	10.0	.900

Ed Walsh and the twenty-four pretenders. The Big Reel was the big story again in 1911, and really the only story. Walsh threw his only no-hitter against Boston on August 27, a walk to Clyde Engle in the fourth providing the sole baserunner. He gave the Sox pride when he stopped Ty Cobb's 40-game hitting streak on July 4, handing the Georgia Peach a comfortable oh-for-four collar. In the 1911 City Series against the Cubs, all Ed Walsh did was win three of the four Sox victories as the Cubs, winners of 92 games in 1911, were swept.

If all this wasn't enough, Walsh was also the winner of "Comiskey Field Day," an exhibition of baseball skill that pitted ballplayers from competing teams in the hundred-yard dash, the shot-put, and a fungo-hitting contest. Walsh captured 1911 honors when he swatted a 419-foot fungo fly, bettering the mark set in 1907 by Mike Mitchell of Cincinnati.

The rest of the season was uneventful, as the Sox climbed into the first division on the last day of the season. Charles Comiskey named Nixey Callahan manager on October 22. The owner wanted a man who lived in Chicago year round (Duffy resided in Dorchester, Massachusetts) to oversee his affairs. Duffy was assigned to the Des Moines club, where he was given the task of developing new talent.

TEAM STATISTICS

	W	L	PCT	GB	R	OR	2B	3B	Batting HR	BA	SA	SB	E	Fielding DP	FA	CG	BB	Pitching SO	ShO	SV	ERA
PHI	101	50	.669		861	601	235	93	32	.296	.396	226	225	100	.965	97	487	739	13	14	3.01
DET	89	65	.578	13.5	831	777	230	96	30	.292	.388	276	318	78	.951	108	460	538	8	6	3.73
CLE	80	73	.523	22	691	709	243	80	21	.282	.370	209	302	108	.954	93	550	673	6	6	3.37
CHI	77	74	.510	24	717	627	179	92	19	.269	.349	201	252	98	.961	86	384	752	14	16	3.01
BOS	78	75	.510	24	680	647	203	66	35	.274	.362	190	323	93	.949	87	475	713	10	12	2.73
NY	76	76	.500	25.5	686	726	190	96	26	.272	.363	270	328	99	.949	91	406	667	5	6	3.54
WAS	64	90	.416	38.5	624	760	159	53	16	.258	.320	215	305	90	.953	106	410	628	13	6	3.52
STL	45	107	.296	56.5	567	810	187	63	16	.238	.310	125	358	104	.945	92	463	383	7	2	3.83
LEAGUE TOTAL					5657	5657	1626	639	195	.273	.358	1712	2411	770	.953	760	3635	5093	76	68	3.34

INDIVIDUAL PITCHING

PITCHER	T	W	L	PCT	ERA	SV	G	GS	CG	IP	H	BB	SO	R	ER	ShO	H9	BB9	SO9
Ed Walsh	R	27	18	.600	2.22	7	56	37	33	368.2	327	72	255	125	91	5	7.98	1.76	6.23
Doc White	L	10	14	.417	2.98	2	34	29	16	214.1	219	35	72	91	71	4	9.20	1.47	3.02
Jim Scott	R	14	11	.560	2.63	2	39	26	14	202	195	81	128	82	59	3	8.69	3.61	5.70
Frank Lange	R	8	8	.500	3.23	0	29	22	8	161.2	151	77	104	77	58	1	8.41	4.29	5.79
Fred Olmstead		6	6	.500	4.21	2	25	11	7	117.2	146	30	45	78	55	1	11.17	2.29	3.44
Jesse Baker	L	2	7	.222	3.93	1	22	8	3	94	101	30	51	52	41	0	9.67	2.87	4.88
Irv Young	L	5	6	.455	4.37	2	24	11	2	92.2	99	25	40	61	45	0	9.62	2.43	3.88
Joe Benz	R	3	2	.600	2.26	0	12	6	2	55.2	52	13	28	23	14	0	8.41	2.10	4.53
Joe Hovlik	R	2	0	1.000	3.06	0	12	3	1	47	47	20	24	21	16	1	9.00	3.83	4.60
George Mogridge	L	0	2	.000	4.97	0	4	1	0	12.2	12	1	5	10	7	0	8.53	0.71	3.55
TEAM TOTAL		77	74	.510	3.01	16	257	154	86	1366.1	1349	384	752	620	457	15	8.89	2.53	4.95

Chicago 1912   Won 78   Lost 76   Pct. .506   4th

MANAGER	W	L	PCT
Nixey Callahan	78	76	.506

POS	Player	B	G	AB	H	2B	3B	HR	HR%	R	RBI	BB	SO	SB	Pinch Hit AB	Pinch Hit H	BA	SA
REGULARS																		
1B	Rollie Zeider	R	129	420	103	12	10	1	0.2	57	42	50		47	3	1	.245	.329
2B	Morrie Rath	L	157	591	161	10	2	1	0.2	104	19	95		30	0	0	.272	.301
SS	Buck Weaver	B	147	523	117	21	8	1	0.2	55	43	9		12	0	0	.224	.300
3B	Harry Lord	L	151	570	152	19	12	5	0.9	81	54	52		28	0	0	.267	.368
RF	Shano Collins	R	153	575	168	34	10	2	0.3	75	81	29		26	2	0	.292	.397
CF	Ping Bodie	R	137	472	139	24	7	5	1.1	58	72	43		12	7	3	.294	.407
LF	Nixey Callahan	R	111	408	111	9	7	1	0.2	45	52	12		19	4	1	.272	.336
C	Walt Kuhn	R	75	178	36	7	0	0	0.0	16	10	20		5	0	0	.202	.242
SUBSTITUTES																		
1B	Babe Borton	L	31	105	39	3	1	0	0.0	15	17	8		1	1	1	.371	.419
1B	Jack Fournier	L	35	73	14	5	2	0	0.0	5	2	4		1	18	5	.192	.315
SS	Ernie Johnson	L	18	42	11	0	1	0	0.0	7	5	1		0	1	1	.262	.310
1B	Mutz Ens	L	3	6	0	0	0	0	0.0	0	0	0		0	0	0	.000	.000
3B	Lee Tannehill	R	3	3	0	0	0	0	0.0	0	0	1		0	0	0	.000	.000
2B	Kid Gleason	L	1	2	1	0	0	0	0.0	0	0	0		0	0	0	.500	.500
S3	Lena Blackburne	R	3	1	0	0	0	0	0.0	0	0	1		1	0	0	.000	.000
OF	Wally Mattick	R	88	285	74	7	9	1	0.4	45	35	27		15	8	3	.260	.358
OF	Matty McIntyre	L	45	84	14	0	0	0	0.0	10	10	14		3	0	0	.167	.167
OF	Cuke Barrows	R	8	13	3	0	0	0	0.0	0	2	2		1	4	1	.231	.231
OF	Joe Berrens		2	4	1	0	0	0	0.0	1	0	0		0	0	0	.250	.250
C	Bruno Block	R	46	136	35	5	6	0	0.0	8	26	7		1	0	0	.257	.382
C	Billy Sullivan	R	39	91	19	2	1	0	0.0	9	15	9		0	0	0	.209	.253
C	Ray Schalk	R	23	63	18	2	0	0	0.0	7	8	3		2	0	0	.286	.317
C	Ted Easterly	L	30	55	20	2	0	0	0.0	5	14	2		1	18*	8*	.364	.400
C	Wally Mayer	R	7	9	0	0	0	0	0.0	1	0	1		0	1	0	.000	.000
PH	Polly McLarry	L	2	2	0	0	0	0	0.0	0	0	0		0	2	0	.000	.000
PH	Del Paddock	L	1	1	0	0	0	0	0.0	0	0	0		0	1	0	.000	.000
PH	Polly Wolfe	L	1	1	0	0	0	0	0.0	0	0	0		0	1	0	.000	.000
PITCHERS																		
P	Ed Walsh	R	64	136	33	4	1	0	0.0	12	12	14		0	2	1	.243	.287
P	Joe Benz	R	41	76	10	0	1	0	0.0	3	4	1		0	0	0	.132	.158
P	Frank Lange	R	40	65	14	4	1	0	0.0	4	7	4		0	9	2	.215	.308
P	Eddie Cicotte	B	20	56	13	2	0	0	0.0	10	3	2		0	0	0	.232	.268
P	Doc White	L	33	56	7	1	1	0	0.0	5	0	7		0	0	0	.125	.179
P	Rube Peters	R	28	31	6	1	0	0	0.0	1	2	1		0	0	0	.194	.226
P	George Mogridge	L	17	16	2	0	0	0	0.0	0	1	3		0	0	0	.125	.125
P	Jim Scott	R	6	12	0	0	0	0	0.0	0	0	0		0	0	0	.000	.000
P	Wiley Taylor	R	3	5	0	0	0	0	0.0	0	0	0		0	0	0	.000	.000
P	Rip Jordan	L	3	4	0	0	0	0	0.0	0	0	0		0	0	0	.000	.000
P	Jim Crabb	R	2	3	0	0	0	0	0.0	0	0	0		0	0	0	.000	.000
P	Ellis Johnson	R	4	3	0	0	0	0	0.0	0	0	1		0	0	0	.000	.000
P	Ralph Bell	L	3	2	0	0	0	0	0.0	0	0	0		0	0	0	.000	.000
P	Phil Douglas	R	3	2	0	0	0	0	0.0	0	0	0		0	0	0	.000	.000
P	Harry Smith		1	1	0	0	0	0	0.0	0	1	0		0	0	0	.000	.000
P	Flame Delhi	R	1	0	0	0	0	0	—	0	0	0		0	0	0	—	—
P	Fred Lamline	R	1	0	0	0	0	—		0	0	0		0	0	0	—	—
TEAM TOTAL				5181	1321	174	80	17	0.3	640	537	423		205	83	27	.255	.329

INDIVIDUAL FIELDING

POS	Player	T	G	PO	A	E	DP	TCG	FA
1B	R. Zeider	R	66	682	54	16	28	11.4	.979
	S. Collins	R	46	455	35	4	24	10.7	.992
	B. Borton	L	30	312	16	1	14	11.0	.997
	J. Fournier	R	17	154	16	2	4	10.1	.988
	M. Ens	L	3	12	0	2	1	4.7	.857
2B	M. Rath	R	157	353	463	31	46	5.4	.963
	K. Gleason	R	1	1	1	1	0	3.0	.667
SS	B. Weaver	R	147	342	425	71	53	5.7	.915
	E. Johnson	R	16	23	37	1	3	3.8	.984
	L. Blackburne	R	2	3	1	1	1	2.5	.800
	R. Zeider	R	1	3	1	0	0	4.0	1.000
3B	H. Lord	R	106	127	172	35	11	3.2	.895
	R. Zeider	R	56	57	108	11	11	3.1	.938
	L. Tannehill	R	3	2	2	2	1	2.0	.667
	L. Blackburne	R	1	0	1	0	0	1.0	1.000

POS	Player	T	G	PO	A	E	DP	TCG	FA
OF	P. Bodie	R	130	208	11	7	3	1.7	.969
	S. Collins	R	105	177	11	6	0	1.8	.969
	N. Callahan	R	107	166	3	11	0	1.7	.939
	W. Mattick	R	78	154	8	3	1	2.1	.982
	H. Lord	R	45	61	5	3	3	1.5	.957
	M. McIntyre	L	45	37	2	0	0	0.9	1.000
	T. Easterly	R	1	0	0	0	0	0.0	.000
	C. Barrows	L	3	1	1	0	0	0.7	1.000
	J. Berrens		2	1	0	0	0	0.5	1.000
C	W. Kuhn	R	75	318	104	15	8	5.8	.966
	B. Block	R	46	222	65	6	4	6.4	.980
	B. Sullivan	R	39	147	52	5	4	5.2	.975
	R. Schalk	R	23	115	40	14	4	7.3	.917
	T. Easterly	R	10	40	13	2	3*	5.5	.964
	W. Mayer	R	6	13	1	0	0	2.3	1.000

It started promisingly enough. Callahan's charges broke away to a 26–8 record, good for first place on May 25. Too bad it didn't end there. An unsettled outfield and a season-long illness to Jim Scott dropped the Sox back into their familiar .500 pattern by August. At various times, the outfield trio consisted of Harry Lord, Chick Mattick, Ping Bodie, Jimmy Callahan, and Matty McIntyre. Pennants aren't won through experimentation.

By July Comiskey and Callahan were searching for new faces. They talked the Red Sox into parting with Ed Cicotte on July 10. He was a malcontent with Boston but became the first of the great White Sox knuckleball pitchers, a list that later included Ted Lyons, Hoyt Wilhelm, and Wilbur Wood. Cicotte lost his Chicago debut to Walter Johnson on July 13 but showed well for the future.

On August 19 Lena Blackburne and Jimmy Block were dealt to Milwaukee of the American Association for catcher Ray Schalk. In his debut on August 11, against Philadelphia, young Schalk went one-for-three. The *Chicago Tribune* said that they "...were pleased to see catcher Ray Schalk go behind the bat in the first game and play like a major leaguer right from the start."

TEAM STATISTICS

	W	L	PCT	GB	R	OR	2B	3B	HR	BA	SA	SB	E	DP	FA	CG	BB	SO	ShO	SV	ERA
BOS	105	47	.691		800	544	269	86	29	.277	.381	185	267	88	.957	110	385	712	18	6	2.76
WAS	91	61	.599	14	698	581	202	86	19	.256	.341	274	297	92	.954	99	525	821	12	8	2.69
PHI	90	62	.592	15	780	656	204	108	22	.282	.377	258	263	115	.959	100	518	601	9	9	3.32
CHI	78	76	.506	28	640	647	174	80	17	.255	.329	205	291	102	.956	84	426	697	14	15	3.06
CLE	75	78	.490	30.5	680	681	218	77	10	.273	.352	194	287	124	.954	96	523	622	7	7	3.30
DET	69	84	.451	36.5	720	768	189	86	19	.267	.349	270	338	91	.950	104	517	506	7	5	3.78
STL	53	101	.344	53	556	790	166	71	19	.249	.320	176	341	127	.947	89	442	547	8	5	3.71
NY	50	102	.329	55	632	839	168	79	18	.259	.334	247	382	77	.940	109	436	637	3	2	4.13
LEAGUE TOTAL					5506	5506	1590	673	153	.265	.348	1809	2466	816	.952	791	3772	5143	78	57	3.34

INDIVIDUAL PITCHING

PITCHER	T	W	L	PCT	ERA	SV	G	GS	CG	IP	H	BB	SO	R	ER	ShO	H9	BB9	SO9
Ed Walsh	R	27	17	.614	2.15	10	62	41	32	393	332	94	254	125	94	6	7.60	2.15	5.82
Joe Benz	R	12	18	.400	2.92	0	41	31	11	237.2	230	70	96	107	77	3	8.71	2.65	3.64
Doc White	L	8	9	.471	3.24	0	32	19	9	172	172	47	57	81	62	1	9.00	2.46	2.98
Frank Lange	R	10	10	.500	3.27	3	31	21	11	165.1	165	68	96	85	60	2	8.98	3.70	5.23
Eddie Cicotte	R	9	7	.563	2.84	0	20	18	13	152	159	37	70	63	48	1	9.41	2.19	4.14
Rube Peters	R	5	6	.455	4.14	0	28	11	4	108.2	134	33	39	72	50	0	11.10	2.73	3.23
George Mogridge	L	3	4	.429	4.04	2	17	7	2	64.2	69	15	31	32	29	0	9.60	2.09	4.31
Jim Scott	R	2	2	.500	2.15	0	6	4	2	37.2	36	15	23	16	9	1	8.60	3.58	5.50
Wiley Taylor	R	1	1	.500	4.95	0	3	3	0	20	21	14	4	12	11	0	9.45	6.30	1.80
Ellis Johnson	R	0	0	–	3.29	0	4	0	0	13.2	11	10	8	6	5	0	7.24	6.59	5.27
Phil Douglas	R	0	1	.000	7.30	0	3	1	0	12.1	21	6	7	17	10	0	15.32	4.38	5.11
Rip Jordan	R	0	0	–	6.10	0	3	0	0	10.1	13	0	0	8	7	0	11.32	0.00	0.00
Jim Crabb	R	0	1	.000	1.04	0	2	1	0	8.2	6	4	3	2	1	0	6.23	4.15	3.12
Ralph Bell	L	0	0	–	9.00	0	3	0	0	6	8	8	5	7	6	0	12.00	12.00	7.50
Harry Smith	R	1	0	1.000	1.80	0	1	1	0	5	6	0	1	1	1	0	10.80	0.00	1.80
Flame Delhi	R	0	0	–	9.00	0	1	0	0	3	7	3	2	6	3	0	21.00	9.00	6.00
Fred Lamline	R	0	0	–	31.50	0	1	1	0	2	7	2	1	7	7	0	31.50	9.00	4.50
TEAM TOTAL		78	76	.506	3.06	15	258	158	84	1412	1397	426	697	647	480	14	8.90	2.72	4.44

Chicago 1913   Won 78 Lost 74 Pct. .513 5th

MANAGER	W	L	PCT
Nixey Callahan	78	74	.513

POS	Player	B	G	AB	H	2B	3B	HR	HR%	R	RBI	BB	SO	SB	Pinch Hit AB	Pinch Hit H	BA	SA
REGULARS																		
1B	Hal Chase	R	102	384	110	11	10	2	0.5	49	39	16	41	9	0	0	.286	.383
2B	Morrie Rath	L	90	295	59	2	0	0	0.0	37	12	46	22	22	2	1	.200	.207
SS	Buck Weaver	B	151	533	145	17	8	4	0.8	51	52	15	60	20	0	0	.272	.356
3B	Harry Lord	L	150	547	144	18	12	1	0.2	62	42	45	39	24	0	0	.263	.346
RF	Shano Collins	R	148	535	128	26	9	1	0.2	53	47	32	60	22	1	1	.239	.327
CF	Ping Bodie	R	127	406	107	14	8	8	2.0	39	48	35	57	5	6	0	.264	.397
LF	Wally Mattick	R	68	207	39	8	1	0	0.0	15	11	18	16	3	3	1	.188	.237
C	Ray Schalk	R	128	401	98	15	5	1	0.2	38	38	27	36	14	3	0	.244	.314
SUBSTITUTES																		
2B	Joe Berger	R	77	223	48	6	2	2	0.9	27	20	36	28	5	2	0	.215	.287
1O	Jack Fournier	L	68	172	40	8	5	1	0.6	20	23	21	23	9	13	1	.233	.355
1B	Babe Borton	L	28	80	22	5	0	0	0.0	9	13	23	5	1	2	0	.275	.338
S3	Jim Breton	R	10	30	5	1	1	0	0.0	1	2	1	5	0	0	0	.167	.267
31	Rollie Zeider	R	13	20	7	0	0	0	0.0	4	2	4	1	3	1	0	.350	.350
OF	Larry Chappell	L	60	208	48	8	1	0	0.0	20	15	18	22	7	1	0	.231	.279
OF	Biff Schaller	L	34	96	21	3	0	0	0.0	12	4	20	16	5	2	0	.219	.250
OF	Johnny Beall	L	17	60	16	0	1	2	3.3	10	3	0	0	1	0	0	.267	.400
OF	Davy Jones	L	10	21	6	0	0	0	0.0	2	0	9	0	1	1	0	.286	.286
OF	Edd Roush	L	9	10	1	0	0	0	0.0	2	0	0	2	0	4	1	.100	.100
OF	Nixey Callahan	R	6	9	2	0	0	0	0.0	0	1	0	2	0	5	1	.222	.222
O3	Don Rader	L	2	3	1	1	0	0	0.0	1	0	0	0	0	0	0	.333	.667
C	Ted Easterly	L	60	97	23	1	0	0	0.0	3	8	4	9	2	37	8	.237	.247
C	Walt Kuhn	R	26	50	8	1	0	0	0.0	5	5	13	8	1	2	0	.160	.180
C	Tom Daly	R	1	3	0	0	0	0	0.0	0	0	0	0	0	0	0	.000	.000
C	Billy Meyer	R	1	1	1	0	0	0	0.0	0	0	0	0	0	0	0	1.000	1.000
PITCHERS																		
P	Reb Russell	L	52	106	20	5	3	0	0.0	9	7	1	29	0	1	1	.189	.292
P	Jim Scott	R	48	97	7	1	0	1	1.0	3	8	3	24	2	0	0	.072	.113
P	Eddie Cicotte	B	41	91	13	2	0	0	0.0	7	2	4	16	0	0	0	.143	.165
P	Joe Benz	R	33	50	9	2	0	0	0.0	3	4	0	14	0	0	0	.180	.220
P	Ed Walsh	R	17	32	5	1	0	0	0.0	1	2	1	7	0	1	0	.156	.188
P	Doc White	L	20	25	3	0	0	0	0.0	1	0	3	1	0	0	0	.120	.120
P	Frank Lange	R	17	18	3	1	0	0	0.0	1	1	3	5	0	5	1	.167	.222
P	Pop Boy Smith	R	15	5	0	0	0	0	0.0	0	0	0	1	0	0	0	.000	.000
P	Bill Lathrop	R	6	4	0	0	0	0	0.0	1	1	0	1	0	0	0	.000	.000
P	Buck O'Brien	R	6	3	0	0	0	0	0.0	0	0	0	0	0	0	0	.000	.000
P	Frank Miller	R	1	0	0	0	0	0	—	0	0	0	0	0	0	0	—	—
P	Jim Scoggins	L	1	0	0	0	0	0	—	0	0	0	0	0	0	0	—	—
P	Bob Smith	R	1	0	0	0	0	0	—	0	0	0	0	0	0	0	—	—
TEAM TOTAL				4822	1139	157	66	23	0.5	486	410	398	550	156	92	16	.236	.310

INDIVIDUAL FIELDING

POS	Player	T	G	PO	A	E	DP	TCG	FA	POS	Player	T	G	PO	A	E	DP	TCG	FA
1B	H. Chase	L	102	1009	71	27*	53	10.9	.976	OF	S. Collins	R	147	244	19	14	3	1.9	.949
	B. Borton	L	26	301	12	3	19	12.2	.991		P. Bodie	R	119	226	14	8	1	2.1	.968
	J. Fournier	R	29	267	16	3	9	9.9	.990		W. Mattick	R	63	116	14	3	2	2.1	.977
	R. Zeider	R	3	7	2	0	0	3.0	1.000		L. Chappell	L	59	114	5	6	1	2.1	.952
	D. White	L	1	2	0	0	0	2.0	1.000		B. Schaller	R	32	45	0	4	0	1.5	.918
2B	M. Rath	R	86	159	251	16	32	5.0	.962		J. Fournier	R	23	39	7	2	1	2.1	.958
	J. Berger	R	69	111	214	14	18	4.9	.959		J. Beall	R	17	38	3	2	0	2.5	.953
	R. Zeider	R	1	0	1	0	0	1.0	1.000		D. Jones	R	8	11	2	2	0	1.9	.867
SS	B. Weaver	R	151	392	520	70	73	6.5	.929		E. Roush	L	2	3	0	0	0	1.5	1.000
	J. Breton	R	7	7	23	2	2	4.6	.938		N. Callahan	R	1	2	0	0	0	2.0	1.000
	J. Berger	R	4	2	8	1	1	2.8	.909		D. Rader	R	1	2	0	0	0	2.0	1.000
3B	H. Lord	R	150	142	221	30	13	2.6	.924	C	R. Schalk	R	125	599	154	15	18	6.1	.980
	R. Zeider	R	6	8	9	0	0	2.8	1.000		T. Easterly	R	19	96	24	3	0	6.5	.976
	J. Breton	R	3	1	7	1	0	3.0	.889		W. Kuhn	R	24	75	22	2	1	4.1	.980
	J. Berger	R	1	1	1	0	0	2.0	1.000		T. Daly	R	1	6	1	0	1	7.0	1.000
	D. Rader	R	1	0	0	1	0	1.0	.000		B. Meyer	R	1	5	1	1	0	7.0	.857

Purchased from the Fort Worth team for $1,200, Ewell "Reb" Russell from Jackson, Mississippi, couldn't throw a decent curveball in spring training. A year earlier he had broken his hand, but coach Kid Gleason taught him a new and better delivery. The results spoke for themselves. The rookie won 21 games with a nifty 1.91 ERA.

The White Sox decided to honor New York manager and longtime Chicago favorite Frank Chance with his own day. Thirty-five thousand fans clamored for tickets to the May 17 contest. Ticket scalpers in the Loop demanded upwards of $10 a ticket, but Comiskey heard of this and bought up $30 worth himself. He then traced the owners and published their names in the paper. "Chance Day" saw a victory for the Sox, but a section of the grandstand collapsed under the weight of pushing fans. There were only four injuries, but the incident convinced Comiskey to add more seats for 1914.

The mysterious and disruptive Hal Chase was acquired on June 1 from New York in exchange for Babe Borton and Rollie Zeider. He was seven days late in reporting. The Sox thought they made quite a deal. Chase, who was once blacklisted for gambling escapades, batted a decent .286. But Frank Chance knew what he was doing; he wasn't about to be fleeced, especially by his former crosstown rivals. The temporarily docile Chase didn't help the Sox escape their .500 doldrums. Once again they finished in fourth, just another also-ran.

TEAM STATISTICS

	W	L	PCT	GB	R	OR	2B	3B	HR	BA	SA	SB	E	DP	FA	CG	BB	SO	ShO	SV	ERA
PHI	96	57	.627		794	593	223	80	33	.280	.375	221	212	108	.966	69	532	630	15	21	3.19
WAS	90	64	.584	6.5	596	566	156	80	20	.252	.327	287	261	122	.960	80	465	757	22	19	2.72
CLE	86	66	.566	9.5	631	529	205	74	16	.268	.348	191	242	124	.962	95	502	689	18	3	2.52
BOS	79	71	.527	15.5	630	607	220	101	17	.269	.364	189	237	84	.961	87	441	709	11	13	2.94
CHI	78	74	.513	17.5	486	492	157	66	23	.236	.310	156	255	104	.960	86	438	602	16	8	2.33
DET	66	87	.431	30	624	720	180	101	24	.265	.355	218	300	105	.954	90	504	468	3	5	3.41
NY	57	94	.377	38	529	669	154	45	9	.237	.293	203	293	94	.954	78	455	530	7	4	3.27
STL	57	96	.373	39	528	642	179	73	18	.237	.312	209	301	125	.954	101	454	476	13	4	3.06
LEAGUE TOTAL					4818	4818	1474	620	160	.256	.336	1674	2101	866	.959	686	3791	4861	105	77	2.93

INDIVIDUAL PITCHING

PITCHER	T	W	L	PCT	ERA	SV	G	GS	CG	IP	H	BB	SO	R	ER	ShO	H9	BB9	SO9
Reb Russell	L	22	16	.579	1.91	4	51	36	25	316	249	79	122	89	67	8	7.09	2.25	3.47
Jim Scott	R	20	20	.500	1.90	1	48	38	27	312.1	252	86	158	96	66	4	7.26	2.48	4.55
Eddie Cicotte	R	18	12	.600	1.58	0	41	30	18	268	224	73	121	77	47	3	7.52	2.45	4.06
Joe Benz	R	7	10	.412	2.74	2	33	17	7	151	146	59	79	64	46	1	8.70	3.52	4.71
Doc White	L	2	4	.333	3.50	0	19	8	2	103	106	39	39	56	40	0	9.26	3.41	3.41
Ed Walsh	R	8	3	.727	2.58	1	16	14	7	97.2	91	39	34	37	28	1	8.39	3.59	3.13
Frank Lange	R	1	3	.250	4.87	0	12	3	0	40.2	46	20	20	24	22	0	10.18	4.43	4.43
Pop Boy Smith	R	0	2	.000	3.38	0	15	2	0	32	31	11	13	15	12	0	8.72	3.09	3.66
Buck O'Brien	R	0	3	.000	3.93	0	6	3	0	18.1	21	13	4	14	8	0	10.31	6.38	1.96
Bill Lathrop	R	0	0	–	4.24	0	6	0	0	17	16	12	9	11	8	0	8.47	6.35	4.76
Bob Smith	R	0	0	–	13.50	0	1	0	0	2	3	3	1	3	3	0	13.50	13.50	4.50
Frank Miller	R	0	1	.000	27.00	0	1	1	0	1.2	4	3	2	5	5	0	21.60	16.20	10.80
TEAM TOTAL		78	74	.513	2.33	8	249	152	86	1359.2	1189	437	602	491	352	17	7.87	2.89	3.98

Chicago 1914   Won 70 Lost 84 Pct .455 6th

MANAGER	W	L	PCT
Nixey Callahan	70	84	.455

POS	Player	B	G	AB	H	2B	3B	HR	HR%	R	RBI	BB	SO	SB	Pinch Hit AB	H	BA	SA
REGULARS																		
1B	Jack Fournier	L	109	379	118	14	9	6	1.6	44	44	31	44	10	6	0	.311	.443
2B	Lena Blackburne	R	144	474	105	10	5	1	0.2	52	35	66	58	25	1	0	.222	.270
SS	Buck Weaver	B	136	541	133	20	9	2	0.4	64	28	20	40	14	2	0	.246	.327
3B	Jim Breton	R	81	231	49	7	2	0	0.0	21	24	24	42	9	0	0	.212	.260
RF	Shano Collins	R	154	598	164	34	9	3	0.5	61	65	27	49	30	0	0	.274	.376
CF	Ping Bodie	R	107	327	75	9	5	3	0.9	21	29	21	35	12	10	2	.229	.315
LF	Ray Demmitt	L	146	515	133	13	12	2	0.4	63	46	61	48	12	3	1	.258	.342
C	Ray Schalk	R	135	392	106	13	2	0	0.0	30	36	38	24	24	9	3	.270	.314
SUBSTITUTES																		
1B	Hal Chase	R	58	206	55	10	5	0	0.0	27	20	23	19	9	0	0	.267	.364
3B	Scotty Alcock	R	54	156	27	4	2	0	0.0	12	7	7	14	4	3	0	.173	.224
UT	Joe Berger	R	47	148	23	3	1	0	0.0	11	3	13	9	2	1	0	.155	.189
3B	Harry Lord	L	21	69	13	1	1	1	1.4	8	3	5	3	2	0	0	.188	.275
3B	Howard Baker	R	15	47	13	1	1	0	0.0	4	5	3	8	2	0	0	.277	.340
2B	Carl Manda	R	9	15	4	0	0	0	0.0	2	1	3	3	1	0	0	.267	.267
UT	Tom Daly	R	61	133	31	2	0	0	0.0	13	8	7	13	3	24	6	.233	.248
OF	Braggo Roth	R	34	126	37	4	6	1	0.8	14	10	8	25	3	0	0	.294	.444
OF	Larry Chappell	L	21	39	9	0	0	0	0.0	3	1	4	11	0	10	1	.231	.231
OF	Polly Wolfe	L	9	28	6	0	0	0	0.0	0	0	3	6	1	1	0	.214	.214
OF	Cecil Coombs	R	7	23	4	1	0	0	0.0	1	1	1	7	0	0	0	.174	.217
OF	Irv Porter	B	1	4	1	0	0	0	0.0	1	0	0	1	0	0	0	.250	.250
OF	Hank Schreiber	R	1	2	0	0	0	0	0.0	0	0	0	1	0	0	0	.000	.000
C	Wally Mayer	R	39	85	14	3	1	0	0.0	7	5	14	23	1	5	0	.165	.224
C	Walt Kuhn	R	17	40	11	1	0	0	0.0	4	0	8	11	2	0	0	.275	.300
C	Billy Sullivan	R	1	0	0	0	0	0	—	0	0	0	0	0	0	0	—	—
PH	Charlie Kavanagh	R	5	5	1	0	0	0	0.0	0	0	0	2	0	5	1	.200	.200
PH	Delos Brown	R	1	1	0	0	0	0	0.0	0	0	0	1	0	1	0	.000	.000
PITCHERS																		
P	Joe Benz	R	48	92	12	3	0	0	0.0	5	1	1	29	1	0	0	.130	.163
P	Eddie Cicotte	B	45	86	14	2	0	0	0.0	5	4	3	18	0	0	0	.163	.186
P	Jim Scott	R	43	86	14	3	0	0	0.0	3	2	3	19	0	0	0	.163	.198
P	Reb Russell	L	43	64	17	1	1	0	0.0	6	7	1	14	0	5	2	.266	.313
P	Red Faber	B	40	55	8	1	0	0	0.0	3	1	10	16	0	0	0	.145	.164
P	Mellie Wolfgang	R	24	40	7	0	0	0	0.0	2	0	2	7	0	0	0	.175	.175
P	Ed Walsh	R	10	16	1	1	0	0	0.0	0	0	1	4	0	2	0	.063	.125
P	Bill Lathrop	R	19	12	0	0	0	0	0.0	0	0	0	4	0	0	0	.000	.000
P	Hi Jasper	R	16	5	0	0	0	0	0.0	0	4	0	1	0	0	0	.000	.000
TEAM TOTAL				5040	1205	161	71	19	0.4	487	390	408	609	167	88	16	.239	.311

INDIVIDUAL FIELDING

POS	Player	T	G	PO	A	E	DP	TCG	FA
1B	J. Fournier	R	97	1025	78	25	30	11.6	.978
	H. Chase	L	58	632	43	13	27	11.9	.981
	T. Daly	R	2	25	1	1	2	13.5	.963
2B	L. Blackburne	R	143	239	433	26	28	4.9	.963
	J. Berger	R	12	14	30	3	4	3.9	.936
	C. Manda	R	7	10	23	1	1	4.9	.971
	S. Alcock	R	1	4	1	0	1	5.0	1.000
SS	B. Weaver	R	134	367	389	59	50	6.1	.928
	J. Berger	R	27	56	74	11	7	5.2	.922
3B	J. Breton	R	79	84	159	24	6	3.4	.910
	S. Alcock	R	48	57	95	16	10	3.5	.905
	H. Lord	R	19	10	32	3	0	2.4	.933
	H. Baker	R	15	7	22	4	1	2.2	.879
	J. Berger	R	7	6	9	1	0	2.3	.938
	T. Daly	R	5	3	2	1	0	1.2	.833
	W. Mayer	R	1	1	0	1	0	2.0	.500

POS	Player	T	G	PO	A	E	DP	TCG	FA
OF	S. Collins	R	154	268	21	19	5	2.0	.938
	R. Demmitt	R	142	217	24	12	3	1.8	.953
	P. Bodie	R	95	175	14	8	2	2.1	.959
	B. Roth	R	34	54	7	5	1	1.9	.924
	T. Daly	R	23	19	1	2	0	1.0	.909
	H. Lord	R	1	0	0	0	0	0.0	.000
	H. Schreiber	R	1	0	0	0	0	0.0	.000
	C. Coombs	R	7	13	2	0	0	2.1	1.000
	L. Chappell	L	9	13	0	1	0	1.6	.929
	J. Fournier	R	6	9	1	2	1	2.0	.833
	P. Wolfe	R	8	7	0	1	0	1.0	.875
	I. Porter	R	1	1	0	0	0	1.0	1.000
C	R. Schalk	R	124	613	183	21	20	6.6	.974
	W. Mayer	R	33	137	47	6	3	5.8	.968
	W. Kuhn	R	16	60	17	1	3	4.9	.987
	T. Daly	R	4	13	2	0	1	3.8	1.000
	B. Sullivan	R	1	1	0	0	0	1.0	1.000

It was a banner winter for Comiskey. Together with his former enemy John McGraw, the Old Roman took the Giants and White Sox on a world tour that included stops in Japan, Egypt, and a command performance before the King of England. It was a dream come true for Comiskey, who was reaching the zenith of his popularity and esteem. When he came home he faced the propects of war with the newly formed Federal League. By reverting to some of his old tactics, Federal raiders lured a number of major leaguers to their third league.

The Sox weren't affected by this until Hal Chase began telling his teammates of the Federal League riches. Team captain Harry Lord jumped the club on May 13 for unexplained reasons. Amid widespread dissension, the team remained in last place through May, and despite no-hitters by Jim Scott and Joe Benz they were lucky to finish sixth.

Chase served the ten-day clause on Comiskey, notifying him of his intention to go to another team, and moved his baggage to Weeghman Park (now Wrigley Field) where he joined the Buffalo Federals on June 21. A subsequent lawsuit by Comiskey failed to restrain Chase, who went on his merry way.

Convinced that the Sox needed an overhaul, Comiskey purchased Eddie Collins from the A's for a cool $50,000. Collins was fresh from having been named winner of the Chalmers Award for excellence in play in 1914. His five year contract was guaranteed.

TEAM STATISTICS

	W	L	PCT	GB	R	OR	2B	3B	HR	BA	SA	SB	E	DP	FA	CG	BB	SO	ShO	SV	ERA
PHI	99	53	.651		749	520	165	80	28	.272	.351	231	213	116	.966	88	521	720	22	12	2.78
BOS	91	62	.595	8.5	588	511	226	85	18	.250	.338	177	242	99	.963	88	397	605	26	9	2.35
WAS	81	73	.526	19	572	519	176	81	18	.244	.320	220	254	116	.961	75	520	784	24	14	2.54
DET	80	73	.523	19.5	615	618	195	84	25	.258	.344	211	286	101	.958	81	498	567	14	9	2.86
STL	71	82	.464	28.5	523	614	185	75	17	.243	.319	233	317	114	.952	80	540	553	14	9	2.85
CHI	70	84	.455	30	487	568	161	71	19	.239	.311	167	299	90	.955	74	401	660	17	12	2.48
NY	70	84	.455	30	536	550	149	52	12	.229	.287	251	238	93	.963	97	390	563	5	5	2.81
CLE	51	102	.333	48.5	538	708	178	69	11	.245	.312	167	300	119	.953	69	666	688	10	2	3.21
LEAGUE TOTAL					4608	4608	1435	597	148	.248	.323	1657	2149	848	.959	652	3933	5140	132	72	2.73

INDIVIDUAL PITCHING

PITCHER	T	W	L	PCT	ERA	SV	G	GS	CG	IP	H	BB	SO	R	ER	ShO	H9	BB9	SO9
Joe Benz	R	14	19	.424	2.26	2	48	35	16	283.1	245	66	142	103	71	4	7.78	2.10	4.51
Eddie Cicotte	R	11	16	.407	2.04	3	45	29	15	269.1	220	72	122	96	61	4	7.35	2.41	4.08
Jim Scott	R	14	18	.438	2.84	0	43	33	12	253.1	228	75	138	109	80	2	8.10	2.66	4.90
Red Faber	R	10	9	.526	2.68	4	40	20	11	181.1	154	64	88	77	54	2	7.64	3.18	4.37
Reb Russell	L	8	12	.400	2.90	1	38	23	8	167.1	168	33	79	80	54	1	9.04	1.77	4.25
Mellie Wolfgang	R	9	5	.643	1.89	2	24	11	9	119.1	96	32	50	42	25	2	7.24	2.41	3.77
Bill Lathrop	R	1	2	.333	2.64	0	19	1	0	47.2	41	19	7	20	14	0	7.74	3.59	1.32
Ed Walsh	R	2	3	.400	2.82	0	8	5	3	44.2	33	20	15	19	14	1	6.65	4.03	3.02
Hi Jasper	R	1	0	1.000	3.34	0	16	0	0	32.1	22	20	19	22	12	0	6.12	5.57	5.29
TEAM TOTAL		70	84	.455	2.48	12	281	157	74	1398.2	1207	401	660	568	385	16	7.77	2.58	4.25

Chicago 1915   Won 93   Lost 61   Pct. .604   3rd   54

MANAGER	W	L	PCT
Pants Rowland	93	61	.604

POS	Player	B	G	AB	H	2B	3B	HR	HR%	R	RBI	BB	SO	SB	Pinch Hit AB	H	BA	SA
REGULARS																		
1B	Jack Fournier	L	126	422	136	20	18	5	1.2	86	77	64	37	21	4	2	.322	.491
2B	Eddie Collins	L	155	521	173	22	10	4	0.8	118	77	119	27	46	0	0	.332	.436
SS	Buck Weaver	B	148	563	151	18	11	3	0.5	83	49	32	58	24	0	0	.268	.355
3B	Lena Blackburne	R	96	283	61	5	1	0	0.0	33	25	35	34	13	2	1	.216	.240
RF	Eddie Murphy	L	70	273	86	11	5	0	0.0	51	26	39	12	20	0	0	.315	.392
CF	Happy Felsch	R	121	427	106	18	11	3	0.7	65	53	51	59	16	3	0	.248	.363
LF	Shano Collins	R	153	576	148	24	17	2	0.3	73	85	28	50	38	2	0	.257	.368
C	Ray Schalk	R	135	413	110	14	4	1	0.2	46	54	62	21	15	1	1	.266	.327
SUBSTITUTES																		
3O	Braggo Roth	R	70	240	60	6	10	3*	1.3*	44	35	29	50	12	4	0	.250	.396
1B	Bunny Brief	R	48	154	33	6	2	2	1.3	13	17	16	28	8	2	0	.214	.318
3B	Pete Johns	R	28	100	21	2	1	0	0.0	7	11	8	11	2	0	0	.210	.250
3B	Jim Breton	R	16	36	5	1	0	0	0.0	3	1	5	9	2	0	0	.139	.167
OF	Joe Jackson	L	46	162	43	4	5	2	1.2	21	36	24	12	6	0	0	.265	.389
OF	Finners Quinlan	L	42	114	22	3	0	0	0.0	11	7	4	11	3	4	0	.193	.219
OF	Nemo Leibold	L	36	74	17	1	0	0	0.0	10	11	15	11	1	12	4	.230	.243
OF	Ray Demmitt	L	9	6	0	0	0	0	0.0	0	0	1	2	0	6	0	.000	.000
C	Wally Mayer	R	22	54	12	3	1	0	0.0	3	5	5	8	0	2	0	.222	.315
C	Tom Daly	R	29	47	9	1	0	0	0.0	5	3	5	9	0	9	1	.191	.213
PH	Howard Baker	R	2	2	0	0	0	0	0.0	0	0	0	2	0	2	0	.000	.000
PH	Larry Chappell	L	1	1	0	0	0	0	0.0	0	0	0	0	0	1	0	.000	.000
PH	Charlie Jackson	L	1	1	0	0	0	0	0.0	0	0	0	1	0	1	0	.000	.000
PITCHERS																		
P	Jim Scott	R	48	95	12	0	0	0	0.0	3	6	8	26	1	0	0	.126	.126
P	Reb Russell	L	45	86	21	2	3	0	0.0	11	7	4	14	1	3	0	.244	.337
P	Red Faber	B	50	84	11	1	2	0	0.0	11	6	20	33	4	0	0	.131	.190
P	Joe Benz	R	39	79	10	0	1	0	0.0	7	1	1	25	0	0	0	.127	.152
P	Eddie Cicotte	B	40	67	14	1	0	0	0.0	10	4	7	16	0	1	0	.209	.224
P	Mellie Wolfgang	R	17	17	2	0	0	0	0.0	3	1	0	2	0	0	0	.118	.118
P	Ed Walsh	R	5	11	4	0	0	0	0.0	0	1	0	1	0	2	1	.364	.364
P	Hi Jasper	R	3	7	2	0	0	0	0.0	0	0	0	4	0	0	0	.286	.286
P	Ed Klepfer	R	3	3	0	0	0	0	0.0	0	0	1	2	0	0	0	.000	.000
P	Dixie Davis	R	2	0	0	0	0	0	–	0	0	0	0	0	0	0	–	–
P	Ellis Johnson	R	1	0	0	0	0	0	–	0	0	0	0	0	0	0	–	–
TEAM TOTAL				4918	1269	163	102	25	0.5	717	598	583	575	233	61	10	.258	.348

INDIVIDUAL FIELDING

POS	Player	T	G	PO	A	E	DP	TCG	FA	POS	Player	T	G	PO	A	E	DP	TCG	FA
1B	J. Fournier	R	65	674	41	10	31	11.2	.986	OF	H. Felsch	R	118	247	9	11	1	2.3	.959
	S. Collins	R	47	516	28	12	26	11.8	.978		S. Collins	R	104	197	13	8	2	2.1	.963
	B. Brief	R	46	458	23	7	21	10.6	.986		J. Fournier	R	57	110	10	7	3	2.2	.945
	T. Daly	R	1	2	0	0	0	2.0	1.000		E. Murphy	R	70	113	7	6	0	1.8	.952
2B	E. Collins	R	155	344	487	22	54	5.5	.974		J. Jackson	R	46	84	6	5	1	2.1	.947
	J. Breton	R	1	1	1	0	0	2.0	1.000		N. Leibold	R	22	57	5	0	0	2.8	1.000
SS	B. Weaver	R	148	281	470	49	54	5.4	.939		B. Roth	R	30	45	5	3	0	1.8	.943
	L. Blackburne	R	9	11	19	3	3	3.7	.909		F. Quinlan	L	32	43	5	0	2	1.5	1.000
	J. Breton	R	1	0	2	0	0	2.0	1.000		R. Demmitt	R	3	1	0	0	0	0.3	1.000
3B	L. Blackburne	R	83	88	134	12	13	2.8	.949	C	R. Schalk	R	134	655	159	13	8	6.2	.984
	P. Johns	R	28	37	62	6	5	3.8	.943		W. Mayer	R	20	89	15	1	0	5.3	.990
	B. Roth	R	35	34	43	15	1	2.6	.837		T. Daly	R	19	59	9	3	0	3.7	.958
	J. Breton	R	14	14	16	4	2	2.4	.882										

Comiskey surprised the baseball world by naming a 33-year-old "busher" named Clarence "Pants" Rowland the new manager on December 18, 1914. Callahan's contract was not renewed, as Comiskey continued his overhaul. Though he was young, the new manager was running a young team. There were five new position players in 1915.

A nine-game winning streak put the Sox in first place on May 23. Included in this skein was an 11–3 rout of Babe Ruth, who made his first Comiskey Park appearance on the mound for Boston on May 22. The Sox remained close to Boston and Detroit for much of the season but found themselves seven and a half games out when September began. Then came another dip before they ran off an eleven-game win streak that closed the season. Too little, too late.

Shoeless Joe Jackson was purchased by the Sox on August 20 from the financially troubled Cleveland Naps. Six days earlier they purchased the contract of a young Pacific Coast League pitcher named Claude "Lefty" Williams. Nobody paid much attention at the time. Comiskey was serious about the overhaul following the Federal League challenge.

But 1915 also marked an end. Big Ed Walsh won his last game for the Sox on October 1, going out with an 8–0 shutout of the Browns. He attempted a comeback in 1916, but the years of overwork had taken their toll. The greatest pitcher in White Sox history was through.

TEAM STATISTICS

	W	L	PCT	GB	R	OR	2B	3B	HR	BA	SA	SB	E	DP	FA	CG	BB	SO	ShO	SV	ERA
BOS	101	50	.669		668	499	202	76	14	.260	.339	118	226	95	.964	82	446	634	16	12	2.39
DET	100	54	.649	2.5	778	573	207	94	23	.268	.358	241	258	107	.961	86	489	550	9	20	2.86
CHI	93	61	.604	9.5	717	509	163	102	25	.258	.348	233	222	95	.965	92	350	635	17	9	2.43
WAS	85	68	.556	17	571	492	152	79	12	.244	.312	186	230	101	.964	87	455	715	19	11	2.31
NY	69	83	.454	32.5	583	596	167	50	31	.233	.305	198	217	118	.966	100	517	559	11	2	3.09
STL	63	91	.409	39.5	521	693	166	65	19	.246	.315	202	335	144	.949	76	612	566	6	5	3.07
CLE	57	95	.375	44.5	539	670	169	79	20	.241	.317	138	280	82	.957	62	518	610	11	10	3.13
PHI	43	109	.283	58.5	545	890	183	72	16	.237	.311	127	338	118	.947	78	827	588	6	1	4.33
LEAGUE TOTAL					4922	4922	1409	617	160	.248	.326	1443	2106	860	.959	663	4214	4857	95	70	2.94

INDIVIDUAL PITCHING

PITCHER	T	W	L	PCT	ERA	SV	G	GS	CG	IP	H	BB	SO	R	ER	ShO	H9	BB9	SO9
Red Faber	R	24	14	.632	2.55	2	50	32	22	299.2	264	99	182	118	85	3	7.93	2.97	5.47
Jim Scott	R	24	11	.686	2.03	2	48	35	23	296.1	256	78	120	98	67	7	7.78	2.37	3.64
Joe Benz	R	15	11	.577	2.11	0	39	28	17	238.1	209	43	81	78	56	2	7.89	1.62	3.06
Reb Russell	L	11	10	.524	2.59	2	41	25	10	229.1	215	47	90	90	66	3	8.44	1.84	3.53
Eddie Cicotte	R	13	12	.520	3.02	3	39	26	15	223.1	216	48	106	89	75	1	8.70	1.93	4.27
Mellie Wolfgang	R	2	2	.500	1.84	0	17	2	0	53.2	39	12	21	18	11	0	6.54	2.01	3.52
Ed Walsh	R	3	0	1.000	1.33	0	3	3	3	27	19	7	12	4	4	1	6.33	2.33	4.00
Hi Jasper	R	0	1	.000	4.60	0	3	2	1	15.2	8	9	15	8	8	0	4.60	5.17	8.62
Ed Klepfer	R	1	0	1.000	2.84	0	3	2	1	12.2	11	5	3	4	4	0	7.82	3.55	2.13
Dixie Davis	R	0	0	—	0.00	0	2	0	0	3	2	2	2	0	0	0	6.00	6.00	6.00
Ellis Johnson	R	0	0	—	9.00	0	1	0	0	2	3	0	3	2	2	0	13.50	0.00	13.50
TEAM TOTAL		93	61	.604	2.43	9	246	155	92	1401	1242	350	635	509	378	17	7.98	2.25	4.08

Chicago 1916   Won 89 Lost 65 Pct. .578 2nd

MANAGER	W	L	PCT
Pants Rowland	89	65	.578

POS	Player	B	G	AB	H	2B	3B	HR	HR%	R	RBI	BB	SO	SB	Pinch Hit AB	H	BA	SA
REGULARS																		
1B	Jack Fournier	L	105	313	75	13	9	3	1.0	36	44	36	40	19	14	2	.240	.367
2B	Eddie Collins	L	155	545	168	14	17	0	0.0	87	52	86	36	40	0	0	.308	.396
SS	Zeb Terry	R	94	269	51	8	4	0	0.0	20	17	33	36	4	1	1	.190	.249
3B	Buck Weaver	B	151	582	132	27	6	3	0.5	78	38	30	48	22	0	0	.227	.309
RF	Shano Collins	R	143	527	128	28	12	0	0.0	74	42	59	51	16	3	0	.243	.342
CF	Happy Felsch	R	146	546	164	24	12	7	1.3	73	70	31	67	13	4	2	.300	.427
LF	Joe Jackson	L	155	592	202	40	21	3	0.5	91	78	46	25	24	0	0	.341	.495
C	Ray Schalk	R	129	410	95	12	9	0	0.0	36	41	41	31	30	3	0	.232	.305
SUBSTITUTES																		
1B	Jack Ness	R	75	258	69	7	5	1	0.4	32	34	9	32	4	6	3	.267	.345
3B	Fred McMullin	R	68	187	48	3	0	0	0.0	8	10	19	30	9	2	1	.257	.273
3B	Fritz Von Kolnitz	R	24	44	10	3	0	0	0.0	1	7	2	6	0	10	3	.227	.295
SS	Ceylon Wright	L	8	18	0	0	0	0	0.0	0	0	1	7	0	0	0	.000	.000
1B	Ziggy Hasbrook	R	9	8	1	0	0	0	0.0	1	0	1	2	0	1	0	.125	.125
13	George Moriarty	R	7	5	1	0	0	0	0.0	1	0	2	0	0	3	1	.200	.200
OF	Eddie Murphy	L	51	105	22	5	1	0	0.0	14	4	9	5	3	20	4	.210	.276
OF	Nemo Leibold	L	45	82	20	1	2	0	0.0	5	13	7	7	7	20	4	.244	.305
C	Jack Lapp	L	40	101	21	0	1	0	0.0	6	7	8	10	1	4	0	.208	.228
C	Byrd Lynn	R	31	40	9	1	0	0	0.0	4	3	4	7	2	15	3	.225	.250
PH	Ted Jourdan	L	3	2	0	0	0	0	0.0	0	0	1	1	2	2	0	.000	.000
PH	Joe Fautsch	R	1	1	0	0	0	0	0.0	0	0	0	0	0	1	0	.000	.000
PH	Ray Shook	R	1	0	0	0	0	0	—	0	0	0	0	0	0	0	—	—
PITCHERS																		
P	Reb Russell	L	56	91	13	2	0	0	0.0	9	6	0	18	1	0	0	.143	.165
P	Lefty Williams	R	43	74	10	2	1	0	0.0	5	4	7	30	0	0	0	.135	.189
P	Red Faber	B	35	63	6	0	0	0	0.0	4	2	5	34	0	0	0	.095	.095
P	Eddie Cicotte	B	44	57	12	2	0	0	0.0	6	4	4	16	0	0	0	.211	.246
P	Jim Scott	R	32	52	6	0	0	0	0.0	2	3	0	13	0	0	0	.115	.115
P	Joe Benz	R	28	46	3	1	0	0	0.0	3	2	2	19	0	0	0	.065	.087
P	Mellie Wolfgang	R	28	40	9	1	0	0	0.0	2	3	0	8	0	0	0	.225	.250
P	Dave Danforth	L	28	23	2	0	0	0	0.0	3	0	4	12	0	0	0	.087	.087
P	Ed Walsh	R	2	0	0	0	0	0	—	0	0	0	0	0	0	0	—	—
TEAM TOTAL				5081	1277	194	100	17	0.3	601	484	447	591	197	109	24	.251	.339

INDIVIDUAL FIELDING

POS	Player	T	G	PO	A	E	DP	TCG	FA
1B	J. Fournier	R	85	855	49	20	47	10.9	.978
	J. Ness	R	69	655	31	15	45	10.2	.979
	S. Collins	R	4	34	4	0	2	9.5	1.000
	Z. Hasbrook	R	7	24	3	0	1	3.9	1.000
	G. Moriarty	R	1	2	1	0	0	3.0	1.000
2B	E. Collins	R	155	346	415	19	75	5.0	**.976**
	F. McMullin	R	1	3	1	0	0	4.0	1.000
SS	Z. Terry	R	93	148	243	27	36	4.5	.935
	B. Weaver	R	66	142	192	16	27	5.3	.954
	C. Wright	R	8	8	19	5	2	4.0	.844
	F. McMullin	R	2	1	0	0	0	0.5	1.000
3B	B. Weaver	R	85	124	193	20	22	4.0	.941
	F. McMullin	R	63	74	115	10	11	3.2	.950
	Von Kolnitz	R	13	9	11	2	1	1.7	.909
	M. Wolfgang	R	1	0	1	1	1	2.0	.500
	G. Moriarty	R	1	0	1	0	0	1.0	1.000
	E. Murphy	R	1	0	0	1	0	1.0	.000

POS	Player	T	G	PO	A	E	DP	TCG	FA
OF	H. Felsch	R	141	340	19	7	5	2.6	**.981**
	J. Jackson	R	155	290	17	8	5	2.0	.975
	S. Collins	R	136	238	20	11	6	2.0	.959
	N. Leibold	R	24	31	1	0	2	1.3	1.000
	E. Murphy	R	24	28	2	0	0	1.3	1.000
	J. Fournier	R	1	2	0	0	0	2.0	1.000
C	R. Schalk	R	124	653	166	10	25	6.7	**.988**
	J. Lapp	R	34	131	41	2	2	5.1	.989
	B. Lynn	R	13	56	24	4	0	6.5	.952

It isn't every club that can remain under .500 until the end of June and still win 89 games. A case of massive overconfidence doomed the Sox in the early going. Eddie Collins was swinging at bad pitches, and first baseman Jack Fournier made the most routine play an adventure. A Boston cartoonist lampooned the Sox in one of the newspapers, prompting a team meeting. The Sox made a secret pact to never give up any game. This followed the published reports of Clarence Rowland's imminent firing. Such comradeship seems unusual, given the nature of this team, for this was the first of the great Black Sox clubs. The fourth epoch of Sox history was underway.

They achieved first place on August 3 and held it for exactly one week. The onrushing Boston Red Sox, led by Babe Ruth, were just too good. But the Sox hung on grimly to the end. The Bostons finally won their flag on October 1 when the White Sox split a doubleheader at Cleveland.

The Sox were a talented bunch, impressive in all categories. They led in team ERA and were second in team batting average, but they did their best hitting when it didn't matter, and were unable to advance runners and convert all their hits into runs. *Tribune* columnist "Si" Sanborn described the Sox as neither "fish, fowl, nor good red herring."

TEAM STATISTICS

	W	L	PCT	GB	R	OR	2B	3B	HR	BA	SA	SB	E	DP	FA	CG	BB	SO	ShO	SV	ERA
BOS	91	63	.591		548	480	196	56	14	.248	.318	129	183	108	.972	76	463	584	23	14	2.48
CHI	89	65	.578	2	601	500	194	100	17	.251	.339	197	203	134	.968	73	405	644	18	15	2.36
DET	87	67	.565	4	673	573	202	96	17	.264	.350	190	211	110	.968	81	578	531	9	10	2.97
NY	80	74	.519	11	575	561	194	60	34	.246	.326	179	219	119	.967	83	476	616	10	16	2.77
STL	79	75	.513	12	591	545	181	50	13	.245	.307	234	248	120	.963	71	478	505	9	12	2.58
CLE	77	77	.500	14	630	621	233	66	16	.250	.331	160	232	130	.965	65	467	537	9	15	2.99
WAS	76	77	.497	14.5	534	543	170	60	12	.242	.306	185	231	119	.964	84	540	706	11	8	2.66
PHI	36	117	.235	54.5	447	776	169	65	19	.242	.313	151	314	126	.951	94	715	575	11	3	3.84
LEAGUE TOTAL					4599	4599	1539	553	142	.248	.324	1425	1841	966	.965	627	4122	4698	100	93	2.83

INDIVIDUAL PITCHING

PITCHER	T	W	L	PCT	ERA	SV	G	GS	CG	IP	H	BB	SO	R	ER	ShO	H9	BB9	SO9
Reb Russell	L	17	11	.607	2.42	4	56	26	16	264.1	207	42	112	88	71	5	7.05	1.43	3.81
Lefty Williams	L	13	7	.650	2.89	1	43	25	10	224.1	220	65	138	99	72	2	8.83	2.61	5.54
Red Faber	R	16	9	.640	2.02	2	35	25	15	205.1	167	61	87	67	46	3	7.32	2.67	3.81
Eddie Cicotte	R	16	7	.697	1.78	4	44	20	11	187	138	70	91	56	37	2	6.64	3.37	4.38
Jim Scott	R	9	14	.391	2.72	2	32	20	8	165.1	155	53	71	63	50	1	8.44	2.89	3.86
Joe Benz	R	9	5	.643	2.03	0	28	16	6	142	108	32	57	42	32	4	6.85	2.03	3.61
Mellie Wolfgang	R	4	6	.400	1.98	0	27	14	6	127	103	42	36	39	28	1	7.30	2.98	2.55
Dave Danforth	L	5	5	.500	3.27	2	28	8	1	93.2	87	37	49	43	34	0	8.36	3.56	4.71
Ed Walsh	R	0	1	.000	2.70	0	2	1	0	3.1	4	3	3	3	1	0	10.80	8.10	8.10
TEAM TOTAL		89	65	.578	2.36	15	295	155	73	1412.1	1189	405	644	500	371	18	7.58	2.58	4.10

Chicago 1917   Won 100   Lost 54   Pct .649   1st

MANAGER	W	L	PCT
Pants Rowland	100	54	.649

POS	Player	B	G	AB	H	2B	3B	HR	HR %	R	RBI	BB	SO	SB	Pinch Hit AB	Pinch Hit H	BA	SA
REGULARS																		
1B	Chick Gandil	R	149	553	151	9	7	0	0.0	53	57	30	36	16	0	0	.273	.315
2B	Eddie Collins	L	156	564	163	18	12	0	0.0	91	67	89	16	53	0	0	.289	.363
SS	Swede Risberg	R	149	474	96	20	8	1	0.2	59	45	59	65	16	2	1	.203	.285
3B	Buck Weaver	B	118	447	127	16	5	3	0.7	64	32	27	29	19	1	0	.284	.362
RF	Nemo Leibold	L	125	428	101	12	6	0	0.0	59	29	74	34	27	3	0	.236	.292
CF	Happy Felsch	R	152	575	177	17	10	6	1.0	75	102	33	52	26	0	0	.308	.403
LF	Joe Jackson	L	146	538	162	20	17	5	0.9	91	75	57	25	13	1	0	.301	.429
C	Ray Schalk	R	140	424	96	12	4	3	0.7	48	51	59	27	19	1	0	.226	.295
SUBSTITUTES																		
3B	Fred McMullin	R	59	194	46	2	1	0	0.0	35	12	27	17	9	5	1	.237	.258
1B	Ted Jourdan	L	17	34	5	0	1	0	0.0	2	2	1	3	0	3	0	.147	.206
2B	Bobby Byrne	R	1	1	0	0	0	0	0.0	0	0	0	0	0	0	0	.000	.000
2B	Ziggy Hasbrook	R	2	1	0	0	0	0	0.0	1	0	0	0	0	0	0	.000	.000
SS	Zeb Terry	R	2	1	0	0	0	0	0.0	0	0	2	0	0	0	0	.000	.000
OF	Shano Collins	R	82	252	59	13	3	1	0.4	38	14	10	27	14	8	2	.234	.321
OF	Eddie Murphy	L	53	51	16	2	1	0	0.0	9	16	5	1	4	32	12	.314	.392
C	Byrd Lynn	R	35	72	16	2	0	0	0.0	7	5	7	11	1	6	1	.222	.250
PH	Joe Jenkins	R	10	9	1	0	0	0	0.0	0	2	0	5	0	9	1	.111	.111
PH	Jack Fournier	L	1	1	0	0	0	0	0.0	0	0	0	1	0	1	0	.000	.000
PITCHERS																		
P	Eddie Cicotte	B	49	112	20	2	0	0	0.0	6	8	12	23	1	0	0	.179	.196
P	Red Faber	B	41	69	4	1	0	0	0.0	1	2	10	38	0	0	0	.058	.072
P	Reb Russell	L	39	68	19	3	3	0	0.0	5	9	2	10	0	3	0	.279	.412
P	Lefty Williams	R	45	67	6	0	1	0	0.0	5	2	8	19	0	0	0	.090	.119
P	Dave Danforth	L	50	46	6	2	1	0	0.0	3	5	6	19	1	0	0	.130	.217
P	Jim Scott	R	24	42	5	0	0	0	0.0	1	0	4	9	0	0	0	.119	.119
P	Joe Benz	R	19	30	5	1	0	0	0.0	4	0	0	11	0	0	0	.167	.200
P	Mellie Wolfgang	R	5	4	0	0	0	0	0.0	0	0	0	1	0	0	0	.000	.000
TEAM TOTAL				5057	1281	152	80	19	0.4	657	535	522	479	219	75	18	.253	.326

INDIVIDUAL FIELDING

POS	Player	T	G	PO	A	E	DP	TCG	FA
1B	C. Gandil	R	149	1405	77	8	84	10.0	**.995**
	T. Jourdan	L	14	68	5	2	2	5.4	.973
2B	E. Collins	R	156	**353**	388	24	68	4.9	.969
	Z. Hasbrook	R	1	0	2	0	1	2.0	1.000
	B. Byrne	R	1	0	1	0	0	1.0	1.000
SS	S. Risberg	R	146	291	352	61	57	4.8	.913
	B. Weaver	R	10	20	39	1	9	6.0	.983
	F. McMullin	R	2	2	2	4	0	4.0	.500
	Z. Terry	R	1	0	1	0	0	1.0	1.000
3B	B. Weaver	R	107	154	218	20	18	3.7	**.949**
	F. McMullin	R	52	61	90	11	4	3.1	.932

POS	Player	T	G	PO	A	E	DP	TCG	FA
OF	H. Felsch	R	152	**440**	24	7	5	**3.1**	.985
	J. Jackson	R	145	341	18	6	4	2.5	.984
	N. Leibold	R	122	204	18	9	3	1.9	.961
	S. Collins	R	73	125	6	1	4	1.8	.992
	R. Russell	L	1	3	0	0	0	3.0	1.000
	E. Murphy	R	9	2	0	0	0	0.2	1.000
C	R. Schalk	R	139	**624**	148	15	13	5.7	.981
	B. Lynn	R	29	104	13	5	4	4.2	.959

Broadway showgirls cried, the Tammany Hall politicians were glum, and John McGraw was a tempest in a teapot. On October 15, 1917, Red Faber put away the New York Giants for his third victory in the World Series. This was Chicago's last World Championship, and it occurred the very same day that Baron Manfred Freiherr von Richthofen registered his record-setting sixtieth kill in the skies over France. That's how long it's been.

The road to the pennant was the usual rocky one for the Sox. Boston snapped at their heels until the first week of September when the Sox won a pair of doubleheaders on successive days from the Tigers. In those games of the second and third, it was alleged that the Tigers "lay down," and that the Sox later collected a pool to reward them for their efforts. All this came out of the Black Sox scandal and its aftermath. But in 1917 such talk was taken lightly. The honor of pitching the clincher fell to Red Faber on September 21 in Boston. With bases full of Red Sox, Faber induced Babe Ruth to hit into a game-ending double play to nail down the flag.

The Sox were popular favorites in the World Series. They didn't disappoint anyone, outclassing New York in every phase of the game. The goat of the Series was Giant infielder Heinie Zimmerman, who hit .120 and chased Eddie Collins across a vacated home plate in the final game.

TEAM STATISTICS

	W	L	PCT	GB	R	OR	2B	3B	HR	BA	SA	SB	E	DP	FA	CG	BB	SO	ShO	SV	ERA
CHI	100	54	.649		657	464	152	80	19	.253	.326	219	204	117	.967	79	413	517	21	19	2.16
BOS	90	62	.592	9	556	453	198	64	14	.246	.319	105	183	116	.972	115	413	509	15	6	2.20
CLE	88	66	.571	12	584	543	218	63	14	.245	.322	210	242	136	.964	74	438	451	19	19	2.52
DET	78	75	.510	21.5	639	577	204	76	26	.259	.344	163	234	95	.964	78	504	516	20	12	2.56
WAS	74	79	.484	25.5	543	566	173	70	4	.241	.304	166	251	127	.961	84	536	637	20	7	2.77
NY	71	82	.464	28.5	524	560	172	52	27	.239	.308	136	225	129	.965	87	427	571	9	6	2.66
STL	57	97	.370	43	511	687	183	63	15	.245	.315	157	280	139	.957	65	537	429	12	12	3.20
PHI	55	98	.359	44.5	527	691	177	62	17	.254	.322	112	251	106	.961	80	562	516	8	5	3.27
LEAGUE TOTAL					4541	4541	1477	530	136	.248	.320	1268	1870	965	.964	662	3830	4146	124	86	2.66

INDIVIDUAL PITCHING

PITCHER	T	W	L	PCT	ERA	SV	G	GS	CG	IP	H	BB	SO	R	ER	ShO	H9	BB9	SO9
Eddie Cicotte	R	28	12	.700	1.53	4	49	35	29	346.2	246	70	150	150	59	7	6.39	1.82	3.89
Red Faber	R	16	13	.552	1.92	3	41	29	17	248	224	85	84	84	53	3	8.13	3.08	3.05
Lefty Williams	L	17	8	.680	2.97	1	45	29	8	230	221	81	85	85	76	1	8.65	3.17	3.33
Reb Russell	L	12	5	.706	1.95	4	35	24	11	189.1	170	32	54	54	41	5	8.08	1.52	2.57
Dave Danforth	L	15	6	.714	2.65	7	50	9	1	173	155	74	79	79	51	1	8.06	3.85	4.11
Jim Scott	R	6	7	.462	1.87	0	24	17	6	125	126	42	37	37	26	2	9.07	3.02	2.66
Joe Benz	R	6	3	.667	2.47	0	19	13	7	94.2	76	23	25	25	26	2	7.23	2.19	2.38
Mellie Wolfgang	R	0	0	–	5.09	0	5	0	0	17.2	18	6	3	3	10	0	9.17	3.06	1.53
TEAM TOTAL		100	54	.649	2.16	19	268	156	79	1424.1	1236	413	517	464	342	21	7.81	2.61	3.27

Chicago 1918   Won 57 Lost 67 Pct .460 6th

MANAGER	W	L	PCT
Pants Rowland	57	67	.460

POS	Player	B	G	AB	H	2B	3B	HR	HR%	R	RBI	BB	SO	SB	Pinch Hit AB	H	BA	SA
REGULARS																		
1B	Chick Gandil	R	114	439	119	18	4	0	0.0	49	55	27	19	9	0	0	.271	.330
2B	Eddie Collins	L	97	330	91	8	2	2	0.6	51	30	73	13	22	1	1	.276	.330
SS	Buck Weaver	B	112	420	126	12	5	0	0.0	37	29	11	24	20	2	1	.300	.352
3B	Fred McMullin	R	70	235	65	7	0	1	0.4	32	16	25	26	7	0	0	.277	.319
RF	Happy Felsch	R	53	206	52	2	5	1	0.5	16	20	15	13	6	0	0	.252	.325
CF	Shano Collins	R	103	365	100	18	1	1	0.3	30	56	17	19	7	5	1	.274	.392
LF	Nemo Leibold	L	116	440	110	14	6	1	0.2	57	31	63	32	13	1	0	.250	.316
C	Ray Schalk	R	108	333	73	6	3	0	0.0	35	22	36	22	12	2	1	.219	.255
SUBSTITUTES																		
UT	Swede Risberg	R	82	273	70	12	3	1	0.4	36	27	23	32	5	4	1	.256	.333
3B	Babe Pinelli	R	24	78	18	1	1	1	1.3	7	7	7	8	3	0	0	.231	.308
2B	Johnny Mostil	R	10	33	9	2	2	0	0.0	4	4	1	6	1	0	0	.273	.455
1B	Ted Jourdan	L	7	10	1	0	0	0	0.0	1	1	0	0	0	5	1	.100	.100
OF	Eddie Murphy	L	91	286	85	9	3	0	0.0	36	23	22	18	6	18	4	.297	.350
OF	Wilbur Good	L	35	148	37	9	4	0	0.0	24	11	11	16	1	0	0	.250	.365
OF	Joe Jackson	L	17	65	23	2	2	1	1.5	9	20	8	1	3	0	0	.354	.492
C	Otto Jacobs	R	29	73	15	3	1	0	0.0	4	3	5	8	0	7	1	.205	.274
C	Al DeVormer	R	8	19	5	2	0	0	0.0	2	0	0	4	1	1	0	.263	.368
C	Byrd Lynn	R	5	8	2	0	0	0	0.0	0	0	2	1	0	1	1	.250	.250
PH	Pat Hargrove	R	2	2	0	0	0	0	0.0	0	0	0	0	0	2	0	.000	.000
PH	Kid Willson	L	4	1	0	0	0	0	0.0	2	0	1	1	0	1	0	.000	.000
PITCHERS																		
P	Eddie Cicotte	B	38	86	14	5	1	0	0.0	6	4	12	12	0	0	0	.163	.244
P	Frank Shellenback	R	29	54	7	1	0	0	0.0	4	1	8	25	0	0	0	.130	.148
P	Joe Benz	R	29	51	11	1	0	0	0.0	3	5	0	14	0	0	0	.216	.235
P	Reb Russell	L	27	50	7	3	0	0	0.0	2	3	0	6	0	6	0	.140	.200
P	Dave Danforth	L	39	42	6	0	0	0	0.0	3	0	2	11	0	0	0	.143	.143
P	Lefty Williams	R	15	38	5	0	0	0	0.0	4	2	1	14	0	0	0	.132	.132
P	Red Faber	B	11	24	1	0	0	0	0.0	1	0	3	11	0	0	0	.042	.042
P	Jack Quinn	R	6	18	4	1	1	0	0.0	1	3	2	2	0	0	0	.222	.389
P	Roy Mitchell	R	2	2	0	0	0	0	0.0	0	0	0	0	0	0	0	.000	.000
P	Mellie Wolfgang	R	5	2	1	0	0	0	0.0	1	2	0	0	0	0	0	.500	.500
P	Ed Corey	R	1	1	0	0	0	0	0.0	0	0	0	0	0	0	0	.000	.000
TEAM TOTAL				4132	1057	136	54	9	0.2	457	375	375	358	116	56	12	.256	.321

INDIVIDUAL FIELDING

POS	Player	T	G	PO	A	E	DP	TCG	FA
1B	C. Gandil	R	114	1123	64	10	70	10.5	.992
	S. Collins	R	7	79	2	2	6	11.9	.976
	S. Collins	R	5	32	2	2	1	7.2	.944
	T. Jourdan	L	2	12	0	0	0	6.0	1.000
2B	E. Collins	R	96	231	285	14	53	5.5	.974
	S. Collins	R	1	0	0	0	0	0.0	.000
	F. McMullin	R	1	0	0	0	0	0.0	.000
	S. Risberg	R	12	28	40	3	5	5.9	.958
	J. Mostil	R	9	15	21	3	4	4.3	.923
	E. Murphy	R	8	13	15	2	1	3.8	.933
	B. Weaver	R	1	0	2	0	1	2.0	1.000
SS	B. Weaver	R	98	191	319	32	50	5.5	.941
	S. Risberg	R	30	29	76	8	12	3.8	.929
3B	F. McMullin	R	69	74	151	14	9	3.5	.941
	S. Risberg	R	24	29	42	8	4	3.3	.899
	B. Pinelli	R	24	28	33	11	4	3.0	.847
	M. Wolfgang	R	1	0	0	0	0	0.0	.000
	B. Weaver	R	11	10	18	1	0	2.6	.966

POS	Player	T	G	PO	A	E	DP	TCG	FA
OF	N. Leibold	R	114	259	16	6	5	2.5	.979
	S. Collins	R	92	230	20	7	1	2.8	.973
	H. Felsch	R	53	149	7	7	5	3.1	.957
	E. Murphy	R	63	111	3	5	1	1.9	.958
	W. Good	L	35	103	4	2	1	3.1	.982
	J. Jackson	R	17	36	1	0	0	2.2	1.000
	Shellenback	R	1	0	0	0	0	0.0	.000
	S. Risberg	R	3	3	0	0	0	1.0	1.000
	R. Russell	L	1	2	0	0	0	2.0	1.000
	A. DeVormer	R	1	1	0	0	0	1.0	1.000
C	R. Schalk	R	106	422	114	12	15	5.2	.978
	O. Jacobs	R	21	64	21	4	3	4.2	.955
	A. DeVormer	R	6	11	4	0	0	2.5	1.000
	B. Lynn	R	4	6	3	0	0	2.3	1.000

Chicago 1918

The "work or fight" edict issued in June of 1918 gave eligible draftees playing in the major leagues the choice of entering the service or becoming a part of wartime industries. While many players like Red Faber joined the Navy, Joe Jackson and Lefty Williams chose to work in East Coast shipyards rather than be exposed to the perils of a sure trip to France. (Jackson in particular was afraid of seasickness.) Comiskey reacted angrily. "I don't consider them fit to play for my club," he fumed. "I hate to see any players, particularly my own, go to the shipyards to escape service." They were suspended.

Spring training was a near disaster, as the Sox' train derailed near Weatherford, Texas, on March 18. Fortunately, the World Champs were not hurt. Two days later, Schalk, Cicotte, Jackson, and Gandil were returning from the golf course in a friend's touring car when they were broadsided by a reckless driver. Cicotte suffered whiplash, further earning Comiskey's wrath. "Their place was on the ball field, not out experimenting with golf sticks and looking at scenery," the boss fumed.

The war effort hit baseball hard. A wartime tax on baseball raised Comiskey Park bleacher seats to $.30, grandstands to $.55, and box seats to $1.10. It was a price not worth paying, as the Sox remained at .500 till mid-June, when the armed forces began rifling the roster.

Comiskey's cordial relationship with Ban Johnson turned ugly when the American League president awarded pitcher John Picus Quinn to the Yankees after he had won his first five decisions for the Sox. Comiskey had negotiatied with Quinn, while the Yankees had dealt with Los Angeles when he was under their employ. This crucial decision split the American League into two warring factions. Casual days of hunting and fishing in Wisconsin were over for the two founders of the American League.

TEAM STATISTICS

	W	L	PCT	GB	R	OR	2B	3B	HR	BA	SA	SB	E	DP	FA	CG	BB	SO	ShO	SV	ERA
BOS	75	51	.595		473	381	159	54	15	.249	.327	110	149	89	.971	105	380	392	25	2	2.31
CLE	73	56	.566	3.5	510	447	176	67	9	.260	.341	165	207	82	.962	80	343	364	6	13	2.64
WAS	72	56	.563	4	461	392	156	48	5	.256	.316	137	226	95	.960	75	395	505	20	7	**2.14**
NY	60	63	.488	13.5	491	474	160	45	20	.257	.330	88	161	**137**	.970	59	463	369	9	10	3.03
STL	60	64	.484	14	426	448	152	40	5	.259	.320	138	190	86	.963	67	402	346	7	7	2.75
CHI	57	67	.460	17	457	443	136	54	9	.256	.321	116	169	98	.967	76	**300**	349	10	6	2.69
DET	55	71	.437	20	473	555	141	56	13	.249	.318	123	211	77	.960	74	437	374	8	5	3.40
PHI	52	76	.406	24	412	563	124	44	**22**	.243	.308	83	228	136	.959	80	479	279	12	7	3.22
LEAGUE TOTAL					3703	3703	1204	408	98	.254	.323	960	1541	800	.964	616	3199	2978	97	57	2.77

INDIVIDUAL PITCHING

PITCHER	T	W	L	PCT	ERA	SV	G	GS	CG	IP	H	BB	SO	R	ER	ShO	H9	BB9	SO9
Eddie Cicotte	R	12	19	.387	2.64	2	38	30	24	266	275	40	104	102	78	1	9.30	**1.35**	3.52
Frank Shellenback	R	10	12	.455	2.66	1	28	20	10	182.2	180	74	47	77	54	3	8.87	3.65	2.32
Joe Benz	R	7	8	.467	2.51	0	29	17	10	154	156	28	30	57	43	1	9.12	1.64	1.75
Dave Danforth	L	6	15	.286	3.43	2	39	13	5	139	148	40	48	73	53	0	9.58	2.59	3.11
Reb Russell	L	6	5	.545	2.60	0	19	14	10	124.2	117	33	38	45	36	2	8.45	2.38	2.74
Lefty Williams	L	6	4	.600	2.73	1	15	14	7	105.2	76	47	30	32	32	2	6.47	4.00	2.56
Red Faber	R	5	1	.833	1.23	0	11	9	5	80.2	70	23	26	23	11	1	7.81	2.57	2.90
Jack Quinn	R	5	1	.833	2.29	0	6	5	5	51	38	7	22	13	13	0	6.71	1.24	3.88
Roy Mitchell	R	0	1	.000	7.50	0	2	2	0	12	18	4	3	14	10	0	13.50	3.00	2.25
Mellie Wolfgang	R	0	1	.000	5.40	0	4	0	0	8.1	12	3	1	6	5	0	12.96	3.24	1.08
Ed Corey	R	0	0	—	4.50	0	1	0	0	2	2	1	0	1	1	0	9.00	4.50	0.00
TEAM TOTAL		57	67	.460	2.69	6	192	124	76	1126	1092	300	349	443	336	10	8.73	2.40	2.79

Chicago 1919   Won 88 Lost 52 Pct .629 1st

MANAGER	W	L	PCT
Kid Gleason	88	52	.629

POS	Player	B	G	AB	H	2B	3B	HR	HR%	R	RBI	BB	SO	SB	Pinch Hit AB	Pinch Hit H	BA	SA
REGULARS																		
1B	Chick Gandil	R	115	441	128	24	7	1	0.2	54	60	20	20	10	0	0	.290	.383
2B	Eddie Collins	L	140	518	165	19	7	4	0.8	87	80	68	27	33	0	0	.319	.405
SS	Swede Risberg	R	119	414	106	19	6	2	0.5	48	38	35	38	19	0	0	.256	.345
3B	Buck Weaver	B	140	571	169	33	9	3	0.5	89	75	11	21	22	0	0	.296	.401
RF	Nemo Leibold	L	122	434	131	18	2	0	0.0	81	26	72	30	17	0	0	.302	.353
CF	Happy Felsch	R	135	502	138	34	11	7	1.4	68	86	40	35	19	0	0	.275	.428
LF	Joe Jackson	L	139	516	181	31	14	7	1.4	79	96	60	10	9	0	0	.351	.506
C	Ray Schalk	R	131	394	111	9	3	0	0.0	57	34	51	25	11	2	0	.282	.320
SUBSTITUTES																		
3B	Fred McMullin	R	60	170	50	8	4	0	0.0	31	19	11	18	4	8	4	.294	.388
3S	Harvey McClellan	R	7	12	4	0	0	0	0.0	2	1	1	1	0	1	0	.333	.333
OF	Shano Collins	R	63	179	50	6	3	1	0.6	21	16	7	11	3	9	2	.279	.363
OF	Eddie Murphy	L	30	35	17	4	0	0	0.0	8	5	7	0	0	21	8	.486	.600
C	Byrd Lynn	R	29	66	15	4	0	0	0.0	4	4	4	9	0	1	1	.227	.288
C	Joe Jenkins	R	11	19	3	1	0	0	0.0	0	1	1	1	1	7	1	.158	.211
PITCHERS																		
P	Eddie Cicotte	B	40	99	20	0	1	0	0.0	5	8	9	18	0	0	0	.202	.222
P	Lefty Williams	R	41	94	17	2	2	0	0.0	10	10	9	28	0	0	0	.181	.245
P	Dickie Kerr	L	39	68	17	3	1	0	0.0	12	4	9	8	1	0	0	.250	.324
P	Red Faber	B	25	54	10	0	0	0	0.0	8	4	6	20	0	0	0	.185	.185
P	Grover Lowdermilk	R	20	34	3	0	0	0	0.0	1	1	0	19	1	0	0	.088	.088
P	Bill James	B	5	14	2	0	0	0	0.0	2	0	0	2	0	0	0	.143	.143
P	Frank Shellenback	R	8	11	1	0	0	0	0.0	0	0	2	5	0	0	0	.091	.091
P	Dave Danforth	L	15	9	1	1	0	0	0.0	0	0	2	2	0	0	0	.111	.222
P	Roy Wilkinson	R	4	8	3	2	0	0	0.0	1	2	1	3	0	0	0	.375	.625
P	Erskine Mayer	R	6	7	0	0	0	0	0.0	0	0	0	3	0	0	0	.000	.000
P	John Sullivan	L	4	3	0	0	0	0	0.0	0	1	1	3	0	0	0	.000	.000
P	Wynn Noyes	R	1	2	1	0	0	0	0.0	0	0	0	0	0	0	0	.500	.500
P	Tom McGuire	R	1	1	0	0	0	0	0.0	0	0	0	1	0	0	0	.000	.000
P	Joe Benz	R	1	0	0	0	0	0	–	0	0	0	0	0	0	0	–	–
P	Pat Ragan	R	1	0	0	0	0	0	–	0	0	0	0	0	0	0	–	–
P	Charlie Robertson	L	1	0	0	0	0	0	–	0	0	0	0	0	0	0	–	–
P	Reb Russell	L	1	0	0	0	0	0	–	0	0	0	0	0	0	0	–	–
TEAM TOTAL				4675	1343	218	70	25	0.5	668	571	427	358	150	49	16	.287	.380

INDIVIDUAL FIELDING

POS	Player	T	G	PO	A	E	DP	TCG	FA
1B	C. Gandil	R	115	1116	60	3	71	10.3	**.997**
	S. Risberg	R	22	204	13	2	10	10.0	.991
	S. Collins	R	8	76	4	0	1	10.0	1.000
2B	E. Collins	R	140	347	401	20	**66**	5.5	.974
	F. McMullin	R	5	9	6	1	1	3.2	.938
SS	S. Risberg	R	97	278	32	39	5.0	.934	
	B. Weaver	R	43	87	141	8	14	5.5	.966
	H. McClellan	R	2	4	1	1	0	3.0	.833
3B	B. Weaver	R	97	113	200	12	14	3.4	.963
	F. McMullin	R	46	45	90	10	10	3.2	.931
	H. McClellan	R	3	2	6	0	1	2.7	1.000

POS	Player	T	G	PO	A	E	DP	TCG	FA
OF	H. Felsch	R	135	360	**32**	13	**15**	3.0	.968
	J. Jackson	R	139	252	15	9	4	2.0	.967
	N. Leibold	R	122	218	26	**19**	4	2.2	.928
	S. Collins	R	46	82	7	4	5	2.0	.957
	E. Murphy	R	6	10	1	1	0	2.0	.917
C	R. Schalk	R	129	**551**	130	13	14	5.4	.981
	B. Lynn	R	28	87	20	2	5	3.9	.982
	J. Jenkins	R	4	10	4	3	0	4.3	.824

Speed, pitching, hitting, and defense. The Sox had all these things in 1919, and old-timers who saw them still maintain that this club was as good as the Yankees of the next decade. Why, then, would Eddie Cicotte, winner of 29 games in 1919, and Joe Jackson, proud owner of a .351 batting average, sell out the Sox in the World Series?

Even in the best of seasons, this was a bitterly divided club. There were two distinct cliques on the team. In 1918 the lily-White Sox did their duty for their country, while certain members of the Black Sox went to the shipyards. There was jealousy over Collins's $15,000 contract, a salary that equaled Felsch's, Jackson's, and Gandil's *combined*. There was a city-slicker attitude among the clean Sox, as contrasted with the rural backgrounds of those who sold out.

It can be surmised that the initial contact with the gamblers was made by Chick Gandil on September 19, when the Sox were in the process of losing two out of three in Boston. Making the initial contact was gambler Sport Sullivan and former Sox pitcher Sleepy Bill Burns.

The lure of some fast money (which proved to be illusory) compelled Weaver, Jackson, Felsch, Gandil, McMullin, Cicotte, Risberg, and Williams to sell out to the Reds in the best-of-nine World Series. It would take another year of conning the public before the whole mess spilled over onto page one.

TEAM STATISTICS

	W	L	PCT	GB	R	OR	2B	3B	HR	BA	SA	SB	E	DP	FA	CG	BB	SO	ShO	SV	ERA
CHI	88	52	.629		668	534	218	70	25	**.287**	.380	**150**	176	116	.969	**87**	**342**	468	14	2	3.04
CLE	84	55	.604	3.5	634	535	**254**	72	24	.278	.381	113	201	102	.965	80	362	432	10	7	2.92
NY	80	59	.576	7.5	582	**514**	193	49	**45**	.267	.356	101	192	108	.968	85	433	500	14	7	**2.78**
DET	80	60	.571	8	620	582	222	**84**	23	.283	**.381**	121	205	81	.964	85	431	428	10	4	3.30
STL	67	72	.482	20.5	535	567	187	73	31	.264	.355	74	216	98	.963	77	421	415	14	5	3.13
BOS	66	71	.482	20.5	565	552	181	49	33	.261	.344	108	**141**	118	**.975**	85	420	380	15	5	3.30
WAS	56	84	.400	32	533	570	177	63	24	.260	.339	142	227	86	.960	69	451	**536**	12	**8**	3.01
PHI	36	104	.257	52	459	742	175	71	35	.244	.334	103	259	96	.956	72	503	417	1	2	4.26
LEAGUE TOTAL					4596	4596	1607	531	240	.268	.359	912	1617	805	.965	640	3363	3576	90	40	3.21

INDIVIDUAL PITCHING

PITCHER	T	W	L	PCT	ERA	SV	G	GS	CG	IP	H	BB	SO	R	ER	ShO	H9	BB9	SO9
Eddie Cicotte	R	**29**	7	**.806**	1.82	1	40	35	**29**	**306.2**	256	49	110	77	62	5	7.51	**1.44**	3.23
Lefty Williams	L	23	11	.676	2.64	0	41	**40**	27	297	265	58	125	104	87	5	8.03	1.76	3.79
Dickie Kerr	L	13	7	.650	2.88	0	39	17	10	212.1	208	64	79	78	68	1	8.82	2.71	3.35
Red Faber	R	11	9	.550	3.83	0	25	20	9	162.1	185	45	45	92	69	0	10.26	2.49	2.49
Grover Lowdermilk	R	5	5	.500	2.79	0	20	11	5	96.2	95	43	43	44	30	0	8.84	4.00	4.00
Dave Danforth	L	1	2	.333	7.78	1	15	1	0	41.2	58	20	17	44	36	0	12.53	4.32	3.67
Bill James	R	3	2	.600	2.52	0	5	5	3	39.1	39	14	11	12	11	2	8.92	3.20	2.52
Frank Shellenback	R	1	3	.250	5.14	0	8	4	2	35	40	16	10	24	20	0	10.29	4.11	2.57
Erskine Mayer	R	1	3	.250	8.37	0	6	2	0	23.2	30	11	9	23	22	0	11.41	4.18	3.42
Roy Wilkinson	R	1	1	.500	2.05	0	4	1	1	22	21	10	5	9	5	1	8.59	4.09	2.05
John Sullivan	L	0	1	.000	4.20	0	4	2	1	15	24	8	9	15	7	0	14.40	4.80	5.40
Wynn Noyes	R	0	0	—	7.50	0	1	1	0	6	10	0	4	5	5	0	15.00	0.00	6.00
Tom McGuire	R	0	0	—	9.00	0	1	0	0	3	5	3	0	4	3	0	15.00	9.00	0.00
Joe Benz	R	0	0	—	0.00	0	1	0	0	2	2	0	0	1	0	0	9.00	0.00	0.00
Charlie Robertson	R	0	1	.000	9.00	0	1	1	0	2	5	0	1	2	2	0	22.50	0.00	4.50
Pat Ragan	R	0	0	—	0.00	0	1	0	0	1	1	0	0	0	0	0	9.00	0.00	0.00
TEAM TOTAL		88	52	.629	3.04	2	212	140	87	1265.2	1244	341	468	534	427	14	8.85	2.42	3.33

Chicago 1920   Won 96   Lost 58   Pct .623   2nd

MANAGER	W	L	PCT
Kid Gleason	96	58	.623

POS	Player	B	G	AB	H	2B	3B	HR	HR%	R	RBI	BB	SO	SB	Pinch Hit AB	H	BA	SA
REGULARS																		
1B	Shano Collins	R	133	495	150	21	10	1	0.2	70	63	23	24	12	4	0	.303	.392
2B	Eddie Collins	L	153	601	222	37	13	3	0.5	115	75	69	19	19	0	0	.369	.489
SS	Swede Risberg	R	126	458	122	21	10	2	0.4	53	65	31	45	12	2	0	.266	.369
3B	Buck Weaver	B	151	630	210	35	8	2	0.3	104	75	28	23	19	0	0	.333	.424
RF	Nemo Leibold	L	108	413	91	16	3	1	0.2	61	28	55	30	7	3	1	.220	.281
CF	Happy Felsch	R	142	556	188	40	15	14	2.5	88	115	37	25	8	0	0	.338	.540
LF	Joe Jackson	L	146	570	218	42	20	12	2.1	105	121	56	14	9	1	0	.382	.589
C	Ray Schalk	R	151	485	131	25	5	1	0.2	64	61	68	19	10	0	0	.270	.348
SUBSTITUTES																		
1B	Ted Jourdan	L	48	150	36	6	1	0	0.0	16	8	17	17	3	8	1	.240	.293
3B	Fred McMullin	R	46	127	25	1	4	0	0.0	14	13	9	13	1	11	1	.197	.268
S3	Harvey McClellan	R	10	18	6	1	1	0	0.0	4	5	4	1	2	2	0	.333	.500
OF	Amos Strunk	L	51	183	42	7	1	1	0.5	32	14	28	15	1	3	0	.230	.295
OF	Eddie Murphy	L	58	118	40	2	1	0	0.0	22	19	12	4	1	33	13	.339	.373
OF	Bibb Falk	L	7	17	5	1	1	0	0.0	1	2	0	5	0	3	1	.294	.471
C	Byrd Lynn	R	16	25	8	2	1	0	0.0	0	3	1	3	0	2	2	.320	.480
C	Bubber Jonnard	R	2	5	0	0	0	0	0.0	0	0	0	1	0	1	0	.000	.000
PITCHERS																		
P	Eddie Cicotte	B	37	112	22	2	0	0	0.0	10	6	5	10	2	0	0	.196	.214
P	Red Faber	B	40	104	11	1	0	0	0.0	10	1	19	39	1	0	0	.106	.115
P	Lefty Williams	R	39	101	22	2	1	0	0.0	5	10	7	16	0	0	0	.218	.257
P	Dickie Kerr	L	46	90	14	1	1	0	0.0	12	5	3	9	1	1	0	.156	.189
P	Roy Wilkinson	R	34	48	7	0	1	0	0.0	5	2	1	12	0	0	0	.146	.188
P	George Payne	R	12	8	1	0	0	0	0.0	2	0	1	2	0	0	0	.125	.125
P	Shovel Hodge	L	4	6	0	0	0	0	0.0	0	0	0	3	0	0	0	.000	.000
P	Spencer Heath	B	4	3	0	0	0	0	0.0	0	0	0	0	0	0	0	.000	.000
P	Joe Kiefer	R	2	2	0	0	0	0	0.0	0	0	0	1	0	0	0	.000	.000
P	Grover Lowdermilk	R	3	0	0	0	0	0	–	0	0	0	0	0	0	0	–	–
TEAM TOTAL				5325	1571	263	97	37	0.7	793	692	474	350	108	74	19	.295	.402

INDIVIDUAL FIELDING

POS	Player	T	G	PO	A	E	DP	TCG	FA	POS	Player	T	G	PO	A	E	DP	TCG	FA
1B	S. Collins	R	117	1146	63	15	69	10.5	.988	OF	H. Felsch	R	142	385	25	8	10	2.9	.981
	T. Jourdan	L	40	369	18	7	35	9.9	.982		J. Jackson	R	145	314	14	12	2	2.3	.965
2B	E. Collins	R	153	449	471	23	76	6.2	**.976**		N. Leibold	R	108	190	18	5	5	2.0	.977
	F. McMullin	R	3	8	3	0	2	3.7	1.000		A. Strunk	L	49	96	3	2	0	2.1	.980*
SS	S. Risberg	R	124	238	400	45	59	5.5	.934		E. Murphy	R	19	23	8	4	0	1.8	.886
	B. Weaver	R	25	56	75	5	18	5.4	.963		S. Collins	R	12	17	0	1	0	1.5	.944
	F. McMullin	R	1	0	0	0	0	0.0	.000		B. Falk	L	4	5	0	0	0	1.3	1.000
	H. McClellan	R	4	6	5	1	0	3.0	.917	C	R. Schalk	R	151	581	138	10	19	4.8	**.986**
3B	B. Weaver	R	126	153	276	31	15	3.7	.933		B. Lynn	R	14	27	5	0	0	2.3	1.000
	F. McMullin	R	29	23	53	3	3	2.7	.962		B. Jonnard	R	1	4	2	1	1	7.0	.857
	E. Murphy	R	3	4	5	1	2	3.3	.900										
	H. McClellan	R	2	1	1	0	0	1.0	1.000										

Chicago 1920

Two tragedies struck the baseball public in 1920: the death of Ray Chapman after being hit by a Carl Mays pitch, and the revelation that the White Sox had thrown the 1919 World Series. Through the summer the Sox locked horns with the emerging Yankees and the talented Cleveland ball club. Williams, Cicotte, Faber, and Dickie Kerr became the first quartet to win 20 games each, a feat not matched until 1971.

The Sox remained in third place until early August, when they challenged for the lead. They gained first place on August 21, throwing a scare into the gamblers who had their money on the Indians this time. Evidence suggests that pressure was put on the Black Sox Eight to throw crucial August games on the 17th, 28th, 29th, and 30th during a road trip to Boston and New York. When the deed was done Eddie Cicotte blamed it all on Chick Gandil and Swede Risberg.

With just three games left in the regular season, and the pennant still hanging in the balance, Cicotte, Williams, Gandil, Felsch, Jackson, McMullin, Weaver, and Risberg were suspended by Comiskey. A makeshift lineup consisting of such venerables as Joe Kiefer, Harvey McClellan, Ted Jourdan, and Amos Strunk took the field where Jackson and Weaver once roamed. In better times the Sox would have won the St. Louis series and clinched the flag. But they lost two out of three, and the taste of victory champagne belonged to others.

TEAM STATISTICS

	W	L	PCT	GB	R	OR	2B	3B	HR	BA	SA	SB	E	DP	FA	CG	BB	SO	ShO	SV	ERA
CLE	98	56	.636		857	642	300	95	35	.303	.417	73	184	124	.971	93	401	466	10	7	3.41
CHI	96	58	.623	2	794	666	267	92	37	.294	.400	111	198	142	.968	112	405	440	8	10	3.59
NY	95	59	.617	3	839	629	268	71	115	.280	.426	64	194	129	.969	88	420	480	16	11	3.31
STL	76	77	.497	21.5	797	766	279	83	50	.308	.419	118	233	119	.963	84	578	444	9	14	4.03
BOS	72	81	.471	25.5	651	699	216	71	22	.269	.350	98	183	131	.972	91	461	481	11	6	3.82
WAS	68	84	.447	29	723	802	233	81	36	.291	.386	160	232	95	.963	80	520	418	10	10	4.17
DET	61	93	.396	37	651	832	228	72	30	.270	.359	76	230	95	.964	76	561	483	7	7	4.04
PHI	48	106	.312	50	555	831	219	49	44	.252	.338	50	265	126	.960	81	461	423	5	2	3.93
LEAGUE TOTAL					5867	5867	2010	614	369	.283	.387	750	1719	961	.966	705	3807	3635	76	67	3.79

INDIVIDUAL PITCHING

PITCHER	T	W	L	PCT	ERA	SV	G	GS	CG	IP	H	BB	SO	R	ER	ShO	H9	BB9	SO9
Red Faber	R	23	13	.639	2.99	1	40	39	28	319	332	88	108	136	106	2	9.37	2.48	3.05
Eddie Cicotte	R	21	10	.677	3.26	2	37	35	28	303.1	316	74	87	128	110	4	9.38	2.20	2.58
Lefty Williams	L	22	14	.611	3.91	0	39	38	26	299	302	90	128	145	130	0	9.09	2.71	3.85
Dickie Kerr	L	21	9	.700	3.37	5	45	28	20	253.2	266	72	72	116	95	3	9.44	2.55	2.55
Roy Wilkinson	R	7	9	.438	4.03	2	34	11	9	145	162	48	30	75	65	0	10.06	2.98	1.86
George Payne	R	1	1	.500	5.46	0	12	0	0	29.2	39	9	9	24	18	0	11.83	2.73	2.73
Shovel Hodge	R	1	1	.500	2.29	0	4	2	1	19.2	15	12	5	14	5	0	6.86	5.49	2.29
Spencer Heath	R	0	0	—	15.43	0	4	0	0	7	19	2	0	12	12	0	24.43	2.57	0.00
Grover Lowdermilk	R	0	0	—	6.75	0	3	0	0	5.1	9	5	0	4	4	0	15.19	8.44	0.00
Joe Kiefer	R	0	1	.000	15.43	0	2	1	0	4.2	7	5	1	8	8	0	13.50	9.64	1.93
TEAM TOTAL		96	58	.623	3.59	10	220	154	112	1386.1	1467	405	440	662	553	9	9.52	2.63	2.86

Chicago 1921   Won 62   Lost 92   Pct. .403   7th

MANAGER	W	L	PCT
Kid Gleason	62	92	.403

POS	Player	B	G	AB	H	2B	3B	HR	HR%	R	RBI	BB	SO	SB	Pinch Hit AB	Pinch Hit H	BA	SA
REGULARS																		
1B	Earl Sheely	R	154	563	171	25	6	11	2.0	68	95	57	34	4	0	0	.304	.428
2B	Eddie Collins	L	139	526	177	20	10	2	0.4	79	58	66	11	12	3	0	.337	.424
SS	Ernie Johnson	L	142	613	181	28	7	1	0.2	93	51	29	24	22	1	1	.295	.369
3B	Eddie Mulligan	R	152	609	153	21	12	1	0.2	82	45	32	53	13	0	0	.251	.330
RF	Harry Hooper	L	108	419	137	26	5	8	1.9	74	58	55	21	13	0	0	.327	.470
CF	Amos Strunk	L	121	401	133	19	10	3	0.7	68	69	38	27	7	8	3	.332	.451
LF	Bibb Falk	L	152	585	167	31	11	5	0.9	62	82	37	69	4	3	1	.285	.402
C	Ray Schalk	R	128	416	105	24	4	0	0.0	32	47	40	36	3	2	0	.252	.329
SUBSTITUTES																		
UT	Harvey McClellan	R	63	196	35	4	1	1	0.5	20	14	14	18	2	3	0	.179	.224
OF	Johnny Mostil	R	100	326	98	21	7	3	0.9	43	42	28	35	10	5	2	.301	.436
OF	Fred Bratchi	R	16	28	8	1	0	0	0.0	0	3	0	2	0	10	3	.286	.321
O3	Elmer Leifer	L	9	10	3	0	0	0	0.0	0	1	0	4	0	7	2	.300	.300
C	Yam Yaryan	R	45	102	31	8	2	0	0.0	11	15	9	16	0	10	1	.304	.422
C	George Lees	R	20	42	9	2	0	0	0.0	3	4	0	3	0	4	0	.214	.262
PH	Red Ostergard	L	12	11	4	0	0	0	0.0	2	0	0	2	0	11	4	.364	.364
PH	Eddie Murphy	L	6	5	1	0	0	0	0.0	1	0	0	0	0	5	1	.200	.200
PH	Frank Pratt	L	1	1	0	0	0	0	0.0	0	0	0	0	0	1	0	.000	.000
PITCHERS																		
P	Red Faber	B	43	108	16	0	0	0	0.0	8	4	17	35	1	0	0	.148	.148
P	Dickie Kerr	L	45	105	25	4	3	0	0.0	14	11	15	8	2	0	0	.238	.333
P	Roy Wilkinson	R	36	65	8	1	2	0	0.0	2	3	4	19	0	0	0	.123	.200
P	Shovel Hodge	L	36	52	17	3	1	0	0.0	6	2	0	10	0	0	0	.327	.423
P	Doug McWeeny	R	27	31	1	1	0	0	0.0	2	1	3	21	0	0	0	.032	.065
P	John Russell	L	11	25	10	2	0	0	0.0	1	1	2	7	0	0	0	.400	.480
P	Dominic Mulrenan	R	12	20	3	0	0	0	0.0	1	1	0	2	0	0	0	.150	.150
P	Lum Davenport	L	13	17	7	1	0	0	0.0	3	2	0	8	0	0	0	.412	.471
P	Cy Twombly	R	7	10	0	0	0	0	0.0	0	0	0	4	0	0	0	.000	.000
P	Jack Wieneke	R	10	9	1	0	0	0	0.0	0	0	0	3	0	0	0	.111	.111
P	Sarge Connally	R	5	8	4	0	1	0	0.0	2	0	0	1	0	0	0	.500	.750
P	Lee Thompson	L	4	7	2	0	0	0	0.0	0	0	0	4	0	0	0	.286	.286
P	Hod Fenner	R	3	6	2	0	0	0	0.0	0	0	0	2	0	0	0	.333	.333
P	Bugs Bennett	R	2	2	0	0	0	0	0.0	0	0	0	1	0	0	0	.000	.000
P	Russ Pence	R	4	1	0	0	0	0	0.0	0	0	0	0	0	0	0	.000	.000
P	Babe Blackburn	R	1	0	0	0	0	0	–	0	0	0	0	0	0	0	–	–
P	John Michaelson	R	2	0	0	0	0	0	–	0	0	0	0	0	0	0	–	–
	TEAM TOTAL			5319	1509	242	82	35	0.7	677	609	446	480	93	73	18	.284	.380

INDIVIDUAL FIELDING

POS	Player	T	G	PO	A	E	DP	TCG	FA
1B	E. Sheely	R	154	1637	119	22	121	11.5	.988
2B	E. Collins	R	136	376	458	28	84	6.3	**.968**
	H. McClellan	R	20	52	69	4	4	6.3	.968
	J. Mostil	R	1	0	2	0	0	2.0	1.000
SS	E. Johnson	R	141	291	494	44	80	5.9	.947
	H. McClellan	R	15	24	60	2	12	5.7	.977
	E. Mulligan	R	1	0	1	0	0	1.0	1.000
3B	E. Mulligan	R	152	162	307	22	28	3.2	.955
	H. McClellan	R	5	4	9	1	5	2.8	.929
	E. Leifer	R	1	1	1	0	0	2.0	1.000

POS	Player	T	G	PO	A	E	DP	TCG	FA
OF	B. Falk	L	149	288	9	13	5	2.1	.958
	J. Mostil	R	91	215	12	13	1	2.6	.946
	A. Strunk	L	111	214	10	7	2	2.1	.970
	H. Hooper	R	108	182	12	5	3	1.8	.975
	H. McClellan	R	15	32	3	1	2	2.4	.972
	E. Leifer	R	1	0	0	0	0	0.0	.000
	F. Bratchi	R	5	7	2	0	0	1.8	1.000
C	R. Schalk	R	126	453	129	9	19	4.7	**.985**
	Y. Yaryan	R	34	72	26	7	1	3.1	.933
	G. Lees	R	16	32	7	2	1	2.6	.951

Chicago 1921

The "darned but clean" White Sox regrouped over the winter. Comiskey purchased an entire infield from Salt Lake City: Eddie Mulligan, Ernie Johnson, and the slow-footed slugger Earl Sheely. On March 4, the Old Roman traded Shano Collins and Nemo Leibold to Boston for Harry Hooper. Harry Frazee seemed intent on burying his Red Sox, and Comiskey was more than willing to help out. Hooper, a perennial .300 hitter, was not pleased. The rest of the roster was composed of college kids, a few holdovers from 1920, and a collection of career minor leaguers given a new lease on life.

Baseball survived and prospered following the scandal. The first sign of this was on opening day, when 25,000 cheering fans turned out to wish the Sox well. An 8–3 win over Detroit was no portent, however; the Sox rose as high as sixth place on May 1 but spent the rest of the year rooted in seventh. By June 17, though, Red Faber had 14 wins. His contribution was memorable, given the woeful state of this pitching staff.

The Black Sox players were out of organized baseball and fell victim to ruthless hustlers trying to capitalize on their names. Chicago broker George Miller put some money up and christened them the "Major Stars," booking them against semi-pro teams in the Midwest. But the national Baseball Federation barred its members from playing against any of the Black Sox.

TEAM STATISTICS

	W	L	PCT	GB	R	OR	2B	3B	HR	BA	SA	SB	E	DP	FA	CG	BB	SO	ShO	SV	ERA
NY	98	55	.641		948	708	285	87	134	.300	.464	89	222	138	.965	92	470	481	7	15	3.79
CLE	94	60	.610	4.5	925	712	355	90	42	.308	.430	58	204	124	.967	81	430	475	11	14	3.90
STL	81	73	.526	17.5	835	845	246	106	66	.304	.425	92	224	127	.964	79	557	478	9	9	4.62
WAS	80	73	.523	18	704	738	240	96	42	.277	.383	111	235	153	.963	80	442	452	8	10	3.97
BOS	75	79	.487	23.5	668	696	248	69	17	.277	.361	83	157	151	.975	88	452	446	9	5	3.98
DET	71	82	.464	27	883	852	268	100	58	.316	.433	95	232	107	.963	73	495	452	4	17	4.40
CHI	62	92	.403	36.5	683	858	242	82	35	.283	.379	97	200	155	.969	86	549	392	7	9	4.94
PHI	53	100	.346	45	657	894	256	64	83	.274	.390	68	274	144	.958	75	548	431	1	7	4.60
LEAGUE TOTAL					6303	6303	2140	694	477	.292	.408	693	1748	1099	.965	654	3943	3607	56	86	4.28

INDIVIDUAL PITCHING

PITCHER	T	W	L	PCT	ERA	SV	G	GS	CG	IP	H	BB	SO	R	ER	ShO	H9	BB9	SO9
Red Faber	R	25	15	.625	2.48	1	43	39	32	330.2	293	87	124	107	91	4	7.97	2.37	3.38
Dickie Kerr	L	19	17	.528	4.72	1	44	37	25	308.2	357	96	80	182	162	3	10.41	2.80	2.33
Roy Wilkinson	R	4	20	.167	5.13	3	36	22	11	198.1	259	78	50	135	113	0	11.75	3.54	2.27
Shovel Hodge	R	6	8	.429	6.56	2	36	11	6	142.2	191	54	25	118	104	0	12.05	3.41	1.58
Doug McWeeny	R	3	6	.333	6.08	2	27	9	4	97.2	127	45	46	76	66	0	11.70	4.15	4.24
John Russell	L	2	5	.286	5.29	0	11	8	4	66.1	82	35	15	42	39	0	11.13	4.75	2.04
Dominic Mulrenan	R	2	8	.200	7.23	0	12	10	3	56	84	36	10	52	45	0	13.50	5.79	1.61
Lum Davenport	L	0	3	.000	6.88	0	13	2	0	35.1	41	32	9	35	27	0	10.44	8.15	2.29
Cy Twombly	R	1	2	.333	5.86	0	7	4	0	27.2	26	25	7	21	18	0	8.46	8.13	2.28
Jack Wieneke	L	0	1	.000	8.17	0	10	3	0	25.1	39	17	10	24	23	0	13.86	6.04	3.55
Sarge Connally	R	0	1	.000	6.45	0	5	2	0	22.1	29	10	6	16	16	0	11.69	4.03	2.42
Lee Thompson	L	0	3	.000	8.27	0	4	4	0	20.2	32	6	4	21	19	0	13.94	2.61	1.74
Bugs Bennett	R	0	3	.000	6.11	0	3	2	1	17.2	19	16	2	14	12	0	9.68	8.15	1.02
Hod Fenner	R	0	0	—	7.71	0	2	1	0	7	14	3	1	6	6	0	18.00	3.86	1.29
Russ Pence	R	0	0	—	8.44	0	4	0	0	5.1	6	7	2	5	5	0	10.13	11.81	3.38
John Michaelson	R	0	0	—	10.13	0	2	0	0	2.2	4	1	1	3	3	0	13.50	3.38	3.38
Babe Blackburn	R	0	0	—	0.00	0	1	0	0	1	0	1	0	0	0	0	0.00	9.00	0.00
TEAM TOTAL		62	92	.403	4.94	9	260	154	86	1365.1	1603	549	392	857	749	7	10.57	3.62	2.58

Chicago 1922   Won 77   Lost 77   Pct. .500   5th

MANAGER

	W	L	PCT
Kid Gleason	77	77	.500

POS	Player	B	G	AB	H	2B	3B	HR	HR%	R	RBI	BB	SO	SB	Pinch Hit AB	H	BA	SA
REGULARS																		
1B	Earl Sheely	R	149	526	167	37	4	6	1.1	72	80	60	27	4	0	0	.317	.437
2B	Eddie Collins	L	154	598	194	20	12	1	0.2	92	69	73	16	20	0	0	.324	.403
SS	Ernie Johnson	L	145	603	153	17	3	0	0.0	85	56	40	30	21	2	0	.254	.292
3B	Eddie Mulligan	R	103	372	87	14	8	0	0.0	39	31	22	32	7	10	2	.234	.315
RF	Harry Hooper	L	152	602	183	35	8	11	1.8	111	80	68	33	16	3	0	.304	.444
CF	Johnny Mostil	R	132	458	139	28	14	7	1.5	74	70	38	39	14	9	4	.303	.472
LF	Bibb Falk	L	131	483	144	27	1	12	2.5	58	79	27	55	2	1	0	.298	.433
C	Ray Schalk	R	142	442	124	22	3	4	0.9	57	60	67	36	12	0	0	.281	.371
SUBSTITUTES																		
3B	Harvey McClellan	R	91	301	68	17	3	2	0.7	28	28	16	32	3	5	4	.226	.322
2B	Johnny Evers	L	1	3	0	0	0	0	0.0	0	1	2	0	0	0	0	.000	.000
S2	John Jenkins	R	5	3	0	0	0	0	0.0	0	1	0	2	0	1	0	.000	.000
OF	Amos Strunk	L	92	311	90	11	4	0	0.0	36	33	33	28	9	10	3	.289	.350
OF	Elmer Pence	R	1	0	0	0	0	0	—	0	0	0	0	0	0	0	—	—
C	Yam Yaryan	R	36	71	14	2	0	2	2.8	9	9	6	10	1	8	0	.197	.310
C	Roy Graham	R	5	3	0	0	0	0	0.0	0	0	0	0	0	1	0	.000	.000
C	Jim Long	R	3	3	0	0	0	0	0.0	0	0	1	0	0	1	0	.000	.000
C	Augie Swentor	R	1	1	0	0	0	0	0.0	0	0	0	1	0	0	0	.000	.000
PH	Hal Bubser	R	3	3	0	0	0	0	0.0	0	0	0	2	0	3	0	.000	.000
PITCHERS																		
P	Red Faber	B	43	125	25	2	0	0	0.0	8	5	7	40	0	0	0	.200	.216
P	Charlie Robertson	L	37	87	16	0	0	0	0.0	3	7	8	10	0	0	0	.184	.184
P	Dixie Leverett	R	33	83	21	8	0	0	0.0	6	12	2	25	0	0	0	.253	.349
P	Shovel Hodge	L	35	58	12	1	0	0	0.0	4	4	1	10	0	0	0	.207	.224
P	Ted Blankenship	R	24	41	7	1	1	0	0.0	3	3	1	8	0	0	0	.171	.244
P	Henry Courtney	L	18	33	9	3	1	0	0.0	3	3	3	2	0	0	0	.273	.424
P	Ferdie Schupp	R	18	25	5	0	0	0	0.0	0	3	4	7	0	0	0	.200	.200
P	Frank Mack	R	8	12	3	0	1	0	0.0	1	0	0	4	0	0	0	.250	.417
P	Jose Acosta	R	5	5	1	0	0	0	0.0	0	0	1	1	0	0	0	.200	.200
P	Larry Duff	L	3	5	2	0	0	0	0.0	2	1	0	1	0	0	0	.400	.400
P	Homer Blankenship	R	4	4	0	0	0	0	0.0	0	0	0	2	0	0	0	.000	.000
P	Lum Davenport	L	11	3	0	0	0	0	0.0	0	0	1	3	0	0	0	.000	.000
P	Roy Wilkinson	R	4	3	0	0	0	0	0.0	0	0	0	2	0	0	0	.000	.000
P	Doug McWeeny	R	4	1	0	0	0	0	0.0	0	0	1	1	0	0	0	.000	.000
P	John Russell	L	4	1	0	0	0	0	0.0	0	0	0	1	0	0	0	.000	.000
P	Emmett Bowles	R	1	0	0	0	0	0	—	0	0	0	0	0	0	0	—	—
P	Ernie Cox	L	1	0	0	0	0	0	—	0	0	0	0	0	0	0	—	—
P	Dick McCabe	R	3	0	0	0	0	0	—	0	0	0	0	0	0	0	—	—
TEAM TOTAL				5269	1464	245	63	45	0.9	691	635	482	460	109	54	13	.278	.374

INDIVIDUAL FIELDING

POS	Player	T	G	PO	A	E	DP	TCG	FA	POS	Player	T	G	PO	A	E	DP	TCG	FA
1B	E. Sheely	R	149	1512	103	12	101	10.9	.993	OF	J. Mostil	R	132	333	9	12	2	2.7	.966
	A. Strunk	L	9	76	4	1	4	9.0	.988		H. Hooper	R	149	288	19	12	7	2.1	.962
2B	E. Collins	R	154	406	451	21	73	5.7	**.976**		B. Falk	L	131	253	10	10	2	2.1	.963
	J. Evers	L	1	3	3	0	1	6.0	1.000		A. Strunk	L	75	170	9	2	2	2.4	.989
	H. McClellan	R	2	1	2	0	0	1.5	1.000		H. McClellan	R	1	0	0	0	0	0.0	.000
	J. Jenkins	R	1	0	0	1	0	1.0	.000		E. Pence	R	1	1	0	0	0	1.0	1.000
SS	E. Johnson	R	141	259	468	37	74	5.4	.952	C	R. Schalk	R	142	591	150	8	16	5.3	**.989**
	H. McClellan	R	8	16	20	5	2	5.1	.878		Y. Yaryan	R	25	71	14	3	1	3.5	.966
	E. Mulligan	R	7	10	16	2	3	4.0	.929		A. Swentor	R	1	0	0	0	0	0.0	.000
	J. Jenkins	R	1	1	1	0	0	2.0	1.000		R. Graham	R	3	3	0	0	0	1.0	1.000
3B	E. Mulligan	R	86	94	200	11	14	3.5	.964		J. Long	R	2	1	0	0	0	0.5	1.000
	H. McClellan	R	71	77	158	7	15	3.4	.971										

68

Chicago 1922

The record is deceiving. The 1922 Sox were a spirited bunch that captured third place on July 1 on the strength of an eight-game winning streak. They won 16 of 19 games in June without Dickie Kerr, who refused to play for the Sox because Comiskey wouldn't give him a multiyear contract calling for $8,500. He chose to play with a semi-pro outfit in Chicago called The Famous Chicagos. As a result, Judge Landis barred him from the majors.

Two individual accomplishments stand out from the 1922 season. Charlie Robertson, a 26-year-old unknown from Sherman, Texas, pitched the only perfect game in Sox history on April 30, besting the Tigers in Detroit, 2–0. While Robertson's achievement cannot be discounted, it kept him in the majors when he might otherwise have been rightfully farmed out. And on June 27, Ray Schalk became the first player in club annals to hit for the cycle, with a homer and a triple off Tiger pitcher Howard Ehmke, and a single and double off Bert Cole.

News items about the Black Sox were appearing less frequently in 1922, but the pathetic reminders were still there. On June 24 the "Ex-Major League Stars" (another fast buck exploitation) were appearing in Merrill, Wisconsin. Swede Risberg, who was managing the "Stars," knocked out two of Ed Cicotte's teeth in a hotel fight after the pitcher demanded some immediate cash. Risberg was still a hard guy.

TEAM STATISTICS

	W	L	PCT	GB	R	OR	2B	3B	HR	BA	SA	SB	E	DP	FA	CG	BB	SO	ShO	SV	ERA
NY	94	60	.610		758	618	220	75	95	.287	.412	62	157	122	.975	98	423	458	7	14	3.39
STL	93	61	.604	1	867	643	291	94	98	.313	.455	132	201	158	.968	79	421	534	8	22	3.38
DET	79	75	.513	15	828	791	250	87	54	.305	.414	78	191	135	.970	67	473	461	7	15	4.27
CLE	78	76	.506	16	768	817	320	73	32	.292	.398	89	202	140	.968	76	464	489	14	7	4.60
CHI	77	77	.500	17	691	691	243	62	45	.278	.373	106	155	132	.975	86	529	484	13	8	3.93
WAS	69	85	.448	25	650	706	229	76	45	.268	.367	94	196	161	.969	84	500	422	11	10	3.81
PHI	65	89	.422	29	705	830	229	63	111	.269	.400	60	215	119	.966	73	469	373	4	6	4.59
BOS	61	93	.396	33	598	769	250	55	45	.263	.357	60	224	139	.965	71	503	359	10	6	4.30
LEAGUE TOTAL					5865	5865	2032	585	525	.284	.397	681	1541	1106	.969	634	3782	3580	74	88	4.03

INDIVIDUAL PITCHING

PITCHER	T	W	L	PCT	ERA	SV	G	GS	CG	IP	H	BB	SO	R	ER	ShO	H9	BB9	SO9
Red Faber	R	21	17	.553	2.80	2	43	38	31	353	334	83	148	128	110	4	8.52	2.12	3.77
Charlie Robertson	R	14	15	.483	3.64	0	37	34	21	272	294	89	83	124	110	3	9.73	2.94	2.75
Dixie Leverett	R	13	10	.565	3.32	2	33	27	16	224.2	224	79	60	95	83	4	8.97	3.16	2.40
Shovel Hodge	R	7	6	.538	4.14	1	35	8	2	139	154	65	37	73	64	0	9.97	4.21	2.40
Ted Blankenship	R	8	10	.444	3.81	1	24	15	7	127.2	124	47	42	58	54	0	8.74	3.31	2.96
Henry Courtney	L	5	6	.455	4.93	0	18	11	5	87.2	100	37	28	52	48	0	10.27	3.80	2.87
Ferdie Schupp	L	4	4	.500	6.08	0	18	12	3	74	79	66	38	61	50	1	9.61	8.03	4.62
Frank Mack	R	2	2	.500	3.67	0	8	4	1	34.1	36	16	11	16	14	1	9.44	4.19	2.88
Lum Davenport	L	1	1	.500	10.80	0	9	1	0	16.2	14	13	9	21	20	0	7.56	7.02	4.86
Jose Acosta	R	0	2	.000	8.40	0	5	1	0	15	25	6	6	14	14	0	15.00	3.60	3.60
Roy Wilkinson	R	0	1	.000	8.79	1	4	1	0	14.1	24	6	3	15	14	0	15.07	3.77	1.88
Homer Blankenship	R	0	0	–	4.85	0	4	0	0	13	21	5	3	7	7	0	14.54	3.46	2.08
Larry Duff	R	1	1	.500	4.97	0	3	1	0	12.2	16	3	7	7	7	0	11.37	2.13	4.97
Doug McWeeny	R	0	1	.000	5.91	0	4	1	0	10.2	13	7	5	8	7	0	10.97	5.91	4.22
John Russell	L	0	1	.000	6.75	1	4	1	0	6.2	7	4	3	5	5	0	9.45	5.40	4.05
Dick McCabe	R	1	0	1.000	5.40	0	3	0	0	3.1	4	0	1	2	2	0	10.80	0.00	2.70
Emmett Bowles	R	0	0	–	27.00	0	1	0	0	1	2	1	0	3	3	0	18.00	9.00	0.00
Ernie Cox	R	0	0	–	18.00	0	1	0	0	1	1	2	0	2	2	0	9.00	18.00	0.00
TEAM TOTAL		77	77	.500	3.93	8	254	155	86	1406.2	1472	529	484	691	614	13	9.42	3.38	3.10

Chicago 1923   Won 69 Lost 85 Pct. .448 7th

MANAGER	W	L	PCT
Kid Gleason	69	85	.448

POS	Player	B	G	AB	H	2B	3B	HR	HR%	R	RBI	BB	SO	SB	Pinch Hit AB	Pinch Hit H	BA	SA
REGULARS																		
1B	Earl Sheely	R	156	570	169	25	3	4	0.7	74	88	79	30	5	0	0	.296	.372
2B	Eddie Collins	L	145	505	182	22	5	5	1.0	89	67	84	8	47	3	0	.360	.453
SS	Harvey McClellan	R	141	550	129	29	3	1	0.2	67	41	27	44	14	1	1	.235	.304
3B	Willie Kamm	R	149	544	159	39	9	6	1.1	57	87	62	82	17	0	0	.292	.430
RF	Harry Hooper	L	145	576	166	32	4	10	1.7	87	65	68	22	18	2	1	.288	.410
CF	Johnny Mostil	R	153	546	159	37	15	3	0.5	91	64	62	51	41	4	0	.291	.430
LF	Bibb Falk	L	87	274	84	18	6	5	1.8	44	38	25	12	4	7	2	.307	.471
C	Ray Schalk	R	123	382	87	12	2	1	0.3	42	44	39	28	6	2	0	.228	.277
SUBSTITUTES																		
2S	John Happenny	R	32	86	19	5	0	0	0.0	7	10	3	13	0	1	0	.221	.279
SS	Ernie Johnson	L	12	53	10	2	0	0	0.0	5	1	3	5	2	0	0	.189	.226
2B	Lou Rosenberg	R	3	4	1	0	0	0	0.0	0	0	0	1	0	1	0	.250	.250
OF	Roy Elsh	R	81	209	52	7	2	0	0.0	28	24	16	23	15	15	4	.249	.301
OF	Bill Barrett	R	42	162	44	7	2	2	1.2	17	23	9	24	12	1	0	.272	.377
OF	Maurice Archdeacon	L	22	87	35	5	1	0	0.0	23	4	6	8	2	1	0	.402	.483
O1	Amos Strunk	L	54	54	17	0	0	0	0.0	7	8	8	5	1	39	12	.315	.315
C	Roy Graham	R	36	82	16	2	0	0	0.0	3	6	9	6	0	2	0	.195	.220
C	Buck Crouse	L	23	70	18	2	1	1	1.4	6	7	3	4	0	0	0	.257	.357
C	Charlie Dorman	R	1	2	1	0	0	0	0.0	0	0	0	0	0	0	0	.500	.500
PH	Shine Cortazzo	R	1	1	0	0	0	0	0.0	0	0	0	0	0	1	0	.000	.000
PH	Roxy Snipes	L	1	1	0	0	0	0	0.0	0	0	0	0	0	1	0	.000	.000
PH	Leo Taylor	R	2	0	0	0	0	0	—	0	0	0	0	0	0	0	—	—
PITCHERS																		
P	Charlie Robertson	L	38	85	21	2	0	0	0.0	4	1	1	3	1	0	0	.247	.271
P	Sloppy Thurston	R	45	79	25	5	1	0	0.0	10	4	2	6	0	1	0	.316	.405
P	Ted Blankenship	R	44	76	16	0	2	3	3.9	8	8	0	13	0	0	0	.211	.382
P	Mike Cvengros	L	41	74	15	0	0	0	0.0	4	4	4	12	0	0	0	.203	.203
P	Red Faber	B	33	69	15	3	0	1	1.4	7	5	10	28	1	0	0	.217	.304
P	Dixie Leverett	R	38	60	16	1	1	0	0.0	8	3	9	18	0	0	0	.267	.317
P	Claral Gillenwater	R	5	6	0	0	0	0	0.0	0	0	0	0	0	0	0	.000	.000
P	Frank Mack	R	11	6	0	0	0	0	0.0	0	0	0	4	0	0	0	.000	.000
P	Ted Lyons	B	9	5	1	0	0	0	0.0	0	1	1	3	0	0	0	.200	.200
P	Paul Castner	L	6	3	0	0	0	0	0.0	0	1	0	0	0	0	0	.000	.000
P	Sarge Connally	R	3	3	1	0	0	0	0.0	1	0	0	1	0	0	0	.333	.333
P	Lum Davenport	L	2	1	1	0	0	0	0.0	0	0	0	0	0	0	0	1.000	1.000
P	Homer Blankenship	R	4	0	0	0	0	0	—	0	0	0	0	0	0	0	—	—
P	Leon Cadore	R	1	1	0	0	0	0	—	0	1	1	0	0	0	0	—	—
P	Slim Embry	R	1	0	0	0	0	0	—	0	0	0	0	0	0	0	—	—
P	Red Proctor	R	2	0	0	0	0	0	—	0	0	0	0	0	0	0	—	—
P	Frank Woodward	R	2	0	0	0	0	0	—	0	0	0	0	0	0	0	—	—
TEAM TOTAL				5225	1459	255	57	42	0.8	690	604	531	454	186	82	20	.279	.374

INDIVIDUAL FIELDING

POS	Player	T	G	PO	A	E	DP	TCG	FA
1B	E. Sheely	R	156	1563	96	14	113	10.7	.992
	A. Strunk	L	3	8	0	1	0	3.0	.889
2B	E. Collins	R	142	347	430	20	77	5.6	.975
	J. Happenny	R	20	22	49	4	10	3.8	.947
	H. McClellan	R	2	5	5	0	2	5.0	1.000
	L. Rosenberg	R	2	1	0	0	0	0.5	1.000
SS	H. McClellan	R	138	217	394	27	63	4.6	.958
	E. Johnson	R	12	24	35	5	9	5.3	.922
	J. Happenny	R	8	17	15	3	3	4.4	.914
	J. Mostil	R	1	2	2	1	1	5.0	.800
3B	W. Kamm	R	149	173	352	22	29	3.7	.960
	J. Mostil	R	6	10	11	2	1	3.8	.913
	B. Barrett	R	1	2	3	0	0	5.0	1.000

POS	Player	T	G	PO	A	E	DP	TCG	FA
OF	J. Mostil	R	143	422	21	12	5	3.2	.974
	H. Hooper	R	143	272	15	12	3	2.1	.960
	B. Falk	L	80	148	6	8	3	2.0	.951
	R. Elsh	R	57	127	7	6	1	2.5	.957
	B. Barrett	R	40	89	5	6	1	2.5	.940
	M. Archdeacon	L	20	44	1	4	0	2.5	.918
	A. Strunk	L	4	10	0	0	0	2.5	1.000
C	R. Schalk	R	121	481	93	10	20	4.8	.983
	R. Graham	R	33	78	15	5	1	3.0	.949
	B. Crouse	R	22	66	18	4	1	4.0	.955
	C. Dorman	R	1	1	1	0	0	2.0	1.000

With high hopes, the Sox looked toward a bright new season. The newest face in camp was Willie Kamm, a third baseman from the San Francisco Seals whom Comiskey had purchased in June of 1922 for a cool $100,000. The owner had seen the error of his ways and was spending money, but it was too late.

The Sox rallied after a miserable start. A late June road trip saw the Pale Hose win 19 of 28 and climb to third place on July 4. Coincidental with this rise was the arrival of Ted Lyons from the Baylor University campus. He was put into a game on July 2, when the Sox were on the short end of a 7–2 score. He showed well, retiring all three batters. But that same day Eddie Collins twisted his knee. The injury doomed the Sox, and they fell to seventh place in September. The entire infield missed games due to injuries, but the decline could more likely be traced to age. Hooper, Collins, Strunk, and Sheely had all slowed down noticeably.

Two rookies made sensational debuts in 1923. One was Lou Gehrig. The other was the Sox' $50,000 investment, Maurice Archdeacon. In September he hit .402, including a pair of five-hit games. Tonsillitis cut short his career a year later.

Kid Gleason had had enough. He waited until the Sox captured yet another City Series before tendering his resignation on October 17. He thought he could rebuild the Sox after 1920, but the task was more than one man could handle. The Kid was a tragic figure, but his successor Frank Chance was even more so.

TEAM STATISTICS

	W	L	PCT	GB	R	OR	2B	3B	HR	BA	SA	SB	E	DP	FA	CG	BB	SO	ShO	SV	ERA
NY	98	54	.645		823	622	231	79	105	.291	.422	69	144	131	.977	102	491	506	9	10	3.66
DET	83	71	.539	16	831	741	270	69	41	.300	.401	87	200	103	.968	61	459	447	9	12	4.09
CLE	82	71	.536	16.5	888	746	301	75	59	.301	.420	79	226	143	.964	76	466	407	10	11	3.91
WAS	75	78	.490	23.5	720	747	224	93	26	.274	.367	102	216	182	.966	70	559	474	8	16	3.99
STL	74	78	.487	24	688	720	248	62	82	.281	.398	64	177	145	.971	83	528	488	10	10	3.93
PHI	69	83	.454	29	661	761	229	65	52	.271	.370	72	221	127	.965	65	550	400	6	12	4.08
CHI	69	85	.448	30	692	741	254	57	42	.279	.373	191	184	138	.971	74	534	467	5	11	4.03
BOS	61	91	.401	37	584	809	253	54	34	.261	.351	77	232	126	.963	78	520	412	3	11	4.20
LEAGUE TOTAL					5887	5887	2010	554	441	.282	.388	741	1600	1095	.968	609	4107	3601	60	93	3.99

INDIVIDUAL PITCHING

PITCHER	T	W	L	PCT	ERA	SV	G	GS	CG	IP	H	BB	SO	R	ER	ShO	H9	BB9	SO9
Charlie Robertson	R	13	18	.419	3.81	0	38	34	18	255	262	104	91	126	108	1	9.25	3.67	3.21
Red Faber	R	14	11	.560	3.41	0	32	31	15	232.1	233	62	91	114	88	2	9.03	2.40	3.53
Mike Cvengros	L	12	13	.480	4.39	3	41	26	14	215.1	216	107	86	110	105	0	9.03	4.47	3.59
Ted Blankenship	R	9	14	.391	4.27	0	44	23	9	208.2	219	100	57	115	99	1	9.45	4.31	2.46
Dixie Leverett	R	10	13	.435	4.06	3	38	24	9	192.2	212	64	64	108	87	0	9.90	2.99	2.99
Sloppy Thurston	R	7	8	.467	3.05	4	44	12	8	191.2	223	36	55	70	65	0	10.47	1.69	2.58
Frank Mack	R	0	1	.000	4.24	0	11	0	0	23.1	23	11	6	13	11	0	8.87	4.24	2.31
Ted Lyons	R	2	1	.667	6.35	0	9	1	0	22.2	30	15	6	21	16	0	11.91	5.96	2.38
Claral Gillenwater	R	1	3	.250	5.48	0	5	3	1	21.1	28	6	2	15	13	1	11.81	2.53	0.84
Paul Castner	L	0	0	—	6.30	0	6	0	0	10	14	5	0	9	7	0	12.60	4.50	0.00
Sarge Connally	R	0	0	—	6.23	0	3	0	0	8.2	7	12	3	6	6	0	7.27	12.46	3.12
Homer Blankenship	R	1	1	.500	3.60	1	4	0	0	5	9	1	1	5	2	0	16.20	1.80	1.80
Lum Davenport	L	0	0	—	6.23	0	2	0	0	4.1	7	4	1	4	3	0	14.54	8.31	2.08
Red Proctor	R	0	0	—	13.50	0	2	0	0	4	11	2	0	8	6	0	24.75	4.50	0.00
Slim Embry	R	0	0	—	10.13	0	1	0	0	2.2	7	2	1	6	3	0	23.63	6.75	3.38
Leon Cadore	R	0	1	.000	23.14	0	1	1	0	2.1	6	2	3	7	6	0	23.14	7.71	11.57
Frank Woodward	R	0	1	.000	13.50	0	2	1	0	2	5	1	0	3	3	0	22.50	4.50	0.00
TEAM TOTAL		69	85	.448	4.03	11	283	156	74	1402	1512	534	467	740	628	5	9.71	3.43	3.00

Chicago 1924   Won 66   Lost 87   Pct. .431   8th

MANAGER	W	L	PCT
Johnny Evers	66	87	.431

POS	Player	B	G	AB	H	2B	3B	HR	HR%	R	RBI	BB	SO	SB	Pinch Hit AB	Pinch Hit H	BA	SA
REGULARS																		
1B	Earl Sheely	R	146	535	171	34	3	3	0.6	84	103	95	28	7	0	0	.320	.411
2B	Eddie Collins	L	152	556	194	27	7	6	1.1	108	86	89	16	42	2	0	.349	.455
SS	Bill Barrett	R	119	406	110	18	5	2	0.5	52	56	30	38	15	7	2	.271	.355
3B	Willie Kamm	R	147	528	134	28	6	6	1.1	58	93	64	59	9	0	0	.254	.364
RF	Harry Hooper	L	130	476	156	27	8	10	2.1	107	62	65	26	16	5	2	.328	.481
CF	Johnny Mostil	R	118	385	125	22	5	4	1.0	75	49	45	41	7	14	5	.325	.439
LF	Bibb Falk	L	138	526	185	37	8	6	1.1	77	99	47	21	6	3	1	.352	.487
C	Buck Crouse	L	94	305	79	10	1	1	0.3	30	44	23	12	3	4	0	.259	.308
SUBSTITUTES																		
SS	Ray French	R	37	112	20	4	0	0	0.0	13	11	10	13	3	5	0	.179	.214
SS	Ray Morehart	L	31	100	20	4	2	0	0.0	10	8	17	7	3	2	0	.200	.280
S2	Harvey McClellan	R	32	85	15	3	0	0	0.0	9	9	6	7	2	1	0	.176	.212
1B	Bud Clancy	L	13	35	9	1	0	0	0.0	5	6	3	2	3	4	1	.257	.286
SS	Ike Davis	R	10	33	8	1	1	0	0.0	5	4	2	5	0	5	0	.242	.333
2B	Bill Black	L	6	5	1	0	0	0	0.0	0	0	0	0	0	0	0	.200	.200
SS	Wally Dashiell	R	1	2	0	0	0	0	0.0	0	0	0	0	0	0	0	.000	.000
SS	Frank Naleway	R	1	2	0	0	0	0	0.0	0	0	1	0	0	0	0	.000	.000
SS	Bernie DeViveiros	R	1	1	0	0	0	0	0.0	0	0	0	0	0	0	0	.000	.000
OF	Maurice Archdeacon	L	95	288	92	9	3	0	0.0	59	25	40	30	11	14	5	.319	.372
OF	Roy Elsh	R	60	147	45	9	1	0	0.0	21	11	10	14	6	16	3	.306	.381
C	Ray Schalk	R	57	153	30	4	2	1	0.7	15	11	21	10	1	1	0	.196	.268
C	Johnny Grabowski	R	20	56	14	3	0	0	0.0	10	3	2	4	0	0	0	.250	.304
C	Joe Burns	R	8	19	2	0	0	0	0.0	1	0	0	2	0	2	0	.105	.105
C	Kettle Wirtz	R	6	12	1	0	0	0	0.0	0	0	2	2	1	0	0	.083	.083
PH	Amos Strunk	L	1	1	0	0	0	0	0.0	0	0	0	0	0	1	0	.000	.000
PITCHERS																		
P	Sloppy Thurston	R	51	122	31	6	3	1	0.8	15	9	5	14	0	10	3	.254	.377
P	Ted Lyons	B	41	77	17	0	1	0	0.0	10	6	5	13	0	0	0	.221	.247
P	Red Faber	B	21	54	8	0	0	0	0.0	6	1	7	15	0	0	0	.148	.148
P	Sarge Connally	R	44	50	11	1	0	0	0.0	3	0	1	10	0	0	0	.220	.240
P	Ted Blankenship	R	25	46	15	2	1	1	2.2	10	5	4	6	0	0	0	.326	.478
P	Charlie Robertson	L	17	33	6	1	0	0	0.0	3	3	2	2	0	0	0	.182	.212
P	Dixie Leverett	R	21	32	6	2	0	0	0.0	2	2	1	10	0	0	0	.188	.250
P	Mike Cvengros	L	26	30	6	2	2	0	0.0	2	4	4	3	0	0	0	.200	.400
P	Leo Mangum	R	13	14	1	0	0	0	0.0	2	0	3	2	0	0	0	.071	.071
P	Doug McWeeny	R	13	9	0	0	0	0	0.0	2	0	4	4	1	0	0	.000	.000
P	Bob Barnes	L	2	2	0	0	0	0	0.0	0	0	0	0	0	0	0	.000	.000
P	Happy Foreman	L	5	2	0	0	0	0	0.0	0	0	0	1	0	2	0	.000	.000
P	Milt Steengrafe	R	3	1	0	0	0	0	0.0	0	0	0	0	0	0	0	.000	.000
P	Lum Davenport	L	1	0	0	0	0	0	–	0	0	0	0	0	0	0	–	–
P	John Dobb	R	2	0	0	0	0	0	–	0	0	0	0	0	0	0	–	–
P	Bob Lawrence	R	1	0	0	0	0	0	–	0	0	0	0	0	0	0	–	–
P	Webb Schultz	R	1	0	0	0	0	0	0.0	0	0	0	0	0	0	0	–	–
TEAM TOTAL				5240	1512	255	59	41	0.8	794	710	608	417	136	98	22	.289	.383

INDIVIDUAL FIELDING

POS	Player	T	G	PO	A	E	DP	TCG	FA
1B	E. Sheely	R	146	1423	79	14	97	10.4	.991
	B. Clancy	L	8	69	3	3	4	9.4	.960
	R. Elsh	R	2	7	0	2	0	4.5	.778
2B	E. Collins	R	150	396	446	20	83	5.7	**.977**
	B. Black	R	1	0	0	0	0	0.0	.000
	H. McClellan	R	7	8	21	1	1	4.3	.967
	R. Morehart	R	2	4	2	1	0	3.5	.857
	R. French	R	3	2	1	0	1	1.0	1.000
SS	B. Barrett	R	77	167	199	39	36	5.3	.904
	R. French	R	28	36	89	10	9	4.8	.926
	R. Morehart	R	27	35	68	15	12	4.4	.873
	H. McClellan	R	21	26	65	6	4	4.6	.938
	I. Davis	R	10	14	33	3	3	5.0	.940
	F. Naleway	R	1	1	2	1	0	4.0	.750
	W. Dashiell	R	1	1	1	1	0	3.0	.667
	DeViveiros	R	1	1	0	2	0	3.0	.333
3B	W. Kamm	R	145	190	312	15	31	3.6	**.971**
	B. Barrett	R	8	11	15	2	2	3.5	.929
	H. McClellan	R	1	1	1	0	0	2.0	1.000

POS	Player	T	G	PO	A	E	DP	TCG	FA
OF	B. Falk	L	134	292	26	10	4	2.4	.970
	J. Mostil	R	102	281	13	8	2	3.0	.974
	H. Hooper	R	123	251	22	4	8	2.3	.986
	M. Archdeacon	L	77	173	8	8	2	2.5	.958
	R. Elsh	R	38	58	3	3	0	1.7	.953
	B. Barrett	R	27	45	6	4	4	2.0	.927
	S. Thurston	R	1	0	0	0	0	0.0	.000
	H. McClellan	R	1	1	0	0	0	1.0	1.000
C	B. Crouse	R	90	298	97	23	9	4.6	.945
	R. Schalk	R	56	179	55	10	8	4.4	.959
	J. Grabowski	R	19	48	22	2	0	3.8	.972
	K. Wirtz	R	5	9	7	0	0	3.2	1.000
	J. Burns	R	6	12	2	1	1	2.5	.933

Charles Comiskey hired Frank Chance to manage the Sox on October 26, 1923. The "Peerless Leader" had just resigned his job in Boston following a last-place showing. The strain of that season left him in a weak condition when he attended the baseball winter meetings in December. There he contracted a cold that developed into a bronchial infection. On February 17 he wired Comiskey of his intention to quit on his doctor's advice. Comiskey refused to accept it, allowing him a leave of absence. The Sox conducted their spring training under Ed Walsh and Chance's old friend Johnny Evers. Finally, on April 8 Chance returned to Chicago determined to manage the Sox. In his one game at the helm the Sox won a 2–1 decision over the New York Giants. During this exhibition game, Chance developed a cold and had to be hospitalized. With his health in a precarious state, Chance quit the Sox for good on April 19, returning to his home in Los Angeles. Five months later, this legendary figure of Chicago sports was dead.

Johnny Evers, himself sickly, took over for Chance. The team hovered near the .500 mark most of the season, despite operations to the pitching arms of Red Faber and Charlie Robertson. Evers missed the middle part of the season, and Eddie Collins ran the team in his absence. It was a dismal year, one that saw Ray Schalk injure his throwing hand the same day he played in his 1,500th game. For his fortitude, Collins was rewarded with the manager's chair on December 11, 1924.

TEAM STATISTICS

	W	L	PCT	GB	R	OR	2B	3B	HR	BA	SA	SB	E	DP	FA	CG	BB	SO	ShO	SV	ERA
WAS	92	62	.597		755	613	255	88	22	.294	.387	115	171	149	.972	74	505	469	12	25	3.35
NY	89	63	.586	2	798	667	248	86	98	.289	.426	69	156	131	.974	76	522	487	13	13	3.86
DET	86	68	.558	6	849	796	315	76	35	.298	.404	100	187	142	.971	60	466	441	5	20	4.19
STL	74	78	.487	17	764	797	265	62	67	.294	.408	85	183	141	.969	66	512	382	11	7	4.55
PHI	71	81	.467	20	685	778	251	59	63	.281	.389	79	180	157	.971	68	597	371	7	10	4.39
CLE	67	86	.438	24.5	755	814	306	59	41	.296	.399	84	205	130	.967	87	503	315	7	7	4.40
BOS	67	87	.435	25	725	801	300	61	30	.277	.374	79	210	124	.967	73	519	414	8	16	4.36
CHI	66	87	.431	25.5	793	858	254	58	41	.288	.382	138	229	136	.963	76	512	360	1	11	4.75
LEAGUE TOTAL					6124	6124	2194	549	397	.290	.396	749	1521	1110	.969	580	4136	3239	64	109	4.23

INDIVIDUAL PITCHING

PITCHER	T	W	L	PCT	ERA	SV	G	GS	CG	IP	H	BB	SO	R	ER	ShO	H9	BB9	SO9
Sloppy Thurston	R	20	14	.588	3.80	1	38	36	28	291	330	60	37	150	123	1	10.21	1.86	1.14
Ted Lyons	R	12	11	.522	4.87	3	41	22	12	216.1	279	72	52	143	117	0	11.61	3.00	2.16
Red Faber	R	9	11	.450	3.85	0	21	20	9	161.1	173	58	47	78	69	0	9.65	3.24	2.62
Sarge Connally	R	7	13	.350	4.05	6	44	13	6	160	177	68	55	95	72	0	9.96	3.83	3.09
Ted Blankenship	R	7	6	.538	5.17	1	25	11	7	125.1	167	38	36	79	72	0	11.99	2.73	2.59
Mike Cvengros	L	3	12	.200	5.88	0	26	15	2	105.2	119	67	36	80	69	0	10.14	5.71	3.07
Dixie Leverett	R	2	3	.400	5.82	0	21	11	4	99	123	41	29	72	64	0	11.18	3.73	2.64
Charlie Robertson	R	4	10	.286	4.99	0	17	14	5	97.1	108	54	29	65	54	0	9.99	4.99	2.68
Leo Mangum	R	1	4	.200	7.09	0	13	7	1	47	69	25	12	43	37	0	13.21	4.79	2.30
Doug McWeeny	R	1	3	.250	4.57	0	13	5	2	43.1	47	17	18	25	22	0	9.76	3.53	3.74
Milt Steengrafe	R	0	0	—	12.71	0	3	0	0	5.2	15	4	3	8	8	0	23.82	6.35	4.76
Bob Barnes	L	0	0	—	19.29	0	2	0	0	4.2	14	0	1	11	10	0	27.00	0.00	1.93
Happy Foreman	L	0	0	—	2.25	0	3	0	0	4	7	4	1	3	1	0	15.75	9.00	2.25
Lum Davenport	L	0	0	—	0.00	0	1	0	0	2	1	2	1	1	0	0	4.50	9.00	4.50
John Dobb	L	0	0	—	9.00	0	2	0	0	2	4	1	2	2	2	0	18.00	4.50	9.00
Bob Lawrence	R	0	0	—	9.00	0	1	0	0	1	1	1	1	1	1	0	9.00	9.00	9.00
Webb Schultz	R	0	0	—	9.00	0	1	0	0	1	1	0	0	1	1	0	9.00	0.00	0.00
TEAM TOTAL		66	87	.431	4.75	11	272	154	76	1366.2	1635	512	360	857	722	1	10.77	3.37	2.37

Chicago 1925   Won 79 Lost 75 Pct. .513 5th

MANAGER	W	L	PCT
Eddie Collins	79	75	.513

POS	Player	B	G	AB	H	2B	3B	HR	HR %	R	RBI	BB	SO	SB	Pinch Hit AB	Pinch Hit H	BA	SA
REGULARS																		
1B	Earl Sheely	R	153	600	189	43	3	9	1.5	93	111	68	23	3	0	0	.315	.442
2B	Eddie Collins	L	118	425	147	26	3	3	0.7	80	80	87	8	19	2	0	.346	.442
SS	Ike Davis	R	146	562	135	31	9	0	0.0	105	61	71	58	19	2	1	.240	.327
3B	Willie Kamm	R	152	509	142	32	4	6	1.2	82	83	90	36	11	0	0	.279	.393
RF	Harry Hooper	L	127	442	117	23	5	6	1.4	62	55	54	21	12	2	0	.265	.380
CF	Johnny Mostil	R	153	605	181	36	16	2	0.3	135	50	90	52	43	0	0	.299	.421
LF	Bibb Falk	L	154	602	181	35	9	4	0.7	80	99	51	25	4	0	0	.301	.409
C	Ray Schalk	R	125	343	94	18	1	0	0.0	44	52	57	27	11	0	0	.274	.332
SUBSTITUTES																		
UT	Bill Barrett	R	81	245	89	23	3	3	1.2	44	40	24	27	5	7	1	.363	.518
S2	John Kane	B	14	56	10	1	0	0	0.0	6	3	0	3	0	0	0	.179	.196
OF	Spence Harris	L	56	92	26	2	0	1	1.1	12	13	14	13	1	24	7	.283	.337
OF	Roy Elsh	R	32	48	9	1	0	0	0.0	6	4	5	7	2	13	3	.188	.208
OF	Maurice Archdeacon	L	10	9	1	0	0	0	0.0	2	0	2	1	0	8	1	.111	.111
OF	Jule Mallonee	L	2	3	0	0	0	0	0.0	1	0	1	0	0	1	0	.000	.000
C	Buck Crouse	L	54	131	46	7	0	2	1.5	18	25	12	4	1	6	2	.351	.450
C	Johnny Grabowski	R	21	46	14	4	1	0	0.0	5	10	2	4	0	0	0	.304	.435
C	John Bischoff	R	7	11	1	0	0	0	0.0	1	0	1	5	0	3	0	.091	.091
C	Leo Tankersley	R	1	3	0	0	0	0	0.0	0	0	0	0	0	0	0	.000	.000
PH	Bud Clancy	L	4	3	0	0	0	0	0.0	0	0	1	0	0	3	0	.000	.000
PITCHERS																		
P	Ted Lyons	R	43	97	18	3	0	0	0.0	6	7	3	13	0	0	0	.186	.216
P	Ted Blankenship	R	40	88	18	2	2	2	2.3	7	15	4	23	0	0	0	.205	.341
P	Sloppy Thurston	R	44	84	24	7	2	0	0.0	2	13	5	13	0	6	2	.286	.417
P	Red Faber	R	34	77	8	1	0	0	0.0	3	4	10	24	0	0	0	.104	.117
P	Charlie Robertson	L	24	45	10	1	0	0	0.0	3	4	3	6	0	0	0	.222	.244
P	Mike Cvengros	L	22	33	5	1	0	0	0.0	6	1	4	4	0	0	0	.152	.182
P	Sarge Connally	R	40	28	7	1	2	0	0.0	4	3	2	3	0	0	0	.250	.429
P	Jim Joe Edwards	R	9	17	3	0	0	0	0.0	0	2	0	2	0	0	0	.176	.176
P	Dickie Kerr	L	13	12	4	0	0	0	0.0	2	1	1	1	0	0	0	.333	.333
P	Leo Mangum	R	7	4	2	0	0	0	0.0	1	1	1	0	0	0	0	.500	.500
P	Frank Mack	R	8	3	1	1	0	0	0.0	1	1	0	0	0	0	0	.333	.667
P	Jake Freeze	R	2	1	0	0	0	0	0.0	0	0	0	1	0	0	0	.000	.000
P	Tink Riviere	R	3	1	0	0	0	0	0.0	0	0	0	1	0	0	0	.000	.000
P	Ken Ash	R	2	0	0	0	0	0	—	0	0	0	0	0	0	0	—	—
P	Chief Bender	R	1	0	0	0	0	0	—	0	0	0	0	0	0	0	—	—
	TEAM TOTAL			5225	1482	299	60	38	0.7	811	738	663	405	131	77	17	.284	.386

INDIVIDUAL FIELDING

POS	Player	T	G	PO	A	E	DP	TCG	FA
1B	E. Sheely	R	153	1565	95	20	136	11.0	.988
	R. Elsh	R	3	12	0	0	2	4.0	1.000
2B	E. Collins	R	116	290	346	20	74	5.7	.970
	B. Barrett	R	41	83	115	15	23	5.2	.930
	J. Kane	R	6	8	20	0	0	4.7	1.000
SS	I. Davis	R	144	313	472	53	97	5.8	.937
	J. Kane	R	8	14	29	3	6	5.8	.935
	B. Barrett	R	4	4	10	2	0	4.0	.875
3B	W. Kamm	R	152	182	310	22	32	3.4	.957
	B. Barrett	R	4	3	5	0	1	2.0	1.000

POS	Player	T	G	PO	A	E	DP	TCG	FA
OF	J. Mostil	R	153	446	11	7	5	3.0	.985
	B. Falk	L	154	306	18	14	4	2.2	.959
	H. Hooper	R	124	231	16	6	4	2.0	.976
	S. Harris	L	27	42	3	2	0	1.7	.957
	B. Barrett	R	27	42	1	2	0	1.7	.956
	R. Elsh	R	16	13	2	1	0	1.0	.938
	M. Archdeacon	L	1	2	0	0	0	2.0	1.000
	J. Mallonee	R	1	1	0	0	0	1.0	1.000
C	R. Schalk	R	125	368	99	8	15	3.8	.983
	B. Crouse	R	48	104	36	7	5	3.1	.952
	J. Grabowski	R	21	48	9	1	0	2.8	.983
	J. Bischoff	R	4	5	3	0	0	2.0	1.000
	L. Tankersley	R	1	1	0	0	0	1.0	1.000

Eddie Collins proved more than ready to assume the awesome task before him. He succeeded where Gleason and Evers failed because he could turn the ball over to his trio of promising young hurlers: Sloppy Thurston, Ted Blankenship, and Ted Lyons. Lyons turned in his first great year, winning 21. On September 19 he tossed eight and one third innings of hitless ball against the champion Senators, ending when Bobby Veach dropped a bleeder over Earl Sheely's head in right. Final count: Lyons and the Sox 17, the Champs 0.

Spring training in Shreveport, Louisiana, featured a 19-game winning streak against Western League teams and a motley crew known as the Shreveport Gassers. The Sox swept the entire spring schedule and opened the season in Detroit with a new sense of purpose. For most of that year, the Sox held down third place as the Yankees suffered an uncharacteristic off-year. The Sox took advantage of various New York misfortunes to capture the season series, 13 games to 9. The next time they would hold any edge over a Yankee team would be 1959.

It was the Roaring Twenties, and the Sox supplied the thrill seekers with their own brand of daffiness. On May 11 Carl Laemmle of Universal Pictures stood atop the Tribune Tower in Chicago and dropped three balls to Ray Schalk on the sidewalk below. A crowd of 10,000 witnessed the stunt, as Michigan Avenue was cordoned off. The first ball bounded off his mitt, the second missed the target, but Schalk hung onto the third one. The stunt was really nothing new. On August 24, 1910, Billy Sullivan had snagged the twenty-fourth ball thrown off the Washington Monument by Doc White. That drop was 542 feet, something to give a manager apoplexy.

TEAM STATISTICS

	W	L	PCT	GB	R	OR	2B	3B	HR	BA	SA	SB	E	DP	FA	CG	BB	SO	ShO	SV	ERA
WAS	96	55	.636		829	669	251	71	56	.303	.411	134	170	166	.972	69	543	464	9	21	3.67
PHI	88	64	.579	8.5	830	714	298	79	76	.307	.434	67	211	148	.966	61	544	495	8	18	3.89
STL	82	71	.536	15	897	909	304	68	110	.298	.439	85	226	164	.964	67	675	419	7	10	4.85
DET	81	73	.526	16.5	903	829	277	84	50	.302	.413	97	173	143	.972	66	556	419	2	18	4.61
CHI	79	75	.513	18.5	811	771	299	59	38	.284	.385	129	200	162	.968	71	489	374	12	13	4.34
CLE	70	84	.455	27.5	782	810	285	58	52	.297	.399	90	210	146	.967	93	493	345	6	9	4.49
NY	69	85	.448	28.5	706	774	247	74	110	.275	.410	67	160	150	.974	80	505	492	8	13	4.33
BOS	47	105	.309	49.5	639	921	257	64	41	.266	.364	42	271	150	.957	68	510	310	6	6	4.97
LEAGUE TOTAL					6397	6397	2218	557	533	.292	.407	711	1621	1229	.968	575	4315	3318	58	108	4.39

INDIVIDUAL PITCHING

PITCHER	T	W	L	PCT	ERA	SV	G	GS	CG	IP	H	BB	SO	R	ER	ShO	H9	BB9	SO9
Ted Lyons	R	21	11	.656	3.26	3	43	32	19	262.2	274	83	45	111	95	5	9.39	2.84	1.54
Red Faber	R	12	11	.522	3.78	0	34	32	16	238	266	59	71	117	100	1	10.06	2.23	2.68
Ted Blankenship	R	17	8	.680	3.16	1	40	23	16	222	218	69	81	90	78	3	8.84	2.80	3.28
Sloppy Thurston	R	10	14	.417	6.17	1	36	25	9	175	250	47	35	143	120	0	12.86	2.42	1.80
Charlie Robertson	R	8	12	.400	5.26	0	24	23	6	137	181	47	27	96	80	2	11.89	3.09	1.77
Sarge Connally	R	6	7	.462	4.64	8	40	2	0	104.2	122	58	45	63	54	0	10.49	4.99	3.87
Mike Cvengros	L	3	9	.250	4.30	0	22	11	4	104.2	109	55	32	56	50	0	9.37	4.73	2.75
Jim Joe Edwards	L	1	2	.333	3.97	0	9	4	1	45.1	46	23	20	25	20	1	9.13	4.57	3.97
Dickie Kerr	L	0	1	.000	5.15	0	12	2	0	36.2	45	18	4	23	21	0	11.05	4.42	0.98
Leo Mangum	R	1	0	1.000	7.80	0	7	0	0	15	25	6	6	15	13	0	15.00	3.60	3.60
Frank Mack	R	0	0	—	9.45	0	8	0	0	13.1	24	13	6	14	14	0	16.20	8.78	4.05
Tink Riviere	R	0	0	—	13.50	0	3	0	0	4.2	6	7	1	7	7	0	11.57	13.50	1.93
Ken Ash	R	0	0	—	9.00	0	2	0	0	4	7	0	0	4	4	0	15.75	0.00	0.00
Jake Freeze	R	0	0	—	2.45	0	2	0	0	3.2	5	3	1	7	1	0	12.27	7.36	2.45
Chief Bender	R	0	0	—	18.00	0	1	0	0	1	1	1	0	2	2	0	9.00	9.00	0.00
TEAM TOTAL		79	75	.513	4.34	13	283	154	71	1367.2	1579	489	374	773	659	12	10.39	3.22	2.46

Chicago 1926   Won 81   Lost 72   Pct. .529   5th

MANAGER	W	L	PCT
Eddie Collins	81	72	.529

POS	Player	B	G	AB	H	2B	3B	HR	HR%	R	RBI	BB	SO	SB	Pinch Hit AB	H	BA	SA
REGULARS																		
1B	Earl Sheely	R	145	525	157	40	2	6	1.1	77	89	75	13	3	0	0	.299	.417
2B	Eddie Collins	L	106	375	129	32	4	1	0.3	66	62	62	8	13	3	0	.344	.459
SS	Bill Hunnefield	B	131	470	129	26	4	3	0.6	81	48	37	28	24	2	0	.274	.366
3B	Willie Kamm	R	143	480	141	24	10	0	0.0	63	62	77	24	14	1	0	.294	.385
RF	Bill Barrett	R	111	368	113	31	4	6	1.6	46	61	25	26	9	6	3	.307	.462
CF	Johnny Mostil	R	148	600	197	41	15	4	0.7	120	42	79	55	35	0	0	.328	.467
LF	Bibb Falk	L	155	566	195	43	4	8	1.4	86	108	66	22	9	0	0	.345	.477
C	Ray Schalk	R	82	226	60	9	1	0	0.0	26	32	27	11	5	1	0	.265	.314
SUBSTITUTES																		
2B	Ray Morehart	L	73	192	61	10	3	0	0.0	27	21	11	15	3	17	6	.318	.401
SS	Everett Scott	R	40	143	36	10	1	0	0.0	15	13	9	8	1	1	0	.252	.336
SS	Moe Berg	R	41	113	25	6	0	0	0.0	4	7	6	9	0	6	1	.221	.274
1B	Bud Clancy	L	12	38	13	2	2	0	0.0	3	7	1	1	0	2	0	.342	.500
SS	Art Veltman	R	5	4	1	0	0	0	0.0	1	0	1	1	0	3	1	.250	.250
OF	Spence Harris	L	80	222	56	11	3	2	0.9	36	27	20	15	8	14	2	.252	.356
OF	Tom Gulley	L	16	35	8	3	1	0	0.0	5	8	5	2	0	4	1	.229	.371
OF	Pid Purdy	L	11	33	6	2	1	0	0.0	5	6	2	1	0	2	0	.182	.303
C	Buck Crouse	L	49	135	32	4	1	0	0.0	10	17	14	7	0	3	0	.237	.281
C	Johnny Grabowski	R	48	122	32	1	1	1	0.8	6	11	4	15	0	8	4	.262	.311
C1	Harry McCurdy	L	44	86	28	7	2	1	1.2	16	11	6	10	0	11	2	.326	.488
PITCHERS																		
P	Ted Lyons	R	41	104	22	1	1	0	0.0	7	3	1	10	0	1	0	.212	.240
P	Tommy Thomas	R	44	86	16	0	0	0	0.0	5	7	5	21	0	0	0	.186	.186
P	Ted Blankenship	R	29	76	10	4	0	0	0.0	8	2	6	18	0	0	0	.132	.184
P	Sloppy Thurston	R	38	61	19	4	0	0	0.0	5	5	3	6	0	5	0	.311	.377
P	Red Faber	B	27	60	9	2	0	0	0.0	7	10	8	21	0	0	0	.150	.183
P	Jim Joe Edwards	R	32	46	5	1	0	0	0.0	2	3	0	12	0	0	0	.109	.130
P	Sarge Connally	R	31	32	5	0	0	0	0.0	3	3	1	7	1	0	0	.156	.156
P	Milt Steengrafe	R	13	14	0	0	0	0	0.0	0	1	0	7	0	0	0	.000	.000
P	Dixie Leverett	R	6	7	1	0	0	0	0.0	1	0	0	4	0	0	0	.143	.143
P	Les Cox	R	2	2	1	0	0	0	0.0	0	0	0	1	0	0	0	.500	.500
P	Pryor McBee	R	1	0	0	0	0	0	—	0	0	0	0	0	0	0	—	—
TEAM TOTAL				5221	1507	314	60	32	0.6	731	666	551	378	125	90	20	.289	.390

INDIVIDUAL FIELDING

POS	Player	T	G	PO	A	E	DP	TCG	FA
1B	E. Sheely	R	144	1380	84	8	87	10.2	**.995**
	B. Clancy	L	10	104	6	1	11	11.1	.991
	H. McCurdy	R	8	20	3	1	2	3.0	.958
	B. Barrett	R	2	11	1	2	1	7.0	.857
	J. Grabowski	R	1	7	0	0	0	7.0	1.000
2B	E. Collins	R	101	228	307	15	53	5.4	.973
	R. Morehart	R	48	71	136	11	13	4.5	.950
	B. Hunnefield	R	15	40	41	2	8	5.5	.976
	M. Berg	R	2	1	3	0	0	2.0	1.000
SS	B. Hunnefield	R	98	185	259	32	44	4.9	.933
	E. Scott	R	39	70	120	9	20	5.1	.955
	M. Berg	R	31	59	86	8	21	4.9	.948
	A. Veltman	R	1	0	1	0	0	1.0	1.000
3B	W. Kamm	R	142	**177**	**323**	11	16	**3.6**	**.978**
	B. Hunnefield	R	17	25	37	2	2	3.8	.969
	M. Berg	R	1	0	0	0	0	0.0	.000

POS	Player	T	G	PO	A	E	DP	TCG	FA
OF	J. Mostil	R	147	**440**	15	**15**	4	3.2	.968
	B. Falk	L	155	338	16	3	4	2.3	**.992**
	B. Barrett	R	102	179	8	6	2	1.9	.969
	S. Harris	L	63	106	6	6	2	1.9	.949
	T. Gulley	R	12	19	0	0	0	1.6	1.000
	P. Purdy	R	9	17	1	0	0	2.0	1.000
C	R. Schalk	R	80	251	45	7	6	3.8	.977
	B. Crouse	R	45	164	34	3	1	4.5	.985
	J. Grabowski	R	38	121	22	4	0	3.9	.973
	H. McCurdy	R	25	64	10	2	1	3.0	.974

There was an optimistic feeling as the 1926 season began that the Sox were a real pennant threat. Thirty-seven thousand fans turned out on opening day, a new team record. On June 20 some 43,000 Ruth-gazers showed up to see Red Faber humble the Yankees, 4–3. The overflow crowds for Yankee games convinced Comiskey that expansion of the ballpark was necessary in order to take advantage of the Ruth phenomenon.

The Sox got as high as second place on June 19, when management saw fit to honor Eddie Collins with his own day. As is the case with most White Sox "Days," two things were sure to happen. First, the player in question would excel (Collins went three for three). Second, the player would be gone after the season. On November 11 Comiskey released Collins without so much as an advance notice. Repeated injuries had kept him out of the lineup for nearly two years, and Comiskey had little faith in him as a bench manager, so Collins was out.

Ted Blankenship's fractured right thumb hurt the pitching staff, and only Lyons and Tommy Thomas showed promise. Lyons finally got his no-hitter on August 21, in Boston. It was a dandy 6–0 decision in which he faced only 29 batters.

The Sox were well out of the race when September rolled around, but a late spurt gave them fifth place, making 1926 a guarded success. One other item of note: the Sox played the first Sunday game in Philadelphia on August 22, defying a local blue law that had been in existence since 1794. Only a judge's injunction prevented Connie Mack and Eddie Collins from being thrown in jail. Predictably, the Sox lost.

TEAM STATISTICS

	W	L	PCT	GB	R	OR	2B	3B	HR	BA	SA	SB	E	DP	FA	CG	BB	SO	ShO	SV	ERA
NY	91	63	.591		847	713	262	75	121	.289	.437	79	210	117	.966	64	478	486	4	20	3.86
CLE	88	66	.571	3	738	612	333	49	27	.289	.386	88	173	153	.972	96	450	381	11	4	3.40
PHI	83	67	.553	6	677	570	259	65	61	.269	.383	56	171	131	.972	62	451	571	10	16	3.00
WAS	81	69	.540	8	802	761	244	97	43	.292	.401	122	184	129	.969	65	566	418	5	26	4.34
CHI	81	72	.529	9.5	730	665	314	60	32	.289	.390	121	165	122	.973	85	506	458	11	12	3.74
DET	79	75	.513	12	793	830	281	90	36	.291	.398	88	193	151	.969	57	555	469	10	18	4.41
STL	62	92	.403	29	682	845	253	78	72	.276	.394	62	235	167	.963	64	654	337	5	9	4.66
BOS	46	107	.301	44.5	562	835	249	54	32	.256	.343	48	193	143	.970	53	546	336	6	5	4.72
LEAGUE TOTAL					5831	5831	2195	568	424	.281	.392	664	1524	1113	.969	546	4206	3456	62	110	4.02

INDIVIDUAL PITCHING

PITCHER	T	W	L	PCT	ERA	SV	G	GS	CG	IP	H	BB	SO	R	ER	ShO	H9	BB9	SO9
Ted Lyons	R	18	16	.529	3.01	2	39	31	24	283.2	268	106	51	108	95	3	8.50	3.36	1.62
Tommy Thomas	R	15	12	.556	3.80	2	44	32	13	249	225	110	127	113	105	2	8.13	3.98	4.59
Ted Blankenship	R	13	10	.565	3.61	1	29	26	15	209.1	217	65	66	96	84	1	9.33	2.79	2.84
Red Faber	R	15	9	.625	3.56	0	27	25	13	184.2	203	57	65	84	73	1	9.89	2.78	3.17
Jim Joe Edwards	L	6	9	.400	4.18	1	32	16	8	142	140	63	41	76	66	3	8.87	3.99	2.60
Sloppy Thurston	R	6	8	.429	5.02	3	31	13	6	134.1	164	36	35	85	75	1	10.99	2.41	2.34
Sarge Connally	R	6	5	.545	3.16	3	31	8	5	108.1	128	35	47	51	38	0	10.63	2.91	3.90
Milt Steengrafe	R	1	1	.500	3.99	0	13	1	0	38.1	43	19	10	22	17	0	10.10	4.46	2.35
Dixie Leverett	R	1	1	.500	6.00	0	6	3	1	24	31	7	12	18	16	0	11.63	2.63	4.50
Les Cox	R	0	1	.000	5.40	0	2	0	0	5	6	5	3	10	3	0	10.80	9.00	5.40
Pryor McBee	L	0	0	—	6.75	0	1	0	0	1.1	1	3	1	2	1	0	6.75	20.25	6.75
TEAM TOTAL		81	72	.529	3.74	12	255	155	85	1380	1426	506	458	665	573	11	9.30	3.30	2.99

Chicago 1927 Won 70 Lost 83 Pct .458 5th

MANAGER	W	L	PCT
Ray Schalk	70	83	.458

POS	Player	B	G	AB	H	2B	3B	HR	HR%	R	RBI	BB	SO	SB	Pinch Hit AB	H	BA	SA
REGULARS																		
1B	Bud Clancy	L	130	464	139	21	2	3	0.6	46	53	24	24	4	5	1	.300	.373
2B	Aaron Ward	R	145	463	125	25	8	5	1.1	75	56	63	56	6	1	0	.270	.391
SS	Bill Hunnefield	B	112	365	104	25	1	2	0.5	45	36	25	24	13	13	3	.285	.375
3B	Willie Kamm	R	148	540	146	32	13	0	0.0	85	59	70	18	7	2	0	.270	.378
RF	Bill Barrett	R	147	556	159	35	9	4	0.7	62	83	52	46	20	0	0	.286	.403
CF	Alex Metzler	L	134	543	173	29	11	3	0.6	87	61	61	39	15	0	0	.319	.429
LF	Bibb Falk	L	145	535	175	35	6	9	1.7	76	83	52	19	5	0	0	.327	.465
C	Harry McCurdy	L	86	262	75	19	3	1	0.4	34	27	32	24	6	3	0	.286	.393
SUBSTITUTES																		
SS	Roger Peckinpaugh	R	68	217	64	6	3	0	0.0	23	23	21	6	2	7	2	.295	.350
1B	Earl Sheely	R	45	129	27	3	0	2	1.6	11	16	20	5	1	8	1	.209	.279
SS	Ray Flaskamper	B	26	95	21	5	0	0	0.0	12	6	3	8	0	1	0	.221	.274
3S	Jim Battle	R	6	8	3	0	1	0	0.0	1	0	0	1	0	0	0	.375	.625
2B	Bob Way	R	5	3	1	0	0	0	0.0	3	1	0	1	0	3	1	.333	.333
OF	Bernie Neis	B	45	76	22	5	0	0	0.0	9	11	10	9	1	18	4	.289	.355
OF	Ike Boone	L	29	53	12	4	0	1	1.9	10	11	3	4	0	16	3	.226	.358
OF	Carl Reynolds	R	14	42	9	3	0	1	2.4	5	7	5	7	1	0	0	.214	.357
OF	Johnny Mostil	R	13	16	2	0	0	0	0.0	3	1	0	1	1	1	0	.125	.125
OF	Randy Moore	L	6	15	0	0	0	0	0.0	0	0	0	2	0	2	0	.000	.000
OF	Kid Willson	L	7	10	1	0	0	0	0.0	1	1	0	2	0	4	0	.100	.100
C	Buck Crouse	L	85	222	53	11	0	0	0.0	22	20	21	10	4	4	2	.239	.288
UT	Moe Berg	R	35	69	17	4	0	0	0.0	4	4	4	10	0	6	1	.246	.304
C	Ray Schalk	R	16	26	6	2	0	0	0.0	2	2	2	1	0	1	0	.231	.308
PH	Lena Blackburne	R	1	1	1	0	0	0	0.0	1	1	0	0	0	1	1	1.000	1.000
PITCHERS																		
P	Ted Lyons	R	41	110	28	6	2	1	0.9	16	9	6	17	0	0	0	.255	.373
P	Tommy Thomas	R	40	95	14	3	1	1	1.1	5	8	4	23	0	0	0	.147	.232
P	Ted Blankenship	R	38	80	15	5	1	3	3.8	9	14	6	22	0	1	0	.188	.388
P	Sarge Connally	R	43	67	22	1	0	0	0.0	5	6	2	10	0	0	0	.328	.343
P	Red Faber	B	18	37	10	3	0	0	0.0	2	4	2	8	0	0	0	.270	.351
P	Elmer Jacobs	R	25	20	3	0	0	0	0.0	4	2	1	5	0	0	0	.150	.150
P	Charlie Barnabe	L	18	19	3	3	0	0	0.0	3	5	4	4	0	1	0	.158	.316
P	Bert Cole	L	27	18	3	0	0	0	0.0	1	0	0	1	0	0	0	.167	.167
P	Frank Stewart	R	1	1	0	0	0	0	0.0	0	0	0	1	0	0	0	.000	.000
P	Joe Brown	R	1	0	0	0	0	0	—	0	0	0	0	0	0	0	—	—
TEAM TOTAL				5157	1433	285	61	36	0.7	662	610	493	408	86	98	19	.278	.378

INDIVIDUAL FIELDING

POS	Player	T	G	PO	A	E	DP	TCG	FA
1B	B. Clancy	L	123	1184	81	11	76	10.4	.991
	E. Sheely	R	36	315	15	6	25	9.3	.982
2B	A. Ward	R	138	275	437	27	66	5.4	.963
	B. Hunnefield	R	17	32	32	3	3	3.9	.955
	M. Berg	R	10	4	16	1	2	2.1	.952
	B. Way	R	1	1	0	0	0	1.0	1.000
SS	B. Hunnefield	R	78	150	210	26	38	4.9	.933
	Peckinpaugh	R	60	101	170	10	30	4.7	.964
	R. Flaskamper	R	25	55	70	5	10	5.2	.962
	M. Berg	R	6	10	17	6	2	5.5	.818
	J. Battle	R	2	2	0	0	0	1.0	1.000
3B	W. Kamm	R	146	**236**	279	15	21	3.6	**.972**
	A. Ward	R	6	8	13	0	0	3.5	1.000
	M. Berg	R	3	2	3	1	0	2.0	.833
	J. Battle	R	4	3	2	0	0	1.3	1.000
	B. Hunnefield	R	1	3	1	0	0	4.0	1.000

POS	Player	T	G	PO	A	E	DP	TCG	FA
OF	A. Metzler	R	134	397	16	15	6	**3.2**	.965
	B. Falk	L	145	372	22	9	9	2.8	.978
	B. Barrett	R	147	289	22	12	6	2.2	.963
	B. Neis	R	21	36	2	3	1	2.0	.927
	C. Reynolds	R	13	37	1	0	0	2.9	1.000
	I. Boone	R	11	15	0	0	0	1.4	1.000
	R. Moore	R	4	8	1	0	0	2.3	1.000
	J. Mostil	R	6	5	1	1	0	1.2	.857
	K. Willson	R	2	6	0	0	0	3.0	1.000
C	H. McCurdy	R	82	261	55	9	8	4.0	.972
	B. Crouse	R	81	202	79	8	10	3.6	.972
	R. Schalk	R	15	24	8	0	1	2.1	1.000
	M. Berg	R	10	23	5	1	0	2.9	.966

Comiskey rewarded Ray Schalk with the manager's job the same day Collins was released. His choice was a purely sentimental one; Schalk was too low-key and too easygoing to motivate the Sox players.

On March 9 he lost the services of the speedy centerfielder Johnny Mostil. Despondent over his painful neuritis condition, Mostil cut himself thirteen times with a razor while alone in his room at the Hotel Youree in Shreveport. Mostil failed in his suicide attempt but missed almost the entire season.

Pronouncing his spring training a failure, Schalk brought the club north. Over the winter Comiskey had spent $600,000 installing an upper deck in the outfield, replacing the wooden seats with a new concrete and steel pavilion. The architects said no man was capable of hitting a ball over the roof, but Babe Ruth was no ordinary man. It only took him until August to do what the architects had declared to be impossible, smashing a homer clear over the roof.

The White Sox season should have ended on June 6, when they were in second place, just a game out of first. But it didn't, and their shortstop problem and weak catching doomed the effort. Over the winter the Sox had traded the promising John Grabowski to New York for infielder Aaron Ward, and Sloppy Thurston to Washington for former MVP Roger Peckinpaugh. Sometimes the best trades you make come back to haunt you. Sometimes you just shouldn't get out of bed in the morning.

TEAM STATISTICS

	W	L	PCT	GB	R	OR	2B	3B	HR	BA	SA	SB	E	DP	FA	CG	BB	SO	ShO	SV	ERA
NY	110	44	.714		975	599	291	103	158	.307	.489	90	195	123	.969	82	409	431	11	20	3.20
PHI	91	63	.591	19	841	726	281	70	56	.303	.414	98	190	124	.970	66	442	553	8	24	3.95
WAS	85	69	.552	25	782	730	268	87	29	.287	.386	133	195	125	.969	62	491	497	10	23	3.95
DET	82	71	.536	27.5	845	805	282	100	51	.289	.409	141	206	173	.968	75	577	421	5	17	4.12
CHI	70	83	.458	39.5	662	708	285	61	36	.278	.378	90	178	131	.971	85	440	365	10	8	3.91
CLE	66	87	.431	43.5	668	766	321	52	26	.283	.379	63	201	146	.968	72	508	366	5	8	4.27
STL	59	94	.386	50.5	724	904	262	59	55	.276	.380	91	248	166	.960	80	604	385	4	8	4.95
BOS	51	103	.331	59	597	856	271	78	28	.259	.357	82	228	162	.964	63	558	381	6	7	4.68
LEAGUE TOTAL					6094	6094	2261	610	439	.285	.399	788	1641	1150	.967	585	4029	3399	59	115	4.12

INDIVIDUAL PITCHING

PITCHER	T	W	L	PCT	ERA	SV	G	GS	CG	IP	H	BB	SO	R	ER	ShO	H9	BB9	SO9
Ted Lyons	R	22	14	.611	2.84	2	39	34	30	307.2	291	67	71	125	97	2	8.51	1.96	2.08
Tommy Thomas	R	19	16	.543	2.98	1	40	36	24	307.2	271	94	107	110	102	3	7.93	2.75	3.13
Ted Blankenship	R	12	17	.414	5.06	0	37	34	11	236.2	280	74	51	156	133	3	10.65	2.81	1.94
Sarge Connally	R	10	15	.400	4.08	5	43	18	11	198.1	217	83	58	108	90	1	9.85	3.77	2.63
Red Faber	R	4	7	.364	4.55	0	18	15	6	110.2	131	41	39	64	56	0	10.65	3.33	3.17
Elmer Jacobs	R	2	4	.333	4.60	0	25	8	2	74.1	105	37	22	49	38	1	12.71	4.48	2.66
Bert Cole	L	1	4	.200	4.73	0	27	2	0	66.2	79	19	12	43	35	0	10.67	2.57	1.62
Charlie Barnabe	L	0	5	.000	5.31	0	17	5	1	61	86	20	5	46	36	0	12.69	2.95	0.74
Frank Stewart	R	0	1	.000	9.00	0	1	1	0	4	5	4	0	4	4	0	11.25	9.00	0.00
TEAM TOTAL		70	83	.458	3.89	8	247	153	85	1367	1465	439	365	705	591	10	9.65	2.89	2.40

Chicago 1928 Won 72 Lost 82 Pct. .468 5th

MANAGER	W	L	PCT
Ray Schalk	32	42	.432
Lena Blackburne	40	40	.500

POS	Player	B	G	AB	H	2B	3B	HR	HR%	R	RBI	BB	SO	SB	Pinch Hit AB	H	BA	SA
REGULARS																		
1B	Bud Clancy	L	130	487	132	19	11	2	0.4	64	37	42	25	6	2	0	.271	.368
2B	Bill Hunnefield	B	94	333	98	8	3	2	0.6	42	24	26	24	16	7	3	.294	.354
SS	Bill Cissell	R	125	443	115	22	3	1	0.2	66	60	29	41	18	1	1	.260	.330
3B	Willie Kamm	R	155	552	170	30	12	1	0.2	70	84	73	22	17	0	0	.308	.411
RF	Alex Metzler	L	139	464	141	18	14	3	0.6	51	36	41	30	16	6	2	.304	.422
CF	Johnny Mostil	R	133	503	136	19	8	0	0.0	69	51	66	54	23	2	0	.270	.340
LF	Bibb Falk	L	98	286	83	18	4	1	0.3	42	37	25	16	5	16	3	.290	.392
C	Buck Crouse	L	78	218	55	5	2	2	0.9	17	20	19	14	3	2	0	.252	.321
SUBSTITUTES																		
2S	Buck Redfern	R	86	261	61	6	3	0	0.0	22	35	12	19	8	1	0	.234	.280
1B	Art Shires	L	33	123	42	6	1	1	0.8	20	11	13	10	0	1	1	.341	.431
2B	Karl Swanson	L	22	64	9	1	0	0	0.0	2	6	4	7	3	0	0	.141	.156
3B	Johnny Mann	R	6	6	2	0	0	0	0.0	0	1	1	0	0	6	2	.333	.333
OF	Carl Reynolds	R	84	291	94	21	11	2	0.7	51	36	17	13	15	10	6	.323	.491
O2	Bill Barrett	R	76	235	65	11	2	3	1.3	34	26	14	30	8	9	2	.277	.379
OF	George Blackerby	R	30	83	21	0	0	0	0.0	8	12	4	10	2	10	4	.253	.253
OF	Randy Moore	L	24	61	13	4	1	0	0.0	6	5	3	5	0	6	2	.213	.311
C	Moe Berg	R	76	224	55	16	0	0	0.0	25	29	14	25	2	3	1	.246	.317
C	Harry McCurdy	L	49	103	27	10	0	2	1.9	12	13	8	15	1	14	3	.262	.417
C	Ray Schalk	R	2	1	1	0	0	0	0.0	0	1	0	0	1	0	0	1.000	1.000
PITCHERS																		
P	Tommy Thomas	R	36	96	21	3	0	2	2.1	9	12	8	28	0	0	0	.219	.313
P	Ted Lyons	B	49	91	23	2	0	0	0.0	10	8	1	9	0	0	0	.253	.275
P	Grady Adkins	R	39	70	10	0	1	0	0.0	3	5	2	16	0	0	0	.143	.171
P	Red Faber	B	27	70	8	2	0	1	1.4	3	10	4	31	0	0	0	.114	.186
P	Ted Blankenship	R	27	59	10	4	0	0	0.0	4	7	0	17	0	0	0	.169	.237
P	Ed Walsh	R	14	27	3	2	0	0	0.0	2	1	0	9	0	0	0	.111	.185
P	George Cox	R	26	26	2	2	0	0	0.0	0	0	1	7	0	0	0	.077	.154
P	Sarge Connally	R	28	19	2	1	0	0	0.0	2	0	0	7	0	0	0	.105	.158
P	Charlie Barnabe	L	11	8	4	1	0	1	12.5	3	6	0	0	0	4	2	.500	1.000
P	Bob Weiland	L	1	3	1	0	0	0	0.0	0	0	0	1	0	0	0	.333	.333
P	Rudy Leopold	L	2	1	0	0	0	0	0.0	0	0	0	0	0	0	0	.000	.000
P	Roy Wilson	L	1	1	0	0	0	0	0.0	0	0	0	0	0	0	0	.000	.000
P	Dan Dugan	L	1	0	0	0	0	0	—	0	0	0	0	0	0	0	—	—
P	John Goodell	R	2	0	0	0	0	0	—	0	0	0	0	0	0	0	—	—
P	Al Williamson	R	1	0	0	0	0	0	—	0	0	0	0	0	0	0	—	—
TEAM TOTAL				5209	1404	231	76	24	0.5	657	592	463	485	144	100	32	.270	.357

INDIVIDUAL FIELDING

POS	Player	T	G	PO	A	E	DP	TCG	FA
1B	B. Clancy	L	128	1175	93	12	104	10.0	.991
	A. Shires	R	32	282	28	3	22	9.8	.990
2B	B. Hunnefield	R	83	160	239	14	47	5.0	.966
	B. Redfern	R	45	83	141	11	20	5.2	.953
	B. Barrett	R	26	50	55	4	7	4.2	.963
	K. Swanson	R	21	33	66	6	9	5.0	.943
SS	B. Cissell	R	123	255	360	41	77	5.3	.938
	B. Redfern	R	33	83	82	13	19	5.4	.927
	B. Hunnefield	R	3	8	10	0	1	6.0	1.000
3B	W. Kamm	R	155	243	278	12	33	3.4	.977
	B. Hunnefield	R	1	0	0	0	0	0.0	.000
	J. Mann	R	2	1	2	0	0	1.5	1.000
	B. Redfern	R	1	1	0	0	0	1.0	1.000

POS	Player	T	G	PO	A	E	DP	TCG	FA
OF	J. Mostil	R	131	394	18	10	3	**3.2**	.976
	A. Metzler	R	134	288	11	10	3	2.3	.968
	B. Falk	L	78	164	9	5	0	2.3	.972
	C. Reynolds	R	74	135	6	3	2	1.9	.979
	B. Barrett	R	37	72	7	1	0	2.2	.988
	G. Blackerby	R	20	40	1	2	0	2.2	.953
	R. Moore	R	16	34	1	2	0	2.3	.946
C	M. Berg	R	73	256	52	3	8	4.3	.990
	B. Crouse	R	76	196	61	11	3	3.5	.959
	H. McCurdy	R	34	95	11	4	2	3.2	.964
	R. Schalk	R	1	4	0	0	0	4.0	1.000

And youth was served. Aaron Ward was shipped to Cleveland, and Roger Peckinpaugh was released from his contract. These moves paved the way for three spotlighted rookies: Bill Cissell, Johnny Mann, and Buck Redfern. "They are all alike, these rookies," observed Sox trainer Billy Buckner. "They want to show the world they're champs, but Ole Buck knows they're only chumps."

Ole Buck knew right. Only Cissell showed well as the whiz kid infield never materialized. Schalk's easygoing way just wasn't suited to the task. The players openly sassed Schalk and ignored his counsel. Not one fine had been levied against a Sox player in over a year and a half. But all that soon changed. Comiskey talked Schalk into resigning in midseason. The new manager was Lena Blackburne, a coach and former Sox player. He introduced a system of fines, and called his players together to lay down the law, and to describe "Lena Ball."

"The one-run idea is bunk in this league," he said. "Three or no count is my slogan." Blackburne soon met his biggest challenge when the Sox called up infielder Arthur Charles Shires from the Waco club of the Texas League. Shires banged out four hits in his first four major league at bats on August 20, in Fenway Park. The tow-headed youngster was cocky, brash, loud, and made for the 1920s. In the spring of 1929, Blackburne appointed him team captain with the hope that his new job might settle him down. How wrong he was!

TEAM STATISTICS

	W	L	PCT	GB	R	OR	2B	3B	HR	BA	SA	SB	E	DP	FA	CG	BB	SO	ShO	SV	ERA
NY	101	53	.656		894	685	269	79	133	.296	.450	51	194	136	.968	83	452	487	13	21	3.74
PHI	98	55	.641	2.5	829	615	323	75	89	.295	.436	59	181	124	.970	81	424	607	15	16	3.36
STL	82	72	.532	19	772	742	276	76	63	.274	.393	76	189	146	.969	80	454	456	6	15	4.17
WAS	75	79	.487	26	718	705	277	93	40	.284	.393	110	178	146	.972	77	466	462	15	10	3.88
CHI	72	82	.468	29	656	725	231	77	24	.270	.358	139	186	149	.970	88	501	418	6	11	3.98
DET	68	86	.442	33	744	804	265	97	62	.279	.401	113	218	140	.965	65	567	451	5	16	4.32
CLE	62	92	.403	39	674	830	299	61	34	.285	.382	50	221	187	.965	71	511	416	4	15	4.47
BOS	57	96	.373	43.5	589	770	260	62	38	.264	.361	99	178	139	.971	70	452	407	5	9	4.39
LEAGUE TOTAL					5876	5876	2200	620	483	.281	.397	697	1545	1167	.969	615	3827	3704	69	113	4.04

INDIVIDUAL PITCHING

PITCHER	T	W	L	PCT	ERA	SV	G	GS	CG	IP	H	BB	SO	R	ER	ShO	H9	BB9	SO9
Tommy Thomas	R	17	16	.515	3.08	2	36	32	24	283	277	76	129	114	97	3	8.81	2.42	4.10
Ted Lyons	R	15	14	.517	3.98	6	39	27	21	240	276	68	60	133	106	0	10.35	2.55	2.25
Grady Adkins	R	10	16	.385	3.73	1	36	27	14	224.2	233	89	54	113	93	0	9.33	3.57	2.16
Red Faber	R	13	9	.591	3.75	0	27	27	16	201.1	223	68	43	98	84	2	9.97	3.04	1.92
Ted Blankenship	R	9	11	.450	4.61	0	27	22	8	158	186	80	36	92	81	0	10.59	4.56	2.05
George Cox	R	1	2	.333	5.26	0	26	2	0	89	110	39	22	58	52	0	11.12	3.94	2.22
Ed Walsh	R	4	7	.364	4.96	0	14	10	3	78	86	42	32	45	43	0	9.92	4.85	3.69
Sarge Connally	R	2	5	.286	4.84	2	28	5	1	74.1	89	29	28	52	40	0	10.78	3.51	3.39
Charlie Barnabe	L	0	2	.000	6.52	0	7	2	0	9.2	17	0	3	9	7	0	15.83	0.00	2.79
Bob Weiland	L	1	0	1.000	0.00	0	1	1	1	9	7	5	9	0	0	1	7.00	5.00	9.00
Roy Wilson	L	0	0	–	0.00	0	1	0	0	3.1	2	3	2	0	0	0	5.40	8.10	5.40
John Goodell	L	0	0	–	18.00	0	2	0	0	3	6	2	0	6	6	0	18.00	6.00	0.00
Rudy Leopold	L	0	0	–	3.86	0	2	0	0	2.1	3	0	0	3	1	0	11.57	0.00	0.00
Al Williamson	R	0	0	–	0.00	0	1	0	0	2	1	0	0	0	0	0	4.50	0.00	0.00
Dan Dugan	L	0	0	–	0.00	0	1	0	0	.1	0	0	0	0	0	0	0.00	0.00	0.00
TEAM TOTAL		72	82	.468	3.98	11	248	155	88	1378	1516	501	418	723	610	6	9.90	3.27	2.73

Chicago 1929 Won 59 Lost 93 Pct. .388 7th

MANAGER	W	L	PCT
Lena Blackburne	59	93	.388

POS	Player	B	G	AB	H	2B	3B	HR	HR %	R	RBI	BB	SO	SB	Pinch Hit AB	H	BA	SA
REGULARS																		
1B	Art Shires	L	100	353	110	20	7	3	0.8	41	41	32	20	4	9	1	.312	.433
2B	John Kerr	R	127	419	108	20	4	1	0.2	50	39	31	24	9	1	1	.258	.332
SS	Bill Cissell	R	152	618	173	27	12	5	0.8	83	62	28	53	26	0	0	.280	.387
3B	Willie Kamm	R	147	523	140	32	6	3	0.6	72	63	75	23	12	2	1	.268	.369
RF	Carl Reynolds	R	131	517	164	24	12	11	2.1	81	67	20	37	19	0	0	.317	.474
CF	Dutch Hoffman	R	103	337	87	16	5	3	0.9	27	37	24	28	6	19	6	.258	.362
LF	Alex Metzler	L	146	568	156	23	13	2	0.4	80	49	80	45	11	4	0	.275	.371
C	Moe Berg	R	106	351	101	7	0	0	0.0	32	47	17	16	5	0	0	.288	.308
SUBSTITUTES																		
1B	Bud Clancy	L	92	290	82	14	6	3	1.0	36	45	16	19	3	16	4	.283	.403
2B	Bill Hunnefield	B	47	127	23	5	0	0	0.0	13	9	7	3	5	10	1	.181	.220
UT	Buck Redfern	R	21	44	6	0	0	0	0.0	3	3	3	3	1	1	0	.136	.136
2B	Frank Sigafoos	R	7	3	1	0	0	0	0.0	1	1	2	1	0	0	0	.333	.333
OF	Cliff Watwood	L	85	278	84	12	6	2	0.7	33	18	22	21	6	7	2	.302	.410
OF	Doug Taitt	L	47	124	21	7	0	0	0.0	11	12	8	13	0	16	5	.169	.226
OF	Johnny Mostil	R	12	35	8	3	0	0	0.0	4	3	6	2	1	0	0	.229	.314
C	Buck Crouse	L	45	107	29	7	0	2	1.9	11	12	5	7	2	4	0	.271	.393
C	Martin Autry	R	43	96	20	6	0	1	1.0	7	12	1	8	0	11	3	.208	.302
PH	Bill Barrett	R	3	1	0	0	0	0	0.0	0	0	2	0	0	1	0	.000	.000
PH	Karl Swanson	L	2	1	0	0	0	0	0.0	0	0	0	0	0	1	0	.000	.000
PITCHERS																		
P	Tommy Thomas	R	37	98	25	4	0	0	0.0	9	10	5	14	0	0	0	.255	.296
P	Ted Lyons	B	40	91	20	4	0	0	0.0	7	11	9	13	0	0	0	.220	.264
P	Red Faber	B	31	78	10	2	0	1	1.3	8	5	8	24	0	0	0	.128	.192
P	Grady Adkins	R	37	46	11	3	2	0	0.0	6	1	4	10	1	0	0	.239	.391
P	Hal McKain	L	34	44	10	1	0	0	0.0	5	1	9	8	0	0	0	.227	.250
P	Ed Walsh	R	25	43	10	2	1	0	0.0	5	6	3	9	0	0	0	.233	.326
P	Dan Dugan	L	19	20	3	1	0	0	0.0	1	3	0	7	0	0	0	.150	.200
P	Bob Weiland	L	15	18	2	0	0	0	0.0	0	0	2	10	0	0	0	.111	.111
P	Dutch Henry	L	2	7	1	0	0	0	0.0	3	1	2	0	1	0	0	.143	.143
P	Ted Blankenship	R	8	4	1	0	0	0	0.0	0	0	0	2	0	0	0	.250	.250
P	Jerry Byrne	R	3	2	0	0	0	0	0.0	0	0	0	0	0	0	0	.000	.000
P	Lena Blackburne	R	1	0	0	0	0	0	—	0	0	0	0	0	0	0	—	—
P	Sarge Connally	R	11	0	0	0	0	0	—	0	0	0	0	0	0	0	—	—
TEAM TOTAL				5243	1406	240	74	37	0.7	626	558	421	420	112	102	24	.268	.363

INDIVIDUAL FIELDING

POS	Player	T	G	PO	A	E	DP	TCG	FA	POS	Player	T	G	PO	A	E	DP	TCG	FA
1B	A. Shires	R	88	815	58	8	78	10.0	.991	OF	A. Metzler	R	141	316	16	14	3	2.5	.960
	B. Clancy	L	74	647	49	6	47	9.5	.991		C. Reynolds	R	131	268	13	15	5	2.3	.949
2B	J. Kerr	R	122	307	459	23	84	6.5	.971		D. Hoffman	R	89	237	4	4	2	2.8	.984
	B. Hunnefield	R	26	65	90	5	18	6.2	.969		C. Watwood	L	77	188	7	12	2	2.7	.942
	B. Redfern	R	11	14	15	1	1	2.7	.967		D. Taitt	R	30	51	4	2	2	1.9	.965
	F. Sigafoos	R	6	1	8	0	1	1.5	1.000		T. Lyons	R	1	0	0	0	0	0.0	.000
	A. Shires	R	2	1	0	1	0	1.0	.500		J. Mostil	R	11	25	1	1	1	2.5	.963
SS	B. Cissell	R	152	357	459	55	90	5.7	.937	C	M. Berg	R	106	290	86	7	12	3.6	.982
	B. Redfern	R	4	2	2	0	1	1.0	1.000		B. Crouse	R	40	111	29	3	5	3.6	.979
	B. Hunnefield	R	2	1	1	1	0	1.5	.667		M. Autry	R	30	64	14	5	1	2.8	.940
3B	W. Kamm	R	145	221	270	11	27	3.5	.978										
	B. Redfern	R	5	7	5	1	1	2.6	.923										
	B. Hunnefield	R	4	2	5	0	0	1.8	1.000										

There was a generation gap in the spring of 1929, and it was no doubt Shires-inspired. Bill Cissell was suspended for drunkenness, and a few days later Shires appeared in the hotel ballroom three sheets to the wind. Blackburne waited up to tell him of his suspension and fine. Shires was sent to Chicago to consult with some doctors, but Comiskey sent him right back. The club would not pay any consultant fees.

A truce was agreed upon, and Shires resumed his role as team captain. The peace lasted one month, ending for good on May 15, when Blackburne objected to Shires's wearing a red felt hat during batting practice. He was ordered to the clubhouse, where he swore that he "would have Blackburne's job." Blackburne fined him $100 just before landing a right hook.

But somehow Shires made it back. He went to New York in July and composed a poem that read, "You may rave about Babe/You may rave about Lou/Why be so snooty?/The Great Shires is good, too." He then signed a ten-week contract to appear in a New York vaudeville show.

In September, with the Sox hobbling along in seventh, Shires again brawled with the manager. He was enjoying a gin nightcap at the Ben Franklin hotel in Philadelphia when house detectives entered his room. He was in violation of Prohibition, and traveling secretary Lou Barbour had tipped them off. When Barbour and Blackburne appeared in the room, the fight became a three-cornered event in which Barbour nearly had his finger bitten off. Shires was down again but still not out.

TEAM STATISTICS

	W	L	PCT	GB	R	OR	2B	3B	Batting HR	BA	SA	SB	E	Fielding DP	FA	CG	BB	Pitching SO	ShO	SV	ERA
PHI	104	46	.693		901	615	288	76	122	.296	.451	61	146	117	.975	72	487	573	8	24	3.44
NY	88	66	.571	18	899	775	262	74	142	.295	.450	51	178	152	.971	64	485	484	12	18	4.17
CLE	81	71	.533	24	717	736	294	79	62	.294	.417	75	198	162	.968	80	488	389	8	10	4.05
STL	79	73	.520	26	733	713	276	63	46	.276	.380	72	156	148	.975	83	462	415	15	10	4.08
WAS	71	81	.467	34	730	776	244	66	48	.276	.375	86	195	156	.968	61	496	494	3	17	4.34
DET	70	84	.455	36	926	928	339	97	110	.299	.453	95	242	149	.961	82	646	467	5	9	4.96
CHI	59	93	.388	46	627	792	240	74	37	.268	.363	106	188	153	.970	78	505	328	5	7	4.41
BOS	58	96	.377	48	605	803	285	69	28	.267	.365	85	218	159	.965	84	496	416	9	5	4.43
LEAGUE TOTAL					6138	6138	2228	598	595	.284	.407	631	1521	1196	.969	604	4065	3566	65	100	4.24

INDIVIDUAL PITCHING

PITCHER	T	W	L	PCT	ERA	SV	G	GS	CG	IP	H	BB	SO	R	ER	ShO	H9	BB9	SO9
Tommy Thomas	R	14	18	.438	3.19	1	36	31	24	259.2	270	60	62	127	92	2	9.36	2.08	2.15
Ted Lyons	R	14	20	.412	4.10	2	37	31	21	259.1	276	76	57	136	118	1	9.58	2.64	1.98
Red Faber	R	13	13	.500	3.88	0	31	31	15	234	241	61	68	119	101	1	9.27	2.35	2.62
Hal McKain	R	6	9	.400	3.65	1	34	10	4	158	158	85	33	84	64	1	9.00	4.84	1.88
Grady Adkins	R	2	11	.154	5.33	0	31	15	5	138.1	168	67	24	98	82	0	10.93	4.36	1.56
Ed Walsh	R	6	11	.353	5.65	0	24	20	7	129	156	64	31	94	81	0	10.88	4.47	2.16
Dan Dugan	L	1	4	.200	6.65	1	19	2	0	65	77	19	15	51	48	0	10.66	2.63	2.08
Bob Weiland	L	2	4	.333	5.81	1	15	9	1	62	62	43	25	42	40	0	9.00	6.24	3.63
Ted Blankenship	R	0	2	.000	8.84	0	8	1	0	18.1	28	9	7	18	18	0	13.75	4.42	3.44
Dutch Henry	L	1	0	1.000	6.00	0	2	1	1	15	20	7	2	12	10	0	12.00	4.20	1.20
Sarge Connally	R	0	0	—	4.76	1	11	0	0	11.1	13	8	3	6	6	0	10.32	6.35	2.38
Jerry Byrne	R	0	1	.000	7.36	0	3	1	0	7.1	11	6	1	6	6	0	13.50	7.36	1.23
Lena Blackburne	R	0	0	—	0.00	0	1	0	0	.1	1	0	0	0	0	0	27.00	0.00	0.00
TEAM TOTAL		59	93	.388	4.41	7	252	152	78	1357.2	1481	505	328	793	666	5	9.82	3.35	2.17

Chicago 1930   Won 62   Lost 92   Pct. .403   7th

MANAGER		W	L	PCT
Donie Bush		62	92	.403

POS	Player	B	G	AB	H	2B	3B	HR	HR%	R	RBI	BB	SO	SB	Pinch Hit AB	H	BA	SA
REGULARS																		
1B	Bud Clancy	L	68	234	57	8	3	3	1.3	28	27	12	18	3	7	1	.244	.342
2B	Bill Cissell	R	141	561	152	28	9	2	0.4	82	48	28	32	16	1	0	.271	.364
SS	Greg Mulleavy	R	77	289	76	14	5	0	0.0	27	28	20	23	5	4	1	.263	.346
3B	Willie Kamm	R	111	331	89	21	6	3	0.9	49	47	51	20	5	5	0	.269	.396
RF	Smead Jolley	L	152	616	193	38	12	16	2.6	76	114	28	52	3	1	1	.313	.492
CF	Red Barnes	L	85	266	66	12	7	1	0.4	48	31	26	20	4	10	1	.248	.357
LF	Carl Reynolds	R	138	563	202	25	18	22	3.9	103	100	20	39	16	5	0	.359	.584
C	Bennie Tate	L	72	230	73	11	2	0	0.0	26	27	18	10	2	1	0	.317	.383
SUBSTITUTES																		
1O	Cliff Watwood	L	133	427	129	25	4	2	0.5	75	51	52	35	5	19	4	.302	.393
2S	John Kerr	R	70	266	77	11	6	3	1.1	37	27	21	23	4	0	0	.289	.410
1B	Art Shires	L	37	128	33	5	1	1	0.8	14	18	6	6	2	4	2	.258	.336
S3	Irv Jeffries	R	40	97	23	3	0	2	2.1	14	11	3	2	1	1	0	.237	.330
3B	Blondy Ryan	R	28	87	18	0	4	1	1.1	9	10	6	13	0	2	0	.207	.333
SS	Bill Hunnefield	B	31	81	22	2	0	1	1.2	11	5	4	10	1	6	1	.272	.333
SS	Ernie Smith	R	24	79	19	3	0	0	0.0	5	3	5	6	2	3	1	.241	.278
SS	Luke Appling	R	6	26	8	2	0	0	0.0	2	2	0	0	2	0	0	.308	.385
2B	Hugh Willingham	R	3	4	1	0	0	0	0.0	2	0	2	1	0	2	1	.250	.250
OF	Bob Fothergill	R	51	131	40	9	0	0	0.0	10	24	4	8	0	19*	6	.305	.374
OF	Dave Harris	R	33	86	21	2	1	5	5.8	16	13	7	22	0	8	3	.244	.465
OF	Alex Metzler	L	56	76	14	4	0	0	0.0	12	5	11	6	0	24	4	.184	.237
OF	Jim Moore	R	16	39	8	2	0	0	0.0	4	2	6	3	0	5	2	.205	.256
OF	Bruce Campbell	L	5	10	5	1	1	0	0.0	4	5	1	2	0	1	1	.500	.800
C	Buck Crouse	L	42	118	30	8	1	0	0.0	14	15	17	10	1	3	0	.254	.339
C	Martin Autry	R	34	71	18	1	1	0	0.0	1	5	4	8	0	5	1	.254	.296
C	Moe Berg	R	20	61	7	3	0	0	0.0	4	7	1	5	0	0	0	.115	.164
C	Johnny Riddle	R	25	58	14	3	1	0	0.0	7	4	3	6	0	0	0	.241	.328
C	Butch Henline	R	3	8	1	0	0	0	0.0	1	2	0	3	0	0	0	.125	.125
C1	Joe Klinger	R	4	8	3	0	0	0	0.0	0	1	0	0	0	0	0	.375	.375
PITCHERS																		
P	Ted Lyons	B	57	122	38	6	3	1	0.8	20	15	2	18	0	9	3	.311	.434
P	Pat Caraway	L	38	64	11	5	1	0	0.0	5	9	3	12	0	0	0	.172	.281
P	Tommy Thomas	R	34	56	7	1	0	0	0.0	3	3	5	6	0	0	0	.125	.143
P	Dutch Henry	L	35	51	12	1	1	0	0.0	2	3	5	10	0	0	0	.235	.294
P	Red Faber	B	29	49	2	0	0	0	0.0	4	2	9	21	0	0	0	.041	.041
P	Ed Walsh	R	39	34	9	0	0	0	0.0	3	0	3	7	0	0	0	.265	.265
P	Hal McKain	L	33	31	13	1	4	0	0.0	9	6	4	6	0	1	1	.419	.710
P	Garland Braxton	L	19	23	2	0	0	0	0.0	2	2	3	11	0	0	0	.087	.087
P	Jim Moore	R	9	13	3	1	0	0	0.0	0	2	0	1	0	0	0	.231	.308
P	Bob Weiland	L	14	8	0	0	0	0	0.0	0	0	1	3	0	0	0	.000	.000
P	Ted Blankenship	R	7	5	1	0	0	0	0.0	0	1	0	0	0	0	0	.200	.200
P	Biggs Wehde	R	4	1	0	0	0	0	0.0	0	0	0	1	0	0	0	.000	.000
TEAM TOTAL				5408	1497	256	91	63	1.2	729	675	391	479	74	144	34	.277	.393

INDIVIDUAL FIELDING

POS	Player	T	G	PO	A	E	DP	TCG	FA
1B	C. Watwood	L	62	590	41	7	59	10.3	.989
	B. Clancy	L	63	583	24	3	38	9.7	.995
	A. Shires	R	33	317	15	7	18	10.3	.979
	J. Klinger	R	2	12	0	0	2	6.0	1.000
	B. Hunnefield	R	1	2	0	0	0	2.0	1.000
2B	B. Cissell	R	106	251	336	32	60	5.8	.948
	J. Kerr	R	51	130	166	6	33	5.9	.980
	D. Harris	R	1	0	0	0	0	0.0	.000
	B. Ryan	R	1	4	1	1	0	6.0	.833
	H. Willingham	R	1	1	3	0	0	4.0	1.000
SS	G. Mulleavy	R	73	137	219	32	41	5.3	.918
	E. Smith	R	21	45	58	9	8	5.3	.920
	J. Kerr	R	19	42	52	3	7	5.1	.969
	B. Hunnefield	R	22	31	37	5	9	3.3	.932
	I. Jeffries	R	13	13	33	5	3	3.9	.902
	B. Cissell	R	10	15	24	6	2	4.5	.867
	L. Appling	R	6	12	17	4	1	5.5	.879
	B. Ryan	R	2	3	3	0	1	3.0	1.000
3B	W. Kamm	R	105	142	209	23	17	3.6	.939
	B. Cissell	R	24	24	62	3	7	3.7	.966
	B. Ryan	R	23	23	40	9	5	3.1	.875
	I. Jeffries	R	10	18	23	1	3	4.2	.976

POS	Player	T	G	PO	A	E	DP	TCG	FA
OF	C. Reynolds	R	132	336	11	9	1	2.7	.975
	S. Jolley	R	151	249	17	14	4	1.9	.950
	R. Barnes	R	72	179	6	12	3	2.7	.939
	C. Watwood	L	43	117	5	4	0	2.9	.968
	B. Fothergill	R	30	49	2	7	0	1.9	.879
	D. Harris	R	23	46	1	0	0	2.0	1.000
	A. Metzler	R	27	30	1	1	0	1.2	.969
	J. Moore	R	9	16	2	2	2	2.2	.900
	B. Campbell	R	4	8	0	0	0	2.0	1.000
C	B. Tate	R	70	219	40	5	5	3.8	.981
	B. Crouse	R	38	155	31	4	3	5.0	.979
	M. Autry	R	29	96	22	1	1	4.1	.992
	M. Berg	R	20	55	14	1	1	3.5	.986
	J. Riddle	R	25	48	13	0	3	2.4	1.000
	B. Henline	R	3	10	2	0	0	4.0	1.000
	J. Klinger	R	2	2	0	0	0	1.0	1.000

Chicago 1930

The Great Shires was right about one thing: he outlasted Blackburne, who was let go after the '29 season. Donie Bush was named manager on September 30. Unfortunately for Bush, he was a man of honor. He stayed with the White Sox even though the Yankees offered them their managerial job just 24 hours after he had agreed to Comiskey's terms.

Bush and Shires got along just fine, though the Great One was a salary holdout and had just been reprimanded by Judge Landis for boxing during the off-season. Comiskey no longer found humor in the situation, and Art the Great was traded to the Senators on June 16 for catcher Bennie Tatem and pitcher Garland Braxton. Both players immediately sustained injuries.

The year was relatively tame after Shires left. The Sox got as high as fifth, but found seventh more to their liking. The season saw the usual parade of rookies and recent recruits Comiskey believed might be the answer. Only two would make a lasting impression. One was Carl Reynolds, a slugging outfielder who had joined the club a few years earlier. Reynolds hit a team record of 22 homers, and in one game in New York hit three home runs, reached base six times, scored four runs and drove in eight. The other was a recruit brought up from Atlanta in September. Ed Munzel of the *Herald* said of him, "There was another newcomer in the Sox front yesterday. Luke Appling, the shortstop from Atlanta, made his bow. He gathered one hit, but had little to do afield, so judgement must be reserved." But not for long.

TEAM STATISTICS

	W	L	PCT	GB	R	OR	2B	3B	HR	BA	SA	SB	E	DP	FA	CG	BB	SO	ShO	SV	ERA
PHI	102	52	.662		951	751	319	74	125	.294	.452	48	145	121	.975	72	488	672	8	21	4.28
WAS	94	60	.610	8	892	689	300	98	57	.302	.426	101	159	150	.974	78	504	524	4	14	3.96
NY	86	68	.558	16	1062	898	298	110	152	.309	.488	91	207	132	.965	65	524	572	6	15	4.88
CLE	81	73	.526	21	890	915	358	59	72	.304	.431	51	237	156	.962	69	528	441	4	14	4.88
DET	75	79	.487	27	783	833	298	90	82	.284	.421	98	192	156	.967	68	570	574	3	17	4.70
STL	64	90	.416	38	751	886	289	67	75	.268	.391	93	188	152	.970	68	449	470	5	10	5.07
CHI	62	92	.403	40	729	884	255	90	63	.276	.391	74	235	136	.962	67	407	471	2	10	4.71
BOS	52	102	.338	50	612	814	257	68	47	.264	.365	42	196	161	.968	78	488	356	4	5	4.70
LEAGUE TOTAL					6670	6670	2374	656	673	.288	.421	598	1559	1164	.968	565	3958	4080	36	106	4.65

INDIVIDUAL PITCHING

PITCHER	T	W	L	PCT	ERA	SV	G	GS	CG	IP	H	BB	SO	R	ER	ShO	H9	BB9	SO9
Ted Lyons	R	22	15	.595	3.78	1	42	36	29	297.2	331	57	69	160	125	1	10.01	1.72	2.09
Pat Caraway	L	10	10	.500	3.86	1	38	21	9	193.1	194	57	83	96	83	1	9.03	2.65	3.86
Red Faber	R	8	13	.381	4.21	1	29	26	10	169	188	49	62	101	79	0	10.01	2.61	3.30
Tommy Thomas	R	5	13	.278	5.22	0	34	27	7	169	229	44	58	125	98	0	12.20	2.34	3.09
Dutch Henry	L	2	17	.105	4.88	0	35	16	4	155	211	48	35	116	84	0	12.25	2.79	2.03
Ed Walsh	R	1	4	.200	5.38	0	37	4	4	103.2	131	30	37	67	62	0	11.37	2.60	3.21
Garland Braxton	L	4	10	.286	6.45	1	19	10	2	90.2	127	33	44	80	65	0	12.61	3.28	4.37
Hal McKain	R	6	4	.600	5.56	5	32	5	0	89	108	42	52	67	55	0	10.92	4.25	5.26
Jim Moore	R	2	1	.667	3.60	1	9	5	2	40	42	12	11	18	16	0	9.45	2.70	2.48
Bob Weiland	L	0	4	.000	6.61	0	14	3	0	32.2	38	21	15	31	24	0	10.47	5.79	4.13
Ted Blankenship	R	2	1	.667	9.20	0	7	1	0	14.2	23	7	2	15	15	0	14.11	4.30	1.23
Biggs Wehde	R	0	0	—	9.95	0	4	0	0	6.1	7	7	3	8	7	0	9.95	9.95	4.26
TEAM TOTAL		62	92	.403	4.71	10	300	154	67	1361	1629	407	471	884	713	2	10.77	2.69	3.11

Chicago 1931　　　Won 56　Lost 97　Pct. .366　8th

MANAGER　　　　　W　L　　PCT
Donie Bush　　　　　56　97　.366

POS	Player	B	G	AB	H	2B	3B	HR	HR %	R	RBI	BB	SO	SB	Pinch Hit AB	H	BA	SA
REGULARS																		
1B	Lu Blue	B	155	589	179	23	15	1	0.2	119	62	127	60	13	0	0	.304	.399
2B	John Kerr	R	128	444	119	17	2	2	0.5	51	50	35	22	9	4	1	.268	.329
SS	Bill Cissell	R	109	409	90	13	5	1	0.2	42	46	16	26	18	0	0	.220	.284
3B	Billy Sullivan	L	92	363	100	16	5	2	0.6	48	33	20	14	4	7	4	.275	.364
RF	Carl Reynolds	R	118	462	134	24	14	6	1.3	71	77	24	26	17	9	3	.290	.442
CF	Cliff Watwood	L	128	367	104	16	6	1	0.3	51	47	56	30	9	17	5	.283	.368
LF	Lew Fonseca	R	121	465	139	26	5	2	0.4	65	71	32	22	4	4	1	.299	.389
C	Bennie Tate	L	89	273	73	12	3	0	0.0	27	22	26	10	1	4	1	.267	.333
SUBSTITUTES																		
SS	Luke Appling	R	96	297	69	13	4	1	0.3	36	28	29	27	9	12	3	.232	.313
3B	Irv Jeffries	R	79	223	50	10	0	2	0.9	29	16	14	9	3	5	0	.224	.296
3B	Willie Kamm	R	18	59	15	4	0	0	0.0	9	9	7	6	1	0	0	.254	.322
OF	Bob Fothergill	R	108	312	88	9	4	3	1.0	25	56	17	17	2	31	8	.282	.365
OF	Mel Simons	L	68	189	52	9	0	0	0.0	24	12	12	17	1	6	1	.275	.323
OF	Fred Eichrodt	R	34	117	25	5	1	0	0.0	9	15	1	8	0	2	1	.214	.274
OF	Smead Jolley	L	54	110	33	11	0	3	2.7	5	28	7	4	0	30	14	.300	.482
OF	Bill Norman	R	24	55	10	2	0	0	0.0	7	6	4	10	0	4	0	.182	.218
OF	Bruce Campbell	L	4	17	7	2	0	2	11.8	4	5	0	4	0	0	0	.412	.882
C	Frank Grube	R	88	265	58	13	2	1	0.4	29	24	22	22	2	6	1	.219	.294
C	Butch Henline	R	11	15	1	1	0	0	0.0	2	2	2	4	0	5	1	.067	.133
C	Hank Garrity	R	8	14	3	1	0	0	0.0	0	2	1	2	0	0	0	.214	.286
PITCHERS																		
P	Tommy Thomas	R	42	87	21	2	0	0	0.0	9	10	3	15	0	0	0	.241	.264
P	Vic Frazier	R	46	86	18	2	0	0	0.0	10	10	7	14	0	0	0	.209	.233
P	Pat Caraway	L	52	72	14	2	1	0	0.0	11	7	2	12	0	0	0	.194	.250
P	Red Faber	B	44	53	4	1	0	0	0.0	4	3	6	26	0	0	0	.075	.094
P	Hal McKain	L	32	42	5	2	1	0	0.0	5	3	5	14	0	5	0	.119	.214
P	Ted Lyons	B	42	33	5	0	0	0	0.0	6	3	2	1	0	2	1	.152	.152
P	Bob Weiland	L	15	22	4	0	0	0	0.0	2	0	5	2	1	0	0	.182	.182
P	Jim Moore	R	33	16	1	1	0	0	0.0	1	0	1	5	0	0	0	.063	.125
P	Garland Braxton	L	17	11	1	0	0	0	0.0	1	0	1	5	0	0	0	.091	.091
P	Grant Bowler	R	13	10	1	1	0	0	0.0	2	2	0	5	0	0	0	.100	.200
P	Lou Garland	R	7	3	0	0	0	0	0.0	0	0	0	1	0	0	0	.000	.000
P	Biggs Wehde	R	8	3	0	0	0	0	0.0	0	0	0	0	0	0	0	.000	.000
TEAM TOTAL				5483	1423	238	68	27	0.5	704	649	485	440	94	153	45	.260	.343

INDIVIDUAL FIELDING

POS	Player	T	G	PO	A	E	DP	TCG	FA
1B	L. Blue	L	155	**1452**	81	16	105	10.0	.990
	C. Watwood	L	4	18	1	0	1	4.8	1.000
	B. Sullivan	R	1	6	0	0	0	6.0	1.000
	L. Fonseca	R	2	5	0	0	1	2.5	1.000
2B	J. Kerr	R	117	297	366	22	78	5.9	.968
	B. Cissell	R	23	57	69	5	11	5.7	.962
	L. Fonseca	R	21	46	49	2	8	4.6	.979
	I. Jeffries	R	6	5	20	4	4	4.8	.862
	L. Appling	R	1	4	1	1	2	6.0	.833
SS	B. Cissell	R	83	168	233	24	47	5.1	.944
	L. Appling	R	76	147	232	42	37	5.5	.900
	I. Jeffries	R	5	9	10	1	1	4.0	.950
	J. Kerr	R	1	1	4	0	0	5.0	1.000
3B	B. Sullivan	R	83	96	152	24	9	3.3	.912
	I. Jeffries	R	61	69	100	9	4	2.9	.949
	W. Kamm	R	18	29*	32	4	4*	3.6*	.938
	B. Cissell	R	1	0	0	0	0	0.0	.000
	L. Fonseca	R	1	0	0	0	0	0.0	.000
	J. Kerr	R	7	9	13	3	1	3.6	.880

POS	Player	T	G	PO	A	E	DP	TCG	FA
OF	C. Watwood	L	102	259	13	16	2	2.8	.944
	C. Reynolds	R	109	233	10	13	3	2.3	.949
	L. Fonseca	R	95	183	4	5	1	2.0	.974
	B. Fothergill	R	74	169	2	5	0	2.4	.972
	M. Simons	R	59	112	3	6	0	2.1	.950
	F. Eichrodt	R	32	70	0	0	0	2.2	1.000
	B. Norman	R	17	41	1	3	0	2.6	.933
	S. Jolley	R	23	29	1	5	1	1.5	.857
	B. Campbell	R	4	9	0	1	0	2.5	.900
	B. Sullivan	R	2	2	0	0	0	1.0	1.000
C	B. Tate	R	85	310	69	5	11	4.5	.987
	F. Grube	R	81	248	50	7	3	3.8	.977
	B. Henline	R	4	14	2	2	0	4.5	.889
	H. Garrity	R	7	11	5	1	1	2.4	.941

Chicago 1931

Tired of unproven rookies and college boys who didn't pan out, Bush entrusted the 1931 Sox hopes to the veterans. Rookie phenom Rip Radcliff was sent back to the Dallas Steers, and veteran first baseman Lu Blue was purchased from the Browns. Blue was a revelation at first base, though he was one of 1931's many walking wounded. Smead Jolley had boils removed in the spring, Ted Lyons was plagued by a mysterious arm ailment, and Carl Reynolds pulled some tendons. The Sox tumbled to the cellar in June and remained there until August. But the rise was an illusion; the crippled team finished last.

The Sox traded Willie Kamm to the Indians on May 17 for Lew Fonseca. In his time, Kamm was the classiest of all White Sox third basemen. But he had feuded with Bush and played listless ball through the 1930 campaign. It was a small irony that Bush campaigned hard to get Fonseca, his eventual replacement as manager.

By August it was apparent that Bush would not be asked back. He resigned to save face on October 9. "I don't mind losing games if there is a prospect of better days ahead," he said, "but I feel that whatever reputation I have would be jeopardized by remaining another year." Thus he avoided the boot, and Fonseca was named.

Charles Comiskey passed away on October 26, at the Eagle River resort. He survived his old enemy Ban Johnson by several months and left an estate valued at $1,529,707.00.

TEAM STATISTICS

	W	L	PCT	GB	R	OR	2B	3B	HR	BA	SA	SB	E	DP	FA	CG	BB	SO	ShO	SV	ERA
PHI	107	45	.704		858	626	311	64	118	.287	.435	27	141	151	.976	97	457	574	12	16	3.47
NY	94	59	.614	13.5	1067	760	277	78	155	.297	.457	138	169	131	.972	78	543	686	4	17	4.20
WAS	92	62	.597	16	843	691	308	93	49	.285	.400	72	142	148	.976	60	498	582	6	24	3.76
CLE	78	76	.506	30	885	833	321	69	71	.296	.419	63	232	143	.963	76	561	470	6	9	4.63
STL	63	91	.409	45	722	870	287	62	76	.271	.390	73	232	160	.963	65	448	436	4	10	4.76
BOS	62	90	.408	45	625	800	289	34	37	.262	.349	43	188	127	.970	61	473	365	5	10	4.60
DET	61	93	.396	47	651	836	292	69	43	.268	.371	117	220	139	.964	93	597	511	5	6	4.56
CHI	56	97	.366	51.5	704	939	238	69	27	.260	.343	94	245	131	.961	54	588	420	6	10	5.05
LEAGUE TOTAL					6355	6355	2323	538	576	.278	.396	627	1569	1130	.968	584	4165	4044	48	102	4.38

INDIVIDUAL PITCHING

PITCHER	T	W	L	PCT	ERA	SV	G	GS	CG	IP	H	BB	SO	R	ER	ShO	H9	BB9	SO9
Vic Frazier	R	13	15	.464	4.46	4	46	29	13	254	258	127	87	156	126	2	9.14	4.50	3.08
Tommy Thomas	R	10	14	.417	4.80	2	42	36	11	242	296	69	71	166	129	2	11.01	2.57	2.64
Pat Caraway	L	10	24	.294	6.22	2	51	32	11	220	268	101	55	177	152	1	10.96	4.13	2.25
Red Faber	R	10	14	.417	3.82	1	44	19	5	184	210	57	49	96	78	1	10.27	2.79	2.40
Hal McKain	R	6	9	.400	5.71	0	27	8	3	112	134	57	39	82	71	0	10.77	4.58	3.13
Ted Lyons	R	4	6	.400	4.01	0	22	12	7	101	117	33	16	50	45	0	10.43	2.94	1.43
Jim Moore	R	0	2	.000	4.95	0	33	4	0	83.2	93	27	15	52	46	0	10.00	2.90	1.61
Bob Weiland	L	2	7	.222	5.16	0	15	8	3	75	75	46	38	55	43	0	9.00	5.52	4.56
Garland Braxton	L	0	3	.000	6.85	1	17	3	0	47.1	71	23	28	43	36	0	13.50	4.37	5.32
Grant Bowler	R	0	1	.000	5.35	0	13	3	1	35.1	40	24	15	26	21	0	10.19	6.11	3.82
Lou Garland	R	0	2	.000	10.26	0	7	2	0	16.2	30	14	4	24	19	0	16.20	7.56	2.16
Biggs Wehde	R	1	0	1.000	6.75	0	8	0	0	16	19	10	3	12	12	0	10.69	5.63	1.69
TEAM TOTAL		56	97	.366	5.05	10	325	156	54	1387	1611	588	420	939	778	6	10.45	3.82	2.73

Chicago 1932   Won 49   Lost 102   Pct. .325   7th

MANAGER	W	L	PCT
Lew Fonseca	49	102	.325

POS	Player	B	G	AB	H	2B	3B	HR	HR%	R	RBI	BB	SO	SB	Pinch Hit AB	H	BA	SA
REGULARS																		
1B	Lu Blue	B	112	373	93	21	2	0	0.0	51	43	64	21	17	6	1	.249	.316
2B	Jackie Hayes	R	117	475	122	20	5	2	0.4	53	54	30	28	7	0	0	.257	.333
SS	Luke Appling	R	139	489	134	20	10	3	0.6	66	63	40	36	9	7	3	.274	.374
3B	Carey Selph	R	116	396	112	19	8	0	0.0	50	51	31	9	7	18	2	.283	.371
RF	Bob Seeds	R	116	434	126	18	6	2	0.5	53	45	31	37	5	4	0	.290	.373
CF	Liz Funk	L	122	440	114	21	5	2	0.5	59	40	43	19	17	1	0	.259	.343
LF	Bob Fothergill	R	116	346	102	24	1	7	2.0	36	50	27	10	4	29	8	.295	.431
C	Frank Grube	R	93	277	78	16	2	0	0.0	36	31	33	13	6	1	0	.282	.354
SUBSTITUTES																		
13	Billy Sullivan	L	93	307	97	16	1	1	0.3	31	45	20	9	1	19	3	.316	.384
3B	Charlie English	R	24	63	20	3	1	1	1.6	7	8	3	7	0	9	2	.317	.444
SS	Bill Cissell	R	12	43	11	1	1	1	2.3	7	5	1	0	0	0	0	.256	.395
P3	Fabian Kowalik	L	6	13	5	2	0	0	0.0	2	2	1	0	0	1	0	.385	.538
2B	Greg Mulleavy	R	1	3	0	0	0	0	0.0	0	0	0	0	0	0	0	.000	.000
UT	Red Kress	R	135	515	147	42	4	9	1.7	83	57	47	36	6	0	0	.285	.435
O2	Johnny Hodapp	R	68	176	40	8	0	3	1.7	21	20	11	3	1	23	2	.227	.324
O3	Jack Rothrock	B	39	64	12	2	1	0	0.0	8	6	5	9	1	7	1	.188	.250
OF	Evar Swanson	R	14	52	16	3	1	0	0.0	9	8	8	3	3	0	0	.308	.404
OF	Cliff Watwood	L	13	49	15	2	0	0	0.0	5	0	1	3	0	0	0	.306	.347
OF	Bill Norman	R	13	48	11	3	1	0	0.0	6	2	2	3	0	0	0	.229	.333
OF	Smead Jolley	L	12	42	15	3	0	0	0.0	3	7	3	0	1	1	1	.357	.429
OF	Lew Fonseca	R	18	37	5	1	0	0	0.0	0	6	1	7	0	7	3	.135	.162
OF	Hal Anderson	R	9	32	8	0	0	0	0.0	4	2	0	1	0	0	0	.250	.250
OF	Bruce Campbell	L	9	26	4	1	0	0	0.0	3	2	0	4*	0	3	0	.154	.192
OF	Mel Simons	L	7	5	0	0	0	0	0.0	0	0	0	1	0	1	0	.000	.000
C	Charlie Berry	R	72	226	69	15	6	4	1.8	33	31	21	23	3	2	0	.305	.478
C	Bennie Tate	L	4	10	1	0	0	0	0.0	1	0	1	0	0	0	0	.100	.100
PITCHERS																		
P	Ted Lyons	B	49	73	19	2	1	1	1.4	11	10	4	10	0	1	0	.260	.356
P	Milt Gaston	R	28	60	14	4	0	0	0.0	6	10	1	15	0	0	0	.233	.300
P	Sad Sam Jones	R	39	57	11	2	0	0	0.0	12	5	9	22	1	0	0	.193	.228
P	Vic Frazier	R	29	44	4	1	0	0	0.0	2	0	3	14	0	0	0	.091	.114
P	Paul Gregory	R	33	38	3	1	0	0	0.0	2	1	3	9	0	0	0	.079	.105
P	Pat Caraway	L	19	21	3	0	0	0	0.0	1	0	1	2	0	0	0	.143	.143
P	Red Faber	B	42	18	4	1	0	0	0.0	0	1	8	7	0	0	0	.222	.278
P	Pete Daglia	R	12	13	1	0	0	0	0.0	0	2	1	3	0	0	0	.077	.077
P	Tommy Thomas	R	12	13	1	1	0	0	0.0	2	0	0	5	0	0	0	.077	.154
P	Bill Chamberlain	R	12	10	1	0	0	0	0.0	1	0	1	2	0	0	0	.100	.100
P	Charlie Biggs	R	6	9	1	0	0	0	0.0	1	1	1	2	0	0	0	.111	.111
P	Phil Gallivan	R	13	8	3	0	0	0	0.0	1	0	0	2	0	0	0	.375	.375
P	Ed Walsh	R	4	7	2	0	0	0	0.0	1	0	0	1	0	0	0	.286	.286
P	Bump Hadley	R	3	6	1	0	0	0	0.0	0	0	1	2	0	0	0	.167	.167
P	Art Evans	B	7	5	0	0	0	0	0.0	0	0	2	3	0	0	0	.000	.000
P	Archie Wise	R	3	4	0	0	0	0	0.0	0	0	0	1	0	1	0	.000	.000
P	Bob Poser	L	5	3	0	0	0	0	0.0	0	0	1	1	0	3	0	.000	.000
P	Grant Bowler	R	4	2	0	0	0	0	0.0	0	0	0	1	0	0	0	.000	.000
P	Chad Kimsey	L	7	2	0	0	0	0	0.0	0	0	0	0	0	0	0	.000	.000
P	Les Bartholomew	R	3	1	0	0	0	0	0.0	0	0	0	1	0	0	0	.000	.000
P	Hal McKain	L	8	1	0	0	0	0	0.0	0	0	0	0	0	0	0	.000	.000
P	Jim Moore	R	1	1	0	0	0	0	0.0	0	0	0	0	0	0	0	.000	.000
P	Art Smith	R	3	1	0	0	0	0	0.0	0	0	0	1	0	0	0	.000	.000
P	Clarence Fieber	L	3	0	0	0	0	0	—	0	0	0	0	0	0	0	—	—
TEAM TOTAL				5338	1425	273	56	36	0.7	667	608	459	386	89	144	26	.267	.359

INDIVIDUAL FIELDING

POS	Player	T	G	PO	A	E	DP	TCG	FA	POS	Player	T	G	PO	A	E	DP	TCG	FA
1B	L. Blue	L	105	1014	88	16	106	10.6	.986	OF	L. Funk	L	120	318	15	7	4	2.8	.979
	B. Sullivan	R	52	485	35	5	42	10.1	.990		B. Seeds	R	112	234	7	9	1	2.2	.964
	J. Rothrock	R	1	1	0	0	0	1.0	1.000		R. Kress	R	64	139	12	7	2	2.5	.956
2B	J. Hayes	R	97	241	346	20	78	6.3	.967		B. Fothergill	R	86	136	4	7	0	1.7	.952
	L. Appling	R	30	62	110	6	16	5.9	.966		J. Hodapp	R	31	58	0	2	0	1.9	.967
	C. Selph	R	26	45	95	8	14	5.7	.946		J. Rothrock	R	19	13	0	1	0	0.7	.929
	J. Hodapp	R	5	16	14	5	5	7.0	.857		C. Watwood	L	13	23	1	1	0	1.9	.960
	G. Mulleavy	R	1	2	2	0	1	4.0	1.000		E. Swanson	R	14	24	0	1	0	1.8	.960
SS	L. Appling	R	85	195	287	37	66	6.1	.929		B. Norman	R	13	20	2	2	0	1.8	.917
	R. Kress	R	53	125	155	19	35	5.6	.936		H. Anderson	R	9	21	1	0	1	2.4	1.000
	B. Cissell	R	12	40	24	5	9	5.8	.928		L. Fonseca	R	8	14	2	0	1	2.0	1.000
	J. Hayes	R	10	20	25	7	5	5.2	.865		S. Jolley	R	11	11	1	1	0	1.2	.923
	C. English	R	1	1	2	1	0	4.0	.750		B. Campbell	R	6	9	1	2*	0	2.0	.833
3B	C. Selph	R	71	83	120	20	14	3.1	.910		M. Simons	R	6	2	0	0	0	0.3	1.000
	R. Kress	R	19	17	34	6	4	3.0	.895	C	F. Grube	R	92	303	55	16	5	4.1	.957
	B. Sullivan	R	17	14	30	6	4	2.9	.880		C. Berry	R	70	212	52	5	5	3.8	.981
	L. Appling	R	14	13	22	6	2	2.9	.854		B. Sullivan	R	5	12	1	2	0	3.0	.867
	C. English	R	13	9	23	7	2	3.0	.821		B. Tate	R	4	9	3	0	0	3.0	1.000
	J. Hayes	R	10	13	15	3	0	3.1	.903										
	J. Rothrock	R	8	9	13	6	1	3.5	.786										
	J. Hodapp	R	4	1	5	1	0	1.8	.857										
	F. Kowalik	R	2	2	0	1	0	1.5	.667										

Chicago 1932

Failing in their attempts to land Tony Lazzeri, the Sox traded Carl Reynolds and Johnny Kerr to Washington for Sad Sam Jones, Bump Hadley, and Jackie Hayes. It was J. Louis Comiskey's first deal as the new owner, and it was a good one.

Lew Fonseca prided himself on being a strategist in the Connie Mack mold. He even imitated Mack's wave of the scorecard to position fielders from his spot in the dugout. But he lacked the patience necessary to the job. The season was barely two weeks old when he issued a "hit or get out" edict. The Sox went through a dry spell where they scored just two runs in 53 innings. Between April 24 and April 29, Fonseca initiated three trades that changed the whole complexion of the team. He traded away Spider Bill Cissell, Jim Moore, Bump Hadley, Bruce Campbell, Smead Jolley, Johnny Watwood, and Benny Tate, acquiring Bob Seed, Johnny Hodapp, Red Kress, Charlie Berry and John Rothrock. Kress was the key man in the moves, but he flopped badly. Bump Hadley went on to be a big winner for the Yankees, and Campbell became one of the better outfielders of the 1930s. Fonseca's panic moves set the Sox' rebuilding program back several years and did little to ward off their seventh-place finish in 1932. The Sox were left with a collection of one-dimensional players lacking motivation and ability. Fats Fothergill and young Billy Sullivan were hitters who couldn't field, and Elias Funk and Jackie Hayes couldn't hit. The Sox lost over 100 games, a dubious milestone reached by only two other White Sox teams.

TEAM STATISTICS

	W	L	PCT	GB	R	OR	2B	3B	HR	BA	SA	SB	E	DP	FA	CG	BB	SO	ShO	SV	ERA
NY	107	47	.695		1002	724	279	82	160	.286	.454	77	188	124	.969	95	561	770	11	15	3.98
PHI	94	60	.610	13	981	752	303	51	173	.290	.457	38	124	142	.979	95	511	595	10	10	4.45
WAS	93	61	.604	14	840	716	303	100	61	.284	.408	70	125	157	.979	66	526	437	10	22	4.16
CLE	87	65	.572	19	845	747	310	74	78	.285	.413	52	191	129	.969	94	446	439	6	8	4.12
DET	76	75	.503	29.5	799	787	291	80	80	.273	.401	106	187	154	.969	67	592	521	9	17	4.30
STL	63	91	.409	44	736	898	274	69	67	.276	.388	69	188	156	.969	63	574	496	8	11	5.01
CHI	49	102	.325	56.5	667	897	274	56	36	.267	.360	89	264	170	.958	50	580	379	2	12	4.82
BOS	43	111	.279	64	566	915	253	57	53	.251	.351	46	233	165	.963	42	612	365	2	7	5.02
LEAGUE TOTAL					6436	6436	2287	569	708	.277	.404	544	1500	1197	.969	572	4402	4002	58	102	4.48

INDIVIDUAL PITCHING

PITCHER	T	W	L	PCT	ERA	SV	G	GS	CG	IP	H	BB	SO	R	ER	ShO	H9	BB9	SO9
Ted Lyons	R	10	15	.400	3.28	2	33	26	19	230.2	243	71	58	104	84	1	9.48	2.77	2.26
Sad Sam Jones	R	10	15	.400	4.22	0	30	28	10	200.1	217	75	64	123	94	0	9.75	3.37	2.88
Milt Gaston	R	7	17	.292	4.00	1	28	25	7	166.2	183	73	44	101	74	1	9.88	3.94	2.38
Vic Frazier	R	3	13	.188	6.23	0	29	21	4	146	180	70	33	121	101	0	11.10	4.32	2.03
Paul Gregory	R	5	3	.625	4.51	0	33	9	3	117.2	125	51	39	75	59	0	9.56	3.90	2.98
Red Faber	R	2	11	.154	3.74	6	42	5	0	106	123	38	26	61	44	0	10.44	3.23	2.21
Pat Caraway	L	2	6	.250	6.82	0	19	9	1	64.2	80	37	13	55	49	0	11.13	5.15	1.81
Pete Daglia	R	2	4	.333	5.76	0	12	5	2	50	67	20	16	35	32	0	12.06	3.60	2.88
Tommy Thomas	R	3	3	.500	6.18	0	12	3	1	43.2	55	15	11	33	30	0	11.34	3.09	2.27
Bill Chamberlain	L	0	5	.000	4.57	0	12	5	0	41.1	39	25	11	30	21	0	8.49	5.44	2.40
Phil Gallivan	R	1	3	.250	7.56	0	13	3	1	33.1	49	24	12	32	28	0	13.23	6.48	3.24
Charlie Biggs	R	1	1	.500	6.93	0	6	4	0	24.2	32	12	1	22	19	0	11.68	4.38	0.36
Ed Walsh	R	0	2	.000	8.41	0	4	4	1	20.1	26	13	7	22	19	0	11.51	5.75	3.10
Bump Hadley	R	1	1*	.500	3.86	1	3	2	1	18.2	17	8*	13	8*	8*	0	8.20	3.86	6.27
Art Evans	L	0	0	–	3.00	0	7	0	0	18	19	10	6	9	6	0	9.50	5.00	3.00
Hal McKain	R	0	0	–	11.12	0	8	0	0	11.1	17	5	7	15	14	0	13.50	3.97	5.56
Chad Kimsey	R	1	1	.500	2.45	2	7	0	0	11	8	5	6	4	3	0	6.55	4.09	4.91
Fabian Kowalik	R	0	1	.000	6.97	0	2	1	0	10.1	16	4	2	11	8	0	13.94	3.48	1.74
Archie Wise	R	0	0	–	4.91	0	2	0	0	7.1	8	5	2	5	4	0	9.82	6.14	2.45
Art Smith	R	0	1	.000	11.57	0	3	2	0	7	17	4	1	13	9	0	21.86	5.14	1.29
Grant Bowler	R	0	0	–	15.63	0	4	0	0	6.1	15	3	2	12	11	0	21.32	4.26	2.84
Les Bartholomew	L	0	0	–	5.06	0	3	0	0	5.1	5	6	1	3	3	0	8.44	10.13	1.69
Clarence Fieber	L	1	0	1.000	1.69	0	3	0	0	5.1	6	3	1	1	1	0	10.13	5.06	1.69
Lew Fonseca	R	0	0	–	0.00	0	1	0	0	1	0	0	0	0	0	0	0.00	0.00	0.00
Jim Moore	R	0	0	–	0.00	0	1	0	0	1	1	1	2	0	0	0	9.00	9.00	18.00
Bob Poser	R	0	0	–	27.00	0	1	0	0	.2	3	2	1	2	2	0	40.50	27.00	13.50
TEAM TOTAL		49	102	.325	4.82	12	318	152	50	1348.2	1551	580	379	897	723	2	10.35	3.87	2.53

Chicago 1933 Won 67 Lost 83 Pct. .447 6th

MANAGER	W	L	PCT
Lew Fonseca	67	83	.447

POS	Player	B	G	AB	H	2B	3B	HR	HR%	R	RBI	BB	SO	SB	Pinch Hit AB	Pinch Hit H	BA	SA
REGULARS																		
1B	Red Kress	R	129	467	116	20	5	10	2.1	47	78	37	40	4	12	6	.248	.377
2B	Jackie Hayes	R	138	535	138	23	5	2	0.4	65	47	55	36	2	0	0	.258	.331
SS	Luke Appling	R	151	612	197	36	10	6	1.0	90	85	56	29	6	0	0	.322	.443
3B	Jimmy Dykes	R	151	554	144	22	6	1	0.2	49	68	69	37	3	0	0	.260	.327
RF	Evar Swanson	R	144	539	165	25	7	1	0.2	102	63	93	35	19	6	2	.306	.384
CF	Mule Haas	L	146	585	168	33	4	1	0.2	97	51	65	41	0	0	0	.287	.362
LF	Al Simmons	R	146	605	200	29	10	14	2.3	85	119	39	49	5	1	0	.331	.481
C	Frank Grube	R	85	256	59	13	0	0	0.0	23	23	38	20	1	1	0	.230	.281
SUBSTITUTES																		
1C	Billy Sullivan	L	54	125	24	0	1	0	0.0	9	13	10	5	0	22	5	.192	.208
23	Hal Rhyne	R	39	83	22	1	1	0	0.0	9	10	5	9	1	6	1	.265	.301
1B	Lew Fonseca	R	23	59	12	2	0	2	3.4	8	15	7	6	1	10	1	.203	.339
2B	Charlie English	R	3	9	4	2	0	0	0.0	2	1	1	1	0	0	0	.444	.667
O1	Earl Webb	L	58	107	31	5	0	1	0.9	16	8	16	13	0	28*	8	.290	.364
OF	John Stoneham	L	10	25	3	0	0	1	4.0	4	3	2	2	0	0	0	.120	.240
OF	Milt Bocek	R	11	22	8	1	0	1	4.5	3	3	4	6	0	5	1	.364	.545
OF	Liz Funk	L	10	9	2	0	0	0	0.0	1	0	1	0	0	8	2	.222	.222
C	Charlie Berry	R	86	271	69	8	3	2	0.7	25	28	17	16	0	3	0	.255	.328
PH	Mem Lovett	R	1	1	0	0	0	0	0.0	0	0	0	0	0	1	0	.000	.000
PITCHERS																		
P	Ted Lyons	B	51	91	26	2	1	1	1.1	11	11	4	6	0	7	1	.286	.363
P	Sad Sam Jones	R	37	58	9	1	0	0	0.0	10	3	8	10	1	0	0	.155	.172
P	Milt Gaston	B	30	52	8	2	0	0	0.0	5	1	5	11	0	0	0	.154	.192
P	Ed Durham	L	24	46	10	1	0	0	0.0	3	5	1	10	0	0	0	.217	.239
P	Joe Heving	R	40	38	8	2	0	0	0.0	3	0	1	4	0	0	0	.211	.263
P	Jake Miller	L	30	37	7	0	0	0	0.0	4	0	0	10	0	0	0	.189	.189
P	Paul Gregory	R	23	35	5	1	0	0	0.0	4	1	1	2	0	0	0	.143	.171
P	Chad Kimsey	L	28	33	5	0	0	0	0.0	1	1	0	9	0	1	0	.152	.152
P	Whit Wyatt	R	26	28	6	1	0	0	0.0	5	2	1	3	0	0	0	.214	.250
P	Red Faber	B	36	18	0	0	0	0	0.0	0	0	0	6	0	0	0	.000	.000
P	Les Tietje	R	3	8	1	1	0	0	0.0	1	2	1	1	0	0	0	.125	.250
P	Vic Frazier	R	10	4	0	0	0	0	0.0	0	0	0	0	0	0	0	.000	.000
P	Hal Haid	R	6	4	1	0	0	0	0.0	0	0	0	1	0	0	0	.250	.250
P	Ira Hutchinson	R	1	2	1	0	0	0	0.0	1	1	0	1	0	0	0	.500	.500
P	George Murray	R	2	0	0	0	0	0	—	0	0	0	0	0	0	0	—	—
TEAM TOTAL				5318	1449	231	53	43	0.8	683	642	537	419	43	111	27	.272	.360

INDIVIDUAL FIELDING

POS	Player	T	G	PO	A	E	DP	TCG	FA	POS	Player	T	G	PO	A	E	DP	TCG	FA
1B	R. Kress	R	111	1169	60	28	83	11.3	.978	OF	A. Simmons	R	145	372	15	4	1	2.7	.990
	B. Sullivan	R	22	211	12	4	22	10.3	.982		M. Haas	R	146	347	9	6	2	2.5	.983
	L. Fonseca	R	12	138	12	0	15	12.5	1.000		E. Swanson	R	139	281	7	8	0	2.1	.973
	E. Webb	R	10	108	3	7	8	11.8	.941		E. Webb	R	16	20	2	0	0	1.4	1.000
2B	J. Hayes	R	138	344	497	16	89	6.2	.981		L. Funk	L	2	0	0	0	0	0.0	.000
	H. Rhyne	R	19	46	61	5	13	5.9	.955		R. Kress	R	8	16	0	1	0	2.1	.941
	C. English	R	3	6	6	1	2	4.3	.923		J. Stoneham	R	9	13	0	0	0	1.4	1.000
SS	L. Appling	R	151	314	534	55	107	6.0	.939		M. Bocek	R	6	6	0	0	0	1.0	1.000
	H. Rhyne	R	2	1	0	0	0	0.5	1.000	C	F. Grube	R	83	266	44	5	5	3.8	.984
3B	J. Dykes	R	151	132	296	21	22	3.0	.953		C. Berry	R	83	260	39	4	1	3.7	.987
	H. Rhyne	R	13	1	11	2	0	1.1	.857		B. Sullivan	R	8	21	3	4	0	3.5	.857

Chicago 1933

When the White Sox first got wind of Connie Mack's desire to break up the A's, they rushed forward with a one-for-two trade proposal. Harry Grabiner offered Ted Lyons for Lefty Grove and Al Simmons, but was turned down. Mack needed cash — fast. On September 28, 1932, Comiskey purchased Jimmy Dykes, Al Simmons, and Mule Haas for $150,000.

Dykes helped stabilize the infield. He showed leadership and patience in his work with the youngsters, notably the uncertain Luke Appling. Simmons gave Southsiders a taste of power when he hit his first White Sox home run in an exhibition match with the Cubs on April 8. Big Al had a banner year. He was the leading vote-getter in the All-Star Game poll, surpassing even the Babe. The All-Star game was played in Comiskey Park in 1933, but was thought to be a one-time thing — just another exhibition in the Century of Progress World's Fair.

The Sox showed well in 1933, given the sad state of affairs just a year earlier. They held third place as late as July 11, but faltered in August and September. Fonseca chided Simmons for what he perceived to be lackadaisical play, and he released Bull Durham when the pitcher just stood on the mound while a Washington Senator runner dashed across the unprotected plate.

Ted Lyons was rewarded with the first of two days that management gave him in his career. The Depression meant hard times for everyone, so newspapers requested that fans hold their donations down to ten cents. Six hundred dollars was collected and given to the ten-year veteran.

TEAM STATISTICS

	W	L	PCT	GB	R	OR	2B	3B	HR	BA	SA	SB	E	DP	FA	CG	BB	SO	ShO	SV	ERA
WAS	99	53	.651		850	665	281	86	60	.287	.402	65	131	149	.979	68	452	447	5	26	3.82
NY	91	59	.607	7	927	768	241	75	144	.283	.440	74	165	122	.972	70	612	711	8	22	4.36
PHI	79	72	.523	19.5	875	853	297	56	140	.285	.441	33	203	121	.966	69	644	423	6	14	4.81
CLE	75	76	.497	23.5	654	669	218	77	50	.261	.360	36	156	127	.974	74	465	437	12	7	3.71
DET	75	79	.487	25	722	733	283	78	57	.269	.380	68	178	167	.971	69	561	575	6	17	3.96
CHI	67	83	.447	31	683	814	231	53	43	.272	.360	43	186	143	.970	53	519	423	8	13	4.45
BOS	63	86	.423	34.5	700	758	294	56	50	.271	.377	62	204	133	.966	60	591	473	4	14	4.35
STL	55	96	.364	43.5	669	820	244	64	64	.253	.360	70	149	162	.976	55	531	426	7	10	4.82
LEAGUE TOTAL					6080	6080	2089	545	608	.273	.390	451	1372	1124	.972	518	4375	3915	56	123	4.28

INDIVIDUAL PITCHING

PITCHER	T	W	L	PCT	ERA	SV	G	GS	CG	IP	H	BB	SO	R	ER	ShO	H9	BB9	SO9
Ted Lyons	R	10	21	.323	4.38	1	36	27	14	228	260	74	74	142	111	2	10.26	2.92	2.92
Sad Sam Jones	R	10	12	.455	3.36	0	27	25	11	176.2	181	65	60	80	66	2	9.22	3.31	3.06
Milt Gaston	R	8	12	.400	4.85	0	30	25	7	167	177	60	39	106	90	1	9.54	3.23	2.10
Ed Durham	R	10	6	.625	4.48	0	24	21	6	138.2	137	46	65	74	69	0	8.89	2.99	4.22
Joe Heving	R	7	5	.583	2.67	6	40	6	3	118	113	27	47	50	35	1	8.62	2.06	3.58
Jake Miller	L	5	6	.455	5.62	0	26	14	4	105.2	130	47	30	75	66	2	11.07	4.00	2.56
Paul Gregory	R	4	11	.267	4.95	0	23	17	5	103.2	124	47	18	75	57	0	10.77	4.08	1.56
Chad Kimsey	R	4	1	.800	5.53	0	28	2	0	96	124	36	19	67	59	0	11.63	3.38	1.78
Whit Wyatt	R	3	4	.429	4.62	1	26	7	2	87.2	91	45	31	51	45	0	9.34	4.62	3.18
Red Faber	R	3	4	.429	3.44	5	36	2	0	86.1	92	28	18	41	33	0	9.59	2.92	1.88
Les Tietje	R	2	0	1.000	2.42	0	3	3	1	22.1	16	15	9	8	6	0	6.45	6.04	3.63
Vic Frazier	R	1	1	.500	8.85	0	10	1	0	20.1	32	11	4	22	20	0	14.16	4.87	1.77
Hal Haid	R	0	0	—	7.98	0	6	0	0	14.2	18	13	7	15	13	0	11.05	7.98	4.30
Ira Hutchinson	R	0	0	—	13.50	0	1	1	0	4	7	3	2	6	6	0	15.75	6.75	4.50
George Murray	R	0	0	—	7.71	0	2	0	0	2.1	3	2	0	2	2	0	11.57	7.71	0.00
TEAM TOTAL		67	83	.447	4.45	13	318	151	53	1371.1	1505	519	423	814	678	8	9.88	3.41	2.78

Chicago 1934   Won 53 Lost 99 Pct. .349 8th

MANAGER	W	L	PCT
Lew Fonseca	4	13	.235
Jimmy Dykes	49	86	.363

POS	Player	B	G	AB	H	2B	3B	HR	HR%	R	RBI	BB	SO	SB	Pinch Hit AB	Pinch Hit H	BA	SA
REGULARS																		
1B	Zeke Bonura	R	127	510	154	35	4	27	5.3	86	110	64	31	0	0	0	.302	.545
2B	Jackie Hayes	R	62	226	58	9	1	1	0.4	19	31	23	20	3	0	0	.257	.319
SS	Luke Appling	R	118	452	137	28	6	2	0.4	75	61	59	27	3	0	0	.303	.405
3B	Jimmy Dykes	R	127	456	122	17	4	7	1.5	52	82	64	28	1	1	1	.268	.368
RF	Evar Swanson	R	117	426	127	9	5	0	0.0	71	34	59	31	10	9	2	.298	.343
CF	Mule Haas	L	106	351	94	16	3	2	0.6	54	22	47	22	1	13	4	.268	.348
LF	Al Simmons	R	138	558	192	36	7	18	3.2	102	104	53	58	3	0	0	.344	.530
C	Ed Madjeski	R	85	281	62	14	2	5	1.8	36	32	14	31	2	4	1	.221	.338
SUBSTITUTES																		
2S	Bob Boken	R	81	297	70	9	1	3	1.0	30	40	15	32	2	1	0	.236	.303
3B	Marty Hopkins	R	67	210	45	7	0	2	1.0	22	28	42	26	0	0	0	.214	.276
S3	Joe Chamberlin	R	43	141	34	5	1	2	1.4	13	17	6	38	1	0	0	.241	.333
3B	Mark Mauldin	R	10	38	10	2	0	1	2.6	3	3	0	3	0	0	0	.263	.395
2B	Red Kress	R	8	14	4	0	0	0	0.0	3	1	3	3	0	4	1	.286	.286
OF	Jocko Conlan	L	63	225	56	11	3	0	0.0	35	16	19	7	2	8	3	.249	.324
OF	Frenchy Uhalt	L	57	165	40	5	1	0	0.0	28	16	29	12	6	13	4	.242	.285
OF	Frenchy Bordagaray	R	29	87	28	3	1	0	0.0	12	2	3	8	1	12	8	.322	.379
OF	Rip Radcliff	L	14	56	15	2	1	0	0.0	7	5	0	2	1	0	0	.268	.339
OF	Milt Bocek	R	19	38	8	1	0	0	0.0	3	3	5	5	0	6	0	.211	.237
OF	Charlie Uhlir	L	14	27	4	0	0	0	0.0	3	3	2	6	0	5	1	.148	.148
C	Merv Shea	R	62	176	28	3	0	0	0.0	8	5	24	19	0	2	0	.159	.176
C	Muddy Ruel	R	22	57	12	3	0	0	0.0	4	7	8	5	0	1	0	.211	.263
C	George Caithamer	R	5	19	6	1	0	0	0.0	1	3	1	5	0	0	0	.316	.368
C	Johnny Pasek	R	4	9	3	0	0	0	0.0	1	0	1	1	0	0	0	.333	.333
C	Bill Fehring	B	1	1	0	0	0	0	0.0	0	0	0	1	0	0	0	.000	.000
PITCHERS																		
P	Ted Lyons	B	50	97	20	4	0	1	1.0	9	16	3	19	0	17	3	.206	.278
P	George Earnshaw	R	33	79	16	3	0	0	0.0	5	6	3	16	0	0	0	.203	.241
P	Milt Gaston	R	29	68	10	1	0	0	0.0	2	7	3	14	0	0	0	.147	.162
P	Sad Sam Jones	R	31	60	12	3	0	0	0.0	9	6	8	13	0	0	0	.200	.250
P	Les Tietje	R	34	59	1	1	0	0	0.0	2	3	1	19	0	0	0	.017	.034
P	Phil Gallivan	R	35	40	9	3	0	0	0.0	3	2	0	5	0	0	0	.225	.300
P	Joe Heving	R	33	27	5	3	0	0	0.0	2	1	3	6	0	0	0	.185	.296
P	Whit Wyatt	R	23	26	6	1	0	0	0.0	1	2	1	5	0	0	0	.231	.269
P	Harry Kinzy	R	13	10	3	0	0	0	0.0	1	0	1	3	0	0	0	.300	.300
P	Vern Kennedy	L	3	7	2	0	0	0	0.0	0	0	0	1	0	0	0	.286	.286
P	Hugo Klaerner	R	3	6	2	2	0	0	0.0	2	0	0	0	0	0	0	.333	.667
P	Monty Stratton	R	1	2	0	0	0	0	0.0	0	0	0	0	0	0	0	.000	.000
P	Lee Stine	R	4	1	0	0	0	0	0.0	0	0	1	1	0	0	0	.000	.000
P	John Pomorski	R	3	0	0	0	0	0	—	0	0	0	0	0	0	0	—	—
TEAM TOTAL				5302	1395	237	40	71	1.3	704	668	565	523	36	96	28	.263	.363

INDIVIDUAL FIELDING

POS	Player	T	G	PO	A	E	DP	TCG	FA
1B	Z. Bonura	R	127	1239	77	5	94	10.4	**.996**
	J. Dykes	R	27	244	11	5	18	9.6	.981
2B	J. Hayes	R	61	147	188	7	35	5.6	.980
	B. Boken	R	57	121	165	22	28	5.4	.929
	J. Dykes	R	27	65	81	8	13	5.7	.948
	L. Appling	R	8	21	16	1	4	4.8	.974
	R. Kress	R	3	6	3	0	0	3.0	1.000
SS	L. Appling	R	110	243	341	34	55	5.6	.945
	B. Boken	R	22	44	79	12	14	6.1	.911
	J. Chamberlin	R	26	32	80	13	10	4.8	.896
3B	J. Dykes	R	74	74	160	14	9	3.4	.944
	M. Hopkins	R	63	63	136	9	4	3.3	.957
	J. Chamberlin	R	14	10	17	7	2	2.4	.794
	M. Mauldin	R	10	12	17	3	3	3.2	.906

POS	Player	T	G	PO	A	E	DP	TCG	FA
OF	A. Simmons	R	138	286	14	4	3	2.2	.987
	M. Haas	R	89	204	5	2	1	2.4	.991
	E. Swanson	R	105	193	4	4	1	1.9	.980
	J. Conlan	L	54	122	5	6	1	2.5	.955
	F. Uhalt	R	40	85	2	6	1	2.3	.935
	F. Bordagaray	R	17	28	2	2	0	1.9	.938
	R. Radcliff	L	14	35	0	2	0	2.6	.946
	M. Bocek	R	10	25	2	0	1	2.7	1.000
	C. Uhlir	L	6	9	0	0	0	1.5	1.000
C	E. Madjeski	R	79	348	49	11	11	5.2	.973
	M. Shea	R	60	240	35	8	4	4.7	.972
	M. Ruel	R	21	75	8	2	1	4.0	.976
	G. Caithamer	R	5	21	2	1	1	4.8	.958
	J. Pasek	R	4	12	1	0	0	3.3	1.000
	B. Fehring	R	1	2	0	0	0	2.0	1.000

Chicago 1934

Simmons made no secret of his dislike of spacious Comiskey Park, so the White Sox accommodated him by moving home plate fourteen feet closer to the walls. The immediate beneficiary of this wasn't Simmons but Zeke Bonura, the colorful Italian first baseman. He reeled off a 23-game hitting streak in spring training and cracked two homers in his Comiskey Park unveiling. Bonura was a man of the people; he lent color to this whole drab era of Sox history. He was the perfect foil for Jimmy Dykes.

Fonseca issued a bold statement to Sox fans at the start of the season. "We do not expect to finish worse than third," he said. Taking Fonseca at his word, J. Lou Comiskey made his first eastern road trip with the Sox in 22 years. He promised Sox fans a shakeup if things didn't immediately improve. They didn't. The trip was a disaster that saw the worst exhibition of baseball by a Sox team since, well, 1932.

On May 8 Fonseca was handed his walking papers, and Jimmy Dykes ushered in a new era. Dykes was the right man for the job, but no manager was going to make much of a difference in 1934. There were no major shakeups in player personnel, because most players were confined to the disabled list at one time or another. From May to September the Sox occupied the cellar.

One bright spot was Monty Stratton's debut on June 2, against Detroit. The rookie's emergence would soon prove the wisdom of relying on one's own home-grown talent and not taking on some other team's mistakes.

TEAM STATISTICS

	W	L	PCT	GB	R	OR	2B	3B	HR	BA	SA	SB	E	DP	FA	CG	BB	SO	ShO	SV	ERA
DET	101	53	.656		958	708	349	53	74	.300	.424	124	159	150	.974	74	488	640	10	14	4.06
NY	94	60	.610	7	842	669	226	61	135	.278	.419	71	157	151	.973	83	542	656	13	10	3.76
CLE	85	69	.552	16	814	763	340	46	100	.287	.423	52	172	164	.972	72	582	554	8	19	4.28
BOS	76	76	.500	24	820	775	287	70	51	.274	.383	116	188	141	.969	68	543	538	8	9	4.32
PHI	68	82	.453	31	764	838	236	50	144	.280	.425	57	196	166	.967	68	693	480	8	8	5.01
STL	67	85	.441	33	674	800	252	59	62	.268	.373	42	187	160	.969	50	632	499	6	20	4.49
WAS	66	86	.434	34	729	806	278	70	51	.278	.382	49	162	167	.974	61	503	412	3	12	4.68
CHI	53	99	.349	47	704	946	237	40	71	.263	.363	36	207	126	.966	72	628	506	4	8	5.41
LEAGUE TOTAL					6305	6305	2205	449	688	.279	.399	547	1428	1225	.970	548	4611	4285	60	100	4.50

INDIVIDUAL PITCHING

PITCHER	T	W	L	PCT	ERA	SV	G	GS	CG	IP	H	BB	SO	R	ER	ShO	H9	BB9	SO9
George Earnshaw	R	14	11	.560	4.52	0	33	30	16	227	242	104	97	128	114	2	9.59	4.12	3.85
Ted Lyons	R	11	13	.458	4.87	1	30	24	21	205.1	249	66	53	138	111	0	10.91	2.89	2.32
Milt Gaston	R	6	19	.240	5.85	0	29	28	10	194	247	84	48	146	126	1	11.46	3.90	2.23
Sad Sam Jones	R	8	12	.400	5.11	0	27	26	11	183.1	217	60	60	120	104	1	10.65	2.95	2.95
Les Tietje	R	5	14	.263	4.81	0	34	22	6	176	174	96	81	106	94	1	8.90	4.91	4.14
Phil Gallivan	R	4	7	.364	5.61	1	35	7	3	126.2	155	64	55	97	79	0	11.01	4.55	3.91
Joe Heving	R	1	7	.125	7.26	4	33	2	0	88	133	48	40	85	71	0	13.60	4.91	4.09
Whit Wyatt	R	4	11	.267	7.18	2	23	6	2	67.2	83	37	36	59	54	0	11.04	4.92	4.79
Harry Kinzy	R	0	1	.000	4.98	0	13	2	1	34.1	38	31	12	23	19	0	9.96	8.13	3.15
Vern Kennedy	R	0	2	.000	3.72	0	3	3	1	19.1	21	9	7	8	8	0	9.78	4.19	3.26
Hugo Klaerner	R	0	2	.000	10.90	0	3	3	1	17.1	24	16	9	21	21	0	12.46	8.31	4.67
Lee Stine	R	0	0	–	8.18	0	4	0	0	11	11	10	8	10	10	0	9.00	8.18	6.55
Monty Stratton	R	0	0	–	5.40	0	1	0	0	3.1	4	1	0	2	2	0	10.80	2.70	0.00
John Pomorski	R	0	0	–	5.40	0	3	0	0	1.2	1	2	0	2	1	0	5.40	10.80	0.00
TEAM TOTAL		53	99	.349	5.41	8	271	153	72	1355	1599	628	506	945	814	5	10.62	4.17	3.36

Chicago 1935   Won 74   Lost 78   Pct .487   5th

MANAGER	W	L	PCT
Jimmy Dykes	74	78	.487

POS	Player	B	G	AB	H	2B	3B	HR	HR%	R	RBI	BB	SO	SB	Pinch Hit AB	Pinch Hit H	BA	SA
REGULARS																		
1B	Zeke Bonura	R	138	550	162	34	4	21	3.8	107	92	57	28	4	0	0	.295	.485
2B	Jackie Hayes	R	89	329	88	14	0	4	1.2	45	45	29	15	3	5	0	.267	.347
SS	Luke Appling	R	153	525	161	28	6	1	0.2	94	71	122	40	12	0	0	.307	.389
3B	Jimmy Dykes	R	117	403	116	24	2	4	1.0	59	28	4	1	0	.288	.387		
RF	Mule Haas	L	92	327	95	22	1	2	0.6	44	40	37	17	4	7	2	.291	.382
CF	Al Simmons	R	128	525	140	22	7	16	3.0	68	79	33	43	4	3	0	.267	.427
LF	Rip Radcliff	L	146	623	178	28	8	10	1.6	95	68	53	21	4	2	0	.286	.404
C	Luke Sewell	R	118	421	120	19	3	2	0.5	52	67	32	18	3	5	0	.285	.359
SUBSTITUTES																		
23	Tony Piet	R	77	292	87	17	5	3	1.0	47	27	33	27	2	0	0	.298	.421
3B	Marty Hopkins	R	59	144	32	3	0	2	1.4	20	17	36	23	1	1	0	.222	.285
2B	Glenn Wright	R	9	25	3	1	0	0	0.0	1	1	0	6	0	2	0	.120	.160
3B	Mike Kreevich	R	6	23	10	2	0	0	0.0	3	2	1	0	1	0	0	.435	.522
OF	George Washington	L	108	339	96	22	3	8	2.4	40	47	10	18	1	29	9	.283	.437
OF	Jocko Conlan	L	65	140	40	7	1	0	0.0	20	15	14	6	3	24	5	.286	.350
OF	Fred Tauby	R	13	32	4	1	0	0	0.0	5	2	2	3	0	4	0	.125	.156
C	Merv Shea	R	46	122	28	2	0	0	0.0	8	13	30	9	0	2	0	.230	.246
C	Frank Grube	R	9	19	7	2	0	0	0.0	1	6	3	2	0	0	0	.368	.474
PH	Bud Hafey	R	2	0	0	0	0	0	–	1	0	0	0	0	0	0	–	–
PITCHERS																		
P	Ted Lyons	B	29	82	18	4	0	0	0.0	5	9	3	4	0	6	1	.220	.268
P	John Whitehead	R	28	82	12	0	0	0	0.0	7	9	4	9	0	0	0	.146	.146
P	Vern Kennedy	L	31	73	18	3	1	0	0.0	5	10	1	18	0	0	0	.247	.315
P	Les Tietje	R	30	61	12	3	0	0	0.0	4	3	3	17	0	0	0	.197	.246
P	Sad Sam Jones	R	22	48	8	1	0	0	0.0	8	1	10	16	0	0	0	.167	.188
P	Ray Phelps	R	27	41	5	0	0	0	0.0	1	0	1	19	0	0	0	.122	.122
P	Carl Fischer	R	24	21	4	0	0	0	0.0	3	1	2	5	0	0	0	.190	.190
P	Jack Salveson	R	20	20	6	2	0	1	5.0	3	4	1	4	0	0	0	.300	.550
P	Monty Stratton	R	5	14	2	1	0	0	0.0	0	1	0	2	0	0	0	.143	.214
P	Whit Wyatt	R	30	13	3	0	1	0	0.0	2	0	4	2	0	0	0	.231	.385
P	Joe Vance	R	10	11	2	0	0	0	0.0	2	1	0	3	0	0	0	.182	.182
P	George Earnshaw	R	3	7	2	0	0	0	0.0	1	1	0	2	0	0	0	.286	.286
P	Italo Chelini	L	2	2	1	0	0	0	0.0	1	0	0	0	0	0	0	.500	.500
P	Lee Stine	R	1	0	0	0	0	0	–	0	0	0	0	0	0	0	–	–
TEAM TOTAL				5314	1460	262	42	74	1.4	738	690	580	405	46	91	17	.275	.382

INDIVIDUAL FIELDING

POS	Player	T	G	PO	A	E	DP	TCG	FA
1B	Z. Bonura	R	138	1421	83	9	109	11.0	.994
	J. Dykes	R	16	180	8	1	15	11.8	.995
2B	J. Hayes	R	85	202	275	17	48	5.8	.966
	T. Piet	R	59	129	216	9	32	6.0	.975
	G. Wright	R	7	13	20	2	3	5.0	.943
	M. Hopkins	R	5	8	14	4	3	5.2	.846
	J. Dykes	R	3	10	11	1	2	7.3	.955
SS	L. Appling	R	153	335	556	39	93	6.1	.958
3B	J. Dykes	R	98	100	166	13	12	2.8	.953
	M. Hopkins	R	49	27	68	4	4	2.0	.960
	T. Piet	R	17	21	29	3	1	3.1	.943
	M. Kreevich	R	6	8	4	0	0	2.0	1.000

POS	Player	T	G	PO	A	E	DP	TCG	FA
OF	A. Simmons	R	126	349	5	7	1	2.9	.981
	R. Radcliff	L	142	231	8	8	1	1.7	.968
	M. Haas	R	84	183	4	2	1	2.3	.989
	G. Washington	R	79	137	10	4	2	1.9	.974
	J. Conlan	L	37	71	3	3	1	2.1	.961
	F. Tauby	R	7	15	2	0	1	2.4	1.000
C	L. Sewell	R	112	399	83	6	10	4.4	.988
	M. Shea	R	43	161	30	2	2	4.5	.990
	F. Grube	R	9	27	5	2	0	3.8	.941

Finally, measurable improvement! Zeke Bonura hit six home runs in twelve games and the Sox won nine of their first twelve. They grabbed first place on May 6 and held fast until Memorial Day. Luke Appling and Jackie Hayes came into their own this year, anchoring an above-average infield. Veteran catcher Luke Sewell demonstrated that he was the best since Schalk, while two rookie pitchers, Vern Kennedy and John Whitehead, lowered the team ERA one full run from 1934.

Whitehead, purchased from the Texas League in 1934, used a sinkerball as his out pitch. In April he won his first eight decisions. He beat Detroit and Boston twice, and St. Louis, Washington, Philadelphia, and Cleveland once each. But Clark Griffith predicted that the second time around the league would be another story. He was right; Whitehead went 5–13 the rest of the way. Meanwhile, Lloyd Vernon Kennedy fashioned the first Sox no-hitter since 1926 when he beat the Indians on August 31. He modestly told reporters that he didn't know he had a no-hitter until he fanned Joe Vosmik to end it.

The Browns came to Chicago on August 2 and swept the Sox. Browns manager Rogers Hornsby invited the Sox back to the second division, where their neighbors, the Senators and A's, could better appreciate them. "I predict they will curl up and be an old-fashioned second division Sox team at the finish," he declared. He was right, but it was great fun while it lasted.

TEAM STATISTICS

	W	L	PCT	GB	R	OR	2B	3B	HR	BA	SA	SB	E	DP	FA	CG	BB	SO	ShO	SV	ERA
DET	93	58	.616		919	665	301	83	106	.290	.435	70	128	154	.978	87	522	584	16	11	3.82
NY	89	60	.597	3	818	632	255	70	104	.280	.416	68	151	114	.974	76	516	594	12	13	3.60
CLE	82	71	.536	12	776	739	324	77	93	.284	.421	63	177	147	.972	67	457	498	11	21	4.15
BOS	78	75	.510	16	718	732	281	63	69	.276	.392	89	194	136	.969	82	520	470	6	11	4.05
CHI	74	78	.487	19.5	738	750	262	42	74	.275	.382	46	146	133	.976	80	574	436	8	8	4.38
WAS	67	86	.438	27	823	903	255	95	32	.285	.381	54	171	186	.972	67	613	456	5	12	5.25
STL	65	87	.428	28.5	718	930	291	51	73	.270	.384	45	187	138	.970	42	640	435	4	15	5.26
PHI	58	91	.389	34	710	869	243	44	112	.279	.406	42	190	150	.968	58	704	469	7	10	5.12
LEAGUE TOTAL					6220	6220	2212	525	663	.280	.402	477	1344	1158	.972	559	4546	3942	69	101	4.45

INDIVIDUAL PITCHING

PITCHER	T	W	L	PCT	ERA	SV	G	GS	CG	IP	H	BB	SO	R	ER	ShO	H9	BB9	SO9
John Whitehead	R	13	13	.500	3.72	0	28	27	18	222.1	209	101	72	101	92	1	8.46	4.09	2.91
Vern Kennedy	R	11	11	.500	3.91	1	31	25	16	211.2	211	95	65	110	92	2	8.97	4.04	2.76
Ted Lyons	R	15	8	.652	3.02	0	23	22	19	190.2	194	56	54	79	64	3	9.16	2.64	2.55
Les Tietje	R	9	15	.375	4.30	0	30	21	9	169.2	184	81	64	88	81	1	9.76	4.30	3.39
Sad Sam Jones	R	8	7	.533	4.05	0	21	19	7	140	162	51	38	77	63	0	10.41	3.28	2.44
Ray Phelps	R	4	8	.333	4.82	1	27	17	4	125	126	55	38	77	67	0	9.07	3.96	2.74
Carl Fischer	L	5	5	.500	6.19	0	24	11	3	88.2	102	39	31	67	61	1	10.35	3.96	3.15
Jack Salveson	R	1	2	.333	4.86	1	20	2	2	66.2	79	23	22	39	36	0	10.67	3.11	2.97
Whit Wyatt	R	4	3	.571	6.75	5	30	1	0	52	65	25	22	41	39	0	11.25	4.33	3.81
Monty Stratton	R	1	2	.333	4.03	0	5	5	2	38	40	9	8	17	17	0	9.47	2.13	1.89
Joe Vance	R	2	2	.500	6.68	0	10	0	0	31	36	21	12	26	23	0	10.45	6.10	3.48
George Earnshaw	R	1	2	.333	9.00	0	3	3	0	18	26	11	8	19	18	0	13.00	5.50	4.00
Italo Chelini	L	0	0	—	12.60	0	2	0	0	5	7	4	1	7	7	0	12.60	7.20	1.80
Lee Stine	R	0	0	—	9.00	0	1	0	0	2	2	3	1	2	2	0	9.00	13.50	4.50
TEAM TOTAL		74	78	.487	4.38	8	255	153	80	1360.2	1443	574	436	750	662	8	9.54	3.80	2.88

Chicago 1936   Won 81 Lost 70 Pct. .536 3rd

MANAGER	W	L	PCT
Jimmy Dykes	81	70	.536

POS	Player	B	G	AB	H	2B	3B	HR	HR%	R	RBI	BB	SO	SB	Pinch Hit AB	Pinch Hit H	BA	SA
REGULARS																		
1B	Zeke Bonura	R	148	587	194	39	7	12	2.0	120	138	94	29	4	1	0	.330	.482
2B	Jackie Hayes	R	108	417	130	34	3	5	1.2	53	84	35	25	4	3	0	.312	.444
SS	Luke Appling	R	138	526	204	31	7	6	1.1	111	128	85	25	10	1	0	**.388**	.508
3B	Jimmy Dykes	R	127	435	116	16	3	7	1.6	62	60	61	36	1	1	0	.267	.366
RF	Mule Haas	L	119	408	116	26	2	0	0.0	75	46	64	29	1	15	3	.284	.358
CF	Mike Kreevich	R	137	550	169	32	11	5	0.9	99	69	61	46	10	3	2	.307	.433
LF	Rip Radcliff	L	138	618	207	31	7	8	1.3	120	82	44	12	6	6	3	.335	.447
C	Luke Sewell	R	128	451	113	20	5	5	1.1	59	73	54	16	11	2	0	.251	.350
SUBSTITUTES																		
23	Tony Piet	R	109	352	96	15	2	7	2.0	69	42	66	48	15	7	1	.273	.386
3S	Jo-Jo Morrissey	R	17	38	7	1	0	0	0.0	3	6	2	3	0	4	2	.184	.211
1B	Les Rock	L	2	1	0	0	0	0	0.0	0	1	0	0	0	0	0	.000	.000
OF	Larry Rosenthal	L	85	317	89	15	8	3	0.9	71	46	59	37	2	4	3	.281	.407
OF	Dixie Walker	L	26	70	19	2	0	0	0.0	12	11	14	6	1	9	2	.271	.300
OF	George Washington	L	20	49	8	2	0	1	2.0	6	5	1	4	0	6	1	.163	.265
OF	George Stumpf	L	10	22	6	1	0	0	0.0	3	5	2	1	0	5	3	.273	.318
C	Frank Grube	R	33	93	15	2	1	0	0.0	6	11	9	15	1	2	0	.161	.204
C	Merv Shea	R	14	24	3	0	0	0	0.0	3	2	6	5	0	0	0	.125	.125
PITCHERS																		
P	Vern Kennedy	L	36	113	32	8	0	0	0.0	12	11	1	13	0	0	0	.283	.354
P	John Whitehead	R	34	87	21	1	0	0	0.0	6	9	5	9	0	0	0	.241	.253
P	Ted Lyons	B	26	70	11	0	0	0	0.0	2	5	5	12	0	0	0	.157	.157
P	Sugar Cain	L	31	68	7	0	0	0	0.0	5	4	7	14	0	0	0	.103	.103
P	Monty Stratton	R	16	37	8	2	0	1	2.7	7	7	2	4	0	0	0	.216	.351
P	Italo Chelini	L	18	32	5	0	0	0	0.0	3	2	2	9	0	0	0	.156	.156
P	Bill Dietrich	R	14	30	8	0	0	0	0.0	3	5	1	8	0	0	0	.267	.267
P	Ray Phelps	R	15	26	6	2	0	0	0.0	3	4	1	6	0	0	0	.231	.308
P	Clint Brown	L	38	25	4	2	0	0	0.0	5	3	2	1	0	0	0	.160	.240
P	Red Evans	R	18	15	2	0	0	0	0.0	1	1	0	3	0	0	0	.133	.133
P	Bill Shores	R	9	5	1	0	0	0	0.0	0	2	0	3	0	0	0	.200	.200
P	Les Tietje	R	2	0	0	0	0	0	—	1	0	1	0	0	0	0	—	—
P	Whit Wyatt	R	3	0	0	0	0	0	—	0	0	0	0	0	0	0	—	—
TEAM TOTAL				5466	1597	282	56	60	1.1	920	862	684	419	66	69	20	.292	.397

INDIVIDUAL FIELDING

POS	Player	T	G	PO	A	E	DP	TCG	FA	POS	Player	T	G	PO	A	E	DP	TCG	FA
1B	Z. Bonura	R	146	1500	107	7	150	11.1	.996	OF	M. Kreevich	R	133	300	17	12	5	2.5	.964
	L. Rock	R	2	0	0	0	0	0.0	.000		L. Rosenthal	L	80	243	7	6	3	3.2	.977
	M. Haas	R	7	77	4	3	6	12.0	.964		R. Radcliff	L	132	213	6	15	2	1.8	.936
2B	J. Hayes	R	89	216	334	12	70	6.3	.979		M. Haas	R	96	176	7	2	2	1.9	.989
	T. Piet	R	68	135	261	14	47	6.0	.966		D. Walker	R	17	46	2	0	0	2.8	1.000
	J. Morrissey	R	1	1	0	0	0	1.0	1.000		G. Washington	R	12	13	2	1	0	1.3	.938
SS	L. Appling	R	137	320	471	41	119	6.1	.951		G. Stumpf	L	4	9	1	0	0	2.5	1.000
	J. Hayes	R	13	33	45	3	12	6.2	.963	C	L. Sewell	R	126	461	87	9	12	4.4	.984
	J. Morrissey	R	4	10	11	1	1	5.5	.955		F. Grube	R	32	89	19	1	2	3.4	.991
3B	J. Dykes	R	125	108	240	18	14	2.9	.951		M. Shea	R	14	32	3	0	0	2.5	1.000
	T. Piet	R	32	32	56	4	2	2.9	.957										
	J. Morrissey	R	9	6	11	2	1	2.1	.895										
	J. Hayes	R	2	4	1	0	0	2.5	1.000										

Al Simmons wanted out so badly that he tore up a White Sox offer sheet calling for $125,000 over several years. That winter, Jimmy Dykes talked Mickey Cochrane of the Tigers into purchasing Simmons at a cost of $75,000. It was less than the Sox wanted, but it helped restore the Depression-torn coffers.

Without Simmons, and with Bonura holding out for $15,000, the Sox weren't given much of a chance in 1936. Zeke eventually came to terms, but was on the bench when the season started. The Sox got away from the gate sluggishly, but this was a strong young club destined for better things. Rip Radcliff from Selma, Alabama, and Luke Appling were the offensive stars. They traded places atop the league leaders in batting throughout the season, but Appling won the honors easily. He finished up at .388, outdistancing Earl Averill by ten points.

In late August the Sox broke away from the second division and from the stigma of Rogers Hornsby's 1935 predictions. They took second place on September 18, and only a rainout on the last day of the season prevented them from at least tying Detroit for the runner-up spot.

On July 26, 50,000 fans packed Comiskey Park to see a Sox-Yankees doubleheader. In the second game, umpire William Summers made an unpopular call involving a close play at first. Fruit, beer cans, and pop bottles were hurled onto the field. One missile struck Summers in the groin, and he had to retire from the field of play. Judge Landis was in attendance that day and offered $5,000 for the name of the culprit. It was never revealed. The temperament of the baseball fan never changes, only the names of the players and the salaries they make.

TEAM STATISTICS

	W	L	PCT	GB	R	OR	2B	3B	HR	BA	SA	SB	E	DP	FA	CG	BB	SO	ShO	SV	ERA
NY	102	51	.667		1065	731	315	83	182	.300	.483	76	163	148	.973	77	663	624	6	21	4.17
DET	83	71	.539	19.5	921	871	326	55	94	.300	.431	72	153	159	.975	76	562	526	13	13	5.00
CHI	81	70	.536	20	920	873	282	56	60	.292	.397	66	168	174	.973	80	578	414	5	8	5.06
WAS	82	71	.536	20	889	799	293	84	62	.295	.414	103	182	163	.970	78	588	462	8	14	4.58
CLE	80	74	.519	22.5	921	862	357	82	123	.304	.461	66	178	154	.971	80	607	619	6	12	4.83
BOS	74	80	.481	28.5	775	764	288	62	86	.276	.400	54	165	139	.972	78	552	584	11	9	4.39
STL	57	95	.375	44.5	804	1064	299	66	79	.279	.403	62	188	143	.969	54	609	399	3	13	6.24
PHI	53	100	.346	49	714	1045	240	60	72	.269	.376	59	209	152	.965	68	696	405	3	12	6.08
LEAGUE TOTAL					7009	7009	2400	548	758	.289	.421	558	1406	1232	.971	591	4855	4033	55	102	5.04

INDIVIDUAL PITCHING

PITCHER	T	W	L	PCT	ERA	SV	G	GS	CG	IP	H	BB	SO	R	ER	ShO	H9	BB9	SO9
Vern Kennedy	R	21	9	.700	4.63	0	35	34	20	274.1	282	147	99	167	141	1	9.25	4.82	3.25
John Whitehead	R	13	13	.500	4.64	1	34	32	15	230.2	254	98	70	137	119	1	9.91	3.82	2.73
Sugar Cain	R	14	10	.583	4.75	0	30	26	14	195.1	228	75	42	112	103	1	10.51	3.46	1.94
Ted Lyons	R	10	13	.435	5.14	0	26	24	15	182	227	45	48	115	104	1	11.23	2.23	2.37
Monty Stratton	R	5	7	.417	5.21	0	16	14	3	95	117	46	37	66	55	0	11.08	4.36	3.51
Italo Chelini	L	4	3	.571	4.95	0	18	6	5	83.2	100	30	16	51	46	0	10.76	3.23	1.72
Clint Brown	R	6	2	.750	4.99	5	38	2	0	83	106	24	19	50	46	0	11.49	2.60	2.06
Bill Dietrich	R	4	4	.500	4.68	0	14	11	6	82.2	93	36	39	50	43	1	10.13	3.92	4.25
Ray Phelps	R	4	6	.400	6.03	0	15	4	2	68.2	91	42	17	54	46	0	11.93	5.50	2.23
Red Evans	R	0	3	.000	7.61	1	17	0	0	47.1	70	22	19	46	40	0	13.31	4.18	3.61
Bill Shores	R	0	0	—	9.53	0	9	0	0	17	26	8	5	18	18	0	13.76	4.24	2.65
Whit Wyatt	R	0	0	—	0.00	1	3	0	0	3	3	0	0	0	0	0	9.00	0.00	0.00
Les Tietje	R	0	0	—	27.00	0	2	0	0	2.1	6	5	3	7	7	0	23.14	19.29	11.57
TEAM TOTAL		81	70	.536	5.06	8	257	153	80	1365	1603	578	414	873	768	5	10.57	3.81	2.73

Chicago 1937   Won 86   Lost 68   Pct. .558   3rd

MANAGER
Jimmy Dykes   W 86   L 68   PCT .558

POS	Player	B	G	AB	H	2B	3B	HR	HR%	R	RBI	BB	SO	SB	Pinch Hit AB	H	BA	SA
REGULARS																		
1B	Zeke Bonura	R	116	447	154	41	2	19	4.3	79	100	49	24	5	1	0	.345	.573
2B	Jackie Hayes	R	143	573	131	27	4	2	0.3	63	79	41	37	1	0	0	.229	.300
SS	Luke Appling	R	154	574	182	42	8	4	0.7	98	77	86	28	18	0	0	.317	.439
3B	Tony Piet	R	100	332	78	15	1	4	1.2	34	38	32	36	14	1	1	.235	.322
RF	Dixie Walker	L	154	593	179	28	16	9	1.5	105	95	78	26	1	0	0	.302	.449
CF	Mike Kreevich	R	144	583	176	29	16	12	2.1	94	73	43	45	10	3	1	.302	.468
LF	Rip Radcliff	L	144	584	190	38	10	4	0.7	105	79	53	25	6	5	3	.325	.445
C	Luke Sewell	R	122	412	111	21	6	1	0.2	51	61	46	18	4	3	2	.269	.357
SUBSTITUTES																		
3B	Boze Berger	R	52	130	31	5	0	5	3.8	19	13	15	24	1	6	2	.238	.392
1B	Mule Haas	L	54	111	23	3	3	0	0.0	8	15	16	10	1	16	2	.207	.288
3B	Merv Connors	R	28	103	24	4	1	2	1.9	12	12	14	19	2	0	0	.233	.350
13	Jimmy Dykes	R	30	85	26	5	0	1	1.2	10	23	9	7	0	4	2	.306	.400
OF	Larry Rosenthal	L	58	97	28	5	3	0	0.0	20	9	9	20	1	29	9	.289	.402
OF	Hank Steinbacher	L	26	73	19	4	1	1	1.4	13	9	4	7	2	11	1	.260	.384
C	Merv Shea	R	25	71	15	1	0	0	0.0	7	5	15	10	1	0	0	.211	.225
C	Tony Rensa	R	26	57	17	5	1	0	0.0	10	5	8	6	3	2	1	.298	.421
PITCHERS																		
P	Vern Kennedy	L	32	87	20	1	1	2	2.3	12	9	0	17	0	0	0	.230	.333
P	Thornton Lee	L	30	71	15	3	2	0	0.0	5	4	1	16	0	0	0	.211	.310
P	Monty Stratton	R	22	60	12	2	0	1	1.7	9	6	0	9	0	0	0	.200	.283
P	John Whitehead	R	26	58	13	1	0	0	0.0	7	5	4	10	0	0	0	.224	.241
P	Ted Lyons	B	23	57	12	0	0	0	0.0	6	3	9	14	0	0	0	.211	.211
P	Bill Dietrich	R	29	44	8	0	1	0	0.0	6	1	7	20	0	0	0	.182	.227
P	Johnny Rigney	R	22	30	5	0	0	0	0.0	4	0	4	9	0	0	0	.167	.167
P	Sugar Cain	L	18	22	4	0	0	0	0.0	2	2	0	4	0	0	0	.182	.182
P	Clint Brown	L	53	18	4	0	0	0	0.0	1	3	5	5	0	0	0	.222	.222
P	Bill Cox	R	3	4	1	0	0	0	0.0	0	0	0	1	0	0	0	.250	.250
P	Italo Chelini	L	4	1	0	0	0	0	0.0	0	0	1	0	0	0	0	.000	.000
P	George Gick	B	1	0	0	0	0	0	—	0	0	0	0	0	0	0	—	—
	TEAM TOTAL			5277	1478	280	76	67	1.3	780	726	549	447	70	81	24	.280	.400

INDIVIDUAL FIELDING

POS	Player	T	G	PO	A	E	DP	TCG	FA
1B	Z. Bonura	R	115	1114	63	13	123	10.3	.989
	M. Haas	R	32	251	19	7	22	8.7	.975
	J. Dykes	R	15	141	5	1	12	9.8	.993
2B	J. Hayes	R	143	353	490	14	115	6.0	.984
	T. Piet	R	13	36	44	0	12	6.2	1.000
	B. Berger	R	1	0	1	1	0	2.0	.500
SS	L. Appling	R	154	280	541	49	111	5.6	.944
	B. Berger	R	1	2	2	1	1	5.0	.800
3B	T. Piet	R	86	83	163	16	12	3.0	.939
	B. Berger	R	40	35	73	8	8	2.9	.931
	M. Connors	R	28	22	53	6	8	2.9	.926
	J. Dykes	R	11	11	22	0	3	3.0	1.000
OF	M. Kreevich	R	138	401	13	5	4	3.0	.988
	D. Walker	R	154	270	10	14	1	1.9	.952
	R. Radcliff	L	139	273	9	10	5	2.1	.966
	L. Rosenthal	L	25	46	3	1	1	2.0	.980
	Steinbacher	R	15	24	0	1	0	1.7	.960
	M. Haas	R	2	3	0	1	0	2.0	.750
C	L. Sewell	R	118	502	72	9	11	4.9	.985
	M. Shea	R	25	91	21	-4	1	4.6	.966
	T. Rensa	R	23	70	9	2	3	3.5	.975

Dykes tried to peddle John Whitehead at the 1936 winter meetings. When proposed deals for Jack Knott and Harlond Clift failed, Dykes pulled off a dandy three-cornered trade. The Sox dealt rookie pitcher Jack Salveson to Washington for Thornton Lee, who arrived via the Cleveland Indians. Lefty Lee was a well-traveled pitcher, a real sleeper who blossomed under coach Muddy Ruel.

Thin in reserves and weak at the hot corner, the Sox began the season in their usual disarray. They didn't win many games in the beginning; only Monty Stratton and his treacherous "gander" pitch helped keep the Sox near .500. Stratton missed seven weeks due to an arm injury but still won 15 games in 1937.

The Sox got going on Memorial Day. They won ten in a row, including Bullfrog Dietrich's June 1st no-hitter against St. Louis. Dietrich was another Dykes bargain, picked up for the waiver price of $7,500 in 1936 and moved into the starting rotation.

The ten-game streak carried the Sox to a first-place tie with New York on June 10, but they lost to Bump Hadley the next day and dipped in and out of second place the rest of the season. This was a high-water mark for the White Sox. They could do no better, for the Yankee dynasty was invincible at this time. Money, good scouting, and an advanced farm system made Joe McCarthy a "push-button manager." Dykes had to be content with his waiver deals with second-division teams.

TEAM STATISTICS

	W	L	PCT	GB	R	OR	2B	3B	HR	BA	SA	SB	E	DP	FA	CG	BB	SO	ShO	SV	ERA
NY	102	52	.662		979	671	282	73	174	.283	.456	60	170	134	.972	82	506	652	15	21	3.65
DET	89	65	.578	13	935	841	309	62	150	.292	.452	89	147	149	.976	70	635	485	6	11	4.87
CHI	86	68	.558	16	780	730	280	76	67	.280	.400	70	174	173	.971	70	532	533	15	21	4.17
CLE	83	71	.539	19	817	768	304	76	103	.280	.423	76	159	153	.974	64	563	630	4	15	4.39
BOS	80	72	.526	21	821	775	269	64	100	.281	.411	79	177	139	.970	74	597	682	6	14	4.48
WAS	73	80	.477	28.5	757	841	245	84	47	.279	.379	61	170	181	.972	75	676	535	5	14	4.58
PHI	54	97	.358	46.5	699	854	278	60	94	.267	.397	95	198	150	.967	65	613	469	6	9	4.85
STL	46	108	.299	56	715	1023	327	44	71	.285	.399	30	173	166	.972	55	653	468	2	8	6.00
LEAGUE TOTAL					6503	6503	2294	539	806	.281	.415	560	1368	1245	.972	555	4775	4454	59	113	4.62

INDIVIDUAL PITCHING

PITCHER	T	W	L	PCT	ERA	SV	G	GS	CG	IP	H	BB	SO	R	ER	ShO	H9	BB9	SO9
Vern Kennedy	R	14	13	.519	5.09	0	32	30	15	221	238	124	114	150	125	1	9.69	5.05	4.64
Thornton Lee	L	12	10	.545	3.52	0	30	25	13	204.2	209	60	80	91	80	2	9.19	2.64	3.52
Ted Lyons	R	12	7	.632	4.15	0	22	22	11	169.1	182	45	45	86	78	0	9.67	2.39	2.39
John Whitehead	R	11	8	.579	4.07	0	26	24	8	165.2	191	56	45	84	75	4	10.38	3.04	2.44
Monty Stratton	R	15	5	.750	2.40	0	22	21	14	164.2	142	37	69	55	44	5	7.76	2.02	3.77
Bill Dietrich	R	8	10	.444	4.90	1	29	20	7	143.1	162	72	62	93	78	1	10.17	4.52	3.89
Clint Brown	R	7	7	.500	3.42	18	53	0	0	100	92	36	51	47	38	0	8.28	3.24	4.59
Johnny Rigney	R	2	5	.286	4.96	1	22	4	1	90.2	107	46	38	65	50	1	10.62	4.57	3.77
Sugar Cain	R	4	2	.667	6.16	0	18	6	1	68.2	88	51	17	48	47	0	11.53	6.68	2.23
Bill Cox	R	1	0	1.000	0.71	0	3	2	1	12.2	9	5	8	1	1	0	6.39	3.55	5.68
Italo Chelini	L	0	1	.000	10.38	0	4	0	0	8.2	15	0	3	10	10	0	15.58	0.00	3.12
George Gick	R	0	0	—	0.00	1	1	0	0	2	0	0	1	0	0	0	0.00	0.00	4.50
TEAM TOTAL		86	68	.558	4.17	21	262	154	71	1351.1	1435	532	533	730	626	14	9.56	3.54	3.55

Chicago 1938   Won 65 Lost 83 Pct. .439 6th

MANAGER	W	L	PCT
Jimmy Dykes	65	83	.439

POS	Player	B	G	AB	H	2B	3B	HR	HR%	R	RBI	BB	SO	SB	Pinch Hit AB	Pinch Hit H	BA	SA
REGULARS																		
1B	Joe Kuhel	L	117	412	110	27	4	8	1.9	67	51	72	35	9	6	0	.267	.410
2B	Jackie Hayes	R	62	238	78	21	2	1	0.4	40	20	24	6	3	1	0	.328	.445
SS	Luke Appling	R	81	294	89	14	0	0	0.0	41	44	42	17	1	2	1	.303	.350
3B	Marv Owen	R	141	577	162	23	6	6	1.0	84	55	45	31	6	1	0	.281	.373
RF	Hank Steinbacher	L	106	399	132	23	8	4	1.0	59	61	41	19	1	4	1	.331	.459
CF	Mike Kreevich	R	129	489	145	26	12	6	1.2	73	73	55	23	13	3	0	.297	.436
LF	Gee Walker	R	120	442	135	23	6	16	3.6	69	87	38	32	9	12	4	.305	.493
C	Luke Sewell	R	65	211	45	4	1	0	0.0	23	27	20	20	0	0	0	.213	.242
SUBSTITUTES																		
S2	Boze Berger	R	118	470	102	15	3	3	0.6	60	36	43	80	4	0	0	.217	.281
2B	Jimmy Dykes	R	26	89	27	4	2	2	2.2	9	13	10	8	0	1	0	.303	.461
2B	George Meyer	R	24	81	24	2	2	0	0.0	10	9	11	17	3	0	0	.296	.370
1B	Merv Connors	R	24	62	22	4	0	6	9.7	14	13	9	17	0	7	2	.355	.710
SS	John Gerlach	R	9	25	7	0	0	0	0.0	2	1	4	2	0	0	0	.280	.280
1B	Tommy Thompson	L	19	18	2	0	0	0	0.0	2	2	1	2	0	17	2	.111	.111
2B	Jesse Landrum	R	4	6	0	0	0	0	0.0	0	1	0	2	0	1	0	.000	.000
OF	Rip Radcliff	L	129	503	166	23	6	5	1.0	64	81	36	17	5	7	2	.330	.429
OF	Larry Rosenthal	L	61	105	30	5	1	1	1.0	14	12	12	13	0	30	6	.286	.381
C	Tony Rensa	R	59	165	41	5	0	3	1.8	15	19	25	16	1	2	0	.248	.333
C	Norm Schlueter	R	35	118	27	5	1	0	0.0	11	7	4	15	1	1	0	.229	.288
C	Mike Tresh	R	10	29	7	2	0	0	0.0	3	2	8	4	0	0	0	.241	.310
PH	Joe Martin	R	1	0	0	0	0	0	–	0	0	0	0	0	0	0	–	–
PITCHERS																		
P	Thornton Lee	L	34	97	25	3	1	4	4.1	14	16	0	23	0	1	1	.258	.433
P	Monty Stratton	R	27	79	21	5	0	2	2.5	17	10	2	9	0	1	0	.266	.405
P	Ted Lyons	B	24	72	14	2	0	0	0.0	9	4	2	2	0	1	0	.194	.222
P	John Whitehead	R	32	60	6	0	0	0	0.0	3	5	5	15	0	0	0	.100	.100
P	Johnny Rigney	R	38	55	8	1	0	0	0.0	1	4	1	17	0	0	0	.145	.164
P	Jack Knott	R	20	40	5	0	0	0	0.0	0	2	2	19	0	0	0	.125	.125
P	Frank Gabler	R	18	21	5	1	0	0	0.0	1	2	0	5	0	0	0	.238	.286
P	Bill Dietrich	R	8	16	1	0	0	0	0.0	3	0	2	5	0	0	0	.063	.063
P	Harry Boyles	R	9	8	1	0	0	0	0.0	0	0	0	2	0	0	0	.125	.125
P	Sugar Cain	L	5	8	0	0	0	0	0.0	0	0	0	5	0	0	0	.000	.000
P	Gene Ford	R	4	6	1	0	0	0	0.0	0	0	0	2	0	0	0	.167	.167
P	Clint Brown	L	8	2	1	1	0	0	0.0	1	0	0	0	0	0	0	.500	1.000
P	Bill Cox	R	7	2	0	0	0	0	0.0	0	0	0	2	0	0	0	.000	.000
P	George Gick	B	1	0	0	0	0	0	–	0	0	0	0	0	0	0	–	–
P	Bob Uhle	B	1	0	0	0	0	0	–	0	0	0	0	0	0	0	–	–
TEAM TOTAL				5199	1439	239	55	67	1.3	709	657	514	489	56	98	19	.277	.383

INDIVIDUAL FIELDING

POS	Player	T	G	PO	A	E	DP	TCG	FA	POS	Player	T	G	PO	A	E	DP	TCG	FA
1B	J. Kuhel	L	111	1136	59	14	97	10.9	.988	OF	M. Kreevich	R	127	379	7	10	2	3.1	.975
	R. Radcliff	L	23	236	10	5	25	10.9	.980		R. Radcliff	L	99	230	5	5	0	2.4	.979
	M. Connors	R	16	129	11	3	17	8.9	.979		Steinbacher	R	101	202	7	8	2	2.1	.963
	T. Thompson	R	1	2	0	0	1	2.0	1.000		G. Walker	R	107	197	9	9	2	2.0	.958
2B	J. Hayes	R	61	146	183	8	51	5.5	.976		L. Rosenthal	L	22	44	3	2	1	2.2	.959
	B. Berger	R	42	86	117	15	23	5.2	.931	C	L. Sewell	R	65	205	55	4	7	4.1	.985
	J. Dykes	R	23	75	68	9	13	6.6	.941		T. Rensa	R	57	185	36	4	4	3.9	.982
	G. Meyer	R	24	61	86	5	12	6.3	.967		N. Schlueter	R	34	107	13	6	3	3.7	.952
	J. Landrum	R	3	0	3	0	1	1.0	1.000		M. Tresh	R	10	37	8	1	1	4.6	.978
SS	L. Appling	R	78	149	258	20	37	5.5	.953										
	B. Berger	R	67	144	224	21	55	5.8	.946										
	J. Dykes	R	0	0	0	0	0	0.0	.000										
	J. Gerlach	R	8	17	20	2	9	4.9	.949										
3B	M. Owen	R	140	136	305	24	29	3.3	.948										
	B. Berger	R	9	9	12	3	1	2.7	.875										
	J. Dykes	R	1	0	4	0	0	4.0	1.000										

Chicago 1938

Given the friendship between Mickey Cochrane and Jimmy Dykes, it's easy to see why the Sox were Detroit's preferred trading partners in the 1930s. This year's deal sent Vern Kennedy, Tony Piet, and Dixie Walker to the Tigers for Marv Owen, Gee Walker, and rookie Mike Tresh. Dykes was called a genius because Marv Owen solved the third base dilemma and Gee Walker was a solid outfielder. It didn't quite work out that way. Dixie Walker proved to be one of the biggest giveaways in Sox history. In the 1940s he was "The People's Cherce" in Brooklyn.

Fed up with Zeke Bonura's annual holdout for $15,000, Harry Grabiner traded him to Washington for Joe Kuhel. Yes, we had no Bonuras, but the Sox now had the best fielding first baseman in the league.

Then came the injuries. On March 27 Luke Appling fractured his right ankle, and Monty Stratton strained his pitching arm in a game with the Cubs. Relief ace Clint Brown had bone chips removed from his arm in May. Not to mention Bill Dietrich's inflamed elbow, Jackie Hayes's season-long battle with a gimpy knee... but you get the idea.

The injury jinx was enough to ensure their eventual sixth-place finish. The patched-up lineup had a few good moments, though. Ted Lyons won his 200th game on May 22 when he beat the Senators, holding the returning Zeke Bonura hitless. Rookie Mervyn Connors pulled three homers in a game on September 17, and missed a fourth by inches. Dykes had his moment, too. He fined twelve-year-old Chuck Comiskey ten dollars one afternoon; the lad was caught eating a sandwich in the dugout.

TEAM STATISTICS

	W	L	PCT	GB	R	OR	2B	3B	HR	BA	SA	SB	E	DP	FA	CG	BB	SO	ShO	SV	ERA
NY	99	53	.651		966	710	283	63	174	.274	.446	91	169	169	.973	91	566	567	10	13	3.91
BOS	88	61	.591	9.5	902	751	298	56	98	.299	.434	55	190	172	.968	67	528	484	10	15	4.46
CLE	86	66	.566	13	847	782	300	89	113	.281	.434	83	151	145	.974	68	681	717	5	17	4.60
DET	84	70	.545	16	862	795	219	52	137	.272	.411	76	147	172	.976	75	608	435	2	11	4.79
WAS	75	76	.497	23.5	814	873	278	72	85	.293	.416	65	180	179	.970	59	655	515	6	11	4.94
CHI	65	83	.439	32	709	752	239	55	67	.277	.383	56	196	155	.967	83	550	432	5	9	4.36
STL	55	97	.362	44	755	962	273	36	92	.281	.397	51	145	163	.975	71	737	632	3	7	5.80
PHI	53	99	.349	46	726	956	243	62	98	.270	.396	65	206	119	.965	56	599	473	4	12	5.48
LEAGUE TOTAL					6581	6581	2133	485	864	.281	.415	542	1384	1274	.971	570	4924	4255	45	95	4.79

INDIVIDUAL PITCHING

PITCHER	T	W	L	PCT	ERA	SV	G	GS	CG	IP	H	BB	SO	R	ER	ShO	H9	BB9	SO9
Thornton Lee	L	13	12	.520	3.49	1	33	30	18	245.1	252	94	77	123	95	1	9.24	3.45	2.82
Ted Lyons	R	9	11	.450	3.70	0	23	23	17	194.2	238	52	54	93	80	1	11.00	2.40	2.50
Monty Stratton	R	15	9	.625	4.01	2	26	22	17	186.1	186	56	82	95	83	0	8.98	2.70	3.96
John Whitehead	R	10	11	.476	4.76	2	32	24	10	183.1	218	80	38	108	97	2	10.70	3.93	1.87
Johnny Rigney	R	9	9	.500	3.56	1	38	12	7	167	164	72	84	74	66	1	8.84	3.88	4.53
Jack Knott	R	5	10	.333	4.05	0	20	18	9	131	135	54	35	70	59	0	9.27	3.71	2.40
Frank Gabler	R	1	7	.125	9.09	0	18	7	3	69.1	101	34	17	74	70	0	13.11	4.41	2.21
Bill Dietrich	R	2	4	.333	5.44	0	8	7	1	48	49	31	11	33	29	0	9.19	5.81	2.06
Harry Boyles	R	0	4	.000	5.22	1	9	2	1	29.1	31	25	18	27	17	0	9.51	7.67	5.52
Sugar Cain	R	0	1	.000	4.58	0	5	3	0	19.2	26	18	6	17	10	0	11.90	8.24	2.75
Gene Ford	R	0	0	—	10.29	0	4	0	0	14	21	12	2	16	16	0	13.50	7.71	1.29
Clint Brown	R	1	3	.250	4.61	2	8	0	0	13.2	16	9	2	8	7	0	10.54	5.93	1.32
Bill Cox	R	0	2	.000	6.94	0	7	1	0	11.2	11	13	5	14	9	0	8.49	10.03	3.86
Bob Uhle	L	0	0	—	0.00	0	1	0	0	2	1	0	0	0	0	0	4.50	0.00	0.00
George Gick	R	0	0	—	0.00	0	1	0	0	1	0	0	1	0	0	0	0.00	0.00	9.00
TEAM TOTAL		65	83	.439	4.36	9	233	149	83	1316.1	1449	550	432	752	638	5	9.91	3.76	2.95

Chicago 1939   Won 85 Lost 69 Pct. .552 4th

MANAGER	W	L	PCT
Jimmy Dykes	85	69	.552

POS	Player	B	G	AB	H	2B	3B	HR	HR%	R	RBI	BB	SO	SB	Pinch Hit AB	H	BA	SA
REGULARS																		
1B	Joe Kuhel	L	139	546	164	24	9	15	2.7	107	56	64	51	18	3	0	.300	.460
2B	Ollie Bejma	R	90	307	77	9	3	8	2.6	52	44	36	27	1	6	1	.251	.378
SS	Luke Appling	R	148	516	162	16	6	0	0.0	82	56	105	37	16	0	0	.314	.368
3B	Eric McNair	R	129	479	155	18	5	7	1.5	62	82	38	41	17	1	0	.324	.426
RF	Larry Rosenthal	L	107	324	86	21	5	10	3.1	50	51	53	46	6	12	1	.265	.454
CF	Mike Kreevich	R	145	541	175	30	8	5	0.9	85	77	59	40	23	3	0	.323	.436
LF	Gee Walker	R	149	598	174	30	11	13	2.2	95	111	28	43	17	2	0	.291	.443
C	Mike Tresh	R	119	352	91	5	2	0	0.0	49	38	64	30	3	0	0	.259	.284
SUBSTITUTES																		
2B	Jackie Hayes	R	72	269	67	12	3	0	0.0	34	23	27	10	0	2	0	.249	.316
3B	Marv Owen	R	58	194	46	9	0	0	0.0	22	15	16	15	4	2	0	.237	.284
3B	Bob Kennedy	R	3	8	2	0	0	0	0.0	0	1	0	0	0	1	0	.250	.250
3B	John Gerlach	R	3	2	2	0	0	0	0.0	0	0	0	0	0	1	1	1.000	1.000
3B	Jimmy Dykes	R	2	1	0	0	0	0	0.0	0	0	0	0	0	0	0	.000	.000
O1	Rip Radcliff	L	113	397	105	25	2	2	0.5	49	53	26	21	6	13	1	.264	.353
OF	Hank Steinbacher	L	71	111	19	2	1	1	0.9	16	15	21	8	0	39	8	.171	.234
C	Ken Silvestri	B	22	75	13	3	0	2	2.7	6	5	6	13	0	2	1	.173	.293
C	Norm Schlueter	R	34	56	13	2	1	0	0.0	5	8	1	11	2	2	0	.232	.304
C	Tony Rensa	R	14	25	5	0	0	0	0.0	3	2	1	2	0	1	1	.200	.200
PH	Tommy Thompson	L	1	0	0	0	0	0	—	0	1	0	0	0	0	0	—	—
PITCHERS																		
P	Thornton Lee	L	33	91	15	3	0	0	0.0	8	4	4	18	0	0	0	.165	.198
P	Johnny Rigney	R	35	80	16	4	0	0	0.0	4	7	2	18	0	0	0	.200	.250
P	Ted Lyons	B	21	61	18	3	0	0	0.0	5	8	5	7	0	0	0	.295	.344
P	Johnny Marcum	L	38	57	16	0	0	0	0.0	7	12	5	1	0	17	3	.281	.281
P	Jack Knott	R	25	53	8	0	0	0	0.0	3	1	0	18	0	0	0	.151	.151
P	Eddie Smith	B	29	52	6	1	0	0	0.0	5	3	9	15	0	0	0	.115	.135
P	Bill Dietrich	R	25	37	8	3	0	1	2.7	5	2	4	12	0	0	0	.216	.378
P	Clint Brown	L	61	19	4	0	0	0	0.0	0	3	4	3	0	0	0	.211	.211
P	John Whitehead	R	7	9	0	0	0	0	0.0	0	0	0	7	0	0	0	.000	.000
P	Vic Frazier	R	10	7	2	0	0	0	0.0	0	1	0	3	0	0	0	.286	.286
P	Vallie Eaves	R	2	6	2	0	0	0	0.0	0	1	0	2	0	0	0	.333	.333
P	Art Herring	R	7	4	0	0	0	0	0.0	1	0	1	1	0	0	0	.000	.000
P	Harry Boyles	R	2	1	0	0	0	0	0.0	0	0	0	1	0	0	0	.000	.000
P	Jess Dobernic	R	4	1	0	0	0	0	0.0	0	0	0	1	0	0	0	.000	.000
TEAM TOTAL				5279	1451	220	56	64	1.2	755	679	579	502	113	107	17	.275	.374

INDIVIDUAL FIELDING

POS	Player	T	G	PO	A	E	DP	TCG	FA
1B	J. Kuhel	L	136	1256	72	11	113	9.8	.992
	R. Radcliff	L	20	170	11	2	11	9.2	.989
2B	J. Hayes	R	69	172	201	10	51	5.6	.974
	O. Bejma	R	81	170	199	7	36	4.6	.981
	E. McNair	R	19	41	68	2	13	5.8	.982
SS	L. Appling	R	148	289	461	39	78	5.3	.951
	E. McNair	R	9	20	37	4	7	6.8	.934
	O. Bejma	R	1	3	1	0	0	4.0	1.000
3B	E. McNair	R	103	90	194	19	23	2.9	.937
	M. Owen	R	55	63	99	8	11	3.1	.953
	M. Kreevich	R	4	6	8	1	0	3.8	.933
	B. Kennedy	R	2	0	3	1	0	2.0	.750
	J. Dykes	R	2	2	0	1	0	1.5	.667
	O. Bejma	R	1	1	1	0	0	2.0	1.000
	J. Gerlach	R	1	0	1	0	0	1.0	1.000

POS	Player	T	G	PO	A	E	DP	TCG	FA
OF	M. Kreevich	R	139	419	18	11	4	3.2	.975
	G. Walker	R	147	365	11	13	3	2.6	.967
	L. Rosenthal	L	93	193	5	2	1	2.2	.990
	R. Radcliff	L	78	130	1	4	0	1.7	.970
	Steinbacher	R	22	38	1	0	0	1.8	1.000
C	M. Tresh	R	119	480	59	8	7	4.6	.985
	K. Silvestri	R	20	74	15	5	3	4.7	.947
	N. Schlueter	R	32	81	2	1	0	2.6	.988
	T. Rensa	R	13	29	6	1	0	2.8	.972

Chicago 1939

Monty Stratton lost a leg and a career in a hunting accident on November 27, 1938. We can only imagine what heights his career might have reached if this tragedy had not occured. He was only 26, and had just registered two brilliant seasons.

A decision to allow major league teams to sign amateur players outright convinced Comiskey that the time was ripe to develop his own talent in a controlled environment. Under the direction of minor-league manager Bob Tarleton, 81 sandlotters went to Longview, Texas, to try out for the Sox. The best of the group were then parceled out to the new Class D Sox affiliates at Lubbock, Texas, Rayne, Louisiana, Jonesboro, Arkansas, and Longview. But Lou Comiskey wouldn't live to see his farm system reach fruition. On July 18 he passed away at Eagle River, Wisconsin, after naming the First National Bank of Chicago the executor of the will. Control of the White Sox was slipping from the Comiskey family, as the bank sought bids from interested parties.

The club took the field on April 18 wearing their snappy new red, white, and blue uniforms with SOX in large block letters. It was one of several fashion changes in the decade, beginning with the replacement of their long-standing navy blue road uniforms in 1932.

Free of injuries, the Sox remained in the first division the entire season. They were never really in it, but neither were they out of it. The first Comiskey Park night game was played on August 14, as the Sox downed the Browns, 5–2. Pitching hero of the night was John Duncan Rigney, the Lake Forest boy who won eleven in a row that season and began courting Lou Comiskey's oldest daughter, Dorothy.

TEAM STATISTICS

	W	L	PCT	GB	R	OR	2B	3B	HR	BA	SA	SB	E	DP	FA	CG	BB	SO	ShO	SV	ERA
NY	106	45	.702		967	556	259	55	166	.287	.451	72	126	159	.978	87	567	565	12	26	3.31
BOS	89	62	.589	17	890	795	287	57	124	.291	.436	42	180	147	.970	52	543	539	4	20	4.56
CLE	87	67	.565	20.5	797	700	291	79	85	.280	.413	72	180	148	.970	69	602	614	9	13	4.08
CHI	85	69	.552	22.5	755	737	220	56	64	.275	.374	113	167	140	.972	62	454	535	5	21	4.31
DET	81	73	.526	26.5	849	762	277	67	124	.279	.426	88	198	147	.967	64	574	633	6	16	4.29
WAS	65	87	.428	41.5	702	797	249	79	44	.278	.379	94	205	167	.966	72	602	521	4	10	4.60
PHI	55	97	.362	51.5	711	1022	282	55	98	.271	.400	60	210	131	.964	50	579	397	5	12	5.79
STL	43	111	.279	64.5	733	1035	242	50	91	.268	.381	48	199	144	.968	56	739	516	3	3	6.01
LEAGUE TOTAL					6404	6404	2107	498	796	.279	.407	589	1465	1183	.969	512	4660	4320	48	121	4.62

INDIVIDUAL PITCHING

PITCHER	T	W	L	PCT	ERA	SV	G	GS	CG	IP	H	BB	SO	R	ER	ShO	H9	BB9	SO9
Thornton Lee	L	15	11	.577	4.21	3	33	29	15	235	260	70	81	121	110	2	9.96	2.68	3.10
Johnny Rigney	R	15	8	.652	3.70	0	35	29	11	218.2	208	84	119	103	90	2	8.56	3.46	4.90
Eddie Smith	L	9	11	.450	3.67	0	29	22	7	176.2	161	90	67	83	72	1	8.20	4.58	3.41
Ted Lyons	R	14	6	.700	2.76	0	21	21	16	172.2	162	26	65	71	53	0	8.44	1.36	3.39
Jack Knott	R	11	6	.647	4.15	0	25	23	8	149.2	157	41	56	71	69	0	9.44	2.47	3.37
Bill Dietrich	R	7	8	.467	5.22	0	25	19	2	127.2	134	56	43	81	74	0	9.45	3.95	3.03
Clint Brown	R	11	10	.524	3.88	18	61	0	0	118.1	127	27	41	58	51	0	9.66	2.05	3.12
Johnny Marcum	R	3	3	.500	6.00	0	19	6	2	90	125	19	32	66	60	0	12.50	1.90	3.20
John Whitehead	R	0	3	.000	8.16	0	7	4	0	32	60	5	9	30	29	0	16.88	1.41	2.53
Vic Frazier	R	0	1	.000	10.27	0	10	1	0	23.2	45	11	7	27	27	0	17.11	4.18	2.66
Art Herring	R	0	0	–	5.65	0	7	0	0	14.1	13	5	8	9	9	0	8.16	3.14	5.02
Vallie Eaves	R	0	1	.000	4.63	0	2	1	1	11.2	11	8	5	7	6	0	8.49	6.17	3.86
Harry Boyles	R	0	0	–	10.80	0	2	0	0	3.1	4	6	1	4	4	0	10.80	16.20	2.70
Jess Dobernic	R	0	1	.000	13.50	0	4	0	0	3.1	3	6	1	6	5	0	8.10	16.20	2.70
TEAM TOTAL		85	69	.552	4.31	21	280	155	62	1377	1470	454	535	737	659	5	9.61	2.97	3.50

Chicago 1940   Won 82 Lost 72 Pct. .532 4th

MANAGER	W	L	PCT
Jimmy Dykes	82	72	.532

POS	Player	B	G	AB	H	2B	3B	HR	HR%	R	RBI	BB	SO	SB	Pinch Hit AB	H	BA	SA
REGULARS																		
1B	Joe Kuhel	L	155	603	169	28	8	27	4.5	111	94	87	59	12	0	0	.280	.488
2B	Skeeter Webb	R	84	334	79	11	2	1	0.3	33	29	30	33	3	2	0	.237	.290
SS	Luke Appling	R	150	566	197	27	13	0	0.0	96	79	69	35	3	0	0	.348	.442
3B	Bob Kennedy	R	154	606	153	23	3	3	0.5	74	52	42	58	3	0	0	.252	.315
RF	Taffy Wright	L	147	581	196	31	9	5	0.9	79	88	43	25	4	2	1	.337	.448
CF	Mike Kreevich	R	144	582	154	27	10	8	1.4	86	55	34	49	15	0	0	.265	.387
LF	Moose Solters	R	116	428	132	28	3	12	2.8	65	80	27	54	3	9	1	.308	.472
C	Mike Tresh	R	135	480	135	15	5	1	0.2	62	64	49	40	3	0	0	.281	.340
SUBSTITUTES																		
2B	Eric McNair	R	66	251	57	13	1	7	2.8	26	31	12	26	1	0	0	.227	.371
2B	Jackie Hayes	R	18	41	8	0	1	0	0.0	2	1	2	11	0	2	0	.195	.244
2B	Don Kolloway	R	10	40	9	1	0	0	0.0	5	3	0	3	1	0	0	.225	.250
OF	Larry Rosenthal	L	107	276	83	14	5	6	2.2	46	42	64	32	2	11	2	.301	.453
C	Tom Turner	R	37	96	20	1	2	0	0.0	11	6	3	12	1	7	1	.208	.260
C	Ken Silvestri	B	28	24	6	2	0	2	8.3	5	10	4	7	0	24	6	.250	.583
PH	Dave Short	L	4	3	1	0	0	0	0.0	1	0	1	2	0	3	1	.333	.333
PITCHERS																		
P	Johnny Rigney	R	40	93	20	4	0	0	0.0	5	7	3	28	1	0	0	.215	.258
P	Thornton Lee	L	28	84	23	4	0	0	0.0	7	5	4	30	0	0	0	.274	.321
P	Ted Lyons	B	22	75	18	4	0	0	0.0	4	7	2	7	0	0	0	.240	.293
P	Eddie Smith	B	32	69	15	3	1	0	0.0	7	4	6	15	0	0	0	.217	.290
P	Jack Knott	R	25	57	5	1	0	0	0.0	2	4	5	17	0	0	0	.088	.105
P	Bill Dietrich	R	23	50	12	1	0	1	2.0	5	8	7	14	0	0	0	.240	.320
P	Pete Appleton	R	25	17	3	0	0	0	0.0	2	0	1	5	0	0	0	.176	.176
P	Clint Brown	L	37	14	1	0	0	0	0.0	0	1	2	2	0	0	0	.071	.071
P	Vallie Eaves	R	5	5	0	0	0	0	0.0	0	0	0	1	0	0	0	.000	.000
P	Jack Hallett	R	2	5	2	0	0	0	0.0	0	1	0	1	0	0	0	.400	.400
P	Ed Weiland	L	5	5	1	0	0	0	0.0	1	0	0	3	0	0	0	.200	.200
P	Orval Grove	R	3	1	0	0	0	0	0.0	0	0	0	0	0	0	0	.000	.000
TEAM TOTAL				5386	1499	238	63	73	1.4	735	671	497	569	52	60	12	.278	.387

INDIVIDUAL FIELDING

POS	Player	T	G	PO	A	E	DP	TCG	FA
1B	J. Kuhel	L	155	1395	91	18	112	9.7	.988
2B	S. Webb	R	74	143	229	12	44	5.2	.969
	E. McNair	R	65	128	170	13	27	4.8	.958
	J. Hayes	R	15	21	32	1	8	3.6	.981
	D. Kolloway	R	10	19	28	4	7	5.1	.922
SS	L. Appling	R	150	307	436	37	83	5.2	.953
	S. Webb	R	7	9	18	1	2	4.0	.964
3B	B. Kennedy	R	154	178	322	33	25	3.5	.938
	S. Webb	R	1	0	0	0	0	0.0	.000
	E. McNair	R	1	2	1	4	0	7.0	.429

POS	Player	T	G	PO	A	E	DP	TCG	FA
OF	M. Kreevich	R	144	428	12	8	3	3.1	.982
	T. Wright	R	144	278	11	11	2	2.1	.963
	M. Solters	R	107	266	6	8	2	2.6	.971
	L. Rosenthal	L	91	208	4	5	0	2.4	.977
C	M. Tresh	R	135	619	69	12	7	5.2	.983
	T. Turner	R	29	110	13	4	0	4.4	.969
	K. Silvestri	R	1	1	0	0	0	1.0	1.000

On February 29, 1940, Grace Comiskey went before Judge John F. O'Connell to renounce her rights in the will and ask for her dower rights to one-third of the Comiskey estate. Judge O'Connell denied the First National Bank's petition to seek outside bids for the Sox and awarded Grace and her daughter, Dorothy, with their rightful shares of the stock. Peace was formally resolved on March 4, 1941, when Grace was elected team president.

Jackie Hayes fought hard to come back from his painful knee problems. When it appeared that he would make it, he developed a mysterious eye infection during spring training. Diagnosed as a cataract, it was more serious than that. Over a period of several years Hayes went blind.

What a year! Bob Feller pitched the only opening day no-hitter in history when he downed the luckless Edgar Smith on April 16. The Yankees began their season in the cellar, but it didn't help the Sox. They didn't win a game in Comiskey Park until May 20, and they even had one victory taken away from them. On June 20, the Sox won a 1–0 extra-inning battle with New York, but Joe McCarthy protested a catch by outfielder Moose Solters, claiming Solters had trapped the ball with his glove and his hat. League president Will Harridge agreed with McCarthy, ruled it an illegal catch, and ordered a replay for September 18.

By that time, the Sox had sliced an eleven-game deficit to just four, but the makeup game settled matters. The Sox led the Yankees 8–7 when the Bombers scored two in the eighth. With the sun still shining, umpire Harry Geisel called the game due to approaching darkness. It was late in the afternoon, but it was still light enough to complete the game. This and other strange decisions that went against the White Sox may have reflected the umpires' personal feelings about Dykes — a man they loved to hate.

TEAM STATISTICS

	W	L	PCT	GB	R	OR	2B	3B	HR	BA	SA	SB	E	DP	FA	CG	BB	SO	ShO	SV	ERA
DET	90	64	.584		888	717	312	65	134	.286	.442	66	194	116	.968	59	570	752	10	23	4.01
CLE	89	65	.578	1	710	637	287	61	101	.265	.398	53	149	164	.975	72	512	686	13	22	3.63
NY	88	66	.571	2	817	671	243	66	155	.259	.418	59	152	158	.975	76	511	559	10	14	3.89
BOS	82	72	.532	8	872	825	301	80	145	.286	.449	55	173	156	.972	51	625	613	4	16	4.89
CHI	82	72	.532	8	735	672	238	63	73	.278	.387	52	185	125	.969	83	480	574	10	18	3.74
STL	67	87	.435	23	757	882	278	58	118	.263	.401	51	158	179	.974	64	646	439	4	9	5.12
WAS	64	90	.416	26	665	811	266	67	52	.271	.374	94	194	166	.968	74	618	618	6	7	4.59
PHI	54	100	.351	36	703	932	242	53	105	.262	.387	48	238	131	.960	72	534	488	4	12	5.22
LEAGUE TOTAL					6147	6147	2167	513	883	.271	.407	478	1443	1195	.970	551	4496	4729	61	121	4.38

INDIVIDUAL PITCHING

PITCHER	T	W	L	PCT	ERA	SV	G	GS	CG	IP	H	BB	SO	R	ER	ShO	H9	BB9	SO9
Johnny Rigney	R	14	18	.438	3.11	3	39	33	19	280.2	240	90	141	117	97	2	7.70	2.89	4.52
Thornton Lee	L	12	13	.480	3.47	0	28	27	24	228	223	56	87	100	88	1	8.80	2.21	3.43
Eddie Smith	L	14	9	.609	3.21	0	32	28	12	207.1	179	95	119	92	74	0	7.77	4.12	5.17
Ted Lyons	R	12	8	.600	3.24	0	22	22	17	186.1	188	37	72	85	67	4	9.08	1.79	3.48
Jack Knott	R	11	9	.550	4.56	0	25	23	4	158	166	52	44	88	80	2	9.46	2.96	2.51
Bill Dietrich	R	10	6	.625	4.03	0	23	17	6	149.2	154	65	43	78	67	1	9.26	3.91	2.59
Clint Brown	R	4	6	.400	3.68	10	37	0	0	66	75	16	23	30	27	0	10.23	2.18	3.14
Pete Appleton	R	4	0	1.000	5.62	5	25	0	0	57.2	54	28	21	39	36	0	8.43	4.37	3.28
Vallie Eaves	R	0	2	.000	6.75	0	5	3	0	18.2	22	24	11	16	14	0	10.61	11.57	5.30
Ed Weiland	R	0	0	—	8.79	0	5	0	0	14.1	15	7	3	15	14	0	9.42	4.40	1.88
Jack Hallett	R	1	1	.500	6.43	0	2	2	1	14	15	6	9	10	10	0	9.64	3.86	5.79
Orval Grove	R	0	0	—	3.00	0	3	0	0	6	4	4	1	2	2	0	6.00	6.00	1.50
TEAM TOTAL		82	72	.532	3.74	18	246	155	83	1386.2	1335	480	574	672	576	10	8.66	3.12	3.73

Chicago 1941 Won 77 Lost 77 Pct. .500 3rd

MANAGER	W	L	PCT
Jimmy Dykes	77	77	.500

POS	Player	B	G	AB	H	2B	3B	HR	HR%	R	RBI	BB	SO	SB	Pinch Hit AB	H	BA	SA
REGULARS																		
1B	Joe Kuhel	L	153	600	150	39	5	12	2.0	99	63	70	55	20	1	0	.250	.392
2B	Bill Knickerbocker	R	89	343	84	23	2	7	2.0	51	29	41	27	6	1	0	.245	.385
SS	Luke Appling	R	154	592	186	26	8	1	0.2	93	57	82	32	12	0	0	.314	.390
3B	Dario Lodigiani	R	87	322	77	19	2	4	1.2	39	40	31	19	0	0	0	.239	.348
RF	Taffy Wright	L	136	513	165	35	5	10	1.9	71	97	60	27	5	1	0	.322	.468
CF	Mike Kreevich	R	121	436	101	16	8	0	0.0	44	37	35	26	17	7	4	.232	.305
LF	Myril Hoag	R	106	380	97	13	3	1	0.3	30	44	27	29	6	5	2	.255	.313
C	Mike Tresh	R	115	390	98	10	1	0	0.0	38	33	38	27	1	0	0	.251	.282
SUBSTITUTES																		
2B	Don Kolloway	R	71	280	76	8	3	3	1.1	33	24	6	12	11	3	1	.271	.354
3B	Bob Kennedy	R	76	257	53	9	3	1	0.4	16	29	17	23	5	0	0	.206	.276
UT	Skeeter Webb	R	29	84	16	2	0	0	0.0	7	6	3	9	1	3	1	.190	.214
1B	Jake Jones	R	3	11	0	0	0	0	0.0	0	0	0	4	0	0	0	.000	.000
OF	Moose Solters	R	76	251	65	9	4	4	1.6	24	43	18	31	3	12	3	.259	.375
OF	Ben Chapman	R	57	190	43	9	1	2	1.1	26	19	19	14	2	8	2	.226	.316
OF	Larry Rosenthal	L	20	59	14	4	0	0	0.0	9	1	12	5	0	2	0	.237	.305
OF	Dave Philley	B	7	9	2	1	0	0	0.0	4	0	3	3	0	4	0	.222	.333
OF	Dave Short	L	3	8	0	0	0	0	0.0	0	0	2	1	0	1	0	.000	.000
C	Tom Turner	R	38	126	30	5	0	0	0.0	7	8	9	15	2	3	1	.238	.278
C	George Dickey	B	32	55	11	1	0	2	3.6	6	8	5	7	0	14	3	.200	.327
PH	Stan Goletz	L	5	5	3	0	0	0	0.0	0	0	0	2	0	5	3	.600	.600
PH	Chet Hajduk	R	1	1	0	0	0	0	0.0	0	0	0	0	0	1	0	.000	.000
PITCHERS																		
P	Thornton Lee	L	35	114	29	5	0	0	0.0	7	8	4	20	0	0	0	.254	.298
P	Eddie Smith	B	34	88	19	4	0	0	0.0	6	3	8	19	0	0	0	.216	.261
P	Johnny Rigney	R	30	84	17	1	1	0	0.0	8	5	6	27	0	0	0	.202	.238
P	Ted Lyons	B	22	74	20	2	0	0	0.0	8	6	2	6	0	0	0	.270	.297
P	Bill Dietrich	R	19	34	3	1	0	0	0.0	4	1	7	11	0	0	0	.088	.118
P	Buck Ross	R	20	32	7	1	0	0	0.0	2	2	2	5	0	0	0	.219	.250
P	Jack Hallett	R	22	26	4	0	1	0	0.0	2	1	2	6	0	0	0	.154	.231
P	John Humphries	R	14	23	2	2	0	0	0.0	1	3	0	12	0	0	0	.087	.174
P	Joe Haynes	R	8	11	3	0	0	0	0.0	3	0	0	1	0	0	0	.273	.273
P	Pete Appleton	R	13	4	1	0	0	0	0.0	0	0	0	0	0	0	0	.250	.250
P	Orval Grove	R	2	2	0	0	0	0	0.0	0	0	0	1	0	0	0	.000	.000
TEAM TOTAL				5404	1376	245	47	47	0.9	638	567	509	476	91	71	20	.255	.343

INDIVIDUAL FIELDING

POS	Player	T	G	PO	A	E	DP	TCG	FA	POS	Player	T	G	PO	A	E	DP	TCG	FA
1B	J. Kuhel	L	151	**1444**	108	10	113	**10.3**	**.994**	OF	M. Kreevich	R	113	302	7	2	2	2.8	**.994**
	D. Kolloway	R	4	34	4	4	6	10.5	.905		T. Wright	R	134	279	8	8	3	2.2	.973
	J. Jones	R	3	25	0	0	0	8.3	1.000		M. Hoag	R	99	215	6	10	1	2.3	.957
2B	Knickerbocker	R	88	204	221	13	58	5.0	.970		M. Solters	R	63	135	7	5	1	2.3	.966
	D. Kolloway	R	62	118	181	14	23	5.0	.955		B. Chapman	R	49	122	4	1	1	2.6	.992
	S. Webb	R	18	45	49	6	12	5.6	.940		L. Rosenthal	L	18	27	3	2	0	1.8	.938
SS	L. Appling	R	154	294	**473**	42	95	5.3	.948		D. Philley	R	2	0	0	0	0	0.0	.000
	S. Webb	R	5	5	11	3	1	3.8	.842		D. Short	R	2	4	0	1	0	2.5	.800
3B	D. Lodigiani	R	86	120	187	12	22	3.7	.962	C	M. Tresh	R	115	**488**	81	11	12	5.0	.981
	B. Kennedy	R	71	88	153	17	12	3.6	.934		T. Turner	R	35	166	21	4	3	5.5	.979
	S. Webb	R	3	5	4	1	0	3.3	.900		G. Dickey	R	17	56	5	0	1	3.6	1.000

106

The same day the Yankees chose to honor Jimmy Dykes on the occasion of his retirement as an active player, The Streak began. The date was May 15, 1941, and Edgar Smith was on the mound. Joe DiMaggio had one hit, a single. It was the first game of the Yankee Clipper's 56-game hitting streak. And to prove there were no hard feelings, Smith obligingly surrendered the hit that extended the streak to 55 on July 15.

The Sox held second through Memorial Day in a generally weak field; only the Red Sox and Yankees won more games than they lost. Taft Wright continued to shine for the Sox. He hit .322 and had been a major find for Chicago, since they had traded the disappointing Gee Walker to Washington in 1939.

Dykes's umpire-baiting tactics caught up with him on July 7, when he was suspended by Will Harridge for use of "obscene and abusive language" against umpire Steven Basil during a July 4th game. It was the same crew that had officiated the 1940 Sox-Yankees protest fiasco. Dykes had a long memory and a short fuse.

"His tactics (are to delay) our games attempting to bulldoze and browbeat umpires while filing protests which have no basis in fact or justification," Harridge's statement said, in part. Dykes was told that he would be reinstated only if he showed a willingness to reform. The manager said nothing for a week, and the suspension was lifted.

TEAM STATISTICS

	W	L	PCT	GB	R	OR	2B	3B	HR	BA	SA	SB	E	DP	FA	CG	BB	SO	ShO	SV	ERA
NY	101	53	.656		830	631	243	60	151	.269	.419	51	165	196	.973	75	598	589	13	26	3.53
BOS	84	70	.545	17	865	750	304	55	124	.283	.430	67	172	139	.972	70	611	574	8	11	4.19
CHI	77	77	.500	24	638	649	245	47	47	.255	.343	91	180	145	.971	106	521	564	14	4	3.52
CLE	75	79	.487	26	677	668	249	84	103	.256	.393	63	142	158	.976	68	660	617	10	19	3.90
DET	75	79	.487	26	686	743	247	55	81	.263	.375	43	186	129	.969	52	645	697	8	16	4.18
STL	70	84	.455	31	765	823	281	58	91	.266	.390	50	151	156	.975	65	549	454	7	10	4.72
WAS	70	84	.455	31	728	798	257	80	52	.272	.376	79	187	169	.969	69	603	544	8	7	4.35
PHI	64	90	.416	37	713	840	240	69	85	.268	.387	27	200	150	.967	64	557	386	3	18	4.83
LEAGUE TOTAL					5902	5902	2066	508	734	.266	.389	471	1383	1242	.972	569	4744	4425	71	111	4.15

INDIVIDUAL PITCHING

PITCHER	T	W	L	PCT	ERA	SV	G	GS	CG	IP	H	BB	SO	R	ER	ShO	H9	BB9	SO9
Thornton Lee	L	22	11	.667	2.37	1	35	34	30	300.1	258	92	130	98	79	3	7.73	2.76	3.90
Eddie Smith	L	13	17	.433	3.18	1	34	33	21	263.1	243	114	111	107	93	1	8.31	3.90	3.79
Johnny Rigney	R	13	13	.500	3.84	0	30	29	18	237	224	92	119	116	101	3	8.51	3.49	4.52
Ted Lyons	R	12	10	.545	3.70	0	22	22	19	187.1	199	37	63	87	77	2	9.56	1.78	3.03
Bill Dietrich	R	5	8	.385	5.35	0	19	15	4	109.1	114	50	26	73	65	1	9.38	4.12	2.14
Buck Ross	R	3	8	.273	3.16	0	20	11	7	108.1	99	43	30	51	38	0	8.22	3.57	2.49
Jack Hallett	R	5	5	.500	6.03	0	22	6	3	74.2	96	38	25	57	50	0	11.57	4.58	3.01
John Humphries	R	4	2	.667	1.84	1	14	6	4	73.1	63	22	25	18	15	4	7.73	2.70	3.07
Joe Haynes	R	0	0	–	3.86	0	8	0	0	28	30	11	18	13	12	0	9.64	3.54	5.79
Pete Appleton	R	0	3	.000	5.27	1	13	0	0	27.1	27	17	12	21	16	0	8.89	5.60	3.95
Orval Grove	R	0	0	–	10.29	0	2	0	0	7	9	5	5	8	8	0	11.57	6.43	6.43
TEAM TOTAL		77	77	.500	3.52	4	219	156	106	1416	1362	521	564	649	554	14	8.66	3.31	3.58

Won 66 Lost 82 Pct .446 6th

	W	L	PCT
	66	82	.446

	Player	B	G	AB	H	2B	3B	HR	HR%	R	RBI	BB	SO	SB	Pinch Hit AB	Pinch Hit H	BA	SA
REGULARS																		
1B	Joe Kuhel	L	115	413	103	14	4	4	1.0	60	52	60	22	22	3	0	.249	.332
2B	Don Kolloway	R	147	601	164	40	4	3	0.5	72	60	30	39	16	0	0	.273	.368
SS	Luke Appling	R	142	543	142	26	4	3	0.6	78	53	63	23	17	0	0	.262	.341
3B	Bob Kennedy	R	113	412	95	18	5	0	0.0	37	38	22	41	11	1	0	.231	.299
RF	Wally Moses	L	146	577	156	28	4	7	1.2	73	49	74	27	16	1	0	.270	.369
CF	Myril Hoag	R	113	412	99	18	2	2	0.5	47	37	36	21	17	1	1	.240	.308
LF	Taffy Wright	L	85	300	100	13	5	0	0.0	43	47	48	9	1	4	1	.333	.410
C	Mike Tresh	R	72	233	54	8	1	0	0.0	21	15	28	24	2	0	0	.232	.275
SUBSTITUTES																		
3B	Dario Lodigiani	R	59	168	47	7	0	0	0.0	9	15	18	10	3	5	1	.280	.321
2B	Skeeter Webb	R	32	94	16	2	1	0	0.0	5	4	4	13	1	0	0	.170	.213
S3	Leo Wells	R	35	62	12	2	0	1	1.6	8	4	4	5	1	13	5	.194	.274
3B	Jimmy Grant	L	12	36	6	1	1	0	0.0	0	1	5	6	0	1	0	.167	.250
1B	Jake Jones	R	7	20	3	1	0	0	0.0	2	0	2	2	1	2	0	.150	.200
OF	Sammy West	L	49	151	35	5	0	0	0.0	14	25	31	18	2	2	0	.232	.265
OF	Bill Mueller	R	26	85	14	1	0	0	0.0	5	5	12	9	2	1	0	.165	.176
OF	Val Heim	L	13	45	9	1	1	0	0.0	6	7	5	3	1	1	0	.200	.267
OF	Bud Sketchley	L	13	36	7	1	0	0	0.0	1	3	7	4	0	1	0	.194	.222
OF	Thurman Tucker	L	7	24	3	0	1	0	0.0	2	1	0	4	0	2	0	.125	.208
C	Tom Turner	R	56	182	44	9	1	3	1.6	18	21	19	15	0	2	1	.242	.352
C	George Dickey	B	59	116	27	3	0	1	0.9	6	17	9	11	0	31	9	.233	.284
PITCHERS																		
P	John Humphries	R	28	80	18	6	1	0	0.0	9	5	4	33	0	0	0	.225	.325
P	Eddie Smith	B	29	73	9	0	1	0	0.0	2	0	3	15	1	0	0	.123	.151
P	Ted Lyons	B	20	67	16	4	0	0	0.0	10	10	3	7	0	0	0	.239	.299
P	Bill Dietrich	R	26	48	5	1	0	0	0.0	2	5	5	22	0	0	0	.104	.125
P	Buck Ross	R	22	38	6	3	0	0	0.0	2	3	1	10	0	0	0	.158	.237
P	Thornton Lee	L	11	30	6	2	0	0	0.0	0	2	0	10	0	0	0	.200	.267
P	Jake Wade	L	15	29	7	0	0	0	0.0	0	1	1	8	0	0	0	.241	.241
P	Joe Haynes	R	40	28	5	0	0	0	0.0	3	5	2	5	0	0	0	.179	.179
P	Orval Grove	R	12	22	5	0	0	1	4.5	2	1	0	5	0	0	0	.227	.364
P	Johnny Rigney	R	7	19	1	0	0	0	0.0	1	0	1	4	0	0	0	.053	.053
P	Len Perme	L	4	3	1	0	0	0	0.0	0	0	0	0	0	0	0	.333	.333
P	Ed Weiland	L	5	2	0	0	0	0	0.0	0	0	0	0	0	0	0	.000	.000
P	Pete Appleton	R	4	0	0	0	0	0	—	0	0	0	0	0	0	0	—	—
TEAM TOTAL				4949	1215	214	36	25	0.5	538	486	497	425	114	71	18	.246	.318

INDIVIDUAL FIELDING

POS	Player	T	G	PO	A	E	DP	TCG	FA	POS	Player	T	G	PO	A	E	DP	TCG	FA
1B	J. Kuhel	L	112	1085	70	11	94	10.4	.991	OF	W. Moses	L	145	323	14	7	3	2.4	.980
	D. Kolloway	R	33	328	15	5	28	10.5	.986		M. Hoag	R	112	266	12	8	4	2.6	.972
	J. Jones	R	5	47	2	2	2	10.2	.961		T. Wright	R	81	176	6	6	1	2.3	.968
2B	D. Kolloway	R	116	308	345	23	80	5.8	.966		S. West	L	45	112	1	2	1	2.6	.983
	S. Webb	R	29	62	87	6	14	5.3	.961		B. Mueller	R	26	81	7	2	1	3.5	.978
	D. Lodigiani	R	7	15	22	1	5	5.4	.974		B. Kennedy	R	16	31	2	1	0	2.1	.971
SS	L. Appling	R	141	269	418	38	77	5.1	.948		V. Heim	R	12	23	0	1	0	2.0	.958
	L. Wells	R	12	17	37	0	8	4.5	1.000		B. Sketchley	L	12	19	1	1	0	1.8	.952
3B	B. Kennedy	R	96	99	207	14	17	3.3	.956		T. Tucker	R	5	8	1	1	0	2.0	.900
	D. Lodigiani	R	43	40	96	8	4	3.3	.944	C	M. Tresh	R	72	258	37	7	2	4.2	.977
	J. Grant	L	10	15	19	2	3	3.6	.944		T. Turner	R	54	199	35	7	5	4.5	.971
	L. Wells	R	6	6	16	2	2	4.0	.917		G. Dickey	R	29	90	11	9	5	3.8	.918

108

Only 9,879 attended the somber opening day at Comiskey Park. Ushers sold 25-cent war stamps while a battalion of Marines paraded about the grounds. The Sox lost to the Browns, 3–0, and won only a handful of games thereafter. Dykes benched his entire infield on May 6, after the team lost for the 17th time in 21 tries. When that failed to do anything, Dykes threatened to activate the coaching staff. "I am serious about this," the manager said. "If our hitters don't show me something, you are going to see Dykes at third, Muddy Ruel behind the plate, Bing Miller and Mule Haas in the outfield." It never got to that, as the Sox staged a belated August rally that temporarily lifted them to fifth place. By 1942 Ted Lyons pitched only on Sundays. Now 41, he posted a nifty 14–6 record while pacing American League hurlers with a 2.10 ERA. Lyons won his 250th game on June 21 when he beat the Red Sox, 6–5, doubling in the winning run himself. At season's end he volunteered for the Marines.

If Lyons was in the castle, then poor Eddie Smith was in the outhouse. Consider Smith's numbers: by June 20, his record stood at 1–11, and he finished at 7–20, leading the league in defeats. But included in those first 11 losses were three 1–0 shutouts and a pair of 2–1 defeats. In one particularly galling defeat, Dom DiMaggio of the Red Sox doubled to right. Wally Moses lost the ball in the tarpaulin while DiMaggio circled the bases. The fans pointed to the ball, but Moses didn't pay attention. Smith and the White Sox lost, 1–0.

TEAM STATISTICS

	W	L	PCT	GB	R	OR	2B	3B	HR	BA	SA	SB	E	DP	FA	CG	BB	SO	ShO	SV	ERA
NY	103	51	.669		801	507	223	57	108	.269	.394	69	142	190	.976	88	431	558	18	17	2.91
BOS	93	59	.612	9	761	594	244	55	103	.276	.403	68	157	156	.974	84	553	500	11	17	3.44
STL	82	69	.543	19.5	730	637	239	62	98	.259	.385	37	167	143	.972	68	505	488	12	13	3.59
CLE	75	79	.487	28	590	659	223	58	50	.253	.345	69	163	175	.974	61	560	448	12	11	3.59
DET	73	81	.474	30	589	587	217	37	76	.246	.344	39	194	142	.969	65	598	671	12	14	3.13
CHI	66	82	.446	34	538	609	214	36	25	.246	.318	114	173	144	.970	86	473	432	8	8	3.58
WAS	62	89	.411	39.5	653	817	224	49	40	.258	.341	98	222	133	.962	68	558	496	12	11	4.58
PHI	55	99	.357	48	549	801	213	46	33	.249	.325	44	188	124	.969	67	639	546	5	9	4.48
LEAGUE TOTAL					5211	5211	1797	400	533	.257	.357	538	1406	1207	.971	587	4317	4139	90	100	3.66

INDIVIDUAL PITCHING

PITCHER	T	W	L	PCT	ERA	SV	G	GS	CG	IP	H	BB	SO	R	ER	ShO	H9	BB9	SO9
John Humphries	R	12	12	.500	2.68	0	28	28	17	228.1	227	59	71	85	68	2	8.95	2.33	2.80
Eddie Smith	L	7	20	.259	3.98	1	29	28	18	215	223	86	78	112	95	2	9.33	3.60	3.27
Ted Lyons	R	14	6	.700	2.10	0	20	20	20	180.1	167	26	50	52	42	1	8.33	1.30	2.50
Bill Dietrich	R	6	11	.353	4.89	0	26	23	6	160	173	70	39	92	87	0	9.73	3.94	2.19
Buck Ross	R	5	7	.417	5.00	1	22	14	4	113.1	118	39	37	63	63	2	9.37	3.10	2.94
Joe Haynes	R	8	5	.615	2.62	6	40	1	1	103	88	47	35	37	30	0	7.69	4.11	3.06
Jake Wade	L	5	5	.500	4.10	0	15	10	3	85.2	84	56	32	45	39	0	8.82	5.88	3.36
Thornton Lee	L	2	6	.250	3.32	0	11	8	6	76	82	31	25	38	28	1	9.71	3.67	2.96
Orval Grove	R	4	6	.400	5.16	0	12	8	4	66.1	77	33	21	47	38	0	10.45	4.48	2.85
Johnny Rigney	R	3	3	.500	3.20	0	7	7	6	59	40	16	34	23	21	0	6.10	2.44	5.19
Len Perme	L	0	1	.000	1.38	0	4	1	1	13	5	4	4	2	2	0	3.46	2.77	2.77
Ed Weiland	R	0	0	–	7.45	0	5	0	0	9.2	18	3	4	11	8	0	16.76	2.79	3.72
Pete Appleton	R	0	0	–	3.86	0	4	0	0	4.2	2	3	2	2	2	0	3.86	5.79	3.86
TEAM TOTAL		66	82	.446	3.58	8	223	148	86	1314.1	1304	473	432	609	523	8	8.93	3.24	2.96

Chicago 1943   Won 82   Lost 72   Pct. .532   4th

MANAGER	W	L	PCT
Jimmy Dykes	82	72	.532

POS	Player	B	G	AB	H	2B	3B	HR	HR%	R	RBI	BB	SO	SB	Pinch Hit AB	H	BA	SA
REGULARS																		
1B	Joe Kuhel	L	153	531	113	21	1	5	0.9	55	46	76	45	14	0	0	.213	.284
2B	Don Kolloway	R	85	348	75	14	4	1	0.3	29	33	9	30	11	0	0	.216	.287
SS	Luke Appling	R	155	585	192	33	2	3	0.5	63	80	90	29	27	0	0	**.328**	.407
3B	Ralph Hodgin	L	117	407	128	22	8	1	0.2	52	50	20	24	3	20	8	.314	.415
RF	Wally Moses	L	150	599	147	22	12	3	0.5	82	48	55	47	56	2	0	.245	.337
CF	Thurman Tucker	L	139	528	124	15	6	3	0.6	81	39	79	72	29	6	1	.235	.303
LF	Guy Curtright	R	138	488	142	20	7	3	0.6	67	48	69	60	13	9	2	.291	.379
C	Mike Tresh	R	86	279	60	3	0	0	0.0	20	20	37	20	2	0	0	.215	.226
SUBSTITUTES																		
2B	Skeeter Webb	R	58	213	50	5	2	0	0.0	15	22	6	19	5	3	0	.235	.277
3B	Jimmy Grant	L	58	197	51	9	2	4	2.0	23	22	18	34	4	7	1	.259	.386
32	Dick Culler	R	53	148	32	5	1	0	0.0	9	11	16	11	4	0	0	.216	.264
3B	Tony Cuccinello	R	34	103	28	5	0	2	1.9	5	11	13	13	3	3	0	.272	.379
1B	Don Hanski	L	9	21	5	1	0	0	0.0	1	2	0	5	0	3	0	.238	.286
3B	Cass Michaels	R	2	7	0	0	0	0	0.0	0	0	0	0	0	0	0	.000	.000
OF	Moose Solters	R	42	97	15	0	0	1	1.0	6	8	7	5	0	19	2	.155	.186
C	Tom Turner	R	51	154	37	7	1	2	1.3	16	11	13	21	1	2	0	.240	.338
C	Vince Castino	R	33	101	23	1	0	2	2.0	14	16	12	11	0	3	0	.228	.297
PH	Frank Kalin	R	4	4	0	0	0	0	0.0	0	0	0	0	0	4	0	.000	.000
PITCHERS																		
P	John Humphries	R	28	69	20	6	0	0	0.0	6	5	3	25	1	0	0	.290	.377
P	Eddie Smith	B	25	69	11	1	0	1	1.4	4	8	2	9	0	0	0	.159	.217
P	Orval Grove	R	32	66	12	0	0	0	0.0	9	7	11	22	0	0	0	.182	.182
P	Bill Dietrich	R	26	56	8	1	0	1	1.8	7	6	5	22	0	0	0	.143	.214
P	Buck Ross	R	21	46	4	1	0	1	2.2	1	4	5	15	0	0	0	.087	.174
P	Thornton Lee	L	19	42	3	0	0	0	0.0	1	3	0	8	0	0	0	.071	.071
P	Joe Haynes	R	35	34	9	0	0	0	0.0	5	4	3	9	0	0	0	.265	.265
P	Jake Wade	L	21	27	4	1	0	0	0.0	2	3	3	9	0	0	0	.148	.185
P	Gordon Maltzberger	R	37	25	3	0	0	0	0.0	0	1	6	14	0	0	0	.120	.120
P	Bill Swift	R	18	10	1	0	0	0	0.0	0	0	3	3	0	0	0	.100	.100
P	Floyd Speer	R	1	0	0	0	0	0	–	0	0	0	0	0	0	0	–	–
TEAM TOTAL				5254	1297	193	46	33	0.6	573	508	561	582	173	81	14	.247	.320

INDIVIDUAL FIELDING

POS	Player	T	G	PO	A	E	DP	TCG	FA	POS	Player	T	G	PO	A	E	DP	TCG	FA
1B	J. Kuhel	L	153	1471	106	8	143	10.4	.995	OF	T. Tucker	R	132	**399**	14	5	1	**3.2**	.988
	D. Hanski	L	5	37	3	2	5	8.4	.952		W. Moses	L	148	370	12	8	2	2.6	.979
2B	D. Kolloway	R	85	246	240	16	71	5.9	.968		G. Curtright	R	128	301	7	9	1	2.5	.972
	S. Webb	R	54	118	169	14	35	5.6	.953		R. Hodgin	R	42	87	2	0	0	2.1	1.000
	D. Culler	R	19	36	71	4	16	5.8	.964		M. Solters	R	21	30	2	2	0	1.6	.941
SS	L. Appling	R	155	300	**500**	36	115	5.4	.957	C	M. Tresh	R	85	321	62	7	4	4.6	.982
	D. Culler	R	3	4	5	0	0	3.0	1.000		T. Turner	R	49	186	34	5	5	4.6	.978
3B	J. Grant	R	51	43	115	19	11	3.5	.893		V. Castino	R	30	90	9	3	3	3.4	.971
	R. Hodgin	R	56	34	120	9	7	2.9	.945										
	T. Cuccinello	R	30	33	50	3	5	2.9	.965										
	D. Culler	R	26	31	45	4	8	3.1	.950										
	C. Michaels	R	2	1	1	0	0	1.0	1.000										

Wartime travel restrictions forced the Sox to conduct their spring training in French Lick, Indiana. When the ballfields at West Baden were flooded, Dykes had his men work out in the hotel ballroom. Imagine the sight of uniformed players doing calisthenics to the sound of big band music in the ballroom! For effect, dirt was strewn across the tiles.

Bone chips in Thornton Lee's arm limited his playing time, but young Orval Grove picked up the slack. The sophomore pitcher won his first nine decisions, a team record shared with Lefty Williams and now LaMarr Hoyt. Included in this skein was a near no-hitter against the Yankees on July 8. Joe Gordon ended the suspense with a ninth-inning, two-out double.

Guy Curtright from St. Paul was one of those wartime players who might not otherwise have made it up to the majors. But he made a mark for himself when he reeled off a 26-game hitting streak that ended on July 2. In Sox history, only Appling's 27-game streak in 1936 was better.

There were no lengthy streaks for Luke in 1943, but his .328 average was good enough for his second batting title. Led by speedsters Wally Moses (56 stolen bases), Thurman Tucker (29), and Appling (27), the Sox overcame an eighth-place start to finish in fourth. The writers called them the "Wild West Boys," an early forerunner of the brand of baseball that would later thrill the nation.

TEAM STATISTICS

	W	L	PCT	GB	R	OR	2B	3B	HR	BA	SA	SB	E	DP	FA	CG	BB	SO	ShO	SV	ERA
NY	98	56	.636		669	542	218	59	100	.256	.376	46	160	166	.974	83	489	653	14	13	2.93
WAS	84	69	.549	13.5	666	595	245	50	47	.254	.347	142	179	145	.971	61	540	495	16	21	3.18
CLE	82	71	.536	15.5	600	577	246	45	55	.255	.350	47	157	183	.975	64	606	585	14	20	3.15
CHI	82	72	.532	16	573	594	193	46	33	.247	.320	173	166	167	.973	70	501	476	12	19	3.20
DET	78	76	.506	20	632	560	200	47	77	.261	.359	40	177	130	.971	67	549	706	18	20	3.00
STL	72	80	.474	25	596	604	229	36	78	.245	.349	37	152	127	.975	64	488	572	10	14	3.41
BOS	68	84	.447	29	563	607	223	42	57	.244	.332	86	153	179	.976	62	615	513	13	16	3.45
PHI	49	105	.318	49	497	717	174	44	26	.232	.297	55	162	148	.973	73	536	503	5	13	4.05
LEAGUE TOTAL					4796	4796	1728	369	473	.249	.341	626	1306	1245	.973	544	4324	4503	102	136	3.30

INDIVIDUAL PITCHING

PITCHER	T	W	L	PCT	ERA	SV	G	GS	CG	IP	H	BB	SO	R	ER	ShO	H9	BB9	SO9
Orval Grove	R	15	9	.625	2.75	2	32	25	18	216.1	192	72	76	84	66	3	7.99	3.00	3.16
John Humphries	R	11	11	.500	3.30	0	28	27	8	188.1	198	54	51	86	69	2	9.46	2.58	2.44
Eddie Smith	L	11	11	.500	3.69	0	25	25	14	187.2	197	76	66	85	77	2	9.45	3.64	3.17
Bill Dietrich	R	12	10	.545	2.80	0	26	26	12	186.2	180	53	52	72	58	2	8.68	2.56	2.51
Buck Ross	R	11	7	.611	3.19	0	21	21	7	149.1	140	56	41	61	53	1	8.44	3.38	2.47
Thornton Lee	L	5	9	.357	4.18	0	19	19	7	127	129	50	35	66	59	1	9.14	3.54	2.48
Joe Haynes	R	7	2	.778	2.96	3	35	2	1	109.1	114	32	37	51	36	0	9.38	2.63	3.05
Gordon Maltzberger	R	7	4	.636	2.46	14	37	0	0	98.2	86	24	48	29	27	0	7.84	2.19	4.38
Jake Wade	L	3	7	.300	3.01	0	21	9	3	83.2	66	54	41	34	28	1	7.10	5.81	4.41
Bill Swift	R	0	2	.000	4.21	0	18	1	0	51.1	48	27	28	25	24	0	8.42	4.73	4.91
Don Hanski	L	0	0	—	0.00	0	1	0	0	1	1	1	0	0	0	0	9.00	9.00	0.00
Floyd Speer	R	0	0	—	9.00	0	1	0	0	1	1	2	1	1	1	0	9.00	18.00	9.00
TEAM TOTAL		82	72	.532	3.20	19	264	155	70	1400.1	1352	501	476	594	498	12	8.69	3.22	3.06

Chicago 1944　　Won 71　Lost 83　Pct. .461　7th

MANAGER	W	L	PCT
Jimmy Dykes	71	83	.461

POS	Player	B	G	AB	H	2B	3B	HR	HR%	R	RBI	BB	SO	SB	Pinch AB	Hit H	BA	SA
REGULARS																		
1B	Hal Trosky	L	135	497	120	32	2	10	2.0	55	70	62	30	3	4	1	.241	.374
2B	Roy Schalk	R	146	587	129	14	4	1	0.2	47	44	45	52	5	0	0	.220	.262
SS	Skeeter Webb	R	139	513	108	19	6	0	0.0	44	30	20	39	7	0	0	.211	.271
3B	Ralph Hodgin	L	121	465	137	25	7	1	0.2	56	51	21	14	3	6	2	.295	.385
RF	Wally Moses	L	136	535	150	26	9	3	0.6	82	34	52	22	21	1	0	.280	.379
CF	Thurman Tucker	L	124	446	128	15	6	2	0.4	59	46	57	40	13	1	0	.287	.361
LF	Eddie Carnett	L	126	457	126	18	8	1	0.2	51	60	26	35	5	10	1	.276	.357
C	Mike Tresh	R	93	312	81	8	1	0	0.0	22	25	37	15	0	0	0	.260	.292
SUBSTITUTES																		
3B	Dick Clarke	R	63	169	44	10	1	0	0.0	14	27	22	6	0	15	1	.260	.331
3B	Tony Cuccinello	R	38	130	34	3	0	0	0.0	5	17	8	16	0	2	0	.262	.285
SS	Cass Michaels	R	27	68	12	4	1	0	0.0	4	5	2	5	0	1	0	.176	.265
2B	Bill Metzig	R	5	16	2	0	0	0	0.0	1	1	1	4	0	0	0	.125	.125
OF	Guy Curtright	R	72	198	50	8	2	2	1.0	22	23	23	21	4	22	6	.253	.343
OF	Johnny Dickshot	L	62	162	41	8	5	0	0.0	18	15	13	10	2	20	5	.253	.364
OF	Myril Hoag	R	17	48	11	1	0	0	0.0	5	4	10	1	1	3	0	.229	.250
C	Tom Turner	R	36	113	26	6	0	2	1.8	9	13	5	16	0	0	0	.230	.336
C	Vince Castino	R	29	78	18	5	0	0	0.0	8	3	10	13	0	2	1	.231	.295
C	Tom Jordan	R	14	45	12	1	1	0	0.0	2	3	1	0	0	0	0	.267	.333
PITCHERS																		
P	Ed Lopat	L	30	81	25	1	1	0	0.0	8	6	5	5	0	2	0	.309	.346
P	Bill Dietrich	R	36	77	9	0	0	1	1.3	8	4	5	33	0	0	0	.117	.156
P	Orval Grove	R	34	77	8	1	1	0	0.0	4	4	5	25	0	0	0	.104	.143
P	John Humphries	R	30	53	10	2	0	0	0.0	5	2	3	16	0	0	0	.189	.226
P	Joe Haynes	R	33	50	10	3	0	0	0.0	6	2	3	5	2	0	0	.200	.260
P	Thornton Lee	L	15	42	4	0	0	0	0.0	2	2	0	8	0	0	0	.095	.095
P	Buck Ross	R	20	26	2	0	0	0	0.0	1	0	0	4	0	0	0	.077	.077
P	Jake Wade	L	19	24	7	0	0	0	0.0	3	0	1	3	0	0	0	.292	.292
P	Gordon Maltzberger	R	46	22	3	0	0	0	0.0	2	3	2	10	0	0	0	.136	.136
P	Don Hanski	L	2	1	0	0	0	0	0.0	0	0	0	0	0	0	0	.000	.000
P	Floyd Speer	R	2	0	0	0	0	0	—	0	0	0	0	0	0	0	—	—
TEAM TOTAL				5292	1307	210	55	23	0.4	543	494	439	448	66	89	17	.247	.320

INDIVIDUAL FIELDING

POS	Player	T	G	PO	A	E	DP	TCG	FA
1B	H. Trosky	R	130	1310	57	9	122	10.6	.993
	E. Carnett	L	25	226	9	1	16	9.4	.996
2B	R. Schalk	R	142	360	391	28	109	5.5	.964
	S. Webb	R	5	19	19	0	7	7.6	1.000
	B. Metzig	R	5	13	15	0	2	5.6	1.000
	T. Cuccinello	R	6	11	10	1	2	3.7	.955
SS	S. Webb	R	135	202	461	39	81	5.2	.944
	C. Michaels	R	21	36	70	8	12	5.4	.930
	R. Schalk	R	5	6	22	1	3	5.8	.966
3B	R. Hodgin	R	82	77	215	18	22	3.8	.942
	D. Clarke	R	45	36	107	9	6	3.4	.941
	T. Cuccinello	R	30	31	63	4	5	3.3	.959
	C. Michaels	R	3	1	1	0	0	0.7	1.000

POS	Player	T	G	PO	A	E	DP	TCG	FA
OF	T. Tucker	R	120	414	12	4	2	3.6	.991
	W. Moses	L	134	267	7	7	2	2.1	.975
	E. Carnett	L	88	199	7	11	0	2.5	.949
	G. Curtright	R	51	101	8	6	3	2.3	.948
	R. Hodgin	R	33	93	1	0	0	2.8	1.000
	J. Dickshot	R	40	72	3	2	1	1.9	.974
	M. Hoag	R	14	29	2	1*	1	2.3	.969
C	M. Tresh	R	93	370	47	8	5	4.6	.981
	T. Turner	R	36	121	15	6	3	3.9	.958
	V. Castino	R	26	85	16	1	4	3.9	.990
	T. Jordan	R	14	48	6	3	0	4.1	.947

Chicago 1944

The war presented more than the usual amounts of hardship for the Sox. The Pale Hose had to share spring training facilities with the Cubs, and there just wasn't enough room in French Lick for both Jimmy Dykes and Jim Gallagher of the Cubs. The Sox frequently used the Cubs' diamond rather than travel several miles to West Baden. "Gallagher better not get too fresh with me," Dykes snapped. "I'm getting the lads in shape to tender the usual drubbings of the Cubs." Too bad the City Series had been discontinued two years earlier.

Given the uncertain times, the writers viewed the Sox' chances with some optimism. Who could foresee the St. Louis Browns winning a pennant? But the Sox did more than their share to help make the Browns' dream a reality. They lost the first four meetings to St. Louis in April, and in September the Sox batted out of order against the Browns, thereby nullifying a run and assuring a St. Louis victory. Eddie Carnett and Guy Curtright had listened to the public address announcer's lineup and not the revised one turned in by coach Mule Haas. Was Dykes asleep at the switch? It was the second time in three years the White Sox had been guilty of baseball's worst *faux pas*. No doubt the ten years of topsy-turvy baseball Sox style were beginning to take their toll on Dykes. He had watched his contending team taken apart by injuries, financial troubles, and, worst of all, World War II.

TEAM STATISTICS

	W	L	PCT	GB	R	OR	2B	3B	HR	BA	SA	SB	E	DP	FA	CG	BB	SO	ShO	SV	ERA
STL	89	65	.578		684	587	223	45	72	.252	.352	44	171	142	.972	71	469	581	16	17	3.17
DET	88	66	.571	1	658	581	220	44	60	.263	.354	61	190	184	.970	87	452	568	20	8	3.09
NY	83	71	.539	6	674	617	216	74	96	.264	.387	91	156	170	.974	78	532	529	9	13	3.39
BOS	77	77	.500	12	739	676	277	56	69	.270	.380	60	171	154	.972	58	592	524	5	17	3.82
CLE	72	82	.468	17	643	677	270	50	70	.266	.372	48	165	192	.974	48	621	524	7	18	3.65
PHI	72	82	.468	17	525	594	169	47	36	.257	.327	42	176	127	.971	72	390	534	9	14	3.26
CHI	71	83	.461	18	543	662	210	55	23	.247	.320	66	183	154	.970	64	420	481	5	17	3.58
WAS	64	90	.416	25	592	664	186	42	33	.261	.330	127	218	156	.964	83	475	503	12	11	3.49
LEAGUE TOTAL					5058	5058	1771	413	459	.260	.353	539	1430	1279	.971	561	3951	4244	83	115	3.43

INDIVIDUAL PITCHING

PITCHER	T	W	L	PCT	ERA	SV	G	GS	CG	IP	H	BB	SO	R	ER	ShO	H9	BB9	SO9
Bill Dietrich	R	16	17	.485	3.62	0	36	36	15	246	269	68	70	132	99	2	9.84	2.49	2.56
Orval Grove	R	14	15	.483	3.72	0	34	33	11	234.2	237	71	105	112	97	2	9.09	2.72	4.03
Ed Lopat	L	11	10	.524	3.26	0	27	25	13	210	217	59	75	96	76	1	9.30	2.53	3.21
John Humphries	R	8	10	.444	3.67	1	30	20	8	169	170	57	42	75	69	0	9.05	3.04	2.24
Joe Haynes	R	5	6	.455	2.57	2	33	12	8	154.1	148	43	44	55	44	0	8.63	2.51	2.57
Thornton Lee	L	3	9	.250	3.02	0	15	14	6	113.1	105	25	39	51	38	0	8.34	1.99	3.10
Gordon Maltzberger	R	10	5	.667	2.96	12	46	0	0	91.1	81	19	49	31	30	0	7.98	1.87	4.83
Buck Ross	R	2	7	.222	5.18	0	20	9	2	90.1	97	35	20	56	52	0	9.66	3.49	1.99
Jake Wade	L	2	4	.333	4.82	2	19	5	1	74.2	75	41	35	46	40	0	9.04	4.94	4.22
Don Hanski	L	0	0	—	12.00	0	2	0	0	3	5	2	0	4	4	0	15.00	6.00	0.00
Eddie Carnett	L	0	0	—	9.00	0	2	0	0	2	3	0	1	2	2	0	13.50	0.00	4.50
Floyd Speer	R	0	0	—	9.00	0	2	0	0	2	4	0	1	2	2	0	18.00	0.00	4.50
TEAM TOTAL		71	83	.461	3.58	17	266	154	64	1390.2	1411	420	481	662	553	5	9.13	2.72	3.11

Chicago 1945 Won 71 Lost 78 Pct .477 6th

MANAGER	W	L	PCT
Jimmy Dykes	71	78	.477

POS	Player	B	G	AB	H	2B	3B	HR	HR%	R	RBI	BB	SO	SB	Pinch Hit AB	Pinch Hit H	BA	SA
REGULARS																		
1B	Kerby Farrell	L	103	396	102	11	3	0	0.0	44	34	24	18	4	6	3	.258	.301
2B	Roy Schalk	R	133	513	127	23	1	1	0.2	50	65	32	41	3	0	0	.248	.302
SS	Cass Michaels	R	129	445	109	8	5	2	0.4	47	54	37	28	8	2	0	.245	.299
3B	Tony Cuccinello	R	118	402	124	25	3	2	0.5	50	49	45	19	6	6	1	.308	.400
RF	Wally Moses	L	140	569	168	35	15	2	0.4	79	50	69	33	11	1	0	.295	.420
CF	Oris Hockett	L	106	417	122	23	4	2	0.5	46	55	27	30	10	0	0	.293	.381
LF	Johnny Dickshot	R	130	486	147	19	10	4	0.8	74	58	48	41	18	5	1	.302	.407
C	Mike Tresh	R	150	458	114	11	0	0	0.0	50	47	65	37	6	0	0	.249	.273
SUBSTITUTES																		
1B	Bill Nagel	R	67	220	46	10	3	3	1.4	21	27	15	41	3	9	0	.209	.323
3B	Floyd Baker	L	82	208	52	8	0	0	0.0	22	19	23	12	3	16	1	.250	.288
S2	Danny Reynolds	R	29	72	12	2	1	0	0.0	6	4	3	8	1	4	0	.167	.222
SS	Luke Appling	R	18	58	21	2	2	1	1.7	12	10	12	7	1	1	0	.362	.517
3B	Joe Orengo	R	17	15	1	0	0	0	0.0	5	1	3	2	0	5	0	.067	.067
OF	Guy Curtright	R	98	324	91	15	2	4	1.2	51	32	39	29	3	13	5	.281	.407
OF	Bill Mueller	R	13	9	0	0	0	0	0.0	3	0	2	1	1	1	0	.000	.000
C	Vince Castino	R	26	37	8	1	0	0	0.0	2	4	3	7	0	1	0	.216	.243
PITCHERS																		
P	Ed Lopat	L	32	82	24	4	0	1	1.2	13	13	2	9	0	5	1	.293	.378
P	Thornton Lee	L	29	78	14	1	0	0	0.0	6	6	5	15	0	0	0	.179	.192
P	Orval Grove	R	33	71	7	1	0	0	0.0	4	4	4	23	0	0	0	.099	.113
P	John Humphries	R	22	54	8	0	0	0	0.0	1	2	2	19	0	0	0	.148	.148
P	Joe Haynes	R	15	40	7	0	0	0	0.0	0	2	0	2	0	0	0	.175	.175
P	Earl Caldwell	R	27	37	8	1	0	0	0.0	4	4	0	8	0	0	0	.216	.243
P	Bill Dietrich	R	18	36	6	0	1	0	0.0	2	0	5	22	0	0	0	.167	.222
P	Frank Papish	R	19	26	6	1	0	0	0.0	3	1	2	7	0	0	0	.231	.269
P	Johnny Johnson	L	29	14	4	2	0	0	0.0	1	2	3	6	0	0	0	.286	.429
P	Buck Ross	R	13	11	2	0	0	0	0.0	0	1	0	2	0	0	0	.182	.182
P	Clay Touchstone	R	6	1	0	0	0	0	0.0	0	0	0	0	0	0	0	.000	.000
TEAM TOTAL				5079	1330	203	55	22	0.4	596	544	470	467	78	75	12	.262	.336

INDIVIDUAL FIELDING

POS	Player	T	G	PO	A	E	DP	TCG	FA
1B	K. Farrell	L	97	913	74	11	76	10.3	.989
	B. Nagel	R	57	503	34	9	42	9.6	.984
2B	R. Schalk	R	133	380	389	18	90	5.9	.977
	J. Orengo	R	1	0	0	0	0	0.0	.000
	D. Reynolds	R	11	20	27	1	7	4.4	.979
	F. Baker	R	11	15	28	1	4	4.0	.977
	C. Michaels	R	1	1	2	0	0	3.0	1.000
SS	C. Michaels	R	126	259	426	47	74	5.8	.936
	L. Appling	R	17	37	56	7	7	5.9	.930
	D. Reynolds	R	14	19	35	3	6	4.1	.947
3B	T. Cuccinello	R	112	73	221	20	22	2.8	.936
	F. Baker	R	58	36	99	4	6	2.4	.971
	J. Orengo	R	7	5	7	1	0	1.9	.923
	B. Nagel	R	1	0	1	0	0	1.0	1.000

POS	Player	T	G	PO	A	E	DP	TCG	FA
OF	W. Moses	L	139	329	12	8	1	2.5	.977
	O. Hockett	R	106	273	7	5	3	2.7	.982
	J. Dickshot	R	124	253	13	8	3	2.2	.971
	G. Curtright	R	84	196	8	3	0	2.5	.986
	B. Mueller	R	7	7	0	2	0	1.3	.778
C	M. Tresh	R	150	575	102	11	7	4.6	.984
	V. Castino	R	25	32	7	2	1	1.6	.951

Tony Cuccinello was another Dykes reclamation project. Since coming to the Sox in a 1943 waiver deal, he had taken over third base, but after missing the batting title by one point in 1945 Cuccinello was released. After all, the boys were coming home. Only Floyd Baker would survive the post-war cuts.

The Sox got off to a hot start; they were in first place on May 21 and still over .500 in late August. Thornton Lee overcame four years of arm miseries to become a big winner again, but 1945 is best remembered for two unrelated occurrences. First, Harry Grabiner announced his resignation as vice president after forty years with the Sox. Harry had started as a soda-pop boy. Ever optimistic, ever faithful, Grabiner said he quit due to poor health. Those on the inside suspected a falling out between the family and the man they always viewed as an outsider. Les O'Connor, a former legal aide to Judge Landis, stepped in.

Then there was the fight. The Sox employed a 23-year-old batting practice pitcher named Karl Scheel, who also doubled as a bench jockey. On June 20 Browns pitcher George Caster sailed a ball in Scheel's direction. A group of angry Brownies then stormed the Sox dugout and beat Scheel to a pulp. Calling it the most brutal thing he had seen in baseball, Dykes demanded justice. Commissioner Chandler fined the Browns' manager Luke Sewell $250, and Caster, Sid Jakucki, and Ellis Clary $100 each. Brutal? Perhaps, but bench jockeys were once a common part of the baseball scene. They were there when players still cared and had a firm identity with the team they played for.

TEAM STATISTICS

	W	L	PCT	GB	R	OR	2B	3B	HR	BA	SA	SB	E	DP	FA	CG	BB	SO	ShO	SV	ERA
DET	88	65	.575		633	565	**227**	47	77	.256	.361	60	158	173	.975	78	538	**588**	**19**	**16**	2.99
WAS	87	67	.565	1.5	622	562	197	**63**	27	.258	.334	**110**	183	124	.970	82	**440**	550	**19**	11	**2.92**
STL	81	70	.536	6	597	548	215	37	63	.249	.341	25	143	123	.976	**91**	506	570	10	8	3.14
NY	81	71	.533	6.5	**676**	606	189	61	**93**	.259	**.373**	64	175	170	.971	78	485	474	9	14	3.45
CLE	73	72	.503	11	557	548	216	48	65	.255	.359	19	**126**	149	**.977**	76	501	497	14	12	3.31
CHI	71	78	.477	15	596	633	204	55	22	**.262**	.337	78	180	139	.970	84	448	486	13	13	3.69
BOS	71	83	.461	17.5	599	674	225	44	50	.260	.346	72	169	**198**	.973	71	656	490	15	13	3.80
PHI	52	98	.347	34.5	494	638	201	37	33	.245	.316	25	168	160	.973	65	571	531	11	8	3.62
LEAGUE TOTAL					4774	4774	1674	392	430	.255	.346	453	1302	1236	.973	625	4145	4186	110	95	3.36

INDIVIDUAL PITCHING

PITCHER	T	W	L	PCT	ERA	SV	G	GS	CG	IP	H	BB	SO	R	ER	ShO	H9	BB9	SO9
Thornton Lee	L	15	12	.556	2.44	0	29	28	19	228.1	208	76	108	81	62	1	8.20	3.00	4.26
Orval Grove	R	14	12	.538	3.44	1	33	30	16	217	233	68	54	100	83	4	9.66	2.82	2.24
Ed Lopat	L	10	13	.435	4.11	1	26	24	17	199.1	226	56	74	101	91	1	10.20	2.53	3.34
John Humphries	R	6	14	.300	4.24	1	22	21	10	153	172	48	33	83	72	1	10.12	2.82	1.94
Bill Dietrich	R	7	10	.412	4.19	0	18	16	6	122.1	136	36	43	61	57	4	10.01	2.65	3.16
Earl Caldwell	R	6	7	.462	3.59	4	27	11	5	105.1	108	37	45	50	42	1	9.23	3.16	3.84
Joe Haynes	R	5	5	.500	3.55	1	14	13	8	104	92	29	34	44	41	1	7.96	2.51	2.94
Frank Papish	L	4	4	.500	3.74	1	19	5	3	84.1	75	40	45	36	35	0	8.00	4.27	4.80
Johnny Johnson	L	3	0	1.000	4.26	4	29	0	0	69.2	85	35	38	39	33	0	10.98	4.52	4.91
Buck Ross	R	1	1	.500	5.79	0	13	2	0	37.1	51	17	8	28	24	0	12.29	4.10	1.93
Clay Touchstone	R	0	0	–	5.40	0	6	0	0	10	14	6	4	10	6	0	12.60	5.40	3.60
TEAM TOTAL		71	78	.477	3.69	13	236	150	84	1330.2	1400	448	486	633	546	13	9.47	3.03	3.29

Chicago 1946　　　Won 74　Lost 80　Pct. .481　5th　　　116

MANAGER

	W	L	PCT
Jimmy Dykes	10	20	.333
Ted Lyons	64	60	.516

POS	Player	B	G	AB	H	2B	3B	HR	HR%	R	RBI	BB	SO	SB	Pinch Hit AB	Pinch Hit H	BA	SA
REGULARS																		
1B	Hal Trosky	B	88	299	76	12	3	2	0.7	22	31	34	37	4	6	1	.254	.334
2B	Don Kolloway	R	123	482	135	23	4	3	0.6	45	53	9	29	14	1	0	.280	.363
SS	Luke Appling	R	149	582	180	27	5	1	0.2	59	55	71	41	6	0	0	.309	.378
3B	Dario Lodigiani	R	44	155	38	8	0	0	0.0	12	13	16	14	4	0	0	.245	.297
RF	Taffy Wright	L	115	422	116	19	4	7	1.7	46	52	42	17	10	7	2	.275	.389
CF	Thurman Tucker	L	121	438	126	20	3	1	0.2	62	36	54	45	9	8	3	.288	.354
LF	Bob Kennedy	R	113	411	106	13	5	5	1.2	43	34	24	42	6	5	2	.258	.350
C	Mike Tresh	R	80	217	47	5	2	0	0.0	28	21	36	24	0	1	0	.217	.258
SUBSTITUTES																		
23	Cass Michaels	R	91	291	75	8	0	1	0.3	37	22	29	36	9	3	0	.258	.296
1B	Joe Kuhel	L	64	238	65	9	3	4	1.7	24	20	21	24	4	1	0	.273	.387
3B	Leo Wells	R	45	127	24	4	1	1	0.8	11	11	12	34	3	2	0	.189	.260
1B	Jake Jones	R	24	79	21	5	1	3	3.8	10	13	2	13	0	4	0	.266	.468
3B	Floyd Baker	L	9	24	6	1	0	0	0.0	2	3	2	3	0	3	0	.250	.292
UT	Frank Whitman	R	17	16	1	0	0	0	0.0	7	1	2	6	0	0	0	.063	.063
OF	Ralph Hodgin	L	87	258	65	10	1	0	0.0	32	25	19	6	0	29	9	.252	.298
OF	Whitey Platt	R	84	247	62	8	5	3	1.2	28	32	17	34	1	24	6	.251	.360
OF	Wally Moses	L	56	168	46	9	1	4	2.4	20	16	17	20	2	20	4	.274	.411
OF	Dave Philley	B	17	68	24	2	3	0	0.0	10	17	4	4	5	0	0	.353	.471
OF	Guy Curtright	R	23	55	11	2	0	0	0.0	7	5	11	14	0	4	2	.200	.236
OF	Joe Smaza	L	2	5	1	0	0	0	0.0	2	0	0	0	0	1	0	.200	.200
C	Frankie Hayes	R	53	179	38	6	0	2	1.1	15	16	29	33	1	1	0	.212	.279
C	George Dickey	B	37	78	15	1	0	0	0.0	8	1	12	13	0	8	3	.192	.205
C	Ed Fernandes	B	14	32	8	2	0	0	0.0	4	4	8	7	0	2	0	.250	.313
C	Tom Jordan	R	10	15	4	2	1	0	0.0	0	1	0	1	0	8	0	.267	.533
PITCHERS																		
P	Ed Lopat	L	30	87	22	2	1	0	0.0	10	10	8	7	0	1	1	.253	.299
P	Orval Grove	R	33	65	7	0	1	0	0.0	2	2	5	27	0	0	0	.108	.138
P	Joe Haynes	R	32	57	14	4	0	0	0.0	4	6	1	10	0	0	0	.246	.316
P	Eddie Smith	B	24	45	8	1	0	0	0.0	2	3	3	9	0	0	0	.178	.200
P	Frank Papish	R	31	43	8	1	0	0	0.0	3	2	1	7	0	0	0	.186	.209
P	Johnny Rigney	R	15	26	4	1	0	0	0.0	2	4	0	7	0	0	0	.154	.192
P	Bill Dietrich	R	11	19	1	0	0	0	0.0	0	0	0	14	0	0	0	.053	.053
P	Earl Caldwell	R	39	18	3	0	0	0	0.0	2	2	5	4	0	0	0	.167	.167
P	Ralph Hamner	R	25	18	3	1	0	0	0.0	1	2	1	7	0	0	0	.167	.222
P	Thornton Lee	L	7	15	4	0	0	0	0.0	0	3	0	4	0	0	0	.267	.267
P	Ted Lyons	B	5	14	0	0	0	0	0.0	0	1	3	0	0	0	0	.000	.000
P	Al Hollingsworth	L	21	12	0	0	0	0	0.0	1	0	1	3	0	0	0	.000	.000
P	Gordon Maltzberger	R	19	6	0	0	0	0	0.0	0	0	2	3	0	0	0	.000	.000
P	Emmett O'Neill	R	2	1	0	0	0	0	0.0	0	0	0	0	0	0	0	.000	.000
P	Len Perme	L	0	0	0	0	0	0	—	0	0	0	0	0	—	—	—	—
TEAM TOTAL				5312	1364	206	44	37	0.7	562	515	499	602	78	138	33	.257	.333

INDIVIDUAL FIELDING

POS	Player	T	G	PO	A	E	DP	TCG	FA	POS	Player	T	G	PO	A	E	DP	TCG	FA
1B	H. Trosky	R	80	729	33	7	63	9.6	.991	OF	T. Tucker	R	110	276	11	3	1	2.6	.990
	J. Kuhel	L	62	596	38	4	65	10.3	.994		T. Wright	R	107	217	5	2	0	2.1	.991
	J. Jones	R	20	201	5	3	18	10.5	.986		B. Kennedy	R	75	157	10	6	1	2.3	.965
	F. Whitman	R	1	8	0	0	2	8.0	1.000		W. Platt	R	61	130	4	4	1	2.3	.971
2B	D. Kolloway	R	90	235	281	15	74	5.9	.972		R. Hodgin	R	57	114	3	2	0	2.1	.983
	C. Michaels	R	66	185	195	17	51	6.0	.957		W. Moses	L	36	84	2	0	0	2.4	1.000
	F. Whitman	R	1	4	2	2	0	8.0	.750		D. Philley	R	17	55	3	1	0	3.5	.983
SS	L. Appling	R	149	252	505	39	99	5.3	.951		G. Curtright	R	15	30	2	0	1	2.1	1.000
	C. Michaels	R	6	14	16	2	8	5.3	.938		J. Smaza	L	1	0	0	0	0	0.0	.000
	F. Whitman	R	6	8	12	0	0	3.3	1.000	C	M. Tresh	R	79	330	48	2	13	4.8	.995
	L. Wells	R	2	1	1	0	0	1.0	1.000		F. Hayes	R	50	199	32	5	4	4.7*	.979
3B	D. Lodigiani	R	44	41	88	9	4	3.1	.935		G. Dickey	R	30	97	14	0	3	3.7	1.000
	L. Wells	R	38	38	91	8	7	3.6	.942		E. Fernandes	R	12	41	6	4	1	4.3	.922
	D. Kolloway	R	31	32	72	9	8	3.6	.920		T. Jordan	R	2	11	1	0	0	6.0	1.000
	B. Kennedy	R	29	19	77	10	6	3.7	.906										
	C. Michaels	R	13	14	24	3	3	3.2	.927										
	F. Baker	R	6	10	15	1	1	4.3	.962										

The Sox began their 1946 spring training without bats. Someone forgot to send the lumber to Pasadena, an impossible situation that the late sportswriter Warren Brown would have said could only have happened to the White Sox. The bats finally arrived, but Jimmy Dykes wouldn't be on hand to direct camp. Dykes underwent surgery in March for a stomach disorder aggravated by his refusal to give up his daily quota of fifteen cigars.

Dykes returned briefly to guide the club, but there was a falling out between Grace Comiskey and the manager when he demanded a multiyear contract. Grace balked at this, so Dykes quit on May 24. After twelve years, Dykes was ready to move on. His tenure as Sox manager saw several years of good competitive baseball. His greatest talent was in procuring journeymen off of major-league rosters and giving them a second life with the Sox. The reclamation project for 1946 was 41-year-old Earl Caldwell, who won 13 games in relief.

Ted Lyons was named manager in a public relations move. Despite the team's August-September flourish, the soft-spoken Lyons was not the man for the job. He won his 260th (and final) game on April 28 against the Browns, and closed out his career on May 19, pitching his 28th complete game in a row. On June 15, he took himself off the active roster.

Lyons was not one of the "Chicago Fourteen," though. On July 19, umpire Red Jones ejected fourteen Sox players who were taunting him from the dugout in Fenway Park. What vile taunts prompted this extreme action? Jones didn't appreciate being called a "meathead."

TEAM STATISTICS

	W	L	PCT	GB	R	OR	2B	3B	Batting HR	BA	SA	SB	E	Fielding DP	FA	CG	BB	Pitching SO	ShO	SV	ERA
BOS	104	50	.675		792	594	268	50	109	.271	.402	45	139	165	.977	79	501	667	15	20	3.38
DET	92	62	.597	12	704	567	212	41	108	.258	.374	65	155	138	.974	94	497	896	18	15	3.22
NY	87	67	.565	17	684	547	208	50	136	.248	.387	48	150	174	.975	68	552	653	17	17	3.13
WAS	76	78	.494	28	608	706	260	63	60	.260	.366	51	211	162	.966	71	547	537	8	10	3.74
CHI	74	80	.481	30	562	595	206	44	37	.257	.333	78	175	170	.972	62	508	550	9	16	3.10
CLE	68	86	.442	36	537	637	233	56	79	.245	.356	57	147	147	.975	63	649	789	16	13	3.62
STL	66	88	.429	38	621	711	220	46	84	.251	.356	23	159	157	.974	63	573	574	13	12	3.95
PHI	49	105	.318	55	529	680	220	51	40	.253	.338	39	167	141	.971	61	577	562	10	5	3.90
LEAGUE TOTAL					5037	5037	1827	401	653	.256	.364	406	1303	1254	.973	561	4404	5228	106	108	3.50

INDIVIDUAL PITCHING

PITCHER	T	W	L	PCT	ERA	SV	G	GS	CG	IP	H	BB	SO	R	ER	ShO	H9	BB9	SO9
Ed Lopat	L	13	13	.500	2.73	0	29	29	20	231	216	48	89	80	70	2	8.42	1.87	3.47
Orval Grove	R	8	13	.381	3.02	0	33	26	10	205.1	213	78	60	96	69	1	9.34	3.42	2.63
Joe Haynes	R	7	9	.438	3.76	2	32	23	9	177.1	203	60	60	80	74	0	10.30	3.05	3.05
Eddie Smith	L	8	11	.421	2.85	1	24	21	3	145.1	135	60	59	71	46	1	8.36	3.72	3.65
Frank Papish	L	7	5	.583	2.74	0	31	15	6	138	122	63	66	52	42	2	7.96	4.11	4.30
Earl Caldwell	R	13	4	.765	2.08	8	39	0	0	90.2	60	29	42	28	21	0	5.96	2.88	4.17
Johnny Rigney	R	5	5	.500	4.03	0	15	11	3	82.2	76	35	51	37	37	2	8.27	3.81	5.55
Ralph Hamner	R	2	7	.222	4.42	1	25	7	1	71.1	80	39	29	47	35	0	10.09	4.92	3.66
Bill Dietrich	R	3	3	.500	2.61	1	11	9	3	62	63	24	20	21	18	0	9.15	3.48	2.90
Al Hollingsworth	L	3	2	.600	4.58	1	21	2	0	55	63	22	22	29	28	0	10.31	3.60	3.60
Thornton Lee	L	2	4	.333	3.53	0	7	7	2	43.1	39	23	23	24	17	0	8.10	4.78	4.78
Ted Lyons	R	1	4	.200	2.32	0	5	5	5	42.2	38	9	10	17	11	0	8.02	1.90	2.11
Gordon Maltzberger	R	2	0	1.000	1.59	2	19	0	0	39.2	30	6	17	7	7	0	6.81	1.36	3.86
Len Perme	L	0	0	–	8.31	0	4	0	0	4.1	6	7	2	4	4	0	12.46	14.54	4.15
Emmett O'Neill	R	0	0	–	0.00	0	2	0	0	3.2	4	5	0	2	0	0	9.82	12.27	0.00
TEAM TOTAL		74	80	.481	3.10	16	297	155	62	1392.1	1348	508	550	595	479	8	8.71	3.28	3.56

Chicago 1947   Won 70 Lost 84 Pct. .455 6th

MANAGER	W	L	PCT
Ted Lyons	70	84	.455

POS	Player	B	G	AB	H	2B	3B	HR	HR%	R	RBI	BB	SO	SB	Pinch Hit AB	H	BA	SA
REGULARS																		
1B	Rudy York	R	102	400	97	18	4	15	3.8	40	64	36	55	1	0	0	.243	.420
2B	Don Kolloway	R	124	485	135	25	4	2	0.4	49	35	17	34	11	7	2	.278	.359
SS	Luke Appling	R	139	503	154	29	0	8	1.6	67	49	64	28	8	7	0	.306	.412
3B	Floyd Baker	L	105	371	98	12	3	0	0.0	61	22	66	28	9	0	0	.264	.313
RF	Bob Kennedy	R	115	428	112	19	3	6	1.4	47	48	18	38	3	4	0	.262	.362
CF	Dave Philley	B	143	551	142	25	11	2	0.4	55	45	35	39	21	6	2	.258	.354
LF	Taffy Wright	L	124	401	130	13	0	4	1.0	48	54	48	17	8	18	3	.324	.387
C	Mike Tresh	R	90	274	66	6	2	0	0.0	19	20	26	26	2	1	0	.241	.277
SUBSTITUTES																		
23	Cass Michaels	R	110	355	97	15	4	3	0.8	31	34	39	28	10	3	0	.273	.363
SO	Jack Wallaesa	R	81	205	40	9	1	7	3.4	25	32	23	51	2	27	4	.195	.351
1B	Jake Jones	R	45	171	41	7	1	3	1.8	15	20	13	25	1	2	0	.240	.345
OF	Thurman Tucker	L	89	254	60	9	4	1	0.4	28	17	38	25	10	19	4	.236	.315
OF	Ralph Hodgin	L	59	180	53	10	3	1	0.6	26	24	13	4	1	16	1	.294	.400
OF	Lloyd Christopher	R	7	23	5	0	1	0	0.0	1	0	2	4	0	0	0	.217	.304
C	George Dickey	B	83	211	47	6	0	1	0.5	15	27	34	25	4	4	2	.223	.265
C	Joe Stephenson	R	16	35	5	0	0	0	0.0	3	3	1	7	0	1	0	.143	.143
PH	Joe Kuhel	L	4	4	0	0	0	0	0.0	0	0	0	3	0	4	0	.000	.000
PITCHERS																		
P	Ed Lopat	L	35	96	19	3	0	0	0.0	5	11	4	6	0	2	1	.198	.229
P	Joe Haynes	R	29	65	17	2	0	0	0.0	7	6	0	7	0	0	0	.262	.292
P	Frank Papish	R	38	58	5	0	0	0	0.0	1	2	1	15	0	0	0	.086	.086
P	Orval Grove	R	25	48	7	2	0	0	0.0	2	1	5	16	0	0	0	.146	.188
P	Bob Gillespie	R	25	33	2	0	0	0	0.0	2	0	3	12	0	0	0	.061	.061
P	Thornton Lee	L	21	29	6	0	0	0	0.0	0	1	2	11	0	0	0	.207	.207
P	Earl Harrist	R	33	24	5	0	0	0	0.0	1	1	0	8	0	0	0	.208	.208
P	Red Ruffing	R	14	24	5	0	0	0	0.0	2	3	1	3	0	4	1	.208	.208
P	Johnny Rigney	R	11	14	0	0	0	0	0.0	0	0	0	3	0	0	0	.000	.000
P	Pete Gebrian	R	27	13	0	0	0	0	0.0	0	0	0	4	0	0	0	.000	.000
P	Earl Caldwell	R	40	7	0	0	0	0	0.0	0	0	0	1	0	0	0	.000	.000
P	Gordon Maltzberger	R	33	7	1	1	0	0	0.0	2	0	2	4	0	0	0	.143	.286
P	Eddie Smith	B	15	6	1	0	0	0	0.0	1	0	0	1	0	0	0	.167	.167
P	Hi Bithorn	R	2	0	0	0	0	0	—	0	0	0	0	0	0	0	—	—
TEAM TOTAL				5275	1350	211	41	53	1.0	553	519	491	528	91	125	20	.256	.342

INDIVIDUAL FIELDING

POS	Player	T	G	PO	A	E	DP	TCG	FA
1B	R. York	R	102	932	71	5	104*	9.9	.995*
	J. Jones	R	43	444*	31	6	49	11.2*	.988
	D. Kolloway	R	11	99	8	1	9	9.8	.991
2B	D. Kolloway	R	99	274	306	23	76	6.1	.962
	C. Michaels	R	60	160	175	6	52	5.7	.982
	F. Baker	R	1	3	2	0	1	5.0	1.000
SS	L. Appling	R	129	232	422	35	86	5.3	.949
	J. Wallaesa	R	27	55	94	5	22	5.7	.968
	C. Michaels	R	2	2	3	0	0	2.5	1.000
	F. Baker	R	1	1	3	0	0	4.0	1.000
3B	F. Baker	R	101	84	253	7	28	3.4	.980
	C. Michaels	R	44	48	89	9	9	3.3	.938
	D. Kolloway	R	8	5	17	3	1	3.1	.880
	D. Philley	R	4	1	6	0	1	1.8	1.000
	B. Kennedy	R	1	1	2	0	0	3.0	1.000
	J. Wallaesa	R	1	1	1	0	0	2.0	1.000
	L. Appling	R	2	1	1	0	0	1.0	1.000
OF	D. Philley	R	133	355	9	5	2	2.8	.986
	B. Kennedy	R	106	204	8	7	3	2.1	.968
	T. Wright	R	100	198	6	6	1	2.1	.971
	T. Tucker	R	65	171	5	4	2	2.8	.978
	R. Hodgin	R	41	99	2	1	0	2.5	.990
	J. Wallaesa	R	22	74	1	0	0	3.4	1.000
	Christopher	R	7	19	1	0	1	2.9	1.000
C	M. Tresh	R	89	313	38	9	10	4.0	.975
	G. Dickey	R	80	285	35	5	5	4.1	.985
	J. Stephenson	R	13	42	5	2	0	3.8	.959

How far had the Sox farm system progressed in eight years? One need only look at the 1947 rookie crop to see that the road ahead was a rocky one. Bill Eckhardt, John Orphal, Fred Vaughn, Ed Gniewek, Bob Gillespie, and Jack Tree came highly advertised, but only Gillespie saw action with the Sox.

In August Luke Appling took over the league lead in hitting: not bad for a 40-year-old! The club gave him a day on June 8, and 29,629 turned out to see Luke collect one single in an eighteen-inning loss to Washington. The fans contributed a dime each to purchase a shiny new sedan. Chuck Comiskey, who was taking an increasing role in Sox affairs, presented Appling with $1,700: one hundred dollars for each of his seventeen seasons with the team.

Lyons's club started promisingly enough but fell to seventh in mid-June. Encouraged by their 1946 success, Les O'Connor had rewarded Lyons with a two-year contract in April. But the O'Connor-Lyons alliance was not nearly as good at squeezing blood from a stone as Harry Grabiner and Dykes had been.

On July 5 young, scared Larry Doby pinch-hit in Comiskey Park. He struck out against Earl Harrist, but tore down the American League color barrier. Doby would later play an important role in Sox affairs, but in the forties he was Cleveland Indians property. The Sox were still blind to the talent-laden Negro Leagues, and were still a second division team.

TEAM STATISTICS

	W	L	PCT	GB	R	OR	2B	3B	HR	BA	SA	SB	E	DP	FA	CG	BB	SO	ShO	SV	ERA
NY	97	57	.630		794	568	230	72	115	.271	.407	27	109	151	.981	73	628	691	14	21	3.39
DET	85	69	.552	12	714	642	234	42	103	.258	.377	52	155	142	.975	77	531	648	15	18	3.57
BOS	83	71	.539	14	720	669	206	54	103	.265	.382	41	137	172	.977	64	575	586	13	19	3.81
CLE	80	74	.519	17	687	588	234	51	112	.259	.385	29	104	178	.983	55	628	590	13	29	3.44
PHI	78	76	.506	19	633	614	218	52	61	.252	.349	37	143	161	.976	70	597	493	12	15	3.51
CHI	70	84	.455	27	553	661	211	41	53	.256	.342	91	155	180	.975	47	603	522	11	27	3.64
WAS	64	90	.416	33	496	675	186	48	42	.241	.321	53	143	151	.976	67	579	551	15	12	3.97
STL	59	95	.383	38	564	744	189	52	90	.241	.350	69	134	169	.977	50	604	552	7	13	4.33
LEAGUE TOTAL					5161	5161	1708	412	679	.256	.364	399	1080	1304	.977	503	4745	4633	100	154	3.71

INDIVIDUAL PITCHING

PITCHER	T	W	L	PCT	ERA	SV	G	GS	CG	IP	H	BB	SO	R	ER	ShO	H9	BB9	SO9
Ed Lopat	L	16	13	.552	2.81	0	31	31	22	252.2	241	73	109	88	79	3	8.58	2.60	3.88
Frank Papish	L	12	12	.500	3.26	3	38	26	6	199	185	98	79	82	72	1	8.37	4.43	3.57
Joe Haynes	R	14	6	.700	2.42	0	29	22	7	182	174	61	50	65	49	2	8.60	3.02	2.47
Orval Grove	R	6	8	.429	4.44	0	25	19	6	135.2	158	70	33	78	67	1	10.48	4.64	2.19
Bob Gillespie	R	5	8	.385	4.73	0	25	17	1	118	133	53	36	71	62	0	10.14	4.04	2.75
Earl Harrist	R	3	8	.273	3.56	5	33	4	0	93.2	85	49	55	48	37	0	8.17	4.71	5.28
Thornton Lee	L	3	7	.300	4.47	1	21	11	2	86.2	86	56	57	50	43	1	8.93	5.82	5.92
Pete Gebrian	R	2	3	.400	4.48	5	27	4	0	66.1	61	33	17	40	33	0	8.28	4.48	2.31
Gordon Maltzberger	R	1	4	.200	3.39	5	33	0	0	63.2	61	25	22	26	24	0	8.62	3.53	3.11
Earl Caldwell	R	1	4	.200	3.64	8	40	0	0	54.1	53	30	22	23	22	0	8.78	4.97	3.64
Red Ruffing	R	3	5	.375	6.11	0	9	9	1	53	63	16	11	39	36	0	10.70	2.72	1.87
Johnny Rigney	R	2	3	.400	1.95	0	11	7	2	50.2	42	15	19	15	11	0	7.46	2.66	3.38
Eddie Smith	L	1	3	.250	7.29	0	15	5	0	33.1	40	24	12	36	27	0	10.80	6.48	3.24
Hi Bithorn	R	1	0	1.000	0.00	0	2	0	0	2	2	0	0	0	0	0	9.00	0.00	0.00
TEAM TOTAL		70	84	.455	3.64	27	339	155	47	1391	1384	603	522	661	562	8	8.95	3.90	3.38

Chicago 1948   Won 51 Lost 101 Pct. .336 8th   120

MANAGER	W	L	PCT
Ted Lyons	51	101	.336

POS	Player	B	G	AB	H	2B	3B	HR	HR%	R	RBI	BB	SO	SB	Pinch Hit AB	H	BA	SA
REGULARS																		
1B	Tony Lupien	L	154	617	152	19	3	6	1.0	69	54	74	38	11	0	0	.246	.316
2B	Don Kolloway	R	119	417	114	14	4	6	1.4	60	38	18	18	2	12	3	.273	.369
SS	Cass Michaels	R	145	484	120	12	6	5	1.0	47	56	69	42	8	4	2	.248	.329
3B	Luke Appling	R	139	497	156	16	2	0	0.0	63	47	94	35	10	3	1	.314	.354
RF	Taffy Wright	L	134	455	127	15	6	4	0.9	50	61	39	18	2	19	6	.279	.365
CF	Dave Philley	B	137	488	140	28	3	5	1.0	51	42	50	33	8	8	1	.287	.387
LF	Pat Seerey	R	95	340	78	11	0	18	5.3	44	64	83	94*	0	2	0	.229	.421
C	Aaron Robinson	L	98	326	82	14	2	8	2.5	47	39	46	30	0	6	1	.252	.380
SUBSTITUTES																		
32	Floyd Baker	L	104	335	72	8	3	0	0.0	47	18	73	26	4	11	4	.215	.257
SS	Jack Wallaesa	B	33	48	9	0	0	1	2.1	2	3	1	12	0	27	6	.188	.250
SS	Frank Whitman	R	3	6	0	0	0	0	0.0	0	0	0	3	0	2	0	.000	.000
OF	Ralph Hodgin	L	114	331	88	11	5	1	0.3	28	34	21	11	0	33	7	.266	.338
OF	Bob Kennedy	R	30	113	28	8	1	0	0.0	4	14	4	17	0	1	1	.248	.336
OF	Jim Delsing	L	20	63	12	0	0	0	0.0	5	5	5	12	0	4	0	.190	.190
OF	Herb Adams	L	5	11	3	1	0	0	0.0	1	0	1	1	0	0	0	.273	.364
OF	Jerry Scala	L	3	6	0	0	0	0	0.0	1	0	0	3	0	0	0	.000	.000
C	Ralph Weigel	R	66	163	38	7	3	0	0.0	8	26	13	18	1	24	6	.233	.313
C	Mike Tresh	R	39	108	27	1	0	1	0.9	10	11	9	9	0	5	2	.250	.287
PITCHERS																		
P	Bill Wight	L	34	73	6	0	0	0	0.0	2	3	3	31	0	0	0	.082	.082
P	Al Gettel	R	24	54	13	2	0	0	0.0	4	3	0	6	0	0	0	.241	.278
P	Joe Haynes	R	27	50	8	2	0	0	0.0	5	1	3	8	0	0	0	.160	.200
P	Marino Pieretti	R	32	39	7	0	0	0	0.0	5	3	4	6	0	0	0	.179	.179
P	Randy Gumpert	R	16	29	4	0	0	0	0.0	0	1	0	10	0	0	0	.138	.138
P	Howie Judson	R	41	29	3	1	0	0	0.0	1	2	1	13	0	0	0	.103	.138
P	Frank Papish	R	32	27	5	2	0	0	0.0	1	4	0	6	0	0	0	.185	.259
P	Orval Grove	R	32	21	2	0	0	0	0.0	0	0	1	9	0	0	0	.095	.095
P	Glen Moulder	R	33	20	6	0	1	0	0.0	3	1	1	1	0	0	0	.300	.400
P	Bob Gillespie	R	25	16	0	0	0	0	0.0	0	1	1	10	0	0	0	.000	.000
P	Ike Pearson	R	23	10	2	0	0	0	0.0	0	0	0	3	0	0	0	.200	.200
P	Earl Caldwell	R	25	5	0	0	0	0	0.0	0	1	2	3	0	0	0	.000	.000
P	Earl Harrist	R	11	4	0	0	0	0	0.0	0	0	0	0	0	0	0	.000	.000
P	Marv Rotblatt	B	7	4	0	0	0	0	0.0	0	0	1	2	0	0	0	.000	.000
P	Jim Goodwin	L	8	2	1	0	0	0	0.0	0	0	0	0	0	0	0	.500	.500
P	Fred Bradley	R	8	1	0	0	0	0	0.0	0	0	0	0	0	0	0	.000	.000
TEAM TOTAL				5192	1303	172	39	55	1.1	558	532	617	528	46	161	40	.251	.331

INDIVIDUAL FIELDING

POS	Player	T	G	PO	A	E	DP	TCG	FA	POS	Player	T	G	PO	A	E	DP	TCG	FA
1B	T. Lupien	L	154	1436	92	11	155	10.0	.993	OF	D. Philley	R	128	381	22	9	6	3.2	.978
2B	D. Kolloway	R	83	241	276	18	62	6.4	.966		T. Wright	R	114	227	9	3	3	2.1	.987
	C. Michaels	R	55	148	171	8	50	5.9	.976		P. Seerey	R	93	198	9	4	5	2.3	.981
	F. Baker	R	18	51	55	3	17	6.1	.972		R. Hodgin	R	79	184	9	6	0	2.5	.970
	A. Gettel	R	1	0	3	0	1	3.0	1.000		B. Kennedy	R	30	61	3	2	0	2.2	.970
SS	C. Michaels	R	85	164	285	20	65	5.5	.957		J. Delsing	R	15	36	1	0	0	2.5	1.000
	L. Appling	R	64	133	210	20	50	5.7	.945		J. Wallaesa	R	1	0	0	0	0	0.0	.000
	J. Wallaesa	R	5	11	17	0	5	5.6	1.000		H. Adams	L	4	10	2	0	0	3.0	1.000
	F. Whitman	R	1	1	2	3	1	6.0	.500		J. Scala	R	2	5	0	0	0	2.5	1.000
	F. Baker	R	1	2	1	0	0	3.0	1.000		C. Michaels	R	1	1	0	0	0	1.0	1.000
3B	L. Appling	R	72	84	163	15	13	3.6	.943		R. Weigel	R	2	1	0	0	0	0.5	1.000
	F. Baker	R	71	78	170	10	17	3.6	.961	C	A. Robinson	R	92	303	50	4	4	3.9	.989
	D. Kolloway	R	18	23	27	4	1	3.0	.926		R. Weigel	R	39	108	19	4	4	3.4	.969
											M. Tresh	R	34	99	16	2	1	3.4	.983

The Leslie O'Connor regime toppled after the 1948 season, the second worst in club history. While the Indians slugged it out with the Boston Braves in the World Series, it was leaked to the press that 52-year-old former Big Ten official Frank Lane would be the next general manager. Taking the tumble with O'Connor was Ted Lyons who, like Schalk, was too nice a guy to be saddled with a team as poor as the White Sox.

Bill Wight was acquired from the Yankees in one of the White Sox' more notorious trades. To get him, O'Connor gave up Ed Lopat, who then registered a 17-11 record for the Yanks while Wight fell to 9-20. Another O'Connor acquisition was Pat Seerey, a portly outfielder with limited speed and a fat strike zone. Seerey did become the only Sox player ever to hit four home runs in a game, an eleven-inning affair in Philadelphia won by the Sox 12-11.

O'Connor had the honor of getting the Sox evicted from the American League by signing a prep star named George Zoeterman from a school not recognized by the National Federation of State High School Associations. When O'Connor refused to pay the $500 fine levied him by Commissioner Chandler, the Sox were technically out of the league. Fortunately, Comiskey paid the fine.

While O'Connor's player moves were disasters, Lane's were brilliant right from the start. Lane completed his first deal on November 10, when he traded catcher Aaron Robinson to Detroit for a little-known pitcher named Billy Pierce.

TEAM STATISTICS

	W	L	PCT	GB	R	OR	2B	3B	HR	BA	SA	SB	E	DP	FA	CG	BB	SO	ShO	SV	ERA
CLE	97	58	.626		840	568	242	54	155	.282	.431	54	114	183	.982	66	628	595	26	30	3.22
BOS	96	59	.619	1	907	720	277	40	121	.274	.409	38	116	174	.981	70	592	513	11	13	4.20
NY	94	60	.610	2.5	857	633	251	75	139	.278	.432	24	120	161	.979	62	641	654	16	24	3.75
PHI	84	70	.545	12.5	729	735	231	47	68	.260	.362	39	113	180	.981	74	638	486	7	18	4.43
DET	78	76	.506	18.5	700	726	219	58	78	.267	.375	22	155	143	.974	60	589	678	5	22	4.15
STL	59	94	.386	37	671	849	251	62	63	.271	.378	63	168	190	.972	35	737	531	4	20	5.01
WAS	56	97	.366	40	578	796	203	75	31	.244	.331	76	154	144	.974	42	734	446	4	22	4.65
CHI	51	101	.336	44.5	559	814	172	39	55	.251	.331	46	160	176	.974	35	673	403	2	23	4.89
LEAGUE TOTAL					5841	5841	1846	450	710	.266	.382	362	1100	1351	.977	444	5232	4306	75	172	4.28

INDIVIDUAL PITCHING

PITCHER	T	W	L	PCT	ERA	SV	G	GS	CG	IP	H	BB	SO	R	ER	ShO	H9	BB9	SO9
Bill Wight	L	9	20	.310	4.80	1	34	32	7	223.1	238	135	68	132	119	1	9.59	5.44	2.74
Joe Haynes	R	9	10	.474	3.97	0	27	22	6	149.2	167	52	40	79	66	0	10.04	3.13	2.41
Al Gettel	R	8	10	.444	4.01	1	22	19	7	148	154	60	49	76	66	0	9.36	3.65	2.98
Marino Pieretti	R	8	10	.444	4.95	1	21	18	4	120	117	52	28	70	66	0	8.78	3.90	2.10
Howie Judson	R	4	5	.444	4.78	8	40	5	1	107.1	102	56	38	60	57	0	8.55	4.70	3.19
Randy Gumpert	R	2	6	.250	3.79	0	16	11	6	97.1	103	13	31	43	41	1	9.52	1.20	2.87
Frank Papish	L	2	8	.200	5.00	4	32	14	2	95.1	97	75	41	65	53	0	9.16	7.08	3.87
Orval Grove	R	2	10	.167	6.16	1	32	11	1	87.2	110	42	18	64	60	0	11.29	4.31	1.85
Glen Moulder	R	3	6	.333	6.41	2	33	9	0	85.2	108	54	26	67	61	0	11.35	5.67	2.73
Bob Gillespie	R	0	4	.000	5.13	0	25	6	1	72	81	33	19	45	41	0	10.13	4.13	2.38
Ike Pearson	R	2	3	.400	4.92	1	23	2	0	53	62	27	12	32	29	0	10.53	4.58	2.04
Earl Caldwell	R	1	5	.167	5.31	3	25	1	0	39	53	22	10	25	23	0	12.23	5.08	2.31
Earl Harrist	R	1	3	.250	5.79	0	11	1	0	23.1	23	13	14	17	15	0	8.87	5.01	5.40
Marv Rotblatt	L	0	1	.000	7.85	0	7	2	0	18.1	19	23	4	16	16	0	9.33	11.29	1.96
Fred Bradley	R	0	0	–	4.60	0	8	0	0	15.2	11	4	2	12	8	0	6.32	2.30	1.15
Jim Goodwin	L	0	0	–	8.71	1	8	1	0	10.1	9	12	3	11	10	0	7.84	10.45	2.61
TEAM TOTAL		51	101	.336	4.89	23	364	154	35	1346	1454	673	403	814	731	2	9.72	4.50	2.69

Chicago 1949   Won 63 Lost 91 Pct. .409 6th

MANAGER	W	L	PCT
Jack Onslow	63	91	.409

POS	Player	B	G	AB	H	2B	3B	HR	HR%	R	RBI	BB	SO	SB	Pinch Hit AB	Pinch Hit H	BA	SA
REGULARS																		
1B	Charlie Kress	L	97	353	98	17	6	1	0.3	45	44	39	44	6	1	1	.278	.368
2B	Cass Michaels	R	154	561	173	27	9	6	1.1	73	83	101	50	5	0	0	.308	.421
SS	Luke Appling	R	142	492	148	21	5	5	1.0	82	58	121	24	7	1	0	.301	.394
3B	Floyd Baker	L	125	388	101	15	4	1	0.3	38	40	84	32	3	0	0	.260	.327
RF	Dave Philley	B	146	598	171	20	8	0	0.0	84	44	54	51	13	1	0	.286	.346
CF	Catfish Metkovich	L	93	338	80	9	4	5	1.5	50	45	41	24	5	5	1	.237	.331
LF	Herb Adams	L	56	208	61	5	3	0	0.0	26	16	9	16	1	5	1	.293	.346
C	Don Wheeler	R	67	192	46	9	2	1	0.5	17	22	27	19	2	8	1	.240	.323
SUBSTITUTES																		
1B	Gordon Goldsberry	L	39	145	36	3	2	1	0.7	25	13	18	9	2	1	0	.248	.317
3B	Bobby Rhawn	R	24	73	15	4	1	0	0.0	12	5	12	8	0	2	1	.205	.288
2B	Rocky Krsnich	R	16	55	12	3	1	1	1.8	7	9	6	4	0	0	0	.218	.364
SS	Fred Hancock	R	39	52	7	2	1	0	0.0	7	9	8	9	0	5	1	.135	.212
SS	Jim Baumer	R	8	10	4	1	1	0	0.0	2	2	2	1	0	0	0	.400	.700
3B	Don Kolloway	R	4	4	0	0	0	0	0.0	0	0	0	1	0	3	0	.000	.000
O1	Steve Souchock	R	84	252	59	13	5	7	2.8	29	37	25	38	5	17	4	.234	.409
OF	Gus Zernial	R	73	198	63	17	2	5	2.5	29	38	15	26	0	25	8	.318	.500
OF	John Ostrowski	R	49	158	42	9	4	5	3.2	19	31	15	41	4	6	1	.266	.468
OF	Jerry Scala	L	37	120	30	7	1	1	0.8	17	13	17	19	3	5	1	.250	.350
OF	Billy Bowers	L	26	78	15	2	1	0	0.0	5	6	4	5	1	6	0	.192	.244
OF	Earl Rapp	L	19	54	14	1	1	0	0.0	3	11	5	6	1	5	1	.259	.315
OF	Dick Lane	R	12	42	5	0	0	0	0.0	4	4	5	3	0	1	0	.119	.119
OF	Bill Higdon	L	11	23	7	3	0	0	0.0	3	1	6	3	1	4	1	.304	.435
OF	Pat Seerey	R	4	4	0	0	0	0	0.0	1	0	3	1	0	2	0	.000	.000
C	Joe Tipton	R	67	191	39	5	3	3	1.6	20	19	27	17	1	14	1	.204	.309
C	Eddie Malone	R	55	170	46	7	2	1	0.6	17	16	29	19	2	3	1	.271	.353
C	George Yankowski	R	12	18	3	1	0	0	0.0	0	2	0	2	0	6	0	.167	.222
PITCHERS																		
P	Bill Wight	L	35	85	14	3	0	0	0.0	7	6	6	27	0	0	0	.165	.200
P	Randy Gumpert	R	34	84	16	1	0	0	0.0	7	6	3	16	0	0	0	.190	.202
P	Bob Kuzava	B	29	56	2	0	0	0	0.0	1	1	3	19	0	0	0	.036	.036
P	Billy Pierce	L	39	51	9	0	0	0	0.0	7	2	5	15	0	0	0	.176	.176
P	Marino Pieretti	R	48	38	9	1	0	0	0.0	6	3	0	7	0	0	0	.237	.263
P	Howie Judson	R	26	31	2	1	0	0	0.0	0	2	1	11	0	0	0	.065	.097
P	Mickey Haefner	L	20	23	6	0	0	0	0.0	0	0	4	7	0	0	0	.261	.261
P	Max Surkont	R	44	22	1	0	0	0	0.0	1	2	4	12	0	0	0	.045	.045
P	Al Gettel	R	19	18	3	0	0	0	0.0	2	0	2	2	0	0	0	.167	.167
P	Eddie Klieman	R	18	8	2	0	0	0	0.0	1	0	0	2	0	0	0	.250	.250
P	Clyde Shoun	L	16	5	1	0	0	0	0.0	1	1	1	0	0	0	0	.200	.200
P	Bob Cain	L	6	3	0	0	0	0	0.0	0	0	1	1	0	0	0	.000	.000
P	Fred Bradley	R	1	1	0	0	0	0	0.0	0	0	0	1	0	0	0	.000	.000
P	Jack Bruner	L	4	1	0	0	0	0	0.0	0	0	0	1	0	0	0	.000	.000
P	Bill Evans	R	4	1	0	0	0	0	0.0	0	0	0	0	0	0	0	.000	.000
P	Alex Carrasquel	R	3	0	0	0	0	0	—	0	0	0	0	0	0	0	—	—
P	Ernie Groth	R	3	0	0	0	0	0	—	0	0	0	0	0	0	0	—	—
P	Orval Grove	R	1	0	0	0	0	0	—	0	0	0	0	0	0	0	—	—
TEAM TOTAL				5204	1340	207	66	43	0.8	648	591	702	593	62	126	24	.257	.347

INDIVIDUAL FIELDING

POS	Player	T	G	PO	A	E	DP	TCG	FA
1B	C. Kress	L	95	907	66	6	103	10.3	.994
	G. Goldsberry	L	38	359	24	4	37	10.2	.990
	S. Souchock	R	30	250	20	1	30	9.0	.996
2B	C. Michaels	R	154	392	484	22	135	5.8	.976
	R. Krsnich	R	16	18	40	4	4	3.9	.935
	F. Baker	R	1	0	0	0	0	0.0	.000
SS	L. Appling	R	141	253	450	26	95	5.2	.964
	F. Hancock	R	27	21	24	1	10	1.7	.978
	F. Baker	R	3	5	11	0	1	5.3	1.000
	J. Baumer	R	7	3	12	1	4	2.3	.938
	B. Rhawn	R	3	2	6	1	1	3.0	.889
3B	F. Baker	R	122	106	269	9	31	3.1	**.977**
	B. Rhawn	R	19	28	43	3	4	3.9	.959
	D. Kolloway	R	2	0	0	0	0	0.0	.000
	J. Ostrowski	R	8	4	9	1	0	1.8	.929
	F. Hancock	R	3	1	4	1	0	2.0	.833
OF	D. Philley	R	145	282	16	7	3	2.1	.977
	C. Metkovich	L	87	212	1	7	0	2.5	.968
	H. Adams	L	48	112	4	3	1	2.5	.975
	S. Souchock	R	39	96	1	5	0	2.6	.951
	J. Ostrowski	R	41	81	3	5	0	2.2	.944
	J. Scala	R	37	83	1	1	0	2.3	.988
	G. Zernial	R	46	73	4	0	0	1.7	1.000
	B. Bowers	R	20	46	2	1	0	2.5	.980
	F. Hancock	R	1	0	0	0	0	0.0	.000
	E. Rapp	R	13	36	2	1	0	3.0	.974
	D. Lane	R	11	25	2	0	0	2.5	1.000
	B. Higdon	R	6	9	1	0	0	1.7	1.000
	P. Seerey	R	2	1	0	0	0	0.5	1.000
C	D. Wheeler	R	58	210	36	6	4	4.3	.976
	J. Tipton	R	53	203	32	2	4	4.5	.992
	E. Malone	R	51	186	22	2	2	4.1	.990
	G. Yankowski	R	6	15	3	0	0	3.0	1.000

Let there be no doubt: the '40s were the worst decade in White Sox history. Though the '20s were pretty bad, the period beginning in 1941 and ending in 1950 saw the club play at a .448 percentage. In the '20s the Sox were a shade better at .454.

Honest Jack Onslow was the manager this year, a stern disciplinarian who attracted the eye of Chuck Comiskey when he managed the Memphis Chicks. Frank Lane wanted to build the club around the hitting talents of his young Pacific Coast League star, Gus Zernial. A makeshift chicken-wire fence was installed in front of the warning track to give Zernial something to shoot at. But when the light-hitting Washington Senators rolled into town on May 3 and administered 14–12 and 8–7 drubbings courtesy of the new fence, an irate Lane decided it had to go.

Zernial was as good as advertised, rapping American League pitchers to a .355 tune, when disaster struck. On May 29 in Cleveland, Zernial broke a collarbone and was out for most of the remainder of the year. The season disintegrated after that. But there were some highlights: Billy Pierce won his first game on April 23, when he downed the Browns 12–5 in relief. Bob Kuzava, another highly regarded rookie, struck out six Red Sox in a row on August 26, but still lost 10–7. And let us not forget Howard Kolls Judson. He won in Detroit on April 21, but lost his next fourteen decisions. That distinction later earned him an invitation to Bill Veeck's "Unsung Heroes of the Sox Day."

TEAM STATISTICS

	W	L	PCT	GB	R	OR	2B	3B	HR	BA	SA	SB	E	DP	FA	CG	BB	SO	ShO	SV	ERA
NY	97	57	.630		829	637	215	60	115	.269	.400	58	138	195	.977	59	812	671	12	36	3.69
BOS	96	58	.623	1	896	667	272	36	131	.282	.420	43	120	207	.980	84	661	598	16	16	3.97
CLE	89	65	.578	8	675	574	194	58	112	.267	.384	44	103	192	.983	65	611	594	10	19	3.36
DET	87	67	.565	10	751	655	215	51	88	.267	.378	39	131	174	.978	70	628	631	19	12	3.77
PHI	81	73	.526	16	726	725	214	49	82	.260	.369	36	140	217	.976	85	758	490	9	11	4.23
CHI	63	91	.409	34	648	737	207	66	43	.257	.347	62	141	180	.977	57	693	502	10	17	4.30
STL	53	101	.344	44	667	913	213	30	117	.254	.377	38	166	154	.971	43	685	432	3	16	5.21
WAS	50	104	.325	47	584	868	207	41	81	.254	.356	46	161	168	.973	44	779	451	9	9	5.10
LEAGUE TOTAL					5776	5776	1737	391	769	.263	.379	366	1100	1487	.977	507	5627	4369	88	136	4.20

INDIVIDUAL PITCHING

PITCHER	T	W	L	PCT	ERA	SV	G	GS	CG	IP	H	BB	SO	R	ER	ShO	H9	BB9	SO9
Bill Wight	L	15	13	.536	3.31	1	35	33	14	245	254	96	78	106	90	3	9.33	3.53	2.87
Randy Gumpert	R	13	16	.448	3.81	1	34	32	18	234	223	83	78	111	99	3	8.58	3.19	3.00
Billy Pierce	L	7	15	.318	3.88	0	32	26	8	171.2	145	112	95	89	74	0	7.60	5.87	4.98
Bob Kuzava	L	10	6	.625	4.02	0	29	18	9	156.2	139	91	83	76	70	1	7.99	5.23	4.77
Marino Pieretti	R	4	6	.400	5.51	4	39	9	0	116	131	54	25	77	71	0	10.16	4.19	1.94
Howie Judson	R	1	14	.067	4.58	1	26	12	3	108	114	70	36	65	55	0	9.50	5.83	3.00
Max Surkont	R	3	5	.375	4.78	4	44	2	0	96	92	60	38	61	51	0	8.63	5.63	3.56
Mickey Haefner	L	4	6	.400	4.37	1	14	12	4	80.1	84	41	17	40	39	1	9.41	4.59	1.90
Al Gettel	R	2	5	.286	6.43	1	19	7	1	63	69	26	22	48	45	1	9.86	3.71	3.14
Eddie Klieman	R	2	0	1.000	3.00	3	18	0	0	33	33	15	9	15	11	0	9.00	4.09	2.45
Clyde Shoun	L	1	1	.500	5.79	0	16	0	0	23.1	37	13	8	17	15	0	14.27	5.01	3.09
Bob Cain	L	0	0	—	2.45	1	6	0	0	11	7	5	5	3	3	0	5.73	4.09	4.09
Jack Bruner	L	1	2	.333	8.22	0	4	2	0	7.2	10	8	4	7	7	0	11.74	9.39	4.70
Bill Evans	R	0	1	.000	7.11	0	4	0	0	6.1	6	8	1	6	5	0	8.53	11.37	1.42
Ernie Groth	R	0	1	.000	5.40	0	3	0	0	5	2	3	1	3	3	0	3.60	5.40	1.80
Alex Carrasquel	R	0	0	—	14.73	0	3	0	0	3.2	8	4	1	6	6	0	19.64	9.82	2.45
Fred Bradley	R	0	0	—	13.50	0	1	1	0	2	4	3	0	3	3	0	18.00	13.50	0.00
Orval Grove	R	0	0	—	54.00	0	1	0	0	.2	4	1	1	4	4	0	54.00	13.50	13.50
TEAM TOTAL		63	91	.409	4.30	17	328	154	57	1363.1	1362	693	502	737	651	9	8.99	4.57	3.31

Chicago 1950   Won 60 Lost 94 Pct. .390 6th

MANAGER	W	L	PCT
Jack Onslow	8	22	.267
Red Corriden	52	72	.419

POS	Player	B	G	AB	H	2B	3B	HR	HR%	R	RBI	BB	SO	SB	Pinch Hit AB	H	BA	SA
REGULARS																		
1B	Eddie Robinson	L	119	428	133	11	2	20	4.7	62	73	60	28	0	0	0	.311	.486
2B	Nellie Fox	L	130	457	113	12	7	0	0.0	45	30	35	17	4	8	2	.247	.304
SS	Chico Carrasquel	R	141	524	148	21	5	4	0.8	72	46	66	46	0	0	0	.282	.365
3B	Hank Majeski	R	122	414	128	18	2	6	1.4	47	46	42	34	1	9	1	.309	.406
RF	Marv Rickert	L	84	278	66	9	2	4	1.4	38	27	21	42	0	6	0	.237	.327
CF	Dave Philley	B	156	619	150	21	5	14	2.3	69	80	52	57	6	1	0	.242	.360
LF	Gus Zernial	R	143	543	152	16	4	29	5.3	75	93	38	110	0	5	1	.280	.484
C	Phil Masi	R	122	377	105	17	2	7	1.9	38	55	49	36	2	9	1	.279	.390
SUBSTITUTES																		
3B	Floyd Baker	L	83	186	59	7	0	0	0.0	26	11	32	10	1	24	6	.317	.355
2B	Cass Michaels	R	36	138	43	6	3	4	2.9	21	19	13	8	0	1	1	.312	.486
S1	Luke Appling	R	50	128	30	3	4	0	0.0	11	13	12	8	2	15	1	.234	.320
1B	Gordon Goldsberry	L	82	127	34	8	2	2	1.6	19	25	26	18	0	39	12	.268	.409
2B	Al Kozar	R	10	10	3	0	0	1	10.0	4	2	0	3	0	2	0	.300	.600
1B	Charlie Kress	L	3	8	0	0	0	0	0.0	0	0	0	2	0	0	0	.000	.000
3B	Joe Kirrene	R	1	4	1	0	0	0	0.0	0	0	0	1	0	0	0	.250	.250
OF	Mike McCormick	R	55	138	32	4	3	0	0.0	16	10	16	6	0	7	1	.232	.304
OF	Herb Adams	L	34	118	24	2	3	0	0.0	12	2	12	7	3	1	0	.203	.271
OF	Jerry Scala	L	40	67	13	2	1	0	0.0	8	6	10	10	0	5	3	.194	.254
OF	John Ostrowski	R	22	49	12	2	1	2	4.1	10	2	9	9	0	7	0	.245	.449
OF	Jim Busby	R	18	48	10	0	0	0	0.0	5	4	1	5	0	0	0	.208	.208
OF	Ed McGhee	R	3	6	1	0	1	0	0.0	0	0	0	1	0	1	0	.167	.500
OF	Bill Wilson	R	3	6	0	0	0	0	0.0	0	0	2	2	0	0	0	.000	.000
C	Gus Niarhos	R	41	105	34	4	0	0	0.0	17	16	14	6	0	2	0	.324	.362
C	Eddie Malone	R	31	71	16	2	0	0	0.0	2	10	10	8	0	10	2	.225	.254
C	Joe Erautt	R	16	18	4	0	0	0	0.0	0	1	1	3	0	10	2	.222	.222
C	Bill Salkeld	L	1	3	0	0	0	0	0.0	0	0	1	0	0	0	0	.000	.000
PITCHERS																		
P	Billy Pierce	L	40	77	20	3	0	0	0.0	10	6	6	13	0	0	0	.260	.299
P	Bob Cain	L	35	61	12	2	0	0	0.0	7	2	3	15	0	1	0	.197	.230
P	Bill Wight	L	30	61	0	0	0	0	0.0	2	2	4	17	0	0	0	.000	.000
P	Ray Scarborough	R	27	46	8	0	0	0	0.0	1	4	3	7	0	0	0	.174	.174
P	Randy Gumpert	R	41	42	3	0	0	0	0.0	2	4	2	10	0	0	0	.071	.071
P	Ken Holcombe	R	24	32	5	1	0	0	0.0	2	0	0	8	0	0	0	.156	.188
P	Mickey Haefner	L	24	20	4	0	0	0	0.0	1	3	3	3	0	0	0	.200	.200
P	Howie Judson	R	46	20	2	1	0	0	0.0	1	0	3	5	0	0	0	.100	.150
P	Luis Aloma	R	42	15	1	0	0	0	0.0	0	1	0	6	0	0	0	.067	.067
P	Bob Kuzava	B	10	12	1	0	0	0	0.0	3	1	3	3	0	0	0	.083	.083
P	Lou Kretlow	R	11	4	0	0	0	0	0.0	0	0	0	1	0	0	0	.000	.000
P	Marv Rotblatt	B	2	2	0	0	0	0	0.0	0	0	0	1	0	0	0	.000	.000
P	Gus Keriazakos	R	1	1	1	0	0	0	0.0	0	0	0	0	0	0	0	1.000	1.000
P	John Perkovich	R	1	1	0	0	0	0	0.0	0	0	0	1	0	0	0	.000	.000
P	Jack Bruner	L	9	0	0	0	0	0	—	0	0	0	0	0	0	0	—	—
P	Bill Connelly	L	2	0	0	0	0	0	—	0	0	0	0	0	0	0	—	—
P	Charlie Cuellar	R	2	0	0	0	0	0	—	0	0	0	0	0	0	0	—	—
TEAM TOTAL				5264	1368	172	47	93	1.8	625	592	549	567	19	164	33	.260	.363

INDIVIDUAL FIELDING

POS	Player	T	G	PO	A	E	DP	TCG	FA
1B	E. Robinson	R	119	982*	60	14	105	8.9	.987
	G. Goldsberry	L	40	235	29	3	37	6.7	.989
	L. Appling	R	13	91	12	0	16	7.9	1.000
	C. Kress	L	2	19	1	0	2	10.0	1.000
	M. Rickert	R	1	4	0	0	0	4.0	1.000
2B	N. Fox	R	121	340	344	18	100	5.8	.974
	C. Michaels	R	35	101	78	7*	36	5.3	.962
	L. Appling	R	1	0	0	0	0	0.0	.000
	A. Kozar	R	4	6	8	0	3	3.5	1.000
	F. Baker	R	3	2	3	0	2	1.7	1.000
SS	C. Carrasquel	R	141	234	458	28	113	5.1	.961
	L. Appling	R	20	37	50	3	13	4.5	.967
3B	H. Majeski	R	112	115	246	11	31	3.3	.970
	F. Baker	R	53	50	102	2	7	2.9	.987
	A. Kozar	R	1	0	0	0	0	0.0	.000
	J. Kirrene	R	1	1	1	0	0	2.0	1.000
OF	D. Philley	R	154	367	19	8	8	2.6	.980
	G. Zernial	R	137	306	9	10	2	2.4	.969
	M. Rickert	R	78	150	3	5	1	2.0	.968
	M. McCormick	R	44	105	4	2	2	2.5	.982
	H. Adams	L	33	90	1	2	0	2.8	.978
	J. Scala	R	23	43	1	0	0	1.9	1.000
	J. Ostrowski	R	16	28	1	0	0	1.8	1.000
	J. Busby	R	12	25	2	1	1	2.3	.964
	B. Wilson	R	2	3	0	0	0	1.5	1.000
	E. McGhee	R	1	1	0	0	0	1.0	1.000
	F. Baker	R	2	1	0	0	0	0.5	1.000
	G. Goldsberry	L	3	1	0	0	0	0.3	1.000
C	P. Masi	R	114	440	52	2	9	4.3	**.996**
	G. Niarhos	R	36	167	14	4	2	5.1	.978
	E. Malone	R	21	79	10	0	3	4.2	1.000
	J. Erautt	R	5	12	2	0	0	2.8	1.000
	B. Salkeld	R	1	4	0	0	0	4.0	1.000

Frank Lane introduced another *wunderkind* to the baseball public in 1950. He was the sprightly Chico Carrasquel, a shortstop Lane had stolen from Branch Rickey for a mere $25,000. With Chico the everyday shortstop, Luke Appling was out of a job for the first time in twenty years. Luke collected his last major-league hit off Stubby Overmire on October 1. Appling's career spanned 2,422 games, and despite some persistent rumors about his imminent appointment as Sox manager, Luke and the Sox parted company. On that same day, Sox power boy Gus Zernial hit four homers in a doubleheader to establish a new team record of 29 for the season, a record that would stand for nineteen years.

The Sox struggled, prompting still another managerial change. Jack Onslow was fired by Chuck Comiskey after the Sox got off to an 8–22 mark. Sixty-two-year-old coach Red Corriden succeeded Onslow, but things didn't get any better. Cass Michaels, Bob Kuzava, and John Ostrowski were dealt to the Senators for Eddie Robinson and Ray Scarborough on May 30. At one point he was knocked out eight straight times, but Scarborough was the only Sox representative on the All-Star team.

At season's end, Lane and Comiskey brought in a new face to manage the Sox. Paul Richards, the lean, tall Texan, was driving from Los Angeles to his home in Waxahachie, Texas, when he heard the news. He reversed direction and headed to Chicago. The thirty-year malaise was about to end.

TEAM STATISTICS

	W	L	PCT	GB	R	OR	2B	3B	HR	BA	SA	SB	E	DP	FA	CG	BB	SO	ShO	SV	ERA
NY	98	56	.636		914	691	234	70	159	.282	.441	41	119	188	.980	66	708	712	12	31	4.15
DET	95	59	.617	3	837	713	285	50	114	.282	.417	23	120	194	.981	72	553	576	9	20	4.12
BOS	94	60	.610	4	1027	804	287	61	161	.302	.464	32	111	181	.981	66	748	630	6	28	4.88
CLE	92	62	.597	6	806	654	222	46	164	.269	.422	40	129	160	.978	69	647	674	11	16	3.74
WAS	67	87	.435	31	690	813	190	53	76	.260	.360	42	167	181	.972	59	648	486	7	18	4.66
CHI	60	94	.390	38	625	749	172	47	93	.260	.364	19	140	181	.977	62	734	566	7	9	4.41
STL	58	96	.377	40	684	916	235	43	106	.246	.370	39	196	155	.967	56	651	448	7	14	5.20
PHI	52	102	.338	46	670	913	204	53	100	.261	.378	42	155	208	.974	50	729	466	3	18	5.49
LEAGUE TOTAL					6253	6253	1829	423	973	.271	.402	278	1137	1448	.976	500	5418	4558	62	154	4.58

INDIVIDUAL PITCHING

PITCHER	T	W	L	PCT	ERA	SV	G	GS	CG	IP	H	BB	SO	R	ER	ShO	H9	BB9	SO9
Billy Pierce	L	12	16	.429	3.98	1	33	29	15	219.1	189	137	118	112	97	1	7.76	5.62	4.84
Bill Wight	L	10	16	.385	3.58	0	30	28	13	206	213	79	62	89	82	3	9.31	3.45	2.71
Bob Cain	L	9	12	.429	3.93	2	34	23	11	171.2	153	109	77	80	75	1	8.02	5.71	4.04
Randy Gumpert	R	5	12	.294	4.75	0	40	17	6	155.1	165	58	48	87	82	1	9.56	3.36	2.78
Ray Scarborough	R	10	13	.435	5.30	1	27	23	8	149.1	160	62	70	95	88	1	9.64	3.74	4.22
Howie Judson	R	2	3	.400	3.94	0	46	3	1	112	105	63	34	53	49	0	8.44	5.06	2.73
Ken Holcombe	R	3	10	.231	4.59	1	24	15	5	96	122	45	37	68	49	0	11.44	4.22	3.47
Luis Aloma	R	7	2	.778	3.80	4	42	0	0	87.2	77	53	49	44	37	0	7.90	5.44	5.03
Mickey Haefner	L	1	6	.143	5.73	0	24	9	2	70.2	83	45	17	49	45	0	10.57	5.73	2.17
Bob Kuzava	L	1	3	.250	5.68	0	10	7	1	44.1	43	27	21	28	28	0	8.73	5.48	4.26
Lou Kretlow	R	0	0	—	3.80	0	11	1	0	21.1	17	27	14	13	9	0	7.17	11.39	5.91
Jack Bruner	L	0	0	—	3.65	0	9	0	0	12.1	7	14	8	6	5	0	5.11	10.22	5.84
Marv Rotblatt	L	0	0	—	6.23	0	2	0	0	8.2	11	5	6	7	6	0	11.42	5.19	6.23
John Perkovich	R	0	0	—	7.20	0	1	0	0	5	7	1	3	4	4	0	12.60	1.80	5.40
Bill Connelly	R	0	0	—	11.57	0	2	0	0	2.1	5	1	0	3	3	0	19.29	3.86	0.00
Gus Keriazakos	R	0	1	.000	19.29	0	1	1	0	2.1	7	5	1	5	5	0	27.00	19.29	3.86
Charlie Cuellar	R	0	0	—	33.75	0	2	0	0	1.1	6	3	1	6	5	0	40.50	20.25	6.75
TEAM TOTAL		60	94	.390	4.41	9	338	156	62	1365.2	1370	734	566	749	669	7	9.03	4.84	3.73

Chicago 1951 Won 81 Lost 73 Pct. .526 4th

MANAGER	W	L	PCT
Paul Richards	81	73	.526

POS	Player	B	G	AB	H	2B	3B	HR	HR%	R	RBI	BB	SO	SB	Pinch Hit AB	Pinch Hit H	BA	SA
REGULARS																		
1B	Eddie Robinson	L	151	564	159	23	5	29	5.1	85	117	77	54	2	2	0	.282	.495
2B	Nellie Fox	L	147	604	189	32	12	4	0.7	93	55	43	11	9	0	0	.313	.425
SS	Chico Carrasquel	R	147	538	142	22	4	2	0.4	41	58	46	39	14	0	0	.264	.331
3B	Bob Dillinger	R	89	299	90	6	4	0	0.0	39	20	15	17	5	14	4	.301	.348
RF	Al Zarilla	L	120	382	98	21	2	10	2.6	56	60	60	57	2	3	0	.257	.401
CF	Jim Busby	R	143	477	135	15	2	5	1.0	59	68	40	46	26	3	0	.283	.354
LF	Minnie Minoso	R	138	516	167	32	14*	10	1.9	109	74	71	41	31*	1	0	.324	.498
C	Phil Masi	R	84	225	61	11	2	4	1.8	24	28	32	27	1	3	0	.271	.391
SUBSTITUTES																		
3B	Floyd Baker	L	82	133	35	6	1	0	0.0	24	14	25	12	0	33	9	.263	.323
UT	Joe DeMaestri	R	56	74	15	0	2	1	1.4	8	3	5	11	0	6	1	.203	.297
1O	Bert Haas	R	25	43	7	0	1	1	2.3	1	2	5	4	0	11	3	.163	.279
3B	Hank Majeski	R	12	35	9	4	0	0	0.0	4	6	1	0	0	3	1	.257	.371
1B	Bob Boyd	L	12	18	3	0	1	0	0.0	3	4	3	3	0	5	1	.167	.278
1B	Gordon Goldsberry	L	10	11	1	0	0	0	0.0	4	1	2	2	0	2	0	.091	.091
OF	Bud Stewart	L	95	217	60	13	5	6	2.8	40	40	29	9	1	31	9	.276	.465
OF	Don Lenhardt	R	64	199	53	9	1	10	5.0	23	45	24	25	1	8	3	.266	.472
OF	Ray Coleman	L	51	181	50	8	7	3	1.7	21	21	15	14	2	1	1	.276	.448
OF	Paul Lehner	L	23	72	15	3	1	0	0.0	9	3	10	4	0	3	1	.208	.278
OF	Dave Philley	B	7	25	6	2	0	0	0.0	0	2	2	3	0	1	0	.240	.320
OF	Gus Zernial	R	4	19	2	0	0	0*	0.0*	2	4*	2	2*	0	0	0	.105	.105
C	Gus Niarhos	R	66	168	43	6	0	1	0.6	27	10	47	9	4	4	2	.256	.310
C	Bud Sheely	L	34	89	16	2	0	0	0.0	2	7	6	7	0	1	0	.180	.202
C	Joe Eraut	R	16	25	4	1	0	0	0.0	3	0	3	2	0	4	1	.160	.200
C	Red Wilson	R	4	11	3	1	0	0	0.0	1	0	1	2	0	0	0	.273	.364
C	Sam Hairston	R	4	5	2	1	0	0	0.0	1	1	2	0	0	1	0	.400	.600
PH	Rocky Nelson	L	6	5	0	0	0	0	0.0	0	0	1	0	0	5	0	.000	.000
PITCHERS																		
P	Billy Pierce	L	39	79	16	1	0	0	0.0	10	3	9	17	0	0	0	.203	.215
P	Saul Rogovin	R	24	74	15	3	0	0	0.0	7	0	5	8	1	2	1	.203	.243
P	Lou Kretlow	R	26	48	4	0	0	0	0.0	1	5	2	24	0	0	0	.083	.083
P	Joe Dobson	R	28	46	3	1	0	0	0.0	2	1	0	20	0	0	0	.065	.087
P	Randy Gumpert	R	37	45	15	1	0	0	0.0	5	9	2	9	0	0	0	.333	.356
P	Ken Holcombe	R	28	44	11	1	0	0	0.0	5	3	3	16	0	0	0	.250	.273
P	Howie Judson	R	27	33	4	0	0	0	0.0	0	1	2	14	0	0	0	.121	.121
P	Harry Dorish	R	32	31	8	2	0	0	0.0	2	0	0	3	0	0	0	.258	.323
P	Luis Aloma	R	25	20	7	1	0	0	0.0	2	2	1	5	0	0	0	.350	.400
P	Bob Cain	L	4	9	3	1	0	0	0.0	1	0	0	3	0	0	0	.333	.444
P	Marv Rotblatt	B	26	9	0	0	0	0	0.0	0	0	1	4	0	0	0	.000	.000
P	Hal Brown	R	4	2	2	0	0	0	0.0	0	1	1	0	0	0	0	1.000	1.000
P	Ross Grimsley	L	7	2	0	0	0	0	0.0	0	0	0	1	0	0	0	.000	.000
P	Dick Littlefield	L	4	1	0	0	0	0	0.0	0	0	2	0	0	0	0	.000	.000
P	Bob Mahoney	R	3	0	0	0	0	0	—	0	0	0	0	0	0	0	—	—
TEAM TOTAL				5378	1453	229	64	86	1.6	714	668	594	525	99	147	37	.270	.385

INDIVIDUAL FIELDING

POS	Player	T	G	PO	A	E	DP	TCG	FA
1B	E. Robinson	R	147	1296	91	17	143	9.6	.988
	B. Haas	R	7	41	4	0	4	6.4	1.000
	B. Boyd	L	6	36	1	0	8	6.2	1.000
	G. Goldsberry	L	8	28	5	0	4	4.1	1.000
	D. Lenhardt	R	2	6	0	0	0	3.0	1.000
2B	N. Fox	R	147	413	449	17	112	6.0	.981
	J. DeMaestri	R	11	16	14	1	2	2.8	.968
	F. Baker	R	5	11	9	0	3	4.0	1.000
SS	C. Carrasquel	R	147	306	477	20	107	5.5	.975
	J. DeMaestri	R	27	26	45	3	12	2.7	.959
	F. Baker	R	3	2	3	0	1	1.7	1.000
	M. Minoso	R	1	0	1	0	0	1.0	1.000
3B	M. Minoso	R	68	82	122	14	10	3.2	.936
	B. Dillinger	R	70	70	116	14	10	2.9	.930
	F. Baker	R	44	27	46	6	4	1.8	.924
	H. Dorish	R	1	0	0	0	0	0.0	.000
	H. Majeski	R	9	4	15	1	2	2.2	.950
	J. DeMaestri	R	8	1	2	1	0	0.5	.750
	B. Haas	R	1	0	1	0	0	1.0	1.000
OF	J. Busby	R	139	360	16	7	4	2.8	.982
	A. Zarilla	R	117	164	7	3	2	1.5	.983
	M. Minoso	R	82	145	4	6	0	1.9	.961
	R. Coleman	R	51	141	3	3	1	2.9	.980
	D. Lenhardt	R	53	116	2	2	0	2.3	.983
	B. Stewart	R	63	111	4	2	0	1.9	.983
	P. Lehner	L	20	47	4	1	0	2.6	.981
	D. Philley	R	6	15	0	1	0	2.7	.938
	G. Zernial	R	4	13	1*	1	0	3.8	.933
	B. Haas	R	4	3	0	0	0	0.8	1.000
C	P. Masi	R	78	299	24	7	7	4.2	.979
	G. Niarhos	R	59	240	31	4	5	4.7	.985
	B. Sheely	R	33	127	11	2	3	4.2	.986
	J. Eraut	R	12	37	6	1	1	3.7	.977
	R. Wilson	R	4	9	2	0	0	2.8	1.000
	S. Hairston	R	2	3	0	0	0	1.5	1.000

126

Chicago 1951

Nobody took the Sox seriously when they won the Grapefruit League title. But Paul Richards "jet propelled" a team that had stolen just 19 bases in 1950 into a daring "Go-Go" outfit that captured the imaginations of baseball fans everywhere. The Go-Go era began on May 1 when Minnie Minoso was acquired from Cleveland for Gus Zernial and Dave Philley. His first game saw his first home run.

Nellie Fox came of age in 1951, while Billy Pierce and Saul Rogovin carried the day for the pitchers. But it was an eastern road trip in May that showed this was a club to be reckoned with. They won 14 games in a row in such unlikely ports of call as Boston, New York, and Cleveland. When they got back to Chicago on June 2, Mayor Martin Kennelly gave them a City Hall reception.

The Sox revived the forgotten art of the stolen base; they led the league as a team, and Minoso and centerfielder Jim Busby ranked one-two in the league. The move to a speed-based offense was a natural one for a team that could not live by the homer.

Lane kept the pot boiling with twenty-nine separate player transactions between opening day and October. But the team was just too young and inexperienced to sustain a drive on the Yankees. No matter, though; the turnstiles clicked to a merry tune of 1,328,238 — a new club record.

TEAM STATISTICS

	W	L	PCT	GB	R	OR	2B	3B	HR	BA	SA	SB	E	DP	FA	CG	BB	SO	ShO	SV	ERA
NY	98	56	.636		798	621	208	48	140	.269	.408	78	144	190	.975	66	562	664	24	22	3.56
CLE	93	61	.604	5	696	594	208	35	140	.256	.389	52	134	151	.978	76	577	642	10	19	3.38
BOS	87	67	.565	11	804	725	233	32	127	.266	.392	20	141	184	.977	46	599	658	7	24	4.14
CHI	81	73	.526	17	714	644	229	64	86	.270	.385	99	151	176	.975	74	549	572	11	14	3.50
DET	73	81	.474	25	685	741	231	35	104	.265	.380	37	163	166	.973	51	602	597	8	17	4.29
PHI	70	84	.455	28	736	745	262	43	102	.262	.386	48	136	204	.978	52	569	437	7	22	4.47
WAS	62	92	.403	36	672	764	242	45	54	.263	.355	45	160	148	.973	58	630	475	6	13	4.49
STL	52	102	.338	46	611	882	223	47	86	.247	.357	35	172	179	.971	56	801	550	5	9	5.17
LEAGUE TOTAL					5716	5716	1836	349	839	.262	.381	414	1201	1398	.975	479	4889	4595	78	140	4.12

INDIVIDUAL PITCHING

PITCHER	T	W	L	PCT	ERA	SV	G	GS	CG	IP	H	BB	SO	R	ER	ShO	H9	BB9	SO9
Billy Pierce	L	15	14	.517	3.03	2	37	28	18	240.1	237	73	113	93	81	1	8.88	2.73	4.23
Saul Rogovin	R	11	7	.611	2.48*	0	22	22	17	192.2	166	67	77	64	53	3	7.75	3.13	3.60
Ken Holcombe	R	11	12	.478	3.78	0	28	23	12	159.1	142	68	39	69	67	2	8.02	3.84	2.20
Joe Dobson	R	7	6	.538	3.62	3	28	21	6	146.2	136	51	67	68	59	0	8.35	3.13	4.11
Randy Gumpert	R	9	8	.529	4.32	2	33	16	7	141.2	156	34	45	74	68	1	9.91	2.16	2.86
Lou Kretlow	R	6	9	.400	4.20	0	26	18	7	137	129	74	89	77	64	1	8.47	4.86	5.85
Howie Judson	R	5	6	.455	3.77	1	27	14	3	121.2	124	55	43	67	51	0	9.17	4.07	3.18
Harry Dorish	R	5	6	.455	3.54	0	32	4	2	96.2	101	31	29	50	38	1	9.40	2.89	2.70
Luis Aloma	R	6	0	1.000	1.82	3	25	1	1	69.1	52	24	25	14	14	1	6.75	3.12	3.25
Marv Rotblatt	L	4	2	.667	3.40	2	26	2	0	47.2	44	23	20	21	18	0	8.31	4.34	3.78
Bob Cain	L	1	2	.333	3.76	0	4	4	1	26.1	25	13	3	14	11	0	8.54	4.44	1.03
Ross Grimsley	L	0	0	—	3.86	0	7	0	0	14	12	10	8	8	6	0	7.71	6.43	5.14
Dick Littlefield	L	1	1	.500	8.38	0	4	2	0	9.2	9	17	7	12	9	0	8.38	15.83	6.52
Hal Brown	R	0	0	—	9.35	1	3	0	0	8.2	15	4	4	9	9	0	15.58	4.15	4.15
Bob Mahoney	R	0	0	—	5.40	0	3	0	0	6.2	5	5	3	4	4	0	6.75	6.75	4.05
TEAM TOTAL		81	73	.526	3.50	14	305	155	74	1418.1	1353	549	572	644	552	10	8.59	3.48	3.63

Chicago 1952　　Won 81　Lost 73　Pct .526　3rd

MANAGER	W	L	PCT
Paul Richards	81	73	.526

POS	Player	B	G	AB	H	2B	3B	HR	HR%	R	RBI	BB	SO	SB	Pinch Hit AB	H	BA	SA
REGULARS																		
1B	Eddie Robinson	L	155	594	176	33	1	22	3.7	79	104	70	49	2	0	0	.296	.466
2B	Nellie Fox	L	152	**648**	**192**	25	10	0	0.0	76	39	34	14	5	1	0	.296	.366
SS	Chico Carrasquel	R	100	359	89	7	4	1	0.3	36	42	33	27	2	1	1	.248	.298
3B	Hec Rodriguez	R	124	407	108	14	0	1	0.2	55	40	47	22	7	8	2	.265	.307
RF	Sam Mele	R	123	423	105	18	2	14	3.3	46	59	48	40	1	10	1	.248	.400
CF	Ray Coleman	L	85	195	42	7	1	2	1.0	19	14	13	17	0	13	1	.215	.292
LF	Minnie Minoso	R	147	569	160	24	9	13	2.3	96	61	71	46	22	0	0	.281	.424
C	Sherm Lollar	R	132	375	90	15	0	13	3.5	35	50	54	34	1	11	2	.240	.384
SUBSTITUTES																		
SS	Willie Miranda	B	70	150	33	4	1	0	0.0	14	7	13	14	1	1	0	.220	.260
UT	Sam Dente	R	62	145	32	0	1	0	0.0	12	11	5	8	0	12	1	.221	.234
3B	Rocky Krsnich	R	40	91	21	7	2	1	1.1	11	15	12	9	0	2	0	.231	.385
3B	Leo Thomas	R	19	24	4	0	0	0	0.0	1	6	6	4	0	5	1	.167	.167
1B	Ken Landenberger	L	2	5	1	0	0	0	0.0	0	0	0	2	0	1	0	.200	.200
SS	Sammy Esposito	R	1	4	1	0	0	0	0.0	0	0	0	2	0	0	0	.250	.250
OF	Bud Stewart	L	92	225	60	10	0	5	2.2	23	30	28	17	3	34	6	.267	.378
OF	Jim Rivera	L	53	201	50	7	3	3	1.5	27	18	21	27	13	0	0	.249	.358
OF	Tom Wright	L	60	132	34	10	2	1	0.8	15	21	16	16	1	23	8*	.258	.386
OF	Al Zarilla	L	39	99	23	4	1	2	2.0	14	7	14	6	1	6	0	.232	.354
OF	Jim Busby	R	16	39	5	0	0	0	0.0	5	0	2	7	0	0	0	.128	.128
OF	Hank Edwards	L	8	18	6	0	0	0	0.0	2	1	0	2	0	5	2	.333	.333
OF	Ted Wilson	L	8	9	1	0	0	0	0.0	0	1	1	2	0	7	1	.111	.111
OF	Don Nicholas	L	3	2	0	0	0	0	0.0	0	0	0	0	0	2	0	.000	.000
C	Bud Sheely	L	36	75	18	2	0	0	0.0	1	3	12	7	0	6	2	.240	.267
C	Phil Masi	R	30	63	16	1	1	0	0.0	9	7	10	10	0	3	1	.254	.302
C	Darrell Johnson	R	22	37	4	0	0	0	0.0	3	1	5	9	1	2	0	.108	.108
C	Red Wilson	R	2	3	0	0	0	0	0.0	0	0	0	1	0	0	0	.000	.000
PITCHERS																		
P	Billy Pierce	L	35	91	17	1	0	0	0.0	11	3	6	20	0	0	0	.187	.198
P	Saul Rogovin	R	33	84	17	3	0	1	1.2	9	7	4	18	1	0	0	.202	.274
P	Joe Dobson	R	29	63	12	0	0	0	0.0	3	3	4	20	0	0	0	.190	.190
P	Marv Grissom	R	28	53	8	4	0	0	0.0	1	4	1	19	0	0	0	.151	.226
P	Chuck Stobbs	L	38	38	3	0	0	0	0.0	1	3	6	11	0	0	0	.079	.079
P	Harry Dorish	R	39	22	2	1	0	0	0.0	2	0	1	4	0	0	0	.091	.136
P	Lou Kretlow	R	19	20	1	1	0	0	0.0	1	0	3	14	0	0	0	.050	.100
P	Hal Brown	R	51	19	3	1	0	1	5.3	6	3	1	8	0	2	0	.158	.368
P	Bill Kennedy	L	47	13	3	0	0	0	0.0	0	0	0	5	0	0	0	.231	.231
P	Ken Holcombe	R	7	10	0	0	0	0	0.0	0	0	0	4	0	0	0	.000	.000
P	Luis Aloma	R	25	7	0	0	0	0	0.0	0	0	0	2	0	0	0	.000	.000
P	Howie Judson	R	21	4	0	0	0	0	0.0	0	0	0	2	0	0	0	.000	.000
P	Hal Hudson	L	2	0	0	0	0	0	—	0	0	0	0	0	0	0	—	—
P	Al Widmar	R	1	0	0	0	0	0	—	0	0	0	0	0	0	0	—	—
TEAM TOTAL				5316	1337	199	38	80	1.5	610	560	541	519	61	155	29	.252	.348

INDIVIDUAL FIELDING

POS	Player	T	G	PO	A	E	DP	TCG	FA	POS	Player	T	G	PO	A	E	DP	TCG	FA
1B	E. Robinson	R	155	**1329**	89	14	145	9.2	.990	OF	M. Minoso	R	143	322	11	7	3	2.4	.979
	S. Dente	R	2	8	2	0	1	5.0	1.000		S. Mele	R	112	157	8	0	1	1.5	1.000
	S. Mele	R	3	10	0	0	0	3.3	1.000		J. Rivera	L	53	157	2	2	1	3.0	.988
	Landenberger	L	1	8	1	0	0	9.0	1.000		R. Coleman	L	73	130	5	3	0	1.9	.978
2B	N. Fox	R	151	**406**	**433**	13	111	5.6	**.985**		B. Stewart	R	60	108	1	2	0	1.9	.982
	S. Dente	R	6	24	20	0	6	7.3	1.000		T. Wright	R	34	60	2	2	0	1.9	.969
	W. Miranda	R	2	1	8	1	0	5.0	.900		J. Busby	R	16	42*	0	0	0	2.6*	1.000
SS	C. Carrasquel	R	99	176	248	16	50	4.4	.964		A. Zarilla	R	32	35	2	1	0	1.2	.974
	W. Miranda	R	54	72	138	5	28	4.0	.977		D. Nicholas	R	3	0	0	0	0	0.0	.000
	S. Dente	R	27	42	56	6	14	3.9	.942		H. Edwards	L	3	8	0	0	0	2.7	1.000
	M. Minoso	R	1	0	0	0	0	0.0	.000		S. Dente	R	6	4	0	0	0	0.7	1.000
	S. Esposito	R	1	1	1	2	0	4.0	.500		T. Wilson	R	1	2	0	0	0	2.0	1.000
3B	H. Rodriguez	R	113	145	232	16	26	3.5	.959	C	S. Lollar	R	120	590	53	7	4	5.4	.989
	R. Krsnich	R	37	45	72	5	6	3.3	.959		B. Sheely	R	31	105	12	1	1	3.8	.992
	S. Dente	R	18	7	17	0	2	1.3	1.000		P. Masi	R	25	101	7	5	2	4.5	.956
	L. Thomas	R	9	5	15	1	1	2.3	.952		D. Johnson	R	21	75	9	4	1	4.2	.955
	M. Minoso	R	9	1	11	0	0	1.3	1.000		R. Wilson	R	2	8	1	0	0	4.5	1.000
	W. Miranda	R	5	1	4	0	1	1.0	1.000										

Chicago 1952

Even though the Sox finished in third with a 81–73 record, the season was a disappointment to many Sox fans who expected continued improvement. There were no lengthy winning streaks or home run heroics as there had been in 1951. At one stretch Sox batsmen went to the plate 99 times in a row without producing an extra-base hit.

Front office feuds not unlike those of the days of the founder characterized 1952. Chuck Comiskey resigned in disgust when his mother wouldn't give him a raise, but he returned as club vice president several months later after a brief stint with the Liberty Broadcasting System.

Frank Lane went shopping again, but dealt himself a losing hand when he traded Jim Busby to Washington for Sam Mele. Better results were achieved when Jim Rivera was reacquired from the Browns on July 28 for Ray Coleman and J.W. Porter. Earlier in the year, Rivera had been traded to St. Louis along with Dick Littlefield, Joe DeMaestri, Gordie Goldsberry, and Gus Niarhos for Sherm Lollar.

If all these St. Louis trades weren't confusing enough, consider that in the same year Frank Lane traded infielder Willie Miranda to the Browns *twice*, first on June 15, then on October 16. All hopes of maintaining this profitable St. Louis shuttle were dashed when Bill Veeck sold the Browns in 1953. The idea of maintaining a farm team in your own league was copied later in the decade by the Yankees, who cultivated Arnold Johnson's friendship and generosity in Kansas City.

TEAM STATISTICS

	W	L	PCT	GB	R	OR	2B	3B	HR	BA	SA	SB	E	DP	FA	CG	BB	SO	ShO	SV	ERA
NY	95	59	.617		727	557	221	56	129	.267	.403	52	127	199	.979	72	581	666	17	27	3.14
CLE	93	61	.604	2	763	606	211	49	148	.262	.404	46	155	141	.975	80	556	671	16	18	3.32
CHI	81	73	.526	14	610	568	199	38	80	.252	.348	61	123	158	.980	53	578	774	13	28	3.25
PHI	79	75	.513	16	664	723	212	35	89	.253	.359	52	140	148	.977	73	526	562	11	16	4.15
WAS	78	76	.506	17	598	608	225	44	50	.239	.326	48	132	152	.978	75	577	574	10	15	3.37
BOS	76	78	.494	19	668	658	233	34	113	.255	.377	59	145	181	.976	53	623	624	7	24	3.80
STL	64	90	.416	31	604	733	225	46	82	.250	.356	30	155	176	.974	48	598	581	6	18	4.12
DET	50	104	.325	45	557	738	190	37	103	.243	.352	27	152	145	.975	51	591	702	10	14	4.25
LEAGUE TOTAL					5191	5191	1716	339	794	.253	.365	375	1129	1300	.977	505	4630	5154	90	160	3.67

INDIVIDUAL PITCHING

PITCHER	T	W	L	PCT	ERA	SV	G	GS	CG	IP	H	BB	SO	R	ER	ShO	H9	BB9	SO9
Billy Pierce	L	15	12	.556	2.57	1	33	32	14	255.1	214	79	144	76	73	4	7.54	2.78	5.08
Saul Rogovin	R	14	9	.609	3.85	1	33	30	12	231.2	224	79	121	104	99	3	8.70	3.07	4.70
Joe Dobson	R	14	10	.583	2.51	1	29	25	11	200.2	164	60	101	66	56	3	7.36	2.69	4.53
Marv Grissom	R	12	10	.545	3.74	0	28	24	7	166	156	79	97	79	69	1	8.46	4.28	5.26
Chuck Stobbs	L	7	12	.368	3.13	1	38	17	2	135	118	72	73	54	47	0	7.87	4.80	4.87
Harry Dorish	R	8	4	.667	2.47	11	39	1	1	91	66	42	47	28	25	0	6.53	4.15	4.65
Lou Kretlow	R	4	4	.500	2.96	1	19	11	4	79	52	56	63	31	26	2	5.92	6.38	7.18
Hal Brown	R	2	3	.400	4.23	0	24	8	1	72.1	82	21	31	39	34	0	10.20	2.61	3.86
Bill Kennedy	L	2	2	.500	2.80	5	47	1	0	70.2	54	38	46	27	22	0	6.88	4.84	5.86
Luis Aloma	R	3	1	.750	4.28	6	25	0	0	40	42	11	18	20	19	0	9.45	2.48	4.05
Ken Holcombe	R	0	5	.000	6.17	0	7	7	1	35	38	18	12	24	24	0	9.77	4.63	3.09
Howie Judson	R	0	1	.000	4.24	1	21	0	0	34	30	22	15	17	16	0	7.94	5.82	3.97
Hal Hudson	L	0	0	–	2.25	0	2	0	0	4	7	1	4	2	1	0	15.75	2.25	9.00
Al Widmar	R	0	0	–	4.50	0	1	0	0	2	4	0	2	1	1	0	18.00	0.00	9.00
TEAM TOTAL		81	73	.526	3.25	28	346	156	53	1416.2	1251	578	774	568	512	13	7.95	3.67	4.92

Chicago 1953   Won 89 Lost 65 Pct. .578 3rd

MANAGER	W	L	PCT
Paul Richards	89	65	.578

POS	Player	B	G	AB	H	2B	3B	HR	HR%	R	RBI	BB	SO	SB	Pinch Hit AB	H	BA	SA
REGULARS																		
1B	Ferris Fain	L	128	446	114	18	2	6	1.3	73	52	108	28	3	1	1	.256	.345
2B	Nellie Fox	L	154	624	178	31	8	3	0.5	92	72	49	18	4	0	0	.285	.375
SS	Chico Carrasquel	R	149	552	154	30	4	2	0.4	72	47	38	47	5	0	0	.279	.359
3B	Bob Elliott	R	67	208	54	11	1	4	1.9	24	32	31	21	1	6	1	.260	.380
RF	Sam Mele	R	140	481	132	26	8	12	2.5	64	82	58	47	3	6	3	.274	.437
CF	Jim Rivera	L	156	567	147	26	16	11	1.9	79	78	53	70	22	0	0	.259	.420
LF	Minnie Minoso	R	157	556	174	24	8	15	2.7	104	104	74	43	25	0	0	.313	.466
C	Sherm Lollar	R	113	334	96	19	0	8	2.4	46	54	47	29	1	5	1	.287	.416
SUBSTITUTES																		
1O	Bob Boyd	L	55	165	49	6	2	3	1.8	20	23	13	11	1	8	4	.297	.412
3B	Rocky Krsnich	R	64	129	26	8	0	1	0.8	9	14	12	11	0	6	1	.202	.287
3B	Vern Stephens	R	44	129	24	6	0	1	0.8	14	14	13	18	2	4	0	.186	.256
UT	Freddie Marsh	R	67	95	19	1	0	2	2.1	22	2	13	26	0	11	2	.200	.274
3B	Connie Ryan	R	17	54	12	1	0	0	0.0	6	6	9	12	2	1	1	.222	.241
2B	Neil Berry	R	5	8	1	0	0	0	0.0	1	0	1	1	0	1	0	.125	.125
SS	Sam Dente	R	2	0	0	0	0	0	—	0	0	0	0	0	0	0	—	—
OF	Tom Wright	L	77	132	33	5	3	2	1.5	14	25	12	21	0	42	13	.250	.379
OF	Bud Stewart	L	53	59	16	2	0	2	3.4	16	13	14	3	1	34	10	.271	.407
OF	Bill Wilson	R	9	17	1	0	0	0	0.0	1	1	0	7	0	4	0	.059	.059
O1	Allie Clark	R	9	15	1	0	0	0	0.0	0	0	0	5	0	8	0	.067	.067
C	Red Wilson	R	71	164	41	6	1	0	0.0	21	10	26	12	2	7	1	.250	.299
C	Bud Sheely	L	31	46	10	1	0	0	0.0	4	2	9	8	0	10	4	.217	.239
PITCHERS																		
P	Billy Pierce	L	42	87	11	0	0	0	0.0	4	4	4	16	0	0	0	.126	.126
P	Virgil Trucks	R	24	63	15	3	0	1	1.6	6	6	0	10	0	0	0	.238	.333
P	Harry Dorish	R	55	41	7	0	0	0	0.0	4	1	0	5	0	0	0	.171	.171
P	Mike Fornieles	R	39	41	4	1	0	0	0.0	2	5	1	5	0	0	0	.098	.122
P	Saul Rogovin	R	22	37	5	0	0	0	0.0	5	3	7	9	1	0	0	.135	.135
P	Sandy Consuegra	R	29	35	2	0	0	0	0.0	1	3	1	7	0	0	0	.057	.057
P	Joe Dobson	R	23	29	2	1	0	0	0.0	0	2	1	11	0	0	0	.069	.103
P	Bob Keegan	R	22	28	9	0	0	0	0.0	4	5	1	5	0	0	0	.321	.321
P	Gene Bearden	L	31	21	4	0	0	0	0.0	2	3	0	4	0	6	1	.190	.190
P	Connie Johnson	R	15	20	1	0	0	0	0.0	4	1	2	7	0	0	0	.050	.050
P	Tommy Byrne	L	18	18	3	0	0	1	5.6	2	5	2	6	0	10	1	.167	.333
P	Luis Aloma	R	24	6	0	0	0	0	0.0	0	0	0	4	0	0	0	.000	.000
P	Lou Kretlow	R	9	4	0	0	0	0	0.0	0	0	1	2	0	0	0	.000	.000
P	Earl Harrist	R	7	1	0	0	0	0	0.0	0	0	0	0	0	0	0	.000	.000
P	Hal Hudson	L	1	0	0	0	0	0	—	0	0	0	0	0	0	0	—	—
TEAM TOTAL				5212	1345	226	53	74	1.4	716	669	600	529	73	170	44	.258	.364

INDIVIDUAL FIELDING

POS	Player	T	G	PO	A	E	DP	TCG	FA
1B	F. Fain	L	127	1108	106	13	98	9.7	.989
	B. Boyd	L	29	275	16	0	25	10.0	1.000
	F. Marsh	R	5	23	2	1	0	5.2	.962
	A. Clark	R	1	5	0	0	2	5.0	1.000
	S. Mele	R	2	4	0	0	0	2.0	1.000
	S. Lollar	R	1	3	0	0	0	3.0	1.000
	B. Pierce	L	1	1	0	0	0	1.0	1.000
2B	N. Fox	R	154	451	426	15	101	5.8	.983
	N. Berry	R	3	5	10	0	1	5.0	1.000
	F. Marsh	R	2	4	3	0	2	3.5	1.000
SS	C. Carrasquel	R	149	278	462	18	87	5.1	.976
	F. Marsh	R	17	17	36	2	5	3.2	.964
	S. Dente	R	1	0	0	0	0	0.0	.000
	V. Stephens	R	3	0	4	0	0	1.3	1.000
3B	B. Elliott	R	58	54	104	6	9	2.8	.963
	R. Krsnich	R	57	31	100	10	7	2.5	.929
	V. Stephens	R	38	30	67	1	7	2.6	.990
	C. Ryan	R	16	20	31	4	1	3.4	.927
	F. Marsh	R	32	17	30	3	5	1.6	.940
	M. Minoso	R	10	3	14	2	0	1.9	.895

POS	Player	T	G	PO	A	E	DP	TCG	FA
OF	J. Rivera	L	156	385	15	10	5	2.6	.976
	M. Minoso	R	147	279	15	10	3	2.1	.967
	S. Mele	R	138	213	14	1	1	1.7	.996
	T. Wright	R	33	44	1	1	0	1.4	.978
	B. Boyd	L	16	26	0	1	0	1.7	.963
	B. Stewart	R	16	12	0	0	0	0.8	1.000
	B. Wilson	R	3	9	0	0	0	3.0	1.000
	A. Clark	R	1	1	0	0	0	1.0	1.000
	B. Elliott	R	2	0	0	1	0	0.5	.000
C	S. Lollar	R	107	470	51	3	2	4.9	.994
	R. Wilson	R	63	282	24	6	1	5.0	.981
	B. Sheely	R	17	60	2	0	1	3.6	1.000

The Yankees kept rolling, and so did the St. Louis express. Just before the trading deadline, Lane sent the washed-up Lou Kretlow to the Brownies for Virgil Trucks and Bob Elliot. Trucks won his first eight Sox decisions while helping the team rise to second place in the first week of July. Elliot was just one of a changing cast of characters to try their hand at third base. Can't anybody play this position? Certainly not Freddie Marsh, Vern Stephens, Rocky Krsnich, Connie Ryan, or even Minnie Minoso. A proposed deal for Andy Carey fell through when the Yankees insisted on a Gil McDougald-for-Billy Pierce swap.

The Sox did have one fine moment against the Yanks in '53. It happened in Yankee Stadium on May 16, when they trailed the leaders by just a game and a half. They came up for their last turn at bat in the ninth inning trailing Vic Raschi, 3–0. Four straight singles and a walk produced a run, but there were two out. Stengel brought in Ewell Blackwell to face Vern Stephens. Paul Richards, in a moment of inspiration, sent up pitcher Tommy Byrne to pinch-hit. On a 2–2 count he lined a 360-foot homer to right, and the Sox won the game 5–3. Vintage Richards.

The Sox held second place till September 6, when they settled into third place for good. It was fitting that the Sox played (and won) the last American League game in St. Louis, on September 27. The new Baltimore Orioles would not be as obliging as the Brownies had been.

TEAM STATISTICS

	W	L	PCT	GB	R	OR	2B	3B	HR	BA	SA	SB	E	DP	FA	CG	BB	SO	ShO	SV	ERA
NY	99	52	.656		801	547	226	52	139	.273	.417	34	126	182	.979	50	500	604	16	39	3.20
CLE	92	62	.597	8.5	770	627	201	29	160	.270	.410	33	127	197	.979	81	519	586	11	15	3.64
CHI	89	65	.578	11.5	716	592	226	53	74	.258	.364	73	125	144	.980	57	583	714	16	33	3.41
BOS	84	69	.549	16	656	632	255	37	101	.264	.384	33	148	173	.975	41	584	642	14	37	3.59
WAS	76	76	.500	23.5	687	614	230	53	69	.263	.368	65	120	173	.979	76	478	515	16	10	3.66
DET	60	94	.390	40.5	695	923	259	44	108	.266	.387	30	135	149	.978	50	585	645	2	16	5.25
PHI	59	95	.383	41.5	632	799	205	38	116	.256	.372	41	137	161	.977	51	594	566	6	11	4.67
STL	54	100	.351	46.5	555	778	214	25	112	.249	.363	17	152	165	.974	28	626	639	7	24	4.48
LEAGUE TOTAL					5512	5512	1816	331	879	.262	.383	326	1070	1344	.978	434	4469	4911	88	185	4.00

INDIVIDUAL PITCHING

PITCHER	T	W	L	PCT	ERA	SV	G	GS	CG	IP	H	BB	SO	R	ER	ShO	H9	BB9	SO9
Billy Pierce	L	18	12	.600	2.72	3	40	33	19	271.1	216	102	186	94	82	7	7.16	3.38	6.17
Virgil Trucks	R	15	6	.714	2.86	1	24	21	13	176.1	151	67	102	60	56	3	7.71	3.42	5.21
Mike Fornieles	R	8	7	.533	3.59	3	39	16	5	153	160	61	72	68	61	0	9.41	3.59	4.24
Harry Dorish	R	10	6	.625	3.40	18	55	6	2	145.2	140	52	69	59	55	0	8.65	3.21	4.26
Saul Rogovin	R	7	12	.368	5.22	1	22	19	4	131	151	48	62	82	76	1	10.37	3.30	4.26
Sandy Consuegra	R	7	5	.583	2.54	3	29	13	5	124	122	28	30	39	35	1	8.85	2.03	2.18
Joe Dobson	R	5	5	.500	3.67	1	23	15	3	100.2	96	37	50	46	41	1	8.58	3.31	4.47
Bob Keegan	R	7	5	.583	2.74	1	22	11	4	98.2	80	33	32	34	30	2	7.30	3.01	2.92
Connie Johnson	R	4	4	.500	3.56	0	14	10	2	60.2	55	38	44	27	24	1	8.16	5.64	6.53
Gene Bearden	L	3	3	.500	2.93	0	25	3	0	58.1	48	33	24	27	19	0	7.41	5.09	3.70
Luis Aloma	R	2	0	1.000	4.70	2	24	0	0	38.1	41	23	23	20	20	0	9.63	5.40	5.40
Lou Kretlow	R	0	0	—	3.48	0	9	3	0	20.2	12	30	15	11	8	0	5.23	13.06	6.53
Tommy Byrne	L	2	0	1.000	10.13	0	6	6	0	16	18	26	4	18	18	0	10.13	14.63	2.25
Earl Harrist	R	1	0	1.000	7.56	0	7	0	0	8.1	9	5	1	7	7	0	9.72	5.40	1.08
Hal Hudson	L	0	0	—	0.00	0	1	0	0	.2	0	0	0	0	0	0	0.00	0.00	0.00
TEAM TOTAL		89	65	.578	3.41	33	340	156	57	1403.2	1299	583	714	592	532	16	8.33	3.74	4.58

Chicago 1954   Won 94 Lost 60 Pct. .610 3rd

MANAGER	W	L	PCT
Paul Richards	91	54	.628
Marty Marion	3	6	.333

POS	Player	B	G	AB	H	2B	3B	HR	HR %	R	RBI	BB	SO	SB	Pinch Hit AB	Pinch Hit H	BA	SA
REGULARS																		
1B	Ferris Fain	L	65	235	71	10	1	5	2.1	30	51	40	14	5	0	0	.302	.417
2B	Nellie Fox	L	155	631	201	24	8	2	0.3	111	47	51	12	16	0	0	.319	.391
SS	Chico Carrasquel	R	155	620	158	28	3	12	1.9	106	62	85	67	7	0	0	.255	.368
3B	Cass Michaels	R	101	282	74	13	2	7	2.5	35	44	56	31	10	7	0	.262	.397
RF	Jim Rivera	L	145	490	140	16	8	13	2.7	62	61	49	68	18	3	0	.286	.431
CF	Johnny Groth	R	125	422	116	20	0	7	1.7	41	60	42	37	3	1	0	.275	.372
LF	Minnie Minoso	R	153	568	182	29	18	19	3.3	119	116	77	46	18	0	0	.320	.535
C	Sherm Lollar	R	107	316	77	13	0	7	2.2	31	34	37	28	0	15	3	.244	.351
SUBSTITUTES																		
13	George Kell	R	71	233	66	10	0	5	2.1	25	48	18	12	1	8	1	.283	.391
1B	Phil Cavarretta	L	71	158	50	6	0	3	1.9	21	24	26	12	4	16	2	.316	.411
3B	Freddie Marsh	R	62	98	30	5	2	0	0.0	21	4	9	16	4	2	0	.306	.398
1B	Ron Jackson	R	40	93	26	4	0	4	4.3	10	10	6	20	2	7	1	.280	.452
31	Grady Hatton	L	13	30	5	1	0	0	0.0	3	3	5	3	1	2	0	.167	.200
3B	Joe Kirrene	R	9	23	7	1	0	0	0.0	4	4	5	2	1	1	0	.304	.348
3B	Stan Jok	R	3	12	2	0	0	0	0.0	1	2	1	2	0	0	0	.167	.167
OF	Ed McGhee	R	42	75	17	1	0	0	0.0	12	5	12	8	5	4	0	.227	.240
OF	Willard Marshall	L	47	71	18	2	0	1	1.4	7	7	11	9	0	19	4	.254	.324
O1	Bob Boyd	L	29	56	10	3	0	0	0.0	10	5	4	3	2	2	0	.179	.232
OF	Bill Wilson	R	20	35	6	1	0	2	5.7	4	5	7	5	0	2	0	.171	.371
OF	Bud Stewart	L	18	13	1	0	0	0	0.0	0	0	3	2	0	12	1	.077	.077
OF	Don Nicholas	L	7	0	0	0	0	0	—	3	0	1	0	0	0	0	—	—
C	Matt Batts	R	55	158	36	7	1	3	1.9	16	19	17	15	0	12	2	.228	.342
C	Carl Sawatski	L	43	109	20	3	3	1	0.9	6	12	15	20	0	8	1	.183	.294
C	Red Wilson	R	8	20	4	0	0	1	5.0	2	1	1	2	0	0	0	.200	.350
PH	Bob Cain	L	1	0	0	0	0	0	—	1	0	0	0	0	0	0	—	—
PITCHERS																		
P	Virgil Trucks	R	40	93	17	2	0	0	0.0	5	8	1	21	0	0	0	.183	.204
P	Bob Keegan	R	32	75	9	2	1	0	0.0	5	7	4	11	0	1	1	.120	.173
P	Billy Pierce	L	38	57	11	0	0	0	0.0	4	5	4	12	0	0	0	.193	.193
P	Jack Harshman	L	36	56	8	1	0	2	3.6	6	5	12	21	0	0	0	.143	.268
P	Sandy Consuegra	R	39	48	11	0	0	0	0.0	4	3	3	11	0	0	0	.229	.229
P	Don Johnson	R	46	35	1	0	0	0	0.0	0	1	2	12	0	0	0	.029	.029
P	Harry Dorish	R	37	27	3	0	0	0	0.0	3	0	0	5	0	0	0	.111	.111
P	Morrie Martin	L	35	15	2	1	0	0	0.0	1	2	0	6	0	0	0	.133	.200
P	Mike Fornieles	R	16	11	3	0	0	0	0.0	2	0	0	0	1	0	0	.273	.273
P	Al Sima	L	5	2	0	0	0	0	0.0	0	0	0	2	0	0	0	.000	.000
P	Dick Strahs	L	9	1	0	0	0	0	0.0	0	0	0	1	0	0	0	.000	.000
P	Tom Flanigan	R	2	0	0	0	0	0	—	0	0	0	0	0	0	0	—	—
P	Vito Valentinetti	R	1	0	0	0	0	0	—	0	0	0	0	0	0	0	—	—
TEAM TOTAL				5168	1382	203	47	94	1.8	711	655	604	536	98	122	16	.267	.379

INDIVIDUAL FIELDING

POS	Player	T	G	PO	A	E	DP	TCG	FA	POS	Player	T	G	PO	A	E	DP	TCG	FA
1B	F. Fain	L	64	565	31	8	54	9.4	.987	OF	M. Minoso	R	146	340	14	8	3	2.5	.978
	P. Cavarretta	L	44	261	17	2	29	6.4	.993		J. Groth	R	125	314	7	4	3	2.6	.988
	G. Kell	R	32	253	8	1	27	8.2	.996		J. Rivera	L	143	255	5	11	0	1.9	.959
	R. Jackson	R	35	244	9	3	15	7.3	.988		E. McGhee	R	34	51	4	1	1	1.6	.982
	B. Boyd	L	12	51	2	1	3	4.5	.981		B. Wilson	R	19	33	0	2	0	1.8	.943
	G. Hatton	R	3	6	0	0	1	2.0	1.000		W. Marshall	R	29	23	1	1	0	0.9	.960
	J. Harshman	L	1	3	0	0	0	3.0	1.000		D. Nicholas	R	7	0	0	0	0	0.0	.000
	F. Marsh	R	2	2	0	0	0	1.0	1.000		B. Boyd	L	13	20	1	1	0	1.7	.955
2B	N. Fox	R	155	400	392	9	103	5.2	.989		P. Cavarretta	L	9	8	0	1	0	1.0	.889
	C. Michaels	R	2	1	2	0	0	1.5	1.000		F. Marsh	R	1	2	0	1	0	3.0	.667
SS	C. Carrasquel	R	155	280	492	20	102	5.1	.975		G. Kell	R	2	3	0	0	0	1.5	1.000
	F. Marsh	R	3	1	3	0	0	1.3	1.000		B. Stewart	R	2	3	0	0	0	1.5	1.000
3B	C. Michaels	R	91	95	180	12	10	3.2	.958	C	S. Lollar	R	93	395	38	3	8	4.7	.993
	F. Marsh	R	36	36	83	8	3.4	.975		M. Batts	R	42	225	19	2	3	5.9	.992
	G. Kell	R	31	19	48	3	4	2.3	.957		C. Sawatski	R	33	133	14	2	4	4.5	.987
	S. Consuegra	R	1	0	0	0	0	0.0	.000		R. Wilson	R	8	44	3	0	1	5.9	1.000
	G. Hatton	R	10	12	15	0	1	2.7	1.000*										
	J. Kirrene	R	9	7	11	1	2	2.1	.947										
	M. Minoso	R	9	7	11	1	1	2.1	.947										
	S. Jok	R	3	3	7	0	1	3.3	1.000										

An ingenious public relations move brought Phil Cavaretta to the South Side after nineteen years with the Cubs. Cavaretta had been fired as Cubs manager in spring training, so the Cubs paid his salary while he hit .316 for the Sox in a utility role. Fortunately, he didn't have to play third.

In a move to finally shore up the festering hole in the infield, Comiskey and Lane purchased the contract of George Kell from the Boston Red Sox for $123,000. It was the biggest outlay of cash by the White Sox since the Simmons-Dykes-Haas purchase in 1933. For Lane it was the 196th transaction since 1948.

Billy Pierce faltered, but Jack Harshman, a converted first baseman, had quite a year. On July 25, the 27-year-old southpaw fanned sixteen Red Sox in a game in Boston. Another relative unknown carved his name into Sox record books: Sandy Consuegra posted an amazing 16-3 record, bettering the best won-lost percentages of Walsh, Faber, Lyons, and Cicotte.

The Sox' record of 94-60 might have won top honors in other years, but the 1954 Cleveland Indians were a one-year wonder with a 111-43 mark. The Sox settled into third on July 2 and remained there the rest of the way. The season wasn't without its usual crisis, though. In late August Paul Richards was given permission to negotiate with the Baltimore Orioles. Fed up with his contract hassles and looking for a chance to escape Frank Lane's shadow, Richards resigned on September 10. Former Browns manager Marty Marion took over four days later. His was a hard task, for Marion had a shadow to escape from, too.

TEAM STATISTICS

	W	L	PCT	GB	R	OR	2B	3B	HR	BA	SA	SB	E	DP	FA	CG	BB	SO	ShO	SV	ERA
CLE	111	43	.721		746	504	188	39	156	.262	.403	30	128	148	.979	77	486	678	12	36	2.78
NY	103	51	.669	8	805	563	215	59	133	.268	.408	34	126	198	.979	51	552	655	15	37	3.26
CHI	94	60	.610	17	711	521	203	47	94	.267	.379	98	108	149	.982	60	517	701	21	33	3.05
BOS	69	85	.448	42	700	728	244	41	123	.266	.395	51	176	163	.972	41	612	707	9	22	4.01
DET	68	86	.442	43	584	664	215	41	90	.258	.367	48	129	131	.978	58	506	603	13	13	3.81
WAS	66	88	.429	45	632	680	188	69	81	.246	.355	37	137	172	.977	69	573	562	10	7	3.84
BAL	54	100	.351	57	483	668	195	49	52	.251	.338	30	147	152	.975	58	688	668	6	8	3.88
PHI	51	103	.331	60	542	875	191	41	94	.236	.342	30	169	163	.972	49	685	555	3	13	5.18
LEAGUE TOTAL					5203	5203	1639	386	823	.257	.373	358	1120	1276	.977	463	4619	5129	89	169	3.72

INDIVIDUAL PITCHING

PITCHER	T	W	L	PCT	ERA	SV	G	GS	CG	IP	H	BB	SO	R	ER	ShO	H9	BB9	SO9
Virgil Trucks	R	19	12	.613	2.79	3	40	33	16	264.2	224	95	152	87	82	5	7.62	3.23	5.17
Bob Keegan	R	16	9	.640	3.09	2	31	27	14	209.2	211	82	61	84	72	2	9.06	3.52	2.62
Billy Pierce	L	9	10	.474	3.48	3	36	26	12	188.2	179	86	148	86	73	4	8.54	4.10	7.06
Jack Harshman	L	14	8	.636	2.95	1	35	21	9	177	157	96	134	61	58	4	7.98	4.88	6.81
Sandy Consuegra	R	16	3	.842	2.69	3	39	17	3	154	142	35	31	52	46	2	8.30	2.05	1.81
Don Johnson	R	8	7	.533	3.13	7	46	16	3	144	129	43	68	53	50	3	8.06	2.69	4.25
Harry Dorish	R	6	4	.600	2.72	6	37	6	2	109	88	29	48	35	33	1	7.27	2.39	3.96
Morrie Martin	L	5	4	.556	2.06	5	35	2	1	70	52	24	31	18	16	0	6.69	3.09	3.99
Mike Fornieles	R	1	2	.333	4.29	1	15	6	0	42	41	14	18	24	20	0	8.79	3.00	3.86
Dick Strahs	R	0	0	—	5.65	1	9	0	0	14.1	16	8	8	10	9	0	10.05	5.02	5.02
Al Sima	L	0	1	.000	5.14	1	5	1	0	7	11	2	1	5	4	0	14.14	2.57	1.29
Tom Flanigan	L	0	0	—	0.00	0	2	0	0	1.2	1	1	0	0	0	0	5.40	5.40	0.00
Vito Valentinetti	R	0	0	—	54.00	0	1	0	0	1	4	2	1	6	6	0	36.00	18.00	9.00
TEAM TOTAL		94	60	.610	3.05	33	331	155	60	1383	1255	517	701	521	469	21	8.17	3.36	4.56

Chicago 1955   Won 91 Lost 63 Pct. .591 3rd

MANAGER	W	L	PCT
Marty Marion	91	63	.591

POS	Player	B	G	AB	H	2B	3B	HR	HR%	R	RBI	BB	SO	SB	Pinch Hit AB	Pinch Hit H	BA	SA
REGULARS																		
1B	Walt Dropo	R	141	453	127	15	2	19	4.2	55	79	42	71	0	2	1	.280	.448
2B	Nellie Fox	L	154	636	198	28	7	6	0.9	100	59	38	15	7	0	0	.311	.406
SS	Chico Carrasquel	R	145	523	134	11	2	11	2.1	83	52	61	59	1	4	1	.256	.348
3B	George Kell	R	128	429	134	24	1	8	1.9	44	81	51	36	2	8	2	.312	.429
RF	Jim Rivera	L	147	454	120	24	4	10	2.2	71	52	62	59	25	7	2	.264	.401
CF	Jim Busby	R	99	337	82	13	4	1	0.3	38	27	25	37	7	0	0	.243	.315
LF	Minnie Minoso	R	139	517	149	26	7	10	1.9	79	70	76	43	19	1	0	.288	.424
C	Sherm Lollar	R	138	426	111	13	1	16	3.8	67	61	68	34	2	4	1	.261	.408
SUBSTITUTES																		
3O	Bob Kennedy	R	83	214	65	10	2	9	4.2	28	43	16	16	0	16	4	.304	.495
1B	Ron Jackson	R	40	74	15	1	1	2	2.7	10	7	8	22	1	7	4	.203	.324
SS	Jim Brideweser	R	34	58	12	3	2	0	0.0	6	4	3	7	0	1	0	.207	.328
3B	Vern Stephens	R	22	56	14	3	0	3	5.4	10	7	7	11	0	5	1	.250	.464
3B	Bobby Adams	R	28	21	2	0	1	0	0.0	8	3	4	4	0	2	0	.095	.190
SS	Buddy Peterson	R	6	21	6	1	0	0	0.0	7	2	3	2	0	1	1	.286	.333
1B	Phil Cavarretta	L	6	4	0	0	0	0	0.0	1	0	0	1	0	2	0	.000	.000
3B	Sammy Esposito	R	3	4	0	0	0	0	0.0	3	0	1	0	0	0	0	.000	.000
3O	Stan Jok	R	6	4	1	0	0	1	25.0	3	2	1	1	0	0	0	.250	1.000
OF	Bob Nieman	R	99	272	77	11	2	11	4.0	36	53	36	37	1	24	7	.283	.460
OF	Johnny Groth	R	32	77	26	7	0	2	2.6	13	11	6	13	1	1	0	.338	.506
OF	Willard Marshall	L	22	41	7	0	0	0	0.0	6	6	13	1	0	7	0	.171	.171
OF	Gil Coan	L	17	17	3	0	0	0	0.0	0	1	0	5	0	11	2	.176	.176
OF	Ron Northey	L	14	14	5	2	0	1	7.1	1	4	3	3	0	10	4	.357	.714
OF	Ed McGhee	R	26	13	1	0	0	0	0.0	6	0	6	1	2	2	1	.077	.077
OF	Ed White	R	3	4	2	0	0	0	0.0	0	0	1	1	0	1	0	.500	.500
C	Les Moss	R	32	59	15	2	0	2	3.4	5	7	6	10	0	1	0	.254	.390
C	Clint Courtney	L	19	37	14	3	0	1	2.7	7	10	7	0	0	2	1	.378	.541
C	Earl Battey	R	5	7	2	0	0	0	0.0	1	0	1	1	0	1	0	.286	.286
PH	Lloyd Merriman	L	1	1	0	0	0	0	0.0	0	0	0	0	0	1	0	.000	.000
PH	Bob Powell	R	1	0	0	0	0	0	—	0	0	0	0	0	0	0	—	—
PITCHERS																		
P	Dick Donovan	L	40	76	17	0	0	1	1.3	10	5	9	26	0	11	2	.224	.263
P	Billy Pierce	L	34	70	12	2	0	0	0.0	5	7	3	10	1	0	0	.171	.200
P	Virgil Trucks	R	32	64	8	1	0	0	0.0	2	6	0	12	0	0	0	.125	.141
P	Jack Harshman	L	32	60	11	1	0	2	3.3	6	8	9	17	0	0	0	.183	.300
P	Connie Johnson	R	19	33	5	2	0	0	0.0	4	5	0	7	0	0	0	.152	.212
P	Harry Byrd	B	25	30	2	0	0	0	0.0	2	0	0	7	0	0	0	.067	.067
P	Sandy Consuegra	R	44	29	3	0	0	0	0.0	1	1	1	8	0	0	0	.103	.103
P	Mike Fornieles	R	28	29	3	1	0	0	0.0	6	1	0	5	0	0	0	.103	.138
P	Dixie Howell	L	35	21	8	0	0	0	0.0	0	1	0	8	0	0	0	.381	.381
P	Bob Keegan	R	18	18	6	0	0	0	0.0	0	2	1	3	0	0	0	.333	.333
P	Morrie Martin	L	37	10	3	0	0	0	0.0	1	0	0	1	0	0	0	.300	.300
P	Harry Dorish	R	13	3	1	0	0	0	0.0	0	0	0	0	0	0	0	.333	.333
P	Bob Chakales	R	7	2	0	0	0	0	0.0	0	0	0	0	0	0	0	.000	.000
P	Al Papai	R	7	2	0	0	0	0	0.0	0	0	0	1	0	0	0	.000	.000
P	Ted Gray	B	2	0	0	0	0	0	—	0	0	0	0	0	0	0	—	—
	TEAM TOTAL			5220	1401	204	36	116	2.2	725	677	568	595	69	132	34	.268	.388

INDIVIDUAL FIELDING

POS	Player	T	G	PO	A	E	DP	TCG	FA	POS	Player	T	G	PO	A	E	DP	TCG	FA
1B	W. Dropo	R	140	1101	62	6	104	8.4	.995	OF	J. Rivera	L	143	288	22	6	7	2.2	.981
	R. Jackson	R	29	162	9	2	14	6.0	.988		M. Minoso	R	138	287	19	9	3	2.3	.971
	G. Kell	R	24	133	5	1	12	5.8	.993		J. Busby	R	99	243	6	4	3	2.6	.984
	B. Kennedy	R	3	7	0	0	1	2.3	1.000		B. Nieman	R	78	118	4	3	2	1.6	.976
	P. Cavarretta	L	3	3	0	0	0	1.0	1.000		J. Groth	R	26	62	1	0	0	2.4	1.000
2B	N. Fox	R	154	399	483	24	110	5.9	.974		B. Kennedy	R	20	16	0	0	0	0.8	1.000
	B. Adams	R	1	3	4	0	1	7.0	1.000		E. McGhee	R	17	12	0	1	0	0.8	.923
	J. Brideweser	R	2	3	2	0	1	2.5	1.000		S. Jok	R	1	0	0	0	0	0.0	.000
SS	C. Carrasquel	R	144	222	424	18	81	4.6	.973		G. Kell	R	1	0	0	0	0	0.0	.000
	J. Brideweser	R	26	27	48	4	12	3.0	.949		W. Marshall	R	12	22	0	1	0	1.9	.957
	B. Peterson	R	6	10	15	1	4	4.3	.962		E. White	R	2	2	0	0	0	1.0	1.000
3B	G. Kell	R	105	83	165	6	8	2.4	.976		G. Coan	R	3	2	0	0	0	0.7	1.000
	B. Kennedy	R	55	32	73	7	10	2.0	.938		R. Northey	R	2	1	0	0	0	0.5	1.000
	V. Stephens	R	18	13	37	0	4	2.8	1.000	C	S. Lollar	R	136	664	62	4	12	5.4	.995
	B. Adams	R	9	5	9	0	1	1.7	.933		L. Moss	R	33	90	5	1	1	2.9	.990
	S. Jok	R	3	2	4	1	0	2.3	.857		C. Courtney	R	17	49	4	0	2	3.1	1.000
	M. Minoso	R	2	2	2	0	1	2.0	1.000		E. Battey	R	5	19	2	0	0	4.2	1.000
	S. Esposito	R	2	1	0	0	0	0.5	1.000										
	J. Brideweser	R	3	0	1	0	0	0.3	1.000										

Unlike previous years, the Sox found themselves in a pennant race in August. On September 3, they enjoyed a half-game lead as they held first for twenty-four hours. A search of the record books revealed that the last time a Sox club was in first place that late was in September of 1920. They got there on the strength of their improved attack. While the stolen base and hit-and-run were still very much a part of their game, the 1955 Sox hit more home runs than any prior team. Nellie Fox continued to demonstrate that he was the best second baseman in the league, hitting .311, while Minnie Minoso reeled off a 23-game hitting streak. Minoso campaigned hard for the Most Valuable Player Award, and for good luck pinned dollar bills to the inside of his jersey.

The newest pitching hero rescued by Lane from obscurity was Dick Donovan. His best pitch was a slider, which he used en route to a 13–4 record by July 30. On that day he reported a minor upset stomach while the team was in Washington. It turned out to be appendicitis, and he was shelved until September. Another example of the "Comiskey Curse."

With five years remaining on a seven-year contract, Frank Lane called it quits as general manager on September 21. The move followed a public reprimand from Chuck Comiskey over remarks Lane made to Cal Hubbard, supervisor of umpires for the league. His seven-year term witnessed 241 deals involving 353 players. Once again, a year couldn't pass without a front office storm.

TEAM STATISTICS

	W	L	PCT	GB	R	OR	2B	3B	HR	BA	SA	SB	E	DP	FA	CG	BB	SO	ShO	SV	ERA
NY	96	58	.623		762	569	179	55	175	.260	.418	55	128	180	.978	52	689	731	18	33	3.23
CLE	93	61	.604	3	698	601	195	31	148	.257	.394	28	108	152	.981	45	558	877	13	36	3.39
CHI	91	63	.591	5	725	557	204	36	116	.268	.388	69	111	147	.981	55	499	720	17	23	3.37
BOS	84	70	.545	12	755	652	241	39	137	.264	.402	43	136	140	.977	44	582	674	9	34	3.72
DET	79	75	.513	17	775	658	211	38	130	.266	.394	41	139	159	.976	66	517	629	15	12	3.79
KC	63	91	.409	33	638	911	189	46	121	.261	.382	22	146	174	.976	29	707	572	7	23	5.35
BAL	57	97	.370	39	540	754	177	39	54	.240	.320	34	167	159	.972	35	625	595	9	22	4.21
WAS	53	101	.344	43	598	789	178	54	80	.248	.351	25	154	170	.974	37	637	607	9	16	4.62
LEAGUE TOTAL					5491	5491	1574	338	961	.258	.381	317	1089	1281	.977	363	4814	5405	97	199	3.96

INDIVIDUAL PITCHING

PITCHER	T	W	L	PCT	ERA	SV	G	GS	CG	IP	H	BB	SO	R	ER	ShO	H9	BB9	SO9
Billy Pierce	L	15	10	.600	1.97	1	33	26	16	205.2	162	64	157	50	45	6	7.09	2.80	6.87
Dick Donovan	R	15	9	.625	3.32	0	29	24	11	187	186	48	88	77	69	5	8.95	2.31	4.24
Jack Harshman	L	11	7	.611	3.36	0	32	23	9	179.1	144	97	116	74	67	0	7.23	4.87	5.82
Virgil Trucks	R	13	8	.619	3.96	0	32	26	7	175	176	61	91	78	77	3	9.05	3.14	4.68
Sandy Consuegra	R	6	5	.545	2.64	7	44	7	3	126.1	120	18	35	42	37	0	8.55	1.28	2.49
Connie Johnson	R	7	4	.636	3.45	0	17	16	5	99	95	52	72	40	38	2	8.64	4.73	6.55
Harry Byrd	R	4	6	.400	4.65	1	25	12	1	91	85	30	44	49	47	1	8.41	2.97	4.35
Mike Fornieles	R	6	3	.667	3.86	2	26	9	2	86.1	84	29	23	37	37	0	8.76	3.02	2.40
Dixie Howell	R	8	3	.727	2.93	9	35	0	0	73.2	70	25	25	27	24	0	8.55	3.05	3.05
Bob Keegan	R	2	5	.286	5.83	0	18	11	1	58.2	83	28	29	39	38	0	12.73	4.30	4.45
Morrie Martin	L	2	3	.400	3.63	2	37	0	0	52	50	22	22	27	21	0	8.65	3.81	3.81
Harry Dorish	R	2	0	1.000	1.59	1	13	0	0	17	16	9	6	4	3	0	8.47	4.76	3.18
Bob Chakales	R	0	0	–	1.46	0	7	0	0	12.1	11	6	6	2	2	0	8.03	4.38	4.38
Al Papai	R	0	0	–	3.86	0	7	0	0	11.2	10	8	5	5	5	0	7.71	6.17	3.86
Ted Gray	L	0	0	–	18.00	0	2	1	0	3	9	2	1	6	6	0	27.00	6.00	3.00
TEAM TOTAL		91	63	.591	3.37	23	357	155	55	1378	1301	499	720	557	516	17	8.50	3.26	4.70

Chicago 1956   Won 85   Lost 69   Pct. .552   3rd   136

MANAGER	W	L	PCT
Marty Marion	85	69	.552

POS	Player	B	G	AB	H	2B	3B	HR	HR %	R	RBI	BB	SO	SB	Pinch Hit AB	H	BA	SA
REGULARS																		
1B	Walt Dropo	R	125	361	96	13	1	8	2.2	42	52	37	51	1	10	2	.266	.374
2B	Nellie Fox	L	154	649	192	20	10	4	0.6	109	52	44	14	8	0	0	.296	.376
SS	Luis Aparicio	R	152	533	142	19	6	3	0.6	69	56	34	63	21	0	0	.266	.341
3B	Fred Hatfield	L	106	321	84	9	1	7	2.2	46	33	37	36	1	11	2	.262	.361
RF	Jim Rivera	L	139	491	125	23	5	12	2.4	76	66	49	75	20	9	2	.255	.395
CF	Larry Doby	L	140	504	135	22	3	24	4.8	89	102	102	105	0	3	1	.268	.466
LF	Minnie Minoso	R	151	545	172	29	11	21	3.9	106	88	86	40	12	3	1	.316	.525
C	Sherm Lollar	R	136	450	132	28	2	11	2.4	55	75	53	34	2	5	2	.293	.438
SUBSTITUTES																		
1O	Dave Philley	B	86	279	74	14	2	4	1.4	44	47	28	27	1	12	0	.265	.373
3S	Sammy Esposito	R	81	184	42	8	2	3	1.6	30	25	41	19	1	8	1	.228	.342
3B	George Kell	R	21	80	25	5	0	1	1.3	7	11	8	6	0	0	0	.313	.413
1B	Ron Jackson	R	22	56	12	3	0	1	1.8	7	4	10	13	1	3	0	.214	.321
3B	Bob Kennedy	R	8	13	1	0	0	0	0.0	0	0	2	4	0	3	0	.077	.077
SS	Jim Brideweser	R	10	11	2	1	0	0	0.0	0	1	0	3	0	0	0	.182	.273
OF	Bubba Phillips	R	67	99	27	6	0	2	2.0	16	11	6	12	1	13	4	.273	.394
OF	Ron Northey	L	53	48	17	2	0	3	6.3	4	23	8	1	0	39	15	.354	.583
OF	Jim Delsing	L	55	41	5	3	0	0	0.0	11	2	10	13	1	17	3	.122	.195
OF	Bob Nieman	R	14	40	12	1	0	2	5.0	3	4	4	4	0	1	1	.300	.475
OF	Cal Abrams	L	4	3	1	0	0	0	0.0	0	0	2	1	0	2	1	.333	.333
C	Les Moss	R	56	127	31	4	0	10	7.9	20	22	18	15	0	8	1	.244	.512
C	Earl Battey	R	4	4	1	0	0	0	0.0	1	0	1	1	0	0	0	.250	.250
PITCHERS																		
P	Billy Pierce	L	39	102	16	0	0	0	0.0	6	3	3	22	0	0	0	.157	.157
P	Dick Donovan	L	44	90	20	4	0	3	3.3	10	15	14	30	0	7	0	.222	.367
P	Jack Harshman	L	36	71	12	1	0	6	8.5	8	19	11	21	0	1	0	.169	.437
P	Jim Wilson	R	28	62	19	2	0	1	1.6	6	8	1	13	0	0	0	.306	.387
P	Bob Keegan	R	20	32	4	0	0	0	0.0	0	2	1	4	7	0	0	.125	.125
P	Gerry Staley	R	26	32	3	0	0	0	0.0	2	1	2	6	0	0	0	.094	.094
P	Dixie Howell	L	34	17	4	0	0	2	11.8	4	3	2	6	0	0	0	.235	.588
P	Howie Pollet	L	12	8	3	0	0	0	0.0	1	1	0	3	0	0	0	.375	.375
P	Paul LaPalme	L	29	6	0	0	0	0	0.0	0	1	0	3	0	0	0	.000	.000
P	Mike Fornieles	R	6	5	1	1	0	0	0.0	0	0	0	1	0	0	0	.200	.400
P	Morrie Martin	L	10	5	1	0	0	0	0.0	1	0	1	1	0	0	0	.200	.200
P	Jim McDonald	R	8	5	0	0	0	0	0.0	1	0	1	3	0	0	0	.000	.000
P	Sandy Consuegra	R	28	4	0	0	0	0	0.0	0	0	0	2	0	0	0	.000	.000
P	Connie Johnson	R	5	3	0	0	0	0	0.0	0	0	0	1	0	0	0	.000	.000
P	Jim Derrington	L	1	2	1	0	0	0	0.0	0	0	0	1	0	0	0	.500	.500
P	Ellis Kinder	R	29	2	0	0	0	0	0.0	0	0	0	1	0	0	0	.000	.000
P	Harry Byrd	R	3	1	0	0	0	0	0.0	0	0	0	0	0	0	0	.000	.000
P	Jerry Dahlke	R	5	0	0	0	0	0	—	0	0	0	0	0	0	0	—	—
P	Bill Fischer	R	3	0	0	0	0	—	—	0	0	0	0	0	0	0	—	—
P	Dick Marlowe	R	1	0	0	0	0	0	—	0	0	0	0	0	0	0	—	—
TEAM TOTAL				5286	1412	218	43	128	2.4	776	726	619	658	70	155	36	.267	.397

INDIVIDUAL FIELDING

POS	Player	T	G	PO	A	E	DP	TCG	FA
1B	W. Dropo	R	117	855	50	6	95	7.8	.993
	D. Philley	R	51	299	17	7	31	6.3	.978
	R. Jackson	R	19	138	11	0	16	7.8	1.000
	G. Kell	R	4	19	3	0	4	5.5	1.000
	M. Minoso	R	1	1	0	0	0	1.0	1.000
2B	N. Fox	R	154	478	396	12	124	5.8	.986
	S. Esposito	R	3	2	2	0	1	1.3	1.000
SS	L. Aparicio	R	152	250	474	35	91	5.0	.954
	S. Esposito	R	19	9	21	0	1	1.6	1.000
	J. Brideweser	R	10	4	11	1	1	1.6	.938
	F. Hatfield	R	3	1	2	0	0	1.0	1.000
3B	F. Hatfield	R	100	83	189	11	21	2.8	.961
	S. Esposito	R	61	41	109	6	17	2.6	.962
	G. Kell	R	18	17	28	0	0	2.5	1.000*
	M. Minoso	R	8	2	6	2	0	1.3	.800
	B. Kennedy	R	6	4	3	0	2	1.2	1.000
	B. Phillips	R	2	2	2	0	1	2.0	1.000

POS	Player	T	G	PO	A	E	DP	TCG	FA
OF	L. Doby	R	137	371	4	5	2	2.8	.987
	M. Minoso	R	148	284	10	8	1	2.0	.974
	J. Rivera	L	134	271	9	7	4	2.1	.976
	B. Phillips	R	35	59	2	0	1	1.7	1.000
	D. Philley	R	30	50	2	0	0	1.7	1.000
	J. Delsing	R	29	21	1	1	0	0.8	.957
	B. Nieman	R	10	24	0	0	0	2.4	1.000
	R. Northey	R	4	4	1	0	0	1.3	1.000
	C. Abrams	L	2	2	0	0	0	1.0	1.000
C	S. Lollar	R	132	679	40	5	6	5.5	.993
	L. Moss	R	49	149	10	1	1	3.3	.994
	E. Battey	R	3	4	0	1	0	1.7	.800

In 1955, Clark Griffith eyeballed a Sox rookie at Memphis. He was shortstop Luis Aparicio, and Griffith couldn't even pronounce his name. But he remembered his brilliant fielding. So sure of Aparicio were the Sox that they traded Chico Carrasquel and Jim Busby for Larry Doby the previous November. While third base had been a sore spot for a generation, shortstop had never been. Swede Risberg, Luke Appling, Chico Carrasquel — and now the 1956 Rookie of the Year, Luis Ernesto Aparicio.

Nineteen fifty-six boiled down to one weekend of thrills for Sox fans. The Yankees came calling on June 22. No ordinary four-loss weekend this time: such unlikely Sox heroes as Sammy Esposito, Dave Philley, and Jim Wilson beat the Yanks with their fists, their bats, and their guts as they swept the Bombers. Some bad blood had spilled over from 1955, when Minnie Minoso was skulled by Yankee pitcher Bob Grim. When Grim tried to make Philley his second victim a melee ensued. The next day, Billy Pierce and Gerry Staley capped off the 1950s' most exciting weekend with a 14–2 drubbing and a 6–3 nightcap win over New York.

But it all ended up as another third-place finish, as the Sox lost three games in the standings from 1955. Comiskey decided that the problem rested with Marion, and so accepted his "resignation" on October 25. From south of the border (well, Tampa-St. Pete), the genial but canny Al Lopez packed his bags.

TEAM STATISTICS

	W	L	PCT	GB	R	OR	2B	3B	HR	BA	SA	SB	E	DP	FA	CG	BB	SO	ShO	SV	ERA
NY	97	57	.630		857	631	193	55	190	.270	.434	51	136	214	.977	50	652	732	9	35	3.63
CLE	88	66	.571	9	712	581	199	23	153	.244	.381	40	129	130	.978	67	564	845	17	24	3.32
CHI	85	69	.552	12	776	634	218	43	128	.267	.397	70	122	160	.979	65	524	722	11	13	3.73
BOS	84	70	.545	13	780	751	261	45	139	.275	.419	28	169	168	.972	50	668	712	8	20	4.17
DET	82	72	.532	15	789	699	209	50	150	.279	.420	43	140	151	.976	62	655	788	10	15	4.06
BAL	69	85	.448	28	571	705	198	34	91	.244	.350	39	137	142	.977	38	547	715	10	24	4.20
WAS	59	95	.383	38	652	924	198	62	112	.250	.377	37	171	173	.972	36	730	663	1	18	5.33
KC	52	102	.338	45	619	831	204	41	112	.252	.370	40	166	187	.973	30	679	636	3	18	4.86
LEAGUE TOTAL					5756	5756	1680	353	1075	.260	.394	348	1170	1325	.975	398	5019	5813	69	167	4.16

INDIVIDUAL PITCHING

PITCHER	T	W	L	PCT	ERA	SV	G	GS	CG	IP	H	BB	SO	R	ER	ShO	H9	BB9	SO9
Billy Pierce	L	20	9	.690	3.32	1	35	33	21	276.1	261	100	192	108	102	1	8.50	3.26	6.25
Dick Donovan	R	12	10	.545	3.64	0	34	31	14	234.2	212	59	120	99	95	3	8.13	2.26	4.60
Jack Harshman	L	15	11	.577	3.10	0	34	30	15	226.2	183	102	143	85	78	4	7.27	4.05	5.68
Jim Wilson	R	9	12	.429	4.06	0	28	21	6	159.2	149	70	82	82	72	3	8.40	3.95	4.62
Bob Keegan	R	5	7	.417	3.93	0	20	16	4	105.1	119	35	32	56	46	0	10.17	2.99	2.73
Gerry Staley	R	8	3	.727	2.92	0	26	10	5	101.2	98	20	25	37	33	0	8.68	1.77	2.21
Dixie Howell	R	5	6	.455	4.62	4	34	1	0	64.1	79	36	28	39	33	0	11.05	5.04	3.92
Paul LaPalme	L	3	1	.750	2.36	2	29	0	0	45.2	31	27	23	14	12	0	6.11	5.32	4.53
Sandy Consuegra	R	1	2	.333	5.17	3	28	1	0	38.1	45	11	7	25	22	0	10.57	2.58	1.64
Ellis Kinder	R	3	1	.750	2.73	3	29	0	0	29.2	33	8	19	10	9	0	10.01	2.43	5.76
Howie Pollet	L	3	1	.750	4.10	0	11	4	0	26.1	27	11	14	15	12	0	9.23	3.76	4.78
Jim McDonald	R	0	2	.000	8.68	0	8	3	0	18.2	29	7	10	18	18	0	13.98	3.38	4.82
Morrie Martin	L	1	0	1.000	4.91	0	10	0	0	18.1	21	7	9	10	10	0	10.31	3.44	4.42
Mike Fornieles	R	0	1	.000	4.60	0	6	0	0	15.2	22	6	6	9	8	0	12.64	3.45	3.45
Connie Johnson	R	0	1	.000	3.65	0	5	2	0	12.1	11	7	6	5	5	0	8.03	5.11	4.38
Jim Derrington	L	0	1	.000	7.50	0	1	1	0	6	9	6	3	6	5	0	13.50	9.00	4.50
Harry Byrd	R	0	1	.000	10.38	0	3	1	0	4.1	9	4	0	6	5	0	18.69	8.31	0.00
Jerry Dahlke	R	0	0	–	19.29	0	5	0	0	2.1	5	6	1	5	5	0	19.29	23.14	3.86
Bill Fischer	R	0	0	–	21.60	0	3	0	0	1.2	6	1	2	4	4	0	32.40	5.40	10.80
Dick Marlowe	R	0	0	–	9.00	0	1	0	0	1	2	1	1	1	1	0	18.00	9.00	0.00
TEAM TOTAL		85	69	.552	3.73	13	350	154	65	1389	1351	524	722	634	575	11	8.75	3.40	4.68

Chicago 1957 Won 90 Lost 64 Pct. .584 2nd

MANAGER	W	L	PCT
Al Lopez	90	64	.584

POS	Player	B	G	AB	H	2B	3B	HR	HR%	R	RBI	BB	SO	SB	Pinch Hit AB	H	BA	SA
REGULARS																		
1B	Earl Torgeson	L	86	251	74	11	2	7	2.8	53	46	49	44	7	16	5	.295	.438
2B	Nellie Fox	L	155	619	196	27	8	6	1.0	110	61	75	13	5	0	0	.317	.415
SS	Luis Aparicio	R	143	575	148	22	6	3	0.5	82	41	52	55	28	1	0	.257	.332
3B	Bubba Phillips	R	121	393	106	13	3	7	1.8	38	42	28	32	5	3	0	.270	.372
RF	Jim Landis	R	96	274	58	11	3	2	0.7	38	16	45	61	14	4	1	.212	.296
CF	Larry Doby	L	119	416	120	27	2	14	3.4	57	79	56	79	2	9	1	.288	.464
LF	Minnie Minoso	R	153	568	176	36	5	12	2.1	96	103	79	54	18	0	0	.310	.454
C	Sherm Lollar	R	101	351	90	11	2	11	3.1	33	70	35	24	2	9	3	.256	.393
SUBSTITUTES																		
1B	Walt Dropo	R	93	223	57	2	0	13	5.8	24	49	16	40	0	31	11	.256	.439
3S	Sammy Esposito	R	94	176	36	3	0	2	1.1	26	15	38	27	5	11	3	.205	.256
3B	Fred Hatfield	L	69	114	23	3	0	0	0.0	14	8	15	20	1	23	4	.202	.228
1B	Ron Jackson	R	13	60	19	3	0	2	3.3	4	8	1	12	0	0	0	.317	.467
O1	Jim Rivera	L	125	402	103	21	6	14	3.5	51	52	40	80	18	11	3	.256	.443
OF	Ted Beard	L	38	78	16	1	0	0	0.0	15	7	18	14	3	3	1	.205	.218
OF	Dave Philley	B	22	71	23	4	0	0	0.0	9	9	4	10	1	4	2	.324	.380
C	Earl Battey	R	48	115	20	2	3	3	2.6	12	6	11	38	0	4	3	.174	.322
C	Les Moss	R	42	115	31	3	0	2	1.7	10	12	20	18	0	4	2	.270	.348
PH	Ron Northey	L	40	27	5	1	0	0	0.0	0	7	11	5	0	27	5	.185	.222
PH	Bob Kennedy	R	4	2	0	0	0	0	0.0	0	0	0	1	0	2	0	.000	.000
PH	Bob Powell	R	1	0	0	0	0	0	—	1	0	0	0	0	0	0	—	—
PITCHERS																		
P	Billy Pierce	L	41	99	17	1	0	0	0.0	7	6	2	25	0	0	0	.172	.182
P	Dick Donovan	L	30	83	12	1	0	3	3.6	8	10	8	32	0	1	0	.145	.265
P	Jim Wilson	R	31	68	10	2	0	0	0.0	4	5	7	14	0	1	0	.147	.176
P	Jack Harshman	L	30	45	10	2	0	2	4.4	5	5	10	17	0	0	0	.222	.400
P	Bill Fischer	R	33	40	6	0	0	0	0.0	1	5	0	8	0	0	0	.150	.150
P	Bob Keegan	R	30	39	4	0	0	0	0.0	3	3	4	5	0	0	0	.103	.103
P	Dixie Howell	L	42	27	5	1	1	3	11.1	4	3	2	6	0	6	0	.185	.630
P	Gerry Staley	R	47	22	1	0	0	0	0.0	1	1	3	6	0	0	0	.045	.045
P	Jim Derrington	L	20	4	0	0	0	0	0.0	1	0	1	2	0	0	0	.000	.000
P	Paul LaPalme	L	36	4	2	0	0	0	0.0	0	1	1	1	0	0	0	.500	.500
P	Don Rudolph	L	5	2	1	1	0	0	0.0	0	0	0	0	0	0	0	.500	1.000
P	Barry Latman	R	7	1	0	0	0	0	0.0	0	0	0	0	0	0	0	.000	.000
P	Jim McDonald	R	10	1	0	0	0	0	0.0	0	0	1	0	0	0	0	.000	.000
P	Jim Hughes	R	4	0	0	0	0	0	—	0	0	0	0	0	0	0	—	—
P	Ellis Kinder	R	1	0	0	0	0	0	—	0	0	0	0	0	0	0	—	—
P	Stover McIlwain	R	1	0	0	0	0	0	—	0	0	0	0	0	0	0	—	—
TEAM TOTAL				5265	1369	209	41	106	2.0	707	670	632	744	109	170	44	.260	.376

INDIVIDUAL FIELDING

POS	Player	T	G	PO	A	E	DP	TCG	FA
1B	E. Torgeson	L	70	612	29	1	72	9.2	.998
	W. Dropo	R	69	483	39	7	49	7.7	.987
	J. Rivera	L	31	233	8	3	22	7.9	.988
	R. Jackson	R	13	125	5	1	10	10.1	.992
	D. Philley	L	2	15	0	0	2	7.5	1.000
2B	N. Fox	R	155	453	453	13	141	5.9	.986
	S. Esposito	R	4	4	3	1	1	2.0	.875
SS	L. Aparicio	R	142	246	449	20	85	5.0	.972
	S. Esposito	R	22	28	73	3	12	4.7	.971
3B	B. Phillips	R	97	91	227	14	17	3.4	.958
	S. Esposito	R	53	52	92	6	10	2.8	.960
	F. Hatfield	R	44	23	74	5	10	2.3	.951
	M. Minoso	R	1	0	0	0	0	0.0	.000

POS	Player	T	G	PO	A	E	DP	TCG	FA
OF	M. Minoso	R	152	293	9	5	2	2.0	.984
	L. Doby	R	110	255	3	4	0	2.4	.985
	J. Landis	R	90	192	8	3	4	2.3	.985
	J. Rivera	L	82	141	6	4	0	1.8	.974
	B. Phillips	R	20	56	3	0	0	3.0	1.000
	D. Philley	R	17	39	0	1	0	2.4	.975
	T. Beard	L	28	33	5	1	0	1.4	.974
	S. Esposito	R	1	0	0	0	0	0.0	.000
	E. Torgeson	L	1	0	0	0	0	0.0	.000
C	S. Lollar	R	96	454	45	1	5	5.2	.998
	E. Battey	R	43	165	19	2	2	4.3	.989
	L. Moss	R	39	138	8	3	2	3.8	.980

The veteran White Sox profited from Al Lopez's calm, reassuring demeanor. His coaching staff reflected this patient, laid-back attitude, as the brain trust experimented with Jim Rivera at first base and Bubba Phillips at third. Both changes were thought to be radical, but the Sox were still tight up the middle and weak at the corners. Despite the infield problem, the Sox got off to a rousing start. They held first place till the last day in June, and their first-place bulge of six games on June 8 was the biggest by any Sox team since 1919.

The Rivera experiment ended in failure when the Sox traded Dave Philley (again) to Detroit for burly Earl Torgeson. Torgy arrived just in time to help the Sox in their annual fistfight with the New York Yankees. On June 14, Yankee hurler Al Cicotte leveled Larry Doby. Polite words were exchanged, then both benches cleared. Fines of $150 were given to Doby, Walt Dropo, Billy Martin, and Enos Slaughter. "The Yankees have been bullying their opponents long enough. I'm glad it happened," Sox vice president John Rigney said.

The Sox finished second, a welcome change of pace from the string of third-place finishes. Minnie Minoso had a fine year at .310 but was shocked and dismayed when Comiskey traded him to Cleveland in December for Early Wynn and Al Smith. It was Frank Lane's first move as Indians' general manager. "I've just traded the Sox into the pennant," Lane said sardonically. As it turned out, he was absolutely right.

TEAM STATISTICS

	W	L	PCT	GB	R	OR	2B	3B	HR	BA	SA	SB	E	DP	FA	CG	BB	SO	ShO	SV	ERA
NY	98	56	.636		723	534	200	54	145	.268	.409	49	123	183	.980	41	580	810	13	42	3.00
CHI	90	64	.584	8	707	566	208	41	106	.260	.375	109	107	169	.982	59	470	665	16	27	3.35
BOS	82	72	.532	16	721	668	231	32	153	.262	.405	29	149	179	.976	55	498	692	9	23	3.88
DET	78	76	.506	20	614	614	224	37	116	.257	.378	36	121	151	.980	52	505	756	9	21	3.56
BAL	76	76	.500	21	597	588	191	39	87	.252	.353	57	112	159	.981	44	493	767	13	25	3.46
CLE	76	77	.497	21.5	682	722	199	26	140	.252	.382	40	153	154	.974	46	618	807	7	23	4.05
KC	59	94	.386	38.5	563	710	195	40	166	.244	.394	35	125	162	.979	26	565	626	6	19	4.19
WAS	55	99	.357	43	603	808	215	38	111	.244	.363	13	128	159	.979	31	580	691	5	16	4.85
LEAGUE TOTAL					5210	5210	1663	307	1024	.255	.382	368	1018	1316	.979	354	4309	5814	78	196	3.79

INDIVIDUAL PITCHING

PITCHER	T	W	L	PCT	ERA	SV	G	GS	CG	IP	H	BB	SO	R	ER	ShO	H9	BB9	SO9
Billy Pierce	L	20	12	.625	3.26	2	37	34	16	257	228	71	171	98	93	4	7.98	2.49	5.99
Dick Donovan	R	16	6	.727	2.77	0	28	28	16	220.2	203	45	88	76	68	2	8.28	1.84	3.59
Jim Wilson	R	15	8	.652	3.48	0	30	29	12	201.2	189	65	100	85	78	5	8.43	2.90	4.46
Jack Harshman	L	8	8	.500	4.10	1	30	26	6	151.1	142	82	83	78	69	0	8.44	4.88	4.94
Bob Keegan	R	10	8	.556	3.53	2	30	20	6	142.2	131	37	36	62	56	2	8.26	2.33	2.27
Bill Fischer	R	7	8	.467	3.48	1	33	11	3	124	139	35	48	50	48	1	10.09	2.54	3.48
Gerry Staley	R	5	1	.833	2.06	7	47	0	0	105	95	27	44	27	24	0	8.14	2.31	3.77
Dixie Howell	R	6	5	.545	3.29	6	37	0	0	68.1	64	30	37	25	25	0	8.43	3.95	4.87
Paul LaPalme	L	1	4	.200	3.35	7	35	0	0	40.1	35	19	19	16	15	0	7.81	4.24	4.24
Jim Derrington	L	0	1	.000	4.86	0	20	5	0	37	29	29	14	21	20	0	7.05	7.05	3.41
Jim McDonald	R	0	1	.000	2.01	0	10	0	0	22.1	18	10	12	8	5	0	7.25	4.03	4.84
Barry Latman	R	1	2	.333	8.03	1	7	2	0	12.1	12	13	9	11	11	0	8.76	9.49	6.57
Don Rudolph	L	1	0	1.000	2.25	0	5	0	0	12	6	2	2	3	3	0	4.50	1.50	1.50
Jim Hughes	R	0	0	–	10.80	0	4	0	0	5	12	3	2	6	6	0	21.60	5.40	3.60
Ellis Kinder	R	0	0	–	0.00	0	1	0	0	1	0	1	0	0	0	0	0.00	9.00	0.00
Stover McIlwain	R	0	0	–	0.00	0	1	0	0	1	2	1	0	0	0	0	18.00	9.00	0.00
TEAM TOTAL		90	64	.584	3.35	27	355	155	59	1401.2	1305	470	665	566	521	14	8.38	3.02	4.27

Chicago 1958　　Won 82　Lost 72　Pct. .532　2nd　　140

MANAGER	W	L	PCT
Al Lopez	82	72	.532

POS	Player	B	G	AB	H	2B	3B	HR	HR %	R	RBI	BB	SO	SB	Pinch Hit AB	H	BA	SA
REGULARS																		
1B	Earl Torgeson	L	96	188	50	8	0	10	5.3	37	30	48	29	7	24	9	.266	.468
2B	Nellie Fox	L	155	623	187	21	6	0	0.0	82	49	47	11	5	0	0	.300	.353
SS	Luis Aparicio	R	145	557	148	20	9	2	0.4	76	40	35	38	29	0	0	.266	.345
3B	Billy Goodman	L	116	425	127	15	5	0	0.0	41	40	37	21	1	4	2	.299	.358
RF	Jim Rivera	L	116	276	62	8	4	9	3.3	37	35	24	49	21	9	0	.225	.380
CF	Jim Landis	R	142	523	145	23	7	15	2.9	72	64	52	80	19	1	0	.277	.434
LF	Al Smith	R	139	480	121	23	5	12	2.5	61	58	48	77	3	3	1	.252	.396
C	Sherm Lollar	R	127	421	115	16	0	20	4.8	53	84	57	37	2	13	5	.273	.454
SUBSTITUTES																		
3O	Bubba Phillips	R	84	260	71	10	0	5	1.9	26	30	15	14	3	4	0	.273	.369
1B	Ray Boone	R	77	246	60	12	1	7	2.8	25	41	18	33	1	14	1	.244	.386
1B	Ron Jackson	R	61	146	34	4	0	7	4.8	19	21	18	46	2	22	4	.233	.404
3S	Sammy Esposito	R	98	81	20	3	0	0	0.0	16	3	12	6	1	7	1	.247	.284
1B	Walt Dropo	R	28	52	10	1	0	2	3.8	3	8	5	11	0	11	2	.192	.327
OF	Don Mueller	L	70	166	42	5	0	0	0.0	7	16	11	9	0	26	9	.253	.283
OF	Tito Francona	L	41	128	33	3	2	1	0.8	10	10	14	24	2	7	3	.258	.336
OF	Johnny Callison	L	18	64	19	4	2	1	1.6	10	12	6	14	1	0	0	.297	.469
OF	Ted Beard	L	19	22	2	0	0	1	4.5	5	2	6	5	3	3	0	.091	.227
OF	Jim McAnany	R	5	13	0	0	0	0	0.0	0	0	0	5	0	1	0	.000	.000
OF	Norm Cash	L	13	8	2	0	0	0	0.0	2	0	0	1	0	5	1	.250	.250
C	Earl Battey	R	68	168	38	8	0	8	4.8	24	26	24	34	1	17	1	.226	.417
C	Johnny Romano	R	4	7	2	0	0	0	0.0	1	1	1	0	0	2	0	.286	.286
C	Charlie Lindstrom	R	1	1	1	0	1	0	0.0	1	1	1	0	0	0	0	1.000	3.000
PH	Les Moss	R	2	1	0	0	0	0	0.0	0	0	1	0	0	1	0	.000	.000
PITCHERS																		
P	Billy Pierce	L	35	83	17	3	0	0	0.0	10	4	4	13	0	0	0	.205	.241
P	Dick Donovan	L	34	80	9	0	0	0	0.0	5	1	10	33	0	0	0	.113	.113
P	Early Wynn	B	40	75	15	1	0	0	0.0	7	11	10	25	0	0	0	.200	.213
P	Jim Wilson	R	28	51	4	0	0	0	0.0	1	0	4	16	0	0	0	.078	.078
P	Ray Moore	R	32	44	9	2	0	1	2.3	1	2	2	13	0	0	0	.205	.318
P	Bob Shaw	R	29	14	0	0	0	0	0.0	0	0	3	7	0	0	0	.000	.000
P	Barry Latman	R	13	12	1	0	0	0	0.0	2	0	2	7	0	0	0	.083	.083
P	Gerry Staley	R	50	11	0	0	0	0	0.0	0	1	1	5	0	0	0	.000	.000
P	Turk Lown	R	27	9	3	0	0	0	0.0	0	2	0	3	0	0	0	.333	.333
P	Bill Fischer	R	17	7	1	1	0	0	0.0	0	1	0	1	0	0	0	.143	.286
P	Bob Keegan	R	14	4	0	0	0	0	0.0	0	1	0	0	0	0	0	.000	.000
P	Tom Qualters	R	26	2	0	0	0	0	0.0	0	0	2	2	0	0	0	.000	.000
P	Stover McIlwain	R	1	1	0	0	0	0	0.0	0	0	0	0	0	0	0	.000	.000
P	Dixie Howell	L	1	0	0	0	0	0	–	0	0	0	0	0	0	0	–	–
P	Jim McDonald	R	3	0	0	0	0	0	–	0	0	0	0	0	0	0	–	–
P	Don Rudolph	L	7	0	0	0	0	0	–	0	0	0	0	0	0	0	–	–
P	Hal Trosky	R	2	0	0	0	0	0	–	0	0	0	0	0	0	0	–	–
TEAM TOTAL				5249	1348	191	42	101	1.9	634	594	518	669	101	174	39	.257	.367

INDIVIDUAL FIELDING

POS	Player	T	G	PO	A	E	DP	TCG	FA	POS	Player	T	G	PO	A	E	DP	TCG	FA
1B	R. Boone	R	63	511	34	8	45	8.8	.986	OF	J. Landis	R	142	331	9	5	1	2.4	.986
	E. Torgeson	L	73	470	30	11	54	7.0	.978		A. Smith	R	138	249	9	8	2	1.9	.970
	R. Jackson	R	38	289	16	1	29	8.1	.997		J. Rivera	L	99	153	7	1	3	1.6	.994
	W. Dropo	R	16	98	8	0	8	6.6	1.000		B. Phillips	R	37	84	1	2	1	2.4	.977
	B. Goodman	R	3	19	2	0	2	7.0	1.000		D. Mueller	R	43	57	3	2	1	1.4	.968
2B	N. Fox	R	155	444	399	13	117	5.5	.985		T. Francona	L	35	49	3	0	1	1.5	1.000
	B. Goodman	R	1	2	2	0	0	4.0	1.000		J. Callison	R	18	39	2	1	1	2.3	.976
	S. Esposito	R	2	1	0	0	0	0.5	1.000		T. Beard	L	15	15	0	0	0	1.0	1.000
SS	L. Aparicio	R	145	289	463	21	90	5.3	.973		S. Esposito	R	1	0	0	0	0	0.0	.000
	S. Esposito	R	22	24	43	4	7	3.2	.944		J. McAnany	R	3	9	0	0	0	3.0	1.000
	B. Goodman	R	1	1	2	0	0	3.0	1.000		N. Cash	L	4	2	0	0	0	0.5	1.000
3B	B. Goodman	R	111	67	209	14	16	2.6	.952	C	S. Lollar	R	116	597	63	9	8	5.8	.987
	B. Phillips	R	47	38	86	6	12	2.8	.954		E. Battey	R	49	220	27	3	6	5.1	.988
	S. Esposito	R	63	11	35	1	2	0.7	.979		J. Romano	R	2	13	0	0	0	6.5	1.000
	A. Smith	R	1	0	0	0	0	0.0	.000		C. Lindstrom	R	1	2	0	0	0	2.0	1.000

Chicago 1958

Were the Yankees that good or the rest of the league that bad? The same question fans asked in the 1920s was posed again in 1958. It was hardly a race as New York led the pack by nine games on May 25. A second-half rally by the Sox lifted them from the nether regions of the league to second place on August 11. There they remained, but so far out that everyone lost count. Early Wynn was a disappointment, as the big winter trade haunted Comiskey in 1958.

Jim Landis was a sucker for outside curves in 1957, but with Nellie Fox helping he opened up his stance and cut down his alarming strikeout total. He hit safely in 33 of 36 games at one point. Uncharacteristic patience on the part of the front office helped make Landis a dandy. Not so lucky was catcher Chuck Lindstrom, who closed out his major-league career on September 28 with a walk and a triple to left-center. Lindstrom went into the record books as the only Sox player to hit 1.000 for a career: one-for-one.

As usual, the larger story this year was in the front office. Chuck Comiskey made a move to acquire his sister Dorothy's controlling interest in the Sox, but was rebuked when he demanded some concessions in the asking price. On December 20, Bill Veeck and friends purchased a sixty-day option to buy Dorothy's 54 percent. Chuck went to court to battle the sale, and through the winter the proceedings were diligently reported by the media. It wasn't until March of 1959 that Veeck finally won out. The show under the big top was about to begin.

TEAM STATISTICS

	W	L	PCT	GB	R	OR	2B	3B	HR	BA	SA	SB	E	DP	FA	CG	BB	SO	ShO	SV	ERA
NY	92	62	.597		759	577	212	39	164	.268	.416	48	128	182	.978	53	557	796	21	33	3.22
CHI	82	72	.532	10	634	615	191	42	101	.257	.367	101	114	160	.981	55	515	751	15	25	3.61
BOS	79	75	.513	13	697	691	229	30	155	.256	.400	29	145	172	.976	44	521	695	5	28	3.92
CLE	77	76	.503	14.5	694	635	210	31	161	.258	.403	50	152	171	.974	51	604	766	2	20	3.73
DET	77	77	.500	15	659	606	229	41	109	.266	.389	48	106	140	.982	59	437	797	8	19	3.59
BAL	74	79	.484	17.5	521	575	195	19	108	.241	.350	33	114	159	.980	55	403	749	15	28	3.40
KC	73	81	.474	19	642	713	196	50	138	.247	.381	22	125	166	.979	42	467	721	9	25	4.15
WAS	61	93	.396	31	553	747	161	38	121	.240	.357	22	118	163	.980	28	558	762	6	28	4.53
LEAGUE TOTAL					5159	5159	1623	290	1057	.254	.383	353	1002	1313	.979	387	4062	6037	81	206	3.77

INDIVIDUAL PITCHING

PITCHER	T	W	L	PCT	ERA	SV	G	GS	CG	IP	H	BB	SO	R	ER	ShO	H9	BB9	SO9
Dick Donovan	R	15	14	.517	3.01	0	34	34	16	248	240	53	127	92	83	4	8.71	1.92	4.61
Billy Pierce	L	17	11	.607	2.68	2	35	32	19	245	204	66	144	83	73	3	7.49	2.42	5.29
Early Wynn	R	14	16	.467	4.13	2	40	34	11	239.2	214	104	179	115	110	4	8.04	3.91	6.72
Jim Wilson	R	9	9	.500	4.10	1	28	23	4	155.2	156	63	70	75	71	1	9.02	3.64	4.05
Ray Moore	R	9	7	.563	3.82	2	32	20	4	136.2	107	70	73	63	58	2	7.05	4.61	4.81
Gerry Staley	R	4	5	.444	3.16	8	50	0	0	85.1	81	24	27	36	30	0	8.54	2.53	2.85
Bob Shaw	R	4	2	.667	4.64	1	29	3	0	64	67	28	18	33	33	0	9.42	3.94	2.53
Barry Latman	R	3	0	1.000	0.76	0	13	3	1	47.2	27	17	28	7	4	1	5.10	3.21	5.29
Tom Qualters	R	0	0	—	4.19	0	26	0	0	43	45	20	14	22	20	0	9.42	4.19	2.93
Turk Lown	R	3	3	.500	3.98	8	27	0	0	40.2	49	28	40	22	18	0	10.84	6.20	8.85
Bill Fischer	R	2	3	.400	6.69	0	17	3	0	36.1	43	13	16	28	27	0	10.65	3.22	3.96
Bob Keegan	R	0	2	.000	6.07	0	14	2	0	29.2	44	18	8	25	20	0	13.35	5.46	2.43
Don Rudolph	L	1	0	1.000	2.57	0	7	0	0	7	4	5	2	2	2	0	5.14	6.43	2.57
Stover McIlwain	R	0	0	—	2.25	0	1	1	0	4	4	0	4	1	1	0	9.00	0.00	9.00
Hal Trosky	R	1	0	1.000	6.00	0	2	0	0	3	5	2	1	3	2	0	15.00	6.00	3.00
Jim McDonald	R	0	0	—	19.29	0	3	0	0	2.1	6	4	0	8	5	0	23.14	15.43	0.00
Dixie Howell	R	0	0	—	0.00	0	1	0	0	1.2	0	0	0	0	0	0	0.00	0.00	0.00
TEAM TOTAL		82	72	.532	3.61	25	359	155	55	1389.2	1296	515	751	615	557	15	8.39	3.34	4.86

Chicago 1959   Won 94 Lost 60 Pct. .610 1st   142

MANAGER	W	L	PCT
Al Lopez	94	60	.610

POS	Player	B	G	AB	H	2B	3B	HR	HR %	R	RBI	BB	SO	SB	Pinch Hit AB	Pinch Hit H	BA	SA
REGULARS																		
1B	Earl Torgeson	L	127	277	61	5	3	9	3.2	40	45	62	55	7	24	5	.220	.357
2B	Nellie Fox	L	156	624	191	34	6	2	0.3	84	70	71	13	5	0	0	.306	.389
SS	Luis Aparicio	R	152	612	157	18	5	6	1.0	98	51	52	40	56	0	0	.257	.332
3B	Bubba Phillips	R	117	379	100	27	1	5	1.3	43	40	27	28	1	1	0	.264	.380
RF	Jim McAnany	R	67	210	58	9	3	0	0.0	22	27	19	26	2	0	0	.276	.348
CF	Jim Landis	R	149	515	140	26	7	5	1.0	78	60	78	68	20	0	0	.272	.379
LF	Al Smith	R	129	472	112	16	4	17	3.6	65	55	46	74	7	1	0	.237	.396
C	Sherm Lollar	R	140	505	134	22	3	22	4.4	63	84	55	49	4	5	3	.265	.451
SUBSTITUTES																		
3B	Billy Goodman	L	104	268	67	14	1	1	0.4	21	28	19	20	3	31	7	.250	.321
1B	Norm Cash	L	58	104	25	0	1	4	3.8	16	16	18	9	1	19	5	.240	.375
1B	Ted Kluszewski	L	31	101	30	2	1	2	2.0	11	10	9	10	0	2	0	.297	.396
3S	Sammy Esposito	R	69	66	11	1	0	1	1.5	12	5	11	16	0	5	1	.167	.227
1B	Ray Boone	R	9	21	5	0	0	1	4.8	3	5	7	5	1	3	1	.238	.381
1B	Ron Jackson	R	10	14	3	1	0	1	7.1	3	2	1	0	0	5	1	.214	.500
3B	J. C. Martin	L	3	4	1	0	0	0	0.0	0	1	0	1	0	1	0	.250	.250
OF	Jim Rivera	L	80	177	39	9	4	4	2.3	18	19	11	19	5	4	0	.220	.384
OF	Johnny Callison	L	49	104	18	3	0	3	2.9	12	12	13	20	0	4	0	.173	.288
OF	Del Ennis	R	26	96	21	6	0	2	2.1	10	7	4	10	0	2	1	.219	.344
OF	Harry Simpson	L	38	75	14	5	1	2	2.7	5	13	4	14	0	24	4	.187	.360
OF	Larry Doby	L	21	58	14	1	1	0	0.0	1	9	2	13	1	8	2	.241	.293
OF	Lou Skizas	R	8	13	1	0	0	0	0.0	3	0	3	2	0	2	0	.077	.077
OF	Joe Hicks	L	6	7	3	0	0	0	0.0	0	1	1	1	0	2	2	.429	.429
C	Johnny Romano	R	53	126	37	5	1	5	4.0	20	25	23	18	0	13	6	.294	.468
C	Earl Battey	R	26	64	14	1	2	2	3.1	9	7	8	13	0	5	0	.219	.391
C	Cam Carreon	R	1	1	0	0	0	0	0.0	0	0	0	0	0	0	0	.000	.000
PH	Don Mueller	L	4	4	2	0	0	0	0.0	0	0	0	0	0	4	2	.500	.500
PITCHERS																		
P	Early Wynn	B	37	90	22	7	0	2	2.2	11	8	9	18	0	0	0	.244	.389
P	Bob Shaw	R	47	73	9	1	0	0	0.0	7	2	5	19	0	0	0	.123	.137
P	Billy Pierce	L	34	68	13	1	2	0	0.0	3	7	7	13	0	0	0	.191	.265
P	Dick Donovan	R	31	61	8	4	0	1	1.6	4	5	5	32	0	0	0	.131	.246
P	Barry Latman	R	37	47	6	1	0	0	0.0	0	3	6	4	4	0	0	.128	.149
P	Ray Moore	R	29	23	2	1	0	0	0:0	0	0	1	11	0	0	0	.087	.130
P	Gerry Staley	R	67	13	2	0	0	0	0.0	0	2	0	3	5	0	0	.154	.154
P	Turk Lown	R	60	12	3	0	0	0	0.0	1	0	1	3	0	0	0	.250	.250
P	Ken McBride	R	11	6	1	0	0	0	0.0	0	0	0	2	0	0	0	.167	.167
P	Rudy Arias	L	34	4	0	0	0	0	0.0	0	0	0	2	0	0	0	.000	.000
P	Joe Stanka	R	2	3	1	0	0	0	0.0	0	1	1	0	0	0	0	.333	.333
P	Gary Peters	L	2	0	0	0	0	0	—	0	0	0	0	0	0	0	—	—
P	Claude Raymond	R	3	0	0	0	0	0	—	0	0	0	0	0	0	0	—	—
P	Don Rudolph	L	4	0	0	0	0	0	—	0	0	0	0	0	0	0	—	—
TEAM TOTAL				5297	1325	220	46	97	1.8	669	620	579	634	113	165	42	.250	.364

INDIVIDUAL FIELDING

POS	Player	T	G	PO	A	E	DP	TCG	FA	POS	Player	T	G	PO	A	E	DP	TCG	FA
1B	E. Torgeson	L	103	717	37	13	58	7.4	.983	OF	J. Landis	R	148	420	10	3	2	2.9	.993
	N. Cash	L	31	231	14	4	19	8.0	.984		A. Smith	R	128	303	8	6	2	2.5	.981
	T. Kluszewski	L	29	220	10	0	13	7.9	1.000		J. McAnany	R	67	106	6	4	4	1.7	.966
	S. Lollar	R	24	177	17	1	19	8.1	.995		J. Rivera	L	69	75	5	2	3	1.2	.976
	R. Boone	R	6	37	5	2	2	7.3	.955		J. Callison	R	41	54	3	1	0	1.4	.983
	R. Jackson	R	5	30	1	0	3	6.2	1.000		B. Phillips	R	23	37	0	0	0	1.6	1.000
	L. Doby	R	2	13	1	1	3	7.5	.933		D. Ennis	R	25	28	2	3	0	1.3	.909
	H. Simpson	R	1	9	0	1	0	10.0	.900		L. Doby	R	12	20	1	1	1	1.8	.955
2B	N. Fox	R	156	364	453	10	93	5.3	.988		H. Simpson	R	12	18	0	1	1	1.6	.947
	S. Esposito	R	2	0	0	0	0	0.0	.000		L. Skizas	R	6	6	1	0	0	1.2	1.000
	B. Goodman	R	3	4	5	0	1	3.0	1.000		J. Hicks	R	4	3	1	0	0	1.0	1.000
SS	L. Aparicio	R	152	282	460	23	87	5.0	.970	C	S. Lollar	R	122	623	51	5	14	5.6	.993
	S. Esposito	R	14	17	32	1	5	3.6	.980		J. Romano	R	38	169	16	4	5	5.0	.979
3B	B. Phillips	R	100	90	202	15	13	3.1	.951		E. Battey	R	20	92	10	1	1	5.2	.990
	B. Goodman	R	74	57	135	10	10	2.7	.950		C. Carreon	R	1	3	0	0	0	3.0	1.000
	S. Esposito	R	45	22	25	1	1	1.1	.979										
	A. Smith	R	1	0	0	0	0	0.0	.000										
	J. Martin	R	2	0	2	1	0	1.5	.667										

It happened quite by surprise. A decade's worth of problems confronted the Sox as they gathered in Tampa for spring training. No one at first, certainly not Ron Jackson or the kid Norm Cash. Who's on third: Bubba Phillips or Billy Goodman? It was anybody's guess. Spring holdouts and the unsettled ownership problem marked the Sox for third place at best.

The Sox played cautious baseball in the early going, allowing the Cleveland Indians an early lead. But the Sox plugged the holes and really got going in June and July. They captured first place for good on July 12, rolling along on Early Wynn's 22–10 record and a surprise showing by Tiger castoff Bob Shaw. The Sox returned to their Go-Go roots; Luis Aparicio swiped 56 bases, matching Wally Moses's club record. A walk, a hit, and a sacrifice was their offense. The key to this pennant was their outstanding 35–15 record in one-run games. And, as with all good White Sox teams, this club led the league in fielding at .979.

Vic Power's ninth-inning double-play ball on September 22 in Cleveland's mammoth stadium gave the Sox the pennant. The World Series was another matter, but in the hearts of most Sox fans the six-game loss to the Dodgers was academic. Getting there was the real story. Individual honors galore awaited the champs. Nellie Fox was named Most Valuable Player, and Early Wynn won the Cy Young. It would be a long time before anyone from the White Sox won either of those awards again.

TEAM STATISTICS

	W	L	PCT	GB	R	OR	2B	3B	Batting HR	BA	SA	SB	Fielding E	DP	FA	CG	BB	Pitching SO	ShO	SV	ERA
CHI	94	60	.610		669	588	220	46	97	.250	.364	113	130	141	.979	44	525	761	13	36	3.29
CLE	89	65	.578	5	745	646	216	25	167	.263	.408	33	127	138	.978	58	635	799	7	23	3.75
NY	79	75	.513	15	687	647	224	40	153	.260	.402	45	131	160	.978	38	594	836	15	28	3.60
DET	76	78	.494	18	713	732	196	30	160	.258	.400	34	124	131	.978	53	432	829	9	24	4.20
BOS	75	79	.487	19	726	696	248	28	125	.256	.385	68	131	167	.978	38	589	724	9	25	4.17
BAL	74	80	.481	20	551	621	182	23	109	.238	.345	36	146	163	.976	45	476	735	15	30	3.56
KC	66	88	.429	28	681	760	231	43	117	.263	.390	34	160	156	.973	44	492	703	8	21	4.35
WAS	63	91	.409	31	619	701	173	32	163	.237	.379	51	162	140	.973	46	467	694	10	21	4.01
LEAGUE TOTAL					5391	5391	1690	267	1091	.253	.384	414	1111	1196	.977	366	4210	6081	86	208	3.86

INDIVIDUAL PITCHING

PITCHER	T	W	L	PCT	ERA	SV	G	GS	CG	IP	H	BB	SO	R	ER	ShO	H9	BB9	SO9
Early Wynn	R	22	10	.688	3.17	0	37	37	14	255.2	202	119	179	106	90	5	7.11	4.19	6.30
Bob Shaw	R	18	6	.750	2.69	3	47	26	8	230.2	217	54	89	72	69	3	8.47	2.11	3.47
Billy Pierce	L	14	15	.483	3.62	0	34	33	12	224	217	62	114	98	90	2	8.72	2.49	4.58
Dick Donovan	R	9	10	.474	3.66	0	31	29	5	179.2	171	58	71	84	73	1	8.57	2.91	3.56
Barry Latman	R	8	5	.615	3.75	0	37	21	5	156	138	72	97	71	65	2	7.96	4.15	5.60
Gerry Staley	R	8	5	.615	2.24	14	67	0	0	116.1	111	25	54	39	29	0	8.59	1.93	4.18
Turk Lown	R	9	2	.818	2.89	15	60	0	0	93.1	73	42	63	32	30	0	7.04	4.05	6.08
Ray Moore	R	3	6	.333	4.12	0	29	8	0	89.2	86	46	49	46	41	0	8.63	4.62	4.92
Rudy Arias	L	2	0	1.000	4.09	2	34	0	0	44	49	20	28	23	20	0	10.02	4.09	5.73
Ken McBride	R	0	1	.000	3.18	1	11	2	0	22.2	20	17	12	11	8	0	7.94	6.75	4.76
Joe Stanka	R	1	0	1.000	3.38	0	2	0	0	5.1	2	4	3	2	2	0	3.38	6.75	5.06
Claude Raymond	R	0	0	—	9.00	0	3	0	0	4	5	2	1	4	4	0	11.25	4.50	2.25
Don Rudolph	L	0	0	—	0.00	0	1	0	0	3	4	2	0	0	0	0	12.00	6.00	0.00
Gary Peters	L	0	0	—	0.00	0	2	0	0	1	2	2	1	0	0	0	18.00	18.00	9.00
TEAM TOTAL		94	60	.610	3.29	36	398	156	44	1425.1	1297	525	761	588	521	13	8.19	3.32	4.81

Chicago 1960 Won 87 Lost 67 Pct. .565 3rd

MANAGER

	W	L	PCT
Al Lopez	87	67	.565

POS	Player	B	G	AB	H	2B	3B	HR	HR%	R	RBI	BB	SO	SB	Pinch Hit AB	Pinch Hit H	BA	SA
REGULARS																		
1B	Roy Sievers	R	127	444	131	22	0	28	6.3	87	93	74	69	1	9	1	.295	.534
2B	Nellie Fox	L	150	605	175	24	10	2	0.3	85	59	50	13	2	1	0	.289	.372
SS	Luis Aparicio	R	153	600	166	20	7	2	0.3	86	61	43	39	51	0	0	.277	.343
3B	Gene Freese	R	127	455	124	32	6	17	3.7	60	79	29	65	10	6	1	.273	.481
RF	Al Smith	R	142	536	169	31	3	12	2.2	80	72	50	65	8	1	0	.315	.451
CF	Jim Landis	R	148	494	125	25	6	10	2.0	89	49	80	84	23	0	0	.253	.389
LF	Minnie Minoso	R	154	591	184	32	4	20	3.4	89	105	52	63	17	0	0	.311	.481
C	Sherm Lollar	R	129	421	106	23	0	7	1.7	43	46	42	39	2	7	2	.252	.356
SUBSTITUTES																		
1B	Ted Kluszewski	L	81	181	53	9	0	5	2.8	20	39	22	10	0	34	8	.293	.425
3S	Sammy Esposito	R	57	77	14	5	0	1	1.3	14	11	10	20	0	4	1	.182	.286
32	Billy Goodman	L	30	77	18	4	0	0	0.0	5	6	12	8	0	6	0	.234	.286
1B	Earl Torgeson	L	68	57	15	2	0	2	3.5	12	9	21	8	1	41	12	.263	.404
3B	J. C. Martin	L	4	20	2	1	0	0	0.0	0	2	0	6	0	0	0	.100	.150
OF	Joe Hicks	L	36	47	9	1	0	0	0.0	3	2	6	3	0	17	4	.191	.213
OF	Floyd Robinson	L	22	46	13	0	0	0	0.0	7	1	11	8	2	4	0	.283	.283
OF	Jim Rivera	L	48	17	5	0	0	1	5.9	17	1	3	3	4	2	0	.294	.471
OF	Stan Johnson	L	5	6	1	0	0	1	16.7	1	1	0	1	0	5	1	.167	.667
C	Joe Ginsberg	L	28	75	19	4	0	0	0.0	8	9	10	8	1	2	0	.253	.307
C	Dick Brown	R	16	43	7	0	0	3	7.0	4	5	3	11	0	2	1	.163	.372
C	Cam Carreon	R	8	17	4	0	0	0	0.0	2	2	1	3	0	1	0	.235	.235
C	Earl Averill	R	10	14	3	0	0	0	0.0	2	2	4	2	0	5	1	.214	.214
PH	Jim McAnany	R	3	2	0	0	0	0	0.0	0	0	0	2	0	2	0	.000	.000
PITCHERS																		
P	Early Wynn	B	36	75	15	2	1	1	1.3	8	7	14	17	0	0	0	.200	.293
P	Billy Pierce	L	32	67	12	1	0	0	0.0	4	7	6	14	0	0	0	.179	.194
P	Bob Shaw	R	36	58	8	1	0	0	0.0	4	2	6	12	0	0	0	.138	.155
P	Frank Baumann	L	44	52	8	1	0	0	0.0	2	6	9	25	0	0	0	.154	.173
P	Herb Score	L	23	30	3	0	1	0	0.0	2	1	3	16	0	0	0	.100	.167
P	Russ Kemmerer	R	36	29	0	0	0	0	0.0	1	1	2	14	0	0	0	.000	.000
P	Dick Donovan	L	33	23	3	1	0	0	0.0	3	2	1	13	0	0	0	.130	.174
P	Gerry Staley	R	64	17	4	0	0	0	0.0	0	3	2	5	0	0	0	.235	.235
P	Turk Lown	R	45	5	1	1	0	0	0.0	0	0	1	0	0	0	0	.200	.400
P	Mike Garcia	R	15	3	1	0	0	0	0.0	0	1	0	0	0	0	0	.333	.333
P	Don Ferrarese	R	5	2	1	0	0	0	0.0	1	0	0	1	0	0	0	.500	.500
P	Ray Moore	R	14	2	0	0	0	0	0.0	0	0	0	1	0	0	0	.000	.000
P	Al Worthington	R	4	2	2	0	0	0	0.0	1	0	0	0	0	0	0	1.000	1.000
P	Bob Rush	R	9	1	1	0	0	0	0.0	1	0	0	0	0	0	0	1.000	1.000
P	Ken McBride	R	5	0	0	0	0	0	–	0	0	0	0	0	0	0	–	–
P	Gary Peters	L	2	0	0	0	0	0	–	0	0	0	0	0	0	0	–	–
P	Jake Striker	L	2	0	0	0	0	0	–	0	0	0	0	0	0	0	–	–
TEAM TOTAL				5191	1402	242	38	112	2.2	741	684	567	648	122	149	32	.270	.396

INDIVIDUAL FIELDING

POS	Player	T	G	PO	A	E	DP	TCG	FA	POS	Player	T	G	PO	A	E	DP	TCG	FA
1B	R. Sievers	R	114	1079	63	8	117	10.1	.993	OF	J. Landis	R	147	372	10	6	3	2.6	.985
	T. Kluszewski	L	39	325	19	1	38	8.8	.997		M. Minoso	R	154	282	14	6	3	2.0	.980
	E. Torgeson	L	10	54	4	1	3	5.9	.983		A. Smith	R	141	252	5	9	2	1.9	.966
	J. Martin	R	1	3	0	0	0	3.0	1.000		F. Robinson	R	17	24	0	1	0	1.5	.960
2B	N. Fox	R	149	412	447	13	126	5.9	.985		J. Rivera	L	24	16	0	0	0	0.7	1.000
	B. Goodman	R	7	9	14	0	5	3.3	1.000		J. Hicks	R	14	14	0	0	0	1.0	1.000
	S. Esposito	R	5	3	4	1	0	1.6	.875		R. Sievers	R	6	6	0	0	0	1.0	1.000
SS	L. Aparicio	R	153	305	551	18	117	5.7	.979		S. Johnson	L	2	1	0	0	0	0.5	1.000
	S. Esposito	R	11	2	7	0	1	0.8	1.000	C	S. Lollar	R	123	555	54	3	12	5.0	.995
3B	G. Freese	R	122	88	263	20	29	3.0	.946		J. Ginsberg	R	25	129	8	1	0	5.5	.993
	B. Goodman	R	20	17	38	1	2	2.8	.982		D. Brown	R	14	66	7	1	1	5.3	.986
	S. Esposito	R	37	12	40	4	4	1.5	.929		E. Averill	R	5	24	2	0	0	5.2	1.000
	J. Martin	R	5	5	8	0	0	2.6	1.000		C. Carreon	R	7	22	2	0	0	3.4	1.000

With no thought to the future, Veeck masterminded a series of bold trades designed to change the Sox' punchless image and ensure a second pennant. On December 6, 1959, Bubba Phillips, John Romano, and Norm Cash were traded to Cleveland for the fading Minnie Minoso and three prospects. Two days later, he sent the promising rookie Johnny Callison to Philadelphia for Gene Freese. Veeck compounded the felony on April 5, trading Earl Battey and Don Mincher to Washington for Roy Sievers. These lead-footed sluggers succeeded in making the Sox the most potent offensive unit in the American League, but at too great an expense in the field.

The season began in high fashion, with Minoso belting a pair of homecoming four-baggers against Kansas City. The event was celebrated by Veeck's latest stunt: the world's first exploding scoreboard. The idea for the board came to Veeck after he saw the William Saroyan play, *The Time of Your Life*, which featured an excitable pinball machine. In a separate move, Bill Veeck put the names of the players on the Sox' road jerseys. It was not a new idea, but one radical enough to outrage the baseball establishment.

The Sox held first through mid-May, but gave way to the improved Orioles and Yankees. A discouraging four-game sweep at the hands of the Yankees on June 17–19 before the season's largest crowds made it difficult to come back. They dropped to third the last two days of the season, an older, sadder, disoriented ballclub.

TEAM STATISTICS

	W	L	PCT	GB	R	OR	2B	3B	HR	BA	SA	SB	E	DP	FA	CG	BB	SO	ShO	SV	ERA
NY	97	57	.630		746	627	215	40	**193**	**.260**	**.426**	37	129	162	.979	38	609	712	**16**	**42**	**3.52**
BAL	89	65	.578	8	682	**606**	206	33	123	.253	.377	37	**108**	172	.982	**48**	552	785	11	22	3.52
CHI	87	67	.565	10	741	617	**242**	38	112	**.270**	.396	**122**	109	175	**.982**	42	533	695	11	26	3.60
CLE	76	78	.494	21	667	693	218	20	127	.267	.388	58	128	165	.978	32	636	771	10	30	3.95
WAS	73	81	.474	24	672	696	205	**43**	147	.244	.384	52	165	159	.973	34	538	775	10	35	3.77
DET	71	83	.461	26	633	644	188	34	150	.239	.375	66	138	138	.977	**40**	**474**	**824**	7	25	3.64
BOS	65	89	.422	32	658	775	234	32	124	.261	.389	34	141	156	.976	34	580	767	6	23	4.62
KC	58	96	.377	39	615	756	212	34	110	.249	.366	16	127	149	.979	44	525	664	4	14	4.38
LEAGUE TOTAL					5414	5414	1720	274	1086	.255	.388	422	1045	1276	.978	312	4447	5993	75	217	3.87

INDIVIDUAL PITCHING

PITCHER	T	W	L	PCT	ERA	SV	G	GS	CG	IP	H	BB	SO	R	ER	ShO	H9	BB9	SO9
Early Wynn	R	13	12	.520	3.49	1	36	35	13	237.1	220	112	158	105	92	4	8.34	4.25	5.99
Billy Pierce	L	14	7	.667	3.62	0	32	30	8	196.1	201	46	108	81	79	1	9.21	2.11	4.95
Bob Shaw	R	13	13	.500	4.06	0	36	32	7	192.2	221	62	46	97	87	1	10.32	2.90	2.15
Frank Baumann	L	13	6	.684	**2.67**	3	47	20	7	185.1	169	53	71	67	55	2	8.21	2.57	3.45
Russ Kemmerer	R	6	3	.667	2.98	2	36	7	2	120.2	111	45	76	45	40	1	8.28	3.36	5.67
Gerry Staley	R	13	8	.619	2.42	10	64	0	0	115.1	94	25	52	40	31	0	7.34	1.95	4.06
Herb Score	L	5	10	.333	3.72	0	23	22	5	113.2	91	87	78	54	47	1	7.21	6.89	6.18
Dick Donovan	R	6	1	.857	5.38	3	33	8	0	78.2	87	25	30	49	47	0	9.95	2.86	3.43
Turk Lown	R	2	3	.400	3.88	5	45	0	0	67.1	60	34	39	31	29	0	8.02	4.54	5.21
Ray Moore	R	1	1	.500	5.66	0	14	0	0	20.2	19	11	3	13	13	0	8.27	4.79	1.31
Mike Garcia	R	0	0	–	4.58	2	15	0	0	17.2	23	10	8	9	9	0	11.72	5.09	4.08
Bob Rush	R	0	0	–	5.65	0	9	0	0	14.1	16	5	12	10	9	0	10.05	3.14	7.53
Al Worthington	R	1	1	.500	3.38	0	4	0	0	5.1	3	4	1	2	2	0	5.06	6.75	1.69
Ken McBride	R	0	1	.000	3.86	0	5	0	0	4.2	6	3	4	2	2	0	11.57	5.79	7.71
Don Ferrarese	L	0	1	.000	18.00	0	5	0	0	4	8	9	4	8	8	0	18.00	20.25	9.00
Jake Striker	L	0	0	–	4.91	0	2	0	0	3.2	5	1	1	3	2	0	12.27	2.45	2.45
Gary Peters	L	0	0	–	2.70	0	2	0	0	3.1	4	1	4	1	1	0	10.80	2.70	10.80
TEAM TOTAL		87	67	.565	3.60	26	408	154	42	1381	1338	533	695	617	553	10	8.72	3.47	4.53

Chicago 1961   Won 86   Lost 76   Pct. .531   4th

MANAGER	W	L	PCT
Al Lopez	86	76	.531

POS	Player	B	G	AB	H	2B	3B	HR	HR%	R	RBI	BB	SO	SB	Pinch Hit AB	Pinch Hit H	BA	SA
REGULARS																		
1B	Roy Sievers	R	141	492	145	26	6	27	5.5	76	92	61	62	1	10	4	.295	.537
2B	Nellie Fox	L	159	606	152	11	5	2	0.3	67	51	59	12	2	2	1	.251	.295
SS	Luis Aparicio	R	156	625	170	24	4	6	1.0	90	45	38	33	53	0	0	.272	.352
3B	Al Smith	R	147	532	148	29	4	28	5.3	88	93	56	67	4	5	2	.278	.506
RF	Floyd Robinson	L	132	432	134	20	7	11	2.5	69	59	52	32	7	23	6	.310	.465
CF	Jim Landis	R	140	534	151	18	8	22	4.1	87	85	65	71	19	2	0	.283	.470
LF	Minnie Minoso	R	152	540	151	28	3	14	2.6	91	82	67	46	9	1	1	.280	.420
C	Sherm Lollar	R	116	337	95	10	1	7	2.1	38	41	37	22	0	10	4	.282	.380
SUBSTITUTES																		
13	J. C. Martin	L	110	274	63	8	3	5	1.8	26	32	21	31	1	11	2	.230	.336
3B	Andy Carey	R	56	143	38	12	3	0	0.0	21	14	11	24	0	1	0	.266	.392
UT	Sammy Esposito	R	63	94	16	5	0	1	1.1	12	8	12	21	0	2	0	.170	.255
31	Billy Goodman	L	41	51	13	4	0	1	2.0	4	10	7	6	0	27	9	.255	.392
1B	Earl Torgeson	L	20	15	1	0	0	0	0.0	1	1	3	5	0	15	1	.067	.067
3B	Ted Lepcio	R	5	2	0	0	0	0	0.0	0	0	1	0	0	2	0	.000	.000
OF	Al Pilarcik	L	47	62	11	1	0	1	1.6	9	6	9	5	1	17	4	.177	.242
OF	Wes Covington	L	22	59	17	1	0	4	6.8	5	15	4	5	0	6	1	.288	.508
OF	Mike Hershberger	R	15	55	17	3	0	0	0.0	9	5	2	2	1	1	0	.309	.364
OF	Dean Look	R	3	6	0	0	0	0	0.0	0	0	0	1	0	2	0	.000	.000
C	Cam Carreon	R	78	229	62	5	1	4	1.7	32	27	21	24	0	7	2	.271	.354
C	Bob Roselli	R	22	38	10	3	0	0	0.0	2	4	0	11	0	12	4	.263	.342
C	Joe Ginsberg	L	6	3	0	0	0	0	0.0	0	0	1	2	0	3	0	.000	.000
PH	Jim Rivera	L	1	0	0	0	0	0	—	0	0	0	0	0	0	0	—	—
PITCHERS																		
P	Juan Pizarro	L	40	69	17	3	0	0	0.0	10	5	5	19	1	0	0	.246	.319
P	Frank Baumann	L	55	61	16	2	0	2	3.3	8	10	5	25	1	0	0	.262	.393
P	Billy Pierce	L	39	56	8	0	0	0	0.0	3	3	1	11	0	0	0	.143	.143
P	Cal McLish	R	31	54	9	1	0	0	0.0	2	5	1	24	0	0	0	.167	.185
P	Ray Herbert	R	21	53	12	1	0	2	3.8	7	3	3	8	0	0	0	.226	.358
P	Early Wynn	B	17	37	6	0	0	0	0.0	4	2	3	11	0	0	0	.162	.162
P	Don Larsen	R	25	25	8	0	0	1	4.0	2	4	0	5	0	0	0	.320	.440
P	Bob Shaw	R	14	18	0	0	0	0	0.0	0	0	3	6	0	0	0	.000	.000
P	Russ Kemmerer	R	47	15	3	1	0	0	0.0	1	1	2	7	0	0	0	.200	.267
P	Turk Lown	R	60	14	0	0	0	0	0.0	0	0	0	5	0	0	0	.000	.000
P	Warren Hacker	R	42	9	1	0	0	0	0.0	0	1	0	1	0	0	0	.111	.111
P	Joe Horlen	R	5	7	0	0	0	0	0.0	0	0	0	2	0	0	0	.000	.000
P	Herb Score	L	8	6	0	0	0	0	0.0	0	0	0	5	0	0	0	.000	.000
P	Gary Peters	L	3	3	1	0	0	0	0.0	1	0	0	1	0	0	0	.333	.333
P	Alan Brice	R	3	0	0	0	0	0	—	0	0	0	0	0	0	0	—	—
P	Mike DeGerick	R	1	0	0	0	0	0	—	0	0	0	0	0	0	0	—	—
P	Gerry Staley	R	16	0	0	0	0	0	—	0	0	0	0	0	0	0	—	—
TEAM TOTAL				5556	1475	216	46	138	2.5	765	704	550	612	100	159	41	.265	.395

INDIVIDUAL FIELDING

POS	Player	T	G	PO	A	E	DP	TCG	FA
1B	R. Sievers	R	132	1096	94	8	93	9.1	.993
	J. Martin	R	60	314	29	4	27	5.8	.988
	B. Goodman	R	2	6	0	0	0	3.0	1.000
	E. Torgeson	L	1	1	0	0	0	1.0	1.000
2B	N. Fox	R	159	413	407	15	97	5.3	.982
	S. Esposito	R	11	23	16	0	3	3.5	1.000
	B. Goodman	R	1	1	1	0	0	2.0	1.000
SS	L. Aparicio	R	156	264	487	30	86	5.0	.962
	S. Esposito	R	20	18	39	2	3	3.0	.966
3B	A. Smith	R	80	58	161	12	12	2.9	.948
	J. Martin	R	36	39	89	6	11	3.7	.955
	A. Carey	R	54	26	73	4	4	1.9	.961
	S. Esposito	R	28	10	30	1	5	1.5	.976
	B. Goodman	R	7	4	13	1	1	2.6	.944
	T. Lepcio	R	1	1	0	1	0	2.0	.500
OF	J. Landis	R	139	389	9	5	3	2.9	.988
	M. Minoso	R	147	273	10	13	2	2.0	.956
	F. Robinson	R	106	218	7	2	0	2.1	.991
	A. Smith	R	71	123	3	3	0	1.8	.977
	A. Pilarcik	L	17	32	2	2	0	2.1	.944
	Hershberger	R	13	29	2	0	0	2.4	1.000
	W. Covington	R	14	16	2	2	0	1.4	.900
	D. Look	R	1	1	0	0	0	1.0	1.000
C	S. Lollar	R	107	464	48	1	6	4.8	.998
	C. Carreon	R	71	395	25	2	6	5.9	.995
	B. Roselli	R	10	32	3	0	0	3.5	1.000
	J. Ginsberg	R	2	3	0	0	0	1.5	1.000

All the optimism and hope of the New Frontier was reflected on April 10, 1961, when John F. Kennedy threw out the first ball at Griffith Stadium. Jungle Jim Rivera pushed aside Hal Woodeshick to retrieve the ball for the presidential autograph. When Kennedy presented the ball to Rivera, the Sox' reigning zany turned it back, saying, "I can't read this John, you'll have to do better than this." And so began the 1960s for the Sox, a decade of mixed reviews.

With the team in last place on June 10, Veeck sold the club to Chicago businessman Arthur Allyn after turning down a bid by actor Danny Thomas and future mayoral candidate Bernard Epton. The move was prompted as much by Veeck's ill health as the club's poor showing. Hank Greenberg completed the first trade of the Allyn era on the very first day of business: Bob Shaw, Gerry Staley, and rookie Stan Johnson were sent to Kansas City for Ray Herbert, Andy Carey, and Al Pilarcik. Herbert showed well as the Sox began a belated surge that saw them win 12 in a row. They played respectable ball the rest of the way to finish in fourth, but that was their poorest showing in a decade.

Hallmarks of an era passed from the scene in 1961. First, Jim Rivera was released in June, then in November Billy Pierce was traded to San Francisco for Eddie Fisher and Dom Zanni. And finally, the Comiskey family was gone, too. Chuck sold his 46 percent of the club to a group of Chicago businessmen on December 15. Peace had seemingly been restored.

TEAM STATISTICS

	W	L	PCT	GB	R	OR	2B	3B	HR	BA	SA	SB	E	DP	FA	CG	BB	SO	ShO	SV	ERA
NY	109	53	.673		827	612	194	40	240	.263	.442	28	124	180	.980	47	542	866	14	39	3.46
DET	101	61	.623	8	841	671	215	53	180	.266	.421	98	146	147	.976	62	469	836	12	30	3.55
BAL	95	67	.586	14	691	588	227	36	149	.254	.390	39	128	173	.980	54	617	926	21	33	3.22
CHI	86	76	.531	23	765	726	216	46	138	.265	.395	100	128	138	.980	39	498	814	3	33	4.06
CLE	78	83	.484	30.5	737	752	257	39	150	.266	.406	34	139	142	.977	35	599	801	12	23	4.15
BOS	76	86	.469	33	729	792	251	37	112	.254	.374	56	144	170	.977	35	679	831	6	30	4.29
MIN	70	90	.438	38	707	778	215	40	167	.250	.397	47	174	150	.972	49	570	914	14	23	4.28
LA	70	91	.435	38.5	744	784	218	22	189	.245	.398	37	192	154	.969	25	713	973	5	34	4.31
KC	61	100	.379	47.5	683	863	216	47	90	.247	.354	58	175	160	.972	32	629	703	5	23	4.74
WAS	61	100	.379	47.5	618	776	217	44	119	.244	.367	81	156	171	.975	39	586	666	8	21	4.23
LEAGUE TOTAL					7342	7342	2226	404	1534	.256	.395	578	1506	1585	.976	417	5902	8330	100	289	4.02

INDIVIDUAL PITCHING

PITCHER	T	W	L	PCT	ERA	SV	G	GS	CG	IP	H	BB	SO	R	ER	ShO	H9	BB9	SO9
Juan Pizarro	L	14	7	.667	3.05	2	39	25	12	194.2	164	89	188	73	66	1	7.58	4.11	8.69
Frank Baumann	L	10	13	.435	5.61	3	53	23	5	187.2	249	59	75	128	117	1	11.94	2.83	3.60
Billy Pierce	L	10	9	.526	3.80	3	39	28	5	180	190	54	106	85	76	1	9.50	2.70	5.30
Cal McLish	R	10	13	.435	4.38	1	31	27	4	162.1	178	47	80	87	79	0	9.87	2.61	4.44
Ray Herbert	R	9	6	.600	4.05	0	21	20	4	137.2	142	36	50	69	62	0	9.28	2.35	3.27
Early Wynn	R	8	2	.800	3.51	0	17	16	5	110.1	88	47	64	43	43	0	7.18	3.83	5.22
Turk Lown	R	7	5	.583	2.76	11	59	0	0	101	87	35	50	37	31	0	7.75	3.12	4.46
Russ Kemmerer	R	3	3	.500	4.38	2	47	2	0	96.2	102	26	35	53	47	0	9.50	2.42	3.26
Don Larsen	R	7	2	.778	4.12	2	25	3	0	74.1	64	29	53	36	34	0	7.75	3.51	6.42
Bob Shaw	R	3	4	.429	3.79	0	14	10	3	71.1	85	20	31	40	30	0	10.72	2.52	3.91
Warren Hacker	R	3	3	.500	3.77	8	42	0	0	57.1	62	8	40	26	24	0	9.73	1.26	6.28
Herb Score	L	1	2	.333	6.66	0	8	5	1	24.1	22	24	14	19	18	0	8.14	8.88	5.18
Gerry Staley	R	0	3	.000	5.00	0	16	0	0	18	17	5	8	10	10	0	8.50	2.50	4.00
Joe Horlen	R	1	3	.250	6.62	0	5	4	0	17.2	25	13	11	15	13	0	12.74	6.62	5.60
Gary Peters	L	0	0	—	1.74	1	3	0	0	10.1	10	2	6	2	2	0	8.71	1.74	5.23
Alan Brice	R	0	1	.000	0.00	0	3	0	0	3.1	4	3	3	2	0	0	10.80	8.10	8.10
Mike DeGerick	R	0	0	—	5.40	0	1	0	0	1.2	2	1	0	1	1	0	10.80	5.40	0.00
TEAM TOTAL		86	76	.531	4.06	33	423	163	39	1448.2	1491	498	814	726	653	3	9.26	3.09	5.06

Chicago 1962   Won 85 Lost 77 Pct. .525 5th   148

MANAGER	W	L	PCT
Al Lopez	85	77	.525

POS	Player	B	G	AB	H	2B	3B	HR	HR%	R	RBI	BB	SO	SB	Pinch Hit AB	H	BA	SA
REGULARS																		
1B	Joe Cunningham	L	149	526	155	32	7	8	1.5	91	70	101	59	3	3	1	.295	.428
2B	Nellie Fox	L	157	621	166	27	7	2	0.3	79	54	38	12	1	3	0	.267	.343
SS	Luis Aparicio	R	153	581	140	23	5	7	1.2	72	40	32	36	31	1	0	.241	.334
3B	Al Smith	R	142	511	149	23	8	16	3.1	62	82	57	60	3	4	2	.292	.462
RF	Mike Hershberger	R	148	427	112	14	2	4	0.9	54	46	37	36	10	13	3	.262	.333
CF	Jim Landis	R	149	534	122	21	6	15	2.8	82	61	80	105	19	4	1	.228	.375
LF	Floyd Robinson	L	156	600	187	45	10	11	1.8	89	109	72	47	4	1	0	.312	.475
C	Cam Carreon	R	106	313	80	19	1	4	1.3	31	37	33	37	1	11	5	.256	.361
SUBSTITUTES																		
3B	Charley Smith	R	65	145	30	4	0	2	1.4	11	17	9	32	0	13	2	.207	.276
32	Bob Sadowski	L	79	130	30	3	3	6	4.6	22	24	13	22	0	44	10	.231	.438
UT	Sammy Esposito	R	75	81	19	1	0	0	0.0	14	4	17	13	0	3	1	.235	.247
1B	Bob Farley	L	35	53	10	1	1	1	1.9	7	4	13	13	0	20	1	.189	.302
1B	Deacon Jones	L	18	28	9	2	0	0	0.0	3	8	4	6	0	8	4	.321	.393
3B	Ramon Conde	R	14	16	0	0	0	0	0.0	0	1	3	3	0	5	0	.000	.000
UT	Al Weis	B	7	12	1	0	0	0	0.0	2	0	2	3	1	0	0	.083	.083
2B	Dick Kenworthy	R	3	4	0	0	0	0	0.0	0	0	0	3	0	1	0	.000	.000
OF	Charlie Maxwell	L	69	206	61	8	3	9	4.4	30	43	34	32	0	9	1	.296	.495
OF	Brian McCall	L	4	8	3	0	0	2	25.0	2	3	0	2	0	3	1	.375	1.125
OF	Ken Berry	R	3	6	2	0	0	0	0.0	2	0	0	0	0	1	1	.333	.333
C	Sherm Lollar	R	84	220	59	12	0	2	0.9	17	26	32	23	1	19	2	.268	.350
C	Bob Roselli	R	35	64	12	3	1	1	1.6	4	5	11	15	1	15	2	.188	.313
UT	J. C. Martin	L	18	26	2	0	0	0	0.0	0	2	0	3	0	11	0	.077	.077
PITCHERS																		
P	Ray Herbert	R	35	82	16	5	0	2	2.4	6	9	5	16	0	0	0	.195	.329
P	Juan Pizarro	L	37	69	11	1	0	0	0.0	10	5	4	17	0	0	0	.159	.174
P	Early Wynn	B	27	54	7	1	0	0	0.0	5	2	7	17	0	0	0	.130	.148
P	John Buzhardt	R	28	51	6	0	0	0	0.0	2	1	2	22	0	0	0	.118	.118
P	Eddie Fisher	R	57	46	6	2	1	0	0.0	2	2	2	12	0	0	0	.130	.217
P	Joe Horlen	R	20	38	2	0	0	0	0.0	1	0	2	11	0	0	0	.053	.053
P	Frank Baumann	L	40	30	8	2	1	0	0.0	3	4	6	9	0	0	0	.267	.400
P	Dom Zanni	R	44	18	5	0	0	0	0.0	2	3	3	3	1	0	0	.278	.278
P	Mike Joyce	R	25	7	3	0	0	0	0.0	1	0	0	2	0	0	0	.429	.429
P	Turk Lown	R	42	3	0	0	0	0	0.0	0	0	0	1	0	0	0	.000	.000
P	Russ Kemmerer	R	20	2	1	0	0	0	0.0	1	0	1	1	0	0	0	.500	.500
P	Dean Stone	L	27	2	1	1	0	0	0.0	0	0	0	1	0	0	0	.500	1.000
P	Dave DeBusschere	R	12	0	0	0	0	0	—	0	0	0	0	0	0	0	—	—
P	Mike DeGerick	R	1	0	0	0	0	0	—	0	0	0	0	0	0	0	—	—
P	Frank Kreutzer	R	1	0	0	0	0	0	—	0	0	0	0	0	0	0	—	—
P	Gary Peters	L	5	0	0	0	0	0	—	0	0	0	0	0	0	0	—	—
P	Herb Score	L	4	0	0	0	0	0	—	0	0	0	0	0	0	0	—	—
P	Verle Tiefenthaler	L	3	0	0	0	0	0	—	0	0	0	0	0	0	0	—	—
TEAM TOTAL				5514	1415	250	56	92	1.7	707	662	620	674	76	192	37	.257	.372

INDIVIDUAL FIELDING

POS	Player	T	G	PO	A	E	DP	TCG	FA
1B	J. Cunningham	L	143	1282	90	8	118	9.7	**.994**
	B. Farley	L	14	84	5	1	8	6.4	.989
	D. Jones	R	6	46	4	2	3	8.7	.962
	C. Maxwell	L	6	47	3	1	6	8.5	.980
	J. Martin	R	1	1	0	0	0	1.0	1.000
2B	N. Fox	R	154	376	428	8	93	5.3	**.990**
	B. Sadowski	R	12	23	30	0	9	4.4	1.000
	S. Esposito	R	7	3	9	1	1	1.9	.923
	D. Kenworthy	R	2	1	4	0	2	2.5	1.000
	A. Weis	R	1	0	1	1	0	2.0	.500
SS	L. Aparicio	R	152	280	452	20	102	4.9	**.973**
	S. Esposito	R	20	20	47	2	5	3.5	.971
	A. Weis	R	4	3	12	2	0	4.3	.882
3B	A. Smith	R	105	76	185	18	8	2.7	.935
	C. Smith	R	54	26	76	6	12	2.0	.944
	B. Sadowski	R	16	10	32	2	0	2.8	.955
	S. Esposito	R	41	6	16	4	1	0.6	.846
	A. Weis	R	1	0	0	0	0	0.0	.000
	R. Conde	R	7	4	4	1	0	1.3	.889
	J. Martin	R	1	0	2	0	0	2.0	1.000

POS	Player	T	G	PO	A	E	DP	TCG	FA
OF	J. Landis	R	144	360	2	2	1	2.5	.995
	F. Robinson	R	155	278	13	8	2	1.9	.973
	Hershberger	R	135	236	7	4	0	1.8	.984
	C. Maxwell	L	56	100	2	1	1	1.8	.990
	A. Smith	R	39	47	6	2	0	1.4	.964
	K. Berry	R	2	4	1	0	1	2.5	1.000
	J. Cunningham	L	5	5	0	0	0	1.0	1.000
	B. McCall	L	1	4	0	0	0	4.0	1.000
C	C. Carreon	R	93	519	30	3	5	5.9	.995
	S. Lollar	R	66	298	23	3	0	4.9	.991
	B. Roselli	R	20	80	5	1	2	4.3	.988
	J. Martin	R	6	18	0	0	0	3.0	1.000

In what has to be considered a low moment in Sox history, management turned Early Wynn's quest for his 300th victory into a three-ring circus. They delayed his September starts so that the gate revenue might be increased by a few extra starts at home. He won number 299 on September 8 against Washington but faltered the next three times out. The Sox had outsmarted themselves; Wynn's 300th win would come while wearing a Cleveland uniform.

Floyd Robinson, a home-grown product, established a club record for doubles in 1962, with 45. On July 22 he went six-for-six against Red Sox pitching, all singles. But individual honors this year went to Ray Herbert, who won 20 games and reeled off 31 scoreless innings in August. Herbert was also the winning pitcher in the All-Star Game.

The veterans continued to fade in 1962. Aparicio reported to camp overweight, bringing back memories of Chico Carrasquel. But there was no new Looie in the minors this time. Nellie Fox was benched in favor of Bob Sadowski in July, as the club never seemed sure of what course to pursue. Youngsters like Gary Peters, Cam Carreon, and Ken Berry waited in the wings, while the Lollars, Foxes, and Wynns nervously counted their days. New general manager Ed Short was commited to youth but still needed some names the fans could identify with. It was an interesting dilemma for Short, who watched the Sox stage an August rally to avoid finishing in the second division for the first time in twelve years.

TEAM STATISTICS

	W	L	PCT	GB	R	OR	2B	3B	HR	BA	SA	SB	E	DP	FA	CG	BB	SO	ShO	SV	ERA
NY	96	66	.593		817	680	240	29	199	**.267**	**.426**	42	131	151	.979	33	499	838	10	42	3.70
MIN	91	71	.562	5	798	713	215	39	185	.260	.412	33	129	**173**	.979	**53**	**493**	**948**	11	27	3.89
LA	86	76	.531	10	718	706	232	35	137	.250	.380	46	175	153	.972	23	616	858	**15**	**47**	3.70
DET	85	76	.528	10.5	758	692	191	36	**209**	.248	.411	69	156	114	.974	46	503	873	8	35	3.81
CHI	85	77	.525	11	707	658	250	56	92	.257	.372	76	110	153	**.982**	50	537	821	13	28	3.73
CLE	80	82	.494	16	682	745	202	22	180	.245	.388	35	139	168	.977	45	594	780	12	31	4.14
BAL	77	85	.475	19	652	680	225	34	156	.248	.387	45	122	152	.980	32	549	898	8	33	**3.69**
BOS	76	84	.475	19	707	756	**257**	53	146	.258	.403	39	131	152	.979	34	632	923	10	40	4.22
KC	72	90	.444	24	745	837	220	**58**	116	.263	.386	76	132	131	.979	32	655	825	4	33	4.79
WAS	60	101	.373	35.5	599	716	206	38	132	.250	.373	**99**	139	160	.978	38	593	771	11	13	4.04
LEAGUE TOTAL					7183	7183	2238	400	1552	.255	.394	560	1364	1507	.978	386	5671	8535	102	329	3.97

INDIVIDUAL PITCHING

PITCHER	T	W	L	PCT	ERA	SV	G	GS	CG	IP	H	BB	SO	R	ER	ShO	H9	BB9	SO9
Ray Herbert	R	20	9	**.690**	3.27	0	35	35	12	236.2	228	74	115	90	86	2	8.67	2.81	4.37
Juan Pizarro	L	12	14	.462	3.81	1	36	32	9	203.1	182	97	173	97	86	1	8.06	4.29	**7.66**
Eddie Fisher	R	9	5	.643	3.10	5	57	12	2	182.2	169	45	88	74	63	1	8.33	2.22	4.34
Early Wynn	R	7	15	.318	4.46	0	27	26	11	167.2	171	56	91	90	83	3	9.18	3.01	4.88
John Buzhardt	R	8	12	.400	4.19	0	28	25	8	152.1	156	59	64	75	71	2	9.22	3.49	3.78
Frank Baumann	L	7	6	.538	3.38	4	40	10	3	119.2	117	36	55	46	45	1	8.80	2.71	4.14
Joe Horlen	R	7	6	.538	4.89	0	20	19	5	108.2	108	43	63	62	59	1	8.94	3.56	5.22
Dom Zanni	R	6	5	.545	3.75	5	44	2	0	86.1	67	31	66	42	36	0	6.98	3.23	6.88
Turk Lown	R	4	2	.667	3.04	6	42	0	0	56.1	58	25	40	21	19	0	9.27	3.99	6.39
Mike Joyce	R	2	1	.667	3.32	2	25	1	0	43.1	40	14	9	17	16	0	8.31	2.91	1.87
Dean Stone	L	1	0	1.000	3.26	5	27	0	0	30.1	28	9	23	11	11	0	8.31	2.67	6.82
Russ Kemmerer	R	2	1	.667	3.86	0	20	0	0	28	30	11	17	14	12	0	9.64	3.54	5.46
Dave DeBusschere	R	0	0	—	2.00	0	12	0	0	18	5	23	8	7	4	0	2.50	11.50	4.00
Gary Peters	L	0	1	.000	5.68	0	5	0	0	6.1	8	1	4	5	4	0	11.37	1.42	5.68
Herb Score	L	0	0	—	4.50	0	4	0	0	6	6	4	3	3	3	0	9.00	6.00	4.50
Verle Tiefenthaler	R	0	0	—	9.82	0	3	0	0	3.2	6	7	1	4	4	0	14.73	17.18	2.45
Frank Kreutzer	L	0	0	—	0.00	0	1	0	0	1.1	0	1	1	0	0	0	0.00	6.75	6.75
Mike DeGerick	R	0	0	—	0.00	0	1	0	0	1	1	1	0	0	0	0	9.00	9.00	0.00
TEAM TOTAL		85	77	.525	3.73	28	427	162	50	1451.2	1380	537	821	658	602	11	8.56	3.33	5.09

Chicago 1963   Won 94   Lost 68   Pct. .580   2nd   150

MANAGER	W	L	PCT
Al Lopez	94	68	.580

POS	Player	B	G	AB	H	2B	3B	HR	HR %	R	RBI	BB	SO	SB	Pinch Hit AB	Pinch Hit H	BA	SA
REGULARS																		
1B	Tom McCraw	L	102	280	71	11	3	6	2.1	38	33	21	46	15	3	1	.254	.379
2B	Nellie Fox	L	137	539	140	19	0	2	0.4	54	42	24	17	0	6	2	.260	.306
SS	Ron Hansen	R	144	482	109	17	2	13	2.7	55	67	78	74	1	0	0	.226	.351
3B	Pete Ward	L	157	600	177	34	6	22	3.7	80	84	52	77	7	3	1	.295	.482
RF	Floyd Robinson	L	146	527	149	21	6	13	2.5	71	71	62	43	4	9	2	.283	.419
CF	Jim Landis	R	133	396	89	6	6	13	3.3	56	45	47	75	8	11	3	.225	.369
LF	Dave Nicholson	R	126	449	103	11	4	22	4.9	53	70	63	175	2	3	1	.229	.419
C	J. C. Martin	L	105	259	53	11	1	5	1.9	25	28	26	35	0	12	3	.205	.313
SUBSTITUTES																		
1B	Joe Cunningham	L	67	210	60	12	1	1	0.5	32	31	33	23	1	6	4	.286	.367
2S	Al Weis	B	99	210	57	9	0	0	0.0	41	19	18	37	15	9	2	.271	.314
1B	Jim Lemon	R	36	80	16	0	1	1	1.3	4	8	12	32	0	9	1	.200	.263
3B	Don Buford	B	12	42	12	1	2	0	0.0	9	5	5	7	1	1	0	.286	.405
1B	Deacon Jones	L	17	16	3	0	1	1	6.3	4	2	2	2	0	12	1	.188	.500
SS	Charley Smith	R	4	7	2	0	1	0	0.0	0	1	0	2	0	3	1	.286	.571
OF	Mike Hershberger	R	135	476	133	26	2	3	0.6	64	45	39	39	9	14	2	.279	.361
O1	Charlie Maxwell	L	71	130	30	4	2	3	2.3	17	17	31	27	0	21	3	.231	.362
OF	Gene Stephens	L	6	18	7	0	0	1	5.6	5	2	1	3	0	0	0	.389	.556
OF	Brian McCall	L	3	7	0	0	0	0	0.0	1	0	1	2	0	0	0	.000	.000
O2	Ken Berry	R	4	5	1	0	0	0	0.0	2	0	1	1	0	0	0	.200	.200
C	Cam Carreon	R	101	270	74	10	1	2	0.7	28	35	23	32	1	7	3	.274	.341
C	Sherm Lollar	R	35	73	17	4	0	0	0.0	4	6	8	7	0	11	2	.233	.288
PH	Sammy Esposito	R	1	0	0	0	0	0	–	0	0	0	0	0	0	0	–	–
PITCHERS																		
P	Gary Peters	L	50	81	21	4	1	3	3.7	12	12	3	19	0	1	0	.259	.444
P	Juan Pizarro	L	32	73	13	2	0	2	2.7	10	10	3	26	0	0	0	.178	.288
P	Ray Herbert	R	33	63	14	4	0	1	1.6	7	10	9	18	0	0	0	.222	.333
P	John Buzhardt	R	20	48	4	2	0	0	0.0	2	1	0	20	0	0	0	.083	.125
P	Joe Horlen	R	33	40	9	0	0	0	0.0	2	3	1	9	0	0	0	.225	.225
P	Eddie Fisher	R	33	36	5	0	0	0	0.0	2	0	2	15	0	0	0	.139	.139
P	Hoyt Wilhelm	R	55	29	2	0	0	0	0.0	3	2	4	11	0	0	0	.069	.069
P	Dave DeBusschere	R	24	22	1	0	0	0	0.0	1	0	1	9	0	0	0	.045	.045
P	Jim Brosnan	R	45	13	4	0	0	0	0.0	0	0	0	4	0	0	0	.308	.308
P	Frank Baumann	L	24	11	1	0	0	0	0.0	1	0	1	2	0	0	0	.091	.091
P	Fritz Ackley	L	2	5	1	0	0	0	0.0	0	0	0	4	0	0	0	.200	.200
P	Bruce Howard	B	7	4	1	0	0	0	0.0	0	0	0	1	0	0	0	.250	.250
P	Frank Kreutzer	R	1	2	0	0	0	0	0.0	0	0	0	0	0	0	0	.000	.000
P	Taylor Phillips	L	9	2	0	0	0	0	0.0	0	0	0	1	0	0	0	.000	.000
P	Joe Shipley	R	3	2	0	0	0	0	0.0	0	0	0	1	0	0	0	.000	.000
P	Fred Talbot	R	1	1	0	0	0	0	0.0	0	0	0	0	0	0	0	.000	.000
P	Mike Joyce	R	6	0	0	0	0	0	–	0	0	0	0	0	0	0	–	–
P	Dom Zanni	R	5	0	0	0	0	0	–	0	0	0	0	0	0	0	–	–
TEAM TOTAL				5508	1379	208	40	114	2.1	683	648	571	896	64	141	32	.250	.365

INDIVIDUAL FIELDING

POS	Player	T	G	PO	A	E	DP	TCG	FA	POS	Player	T	G	PO	A	E	DP	TCG	FA
1B	T. McCraw	L	97	673	47	5	65	7.5	.993	OF	J. Landis	R	124	264	6	2	0	2.2	**.993**
	J. Cunningham	L	58	535	24	6	39	9.7	.989		F. Robinson	R	137	245	8	4	4	1.9	.984
	J. Lemon	R	25	136	7	3	18	5.8	.979		Hershberger	R	119	230	13	6	3	2.1	.976
	C. Maxwell	L	17	107	5	0	14	6.6	1.000		D. Nicholson	R	123	213	10	7	1	1.9	.970
	J. Martin	R	3	8	1	0	0	3.0	1.000		C. Maxwell	L	24	29	2	0	1	1.3	1.000
	D. Jones	R	1	6	1	0	4	7.0	1.000		G. Stephens	R	5	8	2	1	0	2.2	.909
	S. Lollar	R	2	4	0	0	0	2.0	1.000		K. Berry	R	2	6	0	1	0	3.5	.857
2B	N. Fox	R	134	305	342	8	71	4.9	**.988**		B. McCall	L	2	3	0	0	0	1.5	1.000
	A. Weis	R	48	88	103	2	28	4.0	.990	C	J. Martin	R	98	468	48	9	9	5.4	.983
	K. Berry	R	1	0	0	0	0	0.0	.000		C. Carreon	R	92	429	36	6	7	5.1	.987
	D. Buford	R	2	3	1	1	0	2.5	.800		S. Lollar	R	23	94	9	2	2	4.6	.981
	P. Ward	R	1	1	0	0	0	1.0	1.000										
SS	R. Hansen	R	144	247	483	13	95	5.2	.983										
	A. Weis	R	27	35	65	8	13	4.0	.926										
	C. Smith	R	1	3	5	0	4	8.0	1.000										
	P. Ward	R	1	1	1	0	1	2.0	1.000										
3B	P. Ward	R	154	156	302	38	27	3.2	.923										
	J. Martin	R	1	0	0	0	0	0.0	.000										
	A. Weis	R	1	0	0	0	0	0.0	.000										
	D. Buford	R	9	10	11	1	1	2.4	.955										

Short solved his own riddle that winter. The new year was barely two weeks old when the unhappy Aparicio was sent to Baltimore along with Al Smith for Hoyt Wilhelm, Ron Hansen, Pete Ward, and Dave Nicholson. The Sox got half an infield, the 1960s' best relief pitcher, and, in Nicholson, a player who provided a few heroic moments. The Sox had finally established a definite course, and had put the 1950s behind them once and for all. Nellie Fox was still around but was playing fewer games. His very special time ended on December 10, when he was sold to Houston in a waiver deal. Don Buford and Al Weis were waiting in the wings.

The Sox climbed back into second place on the strength of a much improved pitching staff. Gary Peters was a rookie whose options had expired. He was brought north only because the other two lefties, Juan Pizarro and Frank Baumann, were both ailing. He won his first game on May 6, also demonstrating his batting prowess with a home run that gave the Sox the victory. He won 11 games in a row en route to Rookie of the Year honors. Peters barely edged out Pete Ward, who finally gave the Sox something to brag about at third. This ballclub was getting younger all the time.

Joel Horlen, called by some "The All-American Boy," nursed a July 29th no-hitter into the ninth inning in Washington. With one out in the ninth, Chuck Hinton rolled a single up the middle. After the next man was retired, Don Lock hit a home run that gave Hard Luck Horlen a cruel 2–1 loss and another nickname.

TEAM STATISTICS

	W	L	PCT	GB	R	OR	2B	3B	HR	BA	SA	SB	E	DP	FA	CG	BB	SO	ShO	SV	ERA
NY	104	57	.646		714	547	197	35	188	.252	.403	42	110	162	.982	59	476	965	17	31	3.07
CHI	94	68	.580	10.5	683	544	208	40	114	.250	.365	64	131	163	.979	49	440	932	19	39	2.97
MIN	91	70	.565	13	767	602	223	35	225	.255	.430	32	144	140	.976	58	459	941	12	30	3.28
BAL	86	76	.531	18.5	644	621	207	32	146	.249	.380	97	99	157	.984	35	507	913	8	43	3.45
CLE	79	83	.488	25.5	635	702	214	29	169	.239	.381	59	143	129	.977	40	478	1018	11	25	3.79
DET	79	83	.488	25.5	700	703	195	36	148	.252	.382	73	113	124	.981	42	477	930	6	28	3.90
BOS	76	85	.472	28	666	704	247	34	171	.252	.400	27	135	119	.978	29	539	1009	6	32	3.97
KC	73	89	.451	31.5	615	704	225	38	95	.247	.353	47	127	131	.980	35	540	887	9	29	3.92
LA	70	91	.435	34	597	660	208	38	95	.250	.354	43	163	155	.974	30	578	889	9	31	3.52
WAS	56	106	.346	48.5	578	812	190	35	138	.227	.351	68	182	165	.971	29	537	744	8	25	4.42
LEAGUE TOTAL					6599	6599	2114	352	1489	.247	.380	552	1347	1445	.978	406	5031	9228	105	313	3.63

INDIVIDUAL PITCHING

PITCHER	T	W	L	PCT	ERA	SV	G	GS	CG	IP	H	BB	SO	R	ER	ShO	H9	BB9	SO9
Gary Peters	L	19	8	.704	2.33	1	41	30	13	243	192	68	189	69	63	4	7.11	2.52	7.00
Ray Herbert	R	13	10	.565	3.24	0	33	33	14	224.2	230	35	105	86	81	7	9.21	1.40	4.21
Juan Pizarro	L	16	8	.667	2.39	1	32	28	10	214.2	177	63	163	69	57	3	7.42	2.64	6.83
Hoyt Wilhelm	R	5	8	.385	2.64	21	55	3	0	136.1	106	30	111	47	40	0	7.00	1.98	7.33
John Buzhardt	R	9	4	.692	2.42	0	19	18	6	126.1	100	31	59	35	34	3	7.12	2.21	4.20
Joe Horlen	R	11	7	.611	3.27	0	33	21	3	124	122	55	61	50	45	0	8.85	3.99	4.43
Eddie Fisher	R	9	8	.529	3.95	0	33	15	2	120.2	114	28	67	57	53	1	8.50	2.09	5.00
Dave DeBusschere	R	3	4	.429	3.09	0	24	10	1	84.1	80	34	53	35	29	1	8.54	3.63	5.66
Jim Brosnan	R	3	8	.273	2.84	14	45	0	0	73	71	22	46	24	23	0	8.75	2.71	5.67
Frank Baumann	L	2	1	.667	3.04	1	24	1	0	50.1	52	17	31	22	17	0	9.30	3.04	5.54
Bruce Howard	R	2	1	.667	2.65	1	7	0	0	17	12	14	9	7	5	0	6.35	7.41	4.76
Taylor Phillips	L	0	0	–	10.29	0	9	0	0	14	16	13	13	16	16	0	10.29	8.36	8.36
Fritz Ackley	R	1	0	1.000	2.08	0	2	2	0	13	7	7	11	4	3	0	4.85	4.85	7.62
Mike Joyce	R	0	0	–	8.44	0	6	0	0	10.2	13	8	7	10	10	0	10.97	6.75	5.91
Frank Kreutzer	L	1	0	1.000	1.80	0	1	1	0	5	3	1	0	1	1	0	5.40	1.80	0.00
Joe Shipley	R	0	1	.000	5.79	0	3	0	0	4.2	9	6	3	7	3	0	17.36	11.57	5.79
Dom Zanni	R	0	0	–	8.31	0	5	0	0	4.1	5	4	2	4	4	0	10.38	8.31	4.15
Fred Talbot	R	0	0	–	3.00	0	1	0	0	3	2	4	2	1	1	0	6.00	12.00	6.00
TEAM TOTAL		94	68	.580	2.97	39	373	162	49	1469	1311	440	932	544	485	19	8.03	2.70	5.71

Chicago 1964   Won 98   Lost 64   Pct. .605   2nd

MANAGER	W	L	PCT
Al Lopez	98	64	.605

POS	Player	B	G	AB	H	2B	3B	HR	HR %	R	RBI	BB	SO	SB	Pinch Hit AB	H	BA	SA
REGULARS																		
1B	Tom McCraw	L	125	368	96	11	5	6	1.6	47	36	32	65	15	20	2	.261	.367
2B	Al Weis	B	133	328	81	4	4	2	0.6	36	23	22	41	22	6	1	.247	.302
SS	Ron Hansen	R	158	575	150	25	3	20	3.5	85	68	73	73	1	0	0	.261	.419
3B	Pete Ward	L	144	539	152	28	3	23	4.3	61	94	56	76	1	5	1	.282	.473
RF	Mike Hershberger	R	141	452	104	15	3	2	0.4	55	31	48	47	8	10	1	.230	.290
CF	Jim Landis	R	106	298	62	8	4	1	0.3	30	18	36	64	5	7	1	.208	.272
LF	Floyd Robinson	L	141	525	158	17	3	11	2.1	83	59	70	41	9	6	2	.301	.408
C	J. C. Martin	L	122	294	58	10	1	4	1.4	23	22	16	30	0	6	0	.197	.279
SUBSTITUTES																		
23	Don Buford	B	135	442	116	14	6	4	0.9	62	30	46	62	12	10	1	.262	.348
1B	Bill Skowron	R	73	273	80	11	3	4	1.5	19	38	19	36	0	3	0	.293	.399
1B	Joe Cunningham	L	40	108	27	7	0	0	0.0	13	10	14	14	0	7	1	.250	.315
3B	Charley Smith	R	2	7	1	0	1	0	0.0	1	0	1	1	0	0	0	.143	.429
OF	Dave Nicholson	R	97	294	60	6	1	13	4.4	40	39	52	126	0	7	1	.204	.364
OF	Gene Stephens	L	82	141	33	4	2	3	2.1	21	17	21	28	1	19	7	.234	.355
O1	Jeoff Long	R	23	35	5	0	0	0	0.0	0	5	4	15	0	12	1	.143	.143
OF	Ken Berry	R	12	32	12	1	0	1	3.1	4	4	5	3	0	0	0	.375	.500
OF	Minnie Minoso	R	30	31	7	0	0	1	3.2	4	5	5	3	0	22	4	.226	.323
C	Jerry McNertney	R	73	186	40	5	0	3	1.6	16	23	19	24	0	6	0	.215	.290
C	Cam Carreon	R	37	95	26	5	0	0	0.0	12	4	7	13	0	3	0	.274	.326
PH	Smoky Burgess	L	7	5	1	0	0	1	20.0	1	1	2	0	0	5	1	.200	.800
PH	Marv Staehle	L	6	5	2	0	0	0	0.0	0	2	0	0	1	5	2	.400	.400
PH	Dick Kenworthy	R	2	2	0	0	0	0	0.0	0	0	0	1	0	2	0	.000	.000
PH	Charlie Maxwell	L	2	2	0	0	0	0	0.0	0	0	0	0	0	2	0	.000	.000
PH	Jim Hicks	R	2	0	0	0	0	0	—	0	0	0	0	0	0	0	—	—
PITCHERS																		
P	Gary Peters	L	54	120	25	7	0	4	3.3	9	19	2	29	0	15	4	.208	.367
P	Juan Pizarro	L	33	90	19	1	0	3	3.3	6	15	1	34	0	0	0	.211	.322
P	Joe Horlen	R	32	69	11	0	0	0	0.0	2	5	2	11	0	0	0	.159	.159
P	John Buzhardt	R	31	54	11	1	1	0	0.0	3	6	2	22	0	0	0	.204	.259
P	Ray Herbert	R	20	36	5	0	0	0	0.0	2	3	1	10	0	0	0	.139	.139
P	Hoyt Wilhelm	R	73	21	3	0	0	0	0.0	2	3	1	7	0	0	0	.143	.143
P	Fred Talbot	R	18	19	5	2	0	0	0.0	5	3	4	6	0	0	0	.263	.368
P	Eddie Fisher	B	59	18	3	0	0	0	0.0	0	1	0	6	0	0	0	.167	.167
P	Bruce Howard	R	3	8	0	0	0	0	0.0	0	0	0	5	0	0	0	.000	.000
P	Frank Kreutzer	R	17	8	1	1	0	0	0.0	0	1	0	3	0	0	0	.125	.250
P	Don Mossi	L	34	6	1	0	0	0	0.0	0	0	0	2	0	0	0	.167	.167
P	Frank Baumann	L	22	4	0	0	0	0	0.0	0	0	0	3	0	0	0	.000	.000
P	Fritz Ackley	L	3	1	1	1	0	0	0.0	0	1	0	1	0	0	0	1.000	2.000
TEAM TOTAL				5491	1356	184	40	106	1.9	642	586	562	902	75	178	30	.247	.353

INDIVIDUAL FIELDING

POS	Player	T	G	PO	A	E	DP	TCG	FA	POS	Player	T	G	PO	A	E	DP	TCG	FA
1B	B. Skowron	R	70	621	40	1	53	9.5*	.998	OF	Hershberger	R	134	231	10	4	2	1.8	.984
	T. McCraw	L	84	601	37	5	57	7.7	.992		F. Robinson	R	138	225	5	3	0	1.7	.987
	J. Cunningham	L	33	264	16	1	25	8.5	.996		J. Landis	R	101	183	7	1	2	1.9	.995
	J. Long	R	5	30	4	0	3	6.8	1.000		D. Nicholson	R	92	136	4	4	0	1.6	.972
2B	A. Weis	R	116	199	255	16	64	4.1	.966		G. Stephens	R	59	91	2	3	1	1.6	.969
	D. Buford	R	92	196	198	13	60	4.4	.968		T. McCraw	L	36	36	4	2	0	1.2	.952
SS	R. Hansen	R	158	292	514	21	105	5.2	.975		K. Berry	R	12	15	0	0	0	1.3	1.000
	A. Weis	R	9	4	12	5	1	2.3	.762		M. Minoso	R	5	9	0	0	0	1.8	1.000
3B	P. Ward	R	138	126	309	19	24	3.3	.958		J. Long	R	5	4	0	2	0	1.2	.667
	D. Buford	R	37	30	63	3	5	2.6	.969		A. Weis	R	2	2	0	0	0	1.0	1.000
	C. Smith	R	2	2	10	0	2	6.0	1.000	C	J. Martin	R	120	530	43	8	6	4.8	.986
											J. McNertney	R	69	360	30	5	5	5.7	.987
											C. Carreon	R	34	134	13	2	2	4.4	.987

152

When they were good, the 1964 White Sox nearly stole a pennant. When they were bad, they couldn't beat anyone. On the one hand, they beat the Kansas City A's 16 of 18 times. On the other, they lost their first 11 meetings with the Yankees. You can't win a pennant if you can't beat the people in front of you.

Juan Pizarro, the quiet lefty, won 19 games. With Peters winning 20, the Sox had the best lefthanded duo in baseball. An argument can be made for this pitching staff as the best in club history. It was a staff deep in relief pitching to complement four starters capable of throwing a shutout on any given day.

To meet the Yankee challenge, the Sox acquired Moose Skowron and baseball's best pinch hitter, Smoky Burgess. What hurt them the most was the hole behind the plate. J.C. Martin, Cam Carreon, and Gerry McNertney were in and out of the lineup. None of them provided any leadership or direction for the talented young pitching staff.

The Sox finally won some games against New York, taking four straight in August at Comiskey Park. They were inspired, but it was the last chance to see the Yankees in 1964. A nine-game winning streak closed out the season for the ChiSox, but in the end one game separated the two, as the Yankees won their last ten games.

TEAM STATISTICS

	W	L	PCT	GB	R	OR	2B	3B	HR	BA	SA	SB	E	DP	FA	CG	BB	SO	ShO	SV	ERA
NY	99	63	.611		730	577	208	35	162	.253	.387	54	109	158	.983	46	504	989	18	45	3.15
CHI	98	64	.605	1	642	501	184	40	106	.247	.353	75	122	164	.981	44	401	955	20	45	2.72
BAL	97	65	.599	2	679	567	229	20	162	.248	.387	78	95	159	.985	44	456	939	17	41	3.16
DET	85	77	.525	14	699	678	199	57	157	.253	.395	60	111	137	.982	35	536	993	11	35	3.84
LA	82	80	.506	17	544	551	186	27	102	.242	.344	49	138	168	.978	30	530	965	28	41	2.91
CLE	79	83	.488	20	689	693	208	22	164	.247	.380	79	118	149	.981	37	565	1162	16	37	3.75
MIN	79	83	.488	20	737	678	227	46	221	.252	.427	46	145	131	.977	47	545	1099	4	29	3.57
BOS	72	90	.444	27	688	793	253	29	186	.258	.416	18	138	123	.977	21	571	1094	9	38	4.50
WAS	62	100	.383	37	578	733	199	28	125	.231	.348	47	127	145	.979	27	505	794	5	26	3.98
KC	57	105	.352	42	621	836	216	29	166	.239	.379	34	158	152	.974	18	614	966	6	27	4.71
LEAGUE TOTAL					6607	6607	2109	333	1551	.247	.382	540	1261	1486	.980	349	5227	9956	134	364	3.63

INDIVIDUAL PITCHING

PITCHER	T	W	L	PCT	ERA	SV	G	GS	CG	IP	H	BB	SO	R	ER	ShO	H9	BB9	SO9
Gary Peters	L	20	8	.714	2.50	0	37	36	11	273.2	217	104	205	89	76	3	7.14	3.42	6.74
Juan Pizarro	L	19	9	.679	2.56	0	33	33	11	239	193	55	162	78	68	4	7.27	2.07	6.10
Joe Horlen	R	13	9	.591	1.88	0	32	28	9	210.2	142	55	138	54	44	2	6.07	2.35	5.90
John Buzhardt	R	10	8	.556	2.98	0	31	25	8	160	150	35	97	60	53	3	8.44	1.97	5.46
Hoyt Wilhelm	R	12	9	.571	1.99	27	73	0	0	131.1	94	30	95	35	29	0	6.44	2.06	6.51
Eddie Fisher	R	6	3	.667	3.02	9	59	2	0	125	86	32	74	43	42	0	6.19	2.30	5.33
Ray Herbert	R	6	7	.462	3.47	0	20	19	1	111.2	117	17	40	50	43	1	9.43	1.37	3.22
Fred Talbot	R	4	5	.444	3.70	0	17	12	3	75.1	83	20	34	31	31	2	9.92	2.39	4.06
Frank Kreutzer	L	3	1	.750	3.35	1	17	2	0	40.1	37	18	32	15	15	0	8.26	4.02	7.14
Don Mossi	L	3	1	.750	2.93	7	34	0	0	40	37	7	36	16	13	0	8.33	1.58	8.10
Frank Baumann	L	0	3	.000	6.19	1	22	0	0	32	40	16	19	22	22	0	11.25	4.50	5.34
Bruce Howard	R	2	1	.667	0.81	0	3	3	1	22.1	10	8	17	2	2	1	4.03	3.22	6.85
Fritz Ackley	R	0	0	–	8.53	0	3	2	0	6.1	10	4	6	6	6	0	14.21	5.68	8.53
TEAM TOTAL		98	64	.605	2.72	45	381	162	44	1467.2	1216	401	955	501	444	16	7.46	2.46	5.86

Chicago 1965   Won 95   Lost 67   Pct. .586   2nd

MANAGER	W	L	PCT
Al Lopez	95	67	.586

POS	Player	B	G	AB	H	2B	3B	HR	HR%	R	RBI	BB	SO	SB	Pinch Hit AB	Pinch Hit H	BA	SA
REGULARS																		
1B	Bill Skowron	R	146	559	153	24	3	18	3.2	63	78	32	77	1	1	1	.274	.424
2B	Don Buford	B	155	586	166	22	5	10	1.7	93	47	67	76	17	8	2	.283	.389
SS	Ron Hansen	R	162	587	138	23	4	11	1.9	61	66	60	73	1	0	0	.235	.344
3B	Pete Ward	L	138	507	125	25	3	10	2.0	62	57	56	83	2	5	1	.247	.367
CF	Ken Berry	R	157	472	103	17	4	12	2.5	51	42	28	96	4	1	0	.218	.347
LF	Danny Cater	R	142	514	139	18	4	14	2.7	74	55	33	65	3	7	2	.270	.403
C	J. C. Martin	L	119	230	60	12	0	2	0.9	21	21	24	29	2	15	3	.261	.339
SUBSTITUTES																		
1O	Tom McCraw	L	133	273	65	12	1	5	1.8	38	21	25	48	12	22	7	.238	.344
2B	Al Weis	B	103	135	40	4	3	1	0.7	29	12	12	22	4	6	2	.296	.393
3B	Gene Freese	R	17	32	9	0	1	1	3.1	2	4	5	9	0	7	3	.281	.438
OF	Floyd Robinson	L	156	577	153	15	6	14	2.4	70	66	76	51	4	9	2	.265	.385
OF	Dave Nicholson	R	54	85	13	2	1	2	2.4	11	12	9	40	0	12	0	.153	.271
OF	Bill Voss	L	11	33	6	0	1	1	3.0	4	3	3	5	0	0	0	.182	.333
OF	Tommie Agee	R	10	19	3	1	0	0	0.0	2	3	2	6	0	1	0	.158	.211
OF	Jim Hicks	R	13	19	5	1	0	1	5.3	2	2	0	9	0	8	2	.263	.474
C	Johnny Romano	R	122	356	86	11	0	18	5.1	39	48	59	74	0	8	1	.242	.424
C	Smoky Burgess	L	80	77	22	4	0	2	2.6	2	24	11	7	0	65	20	.286	.416
C	Jimmie Schaffer	R	17	31	6	3	1	0	0.0	2	1	3	4	0	3	0	.194	.355
C	Duane Josephson	R	4	9	1	0	0	0	0.0	2	0	2	4	0	0	0	.111	.111
PH	Marv Staehle	L	7	7	3	0	0	0	0.0	0	2	0	0	0	7	3	.429	.429
PH	Bill Heath	L	1	1	0	0	0	0	0.0	0	0	0	0	0	1	0	.000	.000
PH	Dick Kenworthy	R	3	1	0	0	0	0	0.0	0	0	1	0	0	1	0	.000	.000
PITCHERS																		
P	Gary Peters	L	42	72	13	1	0	1	1.4	2	6	2	15	0	7	3	.181	.236
P	Joe Horlen	R	34	68	9	1	0	0	0.0	0	2	5	12	0	0	0	.132	.147
P	Tommy John	R	39	59	10	1	0	1	1.7	4	2	3	22	0	0	0	.169	.237
P	John Buzhardt	R	34	56	7	0	0	0	0.0	2	3	5	23	0	0	0	.125	.125
P	Bruce Howard	B	30	41	6	2	1	0	0.0	1	3	4	18	0	0	0	.146	.244
P	Juan Pizarro	L	19	34	8	0	0	1	2.9	5	4	2	10	0	1	0	.235	.324
P	Eddie Fisher	R	82	29	4	1	0	0	0.0	3	1	1	12	0	0	0	.138	.172
P	Hoyt Wilhelm	R	66	22	0	0	0	0	0.0	1	0	2	12	0	0	0	.000	.000
P	Bob Locker	R	51	14	0	0	0	0	0.0	0	0	0	13	0	0	0	.000	.000
P	Frank Lary	R	14	2	1	0	0	0	0.0	0	2	0	0	0	0	0	.500	.500
P	Ted Wills	L	15	2	0	0	0	0	0.0	1	0	1	1	0	0	0	.000	.000
P	Greg Bollo	R	15	0	0	0	0	0	—	0	0	0	0	0	0	0	—	—
TEAM TOTAL				5509	1354	200	38	125	2.3	647	587	533	916	50	195	52	.246	.364

INDIVIDUAL FIELDING

POS	Player	T	G	PO	A	E	DP	TCG	FA	POS	Player	T	G	PO	A	E	DP	TCG	FA
1B	B. Skowron	R	145	1297	74	8	116	9.5	.994	OF	K. Berry	R	156	331	6	7	1	2.2	.980
	T. McCraw	L	72	251	22	2	18	3.8	.993		F. Robinson	R	153	254	6	4	0	1.7	.985
	J. Romano	R	2	0	0	0	0	0.0	.000		D. Cater	R	127	174	6	4	2	1.4	.978
	J. Martin	R	4	36	0	0	3	9.0	1.000		T. McCraw	L	64	85	2	2	0	1.4	.978
	D. Cater	R	3	14	0	1	0	5.0	.933		D. Nicholson	R	36	30	0	0	0	0.8	1.000
2B	D. Buford	R	139	326	357	13	93	5.0	.981		T. Agee	R	9	13	0	0	0	1.4	1.000
	A. Weis	R	74	109	122	6	27	3.2	.975		B. Voss	L	10	12	0	0	0	1.2	1.000
	R. Hansen	R	1	0	0	0	0	0.0	.000		J. Romano	R	4	6	1	0	0	1.8	1.000
	P. Ward	R	1	0	0	0	0	1.0	1.000		J. Hicks	R	5	3	0	1	0	0.8	.750
SS	R. Hansen	R	161	287	527	26	97	5.2	.969		A. Weis	R	2	1	0	0	0	0.5	1.000
	A. Weis	R	7	6	7	0	4	1.9	1.000	C	J. Romano	R	111	569	61	5	10	5.7	.992
3B	P. Ward	R	134	97	319	21	22	3.3	.952		J. Martin	R	112	348	41	7	4	3.5	.982
	D. Buford	R	41	13	59	1	9	1.8	.986		J. Schaffer	R	14	50	7	0	2	4.1	1.000
	G. Freese	R	8	4	10	3	1	2.1	.824		D. Josephson	R	4	21	1	0	0	5.5	1.000
	D. Cater	R	11	1	15	1	1	1.5	.941		S. Burgess	R	5	17	3	0	0	4.0	1.000
	J. Martin	R	2	1	2	0	0	1.5	1.000										
	A. Weis	R	2	1	1	0	0	1.0	1.000										

A big winter trade involving the White Sox, Indians, and A's brought John Romano, Tommie Agee, and Tommy John to Chicago for Mike Hershberger, Jim Landis, and Cam Carreon. It was Ed Short's shining moment, but he didn't realize it at the time. The Sox viewed the fading catcher Romano as the big prize. But for the time being, the Sox looked like an improved ballclub.

The disappointment came when the Minnesota Twins, and not the White Sox, picked up the Yankees' fallen banner. Through May 28 the Sox held onto first place, but their collapse coincided with Al Lopez's hospitalization on June 30 due to enteritis. A more costly injury had far-reaching consequences. Early in the 1965 campaign, Pete Ward and Tommy John were involved in a car accident on their way to a Chicago Black Hawks game. Neck pain and subsequent back complications caused Ward's promising career to unwind like a cheap polyester suit.

Despite such mishaps, the Sox had a solid, competitive ball club that might have beaten out the Twins if they could have improved on their 7–11 record against them. The 95-win season was encouraging, but many skeptics still saw too many flaws in the club. With his health failing, Al Lopez resigned on November 11. One month later 48-year-old Eddie Stanky was given a three-year contract to guide the Sox. The Brat didn't know the Sox players well, calling the incumbent Sox shortstop "Roy" Hansen.

TEAM STATISTICS

	W	L	PCT	GB	R	OR	2B	3B	HR	BA	SA	SB	E	DP	FA	CG	BB	SO	ShO	SV	ERA
MIN	102	60	.630		774	600	257	42	150	.254	.399	92	172	158	.973	32	503	934	12	45	3.14
CHI	95	67	.586	7	647	555	200	38	125	.246	.364	50	127	156	.980	21	460	946	14	53	2.99
BAL	94	68	.580	8	641	578	227	38	125	.238	.363	67	126	152	.980	32	510	939	15	41	2.98
DET	89	73	.549	13	680	602	190	27	162	.238	.374	57	116	126	.981	45	509	1069	14	31	3.35
CLE	87	75	.537	15	663	613	198	21	156	.250	.379	109	114	127	.981	41	500	1156	13	41	3.30
NY	77	85	.475	25	611	604	196	31	149	.235	.364	35	137	166	.978	41	511	1001	11	31	3.28
CAL	75	87	.463	27	527	569	200	36	92	.239	.341	107	123	149	.981	39	563	847	14	33	3.17
WAS	70	92	.432	32	591	721	179	33	136	.228	.350	47	143	148	.976	21	633	867	8	40	3.93
BOS	62	100	.383	40	669	791	244	40	165	.251	.400	30	162	129	.974	33	543	993	9	25	4.24
KC	59	103	.364	43	585	755	186	59	110	.240	.358	110	139	142	.977	18	574	882	7	32	4.24
LEAGUE TOTAL					6388	6388	2077	365	1370	.242	.369	704	1359	1453	.978	323	5306	9634	117	372	3.46

INDIVIDUAL PITCHING

PITCHER	T	W	L	PCT	ERA	SV	G	GS	CG	IP	H	BB	SO	R	ER	ShO	H9	BB9	SO9
Joe Horlen	R	13	13	.500	2.88	0	34	34	7	219	203	39	125	88	70	4	8.34	1.60	5.14
John Buzhardt	R	13	8	.619	3.01	1	32	30	4	188.2	167	56	108	69	63	1	7.97	2.67	5.15
Tommy John	L	14	7	.667	3.09	3	39	27	6	183.2	162	58	126	67	63	1	7.94	2.84	6.17
Gary Peters	L	10	12	.455	3.62	0	33	30	1	176.1	181	63	95	76	71	0	9.24	3.22	4.85
Eddie Fisher	R	15	7	.682	2.40	24	82	0	0	165.1	118	43	90	51	44	0	6.42	2.34	4.90
Bruce Howard	R	9	8	.529	3.47	0	30	22	1	148	123	72	120	61	57	1	7.48	4.38	7.30
Hoyt Wilhelm	R	7	7	.500	1.81	20	66	0	0	144	88	32	106	34	29	0	5.50	2.00	6.63
Juan Pizarro	L	6	3	.667	3.43	0	18	18	2	97	96	37	65	42	37	1	8.91	3.43	6.03
Bob Locker	R	5	2	.714	3.15	2	51	0	0	91.1	71	30	69	36	32	0	7.00	2.96	6.80
Frank Lary	R	1	0	1.000	4.05	2	14	1	0	26.2	23	7	14	12	12	0	7.76	2.36	4.73
Greg Bollo	R	0	0	—	3.57	0	15	0	0	22.2	12	9	16	11	9	0	4.76	3.57	6.35
Ted Wills	L	2	0	1.000	2.84	1	15	0	0	19	17	14	12	8	6	0	8.05	6.63	5.68
TEAM TOTAL		95	67	.586	2.99	53	429	162	21	1481.2	1261	460	946	555	493	8	7.66	2.79	5.75

Chicago 1966   Won 83 Lost 79 Pct. .512 4th

MANAGER	W	L	PCT
Eddie Stanky	83	79	.512

POS	Player	B	G	AB	H	2B	3B	HR	HR%	R	RBI	BB	SO	SB	Pinch Hit AB	Pinch Hit H	BA	SA
REGULARS																		
1B	Tom McCraw	L	151	389	89	16	4	5	1.3	49	48	29	40	20	7	1	.229	.329
2B	Al Weis	B	129	187	29	4	1	0	0.0	20	9	17	50	3	0	0	.155	.187
SS	Jerry Adair	R	105	370	90	18	2	4	1.1	27	36	17	44	3	1	0	.243	.335
3B	Don Buford	B	163	607	148	26	7	8	1.3	85	52	69	71	51	1	0	.244	.349
RF	Floyd Robinson	L	127	342	81	11	2	5	1.5	44	35	44	32	8	17	0	.237	.325
CF	Tommie Agee	R	160	629	172	27	8	22	3.5	98	86	41	127	44	0	0	.273	.447
LF	Ken Berry	R	147	443	120	20	2	8	1.8	50	34	28	63	7	3	0	.271	.379
C	Johnny Romano	R	122	329	76	12	0	15	4.6	33	47	58	72	0	16	4	.231	.404
SUBSTITUTES																		
1B	Bill Skowron	R	120	337	84	15	2	6	1.8	27	29	26	45	1	23	3	.249	.359
SS	Lee Elia	R	80	195	40	5	2	3	1.5	16	22	15	39	0	1	0	.205	.297
2B	Wayne Causey	L	78	164	40	8	2	0	0.0	23	13	24	13	2	15	5	.244	.317
3B	Gene Freese	R	48	106	22	2	0	3	2.8	8	10	8	20	2	16	2	.208	.311
SS	Ron Hansen	R	23	74	13	1	0	0	0.0	3	4	15	10	0	0	0	.176	.189
3B	Dick Kenworthy	R	9	25	5	0	0	0	0.0	1	0	0	0	0	3	1	.200	.200
2B	Marv Staehle	L	8	15	2	0	0	0	0.0	2	0	4	2	1	2	0	.133	.133
O3	Pete Ward	L	84	251	55	7	1	3	1.2	22	28	24	49	3	9	0	.219	.291
OF	Danny Cater	R	21	60	11	1	1	0	0.0	3	4	0	10	3	1	0	.183	.233
OF	Ed Stroud	L	12	36	6	2	0	0	0.0	3	1	2	8	3	0	0	.167	.222
OF	Buddy Bradford	R	14	28	4	0	0	0	0.0	3	0	2	6	0	0	0	.143	.143
OF	Jim Hicks	R	18	26	5	0	1	0	0.0	3	1	1	5	0	2	0	.192	.269
OF	Bill Voss	L	2	2	0	0	0	0	0.0	0	0	0	2	0	1	0	.000	.000
C	J. C. Martin	L	67	157	40	5	3	2	1.3	13	20	14	24	0	4	1	.255	.363
C	Smoky Burgess	L	79	67	21	5	0	0	0.0	0	15	11	8	0	66	21	.313	.388
C	Jerry McNertney	R	44	59	13	0	0	0	0.0	3	1	7	6	1	5	0	.220	.220
C	Duane Josephson	R	11	38	9	1	0	0	0.0	3	3	3	3	0	0	0	.237	.263
PH	Deacon Jones	L	5	5	2	0	0	0	0.0	0	0	0	0	0	5	2	.400	.400
PITCHERS																		
P	Gary Peters	L	38	81	19	3	2	1	1.2	12	9	0	19	0	5	1	.235	.358
P	Tommy John	R	34	69	10	1	0	2	2.9	6	8	3	21	0	0	0	.145	.246
P	Joe Horlen	R	64	60	4	0	0	0	0.0	6	1	2	12	1	0	0	.067	.067
P	John Buzhardt	R	34	43	5	0	0	0	0.0	0	2	2	18	0	0	0	.116	.116
P	Bruce Howard	B	27	43	3	1	0	0	0.0	2	2	5	13	0	0	0	.070	.093
P	Jack Lamabe	R	34	35	2	0	0	0	0.0	2	0	1	16	0	0	0	.057	.057
P	Juan Pizarro	L	34	26	4	1	0	0	0.0	2	2	1	5	0	0	0	.154	.192
P	Dennis Higgins	R	42	17	3	0	0	0	0.0	1	1	1	4	0	0	0	.176	.176
P	Bob Locker	R	56	16	4	0	0	0	0.0	3	0	2	7	0	0	0	.250	.250
P	Hoyt Wilhelm	R	46	8	1	1	0	0	0.0	0	0	0	4	0	0	0	.125	.250
P	Fred Klages	R	3	6	3	0	0	0	0.0	1	1	0	2	0	0	0	.500	.500
P	Eddie Fisher	R	23	2	0	0	0	0	0.0	0	0	0	1	0	0	0	.000	.000
P	Greg Bollo	R	3	1	0	0	0	0	0.0	0	0	0	1	0	0	0	.000	.000
TEAM TOTAL				5348	1235	193	40	87	1.6	574	524	476	872	153	203	41	.231	.331

INDIVIDUAL FIELDING

POS	Player	T	G	PO	A	E	DP	TCG	FA
1B	T. McCraw	L	121	843	67	9	56	7.6	.990
	B. Skowron	R	98	722	60	7	75	8.1	.991
	P. Ward	R	5	19	5	1	2	5.0	.960
	J. Hicks	R	2	12	0	1	1	6.5	.923
2B	A. Weis	R	96	130	173	4	44	3.2	.987
	W. Causey	R	60	86	110	4	15	3.3	.980
	J. Adair	R	50	89	92	3	19	3.7	.984
	D. Buford	R	37	88	81	8	18	4.8	.955
	M. Staehle	R	6	9	14	0	5	3.8	1.000
SS	J. Adair	R	75	109	236	9	35	4.7	.975
	L. Elia	R	75	103	186	14	39	4.0	.954
	R. Hansen	R	23	49	73	7	17	5.6	.946
	A. Weis	R	18	21	45	6	8	4.0	.917
	W. Causey	R	1	2	3	0	0	5.0	1.000
3B	D. Buford	R	133	98	301	26	24	3.2	.939
	G. Freese	R	34	12	64	9	5	2.5	.894
	P. Ward	R	16	10	34	1	3	2.8	.978
	D. Kenworthy	R	6	0	7	1	0	1.3	.875
	W. Causey	R	1	0	2	0	0	2.0	1.000

POS	Player	T	G	PO	A	E	DP	TCG	FA
OF	T. Agee	R	159	**376**	12	7	**7**	2.5	.982
	K. Berry	R	141	208	10	2	1	1.6	.991
	F. Robinson	R	113	148	2	6	0	1.4	.962
	P. Ward	R	59	83	3	1	1	1.5	.989
	T. McCraw	L	41	50	1	0	0	1.2	1.000
	D. Cater	R	18	20	0	2	0	1.2	.909
	E. Stroud	R	11	20	0	0	0	1.8	1.000
	J. Hicks	R	10	14	0	0	0	1.4	1.000
	D. Buford	R	11	13	1	0	0	1.3	1.000
	B. Bradford	R	9	5	0	1	0	0.7	.833
	B. Voss	L	1	1	0	0	0	1.0	1.000
C	J. Romano	R	102	622	46	4	7	6.6	.994
	J. Martin	R	63	243	23	5	3	4.3	.982
	J. McNertney	R	37	112	14	4	0	3.5	.969
	D. Josephson	R	11	66	8	2	1	6.9	.974
	S. Burgess	R	2	4	0	0	0	2.0	1.000

Strict midnight curfews, team meetings, proper dress on road trips, rigorous calisthenics: the gospel according to Stanky. His was an unpopular regime. In May he ordered John Buzhardt to throw at Minnesota pitcher Jim Perry. Earlier in the month Stanky had taken Bruce Howard out of the game after the pitcher refused to throw at Joe Sparma. When John Romano told a reporter about these incidents he was benched. When Juan Pizarro left the Sox for two days, only to turn up sporting a bandaged head and nine stitches, Stanky said, "Fine him? I'm too nice of a guy."

The Sox developed a reputation for toughness around the league and soon found themselves the target of the American League's headhunters. There was nothing tough about the weak hitting, though. Deadball baseball had returned as Al Weis (.156), Ron Hansen (.176), Pete Ward (.178), Danny Cater (.191), and Don Buford (.178) led the Sox to an eighth-place dive at the end of May. Only rookie centerfielder Tommie Agee provided any thrills. The youngster was fleet afoot and gifted with some power. He was the runaway choice for Rookie of the Year.

"Do you remember a little second baseman for the 1951 Giants?" Stanky asked his team as they sank further behind the Orioles and Twins. "Do you remember the Giants?" Perhaps not, but Sox fans weren't likely to forget the Stanky storm of the otherwise dull 1966 season.

TEAM STATISTICS

	W	L	PCT	GB	R	OR	2B	3B	HR	BA	SA	SB	E	DP	FA	CG	BB	SO	ShO	SV	ERA
BAL	97	63	.606		755	601	243	35	175	.258	.409	55	115	142	.981	23	514	1070	13	51	3.32
MIN	89	73	.549	9	663	581	219	33	144	.249	.382	67	139	118	.977	52	392	1015	11	28	3.13
DET	88	74	.543	10	719	698	224	45	179	.251	.406	41	120	142	.980	36	520	1026	11	38	3.85
CHI	83	79	.512	15	574	517	193	40	87	.231	.331	153	159	149	.976	38	403	896	22	34	2.68
CLE	81	81	.500	17	574	586	156	25	155	.237	.360	53	138	132	.977	49	489	1111	15	28	3.23
CAL	80	82	.494	18	604	643	179	54	122	.232	.354	20	136	186	.979	31	511	836	12	40	3.56
KC	74	86	.463	23	564	648	212	56	70	.236	.337	132	138	154	.977	19	630	854	11	47	3.55
WAS	71	88	.447	25.5	557	659	185	40	126	.234	.355	53	142	139	.977	25	448	866	6	35	3.70
BOS	72	90	.444	26	655	731	228	44	145	.240	.376	35	155	153	.975	32	577	977	10	31	3.92
NY	70	89	.440	26.5	611	612	182	36	162	.235	.374	49	142	142	.977	29	443	842	7	32	3.42
LEAGUE TOTAL					6276	6276	2021	408	1365	.240	.369	718	1384	1457	.978	334	4927	9493	118	364	3.44

INDIVIDUAL PITCHING

PITCHER	T	W	L	PCT	ERA	SV	G	GS	CG	IP	H	BB	SO	R	ER	ShO	H9	BB9	SO9
Tommy John	L	14	11	.560	2.62	0	34	33	10	223	195	57	138	76	65	5	7.87	2.30	5.57
Joe Horlen	R	10	13	.435	2.43	1	37	29	4	211	185	53	124	64	57	2	7.89	2.26	5.29
Gary Peters	L	12	10	.545	1.98	0	30	27	11	204.2	156	45	129	54	45	4	6.86	1.98	5.67
John Buzhardt	R	6	11	.353	3.83	1	33	22	5	150.1	144	30	66	74	64	4	8.62	1.80	3.95
Bruce Howard	R	9	5	.643	2.30	0	27	21	4	149	110	44	85	48	38	2	6.64	2.66	5.13
Jack Lamabe	R	7	9	.438	3.93	0	34	17	3	121.1	116	35	67	55	53	2	8.60	2.60	4.97
Bob Locker	R	9	8	.529	2.46	12	56	0	0	95	73	23	70	32	26	0	6.92	2.18	6.63
Dennis Higgins	R	1	0	1.000	2.52	5	42	1	0	93	66	33	86	27	26	0	6.39	3.19	8.32
Juan Pizarro	L	8	6	.571	3.76	3	34	9	1	88.2	91	39	42	49	37	0	9.24	3.96	4.26
Hoyt Wilhelm	R	5	2	.714	1.66	6	46	0	0	81.1	50	17	61	21	15	0	5.53	1.88	6.75
Eddie Fisher	R	1	3	.250	2.29	6	23*	0	0	35.1	27	17	18	11	9	0	6.88	4.33	4.58
Fred Klages	R	1	0	1.000	1.72	0	3	3	0	15.2	9	7	6	4	3	0	5.17	4.02	3.45
Greg Bollo	R	0	1	.000	2.57	0	3	1	0	7	7	3	4	2	2	0	9.00	3.86	5.14
TEAM TOTAL		83	79	.512	2.68	34	402	163	38	1475.1	1229	403	896	517	440	19	7.50	2.46	5.47

Chicago 1967   Won 89   Lost 73   Pct. .549   4th

MANAGER	W	L	PCT
Eddie Stanky	89	73	.549

POS	Player	B	G	AB	H	2B	3B	HR	HR %	R	RBI	BB	SO	SB	Pinch Hit AB	Pinch Hit H	BA	SA
REGULARS																		
1B	Tom McCraw	L	125	453	107	18	3	11	2.4	55	45	33	55	24	2	0	.236	.362
2B	Wayne Causey	L	124	292	66	10	3	1	0.3	21	28	32	35	2	34	10	.226	.291
SS	Ron Hansen	R	157	498	116	20	0	8	1.6	35	51	64	51	0	0	0	.233	.321
3B	Don Buford	B	156	535	129	10	9	4	0.7	61	32	65	51	34	3	1	.241	.316
RF	Ken Berry	R	147	485	117	14	4	7	1.4	49	41	46	68	9	4	0	.241	.330
CF	Tommie Agee	R	158	529	124	26	2	14	2.6	73	52	44	129	28	2	1	.234	.371
LF	Pete Ward	L	146	467	109	16	2	18	3.9	49	62	61	109	3	6	3	.233	.392
C	J. C. Martin	L	101	252	59	12	1	4	1.6	22	22	30	41	4	6	1	.234	.337
SUBSTITUTES																		
31	Ken Boyer	R	57	180	47	5	1	4	2.2	17	21	7	25	0	8	3	.261	.367
2B	Jerry Adair	R	28	98	20	4	0	0	0.0	6	9	4	17	0	2	0	.204	.245
3B	Dick Kenworthy	R	50	97	22	4	1	4	4.1	9	11	4	17	0	15	0	.227	.412
2S	Marv Staehle	L	32	54	6	1	0	0	0.0	1	1	4	8	1	8	0	.111	.130
2S	Al Weis	B	50	53	13	2	0	0	0.0	9	4	1	7	3	0	0	.245	.283
SS	Sandy Alomar	B	12	15	3	0	0	0	0.0	4	0	2	0	2	1	0	.200	.200
SS	Rich Morales	R	8	10	0	0	0	0	0.0	0	0	0	2	0	0	0	.000	.000
1B	Cotton Nash	R	3	3	0	0	0	0	0.0	1	0	1	0	0	0	0	.000	.000
OF	Walt Williams	R	104	275	66	16	3	3	1.1	35	15	17	20	3	30	4	.240	.353
OF	Rocky Colavito	R	60	190	42	4	1	3	1.6	20	29	25	10	1	1	0	.221	.300
OF	Jim King	L	23	50	6	1	0	0	0.0	2	2	4	16	0	12	3	.120	.140
OF	Ed Stroud	L	20	27	8	0	1	0	0.0	6	3	1	5	7	2	0	.296	.370
OF	Bill Voss	L	13	22	2	0	0	0	0.0	4	0	0	1	1	0	0	.091	.091
OF	Buddy Bradford	R	24	20	2	1	0	0	0.0	0	6	1	7	1	3	1	.100	.150
UT	Jimmy Stewart	B	24	18	3	0	0	0	0.0	5	1	1	6	1	7	0	.167	.167
C	Duane Josephson	R	62	189	45	5	1	1	0.5	11	9	6	24	0	5	0	.238	.291
C	Jerry McNertney	R	56	123	28	6	0	3	2.4	8	13	6	14	0	1	1	.228	.350
C	Ed Herrmann	L	2	3	2	1	0	0	0.0	1	1	1	0	0	0	0	.667	1.000
PH	Smoky Burgess	L	77	60	8	1	0	2	3.3	2	11	14	8	0	60	8	.133	.250
PH	Bill Skowron	R	8	8	0	0	0	0	0.0	0	1	0	1	0	8	0	.000	.000
PITCHERS																		
P	Gary Peters	L	48	99	21	0	2	2	2.0	10	13	2	23	0	6	1	.212	.313
P	Joe Horlen	R	51	83	14	1	0	0	0.0	8	5	1	14	0	0	0	.169	.181
P	Tommy John	R	31	51	8	0	0	0	0.0	0	2	1	12	0	0	0	.157	.157
P	Bruce Howard	B	30	28	5	1	0	0	0.0	1	0	1	9	0	0	0	.179	.214
P	John Buzhardt	R	28	20	4	0	0	0	0.0	2	0	2	7	0	0	0	.200	.200
P	Wilbur Wood	R	51	16	1	1	0	0	0.0	0	1	1	11	0	0	0	.063	.125
P	Cisco Carlos	R	8	16	1	0	0	0	0.0	0	0	0	7	0	0	0	.063	.063
P	Jim O'Toole	B	15	13	1	0	0	0	0.0	0	1	0	5	0	0	0	.077	.077
P	Hoyt Wilhelm	R	49	13	1	0	0	0	0.0	0	1	0	11	0	0	0	.077	.077
P	Fred Klages	R	12	12	0	0	0	0	0.0	1	0	0	8	0	0	0	.000	.000
P	Don McMahon	R	52	11	2	0	0	0	0.0	0	0	0	8	0	0	0	.182	.182
P	Bob Locker	R	77	10	0	0	0	0	0.0	0	0	0	6	0	0	0	.000	.000
P	Steve Jones	L	11	4	1	1	0	0	0.0	0	0	0	1	0	0	0	.250	.500
P	Dennis Higgins	R	9	1	0	0	0	0	0.0	0	0	0	0	0	0	0	.000	.000
P	Jack Lamabe	R	3	0	0	0	0	0	—	0	0	0	0	0	0	0	—	—
P	Aurelio Monteagudo	R	1	0	0	0	0	0	—	0	0	0	0	0	0	0	—	—
P	Roger Nelson	R	5	0	0	0	0	0	—	0	0	0	0	0	0	0	—	—
	TEAM TOTAL			5383	1209	181	34	89	1.7	531	491	480	849	124	226	37	.225	.320

INDIVIDUAL FIELDING

POS	Player	T	G	PO	A	E	DP	TCG	FA
1B	T. McCraw	L	123	1167	110	11	92	10.5	.991
	P. Ward	R	39	295	19	2	23	8.1	.994
	K. Boyer	R	18	132	12	1	12	8.1	.993
	C. Nash	R	3	10	0	2	3	4.0	.833
	J. Martin	R	1	1	0	0	0	1.0	1.000
2B	W. Causey	R	96	153	199	8	36	3.8	.978
	D. Buford	R	51	102	99	8	30	4.1	.962
	J. Adair	R	27	70	61	2	21	4.9	.985
	A. Weis	R	32	25	46	1	2	2.3	.986
	M. Staehle	R	17	27	32	0	3	3.5	1.000
	J. Stewart	R	5	7	6	2	3	3.0	.867
	S. Alomar	R	2	2	3	0	2	2.5	1.000
SS	R. Hansen	R	157	243	482	27	91	4.8	.964
	S. Alomar	R	8	9	11	1	5	2.6	.952
	A. Weis	R	13	5	16	0	3	1.6	1.000
	R. Morales	R	7	6	11	1	1	2.6	.944
	M. Staehle	R	5	2	3	0	1	1.0	1.000
	J. Stewart	R	2	2	1	1	1	2.0	.750
	W. Causey	R	2	0	1	0	0	0.5	1.000
3B	D. Buford	R	121	95	250	19	16	3.0	.948
	K. Boyer	R	33	22	67	4	4	2.8	.957
	D. Kenworthy	R	35	16	51	2	1	2.0	.971
	P. Ward	R	22	7	33	4	3	2.0	.909

POS	Player	T	G	PO	A	E	DP	TCG	FA
OF	T. Agee	R	152	337	6	11	2	2.3	.969
	K. Berry	R	143	233	9	2	1	1.7	.992
	W. Williams	R	73	112	6	2	2	1.6	.983
	P. Ward	R	89	107	3	1	0	1.2	.991
	R. Colavito	R	58	83	2	2	3	1.5	.977
	E. Stroud	R	12	14	2	0	1	1.3	1.000
	J. King	R	12	15	0	0	0	1.3	1.000
	B. Voss	L	11	14	0	0	0	1.3	1.000
	T. McCraw	L	6	10	0	0	0	1.7	1.000
	B. Bradford	R	14	9	0	1	0	0.7	.900
	D. Buford	R	1	1	0	0	0	1.0	1.000
	J. Stewart	R	6	0	1	0	0	0.2	1.000
C	J. Martin	R	96	478	39	7	3	5.5	.987
	D. Josephson	R	59	292	24	0	3	5.4	1.000
	J. McNertney	R	52	229	41	1	4	5.2	.996
	E. Herrmann	R	2	12	1	0	0	6.5	1.000

Chicago 1967

In Boston they celebrated the Impossible Dream. In Chicago they witnessed the final act of a stirring baseball drama that had begun seventeen years earlier. It was fitting that after seventeen consecutive first-division finishes, the Sox should end this era in the same Go-Go fashion that had started it.

Speed, pitching, and defense carried the Sox to the top of the pack on June 10. They did not waver from this position until August 13. The Sox were next to last in hitting with a .225 average, but the league itself wasn't much better at .236. But oh, that pitching! Joel Horlen finally got his no-hitter on September 10, but had to settle for second place in the Cy Young voting despite pacing American League hurlers with a 2.06 earned run average.

It was a lively year for the Brat, who endeared himself around the league by calling Angels manager Bill Rigney "a television manager" and labeling Carl Yastrzemski "an all-star from the neck down." Angry opponents accused Stanky of freezing the baseballs to keep them in the park and the scores low. Well, perhaps. It was a continuing controversy that was never settled one way or the other.

Years later, one can look back at the Sox 1967 season as a memorable but bittersweet experience. But on "Black Wednesday," September 27, 1967, it only seemed bitter. On that night, they lost a doubleheader to the last-place A's, and with it their last chance for the pennant. "All year long the elephants feared the mouse," Stanky said with uncharacteristic quiet.

TEAM STATISTICS

	W	L	PCT	GB	R	OR	2B	3B	HR	BA	SA	SB	E	DP	FA	CG	BB	SO	ShO	SV	ERA
BOS	92	70	.568		722	614	216	39	158	.255	.395	68	142	142	.977	41	477	1010	9	44	3.36
DET	91	71	.562	1	683	587	192	36	152	.243	.376	37	131	126	.979	46	472	1038	17	40	3.32
MIN	91	71	.562	1	671	590	216	48	131	.240	.369	55	132	123	.978	58	396	1089	18	24	3.14
CHI	89	73	.549	3	531	491	181	34	89	.225	.320	124	138	149	.979	36	465	927	24	39	2.45
CAL	84	77	.522	7.5	567	587	170	37	114	.238	.349	40	111	135	.982	19	525	892	14	46	3.19
BAL	76	85	.472	15.5	654	592	215	44	138	.240	.372	54	124	144	.980	29	566	1034	17	36	3.32
WAS	76	85	.472	15.5	550	637	168	25	115	.223	.326	53	144	167	.978	24	495	878	14	39	3.38
CLE	75	87	.463	17	559	613	213	35	131	.235	.359	53	117	138	.981	49	559	1189	14	27	3.25
NY	72	90	.444	20	522	621	166	17	100	.225	.317	63	154	144	.976	37	480	898	16	27	3.24
KC	62	99	.385	29.5	533	660	212	50	69	.233	.330	132	132	120	.978	26	558	990	10	34	3.68
LEAGUE TOTAL					5992	5992	1949	365	1197	.236	.351	679	1325	1388	.979	365	4993	9945	153	356	3.23

INDIVIDUAL PITCHING

PITCHER	T	W	L	PCT	ERA	SV	G	GS	CG	IP	H	BB	SO	R	ER	ShO	H9	BB9	SO9
Gary Peters	L	16	11	.593	2.28	0	38	36	11	260	187	91	215	81	66	3	6.47	3.15	7.44
Joe Horlen	R	19	7	.731	2.06	0	35	35	13	258	188	58	103	66	59	6	6.56	2.02	3.59
Tommy John	L	10	13	.435	2.47	0	31	29	9	178.1	143	47	110	62	49	6	7.22	2.37	5.55
Bob Locker	R	7	5	.583	2.09	20	77	0	0	124.2	102	23	80	34	29	0	7.36	1.66	5.78
Bruce Howard	R	3	10	.231	3.43	0	30	17	1	112.2	102	52	76	55	43	0	8.15	4.15	6.07
Wilbur Wood	L	4	2	.667	2.45	4	51	8	0	95.1	95	28	47	34	26	0	8.97	2.64	4.44
Don McMahon	R	5	0	1.000	1.67	3	52	0	0	91.2	54	27	74	21	17	0	5.30	2.65	7.27
Hoyt Wilhelm	R	8	3	.727	1.31	12	49	0	0	89	58	34	76	21	13	0	5.87	3.44	7.69
John Buzhardt	R	3	9	.250	3.96	0	28	7	0	88.2	100	37	33	44	39	0	10.15	3.76	3.35
Jim O'Toole	L	4	3	.571	2.82	0	15	10	1	54.1	53	18	37	21	17	1	8.78	2.98	6.13
Fred Klages	R	4	4	.500	3.83	0	11	9	0	44.2	43	16	17	19	19	0	8.66	3.22	3.43
Cisco Carlos	R	2	0	1.000	0.86	0	8	7	1	41.2	23	9	27	5	4	1	4.97	1.94	5.83
Steve Jones	L	2	2	.500	4.21	0	11	3	0	25.2	21	12	17	13	12	0	7.36	4.21	5.96
Dennis Higgins	R	1	2	.333	5.84	0	9	0	0	12.1	13	10	8	9	8	0	9.49	7.30	5.84
Roger Nelson	R	0	1	.000	1.29	0	5	0	0	7	4	0	4	1	1	0	5.14	0.00	5.14
Jack Lamabe	R	1	0	1.000	1.80	0	3	0	0	5	7	1	3	2	1	0	12.60	1.80	5.40
Aurelio Monteagudo	R	0	1	.000	20.25	0	1	1	0	1.1	4	2	0	3	3	0	27.00	13.50	0.00
TEAM TOTAL		89	73	.549	2.45	39	454	162	36	1490.1	1197	465	927	491	406	17	7.23	2.81	5.60

Chicago 1968   Won 67 Lost 95 Pct .414 9th

MANAGER	W	L	PCT
Eddie Stanky	34	45	.430
Les Moss	0	2	.000
Al Lopez	33	48	.407

POS	Player	B	G	AB	H	2B	3B	HR	HR%	R	RBI	BB	SO	SB	Pinch Hit AB	H	BA	SA
REGULARS																		
1B	Tom McCraw	L	136	477	112	16	12	9	1.9	51	44	36	58	20	3	0	.235	.375
2B	Sandy Alomar	B	133	363	92	8	2	0	0.0	41	12	20	42	21	4	2	.253	.287
SS	Luis Aparicio	R	155	622	164	24	4	4	0.6	55	36	33	43	17	2	0	.264	.334
3B	Pete Ward	L	125	399	86	15	0	15	3.8	43	50	76	85	4	6	1	.216	.366
RF	Buddy Bradford	R	103	281	61	11	0	5	1.8	32	24	23	67	8	6	1	.217	.310
CF	Ken Berry	R	153	504	127	21	2	7	1.4	49	32	25	64	6	2	1	.252	.343
LF	Tommy Davis	R	132	456	122	5	3	8	1.8	30	50	16	48	4	12	4	.268	.344
C	Duane Josephson	R	128	434	107	16	6	6	1.4	35	45	18	52	2	11	3	.247	.353
SUBSTITUTES																		
2B	Tim Cullen	R	72	155	31	7	0	2	1.3	16	13	15	23	0	2	0	.200	.284
3B	Dick Kenworthy	R	58	122	27	2	0	0	0.0	2	2	5	21	0	19	5	.221	.238
3B	Bill Melton	R	34	109	29	8	0	2	1.8	5	16	10	32	1	1	0	.266	.394
2B	Wayne Causey	L	59	100	18	2	0	0	0.0	8	7	14	7	0	28	6	.180	.200
3S	Ron Hansen	R	40	87	20	3	0	1	1.1	7	4	11	12	0	3	1	.230	.299
1B	Gail Hopkins	L	29	37	8	2	0	0	0.0	4	2	6	3	0	20	4	.216	.270
S2	Rich Morales	R	10	29	5	0	0	0	0.0	2	0	2	5	0	0	0	.172	.172
3B	Ken Boyer	R	10	24	3	0	0	0	0.0	0	0	1	6	0	3	0	.125	.125
OF	Bill Voss	L	61	167	26	2	1	2	1.2	14	15	16	34	5	7	2	.156	.216
OF	Leon Wagner	L	69	162	46	8	0	1	0.6	14	18	21	31	2	22*	5	.284	.352
OF	Walt Williams	R	63	133	32	6	0	1	0.8	6	8	4	17	0	28	5	.241	.308
OF	Russ Snyder	L	38	82	11	2	0	1	1.2	2	5	4	16	0	17	3	.134	.195
OF	Carlos May	L	17	67	12	1	0	0	0.0	4	1	3	15	0	0	0	.179	.194
OF	Woodie Held	R	40	54	9	1	0	0	0.0	5	2	5	14	0	5	1	.167	.185
C	Jerry McNertney	R	74	169	37	4	1	3	1.8	18	18	18	29	0	11	3	.219	.308
C	Buddy Booker	L	5	5	0	0	0	0	0.0	0	0	1	2	0	4	0	.000	.000
PITCHERS																		
P	Gary Peters	L	46	72	15	3	1	2	2.8	10	8	6	13	0	14	2	.208	.361
P	Joe Horlen	R	41	67	7	0	1	0	0.0	2	3	3	13	0	0	0	.104	.134
P	Tommy John	R	25	62	12	1	0	1	1.6	3	9	0	15	0	0	0	.194	.258
P	Jack Fisher	R	35	53	6	1	0	0	0.0	1	2	1	14	0	0	0	.113	.132
P	Cisco Carlos	R	29	31	2	0	0	0	0.0	0	0	1	15	0	0	0	.065	.065
P	Bob Priddy	R	42	24	1	0	0	1	4.2	3	2	0	9	0	0	0	.042	.167
P	Wilbur Wood	R	88	22	2	0	0	0	0.0	0	2	2	17	0	0	0	.091	.091
P	Jerry Nyman	L	8	13	2	0	0	0	0.0	1	0	0	8	0	0	0	.154	.154
P	Bob Locker	B	70	8	0	0	0	0	0.0	0	0	0	5	0	0	0	.000	.000
P	Dennis Ribant	R	17	7	0	0	0	0	0.0	0	0	0	0	0	0	0	.000	.000
P	Don McMahon	R	25	3	1	0	0	0	0.0	0	0	0	1	0	0	0	.333	.333
P	Hoyt Wilhelm	R	72	3	0	0	0	0	0.0	0	0	0	3	0	0	0	.000	.000
P	Danny Lazar	L	8	2	0	0	0	0	0.0	0	1	1	1	0	0	0	.000	.000
P	Billy Wynne	R	1	0	0	0	0	0	–	0	0	0	0	0	0	0	–	–
P	Fred Rath	R	5	0	0	0	0	–	–	0	0	0	0	0	0	0	–	–
TEAM TOTAL				5405	1233	169	33	71	1.3	463	431	397	840	90	230	49	.228	.311

INDIVIDUAL FIELDING

POS	Player	T	G	PO	A	E	DP	TCG	FA	POS	Player	T	G	PO	A	E	DP	TCG	FA
1B	T. McCraw	L	135	1285	93	20	103	10.4	.986	OF	K. Berry	R	151	352	11	7	2	2.5	.981
	P. Ward	R	31	238	18	0	17	8.3	1.000		T. Davis	R	116	171	8	7	2	1.6	.962
	G. Hopkins	R	7	45	1	0	3	6.6	1.000		B. Bradford	R	99	162	4	6	0	1.7	.965
	T. Davis	R	6	40	1	1	3	7.0	.976		B. Voss	L	55	73	5	3	3	1.5	.963
	K. Boyer	R	1	10	1	0	1	11.0	1.000		L. Wagner	R	46	48	0	3	0	1.1	.941
	J. McNertney	R	1	2	0	0	1	2.0	1.000		W. Williams	R	34	47	2	0	1	1.4	1.000
2B	S. Alomar	R	99	188	221	18	48	4.3	.958		W. Held	R	33	30	2	0	1	1.0	1.000
	T. Cullen	R	71	104	150	9	34	3.7	.966		P. Ward	R	22	28	1	0	1	1.3	1.000
	W. Causey	R	41	47	54	3	11	2.5	.971		C. May	R	17	24	0	1	0	1.5	.960
	R. Morales	R	5	5	10	0	1	3.0	1.000		R. Snyder	R	22	22	0	0	0	1.0	1.000
	R. Hansen	R	2	2	1	0	0	1.5	1.000		S. Alomar	R	1	0	0	0	0	0.0	.000
	W. Held	R	1	0	1	0	0	1.0	1.000	C	D. Josephson	R	122	641	86	7	15	6.0	.990
SS	L. Aparicio	R	154	269	535	19	92	5.3	.977		J. McNertney	R	64	299	39	5	8	5.4	.985
	R. Morales	R	7	12	16	1	4	4.1	.966		B. Booker	R	3	2	0	0	0	0.7	1.000
	S. Alomar	R	9	11	16	0	6	3.0	1.000										
	R. Hansen	R	7	3	17	1	2	3.0	.952										
3B	P. Ward	R	77	59	151	12	7	2.9	.946										
	D. Kenworthy	R	38	21	70	6	3	2.6	.938										
	B. Melton	R	33	17	75	3	5	2.9	.968										
	R. Hansen	R	29	23	49	3	4	2.6	.960										
	S. Alomar	R	27	11	27	2	1	1.5	.950										
	K. Boyer	R	5	2	7	1	1	2.0	.900										
	W. Held	R	5	2	3	1	0	1.2	.833										

Attempts to analyze the great collapse of 1968 have usually been traced back to the crushing finish of the '67 season. The roots go back much further. Veeck's 1960 trades set the trend for the decade, as the Sox sacrificed their farm system and committed to making trades to replace their aging regulars. In 1968, the best prospects in camp were pitchers Steve Jones, Danny Lazar, Fred Rath, and Francisco Carlos, and such "sluggers" as Bill Boss, Berke Reichenbach, Cotton Nash, and Dick Kenworthy. With nothing coming up and a lot going down, it's easy to see why the Sox finished in eighth place in 1968. In retrospect, it's a wonder it didn't happen sooner.

A ten-game losing streak opened the campaign. Newcomer Tommy Davis ended the misery with a game-winning homer against the Twins on April 26. But Davis, Pete Ward, Ken Boyer, and Russ Snyder all failed to deliver any kind of punch at all, and the Sox found themselves in ninth place on July 12. Eddie Stanky was fired that day in favor of Al Lopez, who was brought out of retirement.

It was a year of financial stress for Art Allyn as the Sox played ten "home games" in Milwaukee. The ten games drew 265,552, nearly one-third of the entire Sox home attendance. Rumors were afloat that the team was headed north in the next two years. In the face of Cub hysteria, the Sox entered a dark period they were lucky to survive. The three-year period ending with the hiring of Chuck Tanner represented the worst crisis since the Black Sox Scandal.

TEAM STATISTICS

	W	L	PCT	GB	R	OR	2B	3B	HR	BA	SA	SB	E	DP	FA	CG	BB	SO	ShO	SV	ERA
DET	103	59	.636		671	492	190	39	185	.235	.385	26	105	133	.983	59	486	1115	19	29	2.71
BAL	91	71	.562	12	579	497	215	28	133	.225	.352	78	120	131	.981	53	502	1044	16	31	2.66
CLE	86	75	.534	16.5	516	504	210	36	75	.234	.327	115	127	130	.979	48	540	1157	23	32	2.66
BOS	86	76	.531	17	614	611	207	17	125	.236	.352	76	128	147	.979	55	523	972	17	31	3.33
NY	83	79	.512	20	536	531	154	34	109	.214	.318	90	139	142	.979	45	424	831	14	27	2.79
OAK	82	80	.506	21	569	544	192	40	94	.240	.343	147	145	136	.976	45	505	997	18	29	2.94
MIN	79	83	.488	24	562	546	207	41	105	.237	.350	98	170	117	.973	46	414	996	14	29	2.89
CAL	67	95	.414	36	498	615	170	33	83	.227	.318	62	140	156	.977	29	519	869	11	31	3.43
CHI	67	95	.414	36	463	527	169	33	71	.228	.311	90	151	152	.977	20	451	834	11	40	2.75
WAS	65	96	.404	37.5	524	665	160	37	124	.224	.336	29	148	144	.976	26	517	826	11	28	3.64
LEAGUE TOTAL					5532	5532	1874	338	1104	.230	.339	811	1373	1388	.978	426	4881	9641	154	307	2.98

INDIVIDUAL PITCHING

PITCHER	T	W	L	PCT	ERA	SV	G	GS	CG	IP	H	BB	SO	R	ER	ShO	H9	BB9	SO9
Joe Horlen	R	12	14	.462	2.37	0	35	35	4	223.2	197	70	102	75	59	1	7.93	2.82	4.10
Jack Fisher	R	8	13	.381	2.99	0	35	28	2	180.2	176	48	80	68	60	0	8.77	2.39	3.99
Tommy John	L	10	5	.667	1.98	0	25	25	5	177.1	135	49	117	45	39	1	6.85	2.49	5.94
Gary Peters	L	4	13	.235	3.76	1	31	25	6	162.2	146	60	110	79	68	1	8.08	3.32	6.09
Wilbur Wood	L	13	12	.520	1.87	16	88	2	0	159	127	33	74	39	33	0	7.19	1.87	4.19
Cisco Carlos	R	4	14	.222	3.90	0	29	21	0	122.1	121	37	57	64	53	0	8.90	2.72	4.19
Bob Priddy	R	3	11	.214	3.63	0	35	18	2	114	106	41	66	50	46	0	8.37	3.24	5.21
Hoyt Wilhelm	R	4	4	.500	1.73	12	72	0	0	93.2	69	24	72	20	18	0	6.63	2.31	6.92
Bob Locker	R	5	4	.556	2.29	10	70	0	0	90.1	78	27	62	27	23	0	7.77	2.69	6.18
Don McMahon	R	2	1	.667	1.96	0	25	0	0	46	31	20	32	10	10	0	6.07	3.91	6.26
Jerry Nyman	L	2	1	.667	2.01	0	8	7	1	40.1	38	16	27	13	9	1	8.48	3.57	6.02
Dennis Ribant	R	0	2	.000	6.03	1	17	0	0	31.1	42	17	20	24	21	0	12.06	4.88	5.74
Danny Lazar	L	0	1	.000	4.05	0	8	1	0	13.1	14	4	11	6	6	0	9.45	2.70	7.43
Fred Rath	R	0	0	–	1.59	0	5	0	0	11.1	8	3	3	5	2	0	6.35	2.38	2.38
Billy Wynne	R	0	0	–	4.50	0	1	0	0	2	2	2	1	2	1	0	9.00	9.00	4.50
TEAM TOTAL		67	95	.414	2.75	40	484	162	20	1468	1290	451	834	527	448	4	7.91	2.76	5.11

Chicago 1969   Won 68 Lost 94 Pct. .420 15

MANAGER	W	L	PCT
Al Lopez	8	9	.471
Don Gutteridge	60	85	.414

POS	Player	B	G	AB	H	2B	3B	HR	HR %	R	RBI	BB	SO	SB	Pinch Hit AB	H	BA	SA
REGULARS																		
1B	Gail Hopkins	L	124	373	99	13	3	8	2.1	52	46	50	28	2	21	6	.265	.381
2B	Bobby Knoop	R	104	345	79	14	1	6	1.7	34	41	35	68	2	1	0	.229	.328
SS	Luis Aparicio	R	156	599	168	24	5	5	0.8	77	51	66	29	24	1	0	.280	.362
3B	Bill Melton	R	157	556	142	26	2	23	4.1	67	87	56	106	1	1	0	.255	.433
RF	Walt Williams	R	135	471	143	22	1	3	0.6	59	32	26	33	6	24	7	.304	.374
CF	Ken Berry	R	130	297	69	12	2	4	1.3	25	18	24	50	1	2	0	.232	.327
LF	Carlos May	L	100	367	103	18	2	18	4.9	62	62	58	66	1	2	1	.281	.488
C	Ed Herrmann	L	102	290	67	8	0	8	2.8	31	31	30	35	0	11	1	.231	.341
SUBSTITUTES																		
1O	Tom McCraw	L	93	240	62	12	2	2	0.8	21	25	21	24	1	17	4	.258	.350
UT	Pete Ward	L	105	199	49	7	0	6	3.0	22	32	33	38	0	46	17	.246	.372
UT	Ron Hansen	R	85	185	48	6	1	2	1.1	15	22	18	25	2	25	6	.259	.335
2S	Rich Morales	R	55	121	26	0	1	0	0.0	12	6	7	18	1	3	1	.215	.231
2B	Sandy Alomar	B	22	58	13	2	0	0	0.0	8	4	4	6	2	0	0	.224	.259
1B	Bob Spence	L	12	26	4	1	0	0	0.0	0	3	0	9	0	7	0	.154	.192
OF	Buddy Bradford	R	93	273	70	8	2	11	4.0	36	27	34	75	5	5	0	.256	.421
OF	Bob Christian	R	39	129	28	4	0	3	2.3	11	16	10	19	3	1	1	.217	.318
OF	Angel Bravo	L	27	90	26	4	2	1	1.1	10	3	3	5	2	2	0	.289	.411
UT	Woodie Held	R	56	63	9	2	0	3	4.8	9	6	13	19	0	19	2	.143	.317
OF	Jose Ortiz	R	16	11	3	1	0	0	0.0	0	2	1	0	0	1	0	.273	.364
C1	Don Pavletich	R	78	188	46	12	0	6	3.2	26	33	28	45	0	19	4	.245	.404
C	Duane Josephson	R	52	162	39	6	2	1	0.6	19	20	13	17	0	7	3	.241	.321
C	Chuck Brinkman	R	14	15	1	0	0	0	0.0	2	0	1	5	0	1	0	.067	.067
C	Doug Adams	L	8	14	3	0	0	0	0.0	1	1	1	3	0	5	2	.214	.214
PITCHERS																		
P	Tommy John	R	33	79	9	2	0	0	0.0	6	1	7	27	0	0	0	.114	.139
P	Joe Horlen	R	36	77	14	1	0	0	0.0	4	5	0	22	0	0	0	.182	.195
P	Gary Peters	L	37	71	12	4	0	2	2.8	9	4	2	15	0	0	0	.169	.310
P	Billy Wynne	R	20	41	5	0	1	0	0.0	1	2	2	6	0	0	0	.122	.171
P	Paul Edmondson	R	14	29	5	0	0	0	0.0	3	1	0	8	0	0	0	.172	.172
P	Jerry Nyman	L	21	20	1	1	0	0	0.0	1	3	1	15	0	0	0	.050	.100
P	Wilbur Wood	R	76	15	0	0	0	0	0.0	0	0	0	8	0	0	0	.000	.000
P	Cisco Carlos	R	25	10	0	0	0	0	0.0	0	0	1	4	0	0	0	.000	.000
P	Don Secrist	L	19	7	1	0	0	0	0.0	1	0	1	4	0	0	0	.143	.143
P	Sammy Ellis	R	10	6	1	0	0	0	0.0	0	0	1	3	0	0	0	.167	.167
P	Bart Johnson	R	4	6	1	0	0	0	0.0	1	1	2	1	1	0	0	.167	.167
P	Gary Bell	R	23	5	0	0	0	0	0.0	0	1	2	0	0	0	0	.000	.000
P	Danny Lazar	L	9	4	0	0	0	0	0.0	0	0	0	3	0	0	0	.000	.000
P	Dan Osinski	R	51	3	0	0	0	0	0.0	0	0	0	2	0	0	0	.000	.000
P	Fred Rath	R	3	3	0	0	0	0	0.0	0	0	0	0	0	0	0	.000	.000
P	Bob Locker	R	17	1	0	0	0	0	0.0	0	0	0	1	0	0	0	.000	.000
P	Danny Murphy	L	17	1	0	0	0	0	0.0	0	0	2	0	0	0	0	.000	.000
P	Jack Hamilton	R	8	0	0	0	0	0	–	0	0	0	0	0	0	0	–	–
P	Bob Priddy	R	4	0	0	0	0	0	–	0	0	0	0	0	0	0	–	–
P	Denny O'Toole	R	2	0	0	0	0	0	–	0	0	0	0	0	0	0	–	–
TEAM TOTAL				5450	1346	210	27	112	2.1	625	585	552	844	54	224	56	.247	.357

INDIVIDUAL FIELDING

POS	Player	T	G	PO	A	E	DP	TCG	FA
1B	G. Hopkins	R	101	903	51	6	81	9.5	.994
	T. McCraw	L	44	254	14	3	21	6.2	.989
	P. Ward	R	25	167	12	1	12	7.2	.994
	R. Hansen	R	21	151	11	2	14	7.8	.988
	D. Pavletich	R	13	90	2	1	13	7.2	.989
	B. Spence	R	6	40	2	0	5	7.0	1.000
2B	B. Knoop	R	104	271	320	9	76	5.8*	.985
	R. Morales	R	38	68	95	4	18	4.4	.976
	S. Alomar	R	22	50	47	2*	15	4.5	.980
	R. Hansen	R	26	44	44	3	12	3.5	.967
	W. Held	R	1	2	2	0	0	4.0	1.000
SS	L. Aparicio	R	154	248	563	20	94	5.4	.976
	R. Morales	R	13	9	23	0	4	2.5	1.000
	R. Hansen	R	8	14	14	1	1	3.6	.966
	W. Held	R	3	2	4	0	1	2.0	1.000
3B	B. Melton	R	148	112	322	22	36	3.1	.952
	P. Ward	R	21	15	34	2	1	2.4	.961
	R. Morales	R	1	0	0	0	0	0.0	.000
	R. Hansen	R	7	7	14	2	1	3.3	.913
	W. Held	R	3	2	9	0	0	3.7	1.000

POS	Player	T	G	PO	A	E	DP	TCG	FA
OF	K. Berry	R	120	215	7	0	1	1.9	1.000
	W. Williams	R	111	183	13	3	4	1.8	.985
	C. May	R	100	154	10	3	0	1.7	.982
	B. Bradford	R	88	141	5	6	1	1.7	.961
	B. Christian	R	38	66	3	3	0	1.9	.958
	T. McCraw	L	41	48	1	0	0	1.2	1.000
	A. Bravo	L	25	44	0	1	0	1.8	.978
	W. Held	R	18	17	0	0	0	0.9	1.000
	B. Melton	R	11	13	3	0	0	1.5	1.000
	P. Ward	R	9	11	2	0	0	1.4	1.000
	J. Ortiz	R	8	4	1	0	0	0.6	1.000
C	E. Herrmann	R	92	420	41	8	7	5.1	.983
	D. Josephson	R	47	227	27	4	1	5.5	.984
	D. Pavletich	R	51	195	26	6	3	4.5	.974
	C. Brinkman	R	14	28	2	0	1	2.1	1.000
	D. Adams	R	4	9	2	0	0	2.8	1.000

Chicago 1969

Not a good year. The White Sox reluctantly commmitted themselves to youth, and the results were predictable. But they did improve by one game over the previous year and accepted the fact that rebuilding is a baseball reality sooner or later.

Carlos May and Bill Melton were the best of the rookie crop, but May was lost to the team in August when he blew off a thumb during National Guard exercises. But the youngster staged a valiant comeback against unfavorable odds and went on to produce several first-rate seasons for the Sox.

The Sox became the first American League team to feature artificial turf, when Art Allyn had the infield portions of the field re-sodded. This helped the hitters, but the once classy pitching staff found hard times on the hard turf.

In the new divisional alignment, the Sox struggled to remain ahead of the expansion Royals and Pilots. Up to the last game of the season the Sox held fourth place, but saw that last vestige of respectability slip away in a 6–4 loss to the Twins.

In September Charlie Finley offered to swap ballclubs with Allyn. The A's and Sox would trade all their players, and Charlie O would start all over in Chicago. It was rejected outright by Allyn, who listened to offers from Bud Selig's Milwaukee people before deciding to sell to his brother John on September 24. Selig had offered Allyn thirteen million dollars, but it was unlikely that they would get league approval to move to Milwaukee, so Allyn declined.

TEAM STATISTICS

	W	L	PCT	GB	R	OR	2B	3B	HR	BA	SA	SB	E	DP	FA	CG	BB	SO	ShO	SV	ERA
WEST																					
MIN	97	65	.599		790	618	246	32	163	.268	.408	115	150	177	.977	41	524	906	8	43	3.25
OAK	88	74	.543	9	740	678	210	28	148	.249	.376	100	137	162	.978	42	586	887	14	36	3.71
CAL	71	91	.438	26	528	652	151	29	88	.230	.319	54	136	164	.978	25	517	885	9	39	3.55
KC	69	93	.426	28	586	688	179	32	98	.240	.338	129	157	114	.975	42	560	894	10	25	3.72
CHI	68	94	.420	29	625	723	210	27	112	.247	.357	54	122	163	.981	29	564	810	10	25	4.21
SEA	64	98	.395	33	639	799	179	27	125	.234	.346	167	167	149	.974	21	653	963	6	33	4.35
EAST																					
BAL	109	53	.673		779	517	234	29	175	.265	.414	82	101	145	.984	50	498	897	20	36	2.83
DET	90	72	.556	19	701	601	188	29	182	.242	.387	35	130	130	.979	55	586	1032	20	28	3.32
BOS	87	75	.537	22	743	736	234	37	197	.251	.415	41	157	178	.975	30	685	935	7	41	3.93
WAS	86	76	.531	23	694	644	171	40	148	.251	.378	52	140	159	.978	28	656	835	10	41	3.49
NY	80	81	.497	28.5	562	587	210	44	94	.235	.344	119	131	158	.979	53	522	801	13	20	3.23
CLE	62	99	.385	46.5	573	717	173	24	119	.237	.345	85	145	153	.976	35	681	1000	7	22	3.94
LEAGUE TOTAL					7960	7960	2385	378	1649	.246	.369	1033	1673	1852	.978	451	7032	10845	134	389	3.63

INDIVIDUAL PITCHING

PITCHER	T	W	L	PCT	ERA	SV	G	GS	CG	IP	H	BB	SO	R	ER	ShO	H9	BB9	SO9
Joe Horlen	R	13	16	.448	3.78	0	36	35	7	235.2	237	77	121	105	99	2	9.05	2.94	4.62
Tommy John	L	9	11	.450	3.25	0	33	33	6	232.1	230	90	128	91	84	2	8.91	3.49	4.96
Gary Peters	L	10	15	.400	4.53	0	36	32	7	218.2	238	78	140	118	110	3	9.80	3.21	5.76
Billy Wynne	R	7	7	.500	4.06	0	20	20	6	128.2	143	50	67	63	58	1	10.00	3.50	4.69
Wilbur Wood	L	10	11	.476	3.01	15	76	0	0	119.2	113	40	73	48	40	0	8.50	3.01	5.49
Paul Edmondson	R	1	6	.143	3.70	0	14	13	1	87.2	72	39	46	36	36	0	7.39	4.00	4.72
Jerry Nyman	L	4	4	.500	5.29	0	20	10	2	64.2	58	39	40	40	38	1	8.07	5.43	5.57
Dan Osinski	R	5	5	.500	3.56	2	51	0	0	60.2	56	23	27	28	24	0	8.31	3.41	4.01
Cisco Carlos	R	4	3	.571	5.66	0	25	4	0	49.1	52	23	28	33	31	0	9.49	4.20	5.11
Don Secrist	L	0	1	.000	6.08	0	19	0	0	40	35	14	23	28	27	0	7.88	3.15	5.18
Gary Bell	R	0	0	–	6.28	0	23	2	0	38.2	48	23	26	27	27	0	11.17	5.35	6.05
Danny Murphy	R	2	1	.667	2.01	4	17	0	0	31.1	28	10	16	8	7	0	8.04	2.87	4.60
Sammy Ellis	R	0	3	.000	5.83	0	10	5	0	29.1	42	16	15	20	19	0	12.89	4.91	4.60
Bart Johnson	R	1	3	.250	3.22	0	4	3	0	22.1	22	6	18	11	8	4	8.87	2.42	7.25
Bob Locker	R	2	3	.400	6.55	4	17	0	0	22	26	6	15	18	16	0	10.64	2.45	6.14
Danny Lazar	L	0	0	–	6.53	0	9	3	0	20.2	21	11	9	15	15	4	9.15	4.79	3.92
Jack Hamilton	R	0	3	.000	11.68	0	8	0	0	12.1	23	7	5	16	16	0	16.78	5.11	3.65
Fred Rath	R	0	2	.000	7.71	0	3	2	0	11.2	11	8	4	10	10	4	8.49	6.17	3.09
Bob Priddy	R	0	0	–	4.50	0	4	0	0	8	10	2	5	5	4	0	11.25	2.25	5.63
Denny O'Toole	R	0	0	–	6.75	0	2	0	0	4	5	2	4	3	3	0	11.25	4.50	9.00
TEAM TOTAL		68	94	.420	4.21	25	427	162	29	1437.2	1470	564	810	723	672	9	9.20	3.53	5.07

Chicago 1970   Won 56 Lost 106 Pct .346 16

MANAGER	W	L	PCT
Don Gutteridge	49	87	.360
Bill Adair	4	6	.400
Chuck Tanner	3	13	.188

POS	Player	B	G	AB	H	2B	3B	HR	HR %	R	RBI	BB	SO	SB	Pinch Hit AB	H	BA	SA
REGULARS																		
1B	Gail Hopkins	L	116	287	82	8	1	6	2.1	32	29	28	19	0	36	10	.286	.383
2B	Bobby Knoop	R	130	402	92	13	2	5	1.2	34	36	34	79	0	3	1	.229	.308
SS	Luis Aparicio	R	146	552	173	29	3	5	0.9	86	43	53	34	8	3	2	.313	.404
3B	Bill Melton	R	141	514	135	15	1	33	6.4	74	96	56	107	2	0	0	.263	.488
RF	Walt Williams	R	110	315	79	18	1	3	1.0	43	15	19	30	3	29	8	.251	.343
CF	Ken Berry	R	141	463	128	12	2	7	1.5	45	50	43	61	6	2	1	.276	.356
LF	Carlos May	L	150	555	158	28	4	12	2.2	83	68	79	96	12	2	0	.285	.414
C	Ed Herrmann	L	96	297	84	9	0	19	6.4	42	52	31	41	0	7	1	.283	.505
SUBSTITUTES																		
32	Syd O'Brien	R	121	441	109	13	2	8	1.8	48	44	22	62	3	8	2	.247	.340
1O	Tom McCraw	L	129	332	73	11	2	6	1.8	39	31	21	50	12	32	8	.220	.319
1B	Bob Spence	L	46	130	29	4	1	4	3.1	11	15	11	32	0	9	1	.223	.362
3S	Rich McKinney	R	43	119	20	5	0	4	3.4	12	17	11	25	3	8	1	.168	.311
UT	Rich Morales	R	62	112	18	2	0	1	0.9	6	2	9	16	1	9	1	.161	.205
1B	Ossie Blanco	R	34	66	13	0	0	0	0.0	4	8	3	14	0	16	3	.197	.197
O1	John Matias	L	58	117	22	2	0	2	1.7	7	6	3	22	1	27	5	.188	.256
OF	Buddy Bradford	R	32	91	17	3	0	2	2.2	8	8	10	30	1	5	1	.187	.286
OF	Jose Ortiz	R	15	24	8	1	0	0	0.0	4	1	2	2	1	1	0	.333	.375
OF	Bob Christian	R	12	15	4	0	0	1	6.7	3	3	1	4	0	9	3	.267	.467
C	Duane Josephson	R	96	285	90	12	1	4	1.4	28	41	24	28	1	14	5	.316	.407
C	Chuck Brinkman	R	9	20	5	1	0	0	0.0	4	0	3	3	0	0	0	.250	.300
C	Art Kusnyer	R	4	10	1	0	0	0	0.0	0	0	0	4	0	1	0	.100	.100
PH	Lee Maye	L	6	6	1	0	0	0	0.0	0	1	0	1	0	6	1	.167	.167
PITCHERS																		
P	Tommy John	R	38	84	17	1	0	0	0.0	4	5	2	17	0	1	1	.202	.214
P	Gerry Janeski	R	35	66	5	0	0	0	0.0	0	5	2	31	0	0	0	.076	.076
P	Joe Horlen	R	28	52	6	1	0	0	0.0	2	1	2	14	0	0	0	.115	.135
P	Bart Johnson	R	18	29	8	2	0	0	0.0	3	2	1	6	0	0	0	.276	.345
P	Jerry Crider	R	32	24	2	1	0	0	0.0	2	0	0	5	0	0	0	.083	.125
P	Bob Miller	R	16	23	4	0	0	0	0.0	0	2	3	5	0	0	0	.174	.174
P	Barry Moore	L	24	19	5	0	0	0	0.0	2	2	1	4	0	0	0	.263	.263
P	Wilbur Wood	R	77	18	2	1	0	0	0.0	2	3	0	11	0	0	0	.111	.167
P	Billy Wynne	R	12	13	1	0	0	0	0.0	0	0	1	7	0	0	0	.077	.077
P	Jim Magnuson	R	13	11	0	0	0	0	0.0	1	0	0	3	0	0	0	.000	.000
P	Floyd Weaver	R	31	7	0	0	0	0	0.0	1	0	0	2	0	0	0	.000	.000
P	Danny Murphy	L	51	6	2	0	0	1	16.7	3	1	2	2	0	0	0	.333	.833
P	Jerry Arrigo	L	5	4	0	0	0	0	0.0	0	0	0	2	0	0	0	.000	.000
P	Tommie Sisk	R	17	4	1	0	0	0	0.0	0	0	0	2	0	0	0	.250	.250
P	Lee Stange	R	16	1	0	0	0	0	0.0	0	0	0	1	0	0	0	.000	.000
P	Steve Hamilton	L	3	0	0	0	0	0	–	0	0	0	0	0	0	0	–	–
P	Don Secrist	L	9	0	0	0	0	0	–	0	0	0	0	0	0	0	–	–
P	Denny O'Toole	R	3	0	0	0	0	0	–	0	0	0	0	0	0	0	–	–
P	Don Eddy	R	7	0	0	0	0	0	–	0	0	0	0	0	0	0	–	–
P	Rich Moloney	R	1	0	0	0	0	0	–	0	0	0	0	0	0	0	–	–
P	Virle Rounsaville	R	8	0	0	0	0	0	–	0	0	0	0	0	0	0	–	–
	TEAM TOTAL			5514	1394	192	20	123	2.2	633	587	477	872	54	228	55	.253	.362

INDIVIDUAL FIELDING

POS	Player	T	G	PO	A	E	DP	TCG	FA
1B	G. Hopkins	R	77	629	42	9	67	8.8	.987
	T. McCraw	L	59	357	33	5	34	6.7	.987
	B. Spence	R	37	305	28	2	36	9.1	.994
	O. Blanco	R	22	144	8	1	9	7.0	.993
	J. Matias	L	18	118	10	2	13	7.2	.985
	C. May	R	7	73	11	2	6	12.3	.977
2B	B. Knoop	R	126	276	403	11	102	5.5	.984
	S. O'Brien	R	43	96	127	10	31	5.4	.957
	R. Morales	R	12	24	25	1	2	4.2	.980
SS	L. Aparicio	R	146	251	483	18	99	5.2	.976
	R. Morales	R	24	14	45	2	8	2.5	.967
	R. McKinney	R	11	20	41	2	7	5.7	.968
	S. O'Brien	R	5	3	7	2	1	2.4	.833
3B	B. Melton	R	70	47	179	18	19	3.5	.926
	S. O'Brien	R	68	59	137	13	18	3.1	.938
	R. McKinney	R	23	14	40	4	2	2.5	.931
	R. Morales	R	20	11	21	4	4	1.8	.889

POS	Player	T	G	PO	A	E	DP	TCG	FA
OF	K. Berry	R	138	331	9	4	2	2.5	.988
	C. May	R	141	203	12	2	1	1.5	.991
	W. Williams	R	79	119	12	7	1	1.7	.949
	B. Melton	R	71	111	8	0	3	1.7	1.000
	T. McCraw	L	49	70	2	4	0	1.6	.947
	B. Bradford	R	27	46	1	1	0	1.8	.979
	J. Matias	L	22	14	2	1	1	0.8	.941
	O. Blanco	R	1	0	0	0	0	0.0	.000
	J. Ortiz	R	8	10	3	0	0	1.6	1.000
	B. Christian	R	4	2	0	0	0	0.5	1.000
C	E. Herrmann	R	88	433	51	6	10	5.6	.988
	D. Josephson	R	84	353	38	6	7	4.7	.985
	C. Brinkman	R	9	32	5	1	1	4.2	.974
	A. Kusnyer	R	3	12	4	1	0	5.7	.941
	G. Hopkins	R	8	16	0	0	0	2.0	1.000

Chicago 1970

Rookie pitcher Gerry Janeski put the year into perspective when he told reporters on the occasion of his first major league win that "the crowd was so small, I wasn't nervous." Indeed there was nothing to get nervous or excited about this year. The Sox bagged last place on July 7, and except for one bright day they remained in the cellar. The 106 losses were a new team record, the 4.54 team ERA the worst since 1948. Attendance reached a twenty-eight-year low of 495,355.

Those who cared got to see Bill Melton become the first Sox player to smash 30 home runs when he connected off Aurelio Monteagudo on September 21. Two days later, Looie Aparicio broke Luke Appling's record of 2,218 games at shortstop. Little Looie's final year in Chicago was by far his finest. Despite losing a few steps, the seasoned veteran finished at .313. He was traded to Boston for Mike Andrews that winter.

Manager Don Gutteridge was gone by mutual agreement on September 2. A day earlier Ed Short was let go, too. Stuart K. Holcomb was named general manager, and he brought in the right people: the new manager would be a 42-year-old unknown, Charles William Tanner. From the California Angels front office came Roland Hemond, a low-key Frank Lane who didn't suffer from the same personality caprices. And from that same California farm system came Johnny Sain, a pitching coach who would work some magic with the decimated staff in 1971.

TEAM STATISTICS

	W	L	PCT	GB	R	OR	2B	3B	HR	BA	SA	SB	E	DP	FA	CG	BB	SO	ShO	SV	ERA
WEST																					
MIN	98	64	.605		744	605	230	41	153	.262	.403	57	123	130	.980	26	486	940	12	58	3.23
OAK	89	73	.549	9	678	593	208	24	171	.249	.392	131	141	152	.977	33	542	858	15	40	3.30
CAL	86	76	.531	12	631	630	197	40	114	.251	.363	69	127	169	.980	21	559	922	10	49	3.48
KC	65	97	.401	33	611	705	202	41	97	.244	.348	97	152	162	.976	30	641	915	11	25	3.78
MIL	65	97	.401	33	613	751	202	24	126	.242	.358	91	136	142	.978	31	587	895	2	27	4.20
CHI	56	106	.346	42	633	822	192	20	123	.253	.362	54	165	187	.975	20	556	762	6	30	4.54
EAST																					
BAL	108	54	.667		792	574	213	25	179	.257	.401	84	117	148	.981	60	469	941	12	31	3.15
NY	93	69	.574	15	680	612	208	41	111	.251	.365	105	130	146	.980	36	451	777	6	49	3.25
BOS	87	75	.537	21	786	722	252	28	203	.262	.428	50	156	131	.974	38	594	1003	8	44	3.90
DET	79	83	.488	29	666	731	207	38	148	.238	.374	29	133	142	.978	33	623	1045	9	39	4.09
CLE	76	86	.469	32	649	675	197	23	183	.249	.394	25	133	168	.979	34	689	1076	8	35	3.91
WAS	70	92	.432	38	626	689	184	28	138	.238	.358	72	116	173	.982	20	611	823	11	40	3.80
LEAGUE TOTAL					8109	8109	2492	373	1746	.250	.379	864	1629	1850	.978	382	6808	10957	110	467	3.72

INDIVIDUAL PITCHING

PITCHER	T	W	L	PCT	ERA	SV	G	GS	CG	IP	H	BB	SO	R	ER	ShO	H9	BB9	SO9
Tommy John	L	12	17	.414	3.28	0	37	37	10	269	253	101	138	117	98	3	8.46	3.38	4.62
Gerry Janeski	R	10	17	.370	4.76	0	35	35	4	206	247	63	79	125	109	1	10.79	2.75	3.45
Joe Horlen	R	6	16	.273	4.87	0	28	26	4	172	198	41	77	99	93	0	10.36	2.15	4.03
Wilbur Wood	L	9	13	.409	2.80	21	77	0	0	122	118	36	85	50	38	0	8.70	2.66	6.27
Jerry Crider	R	4	7	.364	4.45	4	32	8	0	91	101	34	40	49	45	0	9.99	3.36	3.96
Bart Johnson	R	4	7	.364	4.80	0	18	15	2	90	92	46	71	53	48	1	9.20	4.60	7.10
Danny Murphy	R	2	3	.400	5.67	5	51	0	0	81	82	49	42	55	51	0	9.11	5.44	4.67
Barry Moore	L	0	4	.000	6.37	0	24	7	0	70.2	85	34	34	56	50	0	10.83	4.33	4.33
Bob Miller	R	4	6	.400	5.01	0	15	12	0	70	88	33	36	42	39	0	11.31	4.24	4.63
Floyd Weaver	R	1	2	.333	4.35	0	31	3	0	62	52	31	51	33	30	0	7.55	4.50	7.40
Jim Magnuson	L	1	5	.167	4.80	0	13	6	0	45	45	16	20	28	24	0	9.00	3.20	4.00
Billy Wynne	R	1	4	.200	5.32	0	12	9	0	44	54	22	19	30	26	0	11.05	4.50	3.89
Tommie Sisk	R	1	1	.500	5.45	0	17	1	0	33	37	13	16	28	20	0	10.09	3.55	4.36
Lee Stange	R	1	0	1.000	5.24	0	16	0	0	22.1	28	5	14	13	13	0	11.28	2.01	5.64
Don Secrist	L	0	0	—	5.40	0	9	0	0	15	19	12	9	9	9	0	11.40	7.20	5.40
Jerry Arrigo	L	0	3	.000	13.15	0	5	3	0	13	24	9	12	20	19	0	16.62	6.23	8.31
Don Eddy	L	0	0	—	2.25	0	7	0	0	12	10	6	9	4	3	0	7.50	4.50	6.75
Virle Rounsaville	R	0	1	.000	10.50	0	8	0	0	6	10	2	3	8	7	0	15.00	3.00	4.50
Steve Hamilton	L	0	0	—	6.00	0	3	0	0	3	4	1	3	2	2	0	12.00	3.00	9.00
Denny O'Toole	R	0	0	—	3.00	0	3	0	0	3	5	2	3	1	1	0	15.00	6.00	9.00
Rich Moloney	R	0	0	—	0.00	0	1	0	0	1	2	0	1	0	0	0	18.00	0.00	9.00
TEAM TOTAL		56	106	.346	4.56	30	442	162	20	1431	1554	556	762	822	725	5	9.77	3.50	4.79

Chicago 1971 Won 79 Lost 83 Pct. .488 13

MANAGER	W	L	PCT
Chuck Tanner	79	83	.488

POS	Player	B	G	AB	H	2B	3B	HR	HR%	R	RBI	BB	SO	SB	Pinch Hit AB	H	BA	SA
REGULARS																		
1B	Carlos May	L	141	500	147	21	7	7	1.4	64	70	62	61	16	5	2	.294	.406
2B	Mike Andrews	R	109	330	93	16	0	12	3.6	45	47	67	36	3	12	4	.282	.439
SS	Luis Alvarado	R	99	264	57	14	1	0	0.0	22	8	11	34	1	9	0	.216	.277
3B	Bill Melton	R	150	543	146	18	2	33	6.1	72	86	61	87	3	0	0	.269	.492
RF	Walt Williams	R	114	361	106	17	3	8	2.2	43	35	24	27	5	27	9	.294	.424
CF	Jay Johnstone	L	124	388	101	14	1	16	4.1	53	40	38	50	10	11	3	.260	.425
LF	Rick Reichardt	R	138	496	138	14	2	19	3.8	53	62	37	90	5	7	2	.278	.429
C	Ed Herrmann	L	101	294	63	6	0	11	3.7	32	35	44	48	2	7	0	.214	.347
SUBSTITUTES																		
2O	Rich McKinney	R	114	369	100	11	2	8	2.2	35	46	35	37	0	19	11	.271	.377
SS	Lee Richard	R	87	260	60	7	3	2	0.8	38	17	20	46	8	6	0	.231	.304
S3	Rich Morales	R	84	185	45	8	0	2	1.1	19	14	22	26	2	12	3	.243	.319
UT	Steve Huntz	B	35	86	18	3	1	2	2.3	10	6	7	9	1	12	0	.209	.337
1B	Bob Spence	L	14	27	4	0	0	0	0.0	2	1	5	6	0	5	0	.148	.148
1B	Tony Muser	L	11	16	5	0	1	0	0.0	2	0	1	1	0	7	2	.313	.438
OF	Pat Kelly	L	67	213	62	6	3	3	1.4	32	22	36	29	14	7	4	.291	.390
OF	Mike Hershberger	R	74	177	46	9	0	2	1.1	22	15	30	23	6	20	5	.260	.345
OF	Ed Stroud	L	53	141	25	4	3	0	0.0	19	2	11	20	4	14	2	.177	.248
OF	Lee Maye	L	32	44	9	2	0	1	2.3	6	7	5	7	0	17	5	.205	.318
OF	Ken Hottman	R	6	16	2	0	0	0	0.0	1	0	1	2	0	1	0	.125	.125
OF	Ron Lolich	R	2	8	1	1	0	0	0.0	0	0	0	2	0	0	0	.125	.250
C	Tom Egan	R	85	251	60	11	1	10	4.0	29	34	26	94	1	10	5	.239	.410
C	Chuck Brinkman	R	15	20	4	0	0	0	0.0	0	1	3	5	0	1	0	.200	.200
PITCHERS																		
P	Wilbur Wood	R	44	96	5	0	0	0	0.0	1	0	11	57	1	0	0	.052	.052
P	Tom Bradley	R	48	96	15	0	0	1	1.0	6	6	1	32	0	0	0	.156	.188
P	Tommy John	L	38	69	10	0	0	0	0.0	3	2	3	14	0	0	0	.145	.145
P	Bart Johnson	R	53	57	11	1	0	0	0.0	3	8	0	12	0	0	0	.193	.211
P	Joe Horlen	R	36	40	4	0	0	0	0.0	1	1	0	3	0	0	0	.100	.100
P	Vicente Romo	R	45	11	4	0	0	0	0.0	1	0	1	2	0	0	0	.364	.364
P	Steve Kealey	R	54	10	2	0	0	1	10.0	1	3	0	4	0	0	0	.200	.500
P	Terry Forster	L	45	5	2	1	0	0	0.0	1	0	0	1	0	0	0	.400	.600
P	Jim Magnuson	R	15	4	0	0	0	0	0.0	0	0	0	3	0	0	0	.000	.000
P	Stan Perzanowski	R	5	2	0	0	0	0	0.0	0	0	0	1	0	0	0	.000	.000
P	Don Eddy	R	22	1	1	1	0	0	0.0	0	0	0	0	0	1	1	1.000	2.000
P	Rich Hinton	L	18	1	0	0	0	0	0.0	1	0	0	0	1	0	0	.000	.000
P	Pat Jacquez	R	2	1	0	0	0	0	0.0	0	0	0	1	0	0	0	.000	.000
P	Denny O'Toole	R	1	0	0	0	0	0	—	0	0	0	0	0	0	0	—	—
TEAM TOTAL				5382	1346	185	30	138	2.6	617	568	562	870	83	209	57	.250	.373

INDIVIDUAL FIELDING

POS	Player	T	G	PO	A	E	DP	TCG	FA	POS	Player	T	G	PO	A	E	DP	TCG	FA
1B	C. May	R	130	1189	71	18	90	9.8	.986	OF	R. Reichardt	R	128	283	4	4	0	2.3	.986
	M. Andrews	R	25	197	11	4	17	8.5	.981		J. Johnstone	R	119	232	9	8	1	2.1	.968
	B. Spence	R	7	69	2	1	6	10.3	.986		W. Williams	R	90	157	4	0	2	1.8	1.000
	R. Reichardt	R	9	50	3	1	2	6.0	.981		P. Kelly	L	61	100	7	1	0	1.8	.991
	T. Muser	L	4	23	3	1	1	6.8	.963		Hershberger	R	59	96	1	4	0	1.7	.960
	T. Egan	R	1	2	0	0	1	2.0	1.000		E. Stroud	R	44	51	0	0	0	1.2	1.000
2B	M. Andrews	R	76	177	191	17	51	5.1	.956		R. McKinney	R	25	44	1	0	0	1.8	1.000
	R. McKinney	R	67	148	159	10	34	4.7	.968		L. Richard	R	16	20	3	1	1	1.5	.958
	L. Alvarado	R	16	31	49	1	12	5.1	.988		R. Morales	R	1	0	0	0	0	0.0	.000
	S. Huntz	R	14	21	32	0	7	3.8	1.000		C. May	R	9	17	1	1	0	2.1	.947
	R. Morales	R	3	2	5	1	1	2.7	.875		L. Maye	R	10	11	1	0	0	1.2	1.000
SS	L. Richard	R	68	87	210	26	30	4.8	.920		K. Hottman	R	5	5	0	0	0	1.0	1.000
	L. Alvarado	R	71	89	189	12	34	4.1	.959		R. Lolich	R	2	1	0	0	0	0.5	1.000
	R. Morales	R	57	66	138	5	14	3.7	.976	C	E. Herrmann	R	97	556	56	3	5	6.3	.995
	S. Huntz	R	7	3	9	0	2	1.7	1.000		T. Egan	R	77	443	41	7	2	6.4	.986
3B	B. Melton	R	148	116	371	16	26	3.4	.968		C. Brinkman	R	14	45	4	0	0	3.5	1.000
	R. Morales	R	18	7	16	3	3	1.4	.885										
	S. Huntz	R	6	7	13	0	1	3.3	1.000										
	R. McKinney	R	5	3	11	1	0	3.0	.933										
	W. Williams	R	3	1	0	1	0	1.0	1.000										

Chicago 1971

Roland Hemond had a busy winter. When the dust settled, the Sox had acquired Vicente Romo, Rick Reichardt, Pat Kelly, Mike Andrews, Jay Johnstone, Tom Egan, Luis Alvarado, Tony Muser, Tom Bradley, Steve Kealey, and Ed Stroud. With the exception of Stroud, all made important contributions to the Sox' dramatic 1971 rise. Sain turned Wilbur Wood into a 20-game winner after Joel Horlen twisted a knee in spring training. Sain put Wood on a steady diet of three days' rest, and the great knuckleballer responded to the challenge with a stingy 1.91 ERA.

A record opening crowd of 43,253 turned out to see the "new look" Sox, a tribute to the determination Hemond, Holcomb, and Tanner had shown. Following a memorable home opening win over the Twins, the Sox settled into familiar 1970 patterns. Last place was their resting spot on July 8 before staging a rally that put them in third on August 5. Orchestrating the sometimes madcap proceedings was Harry Caray, the controversial Cardinal announcer who joined the Sox in '71.

The Sox revived the Eddie Stanky era when they precipitated three bench-clearing brawls, two with the Oakland A's and one with Baltimore. But most important, the rising Sox garnered respect from the Chicago media in 1971, as reporters become increasingly disenchanted with Leo Durocher's glamour boys on the North Side.

TEAM STATISTICS

	W	L	PCT	GB	R	OR	2B	3B	HR	BA	SA	SB	E	DP	FA	CG	BB	SO	ShO	SV	ERA
WEST																					
OAK	101	60	.627		691	564	195	25	160	.252	.384	80	117	157	.981	57	501	999	18	36	3.06
KC	85	76	.528	16	603	566	225	40	80	.250	.353	130	134	178	.978	34	496	775	15	44	3.25
CHI	79	83	.488	22.5	617	597	185	30	138	.250	.373	83	160	128	.975	46	468	976	19	32	3.13
CAL	76	86	.469	25.5	511	576	213	18	96	.231	.329	72	131	159	.980	39	607	904	11	32	3.10
MIN	74	86	.463	26.5	654	670	197	31	116	.260	.372	66	118	134	.980	43	529	895	9	25	3.82
MIL	69	92	.429	32	534	609	160	23	104	.229	.329	82	138	152	.977	32	569	795	23	32	3.38
EAST																					
BAL	101	57	.639		742	530	207	25	158	.261	.398	66	112	148	.981	71	416	793	15	22	3.00
DET	91	71	.562	12	701	645	214	38	179	.254	.405	35	106	156	.983	53	609	1000	11	32	3.64
BOS	85	77	.525	18	691	667	246	28	161	.252	.397	51	116	149	.981	44	535	871	11	35	3.83
NY	82	80	.506	21	648	641	195	43	97	.254	.360	75	125	159	.981	67	423	707	15	12	3.45
WAS	63	96	.396	38.5	537	660	189	30	86	.230	.326	68	141	170	.977	30	554	762	10	26	3.70
CLE	60	102	.370	43	543	747	200	20	109	.238	.342	57	116	159	.981	21	770	937	7	32	4.28
LEAGUE TOTAL					7472	7472	2426	351	1484	.247	.364	865	1514	1849	.980	537	6477	10414	164	360	3.47

INDIVIDUAL PITCHING

PITCHER	T	W	L	PCT	ERA	SV	G	GS	CG	IP	H	BB	SO	R	ER	ShO	H9	BB9	SO9
Wilbur Wood	L	22	13	.629	1.91	1	44	42	22	334	272	62	210	95	71	7	7.33	1.67	5.66
Tom Bradley	R	15	15	.500	2.96	2	45	39	7	286	273	74	206	111	94	6	8.59	2.33	6.48
Tommy John	L	13	16	.448	3.62	0	38	35	10	229	244	58	131	115	92	3	9.59	2.28	5.15
Bart Johnson	R	12	10	.545	2.93	14	53	16	4	178	148	111	153	67	58	0	7.48	5.61	7.74
Joe Horlen	R	8	9	.471	4.27	2	34	18	3	137	150	30	82	72	65	0	9.85	1.97	5.39
Steve Kealey	R	2	2	.500	3.86	6	54	1	0	77	69	26	50	40	33	0	8.06	3.04	5.84
Vicente Romo	R	1	7	.125	3.38	5	45	2	0	72	52	37	48	27	27	0	6.50	4.63	6.00
Terry Forster	L	2	3	.400	3.96	1	45	3	0	50	46	23	48	23	22	0	8.28	4.14	8.64
Jim Magnuson	L	2	1	.667	4.50	0	15	4	0	30	30	16	11	18	15	0	9.00	4.80	3.30
Rich Hinton	L	2	4	.333	4.50	0	18	2	0	24	27	6	15	12	12	0	10.13	2.25	5.63
Don Eddy	L	0	2	.000	2.35	0	22	0	0	23	19	19	14	6	6	0	7.43	7.43	5.48
Stan Perzanowski	R	0	1	.000	12.00	1	5	0	0	6	14	3	5	10	8	0	21.00	4.50	7.50
Denny O'Toole	R	0	0	–	0.00	0	1	0	0	2	0	1	2	0	0	0	0.00	4.50	9.00
Pat Jacquez	R	0	0	–	4.50	0	2	0	0	2	4	2	1	1	1	0	18.00	9.00	4.50
TEAM TOTAL		79	83	.488	3.13	32	421	162	46	1450	1348	468	976	597	504	16	8.37	2.90	6.06

Chicago 1972 Won 87 Lost 67 Pct. .565 12th

MANAGER	W	L	PCT
Chuck Tanner	87	67	.565

POS	Player	B	G	AB	H	2B	3B	HR	HR %	R	RBI	BB	SO	SB	Pinch Hit AB	H	BA	SA
REGULARS																		
1B	Richie Allen	R	148	506	156	28	5	37	7.3	90	113	99	126	19	7	1	.308	.603
2B	Mike Andrews	R	148	505	111	18	0	7	1.4	58	50	70	78	2	1	1	.220	.297
SS	Rich Morales	R	110	287	59	7	1	2	0.7	24	20	19	49	2	5	1	.206	.258
3B	Ed Spiezio	R	74	277	66	10	1	2	0.7	20	22	13	43	0	0	0	.238	.303
RF	Pat Kelly	L	119	402	105	14	7	5	1.2	57	24	55	69	32	17	3	.261	.368
CF	Rick Reichardt	R	101	291	73	14	4	8	2.7	31	43	28	63	2	10	1	.251	.409
LF	Carlos May	L	148	523	161	26	3	12	2.3	83	68	79	70	23	0	0	.308	.438
C	Ed Herrmann	L	116	354	88	9	0	10	2.8	23	40	43	37	0	5	2	.249	.359
SUBSTITUTES																		
SS	Luis Alvarado	R	103	254	54	4	1	4	1.6	30	29	13	36	2	7	2	.213	.283
3B	Bill Melton	R	57	208	51	5	0	7	3.4	22	30	23	31	1	1	0	.245	.370
UT	Jorge Orta	L	51	124	25	3	1	3	2.4	20	11	6	37	3	11	1	.202	.315
1B	Tony Muser	L	44	61	17	2	2	1	1.6	6	9	2	6	1	12	4	.279	.426
3B	Hank Allen	R	9	21	3	0	0	0	0.0	1	0	0	2	0	0	0	.143	.143
SS	Rudy Hernandez	R	8	21	4	0	0	0	0.0	0	1	0	3	0	2	1	.190	.190
3B	Hugh Yancy	R	3	9	1	0	0	0	0.0	0	0	0	0	0	0	0	.111	.111
OF	Jay Johnstone	L	113	261	49	9	0	4	1.5	27	17	25	42	2	19	6	.188	.268
OF	Walt Williams	R	77	221	55	7	1	2	0.9	22	11	13	20	6	23	4	.249	.317
OF	Jim Lyttle	L	44	82	19	5	2	0	0.0	8	5	1	28	0	21	6	.232	.341
OF	Buddy Bradford	R	35	48	13	2	0	2	4.2	13	8	4	13	3	10	4	.271	.438
OF	Lee Richard	R	11	29	7	0	0	0	0.0	5	1	0	7	1	1	1	.241	.241
OF	Jim Qualls	B	11	10	0	0	0	0	0.0	0	0	0	2	0	7	0	.000	.000
C	Tom Egan	R	50	141	27	3	0	2	1.4	8	9	4	48	0	11	3	.191	.255
C	Chuck Brinkman	R	35	52	7	0	0	0	0.0	1	0	4	7	0	3	1	.135	.135
PITCHERS																		
P	Wilbur Wood	R	49	125	17	0	0	0	0.0	8	7	6	65	0	0	0	.136	.136
P	Stan Bahnsen	R	44	92	14	2	0	0	0.0	5	2	1	38	0	0	0	.152	.174
P	Tom Bradley	R	43	91	12	2	0	0	0.0	1	3	1	34	0	0	0	.132	.154
P	Dave Lemonds	L	34	25	3	0	0	0	0.0	1	2	1	16	0	0	0	.120	.120
P	Terry Forster	L	63	19	10	0	0	0	0.0	1	3	1	2	1	1	1	.526	.526
P	Goose Gossage	R	36	16	0	0	0	0	0.0	0	0	0	11	0	0	0	.000	.000
P	Vicente Romo	R	28	9	0	0	0	0	0.0	0	0	0	2	0	0	0	.000	.000
P	Eddie Fisher	R	6	7	0	0	0	0	0.0	0	0	0	0	0	0	0	.000	.000
P	Cecilio Acosta	R	26	4	0	0	0	0	0.0	0	0	0	3	0	0	0	.000	.000
P	Steve Kealey	R	40	3	0	0	0	0	0.0	0	0	0	2	0	0	0	.000	.000
P	Moe Drabowsky	R	7	1	0	0	0	0	0.0	0	0	0	0	0	0	0	.000	.000
P	Phil Regan	R	10	1	1	0	0	0	0.0	0	0	0	0	0	1	1	1.000	1.000
P	Bart Johnson	R	9	1	0	0	0	0	0.0	0	0	0	0	0	0	0	.000	.000
P	Jim Geddes	R	6	1	0	0	0	0	0.0	1	0	0	0	0	0	0	.000	.000
P	Dan Neumeier	R	3	1	0	0	0	0	0.0	0	0	0	1	0	0	0	.000	.000
P	Denny O'Toole	R	3	0	0	0	0	0	–	0	0	0	0	0	0	0	–	–
P	Ken Frailing	L	4	0	0	0	0	0	–	0	0	0	0	0	0	0	–	–
TEAM TOTAL				5083	1208	170	28	108	2.1	566	528	511	991	100	174	43	.238	.346

INDIVIDUAL FIELDING

POS	Player	T	G	PO	A	E	DP	TCG	FA
1B	R. Allen	R	143	1234	67	7	94	9.1	.995
	T. Muser	L	29	135	7	2	12	5.0	.986
	M. Andrews	R	5	33	2	0	7	7.0	1.000
	C. May	R	5	32	2	1	0	7.0	.971
2B	M. Andrews	R	145	354	325	19	69	4.8	.973
	L. Alvarado	R	16	8	17	1	1	1.6	.962
	R. Morales	R	16	10	14	0	4	1.5	1.000
	J. Orta	R	14	20	26	2	8	3.4	.958
SS	R. Morales	R	86	120	213	11	32	4.0	.968
	L. Alvarado	R	81	98	213	14	28	4.0	.957
	J. Orta	R	18	28	41	3	13	4.0	.958
	R. Hernandez	R	6	10	16	0	3	4.3	1.000
	L. Richard	R	1	0	1	0	0	1.0	1.000
3B	E. Spiezio	R	74	67	172	12	11	3.4	.952
	B. Melton	R	56	47	125	12	12	3.3	.935
	W. Williams	R	1	0	0	0	0	0.0	.000
	R. Morales	R	14	3	21	0	2	1.7	1.000
	J. Orta	R	9	2	18	3	2	2.6	.870
	H. Allen	R	6	4	15	2	5	3.5	.905
	H. Yancy	R	3	2	6	0	2	2.7	1.000
	L. Alvarado	R	2	1	4	0	1	2.5	1.000
	R. Allen	R	2	1	2	0	0	1.5	1.000

POS	Player	T	G	PO	A	E	DP	TCG	FA
OF	C. May	R	145	215	13	4	2	1.6	.983
	P. Kelly	L	109	173	8	6	3	1.7	.968
	R. Reichardt	R	90	157	2	3	1	1.8	.981
	J. Johnstone	R	97	154	5	2	1	1.7	.988
	W. Williams	R	57	93	6	1	2	1.8	.990
	J. Lyttle	R	21	32	1	0	1	1.6	1.000
	B. Bradford	R	28	32	1	0	0	1.2	1.000
	T. Muser	L	1	0	0	0	0	0.0	.000
	L. Richard	R	6	8	1	0	1	1.5	1.000
	J. Qualls	R	1	3	0	0	0	3.0	1.000
C	E. Herrmann	R	112	641	69	8	10	6.4	.989
	T. Egan	R	46	257	19	4	2	6.1	.986
	C. Brinkman	R	33	118	11	2	3	4.0	.985

Chicago 1972

Dick Allen, one of the most hated but respected baseball players of the decade, joined the Sox on December 2, 1971. The Sox sacrificed Tommy John and Steve Huntz in one of the hardest trades of all time to evaluate. How can one categorize this trade as a failure for Chicago when Allen's presence helped keep the Sox solvent for three years? But do those three years offset the long-term loss of John?

The season belonged to Allen. He hit 37 home runs — none of them cheap — to establish a club home run mark that still stands. His personality conflicts were nonexistent in 1972, as he responded well to Chuck Tanner's patient understanding.

Bill Melton and Bart Johnson both suffered crippling injuries that limited their playing time in 1972. If they had been able to duplicate their successes of a year earlier, perhaps the Sox might have overtaken Oakland. But then, perhaps not. The A's were a solid veteran ballclub, the Sox a young team built around five players: Forster, May, Allen, Wood, and Bahnsen.

For five days in late August, the Sox sat atop the Western Division. Their late season surge was remarkable, as they had trailed Oakland by eight and a half games on July 19. Nobody really believed the Sox would steal a pennant that easily, and they didn't. But Dick Allen carried the season for the Sox. Who else but Dick Allen could hit two inside-the-park home runs in one game? Who else but Allen could win the coveted Most Valuable Player Award?

TEAM STATISTICS

	W	L	PCT	GB	R	OR	2B	3B	HR	BA	SA	SB	E	DP	FA	CG	BB	SO	ShO	SV	ERA
WEST																					
OAK	93	62	.600		604	457	195	29	134	.240	.366	87	130	146	.979	42	418	862	23	43	2.58
CHI	87	67	.565	5.5	566	538	170	28	108	.238	.346	100	135	136	.977	36	431	936	14	42	3.12
MIN	77	77	.500	15.5	537	535	182	31	93	.244	.344	53	159	133	.974	37	444	838	17	34	2.86
KC	76	78	.494	16.5	580	545	220	26	78	.255	.353	85	120	164	.980	44	405	801	16	28	3.24
CAL	75	80	.484	18	454	533	171	26	78	.242	.330	57	114	135	.981	57	620	1000	18	16	3.06
TEX	54	100	.351	38.5	461	628	166	17	56	.217	.290	126	166	147	.972	11	613	868	8	34	3.53
EAST																					
DET	86	70	.551		558	514	179	32	122	.237	.356	17	96	137	.984	46	465	952	11	33	2.96
BOS	85	70	.548	0.5	640	620	229	34	124	.248	.376	66	130	141	.978	48	512	918	20	25	3.47
BAL	80	74	.519	5	519	430	193	29	100	.229	.339	78	100	150	.983	62	395	788	20	21	2.54
NY	79	76	.510	6.5	557	527	201	24	103	.249	.357	71	134	179	.978	35	419	625	19	39	3.05
CLE	72	84	.462	14	472	519	187	18	91	.234	.330	49	116	157	.981	47	534	846	13	25	2.97
MIL	65	91	.417	21	493	595	167	22	88	.235	.328	64	139	145	.977	37	486	740	14	32	3.45
LEAGUE TOTAL					6441	6441	2260	316	1175	.239	.343	853	1539	1770	.979	502	5742	10174	193	372	3.07

INDIVIDUAL PITCHING

PITCHER	T	W	L	PCT	ERA	SV	G	GS	CG	IP	H	BB	SO	R	ER	ShO	H9	BB9	SO9
Wilbur Wood	L	24	17	.585	2.51	0	49	49	20	376.2	325	74	193	119	105	8	7.77	1.77	4.61
Tom Bradley	R	15	14	.517	2.98	0	40	40	11	260	225	65	209	94	86	2	7.79	2.25	7.23
Stan Bahnsen	R	21	16	.568	3.60	0	43	41	5	252.1	263	73	157	107	101	1	9.38	2.60	5.60
Terry Forster	L	6	5	.545	2.25	29	62	0	0	100	75	44	104	31	25	0	6.75	3.96	9.36
Dave Lemonds	L	4	7	.364	2.95	0	31	18	0	94.2	87	38	69	39	31	0	8.27	3.61	6.56
Goose Gossage	R	7	1	.875	4.28	2	36	1	0	80	72	44	57	44	38	0	8.10	4.95	6.41
Steve Kealey	R	3	2	.600	3.30	4	40	0	0	57.1	50	12	37	21	21	0	7.85	1.88	5.81
Vicente Romo	R	3	0	1.000	3.31	1	28	0	0	51.2	47	18	46	19	19	0	8.19	3.14	8.01
Cecilio Acosta	R	3	0	1.000	1.56	5	26	0	0	34.2	25	17	28	6	6	0	6.49	4.41	7.27
Eddie Fisher	R	0	1	.000	4.43	0	6	4	0	22.1	31	9	10	13	11	0	12.49	3.63	4.03
Bart Johnson	R	0	3	.000	9.22	1	9	0	0	13.2	18	13	9	20	14	0	11.85	8.56	5.93
Phil Regan	R	0	1	.000	4.05	0	10	0	0	13.1	18	6	4	7	6	0	12.15	4.05	2.70
Jim Geddes	R	0	0	—	6.97	0	5	1	0	10.1	12	10	3	9	8	0	10.45	8.71	2.61
Moe Drabowsky	R	0	0	—	2.45	0	7	0	0	7.1	6	2	4	2	2	0	7.36	2.45	4.91
Denny O'Toole	R	0	0	—	5.40	0	3	0	0	5	10	2	5	3	3	0	18.00	3.60	9.00
Dan Neumeier	R	0	0	—	7.36	0	3	0	0	3.2	2	3	0	3	3	0	4.91	7.36	0.00
Ken Frailing	L	1	0	1.000	3.00	0	4	0	0	3	3	1	1	1	1	0	9.00	3.00	3.00
TEAM TOTAL		87	67	.565	3.12	42	402	154	36	1386	1269	431	936	538	480	11	8.24	2.80	6.08

Chicago 1973　　Won 77　Lost 85　Pct. .475　15　　　170

MANAGER	W	L	PCT
Chuck Tanner	77	85	.475

POS	Player	B	G	AB	H	2B	3B	HR	HR%	R	RBI	BB	SO	SB	Pinch Hit AB	Pinch Hit H	BA	SA
REGULARS																		
1B	Tony Muser	L	109	309	88	14	3	4	1.3	38	30	33	36	8	9	4	.285	.388
2B	Jorge Orta	L	128	425	113	9	10	6	1.4	46	40	37	87	8	5	2	.266	.376
SS	Eddie Leon	R	127	399	91	10	3	3	0.8	37	30	34	103	1	2	0	.228	.291
3B	Bill Melton	R	152	561	155	29	1	20	3.6	85	87	75	66	4	0	0	.276	.439
RF	Pat Kelly	L	144	550	154	24	5	1	0.2	77	44	65	91	22	7	2	.280	.347
CF	John Jeter	R	89	299	72	14	4	7	2.3	39	26	9	74	5	8	1	.241	.385
LF	Bill Sharp	L	76	196	54	8	3	4	2.0	23	22	19	28	2	5	2	.276	.408
C	Ed Herrmann	L	119	379	85	17	1	10	2.6	42	39	31	55	2	2	0	.224	.354
DH	Carlos May	L	149	553	148	20	0	20	3.6	61	96	53	73	8	2	0	.268	.412
SUBSTITUTES																		
1B	Richie Allen	R	72	250	79	20	3	16	6.4	39	41	33	51	7	3	0	.316	.612
UT	Luis Alvarado	R	79	203	47	7	2	0	0.0	21	20	4	20	6	7	4	.232	.286
UT	Mike Andrews	R	53	159	32	9	0	0	0.0	10	10	23	28	0	6	0	.201	.258
SS	Bucky Dent	R	40	117	29	2	0	0	0.0	17	10	10	18	2	1	0	.248	.265
UT	Hank Allen	R	28	39	4	2	0	0	0.0	2	0	1	9	0	5	0	.103	.154
1B	Sam Ewing	L	11	20	3	1	0	0	0.0	1	2	2	6	0	5	1	.150	.200
32	Rich Morales	R	7	4	0	0	0	0	0.0	1	1	1	1	0	0	0	.000	.000
OD	Ken Henderson	B	73	262	68	13	0	6	2.3	31	32	27	49	3	1	1	.260	.378
UT	Jerry Hairston	B	60	210	57	11	1	0	0.0	25	23	33	30	0	2	0	.271	.333
OF	Buddy Bradford	R	53	168	40	3	1	8	4.8	24	15	17	43	4	5	0	.238	.411
OF	Rick Reichardt	R	46	153	42	8	1	3	2.0	15	16	8	29	2	6	2	.275	.399
UT	Brian Downing	R	34	73	13	1	0	2	2.7	4	4	10	17	0	8	2	.178	.274
C	Chuck Brinkman	R	63	139	26	6	0	1	0.7	13	10	11	37	0	0	0	.187	.252
C	Pete Varney	R	5	4	0	0	0	0	0.0	0	0	1	0	0	0	0	.000	.000
PH	Joe Keough	L	5	1	0	0	0	0	0.0	1	0	0	0	0	1	0	.000	.000
PITCHERS																		
P	Terry Forster	L	52	1	0	0	0	0	0.0	0	0	0	0	0	1	0	.000	.000
P	Cecilio Acosta	R	48	1	0	0	0	0	0.0	0	0	0	1	0	0	0	.000	.000
P	Stan Bahnsen	R	42	0	0	0	0	0	—	0	0	0	0	0	0	0	—	—
P	Dave Baldwin	R	3	0	0	0	0	0	—	0	0	0	0	0	0	0	—	—
P	Eddie Fisher	R	26	0	0	0	0	0	—	0	0	0	0	0	0	0	—	—
P	Jim Kaat	L	7	0	0	0	0	0	—	0	0	0	0	0	0	0	—	—
P	Jim McGlothlin	R	5	0	0	0	0	0	—	0	0	0	0	0	0	0	—	—
P	Wilbur Wood	R	49	0	0	0	0	0	—	0	0	0	0	0	0	0	—	—
P	Steve Kealey	R	7	0	0	0	0	0	—	0	0	0	0	0	0	0	—	—
P	Bart Johnson	R	22	0	0	0	0	0	—	0	0	0	0	0	0	0	—	—
P	Denny O'Toole	R	6	0	0	0	0	0	—	0	0	0	0	0	0	0	—	—
P	Steve Stone	R	36	0	0	0	0	0	—	0	0	0	0	0	0	0	—	—
P	Ken Frailing	L	10	0	0	0	0	0	—	0	0	0	0	0	0	0	—	—
P	Jim Geddes	R	6	0	0	0	0	0	—	0	0	0	0	0	0	0	—	—
P	Goose Gossage	R	20	0	0	0	0	0	—	0	0	0	0	0	0	0	—	—
TEAM TOTAL				5475	1400	228	38	111	2.0	652	598	537	952	84	91	21	.256	.372

INDIVIDUAL FIELDING

POS	Player	T	G	PO	A	E	DP	TCG	FA	POS	Player	T	G	PO	A	E	DP	TCG	FA
1B	T. Muser	L	89	680	38	6	70	8.1	.992	OF	P. Kelly	L	141	254	9	6	2	1.9	.978
	R. Allen	R	67	597	43	4	55	9.6	.994		B. Sharp	L	70	146	10	3	2	2.3	.981
	J. Hairston	L	19	130	10	1	11	7.4	.993		J. Jeter	R	72	144	3	7	0	2.1	.955
	M. Andrews	R	9	61	3	0	1	7.1	1.000		C. May	R	70	118	7	1	0	1.8	.992
	H. Allen	R	8	35	3	1	1	4.9	.974		B. Bradford	R	51	114	9	1	2	2.4	.992
	S. Ewing	R	4	34	4	0	7	9.5	1.000		K. Henderson	R	44	102	1	3	0	2.4	.972
	C. May	R	2	11	1	0	0	6.0	1.000		J. Hairston	L	33	64	3	4	0	2.2	.944
2B	J. Orta	R	122	254	300	18	75	4.7	.969		R. Reichardt	R	37	61	1	0	1	1.7	1.000
	L. Alvarado	R	45	90	107	4	24	4.5	.980		B. Downing	R	13	19	1	0	0	1.5	1.000
	M. Andrews	R	6	13	7	0	2	3.3	1.000		H. Allen	R	5	5	0	0	0	1.0	1.000
	E. Leon	R	3	4	10	0	2	4.7	1.000		T. Muser	L	2	1	0	0	0	0.5	1.000
	R. Allen	R	2	4	3	0	0	3.5	1.000	C	E. Herrmann	R	114	617	70	11	11	6.1	.984
	B. Dent	R	3	4	2	0	1	2.0	1.000		C. Brinkman	R	63	262	36	4	5	4.8	.987
	R. Morales	R	2	2	2	0	0	2.0	1.000		H. Allen	R	1	0	0	0	0	0.0	.000
	H. Allen	R	1	1	0	0	0	1.0	1.000		B. Downing	R	11	46	7	1	0	4.9	.981
SS	E. Leon	R	122	198	382	17	78	4.7	.972		P. Varney	R	5	10	0	0	0	2.0	1.000
	B. Dent	R	36	51	132	7	22	5.3	.963										
	L. Alvarado	R	18	20	38	4	6	3.4	.935										
	J. Orta	R	1	1	1	0	0	2.0	1.000										
3B	B. Melton	R	151	115	347	23	31	3.2	.953										
	B. Dent	R	1	0	0	0	0	0.0	.000										
	L. Alvarado	R	10	10	13	1	1	2.4	.958										
	B. Downing	R	8	7	9	4	0	2.5	.800										
	H. Allen	R	9	1	9	0	0	1.1	1.000										
	M. Andrews	R	5	7	2	0	0	1.8	1.000										
	R. Morales	R	5	1	3	0	0	0.8	1.000										

Injuries, all 38 of them, robbed the Sox of the middle of their lineup for most of the year. Allen fractured a kneecap on June 28 and was out for the year. There went the Sox' season, as a fine 27–15 start was wasted.

The controversy this year centered on Allen himself. Mike Andrews, Rick Reichardt, and Stan Bahnsen saw a few reasons why they should improve their own salaries. They viewed Allen's big contract with some chagrin, especially after he talked Sox officials into allowing his brother Hank to remain on the roster so Hank could qualify for baseball's pension plan. Reichardt was released, but Bahnsen came to terms. "How could that guy win 21 games in 1972?" Ralph Houk wanted to know. Pitching on two days' rest for much of the season, Wood and Bahnsen each *lost* 20 in '73.

Roland Hemond succeeded to the general manager's chair after Stu Holcomb resigned on July 27. There had been a falling out between employer and employee, and John Allyn sided with Hemond and Tanner in the power struggle.

The Sox sank like a rock in July and August, partly due to the shortage of starting pitching. Wilbur Wood was showing signs of fatigue. Rather than shore up this problem area, the Sox acquired Ron Santo from the Cubs on December 11. They now had two third basemen but still just two pitchers.

TEAM STATISTICS

	W	L	PCT	GB	R	OR	2B	3B	HR	BA	SA	SB	E	DP	FA	CG	BB	SO	ShO	SV	ERA
WEST																					
OAK	94	68	.580		758	615	216	28	147	.260	.389	4	137	170	.978	46	494	797	16	41	3.29
KC	88	74	.543	6	754	752	239	40	114	.261	.381	105	167	192	.974	40	617	791	7	41	4.21
MIN	81	81	.500	13	738	692	240	44	120	**.270**	.393	87	139	147	.978	48	519	880	18	34	3.77
CAL	79	83	.488	15	629	657	183	29	93	.253	.348	59	156	153	.975	72	614	1010	13	19	3.57
CHI	77	85	.475	17	652	705	228	38	111	.256	.372	84	144	165	.977	48	574	848	15	35	3.87
TEX	57	105	.352	37	619	844	195	29	110	.255	.361	91	161	164	.974	35	680	831	10	27	4.64
EAST																					
BAL	97	65	.599		754	**561**	230	**48**	119	.266	.390	**146**	119	184	.981	67	475	715	14	26	**3.08**
BOS	89	73	.549	8	738	647	235	30	147	.267	**.401**	114	127	162	.979	67	499	808	10	33	3.65
DET	85	77	.525	12	642	674	213	32	157	.254	.390	28	**112**	144	**.982**	39	493	911	11	**46**	3.90
NY	80	82	.494	17	641	610	213	17	131	.261	.378	45	156	172	.976	47	457	708	16	39	3.33
MIL	74	88	.457	23	708	731	229	40	145	.253	.388	110	145	167	.977	50	623	671	11	28	3.98
CLE	71	91	.438	26	679	826	205	29	**158**	.256	.387	60	139	174	.978	55	602	883	9	21	4.58
LEAGUE TOTAL					8312	8314	2626	404	1552	.259	.381	933	1702	1994	.977	614	6647	9853	150	390	3.82

INDIVIDUAL PITCHING

PITCHER	T	W	L	PCT	ERA	SV	G	GS	CG	IP	H	BB	SO	R	ER	ShO	H9	BB9	SO9
Wilbur Wood	L	24	20	.545	3.46	0	49	**48**	21	359.1	**381**	91	199	**166**	**138**	4	9.54	2.28	4.98
Stan Bahnsen	R	18	21	.462	3.57	0	42	42	14	282.1	290	117	120	128	112	4	9.24	3.73	3.83
Steve Stone	R	6	11	.353	4.29	1	36	22	3	176.1	163	82	138	87	84	0	8.32	4.19	7.04
Terry Forster	L	6	11	.353	3.23	16	51	12	4	172.2	174	78	120	69	62	0	9.07	4.07	6.25
Eddie Fisher	R	6	7	.462	4.88	0	26	16	2	110.2	135	38	57	64	60	0	10.98	3.09	4.64
Cecilio Acosta	R	10	6	.625	2.23	18	48	0	0	97	66	39	60	30	24	0	6.12	3.62	5.57
Bart Johnson	R	3	3	.500	4.13	0	22	9	0	80.2	76	40	56	39	37	0	8.48	4.46	6.25
Goose Gossage	R	0	4	.000	7.43	0	20	4	1	49.2	57	37	33	44	41	0	10.33	6.70	5.98
Jim Kaat	L	4	1	.800	4.22	0	7	7	3	42.2	44	4	16	23	20	1	9.28	0.84*	3.38
Jim McGlothlin	R	0	1	.000	3.93	0	5	1	0	18.1	13	13	14	8	8	0	6.38	6.38	6.87
Ken Frailing	L	0	0	–	1.96	0	10	0	0	18.1	18	7	15	6	4	0	8.84	3.44	7.36
Denny O'Toole	R	0	0	–	5.29	0	6	0	0	17	23	3	8	11	10	0	12.18	1.59	4.24
Jim Geddes	R	0	0	–	2.87	0	6	1	0	15.2	13	14	7	6	5	0	7.47	8.04	4.02
Steve Kealey	R	0	0	–	15.09	0	7	0	0	11.1	23	7	4	22	19	0	18.26	5.56	3.18
Dave Baldwin	R	0	0	–	3.60	0	3	0	0	5	7	4	1	2	2	0	12.60	7.20	1.80
TEAM TOTAL		77	85	.475	3.87	35	338	162	48	1457	1483	574	848	705	626	9	9.16	3.55	5.24

Chicago 1974 Won 80 Lost 80 Pct. .500 14

MANAGER	W	L	PCT
Chuck Tanner	80	80	.500

POS	Player	B	G	AB	H	2B	3B	HR	HR%	R	RBI	BB	SO	SB	Pinch Hit AB	H	BA	SA
REGULARS																		
1B	Richie Allen	R	128	462	139	23	1	32	6.9	84	88	57	89	7	4	0	.301	.563
2B	Jorge Orta	L	139	525	166	31	2	10	1.9	73	67	40	88	9	7	1	.316	.440
SS	Bucky Dent	R	154	496	136	15	3	5	1.0	55	45	28	48	3	0	0	.274	.347
3B	Bill Melton	R	136	495	120	17	0	21	4.2	63	63	59	60	3	1	0	.242	.404
RF	Bill Sharp	L	100	320	81	13	2	4	1.3	45	24	25	37	0	3	1	.253	.344
CF	Ken Henderson	B	162	602	176	35	5	20	3.3	76	95	66	112	12	0	0	.292	.467
LF	Carlos May	L	149	551	137	19	2	8	1.5	66	58	46	76	8	10	0	.249	.334
C	Ed Herrmann	L	107	367	95	13	1	10	2.7	32	39	16	49	1	0	0	.259	.381
DH	Pat Kelly	L	122	424	119	16	3	4	0.9	60	21	46	58	18	3	0	.281	.361
SUBSTITUTES																		
UT	Ron Santo	R	117	375	83	12	1	5	1.3	29	41	37	72	0	5	3	.221	.299
1B	Tony Muser	L	103	206	60	5	1	1	0.5	16	18	6	22	1	13	3	.291	.340
UT	Lee Richard	R	32	67	11	1	0	0	0.0	5	1	5	8	0	0	0	.164	.179
S2	Eddie Leon	R	31	46	5	1	0	0	0.0	1	3	2	12	0	0	0	.109	.130
3B	Bill Stein	R	13	43	12	1	0	0	0.0	5	5	7	8	0	6	0	.279	.302
1D	Lamar Johnson	R	10	29	10	0	0	0	0.0	1	2	0	3	0	0	0	.345	.345
UT	Luis Alvarado	R	8	10	1	0	0	0	0.0	1	0	0	1	0	1	0	.100	.100
DH	Hugh Yancy	R	1	0	0	0	0	0	—	0	0	0	0	0	0	0	—	—
OD	Jerry Hairston	B	45	109	25	7	0	0	0.0	8	8	13	18	0	12	2	.229	.294
OF	Buddy Bradford	R	39	96	32	2	0	5	5.2	16	10	13	11	1	7	2	.333	.510
OF	Nyls Nyman	L	5	14	9	2	1	0	0.0	5	4	0	1	1	1	1	.643	.929
CO	Brian Downing	R	108	293	66	12	1	10	3.4	41	39	51	72	0	5	0	.225	.375
C	Pete Varney	R	9	28	7	0	0	0	0.0	1	2	1	8	0	0	0	.250	.250
C	Chuck Brinkman	R	8	14	2	0	0	0	0.0	1	0	1	3	0	0	0	.143	.143
PITCHERS																		
P	Cecilio Acosta	R	27	2	0	0	0	0	0.0	0	0	0	2	0	0	0	.000	.000
P	Jim Kaat	L	42	1	0	0	0	0	0.0	0	0	0	0	0	0	0	.000	.000
P	Ken Tatum	R	10	1	0	0	0	0	0.0	0	0	0	0	0	0	0	.000	.000
P	Joe Henderson	R	5	1	0	0	0	0	0.0	0	0	0	0	0	0	0	.000	.000
P	Stan Bahnsen	R	38	0	0	0	0	0	—	0	0	0	0	0	0	0	—	—
P	Wilbur Wood	R	42	0	0	0	0	0	—	0	0	0	0	0	0	0	—	—
P	Wayne Granger	R	5	0	0	0	0	0	—	0	0	0	0	0	0	0	—	—
P	Bart Johnson	R	18	0	0	0	0	0	—	0	0	0	0	0	0	0	—	—
P	Lloyd Allen	R	6	0	0	0	0	0	—	0	0	0	0	0	0	0	—	—
P	Francisco Barrios	R	2	0	0	0	0	0	—	0	0	0	0	0	0	0	—	—
P	Jack Kucek	R	9	0	0	0	0	0	—	0	0	0	0	0	0	0	—	—
P	Carl Moran	R	15	0	0	0	0	0	—	0	0	0	0	0	0	0	—	—
P	Jim Otten	R	5	0	0	0	0	0	—	0	0	0	0	0	0	0	—	—
P	Terry Forster	L	59	0	0	0	0	0	—	0	0	0	0	0	0	0	—	—
P	Stan Perzanowski	R	2	0	0	0	0	0	—	0	0	0	0	0	0	0	—	—
P	Skip Pitlock	L	40	0	0	0	0	0	—	0	0	0	0	0	0	0	—	—
P	Goose Gossage	R	39	0	0	0	0	0	—	0	0	0	0	0	0	0	—	—
TEAM TOTAL				5577	1492	225	23	135	2.4	684	633	519	858	64	78	13	.268	.389

INDIVIDUAL FIELDING

POS	Player	T	G	PO	A	E	DP	TCG	FA
1B	R. Allen	R	125	998	49	15	112	8.5	.986
	T. Muser	L	80	419	13	1	46	5.4	.998
	L. Johnson	R	7	40	2	0	8	6.0	1.000
	R. Santo	R	3	13	0	0	3	4.3	1.000
2B	J. Orta	R	123	297	313	18	93	5.1	.971
	R. Santo	R	39	97	99	6	40	5.2	.970
	E. Leon	R	7	20	14	1	10	5.0	.971
	L. Richard	R	3	2	6	0	2	2.7	1.000
	L. Alvarado	R	1	1	4	0	1	5.0	1.000
	R. Allen	R	1	0	1	1	0	2.0	.500
SS	B. Dent	R	154	251	499	22	108	5.0	.972
	E. Leon	R	21	17	33	2	8	2.5	.962
	R. Santo	R	1	0	0	0	0	0.0	.000
	J. Orta	R	3	0	0	0	0	0.0	.000
	L. Richard	R	6	7	15	0	7	3.7	1.000
	L. Alvarado	R	4	2	2	0	0	1.5	.667
3B	B. Melton	R	123	100	272	24	29	3.2	.939
	R. Santo	R	28	25	49	2	6	2.7	.974
	L. Alvarado	R	1	0	0	0	0	0.0	.000
	B. Stein	R	11	7	20	4	0	2.8	.871
	L. Richard	R	12	4	19	5	2	2.3	.821
	E. Leon	R	2	0	2	0	0	1.0	1.000
OF	K. Henderson	R	162	462	7	6	3	2.9	.987
	C. May	R	129	245	11	3	1	2.0	.988
	B. Sharp	L	99	210	3	3	0	2.2	.986
	P. Kelly	L	53	79	2	2	2	1.6	.976
	B. Downing	R	39	59	2	0	2	1.6	1.000
	B. Bradford	R	32	47	2	1	0	1.6	.980
	J. Hairston	L	22	24	1	2	0	1.2	.926
	N. Nyman	L	3	6	1	0	1	2.3	1.000
	L. Richard	R	1	1	0	0	0	1.0	1.000
C	E. Herrmann	R	107	561	55	8	5	5.8	.987
	B. Downing	R	63	278	28	2	3	4.9	.994
	P. Varney	R	9	47	5	1	0	5.9	.000
	C. Brinkman	R	8	19	1	0	0	2.5	1.000

Chicago 1974

There was no shortage of power this time around, as the Sox led the American League in home runs for the first time ever. Allen, Melton, and Ken Henderson provided the thrills, but the team was not the strongest in club history, as Chuck Tanner had boldly stated in spring training.

The season is remembered for several reasons. Once again, Dick Allen was on center stage. He led the league in home runs, but his play in the second half of the season was lackadaisical. In one September game, Allen forgot how many outs there were. Finally, on the 14th of that month, he resigned with one year remaining on his $250,000 contract. The reasons given were vague. Perhaps the six horses he had quartered at Arlington Park were more interesting to him than trying to help the Sox win games.

Jim Kaat's sizzling September helped to ease the pain a bit. In that month the Minnesota castoff won his last seven decisions while posting a 0.31 earned run average. Not bad for a pitcher whose arm was first pronounced dead in 1967.

Despite Kaat, Wood, and a fine showing by Bart Johnson, the staff was weak. It was a telling factor, as the divisional and world champion Oakland A's were next to last in hitting but first in pitching. The White Sox were a near reversal of that and were probably fortunate to finish the season in fourth.

TEAM STATISTICS

	W	L	PCT	GB	R	OR	2B	3B	HR	BA	SA	SB	E	DP	FA	CG	BB	SO	ShO	SV	ERA
WEST																					
OAK	90	72	.556		689	551	205	37	132	.247	.373	164	141	154	.977	49	430	755	12	28	2.95
TEX	84	76	.525	5	690	698	198	39	99	.272	.377	113	163	164	.974	62	449	871	16	12	3.82
MIN	82	80	.506	8	673	669	190	37	111	.272	.378	74	151	164	.976	43	513	934	11	29	3.64
CHI	80	80	.500	9	684	721	225	23	135	.268	.389	64	147	188	.977	55	548	826	11	29	3.94
KC	77	85	.475	13	667	662	232	42	89	.259	.364	146	152	166	.976	54	482	731	14	17	3.51
CAL	68	94	.420	22	618	657	203	31	95	.254	.356	119	147	150	.977	64	649	986	13	12	3.52
EAST																					
BAL	91	71	.562	.	659	612	226	27	116	.256	.370	145	128	174	.980	57	480	701	16	25	3.27
NY	89	73	.549	2	671	623	220	30	101	.263	.368	53	142	158	.977	53	528	829	13	24	3.31
BOS	84	78	.519	7	696	661	236	31	109	.264	.377	104	145	156	.977	71	463	751	12	18	3.72
CLE	77	85	.475	14	662	694	201	19	131	.255	.370	79	146	157	.977	45	479	650	8	27	3.80
MIL	76	86	.469	15	647	660	228	49	120	.244	.369	106	127	168	.980	43	493	621	11	24	3.77
DET	72	90	.444	19	620	768	200	35	131	.247	.366	67	158	155	.975	54	621	869	7	15	4.17
LEAGUE TOTAL					7976	7976	2564	400	1369	.258	.371	1234	1747	1954	.977	650	6135	9524	144	260	3.62

INDIVIDUAL PITCHING

PITCHER	T	W	L	PCT	ERA	SV	G	GS	CG	IP	H	BB	SO	R	ER	ShO	H9	BB9	SO9
Wilbur Wood	L	20	19	.513	3.60	0	42	42	22	320	305	80	169	143	128	1	8.58	2.25	4.75
Jim Kaat	L	21	13	.618	2.92	0	42	39	15	277	263	63	142	106	90	3	8.55	2.05	4.61
Stan Bahnsen	R	12	15	.444	4.71	0	38	35	10	216	230	110	102	128	113	1	9.58	4.58	4.25
Terry Forster	L	7	8	.467	3.63	24	59	1	0	134	120	48	105	57	54	0	8.06	3.22	7.05
Bart Johnson	R	10	4	.714	2.73	0	18	18	8	122	105	32	76	42	37	2	7.75	2.36	5.61
Skip Pitlock	L	3	3	.500	4.42	1	40	5	0	106	103	55	68	58	52	0	8.75	4.67	5.77
Goose Gossage	R	4	6	.400	4.15	1	39	3	0	89	92	47	64	45	41	0	9.30	4.75	6.47
Carl Moran	R	1	3	.250	4.70	0	15	5	0	46	57	23	17	27	24	0	11.15	4.50	3.33
Cecilio Acosta	R	0	3	.000	3.72	3	27	0	0	46	43	18	19	22	19	0	8.41	3.52	3.72
Jack Kucek	R	1	4	.200	5.21	0	9	7	0	38	48	21	25	25	22	0	11.37	4.97	5.92
Ken Tatum	R	0	0	—	4.71	0	10	1	0	21	23	9	5	12	11	0	9.86	3.86	2.14
Jim Otten	R	0	1	.000	5.63	0	5	1	0	16	22	12	11	11	10	0	12.38	6.75	6.19
Joe Henderson	R	1	0	1.000	8.40	4	5	3	0	15	21	11	12	15	14	0	12.60	6.60	7.20
Wayne Granger	R	0	0	—	7.88	0	5	0	0	8	16	3	4	8	7	0	18.00	3.38	4.50
Lloyd Allen	R	0	1	.000	10.29	0	6	2	0	7	7	12	3	9	8	0	9.00	15.43	3.86
Francisco Barrios	R	0	0	—	27.00	0	2	0	0	2	7	2	2	6	6	0	31.50	9.00	9.00
Stan Perzanowski	R	0	0	—	22.50	0	2	1	0	2	8	2	2	7	5	0	36.00	9.00	9.00
TEAM TOTAL		80	80	.500	3.94	29	364	163	55	1465	1470	548	826	721	641	7	9.03	3.37	5.07

Chicago 1975 Won 75 Lost 86 Pct .466 15

MANAGER	W	L	PCT
Chuck Tanner	75	86	.466

POS	Player	B	G	AB	H	2B	3B	HR	HR%	R	RBI	BB	SO	SB	Pinch Hit AB	H	BA	SA
REGULARS																		
1B	Carlos May	L	128	454	123	19	2	8	1.8	55	53	67	46	12	1	0	.271	.374
2B	Jorge Orta	L	140	542	165	26	10	11	2.0	64	83	48	67	16	3	2	.304	.450
SS	Bucky Dent	R	157	602	159	29	4	3	0.5	52	58	36	48	0	0	0	.264	.341
3B	Bill Melton	R	149	512	123	16	0	15	2.9	62	70	78	106	2	0	0	.240	.359
RF	Pat Kelly	L	133	471	129	21	7	9	1.9	73	45	58	69	18	5	1	.274	.406
CF	Nyls Nyman	L	106	327	74	6	3	2	0.6	36	28	11	34	10	3	1	.226	.281
LF	Ken Henderson	B	140	513	129	20	3	9	1.8	65	53	74	65	5	3	1	.251	.355
C	Brian Downing	R	138	420	101	12	1	7	1.7	58	41	76	75	13	0	0	.240	.324
DH	Deron Johnson	R	148	555	129	25	1	18	3.2	66	72	48	117	0	3	2	.232	.378
SUBSTITUTES																		
UT	Bill Stein	R	76	226	61	7	1	3	1.3	23	21	18	32	2	6	0	.270	.350
1B	Tony Muser	L	43	111	27	3	0	0	0.0	11	6	7	8	2	3	0	.243	.270
1B	Mike Squires	L	20	65	15	0	0	0	0.0	5	4	8	5	3	0	0	.231	.231
UT	Lee Richard	R	43	45	9	0	1	0	0.0	11	5	4	7	2	0	0	.200	.244
UT	Chet Lemon	R	9	35	9	2	0	0	0.0	2	1	2	6	1	1	0	.257	.314
1D	Lamar Johnson	R	8	30	6	3	0	1	3.3	2	1	1	5	0	1	0	.200	.400
D1	Gerry Moses	R	2	2	1	0	1	0	0.0	1	0	0	0	0	0	0	.500	1.500
OF	Jerry Hairston	B	69	219	62	8	0	0	0.0	26	23	46	23	1	3	0	.283	.320
OF	Bob Coluccio	R	61	161	33	4	2	4	2.5	22	13	13	34	4	4	0	.205	.329
OF	Buddy Bradford	R	25	58	9	3	1	2	3.4	8	15	8	22	3	4	0	.155	.345
OF	Bill Sharp	L	18	35	7	0	0	0	0.0	1	4	2	3	0	7	1	.200	.200
C	Pete Varney	R	36	107	29	5	1	2	1.9	12	8	6	28	2	3	0	.271	.393
PITCHERS																		
P	Stan Bahnsen	R	12	0	0	0	0	0	—	0	0	0	0	0	0	0	—	—
P	Jim Kaat	L	43	0	0	0	0	0	—	0	0	0	0	0	0	0	—	—
P	Claude Osteen	L	37	0	0	0	0	0	—	0	0	0	0	0	0	0	—	—
P	Cecil Upshaw	R	29	0	0	0	0	0	—	0	0	0	0	0	0	0	—	—
P	Wilbur Wood	R	43	0	0	0	0	0	—	0	0	0	0	2	0	0	—	—
P	Lloyd Allen	R	3	0	0	0	0	0	—	0	0	0	0	0	0	0	—	—
P	Jack Kucek	R	2	0	0	0	0	0	—	0	0	0	0	0	0	0	—	—
P	Jim Otten	R	2	0	0	0	0	0	—	0	0	0	0	0	0	0	—	—
P	Rick Sawyer	R	4	0	0	0	0	0	—	0	0	0	0	0	0	0	—	—
P	Chris Knapp	R	2	0	0	0	0	0	—	0	0	0	0	0	0	0	—	—
P	Ken Kravec	L	2	0	0	0	0	0	—	0	0	0	0	0	0	0	—	—
P	Danny Osborn	R	24	0	0	0	0	0	—	0	0	0	0	0	0	0	—	—
P	Tim Stoddard	R	1	0	0	0	0	0	—	0	0	0	0	0	0	0	—	—
P	Pete Vuckovich	R	4	0	0	0	0	0	—	0	0	0	0	0	0	0	—	—
P	Terry Forster	L	17	0	0	0	0	0	—	0	0	0	0	0	0	0	—	—
P	Bill Gogolewski	L	19	0	0	0	0	0	—	0	0	0	0	0	0	0	—	—
P	Rich Hinton	L	15	0	0	0	0	0	—	0	0	0	0	0	0	0	—	—
P	Skip Pitlock	L	1	0	0	0	0	0	—	0	0	0	0	0	0	0	—	—
P	Goose Gossage	R	62	0	0	0	0	0	—	0	0	0	0	0	0	0	—	—
P	Dave Hamilton	L	30	0	0	0	0	0	—	0	0	0	0	0	0	0	—	—
P	Jesse Jefferson	R	22	0	0	0	0	0	—	0	0	0	0	0	0	0	—	—
TEAM TOTAL				5490	1400	209	38	94	1.7	655	604	611	800	101	50	8	.255	.358

INDIVIDUAL FIELDING

POS	Player	T	G	PO	A	E	DP	TCG	FA
1B	C. May	R	63	508	46	6	54	8.9	.989
	D. Johnson	R	55	456	24	3	38	8.8	.994
	T. Muser	L	41	263	22	2	35	7.0	.993
	M. Squires	L	20	155	12	2	14	8.5	.988
	L. Johnson	R	6	46	2	2	4	8.3	.960
	G. Moses	R	1	1	0	0	0	1.0	1.000
2B	J. Orta	R	135	354	354	16	95	5.4	.978
	B. Stein	R	28	71	79	4	16	5.5	.974
	L. Richard	R	5	7	3	2	0	2.4	.833
SS	B. Dent	R	157	279	543	16	105	5.3	.981
	L. Richard	R	9	8	19	1	3	3.1	.964
3B	B. Melton	R	138	131	313	26	23	3.4	.945
	B. Stein	R	24	16	39	5	5	2.5	.917
	L. Richard	R	12	5	11	0	0	1.3	1.000
	C. Lemon	R	6	5	7	1	0	2.2	.923
OF	K. Henderson	R	137	394	7	4	0	3.0	.990
	P. Kelly	L	115	222	4	2	1	2.0	.991
	N. Nyman	R	94	177	6	8	0	2.0	.958
	J. Hairston	L	59	111	6	6	1	2.1	.951
	B. Coluccio	R	59	92	4	2	0	1.7	.980
	C. May	R	46	72	6	2	1	1.7	.975
	B. Bradford	R	18	27	1	1	0	1.6	.966
	C. Lemon	R	1	0	0	0	0	0.0	.000
	B. Stein	R	1	0	0	0	0	0.0	.000
	B. Sharp	L	14	16	0	1	0	1.2	.941
C	B. Downing	R	137	730	84	8	5	6.0	.990
	P. Varney	R	34	151	14	2	1	4.9	.988

Chicago 1975

Four players from the White Sox made the All-Star team: Bucky Dent, Jim Kaat, Rich Gossage, and Jorge Orta. But this was a team in turmoil, both on and off the field. Bill Melton was benched in June after he failed to lift his batting average over .230. He was Harry Caray's favorite target, as the players and the announcer formed two warring camps; not a unique experience in White Sox annals.

With the Sox resting comfortably in last place on June 15, Roland Hemond pulled off perhaps his best trade. Stan Bahnsen and Skip Pitlock were sent to Oakland for Dave Hamilton and Chet Lemon. An interesting footnote to this trade was Rich McKinney. McKinney had been traded to the Yankees for Bahnsen in 1971. Later, Chet Lemon was traded to Detroit for Steve Kemp. In essence, the Sox got Bahnsen, Hamilton, Lemon, and Kemp for Rich McKinney, whose career batting average wound up at .225.

In June, John Allyn announced that he would entertain offers for the club, but there were few takers for a team that had lost eight million dollars since 1970. With Allyn in danger of not meeting his September payroll, Bill Veeck rode into town. With the club rumored to be heading to Seattle, American League owners turned down Veeck's bid but gave him one extra week to re-capitalize. No one believed that he could raise an extra $1.2 million, but he did just that. A week later, Paul Richards was named manager, and Veeck hung out a sign at the baseball winter meetings. It said "Open for Business."

TEAM STATISTICS

	W	L	PCT	GB	R	OR	2B	3B	HR	BA	SA	SB	E	DP	FA	CG	BB	SO	ShO	SV	ERA
WEST																					
OAK	98	64	.605		758	606	220	33	151	.254	.391	183	143	140	.977	36	523	784	10	44	3.29
KC	91	71	.562	7	710	649	263	58	118	.261	.394	155	154	151	.976	52	498	815	11	25	3.49
TEX	79	83	.488	19	714	733	208	17	134	.256	.371	102	191	173	.971	60	518	792	16	17	3.90
MIN	76	83	.478	20.5	724	736	215	28	121	.271	.386	81	170	147	.973	57	617	846	7	22	4.05
CHI	75	86	.466	22.5	655	703	209	38	94	.255	.358	101	140	155	.978	34	657	802	7	39	3.94
CAL	72	89	.447	25.5	628	723	195	41	55	.246	.328	220	184	164	.971	59	613	975	19	16	3.89
EAST																					
BOS	95	65	.594		796	709	284	44	134	.275	.417	66	139	142	.977	62	490	720	11	31	3.99
BAL	90	69	.566	4.5	682	553	224	33	124	.252	.373	104	107	175	.983	70	500	717	19	21	3.17
NY	83	77	.519	12	681	588	230	39	110	.264	.382	102	135	148	.978	70	502	809	11	20	3.29
CLE	79	80	.497	15.5	688	703	201	25	153	.261	.392	106	134	156	.978	37	599	800	6	32	3.84
MIL	68	94	.420	28	675	792	242	34	146	.250	.389	65	180	162	.971	36	624	643	10	34	4.34
DET	57	102	.358	37.5	570	786	171	39	125	.249	.366	63	173	141	.972	52	533	787	10	17	4.29
LEAGUE TOTAL					8281	8281	2662	429	1465	.258	.379	1348	1850	1854	.975	625	6674	9490	137	318	3.79

INDIVIDUAL PITCHING

PITCHER	T	W	L	PCT	ERA	SV	G	GS	CG	IP	H	BB	SO	R	ER	ShO	H9	BB9	SO9
Jim Kaat	L	20	14	.588	3.11	0	43	41	12	303.2	321	77	142	121	105	1	9.51	2.28	4.21
Wilbur Wood	L	16	20	.444	4.11	0	43	43	14	291.1	309	92	140	148	133	2	9.55	2.84	4.32
Claude Osteen	L	7	16	.304	4.36	0	37	37	5	204.1	237	92	63	110	99	0	10.44	4.05	2.77
Goose Gossage	R	9	8	.529	1.84	26	62	0	0	141.2	99	70	130	32	29	0	6.29	4.45	8.26
Jesse Jefferson	R	5	9	.357	5.10	0	22	21	1	107.2	100	94	67	69	61	0	8.36	7.86	5.60
Dave Hamilton	L	6	5	.545	2.84	6	30	1	0	69.2	63	29	51	23	22	0	8.14	3.75	6.59
Stan Bahnsen	R	4	6	.400	6.01	4	12	12	2	67.1	78	40	31	49	45	0	10.43	5.35	4.14
Danny Osborn	R	3	0	1.000	4.50	0	24	0	0	58	57	37	38	29	29	0	8.84	5.74	5.90
Bill Gogolewski	R	0	0	—	5.24	2	19	0	0	55	61	28	37	35	32	0	9.98	4.58	6.05
Cecil Upshaw	R	1	1	.500	3.23	1	29	0	0	47.1	49	21	22	19	17	0	9.32	3.99	4.18
Rich Hinton	L	1	0	1.000	4.82	0	15	0	0	37.1	41	15	30	22	20	0	9.88	3.62	7.23
Terry Forster	L	3	3	.500	2.19	4	17	1	0	37	30	24	32	12	9	0	7.30	5.84	7.78
Pete Vuckovich	R	0	1	.000	13.06	0	4	2	0	10.1	17	7	5	15	15	0	14.81	6.10	4.35
Rick Sawyer	R	0	0	—	3.00	0	4	0	0	6	7	2	3	4	2	0	10.50	3.00	4.50
Lloyd Allen	R	0	2	.000	11.81	0	3	2	0	5.1	8	6	2	7	7	0	13.50	10.13	3.38
Jim Otten	R	0	0	—	6.75	0	2	0	0	5.1	4	7	3	5	4	0	6.75	11.81	5.06
Ken Kravec	L	0	1	.000	6.23	0	2	1	0	4.1	1	8	1	3	3	0	2.08	16.62	2.08
Jack Kucek	R	0	0	—	4.91	0	2	0	0	3.2	9	4	2	2	2	0	22.09	9.82	4.91
Chris Knapp	R	0	0	—	4.50	0	2	0	0	2	2	4	3	1	1	0	9.00	18.00	13.50
Tim Stoddard	R	0	0	—	9.00	0	1	0	0	1	2	0	0	1	1	0	18.00	0.00	0.00
TEAM TOTAL		75	86	.466	3.93	39	373	161	34	1458.1	1495	657	802	703	636	3	9.23	4.05	4.95

Chicago 1976   Won 64 Lost 97 Pct .398 16   176

MANAGER	W	L	PCT
Paul Richards	64	97	.398

POS	Player	B	G	AB	H	2B	3B	HR	HR%	R	RBI	BB	SO	SB	Pinch Hit AB	H	BA	SA
REGULARS																		
1B	Jim Spencer	L	150	518	131	13	2	14	2.7	53	70	49	52	6	4	0	.253	.367
2B	Jack Brohamer	L	119	354	89	12	2	7	2.0	33	40	44	28	1	1	0	.251	.356
SS	Bucky Dent	R	158	562	138	18	4	2	0.4	44	52	43	45	3	1	0	.246	.302
3B	Kevin Bell	R	68	230	57	7	6	5	2.2	24	20	18	56	2	1	0	.248	.396
RF	Jorge Orta	L	158	636	174	29	8	14	2.2	74	72	38	77	24	3	0	.274	.410
CF	Chet Lemon	R	132	451	111	15	5	4	0.9	46	38	28	65	13	1	0	.246	.328
LF	Ralph Garr	L	136	527	158	22	6	4	0.8	63	36	17	41	14	5	2	.300	.387
C	Brian Downing	R	104	317	81	14	0	3	0.9	38	30	40	55	7	3	1	.256	.328
DH	Pat Kelly	L	107	311	79	20	3	5	1.6	42	34	45	45	15	20	7	.254	.386
SUBSTITUTES																		
23	Bill Stein	R	117	392	105	15	2	4	1.0	32	36	22	67	4	8	2	.268	.347
D1	Lamar Johnson	R	82	222	71	11	1	4	1.8	29	33	19	37	2	18	4	.320	.432
DH	Sam Ewing	L	19	41	9	2	1	0	0.0	3	2	2	8	0	8	3	.220	.317
2B	Hugh Yancy	R	3	10	1	1	0	0	0.0	0	0	0	3	0	0	0	.100	.200
DH	Minnie Minoso	R	3	8	1	0	0	0	0.0	0	0	0	2	0	0	0	.125	.125
OF	Buddy Bradford	R	55	160	35	5	2	4	2.5	20	14	19	37	6	9	0	.219	.350
UT	Alan Bannister	R	73	145	36	6	2	0	0.0	19	8	14	21	12	2	0	.248	.317
OF	Jerry Hairston	B	44	119	27	2	2	0	0.0	20	10	24	19	1	4	1	.227	.277
OF	Rich Coggins	L	32	96	15	2	0	0	0.0	4	5	6	15	3	4	1	.156	.177
OD	Carlos May	L	20	63	11	2	0	0	0.0	7	3	9	5	4	6	0	.175	.206
UT	Wayne Nordhagen	R	22	53	10	2	0	0	0.0	6	5	4	12	0	2	0	.189	.226
OD	Cleon Jones	R	12	40	8	1	0	0	0.0	2	3	5	5	0	1	0	.200	.225
OF	Nyls Nyman	L	8	15	2	1	0	0	0.0	2	1	0	3	1	0	0	.133	.200
C	Jim Essian	R	78	199	49	7	0	0	0.0	20	21	23	28	2	0	0	.246	.281
C	Pete Varney	R	14	41	10	2	0	3	7.3	5	5	2	9	0	0	0	.244	.512
C	Phil Roof	R	4	9	1	0	0	0	0.0	0	0	0	3	0	0	0	.111	.111
C	George Enright	R	2	1	0	0	0	0	0.0	0	0	0	0	0	0	0	.000	.000
PITCHERS																		
P	Ken Brett	L	33	12	1	0	0	0	0.0	0	0	0	1	0	6	1	.083	.083
P	Clay Carroll	R	29	0	0	0	0	0	—	0	0	0	0	0	0	0	—	—
P	Blue Moon Odom	R	8	0	0	0	0	0	—	0	0	0	0	0	0	0	—	—
P	Wilbur Wood	R	7	0	0	0	0	0	—	0	0	0	0	0	0	0	—	—
P	Bart Johnson	R	32	0	0	0	0	0	—	0	0	0	0	0	0	0	—	—
P	Francisco Barrios	R	35	0	0	0	0	0	—	0	0	0	0	0	0	0	—	—
P	Jack Kucek	R	2	0	0	0	0	0	—	0	0	0	0	0	0	0	—	—
P	Jim Otten	R	2	0	0	0	0	0	—	0	0	0	0	0	0	0	—	—
P	Chris Knapp	R	11	0	0	0	0	0	—	0	0	0	0	0	0	0	—	—
P	Ken Kravec	L	9	0	0	0	0	0	—	0	0	0	0	0	0	0	—	—
P	Pete Vuckovich	R	33	0	0	0	0	0	—	0	0	0	0	0	0	0	—	—
P	Terry Forster	L	29	0	0	0	0	0	—	0	0	0	0	0	0	0	—	—
P	Larry Monroe	R	8	0	0	0	0	0	—	0	0	0	0	0	0	0	—	—
P	Goose Gossage	R	31	0	0	0	0	0	—	0	0	0	0	0	0	0	—	—
P	Dave Hamilton	L	45	0	0	0	0	0	—	0	0	0	0	0	0	0	—	—
P	Jesse Jefferson	R	19	0	0	0	0	0	—	0	0	0	0	0	0	0	—	—
TEAM TOTAL				5532	1410	209	46	73	1.3	586	538	471	739	120	107	22	.255	.349

INDIVIDUAL FIELDING

POS	Player	T	G	PO	A	E	DP	TCG	FA	POS	Player	T	G	PO	A	E	DP	TCG	FA
1B	J. Spencer	L	143	1206	112	2	116	9.2	.998	OF	C. Lemon	R	131	353	12	3	1	2.8	.992
	L. Johnson	R	34	210	18	4	20	6.8	.983		R. Garr	R	125	254	7	6	2	2.1	.978
	S. Ewing	R	1	4	0	0	0	4.0	1.000		J. Orta	R	77	156	9	5	1	2.2	.971
	B. Stein	R	1	3	0	0	0	3.0	1.000		B. Bradford	R	48	91	0	2	0	1.9	.978
	J. Essian	R	2	1	0	0	0	0.5	1.000		A. Bannister	R	43	80	1	1	0	1.9	.988
2B	J. Brohamer	R	117	263	334	10	74	5.2	.984		J. Hairston	L	40	71	1	2	0	1.9	.973
	B. Stein	R	58	118	143	11	34	4.7	.960		R. Coggins	L	26	45	1	0	0	1.8	1.000
	A. Bannister	R	4	4	12	0	2	4.0	1.000		P. Kelly	L	26	37	0	2	0	1.5	.950
	H. Yancy	R	3	8	4	0	3	4.0	1.000		L. Johnson	R	1	0	0	0	0	0.0	.000
SS	B. Dent	R	158	279	468	18	96	4.8	.976		W. Nordhagen	R	10	20	1	0	0	2.1	1.000
	A. Bannister	R	14	8	23	4	5	2.5	.886		N. Nyman	L	7	13	0	0	0	1.9	1.000
	B. Stein	R	1	2	2	0	0	4.0	1.000		C. May	L	9	13	0	0	0	1.4	1.000
3B	K. Bell	R	67	70	124	6	10	3.0	.970		C. Jones	L	8	7	0	0	0	0.9	1.000
	J. Orta	R	49	31	102	10	9	2.9	.930		B. Stein	R	1	3	0	0	0	3.0	1.000
	B. Stein	R	58	35	98	8	5	2.4	.943	C	B. Downing	R	93	450	38	6	4	5.3	.988
	A. Bannister	R	1	0	0	0	0	0.0	.000		J. Essian	R	77	319	53	10	10	5.0	.974
	J. Essian	R	1	0	0	0	0	0.0	.000		P. Varney	R	14	76	4	1	0	5.8	.988
	J. Brohamer	R	1	2	4	0	1	6.0	1.000		W. Nordhagen	R	5	15	2	1	0	3.6	.944
											P. Roof	R	4	8	3	0	1	2.8	1.000
											G. Enright	R	2	4	0	0	0	2.0	1.000

Chicago 1976

Whirlwind trades sent away Jim Kaat, Bill Melton, Ken Henderson, and Dan Osborn, bringing in exchange Alan Bannister, Ralph Garr, Jim Spencer and Clay Carroll. Just as they had changed overnight in 1971, they changed again in '76.

It was a weird season that featured a ten-game winning streak in late May and a combined no-hitter by Blue Moon Odom and Francisco Barrios on July 28. Still, the Sox lost 97 games and finished last for the sixth time in their history.

Wilbur Wood saw his season and his career unravel after Ron LeFlore lined a ball off his left kneecap on May 9. He was out for the season, and at age 35, the road back was painful. Ken Brett was acquired from the Yankees on May 18, but it was a stop-gap measure at best. The Sox, desperate for pitching, could not reverse their fate.

Minnie Minoso was activated at age 56, the Sox wore shorts, and Max Patkin was brought in for some gametime highjinks. These Veeckian diversions failed to lift attendance above one million, but Barnum Bill promised fans on his own night that the Sox would be back. He didn't realize how soon it would be.

TEAM STATISTICS

	W	L	PCT	GB	R	OR	2B	3B	HR	BA	SA	SB	E	DP	FA	CG	BB	SO	ShO	SV	ERA
WEST																					
KC	90	72	.556		713	611	**259**	57	65	.269	.371	218	139	147	.978	41	493	735	12	35	3.21
OAK	87	74	.540	2.5	686	598	208	33	113	.246	.361	**341**	144	130	.977	39	415	711	15	29	3.26
MIN	85	77	.525	5	**743**	704	222	51	81	**.274**	.375	146	172	**182**	.973	29	610	762	11	23	3.72
CAL	76	86	.469	14	550	631	210	23	63	.235	.318	126	150	139	.977	**64**	553	**992**	15	17	3.36
TEX	76	86	.469	14	616	652	213	26	80	.250	.341	87	156	142	.976	63	461	773	15	15	3.47
CHI	64	97	.398	25.5	586	745	209	46	73	.255	.349	120	130	155	.979	54	600	802	10	22	4.25
EAST																					
NY	97	62	.610		730	**575**	231	36	120	.269	.389	163	126	141	.980	62	448	674	15	37	**3.19**
BAL	88	74	.543	10.5	619	598	213	28	119	.243	.358	150	**118**	157	**.982**	59	489	678	16	23	3.31
BOS	83	79	.512	15.5	716	660	257	53	**134**	.263	**.402**	95	141	148	.978	49	**409**	673	13	27	3.52
CLE	81	78	.509	16	615	615	189	38	85	.263	.359	75	121	159	.980	30	533	928	**17**	**46**	3.48
DET	74	87	.460	24	609	709	207	38	101	.257	.365	107	168	161	.974	55	550	738	12	20	3.87
MIL	66	95	.410	32	570	655	170	38	88	.246	.340	62	152	160	.975	45	567	677	10	27	**3.64**
LEAGUE TOTAL					7753	7753	2588	467	1122	.256	.361	1690	1717	1821	.977	590	6128	9143	161	321	3.52

INDIVIDUAL PITCHING

PITCHER	T	W	L	PCT	ERA	SV	G	GS	CG	IP	H	BB	SO	R	ER	ShO	H9	BB9	SO9
Goose Gossage	R	9	17	.346	3.94	1	31	29	15	224	214	90	135	104	98	0	8.60	3.62	5.42
Bart Johnson	R	9	16	.360	4.73	0	32	32	8	211	231	62	91	115	111	3	9.85	2.64	3.88
Ken Brett	L	10	12	.455	3.32	1	27	26	16	200.2	171	76	91	82	74	1	7.67	3.41	4.08
Francisco Barrios	R	5	9	.357	4.31	3	35	14	6	142	136	46	81	72	68	0	8.62	2.92	5.13
Terry Forster	L	2	12	.143	4.38	1	29	16	1	111	126	41	70	61	54	0	10.22	3.32	5.68
Pete Vuckovich	R	7	4	.636	4.66	0	33	7	1	110	122	60	62	59	57	0	9.98	4.91	5.07
Dave Hamilton	L	6	6	.500	3.60	10	45	1	0	90	81	45	62	38	36	0	8.10	4.50	6.20
Clay Carroll	R	4	4	.500	2.57	6	29	0	0	77	67	24	38	26	22	0	7.83	2.81	4.44
Jesse Jefferson	R	2	5	.286	8.56	0	19	9	0	62	86	42	30	62	59	0	12.48	6.10	4.35
Wilbur Wood	L	4	3	.571	2.25	0	7	7	5	56	51	11	31	24	14	1	8.20	1.77	4.98
Chris Knapp	R	3	1	.750	4.85	0	11	6	1	52	54	32	41	31	28	0	9.35	5.54	7.10
Ken Kravec	L	1	5	.167	4.86	0	9	8	1	50	49	32	38	28	27	0	8.82	5.76	6.84
Blue Moon Odom	R	2	2	.500	5.79	0	8	4	0	28	31	20	18	21	18	0	9.96	6.43	5.79
Larry Monroe	R	0	1	.000	4.09	0	8	2	0	22	23	13	9	11	10	0	9.41	5.32	3.68
Jim Otten	R	0	0	–	4.50	0	2	0	0	6	9	2	3	6	3	0	13.50	3.00	4.50
Jack Kucek	R	0	0	–	9.00	0	2	0	0	5	9	4	2	5	5	0	16.20	7.20	3.60
TEAM TOTAL		64	97	.398	4.26	22	327	161	54	1446.2	1460	600	802	745	684	5	9.08	3.73	4.99

Chicago 1977   Won 90 Lost 72 Pct. .556   13

MANAGER	W	L	PCT
Bob Lemon	90	72	.556

POS	Player	B	G	AB	H	2B	3B	HR	HR%	R	RBI	BB	SO	SB	Pinch Hit AB	Pinch Hit H	BA	SA
REGULARS																		
1B	Jim Spencer	L	128	470	116	16	1	18	3.8	56	69	36	50	1	2	1	.247	.400
2B	Jorge Orta	L	144	564	159	27	8	11	2.0	71	84	46	49	4	7	1	.282	.417
SS	Alan Bannister	R	139	560	154	20	3	3	0.5	87	57	54	49	4	1	0	.275	.338
3B	Eric Soderholm	R	130	460	129	20	3	25	5.4	77	67	47	47	2	0	0	.280	.500
RF	Ralph Garr	L	134	543	163	29	7	10	1.8	78	54	27	44	12	7	1	.300	.435
CF	Chet Lemon	R	150	553	151	38	4	19	3.4	99	67	52	88	8	0	0	.273	.459
LF	Richie Zisk	R	141	531	154	17	6	30	5.6	78	101	55	98	0	3	0	.290	.514
C	Jim Essian	R	114	322	88	18	2	10	3.1	50	44	52	35	1	0	0	.273	.435
DH	Oscar Gamble	L	137	408	121	22	2	31	7.6	75	83	54	54	1	18	8	.297	.588
SUBSTITUTES																		
D1	Lamar Johnson	R	118	374	113	12	5	18	4.8	52	65	24	53	1	26	10	.302	.505
32	Jack Brohamer	L	59	152	39	10	3	2	1.3	26	20	21	8	0	2	0	.257	.401
UT	Don Kessinger	B	39	119	28	3	2	0	0.0	12	11	13	7	2	0	0	.235	.294
S3	Kevin Bell	R	9	28	5	1	0	1	3.6	4	6	3	8	0	0	0	.179	.321
SD	Tim Nordbrook	R	15	20	5	0	0	0	0.0	2	1	7	4	1	12	3	.250	.250
1B	Mike Squires	L	3	3	0	0	0	0	0.0	0	0	0	1	0	2	0	.000	.000
UT	John Flannery	R	7	2	0	0	0	0	0.0	1	0	1	1	0	0	0	.000	.000
OF	Wayne Nordhagen	R	52	124	39	7	3	4	3.2	16	22	2	12	1	7	2	.315	.516
OD	Royle Stillman	L	56	119	25	7	1	3	2.5	18	13	17	21	2	17	3	.210	.361
OF	Bob Coluccio	R	20	37	10	0	0	0	0.0	4	7	6	2	0	0	0	.270	.270
OF	Jerry Hairston	B	13	26	8	2	0	0	0.0	3	4	5	7	0	1	0	.308	.385
OF	Henry Cruz	L	16	21	6	0	0	2	9.5	3	5	1	3	0	1	0	.286	.571
OF	Bob Molinaro	R	1	2	1	0	0	0	0.0	0	0	0	1	1	0	0	.500	.500
OF	Cirilio Cruz	L	4	2	0	0	0	0	0.0	1	0	0	0	0	1	0	.000	.000
C	Brian Downing	R	69	169	48	4	2	4	2.4	28	25	34	21	1	3	1	.284	.402
C	Bill Nahorodny	R	7	23	6	1	0	1	4.3	3	4	2	3	0	0	0	.261	.435
PITCHERS																		
P	Clay Carroll	R	8	0	0	0	0	0	—	0	0	0	0	0	0	0	—	—
P	Wilbur Wood	R	24	0	0	0	0	0	—	0	0	0	0	0	0	0	—	—
P	Ken Brett	L	13	0	0	0	0	0	—	0	0	0	0	0	0	0	—	—
P	Steve Renko	R	8	0	0	0	0	0	—	0	0	0	0	0	0	0	—	—
P	Bart Johnson	R	29	0	0	0	0	0	—	0	0	0	0	0	0	0	—	—
P	Don Kirkwood	R	16	0	0	0	0	0	—	0	0	0	0	0	0	0	—	—
P	Jack Kucek	R	8	0	0	0	0	0	—	0	0	0	0	0	0	0	—	—
P	Chris Knapp	R	27	0	0	0	0	0	—	0	0	0	0	0	0	0	—	—
P	Ken Kravec	L	26	0	0	0	0	0	—	0	0	0	0	0	0	0	—	—
P	John Verhoeven	R	6	0	0	0	0	0	—	0	0	0	0	0	0	0	—	—
P	Dave Frost	R	4	0	0	0	0	0	—	0	0	0	0	0	0	0	—	—
P	Silvio Martinez	R	10	0	0	0	0	0	—	0	0	0	0	0	0	0	—	—
P	Randy Wiles	L	5	0	0	0	0	0	—	0	0	0	0	0	0	0	—	—
P	Lerrin LaGrow	R	66	0	0	0	0	0	—	0	0	0	0	0	0	0	—	—
P	Steve Stone	R	31	0	0	0	0	0	—	0	0	0	0	0	0	0	—	—
P	Dave Hamilton	L	55	0	0	0	0	0	—	0	0	0	0	0	0	0	—	—
TEAM TOTAL				5632	1568	254	52	192	3.4	844	809	559	666	42	110	30	.278	.444

INDIVIDUAL FIELDING

POS	Player	T	G	PO	A	E	DP	TCG	FA
1B	J. Spencer	L	125	977	90	10	76	8.6	.991
	L. Johnson	R	45	346	32	4	31	8.5	.990
	M. Squires	L	1	8	1	0	0	9.0	1.000
	R. Stillman	L	1	5	0	0	0	5.0	1.000
2B	J. Orta	R	139	287	335	19	64	4.6	.970
	J. Brohamer	R	18	29	29	0	6	3.2	1.000
	D. Kessinger	R	13	27	27	0	10	4.2	1.000
	A. Bannister	R	3	3	5	0	1	2.7	1.000
SS	A. Bannister	R	133	259	325	40	51	4.7	.936
	D. Kessinger	R	21	32	38	3	12	3.5	.959
	T. Nordbrook	R	11	17	17	6	3	3.6	.850
	K. Bell	R	5	7	13	2	5	4.4	.909
	J. Flannery	R	4	1	4	0	1	1.3	1.000
3B	E. Soderholm	R	126	99	249	8	18	2.8	**.978**
	J. Brohamer	R	38	25	71	8	9	2.7	.923
	T. Nordbrook	R	1	0	0	0	0	0.0	.000
	J. Flannery	R	1	0	0	0	0	0.0	.000
	D. Kessinger	R	9	7	16	2	0	2.8	.920
	K. Bell	R	4	4	8	0	3	3.0	1.000
	J. Essian	R	2	1	0	0	0	0.5	1.000
OF	C. Lemon	R	149	512	12	12	2	**3.6**	.978
	R. Garr	R	126	225	10	3	2	1.9	.987
	R. Zisk	R	109	210	9	4	3	2.0	.982
	O. Gamble	R	49	73	1	1	0	1.5	.987
	W. Nordhagen	R	46	50	1	3	0	1.2	.944
	R. Stillman	L	26	42	0	1	0	1.7	.977
	B. Coluccio	R	19	28	1	0	1	1.5	1.000
	J. Hairston	L	11	15	1	0	0	1.5	1.000
	H. Cruz	L	9	5	0	1	0	0.7	.833
	B. Downing	R	3	5	0	0	0	1.7	1.000
	A. Bannister	R	3	3	1	0	0	1.3	1.000
	B. Molinaro	R	1	1	0	0	0	1.0	1.000
	K. Bell	R	1	1	0	0	0	1.0	1.000
	C. Cruz	L	2	1	0	0	0	0.5	1.000
C	J. Essian	R	111	592	62	9	8	6.0	.986
	B. Downing	R	61	320	28	6	5	5.8	.983
	B. Nahorodny	R	7	29	6	0	2	5.0	1.000
	W. Nordhagen	R	3	2	0	2	2	1.3	.500

Chicago 1977

The Sox were on their way to the American League christening of Toronto when Bart Johnson turned to a writer and said, "Hey, we got pretty a good team here." It got better with the trade of Bucky Dent to New York on April 5 for Oscar Gamble, LaMarr Hoyt, and Bob Polinsky. This trade not only gave credibility to Johnson's brash words but paid the Sox some long-range dividends.

Bob Lemon replaced Paul Richards, who had lost touch with the modern player, and right away things improved. There wasn't much pitching, but oh, that hitting! The Sox clubbed 192 homers, a team record not likely to be broken for a millennium. Time and time again, the 1977 Sox spotted opponents a large lead and came storming back.

The Sox claimed first place on July 1 and held it until August 14. The Sox fans turned out in record numbers to watch the "South Side hitmen" and sing the new fight song, "Na-Na-Hey-Hey Goodbye." Led by organist Nancy Faust, it proved to be a raucous torment for the opposing pitchers who heard it ringing in their ears as they trudged back to the dugout. The Kansas City Royals were not amused. They considered it hot-dogging and showboating, but they reverted to the same tactics when the Sox came to town. Everybody in baseball (perhaps even the Sox) knew the Royals would eventually win it. But White Sox fans were enjoying their one-year wonders for all they were worth.

TEAM STATISTICS

	W	L	PCT	GB	R	OR	2B	3B	HR	BA	SA	SB	E	DP	FA	CG	BB	SO	ShO	SV	ERA
WEST																					
KC	102	60	.630		822	651	299	77	146	.277	.436	170	137	145	.978	41	499	850	15	42	3.52
TEX	94	68	.580	8	767	657	265	39	135	.270	.405	154	117	156	.982	49	471	864	17	31	3.56
CHI	90	72	.556	12	844	771	254	52	192	.278	.444	42	159	125	.974	34	516	842	3	40	4.25
MIN	84	77	.522	17.5	867	776	273	60	123	.282	.417	105	143	184	.978	35	507	737	4	25	4.38
CAL	74	88	.457	28	675	695	233	40	131	.255	.386	159	147	137	.976	53	572	965	13	26	3.76
SEA	64	98	.395	38	624	855	218	33	133	.256	.381	110	147	162	.976	18	578	785	1	31	4.83
OAK	63	98	.391	38.5	605	749	176	37	117	.240	.352	176	190	136	.970	32	560	788	4	26	4.05
EAST																					
NY	100	62	.617		831	651	267	47	184	.281	.444	93	132	151	.979	52	486	758	16	34	3.61
BAL	97	64	.602	2.5	719	653	231	25	148	.261	.393	90	106	189	.983	65	494	737	11	23	3.74
BOS	97	64	.602	2.5	859	712	258	56	213	.281	.465	66	133	162	.978	40	378	758	13	40	4.16
DET	74	88	.457	26	714	751	228	45	166	.264	.410	60	142	153	.978	44	470	784	3	23	4.13
CLE	71	90	.441	28.5	676	739	221	46	100	.269	.380	87	130	145	.979	45	550	876	8	30	4.10
MIL	67	95	.414	33	639	765	255	46	125	.258	.389	85	139	165	.978	38	566	719	6	25	4.32
TOR	54	107	.335	45.5	605	822	230	41	100	.252	.365	65	164	133	.974	40	623	771	3	20	4.57
LEAGUE TOTAL					10247	10247	3408	644	2013	.266	.405	1462	1986	2143	.977	586	7270	11234	117	416	4.07

INDIVIDUAL PITCHING

PITCHER	T	W	L	PCT	ERA	SV	G	GS	CG	IP	H	BB	SO	R	ER	ShO	H9	BB9	SO9
Francisco Barrios	R	14	7	.667	4.13	0	33	31	9	231	241	58	119	117	106	0	9.39	2.26	4.64
Steve Stone	R	15	12	.556	4.52	0	31	31	8	207	228	80	124	115	104	0	9.91	3.48	5.39
Ken Kravec	L	11	8	.579	4.10	0	26	25	6	167	161	57	125	87	76	1	8.68	3.07	6.74
Chris Knapp	R	12	7	.632	4.81	0	27	26	4	146	166	61	103	90	78	0	10.23	3.76	6.35
Wilbur Wood	L	7	8	.467	4.98	0	24	18	5	123	139	50	42	75	68	1	10.17	3.66	3.07
Lerrin LaGrow	R	7	3	.700	2.45	25	66	0	0	99	81	35	63	32	27	0	7.36	3.18	5.73
Bart Johnson	R	4	5	.444	4.01	2	29	4	0	92	114	38	46	48	41	0	11.15	3.72	4.50
Ken Brett	L	6	4	.600	4.99	0	13	13	2	83	101	15	39	47	46	0	10.95	1.63	4.23
Dave Hamilton	L	4	5	.444	3.63	9	55	0	0	67	71	33	45	33	27	0	9.54	4.43	6.04
Steve Renko	R	5	0	1.000	3.57	0	8	8	0	53	55	17	36	23	21	0	9.34	2.89	6.11
Don Kirkwood	R	1	1	.500	5.18	0	16	0	0	40	49	10	24	27	23	0	11.03	2.25	5.40
Jack Kucek	R	0	1	.000	3.60	0	8	3	0	35	35	10	25	20	14	0	9.00	2.57	6.43
Bruce Dal Canton	R	0	2	.000	3.75	2	8	0	0	24	20	13	9	11	10	0	7.50	4.88	3.38
Dave Frost	R	1	1	.500	3.00	0	4	3	0	24	30	3	15	9	8	0	11.25	1.13	5.63
Silvio Martinez	R	0	1	.000	5.57	1	10	0	0	21	28	12	10	14	13	0	12.00	5.14	4.29
Clay Carroll	R	1	3	.250	4.91	1	8	0	0	11	14	4	4	7	6	0	11.45	3.27	3.27
John Verhoeven	R	0	0	–	1.74	0	6	0	0	10.1	9	2	6	3	2	0	7.84	1.74	5.23
Larry Anderson	R	1	3	.250	9.00	0	6	0	0	9	10	15	7	10	9	0	10.00	15.00	7.00
Randy Wiles	L	1	1	.500	9.00	0	5	0	0	3	5	3	0	3	3	0	15.00	9.00	0.00
TEAM TOTAL		90	72	.556	4.25	40	383	162	34	1445.1	1557	516	842	771	682	2	9.70	3.21	5.24

Chicago 1978   Won 71 Lost 90 Pct. .441 15

MANAGER	W	L	PCT
Bob Lemon	34	40	.459
Larry Doby	37	50	.425

POS	Player	B	G	AB	H	2B	3B	HR	HR%	R	RBI	BB	SO	SB	Pinch Hit AB	Pinch Hit H	BA	SA
REGULARS																		
1B	Lamar Johnson	R	148	498	136	23	2	8	1.6	52	72	43	46	6	10	2	.273	.376
2B	Jorge Orta	L	117	420	115	19	2	13	3.1	45	53	42	39	1	3	1	.274	.421
SS	Don Kessinger	B	131	431	110	18	1	1	0.2	35	31	36	34	2	1	0	.255	.309
3B	Eric Soderholm	R	143	457	118	17	1	20	4.4	57	67	39	44	2	7	4	.258	.431
RF	Claudell Washington	L	86	314	83	16	5	6	1.9	33	31	12	57	5	5	1	.264	.404
CF	Chet Lemon	R	105	357	107	24	6	13	3.6	51	55	39	46	5	1	0	.300	.510
LF	Ralph Garr	L	118	443	122	18	9	3	0.7	67	29	24	41	7	2	0	.275	.377
C	Bill Nahorodny	R	107	347	82	11	2	8	2.3	29	35	23	52	1	1	0	.236	.349
DH	Bob Molinaro	L	105	286	75	5	5	6	2.1	39	27	19	12	22	12	4	.262	.378
SUBSTITUTES																		
UT	Greg Pryor	R	82	222	58	11	0	2	0.9	27	15	11	18	3	0	0	.261	.338
DH	Ron Blomberg	L	61	156	36	7	0	5	3.2	16	22	11	17	0	16	2	.231	.372
1B	Mike Squires	L	46	150	42	9	2	0	0.0	25	19	16	21	4	1	1	.280	.367
UT	Alan Bannister	R	49	107	24	3	2	0	0.0	16	8	11	12	3	10	0	.224	.290
SS	Harry Chappas	B	20	75	20	1	0	0	0.0	11	6	6	11	1	0	0	.267	.280
1B	Jim Breazeale	L	25	72	15	3	0	3	4.2	8	13	8	10	0	2	1	.208	.375
3B	Kevin Bell	R	54	68	13	0	0	2	2.9	9	5	5	19	1	2	0	.191	.279
UT	Junior Moore	R	24	65	19	0	1	0	0.0	8	4	6	7	1	5	2	.292	.323
2B	Joe Gates	L	8	24	6	0	0	0	0.0	6	1	4	6	1	0	0	.250	.250
S2	Mike Eden	B	10	17	2	0	0	0	0.0	1	0	4	0	0	0	0	.118	.118
OF	Thad Bosley	L	66	219	59	5	1	2	0.9	25	13	13	32	12	1	0	.269	.329
UT	Wayne Nordhagen	R	68	206	62	16	0	5	2.4	28	35	5	18	0	15	6	.301	.451
OF	Bobby Bonds	R	26	90	25	4	0	2	2.2	8	8	10	10	6	1	1	.278	.389
OF	Henry Cruz	L	53	77	17	2	1	2	2.6	13	10	8	11	0	11	1	.221	.351
OF	Tom Spencer	R	29	65	12	1	0	0	0.0	3	4	2	9	0	7	0	.185	.200
OF	Rusty Torres	B	16	44	14	3	0	3	6.8	7	6	6	7	0	1	0	.318	.591
C	Mike Colbern	R	48	141	38	5	1	2	1.4	11	20	1	36	0	0	0	.270	.362
C	Marv Foley	L	11	34	12	0	0	0	0.0	3	6	4	6	0	1	0	.353	.353
CD	Larry Johnson	R	3	8	1	0	0	0	0.0	0	0	1	4	0	0	0	.125	.125
PITCHERS																		
P	Wilbur Wood	R	28	0	0	0	0	0	—	0	0	0	0	0	0	0	—	—
P	Jack Kucek	R	10	0	0	0	0	0	—	0	0	0	0	0	0	0	—	—
P	Ken Kravec	L	30	0	0	0	0	0	—	0	0	0	0	0	0	0	—	—
P	Pablo Torrealba	L	25	0	0	0	0	0	—	0	0	0	0	0	0	0	—	—
P	Mike Proly	R	14	0	0	0	0	0	—	0	0	0	0	0	0	0	—	—
P	Rich Hinton	L	29	0	0	0	0	0	—	0	0	0	0	0	0	0	—	—
P	Lerrin LaGrow	R	52	0	0	0	0	0	—	0	0	0	0	0	0	0	—	—
P	Ross Baumgarten	L	7	0	0	0	0	0	—	0	0	0	0	0	0	0	—	—
P	Britt Burns	R	2	0	0	0	0	0	—	0	0	0	0	0	0	0	—	—
P	Steve Trout	L	4	0	0	0	0	0	—	0	0	0	0	0	0	0	—	—
P	Rich Wortham	R	8	0	0	0	0	0	—	0	0	0	0	0	0	0	—	—
P	Steve Stone	R	30	0	0	0	0	0	—	0	0	0	0	0	0	0	—	—
P	Jim Willoughby	R	59	0	0	0	0	0	—	0	0	0	0	0	0	0	—	—
P	Ron Schueler	R	31	0	0	0	0	0	—	1	0	0	0	0	0	0	—	—
TEAM TOTAL				5393	1423	221	41	106	2.0	634	595	409	625	83	115	26	.264	.379

INDIVIDUAL FIELDING

POS	Player	T	G	PO	A	E	DP	TCG	FA
1B	L. Johnson	R	108	887	71	8	74	8.9	.992
	M. Squires	L	45	361	20	1	29	8.5	.997
	J. Breazeale	R	19	124	3	1	10	6.7	.992
	R. Blomberg	R	7	70	3	1	2	10.6	.986
	B. Nahorodny	R	4	23	2	0	0	6.3	1.000
2B	J. Orta	R	114	275	290	9	62	5.0	.984
	G. Pryor	R	35	54	90	5	16	4.3	.966
	J. Gates	R	8	9	26	1	4	4.5	.972
	D. Kessinger	R	9	12	14	0	2	2.9	1.000
	M. Eden	R	4	5	3	0	2	2.0	1.000
	A. Bannister	R	2	3	2	1	0	3.0	.833
	E. Soderholm	R	1	0	4	0	0	4.0	1.000
SS	D. Kessinger	R	123	171	321	13	60	4.1	.974
	G. Pryor	R	28	34	64	4	9	3.6	.961
	H. Chappas	R	20	28	64	0	8	4.6	1.000
	A. Bannister	R	8	9	14	1	3	3.0	.958
	M. Eden	R	5	9	10	2	3	4.2	.905
3B	E. Soderholm	R	128	128	245	14	17	3.0	.964
	K. Bell	R	52	23	64	5	6	1.8	.946
	G. Pryor	R	20	12	48	2	6	3.1	.968
	J. Moore	R	6	4	8	2	2	2.3	.857

POS	Player	T	G	PO	A	E	DP	TCG	FA
OF	C. Lemon	R	95	284	8	5	2	3.1	.983
	R. Garr	R	109	205	5	9	2	2.0	.959
	C. Washington	L	82	159	6	7	0	2.1	.959
	T. Bosley	L	64	155	3	4	0	2.5	.975
	B. Molinaro	R	62	88	2	0	0	1.5	1.000
	H. Cruz	L	40	55	4	0	2	1.5	1.000
	T. Spencer	R	27	52	2	0	0	2.0	1.000
	W. Nordhagen	R	36	46	2	3	1	1.4	.941
	B. Bonds	R	22	45	3	2	1	2.0	.956
	A. Bannister	R	15	22	0	0	0	1.5	1.000
	R. Torres	R	14	27	0	1	0	2.0	.964
	J. Moore	R	5	8	1	0	0	1.8	1.000
C	B. Nahorodny	R	104	486	53	11	6	5.3	.980
	M. Colbern	R	47	203	19	7	1	4.9	.969
	W. Nordhagen	R	12	41	10	3	1	4.5	.944
	M. Foley	R	10	41	4	3	0	4.8	.938
	L. Johnson	R	2	5	1	1	0	3.5	.857

Chicago 1978

Richie Zisk and Oscar Gamble left for greener pastures, and Veeck attempted to rebuild immediately by signing Ron Blomberg, the flashy, injury-prone Yankee outfielder. The contract called for a guaranteed $600,000 over four years. But the Boomer was an immediate flop at .231 and Bobby Bonds, the other off-season acquisition, wasn't much better. The Sox had traded Dave Frost, Brian Downing, and Chris Knapp to California for Bonds, Thad Bosley, and Richard Dotson. The ex-Sox helped turn the Angels into a division winner in 1979; the Sox went the other way.

On May 16 Bonds was traded to Texas for Claudell Washington as the Sox grasped for a few feet of rope. With Bob Lemon's job in danger, the Sox went on a tear, winning 17 of 19 and seeming to be on the road to recovery. But all the streak did was to help avoid the cellar and create false hopes. Destiny had big plans for Lemon in New York, and he was let go in what has to be viewed as a panic move. Coach Larry Doby took over, giving him the distinction of being both baseball's second black player and its second black manager.

Wilbur Wood was 10–5 at the All-Star break but would not win again. His final Sox victory came on July 13, against the Yankees. In September he suffered the indignity of being "showcased" for the pennant contenders, a sad finale to Woody's long, successful career.

TEAM STATISTICS

	W	L	PCT	GB	R	OR	2B	3B	HR	BA	SA	SB	E	DP	FA	CG	BB	SO	ShO	SV	ERA
WEST																					
KC	92	70	.568		743	634	305	59	98	.268	.399	216	150	152	.976	53	478	657	14	33	3.44
CAL	87	75	.537	5	691	666	226	28	108	.259	.370	86	136	136	.978	44	599	892	13	33	3.65
TEX	87	75	.537	5	692	632	216	36	132	.253	.381	196	153	140	.976	54	421	776	12	25	3.42
MIN	73	89	.451	19	666	678	259	47	82	.267	.375	99	146	171	.977	48	520	703	9	26	3.69
CHI	71	90	.441	20.5	634	731	221	41	106	.264	.379	83	139	130	.977	38	586	710	9	33	4.22
OAK	69	93	.426	23	532	690	200	31	100	.245	.351	144	179	142	.971	26	582	750	11	29	3.62
SEA	56	104	.350	35	614	834	229	37	97	.248	.359	123	141	172	.978	28	567	630	4	20	4.72
EAST																					
NY	100	63	.613		735	582	228	38	125	.267	.388	98	113	136	.982	39	478	817	16	36	3.18
BOS	99	64	.607	1	796	657	270	46	172	.267	.424	74	146	172	.977	57	464	706	15	26	3.54
MIL	93	69	.574	6.5	804	650	265	38	173	.276	.432	95	150	144	.977	62	398	577	19	24	3.65
BAL	90	71	.559	9	659	633	248	19	154	.261	.396	75	110	166	.977	65	509	754	16	33	3.56
DET	86	76	.531	13.5	714	653	218	34	129	.271	.392	90	118	177	.981	60	503	684	12	21	3.64
CLE	69	90	.434	29	639	694	223	45	106	.261	.379	64	123	142	.980	36	568	739	6	28	3.97
TOR	59	102	.366	40	590	775	217	39	98	.250	.359	28	131	163	.979	35	614	758	5	23	4.55
LEAGUE TOTAL					9509	9509	3325	538	1680	.261	.385	1471	1935	2143	.978	645	7287	10153	161	390	3.77

INDIVIDUAL PITCHING

PITCHER	T	W	L	PCT	ERA	SV	G	GS	CG	IP	H	BB	SO	R	ER	ShO	H9	BB9	SO9
Steve Stone	R	12	12	.500	4.37	0	30	30	6	212	196	84	118	110	103	1	8.32	3.57	5.01
Ken Kravec	L	11	16	.407	4.08	0	30	30	7	203	188	95	154	104	92	2	8.33	4.21	6.83
Francisco Barrios	R	9	15	.375	4.05	0	33	32	9	195.2	180	85	79	93	88	2	8.28	3.91	3.63
Wilbur Wood	L	10	10	.500	5.20	0	28	27	4	168	187	74	69	103	97	0	10.02	3.96	3.70
Jim Willoughby	R	1	6	.143	3.86	13	59	0	0	93.1	95	19	36	41	40	0	9.16	1.83	3.47
Lerrin LaGrow	R	6	5	.545	4.40	16	52	0	0	88	85	38	41	47	43	0	8.69	3.89	4.19
Ron Schueler	R	3	5	.375	4.30	0	30	7	0	81.2	76	39	39	50	39	0	8.38	4.30	4.30
Rich Hinton	L	2	6	.250	4.02	1	29	4	2	80.2	78	28	48	38	36	0	8.70	3.12	5.36
Mike Proly	R	5	2	.714	2.74	1	14	6	2	65.2	63	12	19	24	20	0	8.63	1.64	2.60
Rich Wortham	L	3	2	.600	3.05	0	8	8	2	59	59	23	25	24	20	0	9.00	3.51	3.81
Pablo Torrealba	L	2	4	.333	4.71	1	25	3	1	57.1	69	39	23	37	30	1	10.83	6.12	3.61
Jack Kucek	R	2	3	.400	3.29	1	10	5	3	52	42	27	30	23	19	0	7.27	4.67	5.19
Ross Baumgarten	L	2	2	.500	5.87	0	7	4	1	23	29	9	15	15	15	1	11.35	3.52	5.87
Steve Trout	L	3	0	1.000	4.03	0	4	3	1	22.1	19	11	11	10	10	0	7.66	4.43	4.43
Britt Burns	L	0	2	.000	12.91	0	2	2	0	7.2	14	3	3	12	11	0	16.43	3.52	3.52
TEAM TOTAL		71	90	.441	4.23	33	361	161	38	1409.1	1380	586	710	731	663	7	8.81	3.74	4.53

Chicago 1979   Won 73 Lost 87 Pct. .456 15

MANAGER	W	L	PCT
Don Kessinger	46	60	.434
Tony LaRussa	27	27	.500

POS	Player	B	G	AB	H	2B	3B	HR	HR%	R	RBI	BB	SO	SB	Pinch Hit AB	H	BA	SA
REGULARS																		
1B	Lamar Johnson	R	133	479	148	29	1	12	2.5	60	74	41	56	8	7	1	.309	.449
2B	Alan Bannister	R	136	506	144	28	8	2	0.4	71	55	43	40	22	0	0	.285	.383
SS	Greg Pryor	R	143	476	131	23	3	3	0.6	60	34	35	41	3	1	0	.275	.355
3B	Kevin Bell	R	70	200	49	8	1	4	2.0	20	22	15	43	2	2	0	.245	.355
RF	Claudell Washington	L	131	471	132	33	5	13	2.8	79	66	28	93	19	13	4	.280	.454
CF	Chet Lemon	R	148	556	177	44	2	17	3.1	79	86	56	68	7	0	0	.318	.496
LF	Rusty Torres	B	90	170	43	5	0	8	4.7	26	24	23	37	0	12	1	.253	.424
C	Milt May	L	65	202	51	13	0	7	3.5	23	28	14	27	0	1	0	.252	.421
DH	Jorge Orta	L	113	325	85	18	3	11	3.4	49	46	44	33	1	22	4	.262	.437
SUBSTITUTES																		
1B	Mike Squires	L	122	295	78	10	1	2	0.7	44	22	22	9	15	6	1	.264	.325
23	Jim Morrison	R	67	240	66	14	0	14	5.8	38	35	15	48	11	4	0	.275	.508
3B	Eric Soderholm	R	56	210	53	8	2	6	2.9	31	34	19	19	0	1	1	.252	.395
UT	Wayne Nordhagen	R	78	193	54	15	0	7	3.6	20	25	13	22	0	21	7	.280	.466
SS	Don Kessinger	B	56	110	22	6	0	1	0.9	14	7	10	12	1	0	0	.200	.282
SS	Harry Chappas	B	26	59	17	1	0	1	1.7	9	4	5	5	1	1	1	.288	.356
2B	Joe Gates	L	16	16	1	0	1	0	0.0	5	1	2	3	1	3	0	.063	.188
OD	Ralph Garr	L	102	307	86	10	2	9	2.9	34	39	17	19	2	21	6	.280	.414
OF	Junior Moore	R	88	201	53	6	2	1	0.5	24	23	12	20	0	25	6	.264	.328
OF	Thad Bosley	L	36	77	24	1	1	1	1.3	13	8	9	14	4	7	1	.312	.390
OF	Rusty Kuntz	R	5	11	1	0	0	0	0.0	0	0	2	6	0	0	0	.091	.091
C	Bill Nahorodny	R	65	179	46	10	0	6	3.4	20	29	18	23	0	11	6	.257	.413
C	Marv Foley	L	34	97	24	3	0	2	2.1	6	10	7	5	0	2	1	.247	.340
C	Mike Colbern	R	32	83	20	5	1	0	0.0	5	8	4	25	0	1	0	.241	.325
PITCHERS																		
P	Francisco Barrios	R	15	0	0	0	0	0	—	0	0	0	0	0	0	0	—	—
P	Jack Kucek	R	1	0	0	0	0	0	—	0	0	0	0	0	0	0	—	—
P	Ken Kravec	L	36	0	0	0	0	0	—	0	0	0	0	0	0	0	—	—
P	Pablo Torrealba	L	3	0	0	0	0	0	—	0	0	0	0	0	0	0	—	—
P	Ed Farmer	R	42	0	0	0	0	0	—	0	0	0	0	0	0	0	—	—
P	Mike Proly	R	38	0	0	0	0	0	—	0	0	0	0	0	0	0	—	—
P	Gil Rondon	R	4	0	0	0	0	0	—	0	0	0	0	0	0	0	—	—
P	Rich Hinton	L	16	0	0	0	0	0	—	0	0	0	0	0	0	0	—	—
P	Lerrin LaGrow	R	11	0	0	0	0	0	—	0	0	0	0	0	0	0	—	—
P	Ross Baumgarten	L	28	0	0	0	0	0	—	0	0	0	0	0	0	0	—	—
P	Britt Burns	R	6	0	0	0	0	0	—	0	0	0	0	0	0	0	—	—
P	Steve Trout	L	34	0	0	0	0	0	—	0	0	0	0	0	0	0	—	—
P	Rich Wortham	R	34	0	0	0	0	0	—	0	0	0	0	0	0	0	—	—
P	Rich Dotson	R	5	0	0	0	0	0	—	0	0	0	0	0	0	0	—	—
P	Mark Esser	R	2	0	0	0	0	0	—	0	0	0	0	0	0	0	—	—
P	Guy Hoffman	L	24	0	0	0	0	0	—	0	0	0	0	0	0	0	—	—
P	Fred Howard	R	28	0	0	0	0	0	—	0	0	0	0	0	0	0	—	—
P	LaMarr Hoyt	R	2	0	0	0	0	0	—	0	0	0	0	0	0	0	—	—
P	Dewey Robinson	R	11	0	0	0	0	0	—	0	0	0	0	0	0	0	—	—
P	Randy Scarbery	B	45	0	0	0	0	0	—	0	0	0	0	0	0	0	—	—
P	Ron Schueler	R	8	0	0	0	0	0	—	0	0	0	0	0	0	0	—	—
TEAM TOTAL				5463	1505	290	33	127	2.3	730	680	454	668	97	161	40	.275	.410

INDIVIDUAL FIELDING

POS	Player	T	G	PO	A	E	DP	TCG	FA
1B	L. Johnson	R	94	748	63	11	62	8.7	.987
	M. Squires	L	110	741	60	4	62	7.3	.995
	D. Kessinger	R	1	2	0	0	0	2.0	1.000
	A. Bannister	R	1	2	0	0	1	2.0	1.000
2B	A. Bannister	R	65	150	160	12	32	5.0	.963
	J. Morrison	R	48	104	120	4	33	4.8	.982
	J. Orta	R	41	57	75	3	17	3.3	.978
	G. Pryor	R	25	42	48	1	13	3.6	.989
	J. Gates	R	8	12	16	1	3	3.6	.966
	D. Kessinger	R	1	2	6	0	0	8.0	1.000
	J. Moore	R	2	0	2	0	0	1.0	1.000
SS	G. Pryor	R	119	161	362	21	54	4.6	.961
	D. Kessinger	R	54	57	103	2	17	3.0	.988
	H. Chappas	R	23	28	63	7	13	4.3	.929
	K. Bell	R	2	0	2	0	1	0.5	1.000
3B	K. Bell	R	68	51	153	17	11	3.3	.923
	E. Soderholm	R	56	55	154	3	12	3.8	.986
	J. Morrison	R	29	17	65	5	5	3.0	.943
	G. Pryor	R	22	15	37	4	2	2.5	.929
	A. Bannister	R	12	10	24	6	4	3.3	.850
	J. Gates	R	1	0	1	0	0	1.0	1.000

POS	Player	T	G	PO	A	E	DP	TCG	FA
OF	C. Lemon	R	147	411	10	10	2	2.9	.977
	C. Washington	L	122	256	7	7	3	2.2	.974
	R. Torres	R	85	117	4	3	0	1.5	.976
	R. Garr	R	67	94	3	5	1	1.5	.951
	A. Bannister	R	47	88	3	3	0	2.0	.968
	J. Moore	R	61	83	3	3	0	1.5	.966
	T. Bosley	L	28	57	2	2	1	2.2	.967
	W. Nordhagen	R	12	19	4	0	0	1.9	1.000
	R. Kuntz	R	5	12	1	0	1	2.6	1.000
	M. Squires	L	1	3	0	0	0	3.0	1.000
C	M. May	R	65	277	27	6	1	4.8	.981
	B. Nahorodny	R	60	223	25	7	3	4.3	.973
	M. Foley	R	33	128	11	1	1	4.2	.993
	M. Colbern	R	32	121	12	4	4	4.3	.971
	W. Nordhagen	R	5	9	0	3	0	2.4	.750

Chicago 1979

This was the year of "Disco Demolition," the Rock Concert Fiasco as the outfield turf was torn up by concert crowds, and Veeck's infamous statement that the striking umpires were "bums who should be kept on the road." He meant it in jest, but it earned him the wrath of the umpires and their wives.

Don Kessinger was the latest sacrificial lamb at the helm. The ex-Cub had joined the White Sox late in the '77 campaign and turned in a stellar performance as a player in 1978. The fact that the loudest cheers were reserved for Kessinger was not lost on Veeck. (Sox fans always rooted a little harder for ex-Cubs, players they had hated when they played on the North Side. This was true for Kessinger, Ron Santo, and Phil Cavaretta when they moved to the South Side.) But Kessinger had neither the temperament nor the background to run a major-league team. In 1979, he was saddled with a young ball club that included a "kiddie corps" of Ken Kravec, Ross Baumgarten, Steve Trout, and the erratic Rich Wortham. These young arms were thought to be the pitching staff of the eighties, but, except for Trout, none would be around when the 1984 season began. Attitude problems and a general overestimation of their talents accounted for their failures.

In the wake of seven straight losses, Kessinger met with Veeck on August 2 and offered to step down. Veeck accepted, and Tony LaRussa was named manager. At 35, LaRussa had risen rapidly in the Sox farm system. Soon the Sox would be laughable no more.

TEAM STATISTICS

	W	L	PCT	GB	R	OR	2B	3B	HR	BA	SA	SB	E	DP	FA	CG	BB	SO	ShO	SV	ERA
WEST																					
CAL	88	74	.543		866	768	242	43	164	.282	.429	100	135	172	.978	46	573	820	9	33	4.34
KC	85	77	.525	3	851	816	286	79	116	.282	.422	207	146	160	.977	42	536	640	7	27	4.45
TEX	83	79	.512	5	750	698	252	26	140	.278	.409	79	130	151	.979	26	532	773	10	42	3.86
MIN	82	80	.506	6	764	725	256	46	112	.278	.402	66	134	203	.979	31	452	721	6	33	4.13
CHI	73	87	.456	14	730	748	290	33	127	.275	.410	97	173	142	.972	28	618	675	9	37	4.10
SEA	67	95	.414	21	711	820	250	52	132	.269	.404	126	141	170	.978	37	571	736	7	26	4.58
OAK	54	108	.333	34	573	860	188	32	108	.239	.346	104	174	137	.972	41	654	726	4	20	4.75
EAST																					
BAL	102	57	.642		757	582	258	24	181	.261	.419	99	125	161	.980	52	467	786	12	30	3.26
MIL	95	66	.590	8	807	722	291	41	185	.280	.448	100	127	153	.980	61	381	580	12	23	4.03
BOS	91	69	.569	11.5	841	711	310	34	194	.283	.456	60	142	166	.977	47	463	731	11	29	4.03
NY	89	71	.556	13.5	734	672	226	40	150	.266	.406	65	122	183	.981	43	455	731	10	37	3.83
DET	85	76	.528	18	770	738	221	35	164	.269	.415	176	120	184	.981	25	547	802	5	37	4.28
CLE	81	80	.503	22	760	805	206	29	138	.258	.384	143	134	149	.978	28	570	781	7	32	4.57
TOR	53	109	.327	50.5	613	862	253	34	95	.251	.363	75	159	187	.975	44	594	613	7	11	4.82
LEAGUE TOTAL					10527	10527	3529	548	2006	.270	.408	1497	1962	2318	.978	551	7413	10115	116	417	4.22

INDIVIDUAL PITCHING

PITCHER	T	W	L	PCT	ERA	SV	G	GS	CG	IP	H	BB	SO	R	ER	ShO	H9	BB9	SO9
Ken Kravec	L	15	13	.536	3.74	1	36	35	10	250	208	111	132	115	104	3	7.49	4.00	4.75
Rich Wortham	L	14	14	.500	4.90	0	34	33	5	204	195	100	119	126	111	0	8.60	4.41	5.25
Ross Baumgarten	L	13	8	.619	3.53	0	28	28	4	191	175	83	72	82	75	3	8.25	3.91	3.39
Steve Trout	L	11	8	.579	3.89	4	34	18	6	155	165	59	76	77	67	2	9.58	3.43	4.41
Randy Scarbery	R	2	8	.200	4.63	4	45	5	0	101	102	34	45	56	52	0	9.09	3.03	4.01
Francisco Barrios	R	8	3	.727	3.60	0	15	15	2	95	88	33	28	49	38	0	8.34	3.13	2.65
Mike Proly	R	3	8	.273	3.89	9	38	6	0	88	89	40	32	43	38	0	9.10	4.09	3.27
Ed Farmer	R	3	7	.300	2.44	14	42	3	0	81	66	34	48	36	22	0	7.33	3.78	5.33
Fred Howard	R	1	5	.167	3.57	0	28	6	0	68	73	32	36	34	27	0	9.66	4.24	4.76
Rich Hinton	L	1	2	.333	6.00	2	16	2	0	42	57	8	27	30	28	0	12.21	1.71	5.79
Guy Hoffman	L	0	5	.000	5.40	2	24	0	0	30	30	23	18	18	18	0	9.00	6.90	5.40
Rich Dotson	R	2	0	1.000	3.75	0	5	5	1	24	28	6	13	13	10	1	10.50	2.25	4.88
Ron Schueler	R	0	1	.000	7.20	0	8	1	0	20	19	13	6	16	16	0	8.55	5.85	2.70
Lerrin LaGrow	R	0	3	.000	9.00	1	11	2	0	18	27	16	9	21	18	0	13.50	8.00	4.50
Dewey Robinson	R	0	1	.000	6.43	0	11	0	0	14	11	9	5	12	10	0	7.07	5.79	3.21
Gil Rondon	R	0	0	–	3.60	0	4	0	0	10	11	6	3	5	4	0	9.90	5.40	2.70
Pablo Torrealba	L	0	0	–	1.50	0	3	0	0	6	5	2	1	1	1	0	7.50	3.00	1.50
Britt Burns	L	0	0	–	5.40	0	6	0	0	5	10	1	2	5	3	0	18.00	1.80	3.60
LaMarr Hoyt	R	0	0	–	0.00	0	2	0	0	3	2	0	0	0	0	0	6.00	0.00	0.00
Wayne Nordhagen	R	0	0	–	9.00	0	2	0	0	2	2	1	2	2	2	0	9.00	4.50	9.00
Mark Esser	L	0	0	–	13.50	0	2	0	0	2	2	4	1	3	3	0	9.00	18.00	4.50
Jack Kucek	R	0	0	–	0.00	0	1	0	0	1	0	3	0	4	0	0	0.00	27.00	0.00
TEAM TOTAL		73	86	.459	4.13	37	395	159	28	1410	1365	618	675	748	647	9	8.71	3.94	4.31

Chicago 1980 Won 70 Lost 90 Pct. .438 15

MANAGER	W	L	PCT
Tony LaRussa	70	90	.438

POS	Player	B	G	AB	H	2B	3B	HR	HR%	R	RBI	BB	SO	SB	Pinch Hit AB	H	BA	SA
REGULARS																		
1B	Mike Squires	L	131	343	97	11	3	2	0.6	38	33	33	24	8	14	4	.283	.350
2B	Jim Morrison	R	162	604	171	40	0	15	2.5	66	57	36	74	9	0	0	.283	.424
SS	Todd Cruz	R	90	293	68	11	1	2	0.7	23	18	9	54	2	1	0	.232	.297
3B	Kevin Bell	R	92	191	34	5	2	1	0.5	16	11	29	37	0	3	2	.178	.241
RF	Harold Baines	L	141	491	125	23	6	13	2.6	55	49	19	65	2	9	1	.255	.405
CF	Chet Lemon	R	147	514	150	32	6	11	2.1	76	51	71	56	6	1	0	.292	.442
LF	Wayne Nordhagen	R	123	415	115	22	4	15	3.6	45	59	10	45	0	21	5	.277	.458
C	Bruce Kimm	R	100	251	61	10	1	0	0.0	20	19	17	26	1	3	0	.243	.291
DH	Lamar Johnson	R	147	541	150	26	3	13	2.4	51	81	47	53	2	5	1	.277	.409
SUBSTITUTES																		
S3	Greg Pryor	R	122	338	81	18	4	1	0.3	32	29	12	35	2	5	1	.240	.325
3B	Junior Moore	R	45	121	31	4	1	1	0.8	9	10	7	11	0	4	2	.256	.331
3B	Fran Mullins	R	21	62	12	4	0	0	0.0	9	3	9	8	0	0	0	.194	.258
SS	Harry Chappas	B	26	50	8	2	0	0	0.0	6	2	4	10	0	3	0	.160	.200
UT	Randy Johnson	L	12	20	4	0	0	0	0.0	0	3	2	4	0	5	2	.200	.200
OD	Bob Molinaro	L	119	344	100	16	4	5	1.5	48	36	26	29	18	21	7	.291	.404
OF	Thad Bosley	L	70	147	33	2	0	2	1.4	12	14	10	27	3	25	8	.224	.279
O3	Alan Bannister	R	45	130	25	6	0	0	0.0	16	9	12	16	5	6	0	.192	.238
OF	Claudell Washington	L	32	90	26	4	2	1	1.1	15	12	5	19	4	8	1	.289	.411
OF	Leo Sutherland	L	34	89	23	3	0	0	0.0	9	5	1	11	4	10	4	.258	.292
UT	Ron Pruitt	R	33	70	21	2	0	2	2.9	8	11	8	7	0	11	2	.300	.414
OF	Rusty Kuntz	R	36	62	14	4	0	0	0.0	5	3	5	13	1	3	2	.226	.290
C	Marv Foley	L	68	137	29	5	0	4	2.9	14	15	9	22	0	8	3	.212	.336
C	Glenn Borgmann	R	32	87	19	2	0	2	2.3	10	14	14	9	0	1	0	.218	.310
C	Rick Seilheimer	L	21	52	11	3	1	1	1.9	4	3	4	15	1	0	0	.212	.365
PITCHERS																		
P	Francisco Barrios	R	3	0	0	0	0	0	—	0	0	0	0	0	0	0	—	—
P	Ken Kravec	L	20	0	0	0	0	0	—	0	0	0	0	0	0	0	—	—
P	Ed Farmer	R	64	0	0	0	0	0	—	0	0	0	0	0	0	0	—	—
P	Mike Proly	R	62	0	0	0	0	0	—	0	0	0	0	0	0	0	—	—
P	Ross Baumgarten	L	24	0	0	0	0	0	—	0	0	0	0	0	0	0	—	—
P	Britt Burns	R	34	0	0	0	0	0	—	0	0	0	0	0	0	0	—	—
P	Steve Trout	L	32	0	0	0	0	0	—	0	0	0	0	0	0	0	—	—
P	Rich Wortham	R	41	0	0	0	0	0	—	0	0	0	0	0	0	0	—	—
P	Rich Dotson	R	36	0	0	0	0	0	—	0	0	0	0	0	0	0	—	—
P	Guy Hoffman	L	23	0	0	0	0	0	—	0	0	0	0	0	0	0	—	—
P	LaMarr Hoyt	R	25	0	0	0	0	0	—	0	0	0	0	0	0	0	—	—
P	Dewey Robinson	R	15	0	0	0	0	0	—	0	0	0	0	0	0	0	—	—
P	Randy Scarbery	B	15	0	0	0	0	0	—	0	0	0	0	0	0	0	—	—
P	Nardi Contreras	B	8	0	0	0	0	0	—	0	0	0	0	0	0	0	—	—
TEAM TOTAL				5442	1408	255	38	91	1.7	587	547	399	670	68	167	45	.259	.370

INDIVIDUAL FIELDING

POS	Player	T	G	PO	A	E	DP	TCG	FA
1B	M. Squires	L	114	904	68	5	79	8.6	.995
	L. Johnson	R	80	671	56	7	70	9.2	.990
	R. Pruitt	R	1	0	0	0	0	0.0	.000
	R. Johnson	L	1	0	0	0	0	0.0	.000
	M. Foley	R	3	4	0	0	0	1.3	1.000
	J. Moore	R	1	0	1	0	0	1.0	1.000
2B	J. Morrison	R	161	422	481	29	117	5.8	.969
	C. Lemon	R	1	0	0	0	0	0.0	.000
	G. Pryor	R	5	5	11	0	2	3.2	1.000
	H. Chappas	B	1	0	2	0	1	2.0	1.000
SS	T. Cruz	R	90	138	298	20	62	5.1	.956
	G. Pryor	R	76	97	248	9	46	4.7	.975
	H. Chappas	R	19	18	34	1	9	2.8	.981
	K. Bell	R	3	1	2	1	1	1.3	.750
	J. Morrison	R	1	0	1	0	0	1.0	1.000
3B	K. Bell	R	83	35	151	15	12	2.4	.925
	G. Pryor	R	41	28	85	7	7	2.9	.942
	J. Moore	R	34	28	64	7	6	2.9	.929
	A. Bannister	R	17	8	42	6	5	3.3	.893
	F. Mullins	R	21	15	36	1	7	2.5	.981
	R. Pruitt	R	3	0	1	0	0	0.3	1.000
OF	C. Lemon	R	139	347	11	7	2	2.6	.981
	H. Baines	L	137	229	6	9	1	1.8	.963
	W. Nordhagen	R	74	120	6	4	1	1.8	.969
	T. Bosley	L	52	91	1	4	0	1.8	.958
	B. Molinaro	R	49	85	3	4	0	1.9	.957
	L. Sutherland	L	23	50	0	3	0	2.3	.943
	R. Kuntz	R	34	45	2	1	1	1.4	.979
	C. Washington	L	23	41	1	3	1	2.0	.933
	A. Bannister	R	23	35	0	0	0	1.5	1.000
	R. Pruitt	R	11	20	0	0	0	1.8	1.000
	R. Johnson	L	1	2	0	0	0	2.0	1.000
	J. Moore	R	3	2	0	0	0	0.7	1.000
C	B. Kimm	R	98	375	26	6	2	4.2	.985
	M. Foley	R	64	216	17	2	3	3.7	.991
	G. Borgmann	R	32	134	18	0	1	4.8	1.000
	R. Seilheimer	R	21	62	8	4	2	3.5	.946
	R. Pruitt	R	5	5	0	1	0	1.2	.833
	M. Squires	L	2	1	0	0	0	0.5	1.000

184

Five wins in seven games against the Orioles and Yankees opened the 1980 campaign and kept the April optimists buzzing. Britt Burns emerged from the shadows; named Rookie Pitcher of the Year by *The Sporting News,* Burns won 15 games despite being unable to keep his hat in place. Another rookie, Harold Baines, was being touted as Hall of Fame material by Paul Richards. His development over the next few years would be gradual, but remarkable.

The extremes of 1979 helped Veeck realize that the cost of running a ball club was beyond his capacity. He solicited outside bids for the team. On August 22 Veeck announced an agreement with Edward DeBartolo of Youngstown, Ohio, for a payment of twenty million dollars to Veeck for the team and the park. But DeBartolo intimated that he might move the team to New Orleans, and his horse racing interests did not sit well with Commissioner Kuhn. The league voted down the sale twice before approving a sale to Chicago real estate investor Jerry Reinsdorf and CBS Sports executive Edward M. Einhorn on January 29, 1981.

The Sox' nosedive began on June 18, and despite the encouraging debuts of Richard Dotson and LaMarr Hoyt, no reversal of form was forthcoming. But for the Sox, Veeck's departure signaled better times. Losing would no longer be a state of mind.

TEAM STATISTICS

	W	L	PCT	GB	R	OR	2B	3B	HR	BA	SA	SB	E	DP	FA	CG	BB	SO	ShO	SV	ERA
WEST																					
KC	97	65	.599		809	694	266	59	115	.286	.413	185	141	150	.978	37	465	614	10	42	3.83
OAK	83	79	.512	14	686	642	212	35	137	.259	.385	175	130	115	.979	94	521	769	9	13	**3.46**
MIN	77	84	.478	19.5	670	724	252	46	99	.265	.381	62	148	192	.977	35	468	744	9	30	3.93
TEX	76	85	.472	20.5	756	752	263	27	124	.284	.405	91	147	169	.977	35	519	**890**	6	25	4.02
CHI	70	90	.438	26	587	722	255	38	91	.259	.370	68	171	162	.973	32	563	724	12	42	3.92
CAL	65	95	.406	31	698	797	236	32	106	.265	.378	91	134	144	.978	22	529	725	6	30	4.52
SEA	59	103	.364	38	610	793	211	35	104	.248	.356	116	149	189	.977	31	540	703	7	26	4.38
EAST																					
NY	103	59	.636		820	662	239	34	189	.267	.425	86	138	160	.978	29	463	845	15	50	3.58
BAL	100	62	.617	3	805	640	258	29	156	.273	.413	111	95	178	.985	42	507	789	10	41	3.64
MIL	86	76	.531	17	811	682	**298**	36	**203**	.275	**.448**	131	147	189	.977	48	**420**	575	14	30	3.71
BOS	83	77	.519	19	757	767	297	36	162	.283	.436	79	149	**206**	.977	30	481	696	8	43	4.38
DET	84	78	.519	19	**830**	757	232	53	143	.273	.409	75	133	165	.979	40	558	741	9	30	4.25
CLE	79	81	.494	23	738	807	221	40	89	.277	.381	118	105	143	.983	35	552	842	8	32	4.68
TOR	67	95	.414	36	624	762	249	53	126	.251	.383	67	133	**206**	.979	39	635	705	9	23	4.19
LEAGUE TOTAL					10201	10201	3489	553	1844	.269	.399	1455	1920	2368	.978	549	7221	10362	132	457	4.03

INDIVIDUAL PITCHING

PITCHER	T	W	L	PCT	ERA	SV	G	GS	CG	IP	H	BB	SO	R	ER	ShO	H9	BB9	SO9
Britt Burns	L	15	13	.536	2.84	0	34	32	11	238	213	63	133	83	75	1	8.05	2.38	5.03
Steve Trout	L	9	16	.360	3.69	0	32	30	7	200	229	49	89	102	82	2	10.31	2.21	4.01
Rich Dotson	R	12	10	.545	4.27	0	33	32	8	198	185	87	109	105	94	0	8.41	3.95	4.95
Mike Proly	R	5	10	.333	3.06	8	62	3	0	147	136	58	56	67	50	0	8.33	3.55	3.43
Ross Baumgarten	L	2	12	.143	3.44	0	24	23	3	136	127	52	66	60	52	1	8.40	3.44	4.37
LaMarr Hoyt	R	9	3	.750	4.58	0	24	13	3	112	123	41	55	66	57	1	9.88	3.29	4.42
Ed Farmer	R	7	9	.438	3.33	30	64	0	0	100	92	56	54	37	37	0	8.28	5.04	4.86
Rich Wortham	L	4	7	.364	5.97	1	41	10	0	92	102	58	45	73	61	0	9.98	5.67	4.40
Ken Kravec	L	3	6	.333	6.91	0	20	15	0	82	100	44	37	71	63	0	10.98	4.83	4.06
Guy Hoffman	L	1	0	1.000	2.61	1	23	1	0	38	38	17	24	12	11	0	9.00	4.03	5.68
Dewey Robinson	R	1	1	.500	3.09	0	15	0	0	35	26	16	28	13	12	0	6.69	4.11	7.20
Randy Scarbery	R	1	2	.333	4.03	2	15	0	0	29	24	7	18	14	13	0	7.45	2.17	5.59
Francisco Barrios	R	1	1	.500	5.06	0	3	3	0	16	21	8	2	9	9	0	11.81	4.50	1.13
Nardi Contreras	R	0	0	–	5.79	0	8	0	0	14	18	7	8	10	9	0	11.57	4.50	5.14
TEAM TOTAL		70	90	.438	3.91	42	398	162	32	1437	1434	563	724	722	625	5	8.98	3.53	4.53

Chicago 1981   Won 54 Lost 52 Pct. .509 13

MANAGER	W	L	PCT	
Tony LaRussa	31	22	.585	(1st)
Tony LaRussa	23	30	.434	(2nd)

POS	Player	B	G	AB	H	2B	3B	HR	HR%	R	RBI	BB	SO	SB	Pinch Hit AB	H	BA	SA
REGULARS																		
1B	Mike Squires	L	92	294	78	9	0	0	0.0	35	25	22	17	7	6	2	.265	.296
2B	Tony Bernazard	B	106	384	106	14	4	6	1.6	53	34	54	66	4	2	0	.276	.380
SS	Bill Almon	R	103	349	105	10	2	4	1.1	46	41	21	60	16	0	0	.301	.375
3B	Jim Morrison	R	90	290	68	8	1	10	3.4	27	34	10	29	3	2	0	.234	.372
RF	Harold Baines	L	82	280	80	11	7	10	3.6	42	41	12	41	6	5	1	.286	.482
CF	Chet Lemon	R	94	328	99	23	6	9	2.7	50	50	33	48	5	0	0	.302	.491
LF	Ron LeFlore	R	82	337	83	10	4	0	0.0	46	24	28	70	36	0	0	.246	.300
C	Carlton Fisk	R	96	338	89	12	0	7	2.1	44	45	38	37	3	0	0	.263	.361
DH	Greg Luzinski	R	104	378	100	15	1	21	5.6	55	62	58	80	0	0	0	.265	.476
SUBSTITUTES																		
1B	Lamar Johnson	R	41	134	37	7	0	1	0.7	10	15	5	14	0	6	1	.276	.351
UT	Greg Pryor	R	47	76	17	1	0	0	0.0	4	6	6	8	0	1	0	.224	.237
DO	Bob Molinaro	L	47	42	11	1	1	1	2.4	7	9	8	1	1	35	9	.262	.405
UT	Jay Loviglio	R	14	15	4	0	0	0	0.0	5	2	1	1	2	0	0	.267	.267
OF	Wayne Nordhagen	R	65	208	64	8	1	6	2.9	19	33	10	25	0	7	1	.308	.442
OF	Rusty Kuntz	R	67	55	14	2	0	0	0.0	15	4	6	8	1	3	0	.255	.291
OF	Jerry Hairston	B	9	25	7	1	0	1	4.0	5	6	2	4	0	2	1	.280	.440
OF	Jerry Turner	L	10	12	2	0	0	0	0.0	1	2	1	2	0	8	1	.167	.167
OF	Leo Sutherland	L	11	12	2	0	0	0	0.0	6	0	3	1	2	1	0	.167	.167
C	Jim Essian	R	27	52	16	3	0	0	0.0	6	5	4	5	0	2	0	.308	.365
C	Marc Hill	R	16	6	0	0	0	0	0.0	0	0	0	1	0	3	0	.000	.000
PITCHERS																		
P	Jerry Koosman	R	8	0	0	0	0	0	–	0	0	0	0	0	0	0	–	–
P	Francisco Barrios	R	8	0	0	0	0	0	–	0	0	0	0	0	0	0	–	–
P	Ed Farmer	R	42	0	0	0	0	0	–	0	0	0	0	0	0	0	–	–
P	Dennis Lamp	R	27	0	0	0	0	0	–	0	0	0	0	0	0	0	–	–
P	Ross Baumgarten	L	19	0	0	0	0	0	–	0	0	0	0	0	0	0	–	–
P	Britt Burns	R	24	0	0	0	0	0	–	0	0	0	0	0	0	0	–	–
P	Steve Trout	L	20	0	0	0	0	0	–	0	0	0	0	0	0	0	–	–
P	Rich Dotson	R	27	0	0	0	0	0	–	0	0	0	0	0	0	0	–	–
P	LaMarr Hoyt	R	43	0	0	0	0	0	–	0	0	0	0	0	0	0	–	–
P	Dewey Robinson	R	4	0	0	0	0	0	–	0	0	0	0	0	0	0	–	–
P	Juan Agosto	L	2	0	0	0	0	0	–	0	0	0	0	0	0	0	–	–
P	Kevin Hickey	L	41	0	0	0	0	0	–	0	0	0	0	0	0	0	–	–
P	Reggie Patterson	R	6	0	0	0	0	0	–	0	0	0	0	0	0	0	–	–
P	Lynn McGlothen	L	11	0	0	0	0	0	–	0	0	0	0	0	0	0	–	–
TEAM TOTAL				3615	982	135	27	76	2.1	476	438	322	518	86	83	16	.272	.387

INDIVIDUAL FIELDING

POS	Player	T	G	PO	A	E	DP	TCG	FA
1B	M. Squires	L	88	729	58	6	68	9.0	.992
	L. Johnson	R	36	264	15	3	31	7.8	.989
	M. Hill	R	1	0	0	0	0	0.0	.000
	C. Fisk	R	1	7	2	1	4	10.0	.900
2B	T. Bernazard	R	105	228	320	7	66	5.3	.987
	G. Pryor	R	5	8	9	0	5	3.4	1.000
	J. Loviglio	R	3	5	3	0	2	2.7	1.000
	J. Morrison	R	1	0	1	0	1	1.0	1.000
SS	B. Almon	R	103	190	340	17	78	5.3	.969
	G. Pryor	R	13	7	14	2	2	1.8	.913
	T. Bernazard	R	1	0	1	0	0	1.0	1.000
3B	J. Morrison	R	87	64	199	12	14	3.2	.956
	G. Pryor	R	27	12	42	4	1	2.1	.931
	M. Hill	R	1	0	0	0	0	0.0	.000
	J. Loviglio	R	4	4	7	3	2	3.5	.786
	C. Fisk	R	1	1	0	0	0	1.0	1.000
	J. Essian	R	2	0	0	1	0	0.5	.000

POS	Player	T	G	PO	A	E	DP	TCG	FA
OF	C. Lemon	R	94	240	2	4	1	2.6	.984
	R. LeFlore	R	82	162	6	7	2	2.1	.960
	H. Baines	L	80	120	10	2	1	1.7	.985
	W. Nordhagen	R	60	85	4	5	1	1.6	.947
	R. Kuntz	R	51	54	0	0	0	1.1	1.000
	M. Squires	L	1	0	0	0	0	0.0	.000
	J. Hairston	L	7	14	0	1	0	2.1	.933
	L. Sutherland	L	7	6	0	0	0	0.9	1.000
	B. Molinaro	R	2	3	0	0	0	1.5	1.000
	J. Turner	L	1	2	0	0	0	2.0	1.000
	C. Fisk	R	1	1	0	0	0	1.0	1.000
C	C. Fisk	R	95	470	44	5	10	5.5	.990
	J. Essian	R	25	92	9	1	0	4.1	.990
	M. Hill	R	14	11	1	0	0	0.9	1.000

Thanks to a new influx of revenue, the White Sox invested heavily in the free-agent sweepstakes. Carlton Fisk, Jim Essian, and Ron LeFlore were acquired at great expense, while Greg Luzinski was purchased outright from the Phillies on March 30. The new owners signaled a new age by abandoning the Veeck era softball uniforms and tightening up the lax Comiskey Park security.

The Sox made bold steps toward respectability but had their season dashed by the players' strike. Play was halted on June 11 with the Sox trailing Oakland by only two and a half games and headed for a season attendance record. When the season began again on August 10, the club started brilliantly. They won 10 of 16, and climbed to a game and a half lead on August 28. But everything caved in during the September drive. The same old controversies surrounding announcers Harry Caray and Jimmy Piersall re-surfaced, and it seemed for a time as if it were 1979 again.

Eddie Einhorn promised Sox fans "no more September swan songs" and set out to improve a team that had ranked second in hitting and fourth in pitching. From Detroit came Steve Kemp, and from Seattle came Tom Paciorek. It can be argued that the acquisition of the free agent Kemp was just a giveaway of the popular Chet Lemon. But Kemp gave the Sox one productive year and paved the way for Ron Kittle.

TEAM STATISTICS

	W	L	PCT	GB	R	OR	2B	3B	HR	BA	SA	SB	E	DP	FA	CG	BB	SO	ShO	SV	ERA
WEST																					
OAK	64	45	.587		458	403	119	26	104	.247	.379	98	81	74	.980	60	370	505	11	10	3.30
TEX	57	48	.543	5	452	389	178	15	49	.270	.369	46	69	102	.984	23	322	488	13	18	3.40
CHI	54	52	.509	8.5	476	423	135	27	76	.272	.387	86	87	113	.979	20	336	529	8	23	3.47
KC	50	53	.485	11	397	405	169	29	61	.267	.383	100	72	94	.982	24	**273**	404	8	24	3.56
CAL	51	59	.464	13.5	476	453	134	16	97	.256	.380	44	101	120	.977	27	323	426	8	19	3.70
SEA	44	65	.404	20	426	521	148	13	89	.251	.368	100	91	122	.979	10	360	478	5	23	4.23
MIN	41	68	.376	23	378	486	147	**36**	47	.240	.338	34	96	103	.978	13	376	500	6	22	3.98
EAST																					
MIL	62	47	.569		493	459	173	20	96	.257	.391	39	79	**135**	.982	11	352	448	4	**35**	3.91
BAL	59	46	.562	1	429	437	165	11	88	.251	.379	41	68	114	.983	25	347	489	10	23	3.70
NY	59	48	.551	2	421	**343**	148	22	100	.252	.391	46	72	100	.982	16	287	**606**	13	30	**2.90**
DET	60	49	.550	2	427	404	148	29	65	.256	.368	61	**67**	109	**.984**	33	373	476	13	22	3.53
BOS	59	49	.546	2.5	**519**	481	168	17	90	**.275**	**.399**	32	91	108	.979	19	354	536	4	24	3.81
CLE	52	51	.505	7	431	442	150	21	93	.263	.351	**119**	87	91	.978	33	311	569	10	13	3.88
TOR	37	69	.349	23.5	329	466	137	23	61	.226	.330	66	105	102	.975	20	377	451	4	18	3.82
LEAGUE TOTAL					6112	6112	2119	305	1062	.256	.373	912	1166	1487	.980	334	4761	6905	117	304	3.66

INDIVIDUAL PITCHING

PITCHER	T	W	L	PCT	ERA	SV	G	GS	CG	IP	H	BB	SO	R	ER	ShO	H9	BB9	SO9
Britt Burns	L	10	6	.625	2.64	0	24	23	5	157	139	49	108	52	46	1	7.97	2.81	6.19
Rich Dotson	R	9	8	.529	3.77	0	24	24	5	141	145	49	73	67	59	4	9.26	3.13	4.66
Dennis Lamp	R	7	6	.538	2.41	0	27	10	3	127	103	43	71	41	34	0	7.30	3.05	5.03
Steve Trout	L	8	7	.533	3.46	0	20	18	3	125	122	38	54	53	48	0	8.78	2.74	3.89
Ross Baumgarten	L	5	9	.357	4.06	0	19	19	2	102	101	40	52	56	46	1	8.91	3.53	4.59
LaMarr Hoyt	R	9	3	.750	3.56	10	43	1	0	91	80	28	60	40	36	0	7.91	2.77	5.93
Ed Farmer	R	3	3	.500	4.58	10	42	0	0	53	53	34	42	33	27	0	9.00	5.77	7.13
Kevin Hickey	L	0	2	.000	3.68	3	41	0	0	44	38	18	17	22	18	0	7.77	3.68	3.48
Francisco Barrios	R	1	3	.250	4.00	0	8	7	1	36	45	14	12	23	16	0	11.25	3.50	3.00
Jerry Koosman	L	1	4*	.200	3.33	0	8	3	1	27	27	7	21	10	10	0	9.00	2.33	7.00
Lynn McGlothen	R	0	0	–	4.09	0	11	0	0	22	14	7	12	10	10	0	5.73	2.86	4.91
Reggie Patterson	R	0	1	.000	14.14	0	6	1	0	7	14	6	2	11	11	0	18.00	7.71	2.57
Juan Agosto	L	0	0	–	4.50	0	2	0	0	6	5	0	3	3	3	0	7.50	0.00	4.50
Dewey Robinson	R	1	0	1.000	4.50	0	4	0	0	4	5	3	2	2	2	0	11.25	6.75	4.50
TEAM TOTAL		54	52	.509	3.50	23	279	106	20	942	891	336	529	423	366	6	8.51	3.21	5.05

Chicago 1982 Won 87 Lost 75 Pct. .537 13

MANAGER	W	L	PCT
Tony LaRussa	87	75	.537

POS	Player	B	G	AB	H	2B	3B	HR	HR%	R	RBI	BB	SO	SB	Pinch Hit AB	Pinch Hit H	BA	SA
REGULARS																		
1B	Mike Squires	L	116	195	52	9	3	1	0.5	33	21	14	13	3	14	3	.267	.359
2B	Tony Bernazard	B	137	540	138	25	9	11	2.0	90	56	67	88	11	0	0	.256	.396
SS	Bill Almon	R	111	308	79	10	4	4	1.3	40	26	25	49	10	1	0	.256	.354
3B	Aurelio Rodriguez	R	118	257	62	15	1	3	1.2	24	31	11	35	0	1	0	.241	.342
RF	Harold Baines	L	161	608	165	29	8	25	4.1	89	105	49	95	10	1	0	.271	.469
CF	Rudy Law	L	121	336	107	15	8	3	0.9	55	32	23	41	36	17	3	.318	.438
LF	Steve Kemp	L	160	580	166	23	1	19	3.3	91	98	89	83	7	3	1	.286	.428
C	Carlton Fisk	R	135	476	127	17	3	14	2.9	66	65	46	60	17	3	1	.267	.403
DH	Greg Luzinski	R	159	583	170	37	1	18	3.1	87	102	89	120	1	2	1	.292	.451
SUBSTITUTES																		
1B	Tom Paciorek	R	104	382	119	27	4	11	2.9	49	55	24	53	3	0	0	.312	.490
S3	Vance Law	R	114	359	101	20	1	5	1.4	40	54	26	46	4	1	1	.281	.384
3B	Jim Morrison	R	51	166	37	7	3	7	4.2	17	19	13	15	0	0	0	.223	.428
1B	Chris Nyman	R	28	65	16	1	0	0	0.0	6	2	3	9	3	5	0	.246	.262
2B	Steve Dillard	R	16	41	7	3	1	0	0.0	1	5	1	5	0	0	0	.171	.293
2B	Jay Loviglio	R	15	31	6	0	0	0	0.0	5	2	1	4	2	0	0	.194	.194
3B	Lorenzo Gray	R	17	28	8	1	0	0	0.0	4	0	2	4	1	1	0	.286	.321
DH	Greg Walker	L	11	17	7	2	1	2	11.8	3	7	2	3	0	4	2	.412	1.000
OF	Ron LeFlore	R	91	334	96	15	4	4	1.2	58	25	22	91	28	5	1	.287	.392
OF	Jerry Hairston	B	85	90	21	5	0	5	5.6	11	18	9	15	0	47	11	.233	.456
OD	Ron Kittle	R	20	29	7	2	0	1	3.4	3	7	3	12	0	13	2	.241	.414
OF	Rusty Kuntz	R	21	26	5	1	0	0	0.0	4	3	2	8	0	0	0	.192	.231
C	Marc Hill	R	53	88	23	2	0	3	3.4	9	13	6	13	0	2	1	.261	.386
UT	Marv Foley	L	27	36	4	0	0	0	0.0	1	1	6	4	0	11	1	.111	.111
PITCHERS																		
P	Jerry Koosman	R	42	0	0	0	0	0	—	0	0	0	0	0	0	0	—	—
P	Sparky Lyle	L	11	0	0	0	0	0	—	0	0	0	0	0	0	0	—	—
P	Jim Kern	R	13	0	0	0	0	0	—	0	0	0	0	0	0	0	—	—
P	Warren Brusstar	R	10	0	0	0	0	0	—	0	0	0	0	0	0	0	—	—
P	Dennis Lamp	R	44	0	0	0	0	0	—	0	0	0	0	0	0	0	—	—
P	Britt Burns	R	28	0	0	0	0	0	—	0	0	0	0	0	0	0	—	—
P	Steve Trout	L	25	0	0	0	0	0	—	0	0	0	0	0	0	0	—	—
P	Rich Dotson	R	34	0	0	0	0	0	—	0	0	0	0	0	0	0	—	—
P	LaMarr Hoyt	R	39	0	0	0	0	0	—	0	0	0	0	0	0	0	—	—
P	Juan Agosto	L	1	0	0	0	0	0	—	0	0	0	0	0	0	0	—	—
P	Kevin Hickey	L	60	0	0	0	0	0	—	0	0	0	0	0	0	0	—	—
P	Rich Barnes	B	6	0	0	0	0	0	—	0	0	0	0	0	0	0	—	—
P	Salome Barojas	R	61	0	0	0	0	0	—	0	0	0	0	0	0	0	—	—
P	Ernesto Escarrega	R	38	0	0	0	0	0	—	0	0	0	0	0	0	0	—	—
P	Jim Siwy	R	2	0	0	0	0	0	—	0	0	0	0	0	0	0	—	—
P	Eddie Solomon	R	7	0	0	0	0	0	—	0	0	0	0	0	0	0	—	—
TEAM TOTAL				5575	1523	266	52	136	2.4	786	747	533	866	136	131	28	.273	.413

INDIVIDUAL FIELDING

POS	Player	T	G	PO	A	E	DP	TCG	FA
1B	T. Paciorek	R	102	833	66	6	85	8.9	.993
	M. Squires	L	109	512	48	3	59	5.2	.995
	C. Nyman	R	24	160	12	1	16	7.2	.994
	C. Fisk	R	2	9	1	1	1	5.5	.909
	M. Foley	R	1	2	0	0	0	2.0	1.000
	M. Hill	R	1	1	1	0	0	2.0	1.000
2B	T. Bernazard	R	137	353	443	12	116	5.9	.985
	S. Dillard	R	16	29	42	3	5	4.6	.959
	J. Loviglio	R	13	24	30	2	5	4.3	.964
	V. Law	R	10	11	19	3	5	3.3	.909
	A. Rodriguez	R	3	1	4	0	1	1.7	1.000
SS	B. Almon	R	108	164	317	26	72	4.7	.949
	V. Law	R	85	126	239	18	44	4.5	.953
	A. Rodriguez	R	2	0	1	0	0	0.5	1.000
3B	A. Rodriguez	R	112	78	204	9	19	2.6	.969
	J. Morrison	R	50	19	87	10	10	2.3	.914
	V. Law	R	39	19	55	5	3	2.0	.937
	L. Gray	R	16	9	10	3	2	1.4	.864
	M. Hill	R	1	0	0	0	0	0.0	.000
	M. Foley	R	2	0	0	0	0	0.0	.000

POS	Player	T	G	PO	A	E	DP	TCG	FA
OF	H. Baines	L	161	326	10	7	4	2.1	.980
	S. Kemp	L	154	280	6	7	1	1.9	.976
	R. Law	L	94	215	2	6	0	2.4	.973
	R. LeFlore	R	83	179	7	12	1	2.4	.939
	J. Hairston	L	36	34	2	0	1	1.0	1.000
	R. Kuntz	R	21	21	0	0	0	1.0	1.000
	V. Law	R	1	0	0	0	0	0.0	.000
	R. Kittle	R	5	3	0	0	0	0.6	1.000
	T. Paciorek	R	6	2	0	0	0	0.3	1.000
	C. Nyman	R	2	1	0	0	0	0.5	1.000
C	C. Fisk	R	133	639	62	4	7	5.3	.994
	M. Hill	R	49	135	15	1	2	3.1	.993
	M. Foley	R	15	45	4	1	0	3.3	.980

Chicago 1982

The Sox established a club record for consecutive victories at the start of a season by winning their first eight. LaMarr Hoyt won the last game of the streak, the second victory of his own personal nine-game run. Hoyt wound up leading the league in victories, but no one outside Chicago seemed to notice.

Like Clarence Rowland's 1915 edition, the '81 White Sox with all their highs and lows were streaking to nowhere. A hot spell was followed by a cold one, and time and again Tony LaRussa's job was in the balance as he contended not only with Eddie Einhorn's impatience but with the balky Ron LeFlore. LeFlore at one point skipped the team for several days without so much as paying LaRussa a courtesy call.

Nineteen eighty-two marked the first time since 1966–1967 that a White Sox team had strung two winning seasons back to back. The 87–75 record was one most Sox fans could live with. Optimists viewed the new decade as one that shaped up to be a repeat of the 1950s. As in 1950, the Sox had begun a decade in transition and emerged as a solid contender one year later.

With this thought in mind, "Reinhorn" (as pundits labeled the duo) tested the free-agent waters again. On December 13, Seattle fastballer Floyd Bannister signed a White Sox contract that only an accountant could love. With Bannister added to an already complete pitching staff, the Sox were prepared to join some fast company.

TEAM STATISTICS

	W	L	PCT	GB	R	OR	2B	3B	HR	BA	SA	SB	E	DP	FA	CG	BB	SO	ShO	SV	ERA
WEST																					
CAL	93	69	.574		814	**670**	268	26	186	.274	.433	55	109	171	.983	40	482	728	10	27	3.82
KC	90	72	.556	3	784	717	**295**	**58**	132	**.285**	.428	133	127	140	.979	16	471	650	12	45	4.08
CHI	87	75	.537	6	786	710	266	52	136	.273	.413	136	154	173	.976	30	**460**	753	10	41	3.87
SEA	76	86	.469	17	651	712	259	33	130	.254	.381	131	139	157	.978	23	547	**1002**	11	39	3.88
OAK	68	94	.420	25	691	819	211	27	149	.236	.367	**232**	160	135	.974	42	648	697	6	22	4.54
TEX	64	98	.395	29	590	749	204	26	115	.249	.359	63	121	168	.981	32	483	690	5	24	4.28
MIN	60	102	.370	33	657	819	234	44	148	.257	.396	38	107	162	.982	26	643	812	7	30	4.72
EAST																					
MIL	95	67	.586		**891**	717	277	41	**216**	.279	**.455**	84	125	**184**	.980	34	511	717	6	**47**	3.98
BAL	94	68	.580	1	774	687	259	27	179	.266	.419	49	**101**	140	**.984**	38	488	719	8	34	3.99
BOS	89	73	.549	6	753	713	271	31	136	.274	.407	42	121	172	.981	23	478	816	11	33	4.03
DET	83	79	.512	12	729	685	237	40	177	.266	.418	93	117	164	.981	**45**	554	741	5	27	**3.80**
NY	79	83	.488	16	709	716	225	37	161	.256	.398	69	128	157	.979	24	491	939	8	39	3.99
CLE	78	84	.481	17	683	748	225	32	109	.262	.373	151	123	127	.980	31	589	882	9	30	4.11
TOR	78	84	.481	17	651	701	262	45	106	.262	.383	118	136	146	.978	41	493	776	**13**	25	3.95
LEAGUE TOTAL					10163	10163	3493	519	2080	.264	.402	1394	1768	2196	.980	445	7338	10922	121	463	4.07

INDIVIDUAL PITCHING

PITCHER	T	W	L	PCT	ERA	SV	G	GS	CG	IP	H	BB	SO	R	ER	ShO	H9	BB9	SO9
LaMarr Hoyt	R	19	15	.559	3.53	0	39	32	14	239.2	248	48	124	104	94	2	9.31	1.80	4.66
Rich Dotson	R	11	15	.423	3.84	0	34	31	3	196.2	219	73	109	97	84	1	10.02	3.34	4.99
Dennis Lamp	R	11	8	.579	3.99	5	44	27	3	189.2	206	59	78	96	84	2	9.78	2.80	3.70
Jerry Koosman	L	11	7	.611	3.84	3	42	19	3	173.1	194	38	88	81	74	1	10.07	1.97	4.57
Britt Burns	L	13	5	.722	4.04	0	28	28	5	169.1	168	67	116	89	76	1	8.93	3.56	6.17
Steve Trout	L	6	9	.400	4.26	0	25	19	2	120.1	130	50	62	76	57	0	9.72	3.74	4.64
Salome Barojas	R	6	6	.500	3.54	21	61	0	0	106.2	96	46	56	43	42	0	8.10	3.88	4.73
Kevin Hickey	L	4	4	.500	3.00	6	60	0	0	78	73	30	38	32	26	0	8.42	3.46	4.38
Ernesto Escarrega	R	1	3	.250	3.67	1	38	2	0	73.2	73	16	33	33	30	0	8.92	1.95	4.03
Jim Kern	R	2	1	.667	5.14	3	13	1	0	28	20	12	23	16	16	0	6.43	3.86	7.39
Warren Brusstar	R	2	0	1.000	3.44	0	10	0	0	18.1	19	3	8	7	7	0	9.33	1.47	3.93
Rich Barnes	L	0	2	.000	4.76	0	6	2	0	17	21	4	6	15	9	0	11.12	2.12	3.18
Sparky Lyle	L	0	0	—	3.00	1	11	0	0	12	11	7	6	4	4	0	8.25	5.25	4.50
Eddie Solomon	R	1	0	1.000	3.68	0	6	0	0	7.1	7	2	2	5	3	0	8.59	2.45	2.45
Jim Siwy	R	0	0	—	10.29	0	2	1	0	7	10	5	3	8	8	0	12.86	6.43	3.86
Juan Agosto	L	0	0	—	18.00	0	1	0	0	2	7	0	1	4	4	0	31.50	0.00	4.50
TEAM TOTAL		87	75	.537	3.87	41	420	162	30	1439	1502	460	753	710	618	7	9.39	2.88	4.71

Chicago 1983   Won 99 Lost 63 Pct. .611 11th

MANAGER	W	L	PCT
Tony LaRussa	99	63	.960

POS	Player	B	G	AB	H	2B	3B	HR	HR%	R	RBI	BB	SO	SB	Pinch Hit AB	Pinch Hit H	BA	SA
REGULARS																		
1B	Tom Paciorek	R	115	420	129	32	3	9	2.1	65	63	25	58	6	9	3	.307	.462
2B	Julio Cruz	B	99	334	84	9	4	1	0.3	47	40	29	44	24	1	1	.251	.311
SS	Jerry Dybzinski	R	127	256	59	10	1	1	0.4	30	32	18	29	11	1	0	.230	.289
3B	Vance Law	R	145	408	99	21	5	4	1.0	55	42	51	56	3	0	0	.243	.348
RF	Harold Baines	L	156	596	167	33	2	20	3.4	76	99	49	85	7	1	1	.280	.443
CF	Rudy Law	L	141	501	142	20	7	3	0.6	95	34	42	36	77	13	4	.283	.369
LF	Ron Kittle	R	145	520	132	19	3	35	6.7	75	100	39	**150**	8	6	0	.254	.504
C	Carlton Fisk	R	138	488	141	26	4	26	5.3	85	86	46	88	9	6	1	.289	.518
DH	Greg Luzinski	R	144	502	128	26	1	32	6.4	73	95	70	117	2	2	0	.255	.502
SUBSTITUTES																		
1O	Greg Walker	L	118	307	83	16	3	10	3.3	32	55	28	57	2	35	13	.270	.440
SS	Scott Fletcher	R	114	262	62	16	5	3	1.1	42	31	29	22	5	0	0	.237	.370
2B	Tony Bernazard	B	59	233	61	16	2	2	0.9	30	26	17	45	2	0	0	.262	.373
1B	Mike Squires	L	143	153	34	4	1	1	0.7	21	11	22	11	3	23	4	.222	.281
3B	Lorenzo Gray	R	41	78	14	3	0	1	1.3	18	4	8	16	1	3	1	.179	.256
D1	Chris Nyman	R	21	28	8	0	0	2	7.1	12	4	4	7	2	0	0	.286	.500
3B	Aurelio Rodriguez	R	22	20	4	1	0	1	5.0	1	1	0	3	0	0	0	.200	.400
2B	Tim Hulett	R	6	5	1	0	0	0	0.0	0	0	0	0	1	0	0	.200	.200
DO	Miguel Dilone	B	4	3	0	0	0	0	0.0	1	0	0	0	1	2	0	.000	.000
OF	Jerry Hairston	B	101	126	37	9	1	5	4.0	17	22	23	16	0	62	17	.294	.500
OF	Dave Stegman	R	29	53	9	2	0	0	0.0	5	4	10	9	0	3	0	.170	.208
OF	Rusty Kuntz	R	28	42	11	1	0	0	0.0	6	1	6	13	1	4	1	.262	.286
OD	Casey Parsons	L	8	5	1	0	0	0	0.0	1	0	2	1	0	4	0	.200	.200
C	Marc Hill	R	58	133	30	6	0	1	0.8	11	11	9	24	0	4	2	.226	.293
C	Joel Skinner	R	6	11	3	0	0	0	0.0	2	1	0	1	0	0	0	.273	.273
PITCHERS																		
P	Jerry Koosman	R	37	0	0	0	0	0	—	0	0	0	0	0	0	0	—	—
P	Jim Kern	R	1	0	0	0	0	0	—	0	0	0	0	0	0	0	—	—
P	Floyd Bannister	L	34	0	0	0	0	0	—	0	0	0	0	0	0	0	—	—
P	Dennis Lamp	R	49	0	0	0	0	0	—	0	0	0	0	0	0	0	—	—
P	Britt Burns	R	29	0	0	0	0	0	—	0	0	0	0	0	0	0	—	—
P	Steve Mura	R	6	0	0	0	0	0	—	0	0	0	0	0	0	0	—	—
P	Rich Dotson	R	35	0	0	0	0	0	—	0	0	0	0	0	0	0	—	—
P	Guy Hoffman	L	11	0	0	0	0	0	—	0	0	0	0	0	0	0	—	—
P	LaMarr Hoyt	R	36	0	0	0	0	0	—	0	0	0	0	0	0	0	—	—
P	Randy Martz	L	1	0	0	0	0	0	—	0	0	0	0	0	0	0	—	—
P	Juan Agosto	L	39	0	0	0	0	0	—	0	0	0	0	0	0	0	—	—
P	Kevin Hickey	L	23	0	0	0	0	0	—	0	0	0	0	0	0	0	—	—
P	Salome Barojas	R	52	0	0	0	0	0	—	0	0	0	0	0	0	0	—	—
P	Al Jones	R	2	0	0	0	0	0	—	0	0	0	0	0	0	0	—	—
P	Dick Tidrow	R	50	0	0	0	0	0	—	0	0	0	0	0	0	0	—	—
TEAM TOTAL				5484	1439	270	42	157	2.9	800	762	527	888	165	179	48	.262	.413

INDIVIDUAL FIELDING

POS	Player	T	G	PO	A	E	DP	TCG	FA
1B	T. Paciorek	R	67	555	36	0	42	8.8	1.000
	M. Squires	L	124	515	40	2	55	4.5	**.996**
	G. Walker	R	59	426	19	7	40	7.7	.985
	C. Nyman	R	10	87	5	0	8	9.2	1.000
	G. Luzinski	R	2	6	1	0	1	3.5	1.000
	M. Hill	R	1	1	0	0	0	1.0	1.000
2B	J. Cruz	R	97	213	298	9	71	5.4	.983
	T. Bernazard	R	59	96	189	7	38	4.9	.976
	S. Fletcher	R	12	18	26	1	12	3.8	.978
	T. Hulett	R	6	8	6	2	1	2.7	.875
	V. Law	R	3	3	2	0	0	1.7	1.000
SS	J. Dybzinski	R	118	140	252	14	47	3.4	.966
	S. Fletcher	R	100	107	275	14	52	4.0	.965
	V. Law	R	2	0	0	0	0	0.0	.000
3B	V. Law	R	139	91	309	14	28	3.0	.966
	L. Gray	R	31	17	46	4	3	2.2	.940
	A. Rodriguez	R	22	4	22	0	5	1.2	1.000
	M. Squires	L	1	0	0	0	0	0.0	.000
	S. Fletcher	R	7	1	7	1	0	1.3	.889
	J. Dybzinski	R	9	1	6	0	0	0.8	1.000

POS	Player	T	G	PO	A	E	DP	TCG	FA
OF	H. Baines	L	155	312	10	9	3	2.1	.973
	R. Law	L	132	302	5	2	2	2.3	**.994**
	R. Kittle	R	139	234	7	9	0	1.8	.964
	T. Paciorek	R	55	74	2	1	0	1.4	.987
	R. Kuntz	R	27	40	0	1	0	1.5	.976
	D. Stegman	R	28	31	1	0	0	1.1	1.000
	J. Hairston	L	32	29	1	1	0	1.0	.968
	V. Law	R	1	0	0	0	0	0.0	.000
	C. Parsons	R	3	3	0	0	0	1.0	1.000
	M. Dilone	R	2	1	0	0	0	0.5	1.000
C	C. Fisk	R	133	**709**	46	7	5	5.7	.991
	M. Hill	R	55	214	12	2	1	4.1	.991
	J. Skinner	R	6	20	4	1	1	4.2	.960

Chicago 1983

A season's worth of thrills came to a climax on the evening of September 17. Who could tell in April that a September game with the Mariners would mean so much? At 10:55, Harold Baines lofted a sacrifice fly to center field that brought Julio Cruz home from third. With it came a 4–3 victory and the first White Sox championship of any kind since 1959. The din of the crowd would be stilled three weeks later when Tito Landrum's home run gave Baltimore the championship of the league. But 2,132,821 fans (a Chicago attendance record) were not disappointed.

They did not reach the .500 level until June 22, and LaRussa had to sweat out another season of skeptical owners, belligerent fans, and the hostile Jimmy Piersall. Such remarkable composure under fire no doubt was a factor in LaRussa's selection as Manager of the Year by the Associated Press and *The Sporting News*. "Winning Ugly" was their rallying cry. But ugly or not, they kept on winning. When it ended, they led second-place Kansas City by an AL record 20 games.

There were heroes galore in 1983. Ron Kittle became the Sox' fourth Rookie of the Year, as he poled 35 homers. LaMarr Hoyt survived the "John Whitehead Jinx" to lead the league in victories again while earning Cy Young honors. But the finest tribute went to Roland Hemond. The quiet New Englander won Executive of the Year from U.P.I. He had built the ball club around the traditional White Sox roots: pitching and speed. When all was said and done, nothing had changed at all.

TEAM STATISTICS

	W	L	PCT	GB	R	OR	2B	3B	HR	BA	SA	SB	E	DP	FA	CG	BB	SO	ShO	SV	ERA
WEST																					
CHI	99	63	.611		800	650	270	42	157	.262	.413	165	120	158	.981	35	447	877	12	48	3.67
KC	79	83	.488	20	696	767	273	54	109	.271	.397	182	165	178	.974	19	471	593	8	49	4.25
TEX	77	85	.475	22	639	609	242	33	106	.255	.366	119	113	150	.982	43	471	826	11	32	3.31
OAK	74	88	.457	25	708	782	237	28	121	.262	.381	236	157	157	.974	22	626	719	12	33	4.35
CAL	70	92	.432	29	722	779	241	22	154	.260	.393	41	154	190	.977	39	496	668	7	23	4.31
MIN	70	92	.432	29	709	822	280	41	141	.261	.401	44	121	170	.980	20	580	748	5	39	4.67
SEA	60	102	.370	39	558	740	247	31	111	.240	.360	144	136	159	.978	25	544	910	9	39	4.12
EAST																					
BAL	98	64	.605		799	652	283	27	168	.269	.421	61	121	159	.981	36	452	774	15	38	3.63
DET	92	70	.568	6	789	679	283	53	156	.274	.427	93	125	142	.980	42	522	875	9	28	3.80
NY	91	71	.562	7	770	703	269	40	153	.273	.416	84	139	157	.978	47	455	892	12	32	3.85
TOR	89	73	.549	9	795	726	268	58	167	.277	.436	131	115	148	.981	43	517	835	8	32	4.12
MIL	87	75	.537	11	764	708	281	57	132	.277	.418	101	113	162	.982	35	491	689	10	43	4.02
BOS	78	84	.481	20	724	775	287	32	142	.270	.409	30	130	168	.979	29	493	767	7	42	4.34
CLE	70	92	.432	28	704	785	249	31	86	.265	.369	109	122	174	.980	34	529	794	8	25	4.43
LEAGUE TOTAL					10177	10177	3710	549	1903	.266	.401	1540	1831	2272	.979	469	7094	10967	133	503	4.06

INDIVIDUAL PITCHING

PITCHER	T	W	L	PCT	ERA	SV	G	GS	CG	IP	H	BB	SO	R	ER	ShO	H9	BB9	SO9
LaMarr Hoyt	R	24	10	.706	3.66	0	36	36	11	260.2	236	31	148	115	106	1	8.15	1.07	5.11
Rich Dotson	R	22	7	.759	3.23	0	35	35	8	240	209	106	137	92	86	1	7.84	3.98	5.14
Floyd Bannister	L	16	10	.615	3.35	0	34	34	5	217.1	191	71	193	88	81	2	7.91	2.94	7.99
Britt Burns	L	10	11	.476	3.58	0	29	26	8	173.2	165	55	115	79	69	4	8.55	2.85	5.96
Jerry Koosman	L	11	7	.611	4.77	2	37	24	2	169.2	176	53	90	96	90	1	9.34	2.81	4.77
Dennis Lamp	R	7	7	.500	3.71	15	49	5	1	116.1	123	29	44	52	48	0	9.52	2.24	3.40
Dick Tidrow	R	2	4	.333	4.22	7	50	1	0	91.2	86	34	66	50	43	0	8.44	3.34	6.48
Salome Barojas	R	3	3	.500	2.47	12	52	0	0	87.1	70	32	38	24	24	0	7.21	3.30	3.92
Juan Agosto	L	2	2	.500	4.10	7	39	0	0	41.2	41	11	29	20	19	0	8.86	2.38	6.26
Kevin Hickey	L	1	2	.333	5.23	5	23	0	0	20.2	23	11	8	14	12	0	10.02	4.79	3.48
Steve Mura	R	0	0	—	4.38	0	6	0	0	12.1	13	6	4	11	6	0	9.49	4.38	2.92
Guy Hoffman	L	1	0	1.000	7.50	0	11	0	0	6	14	2	2	5	5	0	21.00	3.00	3.00
Randy Martz	R	0	0	—	3.60	0	1	1	0	5	4	4	1	2	2	0	7.20	7.20	1.80
Al Jones	R	0	0	—	3.86	0	2	0	0	2.1	3	2	2	1	1	0	11.57	7.71	7.71
Jim Kern	R	0	0	—	0.00	0	1	0	0	.2	1	0	0	0	0	0	13.50	0.00	0.00
TEAM TOTAL		99	63	.611	3.69	48	405	162	35	1445.1	1355	447	877	650	592	9	8.44	2.78	5.46

White Sox Graphics

Graphs are not everyone's cup of tea. That's a shame, because a clear, well-drawn graph can present an enormous amount of information faster than any other method. And baseball is the perfect subject for a graphic treatment that can make quick sense of the wealth of statistics and measures generated by that most measured of all sports.

The beauty of John Warner Davenport's work is that it paints a clear picture of more than eighty years of accumulated results and communicates them in a glance. Notice the fall and rise of the White Sox through their history below: two great periods in the first two decades of this century, followed by a long decline lasting thirty years in the wake of the Black Sox scandal, with better times through the 1950s and '60s. And there is every reason to believe that the 1983 pennant will be part of a long, consistent stay near the top of the standings.

If the graphic treatment of baseball history in this section strikes your fancy, you will be interested in Davenport's two books, *Baseball Graphics* and *Baseball's Pennant Races: A Graphic Look,* published by First Impressions of Madison, Wisconsin.

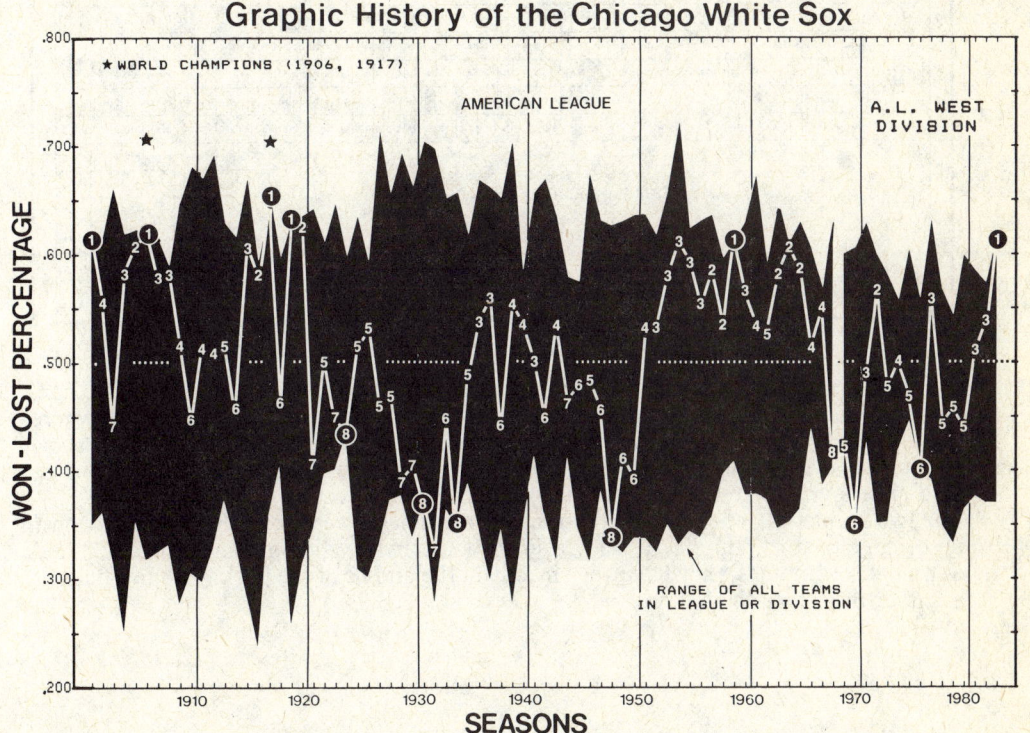

The black space indicates the range of won-lost percentages for all the teams in the league or division in each season; the white numbers represent the White Sox' final placement in each season.

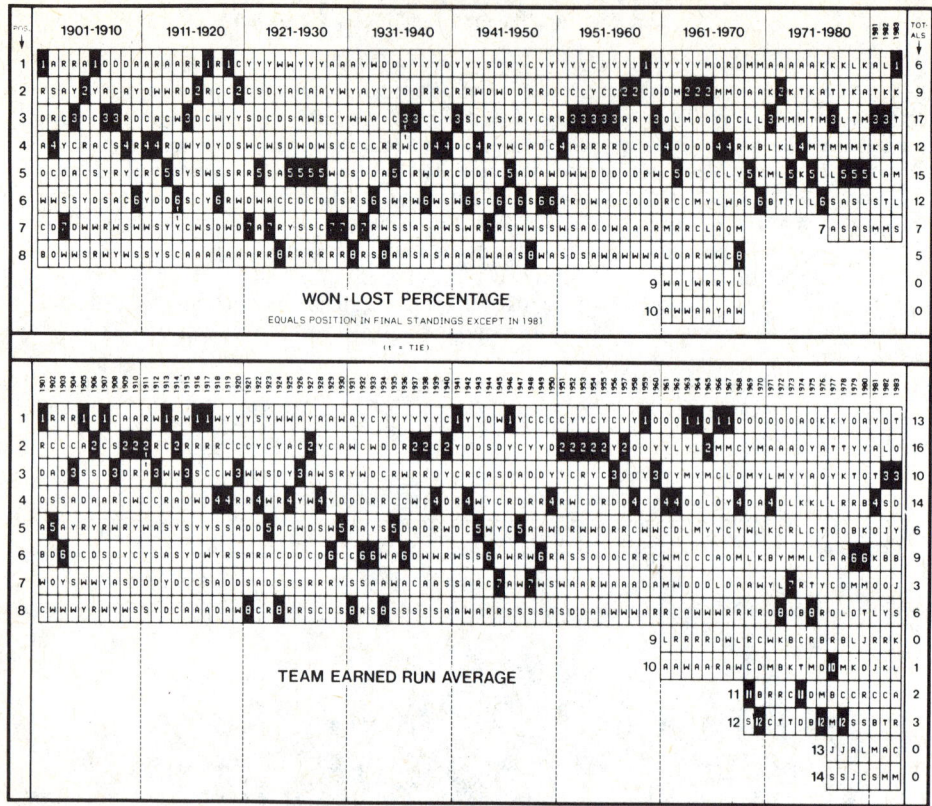

Part graph and part table, these "grables" give as much information as a table can, while maintaining the visual impact of a graph. The black numbered boxes show where the White Sox finished in these categories in each season. The white lettered boxes show the finish of every other team in the league. Following the black boxes through the white field gives a graphlike look at how the White Sox have fared.

The two grables above show a very strong correlation between team ERA and won-lost percentage for the White Sox. They also show that while the Sox have ranged up and down in the standings, they have been mostly in the middle of the pack, with few finishes at either the top or the bottom.

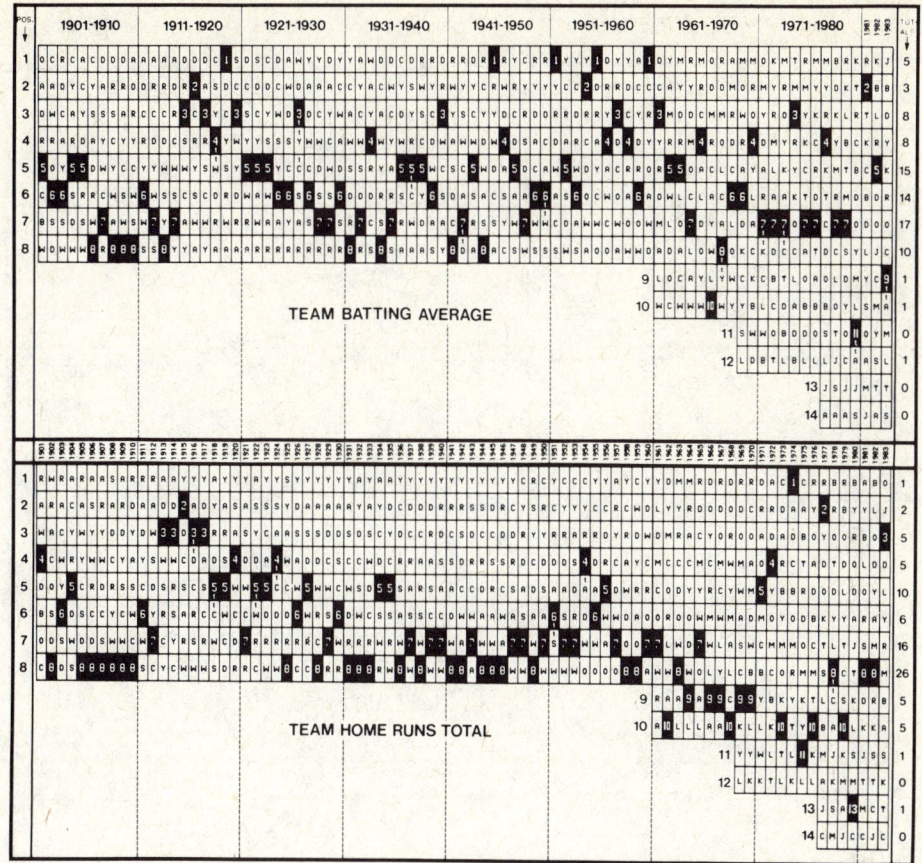

While their pitching statistics closely mirror the pattern of their won-lost record, their batting statistics do not. (Probably just as well, considering those batting statistics!) The Sox ranked in the top half of the league in batting in just two of their five pennant-winning seasons, and of their eight placings in the top three in homers, just three have come since the introduction of the lively ball in 1920. But in the three years since 1980 the Sox have leaped from thirteenth in the league in homers to third; thank you, Messrs. Fisk, Luzinski, Baines, and Kittle!

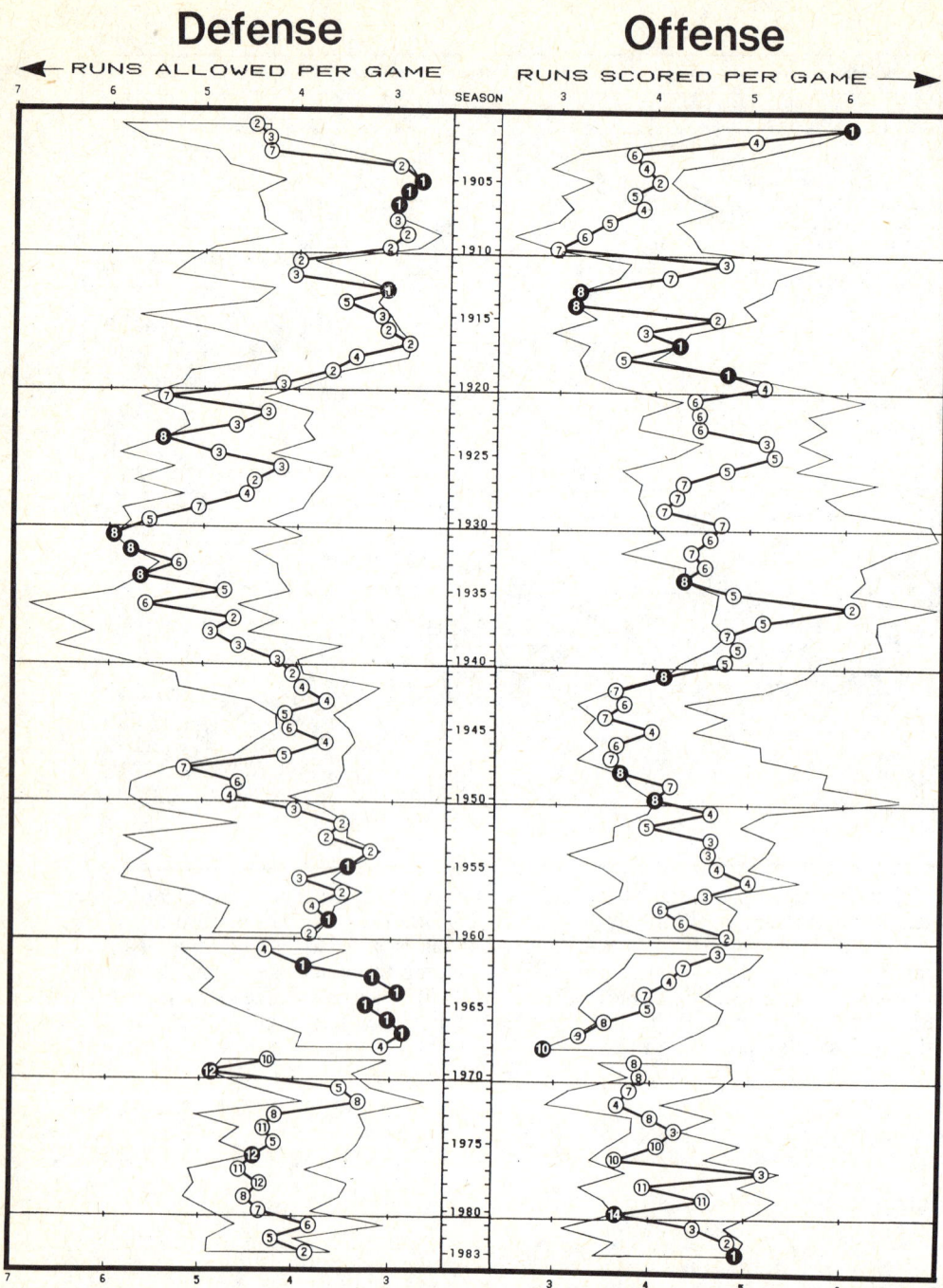

Another look at the White Sox record in scoring and preventing runs shows how closely allied their success has been with their pitching. They have yet to win a pennant without finishing first or second in runs allowed. One can't help sympathizing with the Sox pitchers of the 1960s who led the league in runs allowed for six straight years, but saw their offense fall farther and farther behind.

THE PENNANT RACES

Graphs provide an excellent way of showing the patterns and results of a pennant race. Davenport's method is to chart each team's progress above or below the .500 mark. That way each win is a move up one step, and each loss a step down. It takes a two-game difference in record over or under .500 to make a one-game difference in the standings: A team with a 10–1 mark, nine games over .500, is one game ahead of one with a 9–2 mark, seven games over.

The graph below shows the White Sox' march to the 1983 Western Division title: a slow start, with the club falling to sixth place in late May as the press screamed for LaRussa's scalp; a gradual rise to the top of the standings by late July despite a won-lost record just over .500; the closing hot streak that extended for two months, as the rest of the division fell back. The final twenty-game margin set a new American League record.

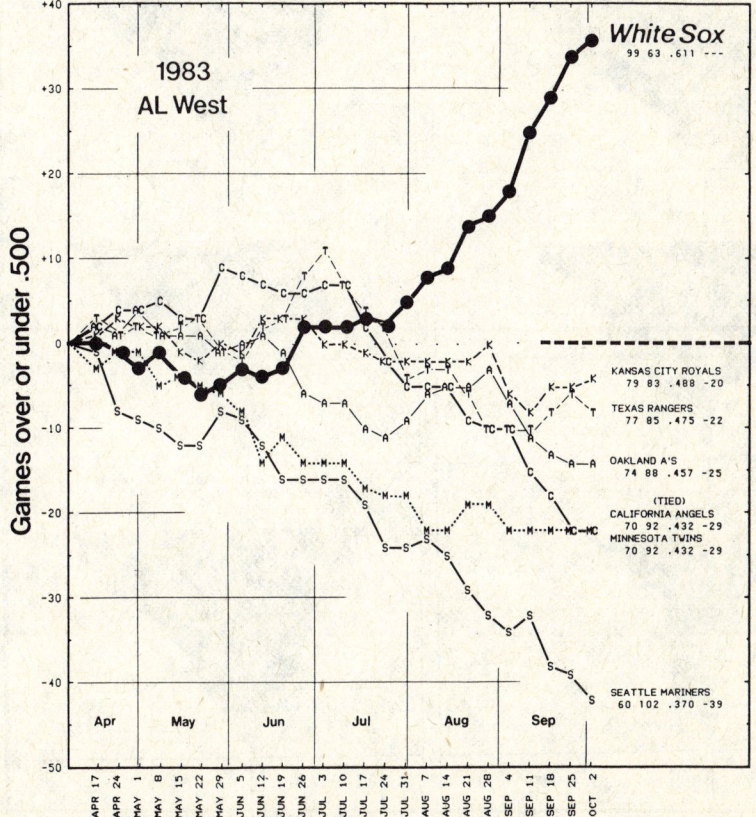

The graphs on the following pages track the White Sox' standing from start to finish for every season since 1901. The black space shows the range of all the clubs in the league (or division since 1969).

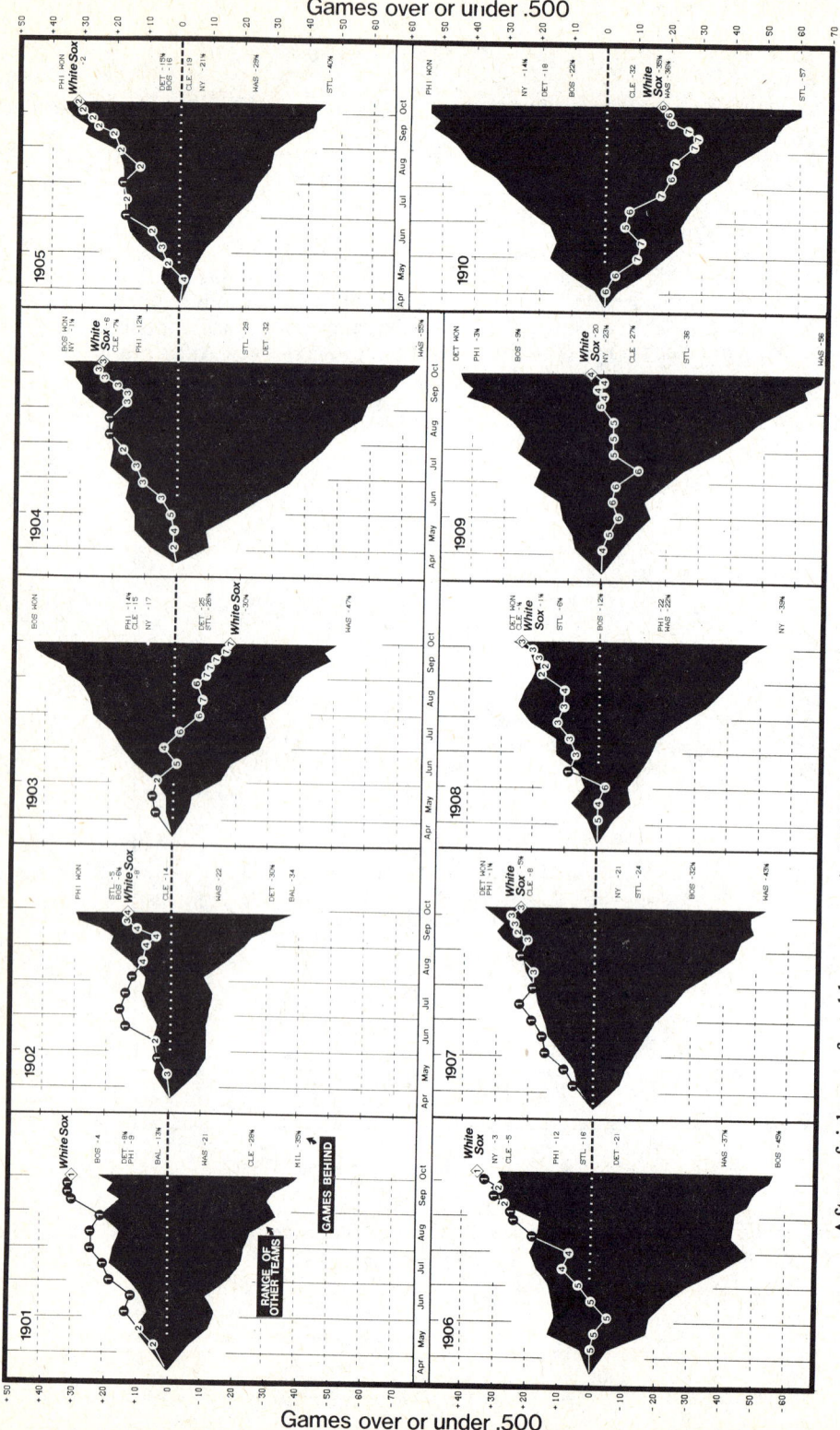

199

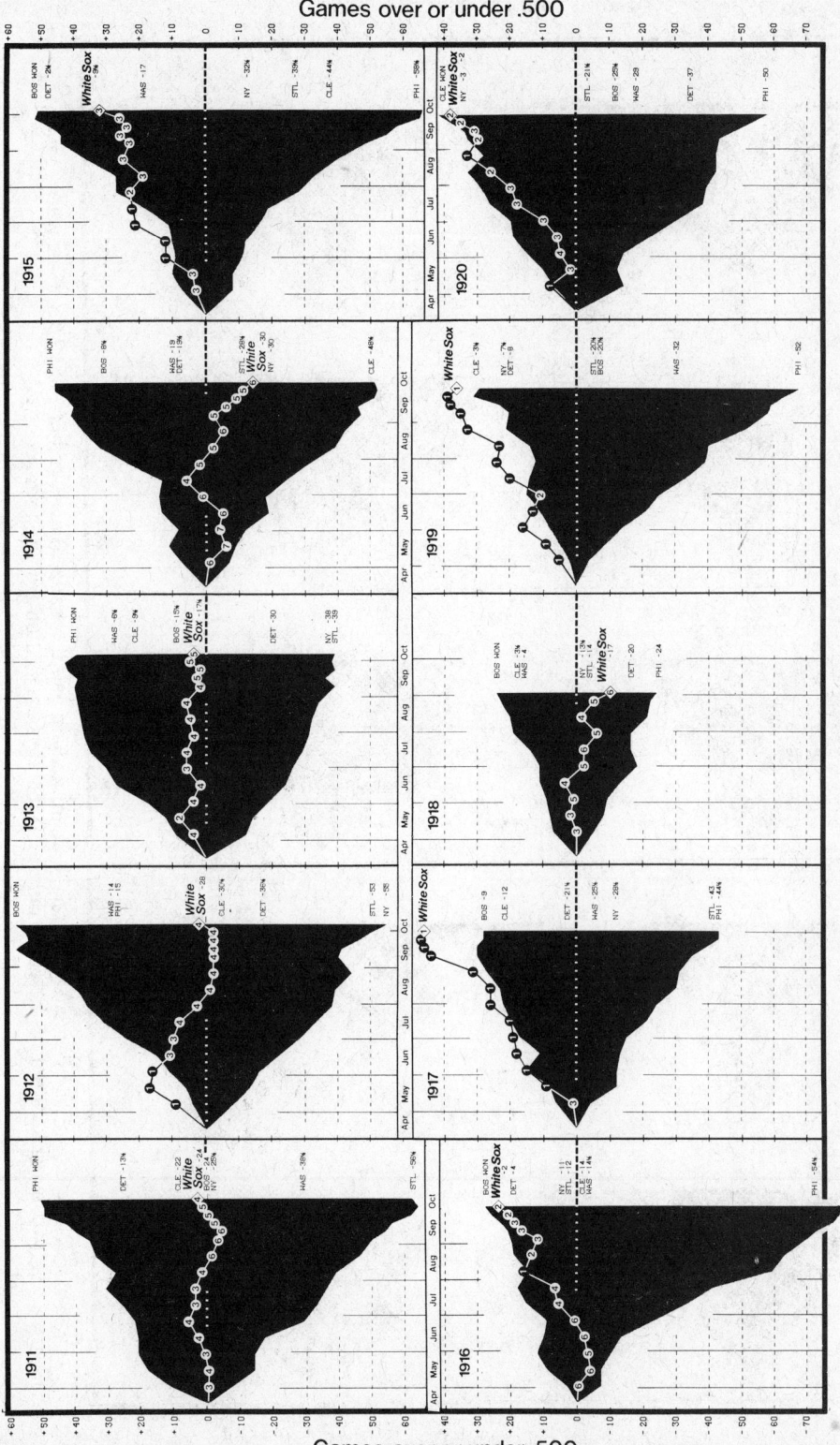

Player losses to World War I accounted for the downturn in White Sox fortunes in 1918; their ascension to first shortly before the Black Sox suspensions in 1920 marked the last time they'd see the top so late in the season until 1959.

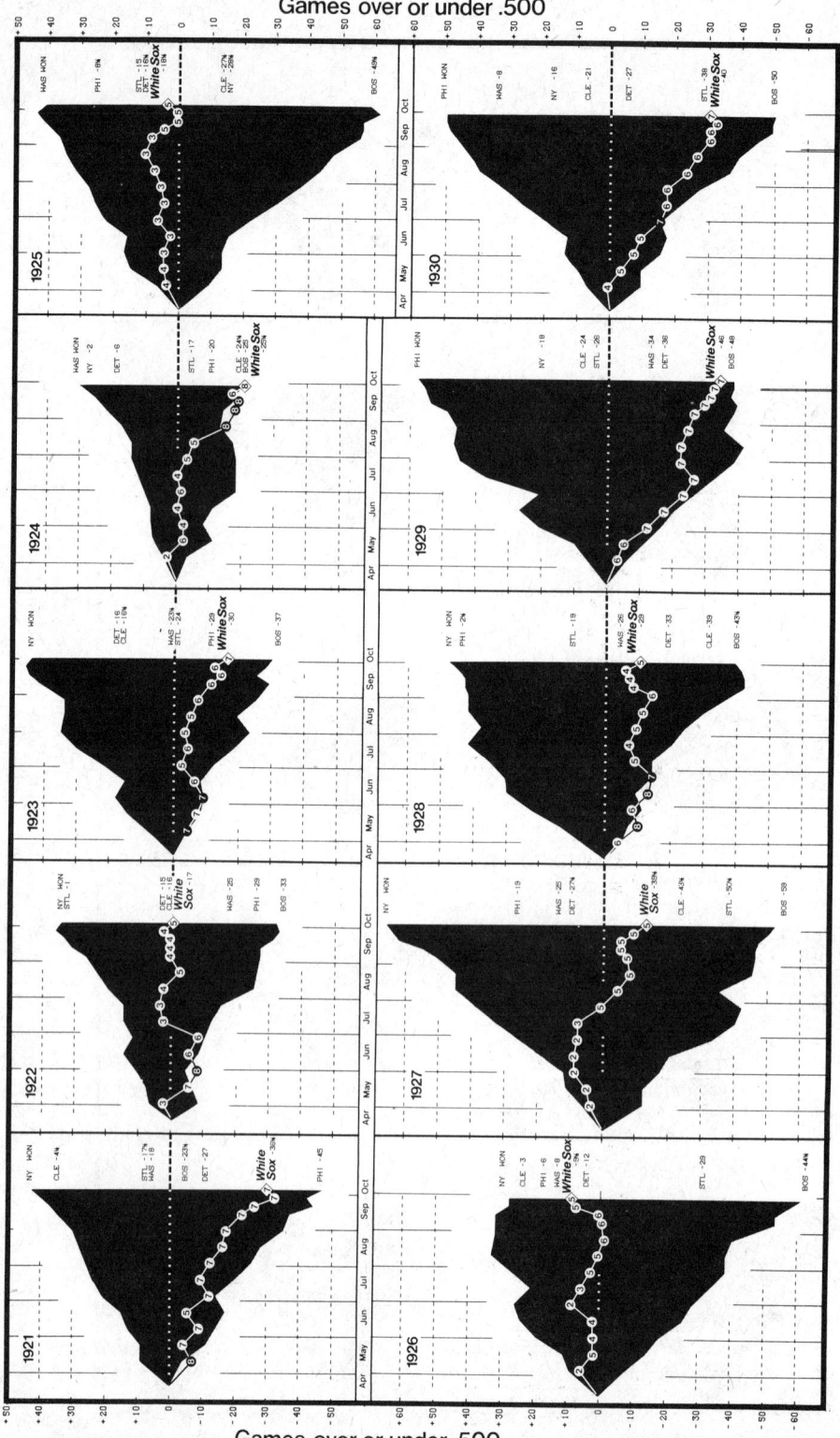

The effect of the Black Sox scandal was immediate and dramatic. By the end of the 1920s, Chicago was being kept out of the cellar only by some abysmal Boston Red Sox squads.

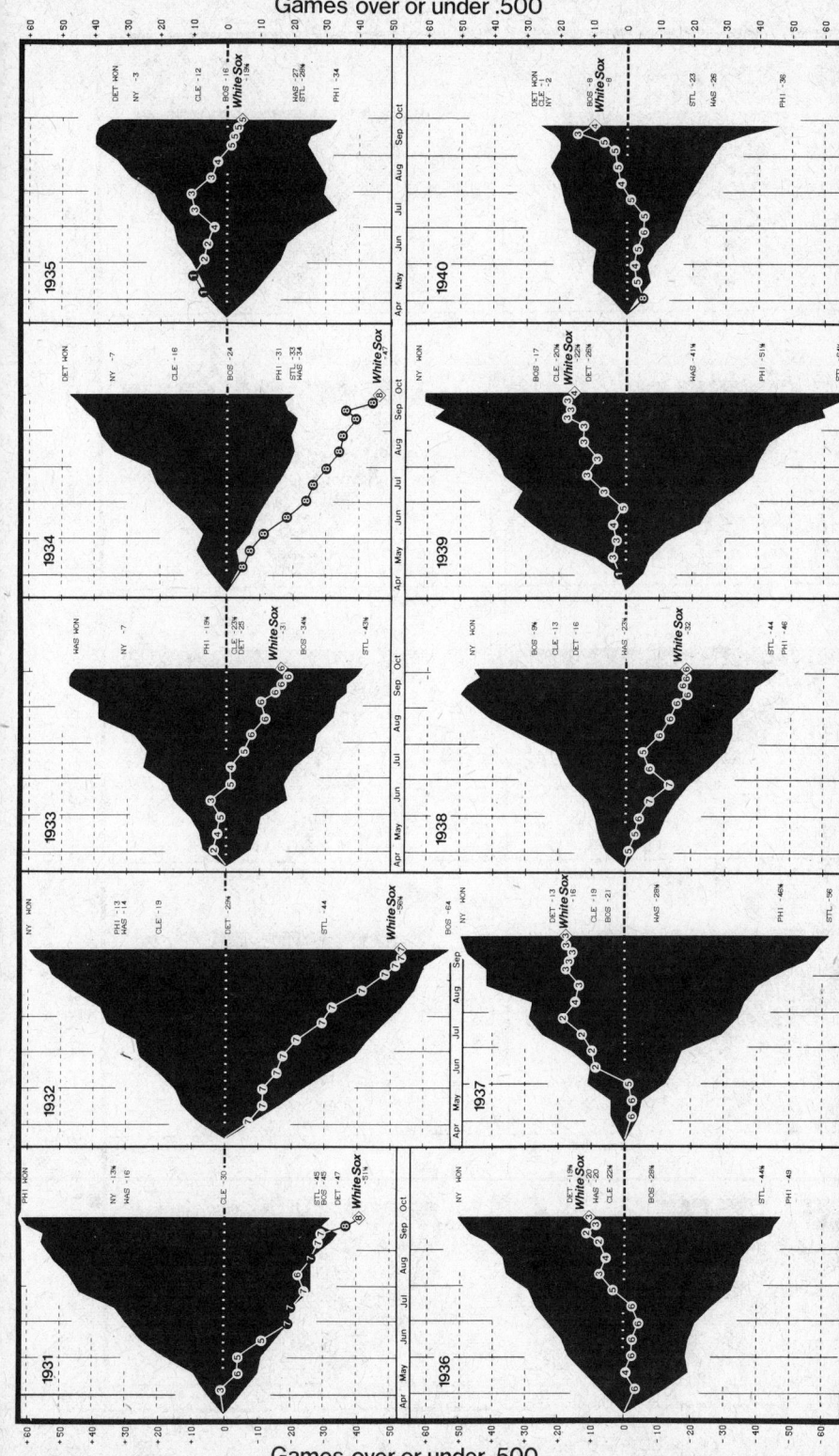

After four more dismal seasons, the Sox achieved respectability (if mediocrity) in 1935 with Jimmy Dykes at the helm.

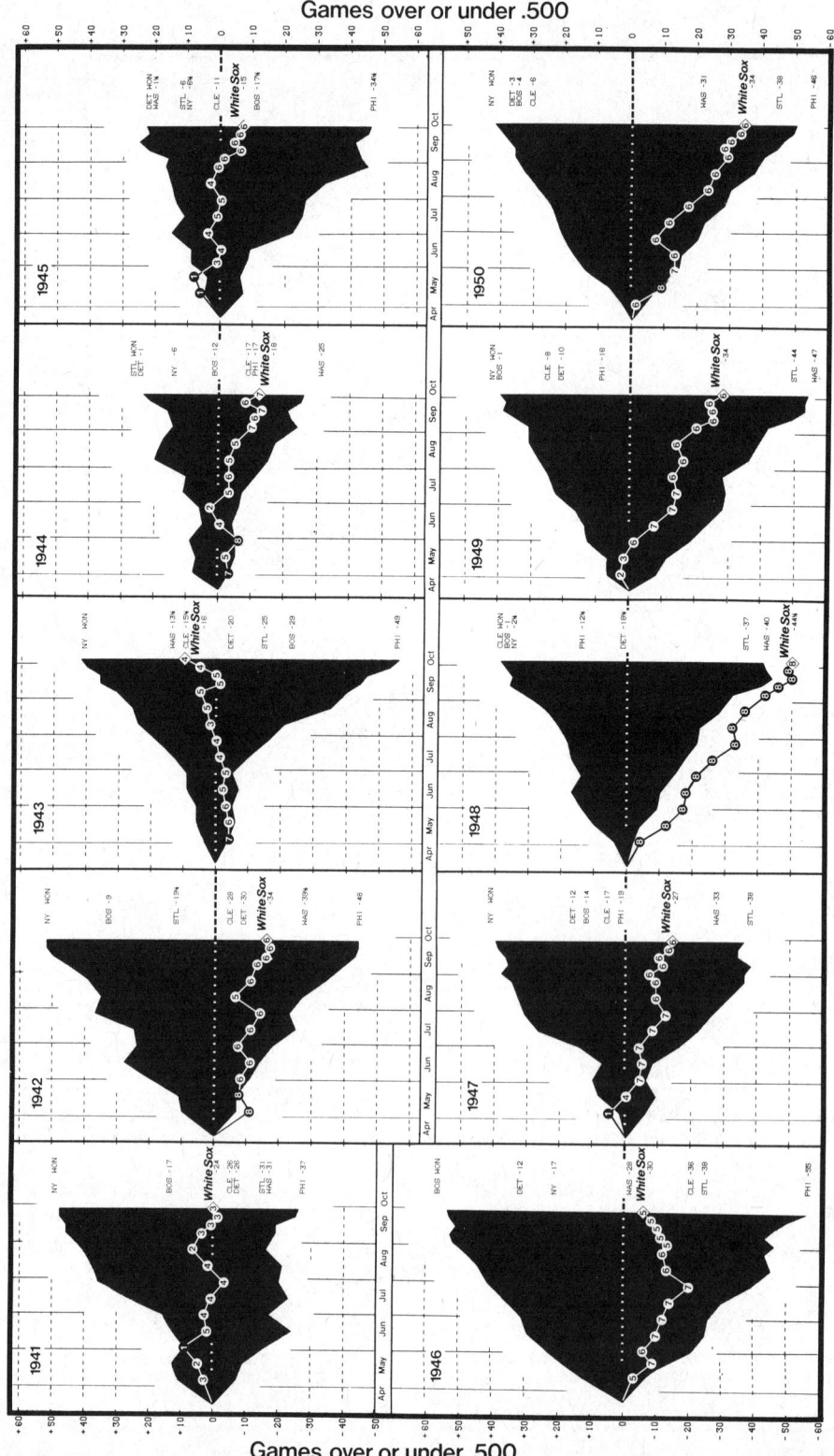

After six years of hugging the .500 mark, topping it just once, the Sox took definitive action—downwards. But better days were just around the corner.

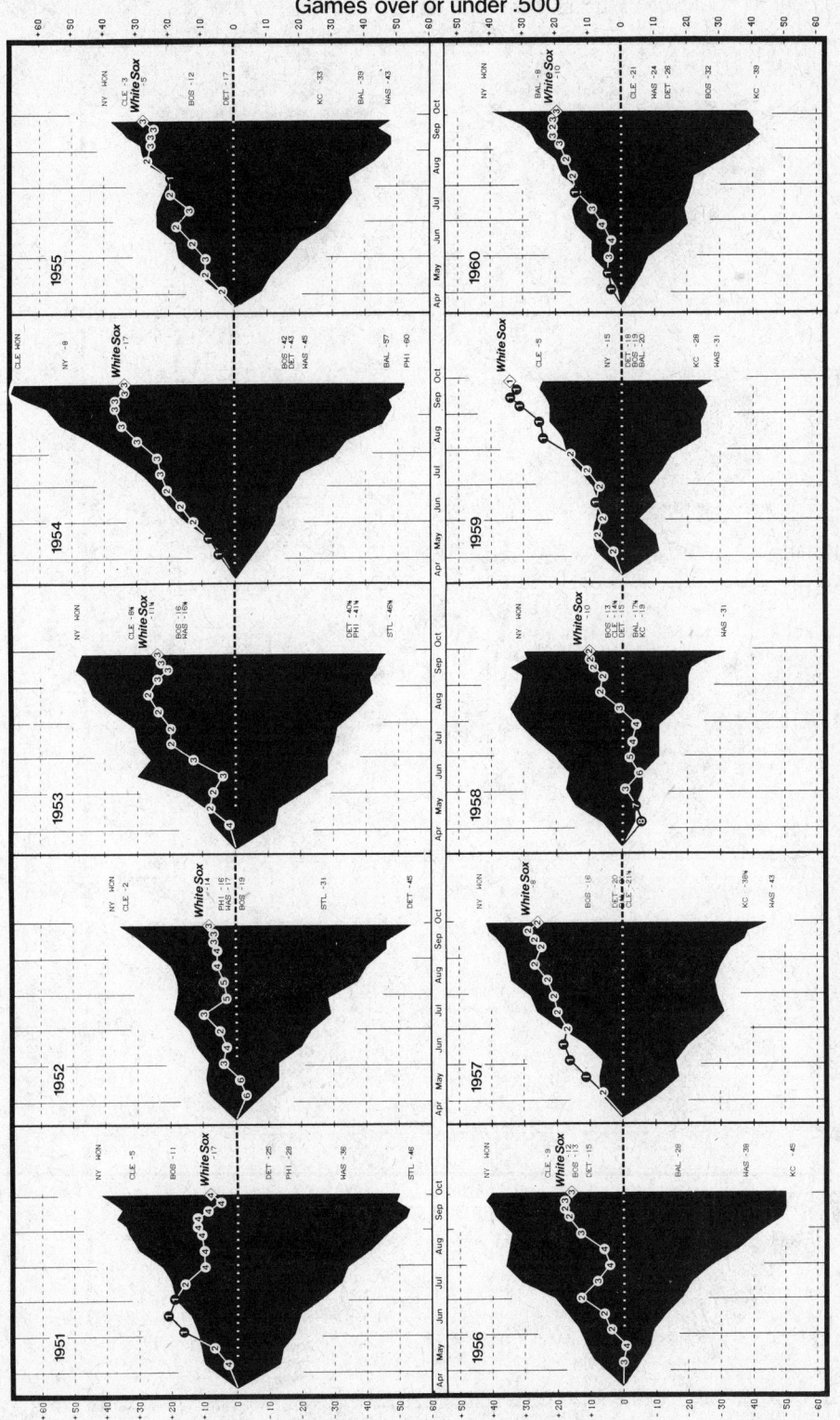

The most exciting decade in White Sox history: the Go-Go Sox were above .500 every year, and hung close to the Yankees and Indians before breaking through to their 1959 pennant.

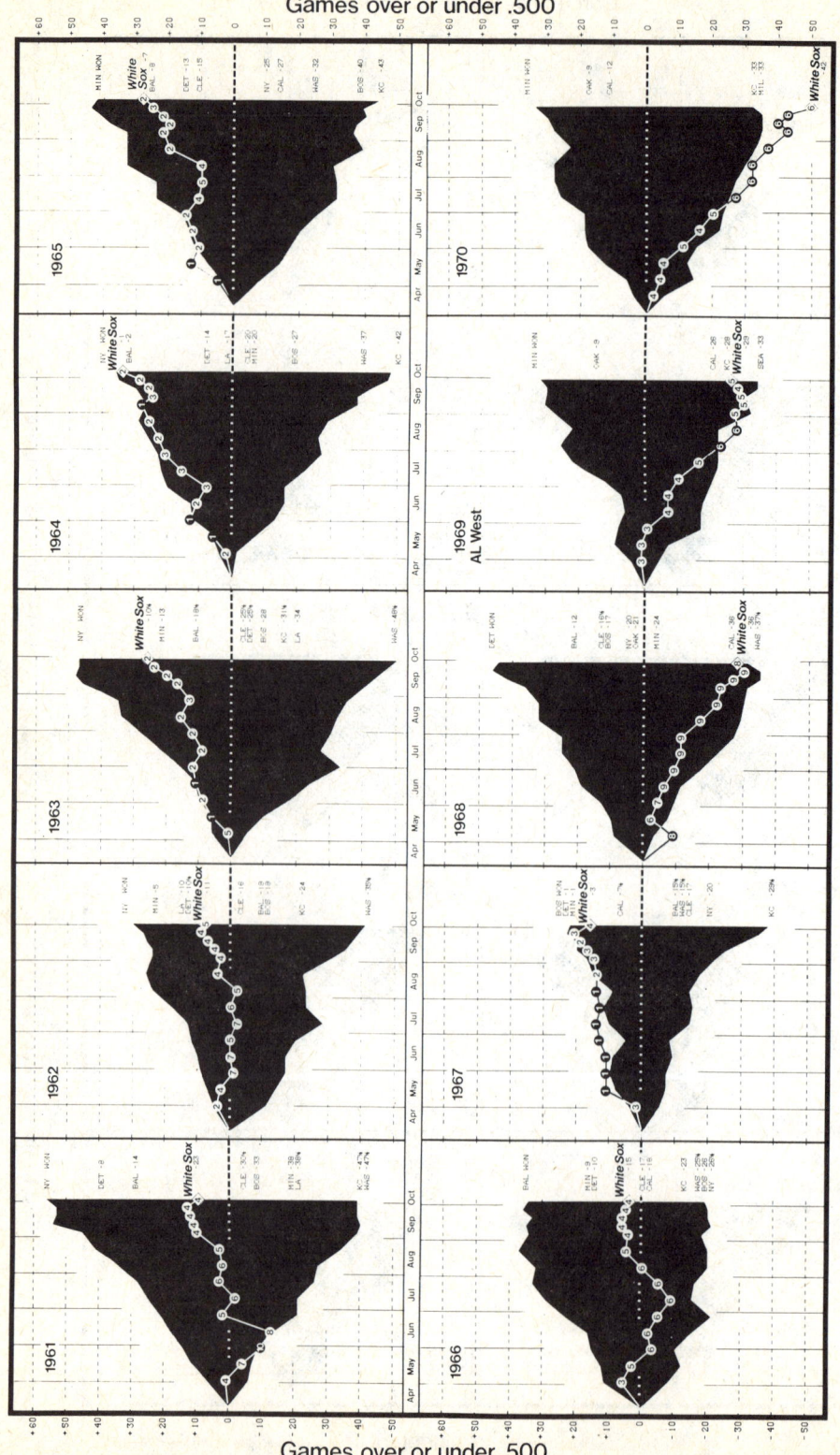

The heartbreaking defeat in 1967 led to the shocking collapse in '68, as the bottom fell out for the team and the franchise teetered on the brink of extinction.

205

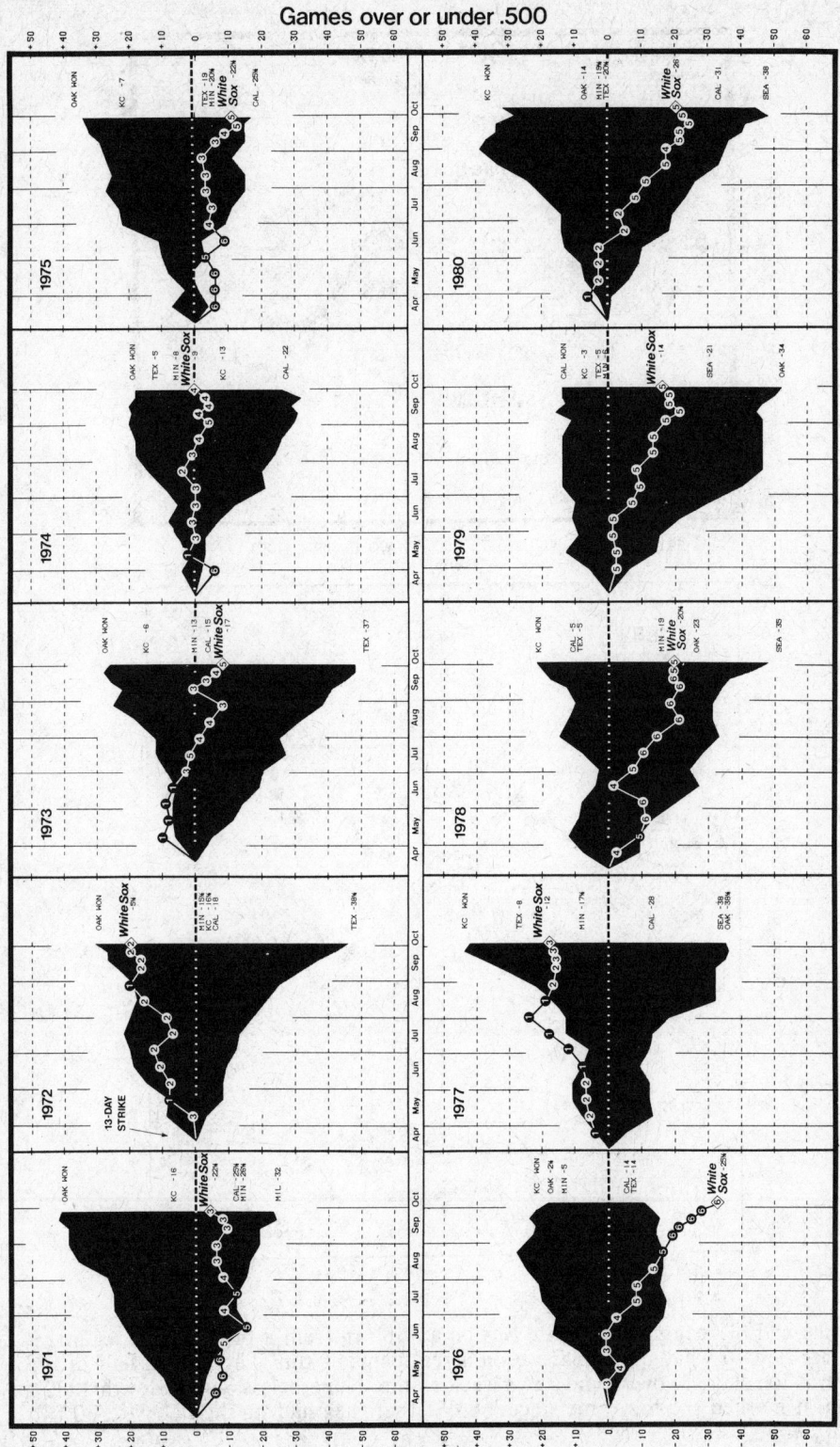

Like bolts from the blue, the strong performances in 1972 and '77 came out of nowhere, and ultimately led nowhere, but they brightened an otherwise dismal period for the Sox.

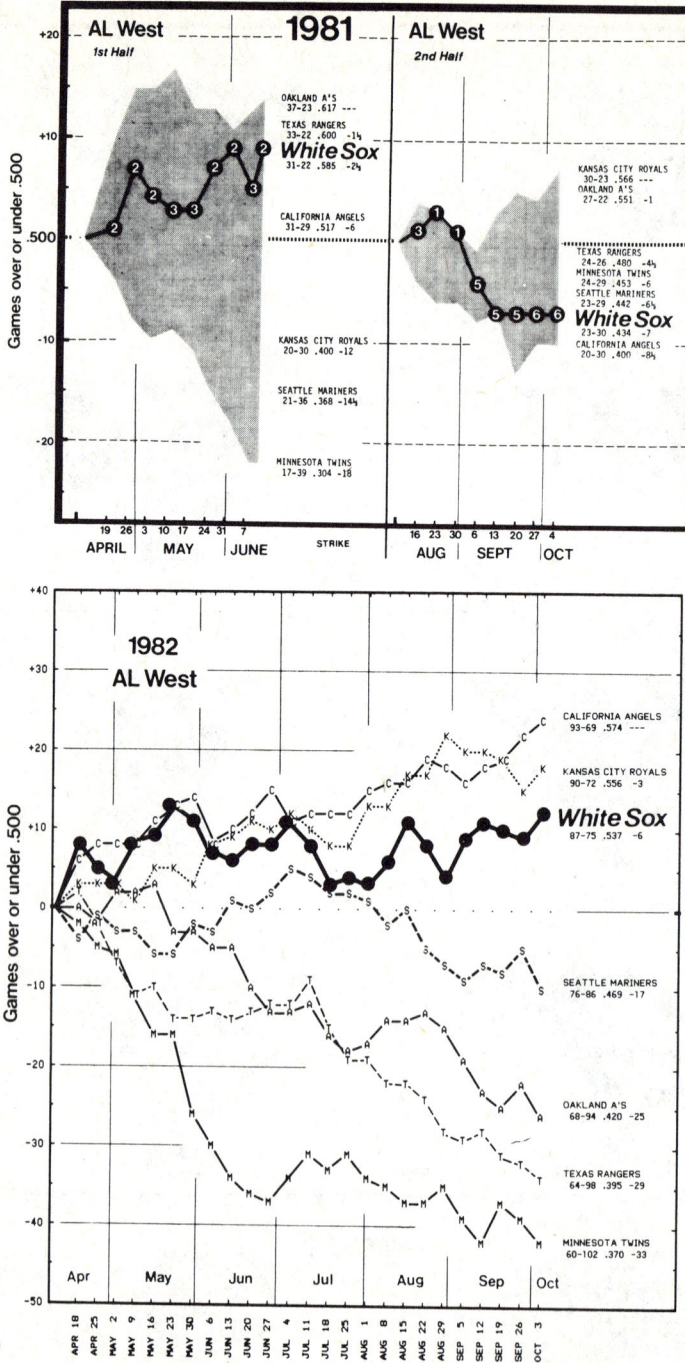

The strike in 1981 caught the White Sox on an upturn from a brief tumble, calling a premature halt to what might have been a real pennant run. The second half of the season was too short to overcome a two-week slump. Nonetheless, coupled with 1982's showing, it marked the first time since '66–'67 that they had finished above .500 two years in a row.

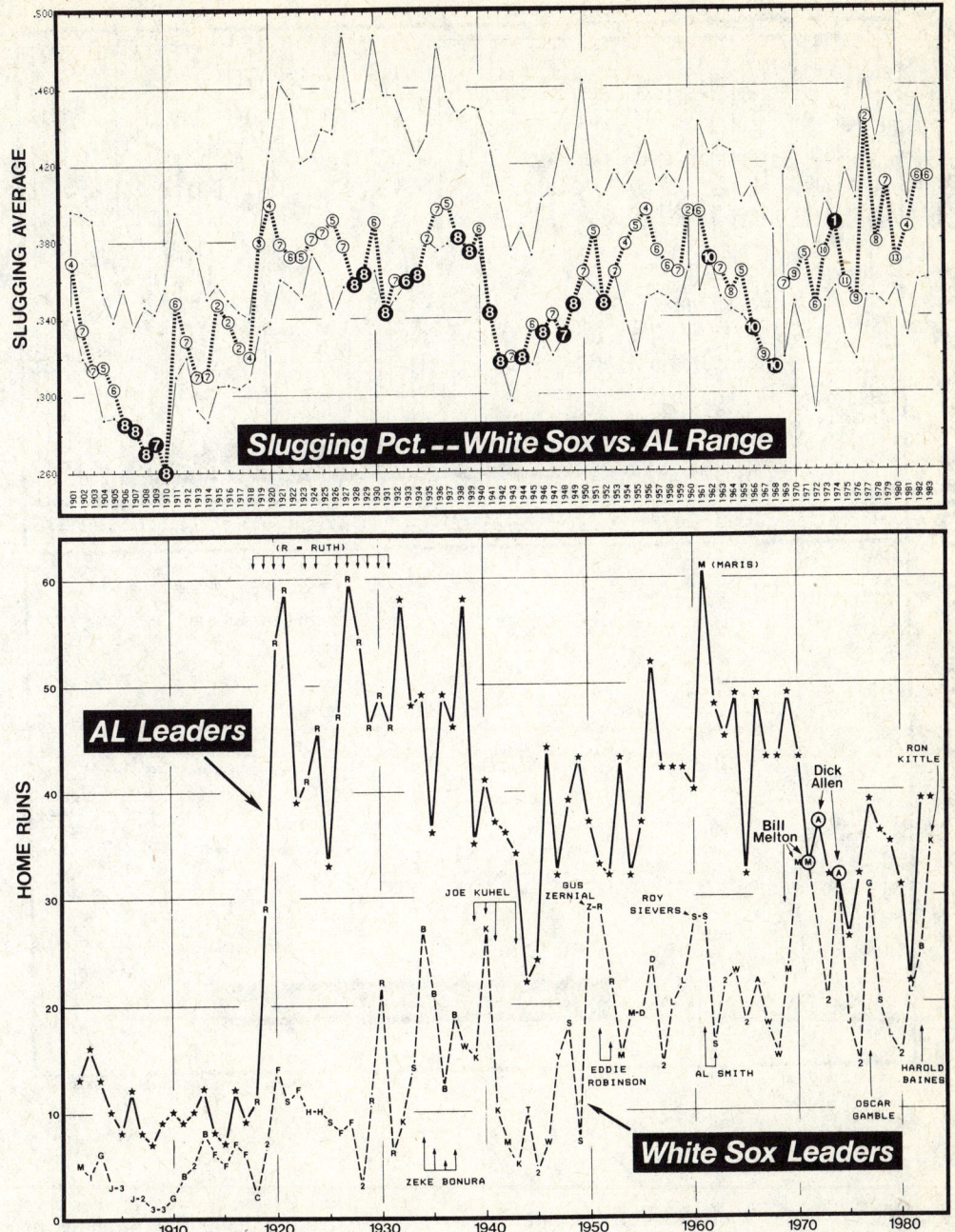

The White Sox' failure over the years to develop hitters who can put the ball in the seats has given the fine pitching staffs too much to overcome. Their first place finish in team slugging in 1974 was only their second finish in the top *three* since 1920. The gap between the club's home run leaders and the league leaders underscores the point: the club is only just reaching parity in this vital department. (Names are listed for those who topped 25 homers for the Sox; other club leaders are indicated by an initial or the number tied for the position.)

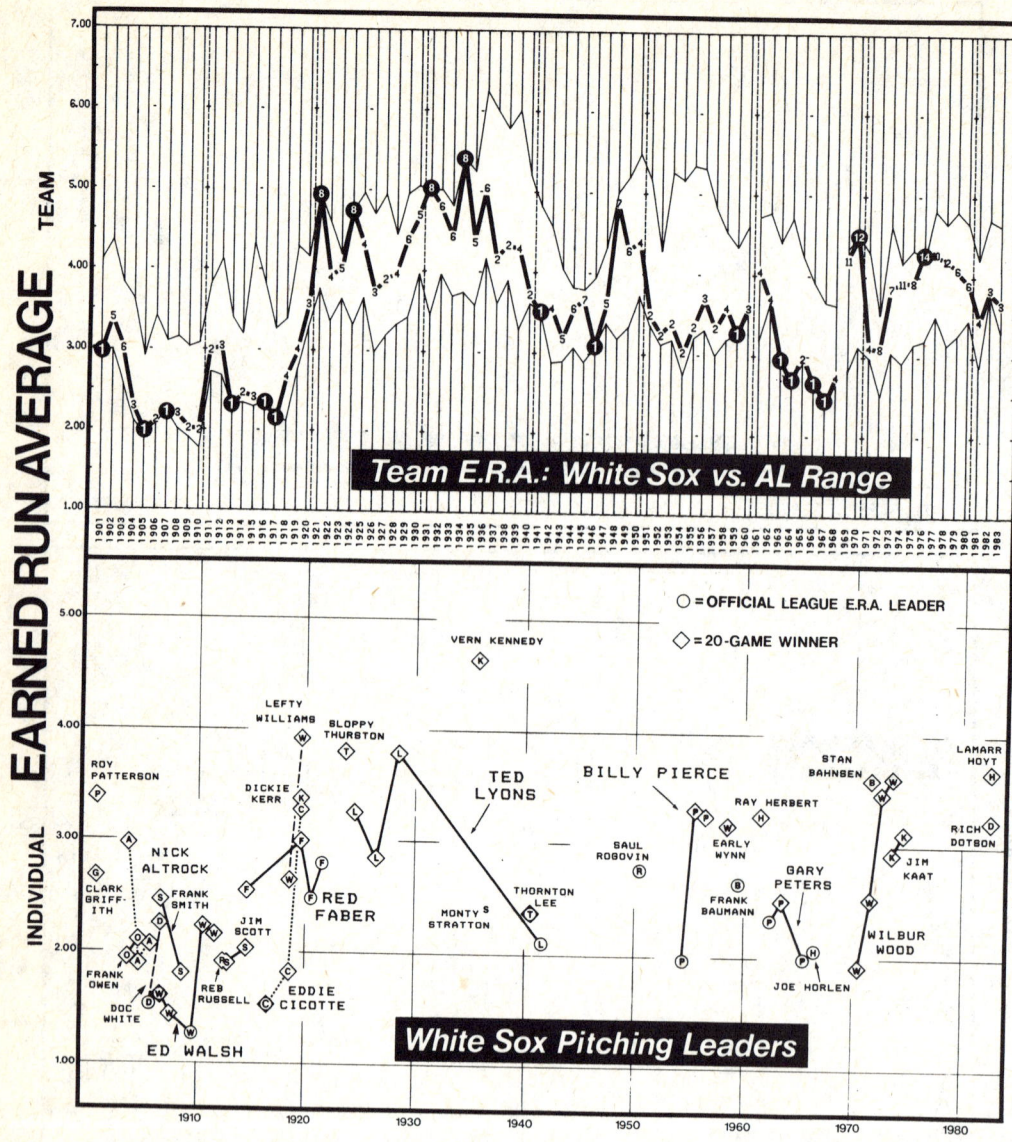

One of the two hallmarks of the traditional White Sox team: outstanding pitching, to go along with strong fielding. The individuals listed in the lower panel are all the White Sox pitchers who ever won twenty games, led the league in ERA, or had Jimmy Stewart play them in the story of their lives.

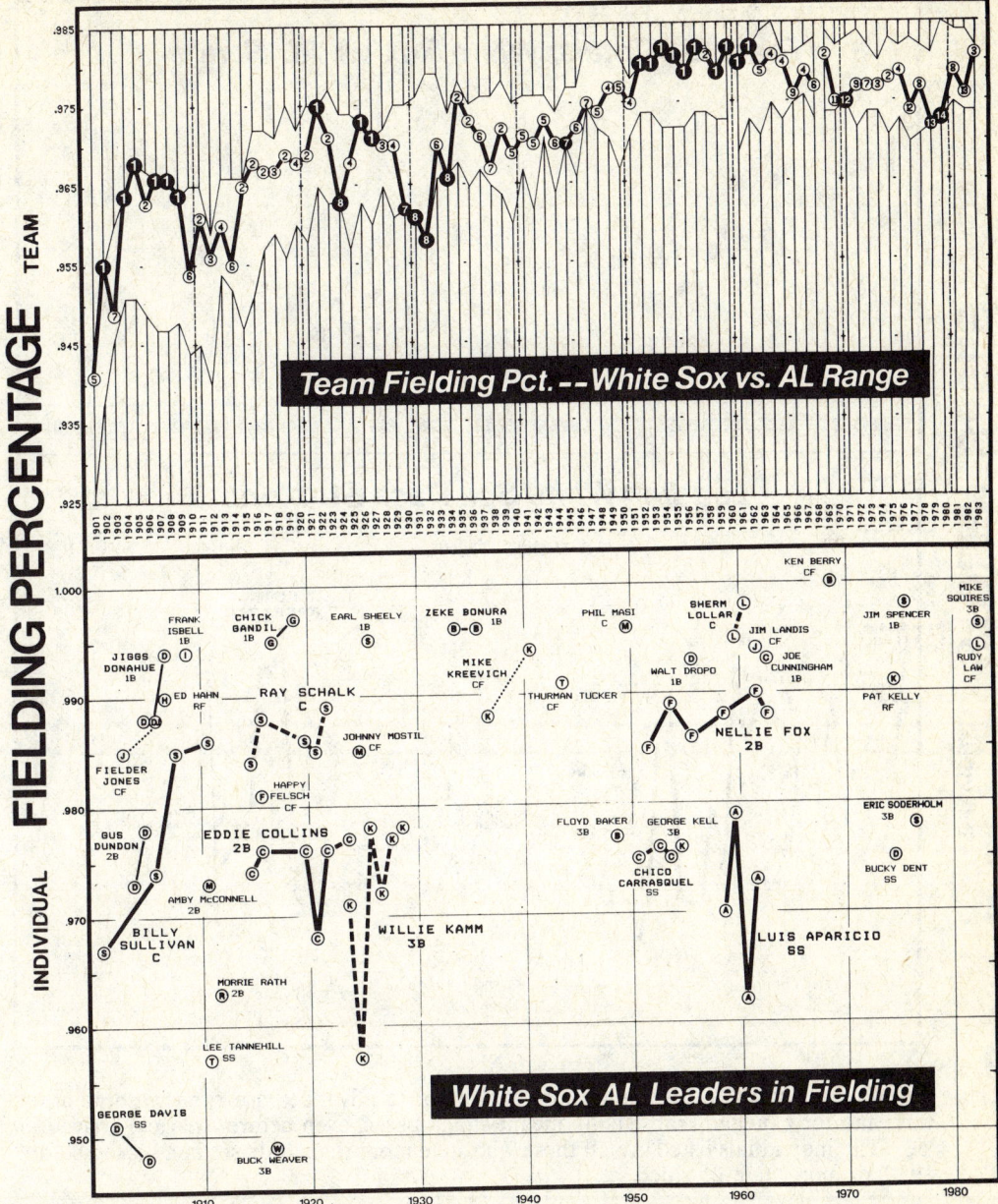

A tip of the cap to the Sox' great glove men; the lower panel shows all the White Sox who have led the league in fielding at their respective positions. Notice the remarkable run from 1952 to 1962: ten firsts and one second in team fielding percentage, aided by the double play combinations of Fox and Carrasquel followed by Fox and Aparicio.

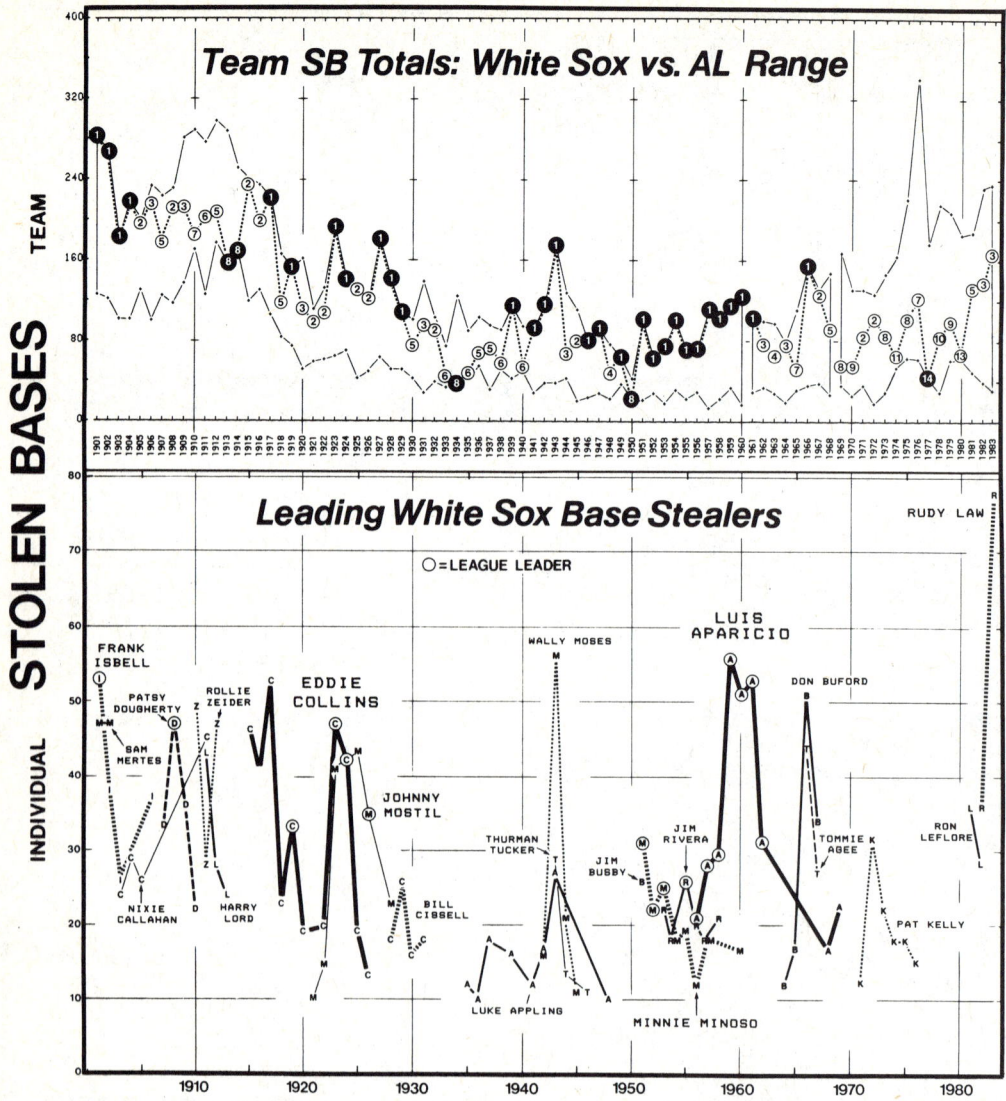

If you're not going to hit home runs, you've got to advance base runners some other way, and for Chicago that usually meant stolen bases, even before Aparicio arrived in '56. (The individuals listed are all those who stole more than 40 bases in a season before 1920, or more than 25 since.)

Player Register

The Player Register is an alphabetical listing of every man who has played in the major leagues and played or managed for the Chicago White Sox from 1901 through today, except those players who were primarily pitchers. However, pitchers who pinch-hit and played in other positions for a total of 25 games or more are listed in this Player Register. Included are facts about the players and their year-by-year batting records and their lifetime totals of League Championship Series and World Series.

Much of this information has never been compiled, especially for the period 1876 through 1919. For certain other years some statistics are still missing or incomplete. Research in this area is still in progress, and the years that lack complete information are indicated. In fact, all information and abbreviations that may appear unfamiliar are explained in the sample format presented below. John Doe, the player used in the sample, is fictitious and serves only to illustrate the information.

		G	AB	H	2B	3B	HR	HR%	R	RBI	BB	SO	SB	BA	SA	Pinch Hit AB	H	G by POS
John Doe					DOE, JOHN LEE (Slim)											BR TR 6'2" 165 lbs.		
					Played as John Cherry part of 1900.											BB 1884 BL 1906		
					Born John Lee Doughnut. Brother of Bill Doe.													
					B. Jan. 1,1850, New York, N. Y. D. July 1, 1855, New York, N. Y.													
					Manager 1908-15.													
					Hall of Fame 1946.													
1884	STL U	125	435	121	18	1	3	0.7	44		37	42	7	.278	.345	9	2	SS-99, P-26
1885	LOU AA	155	547	138	22	3	3	0.6	50	58	42	48	8	.252	.320	8	4	SS-115, P-40
1886	CLE N	147	485	134	38	5	0	0.0	66	54	48	50	8	.276	.375	7	1	SS-107, P-40
1887	BOS N	129	418	117	15	3	1	0.2	38	52	32	37	1	.280	.337	1	0	SS-102, P-27
1888	NY N	144	506	135	26	2	6	1.2	50	63	43	50	1	.267	.362	10	8	SS-105, P-39
1889	3 teams	DET	N (10G - .300)			PIT	N (32G - .241)			PHI	N (41G - .364)							
"	total	83	237	75	31	16	7	3.0	90	42	25	35	3	.316	.671	6	3	SS-61, P-22
1890	NY P	123	430	119	27	5	1	0.2	63	59	39	39	2	.277	.370	12	10	SS-85, P-38
1900	CHI N	146	498	116	29	4	3	0.6	51	46	59	53	1	.233	.325	13	8	SS-111, P-35
1901	NY N	149	540	147	19	6	4	0.7	57	74	49	58	3	.272	.352	23	15	SS-114, P-35
1906	CHI A	144	567	143	26	4	4	0.7	70	43	37	54	1	.252	.333	7	1	SS-113, P-31
1907		134	515	140	31	2	5	1.0	61	70	37	42	0	.272	.369	13	8	SS-97, P-37
1908		106	372	92	10	2	4	1.1	36	40	4	55	1	.247	.317	1	0	SS-105, P-1
1914	CHI F	6	6	0	0	0	0	0.0	0	0	0	1	0	.000	.000	0	0	P-6
1915	NY A	1	0	0	0	0	–	–	0	0	0	0	0	–	–	0	0	SS-1
14 yrs.		1592	5556	1927	292	53 4th	41	0.7	676	601	452	564	36	.266	.360	110	60	SS-1215, P-377
3 yrs.		384	1454	375	67	8	13	0.9	167	153	78	151	2	.258	.342 6th	21	9	SS-315, P-96

LEAGUE CHAMPIONSHIP SERIES

1901	NY N	3	14	5	2	0	3	21.4	3	7	0	1	0	.357	1.143	0	0	OF-3

WORLD SERIES

1901	NY N	7	28	9	1	0	6	21.4	12	14	3	4	0	.321	1.000	0	0	SS-5, P-2
1906	STL N	5	10	5	1	0	1	10.0	3	2	0	2	0	.500	.900	2	0	P-4, SS-1
2 yrs.		12	38	14	2	0	7	18.4 5th	15	16 9th	3	6	0	.368	.974	2	0	SS-6, P-6

211

PLAYER INFORMATION

John Doe	This shortened version of the player's full name is the name most familiar to the fans. All players in this section are alphabetically arranged by the last name part of this name.
DOE, JOHN LEE	Player's full name. The arrangement is last name first, then first and middle name(s).
(Slim)	Player's nickname. Any name or names appearing in parentheses indicates a nickname.

The player's main batting and throwing style. Doe, for instance, batted and threw righthanded. The information listed directly below the main batting information indicates that at various times in a player's career he changed his batting style. The "BB" for Doe in 1884 means he was a switch hitter that year, and the "BL" means he batted lefthanded in 1906. For the years that are not shown it can be assumed that Doe batted right, as his main batting information indicates.	BR TR BB 1884 BL 1906
Player's height.	6'2"
Player's average playing weight.	165 lbs
The player at one time in his major league career played under another name and can be found only in box scores or newspaper stories under that name.	Played as John Cherry part of 1900
The name the player was given at birth. (For the most part, the player never used this name while playing in the major leagues, but, if he did, it would be listed as "played as," which is explained above under the heading "Played as John Cherry part of 1900.")	Born John Lee Doughnut
The player's brother. (Relatives indicated here are fathers, sons, brothers, grandfathers, and grandsons who played or managed in the major leagues and the National Association.)	Brother of Bill Doe

Date and place of birth.   B. Jan. 1, 1850, New York, N.Y.

Date and place of death. (For those players who are listed simply as "deceased," it means that, although no certification of death or other information is presently available, it is reasonably certain they are dead.)   D. July 1, 1955, New York, N.Y.

Doe also served as a major league manager. All men who were managers for the White Sox can be found in the Manager Register, where their complete managerial record is shown.   Manager 1908–15

Doe was elected to the Baseball Hall of Fame in 1946.   Hall of Fame 1946

COLUMN HEADINGS INFORMATION

G	AB	H	2B	3B	HR	HR %	R	RBI	BB	SO	SB	BA	SA	Pinch Hit AB H	G by POS

G	Games
AB	At Bats
H	Hits
2B	Doubles
3B	Triples
HR	Home Runs
HR %	Home Run Percentage (the number of home runs per 100 times at bat)
R	Runs Scored
RBI	Runs Batted In
BB	Bases on Balls
SO	Strikeouts
SB	Stolen Bases
BA	Batting Average
SA	Slugging Average

Pinch Hit

AB	Pinch Hit At Bats
H	Pinch Hits
G by POS	Games by Position. (All fielding positions a man played within the given year are shown. The position where the most games were played is listed first. Any man who pitched, as Doe did, is listed also in the alphabetically arranged Pitcher Register, where his complete pitching record can be found.) If no fielding positions are shown in a particular year, it means the player only pinch-hit, pinch-ran, or was a "designated hitter."

TEAM AND LEAGUE INFORMATION

Doe's record has been exaggerated so that his playing career spans all the years of the six different major leagues. Directly alongside the year and team information is the symbol for the league:

N   National League (1876 to date)
A   American League (1901 to date)
F   Federal League (1914–15)
AA   American Association (1882–91)
P   Players' League (1890)
U   Union Association (1884)

STL—The abbreviation of the city in which the team played. Doe, for example, played for St. Louis in 1884. All teams in this section are listed by an abbreviation of the city in which the team played. The abbreviations follow:

ALT	Altoona		NWK	Newark
ATL	Atlanta		NY	New York
BAL	Baltimore		OAK	Oakland
BOS	Boston		PHI	Philadelphia
BKN	Brooklyn		PIT	Pittsburgh
BUF	Buffalo		PRO	Providence
CAL	California		RIC	Richmond
CHI	Chicago		ROC	Rochester
CIN	Cincinnati		SD	San Diego
CLE	Cleveland		SEA	Seattle
COL	Columbus		SF	San Francisco
DET	Detroit		STL	St. Louis
HAR	Hartford		STP	St. Paul
HOU	Houston		SYR	Syracuse
IND	Indianapolis		TEX	Texas
KC	Kansas City		TOL	Toledo
LA	Los Angeles		TOR	Toronto
LOU	Louisville		TRO	Troy
MIL	Milwaukee		WAS	Washington
MIN	Minnesota		WIL	Wilmington
MON	Montreal		WOR	Worcester

Three franchises in the history of major league baseball changed their location during the season. These teams are designated by the first letter of the two cities they represented. They are:

B-B Brooklyn-Baltimore (American Association, 1890)
C-M Cincinnati-Milwaukee (American Association, 1891)
C-P Chicago-Pittsburgh (Union Association, 1884)

Blank space appearing beneath a team and league indicates that the team and league are the same. Doe, for example, played for Chicago in the American League from 1906 through 1908.

3 Teams Total. Indicates a player played for more than one team in the same year. Doe played for three teams in 1889. The number of games he played and his batting average for each team are also shown. Directly beneath this line, following the word "total," is Doe's combined record for all three teams for 1889.

Total Playing Years. This information, which appears as the first item on the player's lifetime total line, indicates the total number of years in which he played at least one game. Doe, for example, played in at least one game for fourteen years.

White Sox Playing Years. This information, which appears as the first item on the player's White Sox career total line, indicates the total number of years in which he played at least one game for the White Sox.

STATISTICAL INFORMATION

League Leaders. Statistics that appear in bold-faced print indicate the player led his league that year in a particular statistical category. Doe, for example, led the National League in doubles in 1889. When there is a tie for league lead, the figures for all the men who tied are shown in boldface.

All-Time Single Season Leaders. Indicated by the small number that appears next to the statistic. Doe, for example, is shown with a small number "1" next to his doubles total in 1889. This means he is first on the all-time major league list for hitting the most doubles in a single season. All players who tied for first are also shown by the same number.

Lifetime Leaders. Indicated by the figure that appears beneath the line showing the player's lifetime totals. Doe has a "4th" shown below his lifetime triples total. This means that, lifetime, Doe ranks fourth among major league players for hitting the most triples. Once again, only the top ten are indicated, and players who are tied receive the same number.

Unavailable Information. Any time a blank space is shown in a particular statistical column, such as in Doe's 1884 RBI total, it indicates the information was unavailable or incomplete.

Meaningless Averages. Indicated by use of a dash (—). In the case of Doe, a dash is shown for his 1915 batting average. This means that, although he played one game, he had no official at bats. A batting average of .000 would mean he had at least one at bat with no hits.

White Sox Career Totals. The statistical line appearing below Doe's major league career totals indicates his totals for his career with the Chicago White Sox. In Doe's case, the totals are for the years 1906—1908.

White Sox Lifetime Leaders. Indicated by the figure that appears beneath his White Sox career total. Doe has a "6th" shown below his White Sox career pinch hit at bats total. This means that he ranks sixth among White Sox in that category, counting only his years with the club.

World Series Lifetime Leaders. Indicated by the figure that appears beneath the player's lifetime World Series totals. Doe has a "5th" shown below his lifetime home run total. This means that, lifetime, Doe ranks fifth among major league players for hitting the most home runs in total World Series play. Players who tied for a position in the top ten are shown by the same number, so that, if two men tied for fourth and fifth place, the appropriate information for both men would be followed by the small number "4," and the next man would be considered sixth in the ranking. White Sox career totals are not provided for post-season play; the indicated totals are for Doe's entire career.

217 Player Register

	G	AB	H	2B	3B	HR	HR%	R	RBI	BB	SO	SB	BA	SA	Pinch Hit AB	Pinch Hit H	G by POS

Cal Abrams
ABRAMS, CALVIN ROSS
B. Mar. 2, 1924, Philadelphia, Pa.
BL TL 5'11½" 195 lbs.

Year	Team	G	AB	H	2B	3B	HR	HR%	R	RBI	BB	SO	SB	BA	SA	PH-AB	PH-H	G by POS
1949	BKN N	8	24	2	1	0	0	0.0	6	0	7	6	1	.083	.125	1	0	OF-7
1950		38	44	9	1	0	0	0.0	5	4	9	13	0	.205	.227	20	4	OF-15
1951		67	150	42	8	0	3	2.0	27	19	36	26	3	.280	.393	22	5	OF-34
1952	2 teams	BKN N (10G – .200)					CIN N (71G – .278)											
"	total	81	168	46	9	2	2	1.2	24	13	21	29	1	.274	.387	35	6	OF-46
1953	PIT N	119	448	128	10	6	15	3.3	66	43	58	70	4	.286	.435	7	2	OF-112
1954	2 teams	PIT N (17G – .143)					BAL A (115G – .293)											
"	total	132	465	130	23	8	6	1.3	73	27	82	76	1	.280	.402	5	1	OF-128
1955	BAL A	118	309	75	12	3	6	1.9	56	32	89	69	2	.243	.359	16	2	OF-96, 1B-4
1956	CHI A	4	3	1	0	0	0	0.0	0	0	2	1	0	.333	.333	2	1	OF-2
8 yrs.		567	1611	433	64	19	32	2.0	257	138	304	290	12	.269	.392	108	21	OF-440, 1B-4
1 yr.		4	3	1	0	0	0	0.0	0	0	2	1	0	.333	.333	2	1	OF-2

Jerry Adair
ADAIR, KENNETH JERRY
B. Dec. 17, 1936, Sand Springs, Okla.
BR TR 6' 175 lbs.

Year	Team	G	AB	H	2B	3B	HR	HR%	R	RBI	BB	SO	SB	BA	SA	PH-AB	PH-H	G by POS
1958	BAL A	11	19	2	0	0	0	0.0	1	0	1	7	0	.105	.105	0	0	SS-10, 2B-1
1959		12	35	11	0	1	0	0.0	3	2	1	5	0	.314	.371	0	0	2B-11, SS-1
1960		3	5	1	0	0	1	20.0	1	1	0	0	0	.200	.800	0	0	2B-3
1961		133	386	102	21	1	9	2.3	41	37	35	51	5	.264	.394	0	0	2B-107, SS-27, 3B-2
1962		139	538	153	29	4	11	2.0	67	48	27	77	7	.284	.414	4	0	SS-113, 2B-34, 3B-1
1963		109	382	87	21	3	6	1.6	34	30	9	51	3	.228	.346	5	2	2B-103
1964		155	569	141	20	3	9	1.6	56	47	28	72	3	.248	.341	2	1	2B-153
1965		157	582	151	26	3	7	1.2	51	66	35	65	6	.259	.351	0	0	2B-157
1966	2 teams	BAL A (17G – .288)					CHI A (105G – .243)											
"	total	122	422	105	19	2	4	0.9	30	39	21	52	3	.249	.332	4	1	SS-75, 2B-63
1967	2 teams	CHI A (28G – .204)					BOS A (89G – .291)											
"	total	117	414	112	17	1	3	0.7	47	35	17	52	1	.271	.338	8	2	2B-50, 3B-35, SS-30
1968	BOS A	74	208	45	1	0	2	1.0	18	12	9	28	0	.216	.250	13	3	SS-46, 2B-12, 3B-7, 1B-1
1969	KC A	126	432	108	9	1	5	1.2	29	48	20	36	1	.250	.310	6	1	2B-109, SS-8, 3B-1
1970		7	27	4	0	0	0	0.0	0	1	5	3	0	.148	.148	0	0	2B-7
13 yrs.		1165	4019	1022	163	19	57	1.4	378	366	208	499	29	.254	.347	42	10	2B-810, SS-310, 3B-46, 1B-1
2 yrs.		133	468	110	22	2	4	0.9	33	45	21	61	3	.235	.316	3	0	2B-77, SS-75

WORLD SERIES

Year	Team	G	AB	H	2B	3B	HR	HR%	R	RBI	BB	SO	SB	BA	SA	PH-AB	PH-H	G by POS
1967	BOS A	5	16	2	0	0	0	0.0	0	1	0	3	1	.125	.125	0	0	2B-4

Bobby Adams
ADAMS, ROBERT HENRY
Brother of Dick Adams. Father of Mike Adams.
B. Dec. 14, 1921, Tuolumne, Calif.
BR TR 5'10½" 160 lbs.

Year	Team	G	AB	H	2B	3B	HR	HR%	R	RBI	BB	SO	SB	BA	SA	PH-AB	PH-H	G by POS
1946	CIN N	94	311	76	13	3	4	1.3	35	24	18	32	16	.244	.344	13	4	2B-74, OF-2, 3B-1
1947		81	217	59	11	2	4	1.8	39	20	25	23	9	.272	.396	1	1	2B-69
1948		87	262	78	20	3	1	0.4	33	21	25	23	6	.298	.408	14	5	2B-64, 3B-7
1949		107	277	70	16	2	0	0.0	32	25	26	36	4	.253	.325	23	6	2B-63, 3B-14
1950		115	348	98	21	8	3	0.9	57	25	43	29	7	.282	.414	9	1	2B-53, 3B-42
1951		125	403	107	12	5	5	1.2	57	24	43	40	4	.266	.357	30	10	3B-60, 2B-42, OF-1
1952		154	637	180	25	4	6	0.9	85	48	49	67	11	.283	.363	0	0	3B-154
1953		150	607	167	14	6	8	1.3	99	49	58	67	3	.275	.357	0	0	3B-150
1954		110	390	105	25	6	3	0.8	69	42	55	46	2	.269	.387	11	4	3B-93, 2B-2
1955	2 teams	CIN N (64G – .273)					CHI A (28G – .095)											
"	total	92	171	43	11	3	2	1.2	31	23	24	25	2	.251	.386	20	5	3B-51, 2B-6
1956	BAL A	41	111	25	6	1	0	0.0	19	7	25	15	1	.225	.297	0	0	3B-24, 2B-18
1957	CHI N	60	187	47	10	2	1	0.5	21	10	17	28	0	.251	.342	8	1	3B-47, 2B-1
1958		62	96	27	4	4	0	0.0	14	4	6	15	2	.281	.406	35	9	1B-11, 3B-9, 2B-7
1959		3	2	0	0	0	0	0.0	0	0	0	1	0	.000	.000	2	0	1B-1
14 yrs.		1281	4019	1082	188	49	37	0.9	591	303	414	447	67	.269	.368	166	46	3B-652, 2B-399, 1B-12, OF-3
1 yr.		28	21	2	0	1	0	0.0	8	3	4	4	0	.095	.190	2	0	3B-9, 2B-1

Doug Adams
ADAMS, HAROLD DOUGLAS
B. Jan. 27, 1943, Blue River, Wis.
BL TR 6'3" 185 lbs.

Year	Team	G	AB	H	2B	3B	HR	HR%	R	RBI	BB	SO	SB	BA	SA	PH-AB	PH-H	G by POS
1969	CHI A	8	14	3	0	0	0	0.0	1	1	1	3	0	.214	.214	5	2	C-4

Herb Adams
ADAMS, HERBERT LOREN
B. Apr. 14, 1928, Hollywood, Calif.
BL TL 5'9" 160 lbs.

Year	Team	G	AB	H	2B	3B	HR	HR%	R	RBI	BB	SO	SB	BA	SA	PH-AB	PH-H	G by POS
1948	CHI A	5	11	3	1	0	0	0.0	1	0	1	1	0	.273	.364	0	0	OF-4
1949		56	208	61	5	3	0	0.0	26	16	9	16	1	.293	.346	5	1	OF-48
1950		34	118	24	2	3	0	0.0	12	2	12	7	3	.203	.271	1	0	OF-33
3 yrs.		95	337	88	8	6	0	0.0	39	18	22	24	4	.261	.320	6	1	OF-85
3 yrs.		95	337	88	8	6	0	0.0	39	18	22	24	4	.261	.320	6	1	OF-85

Tommie Agee
AGEE, TOMMIE LEE
B. Aug. 9, 1942, Magnolia, Ala.
BR TR 5'11" 195 lbs.

Year	Team	G	AB	H	2B	3B	HR	HR%	R	RBI	BB	SO	SB	BA	SA	PH-AB	PH-H	G by POS
1962	CLE A	5	14	3	0	0	0	0.0	2	0	4	0	.214	.214	2	0	OF-3
1963		13	27	4	1	0	1	3.7	3	3	2	9	0	.148	.296	0	0	OF-13
1964		13	12	2	0	0	0	0.0	0	0	0	3	0	.167	.167	0	0	OF-12
1965	CHI A	10	19	3	1	0	0	0.0	2	3	2	6	0	.158	.211	1	0	OF-9
1966		160	629	172	27	8	22	3.5	98	86	41	127	44	.273	.447	0	0	OF-159
1967		158	529	124	26	2	14	2.6	73	52	44	129	28	.234	.371	2	0	OF-152
1968	NY N	132	368	80	12	3	5	1.4	30	17	15	103	13	.217	.307	3	1	OF-127
1969		149	565	153	23	4	26	4.6	97	76	59	137	12	.271	.464	3	1	OF-146
1970		153	636	182	30	7	24	3.8	107	75	55	156	31	.286	.469	3	1	OF-150
1971		113	425	121	19	0	14	3.3	58	50	50	84	28	.285	.428	6	3	OF-107
1972		114	422	96	23	0	13	3.1	52	47	53	92	8	.227	.374	4	0	OF-109
1973	2 teams	HOU N (83G – .235)					STL N (26G – .177)											
"	total	109	266	59	8	3	11	4.1	38	22	21	68	3	.222	.398	19	4	OF-86
12 yrs.		1129	3912	999	170	27	130	3.3	558	433	342	918	167	.255	.412	43	11	OF-1073
3 yrs.		328	1177	299	54	10	36	3.1	173	141	87	262	72	.254	.409	3	1	OF-320

Player Register

	G	AB	H	2B	3B	HR	HR%	R	RBI	BB	SO	SB	BA	SA	Pinch Hit AB	H	G by POS

Tommie Agee continued
LEAGUE CHAMPIONSHIP SERIES
1969 NY N | 3 | 14 | 5 | 1 | 0 | 2 | 14.3 | 4 | 4 | 2 | 5 | 2 | .357 | .857 | 0 | 0 | OF-3
WORLD SERIES
1969 NY N | 5 | 18 | 3 | 0 | 0 | 1 | 5.6 | 1 | 1 | 2 | 5 | 1 | .167 | .333 | 0 | 0 | OF-5

Scotty Alcock
ALCOCK, JOHN FORBES BR TR 5'9½" 160 lbs.
B. Nov. 29, 1885, Wooster, Ohio D. Jan. 30, 1973, Wooster, Ohio
1914 CHI A | 54 | 156 | 27 | 4 | 2 | 0 | 0.0 | 12 | 7 | 7 | 14 | 4 | .173 | .224 | 3 | 0 | 3B-48, 2B-1

Hank Allen
ALLEN, HAROLD ANDREW BR TR 6' 190 lbs.
Brother of Richie Allen. Brother of Ron Allen.
B. July 23, 1940, Wampum, Pa.

1966 WAS A	9	31	12	0	0	1	3.2	2	6	3	6	0	.387	.484	0	0	OF-9
1967	116	292	68	8	4	3	1.0	34	17	13	53	3	.233	.318	21	7	OF-99
1968	68	128	28	2	2	1	0.8	16	9	7	16	0	.219	.289	22	5	OF-25, 3B-16, 2B-11
1969	109	271	75	9	3	1	0.4	42	17	13	28	12	.277	.343	23	5	OF-91, 3B-6, 2B-3
1970 2 teams	WAS A (22G – .211)				MIL A (28G – .230)												
" total	50	99	22	6	0	0	0.0	7	8	12	14	0	.222	.283	14	2	OF-31, 2B-5, 1B-4
1972 CHI A	9	21	3	0	0	0	0.0	1	0	0	2	0	.143	.143	6	0	3B-6
1973	28	39	4	2	0	0	0.0	2	0	1	9	0	.103	.154	5	0	3B-9, 1B-8, OF-5, 2B-1, C-1
7 yrs.	389	881	212	27	9	6	0.7	104	57	49	128	15	.241	.312	85	19	OF-260, 3B-37, 2B-20, 1B-12, C-1
2 yrs.	37	60	7	2	0	0	0.0	3	0	1	11	0	.117	.150	5	0	3B-15, 1B-8, OF-5, 2B-1, C-1

Richie Allen
ALLEN, RICHARD ANTHONY BR TR 5'11" 187 lbs.
Brother of Hank Allen. Brother of Ron Allen.
B. Mar. 8, 1942, Wampum, Pa.

1963 PHI N	10	24	7	2	1	0	0.0	6	2	0	5	0	.292	.458	2	0	OF-7, 3B-1
1964	162	632	201	38	13	29	4.6	125	91	67	138	3	.318	.557	0	0	3B-162
1965	161	619	187	31	14	20	3.2	93	85	74	150	15	.302	.494	1	0	3B-160, SS-2
1966	141	524	166	25	10	40	7.6	112	110	68	136	10	.317	.632	4	1	3B-91, OF-47
1967	122	463	142	31	10	23	5.0	89	77	75	117	20	.307	.566	5	1	3B-121, SS-1, 2B-1
1968	152	521	137	17	9	33	6.3	87	90	74	161	7	.263	.520	8	0	OF-139, 3B-10
1969	118	438	126	23	3	32	7.3	79	89	64	144	9	.288	.573	1	1	1B-117
1970 STL N	122	459	128	17	5	34	7.4	88	101	71	118	5	.279	.560	3	1	1B-79, 3B-38, OF-3
1971 LA N	155	549	162	24	1	23	4.2	82	90	93	113	8	.295	.468	3	0	3B-67, OF-60, 1B-28
1972 CHI A	148	506	156	28	5	**37**	**7.3**	90	**113**	**99**	126	19	.308	**.603**	7	1	1B-143, 3B-2
1973	72	250	79	20	3	16	6.4	39	41	33	51	7	.316	.612	3	1	1B-67, 2B-2, DH-1
1974	128	462	139	23	1	**32**	**6.9**	84	88	57	89	7	.301	**.563**	4	0	1B-125, DH-1, 2B-1
1975 PHI N	119	416	97	21	3	12	2.9	54	62	58	109	11	.233	.385	5	0	1B-113
1976	85	298	80	16	1	15	5.0	52	49	37	63	11	.268	.480	2	1	1B-85
1977 OAK A	54	171	41	4	0	5	2.9	19	31	24	36	1	.240	.351	2	0	1B-50, DH-1
15 yrs.	1749	6332	1848	320	79	351	5.5	1099	1119	894	1556	133	.292	.534	46	5	1B-807, 3B-652, OF-256, 2B-4, DH-3, SS-3
												9th					
3 yrs.	348	1218	374	71	9	85	7.0	213	242	189	266	33	.307	.589	14	1	1B-335, 2B-3, DH-2, 3B-2
												5th					

LEAGUE CHAMPIONSHIP SERIES
1976 PHI N | 3 | 9 | 2 | 0 | 0 | 0 | 0.0 | 1 | 0 | 3 | 2 | 0 | .222 | .222 | 0 | 0 | 1B-3

Bill Almon
ALMON, WILLIAM FRANCIS BR TR 6'3" 180 lbs.
B. Nov. 21, 1952, Providence, R. I.

1974 SD N	16	38	12	1	0	0	0.0	4	3	2	9	1	.316	.342	0	0	SS-14
1975	6	10	4	0	0	0	0.0	0	0	0	1	0	.400	.400	1	0	SS-2
1976	14	57	14	3	0	1	1.8	6	6	2	9	3	.246	.351	0	0	SS-14
1977	155	613	160	18	11	2	0.3	75	43	37	114	20	.261	.336	0	0	SS-155
1978	138	405	102	19	2	0	0.0	39	21	33	74	17	.252	.309	4	1	3B-114, SS-15, 2B-7
1979	100	198	45	3	0	1	0.5	20	8	21	48	6	.227	.258	3	0	2B-61, SS-25, OF-1
1980 2 teams	MON N (18G – .263)				NY N (48G – .170)												
" total	66	150	29	4	3	0	0.0	15	7	9	32	2	.193	.260	4	0	SS-34, 2B-19, 3B-9
1981 CHI A	103	349	105	12	2	4	1.1	46	41	21	60	16	.301	.375	0	0	SS-103
1982	111	308	79	10	4	4	1.3	40	26	25	49	10	.256	.354	1	0	SS-108, DH-1
1983 OAK A	143	451	120	29	1	4	0.9	45	63	26	67	26	.266	.361	14	3	SS-52, 3B-40, 1B-38, OF-23, 2B-5, DH-4
10 yrs.	852	2579	670	97	23	16	0.6	290	218	176	463	101	.260	.334	27	4	SS-522, 3B-163, 2B-92, 1B-38, OF-24, DH-5
2 yrs.	214	657	184	20	6	8	1.2	86	67	46	109	26	.280	.365	1	0	SS-211, DH-1

Sandy Alomar
ALOMAR, CONDE SANTOS BB TR 5'9" 140 lbs.
B. Oct. 19, 1943, Salinas, Puerto Rico BR 1964-66

1964 MIL N	19	53	13	1	0	0	0.0	3	6	0	11	1	.245	.264	0	0	SS-19
1965	67	108	26	1	1	0	0.0	16	8	4	12	12	.241	.269	0	0	SS-39, 2B-19
1966 ATL N	31	44	4	1	0	0	0.0	4	2	1	10	0	.091	.114	1	0	2B-21, SS-5
1967 2 teams	NY N (15G – .000)				CHI A (12G – .200)												
" total	27	37	3	0	0	0	0.0	5	0	2	6	2	.081	.081	1	0	SS-18, 2B-4, 3B-3
1968 CHI A	133	363	92	8	2	0	0.0	41	12	20	42	21	.253	.287	4	2	2B-99, 3B-27, SS-9, OF-1
1969 2 teams	CHI A (22G – .224)				CAL A (134G – .250)												
" total	156	617	153	12	2	1	0.2	68	34	40	54	20	.248	.279	0	0	2B-156
1970 CAL A	162	672	169	18	2	0	0.3	82	36	49	65	35	.251	.293	0	0	2B-153, SS-10, 3B-1
1971	162	**689**	179	24	3	4	0.6	77	42	41	69	39	.260	.321	0	0	2B-137, SS-28
1972	155	610	146	20	3	1	0.2	65	25	47	55	20	.239	.287	0	0	2B-154, SS-4
1973	136	470	112	7	1	0	0.0	45	28	34	44	25	.238	.257	0	0	2B-110, SS-31
1974 2 teams	CAL A (46G – .222)				NY A (76G – .269)												
" total	122	333	87	8	1	1	0.3	47	28	15	33	8	.261	.300	3	1	2B-91, SS-19, 3B-5, DH-1, OF-1

Player Register

	G	AB	H	2B	3B	HR	HR%	R	RBI	BB	SO	SB	BA	SA	Pinch Hit AB	Pinch Hit H	G by POS

Sandy Alomar continued

1975 NY A	151	489	117	18	4	2	0.4	61	39	26	58	28	.239	.305	0	0	2B-150, SS-1
1976	67	163	39	4	0	1	0.6	20	10	13	12	12	.239	.282	2	0	2B-38, DH-9, SS-6, 3B-3, OF-1, 1B-1
1977 TEX A	69	83	22	3	0	1	1.2	21	11	8	13	4	.265	.337	7	2	DH-26, 2B-18, SS-6, OF-5, 1B-4, 3B-1
1978	24	29	6	1	0	0	0.0	3	1	1	7	0	.207	.241	0	0	1B-9, 2B-6, DH-3, 3B-3, SS-2
15 yrs.	1481	4760	1168	126	19	13	0.3	558	282	301	482	227	.245	.288	18	5	2B-1156, SS-197, 3B-43, DH-39, 1B-14, OF-8
3 yrs.	167	436	108	10	2	0	0.0	53	16	26	48	25	.248	.280	5	2	2B-123, 3B-27, SS-17, OF-1

LEAGUE CHAMPIONSHIP SERIES

1976 NY A	2	1	0	0	0	0	0.0	0	0	0	0	0	.000	.000	0	0	DH-1

Dave Altizer
ALTIZER, DAVID TILDON (Filipino)   BL TR 5'10½" 160 lbs.
B. Nov. 6, 1876, Pearl, Ill.   D. May 14, 1964, Pleasant Hill, Ill.

1906 WAS A	115	433	111	9	5	1	0.2	56	27	35		37	.256	.307	0	0	SS-113, OF-2
1907	147	540	145	15	5	1	0.2	60	42	34		38	.269	.320	0	0	SS-71, 1B-50, OF-26
1908 2 teams	WAS A (67G – .224)				CLE A (29G – .213)												
" total	96	294	65	2	3	0	0.0	30	23	20		15	.221	.248	7	1	2B-38, OF-24, 3B-16, SS-4, 1B-4
1909 CHI A	116	382	89	6	7	1	0.3	47	20	39		27	.233	.293	7	1	OF-62, 1B-45
1910 CIN N	3	10	6	0	0	0	0.0	3	0	3	0	0	.600	.600	0	0	SS-3
1911	37	75	17	4	1	0	0.0	8	4	9	5	2	.227	.307	4	1	SS-23, OF-1, 2B-1, 1B-1
6 yrs.	514	1734	433	36	21	3	0.2	204	116	140	5	119	.250	.300	18	3	SS-214, OF-115, 1B-100, 2B-39, 3B-16
1 yr.	116	382	89	6	7	1	0.3	47	20	39		27	.233	.293	7	1	OF-62, 1B-45

Luis Alvarado
ALVARADO, LUIS CESAR (Pimba)   BR TR 5'9" 162 lbs.
B. Jan. 15, 1949, La Jas, Puerto Rico

1968 BOS A	11	46	6	2	0	0	0.0	3	1	1	11	0	.130	.174	0	0	SS-11
1969	6	5	0	0	0	0	0.0	0	0	0	2	0	.000	.000	1	0	SS-5
1970	59	183	41	11	0	1	0.5	19	10	9	30	1	.224	.301	1	0	3B-29, SS-27
1971 CHI A	99	264	57	14	1	0	0.0	22	8	11	34	1	.216	.277	9	2	SS-71, 2B-16
1972	103	254	54	4	1	4	1.6	30	29	13	36	2	.213	.283	7	2	SS-81, 2B-16, 3B-2
1973	79	203	47	7	2	0	0.0	21	20	4	20	6	.232	.286	7	4	2B-45, SS-18, 3B-10
1974 3 teams	CHI A (8G – .100)				CLE A (61G – .219)				STL N (17G – .139)								
" total	86	160	31	4	0	0	0.0	16	13	8	21	1	.194	.219	5	1	2B-47, SS-28, DH-3, 3B-1
1976 STL N	16	42	12	1	0	0	0.0	5	3	3	6	0	.286	.310	0	0	2B-16
1977 2 teams	DET A (2G – .000)				NY N (1G – .000)												
" total	3	3	0	0	0	0	0.0	0	0	0	0	0	.000	.000	0	0	3B-2, 2B-1
9 yrs.	462	1160	248	43	4	5	0.4	116	84	49	160	11	.214	.271	30	7	SS-241, 2B-141, 3B-44, DH-3
4 yrs.	289	731	159	25	4	4	0.5	74	57	28	91	9	.218	.279	24	6	SS-174, 2B-78, 3B-13

Hal Anderson
ANDERSON, HAROLD   BR TR 5'11" 160 lbs.
B. Feb. 10, 1904, St. Louis, Mo.

1932 CHI A	9	32	8	0	0	0	0.0	4	2	0	1	0	.250	.250	0	0	OF-9

John Anderson
ANDERSON, JOHN JOSEPH (Honest John)   BB TR 6'2" 180 lbs.
B. Dec. 14, 1873, Sasbourg, Norway   D. July 23, 1949, Worcester, Mass.

1894 BKN N	17	63	19	1	3	1	1.6	14	19	3	3		.302	.460	0	0	OF-16, 3B-1
1895	102	419	120	11	14	9	2.1	76	87	12	29	24	.286	.444	0	0	OF-101
1896	108	430	135	23	17	1	0.2	70	55	18	23	37	.314	.453	1	0	OF-68, 1B-42
1897	117	492	160	28	12	4	0.8	93	85	17		29	.325	.455	0	0	OF-115, 1B-3
1898 2 teams	BKN N (25G – .244)				WAS N (110G – .305)												
" total	135	520	153	33	22	9	1.7	82	81	29		20	.294	.494	1	0	OF-115, 1B-19
1899 BKN N	117	439	118	18	7	3	0.7	65	92	27		25	.269	.362	3	0	OF-76, 3B-41
1901 MIL A	138	576	190	46	7	8	1.4	90	99	24		35	.330	.476	0	0	1B-125, OF-13
1902 STL A	126	524	149	29	6	4	0.8	60	85	21		15	.284	.385	0	0	1B-126, OF-3
1903	138	550	156	34	8	2	0.4	65	78	23		16	.284	.385	0	0	1B-133, OF-7
1904 NY A	143	558	155	27	12	3	0.5	62	82	23		20	.278	.385	1	1	OF-111, 1B-33
1905 2 teams	NY A (32G – .232)				WAS A (93G – .290)												
" total	125	499	139	24	7	1	0.2	62	52	30		31	.279	.361	7	1	OF-111, 1B-7
1906 WAS A	151	583	158	25	4	3	0.5	62	70	19		39	.271	.343	0	0	OF-151
1907	87	333	96	12	4	0	0.0	33	44	34		19	.288	.348	0	0	1B-61, OF-26
1908 CHI A	123	355	93	17	1	0	0.0	36	47	30		21	.262	.315	25	5	OF-90, 1B-9
14 yrs.	1627	6341	1841	328	124	48	0.8	870	976	310	55	338	.290	.404	38	7	OF-1003, 1B-599, 3B-1
1 yr.	123	355	93	17	1	0	0.0	36	47	30		21	.262	.315	25	5	OF-90, 1B-9

Mike Andrews
ANDREWS, MICHAEL JAY   BR TR 6'3" 195 lbs.
Brother of Rob Andrews.
B. July 9, 1943, Los Angeles, Calif.

1966 BOS A	5	18	3	0	0	0	0.0	1	0	0	2	0	.167	.167	0	0	2B-5
1967	142	494	130	20	0	8	1.6	79	40	62	72	7	.263	.352	2	0	2B-139, SS-6
1968	147	536	145	22	1	7	1.3	77	45	81	57	3	.271	.354	5	1	2B-139, SS-4, 3B-1
1969	121	464	136	26	2	15	3.2	79	59	71	53	1	.293	.455	1	0	2B-120
1970	151	589	149	28	1	17	2.9	91	65	81	63	2	.253	.390	3	0	2B-148
1971 CHI A	109	330	93	16	0	12	3.6	45	47	67	36	3	.282	.439	12	4	2B-76, 1B-25
1972	148	505	111	18	0	7	1.4	58	50	70	78	2	.220	.297	1	0	2B-145, 1B-5
1973 2 teams	CHI A (53G – .201)				OAK A (18G – .190)												
" total	71	180	36	10	0	0	0.0	11	10	26	29	0	.200	.256	15	1	DH-32, 2B-15, 1B-9, 3B-5
8 yrs.	894	3116	803	140	4	66	2.1	441	316	458	390	18	.258	.369	39	7	2B-787, 1B-39, DH-32, SS-10, 3B-6
3 yrs.	310	994	236	43	0	19	1.9	113	107	160	142	5	.237	.338	19	5	2B-227, 1B-39, DH-30, 3B-5

Player Register 220

	G	AB	H	2B	3B	HR	HR%	R	RBI	BB	SO	SB	BA	SA	Pinch Hit AB	Pinch Hit H	G by POS

Mike Andrews continued

LEAGUE CHAMPIONSHIP SERIES
| 1973 OAK A | 2 | 1 | 0 | 0 | 0 | 0 | 0.0 | 0 | 0 | 0 | 0 | 0 | .000 | .000 | 0 | 0 | 1B-1 |

WORLD SERIES
1967 BOS A	5	13	4	0	0	0	0.0	2	1	0	1	0	.308	.308	2	1	2B-3
1973 OAK A	2	3	0	0	0	0	0.0	0	0	1	1	0	.000	.000	2	0	2B-1
2 yrs.	7	16	4	0	0	0	0.0	2	1	1	2	0	.250	.250	4	1	2B-4

Luis Aparicio

APARICIO, LUIS ERNESTO (Little Looie) BR TR 5'9" 160 lbs.
B. Apr. 29, 1934, Maracaibo, Venezuela
Hall of Fame 1984.

1956 CHI A	152	533	142	19	6	3	0.6	69	56	34	63	21	.266	.341	0	0	SS-152
1957	143	575	148	22	6	3	0.5	82	41	52	55	28	.257	.332	1	0	SS-142
1958	145	557	148	20	9	2	0.4	76	40	35	38	29	.266	.345	0	0	SS-145
1959	152	612	157	18	5	6	1.0	98	51	52	40	56	.257	.332	0	0	SS-152
1960	153	600	166	20	7	2	0.3	86	61	43	39	51	.277	.343	0	0	SS-153
1961	156	625	170	24	4	6	1.0	90	45	38	33	53	.272	.352	0	0	SS-156
1962	153	581	140	23	5	7	1.2	72	40	32	36	31	.241	.334	1	0	SS-152
1963 BAL A	146	601	150	18	8	5	0.8	73	45	36	35	40	.250	.331	0	0	SS-145
1964	146	578	154	20	3	10	1.7	93	37	49	51	57	.266	.363	1	0	SS-145
1965	144	564	127	20	10	8	1.4	67	40	46	56	26	.225	.339	1	0	SS-141
1966	151	659	182	25	8	6	0.9	97	41	33	42	25	.276	.366	0	0	SS-151
1967	134	546	127	22	5	4	0.7	55	31	29	44	18	.233	.313	2	0	SS-131
1968 CHI A	155	622	164	24	4	4	0.6	55	36	33	43	17	.264	.334	2	0	SS-154
1969	156	599	168	24	5	5	0.8	77	51	66	29	24	.280	.362	1	0	SS-154
1970	146	552	173	29	3	5	0.9	86	43	53	34	8	.313	.404	3	2	SS-146
1971 BOS A	125	491	114	23	0	4	0.8	56	45	35	43	6	.232	.303	2	1	SS-121
1972	110	436	112	26	3	3	0.7	47	39	26	28	3	.257	.351	1	0	SS-109
1973	132	499	135	17	1	0	0.0	56	49	43	33	13	.271	.309	0	0	SS-132
18 yrs.	2599	10230	2677	394	92	83	0.8	1335	791	735	742	506	.262	.343	15	3	SS-2581
											10th						
			10th														
10 yrs.	1511	5856	1576	223	54	43	0.7	791	464	438	410	318	.269	.348	8	2	SS-1506
	5th	4th	4th	8th				5th			10th	2nd					

WORLD SERIES
1959 CHI A	6	26	8	1	0	0	0.0	1	0	2	3	1	.308	.346	0	1	SS-6
1966 BAL A	4	16	4	1	0	0	0.0	0	2	0	0	0	.250	.313	0	0	SS-4
2 yrs.	10	42	12	2	0	0	0.0	1	2	2	3	1	.286	.333	0	1	SS-10

Luke Appling

APPLING, LUCIUS BENJAMIN (Old Aches and Pains) BR TR 5'10" 183 lbs.
B. Apr. 2, 1907, High Point, N. C.
Manager 1967.
Hall of Fame 1964.

1930 CHI A	6	26	8	2	0	0	0.0	2	2	0	0	2	.308	.385	0	0	SS-6
1931	96	297	69	13	4	1	0.3	36	28	29	27	9	.232	.313	12	3	SS-76, 2B-1
1932	139	489	134	20	10	3	0.6	66	63	40	36	9	.274	.374	7	3	SS-85, 2B-30, 3B-14
1933	151	612	197	36	10	6	1.0	90	85	56	29	6	.322	.443	0	0	SS-151
1934	118	452	137	28	6	2	0.4	75	61	59	27	3	.303	.405	0	0	SS-110, 2B-8
1935	153	525	161	28	6	1	0.2	94	71	122	40	12	.307	.389	0	0	SS-153
1936	138	526	204	31	7	6	1.1	111	128	85	25	10	.388	.508	1	0	SS-137
1937	154	574	182	42	8	4	0.7	98	77	86	28	18	.317	.439	0	0	SS-154
1938	81	294	89	14	0	0	0.0	41	44	42	17	1	.303	.350	2	1	SS-78
1939	148	516	162	16	6	0	0.0	82	56	105	37	16	.314	.368	0	0	SS-148
1940	150	566	197	27	13	0	0.0	96	79	69	35	3	.348	.442	0	0	SS-150
1941	154	592	186	26	8	1	0.2	93	57	82	32	12	.314	.390	0	0	SS-154
1942	142	543	142	26	4	3	0.6	78	53	63	23	17	.262	.341	0	0	SS-141
1943	155	585	192	33	2	3	0.5	63	80	90	29	27	.328	.407	0	0	SS-155
1945	18	58	21	2	2	1	1.7	12	10	12	7	1	.362	.517	1	0	SS-17
1946	149	582	180	27	5	1	0.2	59	55	71	41	6	.309	.378	0	0	SS-149
1947	139	503	154	29	0	8	1.6	67	49	64	28	8	.306	.412	7	0	SS-129, 3B-2
1948	139	497	156	16	2	0	0.0	63	47	94	35	10	.314	.354	3	1	3B-72, SS-64
1949	142	492	148	21	5	5	1.0	82	58	121	24	7	.301	.394	1	0	SS-141
1950	50	128	30	3	4	0	0.0	11	13	12	8	2	.234	.320	15	1	SS-20, 1B-13, 2B-1
20 yrs.	2422	8857	2749	440	102	45	0.5	1319	1116	1302	528	179	.310	.398	49	9	SS-2218, 3B-88, 2B-40, 1B-13
20 yrs.	2422	8857	2749	440	102	45	0.5	1319	1116	1302	528	179	.310	.398	49	9	SS-2218, 3B-88, 2B-40, 1B-13
		1st	1st	1st	1st	3rd		1st	1st	1st	6th		8th				

Maurice Archdeacon

ARCHDEACON, MAURICE BRUCE (Flash) BL TL 5'8" 153 lbs.
B. Dec. 14, 1897, St. Louis, Mo. D. Sept. 5, 1954, St. Louis, Mo.

1923 CHI A	22	87	35	5	1	0	0.0	23	4	6	8	2	.402	.483	1	0	OF-20
1924	95	288	92	9	3	0	0.0	59	25	40	30	11	.319	.372	14	5	OF-77
1925	10	9	1	0	0	0	0.0	2	0	2	1	0	.111	.111	8	1	OF-1
3 yrs.	127	384	128	14	4	0	0.0	84	29	48	39	13	.333	.391	23	6	OF-98
3 yrs.	127	384	128	14	4	0	0.0	84	29	48	39	13	.333	.391	23	6	OF-98

Charlie Armbruster

ARMBRUSTER, CHARLES A. BR TR 5'9" 180 lbs.
B. Aug. 30, 1880, Cincinnati, Ohio D. Oct. 7, 1964, Grant's Pass, Ore.

1905 BOS A	35	91	18	4	0	0	0.0	13	6	18		3	.198	.242	0	0	C-35
1906	72	201	29	6	1	0	0.0	9	6	25		2	.144	.184	4	0	C-66, 1B-1
1907 2 teams	BOS A (23G – .100)				CHI A (1G – .000)												
" total	24	63	6	1	0	0	0.0	2	0	9		1	.095	.111	1	0	C-22
3 yrs.	131	355	53	11	1	0	0.0	24	12	52		6	.149	.186	5	0	C-123, 1B-1
1 yr.	1	3	0	0	0	0	0.0	0	0	1		0	.000	.000	0	0	C-1

Player Register

	G	AB	H	2B	3B	HR	HR%	R	RBI	BB	SO	SB	BA	SA	Pinch Hit AB	Pinch Hit H	G by POS

Jake Atz
ATZ, JACOB HENRY   BR TR 5'9½" 160 lbs.
B. July 1, 1879, Washington, D. C.   D. May 22, 1945, New Orleans, La.

Year	Team	G	AB	H	2B	3B	HR	HR%	R	RBI	BB	SO	SB	BA	SA	PH AB	PH H	G by POS
1902	WAS A	3	10	1	0	0	0	0.0	1	0	0		0	.100	.100	0	0	2B-3
1907	CHI A	3	7	1	0	0	0	0.0	0	0	0		0	.143	.143	1	0	3B-2
1908		83	206	40	3	0	0	0.0	24	27	31		9	.194	.209	17	4	2B-46, SS-18, 3B-1
1909		119	381	90	18	3	0	0.0	39	22	38		14	.236	.299	1	0	2B-118, OF-3, SS-1
4 yrs.		208	604	132	21	3	0	0.0	64	49	69		23	.219	.263	19	4	2B-167, SS-19, OF-3, 3B-3
3 yrs.		205	594	131	21	3	0	0.0	63	49	69		23	.221	.266	19	4	2B-164, SS-19, OF-3, 3B-3

Martin Autry
AUTRY, MARTIN GORDON (Chick)   BR TR 6' 180 lbs.
B. Mar. 5, 1903, Martindale, Tex.   D. Jan. 26, 1950, Savannah, Ga.

Year	Team	G	AB	H	2B	3B	HR	HR%	R	RBI	BB	SO	SB	BA	SA	PH AB	PH H	G by POS
1924	NY A	2	0	0	0	0	–	–	1	0	0	0	0	–	–	0	0	C-2
1926	CLE A	3	7	1	0	0	0	0.0	1	0	1	0	0	.143	.143	0	0	C-3
1927		16	43	11	4	1	0	0.0	5	7	0	6	0	.256	.395	1	0	C-14
1928		22	60	18	6	1	0	1.7	6	1	9	7	0	.300	.483	4	0	C-18
1929	CHI A	43	96	20	6	0	1	1.0	7	12	1	8	0	.208	.302	11	3	C-30
1930		34	71	18	1	0	0	0.0	1	5	4	8	0	.254	.296	5	1	C-29
6 yrs.		120	277	68	17	3	2	0.7	21	25	15	29	0	.245	.350	21	4	C-96
2 yrs.		77	167	38	7	1	1	0.6	8	17	5	16	0	.228	.299	16	4	C-59

Earl Averill
AVERILL, EARL DOUGLAS   BR TR 5'10" 185 lbs.
Son of Earl Averill.
B. Sept. 9, 1931, Cleveland, Ohio

Year	Team	G	AB	H	2B	3B	HR	HR%	R	RBI	BB	SO	SB	BA	SA	PH AB	PH H	G by POS
1956	CLE A	42	93	22	6	0	3	3.2	12	14	14	25	0	.237	.398	8	2	C-34
1958		17	55	10	1	0	2	3.6	2	7	4	7	1	.182	.309	0	0	3B-17
1959	CHI N	74	186	44	10	0	10	5.4	22	34	15	39	0	.237	.452	25	10	C-32, 3B-13, OF-5, 2B-2
1960	2 teams	CHI N (52G – .235)							CHI A (10G – .214)									
"	total	62	116	27	4	0	1	0.9	16	15	15	18	1	.233	.293	30	6	C-39, OF-1, 3B-1
1961	LA A	115	323	86	9	0	21	6.5	56	59	62	70	1	.266	.489	21	7	C-88, OF-9, 2B-1
1962		92	187	41	9	0	4	2.1	21	22	43	47	0	.219	.332	34	7	OF-49, C-6
1963	PHI N	47	71	19	2	0	3	4.2	8	8	9	14	0	.268	.423	24	4	C-20, OF-8, 3B-1, 1B-1
7 yrs.		449	1031	249	41	0	44	4.3	137	159	162	220	3	.242	.409	142	36	C-219, OF-72, 3B-32, 2B-3, 1B-1
1 yr.		10	14	3	0	0	0	0.0	4	2	1	0	0	.214	.214	5	1	C-5

Harold Baines
BAINES, HAROLD DOUGLASS   BL TL 6'2" 175 lbs.
B. Mar. 15, 1959, St. Michaels, Md.

Year	Team	G	AB	H	2B	3B	HR	HR%	R	RBI	BB	SO	SB	BA	SA	PH AB	PH H	G by POS
1980	CHI A	141	491	125	23	6	13	2.6	55	49	19	65	2	.255	.405	9	1	OF-137, DH-1
1981		82	280	80	11	7	10	3.6	42	41	12	41	6	.286	.482	5	1	OF-80, DH-1
1982		161	608	165	29	8	25	4.1	89	105	49	95	10	.271	.469	1	0	OF-161
1983		156	596	167	33	2	20	3.4	76	99	49	85	7	.280	.443	1	0	OF-155
4 yrs.		540	1975	537	96	23	68	3.4	262	294	129	286	25	.272	.447	16	3	OF-533, DH-2
4 yrs.		540	1975	537	96	23	68	3.4	262	294	129	286	25	.272	.447	16	3	OF-533, DH-2
								4th				8th						

LEAGUE CHAMPIONSHIP SERIES
| 1983 | CHI A | 4 | 16 | 2 | 0 | 0 | 0 | 0.0 | 0 | 0 | 1 | 3 | 0 | .125 | .125 | 0 | 0 | OF-4 |

Floyd Baker
BAKER, FLOYD WILSON   BL TR 5'9" 160 lbs.
B. Oct. 10, 1916, Luray, Va.

Year	Team	G	AB	H	2B	3B	HR	HR%	R	RBI	BB	SO	SB	BA	SA	PH AB	PH H	G by POS
1943	STL A	22	46	8	2	0	0	0.0	5	4	6	4	0	.174	.217	11	2	SS-10, 3B-1
1944		44	97	17	3	0	0	0.0	10	5	11	5	2	.175	.206	11	4	2B-17, SS-16
1945	CHI A	82	208	52	8	0	0	0.0	22	19	23	12	3	.250	.288	16	1	3B-58, 2B-11
1946		9	24	6	1	0	0	0.0	2	3	2	3	0	.250	.292	3	0	3B-6
1947		105	371	98	12	3	0	0.0	61	22	66	28	9	.264	.313	0	0	3B-101, SS-1, 2B-1
1948		104	335	72	8	0	0	0.0	47	18	73	26	4	.215	.257	11	4	3B-71, 2B-18, SS-1
1949		125	388	101	15	4	1	0.3	38	40	84	32	3	.260	.327	0	0	3B-122, SS-3, 2B-1
1950		83	186	59	7	0	0	0.0	26	11	32	10	1	.317	.355	24	6	3B-53, 2B-3, OF-2
1951		82	133	35	6	1	0	0.0	24	14	25	12	0	.263	.323	33	9	3B-44, 2B-5, SS-3
1952	WAS A	79	263	69	8	0	0	0.0	27	33	30	17	1	.262	.293	4	0	2B-68, SS-7, 3B-1
1953	2 teams	WAS A (9G – .000)							BOS A (81G – .273)									
"	total	90	179	47	4	2	0	0.0	22	24	25	10	0	.263	.307	31	3	3B-38, 2B-16
1954	2 teams	BOS A (21G – .200)							PHI N (23G – .227)									
"	total	44	42	9	2	0	0	0.0	1	3	5	5	0	.214	.262	25	7	3B-14, 2B-3
1955	PHI N	5	8	0	0	0	0	0.0	0	0	0	1	0	.000	.000	4	0	3B-1
13 yrs.		874	2280	573	76	13	1	0.0	285	196	382	165	23	.251	.297	173	36	3B-510, 2B-143, SS-41, OF-2
7 yrs.		590	1645	423	57	11	1	0.1	220	127	305	123	20	.257	.307	87	20	3B-455, 2B-39, SS-8, OF-2

WORLD SERIES
| 1944 | STL A | 2 | 2 | 0 | 0 | 0 | 0 | 0.0 | 0 | 2 | 0 | 0 | 0 | .000 | .000 | 2 | 0 | 2B-2 |

Howard Baker
BAKER, HOWARD FRANCIS   BR TR 5'11" 175 lbs.
B. Mar. 1, 1888, Bridgeport, Conn.   D. Jan. 16, 1964, Bridgeport, Conn.

Year	Team	G	AB	H	2B	3B	HR	HR%	R	RBI	BB	SO	SB	BA	SA	PH AB	PH H	G by POS
1912	CLE A	11	30	5	0	0	0	0.0	1	2	5		0	.167	.167	1	0	3B-10
1914	CHI A	15	47	13	1	0	0	0.0	4	5	3	8	2	.277	.340	0	0	3B-15
1915	2 teams	CHI A (2G – .000)							NY N (1G – .000)									
"	total	3	5	0	0	0	0	0.0	0	0	2	0	0	.000	.000	2	0	3B-1
3 yrs.		29	82	18	1	0	0	0.0	5	7	8	10	2	.220	.256	3	0	3B-26
2 yrs.		17	49	13	1	0	0	0.0	4	5	3	10	2	.265	.327	1	0	3B-15

Alan Bannister
BANNISTER, ALAN   BR TR 5'11" 170 lbs.
B. Sept. 3, 1951, Bueno Park, Calif.

Year	Team	G	AB	H	2B	3B	HR	HR%	R	RBI	BB	SO	SB	BA	SA	PH AB	PH H	G by POS
1974	PHI N	26	25	3	0	0	0	0.0	4	1	3	7	0	.120	.120	7	0	OF-8, SS-2
1975		24	61	16	3	1	0	0.0	10	1	1	9	2	.262	.344	1	0	OF-18, SS-1, 2B-1
1976	CHI A	73	145	36	6	3	0	0.0	19	8	14	21	12	.248	.317	2	0	OF-43, SS-14, DH-4, 2B-4, 3B-1

	G	AB	H	2B	3B	HR	HR%	R	RBI	BB	SO	SB	BA	SA	Pinch Hit AB	H	G by POS

Alan Bannister continued
1977	139	560	154	20	3	3	0.5	87	57	54	49	4	.275	.338	1	0	SS-133, OF-3, 2B-3
1978	49	107	24	3	2	0	0.0	16	8	11	12	3	.224	.290	10	0	DH-19, OF-15, SS-8, 2B-2
1979	136	506	144	28	8	2	0.4	71	55	43	40	22	.285	.383	0	0	2B-65, OF-47, 3B-12, DH-9, 1B-1
1980 2 teams		CHI A (45G – .192)				CLE A (81G – .328)											
" total	126	392	111	23	4	1	0.3	57	41	40	41	14	.283	.370	12	0	OF-63, 2B-41, 3B-20, SS-2
1981 CLE A	68	232	61	11	1	1	0.4	36	17	16	19	16	.263	.332	11	4	OF-35, 2B-30, 1B-2, SS-1
1982	101	348	93	16	1	4	1.1	40	41	42	41	18	.267	.353	6	1	OF-55, 2B-48, SS-2, DH-1, 3B-1
1983	117	377	100	25	4	5	1.3	51	45	31	43	6	.265	.393	10	5	OF-91, 2B-27, DH-3, 1B-3
10 yrs.	859	2753	742	135	26	16	0.6	391	273	255	282	97	.270	.355	60	10	OF-378, 2B-221, SS-163, DH-36, 3B-34, 1B-6
5 yrs.	442	1448	383	63	15	5	0.3	209	137	134	138	46	.265	.339	19	0	SS-155, OF-131, 2B-74, DH-32, 3B-30, 1B-1

Red Barnes
BARNES, EMILE DEERING   BL TR 5'10½" 158 lbs.
B. Dec. 25, 1903, Suggsville, Ala.   D. July 3, 1959, Mobile, Ala.

1927 WAS A	3	11	4	1	0	0	0.0	5	0	1	3	0	.364	.455	0	0	OF-3
1928	114	417	126	22	15	6	1.4	82	51	55	38	7	.302	.470	7	2	OF-104
1929	72	130	26	5	2	1	0.8	16	15	13	12	1	.200	.292	36	8	OF-30
1930 2 teams		WAS A (12G – .167)				CHI A (85G – .248)											
" total	97	278	68	13	7	1	0.4	49	31	26	23	4	.245	.353	22	3	OF-72
4 yrs.	286	836	224	41	24	8	1.0	152	97	95	76	12	.268	.403	65	13	OF-209
1 yr.	85	266	66	12	7	1	0.4	48	31	26	20	4	.248	.357	10	1	OF-72

Bill Barrett
BARRETT, WILLIAM JOSEPH (Whispering Bill)   BR TR 6' 175 lbs.
B. May 28, 1900, Cambridge, Mass.   D. Jan. 26, 1951, Cambridge, Mass.

1921 PHI A	14	30	7	2	1	0	0.0	3	3	0	5	0	.233	.367	0	0	SS-7, P-4, 3B-2, 1B-1
1923 CHI A	42	162	44	7	2	2	1.2	17	23	9	24	12	.272	.377	1	0	OF-40, 3B-1
1924	119	406	110	18	5	2	0.5	52	56	30	38	15	.271	.355	7	2	SS-77, OF-27, 3B-8
1925	81	245	89	23	3	3	1.2	44	40	24	27	5	.363	.518	7	1	2B-41, OF-27, SS-4, 3B-4
1926	111	368	113	31	4	6	1.6	46	61	25	26	9	.307	.462	6	3	OF-102, 1B-2
1927	147	556	159	35	9	4	0.7	62	83	52	46	20	.286	.403	0	0	OF-147
1928	76	235	65	11	2	3	1.3	34	26	14	30	8	.277	.379	9	2	OF-37, 2B-26
1929 2 teams		CHI A (3G – .000)				BOS A (111G – .270)											
" total	114	371	100	23	4	3	0.8	57	35	55	38	11	.270	.377	1	0	OF-109, 3B-1
1930 2 teams		BOS A (6G – .167)				WAS A (6G – .000)											
" total	12	22	3	1	0	0	0.0	3	1	2	5	0	.136	.182	5	0	OF-6
9 yrs.	716	2395	690	151	30	23	1.0	318	328	211	239	80	.288	.405	36	8	OF-495, SS-88, 2B-67, 3B-16, P-4, 1B-3
7 yrs.	579	1973	580	125	25	20	1.0	255	289	156	191	69	.294	.413	31	8	OF-380, SS-81, 2B-67, 3B-13, 1B-2

Cuke Barrows
BARROWS, ROLAND   BR TL 5'8" 158 lbs.
B. Oct. 20, 1883, Gray, Me.   D. Feb. 10, 1955, Gorham, Me.

1909 CHI A	5	20	3	0	0	0	0.0	1	2	0		0	.150	.150	0	0	OF-5
1910	6	20	4	0	0	0	0.0	0	1	3		0	.200	.200	0	0	OF-6
1911	13	46	9	2	0	0	0.0	5	4	7		2	.196	.239	0	0	OF-13
1912	8	13	3	0	0	0	0.0	0	2	2		1	.231	.231	4	1	OF-3
4 yrs.	32	99	19	2	0	0	0.0	6	9	12		3	.192	.212	4	1	OF-27
4 yrs.	32	99	19	2	0	0	0.0	6	9	12		3	.192	.212	4	1	OF-27

Earl Battey
BATTEY, EARL JESSE   BR TR 6'1" 205 lbs.
B. Jan. 5, 1935, Los Angeles, Calif.

1955 CHI A	5	7	2	0	0	0	0.0	1	0	1	1	0	.286	.286	1	0	C-5
1956	4	4	1	0	0	0	0.0	1	0	1	1	0	.250	.250	0	0	C-3
1957	48	115	20	2	3	3	2.6	12	6	11	38	0	.174	.322	4	3	C-43
1958	68	168	38	8	0	8	4.8	24	26	24	34	1	.226	.417	17	1	C-49
1959	26	64	14	1	2	2	3.1	9	7	8	13	0	.219	.391	5	0	C-20
1960 WAS A	137	466	126	24	2	15	3.2	49	60	48	68	4	.270	.427	4	2	C-136
1961 MIN A	133	460	139	24	1	17	3.7	70	55	53	66	3	.302	.470	2	0	C-131
1962	148	522	146	20	3	11	2.1	58	57	57	48	0	.280	.393	1	0	C-147
1963	147	508	145	17	1	26	5.1	64	84	61	75	0	.285	.476	2	0	C-146
1964	131	405	110	17	1	12	3.0	33	52	51	49	1	.272	.407	8	2	C-125
1965	131	394	117	22	2	6	1.5	36	60	50	23	0	.297	.409	5	0	C-128
1966	115	364	93	12	1	4	1.1	30	34	43	30	4	.255	.327	2	1	C-113
1967	48	109	18	3	1	0	0.0	6	8	13	24	0	.165	.211	9	3	C-41
13 yrs.	1141	3586	969	150	17	104	2.9	393	449	421	470	13	.270	.409	60	12	C-1087
5 yrs.	151	358	75	11	5	13	3.6	47	39	45	87	1	.209	.377	27	4	C-120

WORLD SERIES
| 1965 MIN A | 7 | 25 | 3 | 0 | 0 | 0 | 0.0 | 1 | 2 | 0 | 5 | 0 | .120 | .200 | 0 | 0 | C-7 |

Jim Battle
BATTLE, JAMES MILTON   BR TR 6'1" 170 lbs.
B. Mar. 26, 1901, Bailer, Tex.   D. Sept. 30, 1965, Chico, Calif.

| 1927 CHI A | 6 | 8 | 3 | 0 | 1 | 0 | 0.0 | 1 | 0 | 0 | 1 | 0 | .375 | .625 | 0 | 0 | 3B-4, SS-2 |

Matt Batts
BATTS, MATTHEW DANIEL   BR TR 5'11" 200 lbs.
B. Oct. 16, 1921, San Antonio, Tex.

1947 BOS A	7	16	8	1	0	1	6.3	3	5	1	1	0	.500	.750	1	0	C-6
1948	46	118	37	12	0	1	0.8	13	24	15	9	0	.314	.441	6	1	C-41
1949	60	157	38	9	1	3	1.9	23	31	25	22	1	.242	.369	11	1	C-50
1950	75	238	65	15	3	4	1.7	27	34	18	19	0	.273	.412	2	1	C-73
1951 2 teams		BOS A (11G – .138)				STL A (79G – .302)											
" total	90	277	79	18	1	5	1.8	27	33	22	23	2	.285	.412	11	1	C-75
1952 DET A	56	173	41	4	0	1	3	1.7	11	13	14	22	1	.237	.324	2	0	C-55

	G	AB	H	2B	3B	HR	HR%	R	RBI	BB	SO	SB	BA	SA	Pinch Hit AB	Pinch Hit H	G by POS

Matt Batts continued

1953	116	374	104	24	3	6	1.6	38	42	24	36	2	.278	.406	12	4	C-103
1954 2 teams		DET	A (12G – .286)			CHI	A (55G – .228)										
" total	67	179	42	8	1	3	1.7	17	24	19	19	0	.235	.341	17	4	C-50
1955 CIN N	26	71	18	4	1	0	0.0	4	13	4	11	0	.254	.338	5	1	C-21
1956	3	2	0	0	0	0	0.0	0	0	1	1	0	.000	.000	2	0	
10 yrs.	546	1605	432	95	11	26	1.6	163	219	143	163	6	.269	.391	69	13	C-474
1 yr.	55	158	36	7	1	3	1.9	16	19	17	15	0	.228	.342	12	2	C-42

Jim Baumer

BAUMER, JAMES SLOAN BR TR 6'2" 185 lbs.
B. Jan. 29, 1931, Tulsa, Okla.

1949 CHI A	8	10	4	1	0	0	0.0	2	2	2	1	0	.400	.700	0	0	SS-7
1961 CIN N	10	24	3	0	0	0	0.0	0	0	0	9	0	.125	.125	0	0	2B-9
2 yrs.	18	34	7	1	0	0	0.0	2	2	2	10	0	.206	.294	0	0	2B-9, SS-7
1 yr.	8	10	4	1	0	0	0.0	2	2	2	1	0	.400	.700	0	0	SS-7

Johnny Beall

BEALL, JOHN WOOLF BL TR 6' 180 lbs.
B. Mar. 12, 1882, Beltsville, Md. D. June 13, 1926, Beltsville, Md.

1913 2 teams		CLE	A (6G – .167)			CHI	A (17G – .267)										
" total	23	66	17	0	1	2	3.0	10	4	0	2	1	.258	.379	6	1	OF-17
1915 CIN N	10	34	8	1	0	0	0.0	3	3	5	10	0	.235	.265	0	0	OF-10
1916	6	21	7	2	0	1	4.8	3	4	3	7	1	.333	.571	0	0	OF-6
1918 STL N	19	49	11	1	0	0	0.0	2	6	3	6	0	.224	.245	5	2	OF-18
4 yrs.	58	170	43	4	1	3	1.8	18	17	11	25	2	.253	.341	12	3	OF-51
1 yr.	17	60	16	0	1	2	3.3	10	3	0	0	1	.267	.400	0	0	OF-17

Ted Beard

BEARD, CRAMER THEODORE BL TL 5'8" 165 lbs.
B. Jan. 7, 1921, Woodsboro, Md.

1948 PIT N	25	81	16	1	3	0	0.0	15	7	12	18	5	.198	.284	2	1	OF-22
1949	14	24	2	0	0	0	0.0	1	1	2	2	0	.083	.083	3	0	OF-10
1950	61	177	41	6	2	4	2.3	32	12	27	45	3	.232	.356	12	3	OF-49
1951	22	48	9	1	0	1	2.1	7	3	6	14	0	.188	.271	6	2	OF-22
1952	15	44	8	2	1	0	0.0	5	3	7	9	2	.182	.273	1	0	OF-13
1957 CHI A	38	78	16	1	0	0	0.0	15	7	18	14	3	.205	.218	3	1	OF-28
1958	19	22	2	0	0	1	4.5	5	2	6	5	3	.091	.227	3	0	OF-15
7 yrs.	194	474	94	11	6	6	1.3	80	35	78	107	16	.198	.285	30	7	OF-159
2 yrs.	57	100	18	1	0	1	1.0	20	9	24	19	6	.180	.220	6	1	OF-43

Ollie Bejma

BEJMA, ALOYSIUS FRANK BR TR 5'10" 115 lbs.
B. Sept. 12, 1907, South Bend, Ind.

1934 STL A	95	262	71	16	3	2	0.8	39	29	40	36	3	.271	.378	22	6	SS-32, 2B-14, 3B-13, OF-9
1935	64	198	38	8	2	2	1.0	18	26	27	21	1	.192	.283	7	2	2B-47, SS-8, 3B-2
1936	67	139	36	2	3	2	1.4	19	18	27	21	0	.259	.345	21	6	2B-32, SS-7, SS-1
1939 CHI A	90	307	77	9	3	8	2.6	52	44	36	27	1	.251	.378	6	1	2B-81, SS-1, 3B-1
4 yrs.	316	906	222	35	11	14	1.5	128	117	130	105	5	.245	.354	56	15	2B-174, SS-42, 3B-23, OF-9
1 yr.	90	307	77	9	3	8	2.6	52	44	36	27	1	.251	.378	6	1	2B-81, SS-1, 3B-1

Kevin Bell

BELL, KEVIN ROBERT BR TR 6' 195 lbs.
B. July 13, 1955, Los Angeles, Calif.

1976 CHI A	68	230	57	7	6	5	2.2	24	20	18	56	2	.248	.396	1	0	3B-67, DH-1
1977	9	28	5	1	0	1	3.6	4	6	3	8	0	.179	.321	0	0	SS-5, 3B-4, OF-1
1978	54	68	13	0	0	2	2.9	9	5	5	19	1	.191	.279	2	0	3B-52, DH-1
1979	70	200	49	8	1	4	2.0	20	22	15	43	2	.245	.355	2	0	3B-68, SS-2
1980	92	191	34	5	2	1	0.5	16	11	29	37	0	.178	.241	3	2	3B-83, DH-3, SS-3
1982 OAK A	4	9	3	1	0	0	0.0	1	0	0	2	0	.333	.444	0	0	3B-3, DH-1
6 yrs.	297	726	161	22	9	13	1.8	74	64	70	165	5	.222	.331	8	2	3B-277, SS-10, DH-6, OF-1
5 yrs.	293	717	158	21	9	13	1.8	73	64	70	163	5	.220	.329	8	2	3B-274, SS-10, DH-5, OF-1

Chief Bender

BENDER, CHARLES ALBERT BR TR 6'2" 185 lbs.
B. May 5, 1883, Brainerd, Minn. D. May 22, 1954, Philadelphia, Pa.
Hall of Fame 1953.

1903 PHI A	43	120	22	4	1	0	0.0	10	8	3		3	.183	.233	3	2	P-36, 1B-3, OF-1
1904	31	79	18	3	2	0	0.0	8	5	5		3	.228	.316	1	0	P-29
1905	38	92	20	3	0	0	0.0	11	14	5		3	.217	.293	3	0	P-35
1906	44	99	25	4	0	3	3.0	9	13	9		2	.253	.384	2	0	P-36, OF-4
1907	45	100	23	6	1	0	0.0	10	8	5		2	.230	.310	7	1	P-33, 1B-2, OF-1, 2B-1
1908	20	50	11	1	0	0	0.0	5	2	10		1	.220	.240	1	0	P-18, 1B-1
1909	40	93	20	5	0	0	0.0	6	9	5		1	.215	.269	5	1	P-34
1910	36	93	25	3	2	0	0.0	6	16	6		0	.269	.344	6	1	P-30
1911	32	79	13	0	0	0	0.0	9	8	2		2	.165	.165	1	0	P-31
1912	27	60	9	1	1	0	0.0	5	4	5		0	.150	.200	0	0	P-27
1913	48	78	12	3	1	0	0.0	7	10	6	17	1	.154	.218	0	0	P-48
1914	28	62	9	1	0	1	1.6	4	8	4	13	0	.145	.210	0	0	P-28
1915 BAL F	26	60	16	2	0	1	1.7	7	2	6		0	.267	.350	0	0	P-26
1916 PHI N	28	43	12	4	0	1	2.3	2	5	3	9	0	.279	.372	0	0	P-27, 3B-1
1917	20	39	8	0	0	1	2.6	2	4	2	3	0	.205	.282	0	0	P-20
1925 CHI A	1	0	0	0	0	0	–	0	0	0	0	0	–	–	0	0	P-1
16 yrs.	507	1147	243	40	10	6	0.5	102	116	75	42	20	.212	.280	29	5	P-459, OF-6, 1B-6, 3B-1, 2B-1
1 yr.	1	0	0	0	0	0	–	0	0	0	0	0	–	–	0	0	P-1

WORLD SERIES

| 1905 PHI A | 2 | 5 | 0 | 0 | 0 | 0 | 0.0 | 0 | 0 | 1 | | 0 | .000 | .000 | 0 | 0 | P-2 |
| 1910 | 2 | 6 | 2 | 0 | 0 | 0 | 0.0 | 1 | 1 | 1 | | 0 | .333 | .333 | 0 | 0 | P-2 |

Player Register 224

	G	AB	H	2B	3B	HR	HR%	R	RBI	BB	SO	SB	BA	SA	Pinch Hit AB	H	G by POS

Chief Bender continued

1911	3	11	1	0	0	0	0.0	0	0	0	1	0	.091	.091	0	0	P-3
1913	2	8	0	0	0	0	0.0	0	1	0	1	0	.000	.000	0	0	P-2
1914	1	2	0	0	0	0	0.0	0	0	0	0	0	.000	.000	0	0	P-1
5 yrs.	10	32	3	0	0	0	0.0	1	2	1	4	0	.094	.094	0	0	P-10

Moe Berg

BERG, MORRIS BR TR 6'1" 185 lbs.
B. Mar. 2, 1902, New York, N. Y. D. May 29, 1972, Belleville, N. J.

1923 BKN N	49	129	24	3	2	0	0.0	9	6	2	5	1	.186	.240	0	0	SS-47, 2B-1
1926 CHI A	41	113	25	6	0	0	0.0	4	7	6	9	0	.221	.274	6	1	SS-31, 2B-2, 3B-1
1927	35	69	17	4	0	0	0.0	4	4	4	10	0	.246	.304	6	1	2B-10, C-10, SS-6, 3B-3
1928	76	224	55	16	0	0	0.0	25	29	14	25	2	.246	.317	3	1	C-73
1929	106	351	101	7	0	0	0.0	32	47	17	16	5	.288	.308	0	0	C-106
1930	20	61	7	3	0	0	0.0	4	7	1	5	0	.115	.164	0	0	C-20
1931 CLE A	10	13	1	1	0	0	0.0	1	0	1	1	0	.077	.154	1	0	C-8
1932 WAS A	75	195	46	8	1	1	0.5	16	26	8	13	1	.236	.303	0	0	C-75
1933	40	65	12	3	0	2	3.1	8	9	4	5	0	.185	.323	4	0	C-35
1934 2 teams		WAS A (33G – .244)				CLE A (29G – .258)											
" total	62	183	46	7	1	0	0.0	9	15	7	11	2	.251	.301	3	0	C-62
1935 BOS A	38	98	28	5	0	2	2.0	13	12	5	3	0	.286	.398	1	0	C-37
1936	39	125	30	4	1	0	0.0	9	19	2	6	0	.240	.288	0	0	C-39
1937	47	141	36	3	1	0	0.0	13	20	5	4	0	.255	.291	0	0	C-47
1938	10	12	4	0	0	0	0.0	0	0	0	1	0	.333	.333	3	2	C-7, 1B-1
1939	14	33	9	1	0	1	3.0	3	5	2	3	0	.273	.394	1	0	C-13
15 yrs.	662	1812	441	71	6	6	0.3	150	206	78	117	11	.243	.299	28	5	C-532, SS-84, 2B-13, 3B-4, 1B-1
5 yrs.	278	818	205	36	0	0	0.0	69	94	42	65	7	.251	.295	15	3	C-209, SS-37, 2B-12, 3B-4

Boze Berger

BERGER, LOUIS WILLIAM BR TR 6'2" 180 lbs.
B. May 13, 1910, Baltimore, Md.

1932 CLE A	1	1	0	0	0	0	0.0	0	0	0	1	0	.000	.000	0	0	SS-1
1935	124	461	119	27	5	5	1.1	62	43	34	97	7	.258	.371	0	0	2B-120, SS-3, 1B-2, 3B-1
1936	28	52	9	2	0	0	0.0	1	3	1	14	0	.173	.212	1	0	2B-8, 1B-8, 3B-7, SS-2
1937 CHI A	52	130	31	5	0	5	3.8	19	13	15	24	1	.238	.392	6	2	3B-40, SS-1, 2B-1
1938	118	470	102	15	3	3	0.6	60	36	43	80	4	.217	.281	0	0	SS-67, 2B-42, 3B-9
1939 BOS A	20	30	9	2	0	0	0.0	4	2	1	10	0	.300	.367	3	1	SS-10, 3B-5, 2B-2
6 yrs.	343	1144	270	51	8	13	1.1	146	97	94	226	12	.236	.329	10	3	2B-173, SS-84, 3B-62, 1B-10
2 yrs.	170	600	133	20	3	8	1.3	79	49	58	104	5	.222	.305	6	2	SS-68, 3B-49, 2B-43

Joe Berger

BERGER, JOSEPH AUGUST (Fats) BR TR 5'10½" 170 lbs.
B. Dec. 20, 1886, St. Louis, Mo. D. Mar. 6, 1956, Rock Island, Ill.

1913 CHI A	77	223	48	6	2	2	0.9	27	20	36	28	5	.215	.287	2	0	2B-69, SS-4, 3B-1
1914	47	148	23	3	1	0	0.0	11	3	13	9	2	.155	.189	1	0	SS-27, 2B-12, 3B-7
2 yrs.	124	371	71	9	3	2	0.5	38	23	49	37	7	.191	.248	3	0	2B-81, SS-31, 3B-8
2 yrs.	124	371	71	9	3	2	0.5	38	23	49	37	7	.191	.248	3	0	2B-81, SS-31, 3B-8

Marty Berghammer

BERGHAMMER, MARTIN ANDREW BL TR 5'9" 172 lbs.
B. Jan. 18, 1886, Pittsburgh, Pa. D. Dec. 21, 1957, Pittsburgh, Pa.

1911 CHI A	2	5	0	0	0	0	0.0	0	0	0	0	0	.000	.000	0	0	2B-2
1913 CIN N	74	188	41	4	1	1	0.5	25	13	10	29	16	.218	.266	0	0	SS-53, 2B-13
1914	77	112	25	2	0	0	0.0	15	6	10	18	4	.223	.241	13	2	SS-33, 2B-13
1915 PIT F	132	469	114	10	6	0	0.0	96	33	83		26	.243	.290	0	0	SS-132
4 yrs.	285	774	180	16	7	1	0.1	136	52	103	47	46	.233	.275	13	2	SS-218, 2B-28
1 yr.	2	5	0	0	0	0	0.0	0	0	0	0	0	.000	.000	0	0	2B-2

Tony Bernazard

BERNAZARD, ANTONIO BB TR 5'9" 150 lbs.
Also known as Antonio Garcia.
B. Aug. 24, 1956, Caguas, Puerto Rico

1979 MON N	22	40	12	2	0	1	2.5	11	8	15	12	1	.300	.425	2	0	2B-14
1980	82	183	41	7	1	5	2.7	26	18	17	41	9	.224	.355	22	4	2B-39, SS-22
1981 CHI A	106	384	106	14	4	6	1.6	53	34	54	66	4	.276	.380	2	0	2B-105, SS-1
1982	137	540	138	25	9	11	2.0	90	56	67	88	11	.256	.396	0	0	2B-137
1983 2 teams		CHI A (59G – .262)				SEA A (80G – .267)											
" total	139	533	141	34	3	8	1.5	65	56	55	97	23	.265	.385	2	0	2B-138
5 yrs.	486	1680	438	82	17	31	1.8	245	172	208	304	48	.261	.385	28	4	2B-433, SS-23
3 yrs.	302	1157	305	55	15	19	1.6	173	116	138	199	17	.264	.386	2	0	2B-301, SS-1

Joe Berrens

BERRENS, JOSEPH
B. Unknown.

| 1912 CHI A | 2 | 4 | 1 | 0 | 0 | 0 | 0.0 | 1 | 0 | 0 | | 0 | .250 | .250 | 0 | 0 | OF-2 |

Charlie Berry

BERRY, CHARLES FRANCIS BR TR 6' 185 lbs.
Son of Charlie Berry.
B. Oct. 18, 1902, Phillipsburg, N. J. D. Sept. 6, 1972, Evanston, Ill.

1925 PHI A	10	14	3	1	0	0	0.0	3	0	2	0	0	.214	.286	6	1	C-4
1928 BOS A	80	177	46	7	3	1	0.6	18	19	21	19	1	.260	.350	14	4	C-63
1929	77	207	50	11	4	1	0.5	19	21	15	29	2	.242	.348	4	3	C-72
1930	88	256	74	9	6	6	2.3	31	35	16	22	2	.289	.441	3	2	C-85
1931	111	357	101	16	2	6	1.7	41	49	29	38	4	.283	.389	9	2	C-102
1932 2 teams		BOS A (10G – .188)				CHI A (72G – .305)											
" total	82	258	75	18	6	4	1.6	33	37	24	25	3	.291	.453	2	0	C-80
1933 CHI A	86	271	69	8	3	2	0.7	25	28	17	16	0	.255	.373	3	0	C-83
1934 PHI A	99	269	72	10	2	0	0.0	14	34	22	23	1	.268	.320	0	0	C-99
1935	62	190	48	7	3	3	1.6	14	29	10	20	0	.253	.368	6	1	C-56
1936	13	17	1	1	0	0	0.0	0	1	6	2	0	.059	.118	1	0	C-12

Player Register

	G	AB	H	2B	3B	HR	HR%	R	RBI	BB	SO	SB	BA	SA	Pinch Hit AB	Pinch Hit H	G by POS

Charlie Berry continued

	G	AB	H	2B	3B	HR	HR%	R	RBI	BB	SO	SB	BA	SA	PH AB	PH H	G by POS
1938	1	2	0	0	0	0	0.0	0	0	0	0	0	.000	.000	0	0	C-1
11 yrs.	709	2018	539	88	29	23	1.1	196	256	160	196	13	.267	.374	48	13	C-657
2 yrs.	158	497	138	23	9	6	1.2	58	59	38	39	3	.278	.396	5	0	C-153

Claude Berry

BERRY, CLAUDE ELZY (Admiral) BR TR 5'7" 165 lbs.
B. Feb. 4, 1880, Losantville, Ind.   D. Feb. 1, 1974, Richmond, Va.

	G	AB	H	2B	3B	HR	HR%	R	RBI	BB	SO	SB	BA	SA	PH AB	PH H	G by POS
1904 CHI A	3	1	0	0	0	0	0.0	1	0	1		0	.000	.000	0	0	C-3
1906 PHI A	10	30	7	0	0	0	0.0	2	2	2		1	.233	.233	0	0	C-10
1907	8	19	4	2	0	0	0.0	2	1	2		0	.211	.316	0	0	C-8
1914 PIT F	124	411	98	18	9	2	0.5	35	36	26		6	.238	.341	1	0	C-122
1915	100	292	56	11	1	1	0.3	32	26	29		7	.192	.247	0	0	C-99
5 yrs.	245	753	165	31	10	3	0.4	72	65	60		14	.219	.299	1	0	C-242
1 yr.	3	1	0	0	0	0	0.0	1	0	1		0	.000	.000	0	0	C-3

Ken Berry

BERRY, ALLEN KEN BR TR 6' 175 lbs.
B. May 10, 1941, Kansas City, Mo.

	G	AB	H	2B	3B	HR	HR%	R	RBI	BB	SO	SB	BA	SA	PH AB	PH H	G by POS
1962 CHI A	3	6	2	0	0	0	0.0	2	0	0	0	0	.333	.333	1	1	OF-2
1963	4	5	1	0	0	0	0.0	2	0	1	0	0	.200	.200	0	0	OF-2, 2B-1
1964	12	32	12	1	0	1	3.1	4	4	5	3	0	.375	.500	0	0	OF-12
1965	157	472	103	17	4	12	2.5	51	42	28	96	4	.218	.347	1	0	OF-156
1966	147	443	120	20	2	8	1.8	50	34	28	63	7	.271	.379	3	0	OF-141
1967	147	485	117	14	4	7	1.4	49	41	46	68	9	.241	.330	4	0	OF-143
1968	153	504	127	21	2	7	1.4	49	32	25	64	6	.252	.343	2	1	OF-151
1969	130	297	69	12	2	4	1.3	25	18	24	50	1	.232	.327	2	0	OF-120
1970	141	463	128	12	2	7	1.5	45	50	43	61	6	.276	.356	2	1	OF-138
1971 CAL A	111	298	66	17	0	3	1.0	29	22	18	33	3	.221	.309	10	5	OF-101
1972	119	409	118	15	3	5	1.2	41	39	35	47	5	.289	.377	4	1	OF-116
1973	136	415	118	11	2	3	0.7	48	36	26	50	1	.284	.342	3	0	OF-129
1974 MIL A	98	267	64	9	2	1	0.4	21	24	18	26	3	.240	.300	9	1	OF-82, DH-13
1975 CLE A	25	40	8	1	0	0	0.0	6	1	1	7	0	.200	.225	1	0	OF-18, DH-5
14 yrs.	1383	4136	1053	150	23	58	1.4	422	343	298	569	45	.255	.344	42	10	OF-1311, DH-18, 2B-1
9 yrs.	894	2707	679	97	16	46	1.7	277	221	200	406	33	.251	.349	15	3	OF-865, 2B-1

Neil Berry

BERRY, CORNELIUS JOHN BR TR 5'10" 168 lbs.
B. Jan. 11, 1922, Kalamazoo, Mich.

	G	AB	H	2B	3B	HR	HR%	R	RBI	BB	SO	SB	BA	SA	PH AB	PH H	G by POS
1948 DET A	87	256	68	8	1	0	0.0	46	16	37	23	1	.266	.305	5	1	SS-41, 2B-26
1949	109	329	78	9	1	0	0.0	38	18	27	24	4	.237	.271	4	0	2B-95, SS-4
1950	38	39	10	1	0	0	0.0	9	7	6	11	0	.256	.282	4	0	SS-11, 2B-2, 3B-1
1951	67	157	36	5	2	0	0.0	17	9	10	15	4	.229	.287	4	0	SS-38, 2B-10, 3B-7
1952	73	189	43	4	3	0	0.0	22	13	22	19	1	.228	.280	1	1	SS-66, 3B-2
1953 2 teams		STL A (57G – .283)				CHI A (5G – .125)											
" total	62	107	29	1	2	0	0.0	15	10	10	11	0	.271	.318	6	1	3B-18, 2B-18, SS-6
1954 BAL A	5	9	1	0	0	0	0.0	1	0	1	2	0	.111	.111	0	0	SS-5
7 yrs.	441	1086	265	28	9	0	0.0	148	74	113	105	11	.244	.286	24	3	SS-171, 2B-151, 3B-28
1 yr.	5	8	1	0	0	0	0.0	1	0	1	1	0	.125	.125	1	0	2B-3

John Bischoff

BISCHOFF, JOHN GEORGE (Smiley) BR TR 5'8" 160 lbs.
B. Oct. 28, 1894, Edwardsville, Ill.

	G	AB	H	2B	3B	HR	HR%	R	RBI	BB	SO	SB	BA	SA	PH AB	PH H	G by POS
1925 2 teams		CHI A (7G – .091)				BOS A (41G – .278)											
" total	48	144	38	9	1	1	0.7	14	16	7	16	1	.264	.361	3	0	C-44
1926 BOS A	59	127	33	11	2	0	0.0	6	19	15	16	1	.260	.378	12	2	C-46
2 yrs.	107	271	71	20	3	1	0.4	20	35	22	32	2	.262	.369	15	2	C-90
1 yr.	7	11	1	0	0	0	0.0	1	0	1	5	0	.091	.091	3	0	C-4

Bill Black

BLACK, JOHN WILLIAM (Jigger) BL TR 5'11" 168 lbs.
B. Aug. 12, 1899, Philadelphia, Pa.   D. Jan. 14, 1968, Philadelphia, Pa.

	G	AB	H	2B	3B	HR	HR%	R	RBI	BB	SO	SB	BA	SA	PH AB	PH H	G by POS
1924 CHI A	6	5	1	0	0	0	0.0	0	0	0	0	0	.200	.200	0	0	2B-1

Lena Blackburne

BLACKBURNE, RUSSELL AUBREY (Slats) BR TR 5'11" 160 lbs.
B. Oct. 23, 1886, Clifton Heights, Pa.   D. Feb. 29, 1968, Riverside, N. J.
Manager 1928-29.

	G	AB	H	2B	3B	HR	HR%	R	RBI	BB	SO	SB	BA	SA	PH AB	PH H	G by POS
1910 CHI A	75	242	42	3	1	0	0.0	16	10	19		4	.174	.194	0	0	SS-74
1912	3	1	0	0	0	0	0.0	0	0	1		1	.000	.000	0	0	SS-2, 3B-1
1914	144	474	105	10	5	1	0.2	52	35	66	58	25	.222	.270	1	0	2B-143
1915	96	283	61	5	1	0	0.0	33	25	35	34	13	.216	.240	2	1	3B-83, SS-9
1918 CIN N	125	435	99	8	10	1	0.2	33	45	25	30	6	.228	.299	0	0	SS-125
1919 2 teams		BOS N (31G – .263)				PHI N (72G – .199)											
" total	103	371	79	13	6	2	0.5	37	23	16	29	5	.213	.296	4	1	3B-96, SS-2, 2B-2, 1B-2
1927 CHI A	1	1	1	0	0	0	0.0	0	1	0	0	0	1.000	1.000	1	1	
1929	1	0	0	0	0	0	–	0	0	0	0	0	–	–	0	0	P-1
8 yrs.	548	1807	387	39	23	4	0.2	174	139	162	151	54	.214	.268	8	3	SS-212, 3B-180, 2B-145, 1B-2, P-1
6 yrs.	320	1001	209	18	7	1	0.1	102	71	121	92	43	.209	.244	4	2	2B-143, SS-85, 3B-84, P-1

George Blackerby

BLACKERBY, GEORGE FRANKLIN
B. Nov. 10, 1903, Gluther, Okla.

	G	AB	H	2B	3B	HR	HR%	R	RBI	BB	SO	SB	BA	SA	PH AB	PH H	G by POS
1928 CHI A	30	83	21	0	0	0	0.0	8	12	4	10	2	.253	.253	10	4	OF-20

Ossie Blanco

BLANCO, CARLOS OSVALDO J. BR TR 6' 185 lbs.
B. Sept. 8, 1945, Caracas, Venezuela

	G	AB	H	2B	3B	HR	HR%	R	RBI	BB	SO	SB	BA	SA	PH AB	PH H	G by POS
1970 CHI A	34	66	13	0	0	0	0.0	4	8	3	14	0	.197	.197	16	3	1B-22, OF-1
1974 CLE A	18	36	7	0	0	0	0.0	1	2	7	4	0	.194	.194	0	0	1B-16, DH-1
2 yrs.	52	102	20	0	0	0	0.0	5	10	10	18	0	.196	.196	16	3	1B-38, DH-1, OF-1
1 yr.	34	66	13	0	0	0	0.0	4	8	3	14	0	.197	.197	16	3	1B-22, OF-1

Player Register

	G	AB	H	2B	3B	HR	HR%	R	RBI	BB	SO	SB	BA	SA	Pinch Hit AB	H	G by POS

Bruno Block
BLOCK, JAMES JOHN
Born James John Blochowitz.
B. Mar. 14, 1885, Wisconsin Rapids, Wis. D. Aug. 6, 1937, S. Milwaukee, Wis.
BR TR 5'9" 185 lbs.

Year	Team	G	AB	H	2B	3B	HR	HR%	R	RBI	BB	SO	SB	BA	SA	PH AB	PH H	G by POS
1907	WAS A	24	57	8	2	1	0	0.0	3	2	2		0	.140	.211	3	0	C-21
1910	CHI A	55	152	32	1	1	0	0.0	12	9	13		3	.211	.230	6	0	C-47
1911		39	115	35	6	1	1	0.9	11	18	6		0	.304	.400	1	0	C-38
1912		46	136	35	5	6	0	0.0	8	26	7		1	.257	.382	0	0	C-46
1914	CHI F	43	100	19	4	1	0	0.0	8	13	11		1	.190	.250	10	2	C-33
5 yrs.		207	560	129	18	10	1	0.2	42	68	39		5	.230	.304	20	2	C-185
3 yrs.		140	403	102	12	8	1	0.2	31	53	26		4	.253	.330	7	0	C-131

Ron Blomberg
BLOMBERG, RONALD MARK
B. Aug. 23, 1948, Atlanta, Ga.
BL TR 6'1½" 195 lbs.

Year	Team	G	AB	H	2B	3B	HR	HR%	R	RBI	BB	SO	SB	BA	SA	PH AB	PH H	G by POS
1969	NY A	4	6	3	0	0	0	0.0	0	0	1	0	0	.500	.500	1	1	OF-2
1971		64	199	64	6	2	7	3.5	30	31	14	23	2	.322	.477	11	2	OF-57
1972		107	299	80	22	1	14	4.7	36	49	38	26	0	.268	.488	15	5	1B-95
1973		100	301	99	13	1	12	4.0	45	57	34	26	2	.329	.498	6	2	DH-55, 1B-41
1974		90	264	82	11	2	10	3.8	39	48	29	33	2	.311	.481	10	5	DH-58, OF-19
1975		34	106	27	8	2	4	3.8	18	17	13	10	0	.255	.481	5	2	DH-27, OF-1
1976		1	2	0	0	0	0	0.0	0	0	0	0	0	.000	.000	1	0	DH-1
1978	CHI A	61	156	36	7	0	5	3.2	16	22	11	17	0	.231	.372	16	2	DH-36, 1B-7
8 yrs.		461	1333	391	67	8	52	3.9	184	224	140	135	6	.293	.473	65	19	DH-177, 1B-143, OF-79
1 yr.		61	156	36	7	0	5	3.2	16	22	11	17	0	.231	.372	16	2	DH-36, 1B-7

Lu Blue
BLUE, LUZERNE ATWELL
B. Mar. 5, 1897, Washington, D. C. D. July 28, 1958, Alexandria, Va.
BB TL 5'10" 165 lbs.

Year	Team	G	AB	H	2B	3B	HR	HR%	R	RBI	BB	SO	SB	BA	SA	PH AB	PH H	G by POS
1921	DET A	153	585	180	33	11	5	0.9	103	75	103	47	13	.308	.427	1	0	1B-152
1922		145	584	175	31	9	6	1.0	131	45	82	48	8	.300	.414	1	1	1B-144
1923		129	504	143	27	7	1	0.2	100	46	96	40	9	.284	.371	0	0	1B-129
1924		108	395	123	26	7	2	0.5	81	50	64	26	9	.311	.428	0	0	1B-108
1925		150	532	163	18	9	3	0.6	91	94	83	29	19	.306	.391	2	0	1B-148
1926		128	429	123	24	14	1	0.2	92	52	90	18	13	.287	.415	12	5	1B-109, OF-1
1927		112	365	95	17	9	1	0.3	71	42	71	28	13	.260	.364	5	2	1B-104
1928	STL A	154	549	154	32	11	14	2.6	116	80	105	43	12	.281	.455	0	0	1B-154
1929		151	573	168	40	10	6	1.0	111	61	126	32	12	.293	.429	0	0	1B-151
1930		117	425	100	27	5	4	0.9	85	42	81	44	12	.235	.351	4	1	1B-111
1931	CHI A	155	589	179	23	15	1	0.2	119	62	127	60	13	.304	.399	0	0	1B-155
1932		112	373	93	21	2	0	0.0	51	43	64	21	17	.249	.316	6	1	1B-105
1933	BKN N	1	1	0	0	0	0	0.0	0	0	0	0	0	.000	.000	0	0	1B-1
13 yrs.		1615	5904	1696	319	109	44	0.7	1151	692	1092	436	150	.287	.401	31	10	1B-1571, OF-1
2 yrs.		267	962	272	44	17	1	0.1	170	105	191	81	30	.283	.367	6	1	1B-260

Milt Bocek
BOCEK, MILTON FRANK
B. July 16, 1912, Chicago, Ill.
BR TR 6'1" 185 lbs.

Year	Team	G	AB	H	2B	3B	HR	HR%	R	RBI	BB	SO	SB	BA	SA	PH AB	PH H	G by POS
1933	CHI A	11	22	8	1	0	1	4.5	3	3	4	6	0	.364	.545	5	1	OF-6
1934		19	38	8	1	0	0	0.0	3	3	5	5	0	.211	.237	6	0	OF-10
2 yrs.		30	60	16	2	0	1	1.7	6	6	9	11	0	.267	.350	11	1	OF-16
2 yrs.		30	60	16	2	0	1	1.7	6	6	9	11	0	.267	.350	11	1	OF-16

Ping Bodie
BODIE, FRANK STEPHAN
Born Francesco Stephano Pezzolo.
B. Oct. 8, 1887, San Francisco, Calif. D. Dec. 17, 1961, San Francisco, Calif.
BR TR 5'8" 195 lbs.

Year	Team	G	AB	H	2B	3B	HR	HR%	R	RBI	BB	SO	SB	BA	SA	PH AB	PH H	G by POS
1911	CHI A	145	551	159	27	13	4	0.7	75	97	49		14	.289	.407	1	0	OF-128, 2B-16
1912		137	472	139	24	7	5	1.1	58	72	43		12	.294	.407	7	3	OF-130
1913		127	406	107	14	8	8	2.0	39	48	35	57	5	.264	.397	6	0	OF-119
1914		107	327	75	9	5	3	0.9	21	29	21	35	12	.229	.315	10	2	OF-95
1917	PHI A	148	557	162	28	11	7	1.3	50	74	53	40	13	.291	.418	2	0	OF-145, 1B-1
1918	NY A	91	324	83	12	6	3	0.9	36	46	27	24	6	.256	.358	1	0	OF-90
1919		134	475	132	27	8	6	1.3	45	59	36	46	15	.278	.406	0	0	OF-134
1920		129	471	139	26	12	7	1.5	63	79	40	30	6	.295	.446	0	0	OF-129
1921		31	87	15	2	2	0	0.0	5	12	8	8	0	.172	.241	6	0	OF-25
9 yrs.		1049	3670	1011	169	72	43	1.2	392	516	312	240	83	.275	.396	33	5	OF-995, 2B-16, 1B-1
4 yrs.		516	1756	480	74	33	20	1.1	193	246	148	92	43	.273	.387	24	5	OF-472, 2B-16

Bob Boken
BOKEN, ROBERT ANTHONY
B. Feb. 23, 1908, Maryville, Ill.
BR TR 6'2" 165 lbs.

Year	Team	G	AB	H	2B	3B	HR	HR%	R	RBI	BB	SO	SB	BA	SA	PH AB	PH H	G by POS
1933	WAS A	55	133	37	5	2	3	2.3	19	26	9	16	0	.278	.414	7	2	2B-31, 3B-19, SS-10
1934	2 teams	WAS A (11G – .222)						CHI A (81G – .236)										
"	total	92	324	76	10	2	3	0.9	35	46	18	33	4	.235	.306	5	2	2B-58, SS-22, 3B-6
2 yrs.		147	457	113	15	4	6	1.3	54	72	27	49	4	.247	.337	12	4	2B-89, SS-32, 3B-25
1 yr.		81	297	70	9	1	3	1.0	30	40	15	32	2	.236	.303	1	0	2B-57, SS-22

Bobby Bonds
BONDS, BOBBY LEE
B. Mar. 15, 1946, Riverside, Calif.
BR TR 6'1" 190 lbs.

Year	Team	G	AB	H	2B	3B	HR	HR%	R	RBI	BB	SO	SB	BA	SA	PH AB	PH H	G by POS
1968	SF N	81	307	78	10	5	9	2.9	55	35	38	84	16	.254	.407	0	0	OF-80
1969		158	622	161	25	6	32	5.1	120	90	81	187	45	.259	.473	1	0	OF-155
1970		157	663	200	36	10	26	3.9	134	78	77	189	48	.302	.504	2	0	OF-157
1971		155	619	178	32	4	33	5.3	110	102	62	137	26	.288	.512	3	1	OF-154
1972		153	626	162	29	5	26	4.2	118	80	60	137	44	.259	.446	0	0	OF-153
1973		160	643	182	34	4	39	6.1	131	96	87	148	43	.283	.530	2	1	OF-158
1974		150	567	145	22	8	21	3.7	97	71	95	134	41	.256	.434	3	1	OF-148
1975	NY A	145	529	143	26	3	32	6.0	93	85	89	137	30	.270	.512	4	1	OF-129, DH-12
1976	CAL A	99	378	100	10	3	10	2.6	48	54	41	90	30	.265	.386	1	0	OF-98, DH-1
1977		158	592	156	23	9	37	6.3	103	115	74	141	41	.264	.520	1	0	OF-140, DH-18
1978	2 teams	CHI A (26G – .278)						TEX A (130G – .265)										
"	total	156	565	151	19	4	31	5.5	93	90	79	120	43	.267	.480	2	1	OF-133, DH-21
1979	CLE A	146	538	148	24	1	25	4.6	93	85	74	135	34	.275	.463	1	0	OF-116, DH-29

Player Register

	G	AB	H	2B	3B	HR	HR%	R	RBI	BB	SO	SB	BA	SA	Pinch Hit AB	Pinch Hit H	G by POS

Bobby Bonds continued
	G	AB	H	2B	3B	HR	HR%	R	RBI	BB	SO	SB	BA	SA	AB	H	G by POS
1980 STL N	86	231	47	5	3	5	2.2	37	24	33	74	15	.203	.316	15	2	OF-70
1981 CHI N	45	163	35	7	1	6	3.7	26	19	24	44	5	.215	.380	0	0	OF-45
14 yrs.	1849	7043	1886	302	66	332	4.7	1258	1024	914	1757 4th	461	.268	.471	35	7	OF-1736, DH-81
1 yr.	26	90	25	4	0	2	2.2	8	8	10	10	6	.278	.389	1	1	OF-22, DH-3

LEAGUE CHAMPIONSHIP SERIES
| 1971 SF N | 3 | 8 | 2 | 0 | 0 | 0 | 0.0 | 0 | 0 | 2 | 4 | 0 | .250 | .250 | 0 | 0 | OF-3 |

Zeke Bonura
BONURA, HENRY JOHN
B. Sept. 20, 1908, New Orleans, La.
BR TR 6' 210 lbs.

	G	AB	H	2B	3B	HR	HR%	R	RBI	BB	SO	SB	BA	SA	AB	H	G by POS
1934 CHI A	127	510	154	35	4	27	5.3	86	110	64	31	0	.302	.545	0	0	1B-127
1935	138	550	162	34	4	21	3.8	107	92	57	28	4	.295	.485	0	0	1B-138
1936	148	587	194	39	7	12	2.0	120	138	94	29	4	.330	.482	1	0	1B-146
1937	116	447	154	41	2	19	4.3	79	100	49	24	5	.345	.573	0	0	1B-115
1938 WAS A	137	540	156	27	3	22	4.1	72	114	44	29	2	.289	.472	8	2	1B-129
1939 NY N	123	455	146	26	6	11	2.4	75	85	46	22	1	.321	.477	0	0	1B-122
1940 2 teams	WAS A (79G − .273)					CHI N (49G − .264)											
" total	128	493	133	30	3	7	1.4	61	65	50	17	3	.270	.385	5	1	1B-123
7 yrs.	917	3582	1099	232	29	119	3.3	600	704	404	180	19	.307	.487	15	3	1B-900
4 yrs.	529	2094	664	149	17	79 9th	3.8 3rd	392	440	264	112	13	.317	.518 4th	2 1st	0	1B-526

Buddy Booker
BOOKER, RICHARD LEE
B. May 28, 1942, Lynchburg, Va.
BL TR 5'10" 170 lbs.

	G	AB	H	2B	3B	HR	HR%	R	RBI	BB	SO	SB	BA	SA	AB	H	G by POS
1966 CLE A	18	28	6	1	0	2	7.1	6	5	2	6	0	.214	.464	8	0	C-12
1968 CHI A	5	5	0	0	0	0	0.0	0	0	1	2	0	.000	.000	4	0	C-3
2 yrs.	23	33	6	1	0	2	6.1	6	5	3	8	0	.182	.394	12	0	C-15
1 yr.	5	5	0	0	0	0	0.0	0	0	1	2	0	.000	.000	4	0	C-3

Ike Boone
BOONE, ISAAC MORGAN
Brother of Danny Boone.
B. Feb. 17, 1897, Samantha, Ala.   D. Aug. 1, 1958, Northport, Ala.
BL TR 6' 195 lbs.

	G	AB	H	2B	3B	HR	HR%	R	RBI	BB	SO	SB	BA	SA	AB	H	G by POS
1922 NY N	2	2	1	0	0	0	0.0	0	0	0	1	0	.500	.500	2	1	
1923 BOS A	5	15	4	0	1	0	0.0	1	2	1	0	0	.267	.400	1	0	OF-4
1924	128	486	162	29	3	13	2.7	71	96	55	32	2	.333	.486	4	1	OF-123
1925	133	476	157	34	5	9	1.9	79	68	60	19	1	.330	.479	11	3	OF-118
1927 CHI A	29	53	12	4	0	1	1.9	10	11	3	4	0	.226	.358	16	3	OF-11
1930 BKN N	40	101	30	9	1	3	3.0	13	13	14	8	0	.297	.495	9	3	OF-27
1931	6	5	1	0	0	0	0.0	0	0	2	0	0	.200	.200	5	1	
1932	13	21	3	1	0	0	0.0	2	2	5	2	0	.143	.190	5	0	OF-8
8 yrs.	356	1159	370	77	10	26	2.2	176	192	140	68	3	.319	.470	53	12	OF-291
1 yr.	29	53	12	4	0	1	1.9	10	11	3	4	0	.226	.358	16	3	OF-11

Ray Boone
BOONE, RAYMOND OTIS (Ike)
Father of Bob Boone.
B. July 27, 1923, San Diego, Calif.
BR TR 6' 172 lbs.

	G	AB	H	2B	3B	HR	HR%	R	RBI	BB	SO	SB	BA	SA	AB	H	G by POS
1948 CLE A	6	5	2	1	0	0	0.0	0	1	0	1	0	.400	.600	1	0	SS-4
1949	86	258	65	4	4	4	1.6	39	26	38	17	0	.252	.345	7	1	SS-76
1950	109	365	110	14	6	7	1.9	53	58	56	27	4	.301	.430	6	0	SS-102
1951	151	544	127	14	1	12	2.2	65	51	48	36	5	.233	.329	0	0	SS-151
1952	103	316	83	8	2	7	2.2	57	45	53	33	0	.263	.367	4	0	SS-96, 3B-2, 2B-1
1953 2 teams	CLE A (34G − .241)					DET A (101G − .312)											
" total	135	497	147	17	8	26	5.2	94	114	72	68	3	.296	.519	4	1	3B-97, SS-34
1954 DET A	148	543	160	19	2	20	3.7	76	85	71	53	4	.295	.466	0	0	3B-148, SS-1
1955	135	500	142	28	7	20	4.0	68	116	50	49	1	.284	.476	8	2	3B-126
1956	131	481	148	14	6	25	5.2	77	81	77	46	0	.308	.518	0	0	3B-130
1957	129	462	126	25	3	12	2.6	48	65	57	47	1	.273	.418	5	1	1B-117, 3B-4
1958 2 teams	DET A (39G − .237)					CHI A (77G − .244)											
" total	116	360	87	16	2	13	3.6	41	61	32	46	1	.242	.406	21	2	1B-95
1959 3 teams	CHI A (9G − .238)					KC A (61G − .273)				MIL N (13G − .200)							
" total	83	168	44	6	0	4	2.4	25	19	38	24	2	.262	.369	37	11	1B-47, 3B-3
1960 2 teams	MIL N (7G − .250)					BOS A (34G − .205)											
" total	41	90	19	2	0	1	1.1	9	15	16	16	0	.211	.267	15	3	1B-26
13 yrs.	1373	4589	1260	162	46	151	3.3	645	737	608	463	21	.275	.429	108	21	3B-510, SS-464, 1B-285, 2B-1
2 yrs.	86	267	65	12	1	8	3.0	28	46	25	38	2	.243	.386	17	2	1B-69

WORLD SERIES
| 1948 CLE A | 1 | 1 | 0 | 0 | 0 | 0 | 0.0 | 0 | 0 | 0 | 1 | 0 | .000 | .000 | 1 | 0 | |

Frenchy Bordagaray
BORDAGARAY, STANLEY GEORGE
B. Jan. 3, 1912, Coalinga, Calif.
BR TR 5'7½" 175 lbs.

	G	AB	H	2B	3B	HR	HR%	R	RBI	BB	SO	SB	BA	SA	AB	H	G by POS
1934 CHI A	29	87	28	3	1	0	0.0	12	2	3	8	1	.322	.379	12	8	OF-17
1935 BKN N	120	422	119	19	6	1	0.2	69	39	17	29	18	.282	.363	9	2	OF-105
1936	125	372	117	21	3	4	1.1	63	31	17	42	12	.315	.419	6	2	OF-92, 2B-11
1937 STL N	96	300	88	11	4	1	0.3	43	37	15	25	11	.293	.367	16	1	OF-50, OF-28
1938	81	156	44	5	1	0	0.0	19	21	8	9	2	.282	.327	43	20	OF-29, 3B-4
1939 CIN N	63	122	24	5	1	0	0.0	19	12	9	10	3	.197	.254	11	0	OF-43, 2B-2
1941 NY A	36	73	19	1	0	0	0.0	10	4	6	8	1	.260	.274	13	4	OF-19
1942 BKN N	48	58	14	2	0	0	0.0	11	5	3	3	2	.241	.276	15	4	OF-17
1943	89	268	81	18	2	0	0.0	47	19	30	15	6	.302	.384	6	2	OF-53, 3B-25
1944	130	501	141	26	4	6	1.2	85	51	36	22	2	.281	.385	10	3	OF-98, 3B-25
1945	113	273	70	9	6	2	0.7	32	49	29	15	7	.256	.355	32	8	3B-57, OF-22
11 yrs.	930	2632	745	120	28	14	0.5	410	270	173	186	65	.283	.366	173	54	OF-450, 3B-234, 2B-13
1 yr.	29	87	28	3	1	0	0.0	12	2	3	8	1	.322	.379	12	8	OF-17

WORLD SERIES
| 1939 CIN N | 2 | 0 | 0 | 0 | 0 | 0 | − | 0 | 0 | 0 | 0 | 0 | − | − | 0 | 0 | |

Player Register

	G	AB	H	2B	3B	HR	HR%	R	RBI	BB	SO	SB	BA	SA	Pinch Hit AB H	G by POS

Frenchy Bordagaray continued

| 1941 NY A | 1 | 0 | 0 | 0 | 0 | 0 | — | 0 | 0 | 0 | 0 | 0 | — | — | 0 0 | |
| 2 yrs. | 3 | 0 | 0 | 0 | 0 | 0 | — | 0 | 0 | 0 | 0 | 0 | — | — | 0 0 | |

Glenn Borgmann
BORGMANN, GLENN DENNIS
B. May 25, 1950, Paterson, N. J.
BR TR 6'4" 210 lbs.

1972 MIN A	56	175	41	4	0	3	1.7	19	14	25	25	0	.234	.309	0 0	C-56
1973	12	34	9	2	0	0	0.0	7	9	6	10	0	.265	.324	0 0	C-12
1974	128	345	87	8	1	3	0.9	33	45	39	44	2	.252	.307	4 0	C-128
1975	125	352	73	15	2	2	0.6	34	33	47	59	0	.207	.278	2 0	C-125
1976	24	65	16	3	0	1	1.5	10	6	19	7	1	.246	.338	1 1	C-24
1977	17	43	11	1	0	2	4.7	12	7	11	9	0	.256	.419	0 0	C-17
1978	49	123	26	4	1	3	2.4	16	15	18	17	0	.211	.333	3 1	C-46, DH-1
1979	31	70	14	3	0	0	0.0	4	8	12	11	1	.200	.243	0 0	C-31
1980 CHI A	32	87	19	2	0	2	2.3	10	14	14	9	0	.218	.310	1 0	C-32
9 yrs.	474	1294	296	42	4	16	1.2	137	151	191	191	4	.229	.304	11 2	C-471, DH-1
1 yr.	32	87	19	2	0	2	2.3	10	14	14	9	0	.218	.310	1 0	C-32

Babe Borton
BORTON, WILLIAM BAKER
B. Aug. 14, 1888, Marion, Ill.   D. July 29, 1954, Berkeley, Calif.
BL TL 6' 178 lbs.

1912 CHI A	31	105	39	3	1	0	0.0	15	17	8		1	.371	.419	1 1	1B-30
1913 2 teams	CHI A (28G – .275)					NY A (33G – .130)										
" total	61	188	36	6	0	1	0.5	17	24	41	24	2	.191	.239	2 0	1B-59
1915 STL F	159	549	157	20	14	3	0.5	97	83	92		17	.286	.390	7 1	1B-159
1916 STL A	66	98	22	1	2	1	1.0	10	12	19	13	1	.224	.306	35 6	1B-22
4 yrs.	317	940	254	30	17	5	0.5	139	136	160	37	21	.270	.354	38 7	1B-270
2 yrs.	59	185	61	8	1	0	0.0	24	30	31	5	2	.330	.384	3 1	1B-56

Thad Bosley
BOSLEY, THADDIS
B. Sept. 17, 1956, Oceanside, Calif.
BL TL 6'3" 175 lbs.

1977 CAL A	58	212	63	10	2	0	0.0	19	19	16	32	5	.297	.363	4 2	OF-55
1978 CHI A	66	219	59	5	1	2	0.9	25	13	13	32	12	.269	.329	1 0	OF-64
1979	36	77	24	1	1	1	1.3	13	8	9	14	4	.312	.390	7 1	OF-28, DH-1
1980	70	147	33	2	0	2	1.4	12	14	10	27	3	.224	.279	25 8	OF-52
1981 MIL A	42	105	24	2	0	0	0.0	11	3	6	13	2	.229	.248	4 0	OF-37, DH-1
1982 SEA A	22	46	8	1	0	0	0.0	3	2	4	8	3	.174	.196	3 0	OF-19
1983 CHI N	43	72	21	4	1	2	2.8	12	12	10	12	1	.292	.458	18 4	OF-20
7 yrs.	337	878	232	25	5	7	0.8	95	71	68	138	30	.264	.328	62 15	OF-275, DH-2
3 yrs.	172	443	116	8	2	5	1.1	50	35	32	73	19	.262	.323	33 9	OF-144, DH-1

DIVISIONAL PLAYOFF SERIES

| 1981 MIL A | 1 | 0 | 0 | 0 | 0 | 0 | — | 0 | 0 | 0 | 0 | 0 | — | — | 0 0 | DH-1 |

Billy Bowers
BOWERS, GROVER BILL
B. Mar. 25, 1923, Parkin, Ark.
BL TR 5'9½" 176 lbs.

| 1949 CHI A | 26 | 78 | 15 | 2 | 1 | 0 | 0.0 | 9 | 6 | 4 | 5 | 1 | .192 | .244 | 6 0 | OF-20 |

Red Bowser
BOWSER, JAMES H.
B. 1886, Greensburg, Pa.

| 1910 CHI A | 1 | 2 | 0 | 0 | 0 | 0 | 0.0 | 0 | 0 | 0 | | 0 | .000 | .000 | 0 0 | OF-1 |

Bob Boyd
BOYD, ROBERT RICHARD (The Rope)
B. Oct. 1, 1926, Potts Camp, Miss.
BL TL 5'10" 170 lbs.

1951 CHI A	12	18	3	0	1	0	0.0	3	4	3	3	0	.167	.278	5 1	1B-6
1953	55	165	49	6	2	3	1.8	20	23	13	11	1	.297	.412	8 4	1B-29, OF-16
1954	29	56	10	3	0	0	0.0	10	5	4	3	2	.179	.232	2 0	OF-13, 1B-12
1956 BAL A	70	225	70	8	3	2	0.9	28	11	30	14	0	.311	.400	10 3	1B-60, OF-8
1957	141	485	154	16	8	4	0.8	73	34	55	31	2	.318	.408	15 6	1B-132, OF-1
1958	125	401	124	21	5	7	1.7	58	36	25	24	1	.309	.439	32 4	1B-99
1959	128	415	110	20	2	3	0.7	42	41	29	14	3	.265	.345	20 4	1B-109
1960	71	82	26	5	2	0	0.0	9	9	6	5	0	.317	.402	56 17	1B-17
1961 2 teams	KC A (26G – .229)					MIL N (36G – .244)										
" total	62	89	21	2	0	0	0.0	10	12	2	9	0	.236	.258	49 9	1B-11
9 yrs.	693	1936	567	81	23	19	1.0	253	175	167	114	9	.293	.388	197 48	1B-475, OF-38
3 yrs.	96	239	62	9	3	3	1.3	33	32	20	17	3	.259	.360	15 5	1B-47, OF-29

Ken Boyer
BOYER, KENTON LLOYD
Brother of Cloyd Boyer.   Brother of Clete Boyer.
B. May 20, 1931, Liberty, Mo.   D. Sept. 7, 1982, St. Louis, Mo.
Manager 1978-80.
BR TR 6'1½" 190 lbs.

1955 STL N	147	530	140	27	2	18	3.4	78	62	37	67	22	.264	.425	1 0	3B-139, SS-18
1956	150	595	182	30	2	26	4.4	91	98	38	65	8	.306	.494	1 0	3B-149
1957	142	544	144	18	3	19	3.5	79	62	44	77	12	.265	.414	1 0	OF-105, 3B-41
1958	150	570	175	21	9	23	4.0	101	90	49	53	11	.307	.496	1 0	3B-144, OF-6, SS-1
1959	149	563	174	18	5	28	5.0	86	94	67	77	12	.309	.508	1 0	3B-143, SS-12
1960	151	552	168	26	10	32	5.8	95	97	56	77	8	.304	.562	5 1	3B-146
1961	153	589	194	26	11	24	4.1	109	95	68	91	6	.329	.533	0 0	3B-153
1962	160	611	178	27	5	24	3.9	92	98	75	104	12	.291	.470	0 0	3B-160
1963	159	617	176	28	2	24	3.9	86	111	70	90	1	.285	.454	0 0	3B-159
1964	162	628	185	30	10	24	3.8	100	119	70	85	3	.295	.489	0 0	3B-162
1965	144	535	139	18	2	13	2.4	71	75	57	73	2	.260	.374	3 0	3B-143
1966 NY N	136	496	132	28	2	14	2.8	62	61	30	64	6	.266	.415	7 3	3B-130, 1B-2
1967 2 teams	NY N (56G – .235)					CHI A (57G – .261)										
" total	113	346	86	12	3	7	2.0	34	34	33	47	2	.249	.361	15 4	3B-77, 1B-26

228

Player Register
229

	G	AB	H	2B	3B	HR	HR%	R	RBI	BB	SO	SB	BA	SA	Pinch Hit AB	H	G by POS

Ken Boyer continued

1968 2 teams	CHI A (10G – .125)					LA N (83G – .271)											
" total	93	245	63	7	2	6	2.4	20	41	17	40	2	.257	.376	29	6	3B-39, 1B-33
1969 LA N	25	34	7	2	0	0	0.0	0	4	2	7	0	.206	.265	19	4	1B-4
15 yrs.	2034	7455	2143	318	68	282	3.8	1104	1141	713	1017	105	.287	.462	83	18	3B-1785, OF-111, 1B-65, SS-31
2 yrs.	67	204	50	5	1	4	2.0	17	21	8	31	0	.245	.338	11	3	3B-38, 1B-19
WORLD SERIES																	
1964 STL N	7	27	6	1	0	2	7.4	5	6	1	5	0	.222	.481	0	0	3B-7

Buddy Bradford
BRADFORD, CHARLES WILLIAM
B. July 25, 1944, Mobile, Ala.   BR TR 5'11" 170 lbs.

1966 CHI A	14	28	4	0	0	0	0.0	3	0	2	6	0	.143	.143	0	0	OF-9
1967	24	20	2	1	0	0	0.0	6	1	1	7	1	.100	.150	3	1	OF-14
1968	103	281	61	11	0	5	1.8	32	24	23	67	8	.217	.310	6	1	OF-99
1969	93	273	70	8	2	11	4.0	36	27	34	75	5	.256	.421	5	0	OF-88
1970 2 teams	CHI A (32G – .187)					CLE A (75G – .196)											
" total	107	254	49	9	1	9	3.5	33	31	31	73	1	.193	.343	18	3	OF-91, 3B-1
1971 2 teams	CLE A (20G – .158)					CIN N (79G – .200)											
" total	99	138	26	5	1	2	1.4	21	15	20	33	4	.188	.283	14	2	OF-84
1972 CHI A	35	48	13	2	0	2	4.2	15	8	4	13	3	.271	.438	10	4	OF-28
1973	53	168	40	3	1	8	4.8	24	15	17	43	0	.238	.411	5	0	OF-51
1974	39	96	32	2	0	5	5.2	16	10	13	11	1	.333	.510	7	2	OF-32, DH-1
1975 2 teams	CHI A (25G – .155)					STL N (50G – .272)											
" total	75	139	31	4	1	6	4.3	20	30	20	46	3	.223	.396	27	6	OF-43, DH-4
1976 CHI A	55	160	35	5	2	4	2.5	20	14	19	37	6	.219	.350	9	0	OF-48, DH-3
11 yrs.	697	1605	363	50	8	52	3.2	224	175	184	411	36	.226	.364	104	19	OF-587, DH-8, 3B-1
10 yrs.	473	1223	283	38	6	39	3.2	166	122	131	311	32	.231	.368	54	9	OF-414, DH-8

Dave Brain
BRAIN, DAVID LEONARD
B. Jan. 24, 1879, Hereford, England   D. May 25, 1959, Los Angeles, Calif.   BR TR 5'10" 170 lbs.

1901 CHI A	5	20	7	1	0	0	0.0	2	5	1		0	.350	.400	0	0	2B-5
1903 STL N	119	464	107	8	15	1	0.2	44	60	25		21	.231	.319	0	0	SS-72, 3B-46
1904	127	488	130	24	12	7	1.4	57	72	17		18	.266	.408	2	0	SS-59, 3B-30, OF-19, 2B-13, 1B-4
1905 2 teams	STL N (44G – .228)					PIT N (85G – .257)											
" total	129	465	115	21	11	4	0.9	42	63	23		12	.247	.366	3	1	3B-84, SS-33, OF-6
1906 BOS N	139	525	131	19	5	5	1.0	43	45	29		11	.250	.333	0	0	3B-139
1907	133	509	142	24	9	10	2.0	60	56	29		10	.279	.420	0	0	3B-130, OF-3
1908 2 teams	CIN N (16G – .109)					NY N (11G – .176)											
" total	27	72	9	0	0	0	0.0	6	2	10		1	.125	.125	2	0	OF-19, 2B-3, 3B-2, SS-1
7 yrs.	679	2543	641	97	52	27	1.1	254	303	134		73	.252	.363	7	1	3B-431, SS-165, OF-47, 2B-21, 1B-4
1 yr.	5	20	7	1	0	0	0.0	2	5	1		0	.350	.400	0	0	2B-5

Fred Bratchi
BRATCHI, FREDERICK OSCAR (Fritz)
B. Jan. 16, 1892, Alliance, Ohio   D. Jan. 10, 1962, Massillon, Ohio   BR TR 5'10" 170 lbs.

1921 CHI A	16	28	8	1	0	0	0.0	3	0	0	2	0	.286	.321	10	3	OF-5
1926 BOS A	72	167	46	10	1	0	0.0	12	19	14	15	0	.275	.347	30	7	OF-37
1927	1	1	0	0	0	0	0.0	0	0	0	0	0	.000	.000	1	0	
3 yrs.	89	196	54	11	1	0	0.0	12	22	14	17	0	.276	.342	41	10	OF-42
1 yr.	16	28	8	1	0	0	0.0	3	0	0	2	0	.286	.321	10	3	OF-5

Angel Bravo
BRAVO, ANGEL ALFONSO
B. Aug. 4, 1942, Maracaibo, Venezuela   BL TL 5'8" 150 lbs.

1969 CHI A	27	90	26	4	2	1	1.1	10	3	5	2	.289	.411	2	0	OF-25	
1970 CIN N	65	65	18	1	1	0	0.0	10	3	9	13	0	.277	.323	42	13	OF-22
1971 2 teams	CIN N (5G – .200)					SD N (52G – .155)											
" total	57	63	10	2	0	0	0.0	6	6	8	13	0	.159	.190	40	7	OF-9
3 yrs.	149	218	54	7	3	1	0.5	26	12	20	31	2	.248	.321	84	20	OF-56
1 yr.	27	90	26	4	2	1	1.1	10	3	3	5	2	.289	.411	2	0	OF-25
LEAGUE CHAMPIONSHIP SERIES																	
1970 CIN N	1	1	0	0	0	0	0.0	0	0	0	0	0	.000	.000	1	0	
WORLD SERIES																	
1970 CIN N	4	2	0	0	0	0	0.0	0	0	1	1	0	.000	.000	2	0	

Jim Breazeale
BREAZEALE, JAMES LEO
B. Oct. 3, 1949, Houston, Tex.   BL TR 6'2" 210 lbs.

1969 ATL N	2	1	0	0	0	0	0.0	1	0	2	0	0	.000	.000	0	0	1B-1
1971	10	21	4	0	0	1	4.8	1	3	0	3	0	.190	.333	5	3	1B-4
1972	52	85	21	2	0	5	5.9	10	17	6	12	0	.247	.447	33	10	1B-16, 3B-1
1978 CHI A	25	72	15	3	0	3	4.2	8	13	8	10	0	.208	.375	2	1	1B-19, DH-4
4 yrs.	89	179	40	5	0	9	5.0	20	33	16	25	0	.223	.402	40	14	1B-40, DH-4, 3B-1
1 yr.	25	72	15	3	0	3	4.2	8	13	8	10	0	.208	.375	2	1	1B-19, DH-4

Jim Breton
BRETON, JOHN FREDERICK
B. July 15, 1891, Chicago, Ill.   D. May 30, 1973, Beloit, Wis.   BR TR 5'10½" 178 lbs.

1913 CHI A	10	30	5	1	1	0	0.0	1	2	1	5	0	.167	.267	0	0	SS-7, 3B-3
1914	81	231	49	7	2	0	0.0	21	24	24	42	9	.212	.260	0	0	3B-79
1915	16	36	5	1	0	0	0.0	3	1	5	9	2	.139	.167	0	0	3B-14, SS-1, 2B-1
3 yrs.	107	297	59	9	3	0	0.0	25	27	30	56	11	.199	.249	0	0	3B-96, SS-8, 2B-1
3 yrs.	107	297	59	9	3	0	0.0	25	27	30	56	11	.199	.249	0	0	3B-96, SS-8, 2B-1

Ken Brett
BRETT, KENNETH ALVIN
Brother of George Brett.
B. Sept. 18, 1948, Brooklyn, N.Y.   BL TL 6' 190 lbs.

1967 BOS A	1	0	0	0	0	0	–	0	0	0	0	0	–	–	0	0	P-1

Player Register

	G	AB	H	2B	3B	HR	HR %	R	RBI	BB	SO	SB	BA	SA	Pinch Hit AB	H	G by POS

Ken Brett continued

1969		8	10	3	1	0	1	10.0	1	3	1	1	0	.300	.700	0	0	P-8
1970		41	41	13	3	0	2	4.9	8	3	2	7	0	.317	.537	0	0	P-41
1971		29	10	2	0	0	0	0.0	0	0	0	2	0	.200	.200	0	0	P-29
1972 MIL A	31	44	10	1	0	0	0.0	6	1	2	10	0	.227	.250	1	0	P-26
1973 PHI N	37	80	20	5	0	4	5.0	6	16	4	17	0	.250	.463	2	0	P-31
1974 PIT N	43	87	27	4	1	2	2.3	13	15	4	20	0	.310	.448	15	3	P-27
1975	26	52	12	4	0	1	1.9	5	4	1	7	0	.231	.365	3	0	P-23
1976 2 teams	NY A (2G – .000)					CHI A (33G – .083)											
" total	35	12	1	0	0	0	0.0	0	0	0	1	0	.083	.083	6	1	P-29
1977 2 teams	CHI A (13G – .000)					CAL A (21G – .000)											
" total	34	0	0	0	0	0	–	0	0	0	0	0	–	–	0	0	P-34
1978 CAL A	31	0	0	0	0	0	0.0	0	0	0	0	0	–	–	0	0	P-31
1979 2 teams	MIN A (9G – .000)					LA N (30G – .273)											
" total	39	11	3	0	0	0	0.0	0	2	0	2	0	.273	.273	0	0	P-39
1980 KC A	8	0	0	0	0	0	–	0	0	0	0	0	–	–	0	0	P-8
1981	22	0	0	0	0	0	–	0	0	0	0	0	–	–	0	0	P-22
14 yrs.	385	347	91	18	1	10	2.9	39	44	14	67	0	.262	.406	27	4	P-349
2 yrs.	46	12	1	0	0	0	0.0	0	0	0	1	0	.083	.083	6	1	P-40

LEAGUE CHAMPIONSHIP SERIES

1974 PIT N	1	1	0	0	0	0	0.0	0	0	0	1	0	.000	.000	0	0	P-1
1975	2	0	0	0	0	0	–	0	0	0	0	0	–	–	0	0	P-2
2 yrs.	3	1	0	0	0	0	0.0	0	0	0	1	0	.000	.000	0	0	P-3

WORLD SERIES

| 1967 BOS A | 2 | 0 | 0 | 0 | 0 | 0 | – | 0 | 0 | 0 | 0 | 0 | – | – | 0 | 0 | P-2 |

Jim Brideweser
BRIDEWESER, JAMES EHRENFELD
B. Feb. 13, 1927, Lancaster, Ohio
BR TR 6' 165 lbs.

1951 NY A	2	8	3	0	0	0	0.0	1	0	0	1	0	.375	.375	0	0	SS-2
1952	42	38	10	0	0	0	0.0	12	2	3	5	0	.263	.263	9	1	SS-22, 2B-4, 3B-1
1953	7	3	3	0	1	0	0.0	3	3	1	0	0	1.000	1.667	2	2	SS-3
1954 BAL A	73	204	54	7	2	0	0.0	18	12	15	27	1	.265	.319	11	2	SS-48, 2B-19
1955 CHI A	34	58	12	3	2	0	0.0	6	4	3	7	0	.207	.328	1	0	SS-26, 3B-3, 2B-2
1956 2 teams	CHI A (10G – .182)					DET A (70G – .218)											
" total	80	167	36	5	0	0	0.0	23	11	20	22	3	.216	.246	1	1	SS-42, 2B-31, 3B-4
1957 BAL A	91	142	38	6	1	1	0.7	16	18	21	16	2	.268	.345	5	1	SS-74, 3B-3, 2B-1
7 yrs.	329	620	156	21	6	1	0.2	79	50	63	78	6	.252	.310	29	7	SS-217, 2B-57, 3B-11
2 yrs.	44	69	14	4	2	0	0.0	6	5	3	10	0	.203	.319	1	0	SS-36, 3B-3, 2B-2

Bunny Brief
BRIEF, ANTHONY VINCENT
Born Antonio Bordetzki.
B. July 3, 1892, Remus, Mich. D. Feb. 10, 1963, Milwaukee, Wis.
BR TR 6' 185 lbs.

1912 STL A	15	42	13	3	0	0	0.0	9	5	6		2	.310	.381	2	0	OF-9, 1B-4
1913	84	258	56	11	6	1	0.4	24	26	21	46	3	.217	.318	14	1	1B-62, OF-8
1915 CHI A	48	154	33	6	2	2	1.3	13	17	16	28	8	.214	.318	2	0	1B-46
1917 PIT N	36	115	25	5	1	2	1.7	15	11	15	21	4	.217	.330	2	2	1B-34
4 yrs.	183	569	127	25	9	5	0.9	61	59	58	95	17	.223	.325	20	3	1B-146, OF-17
1 yr.	48	154	33	6	2	2	1.3	13	17	16	28	8	.214	.318	2	0	1B-46

Chuck Brinkman
BRINKMAN, CHARLES ERNEST
Brother of Ed Brinkman.
B. Sept. 16, 1944, Cincinnati, Ohio
BR TR 6'1" 185 lbs.

1969 CHI A	14	15	1	0	0	0	0.0	2	0	1	5	0	.067	.067	1	0	C-14
1970	9	20	5	1	0	0	0.0	4	0	3	3	0	.250	.300	0	0	C-9
1971	15	20	4	0	0	0	0.0	0	1	3	5	0	.200	.200	1	0	C-14
1972	35	52	7	0	0	0	0.0	1	0	4	7	0	.135	.135	3	1	C-33
1973	63	139	26	6	0	1	0.7	13	10	11	37	0	.187	.252	0	0	C-63
1974 2 teams	CHI A (8G – .143)					PIT N (4G – .143)											
" total	12	21	3	0	0	0	0.0	2	1	1	3	0	.143	.143	0	0	C-12
6 yrs.	148	267	46	7	0	1	0.4	22	12	23	60	0	.172	.210	5	1	C-145
6 yrs.	144	260	45	7	0	1	0.4	21	11	23	60	0	.173	.212	5	1	C-141

Jack Brohamer
BROHAMER, JOHN ANTHONY
B. Feb. 26, 1950, Maywood, Calif.
BL TR 5'10" 165 lbs.

1972 CLE A	136	527	123	13	2	5	0.9	49	35	27	46	3	.233	.294	6	1	2B-132, 3B-1
1973	102	300	66	12	1	4	1.3	29	29	32	23	0	.220	.307	10	3	2B-97
1974	101	315	85	11	1	2	0.6	33	30	26	22	2	.270	.330	9	4	2B-99
1975	69	217	53	5	0	6	2.8	15	16	14	14	2	.244	.350	3	1	2B-66
1976 CHI A	119	354	89	12	2	7	2.0	33	40	44	28	1	.251	.356	1	0	2B-117, 3B-1
1977	59	152	39	10	3	2	1.3	26	20	21	8	0	.257	.401	2	0	3B-38, 2B-18, DH-1
1978 BOS A	81	244	57	14	1	1	0.4	34	25	25	13	1	.234	.311	11	3	3B-30, DH-25, 2B-23
1979	64	192	51	7	1	1	0.5	25	11	15	15	0	.266	.328	8	1	2B-36, 3B-22
1980 2 teams	BOS A (21G – .316)					CLE A (53G – .225)											
" total	74	199	50	7	1	2	1.0	18	21	18	9	0	.251	.327	15	3	2B-51, 3B-13, DH-4
9 yrs.	805	2500	613	91	12	30	1.2	262	227	222	178	9	.245	.327	65	16	2B-639, 3B-105, DH-30
2 yrs.	178	506	128	22	5	9	1.8	59	60	65	36	1	.253	.370	3	0	2B-135, 3B-39, DH-1

Delos Brown
BROWN, DELOS HIGHT
B. Oct. 4, 1892, Anna, Ill. D. Dec. 21, 1964, Carbondale, Ill.
BR TR 5'9" 160 lbs.

| 1914 CHI A | 1 | 1 | 0 | 0 | 0 | 0 | 0.0 | 0 | 0 | 0 | 1 | 0 | .000 | .000 | 1 | 0 | |

Dick Brown
BROWN, RICHARD ERNEST
Brother of Larry Brown.
B. Jan. 17, 1935, Shinnston, W. Va. D. Apr. 12, 1970, Baltimore, Md.
BR TR 6'2" 176 lbs.

1957 CLE A	34	114	30	4	0	4	3.5	10	22	4	23	1	.263	.404	1	0	C-33
1958	68	173	41	5	0	7	4.0	20	20	12	27	0	.237	.387	6	0	C-62
1959	48	141	31	7	0	5	3.5	15	16	11	39	0	.220	.376	2	0	C-48

Player Register

	G	AB	H	2B	3B	HR	HR%	R	RBI	BB	SO	SB	BA	SA	Pinch Hit AB	H	G by POS

Dick Brown continued
1960 CHI A	16	43	7	0	0	3	7.0	4	5	3	11	0	.163	.372	2	1	C-14
1961 DET A	98	308	82	12	2	16	5.2	32	45	22	57	0	.266	.474	3	2	C-91
1962	134	431	104	12	0	12	2.8	40	40	21	66	0	.241	.353	3	1	C-132
1963 BAL A	59	171	42	7	0	2	1.2	13	13	15	35	1	.246	.322	1	1	C-58
1964	88	230	59	6	0	8	3.5	24	32	12	45	2	.257	.387	7	0	C-84
1965	96	255	59	9	1	5	2.0	17	30	17	53	2	.231	.333	7	1	C-92
9 yrs.	641	1866	455	62	3	62	3.3	175	223	117	356	7	.244	.380	32	6	C-614
1 yr.	16	43	7	0	0	3	7.0	4	5	3	11	0	.163	.372	2	1	C-14

George Browne
BROWNE, GEORGE EDWARD BL TR 5'10½" 160 lbs.
B. Jan. 9, 1876, Richmond, Va. D. Dec. 9, 1920, Hyde Park, N. Y.

1901 PHI N	8	26	5	1	0	0	0.0	2	4	1		2	.192	.231	0	0	OF-8
1902 2 teams	PHI N (70G – .260)		NY N (53G – .319)														
" total	123	497	142	16	6	0	0.0	71	40	25		24	.286	.342	0	0	OF-123
1903 NY N	141	591	185	20	3	3	0.5	105	45	43		27	.313	.372	0	0	OF-141
1904	150	596	169	16	5	4	0.7	99	39	39		24	.284	.347	1	0	OF-149
1905	127	536	157	16	14	4	0.7	95	43	20		26	.293	.397	0	0	OF-127
1906	122	477	126	10	4	0	0.0	61	38	27		32	.264	.302	1	0	OF-121
1907	127	458	119	11	10	5	1.1	54	37	31		15	.260	.360	4	0	OF-121
1908 BOS N	138	536	122	10	6	1	0.2	61	34	36		17	.228	.274	3	1	OF-138
1909 2 teams	CHI N (12G – .205)		WAS A (103G – .272)														
" total	115	432	115	15	6	1	0.2	47	17	22		16	.266	.336	2	0	OF-113
1910 2 teams	WAS A (7G – .182)		CHI A (30G – .241)														
" total	37	134	31	4	1	0	0.0	18	4	13		5	.231	.276	3	0	OF-34
1911 BKN N	8	12	4	0	0	0	0.0	1	2	1		2	.333	.333	4	0	OF-2
1912 PHI N	6	5	1	0	0	0	0.0	0	0	1		0	.200	.200	4	1	3B-1
12 yrs.	1102	4300	1176	119	55	18	0.4	614	303	259	1	190	.273	.339	22	2	OF-1077, 3B-1
1 yr.	30	112	27	4	1	0	0.0	17	4	12		5	.241	.295	1	0	OF-29

WORLD SERIES
| 1905 NY N | 5 | 22 | 4 | 0 | 0 | 0 | 0.0 | 2 | 1 | 0 | 2 | 2 | .182 | .182 | 0 | 0 | OF-5 |

Hal Bubser
BUBSER, HAROLD FRED BR TR 5'11" 170 lbs.
B. Sept. 28, 1895, Chicago, Ill.

| 1922 CHI A | 3 | 3 | 0 | 0 | 0 | 0 | 0.0 | | | 0 | 2 | 0 | .000 | .000 | 3 | 0 | |

Don Buford
BUFORD, DONALD ALVIN BB TR 5'7" 160 lbs.
B. Feb. 2, 1937, Linden, Tex.

1963 CHI A	12	42	12	1	2	0	0.0	9	5	5	7	1	.286	.405	1	0	3B-9, 2B-2
1964	135	442	116	14	6	4	0.9	62	30	46	62	12	.262	.348	10	1	2B-92, 3B-37
1965	155	586	166	22	5	10	1.7	93	47	67	76	17	.283	.389	8	2	2B-139, 3B-41
1966	163	607	148	26	7	8	1.3	85	52	69	71	51	.244	.349	1	0	3B-133, 2B-37, OF-11
1967	156	535	129	10	9	4	0.7	61	32	65	51	34	.241	.316	3	1	3B-121, 2B-51, OF-1
1968 BAL A	130	426	120	13	4	15	3.5	65	46	57	46	27	.282	.437	20	6	OF-65, 2B-58, 3B-1
1969	144	554	161	31	3	11	2.0	99	64	96	62	19	.291	.417	5	1	OF-128, 2B-10, 3B-6
1970	144	504	137	15	2	17	3.4	99	66	109	55	16	.272	.411	10	2	OF-130, 3B-3, 2B-3
1971	122	449	130	19	4	19	4.2	99	54	89	62	15	.290	.477	8	2	OF-115
1972	125	408	84	6	2	5	1.2	46	22	69	83	6	.206	.267	19	2	OF-105
10 yrs.	1286	4553	1203	157	44	93	2.0	718	418	672	575	200	.264	.379	85	17	OF-555, 2B-392, 3B-352
5 yrs.	621	2212	571	73	29	26	1.2	310	166	252	267	115	.258	.353	23	4	3B-341, 2B-321, OF-12

LEAGUE CHAMPIONSHIP SERIES
1969 BAL A	3	14	4	1	0	1	7.1	3	1	3	0	0	.286	.357	0	0	OF-3
1970	2	7	3	1	0	1	14.3	2	3	2	0	0	.429	1.000	0	0	OF-2
1971	2	7	3	0	1	0	0.0	1	0	2	1	0	.429	.714	0	0	OF-2
3 yrs.	7	28	10	2	1	1	3.6	6	4	7	1	0	.357	.607	0	0	OF-7

WORLD SERIES
1969 BAL A	5	20	2	0	1	0	5.0	1	2	2	4	0	.100	.300	0	0	OF-5
1970	4	15	4	0	0	1	6.7	3	1	3	2	0	.267	.467	0	0	OF-4
1971	6	23	6	1	0	2	8.7	3	4	3	3	0	.261	.565	0	0	OF-6
3 yrs.	15	58	12	1	1	3	6.9	7	7	8	9	0	.207	.448	0	0	OF-15

Smoky Burgess
BURGESS, FORREST HARRILL BL TR 5'8½" 185 lbs.
B. Feb. 6, 1927, Caroleen, N. C.

1949 CHI N	46	56	15	0	0	1	1.8	4	12	4	4	0	.268	.321	37	12	C-8
1951	94	219	55	4	2	2	0.9	21	20	21	12	2	.251	.315	30	5	C-64
1952 PHI N	110	371	110	27	2	6	1.6	49	56	49	21	3	.296	.429	6	3	C-104
1953	102	312	91	17	5	4	1.3	31	36	37	17	3	.292	.417	9	3	C-95
1954	108	345	127	27	5	4	1.2	41	46	42	11	5	.368	.510	17	6	C-91
1955 2 teams	PHI N (7G – .190)		CIN N (116G – .306)														
" total	123	442	133	17	3	21	4.8	57	78	50	36	1	.301	.495	9	3	C-113
1956 CIN N	90	229	63	10	0	12	5.2	28	39	26	18	0	.275	.476	29	7	C-55
1957	90	205	58	14	1	14	6.8	29	39	24	16	0	.283	.566	39	11	C-45
1958	99	251	71	12	0	6	2.4	28	31	22	20	0	.283	.410	40	11	C-58
1959 PIT N	114	377	112	28	5	11	2.9	41	59	31	16	0	.297	.485	17	7	C-101
1960	110	337	99	15	2	7	2.1	33	39	35	13	0	.294	.412	20	9	C-89
1961	100	323	98	17	3	12	3.7	37	52	30	16	1	.303	.486	14	4	C-92
1962	130	360	118	19	3	13	3.6	38	61	31	19	0	.328	.500	5	1	C-101
1963	91	264	74	10	1	6	2.3	20	37	24	14	0	.280	.394	18	6	C-72
1964 2 teams	PIT N (68G – .246)		CHI A (7G – .200)														
" total	75	176	43	3	1	3	1.7	10	18	15	14	2	.244	.324	26	8	C-44
1965 CHI A	80	77	22	4	0	2	2.6	2	24	11	7	0	.286	.416	65	20	C-5
1966	79	67	21	5	0	0	0.0	0	15	11	8	0	.313	.388	66	21	C-2
1967	77	60	8	1	0	2	3.3	2	11	14	8	0	.133	.250	60	8	
18 yrs.	1718	4471	1318	230	33	126	2.8	485	673	477	270	13	.295	.446	507 1st	145 2nd	C-1139
4 yrs.	243	209	52	10	0	5	2.4	5	51	38	23	0	.249	.368	196 1st	50 1st	C-7

Player Register

	G	AB	H	2B	3B	HR	HR%	R	RBI	BB	SO	SB	BA	SA	Pinch Hit AB H	G by POS

Smoky Burgess continued
WORLD SERIES
| 1960 PIT N | 5 | 18 | 6 | 1 | 0 | 0 | 0.0 | 2 | 0 | 2 | 1 | 0 | .333 | .389 | 0 0 | C-5 |

Jimmy Burke
BURKE, JAMES TIMOTHY (Sunset Jimmy) BR TR
B. Oct. 12, 1874, St. Louis, Mo. D. Mar. 26, 1942, St. Louis, Mo.
Manager 1905, 1918-20.

1898 CLE N	13	38	4	1	0	0	0.0	1		1		2	.105	.132	0 0	3B-13
1901 3 teams	MIL A (64G – .206)					CHI A (42G – .264)			PIT N (14G – .196)							
" total	120	432	97	13	0	0	0.0	48	51	33		17	.225	.255	0 0	3B-89, SS-31
1902 PIT N	60	203	60	12	2	0	0.0	24	26	17		9	.296	.374	2 0	2B-27, OF-18, 3B-9, SS-4
1903 STL N	115	431	123	13	3	0	0.0	55	42	23		28	.285	.329	1 0	3B-93, 2B-15, OF-5
1904	118	406	92	10	3	0	0.0	37	37	15		17	.227	.266	0 0	3B-118
1905	122	431	97	9	5	1	0.2	34	30	21		15	.225	.276	0 0	3B-122
6 yrs.	548	1941	473	58	13	1	0.1	199	187	111		87	.244	.289	3 0	3B-444, 2B-42, SS-35, OF-23
1 yr.	42	148	39	5	0	0	0.0	20	21	12		11	.264	.297	0 0	SS-31, 3B-11

Joe Burns
BURNS, JOSEPH FRANCIS BR TR 6' 175 lbs.
B. Feb. 25, 1900, Trenton, N. J.

| 1924 CHI A | 8 | 19 | 2 | 0 | 0 | 0 | 0.0 | 1 | 0 | 1 | 2 | 0 | .105 | .105 | 2 0 | C-6 |

Jim Busby
BUSBY, JAMES FRANKLIN BR TR 6'1" 175 lbs.
B. Jan. 8, 1927, Kenedy, Tex.

1950 CHI A	18	48	10	0	0	0	0.0	5	4	1	5	0	.208	.208	0 0	OF-12
1951	143	477	135	15	2	5	1.0	59	68	40	46	26	.283	.354	3 0	OF-139
1952 2 teams	CHI A (16G – .128)					WAS A (129G – .244)										
" total	145	551	130	24	4	2	0.4	63	47	24	55	5	.236	.305	1 0	OF-144
1953 WAS A	150	586	183	28	7	6	1.0	68	82	38	45	13	.312	.415	0 0	OF-150
1954	155	628	187	22	7	7	1.1	83	80	43	56	17	.298	.389	0 0	OF-155
1955 2 teams	WAS A (47G – .230)					CHI A (99G – .243)										
" total	146	528	126	19	6	7	1.3	61	41	38	59	12	.239	.337	0 0	OF-146
1956 CLE A	135	494	116	17	3	12	2.4	72	50	43	47	8	.235	.354	5 1	OF-133
1957 2 teams	CLE A (30G – .189)					BAL A (86G – .250)										
" total	116	362	86	12	2	5	1.4	40	23	24	44	6	.238	.323	8 2	OF-111
1958 BAL A	113	215	51	7	2	3	1.4	32	19	24	37	6	.237	.330	6 1	OF-103, 3B-1
1959 BOS A	61	102	23	8	0	1	1.0	16	5	7	18	0	.225	.333	18 1	OF-34
1960 2 teams	BOS A (1G – .000)					BAL A (79G – .258)										
" total	80	159	41	7	1	0	0.0	25	12	20	14	2	.258	.314	3 1	OF-72
1961 BAL A	75	89	23	3	1	0	0.0	15	6	8	10	2	.258	.315	4 1	OF-71
1962 HOU N	15	11	2	0	0	0	0.0	2	1	2	3	0	.182	.182	3 1	OF-10, C-1
13 yrs.	1352	4250	1113	162	35	48	1.1	541	438	310	439	97	.262	.350	51 8	OF-1280, 3B-1, C-1
4 yrs.	276	901	232	28	6	6	0.7	107	99	68	95	33	.257	.322	3 0	OF-266

Donie Bush
BUSH, OWEN JOSEPH BB TR 5'6" 140 lbs.
B. Oct. 8, 1887, Indianapolis, Ind. D. Mar. 28, 1972, Indianapolis, Ind.
Manager 1923, 1927-31, 1933.

1908 DET A	20	68	20	1	1	0	0.0	13	4	7		2	.294	.338	0 0	SS-20
1909	157	532	145	18	2	0	0.0	114	33	88		53	.273	.314	0 0	SS-157
1910	142	496	130	13	4	3	0.6	90	34	78		49	.262	.323	0 0	SS-141, 3B-1
1911	150	561	130	18	5	1	0.2	126	36	98		40	.232	.287	0 0	SS-150
1912	144	511	118	14	8	2	0.4	107	38	117		35	.231	.301	0 0	SS-144
1913	153	597	150	19	10	1	0.2	98	40	80	32	44	.251	.322	0 0	SS-153
1914	157	596	150	18	4	0	0.0	97	32	112	54	35	.252	.295	0 0	SS-157
1915	155	561	128	12	8	1	0.2	99	44	118	44	35	.228	.283	0 0	SS-155
1916	145	550	124	5	9	0	0.0	73	34	75	42	19	.225	.267	0 0	SS-144
1917	147	581	163	18	3	0	0.0	112	24	80	40	34	.281	.322	0 0	SS-147
1918	128	500	117	10	3	0	0.0	74	22	79	31	9	.234	.266	0 0	SS-128
1919	129	509	124	11	6	0	0.0	82	26	75	36	22	.244	.289	0 0	SS-129
1920	141	506	133	18	5	1	0.2	85	33	73	32	15	.263	.324	1 1	SS-140
1921 2 teams	DET A (104G – .281)					WAS A (23G – .214)										
" total	127	486	131	7	5	0	0.0	87	29	57	27	10	.270	.305	2 1	SS-102, 2B-23
1922 WAS A	41	134	32	4	1	0	0.0	17	7	21	7	1	.239	.284	3 0	SS-37, 2B-1
1923	10	22	9	0	0	0	0.0	6	0	0	1	0	.409	.409	1 0	3B-6, 2B-1
16 yrs.	1946	7210	1804	186	74	9	0.1	1280	436	1158	346	403	.250	.300	7 2	SS-1867, 3B-44, 2B-25

WORLD SERIES
| 1909 DET A | 7 | 23 | 6 | 1 | 0 | 0 | 0.0 | 5 | 2 | 5 | 3 | 1 | .261 | .304 | 0 0 | SS-7 |

Bobby Byrne
BYRNE, ROBERT MATTHEW BR TR 5'7½" 145 lbs.
B. Dec. 31, 1884, St. Louis, Mo. D. Dec. 31, 1964, Wayne, Pa.

1907 STL N	148	558	143	11	5	0	0.0	55	29	35		21	.256	.294	0 0	3B-147, SS-1
1908	127	439	84	7	1	0	0.0	27	14	23		16	.191	.212	1 0	3B-122, SS-4
1909 2 teams	STL N (105G – .214)					PIT N (46G – .256)										
" total	151	589	133	19	8	1	0.2	92	40	78		29	.226	.290	0 0	3B-151
1910 PIT N	148	602	178	43	12	2	0.3	101	52	66	27	36	.296	.417	0 0	3B-148
1911	153	598	155	24	17	2	0.3	96	52	67	41	23	.259	.366	1 0	3B-152
1912	130	528	152	31	11	3	0.6	99	35	54	40	20	.288	.405	0 0	3B-130
1913 2 teams	PIT N (113G – .270)					PHI N (19G – .224)										
" total	132	506	134	23	0	2	0.4	63	51	34	31	12	.265	.322	5 1	3B-125
1914 PHI N	126	467	127	12	1	0	0.0	61	26	45	44	9	.272	.302	4 2	3B-101, 3B-22
1915	105	387	81	6	4	0	0.0	50	21	39	28	4	.209	.245	0 0	3B-105
1916	48	141	33	10	1	0	0.0	22	9	14	7	6	.234	.319	6 1	3B-40
1917 2 teams	PHI N (13G – .357)					CHI A (1G – .000)										
" total	14	15	5	0	0	0	0.0	1	0	1	2	0	.333	.333	9 2	3B-4, 2B-1
11 yrs.	1282	4830	1225	186	60	10	0.2	667	329	456	220	176	.254	.323	26 6	3B-1146, 2B-102, SS-5
1 yr.	1	1	0	0	0	0	0.0	0	0	0	0	0	.000	.000	0 0	2B-1

WORLD SERIES
| 1909 PIT N | 7 | 24 | 6 | 1 | 0 | 0 | 0.0 | 5 | 0 | 4 | 1 | 0 | .250 | .292 | 0 0 | 3B-7 |

Player Register

	G	AB	H	2B	3B	HR	HR%	R	RBI	BB	SO	SB	BA	SA	Pinch Hit AB	H	G by POS

Bobby Byrne continued
1915 PHI N	1	1	0	0	0	0	0.0	0	0	0	0	0	.000	.000	1	0	
2 yrs.	8	25	6	1	0	0	0.0	5	0	1	4	1	.240	.280	1	0	3B-7

Tommy Byrne
BYRNE, THOMAS JOSEPH
B. Dec. 31, 1919, Baltimore, Md. BL TL 6'1" 182 lbs.

	G	AB	H	2B	3B	HR	HR%	R	RBI	BB	SO	SB	BA	SA	PH AB	H	G by POS
1943 NY A	13	11	1	0	0	0	0.0	0	0	2	3	0	.091	.091	1	0	P-11
1946	14	9	2	0	0	0	0.0	2	0	1	0	0	.222	.222	6	1	P-4
1947	4	0	0	0	0	0	-	1	0	1	0	0	-	-	0	0	P-4
1948	31	46	15	3	1	1	2.2	8	7	1	7	0	.326	.500	0	0	P-31
1949	35	83	16	4	2	0	0.0	8	13	2	20	0	.193	.289	1	0	P-32
1950	34	81	22	3	1	2	2.5	14	16	4	15	1	.272	.407	1	0	P-31
1951 2 teams	NY A (9G – .222)			STL A (34G – .281)													
" total	43	66	18	3	0	2	3.0	9	15	4	10	0	.273	.409	13	2	P-28
1952 STL A	40	84	21	5	1	1	1.2	9	12	5	18	0	.250	.369	9	0	P-29
1953 2 teams	CHI A (18G – .167)			WAS A (14G – .059)													
" total	32	35	4	0	0	1	2.9	2	5	5	13	0	.114	.200	18	1	P-12
1954 NY A	7	19	7	4	1	0	0.0	2	6	0	3	0	.368	.684	2	0	P-5
1955	45	78	16	1	1	1	1.3	6	6	8	15	0	.205	.282	14	0	P-27
1956	44	52	14	1	1	3	5.8	8	10	2	11	0	.269	.500	8	0	P-37
1957	35	37	7	2	0	3	8.1	5	8	3	11	0	.189	.486	7	2	P-30
13 yrs.	377	601	143	26	8	14	2.3	73	98	38	126	1	.238	.378	80	6	P-281
1 yr.	18	18	3	0	0	1	5.6	2	5	2	6	0	.167	.333	10	1	P-6
WORLD SERIES																	
1949 NY A	1	1	1	0	0	0	0.0	0	0	0	0	0	1.000	1.000	0	0	P-1
1955	3	6	1	0	0	0	0.0	0	2	0	2	0	.167	.167	1	0	P-2
1956	2	1	0	0	0	0	0.0	0	0	0	0	0	.000	.000	1	0	P-1
1957	2	2	1	0	0	0	0.0	0	0	0	1	0	.500	.500	0	0	P-2
4 yrs.	8	10	3	0	0	0	0.0	0	2	0	3	0	.300	.300	2	0	P-6

George Caithamer
CAITHAMER, GEORGE THEODORE
B. July 22, 1910, Chicago, Ill. D. June 1, 1954, Chicago, Ill. BR TR 5'7½" 160 lbs.

	G	AB	H	2B	3B	HR	HR%	R	RBI	BB	SO	SB	BA	SA	PH AB	H	G by POS
1934 CHI A	5	19	6	1	0	0	0.0	1	3	1	5	0	.316	.368	0	0	C-5

Nixey Callahan
CALLAHAN, JAMES JOSEPH
B. Mar. 18, 1874, Fitchburg, Mass. D. Oct. 4, 1934, Boston, Mass.
Manager 1903-04, 1912-14, 1916-17. BR TR 5'10½" 180 lbs.

	G	AB	H	2B	3B	HR	HR%	R	RBI	BB	SO	SB	BA	SA	PH AB	H	G by POS
1894 PHI N	9	21	5	0	0	0	0.0	4	0	0	7	0	.238	.238	0	0	P-9
1897 CHI N	94	360	105	18	6	3	0.8	60	47	10		12	.292	.400	2	0	2B-30, P-23, OF-21, SS-18, 3B-2
1898	43	164	43	7	5	0	0.0	27	22	4		3	.262	.366	0	0	P-31, OF-9, SS-1, 2B-1, 1B-1
1899	47	150	39	4	3	0	0.0	21	18	8		9	.260	.327	1	0	P-35, OF-9, SS-2, 2B-1
1900	32	115	27	3	2	0	0.0	16	9	6		5	.235	.296	0	0	P-32
1901 CHI A	45	118	39	7	3	1	0.8	15	19	10		10	.331	.466	10	3	P-27, 3B-6, 2B-2
1902	70	218	51	7	2	0	0.0	27	13	6		4	.234	.284	12	2	P-35, OF-23, SS-1
1903	118	439	128	26	5	2	0.5	47	56	20		24	.292	.387	5	3	3B-102, OF-8, P-3
1904	132	482	126	23	2	0	0.0	66	54	39		29	.261	.317	1	0	OF-104, 2B-28
1905	96	345	94	18	6	1	0.3	50	43	29		26	.272	.368	3	1	OF-93
1911	120	466	131	13	5	3	0.6	64	60	15		45	.281	.350	5	1	OF-114
1912	111	408	111	9	7	1	0.2	45	52	12		19	.272	.336	4	1	OF-107
1913	6	9	2	0	0	0	0.0	0	1	0		2	.222	.222	5	1	OF-1
13 yrs.	923	3295	901	135	46	11	0.3	442	394	159	9	186	.273	.352	48	12	OF-489, P-195, 3B-110, 2B-62, SS-22, 1B-1
8 yrs.	698	2485	682	103	30	8	0.3	314	298	131	2	157	.274	.350	45	12	OF-450, 3B-108, P-65, 2B-30, SS-1

Johnny Callison
CALLISON, JOHN WESLEY
B. Mar. 12, 1939, Qualls, Okla. BL TR 5'10" 175 lbs.

	G	AB	H	2B	3B	HR	HR%	R	RBI	BB	SO	SB	BA	SA	PH AB	H	G by POS
1958 CHI A	18	64	19	4	2	1	1.6	10	12	6	14	1	.297	.469	0	0	OF-18
1959	49	104	18	3	0	3	2.9	12	12	13	20	0	.173	.288	4	0	OF-41
1960 PHI N	99	288	75	11	5	9	3.1	36	30	45	70	0	.260	.427	15	3	OF-86
1961	138	455	121	20	11	9	2.0	74	47	69	76	10	.266	.418	14	3	OF-124
1962	157	603	181	26	10	23	3.8	107	83	54	96	10	.300	.491	9	4	OF-157
1963	157	626	178	36	11	26	4.2	96	78	50	111	8	.284	.502	2	0	OF-157
1964	162	654	179	30	10	31	4.7	101	104	36	95	6	.274	.492	2	1	OF-162
1965	160	619	162	25	16	32	5.2	93	101	57	117	6	.262	.509	6	0	OF-159
1966	155	612	169	40	7	11	1.8	93	55	56	83	8	.276	.418	3	1	OF-154
1967	149	556	145	29	5	14	2.5	62	64	55	63	6	.261	.408	3	0	OF-147
1968	121	398	97	18	4	14	3.5	46	40	42	70	4	.244	.415	11	3	OF-109
1969	134	495	131	29	5	16	3.2	66	64	49	73	2	.265	.440	6	1	OF-129
1970 CHI N	147	477	126	23	2	19	4.0	65	68	60	63	7	.264	.440	3	1	OF-144
1971	103	290	61	12	1	8	2.8	27	38	36	55	2	.210	.341	14	1	OF-89
1972 NY A	92	275	71	10	0	9	3.3	28	34	18	34	3	.258	.393	19	4	OF-74
1973	45	136	24	4	0	1	0.7	10	10	4	24	1	.176	.228	5	2	OF-32, DH-10
16 yrs.	1886	6652	1757	321	89	226	3.4	926	840	650	1064	74	.264	.441	116	24	OF-1777, DH-10
2 yrs.	67	168	37	7	2	4	2.4	22	24	19	34	1	.220	.357	4	0	OF-59

Bruce Campbell
CAMPBELL, BRUCE DOUGLAS
B. Oct. 20, 1909, Chicago, Ill. BL TR 6'1" 185 lbs.

	G	AB	H	2B	3B	HR	HR%	R	RBI	BB	SO	SB	BA	SA	PH AB	H	G by POS
1930 CHI A	5	10	5	1	1	0	0.0	4	5	1	2	0	.500	.800	1	1	OF-4
1931	4	17	7	2	0	2	11.8	4	5	0	4	0	.412	.882	0	0	OF-4
1932 2 teams	CHI A (9G – .154)			STL A (137G – .289)													
" total	146	611	173	36	11	14	2.3	86	87	40	104	1	.283	.447	3	0	OF-143
1933 STL A	148	567	157	38	8	16	2.8	87	106	69	77	10	.277	.457	4	1	OF-144
1934	138	481	134	25	6	9	1.9	62	74	51	64	5	.279	.412	14	4	OF-123
1935 CLE A	80	308	100	26	3	7	2.3	56	54	31	33	2	.325	.497	4	1	OF-75

Player Register

	G	AB	H	2B	3B	HR	HR%	R	RBI	BB	SO	SB	BA	SA	Pinch Hit AB	H	G by POS

Bruce Campbell continued

	G	AB	H	2B	3B	HR	HR%	R	RBI	BB	SO	SB	BA	SA	PH AB	PH H	G by POS
1936	76	172	64	15	2	6	3.5	35	30	19	17	2	.372	.587	25	9	OF-47
1937	134	448	135	42	11	4	0.9	82	61	67	49	4	.301	.471	11	5	OF-123
1938	133	511	148	27	12	12	2.3	90	72	53	57	11	.290	.460	11	2	OF-122
1939	130	450	129	23	13	8	1.8	84	72	67	48	9	.287	.449	14	2	OF-115
1940 DET A	103	297	84	15	5	8	2.7	56	44	45	28	2	.283	.448	23	9	OF-74
1941	141	512	141	28	10	15	2.9	72	93	68	67	3	.275	.457	5	2	OF-133
1942 WAS A	122	378	105	17	5	5	1.3	41	63	37	34	0	.278	.389	29	5	OF-87
13 yrs.	1360	4762	1382	295	87	106	2.2	759	766	548	584	53	.290	.455	144	41	OF-1194
3 yrs.	18	53	16	4	1	2	3.8	11	12	1	10	0	.302	.528	4	1	OF-14

WORLD SERIES
| 1940 DET A | 7 | 25 | 9 | 1 | 0 | 1 | 4.0 | 4 | 5 | 4 | 4 | 0 | .360 | .520 | 0 | 0 | OF-7 |

Andy Carey

CAREY, ANDREW ARTHUR
Born Andrew Arthur Nordstrom.
B. Oct. 18, 1931, Oakland, Calif.
BR TR 6'1½" 190 lbs.

	G	AB	H	2B	3B	HR	HR%	R	RBI	BB	SO	SB	BA	SA	PH AB	PH H	G by POS
1952 NY A	16	40	6	0	0	0	0.0	6	1	3	10	0	.150	.150	0	0	3B-14, SS-1
1953	51	81	26	5	0	4	4.9	14	8	9	12	2	.321	.531	7	1	3B-40, SS-2, 2B-1
1954	122	411	124	14	6	8	1.9	60	65	43	38	5	.302	.423	3	0	3B-120
1955	135	510	131	19	11	7	1.4	73	47	44	51	3	.257	.378	0	0	3B-135
1956	132	422	100	18	2	7	1.7	54	50	45	53	9	.237	.339	1	0	3B-131
1957	85	247	63	6	5	6	2.4	30	33	15	42	2	.255	.393	6	1	3B-81
1958	102	315	90	19	4	12	3.8	39	45	34	43	1	.286	.486	7	2	3B-99
1959	41	101	26	1	0	3	3.0	11	9	7	17	1	.257	.356	8	3	3B-34
1960 2 teams	NY	A (4G –	.333)		KC	A (102G –	.233)										
" total	106	346	81	14	4	12	3.5	31	54	26	53	0	.234	.402	15	1	3B-93, OF-1
1961 2 teams	KC	A (39G –	.244)		CHI	A (56G –	.266)										
" total	95	266	68	18	5	3	1.1	41	25	26	47	0	.256	.395	1	0	3B-93
1962 LA N	53	111	26	5	1	2	1.8	12	13	16	23	0	.234	.351	13	2	3B-42
11 yrs.	938	2850	741	119	38	64	2.2	371	350	268	389	23	.260	.396	61	10	3B-882, SS-3, OF-1, 2B-1
1 yr.	56	143	38	12	3	0	0.0	21	14	11	24	0	.266	.392	1	0	3B-54

WORLD SERIES
1955 NY A	2	2	1	0	1	0	0.0	0	1	0	0	0	.500	1.500	2	1	
1956	7	19	3	0	0	0	0.0	2	0	1	6	0	.158	.158	0	0	3B-7
1957	2	7	2	1	0	0	0.0	0	1	1	0	0	.286	.429	1	0	3B-2
1958	5	12	1	0	0	0	0.0	1	0	0	3	0	.083	.083	0	0	3B-12
4 yrs.	16	40	7	1	1	0	0.0	3	2	2	9	0	.175	.250	2	1	3B-21

Eddie Carnett

CARNETT, EDWIN ELLIOTT (Lefty)
B. Oct. 21, 1916, Springfield, Mo.
BL TL 6' 185 lbs.

	G	AB	H	2B	3B	HR	HR%	R	RBI	BB	SO	SB	BA	SA	PH AB	PH H	G by POS
1941 BOS N	2	0	0	0	0	0	–	0	0	0	0	0			0	0	P-2
1944 CHI A	126	457	126	18	8	1	0.2	51	60	26	35	5	.276	.357	10	1	OF-88, 1B-25, P-2
1945 CLE A	30	73	16	7	0	0	0.0	5	7	2	9	0	.219	.315	11	3	OF-16, P-2
3 yrs.	158	530	142	25	8	1	0.2	56	67	28	44	5	.268	.351	21	4	OF-104, 1B-25, P-6
1 yr.	126	457	126	18	8	1	0.2	51	60	26	35	5	.276	.357	10	1	OF-88, 1B-25, P-2

Chico Carrasquel

CARRASQUEL, ALFONSO COLON
B. Jan. 23, 1928, Caracas, Venezuela
BR TR 6' 170 lbs.

	G	AB	H	2B	3B	HR	HR%	R	RBI	BB	SO	SB	BA	SA	PH AB	PH H	G by POS
1950 CHI A	141	524	148	21	5	4	0.8	72	46	66	46	0	.282	.365	0	0	SS-141
1951	147	538	142	22	4	2	0.4	61	58	46	39	14	.264	.331	0	0	SS-147
1952	100	359	89	7	4	1	0.3	36	42	33	27	2	.248	.298	1	1	SS-99
1953	149	552	154	30	4	2	0.4	72	47	38	47	5	.279	.359	0	0	SS-149
1954	155	620	158	28	3	12	1.9	106	62	85	67	7	.255	.368	0	0	SS-155
1955	145	523	134	11	2	11	2.1	83	52	61	59	1	.256	.348	4	1	SS-144
1956 CLE A	141	474	115	15	1	7	1.5	60	48	52	61	0	.243	.323	0	0	SS-141, 3B-1
1957	125	392	108	14	1	8	2.0	37	57	41	53	0	.276	.378	3	1	SS-122
1958 2 teams	CLE	A (49G –	.256)		KC	A (59G –	.213)										
" total	108	316	74	11	4	4	1.3	33	34	35	27	0	.234	.313	11	4	SS-54, 3B-46
1959 BAL A	114	346	77	13	0	4	1.2	28	28	34	41	2	.223	.295	6	2	SS-89, 2B-22, 3B-2, 1B-1
10 yrs.	1325	4644	1199	172	25	55	1.2	568	474	491	467	31	.258	.342	25	9	SS-1241, 3B-49, 2B-22, 1B-1
6 yrs.	837	3116	825	119	22	32	1.0	410	307	329	285	29	.265	.348	5	2	SS-835

Cam Carreon

CARREON, CAMILO GARCIA
B. Aug. 6, 1937, Colton, Calif.
BR TR 6'1½" 190 lbs.

	G	AB	H	2B	3B	HR	HR%	R	RBI	BB	SO	SB	BA	SA	PH AB	PH H	G by POS
1959 CHI A	1	1	0	0	0	0	0.0	0	0	0	0	0	.000	.000	0	0	C-1
1960	8	17	4	0	0	0	0.0	2	2	1	3	0	.235	.235	1	0	C-7
1961	78	229	62	5	1	4	1.7	32	27	21	24	0	.271	.354	7	2	C-71
1962	106	313	80	19	1	4	1.3	31	37	33	37	1	.256	.361	11	5	C-93
1963	101	270	74	10	1	2	0.7	28	35	23	32	1	.274	.341	7	3	C-92
1964	37	95	26	5	0	0	0.0	12	4	7	13	0	.274	.326	3	0	C-34
1965 CLE A	19	52	12	2	1	1	1.9	6	7	9	6	1	.231	.365	0	0	C-19
1966 BAL A	4	9	2	0	0	0	0.0	2	2	3	2	0	.222	.444	1	1	C-3
8 yrs.	354	986	260	43	4	11	1.1	113	114	97	117	3	.264	.349	30	11	C-320
6 yrs.	331	925	246	39	3	10	1.1	105	105	85	109	2	.266	.347	29	10	C-298

Norm Cash

CASH, NORMAN DALTON
B. Nov. 10, 1934, Justiceburg, Tex.
BL TL 6' 185 lbs.

	G	AB	H	2B	3B	HR	HR%	R	RBI	BB	SO	SB	BA	SA	PH AB	PH H	G by POS
1958 CHI A	13	8	2	0	0	0	0.0	2	0	0	1	0	.250	.250	5	1	OF-4
1959	58	104	25	0	1	4	3.8	16	16	18	9	1	.240	.375	19	5	1B-31
1960 DET A	121	353	101	16	3	18	5.1	64	63	65	58	0	.286	.501	23	9	1B-99, OF-4
1961	159	535	193	22	8	41	7.7	119	132	124	85	11	.361	.662	1	0	1B-157
1962	148	507	123	16	2	39	7.7	94	89	104	82	6	.243	.513	2	1	1B-146, OF-3
1963	147	493	133	19	1	26	5.3	67	79	89	76	2	.270	.471	7	0	1B-142
1964	144	479	123	15	5	23	4.8	63	83	70	66	2	.257	.453	10	1	1B-137
1965	142	467	124	23	1	30	6.4	79	82	77	62	6	.266	.512	5	0	1B-139

235　　　　　　　　　　　　　　　　　　　　　　　　　　　　　　　　　　　　*Player Register*

	G	AB	H	2B	3B	HR	HR%	R	RBI	BB	SO	SB	BA	SA	Pinch Hit AB	H	G by POS

Norm Cash continued

	G	AB	H	2B	3B	HR	HR%	R	RBI	BB	SO	SB	BA	SA	PH AB	PH H	G by POS
1966	160	603	168	18	3	32	5.3	98	93	66	91	2	.279	.478	3	1	1B-158
1967	152	488	118	16	5	22	4.5	64	72	81	100	3	.242	.430	7	1	1B-146
1968	127	411	108	15	1	25	6.1	50	63	39	70	1	.263	.487	15	2	1B-117
1969	142	483	135	15	4	22	4.6	81	74	63	80	2	.280	.464	9	2	1B-134
1970	130	370	96	18	2	15	4.1	58	53	72	58	0	.259	.441	17	6	1B-114
1971	135	452	128	10	3	32	7.1	72	91	59	86	1	.283	.531	7	1	1B-131
1972	137	440	114	16	0	22	5.0	51	61	50	64	0	.259	.445	11	0	1B-134
1973	121	363	95	19	0	19	5.2	51	40	47	73	1	.262	.471	8	2	1B-114, DH-3
1974	53	149	34	3	2	7	4.7	17	12	19	30	1	.228	.416	9	3	1B-44
17 yrs.	2089	6705	1820	241	41	377	5.6	1046	1103	1043	1091	43	.271	.488	158	35	1B-1943, OF-11, DH-3
2 yrs.	71	112	27	0	1	4	3.6	18	16	18	10	1	.241	.366	24	6	1B-31, OF-4

LEAGUE CHAMPIONSHIP SERIES
| 1972 DET A | 5 | 15 | 4 | 0 | 0 | 1 | 6.7 | 1 | 2 | 2 | 3 | 0 | .267 | .467 | 1 | 0 | 1B-5 |

WORLD SERIES
1959 CHI A	4	4	0	0	0	0	0.0	0	0	0	2	0	.000	.000	4	0	
1968 DET A	7	26	10	0	0	1	3.8	5	5	3	5	0	.385	.500	0	0	1B-7
2 yrs.	11	30	10	0	0	1	3.3	5	5	3	7	0	.333	.433	4	0	1B-7

Vince Castino
CASTINO, VINCENT CHARLES　　　　BR TR 5'9" 175 lbs.
B. Oct. 11, 1917, Willisville, Ill.　D. Mar. 6, 1967, Sacramento, Calif.

	G	AB	H	2B	3B	HR	HR%	R	RBI	BB	SO	SB	BA	SA	PH AB	PH H	G by POS
1943 CHI A	33	101	23	1	0	2	2.0	14	16	12	11	0	.228	.297	3	0	C-30
1944	29	78	18	5	0	0	0.0	8	3	10	13	0	.231	.295	2	1	C-26
1945	26	37	8	1	0	0	0.0	2	4	3	7	0	.216	.243	1	0	C-25
3 yrs.	88	216	49	7	0	2	0.9	24	23	25	31	0	.227	.287	6	1	C-81
3 yrs.	88	216	49	7	0	2	0.9	24	23	25	31	0	.227	.287	6	1	C-81

Danny Cater
CATER, DANNY ANDERSON　　　　BR TR 6' 170 lbs.
B. Feb. 25, 1940, Austin, Tex.

	G	AB	H	2B	3B	HR	HR%	R	RBI	BB	SO	SB	BA	SA	PH AB	PH H	G by POS
1964 PHI N	60	152	45	9	1	1	0.7	13	13	7	15	1	.296	.388	18	6	OF-39, 1B-7, 3B-1
1965 CHI A	142	514	139	18	4	14	2.7	74	55	33	65	3	.270	.403	7	2	OF-127, 3B-11, 1B-3
1966 2 teams		CHI	A (21G –	.183)		KC	A (116G –	.292)									
" total	137	485	135	17	4	7	1.4	50	56	28	47	4	.278	.373	5	1	1B-53, 3B-42, OF-40
1967 KC A	142	529	143	17	7	4	0.8	55	46	34	56	4	.270	.340	2	1	3B-56, OF-55, 1B-44
1968 OAK A	147	504	146	28	3	6	1.2	53	62	35	43	8	.290	.393	11	4	1B-121, OF-20, 3B-8
1969	152	584	153	24	2	10	1.7	64	76	28	40	1	.262	.361	8	1	1B-132, OF-20, 2B-4
1970 NY A	155	582	175	26	5	6	1.0	64	76	34	44	4	.301	.393	3	0	1B-131, 3B-42, OF-7
1971	121	428	118	16	5	4	0.9	39	50	19	25	0	.276	.364	10	3	1B-78, 3B-52
1972 BOS A	92	317	75	17	1	8	2.5	32	39	15	33	0	.237	.372	6	1	1B-90
1973	63	195	61	12	0	1	0.5	30	24	10	22	0	.313	.390	7	2	1B-37, 3B-21, DH-3
1974	56	126	31	5	0	5	4.0	14	20	10	13	1	.246	.405	18	5	1B-23, DH-14
1975 STL N	22	35	8	2	0	0	0.0	3	2	1	3	0	.229	.286	13	2	1B-12
12 yrs.	1289	4451	1229	191	29	66	1.5	491	519	254	406	26	.276	.377	108	28	1B-731, OF-308, 3B-225, DH-17, 2B-5
2 yrs.	163	574	150	19	5	14	2.4	77	59	33	75	6	.261	.385	8	2	OF-145, 3B-11, 1B-3

Wayne Causey
CAUSEY, JAMES WAYNE　　　　BL TR 5'10½" 175 lbs.
B. Dec. 26, 1936, Ruston, La.

	G	AB	H	2B	3B	HR	HR%	R	RBI	BB	SO	SB	BA	SA	PH AB	PH H	G by POS
1955 BAL A	68	175	34	2	1	1	0.6	14	9	17	25	0	.194	.234	8	0	3B-55, 2B-7, SS-1
1956	53	88	15	0	1	1	1.1	7	4	8	23	0	.170	.227	16	5	3B-30, 2B-7
1957	14	10	2	0	0	0	0.0	2	1	5	2	0	.200	.200	3	0	2B-6, 3B-5
1961 KC A	104	312	86	14	1	8	2.6	37	49	37	28	0	.276	.404	2	0	3B-88, SS-11, 2B-9
1962	117	305	77	14	1	4	1.3	40	38	41	30	2	.252	.344	28	9	SS-51, 3B-26, 2B-9
1963	139	554	155	32	4	8	1.4	72	44	56	54	4	.280	.395	1	1	SS-135, 3B-2
1964	157	604	170	31	4	8	1.3	82	49	88	65	0	.281	.386	3	2	SS-131, 2B-17, 3B-9
1965	144	513	134	17	8	3	0.6	48	34	61	48	1	.261	.343	8	1	SS-62, 2B-45, 3B-35
1966 2 teams		KC	A (28G –	.228)		CHI	A (78G –	.244)									
" total	106	243	58	8	2	0	0.0	24	18	31	19	3	.239	.288	19	7	2B-60, 3B-16, SS-11
1967 CHI A	124	292	66	10	3	1	0.3	21	28	32	35	2	.226	.291	34	10	2B-96, SS-2
1968 3 teams		CHI	A (59G –	.180)		CAL	A (4G –	.000)		ATL	N (16G –	.108)					
" total	79	148	22	1	0	1	0.7	10	11	14	12	0	.149	.196	36	6	2B-51, SS-2, 3B-2
11 yrs.	1105	3244	819	130	26	35	1.1	357	285	390	341	12	.252	.341	158	41	SS-406, 2B-307, 3B-268
3 yrs.	261	556	124	20	5	1	0.2	52	48	70	55	4	.223	.282	77	21	2B-197, SS-3, 3B-1

Phil Cavarretta
CAVARRETTA, PHILIP JOSEPH　　　　BL TL 5'11½" 175 lbs.
B. July 19, 1916, Chicago, Ill.
Manager 1951-53.

	G	AB	H	2B	3B	HR	HR%	R	RBI	BB	SO	SB	BA	SA	PH AB	PH H	G by POS
1934 CHI N	7	21	8	0	1	1	4.8	5	6	2	3	1	.381	.619	2	0	1B-5
1935	146	589	162	28	12	8	1.4	85	82	39	61	4	.275	.404	1	0	1B-145
1936	124	458	125	18	1	9	2.0	55	56	17	36	8	.273	.376	8	4	1B-115
1937	106	329	94	18	7	5	1.5	43	56	32	35	7	.286	.429	11	4	OF-53, 1B-43
1938	92	268	64	11	4	1	0.4	29	28	14	27	4	.239	.321	13	1	OF-52, 1B-28
1939	22	55	15	3	1	0	0.0	4	0	4	3	2	.273	.364	7	3	1B-13, OF-1
1940	65	193	54	11	4	2	1.0	34	22	31	18	3	.280	.409	10	0	1B-52
1941	107	346	99	18	4	6	1.7	46	40	53	28	2	.286	.413	5	2	OF-66, 1B-33
1942	136	482	130	28	4	3	0.6	59	54	71	42	7	.270	.363	6	0	OF-70, 1B-61
1943	143	530	154	27	9	8	1.5	93	73	75	42	3	.291	.421	5	0	1B-134, OF-7
1944	152	614	197	35	15	5	0.8	106	82	67	42	4	.321	.451	0	0	1B-139, OF-13
1945	132	498	177	34	10	6	1.2	94	97	81	34	5	.355	.500	0	0	1B-120, OF-11
1946	139	510	150	28	10	8	1.6	89	78	88	54	2	.294	.435	2	0	OF-86, 1B-51
1947	127	459	144	22	5	2	0.4	56	63	58	35	2	.314	.397	3	2	OF-100, 1B-24
1948	111	334	93	16	5	3	0.9	41	40	35	29	4	.278	.383	23	3	1B-41, OF-40
1949	105	360	106	22	4	8	2.2	46	49	45	31	2	.294	.444	9	2	1B-70, OF-25
1950	82	256	70	11	4	10	3.9	49	31	40	31	1	.273	.441	9	2	1B-67, OF-3
1951	89	206	64	7	1	6	2.9	24	28	27	28	0	.311	.442	33	12	1B-53
1952	41	63	15	1	1	1	1.6	7	8	9	3	0	.238	.333	26	5	1B-13

	G	AB	H	2B	3B	HR	HR%	R	RBI	BB	SO	SB	BA	SA	Pinch Hit AB	H	G by POS

Phil Cavarretta continued

1953		27	21	6	3	0	0	0.0	3	3	6	3	0	.286	.429	21	6	
1954 CHI A		71	158	50	6	0	3	1.9	21	24	26	12	4	.316	.411	16	2	1B-44, OF-9
1955		6	4	0	0	0	0	0.0	0	0	0	1	0	.000	.000	2	0	1B-3
22 yrs.		2030	6754	1977	347	99	95	1.4	990	920	820	598	65	.293	.416	209	48	1B-1254, OF-536
2 yrs.		77	162	50	6	0	3	1.9	22	24	26	13	4	.309	.401	18	2	1B-47, OF-9

WORLD SERIES

1935 CHI N	6	24	3	0	0	0	0.0	1	1	0	5	0	.125	.125	0	0	1B-6
1938	4	13	6	1	0	0	0.0	1	0	0	1	0	.462	.538	1	1	OF-3
1945	7	26	11	2	0	1	3.8	7	5	4	3	0	.423	.615	0	0	1B-7
3 yrs.	17	63	20	3	0	1	1.6	9	5	4	9	0	.317	.413	1	1	1B-13, OF-3

Joe Chamberlin

CHAMBERLIN, JOSEPH JEREMIAH BR TR 6'1" 175 lbs.
B. May 10, 1910, San Francisco, Calif.

| 1934 CHI A | 43 | 141 | 34 | 5 | 1 | 2 | 1.4 | 13 | 17 | 6 | 38 | 1 | .241 | .333 | 0 | 0 | SS-26, 3B-14 |

Ben Chapman

CHAPMAN, WILLIAM BENJAMIN BR TR 6' 190 lbs.
B. Dec. 25, 1908, Nashville, Tenn.
Manager 1945-48.

1930 NY A		138	513	162	31	10	10	1.9	74	81	43	58	14	.316	.474	2	0	3B-91, 2B-45
1931		149	600	189	28	11	17	2.8	120	122	75	77	61	.315	.483	1	0	OF-137, 2B-11
1932		150	581	174	41	15	10	1.7	101	107	71	55	38	.299	.473	1	0	OF-149
1933		147	565	176	36	4	9	1.6	112	98	72	45	27	.312	.437	0	0	OF-147
1934		149	588	181	21	13	5	0.9	82	86	67	68	26	.308	.413	0	0	OF-149
1935		140	553	160	38	8	8	1.4	118	74	61	39	17	.289	.430	2	0	OF-138
1936 2 teams	NY A (36G – .266)							WAS A (97G – .332)									
" total	133	540	170	50	10	5	0.9	110	81	84	38	20	.315	.472	0	0	OF-133
1937 2 teams	WAS A (35G – .262)							BOS A (113G – .307)									
" total	148	553	164	30	12	7	1.3	99	69	83	42	35	.297	.432	2	1	OF-144, SS-1
1938 BOS A		127	480	163	40	8	6	1.3	92	80	65	33	13	.340	.494	1	0	OF-126, 3B-1
1939 CLE A		149	545	158	31	9	6	1.1	101	82	87	30	18	.290	.413	2	1	OF-146
1940		143	548	157	40	6	4	0.7	82	50	78	45	13	.286	.403	3	1	OF-140
1941 2 teams	WAS A (28G – .255)							CHI A (57G – .226)									
" total	85	300	71	15	1	3	1.0	35	29	29	20	4	.237	.323	10	2	OF-75
1944 BKN N		20	38	14	4	0	0	0.0	11	11	5	4	1	.368	.474	9	3	P-11
1945 2 teams	BKN N (13G – .136)							PHI N (24G – .314)									
" total	37	73	19	2	0	0	0.0	6	7	4	2	0	.260	.288	10	4	P-13, OF-10, 3B-4
1946 PHI N		1	1	0	0	0	0	0.0	1	0	0	0	0	.000	.000	0	0	P-1
15 yrs.		1716	6478	1958	407	107	90	1.4	1144	977	824	556	287	.302	.440	43	13	OF-1494, 3B-96, 2B-56, P-25, SS-1
1 yr.		57	190	43	9	1	2	1.1	26	19	19	14	2	.226	.316	8	2	OF-49

WORLD SERIES

| 1932 NY A | 4 | 17 | 5 | 1 | 0 | 0 | 0.0 | 1 | 6 | 2 | 4 | 0 | .294 | .353 | 0 | 0 | OF-4 |

Harry Chappas

CHAPPAS, HAROLD PERRY BB TR 5'3" 150 lbs.
B. Oct. 26, 1957, Mt. Rainier, Md.

1978 CHI A	20	75	20	1	0	0	0.0	11	6	6	11	1	.267	.280	0	0	SS-20
1979	26	59	17	1	0	1	1.7	9	4	5	5	1	.288	.356	1	1	SS-23
1980	26	50	8	2	0	0	0.0	6	2	4	10	0	.160	.200	3	0	SS-19, DH-2, 2B-1
3 yrs.	72	184	45	4	0	1	0.5	26	12	15	26	2	.245	.283	4	1	SS-62, DH-2, 2B-1
3 yrs.	72	184	45	4	0	1	0.5	26	12	15	26	2	.245	.283	4	1	SS-62, DH-2, 2B-1

Larry Chappell

CHAPPELL, LAWRENCE ASHFORD BL TL 6' 186 lbs.
B. Feb. 19, 1891, Jerseyville, Ill.   D. Nov. 8, 1918, San Francisco, Calif.

1913 CHI A		60	208	48	8	1	0	0.0	20	15	18	22	7	.231	.279	1	0	OF-59
1914		21	39	9	0	0	0	0.0	3	1	4	11	0	.231	.231	10	1	OF-9
1915		1	1	0	0	0	0	0.0	0	0	0	0	0	.000	.000	1	0	
1916 2 teams	CLE A (3G – .000)							BOS N (20G – .226)									
" total	23	55	12	1	1	0	0.0	4	9	3	8	2	.218	.273	8	1	OF-14
1917 BOS N		4	2	0	0	0	0	0.0	0	1	0	1	0	.000	.000	2	0	OF-1
5 yrs.		109	305	69	9	2	0	0.0	27	26	25	42	9	.226	.269	22	2	OF-83
3 yrs.		82	248	57	8	1	0	0.0	23	16	22	33	7	.230	.270	12	1	OF-68

Hal Chase

CHASE, HAROLD HARRIS (Prince Hal) BR TL 6' 175 lbs.
B. Feb. 13, 1883, Los Gatos, Calif.   D. May 18, 1947, Colusa, Calif.
Manager 1910-11.

1905 NY A		126	465	116	16	6	3	0.6	60	49	15		22	.249	.329	1	1	1B-122, SS-1, 2B-1
1906		151	597	193	23	10	0	0.0	84	76	13		28	.323	.395	0	0	1B-150, 2B-1
1907		125	498	143	23	3	2	0.4	72	68	19		32	.287	.357	0	0	1B-121, OF-4
1908		106	405	104	11	3	1	0.2	50	36	15		27	.257	.306	1	1	1B-96, OF-3, 2B-3, 3B-1
1909		118	474	134	17	3	4	0.8	60	63	20		25	.283	.357	0	0	1B-118
1910		130	524	152	20	5	3	0.6	67	73	16		40	.290	.365	0	0	1B-130
1911		133	527	166	32	7	3	0.6	82	62	21		36	.315	.419	0	0	1B-124, OF-7, 2B-2, SS-1
1912		131	522	143	21	9	4	0.8	61	58	17		33	.274	.372	2	0	1B-121, 2B-8
1913 2 teams	NY A (39G – .212)					CHI A (102G – .286)											
" total	141	530	141	13	14	2	0.4	64	48	27		54	14	.266	.355	0	0	1B-131, OF-5, 2B-5
1914 2 teams	CHI A (58G – .267)					BUF F (75G – .347)											
" total	133	497	156	29	14	3	0.6	70	68	29	19	19	.314	.447	2	1	1B-131
1915 BUF F		145	567	165	31	10	17	3.0	85	89	20		23	.291	.471	1	0	1B-143, OF-1
1916 CIN N		142	542	184	29	12	4	0.7	66	82	19	48	22	.339	.459	7	2	1B-98, OF-25, 2B-16
1917		152	602	167	28	15	4	0.7	71	86	15	49	21	.277	.394	0	0	1B-151
1918		74	259	78	12	6	2	0.8	30	38	13	15	5	.301	.417	5	0	1B-67, OF-2
1919 NY N		110	408	116	17	7	5	1.2	58	45	17	40	16	.284	.397	2	0	1B-107
15 yrs.		1917	7417	2158	322	124	57	0.8	980	941	276	225	363	.291	.391	21	6	1B-1810, OF-47, 2B-36, SS-2, 3B-1
2 yrs.		160	590	165	21	15	2	0.3	76	59	39	60	18	.280	.376	0	0	1B-160

	G	AB	H	2B	3B	HR	HR%	R	RBI	BB	SO	SB	BA	SA	Pinch Hit AB H	G by POS

Felix Chouinard
CHOUINARD, FELIX GEORGE   BB TR
B. 1888, Chicago, Ill.   D. Chicago, Ill.

1910 CHI A	24	82	16	3	2	0	0.0	6	9	8		4	.195	.280	0 0	OF-23, 2B-1
1911 "	14	17	3	0	0	0	0.0	3	0	0		1	.176	.176	0 0	OF-4, 2B-4
1914 3 teams	PIT	F (9G – .300)		BKN	F (32G – .253)		BAL	F (5G – .444)								
" total	46	118	33	2	2	1	0.8	12	12	4		4	.280	.356	11 2	OF-25, 2B-4, SS-1
1915 BKN F	4	4	2	0	0	0	0.0	1	2	0		0	.500	.500	1 0	OF-2
4 yrs.	88	221	54	5	4	1	0.5	22	23	12		8	.244	.317	12 2	OF-54, 2B-9, SS-1
2 yrs.	38	99	19	3	2	0	0.0	9	9	8		4	.192	.263	0 0	OF-27, 2B-5

Bob Christian
CHRISTIAN, ROBERT CHARLES   BR TR 5'10" 180 lbs.
B. Oct. 17, 1945, Chicago, Ill.   D. Feb. 20, 1974, San Diego, Calif.

1968 DET A	3	3	1	1	0	0	0.0	0	0	0	0	0	.333	.667	1 0	OF-1, 1B-1
1969 CHI A	39	129	28	4	0	3	2.3	11	16	10	19	3	.217	.318	1 1	OF-38
1970	12	15	4	0	0	1	6.7	3	3	1	4	0	.267	.467	9 3	OF-4
3 yrs.	54	147	33	5	0	4	2.7	14	19	11	23	3	.224	.340	11 4	OF-43, 1B-1
2 yrs.	51	144	32	4	0	4	2.8	14	19	11	23	3	.222	.333	10 4	OF-42

Lloyd Christopher
CHRISTOPHER, LLOYD EUGENE   BR TR 6'2" 190 lbs.
Brother of Russ Christopher.
B. Dec. 31, 1919, Richmond, Calif.

1945 2 teams	BOS	A (8G – .286)		CHI	N (1G – .000)											
" total	9	14	4	0	0	0	0.0	4	4	3	2	0	.286	.286	3 0	OF-4
1947 CHI A	7	23	5	0	1	0	0.0	1	0	2	4	0	.217	.304	0 0	OF-7
2 yrs.	16	37	9	0	1	0	0.0	5	4	5	6	0	.243	.297	3 0	OF-11
1 yr.	7	23	5	0	1	0	0.0	1	0	2	4	0	.217	.304	0 0	OF-7

Bill Cissell
CISSELL, CHALMER WILLIAM   BR TR 5'11" 170 lbs.
B. Jan. 3, 1904, Perryville, Mo.   D. Mar. 15, 1949, Chicago, Ill.

1928 CHI A	125	443	115	22	3	1	0.2	66	60	29	41	18	.260	.330	1 1	SS-123
1929 "	152	618	173	27	12	5	0.8	83	62	28	53	26	.280	.387	0 0	SS-152
1930 "	141	561	152	28	9	2	0.4	82	48	28	32	16	.271	.364	1 0	2B-106, 3B-24, SS-10
1931 "	109	409	90	13	5	1	0.2	42	46	16	26	18	.220	.284	0 0	SS-83, 2B-23, 3B-1
1932 2 teams	CHI	A (12G – .256)		CLE	A (131G – .320)											
" total	143	584	184	36	7	7	1.2	85	98	29	25	18	.315	.437	0 0	2B-129, SS-18
1933 CLE A	112	409	94	21	3	6	1.5	53	33	31	29	6	.230	.340	2 1	2B-62, SS-46, 3B-1
1934 BOS A	102	416	111	13	4	4	1.0	71	44	28	23	11	.267	.346	2 1	2B-96, SS-7, 3B-2
1937 PHI A	34	117	31	7	0	1	0.9	15	14	17	10	0	.265	.350	1 0	2B-33
1938 NY N	38	149	40	6	0	2	1.3	19	18	6	11	1	.268	.349	0 0	2B-33, 3B-6
9 yrs.	956	3706	990	173	43	29	0.8	516	423	212	250	114	.267	.360	7 3	2B-482, SS-439, 3B-34
5 yrs.	539	2074	541	91	30	10	0.5	280	221	102	152	78	.261	.348	2 1	SS-380, 2B-129, 3B-25

Bud Clancy
CLANCY, JOHN WILLIAM   BL TL 6' 170 lbs.
B. Sept. 15, 1900, Odell, Ill.   D. Sept. 27, 1968, Ottumwa, Iowa

1924 CHI A	13	35	9	1	0	0	0.0	5	6	3	2	3	.257	.286	4 1	1B-8
1925 "	4	3	0	0	0	0	0.0	0	0	1	0	0	.000	.000	3 0	
1926 "	12	38	13	2	2	0	0.0	3	7	1	1	0	.342	.500	2 0	1B-10
1927 "	130	464	139	21	2	3	0.6	46	53	24	24	4	.300	.373	5 1	1B-123
1928 "	130	487	132	19	11	2	0.4	64	37	42	25	6	.271	.368	2 0	1B-128
1929 "	92	290	82	14	6	3	1.0	36	45	16	19	3	.283	.403	16 4	1B-74
1930 "	68	234	57	8	3	3	1.3	28	27	12	18	3	.244	.342	7 1	1B-63
1932 BKN N	53	196	60	4	2	0	0.0	14	16	6	13	0	.306	.347	0 0	1B-53
1934 PHI N	20	49	12	0	0	1	2.0	8	7	6	4	0	.245	.306	9 2	1B-10
9 yrs.	522	1796	504	69	26	12	0.7	204	198	111	106	19	.281	.368	48 9	1B-469
7 yrs.	449	1551	432	65	24	11	0.7	182	175	99	89	19	.279	.373	39 7	1B-406

Allie Clark
CLARK, ALFRED ALOYSIUS   BR TR 6' 185 lbs.
B. June 16, 1923, South Amboy, N. J.

1947 NY A	24	67	25	5	0	1	1.5	9	14	5	2	0	.373	.493	7 2	OF-16
1948 CLE A	81	271	84	5	2	9	3.3	43	38	23	13	0	.310	.443	11 3	OF-65, 3B-5, 1B-1
1949 "	35	74	13	4	0	1	1.4	8	9	4	7	0	.176	.270	19 2	OF-17, 1B-1
1950 "	59	163	35	6	1	6	3.7	19	21	11	10	0	.215	.374	15 2	OF-41
1951 2 teams	CLE	A (3G – .300)		PHI	A (56G – .248)											
" total	59	171	43	12	1	5	2.9	23	25	16	9	2	.251	.421	13 4	OF-35, 3B-10
1952 PHI A	71	186	51	12	0	7	3.8	23	29	10	19	0	.274	.452	21 7	OF-48, 1B-2
1953 2 teams	PHI	A (20G – .203)		CHI	A (9G – .067)											
" total	29	89	16	4	0	3	3.4	6	13	3	10	0	.180	.326	9 1	OF-20, 1B-1
7 yrs.	358	1021	267	48	4	32	3.1	131	149	72	70	2	.262	.410	95 21	OF-242, 3B-15, 1B-5
1 yr.	9	15	1	0	0	0	0.0	0	0	5	0	0	.067	.067	8 0	OF-1, 1B-1
WORLD SERIES																
1947 NY A	3	2	1	0	0	0	0.0	1	1	1	0	0	.500	.500	2 1	OF-1
1948 CLE A	1	3	0	0	0	0	0.0	0	0	0	1	0	.000	.000	0 0	OF-1
2 yrs.	4	5	1	0	0	0	0.0	1	1	1	1	0	.200	.200	2 1	OF-2

Pep Clark
CLARK, HARRY   BR TR 5'7½" 175 lbs.
B. Mar. 18, 1883, Union City, Ohio   D. June 8, 1965, Milwaukee, Wis.

1903 CHI A	15	65	20	4	2	0	0.0	7	9	2		5	.308	.431	0 0	3B-15

Dick Clarke
CLARKE, RICHARD GREY (Noisy)   BR TR 5'9" 183 lbs.
B. Sept. 26, 1912, Fulton, Ala.

1944 CHI A	63	169	44	10	1	0	0.0	14	27	22	6	0	.260	.331	15 1	3B-45

Gil Coan
COAN, GILBERT FITZGERALD   BL TR 6' 180 lbs.
B. May 18, 1922, Monroe, N. C.

1946 WAS A	59	134	28	3	2	3	2.2	17	9	7	37	2	.209	.328	24 4	OF-29
1947 "	11	42	21	3	2	0	0.0	5	3	5	6	2	.500	.667	0 0	OF-11
1948 "	138	513	119	13	9	7	1.4	56	60	41	78	23	.232	.333	8 1	OF-131
1949 "	111	358	78	7	8	3	0.8	36	25	29	58	9	.218	.307	11 2	OF-97

Player Register 238

	G	AB	H	2B	3B	HR	HR%	R	RBI	BB	SO	SB	BA	SA	Pinch Hit AB	Pinch Hit H	G by POS

Gil Coan continued

	G	AB	H	2B	3B	HR	HR%	R	RBI	BB	SO	SB	BA	SA	PH AB	PH H	G by POS
1950	104	366	111	17	4	7	1.9	58	50	28	46	10	.303	.429	5	3	OF-98
1951	135	538	163	25	7	9	1.7	85	62	39	62	8	.303	.426	5	0	OF-132
1952	107	332	68	11	6	5	1.5	50	20	32	35	9	.205	.319	16	3	OF-86
1953	68	168	33	1	4	2	1.2	28	17	22	23	7	.196	.286	22	4	OF-46
1954 BAL A	94	265	74	11	1	2	0.8	29	20	16	17	9	.279	.351	25	2	OF-67
1955 3 teams	BAL A (61G – .238)				CHI A (17G – .176)			NY N (9G – .154)									
" total	87	160	36	7	1	1	0.6	18	12	13	21	4	.225	.300	29	11	OF-51
1956 NY N	4	1	0	0	0	0	0.0	2	0	0	1	0	.000	.000	1	0	
11 yrs.	918	2877	731	98	44	39	1.4	384	278	232	384	83	.254	.359	146	30	OF-748
1 yr.	17	17	3	0	0	0	0.0	1	0	0	5	0	.176	.176	11	2	OF-3

Rich Coggins

COGGINS, RICHARD ALLEN BL TL 5'8" 170 lbs.
B. Dec. 7, 1950, Indianapolis, Ind.

	G	AB	H	2B	3B	HR	HR%	R	RBI	BB	SO	SB	BA	SA	PH AB	PH H	G by POS
1972 BAL A	16	39	13	4	0	0	0.0	5	1	1	6	0	.333	.436	2	1	OF-13
1973	110	389	124	19	9	7	1.8	54	41	28	24	17	.319	.468	7	1	OF-101, DH-1
1974	113	411	100	13	3	4	1.0	53	32	29	31	26	.243	.319	12	1	OF-105
1975 2 teams	MON N (13G – .270)				NY A (51G – .224)												
" total	64	144	34	4	1	1	0.7	8	10	8	23	3	.236	.299	5	1	OF-46, DH-9
1976 2 teams	NY A (7G – .250)				CHI A (32G – .156)												
" total	39	100	16	2	0	0	0.0	5	6	6	16	4	.160	.180	5	1	OF-28, DH-1
5 yrs.	342	1083	287	42	13	12	1.1	125	90	72	100	50	.265	.361	31	5	OF-293, DH-11
1 yr.	32	96	15	2	0	0	0.0	4	5	6	15	3	.156	.177	4	1	OF-26

LEAGUE CHAMPIONSHIP SERIES

	G	AB	H	2B	3B	HR	HR%	R	RBI	BB	SO	SB	BA	SA	PH AB	PH H	G by POS
1973 BAL A	2	9	4	1	0	0	0.0	1	0	0	0	0	.444	.556	0	0	OF-2
1974	3	11	0	0	0	0	0.0	0	0	0	3	0	.000	.000	0	0	OF-3
2 yrs.	5	20	4	1	0	0	0.0	1	0	0	3	0	.200	.250	0	0	OF-5

Rocky Colavito

COLAVITO, ROCCO DOMENICO BR TR 6'3" 190 lbs.
B. Aug. 10, 1933, New York, N.Y.

	G	AB	H	2B	3B	HR	HR%	R	RBI	BB	SO	SB	BA	SA	PH AB	PH H	G by POS
1955 CLE A	5	9	4	2	0	0	0.0	3	0	0	2	0	.444	.667	2	0	OF-2
1956	101	322	89	11	4	21	6.5	55	65	49	46	0	.276	.531	5	0	OF-98
1957	134	461	116	26	0	25	5.4	66	84	71	80	1	.252	.471	3	1	OF-130
1958	143	489	148	26	3	41	8.4	80	113	84	89	0	.303	**.620**	5	1	OF-129, 1B-11, P-1
1959	154	588	151	24	0	42	7.1	90	111	71	86	3	.257	.512	0	0	OF-154
1960 DET A	145	555	138	18	1	35	6.3	67	87	53	80	3	.249	.474	2	0	OF-144
1961	163	583	169	30	2	45	7.7	129	140	113	75	1	.290	.580	2	0	OF-161
1962	161	601	164	30	2	37	6.2	90	112	96	68	2	.273	.514	0	0	OF-161
1963	160	597	162	29	2	22	3.7	91	91	84	78	0	.271	.437	1	0	OF-159
1964 KC A	160	588	161	31	2	34	5.8	89	102	83	56	3	.274	.507	1	1	OF-159
1965 CLE A	162	592	170	25	2	26	4.4	92	**108**	93	63	1	.287	.468	0	0	OF-162
1966	151	533	127	13	0	30	5.6	68	72	76	81	2	.238	.432	5	3	OF-146
1967 2 teams	CLE A (63G – .241)				CHI A (60G – .221)												
" total	123	381	88	13	1	8	2.1	30	50	49	41	3	.231	.333	12	3	OF-108
1968 2 teams	LA N (40G – .204)				NY A (39G – .220)												
" total	79	204	43	5	2	8	3.9	21	24	29	35	0	.211	.373	17	2	OF-61, P-1
14 yrs.	1841	6503	1730	283	21	374	5.8	971	1159	951	880	19	.266	.489	55	11	OF-1774, 1B-11, P-2
1 yr.	60	190	42	4	1	3	1.6	20	29	25	10	1	.221	.300	1	0	OF-58

Mike Colbern

COLBERN, MICHAEL MALLOY BR TR 6'3" 205 lbs.
B. Apr. 19, 1955, Santa Monica, Calif.

	G	AB	H	2B	3B	HR	HR%	R	RBI	BB	SO	SB	BA	SA	PH AB	PH H	G by POS
1978 CHI A	48	141	38	5	1	2	1.4	11	20	1	36	0	.270	.362	0	0	C-47, DH-1
1979	32	83	20	5	1	0	0.0	5	8	4	25	0	.241	.325	1	0	C-32
2 yrs.	80	224	58	10	2	2	0.9	16	28	5	61	0	.259	.348	1	0	C-79, DH-1
2 yrs.	80	224	58	10	2	2	0.9	16	28	5	61	0	.259	.348	1	0	C-79, DH-1

Willis Cole

COLE, WILLIS RUSSELL BR TR 5'8" 170 lbs.
B. Jan. 6, 1882, Milton Junction, Wis. D. Oct. 11, 1965, Madison, Wis.

	G	AB	H	2B	3B	HR	HR%	R	RBI	BB	SO	SB	BA	SA	PH AB	PH H	G by POS
1909 CHI A	46	165	39	7	3	0	0.0	17	16	16		3	.236	.315	0	0	OF-46
1910	22	80	14	2	1	0	0.0	6	2	4		0	.175	.225	0	0	OF-22
2 yrs.	68	245	53	9	4	0	0.0	23	18	20		3	.216	.286	0	0	OF-68
2 yrs.	68	245	53	9	4	0	0.0	23	18	20		3	.216	.286	0	0	OF-68

Ray Coleman

COLEMAN, RAYMOND LeROY BL TR 5'11" 170 lbs.
B. June 4, 1922, Dunsmuir, Calif.

	G	AB	H	2B	3B	HR	HR%	R	RBI	BB	SO	SB	BA	SA	PH AB	PH H	G by POS
1947 STL A	110	343	89	9	7	2	0.6	34	30	26	32	2	.259	.344	18	3	OF-93
1948 2 teams	STL A (17G – .172)				PHI A (68G – .243)												
" total	85	239	56	6	7	0	0.0	34	23	33	22	5	.234	.318	24	2	OF-58
1950 STL A	117	384	104	25	6	8	2.1	54	55	32	37	7	.271	.430	17	6	OF-98
1951 2 teams	STL A (91G – .282)				CHI A (51G – .276)												
" total	142	522	146	24	12	8	1.5	62	76	39	46	5	.280	.418	6	2	OF-138
1952 2 teams	CHI A (85G – .215)				STL A (20G – .196)												
" total	105	241	51	10	2	2	0.8	24	15	18	21	0	.212	.286	16	1	OF-89
5 yrs.	559	1729	446	74	33	20	1.2	208	199	148	158	19	.258	.374	81	14	OF-476
2 yrs.	136	376	92	15	8	5	1.3	40	35	28	31	2	.245	.367	14	2	OF-124

Eddie Collins

COLLINS, EDWARD TROWBRIDGE, SR. (Cocky) BL TR 5'9" 175 lbs.
Played as Eddie Sullivan 1906. Father of Eddie Collins.
B. May 2, 1887, Millerton, N.Y. D. Mar. 25, 1951, Boston, Mass.
Manager 1925-26.
Hall of Fame 1939.

	G	AB	H	2B	3B	HR	HR%	R	RBI	BB	SO	SB	BA	SA	PH AB	PH H	G by POS
1906 PHI A	6	17	4	0	0	0	0.0	1	0	0		1	.235	.235	1	0	SS-3, 3B-1, 2B-1
1907	14	20	5	0	1	0	0.0	0	2	0		0	.250	.350	6	1	SS-6
1908	102	330	90	18	7	1	0.3	39	40	16		8	.273	.373	11	4	2B-47, SS-28, OF-1
1909	153	572	198	30	10	3	0.5	104	56	62		67	.346	.449	0	0	2B-152, SS-1
1910	153	583	188	16	15	3	0.5	81	81	49		**81**	.322	.417	0	0	2B-153
1911	132	493	180	22	13	3	0.6	92	73	62		38	.365	.481	0	0	2B-132

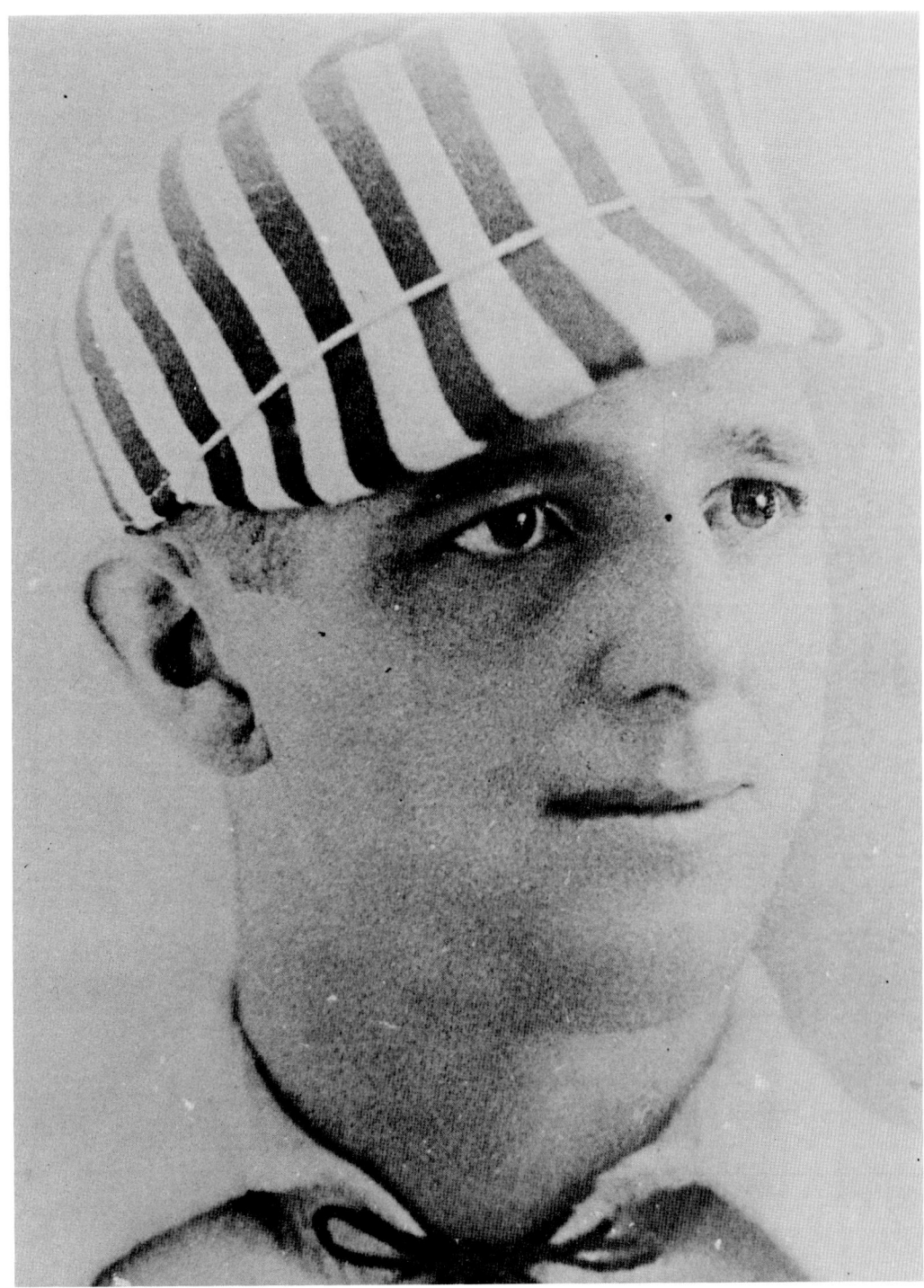

Founder, owner, Hall of Famer, Charles Comiskey defined the White Sox for a generation and headed a family that held onto the club for almost six decades. *(George Brace photo)*

Red Faber and Ted Lyons each won more than 250 games for the White Sox. Faber *(left)* pitched in one World Series, winning three games for the 1917 world champs. Lyons, a Chicago favorite honored twice with his own day at Comiskey Park *(below)*, never came near a Series in twenty-two seasons. *(Chicago White Sox photos)*

Jimmy Dykes *(above)* accepts good luck wishes from his old manager, Connie Mack. As manager of the Sox through the '30s and '40s, he needed all the luck he could get. *(Chicago White Sox photo)* What he didn't need, though, was a new shortstop: Luke Appling *(right)* owned that position for twenty years, picking up two batting titles along the way. *(George Brace photo)*

Nellie Fox *(left)* was another of Frank Lane's thefts, coming from Philadelphia for Joe Tipton. For fourteen seasons he was among the league leaders in hits, range, fielding percentage, and size of chaw. *(Chicago White Sox photo)* Early Wynn *(below)* also came to Chicago through the good graces of Mr. Lane, but this time it was while Lane was running the Cleveland Indians. *(George Brace photo)*

Al Lopez, the only manager besides Casey Stengel to win an AL pennant in the '50s, directed the White Sox' fortunes for nine years, never once falling into the second division. *(Chicago White Sox photo)*

Tommy John, Gary Peters, and Joel Horlen formed the heart of the outstanding White Sox rotations through the middle '60s, combining for a 2.56 ERA in their three prime years together. *(Chicago White Sox photo)*

Beanball wars and bench-clearing brawls typified baseball Stanky-style. Eddie Stanky's tactics had the Sox in first for most of 1967, but by season's end the Brat *(left)* was looking up at Boston, Detroit, and Minnesota. *(Chicago White Sox photos)*

Two of Chicago's masters of the butterfly. Hoyt Wilhelm *(left)* threw his knuckler in over a thousand games, more than any other pitcher. His ERA for his six years with the Pale Hose was a stingy 1.92. Wilbur Wood *(below)* started 49 games in 1972, more than any pitcher since Ed Walsh in 1908. He also became the first in over fifty years to win 20 and lose 20 in the same season. *(Chicago White Sox photos)*

The Sox showed uncharacteristic muscle in the early '70s. Third baseman Bill Melton *(above)* was the club's first homer champ ever in 1971. *(Chicago White Sox photo)* Dick Allen *(right)* became the second just one year later en route to winning the Most Valuable Player Award.

An unexpected burst came from Bill Veeck's "rent-a-stars" in 1977: Oscar Gamble *(left)* and Richie Zisk *(below)* each topped the 30-homer mark for the "South Side Hitmen." Both would take the free-agent road to millions with other clubs in 1978. *(Chicago White Sox photos)*

The cornerstone of the 1983 Western Division champions: *(clockwise from above left)* Carlton Fisk, who went on a tear after being moved into the second slot in the order in June; Greg Luzinski, who slugged 32 homers; and LaMarr Hoyt, league leader in wins in '82 and '83, who won 24 while walking just 31 in 260.2 innings. *(Chicago White Sox photos)*

The future is now. Greg Walker congratulates Ron Kittle after one of Kittle's 35 homers in 1983. Kittle was named AL Rookie of the Year, and he and Walker figure to be a part of a powerful White Sox team for years to come. *(Chicago White Sox photo)*

Player Register

	G	AB	H	2B	3B	HR	HR%	R	RBI	BB	SO	SB	BA	SA	Pinch Hit AB	H	G by POS

Eddie Collins continued

	G	AB	H	2B	3B	HR	HR%	R	RBI	BB	SO	SB	BA	SA	PH AB	H	G by POS
1912	153	543	189	25	11	0	0.0	137	64	101		63	.348	.435	0	0	2B-153
1913	148	534	184	23	13	3	0.6	125	73	85	37	55	.345	.453	0	0	2B-148
1914	152	526	181	23	14	2	0.4	122	85	97	31	58	.344	.452	0	0	2B-152
1915 CHI A	155	521	173	22	10	4	0.8	118	77	119	27	46	.332	.436	0	0	2B-155
1916	155	545	168	14	17	0	0.0	87	52	86	36	40	.308	.396	0	0	2B-155
1917	156	564	163	18	12	0	0.0	91	67	89	16	53	.289	.363	0	0	2B-156
1918	97	330	91	8	2	2	0.6	51	30	73	13	22	.276	.330	1	1	2B-96
1919	140	518	165	19	7	4	0.8	87	80	68	27	33	.319	.405	0	0	2B-140
1920	153	601	222	37	13	3	0.5	115	75	69	19	19	.369	.489	0	0	2B-153
1921	139	526	177	20	10	2	0.4	79	58	66	11	12	.337	.424	3	0	2B-136
1922	154	598	194	20	12	1	0.2	92	69	73	16	20	.324	.403	0	0	2B-154
1923	145	505	182	22	5	5	1.0	89	67	84	8	47	.360	.453	3	0	2B-142
1924	152	556	194	27	7	6	1.1	108	86	89	16	42	.349	.455	2	0	2B-150
1925	118	425	147	26	3	3	0.7	80	80	87	8	19	.346	.442	2	0	2B-116
1926	106	375	129	32	4	1	0.3	66	62	62	8	13	.344	.459	3	0	2B-101
1927 PHI A	95	225	76	12	1	1	0.4	50	15	60	9	6	.338	.413	34	12	2B-56, SS-1
1928	36	33	10	3	0	0	0.0	3	7	4	4	0	.303	.394	29	8	2B-2, SS-1
1929	9	7	0	0	0	0	0.0	0	0	2	0	0	.000	.000	7	0	
1930	3	2	1	0	0	0	0.0	1	0	0	0	0	.500	.500	2	1	
25 yrs.	2826	9949	3311	437	187	47	0.5	1818	1299	1503	286	743	.333	.428	104	27	2B-2650, SS-40, OF-10, 3B-1
	9th		8th									3rd					
12 yrs.	1670	6064	2005	265	102	31	0.5	1063	803	965	205	366	.331	.423	14	1	2B-1654
	4th	3rd	3rd	3rd	3rd			3rd	3rd	2nd		1st	2nd				

WORLD SERIES

	G	AB	H	2B	3B	HR	HR%	R	RBI	BB	SO	SB	BA	SA	PH AB	H	G by POS
1910 PHI A	5	21	9	4	0	0	0.0	5	3	2	0	4	.429	.619	0	0	2B-5
1911	6	21	6	1	0	0	0.0	4	1	2	2	2	.286	.333	0	0	2B-6
1913	5	19	8	0	2	0	0.0	5	3	1	2	3	.421	.632	0	0	2B-5
1914	4	14	3	0	0	0	0.0	0	1	2	1	1	.214	.214	0	0	2B-4
1917 CHI A	6	22	9	1	0	0	0.0	4	2	2	3	3	.409	.455	0	0	2B-6
1919	8	31	7	1	0	0	0.0	2	1	1	2	1	.226	.258	0	0	2B-8
6 yrs.	34	128	42	7	2	0	0.0	20	11	10	10	14	.328	.414	0	0	2B-34
			10th	8th								1st					

Shano Collins

COLLINS, JOHN FRANCIS
B. Dec. 4, 1885, Charlestown, Mass. D. Sept. 10, 1955, Newton, Mass.
Manager 1931-32.
BR TR 6' 185 lbs.

	G	AB	H	2B	3B	HR	HR%	R	RBI	BB	SO	SB	BA	SA	PH AB	H	G by POS
1910 CHI A	97	315	62	10	8	1	0.3	29	24	25		10	.197	.289	4	1	OF-65, 1B-27
1911	106	370	97	16	12	3	0.8	48	48	20		14	.262	.395	3	0	1B-97, OF-3, 2B-3
1912	153	575	168	34	10	2	0.3	75	81	29		26	.292	.397	2	0	OF-105, 1B-46
1913	148	535	128	26	9	1	0.2	53	47	32	60	22	.239	.327	1	1	OF-147
1914	154	598	164	34	9	3	0.5	61	65	27	49	30	.274	.376	0	0	OF-154
1915	153	576	148	24	17	2	0.3	73	85	28	50	38	.257	.368	2	0	OF-104, 1B-47
1916	143	527	128	28	12	0	0.0	74	42	59	51	16	.243	.342	3	0	OF-136, 1B-4
1917	82	252	59	13	3	1	0.4	38	14	10	27	14	.234	.321	8	2	OF-73
1918	103	365	100	18	11	1	0.3	30	56	17	19	7	.274	.392	5	1	OF-92, 1B-5, 2B-1
1919	63	179	50	6	3	1	0.6	21	16	7	11	3	.279	.363	9	2	OF-46, 1B-8
1920	133	495	150	21	10	1	0.2	70	63	23	24	12	.303	.392	4	0	1B-117, OF-12
1921 BOS A	141	542	155	29	12	4	0.7	63	65	18	38	15	.286	.406	0	0	OF-138, 1B-3
1922	135	472	128	24	7	1	0.2	33	52	7	16	7	.271	.358	16	5	OF-117, 1B-1
1923	97	342	79	10	5	0	0.0	41	18	11	29	7	.231	.289	6	1	OF-89
1924	88	240	70	16	5	0	0.0	36	28	18	17	4	.292	.400	20	7	OF-55, 1B-12
1925	2	3	1	0	0	0	0.0	1	0	0	0	0	.333	.333	1	0	OF-1
16 yrs.	1798	6386	1687	309	133	21	0.3	746	705	331	391	225	.264	.364	84	20	OF-1337, 1B-367, 2B-4
11 yrs.	1335	4787	1254	230	104	16	0.3	572	541	277	291	192	.262	.363	41	7	OF-937, 1B-351, 2B-4
	8th	8th	8th	7th	1st			10th	10th			5th					

WORLD SERIES

	G	AB	H	2B	3B	HR	HR%	R	RBI	BB	SO	SB	BA	SA	PH AB	H	G by POS
1917 CHI A	6	21	6	1	0	0	0.0	2	0	0	2	0	.286	.333	0	0	OF-6
1919	4	16	4	1	0	0	0.0	2	0	0	0	0	.250	.313	0	0	OF-4
2 yrs.	10	37	10	2	0	0	0.0	4	0	0	2	0	.270	.324	0	0	OF-10

Bob Coluccio

COLUCCIO, ROBERT PASQUALI
B. Oct. 2, 1951, Centralia, Wash.
BR TR 5'11" 183 lbs.

	G	AB	H	2B	3B	HR	HR%	R	RBI	BB	SO	SB	BA	SA	PH AB	H	G by POS
1973 MIL A	124	438	98	21	8	15	3.4	64	58	54	92	13	.224	.411	5	0	OF-108, DH-11
1974	138	394	88	13	4	6	1.5	42	31	43	61	15	.223	.322	2	0	OF-131, DH-2
1975 2 teams	MIL A (22G – .194)				CHI A (61G – .205)												
" total	83	223	45	4	3	5	2.2	30	18	24	45	5	.202	.314	4	0	OF-81, DH-1
1977 CHI A	20	37	10	0	0	0	0.0	4	7	6	2	0	.270	.270	0	0	OF-19
1978 STL N	5	3	0	0	0	0	0.0	0	0	1	2	0	.000	.000	3	0	OF-2
5 yrs.	370	1095	241	38	15	26	2.4	140	114	128	202	33	.220	.353	14	0	OF-341, DH-14
2 yrs.	81	198	43	4	2	4	2.0	26	20	19	36	4	.217	.318	4	0	OF-78, DH-1

Ramon Conde

CONDE, RAMON LUIS (Wito)
B. Dec. 29, 1934, Juana Diaz, Puerto Rico
BR TR 5'8" 172 lbs.

	G	AB	H	2B	3B	HR	HR%	R	RBI	BB	SO	SB	BA	SA	PH AB	H	G by POS
1962 CHI A	14	16	0	0	0	0	0.0	0	1	3	3	0	.000	.000	5	0	3B-7

Jocko Conlan

CONLAN, JOHN BERTRAND
B. Dec. 6, 1899, Chicago, Ill.
Hall of Fame 1974.
BL TL 5'7½" 165 lbs.

	G	AB	H	2B	3B	HR	HR%	R	RBI	BB	SO	SB	BA	SA	PH AB	H	G by POS
1934 CHI A	63	225	56	11	3	0	0.0	35	16	19	7	2	.249	.324	8	3	OF-54
1935	65	140	40	7	1	0	0.0	20	15	14	6	3	.286	.350	24	5	OF-37
2 yrs.	128	365	96	18	4	0	0.0	55	31	33	13	5	.263	.334	32	8	OF-91
2 yrs.	128	365	96	18	4	0	0.0	55	31	33	13	5	.263	.334	32	8	OF-91

Player Register 240

	G	AB	H	2B	3B	HR	HR%	R	RBI	BB	SO	SB	BA	SA	Pinch Hit AB	H	G by POS

Merv Connors
CONNORS, MERVYN JAMES BR TR 6'2" 192 lbs.
B. Jan. 23, 1914, Berkeley, Calif.

		G	AB	H	2B	3B	HR	HR%	R	RBI	BB	SO	SB	BA	SA	AB	H	G by POS
1937	CHI A	28	103	24	4	1	2	1.9	12	12	14	19	2	.233	.350	0	0	3B-28
1938		24	62	22	4	0	6	9.7	14	13	9	17	0	.355	.710	7	2	1B-16
2 yrs.		52	165	46	8	1	8	4.8	26	25	23	36	2	.279	.485	7	2	3B-28, 1B-16
2 yrs.		52	165	46	8	1	8	4.8	26	25	23	36	2	.279	.485	7	2	3B-28, 1B-16

Cecil Coombs
COOMBS, CECIL LYSANDER BR TR 5'9" 160 lbs.
B. Mar. 18, 1888, Moweaqua, Ill. D. Nov. 25, 1975, Ft. Worth, Tex.

1914	CHI A	7	23	4	1	0	0	0.0	1	1	1	7	0	.174	.217	0	0	OF-7

Roy Corhan
CORHAN, ROY GEORGE (Irish) BR TR 5'9½" 165 lbs.
B. Oct. 21, 1887, Indianapolis, Ind. D. Nov. 24, 1958, San Francisco, Calif.

1911	CHI A	43	131	28	6	2	0	0.0	14	8	15		2	.214	.290	0	0	SS-43
1916	STL N	92	295	62	6	3	0	0.0	30	18	20	31	15	.210	.251	7	3	SS-84
2 yrs.		135	426	90	12	5	0	0.0	44	26	35	31	17	.211	.263	7	3	SS-127
1 yr.		43	131	28	6	2	0	0.0	14	8	15		2	.214	.290	0	0	SS-43

Red Corriden
CORRIDEN, JOHN MICHAEL, SR. BR TR 5'9" 165 lbs.
Father of John Corriden.
B. Sept. 4, 1887, Logansport, Ind. D. Sept. 28, 1959, Indianapolis, Ind.
Manager 1950.

1910	STL A	26	84	13	3	0	1	1.2	19	4	13		5	.155	.226	0	0	SS-14, 3B-12
1912	DET A	38	138	28	6	0	0	0.0	22	5	15		4	.203	.246	3	0	3B-25, 2B-7, SS-3
1913	CHI N	45	97	17	3	0	2	2.1	13	9	9	14	4	.175	.268	4	1	SS-36, 2B-2, 3B-1
1914		107	318	73	9	5	3	0.9	42	29	35	33	13	.230	.318	6	2	SS-96, 3B-8, 2B-3
1915		6	3	0	0	0	0	0.0	1	0	2	1	0	.000	.000	2	0	OF-1, 3B-1
5 yrs.		222	640	131	21	5	6	0.9	97	47	74	48	26	.205	.281	15	3	SS-149, 3B-47, 2B-12, OF-1

Shine Cortazzo
CORTAZZO, JOHN FRANCIS BR TR 5'3½" 142 lbs.
B. Sept. 26, 1904, Wilmerding, Pa. D. Mar. 4, 1963, Braddock, Pa.

1923	CHI A	1	1	0	0	0	0	0.0	0	0	0	0	0	.000	.000	1	0	

Clint Courtney
COURTNEY, CLINTON DAWSON (Scrap Iron) BL TR 5'8" 180 lbs.
B. Mar. 16, 1927, Hall Summit, La. D. June 16, 1975, Rochester, N. Y.

1951	NY A	1	2	0	0	0	0	0.0	0	0	1	1	0	.000	.000	0	0	C-1
1952	STL A	119	413	118	24	3	5	1.2	38	50	39	26	0	.286	.395	6	0	C-113
1953		106	355	89	12	2	4	1.1	28	19	25	20	0	.251	.330	7	2	C-103
1954	BAL A	122	397	107	18	3	4	1.0	25	37	30	7	2	.270	.360	14	5	C-111
1955	2 teams		CHI A (19G – .378)				WAS A (75G – .298)											
"	total	94	275	85	12	4	3	1.1	33	40	26	9	0	.309	.415	11	6	C-84
1956	WAS A	101	283	85	20	3	5	1.8	31	44	20	10	0	.300	.445	31	8	C-76
1957		91	232	62	14	1	6	2.6	23	27	16	11	0	.267	.414	27	11	C-59
1958		134	450	113	18	0	8	1.8	46	62	48	23	1	.251	.344	7	2	C-128
1959		72	189	44	4	1	2	1.1	19	18	20	19	0	.233	.296	19	3	C-53
1960	BAL A	83	154	35	3	0	1	0.6	14	12	30	14	0	.227	.266	18	7	C-58
1961	2 teams		KC A (1G – .000)				BAL A (22G – .267)											
"	total	23	46	12	2	0	0	0.0	3	4	10	3	0	.261	.304	7	2	C-16
11 yrs.		946	2796	750	127	17	38	1.4	260	313	265	143	3	.268	.367	147	46	C-802
1 yr.		19	37	14	3	0	1	2.7	7	10	7	0	0	.378	.541	2	1	C-17

Wes Covington
COVINGTON, JOHN WESLEY BL TR 6'1" 205 lbs.
B. Mar. 27, 1932, Laurinburg, N. C.

1956	MIL N	75	138	39	4	0	2	1.4	17	16	16	20	1	.283	.355	31	10	OF-35
1957		96	328	93	4	8	21	6.4	51	65	29	44	4	.284	.537	8	1	OF-89
1958		90	294	97	12	1	24	8.2	43	74	20	35	0	.330	.622	7	0	OF-82
1959		103	373	104	17	3	7	1.9	38	45	26	41	0	.279	.397	9	2	OF-94
1960		95	281	70	16	1	10	3.6	25	35	15	37	1	.249	.420	22	5	OF-72
1961	4 teams		MIL N (9G – .190)				CHI A (22G – .288)				KC A (17G – .159)			PHI N (57G – .303)				
"	total	105	289	78	11	0	12	4.2	34	42	25	33	0	.270	.433	28	6	OF-76
1962	PHI N	116	304	86	12	1	9	3.0	36	44	19	44	0	.283	.418	30	9	OF-88
1963		119	353	107	24	1	17	4.8	46	64	26	56	1	.303	.521	25	8	OF-101
1964		129	339	95	18	0	13	3.8	37	58	38	50	0	.280	.448	31	5	OF-108
1965		101	235	58	10	1	15	6.4	27	45	26	47	0	.247	.489	35	7	OF-64
1966	2 teams		CHI N (9G – .091)				LA N (37G – .121)											
"	total	46	44	5	0	1	1	2.3	1	6	7	7	0	.114	.227	34	4	OF-3
11 yrs.		1075	2978	832	128	17	131	4.4	355	499	247	414	7	.279	.466	260	57	OF-812
1 yr.		22	59	17	1	0	4	6.8	5	15	4	5	0	.288	.508	6	1	OF-14

WORLD SERIES

1957	MIL N	7	24	5	1	0	0	0.0	1	1	2	6	1	.208	.250	0	0	OF-7
1958		7	26	7	0	0	0	0.0	2	4	2	4	0	.269	.269	0	0	OF-7
1966	LA N	1	1	0	0	0	0	0.0	0	0	0	1	0	.000	.000	1	0	
3 yrs.		15	51	12	1	0	0	0.0	3	5	4	11	1	.235	.255	1	0	OF-14

Gavvy Cravath
CRAVATH, CLIFFORD CARLTON (Cactus) BR TR 5'10½" 186 lbs.
B. Mar. 23, 1881, Escondido, Calif. D. May 23, 1963, Laguna Beach, Calif.
Manager 1919-20.

1908	BOS A	94	277	71	10	11	1	0.4	43	34	32		6	.256	.383	14	5	OF-77, 1B-5
1909	2 teams		CHI A (19G – .180)				WAS A (3G – .000)											
"	total	22	55	9	0	0	1	1.8	7	9	20		3	.164	.218	2	0	OF-19
1912	PHI N	130	436	124	30	9	11	2.5	63	70	47	77	15	.284	.470	16	4	OF-113
1913		147	525	179	34	14	19	3.6	78	128	55	63	10	.341	.568	5	4	OF-141
1914		149	499	149	27	8	19	3.8	76	100	83	72	14	.299	.499	6	0	OF-143
1915		150	522	149	31	7	24	4.6	89	115	86	77	11	.285	.510	0	0	OF-150
1916		137	448	127	21	8	11	2.5	70	70	64	89	9	.283	.440	7	1	OF-130
1917		140	503	141	29	16	12	2.4	70	83	70	57	6	.280	.473	1	0	OF-139
1918		121	426	99	27	5	8	1.9	43	54	54	46	7	.232	.376	2	0	OF-118

	G	AB	H	2B	3B	HR	HR%	R	RBI	BB	SO	SB	BA	SA	Pinch Hit AB	H	G by POS

Gavvy Cravath continued

	G	AB	H	2B	3B	HR	HR%	R	RBI	BB	SO	SB	BA	SA	PH AB	PH H	G by POS
1919	83	214	73	18	5	12	5.6	34	45	35	21	8	.341	.640	19	6	OF-56
1920	46	45	13	5	0	1	2.2	2	11	9	12	0	.289	.467	34	12	OF-5
11 yrs.	1219	3950	1134	232	83	119	3.0	575	719	561	514	89	.287	.478	106	32	OF-1091, 1B-5
1 yr.	19	50	9	0	0	1	2.0	7	8	19		3	.180	.240	0	0	OF-18

WORLD SERIES

| 1915 PHI N | 5 | 16 | 2 | 1 | 1 | 0 | 0.0 | 2 | 1 | 2 | 6 | 0 | .125 | .313 | 0 | 0 | OF-5 |

Buck Crouse

CROUSE, CLYDE ELSWORTH BL TR 5'8" 158 lbs.
B. Jan. 6, 1897, Anderson, Ind.

	G	AB	H	2B	3B	HR	HR%	R	RBI	BB	SO	SB	BA	SA	PH AB	PH H	G by POS
1923 CHI A	23	70	18	2	1	1	1.4	6	7	3	4	0	.257	.357	0	0	C-22
1924	94	305	79	10	1	1	0.3	30	44	23	12	3	.259	.308	4	0	C-90
1925	54	131	46	7	0	2	1.5	18	25	12	4	1	.351	.450	6	2	C-48
1926	49	135	32	4	1	0	0.0	10	17	14	7	0	.237	.281	3	0	C-45
1927	85	222	53	11	0	0	0.0	22	20	21	10	4	.239	.288	4	2	C-81
1928	78	218	55	5	2	2	0.9	17	20	19	14	3	.252	.321	2	0	C-76
1929	45	107	29	7	0	2	1.9	11	12	5	7	2	.271	.393	4	0	C-40
1930	42	118	30	8	1	0	0.0	14	15	17	10	1	.254	.339	3	0	C-38
8 yrs.	470	1306	342	54	6	8	0.6	128	160	114	68	14	.262	.331	26	4	C-440
8 yrs.	470	1306	342	54	6	8	0.6	128	160	114	68	14	.262	.331	26	4	C-440

Cirilio Cruz

CRUZ, CIRILIO DILAN (Tommy) BL TL 5'9" 165 lbs.
Brother of Jose Cruz. Brother of Hector Cruz.
B. Feb. 15, 1951, Arroyo, Puerto Rico

	G	AB	H	2B	3B	HR	HR%	R	RBI	BB	SO	SB	BA	SA	PH AB	PH H	G by POS
1973 STL N	3	0	0	0	0	0	—	1	0	0	0	0	—	—	0	0	OF-1
1977 CHI A	4	2	0	0	0	0	0.0	1	0	0	0	0	.000	.000	1	0	OF-2
2 yrs.	7	2	0	0	0	0	0.0	2	0	0	0	0	.000	.000	1	0	OF-3
1 yr.	4	2	0	0	0	0	0.0	1	0	0	0	0	.000	.000	1	0	OF-2

Henry Cruz

CRUZ, HENRY BL TL 6' 175 lbs.
B. Feb. 27, 1952, St Croix, Virgin Islands

	G	AB	H	2B	3B	HR	HR%	R	RBI	BB	SO	SB	BA	SA	PH AB	PH H	G by POS
1975 LA N	53	94	25	3	1	0	0.0	8	5	7	6	1	.266	.319	14	2	OF-41
1976	49	88	16	2	1	4	4.5	8	14	9	11	0	.182	.364	20	3	OF-23
1977 CHI A	16	21	6	0	0	2	9.5	3	5	1	3	0	.286	.571	1	0	OF-9
1978	53	77	17	2	1	2	2.6	13	10	8	11	0	.221	.351	11	1	OF-40, DH-1
4 yrs.	171	280	64	7	3	8	2.9	32	34	25	31	1	.229	.361	46	6	OF-113, DH-1
2 yrs.	69	98	23	2	1	4	4.1	16	15	9	14	0	.235	.398	12	1	OF-49, DH-1

Julio Cruz

CRUZ, JULIO LUIS BB TR 5'9" 165 lbs.
B. Dec. 2, 1954, Brooklyn, N.Y.

	G	AB	H	2B	3B	HR	HR%	R	RBI	BB	SO	SB	BA	SA	PH AB	PH H	G by POS
1977 SEA A	60	199	51	3	1	1	0.5	25	7	24	29	15	.256	.296	2	0	2B-54
1978	147	550	129	14	1	1	0.2	77	25	69	66	59	.235	.269	0	0	2B-141, SS-5, DH-1
1979	107	414	112	16	2	1	0.2	70	29	62	61	49	.271	.326	0	0	2B-107
1980	119	422	88	9	3	2	0.5	66	16	59	49	45	.209	.258	0	0	2B-115, DH-3
1981	94	352	90	12	3	2	0.6	57	24	39	40	43	.256	.324	1	0	2B-92, SS-1
1982	154	549	133	22	5	8	1.5	83	49	57	71	46	.242	.344	0	0	2B-151, DH-2, SS-2, 3B-1
1983 2 teams	SEA A (61G – .254)					CHI A (99G – .251)											
" total	160	515	130	19	5	3	0.6	71	52	49	66	57	.252	.326	1	1	2B-157, DH-1
7 yrs.	841	3001	733	95	20	18	0.6	449	202	359	382	314	.244	.307	4	1	2B-817, SS-8, DH-7, 3B-1
1 yr.	99	334	84	9	4	1	0.3	47	40	29	44	24	.251	.311	1	1	2B-97, DH-1

LEAGUE CHAMPIONSHIP SERIES

| 1983 CHI A | 4 | 12 | 4 | 0 | 0 | 0 | 0.0 | 0 | 0 | 3 | 4 | 2 | .333 | .333 | 0 | 0 | 2B-4 |

Todd Cruz

CRUZ, TODD RUBEN BR TR 6' 175 lbs.
B. Nov. 23, 1955, Highland Park, Mich.

	G	AB	H	2B	3B	HR	HR%	R	RBI	BB	SO	SB	BA	SA	PH AB	PH H	G by POS
1978 PHI N	3	4	2	0	0	0	0.0	0	2	0	0	0	.500	.500	0	0	SS-2
1979 KC A	55	118	24	7	0	2	1.7	9	15	3	19	0	.203	.314	0	0	SS-48, 3B-9
1980 2 teams	CAL A (18G – .275)					CHI A (90G – .232)											
" total	108	333	79	14	1	3	0.9	28	23	14	62	2	.237	.312	2	1	SS-102, 3B-4, OF-1, 2B-1
1982 SEA A	136	492	113	20	2	16	3.3	44	57	12	95	2	.230	.376	0	0	SS-136
1983 2 teams	SEA A (65G – .190)					BAL A (81G – .208)											
" total	146	437	87	13	3	10	2.3	37	48	22	108	4	.199	.311	5	2	3B-79, SS-63, 2B-2
5 yrs.	448	1384	305	54	6	31	2.2	118	145	51	284	8	.220	.335	7	3	SS-351, 3B-92, 2B-3, OF-1
1 yr.	90	293	68	11	1	2	0.7	23	18	9	54	2	.232	.297	1	0	SS-90

LEAGUE CHAMPIONSHIP SERIES

| 1983 BAL A | 4 | 15 | 2 | 0 | 0 | 0 | 0.0 | 0 | 1 | 0 | 5 | 0 | .133 | .133 | 0 | 0 | 3B-4 |

WORLD SERIES

| 1983 BAL A | 5 | 16 | 2 | 0 | 0 | 0 | 0.0 | 1 | 0 | 1 | 3 | 0 | .125 | .125 | 0 | 0 | 3B-5 |

Tony Cuccinello

CUCCINELLO, ANTHONY FRANCIS (Chick) BR TR 5'7" 160 lbs.
Brother of Al Cuccinello.
B. Nov. 8, 1907, Long Island City, N.Y.

	G	AB	H	2B	3B	HR	HR%	R	RBI	BB	SO	SB	BA	SA	PH AB	PH H	G by POS
1930 CIN N	125	443	138	22	5	10	2.3	64	78	47	44	5	.312	.451	3	1	3B-109, 2B-15, SS-4
1931	154	575	181	39	11	2	0.3	79	93	54	28	5	.315	.431	0	0	2B-154
1932 BKN N	154	597	168	32	6	12	2.0	76	77	46	47	5	.281	.415	0	0	2B-154
1933	134	485	122	31	4	9	1.9	58	65	44	40	4	.252	.388	0	0	2B-120, 3B-14
1934	140	528	138	32	2	14	2.7	59	94	49	45	0	.261	.409	1	1	2B-101, 3B-43
1935	102	360	105	20	3	8	2.2	49	53	40	35	3	.292	.431	4	1	2B-64, 3B-36
1936 BOS N	150	565	174	26	3	7	1.2	68	86	58	49	1	.308	.402	0	0	2B-150
1937	152	575	156	36	4	11	1.9	77	80	61	40	2	.271	.405	1	0	2B-151
1938	147	555	147	25	2	9	1.6	62	76	52	32	4	.265	.366	0	0	2B-147
1939	81	310	95	17	1	2	0.6	42	40	26	26	5	.306	.387	1	0	2B-80

	G	AB	H	2B	3B	HR	HR%	R	RBI	BB	SO	SB	BA	SA	Pinch Hit AB	H	G by POS

Tony Cuccinello continued
1940 2 teams	BOS N (34G – .270)							NY N (88G – .208)									
" total	122	433	98	18	2	5	1.2	40	55	24	51	2	.226	.312	6	1	3B-70, 2B-47
1942 BOS N	40	104	21	3	0	1	1.0	8	8	9	11	1	.202	.260	5	2	3B-20, 2B-14
1943 2 teams	BOS N (13G – .000)							CHI A (34G – .272)									
" total	47	122	28	5	0	2	1.6	5	13	16	14	3	.230	.320	7	0	3B-34, 2B-2, SS-1
1944 CHI A	38	130	34	3	0	0	0.0	5	17	8	16	0	.262	.285	2	0	3B-30, 2B-6
1945	118	402	124	25	3	2	0.5	50	49	45	19	6	.308	.400	6	1	3B-112
15 yrs.	1704	6184	1729	334	46	94	1.5	730	884	579	497	42	.280	.394	36	7	2B-1205, 3B-468, SS-5
3 yrs.	190	635	186	33	3	4	0.6	60	77	66	48	9	.293	.373	11	1	3B-172, 2B-6

Tim Cullen
CULLEN, TIMOTHY LEO
B. Feb. 16, 1942, San Francisco, Calif.
BR TR 6'1" 185 lbs.

	G	AB	H	2B	3B	HR	HR%	R	RBI	BB	SO	SB	BA	SA	PH AB	H	G by POS
1966 WAS A	18	34	8	1	0	0	0.0	8	0	2	8	0	.235	.265	6	1	3B-8, 2B-5
1967	124	402	95	7	0	2	0.5	35	31	40	47	4	.236	.269	2	0	SS-69, 2B-46, 3B-15, OF-1
1968 2 teams	CHI A (72G – .200)							WAS A (47G – .272)									
" total	119	269	62	11	2	3	1.1	24	29	22	35	0	.230	.320	4	2	2B-87, SS-33, 3B-3
1969 WAS A	119	249	52	7	0	1	0.4	22	15	14	27	1	.209	.249	10	2	2B-105, SS-9, 3B-1
1970	123	262	56	10	2	1	0.4	22	18	31	38	3	.214	.279	12	1	2B-112, SS-6
1971	125	403	77	13	4	2	0.5	34	26	33	47	2	.191	.258	1	0	2B-78, SS-62
1972 OAK A	72	142	37	8	1	0	0.0	10	15	5	17	0	.261	.331	3	1	2B-65, 3B-4, SS-1
7 yrs.	700	1761	387	57	9	9	0.5	155	134	147	219	10	.220	.278	38	7	2B-498, SS-180, 3B-31, OF-1
1 yr.	72	155	31	7	0	2	1.3	16	13	15	23	0	.200	.284	2	0	2B-71

LEAGUE CHAMPIONSHIP SERIES
| 1972 OAK A | 2 | 1 | 0 | 0 | 0 | 0 | 0.0 | 0 | 0 | 0 | 0 | 0 | .000 | .000 | 0 | 0 | SS-2 |

Dick Culler
CULLER, RICHARD BROADUS
B. Jan. 25, 1915, High Point, N. C.   D. June 16, 1964, Chapel Hill, N. C.
BR TR 5'9½" 155 lbs.

	G	AB	H	2B	3B	HR	HR%	R	RBI	BB	SO	SB	BA	SA	PH AB	H	G by POS
1936 PHI A	9	38	9	0	0	0	0.0	3	1	1	3	0	.237	.237	0	0	2B-7, SS-2
1943 CHI A	53	148	32	5	1	0	0.0	9	11	16	11	4	.216	.264	0	0	3B-26, 2B-19, SS-3
1944 BOS N	8	28	2	0	0	0	0.0	2	0	4	2	0	.071	.071	0	0	SS-8
1945	136	527	138	12	1	2	0.4	87	30	50	35	7	.262	.300	1	0	SS-126, 3B-6
1946	134	482	123	15	3	0	0.0	70	33	62	18	7	.255	.299	2	1	SS-132
1947	77	214	53	5	1	0	0.0	20	19	19	15	1	.248	.280	1	1	SS-75
1948 CHI N	48	89	15	2	0	0	0.0	4	5	13	3	0	.169	.191	1	0	SS-43, 2B-2
1949 NY N	7	1	0	0	0	0	0.0	0	0	1	0	0	.000	.000	0	0	SS-7
8 yrs.	472	1527	372	39	6	2	0.1	195	99	166	87	19	.244	.281	5	2	SS-396, 3B-32, 2B-28
1 yr.	53	148	32	5	1	0	0.0	9	11	16	11	4	.216	.264	0	0	3B-26, 2B-19, SS-3

Joe Cunningham
CUNNINGHAM, JOSEPH ROBERT
B. Aug. 27, 1931, Paterson, N. J.
BL TL 6' 180 lbs.

	G	AB	H	2B	3B	HR	HR%	R	RBI	BB	SO	SB	BA	SA	PH AB	H	G by POS
1954 STL N	85	310	88	11	3	11	3.5	40	50	43	40	1	.284	.445	0	0	1B-85
1956	4	3	0	0	0	0	0.0	1	0	1	1	0	.000	.000	2	0	1B-1
1957	122	261	83	15	0	9	3.4	50	52	56	29	3	.318	.479	29	11	1B-57, OF-46
1958	131	337	105	20	3	12	3.6	61	57	82	23	4	.312	.496	19	5	1B-67, OF-66
1959	144	458	158	28	6	7	1.5	65	60	88	47	2	.345	.478	8	2	OF-121, 1B-35
1960	139	492	138	28	3	6	1.2	68	39	59	59	1	.280	.386	9	2	OF-116, 1B-15
1961	113	322	92	11	2	7	2.2	60	40	53	32	1	.286	.398	20	5	OF-86, 1B-10
1962 CHI A	149	526	155	32	7	8	1.5	91	70	101	59	3	.295	.428	3	1	1B-143, OF-5
1963	67	210	60	12	1	1	0.5	32	31	33	23	1	.286	.367	6	4	1B-58
1964 2 teams	CHI A (40G – .250)							WAS A (49G – .214)									
" total	89	234	54	11	0	0	0.0	28	17	37	27	0	.231	.278	14	1	1B-74
1965 WAS A	95	201	46	9	1	3	1.5	29	20	46	27	0	.229	.328	27	5	1B-59
1966	3	8	1	0	0	0	0.0	0	0	0	1	0	.125	.125	0	0	1B-3
12 yrs.	1141	3362	980	177	26	64	1.9	525	436	599	368	16	.291	.417	137	36	1B-607, OF-440
3 yrs.	256	844	242	51	8	9	1.1	136	111	148	96	4	.287	.398	16	6	1B-234, OF-5

Guy Curtright
CURTRIGHT, GUY PAXTON
B. Oct. 18, 1912, Holliday, Mo.
BR TR 5'11" 200 lbs.

	G	AB	H	2B	3B	HR	HR%	R	RBI	BB	SO	SB	BA	SA	PH AB	H	G by POS
1943 CHI A	138	488	142	20	7	3	0.6	67	48	69	60	13	.291	.379	9	2	OF-128
1944	72	198	50	8	2	2	1.0	22	23	23	21	4	.253	.343	22	6	OF-51
1945	98	324	91	15	7	4	1.2	51	32	39	29	3	.281	.407	13	5	OF-84
1946	23	55	11	2	0	0	0.0	7	5	11	14	0	.200	.236	4	2	OF-15
4 yrs.	331	1065	294	45	16	9	0.8	147	108	142	124	20	.276	.374	48	15	OF-278
4 yrs.	331	1065	294	45	16	9	0.8	147	108	142	124	20	.276	.374	48	15	OF-278

Tom Daly
DALY, THOMAS DANIEL
B. Dec. 12, 1891, St. John, N. B., Canada   D. Nov. 7, 1946, Bedford, Mass.
BR TR 5'11½" 171 lbs.

	G	AB	H	2B	3B	HR	HR%	R	RBI	BB	SO	SB	BA	SA	PH AB	H	G by POS
1913 CHI A	1	3	0	0	0	0	0.0	0	0	0	0	0	.000	.000	0	0	C-1
1914	61	133	31	2	0	0	0.0	13	8	7	13	3	.233	.248	24	6	OF-23, 3B-5, C-4, 1B-2
1915	29	47	9	1	0	0	0.0	5	3	5	9	0	.191	.213	9	1	C-19, 1B-1
1916 CLE A	31	73	16	1	1	0	0.0	3	8	1	2	0	.219	.260	5	1	C-25, OF-1
1918 CHI N	1	1	0	0	0	0	0.0	0	0	0	0	0	.000	.000	0	0	C-1
1919	25	50	11	0	1	0	0.0	4	1	2	5	0	.220	.260	6	0	C-18
1920	44	90	28	6	0	0	0.0	12	13	2	6	1	.311	.378	14	4	C-29
1921	51	143	34	7	1	0	0.0	12	22	8	8	1	.238	.301	4	1	C-47
8 yrs.	243	540	129	17	3	0	0.0	49	55	25	43	5	.239	.278	62	13	C-144, OF-24, 3B-5, 1B-3
3 yrs.	91	183	40	3	0	0	0.0	18	11	12	22	3	.219	.235	33	7	C-24, OF-23, 3B-5, 1B-3

Tom Daly
DALY, THOMAS PETER (Tido)
Brother of Joe Daly.
B. Feb. 7, 1866, Philadelphia, Pa.   D. Oct. 29, 1939, Brooklyn, N. Y.
BB TR 5'7" 170 lbs.

	G	AB	H	2B	3B	HR	HR%	R	RBI	BB	SO	SB	BA	SA	PH AB	H	G by POS
1887 CHI N	74	256	53	10	4	2	0.8	45	17	22	25	29	.207	.301	0	0	C-64, OF-8, SS-2, 2B-2, 1B-2
1888	65	219	42	2	6	0	0.0	34	29	10	26	10	.192	.256	0	0	C-62, OF-4

Player Register

	G	AB	H	2B	3B	HR	HR%	R	RBI	BB	SO	SB	BA	SA	Pinch Hit AB	Pinch Hit H	G by POS

Tom Daly continued

	G	AB	H	2B	3B	HR	HR%	R	RBI	BB	SO	SB	BA	SA	PH AB	PH H	G by POS
1889 WAS N	71	250	75	13	5	1	0.4	39	40	38	28	18	.300	.404	0	0	C-57, 1B-8, 2B-4, OF-3, SS-1
1890 BKN N	82	292	71	9	4	5	1.7	55	43	32	43	20	.243	.353	0	0	C-69, 1B-12, OF-1
1891	58	200	50	11	5	2	1.0	29	27	21	34	7	.250	.385	0	0	C-26, 1B-15, SS-11, OF-7
1892	124	446	114	15	6	4	0.9	76	51	64	61	34	.256	.343	0	0	3B-57, OF-30, C-27, 2B-10
1893	126	470	136	21	14	8	1.7	94	70	76	65	32	.289	.445	0	0	2B-82, 3B-45
1894	123	492	168	22	10	8	1.6	135	82	77	42	51	.341	.476	0	0	2B-123
1895	120	455	128	17	8	2	0.4	89	68	52	52	28	.281	.367	0	0	2B-120
1896	67	224	63	13	6	3	1.3	43	29	33	25	19	.281	.433	0	0	2B-66, C-1
1898	23	73	24	3	1	0	0.0	11	11	14		6	.329	.397	0	0	2B-23
1899	141	498	156	24	9	5	1.0	95	88	69		43	.313	.428	0	0	2B-141
1900	97	343	107	17	3	4	1.2	72	55	46		27	.312	.414	0	0	2B-93, 1B-3, OF-2
1901	133	520	164	38	10	3	0.6	88	90	42		31	.315	.444	0	0	2B-133
1902 CHI A	137	489	110	22	3	1	0.2	57	54	55		19	.225	.288	0	0	2B-137
1903 2 teams	CHI A (43G – .207)				CIN N (80G – .293)												
" total	123	457	121	25	9	1	0.2	62	57	36		11	.265	.365	1	0	2B-122
16 yrs.	1564	5684	1582	262	103	49	0.9	1024	811	687	401	385	.278	.387	1	0	2B-1056, C-306, 3B-102, OF-55, 1B-40, SS-14
2 yrs.	180	639	141	33	3	1	0.2	77	73	75		25	.221	.286	0	0	2B-180

Wally Dashiell
DASHIELL, JOHN WALLACE   BR TR 5'9½" 170 lbs.
B. May 9, 1901, Jewett, Tex.   D. May 20, 1972, Pensacola, Fla.

	G	AB	H	2B	3B	HR	HR%	R	RBI	BB	SO	SB	BA	SA	PH AB	PH H	G by POS
1924 CHI A	1	2	0	0	0	0	0.0	0	0	0	0	0	.000	.000	0	0	SS-1

George Davis
DAVIS, GEORGE STACEY   BB TR 5'9" 180 lbs.
B. Aug. 23, 1870, Cohoes, N.Y.   D. Oct. 17, 1940, Philadelphia, Pa.
Manager 1895, 1900-01.

	G	AB	H	2B	3B	HR	HR%	R	RBI	BB	SO	SB	BA	SA	PH AB	PH H	G by POS
1890 CLE N	136	526	139	22	9	6	1.1	98	73	53	34	22	.264	.375	0	0	OF-133, 2B-2, SS-1
1891	136	571	167	35	12	3	0.5	115	89	53	29	42	.292	.412	0	0	OF-116, 3B-22, P-3
1892	144	597	151	27	12	5	0.8	96	82	58	51	36	.253	.363	0	0	3B-79, OF-44, SS-20, 2B-3
1893 NY N	133	549	199	22	27	11	2.0	112	119	42	20	37	.362	.561	0	0	3B-133, SS-1
1894	124	492	170	28	20	9	1.8	124	91	66	10	40	.346	.539	0	0	3B-124
1895	110	433	143	32	11	5	1.2	106	101	55	12	48	.330	.490	0	0	3B-81, 1B-14, 2B-10, OF-7
1896	124	494	158	25	12	6	1.2	98	99	50	24	48	.320	.455	0	0	3B-74, SS-45, OF-3, 1B-3
1897	131	525	188	34	11	9	1.7	114	134	41		65	.358	.516	0	0	SS-130
1898	121	486	149	20	5	2	0.4	80	86	32		26	.307	.381	0	0	SS-121
1899	108	416	144	21	5	1	0.2	68	57	37		34	.346	.428	0	0	SS-108
1900	114	426	138	20	4	3	0.7	69	61	35		29	.324	.411	0	0	SS-114
1901	130	495	153	26	7	7	1.4	69	65	40		27	.309	.432	0	0	SS-113, 3B-17
1902 CHI A	132	485	145	27	7	3	0.6	76	93	65		31	.299	.402	1	1	SS-129, 1B-3
1903 NY N	4	15	4	0	0	0	0.0	2	1	1		0	.267	.267	0	0	SS-4
1904 CHI A	152	563	142	27	15	1	0.2	75	69	43		32	.252	.359	0	0	SS-152
1905	157	550	153	29	1	1	0.2	74	55	60		31	.278	.340	0	0	SS-157
1906	133	484	134	26	6	0	0.0	63	80	41		27	.277	.355	3	1	SS-129, 2B-1
1907	132	466	111	16	2	1	0.2	59	52	47		15	.238	.288	0	0	SS-131
1908	128	419	91	14	1	0	0.0	41	26	41		22	.217	.255	5	1	2B-95, SS-23, 1B-4
1909	28	68	9	1	0	0	0.0	5	2	10		4	.132	.147	14	0	1B-17, 2B-2
20 yrs.	2377	9060	2688	452	167	73	0.8	1544	1435	870	180	616	.297	.408	23	4	SS-1378, 3B-530, OF-303, 2B-113, 1B-41, P-3
7 yrs.	862	3035	785	140	32	6	0.2	393	377	307		162	.259	.332	23	4	SS-721, 2B-98, 1B-24

WORLD SERIES
| 1906 CHI A | 3 | 13 | 4 | 3 | 0 | 0 | 0.0 | 4 | 6 | 0 | 1 | 1 | .308 | .538 | 0 | 0 | SS-3 |

Ike Davis
DAVIS, ISAAC MARION   BR TR 5'7" 155 lbs.
B. June 14, 1895, Pueblo, Colo.

	G	AB	H	2B	3B	HR	HR%	R	RBI	BB	SO	SB	BA	SA	PH AB	PH H	G by POS
1919 WAS A	8	14	0	0	0	0	0.0	0	0	0	6	0	.000	.000	0	0	SS-4
1924 CHI A	10	33	8	1	1	0	0.0	5	4	2	5	0	.242	.333	5	0	SS-10
1925	146	562	135	31	9	0	0.0	105	61	71	58	19	.240	.327	2	1	SS-144
3 yrs.	164	609	143	32	10	0	0.0	110	65	73	69	19	.235	.320	7	1	SS-158
2 yrs.	156	595	143	32	10	0	0.0	110	65	73	63	19	.240	.328	7	1	SS-154

Tommy Davis
DAVIS, HERMAN THOMAS   BR TR 6'2" 195 lbs.
B. Mar. 21, 1939, Brooklyn, N.Y.

	G	AB	H	2B	3B	HR	HR%	R	RBI	BB	SO	SB	BA	SA	PH AB	PH H	G by POS
1959 LA N	1	1	0	0	0	0	0.0	0	1	0	.000		.000	1	0		
1960	110	352	97	18	1	11	3.1	49	44	13	35	6	.276	.426	21	7	OF-87, 3B-5
1961	132	460	128	13	2	15	3.3	60	58	32	53	10	.278	.413	10	3	OF-86, 3B-59
1962	163	665	230	27	9	27	4.1	120	153	33	65	18	.346	.535	2	0	OF-146, 3B-39
1963	146	556	181	19	3	16	2.9	69	88	29	59	15	.326	.457	3	0	OF-129, 3B-40
1964	152	592	163	20	5	14	2.4	70	86	29	68	11	.275	.397	4	2	OF-148
1965	17	60	15	1	1	0	0.0	3	9	2	4	2	.250	.300	1	0	OF-16
1966	100	313	98	16	1	3	1.0	27	27	16	36	3	.313	.383	22	5	OF-79, 3B-2
1967 NY N	154	577	174	32	0	16	2.8	72	73	31	71	9	.302	.440	4	0	OF-149, 1B-1
1968 CHI A	132	456	122	5	3	8	1.8	30	50	16	48	4	.268	.344	12	4	OF-116, 1B-6
1969 2 teams	SEA A (123G – .271)				HOU N (24G – .241)												
" total	147	533	142	32	1	7	1.3	54	89	38	55	20	.266	.370	16	7	OF-133, 1B-1
1970 3 teams	HOU N (57G – .282)				OAK A (66G – .290)				CHI N (11G – .262)								
" total	134	455	129	23	3	6	1.3	45	65	16	44	10	.284	.387	23	5	OF-108, 1B-8
1971 OAK A	79	219	71	8	1	3	1.4	26	42	15	19	7	.324	.411	28	13	1B-35, OF-16, 2B-3, 3B-2
1972 2 teams	CHI N (15G – .269)				BAL A (26G – .256)												
" total	41	108	28	4	0	0	0.0	12	12	8	21	2	.259	.296	15	3	OF-20, 1B-6
1973 BAL A	137	552	169	21	3	7	1.3	52	89	30	56	11	.306	.393	6	4	DH-127, 1B-4
1974	158	626	181	20	1	11	1.8	67	84	34	49	6	.289	.377	4	1	DH-155
1975	116	460	130	14	1	6	1.3	43	57	23	52	2	.283	.357	4	1	DH-111

Player Register

	G	AB	H	2B	3B	HR	HR%	R	RBI	BB	SO	SB	BA	SA	Pinch Hit AB	H	G by POS

Tommy Davis continued

	G	AB	H	2B	3B	HR	HR%	R	RBI	BB	SO	SB	BA	SA	PH AB	PH H	G by POS
1976 2 teams	CAL A (72G – .265)					KC A (8G – .263)											
" total	80	238	63	5	0	3	1.3	17	26	16	18	0	.265	.324	21	8	DH-56, 1B-1
18 yrs.	1999	7223	2121	273	35	153	2.1	810	1052	381	754	136	.294	.405	197	63	OF-1233, DH-449, 3B-147, 1B-62, 2B-3
1 yr.	132	456	122	5	3	8	1.8	30	50	16	48	4	.268	.344	12	4	OF-116, 1B-6

LEAGUE CHAMPIONSHIP SERIES

1971 OAK A	3	8	3	1	0	0	0.0	1	0	0	0	0	.375	.500	1	0	1B-2
1973 BAL A	5	21	6	1	0	0	0.0	1	2	1	0	0	.286	.333	0	0	DH-5
1974	4	15	4	0	0	0	0.0	0	1	0	1	0	.267	.267	0	0	DH-4
3 yrs.	12	44	13	2	0	0	0.0	2	3	1	1	0	.295	.341	1	0	DH-9, 1B-2

WORLD SERIES

1963 LA N	4	15	6	2	0	0	0.0	0	2	0	2	1	.400	.667	0	0	OF-4
1966	4	8	2	0	0	0	0.0	0	0	1	1	0	.250	.250	2	2	OF-3
2 yrs.	8	23	8	2	0	0	0.0	0	2	1	3	1	.348	.522	2	2	OF-7

Jim Delsing

DELSING, JAMES HENRY
B. Nov. 13, 1925, Rudolph, Wis.   BL TR 5'10" 175 lbs.

1948 CHI A	20	63	12	0	0	0	0.0	5	5	5	12	0	.190	.190	4	0	OF-15
1949 NY A	9	20	7	1	0	1	5.0	5	3	1	2	0	.350	.550	4	2	OF-5
1950 2 teams	NY A (12G – .400)					STL A (69G – .263)											
" total	81	219	59	5	2	0	0.0	27	17	22	23	1	.269	.311	24	8	OF-53
1951 STL A	131	449	112	20	2	8	1.8	59	45	56	39	2	.249	.356	4	1	OF-124
1952 2 teams	STL A (93G – .255)					DET A (33G – .274)											
" total	126	411	107	15	7	4	1.0	48	49	36	37	4	.260	.360	11	4	OF-117
1953 DET A	138	479	138	26	6	11	2.3	77	62	66	39	1	.288	.436	6	1	OF-133
1954	122	371	92	24	2	6	1.6	39	38	49	38	4	.248	.372	13	5	OF-108
1955	114	356	85	14	2	10	2.8	49	60	48	40	2	.239	.374	14	3	OF-101
1956 2 teams	DET A (10G – .000)					CHI A (55G – .122)											
" total	65	53	5	3	0	0	0.0	11	2	13	16	1	.094	.151	21	3	OF-32
1960 KC A	16	40	10	3	0	0	0.0	2	5	3	5	0	.250	.325	6	1	OF-10
10 yrs.	822	2461	627	111	21	40	1.6	322	286	299	251	15	.255	.366	107	28	OF-698
2 yrs.	75	104	17	3	0	0	0.0	16	7	15	25	1	.163	.192	21	3	OF-44

Joe DeMaestri

DeMAESTRI, JOSEPH PAUL (Oats)
B. Dec. 9, 1928, San Francisco, Calif.   BR TR 6' 170 lbs.

1951 CHI A	56	74	15	0	2	1	1.4	8	3	5	11	0	.203	.297	6	1	SS-27, 2B-11, 3B-8
1952 STL A	81	186	42	9	1	1	0.5	13	18	8	25	0	.226	.301	1	0	SS-77, 3B-1, 2B-1
1953 PHI A	111	420	107	17	3	6	1.4	53	35	24	39	0	.255	.352	0	0	SS-108
1954	146	539	124	16	3	8	1.5	49	40	20	63	1	.230	.315	3	0	SS-142, 3B-1, 2B-1
1955 KC A	123	457	114	14	1	6	1.3	42	37	20	47	3	.249	.324	1	1	SS-122
1956	133	434	101	16	1	6	1.4	41	39	25	73	3	.233	.316	1	0	SS-132, 2B-2
1957	135	461	113	14	6	9	2.0	44	33	22	82	6	.245	.360	1	0	SS-134
1958	139	442	97	11	1	6	1.4	32	38	16	84	1	.219	.290	2	1	SS-137
1959	118	352	86	16	5	6	1.7	31	34	28	65	1	.244	.369	2	0	SS-115
1960 NY A	49	35	8	1	0	0	0.0	8	2	0	9	0	.229	.257	7	1	2B-19, SS-17
1961	30	41	6	0	0	0	0.0	1	2	0	13	0	.146	.146	0	0	SS-18, 2B-5, 3B-4
11 yrs.	1121	3441	813	114	23	49	1.4	322	281	168	511	15	.236	.325	24	4	SS-1029, 2B-39, 3B-14
1 yr.	56	74	15	0	2	1	1.4	8	3	5	11	0	.203	.297	6	1	SS-27, 2B-11, 3B-8

WORLD SERIES

| 1960 NY A | 4 | 2 | 1 | 0 | 0 | 0 | 0.0 | 1 | 0 | 0 | 1 | 0 | .500 | .500 | 0 | 0 | SS-3 |

Ray Demmitt

DEMMITT, CHARLES RAYMOND
B. Feb. 2, 1884, Illiopolis, Ill. D. Feb. 19, 1956, Glen Ellyn, Ill.   BL TR

1909 NY A	123	427	105	12	12	4	0.9	68	30	55		16	.246	.358	0	0	OF-109
1910 STL A	10	23	4	1	0	0	0.0	4	2	3		0	.174	.217	2	0	OF-8
1914 2 teams	DET A (1G – .000)					CHI A (146G – .258)											
" total	147	515	133	13	12	2	0.4	63	46	61	48	12	.258	.342	3	1	OF-142
1915 CHI A	9	6	0	0	0	0	0.0	0	0	1	2	0	.000	.000	6	0	OF-3
1917 STL A	14	53	15	1	2	0	0.0	6	7	0	8	1	.283	.377	0	0	OF-14
1918	116	405	114	23	5	1	0.2	45	61	38	35	10	.281	.370	1	0	OF-114
1919	79	202	48	11	2	1	0.5	19	19	14	27	3	.238	.327	27	6	OF-49
7 yrs.	498	1631	419	61	33	8	0.5	205	165	172	120	42	.257	.349	39	7	OF-439
2 yrs.	155	521	133	13	12	2	0.4	63	46	62	50	12	.255	.338	9	1	OF-145

Bucky Dent

DENT, RUSSELL EARL
B. Nov. 25, 1951, Savannah, Ga.   BR TR 5'9" 170 lbs.

1973 CHI A	40	117	29	2	0	0	0.0	17	10	10	18	2	.248	.265	1	0	SS-36, 2B-3, 3B-1
1974	154	496	136	15	3	5	1.0	55	45	28	48	3	.274	.347	0	0	SS-154
1975	157	602	159	29	4	3	0.5	52	58	36	48	2	.264	.341	0	0	SS-157
1976	158	562	138	18	4	2	0.4	44	52	43	45	3	.246	.302	1	0	SS-158
1977 NY A	158	477	118	18	4	8	1.7	54	49	39	28	1	.247	.352	0	0	SS-157
1978	123	379	92	11	1	5	1.3	40	40	23	24	3	.243	.317	0	0	SS-123
1979	141	431	99	14	2	2	0.5	47	32	37	30	0	.230	.285	0	0	SS-141
1980	141	489	128	26	2	5	1.0	57	52	48	37	0	.262	.354	0	0	SS-141
1981	73	227	54	11	0	7	3.1	22	27	19	17	0	.238	.379	0	0	SS-73
1982 2 teams	NY A (59G – .169)					TEX A (46G – .219)											
" total	105	306	59	10	1	1	0.3	27	23	21	21	0	.193	.242	2	0	SS-103
1983 TEX A	131	417	99	15	2	2	0.5	36	34	23	31	3	.237	.297	0	0	SS-129, DH-1
11 yrs.	1381	4503	1111	169	23	40	0.9	449	422	327	347	17	.247	.321	4	0	SS-1372, 2B-3, DH-1, 3B-1
4 yrs.	509	1777	462	64	11	10	0.6	168	165	117	159	10	.260	.325	2	0	SS-505, 2B-3, 3B-2

LEAGUE CHAMPIONSHIP SERIES

| 1977 NY A | 5 | 14 | 3 | 1 | 0 | 0 | 0.0 | 1 | 2 | 1 | 0 | 0 | .214 | .286 | 0 | 0 | SS-5 |
| 1978 | 4 | 15 | 3 | 0 | 0 | 0 | 0.0 | 0 | 4 | 0 | 0 | 0 | .200 | .200 | 0 | 0 | SS-4 |

244

Player Register

245

	G	AB	H	2B	3B	HR	HR%	R	RBI	BB	SO	SB	BA	SA	Pinch Hit AB	H	G by POS

Bucky Dent continued

| 1980 | 3 | 11 | 2 | 0 | 0 | 0 | 0.0 | 0 | 0 | 0 | 1 | 0 | .182 | .182 | 0 | 0 | SS-3 |
| 3 yrs. | 12 | 40 | 8 | 1 | 0 | 0 | 0.0 | 1 | 6 | 1 | 1 | 0 | .200 | .225 | 0 | 0 | SS-12 |

WORLD SERIES

1977 NY A	6	19	5	0	0	0	0.0	0	2	2	1	0	.263	.263	0	0	SS-6
1978	6	24	10	1	0	0	0.0	3	7	1	2	0	.417	.458	0	0	SS-6
2 yrs.	12	43	15	1	0	0	0.0	3	9	3	3	0	.349	.372	0	0	SS-12

Sam Dente

DENTE, SAMUEL JOSEPH (Blackie)
B. Apr. 26, 1922, Harrison, N. J.   BR TR 5'11" 175 lbs.

1947 BOS A	46	168	39	4	2	0	0.0	14	11	19	15	0	.232	.280	0	0	3B-46
1948 STL A	98	267	72	11	2	0	0.0	26	22	22	8	1	.270	.326	17	5	SS-76, 3B-6
1949 WAS A	153	590	161	24	4	1	0.2	48	53	31	24	4	.273	.332	0	0	SS-153
1950	155	603	144	20	5	2	0.3	56	59	39	19	1	.239	.299	0	0	SS-128, 2B-29
1951	88	273	65	8	1	0	0.0	21	29	25	10	3	.238	.275	14	2	SS-65, 2B-10, 3B-5
1952 CHI A	62	145	32	0	1	0	0.0	12	11	5	8	0	.221	.234	12	1	SS-27, 3B-18, OF-6, 2B-6, 1B-2
1953	2	0	0	0	0	0	—	0	0	0	0	0	—	—	0	0	SS-1
1954 CLE A	68	169	45	7	1	1	0.6	18	19	14	4	0	.266	.337	1	1	SS-60, 2B-7
1955	73	105	27	4	0	0	0.0	10	10	12	8	0	.257	.295	3	1	SS-53, 3B-13, 2B-4
9 yrs.	745	2320	585	78	16	4	0.2	205	214	167	96	9	.252	.305	47	10	SS-563, 3B-88, 2B-56, OF-6, 1B-2
2 yrs.	64	145	32	0	1	0	0.0	12	11	5	8	0	.221	.234	12	1	SS-28, 3B-18, OF-6, 2B-6, 1B-2

WORLD SERIES

| 1954 CLE A | 3 | 3 | 0 | 0 | 0 | 0 | 0.0 | 1 | 0 | 1 | 0 | 0 | .000 | .000 | 0 | 0 | SS-3 |

Bernie DeViveiros

DeVIVEIROS, BERNARD JOHN
B. Apr. 19, 1901, Oakland, Calif.   BR TR 5'7" 160 lbs.

1924 CHI A	1	1	0	0	0	0	0.0	0	0	0	0	0	.000	.000	0	0	SS-1
1927 DET A	24	22	5	1	0	0	0.0	4	2	2	8	1	.227	.273	2	0	SS-14, 3B-1
2 yrs.	25	23	5	1	0	0	0.0	4	2	2	8	1	.217	.261	2	0	SS-15, 3B-1
1 yr.	1	1	0	0	0	0	0.0	0	0	0	0	0	.000	.000	0	0	SS-1

Al DeVormer

DeVORMER, ALBERT E.
B. Aug. 19, 1891, Grand Rapids, Mich.   D. Aug. 29, 1966, Grand Rapids, Mich.   BR TR 6'½" 175 lbs.

1918 CHI A	8	19	5	2	0	0	0.0	2	0	0	4	1	.263	.368	1	0	C-6, OF-1
1921 NY A	22	49	17	4	0	0	0.0	6	7	2	4	2	.347	.429	5	1	C-17
1922	24	59	12	4	1	0	0.0	8	11	1	6	0	.203	.305	4	1	C-17, 1B-1
1923 BOS A	74	209	54	7	3	0	0.0	20	18	6	21	3	.258	.321	12	3	C-55, 1B-2
1927 NY N	68	141	35	3	1	2	1.4	14	21	11	11	1	.248	.326	8	4	C-54, 1B-3
5 yrs.	196	477	123	20	5	2	0.4	50	57	20	46	7	.258	.333	30	9	C-149, 1B-6, OF-1
1 yr.	8	19	5	2	0	0	0.0	2	0	0	4	1	.263	.368	1	0	C-6, OF-1

WORLD SERIES

| 1921 NY A | 2 | 1 | 0 | 0 | 0 | 0 | 0.0 | 0 | 0 | 0 | 0 | 0 | .000 | .000 | 0 | 0 | C-1 |

George Dickey

DICKEY, GEORGE WILLARD (Skeets)
Brother of Bill Dickey.
B. July 10, 1915, Kensett, Ark.   D. June 16, 1976, DeWitt, Ark.   BB TR 6'2" 180 lbs.

1935 BOS A	5	11	0	0	0	0	0.0	1	1	1	3	0	.000	.000	1	0	C-4
1936	10	23	1	0	0	0	0.0	0	0	2	3	0	.043	.087	0	0	C-10
1941 CHI A	32	55	11	2	0	2	3.6	6	8	5	7	0	.200	.327	14	3	C-17
1942	59	116	27	3	0	1	0.9	6	17	9	11	0	.233	.284	31	9	C-29
1946	37	78	15	1	0	0	0.0	8	1	12	13	0	.192	.205	8	3	C-30
1947	83	211	47	6	0	1	0.5	15	27	34	25	4	.223	.265	4	2	C-80
6 yrs.	226	494	101	12	0	4	0.8	36	54	63	62	4	.204	.253	58	17	C-170
4 yrs.	211	460	100	11	0	4	0.9	35	53	60	56	4	.217	.267	57	17	C-156

Johnny Dickshot

DICKSHOT, JOHN OSCAR
Born John Oscar Dicksus.
B. Jan. 24, 1910, Waukegan, Ill.   BR TR 6' 195 lbs.

1936 PIT N	9	9	2	0	0	0	0.0	2	1	1	2	0	.222	.222	7	1	OF-1
1937	82	264	67	8	4	3	1.1	42	33	26	36	0	.254	.348	15	3	OF-64
1938	29	35	8	0	0	0	0.0	3	4	8	5	3	.229	.229	9	3	OF-10
1939 NY N	10	34	8	0	0	0	0.0	3	5	3	0	0	.235	.235	0	0	OF-10
1944 CHI A	62	162	41	8	5	0	0.0	18	15	13	10	2	.253	.364	20	5	OF-40
1945	130	486	147	19	10	4	0.8	74	58	48	41	18	.302	.407	5	1	OF-124
6 yrs.	322	990	273	35	19	7	0.7	142	116	101	97	23	.276	.371	56	13	OF-249
2 yrs.	192	648	188	27	15	4	0.6	92	73	61	51	20	.290	.397	25	6	OF-164

Steve Dillard

DILLARD, STEPHEN BRADLEY
B. Dec. 8, 1951, Memphis, Tenn.   BR TR 6'1" 180 lbs.

1975 BOS A	1	5	2	0	0	0	0.0	2	0	0	0	1	.400	.400	0	0	2B-1
1976	57	167	46	14	0	1	0.6	22	15	17	20	6	.275	.377	3	1	3B-18, 2B-17, SS-12, DH-7
1977	66	141	34	7	0	1	0.7	22	13	7	13	4	.241	.312	7	1	2B-45, SS-9, DH-6
1978 DET A	56	130	29	5	2	0	0.0	21	7	6	11	1	.223	.292	4	1	2B-41, DH-4
1979 CHI N	89	166	47	6	1	5	3.0	31	24	17	24	1	.283	.422	17	6	2B-60, 3B-9
1980	100	244	55	8	1	4	1.6	31	27	20	54	2	.225	.316	13	3	3B-51, 2B-38, SS-2
1981	53	119	26	7	1	2	1.7	18	11	8	20	0	.218	.345	11	3	2B-32, 3B-7, SS-2
1982 CHI A	16	41	7	3	1	0	0.0	1	5	1	5	0	.171	.293	0	0	2B-16
8 yrs.	438	1013	246	50	6	13	1.3	148	102	76	147	15	.243	.343	52	14	2B-250, 3B-85, SS-25, DH-17
1 yr.	16	41	7	3	1	0	0.0	1	5	1	5	0	.171	.293	0	0	2B-16

Player Register

	G	AB	H	2B	3B	HR	HR%	R	RBI	BB	SO	SB	BA	SA	Pinch Hit AB	Pinch Hit H	G by POS

Bob Dillinger
DILLINGER, ROBERT BERNARD
B. Sept. 17, 1918, Glendale, Calif.
BR TR 5'11½" 170 lbs.

1946 STL A	83	225	63	6	3	0	0.0	33	11	19	32	8	.280	.333	18	8	3B-54, SS-1
1947	137	571	168	23	6	3	0.5	70	37	56	38	34	.294	.371	0	0	3B-137
1948	153	644	207	34	10	2	0.3	110	44	65	34	28	.321	.415	1	0	3B-153
1949	137	544	176	22	13	1	0.2	68	51	51	40	20	.324	.417	4	1	3B-133
1950 2 teams	PHI	A	(84G	–	.309)	PIT	N	(58G	–	.288)							
" total	142	578	174	29	11	4	0.7	78	50	42	42	9	.301	.410	5	0	3B-135
1951 2 teams	PIT	N	(12G	–	.233)	CHI	A	(89G	–	.301)							
" total	101	342	100	9	4	0	0.0	42	20	16	19	5	.292	.342	15	4	3B-80
6 yrs.	753	2904	888	123	47	10	0.3	401	213	249	205	104	.306	.391	43	13	3B-692, SS-1
1 yr.	89	299	90	6	4	0	0.0	39	20	15	17	5	.301	.348	14	4	3B-70

Miguel Dilone
DILONE, MIGUEL ANGEL
Also known as Miguel Angel Reyes.
B. Nov. 1, 1954, Santiago, Dominican Republic
BB TR 6' 160 lbs.

1974 PIT N	12	2	0	0	0	0	0.0	3	0	1	0	2	.000	.000	2	0	OF-2
1975	18	6	0	0	0	0	0.0	8	0	0	1	2	.000	.000	1	0	OF-2
1976	16	17	4	0	0	0	0.0	7	0	0	0	5	.235	.235	4	0	OF-3
1977	29	44	6	0	0	0	0.0	5	0	2	3	12	.136	.136	10	1	OF-17
1978 OAK A	135	258	59	8	0	1	0.4	34	14	23	30	50	.229	.271	1	0	OF-99, 3B-3, DH-1
1979 2 teams	OAK	A	(30G	–	.187)	CHI	A	(43G	–	.306)							
" total	73	127	28	1	2	1	0.8	29	7	8	12	21	.220	.283	2	1	OF-47
1980 CLE A	132	528	180	30	9	0	0.0	82	40	28	45	61	.341	.432	3	0	OF-118, DH-11
1981	72	269	78	5	5	0	0.0	33	19	18	28	29	.290	.346	4	2	OF-56, DH-11
1982	104	379	89	12	3	3	0.8	50	25	25	36	33	.235	.306	12	1	OF-97, DH-1
1983 3 teams	CLE	A	(32G	–	.191)	CHI	A	(4G	–	.000)	PIT	N	(7G	–	.000)		
" total	43	71	13	3	1	0	0.0	17	7	10	9	8	.183	.254	4	0	OF-21, DH-2
10 yrs.	634	1701	457	59	20	5	0.3	268	112	115	160	223	.269	.336	43	5	OF-462, DH-26, 3B-3
1 yr.	4	3	0	0	0	0	0.0	1	0	0	0	1	.000	.000	2	0	DH-2, OF-2

Larry Doby
DOBY, LAWRENCE EUGENE
B. Dec. 13, 1923, Camden, S. C.
Manager 1978
BL TR 6'1" 180 lbs.

1947 CLE A	29	32	5	1	0	0	0.0	3	2	1	11	0	.156	.188	21	4	2B-4, SS-1, 1B-1
1948	121	439	132	23	9	14	3.2	83	66	54	77	9	.301	.490	6	2	OF-114
1949	147	547	153	25	3	24	4.4	106	85	91	90	10	.280	.468	0	0	OF-147
1950	142	503	164	25	5	25	5.0	110	102	98	71	8	.326	.545	2	1	OF-140
1951	134	447	132	27	5	20	4.5	84	69	101	81	4	.295	.512	2	0	OF-132
1952	140	519	143	26	8	32	6.2	104	104	90	111	5	.276	.541	3	1	OF-136
1953	149	513	135	18	5	29	5.7	92	102	96	121	3	.263	.487	3	1	OF-146
1954	153	577	157	18	4	32	5.5	94	126	85	94	3	.272	.484	0	0	OF-153
1955	131	491	143	17	5	26	5.3	91	75	61	100	2	.291	.505	2	0	OF-129
1956 CHI A	140	504	135	22	3	24	4.8	89	102	102	105	0	.268	.466	3	1	OF-137
1957	119	416	120	27	2	14	3.4	57	79	56	79	2	.288	.464	9	1	OF-110
1958 CLE A	89	247	70	10	1	13	5.3	41	45	26	49	0	.283	.490	18	5	OF-68
1959 2 teams	DET	A	(18G	–	.218)	CHI	A	(21G	–	.241)							
" total	39	113	26	4	2	0	0.0	6	12	10	22	1	.230	.301	9	2	OF-28, 1B-2
13 yrs.	1533	5348	1515	243	52	253	4.7	960	969	871	1011	47	.283	.490	78	18	OF-1440, 2B-4, 1B-3, SS-1
3 yrs.	280	978	269	50	6	38	3.9	147	190	160	197	3	.275	.455	20	4	OF-259, 1B-2

WORLD SERIES

1948 CLE A	6	22	7	1	0	1	4.5	1	2	2	4	0	.318	.500	0	0	OF-6
1954	4	16	2	0	0	0	0.0	0	0	2	4	0	.125	.125	0	0	OF-4
2 yrs.	10	38	9	1	0	1	2.6	1	2	4	8	0	.237	.342	0	0	OF-10

Cozy Dolan
DOLAN, PATRICK HENRY
B. Dec. 3, 1872, Cambridge, Mass.   D. Mar. 29, 1907, Louisville, Ky.
BL TL 5'10" 160 lbs.

1895 BOS N	26	83	20	4	1	0	0.0	12	7	6	7	3	.241	.313	0	0	P-25, OF-1
1896	6	14	2	0	0	0	0.0	4	0	0		1	.143	.143	0	0	P-6
1900 CHI N	13	48	13	1	0	0	0.0	5	2	2		2	.271	.292	0	0	OF-13
1901 2 teams	CHI	N	(43G	–	.263)	BKN	N	(66G	–	.261)							
" total	109	424	111	12	3	0	0.0	62	45	24		10	.262	.304	4	1	OF-105
1902 BKN N	141	592	166	16	7	1	0.2	72	54	33		24	.280	.336	0	0	OF-141
1903 2 teams	CHI	A	(27G	–	.260)	CIN	N	(93G	–	.288)							
" total	120	489	138	25	4	0	0.0	80	65	34		16	.282	.350	4	0	OF-97, 1B-19
1904 CIN N	129	465	132	8	10	6	1.3	88	51	39		19	.284	.383	3	0	OF-102, 1B-24
1905 2 teams	CIN	N	(22G	–	.234)	BOS	N	(112G	–	.275)							
" total	134	510	137	13	8	0	0.0	51	52	34		23	.269	.343	0	0	OF-120, 1B-15, P-2
1906 BOS N	152	549	136	20	4	0	0.0	54	39	55		17	.248	.299	0	0	OF-144, 2B-7, P-2, 1B-1
9 yrs.	830	3174	855	99	37	7	0.2	428	315	227	8	114	.269	.333	11	1	OF-723, 1B-59, P-35, 2B-7
1 yr.	27	104	27	5	1	0	0.0	16	7	6		5	.260	.327	4	0	1B-19, OF-4

Jiggs Donahue
DONAHUE, JOHN AUGUSTUS
Brother of Pat Donahue.
B. July 13, 1879, Springfield, Ohio   D. July 19, 1913, Columbus, Ohio
BL TL 6'1" 178 lbs.

1900 PIT N	3	10	2	0	1	0	0.0	1	3	0		1	.200	.400	0	0	C-2, OF-1
1901 2 teams	PIT	N	(2G	–	.000)	MIL	A	(37G	–	.318)							
" total	39	107	34	5	4	0	0.0	10	16	10		4	.318	.439	5	0	C-20, 1B-13, OF-1
1902 STL A	30	89	21	1	4	1	1.1	11	7	12		2	.236	.303	2	0	C-23, 1B-5
1904 CHI A	102	367	91	9	7	1	0.3	46	48	25		18	.248	.319	1	1	1B-101
1905	149	533	153	22	4	1	0.2	71	76	44		32	.287	.349	0	0	1B-149
1906	154	556	143	17	7	1	0.2	70	57	48		36	.257	.318	0	0	1B-154
1907	157	609	158	16	4	0	0.0	75	68	28		27	.259	.299	0	0	1B-157
1908	93	304	62	8	2	0	0.0	22	22	25		14	.204	.243	10	1	1B-83
1909 2 teams	CHI	A	(2G	–	.000)	WAS	A	(84G	–	.237)							
" total	86	287	67	12	1	0	0.0	13	30	23		9	.233	.282	3	2	1B-83
9 yrs.	813	2862	731	90	31	4	0.1	319	327	215		143	.255	.313	21	4	1B-745, C-45, OF-2
6 yrs.	657	2373	607	72	24	3	0.1	284	273	171		127	.256	.310	11	2	1B-646

Player Register

	G	AB	H	2B	3B	HR	HR%	R	RBI	BB	SO	SB	BA	SA	Pinch Hit AB H	G by POS

Jiggs Donahue continued
WORLD SERIES
| 1906 CHI A | 6 | 18 | 6 | 2 | 1 | 0 | 0.0 | 0 | 4 | 3 | 4 | 0 | .333 | .556 | 0 0 | 1B-6 |

Charlie Dorman
DORMAN, DWIGHT DEXTER (Red)   BR TR 5'10½" 180 lbs.
B. Oct. 3, 1903, Merritt, Ill.

1923 CHI A	1	2	1	0	0	0	0.0	0	0	0	0	0	.500	.500	0 0	C-1
1928 CLE A	25	77	28	6	0	0	0.0	12	11	9	6	1	.364	.442	1 1	OF-24
2 yrs.	26	79	29	6	0	0	0.0	12	11	9	6	1	.367	.443	1 1	OF-24, C-1
1 yr.	1	2	1	0	0	0	0.0	0	0	0	0	0	.500	.500	0 0	C-1

Patsy Dougherty
DOUGHERTY, PATRICK HENRY   BL TR 6'2" 190 lbs.
B. Oct. 27, 1876, Andover, N.Y.   D. Apr. 30, 1940, Bolivar, N.Y.

1902 BOS A	108	438	150	12	6	0	0.0	77	34	42		20	.342	.397	3 2	OF-102, 3B-1
1903	139	590	195	19	12	4	0.7	108	59	33		35	.331	.424	0 0	OF-139
1904 2 teams		BOS A (49G – .272)				NY A (106G – .283)										
" total	155	647	181	18	14	5	0.8	113	26	44		21	.280	.374	0 0	OF-155
1905 NY A	116	418	110	9	6	3	0.7	56	29	28		17	.263	.335	5 1	OF-108, 3B-1
1906 2 teams		NY A (12G – .192)				CHI A (75G – .233)										
" total	87	305	69	11	4	1	0.3	33	31	19		11	.226	.298	0 0	OF-86
1907 CHI A	148	533	144	17	2	2	0.4	69	59	36		33	.270	.321	0 0	OF-148
1908	138	482	134	11	6	0	0.0	68	45	58		47	.278	.326	9 2	OF-138
1909	139	491	140	23	13	1	0.2	71	55	51		36	.285	.391	1 0	OF-138
1910	127	443	110	8	6	1	0.2	45	43	41		22	.248	.303	3 1	OF-121
1911	76	211	61	10	9	0	0.0	39	32	26		19	.289	.422	19 3	OF-56
10 yrs.	1233	4558	1294	138	78	17	0.4	679	413	378		261	.284	.360	40 9	OF-1191, 3B-2
6 yrs.	703	2413	648	78	40	5	0.2	322	261	231		168	.269	.340	32 6	OF-675

WORLD SERIES
1903 BOS A	8	34	8	0	2	2	5.9	3	5	2	5	0	.235	.529	0 0	OF-8
1906 CHI A	6	20	2	0	0	0	0.0	1	1	3	3	2	.100	.100	0 0	OF-6
2 yrs.	14	54	10	0	2	2	3.7	4	6	5	8	2	.185	.370	0 0	OF-14

Brian Downing
DOWNING, BRIAN JAY   BR TR 5'10" 170 lbs.
B. Oct. 9, 1950, Los Angeles, Calif.

1973 CHI A	34	73	13	1	0	2	2.7	4	4	10	17	0	.178	.274	8 2	OF-13, C-11, 3B-8
1974	108	293	66	12	1	10	3.4	41	39	51	72	0	.225	.375	5 0	C-63, OF-39, DH-9
1975	138	420	101	12	1	7	1.7	58	41	76	75	13	.240	.324	0 0	C-137, DH-1
1976	104	317	81	14	0	3	0.9	38	30	40	55	7	.256	.328	3 1	C-93, DH-11
1977	69	169	48	4	2	4	2.4	28	25	34	21	1	.284	.402	3 1	C-61, OF-3, DH-2
1978 CAL A	133	412	105	15	0	7	1.7	42	46	52	47	3	.255	.342	3 1	C-128, DH-2
1979	148	509	166	27	3	12	2.4	87	75	77	57	3	.326	.462	3 1	C-129, DH-18
1980	30	93	27	6	0	2	2.2	5	25	12	12	0	.290	.419	2 0	C-16, DH-13
1981	93	317	79	14	0	9	2.8	47	41	46	35	1	.249	.379	2 1	OF-56, C-37, DH-5
1982	158	623	175	37	2	28	4.5	109	84	86	58	2	.281	.482	1 0	OF-158
1983	113	403	99	15	1	19	4.7	68	53	62	59	1	.246	.429	3 1	OF-84, DH-26
11 yrs.	1128	3629	960	157	10	103	2.8	527	463	546	508	31	.265	.398	33 7	C-675, OF-353, DH-87, 3B-8
5 yrs.	453	1272	309	43	4	26	2.0	169	139	211	240	21	.243	.344	19 4	C-365, OF-55, DH-23, 3B-8

LEAGUE CHAMPIONSHIP SERIES
1979 CAL A	4	15	3	0	0	0	0.0	1	1	1	1	0	.200	.200	0 0	C-4
1982	5	19	3	1	0	0	0.0	4	0	3	2	0	.158	.211	0 0	OF-5
2 yrs.	9	34	6	1	0	0	0.0	5	1	4	3	0	.176	.206	0 0	OF-5, C-4

Walt Dropo
DROPO, WALTER (Moose)   BR TR 6'5" 220 lbs.
B. Jan. 30, 1923, Moosup, Conn.

1949 BOS A	11	41	6	2	0	0	0.0	3	1	3	7	0	.146	.195	0 0	1B-11
1950	136	559	180	28	8	34	6.1	101	144	45	75	0	.322	.583	2 0	1B-134
1951	99	360	86	14	0	11	3.1	37	57	38	52	0	.239	.369	7 2	1B-93
1952 2 teams		BOS A (37G – .265)				DET A (115G – .279)										
" total	152	591	163	24	4	29	4.9	69	97	37	85	2	.276	.477	2 0	1B-150
1953 DET A	152	606	150	30	3	13	2.1	61	96	29	69	2	.248	.371	2 1	1B-150
1954	107	320	90	14	2	4	1.3	27	44	24	41	0	.281	.375	18 5	1B-95
1955 CHI A	141	453	127	15	2	19	4.2	55	79	42	71	0	.280	.448	2 1	1B-140
1956	125	361	96	13	1	8	2.2	42	52	37	51	1	.266	.374	10 2	1B-117
1957	93	223	57	2	0	13	5.8	24	49	16	40	0	.256	.439	31 11	1B-69
1958 2 teams		CHI A (28G – .192)				CIN N (63G – .290)										
" total	91	214	57	8	2	9	4.2	21	39	17	42	0	.266	.449	31 7	1B-59
1959 2 teams		CIN N (26G – .103)				BAL A (62G – .278)										
" total	88	190	46	10	0	4	2.1	21	23	16	27	0	.242	.405	11 1	1B-77, 3B-2
1960 BAL A	79	179	48	8	0	4	2.2	16	21	20	19	0	.268	.380	14 2	1B-67, 3B-1
1961	14	27	7	0	0	1	3.7	1	2	4	4	3	.259	.370	2 1	1B-12
13 yrs.	1288	4124	1113	168	22	152	3.7	478	704	328	582	5	.270	.432	132 33	1B-1174, 3B-3
4 yrs.	387	1089	290	31	3	42	3.9	124	188	100	173	1	.266	.416	54 16	1B-342

Hugh Duffy
DUFFY, HUGH   BR TR 5'7" 168 lbs.
B. Nov. 26, 1866, Cranston, R.I.   D. Oct. 19, 1954, Allston, Mass.
Manager 1901, 1904-06, 1910-11, 1921-22.
Hall of Fame 1945.

1888 CHI N	71	298	84	10	4	7	2.3	60	41	9	32	13	.282	.413	0 0	OF-67, SS-3, 3B-1
1889	136	584	182	21	7	12	2.1	144	89	46	30	52	.312	.433	0 0	OF-126, SS-10
1890 CHI P	137	596	194	36	16	7	1.2	161	82	59	20	79	.326	.475	0 0	OF-137
1891 BOS AA	127	536	180	20	8	8	1.5	134	108	61	29	85	.336	.448	0 0	OF-124, 3B-3, SS-1
1892 BOS N	147	612	184	28	12	5	0.8	125	81	60	37	61	.301	.410	0 0	OF-146, 3B-2
1893	131	560	203	23	7	6	1.1	147	118	50	13	50	.363	.461	0 0	OF-131
1894	124	539	236	50	13	18	3.3	160	145	66	15	49	.438[1]	.679	0 0	OF-124, SS-2
1895	131	540	190	30	6	9	1.7	113	100	63	16	42	.352	.480	0 0	OF-130

Player Register

	G	AB	H	2B	3B	HR	HR%	R	RBI	BB	SO	SB	BA	SA	Pinch Hit AB	H	G by POS

Hugh Duffy continued

	G	AB	H	2B	3B	HR	HR%	R	RBI	BB	SO	SB	BA	SA	PH AB	H	G by POS
1896	131	533	161	16	8	5	0.9	93	112	52	19	45	.302	.390	0	0	OF-126, 2B-9, SS-2
1897	134	554	189	25	10	11	2.0	131	129	52		45	.341	.482	0	0	OF-129, 2B-6, SS-2
1898	152	568	179	13	3	8	1.4	97	108	59		32	.315	.391	0	0	OF-152, 3B-1, 1B-1, C-1
1899	147	588	164	29	7	3	0.5	103	102	39		18	.279	.367	0	0	OF-147
1900	55	181	55	5	4	2	1.1	27	31	16		12	.304	.409	4	1	OF-49, 2B-1
1901 MIL A	79	286	88	15	9	2	0.7	41	45	16		13	.308	.444	2	0	OF-77
1904 PHI N	18	46	13	1	1	0	0.0	10	5	13		3	.283	.348	4	1	OF-14
1905	15	40	12	2	1	0	0.0	7	3	1		0	.300	.400	7	3	OF-8
1906	1	1	0	0	0	0	0.0	0	0	0			.000	.000	1	0	
17 yrs.	1736	7062	2314	324	116	103	1.5	1553	1299	662	211	599	.328	.450	18	5	OF-1687, SS-20, 2B-16, 3B-7, 1B-1, C-1

Gus Dundon

DUNDON, AUGUSTUS TR
B. July 10, 1875, Columbus, Ohio D. Sept. 1, 1940, Columbus, Ohio

	G	AB	H	2B	3B	HR	HR%	R	RBI	BB	SO	SB	BA	SA	PH AB	H	G by POS
1904 CHI A	108	373	85	9	3	0	0.0	40	36	30		19	.228	.268	0	0	2B-103, 3B-3, SS-2
1905	106	364	70	7	3	0	0.0	30	22	23		14	.192	.228	0	0	2B-104, SS-2
1906	33	96	13	1	0	0	0.0	7	4	11		4	.135	.146	1	0	2B-18, SS-14
3 yrs.	247	833	168	17	6	0	0.0	77	62	64		37	.202	.236	1	0	2B-225, SS-18, 3B-3
3 yrs.	247	833	168	17	6	0	0.0	77	62	64		37	.202	.236	1	0	2B-225, SS-18, 3B-3

Jerry Dybzinski

DYBZINSKI, JEROME MATHEW BR TR 6'2" 180 lbs.
B. July 7, 1955, Cleveland, Ohio

	G	AB	H	2B	3B	HR	HR%	R	RBI	BB	SO	SB	BA	SA	PH AB	H	G by POS
1980 CLE A	114	248	57	11	1	1	0.4	32	23	13	35	4	.230	.294	3	0	SS-73, 2B-29, 3B-4, DH-2
1981	48	57	17	0	0	0	0.0	10	6	5	8	7	.298	.298	1	0	SS-34, 3B-3, 2B-3, DH-1
1982	80	212	49	6	2	0	0.0	19	22	21	25	3	.231	.278	2	0	3B-77, 2B-44, SS-1
1983 CHI A	127	256	59	10	1	1	0.4	30	32	18	29	11	.230	.289	1	0	SS-118, 3B-9
4 yrs.	369	773	182	27	4	2	0.3	91	83	57	97	25	.235	.288	7	0	SS-302, 2B-32, 3B-19, DH-3
1 yr.	127	256	59	10	1	1	0.4	30	32	18	29	11	.230	.289	1	0	SS-118, 3B-9

LEAGUE CHAMPIONSHIP SERIES
| 1983 CHI A | 2 | 4 | 1 | 0 | 0 | 0 | 0.0 | 0 | 0 | 0 | 0 | 0 | .250 | .250 | 0 | 0 | SS-2 |

Jimmy Dykes

DYKES, JAMES JOSEPH BR TR 5'9" 185 lbs.
B. Nov. 10, 1896, Philadelphia, Pa. D. June 15, 1976, Philadelphia, Pa.
Manager 1934-46, 1951-54, 1958-61.

	G	AB	H	2B	3B	HR	HR%	R	RBI	BB	SO	SB	BA	SA	PH AB	H	G by POS
1918 PHI A	59	186	35	3	3	0	0.0	13	13	19	32	3	.188	.237	2	0	2B-56, 3B-1
1919	17	49	9	1	0	0	0.0	4	1	7	11	0	.184	.204	0	0	2B-16
1920	142	546	140	25	4	8	1.5	81	35	52	73	6	.256	.361	0	0	2B-108, 3B-36
1921	155	613	168	32	13	17	2.8	88	77	60	75	6	.274	.452	0	0	2B-155
1922	145	501	138	23	7	12	2.4	66	68	55	98	6	.275	.421	0	0	3B-140, 2B-5
1923	124	416	105	28	1	4	1.0	50	43	35	40	6	.252	.353	0	0	2B-102, SS-20, 3B-2
1924	110	410	128	26	6	3	0.7	68	50	38	59	1	.312	.427	2	1	2B-78, 3B-27, SS-4
1925	122	465	150	32	11	5	1.1	93	55	46	49	3	.323	.471	3	2	3B-64, 2B-58, SS-2
1926	124	429	123	32	5	1	0.2	54	44	49	34	6	.287	.392	1	0	3B-77, 2B-44, SS-1
1927	121	417	135	33	6	3	0.7	61	60	44	23	2	.324	.453	5	3	1B-82, 3B-25, OF-5, SS-5, 2B-5, P-2
1928	85	242	67	11	0	5	2.1	39	30	27	21	2	.277	.384	3	0	2B-32, SS-23, 3B-20, 1B-8, OF-1
1929	119	401	131	34	6	13	3.2	76	79	51	25	8	.327	.539	2	0	SS-60, 3B-48, 2B-13
1930	125	435	131	28	4	6	1.4	69	73	74	53	3	.301	.425	1	0	3B-123, OF-1
1931	101	355	97	28	2	3	0.8	48	46	48	47	1	.273	.389	0	0	3B-87, SS-15
1932	153	558	148	29	5	7	1.3	71	90	77	65	8	.265	.373	1	0	3B-141, SS-10, 2B-1
1933 CHI A	151	554	144	22	6	1	0.2	49	68	69	37	3	.260	.327	0	0	3B-151
1934	127	456	122	17	4	7	1.5	52	82	64	28	1	.268	.368	1	1	3B-74, 2B-27, 1B-8
1935	117	403	116	24	2	4	1.0	45	61	59	28	4	.288	.387	1	0	3B-98, 1B-16, 2B-3
1936	127	435	116	16	3	7	1.6	62	60	61	36	1	.267	.366	1	0	3B-125
1937	30	85	26	5	0	1	1.2	10	23	9	7	0	.306	.400	4	2	1B-15, 3B-11
1938	26	89	27	4	2	2	2.2	9	13	10	8	0	.303	.461	1	0	2B-23, 3B-1
1939	2	1	0	0	0	0	0.0	0	0	0	0	0	.000	.000	0	0	3B-2
22 yrs.	2282	8046	2256	453	90	109	1.4	1108	1071	954	849	70	.280	.400	28	9	3B-1253, 2B-726, 1B-148, SS-140, OF-7, P-2
7 yrs.	580	2023	551	88	17	22	1.1	227	307	272	144	9	.272	.365	8	3	3B-462, 1B-58, 2B-5

WORLD SERIES
1929 PHI A	5	19	8	1	0	0	0.0	2	4	1	1	0	.421	.474	0	0	3B-5
1930	6	18	4	3	0	1	5.6	2	5	5	3	0	.222	.556	0	0	3B-6
1931	7	22	5	0	0	0	0.0	2	2	5	1	0	.227	.227	0	0	3B-7
3 yrs.	18	59	17	4	0	1	1.7	6	11	11	5	0	.288	.407	0	0	3B-18

Ted Easterly

EASTERLY, THEODORE HARRISON BL TR
B. Apr. 20, 1886, Lincoln, Neb. D. July 6, 1951, Clear Lake, Calif.

	G	AB	H	2B	3B	HR	HR%	R	RBI	BB	SO	SB	BA	SA	PH AB	H	G by POS
1909 CLE A	98	287	75	14	10	1	0.3	32	27	13		8	.261	.390	22	4	C-76
1910	110	363	111	16	6	0	0.0	34	55	21		10	.306	.383	14	4	C-66, OF-30
1911	99	287	93	19	5	1	0.3	34	37	8		6	.324	.436	23	8	OF-54, C-23
1912 2 teams	CLE A (63G – .296)					CHI A (30G – .364)											
" total	93	241	75	6	0	1	0.4	22	35	9		4	.311	.349	30	13	C-61, OF-1
1913 CHI A	60	97	23	1	0	0	0.0	3	8	4	9	2	.237	.247	37	8	C-19
1914 KC F	134	436	146	20	12	0	0.0	58	67	31		10	.335	.443	6	0	C-128
1915	110	309	84	12	5	3	1.0	32	32	21		2	.272	.372	20	8	C-88
7 yrs.	704	2020	607	88	38	7	0.3	215	261	107	9	42	.300	.392	152	45	C-461, OF-85
2 yrs.	90	152	43	3	0	0	0.0	8	22	6	9	3	.283	.303	55	16	C-29, OF-1

Mike Eden

EDEN, EDWARD MICHAEL BB TR 5'10" 170 lbs.
B. May 22, 1949, Fort Clayton, Canal Zone

	G	AB	H	2B	3B	HR	HR%	R	RBI	BB	SO	SB	BA	SA	PH AB	H	G by POS
1976 ATL N	5	8	0	0	0	0	0.0	0	1	0	0	0	.000	.000	2	0	2B-2

Player Register

	G	AB	H	2B	3B	HR	HR%	R	RBI	BB	SO	SB	BA	SA	Pinch Hit AB H	G by POS

Mike Eden continued
1978 CHI A	10	17	2	0	0	0	0.0	1	0	4	0	0	.118	.118	0 0	SS-5, 2B-4
2 yrs.	15	25	2	0	0	0	0.0	1	1	4	0	0	.080	.080	2 0	2B-6, SS-5
1 yr.	10	17	2	0	0	0	0.0	1	0	4	0	0	.118	.118	0 0	SS-5, 2B-4

Hank Edwards
EDWARDS, HENRY ALBERT BL TL 6' 190 lbs.
B. Jan. 29, 1919, Elmwood Place, Ohio

	G	AB	H	2B	3B	HR	HR%	R	RBI	BB	SO	SB	BA	SA	PH AB H	G by POS
1941 CLE A	16	68	15	1	1	1	1.5	10	6	2	4	0	.221	.309	0 0	OF-16
1942	13	48	12	2	1	0	0.0	6	7	5	8	2	.250	.333	1 0	OF-12
1943	92	297	82	18	6	3	1.0	38	28	30	34	4	.276	.407	15 4	OF-74
1946	124	458	138	33	16	10	2.2	62	54	43	48	1	.301	.509	2 1	OF-123
1947	108	393	102	12	3	15	3.8	54	59	31	55	1	.260	.420	8 3	OF-100
1948	55	160	43	9	2	3	1.9	27	18	18	18	1	.269	.406	12 2	OF-41
1949 2 teams		CLE A (5G – .267)			CHI N (58G – .290)											
" total	63	191	55	8	4	8	4.2	28	22	20	24	0	.288	.497	6 1	OF-56
1950 CHI N	41	110	40	11	1	2	1.8	13	21	10	13	0	.364	.536	10 0	OF-29
1951 2 teams		BKN N (35G – .226)			CIN N (41G – .315)											
" total	76	158	47	12	1	3	1.9	15	23	17	26	0	.297	.443	37 8	OF-34
1952 2 teams		CIN N (74G – .283)			CHI A (8G – .333)											
" total	82	202	58	7	6	6	3.0	26	29	19	24	0	.287	.470	26 4	OF-54
1953 STL A	65	106	21	3	0	0	0.0	6	9	13	10	0	.198	.226	40 12	OF-21
11 yrs.	735	2191	613	116	41	51	2.3	285	276	208	264	9	.280	.440	157 35	OF-560
1 yr.	8	18	6	0	0	0	0.0	0	2	0	2	0	.333	.333	5 2	OF-3

Tom Egan
EGAN, THOMAS PATRICK BR TR 6'4" 218 lbs.
B. June 9, 1946, Los Angeles, Calif.

	G	AB	H	2B	3B	HR	HR%	R	RBI	BB	SO	SB	BA	SA	PH AB H	G by POS
1965 CAL A	18	38	10	0	1	0	0.0	3	1	3	12	0	.263	.316	2 1	C-16
1966	7	11	0	0	0	0	0.0	0	0	1	5	0	.000	.000	0 0	C-6
1967	1	1	0	0	0	0	0.0	0	0	0	0	0	.000	.000	0 0	C-1
1968	16	43	5	1	0	1	2.3	2	4	2	15	0	.116	.209	3 0	C-14
1969	46	120	17	1	0	5	4.2	7	16	17	41	0	.142	.275	1 0	C-46
1970	79	210	50	6	0	4	1.9	14	20	14	67	0	.238	.324	1 0	C-79
1971 CHI A	85	251	60	11	1	10	4.0	29	34	26	94	1	.239	.410	10 5	C-77, 1B-1
1972	50	141	27	3	0	2	1.4	9	8	4	48	0	.191	.255	3 0	C-46
1974 CAL A	43	94	11	0	0	0	0.0	4	4	8	40	1	.117	.117	0 0	C-41
1975	28	70	16	3	1	0	0.0	7	3	5	14	0	.229	.300	0 0	C-28
10 yrs.	373	979	196	25	3	22	2.2	74	91	80	336	2	.200	.299	30 9	C-354, 1B-1
2 yrs.	135	392	87	14	1	12	3.1	37	43	30	142	1	.222	.355	21 8	C-123, 1B-1

Fred Eichrodt
EICHRODT, FREDERICK GEORGE (Ike) BR TR 5'11½" 167 lbs.
B. Jan. 6, 1903, Chicago, Ill. D. July 14, 1965, Indianapolis, Ind.

	G	AB	H	2B	3B	HR	HR%	R	RBI	BB	SO	SB	BA	SA	PH AB H	G by POS
1925 CLE A	15	52	12	3	1	0	0.0	4	4	2	7	0	.231	.327	2 0	OF-13
1926	37	80	25	7	1	0	0.0	14	7	2	11	1	.313	.425	10 2	OF-27
1927	85	267	59	19	2	0	0.0	24	25	16	25	2	.221	.307	4 0	OF-81
1931 CHI A	34	117	25	5	1	0	0.0	9	15	1	8	0	.214	.274	2 1	OF-32
4 yrs.	171	516	121	34	5	0	0.0	51	51	21	51	3	.234	.320	18 3	OF-153
1 yr.	34	117	25	5	1	0	0.0	9	15	1	8	0	.214	.274	2 1	OF-32

Lee Elia
ELIA, LEE CONSTANTINE BR TR 5'11" 175 lbs.
B. July 16, 1937, Philadelphia, Pa.
Manager 1982-83.

	G	AB	H	2B	3B	HR	HR%	R	RBI	BB	SO	SB	BA	SA	PH AB H	G by POS
1966 CHI A	80	195	40	5	2	3	1.5	16	22	15	39	0	.205	.297	1 0	SS-75
1968 CHI N	15	17	3	0	0	0	0.0	1	3	0	6	0	.176	.176	10 2	SS-2, 3B-1, 2B-1
2 yrs.	95	212	43	5	2	3	1.4	17	25	15	45	0	.203	.288	11 2	SS-77, 3B-1, 2B-1
1 yr.	80	195	40	5	2	3	1.5	16	22	15	39	0	.205	.297	1 0	SS-75

Bob Elliott
ELLIOTT, ROBERT IRVING BR TR 6' 185 lbs.
B. Nov. 26, 1916, San Francisco, Calif. D. May 4, 1966, San Diego, Calif.
Manager 1960.

	G	AB	H	2B	3B	HR	HR%	R	RBI	BB	SO	SB	BA	SA	PH AB H	G by POS
1939 PIT N	32	129	43	10	3	3	2.3	18	19	9	4	0	.333	.527	2 0	OF-30
1940	148	551	161	34	11	5	0.9	88	64	45	28	13	.292	.421	1 0	OF-147
1941	141	527	144	24	10	3	0.6	74	76	64	52	6	.273	.374	2 0	OF-139
1942	143	560	166	26	7	9	1.6	75	89	52	35	2	.296	.416	1 0	3B-142, OF-1
1943	156	581	183	30	12	7	1.2	82	101	56	24	4	.315	.444	4 0	3B-141, 2B-2, SS-1
1944	143	538	160	28	16	10	1.9	85	108	75	42	9	.297	.465	3 0	3B-140, SS-1
1945	144	541	157	36	6	8	1.5	80	108	64	38	5	.290	.423	3 0	3B-81, OF-61
1946	140	486	128	25	3	5	1.0	50	68	64	44	6	.263	.358	4 2	OF-92, 3B-43
1947 BOS N	150	555	176	35	5	22	4.0	93	113	87	60	3	.317	.517	2 0	3B-148
1948	151	540	153	24	5	23	4.3	99	100	131	57	6	.283	.474	1 0	3B-150
1949	139	482	135	29	5	17	3.5	77	76	90	38	0	.280	.467	10 5	3B-130
1950	142	531	162	28	5	24	4.5	94	107	68	67	2	.305	.512	5 1	3B-137
1951	136	480	137	29	2	15	3.1	73	70	65	56	2	.285	.448	7 1	3B-127
1952 NY N	98	272	62	6	2	10	3.7	33	35	36	20	1	.228	.375	18 5	OF-65, 3B-13
1953 2 teams		STL A (48G – .250)			CHI A (67G – .260)											
" total	115	368	94	19	2	9	2.4	43	61	61	39	1	.255	.391	8 2	3B-103, OF-2
15 yrs.	1978	7141	2061	383	94	170	2.4	1064	1195	967	604	60	.289	.440	71 14	3B-1365, OF-537, SS-2, 2B-2
1 yr.	67	208	54	11	1	4	1.9	24	32	31	21	1	.260	.380	6 0	3B-58, OF-2

WORLD SERIES
1948 BOS N	6	21	7	0	0	2	9.5	4	5	2	0	0	.333	.619	0 0	3B-6

Roy Elsh
ELSH, EUGENE ROY BR TR 5'9" 165 lbs.
B. Mar. 1, 1896, Pennsgrove, N. J.

	G	AB	H	2B	3B	HR	HR%	R	RBI	BB	SO	SB	BA	SA	PH AB H	G by POS
1923 CHI A	81	209	52	7	2	0	0.0	28	24	16	23	15	.249	.301	15 4	OF-57
1924	60	147	45	9	1	0	0.0	21	11	10	14	6	.306	.381	16 3	OF-38, 1B-2

Player Register

	G	AB	H	2B	3B	HR	HR%	R	RBI	BB	SO	SB	BA	SA	Pinch Hit AB H	G by POS

Roy Elsh continued

1925	32	48	9	1	0	0	0.0	6	4	5	7	2	.188	.208	13 3	OF-16, 1B-3
3 yrs.	173	404	106	17	3	0	0.0	55	39	31	44	23	.262	.319	44 10	OF-111, 1B-5
3 yrs.	173	404	106	17	3	0	0.0	55	39	31	44	23	.262	.319	44 10	OF-111, 1B-5

Charlie English

ENGLISH, CHARLES DEWIE
B. Apr. 8, 1910, Darlington, S. C.
BR TR 5'9½" 160 lbs.

1932 CHI A	24	63	20	3	1	1	1.6	7	8	3	7	0	.317	.444	9 2	3B-13, SS-1
1933	3	9	4	2	0	0	0.0	2	1	1	1	0	.444	.667	0 0	2B-3
1936 NY N	6	1	0	0	0	0	0.0	0	0	0	0	0	.000	.000	1 0	2B-1
1937 CIN	17	63	15	3	1	0	0.0	1	4	0	2	0	.238	.317	0 0	3B-15, 2B-2
4 yrs.	50	136	39	8	2	1	0.7	10	13	4	10	0	.287	.397	10 2	3B-28, 2B-6, SS-1
2 yrs.	27	72	24	5	1	1	1.4	9	9	4	8	0	.333	.472	9 2	3B-13, 2B-3, SS-1

Del Ennis

ENNIS, DELMER
B. June 8, 1925, Philadelphia, Pa.
BR TR 6' 195 lbs.

1946 PHI N	141	540	169	30	6	17	3.1	70	73	39	65	5	.313	.485	3 0	OF-138
1947	139	541	149	25	6	12	2.2	71	81	37	51	9	.275	.410	4 1	OF-135
1948	152	589	171	40	4	30	5.1	86	95	47	58	2	.290	.525	2 1	OF-151
1949	154	610	184	39	11	25	4.1	92	110	59	61	2	.302	.525	0 0	OF-154
1950	153	595	185	34	8	31	5.2	92	126	56	59	2	.311	.551	4 0	OF-149
1951	144	532	142	20	5	15	2.8	66	73	68	42	4	.267	.408	8 2	OF-144
1952	151	592	171	30	10	20	3.4	90	107	47	65	6	.289	.475	2 0	OF-149
1953	152	578	165	22	3	29	5.0	79	125	57	53	1	.285	.484	2 0	OF-150
1954	145	556	145	23	2	25	4.5	73	119	50	60	2	.261	.444	1 0	OF-142, 1B-1
1955	146	564	167	24	7	29	5.1	82	120	46	46	4	.296	.518	1 0	OF-145
1956	153	630	164	23	3	26	4.1	80	95	33	62	7	.260	.430	0 0	OF-153
1957 STL N	136	490	140	24	3	24	4.9	61	105	37	50	1	.286	.494	8 3	OF-127
1958	106	329	86	18	1	3	0.9	22	47	15	35	0	.261	.350	22 2	OF-84
1959 2 teams	CIN N (5G – .333)					CHI A (26G – .219)										
" total	31	108	25	6	0	2	1.9	11	8	6	12	0	.231	.343	3 1	OF-28
14 yrs.	1903	7254	2063	358	69	288	4.0	985	1284	597	719	45	.284	.472	60 10	OF-1849, 1B-1
1 yr.	26	96	21	6	0	2	2.1	10	7	4	10	0	.219	.344	2 1	OF-25

WORLD SERIES
| 1950 PHI N | 4 | 14 | 2 | 1 | 0 | 0 | 0.0 | 1 | 0 | 0 | 1 | 0 | .143 | .214 | 0 0 | OF-4 |

George Enright

ENRIGHT, GEORGE ALBERT
B. May 9, 1954, New Britain, Conn.
BR TR 5'11" 175 lbs.

| 1976 CHI A | 2 | 1 | 0 | 0 | 0 | 0 | 0.0 | 0 | 0 | 0 | 0 | 0 | .000 | .000 | 0 0 | C-2 |

Mutz Ens

ENS, ANTON
Brother of Jewel Ens.
B. Nov. 8, 1884, St. Louis, Mo.   D. June 28, 1950, St. Louis, Mo.
BL TL 6'1" 185 lbs.

| 1912 CHI A | 3 | 6 | 0 | 0 | 0 | 0 | 0.0 | 0 | | 0 | | 0 | .000 | .000 | 0 0 | 1B-3 |

Joe Erautt

ERAUTT, JOSEPH MICHAEL (Stubby)
Brother of Eddie Erautt.
B. Sept. 1, 1921, Vibank, Sask., Canada
BR TR 5'9" 175 lbs.

1950 CHI A	16	18	4	0	0	0	0.0	0	1	1	3	0	.222	.222	10 2	C-5
1951	16	25	4	1	0	0	0.0	3	0	3	2	0	.160	.200	4 1	C-12
2 yrs.	32	43	8	1	0	0	0.0	3	1	4	5	0	.186	.209	14 3	C-17
2 yrs.	32	43	8	1	0	0	0.0	3	1	4	5	0	.186	.209	14 3	C-17

Sammy Esposito

ESPOSITO, SAMUEL
B. Dec. 15, 1931, Chicago, Ill.
BR TR 5'9" 165 lbs.

1952 CHI A	1	4	1	0	0	0	0.0	0	0	0	2	0	.250	.250	0 0	SS-1
1955	3	4	0	0	0	0	0.0	3	0	1	0	0	.000	.000	0 0	3B-2
1956	81	184	42	8	2	3	1.6	30	25	41	19	1	.228	.342	8 1	3B-61, SS-19, 2B-3
1957	94	176	36	5	0	2	1.1	26	15	38	27	5	.205	.256	11 3	3B-53, SS-22, 2B-4, OF-1
1958	98	81	20	3	0	0	0.0	16	3	12	6	1	.247	.284	7 1	3B-63, SS-22, 2B-2, OF-1
1959	69	66	11	1	0	1	1.5	12	5	11	16	0	.167	.227	5 1	3B-45, SS-14, 2B-2
1960	57	77	14	5	0	1	1.3	14	11	10	20	0	.182	.286	4 1	3B-37, SS-11, 2B-5
1961	63	94	16	5	0	1	1.1	12	8	12	21	0	.170	.255	2 0	3B-28, SS-20, 2B-1
1962	75	81	19	1	0	0	0.0	14	4	17	13	0	.235	.247	3 1	3B-41, SS-20, 2B-7
1963 2 teams	CHI A (1G – .000)					KC A (18G – .200)										
" total	19	25	5	1	0	0	0.0	3	2	3	3	0	.200	.240	1 1	2B-7, SS-4, 3B-3
10 yrs.	560	792	164	27	2	8	1.0	130	73	145	127	7	.207	.277	41 9	3B-333, SS-133, 2B-41, OF-2
10 yrs.	542	767	159	26	2	8	1.0	127	71	142	124	7	.207	.278	40 8	3B-330, SS-129, 2B-34, OF-2

WORLD SERIES
| 1959 CHI A | 2 | 2 | 0 | 0 | 0 | 0 | 0.0 | 0 | 0 | 1 | 0 | 0 | .000 | .000 | 0 0 | 3B-2 |

Jim Essian

ESSIAN, JAMES SARKIS
B. Jan. 2, 1951, Detroit, Mich.
BR TR 6'2" 195 lbs.

1973 PHI N	2	3	0	0	0	0	0.0	0	0	0	1	0	.000	.000	2 0	C-1
1974	17	20	2	0	0	0	0.0	1	0	2	1	0	.100	.100	1 0	C-15, 3B-1, 1B-1
1975	2	1	1	0	0	0	0.0	1	1	0	0	0	1.000	1.000	1 1	C-2
1976 CHI A	78	199	49	7	0	0	0.0	20	21	23	28	2	.246	.281	0 0	C-77, 1B-2, 3B-1
1977	114	322	88	18	2	10	3.1	50	44	52	35	1	.273	.435	0 0	C-111, 3B-2
1978 OAK A	126	278	62	9	1	3	1.1	21	26	44	22	2	.223	.295	4 0	C-119, 1B-3, 2B-1
1979	98	313	76	16	0	8	2.6	34	40	25	29	0	.243	.371	8 2	C-70, 3B-10, OF-4, 1B-4, DH-3
1980	87	285	66	11	0	5	1.8	19	29	30	18	1	.232	.323	8 1	C-68, DH-11, 1B-1
1981 CHI A	27	52	16	3	0	0	0.0	6	5	4	5	0	.308	.365	9 2	C-25, 3B-2

	G	AB	H	2B	3B	HR	HR%	R	RBI	BB	SO	SB	BA	SA	Pinch Hit AB	Pinch Hit H	G by POS

Jim Essian continued

	G	AB	H	2B	3B	HR	HR%	R	RBI	BB	SO	SB	BA	SA	PH AB	PH H	G by POS
1982 SEA A	48	153	42	8	0	3	2.0	14	20	11	7	2	.275	.386	1	1	C-48
1983 CLE A	48	93	19	4	0	2	2.2	11	11	16	8	0	.204	.312	0	0	C-47, 3B-1
11 yrs.	647	1719	421	76	3	31	1.8	177	197	208	154	8	.245	.347	27	5	C-583, 3B-17, DH-14, 1B-11, OF-4, 2B-1
3 yrs.	219	573	153	28	2	10	1.7	76	70	79	68	3	.267	.375	2	0	C-213, 3B-5, 1B-2

Johnny Evers

EVERS, JOHN JOSEPH (The Trojan, The Crab) BL TR 5'9" 125 lbs.
Brother of Joe Evers.
B. July 21, 1881, Troy, N. Y.   D. Mar. 28, 1947, Albany, N. Y.
Manager 1913, 1921, 1924.
Hall of Fame 1946.

	G	AB	H	2B	3B	HR	HR%	R	RBI	BB	SO	SB	BA	SA	PH AB	PH H	G by POS
1902 CHI N	26	90	20	0	0	0	0.0	7	2	3		1	.222	.222	0	0	2B-18, SS-8
1903	124	464	136	27	7	0	0.0	70	52	19		25	.293	.381	0	0	2B-110, SS-11, 3B-2
1904	152	532	141	14	7	0	0.0	49	47	28		26	.265	.318	0	0	2B-152
1905	99	340	94	11	2	1	0.3	44	37	27		19	.276	.329	0	0	2B-99
1906	154	533	136	17	6	1	0.2	65	51	36		49	.255	.315	0	0	2B-153, 3B-1
1907	150	507	127	18	4	2	0.4	66	51	38		46	.250	.314	0	0	2B-150
1908	126	416	125	19	6	0	0.0	83	37	66		36	.300	.375	2	1	2B-123
1909	127	463	122	19	6	1	0.2	88	24	73		28	.263	.337	0	0	2B-126
1910	125	433	114	11	7	0	0.0	87	28	108	18	28	.263	.321	0	0	2B-125
1911	46	155	35	4	3	0	0.0	29	7	34	10	6	.226	.290	2	0	2B-33, 3B-11
1912	143	478	163	23	11	1	0.2	73	63	74	18	16	.341	.441	0	0	2B-143
1913	135	444	126	20	5	3	0.7	81	49	50	14	11	.284	.372	0	0	2B-135
1914 BOS N	139	491	137	20	3	1	0.2	81	40	87	26	12	.279	.338	0	0	2B-139
1915	83	278	73	4	1	1	0.4	38	22	50	16	7	.263	.295	0	0	2B-83
1916	71	241	52	4	1	0	0.0	33	15	40	19	5	.216	.241	0	0	2B-71
1917 2 teams		BOS N (24G – .193)				PHI N (56G – .224)											
" total	80	266	57	5	1	1	0.4	25	12	43	21	9	.214	.252	0	0	2B-73, 3B-7
1922 CHI A	1	3	0	0	0	0	0.0	0	1	2	0	0	.000	.000	0	0	2B-1
1929 BOS N	1	0	0	0	0	0	–	0	0	0	0	0	–	–	0	0	2B-1
18 yrs.	1782	6134	1658	216	70	12	0.2	919	538	778	142	324	.270	.334	4	1	2B-1735, 3B-21, SS-19
1 yr.	1	3	0	0	0	0	0.0	0	1	2	0	0	.000	.000	0	0	2B-1

WORLD SERIES

	G	AB	H	2B	3B	HR	HR%	R	RBI	BB	SO	SB	BA	SA	PH AB	PH H	G by POS
1906 CHI N	6	20	3	1	0	0	0.0	2	1	1	3	2	.150	.200	0	0	2B-6
1907	5	20	7	2	0	0	0.0	2	1	0	1	3	.350	.450	0	0	2B-5
1908	5	20	7	1	0	0	0.0	5	2	1	2	2	.350	.400	0	0	2B-5
1914 BOS N	4	16	7	0	0	0	0.0	2	2	2	2	1	.438	.438	0	0	2B-4
4 yrs.	20	76	24	4	0	0	0.0	11	6	4	8	8	.316	.368	0	0	2B-20
												8th					

Sam Ewing

EWING, SAMUEL JAMES BL TR 6'3" 200 lbs.
B. Apr. 9, 1949, Nashville, Tenn.

	G	AB	H	2B	3B	HR	HR%	R	RBI	BB	SO	SB	BA	SA	PH AB	PH H	G by POS
1973 CHI A	11	20	3	1	0	0	0.0	1	2	2	6	0	.150	.200	5	1	1B-4
1976	19	41	9	2	1	0	0.0	3	2	2	8	0	.220	.317	8	3	DH-12, 1B-1
1977 TOR A	97	244	70	8	2	4	1.6	24	34	19	42	1	.287	.385	27	9	OF-46, DH-27, 1B-2
1978	40	56	10	0	0	2	3.6	3	9	5	9	0	.179	.286	29	5	DH-9, OF-3
4 yrs.	167	361	92	11	3	6	1.7	31	47	28	65	1	.255	.352	69	18	OF-49, DH-48, 1B-7
2 yrs.	30	61	12	3	1	0	0.0	4	4	4	14	0	.197	.279	13	4	DH-12, 1B-5

Ferris Fain

FAIN, FERRIS ROY (Burrhead) BL TL 5'11" 180 lbs.
B. Mar. 29, 1921, San Antonio, Tex.

	G	AB	H	2B	3B	HR	HR%	R	RBI	BB	SO	SB	BA	SA	PH AB	PH H	G by POS
1947 PHI A	136	461	134	28	6	7	1.5	70	71	95	34	4	.291	.423	4	0	1B-132
1948	145	520	146	27	6	7	1.3	81	88	113	37	10	.281	.396	0	0	1B-145
1949	150	525	138	21	5	3	0.6	81	78	136	51	8	.263	.339	0	0	1B-150
1950	151	522	147	25	4	10	1.9	83	83	132	26	8	.282	.402	0	0	1B-151
1951	117	425	146	30	3	6	1.4	63	57	80	20	0	.344	.471	0	0	1B-108, OF-11
1952	145	538	176	43	3	2	0.4	82	59	105	26	3	.327	.429	1	0	1B-144
1953 CHI A	128	446	114	18	2	6	1.3	73	52	108	28	3	.256	.345	1	1	1B-127
1954	65	235	71	10	1	5	2.1	30	51	40	14	5	.302	.417	0	0	1B-64
1955 2 teams		DET A (58G – .264)				CLE A (56G – .254)											
" total	114	258	67	11	0	2	0.8	32	31	94	25	5	.260	.326	13	4	1B-95
9 yrs.	1151	3930	1139	213	30	48	1.2	595	570	903	261	46	.290	.396	19	5	1B-1116, OF-11
2 yrs.	193	681	185	28	3	11	1.6	103	103	148	42	8	.272	.370	1	1	1B-191

Bibb Falk

FALK, BIBB AUGUST (Jockey) BL TL 6' 175 lbs.
Brother of Chet Falk.
B. Jan. 27, 1899, Austin, Tex.

	G	AB	H	2B	3B	HR	HR%	R	RBI	BB	SO	SB	BA	SA	PH AB	PH H	G by POS
1920 CHI A	7	17	5	1	1	0	0.0	1	2	0	5	0	.294	.471	3	1	OF-4
1921	152	585	167	31	11	5	0.9	62	82	37	69	4	.285	.402	3	1	OF-149
1922	131	483	144	27	1	12	2.5	58	79	27	55	2	.298	.433	1	0	OF-131
1923	87	274	84	18	6	5	1.8	44	38	25	12	4	.307	.471	7	2	OF-80
1924	138	526	185	37	8	6	1.1	77	99	47	21	6	.352	.487	3	1	OF-134
1925	154	602	181	35	9	4	0.7	80	99	51	25	0	.301	.409	0	0	OF-154
1926	155	566	195	43	4	8	1.4	86	108	66	22	9	.345	.477	0	0	OF-155
1927	145	535	175	35	6	9	1.7	76	83	52	19	5	.327	.465	0	0	OF-145
1928	98	286	83	18	4	1	0.3	42	37	25	16	4	.290	.392	16	3	OF-78
1929 CLE A	126	430	133	30	7	13	3.0	66	94	42	14	4	.309	.502	4	1	OF-121
1930	82	191	62	12	1	4	2.1	34	36	23	8	2	.325	.461	34	13	OF-42
1931	79	161	49	13	1	2	1.2	30	28	17	13	1	.304	.435	43	14	OF-33
12 yrs.	1354	4656	1463	300	59	69	1.5	656	785	412	279	46	.314	.448	114	36	OF-1226
9 yrs.	1067	3874	1219	245	50	50	1.3	526	627	330	244	39	.315	.442	33	8	OF-1030
			9th	5th				6th				6th	10th				

Player Register   252

	G	AB	H	2B	3B	HR	HR %	R	RBI	BB	SO	SB	BA	SA	Pinch Hit AB H	G by POS

Bob Farley
FARLEY, ROBERT JACOB BL TL 6'2" 200 lbs.
B. Nov. 15, 1937, Watsontown, Pa.

1961 SF N	13	20	2	0	0	0	0.0	3	1	3	5	0	.100	.100	8	1	OF-3, 1B-1
1962 2 teams	CHI A (35G – .189)							DET A (36G – .160)									
" total	71	103	18	3	1	2	1.9	16	8	27	23	0	.175	.282	33	4	1B-20, OF-6
2 yrs.	84	123	20	3	1	2	1.6	19	9	30	28	0	.163	.252	41	5	1B-21, OF-9
1 yr.	35	53	10	1	1	1	1.9	7	4	13	13	0	.189	.302	20	1	1B-14

Kerby Farrell
FARRELL, KERBY BL TL 5'11" 172 lbs.
B. Sept. 3, 1913, Leapwood, Tenn. D. Dec. 17, 1975, Nashville, Tenn.
Manager 1957.

1943 BOS N	85	280	75	14	1	0	0.0	11	21	16	15	1	.268	.325	11	2	1B-69, P-5
1945 CHI A	103	396	102	11	3	0	0.0	44	34	24	18	4	.258	.301	6	3	1B-97
2 yrs.	188	676	177	25	4	0	0.0	55	55	40	33	5	.262	.311	17	5	1B-166, P-5
1 yr.	103	396	102	11	3	0	0.0	44	34	24	18	4	.258	.301	6	3	1B-97

Joe Fautsch
FAUTSCH, JOSEPH R. BR TR 5'10" 162 lbs.
B. 1886, Minneapolis, Minn. D. Mar. 16, 1971, Newhope, Minn.

| 1916 CHI A | 1 | 1 | 0 | 0 | 0 | 0 | 0.0 | 0 | 0 | 0 | 0 | 0 | .000 | .000 | 1 | 0 | |

Bill Fehring
FEHRING, WILLIAM PAUL (Dutch) BB TR 6' 195 lbs.
B. May 31, 1912, Columbus, Ind.

| 1934 CHI A | 1 | 1 | 0 | 0 | 0 | 0 | 0.0 | 0 | 0 | 0 | 1 | 0 | .000 | .000 | 0 | 0 | C-1 |

Happy Felsch
FELSCH, OSCAR EMIL BR TR 5'11" 175 lbs.
B. Aug. 22, 1891, Milwaukee, Wis. D. Aug. 17, 1964, Milwaukee, Wis.

1915 CHI A	121	427	106	18	11	3	0.7	65	53	51	59	16	.248	.363	3	0	OF-118
1916	146	546	164	24	12	7	1.3	73	70	31	67	13	.300	.427	4	2	OF-141
1917	152	575	177	17	10	6	1.0	75	102	33	52	26	.308	.403	0	0	OF-152
1918	53	206	52	2	5	1	0.5	16	20	15	13	6	.252	.325	0	0	OF-53
1919	135	502	138	34	11	7	1.4	68	86	40	35	19	.275	.428	0	0	OF-135
1920	142	556	188	40	15	14	2.5	88	115	37	25	8	.338	.540	0	0	OF-142
6 yrs.	749	2812	825	135	64	38	1.4	385	446	207	251	88	.293	.427	7	2	OF-741
6 yrs.	749	2812	825	135	64	38	1.4	385	446	207	251	88	.293	.427	7	2	OF-741

WORLD SERIES

1917 CHI A	6	22	6	1	0	1	4.5	4	3	1	5	0	.273	.455	0	0	OF-6
1919	8	26	5	1	0	0	0.0	2	3	1	4	0	.192	.231	0	0	OF-8
2 yrs.	14	48	11	2	0	1	2.1	6	6	2	9	0	.229	.333	0	0	OF-14

Ed Fernandes
FERNANDES, EDWARD PAUL BB TR 5'9" 185 lbs.
B. Mar. 11, 1918, Oakland, Calif. D. Nov. 27, 1968, Hayward, Calif.

1940 PIT N	28	33	4	1	0	0	0.0	1	2	7	6	0	.121	.152	1	0	C-27
1946 CHI A	14	32	8	2	0	0	0.0	4	2	8	7	0	.250	.313	2	0	C-12
2 yrs.	42	65	12	3	0	0	0.0	5	6	15	13	0	.185	.231	3	0	C-39
1 yr.	14	32	8	2	0	0	0.0	4	4	8	7	0	.250	.313	2	0	C-12

Carlton Fisk
FISK, CARLTON ERNEST (Pudge) BR TR 6'3" 200 lbs.
B. Dec. 26, 1948, Bellows Falls, Vt.

1969 BOS A	2	5	0	0	0	0	0.0	0	0	0	2	0	.000	.000	1	0	C-1
1971	14	48	15	2	1	2	4.2	7	6	1	10	0	.313	.521	0	0	C-14
1972	131	457	134	28	9	22	4.8	74	61	52	83	5	.293	.538	0	0	C-131
1973	135	508	125	21	0	26	5.1	65	71	37	99	7	.246	.441	1	0	C-131, DH-3
1974	52	187	56	12	1	11	5.9	36	26	24	23	5	.299	.551	0	0	C-50, DH-2
1975	79	263	87	14	4	10	3.8	47	52	27	32	4	.331	.529	2	0	C-71, DH-6
1976	134	487	124	17	5	17	3.5	76	58	56	71	12	.255	.415	1	0	C-133, DH-1
1977	152	536	169	26	3	26	4.9	106	102	75	85	7	.315	.521	2	0	C-151
1978	157	571	162	39	5	20	3.5	94	88	71	83	7	.284	.475	2	1	C-154, DH-1, OF-1
1979	91	320	87	23	2	10	3.1	49	42	10	38	3	.272	.450	13	1	DH-42, C-39, OF-1
1980	131	478	138	25	3	18	3.8	73	62	36	62	11	.289	.467	0	0	C-115, DH-5, OF-5, 3B-3, 1B-3
1981 CHI A	96	338	89	12	0	7	2.1	44	45	38	37	3	.263	.361	0	0	C-95, OF-1, 3B-1, 1B-1
1982	135	476	127	17	3	14	2.9	66	65	46	60	17	.267	.403	3	1	C-133, 1B-2
1983	138	488	141	26	4	26	5.3	85	86	46	88	9	.289	.518	6	1	C-133, DH-2
14 yrs.	1447	5162	1454	262	40	209	4.0	822	764	519	773	90	.282	.469	31	7	C-1351, DH-62, OF-8, 1B-6, 3B-4
3 yrs.	369	1302	357	55	7	47	3.6	195	196	130	185	29	.274	.435	9	2	C-361, 1B-3, DH-2, OF-1, 3B-1

LEAGUE CHAMPIONSHIP SERIES

1975 BOS A	3	12	5	1	0	0	0.0	4	2	0	2	1	.417	.500	0	0	C-3
1983 CHI A	4	17	3	1	0	0	0.0	0	0	1	3	0	.176	.235	0	0	C-4
2 yrs.	7	29	8	2	0	0	0.0	4	2	1	5	1	.276	.345	0	0	C-7

WORLD SERIES

| 1975 BOS A | 7 | 25 | 6 | 0 | 0 | 2 | 8.0 | 5 | 4 | 7 | 7 | 0 | .240 | .480 | 0 | 0 | C-7 |

Patsy Flaherty
FLAHERTY, PATRICK JOSEPH BL TL
B. June 29, 1876, Carnegie, Pa. D. Jan. 23, 1968, Alexandria, La.

1899 LOU N	7	24	5	1	0	0	0.0	3	6	3		0	.208	.333	0	0	P-5, OF-2
1900 PIT N	4	9	1	0	0	0	0.0	0	0	1		0	.111	.111	0	0	P-4
1903 CHI A	40	102	14	4	0	0	0.0	7	5	5		4	.137	.176	0	0	P-40
1904 2 teams	CHI A (5G – .333)					PIT N (36G – .212)											
" total	41	116	26	4	4	2	1.7	10	19	12		0	.224	.379	5	1	P-34, OF-2
1905 PIT N	30	76	15	4	2	0	0.0	7	4	3		0	.197	.303	1	0	P-27, OF-2
1907 BOS N	41	115	22	3	2	1	1.7	9	11	2		0	.191	.304	4	1	P-27, OF-8
1908	32	86	12	0	0	0	0.0	8	5	6		2	.140	.186	0	0	P-31
1910 PHI N	2	2	1	0	0	0	0.0	0	0	0		0	.500	.500	1	0	OF-1, P-1

Player Register

	G	AB	H	2B	3B	HR	HR%	R	RBI	BB	SO	SB	BA	SA	Pinch Hit AB	H	G by POS

Patsy Flaherty continued
1911 BOS N	38	94	27	3	2	2	2.1	9	20	8	11	2	.287	.426	17	6	OF-19, P-4
9 yrs.	235	624	123	19	13	6	1.0	53	70	40	11	9	.197	.298	28	8	P-173, OF-34
2 yrs.	45	114	18	5	0	0	0.0	5	9			4	.158	.202	0	0	P-45

John Flannery
FLANNERY, JOHN MICHAEL
B. Jan. 25, 1957, Long Beach, Calif.   BR TR 6'3" 173 lbs.

| 1977 CHI A | 7 | 2 | 0 | 0 | 0 | 0 | 0.0 | 1 | 0 | 1 | 1 | 0 | .000 | .000 | 0 | 0 | SS-4, DH-1, 3B-1 |

Ray Flaskamper
FLASKAMPER, RAY HAROLD (Flash)   BB TR 5'7" 140 lbs.
B. Oct. 31, 1901, St. Louis, Mo.   D. Feb. 3, 1978, San Antonio, Tex.

| 1927 CHI A | 26 | 95 | 21 | 5 | 0 | 0 | 0.0 | 12 | 6 | 3 | 8 | 0 | .221 | .274 | 1 | 0 | SS-25 |

Scott Fletcher
FLETCHER, SCOTT   BR TR 5'11" 168 lbs.
B. July 30, 1958, Ft. Walton, Fla.

1981 CHI N	19	46	10	4	0	0	0.0	6	1	2	4	0	.217	.304	0	0	2B-13, SS-4, 3B-1
1982	11	24	4	0	0	0	0.0	4	1	4	5	1	.167	.167	0	0	SS-11
1983 CHI A	114	262	62	16	5	3	1.1	42	31	29	22	5	.237	.370	0	0	SS-100, 2B-12, 3B-7, DH-1
3 yrs.	144	332	76	20	5	3	0.9	52	33	35	31	6	.229	.346	0	0	SS-115, 2B-25, 3B-8, DH-1
1 yr.	114	262	62	16	5	3	1.1	42	31	29	22	5	.237	.370	0	0	SS-100, 2B-12, 3B-7, DH-1

LEAGUE CHAMPIONSHIP SERIES
| 1983 CHI A | 3 | 7 | 0 | 0 | 0 | 0 | 0.0 | 0 | 0 | 1 | 0 | 0 | .000 | .000 | 0 | 0 | SS-3 |

Marv Foley
FOLEY, MARVIS EDWIN   BL TR 6' 195 lbs.
B. Aug. 29, 1953, Stanford, Ky.

1978 CHI A	11	34	12	0	0	0	0.0	3	6	4	6	0	.353	.353	1	0	C-10
1979	34	97	24	3	0	2	2.1	6	10	7	5	0	.247	.340	2	1	C-33
1980	68	137	29	5	0	4	2.9	14	15	9	22	0	.212	.336	8	3	C-64, 1B-3
1982	27	36	4	0	0	0	0.0	1	1	6	4	0	.111	.111	11	1	C-15, 3B-2, DH-1, 1B-1
4 yrs.	140	304	69	8	0	6	2.0	24	32	26	37	0	.227	.313	22	5	C-122, 1B-4, 3B-2, DH-1
4 yrs.	140	304	69	8	0	6	2.0	24	32	26	37	0	.227	.313	22	5	C-122, 1B-4, 3B-2, DH-1

Lew Fonseca
FONSECA, LEWIS ALBERT   BR TR 5'10½" 180 lbs.
B. Jan. 21, 1899, Oakland, Calif.
Manager 1932-34.

1921 CIN N	82	297	82	10	3	1	0.3	38	41	8	13	2	.276	.340	2	0	2B-50, OF-16, 1B-16
1922	91	291	105	20	3	4	1.4	55	45	14	18	7	.361	.491	18	8	2B-71
1923	65	237	66	11	4	3	1.3	33	28	9	16	4	.278	.397	6	2	2B-45, 1B-14
1924	20	57	13	2	1	0	0.0	5	9	4	4	1	.228	.298	4	0	2B-10, 1B-6
1925 PHI N	126	467	149	30	5	7	1.5	78	60	21	42	6	.319	.450	5	1	2B-69, 1B-55
1927 CLE A	112	428	133	20	7	2	0.5	60	40	12	17	12	.311	.404	6	1	2B-96, 1B-13
1928	75	263	86	19	4	3	1.1	38	36	13	17	4	.327	.464	0	0	1B-56, 3B-15, SS-4, 2B-1
1929	148	566	209	44	15	6	1.1	97	103	50	23	19	.369	.532	1	0	1B-147
1930	40	129	36	9	2	0	0.0	20	17	7	7	1	.279	.380	5	0	1B-28, 3B-6
1931 2 teams			CLE A (26G – .370)			CHI A (121G – .299)											
" total	147	573	179	35	6	3	0.5	86	85	40	29	7	.312	.410	4	1	OF-95, 1B-28, 2B-21, 3B-1
1932 CHI A	18	37	5	1	0	0	0.0	0	6	1	7	0	.135	.162	7	3	OF-8, P-1
1933	23	59	12	2	0	2	3.4	8	15	7	6	1	.203	.339	10	1	1B-12
12 yrs.	947	3404	1075	203	50	31	0.9	518	485	186	199	64	.316	.432	68	17	1B-375, 2B-363, OF-119, 3B-22, SS-4, P-1
3 yrs.	162	561	156	29	5	4	0.7	73	92	40	35	5	.278	.369	21	5	OF-103, 2B-21, 1B-14, 3B-1, P-1

Pop Foster
FOSTER, CLARENCE FRANCIS   TR
B. Apr. 8, 1878, New Haven, Conn.   D. Apr. 16, 1944, Princeton, N.J.

1898 NY N	32	112	30	6	1	0	0.0	10	9	0		0	.268	.339	0	0	OF-21, 3B-10, SS-2
1899	84	301	89	9	7	3	1.0	48	57	20		7	.296	.402	0	0	OF-84, SS-1, 3B-1
1900	31	84	22	3	1	0	0.0	19	11	11		0	.262	.321	5	0	OF-12, SS-7, 2B-5
1901 2 teams			WAS A (103G – .278)			CHI A (12G – .286)											
" total	115	427	119	18	11	7	1.6	69	59	45		10	.279	.422	3	1	OF-111, SS-2
4 yrs.	262	924	260	36	20	10	1.1	146	136	76		17	.281	.396	8	1	OF-228, SS-12, 3B-11, 2B-5
1 yr.	12	35	10	2	2	1	2.9	4	6	4		0	.286	.543	3	1	OF-9

Bob Fothergill
FOTHERGILL, ROBERT ROY (Fats)   BR TR 5'10½" 230 lbs.
B. Aug. 16, 1897, Massillon, Ohio   D. Mar. 1, 1976, Bokoshe, Okla.

1922 DET A	42	152	49	12	4	0	0.0	20	29	8	9	1	.322	.454	3	1	OF-39
1923	101	241	76	18	3	1	0.4	34	49	12	19	4	.315	.419	30	9	OF-68
1924	54	166	50	8	3	0	0.0	28	15	5	13	2	.301	.386	9	3	OF-45
1925	71	204	72	14	0	2	1.0	38	28	6	3	2	.353	.451	11	5	OF-59
1926	110	387	142	31	7	3	0.8	63	73	33	23	4	.367	.506	6	4	OF-103
1927	143	527	189	38	9	9	1.7	93	114	47	31	9	.359	.516	5	2	OF-137
1928	111	347	110	28	10	3	0.9	49	63	24	19	8	.317	.481	19	4	OF-90
1929	115	277	98	24	9	6	2.2	42	62	11	11	3	.354	.570	53	19	OF-59
1930 2 teams			DET A (55G – .259)			CHI A (51G – .305)											
" total	106	274	77	18	3	2	0.7	24	38	10	18	1	.281	.391	34	6	OF-68
1931 CHI A	108	312	88	21	8	3	1.0	25	56	17	17	2	.282	.365	31	8	OF-74
1932	116	346	102	24	1	7	2.0	36	50	27	10	4	.295	.431	29	8	OF-86
1933 BOS A	28	32	11	1	0	0	0.0	1	5	2	4	0	.344	.375	23	7	OF-4
12 yrs.	1105	3265	1064	225	52	36	1.1	453	582	202	177	40	.326	.460	253	76	OF-832
3 yrs.	275	789	230	42	5	10	1.3	71	130	48	35	6	.292	.395	79	22	OF-190

Player Register 254

	G	AB	H	2B	3B	HR	HR%	R	RBI	BB	SO	SB	BA	SA	Pinch Hit AB	H	G by POS

Jack Fournier
FOURNIER, JOHN FRANK (Jacques) BL TR 6' 195 lbs.
B. Sept. 28, 1892, Au Sable, Mich. D. Sept. 5, 1973, Tacoma, Wash.

Year	Team	G	AB	H	2B	3B	HR	HR%	R	RBI	BB	SO	SB	BA	SA	PH AB	PH H	G by POS
1912	CHI A	35	73	14	5	2	0	0.0	5	2	4		1	.192	.315	18	5	1B-17
1913		68	172	40	8	5	1	0.6	20	23	21	23	9	.233	.355	13	1	1B-29, OF-23
1914		109	379	118	14	9	6	1.6	44	44	31	44	10	.311	.443	6	0	1B-97, OF-6
1915		126	422	136	20	18	5	1.2	86	77	64	37	21	.322	.491	4	2	1B-65, OF-57
1916		105	313	75	13	9	3	1.0	36	44	36	40	19	.240	.367	14	2	1B-85, OF-1
1917		1	1	0	0	0	0	0.0	0	0	0	1	0	.000	.000	1	0	
1918	NY A	27	100	35	6	1	0	0.0	9	12	7	7	7	.350	.430	0	0	1B-27
1920	STL N	141	530	162	33	14	3	0.6	77	61	42	42	26	.306	.438	3	2	1B-138
1921		149	574	197	27	9	16	2.8	103	86	56	48	20	.343	.505	0	0	1B-149
1922		128	404	119	23	9	10	2.5	64	61	40	21	6	.295	.470	12	5	1B-109, P-1
1923	BKN N	133	515	181	30	13	22	4.3	91	102	43	28	11	.351	.588	0	0	1B-133
1924		154	563	188	25	4	27	4.8	93	116	83	46	7	.334	.536	1	0	1B-153
1925		145	545	191	21	16	22	4.0	99	130	86	39	4	.350	.569	0	0	1B-145
1926		87	243	69	9	2	11	4.5	39	48	30	16	0	.284	.473	18	4	1B-64
1927	BOS N	122	374	106	18	2	10	2.7	55	53	44	16	4	.283	.422	19	8	1B-102
15 yrs.		1530	5208	1631	252	113	136	2.6	821	859	587	408	145	.313	.483	109	29	1B-1313, OF-87, P-1
6 yrs.		444	1360	383	60	43	15	1.1	191	190	156	145	60	.282	.422	56	10	1B-293, OF-87

Nellie Fox
FOX, JACOB NELSON BL TR 5'10" 160 lbs.
B. Dec. 25, 1927, St. Thomas, Pa. D. Dec. 1, 1975, Baltimore, Md.

Year	Team	G	AB	H	2B	3B	HR	HR%	R	RBI	BB	SO	SB	BA	SA	PH AB	PH H	G by POS
1947	PHI A	7	3	0	0	0	0	0.0	2	0	1	0	0	.000	.000	2	0	2B-1
1948		3	13	2	0	0	0	0.0	0	0	1	0	1	.154	.154	0	0	2B-3
1949		88	247	63	6	2	0	0.0	42	21	32	9	2	.255	.296	2	0	2B-77
1950	CHI A	130	457	113	12	7	0	0.0	45	30	35	17	4	.247	.304	8	2	2B-121
1951		147	604	189	32	12	4	0.7	93	55	43	11	9	.313	.425	0	0	2B-147
1952		152	648	192	25	10	0	0.0	76	39	34	14	5	.296	.366	1	0	2B-151
1953		154	624	178	31	8	3	0.5	92	72	49	18	4	.285	.375	0	0	2B-154
1954		155	631	201	24	8	2	0.3	111	47	51	12	16	.319	.391	0	0	2B-155
1955		154	636	198	28	7	6	0.9	100	59	38	15	7	.311	.406	0	0	2B-154
1956		154	649	192	20	10	4	0.6	109	52	44	14	8	.296	.376	0	0	2B-154
1957		155	619	196	27	8	6	1.0	110	61	75	13	5	.317	.415	0	0	2B-155
1958		155	623	187	21	6	0	0.0	82	49	47	11	5	.300	.353	0	0	2B-155
1959		156	624	191	34	6	2	0.3	84	70	71	13	5	.306	.389	0	0	2B-156
1960		150	605	175	24	10	2	0.3	85	59	50	13	2	.289	.372	1	0	2B-149
1961		159	606	152	11	5	2	0.3	67	51	59	12	2	.251	.295	2	1	2B-159
1962		157	621	166	27	7	2	0.3	79	54	38	12	1	.267	.343	3	0	2B-154
1963		137	539	140	19	0	2	0.4	54	42	24	17	0	.260	.306	6	2	2B-134
1964	HOU N	133	442	117	12	6	0	0.0	45	28	27	13	0	.265	.319	13	1	2B-115
1965		21	41	11	2	0	0	0.0	3	1	0	2	0	.268	.317	12	4	3B-6, 1B-2, 2B-1
19 yrs.		2367	9232	2663	355	112	35	0.4	1279	790	719	216	76	.288	.363	50	10	2B-2295, 3B-6, 1B-2
14 yrs.		2115	8486	2470	335	104	35	0.4	1187	740	658	192	73	.291	.367	21	5	2B-2098
		2nd	2nd	2nd	2nd	1st		0.4	2nd	4th	3rd							

WORLD SERIES
| 1959 | CHI A | 6 | 24 | 9 | 3 | 0 | 0 | 0.0 | 4 | 0 | 4 | 1 | 0 | .375 | .500 | 0 | 1 | 2B-6 |

Tito Francona
FRANCONA, JOHN PATSY BL TL 5'11" 190 lbs.
Father of Terry Francona.
B. Nov. 4, 1933, Aliquippa, Pa.

Year	Team	G	AB	H	2B	3B	HR	HR%	R	RBI	BB	SO	SB	BA	SA	PH AB	PH H	G by POS
1956	BAL A	139	445	115	16	4	9	2.0	62	57	51	60	11	.258	.373	18	4	OF-122, 1B-21
1957		97	279	65	8	3	7	2.5	35	38	29	48	7	.233	.358	23	3	OF-73, 1B-4
1958	2 teams	CHI A (41G – .258)					DET A (45G – .246)											
"	total	86	197	50	8	2	1	0.5	21	20	29	40	2	.254	.330	29	11	OF-72
1959	CLE A	122	399	145	17	2	20	5.0	68	79	35	42	2	.363	.566	20	5	OF-64, 1B-35
1960		147	544	159	36	2	17	3.1	84	79	67	67	4	.292	.460	3	0	OF-138, 1B-13
1961		155	592	178	30	8	16	2.7	87	85	56	52	2	.301	.459	7	1	OF-138, 1B-14
1962		158	621	169	28	5	14	2.3	82	70	47	74	3	.272	.401	0	0	1B-158
1963		142	500	114	29	0	10	2.0	57	41	47	77	9	.228	.346	13	3	OF-122, 1B-11
1964		111	270	67	13	2	8	3.0	35	24	44	46	1	.248	.400	29	6	OF-69, 1B-17
1965	STL N	81	174	45	6	2	5	2.9	15	19	17	30	0	.259	.402	35	9	OF-34, 1B-13
1966		83	156	33	4	1	4	2.6	14	17	7	27	0	.212	.327	41	6	1B-30, OF-9
1967	2 teams	PHI N (27G – .205)					ATL N (82G – .248)											
"	total	109	327	78	6	1	6	1.8	35	28	27	44	1	.239	.318	27	3	1B-80, OF-7
1968	ATL N	122	346	99	13	1	2	0.6	32	47	51	45	3	.286	.347	24	5	OF-65, 1B-33
1969	2 teams	ATL N (51G – .295)					OAK A (32G – .341)											
"	total	83	173	55	7	1	5	2.9	17	42	25	21	0	.318	.457	32	8	1B-26, OF-16
1970	2 teams	OAK A (32G – .242)					MIL A (52G – .231)											
"	total	84	98	23	3	0	1	1.0	6	10	12	21	1	.235	.296	64	15	1B-19, OF-1
15 yrs.		1719	5121	1395	224	34	125	2.4	650	656	544	694	46	.272	.403	365	81	OF-930, 1B-474
1 yr.		41	128	33	3	2	1	0.8	10	10	14	24	2	.258	.336	7	3	OF-35

Gene Freese
FREESE, EUGENE LEWIS (Augie) BR TR 5'11" 175 lbs.
Brother of George Freese.
B. Jan. 8, 1934, Wheeling, W. Va.

Year	Team	G	AB	H	2B	3B	HR	HR%	R	RBI	BB	SO	SB	BA	SA	PH AB	PH H	G by POS
1955	PIT N	134	455	115	21	8	14	3.1	69	44	34	57	5	.253	.426	12	3	3B-65, 2B-57
1956		65	207	43	9	0	3	1.4	19	14	16	45	2	.208	.295	10	0	3B-47, 2B-26
1957		114	346	98	18	2	6	1.7	44	31	17	42	9	.283	.399	30	9	3B-74, OF-10, 2B-10
1958	2 teams	PIT N (17G – .167)					STL N (62G – .257)											
"	total	79	209	52	11	1	7	3.3	29	18	11	34	1	.249	.411	29	6	SS-28, 2B-14, 3B-4
1959	PHI N	132	400	107	14	5	23	5.8	60	70	43	61	8	.268	.500	20	7	3B-109, 2B-6
1960	CHI A	127	455	124	32	6	17	3.7	60	79	29	65	10	.273	.481	6	1	3B-122
1961	CIN N	152	575	159	27	2	26	4.5	78	87	27	78	8	.277	.466	1	0	3B-151, 2B-1
1962		18	42	6	1	0	0	0.0	2	1	6	8	0	.143	.167	5	0	3B-10
1963		66	217	53	9	1	6	2.8	20	26	17	42	4	.244	.378	3	0	3B-62, OF-1
1964	PIT N	99	289	65	13	2	9	3.1	33	40	19	45	1	.225	.377	30	5	3B-72

	G	AB	H	2B	3B	HR	HR %	R	RBI	BB	SO	SB	BA	SA	Pinch Hit AB	Pinch Hit H	G by POS

Gene Freese continued

1965 2 teams	PIT N (43G – .263)			CHI A (17G – .281)													
" total	60	112	30	4	1	1	0.9	8	12	11	27	0	.268	.348	31	12	3B-27
1966 2 teams	CHI A (48G – .208)			HOU N (21G – .091)													
" total	69	139	25	2	0	3	2.2	9	10	13	31	3	.180	.259	29	2	3B-38, 2B-3, OF-1
12 yrs.	1115	3446	877	161	28	115	3.3	429	432	243	535	51	.254	.418	206	45	3B-781, 2B-117, SS-28, OF-12
3 yrs.	192	593	155	34	7	21	3.5	70	93	42	94	12	.261	.449	29	6	3B-164

WORLD SERIES
1961 CIN N	5	16	1	1	0	0	0.0	0	0	3	4	0	.063	.125	0	0	3B-5

Charlie French

FRENCH, CHARLES CALVIN BL TR 5'6" 140 lbs.
B. Oct. 12, 1883, Indianapolis, Ind. D. Mar. 30, 1962, Indianapolis, Ind.

1909 BOS A	51	167	42	3	1	0	0.0	13	13	15		8	.251	.281	0	0	2B-28, SS-23
1910 2 teams	BOS A (9G – .200)			CHI A (45G – .165)													
" total	54	210	36	2	1	0	0.0	21	7	11		5	.171	.190	0	0	2B-36, OF-16
2 yrs.	105	377	78	5	2	0	0.0	34	20	26		13	.207	.231	0	0	2B-64, SS-23, OF-16
1 yr.	45	170	28	1	1	0	0.0	17	4	10		5	.165	.182	0	0	2B-28, OF-16

Ray French

FRENCH, RAYMOND EDWARD BR TR 5'9½" 158 lbs.
B. Jan. 9, 1897, Alameda, Calif. D. Apr. 3, 1978, Alameda, Calif.

1920 NY A	2	2	0	0	0	0	0.0	2	1	0	1	0	.000	.000	0	0	SS-1
1923 BKN N	43	73	16	2	1	0	0.0	14	7	4	7	0	.219	.274	1	0	SS-30
1924 CHI A	37	112	20	4	0	0	0.0	13	11	10	13	3	.179	.214	5	0	SS-28, 2B-3
3 yrs.	82	187	36	6	1	0	0.0	29	19	14	21	3	.193	.235	6	0	SS-59, 2B-3
1 yr.	37	112	20	4	0	0	0.0	13	11	10	13	3	.179	.214	5	0	SS-28, 2B-3

Liz Funk

FUNK, ELIAS CALVIN BL TL 5'8½" 160 lbs.
B. Oct. 28, 1904, La Cygne, Kans. D. Jan. 16, 1968, Norman, Okla.

1929 NY A	1	0	0	0	0	0	–	0	0	0	0	–	–	–	0	0	
1930 DET A	140	527	145	26	11	4	0.8	74	65	29	39	12	.275	.389	10	0	OF-129
1932 CHI A	122	440	114	21	5	2	0.5	59	40	43	19	17	.259	.343	1	0	OF-120
1933	10	9	2	0	0	0	0.0	1	0	1	0	0	.222	.222	8	2	OF-2
4 yrs.	273	976	261	47	16	6	0.6	134	105	73	58	29	.267	.367	19	2	OF-251
2 yrs.	132	449	116	21	5	2	0.4	60	40	44	19	17	.258	.341	9	2	OF-122

Oscar Gamble

GAMBLE, OSCAR CHARLES BL TR 5'11" 160 lbs.
B. Dec. 20, 1949, Ramer, Ala.

1969 CHI N	24	71	16	1	1	1	1.4	6	5	10	12	0	.225	.310	0	0	OF-24
1970 PHI N	88	275	72	12	4	1	0.4	31	19	27	37	5	.262	.345	14	4	OF-74
1971	92	280	62	11	1	6	2.1	24	23	21	35	5	.221	.332	13	4	OF-80
1972	74	135	32	5	2	1	0.7	17	13	19	16	0	.237	.326	30	9	OF-35, 1B-1
1973 CLE A	113	390	104	11	3	20	5.1	56	44	34	37	3	.267	.464	8	2	DH-70, OF-37
1974	135	454	132	16	4	19	4.2	74	59	48	51	5	.291	.469	7	0	DH-115, OF-13
1975	121	348	91	16	3	15	4.3	60	45	53	39	11	.261	.454	11	2	DH-82, DH-29
1976 NY A	110	340	79	13	1	17	5.0	43	57	38	38	5	.232	.426	16	6	OF-104, DH-1
1977 CHI A	137	408	121	22	2	31	7.6	75	83	54	54	1	.297	.588	18	8	DH-79, OF-49
1978 SD N	126	375	103	15	3	7	1.9	46	47	51	45	1	.275	.387	13	6	OF-107
1979 2 teams	TEX A (64G – .335)			NY A (36G – .389)													
" total	100	274	98	10	1	19	6.9	48	64	50	28	2	.358	.609	18	5	OF-48, DH-43
1980 NY A	78	194	54	10	2	14	7.2	40	50	28	21	2	.278	.567	17	4	OF-49, DH-20
1981	80	189	45	8	0	10	5.3	24	27	35	23	0	.238	.439	15	5	OF-43, DH-33
1982	108	316	86	21	2	18	5.7	49	57	58	47	6	.272	.522	18	2	DH-74, OF-29
1983	74	180	47	10	2	7	3.9	26	26	25	23	0	.261	.456	20	6	OF-32, DH-21
15 yrs.	1460	4229	1142	181	31	186	4.4	619	619	551	506	46	.270	.459	218	63	OF-806, DH-485, 1B-1
1 yr.	137	408	121	22	2	31	7.6	75	83	54	54	1	.297	.588	18	8	DH-79, OF-49

DIVISIONAL PLAYOFF SERIES
1981 NY A	4	9	5	1	0	2	22.2	2	3	1	2	0	.556	1.333	1	1	DH-4

LEAGUE CHAMPIONSHIP SERIES
1976 NY A	3	8	2	1	0	0	0.0	1	1	1	1	0	.250	.375	1	1	OF-3
1980	2	5	1	0	0	0	0.0	1	0	1	1	0	.200	.200	1	1	OF-1
1981	3	6	1	0	0	0	0.0	2	1	5	3	0	.167	.167	0	0	OF-1
3 yrs.	8	19	4	1	0	0	0.0	4	2	7	5	0	.211	.263	2	2	OF-5

WORLD SERIES
1976 NY A	3	8	1	0	0	0	0.0	0	1	0	0	0	.125	.125	1	0	OF-2
1981	3	6	2	0	0	0	0.0	1	1	1	0	0	.333	.333	0	0	OF-2
2 yrs.	6	14	3	0	0	0	0.0	1	2	1	0	0	.214	.214	1	0	OF-4

Chick Gandil

GANDIL, CHARLES ARNOLD BR TR 6'1½" 190 lbs.
B. Jan. 19, 1888, St. Paul, Minn. D. Dec. 13, 1970, Calistoga, Calif.

1910 CHI A	77	275	53	7	3	2	0.7	21	21	24		12	.193	.262	0	0	1B-74, OF-2
1912 WAS A	117	443	135	20	15	2	0.5	59	81	27		21	.305	.431	0	0	1B-117
1913	148	550	175	25	8	1	0.2	61	72	36	33	22	.318	.398	3	0	1B-145
1914	145	526	136	24	10	3	0.6	48	75	44	44	30	.259	.359	0	0	1B-145
1915	136	485	141	20	15	2	0.4	53	64	29	33	20	.291	.406	2	1	1B-134
1916 CLE A	146	533	138	26	9	0	0.0	51	72	36	48	13	.259	.341	1	1	1B-145
1917 CHI A	149	553	151	9	7	0	0.0	53	57	30	36	16	.273	.315	0	0	1B-149
1918	114	439	119	18	4	0	0.0	49	55	27	19	9	.271	.330	0	0	1B-114
1919	115	441	128	24	7	1	0.2	54	60	20	20	10	.290	.383	0	0	1B-115
9 yrs.	1147	4245	1176	173	78	11	0.3	449	557	273	233	153	.277	.362	6	2	1B-1138, OF-2
4 yrs.	455	1708	451	58	21	3	0.2	177	193	101	75	47	.264	.328	0	0	1B-452, OF-2

WORLD SERIES
1917 CHI A	6	23	6	1	0	0	0.0	1	5	0	2	1	.261	.304	0	0	1B-6

Player Register

	G	AB	H	2B	3B	HR	HR%	R	RBI	BB	SO	SB	BA	SA	Pinch Hit AB	H	G by POS

Chick Gandil continued
1919	8	30	7	0	1	0	0.0	1	5	1	3	1	.233	.300	0	0	1B-8
2 yrs.	14	53	13	1	1	0	0.0	2	10	1	5	2	.245	.302	0	0	1B-14

Ralph Garr
GARR, RALPH ALLEN
B. Dec. 12, 1945, Ruston, La.
BL TR 5'11" 185 lbs.

	G	AB	H	2B	3B	HR	HR%	R	RBI	BB	SO	SB	BA	SA	PH AB	PH H	G by POS
1968 ATL N	11	7	2	0	0	0	0.0	3	0	1	0	1	.286	.286	7	2	
1969	22	27	6	1	0	0	0.0	6	2	2	4	1	.222	.259	5	2	OF-7
1970	37	96	27	3	0	0	0.0	18	8	5	12	5	.281	.313	10	1	OF-21
1971	154	639	219	24	6	9	1.4	101	44	30	68	30	.343	.441	1	1	OF-153
1972	134	554	180	22	0	12	2.2	87	53	25	41	25	.325	.430	3	0	OF-131
1973	148	668	200	32	6	11	1.6	94	55	22	64	35	.299	.415	0	0	OF-148
1974	143	606	214	24	17	11	1.8	87	54	28	52	26	.353	.503	1	1	OF-139
1975	151	625	174	26	11	6	1.0	74	31	44	50	14	.278	.384	3	2	OF-148
1976 CHI A	136	527	158	22	6	4	0.8	63	36	17	41	14	.300	.387	5	2	OF-125
1977	134	543	163	29	7	10	1.8	78	54	27	44	12	.300	.435	7	1	OF-126, DH-2
1978	118	443	122	18	9	3	0.7	67	29	24	41	7	.275	.377	2	0	OF-109, DH-9
1979 2 teams	CHI	A	(102G –	.280)		CAL	A	(6G –	.125)								
" total	108	331	89	10	2	9	2.7	34	39	17	22	2	.269	.393	23	6	OF-67, DH-23
1980 CAL A	21	42	8	1	0	0	0.0	5	3	4	6	0	.190	.214	9	1	DH-8, OF-2
13 yrs.	1317	5108	1562	212	64	75	1.5	717	408	246	445	172	.306	.416	76	19	OF-1176, DH-42
4 yrs.	490	1820	529	79	24	26	1.4	242	158	85	145	35	.291	.403	35	9	OF-427, DH-30

Hank Garrity
GARRITY, FRANCIS JOSEPH
B. Feb. 4, 1908, Boston, Mass. D. Sept. 1, 1962, Boston, Mass.
BR TR 6'1" 185 lbs.

	G	AB	H	2B	3B	HR	HR%	R	RBI	BB	SO	SB	BA	SA	PH AB	PH H	G by POS
1931 CHI A	8	14	3	1	0	0	0.0	0	2	1	2	0	.214	.286	0	0	C-7

Joe Gates
GATES, JOSEPH DANIEL
B. Oct. 3, 1954, Gary, Ind.
BL TR 5'7" 175 lbs.

	G	AB	H	2B	3B	HR	HR%	R	RBI	BB	SO	SB	BA	SA	PH AB	PH H	G by POS
1978 CHI A	8	24	6	0	0	0	0.0	6	1	4	6	1	.250	.250	0	0	2B-8
1979	16	16	1	0	1	0	0.0	5	1	2	3	1	.063	.188	3	0	2B-8, DH-1, 3B-1
2 yrs.	24	40	7	0	1	0	0.0	11	2	6	9	2	.175	.225	3	0	2B-16, DH-1, 3B-1
2 yrs.	24	40	7	0	1	0	0.0	11	2	6	9	2	.175	.225	3	0	2B-16, DH-1, 3B-1

John Gerlach
GERLACH, JOHN GLENN (Johnny)
B. May 11, 1917, Shullsburg, Wis.
BR TR 5'9" 165 lbs.

	G	AB	H	2B	3B	HR	HR%	R	RBI	BB	SO	SB	BA	SA	PH AB	PH H	G by POS
1938 CHI A	9	25	7	0	0	0	0.0	2	1	4	2	0	.280	.280	0	0	SS-8
1939	3	2	2	0	0	0	0.0	0	0	0	0	0	1.000	1.000	1	1	3B-1
2 yrs.	12	27	9	0	0	0	0.0	2	1	4	2	0	.333	.333	1	1	SS-8, 3B-1
2 yrs.	12	27	9	0	0	0	0.0	2	1	4	2	0	.333	.333	1	1	SS-8, 3B-1

Joe Ginsberg
GINSBERG, MYRON NATHAN
B. Oct. 11, 1926, New York, N.Y.
BL TR 5'11" 180 lbs.

	G	AB	H	2B	3B	HR	HR%	R	RBI	BB	SO	SB	BA	SA	PH AB	PH H	G by POS
1948 DET A	11	36	13	0	0	0	0.0	7	1	3	1	0	.361	.361	0	0	C-11
1950	36	95	22	6	0	0	0.0	12	12	11	6	1	.232	.295	4	1	C-31
1951	102	304	79	10	2	8	2.6	44	37	43	21	0	.260	.385	8	2	C-95
1952	113	307	68	13	2	6	2.0	29	36	51	21	1	.221	.336	16	2	C-101
1953 2 teams	DET	A	(18G –	.302)		CLE	A	(46G –	.284)								
" total	64	162	47	6	0	0	0.0	16	13	24	5	0	.290	.327	12	2	C-54
1954 CLE A	3	2	1	0	1	0	0.0	0	0	0	1	0	.500	1.500	2	1	C-1
1956 2 teams	KC	A	(71G –	.246)		BAL	A	(15G –	.071)								
" total	86	223	50	8	1	1	0.4	15	14	25	21	1	.224	.283	18	2	C-65
1957 BAL A	85	175	48	8	2	1	0.6	15	18	18	19	2	.274	.360	18	3	C-66
1958	61	109	23	1	0	3	2.8	4	16	13	14	0	.211	.303	20	4	C-39
1959	65	166	30	2	0	1	0.6	14	14	21	13	1	.181	.211	5	1	C-62
1960 2 teams	BAL	A	(14G –	.267)		CHI	A	(28G –	.253)								
" total	42	105	27	5	0	0	0.0	11	15	16	9	0	.257	.305	2	0	C-39
1961 2 teams	CHI	A	(6G –	.000)		BOS	A	(19G –	.250)								
" total	25	27	6	0	0	0	0.0	1	5	1	4	0	.222	.222	16	3	C-8
1962 NY N	2	5	0	0	0	0	0.0	0	0	1	0	0	.000	.000	0	0	C-2
13 yrs.	695	1716	414	59	8	20	1.2	168	182	226	135	7	.241	.320	121	22	C-574
2 yrs.	34	78	19	4	0	0	0.0	8	9	11	10	1	.244	.295	5	0	C-27

Kid Gleason
GLEASON, WILLIAM J.
Brother of Harry Gleason.
B. Oct. 26, 1866, Camden, N.J. D. Jan. 2, 1933, Philadelphia, Pa.
Manager 1919-23.
BL TR 5'7" 158 lbs.

	G	AB	H	2B	3B	HR	HR%	R	RBI	BB	SO	SB	BA	SA	PH AB	PH H	G by POS
1888 PHI N	24	83	17	2	0	0	0.0	4	5	3	16	3	.205	.229	0	0	P-24, OF-1
1889	30	99	25	5	0	0	0.0	11	8	8	12	4	.253	.303	0	0	P-28, OF-3, 2B-2
1890	63	224	47	3	0	0	0.0	22	17	12	21	10	.210	.223	0	0	P-60, 2B-2
1891	65	214	53	5	2	0	0.0	31	17	20	17	6	.248	.290	0	0	P-53, OF-9, SS-4
1892 STL N	66	233	50	4	2	3	1.3	35	25	34	23	7	.215	.288	0	0	P-47, OF-11, 2B-10, 1B-1, C-1
1893	59	199	51	6	4	0	0.0	25	20	19	8	2	.256	.327	2	1	P-48, OF-11, SS-1
1894 2 teams	STL	N	(9G –	.250)		BAL	N	(26G –	.349)								
" total	35	114	37	5	2	0	0.0	25	18	9	3	1	.325	.404	4	2	P-29, 1B-2
1895 BAL N	112	421	130	14	12	0	0.0	90	74	33	18	19	.309	.399	3	0	2B-85, 3B-12, P-9, OF-4
1896 NY N	133	541	162	17	5	4	0.7	79	89	42	13	46	.299	.372	0	0	2B-130, 3B-3, OF-1
1897	131	540	172	16	4	1	0.2	85	106	26		43	.319	.369	0	0	2B-129, SS-3
1898	150	570	126	8	5	0	0.0	78	62	39		21	.221	.253	0	0	2B-144, SS-6
1899	146	576	152	14	4	0	0.0	72	59	24		29	.264	.302	0	0	2B-146
1900	111	420	104	11	3	1	0.2	60	29	17		23	.248	.295	0	0	2B-111, SS-1
1901 DET A	135	547	150	16	12	3	0.5	82	75	41		32	.274	.364	0	0	2B-135
1902	118	441	109	11	4	1	0.2	42	38	25		17	.247	.297	0	0	2B-118
1903 PHI N	106	412	117	19	6	1	0.2	65	49	23		12	.284	.367	0	0	2B-102, OF-4
1904	153	587	161	23	6	0	0.0	61	42	37		17	.274	.334	0	0	2B-152, 3B-1
1905	155	608	150	17	7	1	0.2	95	50	45		16	.247	.303	0	0	2B-155

256

Player Register — 257

	G	AB	H	2B	3B	HR	HR %	R	RBI	BB	SO	SB	BA	SA	Pinch Hit AB	H	G by POS

Kid Gleason continued
1906	135	494	112	17	2	0	0.0	47	34	36		17	.227	.269	0	0	2B-135
1907	36	126	18	3	0	0	0.0	11	6	7		3	.143	.167	1	0	2B-26, SS-4, 1B-4, OF-1
1908	2	1	0	0	0	0	0.0	0	0	0		0	.000	.000	0	0	OF-1, 2B-1
1912 CHI A	1	2	1	0	0	0	0.0	0	0	0		0	.500	.500	0	0	2B-1
22 yrs.	1966	7452	1944	216	80	15	0.2	1020	823	500	131	328	.261	.317	10	3	2B-1584, P-298, OF-46, SS-19, 3B-16, 1B-7, C-1
1 yr.	1	2	1	0	0	0	0.0	0	0	0		0	.500	.500	0	0	2B-1

Gordon Goldsberry
GOLDSBERRY, GORDON FREDERICK BL TL 6' 170 lbs.
B. Aug. 30, 1927, Sacramento, Calif.

1949 CHI A	39	145	36	3	2	1	0.7	25	13	18	9	2	.248	.317	1	0	1B-38
1950	82	127	34	8	2	2	1.6	19	25	26	18	0	.268	.409	39	12	1B-40, OF-3
1951	10	11	1	0	0	0	0.0	4	1	2	2	0	.091	.091	2	0	1B-8
1952 STL A	86	227	52	9	3	3	1.3	30	17	34	37	0	.229	.335	10	2	1B-72, OF-2
4 yrs.	217	510	123	20	7	6	1.2	78	56	80	66	2	.241	.343	52	14	1B-158, OF-5
3 yrs.	131	283	71	11	4	3	1.1	48	39	46	29	2	.251	.350	42	12	1B-86, OF-3

Stan Goletz
GOLETZ, STANLEY (Stash) BL TL 6'3" 200 lbs.
B. May 21, 1918, Crescent, Ohio

| 1941 CHI A | 5 | 5 | 3 | 0 | 0 | 0 | 0.0 | 0 | 2 | 0 | | 0 | .600 | .600 | 5 | 3 | |

Wilbur Good
GOOD, WILBUR DAVID (Lefty) BL TL 5'6" 165 lbs.
B. Sept. 28, 1885, Punxsutawney, Pa. D. Dec. 30, 1963, Brooksville, Fla.

1905 NY A	6	8	3	0	0	0	0.0	2	0	0		0	.375	.375	0	0	P-5
1908 CLE A	46	154	43	1	3	1	0.6	23	14	13		7	.279	.344	2	1	OF-42
1909	94	318	68	6	5	0	0.0	33	17	28	13	13	.214	.264	10	1	OF-80
1910 BOS N	23	86	29	5	4	0	0.0	15	11	6	13	5	.337	.488	0	0	OF-23
1911 2 teams	BOS N (43G – .267)						CHI N (58G – .269)										
" total	101	310	83	14	7	2	0.6	48	36	23	39	13	.268	.377	12	1	OF-83
1912 CHI N	39	35	5	0	0	0	0.0	7	1	3	7	3	.143	.143	21	3	OF-10
1913	49	91	23	3	2	1	1.1	11	12	11	16	5	.253	.363	16	4	OF-26
1914	154	580	158	24	7	2	0.3	70	43	53	74	31	.272	.348	0	0	OF-154
1915	128	498	126	18	9	2	0.4	66	27	34	65	19	.253	.337	2	1	OF-125
1916 PHI N	75	136	34	4	3	1	0.7	25	15	8	13	7	.250	.346	22	3	OF-46
1918 CHI N	35	148	37	9	4	0	0.0	24	11	11	16	1	.250	.365	0	0	OF-35
11 yrs.	750	2364	609	84	44	9	0.4	324	187	190	243	104	.258	.342	85	14	OF-624, P-5
1 yr.	35	148	37	9	4	0	0.0	24	11	11	16	1	.250	.365	0	0	OF-35

Billy Goodman
GOODMAN, WILLIAM DALE BL TR 5'11" 165 lbs.
B. Mar. 22, 1926, Concord, N. C.

1947 BOS A	12	11	2	0	0	0	0.0	1	1	1	2	0	.182	.182	9	1	OF-1
1948	127	445	138	27	2	1	0.2	65	66	74	44	5	.310	.387	4	2	1B-117, 3B-2, 2B-2
1949	122	443	132	23	3	0	0.0	54	56	58	21	2	.298	.363	3	2	1B-117
1950	110	424	150	25	3	4	0.9	91	68	52	25	2	.354	.455	11	2	OF-45, 3B-27, 1B-21, 2B-5, SS-1
1951	141	546	162	34	4	0	0.0	92	50	79	37	7	.297	.374	1	0	1B-62, 2B-44, OF-38, 3B-1
1952	138	513	157	27	3	4	0.8	79	56	48	23	8	.306	.394	6	1	2B-103, 1B-23, 3B-5, OF-4
1953	128	514	161	33	5	2	0.4	73	41	57	11	1	.313	.409	2	2	2B-112, 1B-20
1954	127	489	148	25	4	1	0.2	71	36	51	15	3	.303	.376	10	3	2B-72, 1B-27, OF-13, 3B-12
1955	149	599	176	31	2	0	0.0	100	52	99	44	5	.294	.352	0	0	2B-143, 1B-5, OF-1
1956	105	399	117	22	8	2	0.5	61	38	40	22	0	.293	.404	9	2	2B-95
1957 2 teams	BOS A (18G – .063)						BAL A (73G – .308)										
" total	91	279	82	11	3	3	1.1	37	33	23	19	0	.294	.387	22	2	3B-54, OF-9, 1B-8, SS-5, 2B-5
1958 CHI A	116	425	127	15	5	0	0.0	41	40	37	21	1	.299	.358	4	2	3B-111, 1B-3, SS-1, 2B-1
1959	104	268	67	14	1	1	0.4	21	28	19	20	3	.250	.321	31	7	3B-74, 2B-3
1960	30	77	18	4	0	0	0.0	5	6	12	8	0	.234	.286	6	0	3B-20, 2B-7
1961	41	51	13	4	0	1	2.0	4	10	7	6	0	.255	.392	27	9	3B-7, 1B-2, 2B-1
1962 HOU N	82	161	41	4	1	0	0.0	12	10	12	11	0	.255	.292	53	14	2B-31, 3B-17, 1B-1
16 yrs.	1623	5644	1691	299	44	19	0.3	807	591	669	329	37	.300	.378	198	49	2B-624, 1B-406, 3B-330, OF-111, SS-7
4 yrs.	291	821	225	37	6	2	0.2	71	84	75	55	4	.274	.341	68	18	3B-212, 2B-12, 1B-5, SS-1

WORLD SERIES
| 1959 CHI A | 5 | 13 | 3 | 0 | 0 | 0 | 0.0 | 1 | 1 | 0 | 5 | 0 | .231 | .231 | 2 | 0 | 3B-5 |

Johnny Grabowski
GRABOWSKI, JOHN PATRICK (Nig) BR TR 5'10" 185 lbs.
B. Jan. 7, 1900, Ware, Mass. D. May 23, 1946, Albany, N. Y.

1924 CHI A	20	56	14	3	0	0	0.0	10	3	2	4	0	.250	.304	0	0	C-19
1925	21	46	14	4	1	0	0.0	5	10	2	3	0	.304	.435	0	0	C-21
1926	48	122	32	1	1	1	0.8	6	11	4	15	0	.262	.311	8	4	C-38, 1B-1
1927 NY A	70	195	54	2	4	0	0.0	29	25	20	15	0	.277	.328	2	0	C-68
1928	75	202	48	7	1	1	0.5	21	21	10	21	0	.238	.297	0	0	C-75
1929	22	59	12	0	0	0	0.0	4	2	3	6	1	.203	.220	0	0	C-22
1931 DET A	40	136	32	7	1	1	0.7	9	14	6	19	0	.235	.324	1	1	C-39
7 yrs.	296	816	206	25	8	3	0.4	84	86	47	84	1	.252	.314	11	5	C-282, 1B-1
3 yrs.	89	224	60	8	2	1	0.4	21	24	8	23	0	.268	.335	8	4	C-78, 1B-1

WORLD SERIES
| 1927 NY A | 1 | 2 | 0 | 0 | 0 | 0 | 0.0 | 0 | 0 | 0 | 0 | 0 | .000 | .000 | 0 | 0 | C-1 |

Roy Graham
GRAHAM, ROY VINCENT BR TR 5'10½" 175 lbs.
B. Feb. 22, 1895, San Francisco, Calif. D. Apr. 26, 1933, Manila, Philippines

| 1922 CHI A | 5 | 3 | 0 | 0 | 0 | 0 | 0.0 | 0 | 0 | 0 | 0 | 0 | .000 | .000 | 1 | 0 | C-3 |

	G	AB	H	2B	3B	HR	HR %	R	RBI	BB	SO	SB	BA	SA	Pinch Hit AB	H	G by POS

Roy Graham continued
1923	36	82	16	2	0	0	0.0	3	6	9	6	0	.195	.220	2	1	C-33
2 yrs.	41	85	16	2	0	0	0.0	3	6	9	6	0	.188	.212	3	0	C-36
2 yrs.	41	85	16	2	0	0	0.0	3	6	9	6	0	.188	.212	3	0	C-36

Jimmy Grant
GRANT, JAMES CHARLES BL TR 5'8" 166 lbs.
B. Oct. 6, 1918, Racine, Wis.

1942 CHI A	12	36	6	1	1	0	0.0	0	1	5	6	0	.167	.250	1	0	3B-10
1943 2 teams	CHI	A (58G – .259)			CLE	A (15G – .136)											
" total	73	219	54	11	2	4	1.8	26	23	22	41	4	.247	.370	19	2	3B-56
1944 CLE A	61	99	27	4	3	1	1.0	12	12	11	20	1	.273	.404	32	5	2B-20, 3B-4
3 yrs.	146	354	87	16	6	5	1.4	38	36	38	67	5	.246	.367	52	7	3B-70, 2B-20
2 yrs.	70	233	57	10	3	4	1.7	23	23	23	40	4	.245	.365	8	1	3B-61

Lorenzo Gray
GRAY, LORENZO BR TR 6'1" 180 lbs.
B. Mar. 4, 1958, Mound Bayou, Miss.

1982 CHI A	17	28	8	1	0	0	0.0	4	0	2	4	1	.286	.321	1	0	3B-16
1983	41	78	14	3	0	1	1.3	18	4	8	16	1	.179	.256	3	1	3B-31, DH-7
2 yrs.	58	106	22	4	0	1	0.9	22	4	10	20	2	.208	.274	4	1	3B-47, DH-7
2 yrs.	58	106	22	4	0	1	0.9	22	4	10	20	2	.208	.274	4	1	3B-47, DH-7

Danny Green
GREEN, EDWARD BL
B. Nov. 6, 1876, Burlington, N. J. D. Nov. 9, 1914, Camden, N. J.

1898 CHI N	47	188	59	4	3	4	2.1	26	27	7		12	.314	.431	0	0	OF-47
1899	117	475	140	12	11	6	1.3	90	56	35		18	.295	.404	2	0	OF-115
1900	103	389	116	21	5	5	1.3	63	49	17		28	.298	.416	2	1	OF-101
1901	133	537	168	16	12	5	0.9	82	60	40		31	.313	.415	0	0	OF-133
1902 CHI A	129	481	150	16	11	0	0.0	77	62	53		35	.312	.391	0	0	OF-129
1903	135	499	154	26	7	6	1.2	75	62	47		29	.309	.425	1	0	OF-133
1904	147	536	142	16	10	2	0.4	83	62	63		28	.265	.343	1	1	OF-146
1905	112	379	92	13	6	0	0.0	56	44	53		11	.243	.309	5	0	OF-107
8 yrs.	923	3484	1021	124	65	28	0.8	552	422	315		192	.293	.390	12	2	OF-911
4 yrs.	523	1895	538	71	34	8	0.4	291	230	216		103	.284	.370	8	1	OF-515

Clark Griffith
GRIFFITH, CLARK CALVIN (The Old Fox) BR TR 5'6½" 156 lbs.
B. Nov. 20, 1869, Stringtown, Mo. D. Oct. 27, 1955, Washington, D. C.
Manager 1901-20.
Hall of Fame 1946.

1891 2 teams	STL	AA (27G – .156)			BOS	AA (10G – .174)											
" total	37	100	16	2	1	2	2.0	17	11	14	20	3	.160	.260	1	0	P-34, OF-3
1893 CHI N	4	11	2	0	0	0	0.0	1	2	0	1	0	.182	.182	0	0	P-4
1894	46	142	33	5	4	0	0.0	27	15	23	9	6	.232	.324	2	1	P-36, OF-7, SS-1
1895	43	144	46	3	0	1	0.7	20	27	16	9	2	.319	.361	1	0	P-42, OF-1
1896	38	135	36	5	2	1	0.7	22	16	9	7	3	.267	.356	2	0	P-36
1897	46	162	38	8	4	0	0.0	27	21	18		2	.235	.333	1	0	P-41, OF-2, SS-2, 3B-1, 1B-1
1898	38	122	20	2	3	0	0.0	15	15	13		1	.164	.230	0	0	P-38
1899	39	120	31	5	0	0	0.0	15	14	14		2	.258	.300	0	0	P-38, SS-1
1900	30	95	24	4	1	1	1.1	16	7	8		2	.253	.347	0	0	P-30
1901 CHI A	35	89	27	3	1	2	2.2	21	14	23		0	.303	.427	0	0	P-35
1902	35	92	20	3	0	0	0.0	11	8	7		0	.217	.250	4	0	P-28, OF-3
1903 NY A	25	69	11	4	0	1	1.4	5	7	11		0	.159	.261	0	0	P-25
1904	16	42	6	2	0	0	0.0	2	1	4		0	.143	.190	0	0	P-16
1905	26	32	7	1	1	0	0.0	2	5	3		0	.219	.313	0	0	P-25, OF-1
1906	17	18	2	0	0	0	0.0	0	1	3		0	.111	.111	0	0	P-17
1907	4	2	0	0	0	0	0.0	0	0	0		0	.000	.000	0	0	P-4
1909 CIN N	1	2	0	0	0	0	0.0	0	0	0		0	.000	.000	0	0	P-1
1910	1	0	0	0	0	0	–	1	0	0		0	–	–	0	0	
1912 WAS A	1	1	0	0	0	0	0.0	0	0	0	0	0	.000	.000	0	0	2B-1, P-1
1913	1	1	1	1	0	0	0.0	0	1	0	0	0	1.000	2.000	0	0	OF-1, P-1
1914	1	1	1	1	0	0	0.0	0	1	0	0	0	1.000	2.000	0	0	P-1
21 yrs.	484	1380	321	49	17	8	0.6	202	166	166	46	22	.233	.310	9	1	P-453, OF-18, SS-4, 3B-1, 2B-1, 1B-1
2 yrs.	70	181	47	6	1	2	1.1	32	22	30		0	.260	.337	4	0	P-63, OF-3

Johnny Groth
GROTH, JOHN THOMAS BR TR 6' 182 lbs.
B. July 23, 1926, Chicago, Ill.

1946 DET A	4	9	0	0	0	0	0.0	1	0	3	0	0	.000	.000	0	0	OF-4
1947	2	4	1	0	0	0	0.0	1	0	2	1	0	.250	.250	1	0	OF-1
1948	6	17	8	3	0	1	5.9	3	5	1	1	0	.471	.824	1	0	OF-4
1949	103	348	102	19	5	11	3.2	60	73	65	27	3	.293	.471	3	0	OF-99
1950	157	566	173	30	8	12	2.1	95	85	95	27	1	.306	.451	0	0	OF-157
1951	118	428	128	29	1	3	0.7	41	49	31	32	1	.299	.393	6	2	OF-112
1952	141	524	149	22	2	4	0.8	56	51	51	39	2	.284	.357	3	0	OF-139
1953 STL A	141	557	141	27	4	10	1.8	65	57	42	53	5	.253	.370	0	0	OF-141
1954 CHI A	125	422	116	20	0	7	1.7	41	60	42	37	3	.275	.372	1	0	OF-125
1955 2 teams	CHI	A (32G – .338)			WAS	A (63G – .219)											
" total	95	260	66	11	5	4	1.5	35	28	24	31	3	.254	.381	14	5	OF-74
1956 KC A	95	244	63	13	5	2	2.0	22	37	30	31	1	.258	.398	13	4	OF-84
1957 2 teams	KC	A (55G – .254)			DET	A (38G – .291)											
" total	93	162	45	10	0	0	0.0	21	18	13	13	0	.278	.340	4	0	OF-86
1958 DET A	88	146	41	5	2	2	1.4	24	11	13	19	0	.281	.384	16	6	OF-80
1959	55	102	24	7	1	1	1.0	12	10	7	14	0	.235	.353	13	3	OF-41
1960	25	19	7	1	0	0	0.0	3	2	3	1	0	.368	.421	8	3	OF-8
15 yrs.	1248	3808	1064	197	31	60	1.6	480	486	419	329	19	.279	.395	83	24	OF-1155
2 yrs.	157	499	142	27	0	9	1.8	54	71	48	50	4	.285	.393	2	0	OF-151

Player Register

	G	AB	H	2B	3B	HR	HR%	R	RBI	BB	SO	SB	BA	SA	Pinch Hit AB	Pinch Hit H	G by POS

Frank Grube
GRUBE, FRANKLIN THOMAS (Hans)   BR TR 5'9" 190 lbs.
B. Jan. 7, 1905, Easton, Pa.   D. July 2, 1945, New York, N.Y.

	G	AB	H	2B	3B	HR	HR%	R	RBI	BB	SO	SB	BA	SA	PH-AB	PH-H	G by POS
1931 CHI A	88	265	58	13	2	1	0.4	29	24	22	22	2	.219	.294	6	1	C-81
1932	93	277	78	16	2	0	0.0	36	31	33	13	6	.282	.354	1	0	C-92
1933	85	256	59	13	0	0	0.0	23	23	38	20	1	.230	.281	1	0	C-83
1934 STL A	65	170	49	10	0	0	0.0	22	11	24	11	2	.288	.347	9	0	C-55
1935 2 teams	STL A (3G – .333)			CHI A (9G – .368)													
" total	12	25	9	3	0	0	0.0	4	6	3	3	0	.360	.480	0	0	C-12
1936 CHI A	33	93	15	2	1	0	0.0	6	11	9	15	1	.161	.204	2	0	C-32
1941 STL A	18	39	6	2	0	0	0.0	1	1	2	4	0	.154	.205	0	0	C-18
7 yrs.	394	1125	274	59	5	1	0.1	121	107	131	88	12	.244	.308	19	1	C-373
5 yrs.	308	910	217	46	5	1	0.1	95	95	105	72	10	.238	.303	10	1	C-297

Tom Gulley
GULLEY, THOMAS JEFFERSON   BL TR 5'11" 178 lbs.
B. Dec. 25, 1899, Garner, N.C.   D. Nov. 24, 1966, St. Charles, Ark.

	G	AB	H	2B	3B	HR	HR%	R	RBI	BB	SO	SB	BA	SA	PH-AB	PH-H	G by POS
1923 CLE A	2	3	1	1	0	0	0.0	1	0	0	0	0	.333	.667	1	1	OF-1
1924	8	20	3	0	1	0	0.0	4	1	3	2	0	.150	.250	3	0	OF-5
1926 CHI A	16	35	8	3	1	0	0.0	5	8	5	2	0	.229	.371	4	1	OF-12
3 yrs.	26	58	12	4	2	0	0.0	10	9	8	4	0	.207	.345	8	1	OF-18
1 yr.	16	35	8	3	1	0	0.0	5	8	5	2	0	.229	.371	4	1	OF-12

Don Gutteridge
GUTTERIDGE, DONALD JOSEPH   BR TR 5'10½" 165 lbs.
B. June 19, 1912, Pittsburg, Kans. Manager 1969-70.

	G	AB	H	2B	3B	HR	HR%	R	RBI	BB	SO	SB	BA	SA	PH-AB	PH-H	G by POS
1936 STL N	23	91	29	3	4	3	3.3	13	16	1	14	3	.319	.538	0	0	3B-23
1937	119	447	121	26	10	7	1.6	66	61	25	66	12	.271	.421	8	1	3B-105, SS-8
1938	142	552	141	21	15	9	1.6	61	64	29	49	14	.255	.397	2	0	3B-73, SS-68
1939	148	524	141	27	4	7	1.3	71	54	27	70	5	.269	.376	2	0	3B-143, SS-2
1940	69	108	29	5	0	3	2.8	19	14	5	15	3	.269	.398	20	2	3B-39
1942 STL A	147	616	157	27	11	1	0.2	90	50	59	54	16	.255	.339	1	1	2B-145, 3B-2
1943	132	538	147	35	6	1	0.2	77	36	50	46	10	.273	.366	1	0	2B-132
1944	148	603	148	27	11	3	0.5	89	36	51	63	20	.245	.342	1	0	2B-146
1945	143	543	129	24	3	2	0.4	72	49	43	46	9	.238	.304	1	0	2B-128, OF-14
1946 BOS A	22	47	11	3	0	1	2.1	8	6	2	7	0	.234	.362	1	0	2B-9, 3B-8
1947	54	131	22	2	0	2	1.5	20	5	17	13	3	.168	.229	5	1	2B-20, 3B-19
1948 PIT N	4	2	0	0	0	0	0.0	0	0	0	1	0	.000	.000	2	0	
12 yrs.	1151	4202	1075	200	64	39	0.9	586	391	309	444	95	.256	.362	44	5	2B-580, 3B-412, SS-78, OF-14

WORLD SERIES

	G	AB	H	2B	3B	HR	HR%	R	RBI	BB	SO	SB	BA	SA	PH-AB	PH-H	G by POS
1944 STL A	6	21	3	1	0	0	0.0	1	0	3	5	0	.143	.190	0	0	2B-6
1946 BOS A	3	5	2	0	0	0	0.0	1	0	0	0	0	.400	.400	0	0	2B-2
2 yrs.	9	26	5	1	0	0	0.0	2	0	3	5	0	.192	.231	0	0	2B-8

Bert Haas
HAAS, BERTHOLD JOHN   BR TR 5'11" 178 lbs.
B. Feb. 8, 1914, Naperville, Ill.

	G	AB	H	2B	3B	HR	HR%	R	RBI	BB	SO	SB	BA	SA	PH-AB	PH-H	G by POS
1937 BKN N	16	25	10	3	0	0	0.0	2	2	1	1	0	.400	.520	9	4	OF-4, 1B-3
1938	1	0	0	0	0	0	–	0	0	0	0	0			0	0	
1942 CIN N	154	585	140	21	6	6	1.0	59	54	59	54	6	.239	.326	0	0	3B-146, 1B-6, OF-2
1943	101	332	87	17	6	4	1.2	39	44	22	26	6	.262	.386	16	4	1B-44, 3B-23, OF-18
1946	140	535	141	24	7	3	0.6	57	50	33	42	22	.264	.351	2	1	1B-131, 3B-6
1947	135	482	138	17	7	3	0.6	58	67	42	27	9	.286	.369	11	2	OF-69, 1B-53
1948 PHI N	95	333	94	9	2	4	1.2	35	34	26	25	8	.282	.357	9	2	3B-54, 1B-35
1949 2 teams	PHI N (2G – .000)			NY N (54G – .260)													
" total	56	105	27	2	1	0	0.0	12	10	6	9	0	.257	.362	19	4	1B-23, 3B-11
1951 CHI A	25	43	7	0	1	1	2.3	1	2	5	4	0	.163	.279	11	3	1B-7, OF-4, 3B-1
9 yrs.	723	2440	644	93	32	22	0.9	263	263	204	188	51	.264	.355	77	20	1B-302, 3B-241, OF-97
1 yr.	25	43	7	0	1	1	2.3	1	2	5	4	0	.163	.279	11	3	1B-7, OF-4, 3B-1

Mule Haas
HAAS, GEORGE WILLIAM   BL TR 6'1" 175 lbs.
B. Oct. 15, 1903, Montclair, N.J.   D. June 30, 1974, New Orleans, La.

	G	AB	H	2B	3B	HR	HR%	R	RBI	BB	SO	SB	BA	SA	PH-AB	PH-H	G by POS
1925 PIT N	4	3	0	0	0	0	0.0	1	0	0	1	0	.000	.000	1	0	OF-2
1928 PHI A	91	332	93	21	4	6	1.8	41	39	23	20	2	.280	.422	8	0	OF-82
1929	139	578	181	41	9	16	2.8	115	82	34	38	0	.313	.498	0	0	OF-139
1930	132	532	159	33	7	2	0.4	91	68	43	33	2	.299	.398	1	0	OF-131
1931	102	440	142	29	7	8	1.8	82	56	30	29	0	.323	.475	0	0	OF-102
1932	143	558	170	28	5	6	1.1	91	65	62	49	1	.305	.405	6	3	OF-137
1933 CHI A	146	585	168	33	4	1	0.2	97	51	65	41	0	.287	.362	0	0	OF-146
1934	106	351	94	16	3	2	0.6	54	22	47	22	1	.268	.348	13	4	OF-89
1935	92	327	95	22	1	2	0.6	44	40	37	17	4	.291	.382	7	2	OF-84
1936	119	408	116	26	2	0	0.0	75	46	64	29	1	.284	.358	15	3	OF-96, 1B-7
1937	54	111	23	3	0	0	0.0	8	15	16	10	1	.207	.288	16	2	1B-32, OF-2
1938 PHI A	40	78	16	2	0	0	0.0	7	12	12	10	0	.205	.231	20	1	OF-12, 1B-6
12 yrs.	1168	4303	1257	254	45	43	1.0	706	496	433	299	12	.292	.402	87	15	OF-1022, 1B-45
5 yrs.	517	1782	496	100	13	5	0.3	278	174	229	119	7	.278	.357	51	11	OF-417, 1B-39

WORLD SERIES

	G	AB	H	2B	3B	HR	HR%	R	RBI	BB	SO	SB	BA	SA	PH-AB	PH-H	G by POS
1929 PHI A	5	21	5	0	0	2	9.5	3	6	1	3	0	.238	.524	0	0	OF-5
1930	6	18	2	0	0	0	0.0	1	1	1	3	0	.111	.222	0	0	OF-6
1931	7	23	3	1	0	0	0.0	1	3	5	5	0	.130	.174	0	0	OF-7
3 yrs.	18	62	10	1	0	2	3.2	5	9	5	11	0	.161	.306	0	0	OF-18

Bud Hafey
HAFEY, DANIEL ALBERT   BR TR 6' 185 lbs.
Brother of Tom Hafey.
B. Aug. 6, 1912, Berkeley, Calif.

	G	AB	H	2B	3B	HR	HR%	R	RBI	BB	SO	SB	BA	SA	PH-AB	PH-H	G by POS
1935 2 teams	CHI A (2G – .000)			PIT N (58G – .228)													
" total	60	184	42	11	2	6	3.3	30	16	16	48	0	.228	.408	5	1	OF-47
1936 PIT N	39	118	25	6	1	4	3.4	19	13	10	27	0	.212	.381	9	0	OF-29

Player Register　260

	G	AB	H	2B	3B	HR	HR%	R	RBI	BB	SO	SB	BA	SA	Pinch Hit AB	H	G by POS

Bud Hafey continued

1939 2 teams	CIN N (6G – .154)			PHI N (18G – .176)													
" total	24	64	11	2	0	0	0.0	4	4	4	16	2	.172	.203	5	1	OF-17, P-2
3 yrs.	123	366	78	19	3	10	2.7	53	33	30	91	2	.213	.363	19	2	OF-93, P-2
1 yr.	2	0	0	0	0	0	–	1	0	0	0	0	–	–	0	0	

Ed Hahn
HAHN, EDGAR WILLIAM
B. Aug. 27, 1880, Nevada, Ohio　D. Nov. 29, 1941, Des Moines, Iowa　BL TR

1905 NY A	43	160	51	5	0	0	0.0	32		11		25		1	.319	.350	0	0	OF-43
1906 2 teams	NY A (11G – .091)				CHI A (130G – .227)														
" total	141	506	112	8	5	0	0.0	82	28	72		21	.221	.257	1	0	OF-137		
1907 CHI A	156	592	151	9	7	0	0.0	87	45	84		17	.255	.294	0	0	OF-156		
1908	122	447	112	12	8	0	0.0	58	21	39		11	.251	.313	3	1	OF-118		
1909	76	287	52	6	0	1	0.3	30	16	31		9	.181	.213	0	0	OF-76		
1910	15	53	6	2	0	0	0.0	2	1	7		0	.113	.151	0	0	OF-15		
6 yrs.	553	2045	484	42	20	1	0.0	291	122	258		59	.237	.278	4	1	OF-545		
5 yrs.	499	1863	431	36	20	1	0.1	257	110	230		56	.231	.274	3	1	OF-495		

WORLD SERIES

1906 CHI A	6	22	6	0	0	0	0.0	4	0	1	1	0	.273	.273	0	0	OF-6

Jerry Hairston
HAIRSTON, JERRY WAYNE
Brother of John Hairston.　Son of Sam Hairston.
B. Feb. 16, 1952, Birmingham, Ala.　BB TL 5'10" 170 lbs.

1973 CHI A	60	210	57	11	1	0	0.0	25	23	33	30	0	.271	.333	2	0	OF-33, 1B-19, DH-8
1974	45	109	25	7	0	0	0.0	8	8	13	18	0	.229	.294	12	2	OF-22, DH-10
1975	69	219	62	8	0	0	0.0	26	23	46	23	1	.283	.320	3	0	OF-59, DH-8
1976	44	119	27	2	2	0	0.0	20	10	24	19	1	.227	.277	4	1	OF-40
1977 2 teams	CHI A (13G – .308)				PIT N (51G – .192)												
" total	64	78	18	4	0	2	2.6	8	10	11	17	0	.231	.359	34	7	OF-25, 2B-1
1981 CHI A	9	25	7	1	0	1	4.0	5	6	2	4	0	.280	.440	2	1	OF-7
1982	85	90	21	5	0	5	5.6	11	18	9	15	0	.233	.456	47	11	OF-36, DH-2
1983	101	126	37	9	1	5	4.0	17	22	23	16	0	.294	.500	62	17	OF-32, DH-4
8 yrs.	477	976	254	47	4	13	1.3	120	120	161	142	2	.260	.357	166	39	OF-254, DH-32, 1B-19, 2B-1
8 yrs.	426	924	244	45	4	11	1.2	115	114	155	132	2	.264	.357	133 3rd	32 4th	OF-240, DH-32, 1B-19

LEAGUE CHAMPIONSHIP SERIES

1983 CHI A	2	3	0	0	0	0	0.0	0	0	1	1	0	.000	.000	2	0	OF-2

Sam Hairston
HAIRSTON, SAMUEL
Father of Jerry Hairston.　Father of John Hairston.
B. Jan. 28, 1920, Crawford, Miss.　BR TR 5'10½" 187 lbs.

1951 CHI A	4	5	2	1	0	0	0.0	1	1	2	0	0	.400	.600	1	0	C-2

Chet Hajduk
HAJDUK, CHESTER
B. July 21, 1918, Chicago, Ill.　BR TR 6' 195 lbs.

1941 CHI A	1	1	0	0	0	0	0.0	0	0	0	0	0	.000	.000	1	0	

Bill Hallman
HALLMAN, WILLIAM HARRY
B. Mar. 15, 1876, Philadelphia, Pa.　D. Apr. 23, 1950, Philadelphia, Pa.

1901 MIL A	139	549	135	27	6	2	0.4	70	47	41		12	.246	.328	0	0	OF-139
1903 PHI A	63	207	43	7	4	0	0.0	29	18	31		11	.208	.280	6	0	OF-57
1906 PIT N	23	89	24	3	1	1	1.1	12	6	15		3	.270	.360	0	0	OF-23
1907	94	302	67	6	2	0	0.0	39	15	33		21	.222	.255	9	2	OF-84
4 yrs.	319	1147	269	43	13	3	0.3	150	86	120		47	.235	.303	15	2	OF-303
1 yr.	63	207	43	7	4	0	0.0	29	18	31		11	.208	.280	6	0	OF-57

Fred Hancock
HANCOCK, FRED JAMES
B. Mar. 28, 1920, Allenport, Pa.　BR TR 5'8" 170 lbs.

1949 CHI A	39	52	7	2	1	0	0.0	7	9	8	9	0	.135	.212	5	1	SS-27, 3B-3, OF-1

Ron Hansen
HANSEN, RONALD LAVERN
B. Apr. 5, 1938, Oxford, Neb.　BR TR 6'3" 190 lbs.

1958 BAL A	12	19	0	0	0	0	0.0	1		0	7	0	.000	.000	0	0	SS-12
1959	2	4	0	0	0	0	0.0	0	0	1	1	0	.000	.000	0	0	SS-2
1960	153	530	135	22	5	22	4.2	72	86	69	94	3	.255	.440	1	0	SS-153
1961	155	533	132	13	2	12	2.3	51	51	66	96	1	.248	.347	0	0	SS-149, 2B-7
1962	71	196	34	7	0	3	1.5	12	17	30	36	0	.173	.255	6	2	SS-64
1963 CHI A	144	482	109	17	2	13	2.7	55	67	78	74	1	.226	.351	0	0	SS-144
1964	158	575	150	25	3	20	3.5	85	68	73	73	1	.261	.419	0	0	SS-158
1965	162	587	138	23	4	11	1.9	61	66	60	73	1	.235	.344	0	0	SS-161, 2B-1
1966	23	74	13	1	0	0	0.0	3	4	15	10	0	.176	.189	0	0	SS-23
1967	157	498	116	20	0	8	1.6	35	51	64	51	0	.233	.321	0	0	SS-157
1968 2 teams	WAS A (86G – .185)				CHI A (40G – .230)												
" total	126	362	71	15	0	9	2.5	35	32	46	61	0	.196	.312	6	2	SS-88, 3B-34, 2B-2
1969 CHI A	85	185	48	6	1	2	1.1	15	22	18	25	2	.259	.335	25	6	2B-26, 1B-21, SS-8, 3B-7
1970 NY A	59	91	27	4	0	4	4.4	19	9	10	9	0	.297	.495	28	4	SS-15, 3B-11, 2B-1
1971	61	145	30	3	0	2	1.4	6	20	9	27	0	.207	.269	22	4	3B-30, 2B-9, SS-3
1972 KC A	16	30	4	0	0	0	0.0	2	2	3	6	0	.133	.133	7	1	SS-6, 3B-4, 2B-1
15 yrs.	1384	4311	1007	156	17	106	2.5	446	501	551	643	9	.234	.351	95	19	SS-1143, 3B-86, 2B-47, 1B-21
7 yrs.	769	2488	594	95	10	55	2.2	261	282	319	318	5	.239	.351	28	7	SS-658, 3B-36, 2B-29, 1B-21

Player Register

	G	AB	H	2B	3B	HR	HR %	R	RBI	BB	SO	SB	BA	SA	Pinch Hit AB H	G by POS

Don Hanski
HANSKI, DONALD THOMAS BL TL 5'11" 180 lbs.
Born Donald Thomas Hanyzewski.
B. Feb. 27, 1916, LaPorte, Ind.   D. Sept. 2, 1957, Worth, Ill.

Year		G	AB	H	2B	3B	HR	HR%	R	RBI	BB	SO	SB	BA	SA	PH AB	PH H	G by POS
1943	CHI A	9	21	5	1	0	0	0.0	0	2	0	5	0	.238	.286	3	0	1B-5, P-1
1944		2	1	0	0	0	0	0.0	0	0	0	0	0	.000	.000	0	0	P-2
2 yrs.		11	22	5	1	0	0	0.0	1	2	0	5	0	.227	.273	3	0	1B-5, P-3
2 yrs.		11	22	5	1	0	0	0.0	1	2	0	5	0	.227	.273	3	0	1B-5, P-3

John Happenny
HAPPENNY, JOHN CLIFFORD (Cliff) BR TR 5'11" 165 lbs.
B. May 18, 1901, Waltham, Mass.

Year		G	AB	H	2B	3B	HR	HR%	R	RBI	BB	SO	SB	BA	SA	PH AB	PH H	G by POS
1923	CHI A	32	86	19	5	0	0	0.0	7	10	3	13	0	.221	.279	1	0	2B-20, SS-8

Pat Hargrove
HARGROVE, WILLIAM PATRICK BR TR 5'10" 158 lbs.
B. May 10, 1896, Palmyra Ct. House, Kans.

Year		G	AB	H	2B	3B	HR	HR%	R	RBI	BB	SO	SB	BA	SA	PH AB	PH H	G by POS
1918	CHI A	2	2	0	0	0	0	0.0	0	0	0	0	0	.000	.000	2	0	

Dave Harris
HARRIS, DAVID STANLEY (Sheriff) BR TR 5'11" 170 lbs.
B. June 14, 1900, Summerfield, N. C.   D. Sept. 18, 1973, Atlanta, Ga.

Year		G	AB	H	2B	3B	HR	HR%	R	RBI	BB	SO	SB	BA	SA	PH AB	PH H	G by POS
1925	BOS N	92	340	90	8	7	5	1.5	49	36	27	44	6	.265	.374	1	0	OF-90
1928		7	17	2	1	0	0	0.0	0	2	6	0	0	.118	.176	1	0	OF-6
1930	2 teams	CHI A (33G – .244)							WAS A (73G – .317)										
"	total	106	291	86	21	9	9	3.1	56	57	35	57	6	.296	.522	21	9	OF-82, 2B-1
1931	WAS A	77	231	72	14	8	5	2.2	49	50	49	38	7	.312	.506	13	5	OF-60
1932		81	156	51	7	4	6	3.8	26	29	19	34	4	.327	.538	43	14	OF-34
1933		82	177	46	9	2	5	2.8	33	38	25	26	3	.260	.418	24	8	OF-45, 1B-6, 3B-2
1934		97	235	59	14	3	2	0.9	28	37	39	40	2	.251	.362	26	4	OF-64, 3B-5
7 yrs.		542	1447	406	74	33	32	2.2	243	247	196	245	28	.281	.444	129	40	OF-381, 3B-7, 1B-6, 2B-1
1 yr.		33	86	21	2	1	5	5.8	16	13	7	22	0	.244	.465	8	3	OF-23, 2B-1

WORLD SERIES
| 1933 | WAS A | 3 | 2 | 0 | 0 | 0 | 0 | 0.0 | 0 | 0 | 2 | 0 | 0 | .000 | .000 | 1 | 0 | OF-1 |

Spence Harris
HARRIS, ANTHONY SPENCER BL TL 5'9" 145 lbs.
B. Aug. 12, 1900, Duluth, Minn.

Year		G	AB	H	2B	3B	HR	HR%	R	RBI	BB	SO	SB	BA	SA	PH AB	PH H	G by POS
1925	CHI A	56	92	26	2	1	1	1.1	12	13	14	13	1	.283	.337	24	7	OF-27
1926		80	222	56	11	3	2	0.9	36	27	20	15	8	.252	.356	14	2	OF-64
1929	WAS A	6	14	3	1	0	0	0.0	1	1	0	3	1	.214	.286	0	0	OF-4
1930	PHI A	22	49	9	1	0	0	0.0	4	5	5	2	0	.184	.204	7	1	OF-13
4 yrs.		164	377	94	15	3	3	0.8	53	46	39	33	10	.249	.329	45	10	OF-107
2 yrs.		136	314	82	13	3	3	1.0	48	40	34	28	9	.261	.350	38	9	OF-90

Jack Harshman
HARSHMAN, JOHN ELVIN BL TL 6'2" 178 lbs.
B. July 12, 1927, San Diego, Calif.

Year		G	AB	H	2B	3B	HR	HR%	R	RBI	BB	SO	SB	BA	SA	PH AB	PH H	G by POS
1948	NY N	5	8	2	0	0	0	0.0	0	1	1	3	0	.250	.250	2	0	1B-3
1950		9	32	4	0	0	2	6.3	3	4	3	6	0	.125	.313	0	0	1B-9
1952		3	2	0	0	0	0	0.0	0	0	0	0	0	.000	.000	1	0	P-2
1954	CHI A	36	56	8	1	0	2	3.6	6	5	12	21	0	.143	.268	0	0	P-35, 1B-1
1955		32	60	11	1	0	2	3.3	6	8	9	17	0	.183	.300	0	0	P-32
1956		36	71	12	1	0	6	8.5	8	19	11	21	0	.169	.437	1	0	P-34
1957		30	45	10	2	0	2	4.4	5	5	10	17	0	.222	.400	0	0	P-30
1958	BAL A	47	82	16	1	0	6	7.3	11	14	17	22	0	.195	.427	9	2	P-34, OF-1
1959	3 teams	BAL A (15G – .200)			BOS N (9G – .143)				CLE A (21G – .206)										
"	total	45	51	10	1	0	1	2.0	7	8	9	8	0	.196	.275	9	1	P-35
1960	CLE A	15	17	3	1	0	0	0.0	0	1	0	4	0	.176	.235	0	0	P-15
10 yrs.		258	424	76	8	0	21	5.0	46	65	72	119	0	.179	.347	22	3	P-217, 1B-13, OF-1
4 yrs.		134	232	41	5	0	12	5.2	25	37	42	76	0	.177	.353	1	0	P-131, 1B-1

Hub Hart
HART, JAMES HENRY BL TR 5'11" 170 lbs.
B. Feb. 2, 1878, Everett, Mass.   D. Oct. 10, 1960, Fort Wayne, Ind.

Year		G	AB	H	2B	3B	HR	HR%	R	RBI	BB	SO	SB	BA	SA	PH AB	PH H	G by POS
1905	CHI A	10	17	2	0	0	0	0.0	2	4	3		0	.118	.118	4	1	C-6
1906		17	37	6	0	0	0	0.0	1	0	2		0	.162	.162	2	0	C-15
1907		29	70	19	1	0	0	0.0	6	7	5		1	.271	.286	4	0	C-25
3 yrs.		56	124	27	1	0	0	0.0	9	11	10		1	.218	.226	10	1	C-46
3 yrs.		56	124	27	1	0	0	0.0	9	11	10		1	.218	.226	10	1	C-46

Fred Hartman
HARTMAN, FREDERICK ORRIN (Dutch) TR
B. Apr. 25, 1868, Pittsburgh, Pa.   D. Nov. 11, 1938, McKeesport, Pa.

Year		G	AB	H	2B	3B	HR	HR%	R	RBI	BB	SO	SB	BA	SA	PH AB	PH H	G by POS
1894	PIT N	49	182	58	4	7	2	1.1	41	20	16	11	12	.319	.451	0	0	3B-49
1897	STL N	124	516	158	21	8	2	0.4	67	67	26		18	.306	.390	0	0	3B-124
1898	NY N	123	475	129	16	11	2	0.4	57	88	25		11	.272	.364	0	0	3B-123
1899		50	174	41	3	5	1	0.6	25	16	12		2	.236	.328	0	0	3B-50
1901	CHI N	120	473	146	23	13	3	0.6	77	89	25		31	.309	.431	1	1	3B-119
1902	STL N	114	416	90	10	3	0	0.0	30	52	14		14	.216	.255	2	1	3B-105, SS-4, 1B-3
6 yrs.		580	2236	622	77	47	10	0.4	297	332	118	11	88	.278	.368	3	2	3B-570, SS-4, 1B-3
1 yr.		120	473	146	23	13	3	0.6	77	89	25		31	.309	.431	1	1	3B-119

Erwin Harvey
HARVEY, ERWIN KING (Zaza) TL
B. Jan. 5, 1879, Saratoga, Calif.   D. June 3, 1954, Santa Monica, Calif.

Year		G	AB	H	2B	3B	HR	HR%	R	RBI	BB	SO	SB	BA	SA	PH AB	PH H	G by POS
1900	CHI N	2	3	0	0	0	0	0.0	0	0	0		0	.000	.000	1	0	P-1
1901	2 teams	CHI A (17G – .250)			CLE A (45G – .353)														
"	total	62	210	70	8	1	1	0.5	32	27	11		16	.333	.443	1	0	OF-45, P-16
1902	CLE A	12	46	16	2	0	0	0.0	5	5	3		1	.348	.391	0	0	OF-12
3 yrs.		76	259	86	10	6	1	0.4	37	32	14		17	.332	.429	2	0	OF-57, P-17
1 yr.		17	40	10	3	1	0	0.0	11	3	2		1	.250	.375	1	0	P-16

Player Register 262

	G	AB	H	2B	3B	HR	HR%	R	RBI	BB	SO	SB	BA	SA	Pinch Hit AB	H	G by POS

Ziggy Hasbrook
HASBROOK, ROBERT LYNDON BR TR 6'1" 180 lbs.
B. Nov. 21, 1893, Grundy Center, Iowa D. Feb. 9, 1976, Garland, Tex.

1916 CHI A	9	8	1	0	0	0	0.0	1	0	1	2	0	.125	.125	1	0	1B-7
1917 "	2	1	0	0	0	0	0.0	0	0	0	0	0	.000	.000	0	0	2B-1
2 yrs.	11	9	1	0	0	0	0.0	2	0	1	2	0	.111	.111	1	0	1B-7, 2B-1
2 yrs.	11	9	1	0	0	0	0.0	0	0	1	2	0	.111	.111	1	0	1B-7, 2B-1

Fred Hatfield
HATFIELD, FRED JAMES BL TR 6'1" 171 lbs.
B. Mar. 18, 1925, Lanett, Ala.

1950 BOS A	10	12	3	0	0	0	0.0	3	2	3	1	0	.250	.250	1	0	3B-3
1951 "	80	163	28	4	2	2	1.2	23	14	22	27	1	.172	.258	14	2	3B-49
1952 2 teams	BOS A (19G – .320)				DET A (112G – .236)												
" total	131	466	112	13	3	3	0.6	48	28	39	54	2	.240	.300	0	0	3B-124, SS-9
1953 DET A	109	311	79	11	1	3	1.0	41	19	40	34	3	.254	.325	19	7	3B-54, 2B-28, SS-1
1954 "	81	218	64	12	0	2	0.9	31	25	28	24	4	.294	.376	17	5	2B-54, 3B-15
1955 "	122	413	96	15	3	8	1.9	51	33	61	49	3	.232	.341	3	0	2B-92, 3B-16, SS-14
1956 2 teams	DET A (8G – .250)				CHI A (106G – .262)												
" total	114	333	87	9	1	7	2.1	48	35	39	37	1	.261	.357	12	2	3B-100, 2B-4, SS-3
1957 CHI A	69	114	23	3	0	0	0.0	14	8	15	20	1	.202	.228	23	4	3B-44
1958 2 teams	CLE A (3G – .125)				CIN N (3G – .000)												
" total	6	9	1	0	0	0	0.0	0	1	1	1	0	.111	.111	2	0	3B-2
9 yrs.	722	2039	493	67	10	25	1.2	259	165	248	247	15	.242	.321	91	20	3B-407, 2B-178, SS-27
2 yrs.	175	435	107	12	1	7	1.6	60	41	52	56	2	.246	.326	34	6	3B-144, SS-3

Grady Hatton
HATTON, GRADY EDGEBERT BL TR 5'8½" 170 lbs.
B. Oct. 7, 1922, Beaumont, Tex.
Manager 1966-68.

1946 CIN N	116	436	118	18	3	14	3.2	56	69	66	53	6	.271	.422	0	0	3B-116, OF-2
1947 "	146	524	147	24	8	16	3.1	91	77	81	50	7	.281	.448	7	2	3B-136
1948 "	133	458	110	17	2	9	2.0	58	44	72	50	7	.240	.345	3	1	3B-123, 2B-3, SS-2, OF-1
1949 "	137	537	141	38	5	11	2.0	71	69	62	48	4	.263	.413	1	0	3B-136
1950 "	130	438	114	17	1	11	2.5	67	54	70	39	6	.260	.379	4	1	3B-126, SS-1, 2B-1
1951 "	96	331	84	9	3	4	1.2	41	37	33	32	4	.254	.335	7	2	3B-87, OF-2
1952 "	128	433	92	14	1	9	2.1	48	57	66	60	5	.212	.312	7	1	2B-120
1953 "	83	159	37	3	1	7	4.4	22	22	29	24	0	.233	.396	38	7	2B-35, 1B-10, 3B-5
1954 3 teams	CIN N (1G – .000)				CHI A (13G – .167)				BOS A (99G – .281)								
" total	113	333	90	13	3	5	1.5	43	36	63	28	2	.270	.372	8	0	3B-103, 1B-4, SS-1
1955 BOS A	126	380	93	11	4	4	1.1	48	49	76	28	0	.245	.326	12	1	3B-111, 2B-1
1956 3 teams	BOS A (5G – .400)				STL N (44G – .247)				BAL A (27G – .148)								
" total	76	139	29	2	2	1	0.7	14	12	26	13	1	.209	.273	35	9	2B-28, 3B-13
1960 CHI N	28	38	13	0	0	0	0.0	3	7	2	5	0	.342	.342	16	3	2B-8
12 yrs.	1312	4206	1068	166	33	91	2.2	562	533	646	430	42	.254	.374	138	27	3B-956, 2B-196, 1B-14, OF-5, SS-4
1 yr.	13	30	5	1	0	0	0.0	3	3	5	3	1	.167	.200	2	0	3B-10, 1B-3

Frankie Hayes
HAYES, FRANKLIN WITMAN (Blimp) BR TR 6'1" 190 lbs.
B. Oct. 13, 1914, Jamesburg, N. J. D. June 22, 1955, Point Pleasant, N. J.

1933 PHI A	3	5	0	0	0	0	0.0	0	0	0	2	0	.000	.000	0	0	C-3
1934 "	92	248	56	10	0	6	2.4	24	30	20	44	2	.226	.339	4	3	C-89
1936 "	144	505	137	25	2	10	2.0	59	67	46	58	3	.271	.388	1	0	C-143
1937 "	60	188	49	11	1	10	5.3	24	38	29	34	0	.261	.489	4	1	C-56
1938 "	99	316	92	19	3	11	3.5	56	55	54	51	2	.291	.475	7	3	C-90
1939 "	124	431	122	28	5	20	4.6	66	83	40	55	4	.283	.510	10	5	C-114
1940 "	136	465	143	23	4	16	3.4	73	70	61	59	9	.308	.477	2	1	C-134, 1B-2
1941 "	126	439	123	27	4	12	2.7	66	63	62	56	2	.280	.442	3	0	C-123
1942 2 teams	PHI A (21G – .238)				STL A (56G – .252)												
" total	77	222	55	10	0	2	0.9	22	22	37	47	1	.248	.320	6	2	C-71
1943 STL A	88	250	47	7	0	5	2.0	16	30	37	36	1	.188	.276	9	3	C-76, 1B-1
1944 PHI A	155	581	144	18	6	13	2.2	62	78	57	59	2	.248	.367	0	0	C-155, 1B-1
1945 2 teams	PHI A (32G – .227)				CLE A (119G – .236)												
" total	151	495	116	17	7	9	1.8	51	57	71	66	2	.234	.352	0	0	C-151
1946 2 teams	CLE A (51G – .256)				CHI A (53G – .212)												
" total	104	335	78	18	0	5	1.5	26	34	50	59	2	.233	.331	2	1	C-100
1947 BOS A	5	13	2	0	0	0	0.0	0	1	0	1	0	.154	.154	1	0	C-4
14 yrs.	1364	4493	1164	213	32	119	2.6	545	628	564	627	30	.259	.400	49	19	C-1309, 1B-4
1 yr.	53	179	38	6	0	2	1.1	15	16	29	33	1	.212	.279	1	0	C-50

Jackie Hayes
HAYES, MINTER CARNEY BR TR 5'10½" 165 lbs.
B. July 19, 1906, Clanton, Ala.

1927 WAS A	10	29	7	0	0	0	0.0	2	2	1	2	0	.241	.241	0	0	SS-8, 3B-1
1928 "	60	210	54	7	3	0	0.0	30	22	5	10	3	.257	.319	2	1	2B-41, SS-15, 3B-2
1929 "	123	424	117	20	3	2	0.5	52	57	24	29	4	.276	.351	2	0	3B-63, 2B-56, SS-2
1930 "	51	166	47	7	2	1	0.6	25	20	7	8	2	.283	.367	5	1	2B-29, 3B-9, 1B-8
1931 "	38	108	24	2	1	0	0.0	11	8	6	4	2	.222	.259	7	1	2B-19, 3B-8, SS-3
1932 CHI A	117	475	122	20	5	2	0.4	53	54	30	28	7	.257	.333	0	0	2B-97, SS-10, 3B-10
1933 "	138	535	138	23	5	2	0.4	65	47	55	36	2	.258	.331	0	0	2B-138
1934 "	62	226	58	9	1	1	0.4	19	31	23	20	3	.257	.319	0	0	2B-61
1935 "	89	329	88	14	0	4	1.2	45	45	29	15	3	.267	.347	5	0	2B-85
1936 "	108	417	130	34	3	5	1.2	53	84	35	25	4	.312	.444	3	0	2B-89, SS-13, 3B-2
1937 "	143	573	131	27	4	2	0.3	63	79	41	37	5	.229	.300	0	0	2B-143
1938 "	62	238	78	21	2	1	0.4	40	20	24	6	3	.328	.445	1	0	2B-61
1939 "	72	269	67	12	3	0	0.0	34	23	27	10	0	.249	.316	2	0	2B-69
1940 "	18	41	8	0	1	0	0.0	2	1	2	11	0	.195	.244	2	0	2B-15
14 yrs.	1091	4040	1069	196	33	20	0.5	494	493	309	241	34	.265	.344	29	3	2B-903, 3B-95, SS-51, 1B-8
9 yrs.	809	3103	820	160	24	17	0.5	374	384	266	188	23	.264	.348	13	0	2B-758, SS-23, 3B-12

	G	AB	H	2B	3B	HR	HR%	R	RBI	BB	SO	SB	BA	SA	Pinch Hit AB H	G by POS

Bill Heath
HEATH, WILLIAM CHRIS
B. Mar. 10, 1939, Yuba City, Calif.
BL TR 5'8" 175 lbs.

	G	AB	H	2B	3B	HR	HR%	R	RBI	BB	SO	SB	BA	SA	PH AB	PH H	G by POS
1965 CHI A	1	1	0	0	0	0	0.0	0	0	0	0	0	.000	.000	1	0	
1966 HOU N	55	123	37	6	0	0	0.0	12	8	9	11	1	.301	.350	16	4	C-37
1967 2 teams	HOU N (9G – .091)				DET A (20G – .125)												
" total	29	43	5	0	0	0	0.0	0	4	5	7	0	.116	.116	19	2	C-12
1969 CHI N	27	32	5	0	0	0	0.0	1	1	12	4	0	.156	.219	12	2	C-9
4 yrs.	112	199	47	6	0	0	0.0	13	13	26	22	1	.236	.276	48	8	C-58
1 yr.	1	1	0	0	0	0	0.0	0	0	0	0	0	.000	.000	1	0	

Val Heim
HEIM, VAL RAYMOND
B. Nov. 4, 1920, Plymouth, Wis.
BL TR 5'11" 170 lbs.

	G	AB	H	2B	3B	HR	HR%	R	RBI	BB	SO	SB	BA	SA	PH AB	PH H	G by POS
1942 CHI A	13	45	9	1	1	0	0.0	6	7	5	3	1	.200	.267	1	0	OF-12

Woodie Held
HELD, WOODSON GEORGE
B. Mar. 25, 1932, Sacramento, Calif.
BR TR 5'10½" 167 lbs.

	G	AB	H	2B	3B	HR	HR%	R	RBI	BB	SO	SB	BA	SA	PH AB	PH H	G by POS
1954 NY A	4	3	0	0	0	0	0.0	2	0	2	1	0	.000	.000	0	0	SS-4, 3B-1
1957 2 teams	NY A (1G – .000)			KC A (92G – .239)													
" total	93	327	78	14	3	20	6.1	48	50	37	81	4	.239	.483	1	0	OF-92
1958 2 teams	KC A (47G – .214)			CLE A (67G – .194)													
" total	114	275	56	6	1	7	2.5	25	33	25	64	1	.204	.309	11	1	OF-84, SS-15, 3B-8
1959 CLE A	143	525	132	19	3	29	5.5	82	71	47	118	1	.251	.465	1	0	SS-103, 3B-40, OF-6, 2B-3
1960	109	376	97	15	1	21	5.6	45	67	44	73	0	.258	.471	0	0	SS-109
1961	146	509	136	23	5	23	4.5	67	78	69	111	0	.267	.468	2	1	SS-144
1962	139	466	116	12	2	19	4.1	55	58	73	107	5	.249	.406	3	1	SS-133, 3B-5, OF-1
1963	133	416	103	19	4	17	4.1	61	61	61	96	2	.248	.435	9	2	2B-96, OF-35, SS-5, 3B-3
1964	118	364	86	13	0	18	4.9	50	49	43	88	1	.236	.420	8	0	2B-52, OF-41, 3B-30
1965 WAS A	122	332	82	16	2	16	4.8	46	54	49	74	0	.247	.452	15	2	OF-106, 3B-5, 2B-4, SS-2
1966 BAL A	56	82	17	3	1	1	1.2	6	7	12	30	0	.207	.305	34	6	OF-10, 2B-5, SS-3, 3B-3
1967 2 teams	BAL A (26G – .146)			CAL A (58G – .220)													
" total	84	182	37	6	0	5	2.7	19	23	24	53	0	.203	.319	22	1	3B-24, OF-19, SS-13, 2B-12
1968 2 teams	CAL A (33G – .111)			CHI A (40G – .167)													
" total	73	99	14	2	0	0	0.0	9	2	10	29	0	.141	.162	22	3	OF-36, 3B-10, 2B-6, SS-5
1969 CHI A	56	63	9	2	0	3	4.8	9	6	13	19	0	.143	.317	19	2	OF-18, SS-3, 3B-3, 2B-1
14 yrs.	1390	4019	963	150	22	179	4.5	524	559	509	944	14	.240	.421	147	19	SS-539, OF-448, 2B-179, 3B-132
2 yrs.	96	117	18	3	0	3	2.6	14	8	18	33	0	.154	.256	24	3	OF-51, 3B-8, SS-3, 2B-2

Frank Hemphill
HEMPHILL, FRANK VERNON
Brother of Charlie Hemphill.
B. May 13, 1878, Greenville, Mich. D. Nov. 16, 1950, Chicago, Ill.
BR TR 5'11" 165 lbs.

	G	AB	H	2B	3B	HR	HR%	R	RBI	BB	SO	SB	BA	SA	PH AB	PH H	G by POS
1906 CHI A	13	40	3	0	0	0	0.0	0	2	9		1	.075	.075	0	0	OF-13
1909 WAS A	1	3	0	0	0	0	0.0	0	0	0		0	.000	.000	0	0	OF-1
2 yrs.	14	43	3	0	0	0	0.0	0	2	9		1	.070	.070	0	0	OF-14
1 yr.	13	40	3	0	0	0	0.0	0	2	9		1	.075	.075	0	0	OF-13

Ken Henderson
HENDERSON, KENNETH JOSEPH
B. June 15, 1946, Carroll, Iowa
BB TR 6'2" 180 lbs.
BL 1967

	G	AB	H	2B	3B	HR	HR%	R	RBI	BB	SO	SB	BA	SA	PH AB	PH H	G by POS
1965 SF N	63	73	14	1	1	0	0.0	10	7	9	19	1	.192	.233	7	0	OF-48
1966	11	29	9	1	1	1	3.4	4	1	2	3	0	.310	.517	1	0	OF-10
1967	65	179	34	3	0	4	2.2	15	14	19	52	0	.190	.274	11	3	OF-52
1968	3	3	1	0	0	0	0.0	1	0	2	1	0	.333	.333	0	0	OF-2
1969	113	374	84	14	4	6	1.6	42	44	42	64	6	.225	.332	1	0	OF-111, 3B-3
1970	148	554	163	35	3	17	3.1	104	88	87	78	20	.294	.460	4	1	OF-140
1971	141	504	133	26	6	15	3.0	80	65	84	76	18	.264	.429	2	0	OF-138, 1B-1
1972	130	439	113	21	2	18	4.1	60	51	38	66	14	.257	.437	7	1	OF-123
1973 CHI A	73	262	68	13	0	6	2.3	31	32	27	49	3	.260	.378	1	1	OF-44, DH-26
1974	162	602	176	35	5	20	3.3	76	95	66	112	12	.292	.467	0	0	OF-162
1975	140	513	129	20	3	9	1.8	65	53	74	65	5	.251	.355	3	1	OF-137, DH-1
1976 ATL N	133	435	114	19	0	13	3.0	52	61	62	68	5	.262	.395	10	2	OF-122
1977 TEX A	75	244	63	14	0	5	2.0	28	23	23	37	2	.258	.377	9	2	OF-65, DH-3
1978 2 teams	NY N (7G – .227)			CIN N (64G – .167)													
" total	71	166	29	8	1	4	2.4	12	23	27	36	0	.175	.307	28	6	OF-45
1979 2 teams	CIN N (10G – .231)			CHI N (62G – .235)													
" total	72	94	22	3	0	2	2.1	12	10	15	18	0	.234	.330	50	9	OF-25
1980 CHI N	44	82	16	3	0	2	2.4	7	9	17	19	0	.195	.305	19	3	OF-22
16 yrs.	1444	4553	1168	216	26	122	2.7	594	576	589	763	86	.257	.396	153	29	OF-1246, DH-30, 3B-3, 1B-1
3 yrs.	375	1377	373	68	8	35	2.5	172	180	167	226	20	.271	.408	4	2	OF-343, DH-27

LEAGUE CHAMPIONSHIP SERIES

	G	AB	H	2B	3B	HR	HR%	R	RBI	BB	SO	SB	BA	SA	PH AB	PH H	G by POS
1971 SF N	4	16	5	1	0	0	0.0	3	2	2	1	1	.313	.375	0	0	OF-4

Butch Henline
HENLINE, WALTER JOHN
B. Dec. 20, 1894, Fort Wayne, Ind. D. Oct. 9, 1957, Sarasota, Fla.
BR TR 5'10" 175 lbs.

	G	AB	H	2B	3B	HR	HR%	R	RBI	BB	SO	SB	BA	SA	PH AB	PH H	G by POS
1921 2 teams	NY N (1G – .000)			PHI N (33G – .306)													
" total	34	112	34	2	0	0	0.0	8	8	2	7	1	.304	.321	2	0	C-32
1922 PHI N	125	430	136	20	4	14	3.3	57	64	36	33	2	.316	.479	4	2	C-119
1923	111	330	107	14	3	7	2.1	45	46	37	33	7	.324	.448	12	3	C-96, OF-1
1924	115	289	82	18	4	5	1.7	41	35	27	15	1	.284	.426	28	7	C-83, OF-2
1925	93	263	80	12	5	8	3.0	43	48	24	16	3	.304	.479	18	6	C-68, OF-1
1926	99	283	80	14	1	2	0.7	32	30	21	18	1	.283	.360	17	4	C-77, 1B-4, OF-2
1927 BKN N	67	177	47	10	3	1	0.6	12	18	17	10	1	.266	.373	7	1	C-60
1928	55	132	28	3	1	2	1.5	12	9	17	8	2	.212	.295	8	2	C-45
1929	27	62	15	2	0	1	1.6	5	7	9	9	0	.242	.323	5	0	C-21
1930 CHI A	3	8	1	0	0	0	0.0	1	2	0	3	0	.125	.125	3	0	C-3

Player Register

	G	AB	H	2B	3B	HR	HR%	R	RBI	BB	SO	SB	BA	SA	Pinch Hit AB	H	G by POS

Butch Henline continued

1931		11	15	1	1	0	0	0.0	2	2	2	4	0	.067	.133	5	1	C-4
11 yrs.		740	2101	611	96	21	40	1.9	258	268	192	156	18	.291	.414	106	22	C-608, OF-6, 1B-4
2 yrs.		14	23	2	1	0	0	0.0	3	4	2	7	0	.087	.130	5	1	C-7

Rudy Hernandez

HERNANDEZ, RODOLFO
Also known as Rodolfo Acosta.
B. Oct. 18, 1952, Empalme, Mexico

BR TR 5'9" 150 lbs.

1972 CHI A	8	21	4	0	0	0	0.0	0	1	0	3	0	.190	.190	2	1	SS-6

Ed Herrmann

HERRMANN, EDWARD MARTIN
B. Aug. 27, 1946, San Diego, Calif.

BL TR 6'1" 195 lbs.

1967 CHI A	2	3	2	1	0	0	0.0	1	1	1	0	0	.667	1.000	0	0	C-2
1969	102	290	67	8	0	8	2.8	31	31	30	35	0	.231	.341	11	1	C-92
1970	96	297	84	9	0	19	6.4	42	52	31	41	0	.283	.505	7	1	C-88
1971	101	294	63	6	0	11	3.7	32	35	44	48	2	.214	.347	7	0	C-97
1972	116	354	88	9	0	10	2.8	23	40	43	37	0	.249	.359	5	2	C-112
1973	119	379	85	17	1	10	2.6	42	39	31	55	2	.224	.354	6	0	C-114, DH-2
1974	107	367	95	13	1	10	2.7	32	39	16	49	1	.259	.381	0	0	C-107
1975 NY A	80	200	51	9	2	6	3.0	16	30	16	23	0	.255	.410	19	3	DH-35, C-24
1976 2 teams	CAL A (29G − .174)				HOU N (79G − .204)												
" total	108	311	62	11	0	5	1.6	19	33	29	48	0	.199	.283	4	0	C-106
1977 HOU N	56	158	46	7	0	1	0.6	7	17	15	18	1	.291	.354	7	2	C-49
1978 2 teams	HOU N (16G − .111)				MON N (19G − .175)												
" total	35	76	11	2	0	0	0.0	2	3	4	7	0	.145	.171	10	3	C-26
11 yrs.	922	2729	654	92	4	80	2.9	247	320	260	361	6	.240	.364	72	12	C-817, DH-37
7 yrs.	643	1984	484	63	2	68	3.4	203	237	196	265	5	.244	.381	32	4	C-612, DH-2
							5th										

Mike Hershberger

HERSHBERGER, NORMAN MICHAEL
B. Oct. 9, 1939, Massillon, Ohio

BR TR 5'10" 175 lbs.

1961 CHI A	15	55	17	3	0	0	0.0	9	5	2	2	1	.309	.364	1	0	OF-13
1962	148	427	112	14	2	4	0.9	54	46	37	36	10	.262	.333	13	3	OF-135
1963	135	476	133	26	2	3	0.6	64	45	39	39	9	.279	.361	14	2	OF-119
1964	141	452	104	15	3	2	0.4	55	31	48	47	8	.230	.290	10	1	OF-134
1965 KC A	150	494	114	15	5	5	1.0	43	48	37	42	7	.231	.312	9	5	OF-144
1966	146	538	136	27	7	2	0.4	55	57	47	37	13	.253	.340	5	0	OF-143
1967	142	480	122	25	1	1	0.2	55	49	38	40	10	.254	.317	12	5	OF-130
1968 OAK A	99	246	67	9	2	5	2.0	23	32	21	22	8	.272	.386	12	5	OF-90
1969	51	129	26	2	0	1	0.8	11	10	10	15	1	.202	.240	15	3	OF-35
1970 MIL A	49	98	23	5	0	1	1.0	7	6	10	8	1	.235	.316	16	3	OF-35
1971 CHI A	74	177	46	9	0	2	1.1	22	15	30	23	6	.260	.345	20	5	OF-59
11 yrs.	1150	3572	900	150	22	26	0.7	398	344	319	311	74	.252	.328	127	32	OF-1037
5 yrs.	513	1587	412	67	7	11	0.7	204	142	156	147	34	.260	.331	58	11	OF-460

Mike Heydon

HEYDON, MICHAEL EDWARD
B. July 15, 1874, Indianapolis, Ind.   D. Oct. 13, 1913, Indianapolis, Ind.

TR

1898 BAL N	3	9	1	0	0	0	0.0	2	1	2		0	.111	.111	0	0	C-3
1899 WAS N	3	3	0	0	0	0	0.0	0	0	2		0	.000	.000	1	0	C-2
1901 STL N	16	43	9	1	1	1	2.3	2	6	5		2	.209	.349	1	0	C-13, OF-1
1904 CHI A	4	10	1	1	0	0	0.0	0	1	1		0	.100	.200	0	0	C-4
1905 WAS A	77	245	47	7	4	1	0.4	20	26	21		5	.192	.265	0	0	C-77
1906	49	145	23	7	1	0	0.0	14	10	14		2	.159	.221	0	0	C-49
1907	62	164	30	3	0	0	0.0	14	9	25		3	.183	.201	4	0	C-57
7 yrs.	214	619	111	19	6	2	0.3	52	53	70		12	.179	.239	6	0	C-205, OF-1
1 yr.	4	10	1	1	0	0	0.0	0	1	1		0	.100	.200	0	0	C-4

Piano Legs Hickman

HICKMAN, CHARLES TAYLOR
B. Mar. 4, 1876, Dunkirk, N.Y.   D. Apr. 19, 1934, Morgantown, W. Va.

BR TR 5'11½" 215 lbs.

1897 BOS N	2	3	2	0	1	1	33.3	2	2	0		0	.667	1.667	0	0	P-2
1898	19	58	15	2	0	0	0.0	4	7	1		0	.259	.293	0	0	OF-7, 1B-6, P-6
1899	19	63	25	2	7	0	0.0	15	15	2		0	.397	.651	0	0	P-11, OF-7, 1B-1
1900 NY N	127	473	148	19	17	9	1.9	65	91	17		10	.313	.482	0	0	3B-120, OF-7
1901	128	406	113	20	4	4	1.0	44	62	15		5	.278	.387	8	1	OF-50, SS-23, 3B-15, P-9, 2B-7, 1B-2
1902 2 teams	BOS A (28G − .296)				CLE A (102G − .378)												
" total	130	534	193	36	13	11	2.1	74	110	15		9	.361	.539	1	0	1B-98, OF-27, 2B-3, P-1
1903 CLE A	131	522	171	31	11	12	2.3	67	97	17		14	.328	.498	0	0	1B-125, 2B-7
1904 2 teams	CLE A (86G − .288)				DET A (42G − .243)												
" total	128	481	132	28	16	6	1.2	52	67	24		12	.274	.437	1	1	1B-79, 2B-45, OF-1
1905 2 teams	DET A (59G − .221)				WAS A (88G − .311)												
" total	147	573	159	37	12	4	0.7	69	66	21		6	.277	.405	0	0	2B-85, OF-47, 1B-15
1906 WAS A	120	451	128	25	5	9	2.0	53	57	21		9	.284	.421	1	0	OF-95, 1B-18, 3B-5, 2B-1
1907 2 teams	WAS A (60G − .285)				CHI A (21G − .261)												
" total	81	216	61	12	4	1	0.5	21	24	18		4	.282	.389	22	4	1B-30, OF-21, 2B-3, P-1
1908 CLE A	65	197	46	6	1	2	1.0	16	16	9		2	.234	.305	16	4	OF-28, 1B-20, 2B-1
12 yrs.	1081	3977	1193	218	92	59	1.5	481	614	153		72	.300	.446	49	10	1B-394, OF-290, 2B-152, 3B-140, P-30, SS-23
1 yr.	21	23	6	2	0	0	0.0	1	1	4		0	.261	.348	16	4	OF-3

Jim Hicks

HICKS, JAMES EDWARD
B. May 18, 1940, East Chicago, Ind.

BR TR 6'3" 205 lbs.

1964 CHI A	2	0	0	0	0	0	−	0	0	0	0	0	−	−	0	0	
1965	13	19	5	1	0	1	5.3	2	2	0	9	0	.263	.474	8	2	OF-5
1966	18	26	5	0	1	0	0.0	3	1	5	1	0	.192	.269	2	0	OF-10, 1B-2

	G	AB	H	2B	3B	HR	HR%	R	RBI	BB	SO	SB	BA	SA	Pinch Hit AB H	G by POS

Jim Hicks continued
1969 2 teams	STL N (19G – .182)			CAL A (37G – .083)												
" total	56	92	12	0	2	4	4.3	11	11	17	32	0	.130	.304	17 0	OF-25, 1B-8
1970 CAL A	4	4	1	0	0	0	0.0	0	0	0	2	0	.250	.250	4 1	
5 yrs.	93	141	23	1	3	5	3.5	16	14	18	48	0	.163	.319	31 3	OF-40, 1B-10
3 yrs.	33	45	10	1	1	1	2.2	5	3	1	14	0	.222	.356	10 2	OF-15, 1B-2

Joe Hicks
HICKS, WILLIAM JOSEPH B. Apr. 7, 1933, Ivy, Va. BL TR 6' 180 lbs.

1959 CHI N	6	7	3	0	0	0	0.0	0	1	1	0	0	.429	.429	2 2	OF-4
1960 "	36	47	9	1	0	0	0.0	3	2	6	3	0	.191	.213	17 4	OF-14
1961 WAS A	12	29	5	0	0	1	3.4	2	1	0	4	0	.172	.276	6 2	OF-7
1962 "	102	174	39	4	2	6	3.4	20	14	15	34	3	.224	.374	61 9	OF-42
1963 NY N	56	159	36	6	1	5	3.1	16	22	7	31	0	.226	.371	16 3	OF-41
5 yrs.	212	416	92	11	3	12	2.9	41	39	29	73	3	.221	.349	102 20	OF-108
2 yrs.	42	54	12	1	0	0	0.0	3	2	7	4	0	.222	.241	19 6	OF-18

Bill Higdon
HIGDON, WILLIAM TRAVIS B. Apr. 27, 1925, Camp Hill, Ala. BL TR 6'1" 193 lbs.

1949 CHI N	11	23	7	3	0	0	0.0	3	1	6	3	1	.304	.435	4 1	OF-6

Marc Hill
HILL, MARC KEVIN B. Feb. 18, 1952, Louisiana, Mo. BR TR 6'3" 205 lbs.

1973 STL N	1	3	0	0	0	0	0.0	0	0	0	1	0	.000	.000	0 0	C-1
1974 "	10	21	5	1	0	0	0.0	2	2	4	5	0	.238	.286	1 0	C-9
1975 SF N	72	182	39	4	0	5	2.7	14	23	25	27	0	.214	.319	16 3	C-60, 3B-1
1976 "	54	131	24	5	0	3	2.3	11	15	10	19	0	.183	.290	4 1	C-49, 1B-1
1977 "	108	320	80	10	0	9	2.8	28	50	34	34	0	.250	.366	7 2	C-102
1978 "	117	358	87	15	1	3	0.8	20	36	45	39	1	.243	.316	5 3	C-116, 1B-2
1979 "	63	169	35	3	0	3	1.8	20	15	26	25	0	.207	.278	6 1	C-58, 1B-1
1980 2 teams	SF N (17G – .171)			SEA A (29G – .229)												
" total	46	111	23	4	1	2	1.8	9	9	4	17	0	.207	.315	3 0	C-43
1981 CHI A	16	6	0	0	0	0	0.0	0	0	1	0	0	.000	.000	2 0	C-14, 3B-1, 1B-1
1982 "	53	88	23	2	0	3	3.4	9	13	6	13	0	.261	.386	2 1	C-49, 3B-1, 1B-1
1983 "	58	133	30	6	0	1	0.8	11	11	9	24	0	.226	.293	4 2	C-55, DH-2, 1B-1
11 yrs.	598	1522	346	50	2	29	1.9	124	174	163	205	1	.227	.320	51 13	C-556, 1B-7, 3B-3, DH-2
3 yrs.	127	227	53	8	0	4	1.8	20	24	15	38	0	.233	.322	9 3	C-118, 1B-3, DH-2, 3B-2

Myril Hoag
HOAG, MYRIL OLIVER B. Mar. 9, 1908, Davis, Calif. D. July 28, 1971, High Springs, Fla. BR TR 5'11" 180 lbs.

1931 NY A	44	28	4	2	0	0	0.0	6	3	1	8	0	.143	.214	10 1	OF-23, 3B-1
1932 "	46	54	20	5	0	1	1.9	18	7	7	13	1	.370	.519	3 1	OF-35, 1B-1
1934 "	97	251	67	8	2	3	1.2	45	34	21	21	1	.267	.351	7 0	OF-86
1935 "	48	110	28	4	1	1	0.9	13	13	12	19	4	.255	.336	5 0	OF-37
1936 "	45	156	47	9	4	3	1.9	23	34	7	16	3	.301	.468	3 1	OF-39
1937 "	106	362	109	19	8	3	0.8	48	46	33	33	4	.301	.423	7 2	OF-99
1938 "	85	267	74	14	3	0	0.0	28	48	25	31	4	.277	.352	15 3	OF-70
1939 STL A	129	482	142	23	4	10	2.1	58	75	24	35	9	.295	.421	12 4	OF-117, P-1
1940 "	76	191	50	11	0	3	1.6	20	26	13	30	2	.262	.366	28 5	OF-46
1941 2 teams	STL A (1G – .000)			CHI A (106G – .255)												
" total	107	381	97	13	3	1	0.3	30	44	27	29	6	.255	.312	6 2	OF-99
1942 CHI A	113	412	99	18	3	2	0.5	47	37	36	21	17	.240	.308	1 0	OF-112
1944 2 teams	CHI A (17G – .229)			CLE A (67G – .285)												
" total	84	325	90	10	3	1	0.3	38	31	35	24	7	.277	.335	4 0	OF-80
1945 CLE A	40	128	27	5	3	0	0.0	10	3	11	18	1	.211	.297	1 0	OF-33, P-2
13 yrs.	1020	3147	854	141	33	28	0.9	384	401	252	298	59	.271	.364	102 20	OF-876, P-3, 3B-1, 1B-1
3 yrs.	236	840	207	32	5	3	0.4	82	85	73	51	24	.246	.307	9 3	OF-225

WORLD SERIES
1932 NY A	1	0	0	0	0	0	–	1	0	0	0	0	–	–	0 0	
1937 "	5	20	6	1	0	1	5.0	4	2	0	1	0	.300	.500	0 0	OF-5
1938 "	2	5	2	1	0	0	0.0	3	1	0	0	0	.400	.600	1 0	OF-1
3 yrs.	8	25	8	2	0	1	4.0	8	3	0	1	0	.320	.520	1 0	OF-6

Oris Hockett
HOCKETT, ORIS LEON B. Sept. 29, 1909, Bluffton, Ind. D. Mar. 23, 1969, Hawthorne, Calif. BL TR 5'9" 182 lbs.

1938 BKN N	21	70	23	5	1	1	1.4	8	8	4	9	0	.329	.471	4 2	OF-17
1939 "	9	13	3	0	0	0	0.0	3	1	1	0	0	.231	.231	7 2	OF-1
1941 CLE A	2	6	2	0	0	0	0.0	0	1	2	0	0	.333	.333	1 0	OF-2
1942 "	148	601	150	22	7	1	0.2	85	48	45	45	12	.250	.344	1 0	OF-145
1943 "	141	601	166	33	4	2	0.3	70	51	45	45	13	.276	.354	2 0	OF-139
1944 "	124	457	132	29	5	1	0.2	47	50	35	27	8	.289	.381	14 2	OF-110
1945 CHI A	106	417	122	23	4	0	0.0	45	55	27	30	10	.293	.381	0 0	OF-106
7 yrs.	551	2165	598	112	21	13	0.6	259	214	159	157	43	.276	.365	28 6	OF-520
1 yr.	106	417	122	23	4	0	0.0	45	55	27	30	10	.293	.381	0 0	OF-106

Johnny Hodapp
HODAPP, URBAN JOHN B. Sept. 26, 1905, Cincinnati, Ohio D. June 14, 1980, Cincinnati, Ohio BR TR 6' 185 lbs.

1925 CLE A	37	130	31	5	1	0	0.0	12	14	11	7	2	.238	.292	0 0	3B-37
1926 "	3	5	1	0	0	0	0.0	0	0	0	0	0	.200	.200	0 0	3B-3
1927 "	75	240	73	15	3	5	2.1	25	40	14	23	2	.304	.454	7 3	3B-67, 1B-4
1928 "	116	449	145	31	6	2	0.4	51	73	20	20	2	.323	.432	3 2	3B-101, 1B-13
1929 "	90	294	96	12	7	4	1.4	30	51	15	14	3	.327	.456	16 4	2B-72
1930 "	154	635	225	51	8	9	1.4	111	121	32	29	6	.354	.502	0 0	2B-154
1931 "	122	468	138	19	3	2	0.4	71	56	27	23	1	.295	.365	1 0	2B-121

Player Register 266

	G	AB	H	2B	3B	HR	HR%	R	RBI	BB	SO	SB	BA	SA	Pinch Hit AB	Pinch Hit H	G by POS

Johnny Hodapp continued

1932 2 teams	CLE A (7G – .125)					CHI A (68G – .227)											
" total	75	192	42	9	0	3	1.6	23	20	11	5	1	.219	.313	23	2	OF-31, 2B-12, 3B-4
1933 BOS A	115	413	129	27	5	3	0.7	55	54	33	14	1	.312	.424	6	3	2B-101, 1B-10
9 yrs.	787	2826	880	169	34	28	1.0	378	429	163	136	18	.311	.425	56	14	2B-460, 3B-212, OF-31, 1B-27
1 yr.	68	176	40	8	0	3	1.7	21	20	11	3	1	.227	.324	23	2	OF-31, 2B-5, 3B-4

Ralph Hodgin

HODGIN, ELMER RALPH   BL TR 5'10" 167 lbs.
B. Feb. 10, 1916, Greensboro, N. C.

1939 BOS N	32	48	10	1	0	0	0.0	4	4	3	4	0	.208	.229	20	4	OF-9
1943 CHI A	117	407	128	22	8	1	0.2	52	50	20	24	3	.314	.415	20	8	3B-56, OF-42
1944	121	465	137	25	7	1	0.2	56	51	21	14	3	.295	.385	6	2	3B-82, OF-33
1946	87	258	65	10	1	0	0.0	32	25	19	6	0	.252	.298	29	9	OF-57
1947	59	180	53	10	3	1	0.6	26	24	13	4	1	.294	.400	16	1	OF-41
1948	114	331	88	11	5	1	0.3	28	34	21	11	0	.266	.338	33	7	OF-79
6 yrs.	530	1689	481	79	24	4	0.2	198	188	97	63	7	.285	.367	124	31	OF-261, 3B-138
5 yrs.	498	1641	471	78	24	4	0.2	194	184	94	59	7	.287	.371	104	27	OF-252, 3B-138
													9th	7th			

Dutch Hoffman

HOFFMAN, CLARENCE CASPER   BR TR 6' 175 lbs.
B. Jan. 28, 1904, Freeburg, Ill.   D. Dec. 6, 1962, Beneville, Ill.

1929 CHI A	103	337	87	16	5	3	0.9	27	37	24	28	6	.258	.362	19	6	OF-89

Ducky Holmes

HOLMES, JAMES WILLIAM   BL TR 5'6" 170 lbs.
B. Jan. 28, 1869, Des Moines, Iowa   D. Aug. 6, 1932, Truro, Iowa

1895 LOU N	40	161	60	10	2	3	1.9	33	20	12	9	9	.373	.516	0	0	OF-29, SS-8, 3B-4, P-2
1896	47	141	38	3	2	0	0.0	22	18	13	5	8	.270	.319	10	3	OF-33, P-2, SS-1, 2B-1
1897 2 teams	LOU N (2G – .000)					NY N (79G – .268)											
" total	81	310	82	8	6	1	0.3	51	44	19		30	.265	.339	2	0	OF-77, SS-2
1898 2 teams	STL N (23G – .238)					BAL N (113G – .285)											
" total	136	543	150	11	10	1	0.2	63	64	25		29	.276	.339	1	1	OF-135
1899 BAL N	138	553	177	31	7	4	0.7	80	66	39		50	.320	.423	0	0	OF-138
1901 DET A	131	537	158	28	10	4	0.7	90	62	37		35	.294	.406	0	0	OF-131
1902	92	362	93	15	4	2	0.6	50	33	28		16	.257	.337	0	0	OF-92
1903 2 teams	WAS A (21G – .225)					CHI A (86G – .279)											
" total	107	415	112	10	6	1	0.2	66	26	30		35	.270	.330	3	0	OF-96, 3B-7, 2B-2
1904 CHI A	68	251	78	11	9	1	0.4	42	19	14		13	.311	.438	5	2	OF-63
1905	92	328	66	15	2	0	0.0	42	22	19		11	.201	.259	3	2	OF-89
10 yrs.	932	3601	1014	142	58	17	0.5	539	374	236	14	236	.282	.367	24	8	OF-883, SS-11, 3B-11, P-4, 2B-3
3 yrs.	246	923	240	33	16	1	0.1	137	59	58		49	.260	.334	10	4	OF-234, 3B-3

Harry Hooper

HOOPER, HARRY BARTHOLOMEW   BL TR 5'10" 168 lbs.
B. Aug. 24, 1887, Bell Station, Calif.   D. Dec. 18, 1974, Santa Cruz, Calif.
Hall of Fame 1971.

1909 BOS A	81	255	72	3	4	0	0.0	29	12	16		15	.282	.325	4	2	OF-74
1910	155	584	156	9	10	2	0.3	81	27	62		40	.267	.327	0	0	OF-155
1911	130	524	163	20	6	4	0.8	93	45	73		38	.311	.395	0	0	OF-130
1912	147	590	143	20	12	2	0.3	98	53	66		29	.242	.327	0	0	OF-147
1913	148	586	169	29	12	4	0.7	100	40	60	51	26	.288	.399	1	0	OF-147, P-1
1914	141	530	137	23	15	1	0.2	85	41	58	47	19	.258	.364	1	0	OF-140
1915	149	566	133	20	13	2	0.4	90	51	89	36	22	.235	.327	0	0	OF-147
1916	151	575	156	20	11	1	0.2	75	37	80	35	27	.271	.350	0	0	OF-151
1917	151	559	143	21	11	3	0.5	89	45	80	40	21	.256	.349	0	0	OF-151
1918	126	474	137	26	13	1	0.2	81	44	75	25	24	.289	.405	0	0	OF-126
1919	128	491	131	25	6	3	0.6	76	49	79	28	23	.267	.360	1	0	OF-128
1920	139	536	167	30	17	7	1.3	91	53	88	27	16	.312	.470	0	0	OF-139
1921 CHI A	108	419	137	26	5	8	1.9	74	58	55	21	13	.327	.470	0	0	OF-108
1922	152	602	183	35	8	11	1.8	111	80	68	33	16	.304	.444	3	0	OF-149
1923	145	576	166	32	4	10	1.7	87	65	68	22	18	.288	.410	2	1	OF-143
1924	130	476	156	27	8	10	2.1	107	62	65	26	16	.328	.481	5	2	OF-123
1925	127	442	117	23	5	6	1.4	62	55	54	21	12	.265	.380	2	0	OF-124
17 yrs.	2308	8785	2466	389	160	75	0.9	1429	817	1136	412	375	.281	.387	18	5	OF-2282, P-1
5 yrs.	662	2515	759	143	30	45	1.8	441	320	310	123	75	.302	.436	12	3	OF-647

WORLD SERIES

1912 BOS A	8	31	9	2	1	0	0.0	3	2	4	4	2	.290	.419	0	0	OF-8
1915	5	20	7	0	0	2	10.0	4	3	2	4	0	.350	.650	0	0	OF-5
1916	5	21	7	1	1	0	0.0	6	1	3	1	1	.333	.476	0	0	OF-5
1918	6	20	4	0	0	0	0.0	0	0	2	2	0	.200	.200	0	0	OF-6
4 yrs.	24	92	27	3	2	2	2.2	13	6	11	11	3	.293	.435	0	0	OF-24

Gail Hopkins

HOPKINS, GAIL EASON   BL TR 5'10" 198 lbs.
B. Feb. 19, 1943, Tulsa, Okla.

1968 CHI A	29	37	8	2	0	0	0.0	4	2	6	3	0	.216	.270	20	4	1B-7
1969	124	373	99	13	3	8	2.1	52	46	50	28	2	.265	.381	21	6	1B-101
1970	116	287	82	8	1	6	2.1	32	29	28	19	0	.286	.383	36	10	1B-77, C-8
1971 KC A	103	295	82	16	1	9	3.1	35	47	37	13	3	.278	.431	17	5	1B-83
1972	53	71	15	2	0	0	0.0	7	5	7	4	0	.211	.239	34	6	1B-13, 3B-1
1973	74	138	34	6	1	2	1.4	17	16	29	15	1	.246	.348	19	7	DH-36, 1B-10
1974 LA N	15	18	4	0	0	0	0.0	1	0	3	1	0	.222	.222	11	4	1B-2, C-2
7 yrs.	514	1219	324	47	6	25	2.1	142	145	160	83	6	.266	.376	158	42	1B-293, DH-36, C-10, 3B-1
3 yrs.	269	697	189	23	4	14	2.0	88	77	84	50	2	.271	.376	77	20	1B-185, C-8

267 Player Register

	G	AB	H	2B	3B	HR	HR%	R	RBI	BB	SO	SB	BA	SA	Pinch Hit AB	Pinch Hit H	G by POS

Marty Hopkins
HOPKINS, MEREDITH HILLIARD BR TR 5'11" 175 lbs.
B. Feb. 22, 1907, Wolfe City, Tex. D. Nov. 20, 1963, Dallas, Tex.

1934 2 teams	PHI N (10G – .120)					CHI A (67G – .214)											
" total	77	235	48	9	0	2	0.9	28	31	49	31	0	.204	.268	1	0	3B-72
1935 CHI A	59	144	32	3	0	2	1.4	20	17	36	23	1	.222	.285	1	0	3B-49, 2B-5
2 yrs.	136	379	80	12	0	4	1.1	48	48	85	54	1	.211	.274	2	0	3B-121, 2B-5
2 yrs.	126	354	77	10	0	4	1.1	42	45	78	49	1	.218	.280	1	0	3B-112, 2B-5

Ken Hottman
HOTTMAN, KENNETH ROGER BR TR 5'11" 190 lbs.
B. May 7, 1948, Stockton, Calif.

| 1971 CHI A | 6 | 16 | 2 | 0 | 0 | 0 | 0.0 | 1 | 0 | 1 | 2 | 0 | .125 | .125 | 1 | 0 | OF-5 |

Dummy Hoy
HOY, WILLIAM ELLSWORTH BL TR 5'4" 148 lbs.
B. May 23, 1862, Houckstown, Ohio D. Dec. 15, 1961, Cincinnati, Ohio

1888 WAS N	136	503	138	10	8	2	0.4	77	29	69	48	82	.274	.338	0	0	OF-136
1889	127	507	139	11	6	0	0.0	98	39	75	30	35	.274	.320	0	0	OF-127
1890 BUF P	122	493	147	17	8	1	0.2	107	53	94	36	39	.298	.371	0	0	OF-122, 2B-1
1891 STL AA	141	567	165	14	5	5	0.9	136	66	119	25	59	.291	.360	0	0	OF-141
1892 WAS N	152	593	166	19	8	3	0.5	108	75	86	23	60	.280	.354	0	0	OF-152
1893	130	564	138	12	6	0	0.0	106	45	66	9	48	.245	.287	0	0	OF-130
1894 CIN N	128	506	158	22	13	5	1.0	114	70	87	18	30	.312	.437	0	0	OF-128
1895	107	429	119	21	12	3	0.7	93	55	52	8	50	.277	.403	0	0	OF-107
1896	121	443	132	23	7	4	0.9	120	57	65	13	50	.298	.409	1	1	OF-120
1897	128	497	145	24	6	2	0.4	87	42	54		37	.292	.376	0	0	OF-128
1898 LOU N	148	582	177	15	16	6	1.0	104	66	49		37	.304	.416	0	0	OF-148
1899	154	633	194	17	13	5	0.8	116	49	61		32	.306	.398	0	0	OF-154
1901 CHI A	132	527	155	28	11	2	0.4	112	60	86		27	.294	.400	0	0	OF-132
1902 CIN N	72	279	81	15	2	2	0.7	48	20	41		11	.290	.380	0	0	OF-72
14 yrs.	1798	7123	2054	248	121	40	0.6	1426	726	1004	210	597	.288	.374	1	1	OF-1797, 2B-1
1 yr.	132	527	155	28	11	2	0.4	112	60	86		27	.294	.400	0	0	OF-132

Frank Huelsman
HUELSMAN, FRANK ELMER BR TR 6'2" 210 lbs.
B. June 5, 1874, St. Louis, Mo. D. June 9, 1959, Affton, Mo.

1897 STL N	2	7	2	1	0	0	0.0	0	0	0		0	.286	.429	1	0	OF-2
1904 4 teams	CHI A (4G – .143)					DET A (4G – .333)					STL A (20G – .221)		WAS A (84G – .248)				
" total	112	396	97	23	5	2	0.5	28	35	31		7	.245	.343	4	0	OF-107
1905 WAS A	126	421	114	28	8	3	0.7	48	62	31		11	.271	.397	4	0	OF-123
3 yrs.	240	824	213	52	13	5	0.6	76	97	62		18	.258	.371	8	1	OF-232
1 yr.	4	7	1	1	0	0	0.0	0	0	0		0	.143	.286	3	0	OF-1

Ed Hughes
HUGHES, EDWARD TR
B. Chicago, Ill.

| 1902 CHI A | 1 | 4 | 1 | 0 | 0 | 0 | 0.0 | 0 | 0 | 0 | | 0 | .250 | .250 | 0 | 0 | C-1 |

Tim Hulett
HULETT, TIMOTHY CRAIG BR TR 6'1" 180 lbs.
B. Jan. 12, 1960, Springfield, Ill.

| 1983 CHI A | 6 | 5 | 1 | 0 | 0 | 0 | 0.0 | 0 | 0 | 0 | 1 | 1 | .200 | .200 | 0 | 0 | 2B-6 |

Bill Hunnefield
HUNNEFIELD, WILLIAM FENTON (Wild Bill) BB TR 5'10" 165 lbs.
B. Jan. 5, 1899, Dedham, Mass.

1926 CHI A	131	470	129	26	4	3	0.6	79	48	37	28	24	.274	.366	2	0	SS-98, 3B-17, 2B-15
1927	112	365	104	25	1	2	0.5	45	36	25	24	13	.285	.375	13	3	SS-78, 2B-17, 3B-1
1928	94	333	98	8	3	2	0.6	42	24	26	24	16	.294	.354	7	3	2B-83, SS-3, 3B-1
1929	47	127	23	5	0	0	0.0	13	9	7	3	5	.181	.220	10	1	2B-26, 3B-4, SS-2
1930	31	81	22	2	0	1	1.2	11	5	4	10	1	.272	.333	6	1	SS-22, 1B-1
1931 3 teams	CLE A (21G – .239)					BOS N (11G – .286)					NY N (64G – .270)						
" total	96	288	76	9	1	0	0.3	38	22	18	22	6	.264	.313	1	0	2B-61, SS-26, 3B-5
6 yrs.	511	1664	452	75	9	9	0.5	230	144	117	111	65	.272	.344	39	8	SS-229, 2B-202, 3B-28, 1B-1
5 yrs.	415	1376	376	66	8	8	0.6	192	122	99	89	59	.273	.350	38	8	SS-203, 2B-141, 3B-23, 1B-1

Steve Huntz
HUNTZ, STEPHEN MICHAEL BB TR 6'1" 204 lbs.
B. Dec. 3, 1945, Cleveland, Ohio

1967 STL N	3	6	1	0	0	0	0.0	1	0	1	2	0	.167	.167	1	0	2B-2
1969	71	139	27	4	0	3	2.2	13	13	27	34	0	.194	.288	3	0	SS-52, 2B-12, 3B-6
1970 SD N	106	352	77	8	0	11	3.1	54	37	66	69	0	.219	.335	9	1	SS-57, 3B-51
1971 CHI A	35	86	18	3	1	2	2.3	10	6	7	9	1	.209	.337	12	0	2B-14, SS-7, 3B-6
1975 SD N	22	53	8	4	0	0	0.0	3	4	7	8	0	.151	.226	6	1	3B-16, 2B-2
5 yrs.	237	636	131	19	1	16	2.5	81	60	108	122	1	.206	.314	31	2	SS-116, 3B-79, 2B-30
1 yr.	35	86	18	3	1	2	2.3	10	6	7	9	1	.209	.337	12	0	2B-14, SS-7, 3B-6

Frank Isbell
ISBELL, WILLIAM FRANK (Bald Eagle) BL TR 5'11" 190 lbs.
B. Aug. 21, 1875, Delavan, N. Y. D. July 15, 1941, Wichita, Kans.

1898 CHI N	45	159	37	4	0	0	0.0	17	8	3		3	.233	.258	0	0	OF-28, P-13, 3B-3, 2B-3, SS-2
1901 CHI A	137	556	143	15	8	3	0.5	93	70	36		52	.257	.329	0	0	1B-137, 2B-2, SS-1, 3B-1, P-1
1902	137	520	133	14	4	4	0.8	65	59	14		38	.256	.321	0	0	1B-133, SS-4, C-1, P-1
1903	138	546	139	25	9	2	0.4	52	59	12		26	.255	.344	0	0	1B-119, 3B-19, 2B-2, OF-1, SS-1
1904	96	314	66	10	3	1	0.3	27	34	16		19	.210	.271	3	0	1B-57, 2B-27, OF-5, SS-4
1905	94	341	101	21	11	2	0.6	55	45	15		15	.296	.440	0	0	2B-42, OF-40, 1B-9, SS-2
1906	143	549	153	21	11	0	0.0	71	57	30		37	.279	.357	0	0	2B-132, OF-14, P-10, C-1
1907	125	486	118	22	8	0	0.0	60	55	22		22	.243	.321	1	0	2B-119, OF-5, SS-1, P-1
1908	84	320	79	15	3	1	0.3	31	49	19		18	.247	.322	1	0	1B-65, 2B-18

Player Register

	G	AB	H	2B	3B	HR	HR %	R	RBI	BB	SO	SB	BA	SA	Pinch Hit AB	H	G by POS

Frank Isbell continued
1909	120	433	97	17	6	0	0.0	33	39	23		23	.224	.291	5	2	1B-101, OF-9, 2B-5
10 yrs.	1119	4224	1066	164	63	13	0.3	504	475	190		253	.252	.330	10	2	1B-619, 2B-350, OF-102, P-26, 3B-23, SS-15, C-2
9 yrs.	1074	4065	1029	160	63	13	0.3	487	467	187		250 3rd	.253	.333	10	2	1B-619, 2B-347, OF-74, 3B-20, SS-13, P-13, C-2

WORLD SERIES
| 1906 CHI A | 6 | 26 | 8 | 4 | 0 | 0 | 0.0 | 4 | 4 | 0 | 6 | 1 | .308 | .462 | 0 | 0 | 2B-6 |

Pete Jablonowski
Playing record listed under Pete Appleton

Charlie Jackson
JACKSON, CHARLES HERBERT (Lefty)   BL TL 5'9" 150 lbs.
B. Feb. 7, 1894, Granite City, Ill.   D. May 27, 1968, Radford, Va.

1915 CHI A	1	1	0	0	0	0	0.0	0	0	0	1	0	.000	.000	1	0	
1917 PIT N	41	121	29	3	2	0	0.0	7	1	10	22	4	.240	.298	2	0	OF-36
2 yrs.	42	122	29	3	2	0	0.0	7	1	10	23	4	.238	.295	3	0	OF-36
1 yr.	1	1	0	0	0	0	0.0	0	0	0	1	0	.000	.000	1	0	

Joe Jackson
JACKSON, JOSEPH JEFFERSON (Shoeless Joe)   BL TR 6'1" 200 lbs.
B. July 16, 1887, Brandon Mills, S. C.   D. Dec. 5, 1951, Greenville, S. C.

1908 PHI A	5	23	3	0	0	0	0.0	0	3			0	.130	.130	0	0	OF-5
1909	5	17	5	0	0	0	0.0	3	3	1		0	.294	.294	1	0	OF-4
1910 CLE A	20	75	29	2	5	1	1.3	15	11	8		4	.387	.587	0	0	OF-20
1911	147	571	233	45	19	7	1.2	126	83	56		41	.408	.590	0	0	OF-147
1912	152	572	226	44	26	3	0.5	121	90	54		35	.395	.579	2	1	OF-150
1913	148	528	197	39	17	7	1.3	109	71	80	26	26	.373	.551	0	0	OF-148
1914	122	453	153	22	13	3	0.7	61	53	41	34	22	.338	.464	2	0	OF-119
1915 2 teams	CLE A (82G – .331)					CHI A (46G – .265)											
" total	128	461	142	20	14	5	1.1	63	81	52	23	16	.308	.445	4	2	OF-95, 1B-27
1916 CHI A	155	592	202	40	21	3	0.5	91	78	46	25	24	.341	.495	0	0	OF-155
1917	146	538	162	20	17	5	0.9	91	75	57	25	13	.301	.429	1	0	OF-145
1918	17	65	23	2	2	1	1.5	9	20	8	1	3	.354	.492	0	0	OF-17
1919	139	516	181	31	14	7	1.4	79	96	60	10	9	.351	.506	0	0	OF-139
1920	146	570	218	42	20	12	2.1	105	121	56	14	9	.382	.589	1	0	OF-145
13 yrs.	1330	4981	1774	307	168	54	1.1	873	785	519	158	202	.356 3rd	.518	11	4	OF-1289, 1B-27
6 yrs.	649	2443	829	139	79 6th	30	1.2	396	426	251	87	64	.339	.498	2	0	OF-647

WORLD SERIES
1917 CHI A	6	23	7	0	0	0	0.0	4	2	1	0	1	.304	.304	0	0	OF-6
1919	8	32	12	3	0	1	3.1	5	6	1	2	0	.375	.563	0	0	OF-8
2 yrs.	14	55	19	3	0	1	1.8	9	8	2	2	1	.345	.455	0	0	OF-14

Ron Jackson
JACKSON, RONALD HARRIS   BR TR 6'7" 225 lbs.
B. Oct. 22, 1933, Kalamazoo, Mich.

1954 CHI A	40	93	26	4	0	4	4.3	10	10	6	20	2	.280	.452	7	1	1B-35
1955	40	74	15	1	1	2	2.7	10	7	8	22	1	.203	.324	7	4	1B-29
1956	22	56	12	3	0	1	1.8	7	4	10	13	1	.214	.321	3	0	1B-19
1957	13	60	19	3	0	2	3.3	4	8	1	12	0	.317	.467	0	0	1B-13
1958	61	146	34	4	0	7	4.8	19	21	18	46	2	.233	.404	22	4	1B-38
1959	10	14	3	1	0	1	7.1	3	2	1	0	0	.214	.500	5	1	1B-5
1960 BOS A	10	31	7	2	0	0	0.0	1	0	1	6	0	.226	.290	1	0	1B-9
7 yrs.	196	474	116	18	1	17	3.6	54	52	45	119	6	.245	.395	45	10	1B-148
6 yrs.	186	443	109	16	1	17	3.8	53	52	44	113	6	.246	.402	44	10	1B-139

Otto Jacobs
JACOBS, OTTO ALBERT   BR TR 5'9" 180 lbs.
B. Apr. 19, 1889, Chicago, Ill.   D. Nov. 19, 1955, Chicago, Ill.

| 1918 CHI A | 29 | 73 | 15 | 3 | 1 | 0 | 0.0 | 4 | 3 | 5 | 8 | 0 | .205 | .274 | 7 | 1 | C-21 |

Irv Jeffries
JEFFRIES, IRVINE FRANKLIN   BR TR 5'10" 175 lbs.
B. Sept. 10, 1905, Louisville, Ky.   D. June 8, 1982, Louisville, Ky.

1930 CHI A	40	97	23	3	0	2	2.1	14	11	3	2	1	.237	.330	1	0	SS-13, 3B-10
1931	79	223	50	10	0	2	0.9	29	16	14	9	3	.224	.296	5	0	3B-61, 2B-6, SS-5
1934 PHI N	56	175	43	6	0	4	2.3	28	19	15	10	2	.246	.349	2	0	2B-52, 3B-1
3 yrs.	175	495	116	19	0	8	1.6	71	46	32	21	6	.234	.321	8	0	3B-72, 2B-58, SS-18
2 yrs.	119	320	73	13	0	4	1.3	43	27	17	11	4	.228	.306	6	0	3B-71, SS-18, 2B-6

Joe Jenkins
JENKINS, JOSEPH DANIEL   BR TR 5'11" 170 lbs.
B. Oct. 12, 1890, Shelbyville, Tenn.   D. June 21, 1974, Fresno, Calif.

1914 STL A	19	32	4	1	1	0	0.0	0	0	1	11	2	.125	.219	9	1	C-9
1917 CHI A	10	9	1	0	0	0	0.0	0	2	0	5	0	.111	.111	9	1	
1919	11	19	3	1	0	0	0.0	0	1	1	1	0	.158	.211	7	1	C-4
3 yrs.	40	60	8	2	1	0	0.0	0	3	2	17	2	.133	.200	25	3	C-13
2 yrs.	21	28	4	1	0	0	0.0	0	3	1	6	0	.143	.179	16	2	C-4

John Jenkins
JENKINS, JOHN ROBERT   BR TR 5'8" 160 lbs.
B. July 7, 1896, Bosworth, Mo.   D. Aug. 3, 1968, Columbia, Mo.

| 1922 CHI A | 5 | 3 | 0 | 0 | 0 | 0 | 0.0 | 1 | 0 | 2 | 0 | .000 | .000 | 1 | 0 | SS-1, 2B-1 |

John Jeter
JETER, JOHN   BR TR 6'1" 180 lbs.
B. Oct. 24, 1944, Shreveport, La.

1969 PIT N	28	29	9	1	1	1	3.4	7	6	3	15	1	.310	.517	3	1	OF-20
1970	85	126	30	3	2	2	1.6	27	12	13	34	9	.238	.341	17	5	OF-56
1971 SD N	18	75	24	4	0	1	1.3	8	3	2	16	2	.320	.413	1	0	OF-17

268

	G	AB	H	2B	3B	HR	HR%	R	RBI	BB	SO	SB	BA	SA	Pinch Hit AB	Pinch Hit H	G by POS

John Jeter continued
1972		110	326	72	4	3	7	2.1	25	21	18	92	11	.221	.316	20	5	OF-91
1973 CHI	A	89	299	72	14	4	7	2.3	39	26	9	74	5	.241	.385	8	1	OF-72, DH-3
1974 CLE	A	6	17	6	1	0	0	0.0	3	1	1	6	0	.353	.412	1	0	OF-6
6 yrs.		336	872	213	27	10	18	2.1	109	69	46	237	29	.244	.360	50	12	OF-262, DH-3
1 yr.		89	299	72	14	4	7	2.3	39	26	9	74	5	.241	.385	8	1	OF-72, DH-3

LEAGUE CHAMPIONSHIP SERIES
1970 PIT	N	3	2	0	0	0	0	0.0	0	0	0	2	0	.000	.000	1	0	OF-1

Pete Johns
JOHNS, WILLIAM R. BR TR 5'10" 165 lbs.
B. Jan. 17, 1889, Cleveland, Ohio   D. Aug. 9, 1964, Cleveland, Ohio

1915 CHI	A	28	100	21	2	1	0	0.0	7	11	8	11	2	.210	.250	0	0	3B-28
1918 STL	A	46	89	16	1	1	0	0.0	5	11	4	6	0	.180	.213	20	2	1B-10, OF-4, SS-4, 3B-4, 2B-2
2 yrs.		74	189	37	3	2	0	0.0	12	22	12	17	2	.196	.233	20	2	3B-32, 1B-10, OF-4, SS-4, 2B-2
1 yr.		28	100	21	2	1	0	0.0	7	11	8	11	2	.210	.250	0	0	3B-28

Darrell Johnson
JOHNSON, DARRELL DEAN BR TR 6'1" 180 lbs.
B. Aug. 25, 1928, Horace, Neb.
Manager 1974-80, 1982

1952 2 teams		STL A (29G – .282)			CHI A (22G – .108)													
" total		51	115	26	2	1	0	0.0	12	10	16	13	1	.226	.261	10	4	C-43
1957 NY	A	21	46	10	1	0	1	2.2	4	8	3	10	0	.217	.304	1	0	C-20
1958		5	16	4	0	0	0	0.0	1	0	0	2	0	.250	.250	1	0	C-4
1960 STL	N	8	2	0	0	0	0	0.0	0	1	0	0	0	.000	.000	0	0	C-8
1961 2 teams		PHI N (21G – .230)			CIN N (20G – .315)													
" total		41	115	31	3	0	1	0.9	7	9	4	10	0	.270	.322	0	0	C-41
1962 2 teams		CIN N (2G – .000)			BAL A (6G – .182)													
" total		8	26	4	0	0	0	0.0	0	1	2	4	0	.154	.154	0	0	C-8
6 yrs.		134	320	75	6	1	2	0.6	24	28	26	39	1	.234	.278	12	4	C-124
1 yr.		22	37	4	0	0	0	0.0	3	1	5	9	1	.108	.108	2	0	C-21

WORLD SERIES
1961 CIN	N	2	4	2	0	0	0	0.0	0	0	0	0	0	.500	.500	0	0	C-2

Deron Johnson
JOHNSON, DERON ROGER BR TR 6'2" 200 lbs.
B. July 17, 1938, San Diego, Calif.

1960 NY	A	6	4	2	1	0	0	0.0	0	0	0	0	0	.500	.750	1	0	3B-5
1961 2 teams		NY A (13G – .105)			KC A (83G – .216)													
" total		96	302	63	11	3	8	2.6	32	44	16	49	0	.209	.344	10	2	OF-59, 3B-27, 1B-3
1962 KC	A	17	19	2	1	0	0	0.0	1	0	3	8	0	.105	.158	9	0	OF-2, 3B-2, 1B-2
1964 CIN	N	140	477	130	24	4	21	4.4	63	79	37	98	4	.273	.472	13	5	1B-131, OF-10, 3B-1
1965		159	616	177	30	7	32	5.2	92	130	52	97	0	.287	.515	0	0	3B-159
1966		142	505	130	25	3	24	4.8	75	81	39	87	1	.257	.461	5	1	OF-106, 1B-71, 3B-18
1967		108	361	81	18	1	13	3.6	39	53	22	104	0	.224	.388	10	3	1B-81, 3B-24
1968 ATL	N	127	342	71	11	1	8	2.3	29	33	35	79	0	.208	.316	13	3	1B-97, 3B-21
1969 PHI	N	138	475	121	19	4	17	3.6	51	80	60	111	4	.255	.419	6	1	OF-72, 3B-50, 1B-18
1970		159	574	147	28	3	27	4.7	66	93	72	132	0	.256	.456	5	2	1B-154, 3B-3
1971		158	582	154	29	0	34	5.8	74	95	72	146	0	.265	.490	3	1	1B-136, 3B-22
1972		96	230	49	4	1	9	3.9	19	31	26	69	0	.213	.357	30	6	1B-62
1973 2 teams		PHI N (12G – .167)			OAK A (131G – .246)													
" total		143	500	120	16	2	20	4.0	64	86	64	126	0	.240	.400	3	0	DH-107, 1B-33
1974 3 teams		OAK A (50G – .195)			MIL A (49G – .151)			BOS A (11G – .120)										
" total		110	351	60	4	2	13	3.7	30	43	32	84	2	.171	.305	6	0	DH-77, 1B-30
1975 2 teams		CHI A (148G – .232)			BOS A (3G – .600)													
" total		151	565	135	25	1	19	3.4	68	75	50	117	0	.239	.388	3	2	DH-94, 1B-57
1976 BOS	A	15	38	5	1	0	0	0.0	3	0	5	11	0	.132	.211	3	0	OF-5
16 yrs.		1765	5941	1447	247	33	245	4.1	706	923	585	1318	11	.244	.420	120	26	1B-875, 3B-332, DH-278, OF-254
1 yr.		148	555	129	25	1	18	3.2	66	72	48	117	0	.232	.378	3	2	DH-93, 1B-55

LEAGUE CHAMPIONSHIP SERIES
1973 OAK A		4	10	1	0	0	0	0.0	0	0	0	0	0	.100	.100	0	0	DH-4

WORLD SERIES
1973 OAK A		6	10	3	1	0	0	0.0	0	0	1	4	0	.300	.400	3	2	1B-2

Ernie Johnson
JOHNSON, ERNEST RUDOLPH BL TR 5'9" 151 lbs.
Father of Don Johnson.
B. Apr. 29, 1888, Chicago, Ill.   D. May 1, 1952, Monrovia, Calif.

1912 CHI	A	18	42	11	0	1	0	0.0	7	5	1	0	0	.262	.310	1	0	SS-16
1915 STL	F	152	512	123	18	10	7	1.4	58	67	46	0	32	.240	.355	0	0	SS-152
1916 STL	A	74	236	54	9	3	0	0.0	29	19	30	23	13	.229	.292	1	0	SS-60, 3B-12
1917		80	199	49	6	2	2	1.0	28	20	12	16	13	.246	.327	2	0	SS-39, 2B-18, 3B-14
1918		29	34	9	1	0	0	0.0	7	0	0	2	4	.265	.294	9	2	SS-11, 3B-1
1921 CHI	A	142	613	181	28	7	1	0.2	93	51	29	24	22	.295	.369	1	1	SS-141
1922		145	603	153	17	3	0	0.0	85	56	40	30	21	.254	.292	2	0	SS-141
1923 2 teams		CHI A (12G – .189)			NY A (17G – .354)													
" total		29	101	27	3	1	1	1.0	11	9	4	6	2	.267	.347	3	3	SS-24, 3B-1
1924 NY	A	64	119	42	4	8	3	2.5	24	12	11	7	1	.353	.597	13	3	2B-27, SS-9, 3B-2
1925		76	170	48	5	1	5	2.9	30	17	8	10	6	.282	.412	14	1	2B-34, SS-28, 3B-2
10 yrs.		809	2629	697	91	36	19	0.7	372	256	181	118	114	.265	.349	46	11	SS-621, 2B-79, 3B-32
4 yrs.		317	1311	355	47	11	1	0.1	190	113	73	59	45	.271	.326	4	2	SS-310

WORLD SERIES
1923 NY	A	2	0	0	0	0	0	–	1	0	0	0	0	–	–	0	0	SS-1

Player Register

	G	AB	H	2B	3B	HR	HR%	R	RBI	BB	SO	SB	BA	SA	Pinch Hit AB	Pinch Hit H	G by POS

Lamar Johnson
JOHNSON, LAMAR
B. Sept. 2, 1950, Bessemer, Ala.
BR TR 6'2" 215 lbs.

	G	AB	H	2B	3B	HR	HR%	R	RBI	BB	SO	SB	BA	SA	PH AB	PH H	G by POS
1974 CHI A	10	29	10	0	0	0	0.0	1	2	0	3	0	.345	.345	0	0	1B-7, DH-3
1975	8	30	6	3	0	1	3.3	2	1	1	5	0	.200	.400	1	0	1B-6, DH-2
1976	82	222	71	11	1	4	1.8	29	33	19	37	2	.320	.432	18	4	DH-35, 1B-34, OF-1
1977	118	374	113	12	5	18	4.8	52	65	24	53	1	.302	.505	26	10	DH-68, 1B-45
1978	148	498	136	23	2	8	1.6	52	72	43	46	6	.273	.376	10	2	1B-108, DH-36
1979	133	479	148	29	1	12	2.5	60	74	41	56	8	.309	.449	7	1	1B-94, DH-37
1980	147	541	150	26	3	13	2.4	51	81	47	53	2	.277	.409	5	1	1B-80, DH-66
1981	41	134	37	7	0	1	0.7	10	15	5	14	0	.276	.351	6	1	1B-36, DH-2
1982 TEX A	105	324	84	11	0	7	2.2	37	38	31	40	3	.259	.358	19	5	DH-77, 1B-12
9 yrs.	792	2631	755	122	12	64	2.4	294	381	211	307	22	.287	.415	92	24	1B-422, DH-326, OF-1
8 yrs.	687	2307	671	111	12	57	2.5	257	343	180	267	19	.291	.423	73	19	1B-410, DH-249, OF-1

Larry Johnson
JOHNSON, LARRY DOBY
B. Aug. 19, 1950, Cleveland, Ohio
BR TR 6' 185 lbs.

	G	AB	H	2B	3B	HR	HR%	R	RBI	BB	SO	SB	BA	SA	PH AB	PH H	G by POS
1972 CLE A	1	2	1	0	0	0	0.0	0	0	0	1	0	.500	.500	1	0	C-1
1974	1	0	0	0	0	0	—	1	0	0	0	0	—	—	0	0	
1975 MON N	1	3	1	1	0	0	0.0	0	1	1	1	0	.333	.667	1	0	C-1
1976	6	13	2	1	0	0	0.0	0	0	0	2	0	.154	.231	0	0	C-5
1978 CHI A	3	8	1	0	0	0	0.0	0	0	1	4	0	.125	.125	0	0	C-2, DH-1
5 yrs.	12	26	5	2	0	0	0.0	1	1	2	8	0	.192	.269	2	0	C-9, DH-1
1 yr.	3	8	1	0	0	0	0.0	0	0	1	4	0	.125	.125	0	0	C-2, DH-1

Randy Johnson
JOHNSON, RANDALL STUART
B. Aug. 15, 1958, Miami, Fla.
BL TL 6'2" 195 lbs.

	G	AB	H	2B	3B	HR	HR%	R	RBI	BB	SO	SB	BA	SA	PH AB	PH H	G by POS
1980 CHI A	12	20	4	0	0	0	0.0	0	3	2	4	0	.200	.200	5	2	DH-4, OF-1, 1B-1
1982 MIN A	89	234	58	10	0	10	4.3	26	33	30	46	0	.248	.419	22	2	DH-67, OF-3, 1B-1
2 yrs.	101	254	62	10	0	10	3.9	26	36	32	50	0	.244	.402	27	4	DH-71, OF-3, 1B-1
1 yr.	12	20	4	0	0	0	0.0	0	3	2	4	0	.200	.200	5	2	DH-4, OF-1, 1B-1

Stan Johnson
JOHNSON, STANLEY LUCIUS
B. Feb. 12, 1937, Dallas, Tex.
BL TL 5'10" 180 lbs.

	G	AB	H	2B	3B	HR	HR%	R	RBI	BB	SO	SB	BA	SA	PH AB	PH H	G by POS
1960 CHI A	5	6	1	0	0	1	16.7	1	1	0	1	0	.167	.667	5	1	OF-2
1961 KC A	3	3	0	0	0	0	0.0	1	0	2	1	0	.000	.000	1	0	OF-2
2 yrs.	8	9	1	0	0	1	11.1	2	1	2	2	0	.111	.444	6	1	OF-4
1 yr.	5	6	1	0	0	1	16.7	1	1	0	1	0	.167	.667	5	1	OF-2

Jimmy Johnston
JOHNSTON, JAMES HARLE
Brother of Doc Johnston.
B. Dec. 10, 1889, Cleveland, Tenn. D. Feb. 14, 1967, Chattanooga, Tenn.
BR TR 5'10" 160 lbs.

	G	AB	H	2B	3B	HR	HR%	R	RBI	BB	SO	SB	BA	SA	PH AB	PH H	G by POS
1911 CHI A	1	2	0	0	0	0	0.0	0	2	0		0	.000	.000	0	0	OF-1
1914 CHI N	50	101	23	3	2	1	1.0	9	8	4	9	3	.228	.327	11	2	OF-28, 2B-4
1916 BKN N	118	425	107	13	8	1	0.2	58	26	35	38	22	.252	.327	1	1	OF-106
1917	103	330	89	10	4	0	0.0	33	25	23	28	16	.270	.324	8	1	OF-92, 1B-14, SS-4, 3B-3, 2B-3
1918	123	484	136	16	8	0	0.0	54	27	33	31	22	.281	.347	1	0	OF-96, 1B-21, 3B-4, 2B-1
1919	117	405	114	11	4	1	0.2	56	23	29	26	11	.281	.336	9	1	2B-87, OF-14, 1B-2, SS-1
1920	155	635	185	17	12	1	0.2	87	52	43	23	19	.291	.361	0	0	3B-146, OF-7, SS-3
1921	152	624	203	41	14	5	0.8	104	56	45	26	28	.325	.460	0	0	3B-150, SS-3
1922	138	567	181	20	7	4	0.7	110	49	38	17	18	.319	.400	0	0	2B-62, SS-50, 3B-26
1923	151	625	203	29	11	4	0.6	111	60	53	15	16	.325	.426	1	0	2B-84, SS-52, 3B-14
1924	86	315	94	11	2	2	0.6	51	29	27	10	5	.298	.365	7	4	SS-63, 3B-10, 1B-4, OF-1
1925	123	431	128	13	2	2	0.5	63	43	45	15	7	.297	.355	12	4	3B-81, OF-20, 1B-8, SS-2
1926 2 teams	BOS N (23G – .246)					NY N (37G – .232)											
" total	60	126	30	1	0	1	0.8	18	10	16	8	2	.238	.270	25	5	OF-15, 3B-14, 2B-2
13 yrs.	1377	5070	1493	185	75	22	0.4	754	410	391	246	169	.294	.374	75	18	3B-448, OF-380, 2B-243, SS-178, 1B-49
1 yr.	1	2	0	0	0	0	0.0	0	2	0		0	.000	.000	0	0	OF-1

WORLD SERIES

	G	AB	H	2B	3B	HR	HR%	R	RBI	BB	SO	SB	BA	SA	PH AB	PH H	G by POS
1916 BKN N	3	10	3	0	1	0	0.0	0	1	0	1	0	.300	.500	1	1	OF-2
1920	4	14	3	0	0	0	0.0	2	0	0	2	1	.214	.214	0	0	3B-4
2 yrs.	7	24	6	0	1	0	0.0	3	0	1	2	1	.250	.333	1	1	3B-4, OF-2

Jay Johnstone
JOHNSTONE, JOHN WILLIAM
B. Nov. 20, 1945, Manchester, Conn.
BL TR 6'1" 175 lbs.
BB 1966

	G	AB	H	2B	3B	HR	HR%	R	RBI	BB	SO	SB	BA	SA	PH AB	PH H	G by POS
1966 CAL A	61	254	67	12	4	3	1.2	35	17	11	36	3	.264	.378	0	0	OF-61
1967	79	230	48	7	1	2	0.9	18	10	5	37	3	.209	.274	21	5	OF-63
1968	41	115	30	4	1	0	0.0	11	3	7	15	2	.261	.313	8	0	OF-29
1969	148	540	146	20	5	10	1.9	64	59	38	75	3	.270	.381	4	1	OF-144
1970	119	320	76	10	5	11	3.4	34	39	24	53	1	.238	.403	23	5	OF-100
1971 CHI A	124	388	101	14	1	16	4.1	53	40	38	50	10	.260	.425	11	3	OF-119
1972	113	261	49	9	0	4	1.5	27	17	25	42	2	.188	.268	19	6	OF-97
1973 OAK A	23	28	3	1	0	0	0.0	1	3	2	4	0	.107	.143	11	0	OF-7, DH-4, 2B-2
1974 PHI N	64	200	59	10	4	6	3.0	30	30	24	28	5	.295	.475	6	4	OF-59
1975	122	350	115	19	2	7	2.0	50	54	42	39	7	.329	.454	25	10	OF-101
1976	129	440	140	38	4	5	1.1	62	53	41	39	5	.318	.457	12	2	OF-122, 1B-6
1977	112	363	103	18	4	15	4.1	64	59	38	38	3	.284	.479	14	5	OF-91, 1B-19
1978 2 teams	PHI N (35G – .179)					NY A (36G – .262)											
" total	71	121	27	2	0	1	0.8	9	10	10	19	0	.223	.264	28	2	OF-29, 1B-8, DH-5
1979 2 teams	NY A (23G – .208)					SD N (75G – .294)											
" total	98	249	69	9	2	1	0.4	17	39	20	28	2	.277	.341	25	6	OF-64, 1B-22, DH-3
1980 LA N	109	251	77	15	2	2	0.8	31	20	24	29	3	.307	.406	41	11	OF-57
1981	61	83	17	3	0	3	3.6	8	6	7	13	0	.205	.349	38	11	OF-16, 1B-2
1982 2 teams	LA N (21G – .077)					CHI N (98G – .249)											
" total	119	282	68	14	1	10	3.5	40	45	45	43	0	.241	.404	26	3	OF-86

	G	AB	H	2B	3B	HR	HR%	R	RBI	BB	SO	SB	BA	SA	Pinch Hit AB	H	G by POS

Jay Johnstone continued
1983 CHI N	86	140	36	7	0	6	4.3	16	22	20	24	1	.257	.436	38	6	OF-44
18 yrs.	1679	4615	1231	212	36	102	2.2	570	526	421	612	50	.267	.395	350	80	OF-1293, 1B-57, DH-12, 2B-2
2 yrs.	237	649	150	23	1	20	3.1	80	57	63	92	12	.231	.362	30	9	OF-216

DIVISIONAL PLAYOFF SERIES
1981 LA N	1	1	0	0	0	0	0.0	0	0	0	0	0	.000	.000	1	0	

LEAGUE CHAMPIONSHIP SERIES
1976 PHI N	3	9	7	1	1	0	0.0	1	2	1	0	0	.778	1.111	1	1	OF-2
1977	2	5	1	0	0	0	0.0	0	0	0	1	0	.200	.200	1	0	OF-2
1981 LA N	2	2	0	0	0	0	0.0	0	0	0	0	0	.000	.000	2	0	
3 yrs.	7	16	8	1	1	0	0.0	1	2	1	1	0	.500	.688	4	1	OF-4

WORLD SERIES
1978 NY A	2	0	0	0	0	—	—	0	0	0	0	0	—	—	0	0	OF-2
1981 LA N	3	3	2	0	0	1	33.3	1	3	0	0	0	.667	1.667	3	2	
2 yrs.	5	3	2	0	0	1	33.3	1	3	0	0	0	.667	1.667	3	2	OF-2

Stan Jok
JOK, STANLEY EDWARD (Tucker)
B. May 3, 1926, Buffalo, N. Y. D. Mar. 6, 1972, Buffalo, N. Y. BR TR 6' 190 lbs.

1954 2 teams	PHI N (3G – .000)				CHI A (3G – .167)												
" total	6	15	2	0	0	0	0.0	1	2	1	4	0	.133	.133	3	0	3B-3
1955 CHI A	6	4	1	0	0	1	25.0	3	2	1	1	0	.250	1.000	0	0	3B-3, OF-1
2 yrs.	12	19	3	0	0	1	5.3	4	4	2	5	0	.158	.316	3	0	3B-6, OF-1
2 yrs.	9	16	3	0	0	1	6.3	4	4	2	3	0	.188	.375	0	0	3B-6, OF-1

Smead Jolley
JOLLEY, SMEAD POWELL (Smudge)
B. Jan. 14, 1902, Wesson, Ark. BL TR 6'3½" 210 lbs.

1930 CHI A	152	616	193	38	12	16	2.6	76	114	28	52	3	.313	.492	1	1	OF-151
1931	54	110	33	11	0	3	2.7	5	28	7	4	0	.300	.482	30	14	OF-23
1932 2 teams	CHI A (12G – .357)				BOS A (137G – .309)												
" total	149	573	179	30	5	18	3.1	60	106	30	29	1	.312	.476	6	1	OF-137, C-5
1933 BOS A	118	411	116	32	4	9	2.2	47	65	24	20	1	.282	.445	15	4	OF-102
4 yrs.	473	1710	521	111	21	46	2.7	188	313	89	105	5	.305	.475	52	20	OF-413, C-5
3 yrs.	218	768	241	52	12	19	2.5	84	149	38	56	4	.314	.487	32	16	OF-185

Cleon Jones
JONES, CLEON JOSEPH
B. Aug. 4, 1942, Plateau, Ala. BR TL 6' 185 lbs.

1963 NY N	6	15	2	0	0	0	0.0	1	1	0	4	0	.133	.133	2	0	OF-5
1965	30	74	11	1	0	1	1.4	2	9	2	23	1	.149	.203	9	2	OF-23
1966	139	495	136	16	4	8	1.6	74	57	30	62	16	.275	.372	11	0	OF-129
1967	129	411	101	10	5	5	1.2	46	30	19	57	12	.246	.331	13	2	OF-115
1968	147	509	151	29	4	14	2.8	63	55	31	98	23	.297	.452	10	1	OF-139
1969	137	483	164	25	4	12	2.5	92	75	64	60	16	.340	.482	4	2	OF-122, 1B-15
1970	134	506	140	25	8	10	2.0	71	63	57	87	12	.277	.417	5	0	OF-130
1971	136	505	161	24	6	14	2.8	63	69	53	87	6	.319	.473	5	1	OF-132
1972	106	375	92	15	1	5	1.3	39	52	30	83	1	.245	.331	3	0	OF-84, 1B-20
1973	92	339	88	13	0	11	3.2	28	48	28	51	1	.260	.395	4	3	OF-92
1974	124	461	130	23	1	13	2.8	62	60	38	79	3	.282	.421	6	1	OF-120
1975	21	50	12	1	0	0	0.0	2	2	3	6	0	.240	.260	9	3	OF-12
1976 CHI A	12	40	8	1	0	0	0.0	2	3	5	5	0	.200	.225	1	0	OF-8, DH-3
13 yrs.	1213	4263	1196	183	33	93	2.2	565	524	360	702	91	.281	.404	82	15	OF-1111, 1B-35, DH-3
1 yr.	12	40	8	1	0	0	0.0	2	3	5	5	0	.200	.225	1	0	OF-8, DH-3

LEAGUE CHAMPIONSHIP SERIES
1969 NY N	3	14	6	2	0	1	7.1	4	4	1	2	2	.429	.786	0	0	OF-3
1973	5	20	6	2	0	0	0.0	3	3	2	4	0	.300	.400	0	0	OF-5
2 yrs.	8	34	12	4	0	1	2.9	7	7	3	6	2	.353	.559	0	0	OF-8

WORLD SERIES
1969 NY N	5	19	3	1	0	0	0.0	2	0	0	1	0	.158	.211	0	0	OF-5
1973	7	28	8	2	0	1	3.6	5	1	4	2	0	.286	.464	0	0	OF-7
2 yrs.	12	47	11	3	0	1	2.1	7	1	4	3	0	.234	.362	0	0	OF-12

Davy Jones
JONES, DAVID JEFFERSON (Kangaroo)
B. June 30, 1880, Cambria, Wis. D. Mar. 30, 1972, Mankato, Minn. BL TR 5'10" 165 lbs.

1901 MIL A	14	52	9	0	0	3	5.8	12	5	11		4	.173	.346	0	0	OF-14
1902 2 teams	STL A (15G – .224)				CHI N (64G – .305)												
" total	79	292	85	13	4	0	0.0	45	17	44		17	.291	.363	0	0	OF-79
1903 CHI N	130	497	140	18	3	1	0.2	64	62	53		15	.282	.336	0	0	OF-130
1904	98	336	82	11	5	3	0.9	44	39	41		14	.244	.333	0	0	OF-97
1906 DET A	84	323	84	12	2	0	0.0	41	24	41		21	.260	.310	0	0	OF-84
1907	126	491	134	10	6	0	0.0	101	27	60		30	.273	.318	0	0	OF-126
1908	56	121	25	2	1	0	0.0	17	10	13		11	.207	.240	21	3	OF-32
1909	69	204	57	2	2	0	0.0	44	10	28		12	.279	.309	10	1	OF-57
1910	113	377	100	6	6	0	0.0	77	24	51		25	.265	.313	9	0	OF-101
1911	98	341	93	10	0	0	0.0	78	19	41		25	.273	.302	4	1	OF-92
1912	97	316	93	5	2	0	0.0	54	24	38		16	.294	.323	15	4	OF-81
1913 CHI A	10	21	6	0	0	0	0.0	0	0	9		1	.286	.286	1	0	OF-8
1914 PIT F	97	352	96	9	8	2	0.6	58	24	42		15	.273	.361	4	2	OF-93
1915	14	49	16	0	1	0	0.0	6	4	6		1	.327	.367	0	0	OF-13
14 yrs.	1085	3772	1020	98	40	9	0.2	643	289	478		207	.270	.325	64	11	OF-1007
1 yr.	10	21	6	0	0	0	0.0	0	0	9		1	.286	.286	1	0	OF-8

WORLD SERIES
1907 DET A	5	17	6	0	0	0	0.0	1	0	4		3	.353	.353	0	0	OF-5
1908	3	2	0	0	0	0	0.0	1	0	1	1	0	.000	.000	2	0	

Player Register

	G	AB	H	2B	3B	HR	HR%	R	RBI	BB	SO	SB	BA	SA	Pinch Hit AB	H	G by POS

Davy Jones continued

| 1909 | 7 | 30 | 7 | 0 | 0 | 1 | 3.3 | 6 | 2 | 2 | 1 | 1 | .233 | .333 | 0 | 0 | OF-7 |
| 3 yrs. | 15 | 49 | 13 | 0 | 0 | 1 | 2.0 | 8 | 2 | 7 | 2 | 4 | .265 | .327 | 2 | 0 | OF-12 |

Deacon Jones

JONES, GROVER WILLIAM
B. Apr. 18, 1934, White Plains, N.Y.
BL TR 5'10" 185 lbs.

1962 CHI A	18	28	9	2	0	0	0.0	3	8	4	6	0	.321	.393	8	4	1B-6
1963	17	16	3	0	1	1	6.3	4	2	2	2	0	.188	.500	12	1	1B-1
1966	5	5	2	0	0	0	0.0	0	0	0	0	0	.400	.400	5	2	
3 yrs.	40	49	14	2	1	1	2.0	7	10	6	8	0	.286	.429	25	7	1B-7
3 yrs.	40	49	14	2	1	1	2.0	7	10	6	8	0	.286	.429	25	7	1B-7

Fielder Jones

JONES, FIELDER ALLISON
B. Aug. 13, 1874, Shinglehouse, Pa. D. Mar. 13, 1934, Portland, Ore.
Manager 1904-08, 1914-18.
BL TR 5'11" 180 lbs.

1896 BKN N	104	399	141	10	8	3	0.8	82	46	48	15	18	.353	.441	0	0	OF-103
1897	135	553	178	14	10	2	0.4	134	49	61		48	.322	.394	0	0	OF-135
1898	147	599	181	15	9	1	0.2	89	69	46		36	.302	.362	0	0	OF-144, SS-2
1899	102	365	104	8	2	2	0.5	75	38	54		18	.285	.334	5	2	OF-96
1900	136	556	172	26	4	4	0.7	108	54	57		33	.309	.392	0	0	OF-136
1901 CHI A	133	521	177	16	3	2	0.4	120	65	84		38	.340	.393	0	0	OF-133
1902	135	532	171	16	5	0	0.0	98	54	57		33	.321	.370	0	0	OF-135
1903	136	530	152	18	5	0	0.0	71	45	47		21	.287	.340	0	0	OF-136
1904	154	564	137	14	6	3	0.5	74	43	54		25	.243	.305	0	0	OF-154
1905	153	568	139	17	12	2	0.4	91	38	73		20	.245	.327	0	0	OF-153
1906	144	496	114	22	4	2	0.4	77	34	83		26	.230	.302	0	0	OF-144
1907	154	559	146	18	1	0	0.0	70	42	67		17	.261	.297	0	0	OF-154
1908	149	529	134	11	7	1	0.2	92	50	86		26	.253	.306	0	0	OF-149
1914 STL F	5	3	1	0	0	0	0.0	0	0	1		0	.333	.333	3	1	
1915	7	6	0	0	0	0	0.0	1	0	0		0	.000	.000	3	0	OF-3
15 yrs.	1794	6780	1947	205	76	22	0.3	1184	632	818	15	359	.287	.350	11	3	OF-1775, SS-2
8 yrs.	1158	4299	1170	132	43	10	0.2	695	376	551		206	.272	.330	0	0	OF-1158
			9th	10th				6th		7th		4th					

WORLD SERIES

| 1906 CHI A | 6 | 21 | 2 | 0 | 0 | 0 | 0.0 | 4 | 0 | 3 | 3 | 0 | .095 | .095 | 0 | 0 | OF-6 |

Jake Jones

JONES, JAMES MURRELL
B. Nov. 23, 1920, Epps, La.
BR TR 6'3" 197 lbs.

1941 CHI A	3	11	0	0	0	0	0.0	0	0	4	0	.000	.000	0	0	1B-3
1942	7	20	3	1	0	0	0.0	2	0	2	2	1	.150	.200	2	0	1B-5
1946	24	79	21	5	1	3	3.8	10	13	2	13	0	.266	.468	4	0	1B-20
1947 2 teams	CHI A (45G — .240)				BOS A (109G — .235)											
" total	154	575	136	21	4	19	3.3	65	96	54	85	6	.237	.386	2	0	1B-152
1948 BOS A	36	105	21	4	0	1	1.0	3	8	11	26	1	.200	.267	4	0	1B-31
5 yrs.	224	790	181	31	5	23	2.9	80	117	69	130	8	.229	.368	12	0	1B-211
4 yrs.	79	281	65	13	2	6	2.1	27	33	17	44	2	.231	.356	8	0	1B-71

Tex Jones

JONES, WILLIAM RODERICK
B. Aug. 4, 1885, Marion, Kans. D. Feb. 26, 1938, Wichita, Kans.
BR TR 6' 192 lbs.

| 1911 CHI A | 9 | 31 | 6 | 1 | 0 | 0 | 0.0 | 4 | 4 | 3 | | 1 | .194 | .226 | 0 | 0 | 1B-9 |

Bubber Jonnard

JONNARD, CLARENCE JAMES
Brother of Claude Jonnard.
B. Nov. 23, 1897, Nashville, Tenn. D. Aug. 23, 1977, New York, N.Y.
BR TR 6'1" 185 lbs.

1920 CHI A	2	5	0	0	0	0	0.0	0	0	1		0	.000	.000	1	0	C-1
1922 PIT N	10	21	5	0	1	0	0.0	4	2	2	4	0	.238	.333	0	0	C-10
1926 PHI N	19	34	4	1	0	0	0.0	3	2	3	4	0	.118	.147	4	0	C-15
1927	53	143	42	6	0	0	0.0	18	14	7	7	0	.294	.336	7	5	C-41
1929 STL N	18	31	3	0	0	0	0.0	1	2	0	6	0	.097	.097	0	0	C-18
1935 PHI N	1	1	0	0	0	0	0.0	0	0	0		1	.000	.000	0	0	C-1
6 yrs.	103	235	54	7	1	0	0.0	26	20	12	23	0	.230	.268	12	5	C-86
1 yr.	2	5	0	0	0	0	0.0	0	0	0		1	.000	.000	1	0	C-1

Tom Jordan

JORDAN, THOMAS JEFFERSON
B. Sept. 5, 1919, Lawton, Okla.
BR TR 6'1½" 195 lbs.

1944 CHI A	14	45	12	1	1	0	0.0	2	3	1	0	0	.267	.333	0	0	C-14
1946 2 teams	CHI A (10G — .267)				CLE A (14G — .200)											
" total	24	50	11	3	1	0	2.0	3	3	3	2	1	.220	.380	10	1	C-15
1948 STL A	1	0	0	0	0	0	0.0	0	0	0	0	0	.000	.000	1	0	
3 yrs.	39	96	23	4	2	1	1.0	5	6	4	2	1	.240	.354	11	1	C-29
2 yrs.	24	60	16	3	2	0	0.0	3	3	1	1	0	.267	.383	8	0	C-16

Duane Josephson

JOSEPHSON, DUANE CHARLES
B. June 3, 1942, New Hampton, Iowa
BR TR 6' 190 lbs.

1965 CHI A	4	9	1	0	0	0	0.0	2	0	2	4	0	.111	.111	0	0	C-4
1966	11	38	9	1	0	0	0.0	3	3	3	3	0	.237	.263	0	0	C-11
1967	62	189	45	5	1	1	0.5	19	9	6	24	0	.238	.291	5	0	C-59
1968	128	434	107	16	6	6	1.4	35	45	18	52	2	.247	.353	11	3	C-122
1969	52	162	39	6	2	1	0.6	19	20	13	17	0	.241	.321	7	3	C-47
1970	96	285	90	12	1	4	1.4	28	41	24	28	1	.316	.407	5	1	C-84
1971 BOS A	91	306	75	14	1	10	3.3	38	39	22	35	2	.245	.395	5	1	C-87
1972	26	82	22	4	1	1	1.2	11	7	4	11	0	.268	.378	4	1	1B-16, C-6
8 yrs.	470	1505	388	58	12	23	1.5	147	164	92	174	5	.258	.358	46	13	C-420, 1B-16
6 yrs.	353	1117	291	40	10	12	1.1	98	118	66	128	3	.261	.346	37	11	C-327

Player Register

	G	AB	H	2B	3B	HR	HR%	R	RBI	BB	SO	SB	BA	SA	Pinch Hit AB	Pinch Hit H	G by POS

Ted Jourdan
JOURDAN, THEODORE CHARLES   BL TL 6'   175 lbs.
B. Sept. 5, 1895, New Orleans, La.   D. Sept. 23, 1961, New Orleans, La.

	G	AB	H	2B	3B	HR	HR%	R	RBI	BB	SO	SB	BA	SA	PH AB	PH H	G by POS
1916 CHI A	3	2	0	0	0	0	0.0	0	0	1	1	2	.000	.000	2	0	
1917	17	34	5	0	1	0	0.0	2	2	1	3	0	.147	.206	3	0	1B-14
1918	7	10	1	0	0	0	0.0	1	1	0	0	0	.100	.100	5	1	1B-2
1920	48	150	36	6	1	0	0.0	16	8	17	17	3	.240	.293	8	1	1B-40
4 yrs.	75	196	42	6	2	0	0.0	19	11	19	21	5	.214	.265	18	2	1B-56
4 yrs.	75	196	42	6	2	0	0.0	19	11	19	21	5	.214	.265	18	2	1B-56

Frank Kalin
KALIN, FRANK BRUNO (Fats)   BR TR 6'   200 lbs.
Born Frank Bruno Kalinkiewicz.
B. Oct. 3, 1917, Steubenville, Ohio

	G	AB	H	2B	3B	HR	HR%	R	RBI	BB	SO	SB	BA	SA	PH AB	PH H	G by POS
1940 PIT N	3	3	0	0	0	0	0.0	0	1	2	0	0	.000	.000	1	0	OF-2
1943 CHI A	4	4	0	0	0	0	0.0	0	0	0	2	0	.000	.000	4	0	
2 yrs.	7	7	0	0	0	0	0.0	0	1	2	2	0	.000	.000	5	0	OF-2
1 yr.	4	4	0	0	0	0	0.0	0	0	0	2	0	.000	.000	4	0	

Willie Kamm
KAMM, WILLIAM EDWARD   BR TR 5'10½" 170 lbs.
B. Feb. 2, 1900, San Francisco, Calif.

	G	AB	H	2B	3B	HR	HR%	R	RBI	BB	SO	SB	BA	SA	PH AB	PH H	G by POS
1923 CHI A	149	544	159	39	9	6	1.1	57	87	62	82	17	.292	.430	0	0	3B-149
1924	147	528	134	28	6	6	1.1	58	93	64	59	9	.254	.364	0	0	3B-145
1925	152	509	142	32	4	6	1.2	82	83	90	36	11	.279	.393	0	0	3B-152
1926	143	480	141	24	10	0	0.0	63	62	77	24	14	.294	.385	1	0	3B-142
1927	148	540	146	32	13	0	0.0	85	59	70	18	7	.270	.378	2	0	3B-146
1928	155	552	170	30	12	1	0.2	70	84	73	22	17	.308	.411	0	0	3B-155
1929	147	523	140	32	6	3	0.6	72	63	75	23	12	.268	.369	2	1	3B-145
1930	111	331	89	21	6	3	0.9	49	47	51	20	5	.269	.396	5	0	3B-105
1931 2 teams	CHI A (18G – .254)			CLE A (114G – .295)													
" total	132	469	136	35	5	0	0.0	77	75	71	19	14	.290	.386	0	0	3B-132
1932 CLE A	148	524	150	34	9	3	0.6	76	83	75	36	6	.286	.403	0	0	3B-148
1933	133	447	126	17	2	1	0.2	59	47	54	27	7	.282	.336	2	0	3B-131
1934	121	386	104	23	3	0	0.0	52	42	62	38	7	.269	.345	4	2	3B-118
1935	6	18	6	0	0	0	0.0	2	1	0	1	0	.333	.333	2	0	3B-4
13 yrs.	1692	5851	1643	347	85	29	0.5	802	826	824	405	126	.281	.384	18	3	3B-1672
9 yrs.	1170	4066	1136	242	66	25	0.6	545	587	569	290	93	.279	.390	10	1	3B-1157
		10th		6th	9th				8th	6th							

John Kane
KANE, JOHN FRANCIS   BB TR 5'10½" 162 lbs.
B. Feb. 19, 1900, Chicago, Ill.

	G	AB	H	2B	3B	HR	HR%	R	RBI	BB	SO	SB	BA	SA	PH AB	PH H	G by POS
1925 CHI A	14	56	10	1	0	0	0.0	6	3	0	3	0	.179	.196	0	0	SS-8, 2B-6

Charlie Kavanagh
KAVANAGH, CHARLES HUGH (Silk)   BR TR 5'9"   165 lbs.
B. June 9, 1893, Chicago, Ill.

	G	AB	H	2B	3B	HR	HR%	R	RBI	BB	SO	SB	BA	SA	PH AB	PH H	G by POS
1914 CHI A	5	5	1	0	0	0	0.0	0	0	0	2	0	.200	.200	5	1	

George Kell
KELL, GEORGE CLYDE   BR TR 5'9"   175 lbs.
Brother of Skeeter Kell.
B. Aug. 23, 1922, Swifton, Ark.
Hall of Fame 1983.

	G	AB	H	2B	3B	HR	HR%	R	RBI	BB	SO	SB	BA	SA	PH AB	PH H	G by POS
1943 PHI A	1	5	1	0	0	0	0.0	0	0	0	0	0	.200	.600	0	0	3B-1
1944	139	514	138	15	3	0	0.0	51	44	22	23	5	.268	.309	0	0	3B-139
1945	147	567	154	30	5	4	0.7	50	56	27	15	2	.272	.356	0	0	3B-147
1946 2 teams	PHI A (26G – .299)			DET A (105G – .327)													
" total	131	521	168	25	10	4	0.8	70	52	40	20	3	.322	.432	0	0	3B-131, 1B-1
1947 DET A	152	588	188	29	5	5	0.9	75	93	61	16	9	.320	.412	0	0	3B-152
1948	92	368	112	24	3	2	0.5	47	44	33	15	2	.304	.402	0	0	3B-92
1949	134	522	179	38	9	3	0.6	97	59	71	13	7	.343	.467	0	0	3B-134
1950	157	641	218	56	6	8	1.2	114	101	66	18	3	.340	.484	0	0	3B-157
1951	147	598	191	36	3	2	0.3	92	59	61	18	10	.319	.400	0	0	3B-147
1952 2 teams	DET A (39G – .296)			BOS A (75G – .319)													
" total	114	428	133	23	2	7	1.6	52	57	45	23	0	.311	.423	1	0	3B-112
1953 BOS A	134	460	141	41	2	12	2.6	68	73	52	22	5	.307	.483	8	4	3B-124, OF-7
1954 2 teams	BOS A (26G – .258)			CHI A (71G – .283)													
" total	97	326	90	13	0	5	1.5	40	58	33	15	1	.276	.362	9	1	3B-56, 1B-32, OF-2
1955 CHI A	128	429	134	24	1	8	1.9	44	81	51	36	0	.312	.429	8	2	3B-105, 1B-24, OF-1
1956 2 teams	CHI A (21G – .313)			BAL A (102G – .261)													
" total	123	425	115	22	2	9	2.1	52	48	33	37	0	.271	.395	6	0	3B-115, 1B-6, 2B-1
1957 BAL A	99	310	92	9	0	9	2.9	28	44	25	16	2	.297	.413	11	4	3B-80, 1B-22
15 yrs.	1795	6702	2054	385	50	78	1.2	881	870	620	287	51	.306	.414	43	11	3B-1692, 1B-85, OF-10, 2B-1
3 yrs.	220	742	225	39	1	14	1.9	76	140	77	54	3	.303	.415	16	3	3B-154, 1B-60, OF-3

Pat Kelly
KELLY, HAROLD PATRICK   BL TL 6'1"   185 lbs.
B. July 30, 1944, Philadelphia, Pa.

	G	AB	H	2B	3B	HR	HR%	R	RBI	BB	SO	SB	BA	SA	PH AB	PH H	G by POS
1967 MIN A	8	1	0	0	0	0	0.0	0	1	0	0	0	.000	.000	1	0	
1968	12	35	4	2	0	1	2.9	2	2	3	10	0	.114	.257	2	0	OF-10
1969 KC A	112	417	110	20	8	8	1.9	61	32	49	70	40	.264	.388	3	0	OF-107
1970	136	452	106	16	1	6	1.3	56	38	76	105	34	.235	.314	17	1	OF-118
1971 CHI A	67	213	62	6	3	3	1.4	32	22	36	29	14	.291	.390	7	4	OF-61
1972	119	402	105	14	7	5	1.2	57	24	55	69	32	.261	.368	3	3	OF-109
1973	144	550	154	24	5	1	0.2	77	44	65	91	22	.280	.347	7	2	OF-141, DH-1
1974	122	424	119	16	3	4	0.9	60	21	46	58	18	.281	.361	3	0	DH-67, OF-53
1975	133	471	129	21	7	9	1.9	73	45	58	69	18	.274	.406	5	1	OF-115, DH-14
1976	107	311	79	20	3	5	1.6	42	34	45	15	0	.254	.386	20	7	DH-63, OF-26
1977 BAL A	120	360	92	13	0	10	2.8	50	49	55	75	25	.256	.375	11	5	OF-109, OF-11
1978	100	274	75	12	1	11	4.0	38	40	34	58	10	.274	.445	18	6	OF-80, DH-2
1979	68	153	44	11	0	9	5.9	25	25	20	25	4	.288	.536	23	11	OF-24, DH-18
1980	89	200	52	10	0	3	1.5	38	26	34	54	16	.260	.365	29	8	OF-36, DH-30

Player Register 274

	G	AB	H	2B	3B	HR	HR%	R	RBI	BB	SO	SB	BA	SA	Pinch Hit AB	H	G by POS

Pat Kelly continued
1981 CLE A	48	75	16	4	0	1	1.3	8	16	14	9	2	.213	.307	24	3	DH-18, OF-8
15 yrs.	1385	4338	1147	189	35	76	1.8	620	418	588	768	250	.264	.377	187	51	OF-997, DH-214
6 yrs.	692	2371	648	101	28	27	1.1	341	190	305	361	119	.273	.374	59	17	OF-505, DH-145

LEAGUE CHAMPIONSHIP SERIES
| 1979 BAL A | 3 | 11 | 4 | 0 | 0 | 1 | 9.1 | 3 | 4 | 1 | 3 | 2 | .364 | .636 | 0 | 0 | OF-2 |

WORLD SERIES
| 1979 BAL A | 5 | 4 | 1 | 0 | 0 | 0 | 0.0 | 0 | 0 | 1 | 1 | 0 | .250 | .250 | 4 | 1 | |

Red Kelly
KELLY, ALBERT MICHAEL BR TR 5'11½" 165 lbs.
B. Nov. 15, 1884, Union, Ill. D. Feb. 4, 1961, Zephyr Hills, Fla.
| 1910 CHI A | 14 | 45 | 7 | 0 | 1 | 0 | 0.0 | 6 | 1 | 7 | | 0 | .156 | .200 | 0 | 0 | OF-14 |

Steve Kemp
KEMP, STEVEN F. BL TL 6' 195 lbs.
B. Aug. 4, 1954, San Angelo, Tex.
1977 DET A	151	552	142	29	4	18	3.3	75	88	71	93	3	.257	.422	3	0	OF-148
1978	159	582	161	18	4	15	2.6	75	79	97	87	2	.277	.399	2	1	OF-157
1979	134	490	156	26	3	26	5.3	88	105	68	70	5	.318	.543	4	1	OF-120, DH-11
1980	135	508	149	23	3	21	4.1	88	101	69	64	5	.293	.474	6	2	OF-85, DH-46
1981	105	372	103	18	4	9	2.4	52	49	70	48	9	.277	.419	3	1	OF-92, DH-12
1982 CHI A	160	580	166	23	1	19	3.3	91	98	89	83	7	.286	.428	3	1	OF-154, DH-2
1983 NY A	109	373	90	17	3	12	3.2	53	49	41	37	1	.241	.399	9	2	OF-101, DH-2
7 yrs.	953	3457	967	154	22	120	3.5	522	569	505	482	32	.280	.441	30	8	OF-857, DH-73
1 yr.	160	580	166	23	1	19	3.3	91	98	89	83	7	.286	.428	3	1	OF-154, DH-2

Bob Kennedy
KENNEDY, ROBERT DANIEL BR TR 6'2" 193 lbs.
B. Aug. 18, 1920, Chicago, Ill.
Manager 1963-65, 1968.
1939 CHI A	3	8	2	0	0	0	0.0	0	1	0	0	0	.250	.250	1	0	3B-2
1940	154	606	153	23	3	3	0.5	74	52	42	58	3	.252	.315	0	0	3B-154
1941	76	257	53	9	3	1	0.4	16	29	17	23	5	.206	.276	0	0	3B-71
1942	113	412	95	18	5	0	0.0	37	38	22	41	11	.231	.299	1	0	3B-96, OF-16
1946	113	411	106	13	5	5	1.2	43	34	24	42	6	.258	.350	5	2	OF-75, 3B-29
1947	115	428	112	19	8	6	1.4	47	48	18	38	3	.262	.362	4	0	OF-106, 3B-1
1948 2 teams	CHI A (30G – .248)				CLE A (66G – .301)												
" total	96	186	50	11	3	0	0.0	14	19	8	23	0	.269	.360	12	6	OF-80, 2B-2, 1B-1
1949 CLE A	121	424	117	23	5	9	2.1	49	57	37	40	5	.276	.417	2	0	OF-98, 3B-21
1950	146	540	157	27	5	9	1.7	79	54	53	31	3	.291	.409	2	0	OF-144
1951	108	321	79	15	4	7	2.2	30	29	34	33	4	.246	.383	4	0	OF-106
1952	22	40	12	3	1	0	0.0	6	12	9	5	1	.300	.425	5	0	OF-13, 3B-3
1953	100	161	38	5	0	3	1.9	22	22	19	11	0	.236	.323	6	2	OF-89
1954 2 teams	CLE A (1G – .000)				BAL A (106G – .251)												
" total	107	323	81	13	2	6	1.9	37	45	28	43	2	.251	.359	17	4	3B-71, OF-22
1955 2 teams	BAL A (26G – .143)				CHI A (83G – .304)												
" total	109	284	75	11	2	9	3.2	38	48	26	26	0	.264	.412	23	4	3B-56, OF-34, 1B-9
1956 2 teams	CHI A (8G – .077)				DET A (69G – .232)												
" total	77	190	42	5	0	4	2.1	17	22	26	23	2	.221	.311	19	2	3B-33, OF-29
1957 2 teams	CHI A (4G – .000)				BKN N (19G – .129)												
" total	23	33	4	1	0	1	3.0	5	4	1	6	0	.121	.242	7	1	OF-9, 3B-3
16 yrs.	1483	4624	1176	196	41	63	1.4	514	514	364	443	45	.254	.355	108	21	OF-821, 3B-540, 1B-10, 2B-2
10 yrs.	699	2464	615	100	22	24	1.0	249	259	145	240	28	.250	.337	33	7	3B-414, OF-247, 1B-3

WORLD SERIES
| 1948 CLE A | 3 | 2 | 1 | 0 | 0 | 0 | 0.0 | 0 | 1 | 0 | 1 | 0 | .500 | .500 | 0 | 0 | OF-3 |

Dick Kenworthy
KENWORTHY, RICHARD LEE BR TR 5'9" 170 lbs.
B. Apr. 1, 1941, Red Oak, Iowa
1962 CHI A	3	4	0	0	0	0	0.0	0	0	0	3	0	.000	.000	1	0	2B-2
1964	2	2	0	0	0	0	0.0	0	0	0	1	0	.000	.000	2	0	
1965	3	1	0	0	0	0	0.0	0	0	1	0	0	.000	.000	1	0	
1966	9	25	5	0	0	0	0.0	1	0	0	0	0	.200	.200	3	1	3B-6
1967	50	97	22	4	1	4	4.1	9	11	4	17	0	.227	.412	15	0	3B-35
1968	58	122	27	2	0	0	0.0	2	2	5	21	0	.221	.238	19	5	3B-38
6 yrs.	125	251	54	6	1	4	1.6	12	13	10	42	0	.215	.295	41	6	3B-79, 2B-2
6 yrs.	125	251	54	6	1	4	1.6	12	13	10	42	0	.215	.295	41	6	3B-79, 2B-2

Joe Keough
KEOUGH, JOSEPH WILLIAM BL TL 6' 185 lbs.
Brother of Marty Keough.
B. Jan. 7, 1946, Pomona, Calif.
1968 OAK A	34	98	21	2	1	2	2.0	7	8	8	11	1	.214	.316	3	1	OF-29, 1B-1
1969 KC A	70	166	31	2	0	0	0.0	17	7	13	13	5	.187	.199	20	3	OF-49, 1B-1
1970	57	183	59	6	2	4	2.2	28	21	23	18	1	.322	.443	8	2	OF-34, 1B-18
1971	110	351	87	14	2	3	0.9	34	30	35	26	0	.248	.325	11	0	OF-100
1972	56	64	14	2	0	0	0.0	8	5	8	7	2	.219	.250	31	8	OF-16
1973 CHI A	5	1	0	0	0	0	0.0	1	0	0	0	0	.000	.000	1	0	
6 yrs.	332	863	212	26	5	9	1.0	95	81	87	75	9	.246	.319	74	18	OF-228, 1B-20
1 yr.	5	1	0	0	0	0	0.0	1	0	0	0	0	.000	.000	1	0	

John Kerr
KERR, JOHN FRANCIS BR TR 5'8" 158 lbs.
B. Nov. 26, 1898, San Francisco, Calif. BB 1923-24
1923 DET A	19	42	9	1	0	0	0.0	4	1	4	5	0	.214	.238	1	0	SS-15
1924	17	11	3	0	0	0	0.0	3	1	0	0	0	.273	.273	7	2	3B-3, OF-2
1929 CHI A	127	419	108	20	4	1	0.2	50	39	31	24	9	.258	.332	1	1	2B-122
1930	70	266	77	11	6	3	1.1	37	27	21	23	4	.289	.410	0	0	2B-51, SS-19
1931	128	444	119	17	2	2	0.5	51	50	35	22	9	.268	.329	4	0	2B-117, 3B-7, SS-1
1932 WAS A	51	132	36	6	1	0	0.0	14	15	13	3	3	.273	.333	10	1	2B-17, SS-14, 3B-8

Player Register

	G	AB	H	2B	3B	HR	HR%	R	RBI	BB	SO	SB	BA	SA	Pinch Hit AB	Pinch Hit H	G by POS

John Kerr continued

1933	28	40	8	0	0	0	0.0	5	0	3	2	0	.200	.200	5	1	2B-16, 3B-1
1934	31	103	28	4	0	0	0.0	8	12	8	13	1	.272	.311	1	1	3B-17, 2B-13
8 yrs.	471	1457	388	59	13	6	0.4	172	145	115	92	26	.266	.337	29	7	2B-336, SS-49, 3B-36, OF-2
3 yrs.	325	1129	304	48	12	6	0.5	138	116	87	69	22	.269	.349	5	2	2B-290, SS-20, 3B-7

WORLD SERIES
| 1933 WAS A | 1 | 0 | 0 | 0 | 0 | 0 | — | 0 | 0 | 0 | 0 | 0 | — | — | 0 | 0 | |

Don Kessinger

KESSINGER, DONALD EULON
B. July 17, 1942, Forrest City, Ark.
Manager 1979

BB TR 6'1" 170 lbs.
BR 1964-65

1964 CHI N	4	12	2	0	0	0	0.0	1	0	0	1	0	.167	.167	2	0	SS-4
1965	106	309	62	4	3	0	0.0	19	14	20	44	1	.201	.233	0	0	SS-105
1966	150	533	146	8	2	1	0.2	50	43	26	46	13	.274	.302	0	0	SS-148
1967	145	580	134	10	7	0	0.0	61	42	33	80	6	.231	.272	0	0	SS-143
1968	160	655	157	14	7	1	0.2	63	32	38	86	9	.240	.287	1	0	SS-159
1969	158	664	181	38	6	4	0.6	109	53	61	70	11	.273	.366	1	0	SS-157
1970	154	631	168	21	14	1	0.2	100	39	66	59	12	.266	.349	0	0	SS-154
1971	155	617	159	18	6	2	0.3	77	38	52	54	15	.258	.316	2	0	SS-154
1972	149	577	158	20	6	1	0.2	77	39	67	44	8	.274	.334	3	0	SS-146
1973	160	577	151	22	3	0	0.0	52	43	57	44	6	.262	.310	2	0	SS-158
1974	153	599	155	20	7	1	0.2	83	42	62	54	7	.259	.321	3	0	SS-150
1975	154	601	146	26	10	0	0.0	77	46	68	47	4	.243	.319	2	0	SS-154
1976 STL N	145	502	120	22	6	1	0.2	55	40	61	51	3	.239	.313	1	0	SS-113, 2B-31, 3B-2
1977 2 teams		STL N (59G – .239)				CHI A (39G – .235)											
" total	98	253	60	7	2	0	0.0	26	18	27	33	2	.237	.281	15	0	SS-47, 2B-37, 3B-13
1978 CHI A	131	431	110	18	1	1	0.2	35	31	36	34	2	.255	.309	1	0	SS-123, 2B-9
1979	56	110	22	6	0	1	0.9	14	7	10	12	1	.200	.282	0	0	SS-54, 2B-1, 1B-1
16 yrs.	2078	7651	1931	254	80	14	0.2	899	527	684	759	100	.252	.312	33	0	SS-1955, 2B-78, 3B-28, 1B-1
3 yrs.	226	660	160	27	3	2	0.3	61	49	59	53	5	.242	.302	1	0	SS-198, 2B-23, 3B-9, 1B-1

Bruce Kimm

KIMM, BRUCE EDWARD
B. June 29, 1951, Norway, Iowa

BR TR 5'11" 175 lbs.

1976 DET A	63	152	40	8	0	1	0.7	13	6	15	20	4	.263	.336	0	0	C-61, DH-2
1977	14	25	2	1	0	0	0.0	2	1	0	4	0	.080	.120	0	0	C-12, DH-2
1979 CHI N	9	11	1	0	0	0	0.0	0	0	0	0	0	.091	.091	0	0	C-9
1980 CHI A	100	251	61	10	1	0	0.0	20	19	17	26	1	.243	.291	3	0	C-98
4 yrs.	186	439	104	19	1	1	0.2	35	26	32	50	5	.237	.292	3	0	C-180, DH-4
1 yr.	100	251	61	10	1	0	0.0	20	19	17	26	1	.243	.291	3	0	C-98

Chad Kimsey

KIMSEY, CLYDE ELIAS
B. Aug. 6, 1905, Copperhill, Tenn. D. Dec. 3, 1942, Pryor, Okla.

BL TR 6'2" 200 lbs.

1929 STL A	29	30	8	2	0	2	6.7	6	4	1	8	0	.267	.533	5	1	P-24
1930	60	70	24	4	1	2	2.9	14	14	5	16	1	.343	.514	16	2	P-42
1931	47	37	10	1	0	2	5.4	5	5	8	11	1	.270	.459	4	0	P-42
1932 2 teams		STL A (34G – .333)				CHI A (7G – .000)											
" total	41	20	6	1	0	0	0.0	1	1	1	4	0	.300	.350	1	0	P-40
1933 CHI A	28	33	5	0	1	0	0.0	1	1	0	9	0	.152	.152	1	0	P-28
1936 DET A	22	16	5	1	1	0	0.0	3	1	1	5	0	.313	.500	0	0	P-22
6 yrs.	227	206	58	9	3	6	2.9	30	26	16	53	2	.282	.432	27	3	P-198
2 yrs.	35	35	5	0	0	0	0.0	1	1	0	9	0	.143	.143	1	0	P-35

Jim King

KING, JAMES HUBERT
B. Aug. 27, 1932, Elkins, Ark.

BL TR 6' 185 lbs.

1955 CHI N	113	301	77	12	3	11	3.7	43	45	24	39	2	.256	.425	18	4	OF-93
1956	118	317	79	13	2	15	4.7	32	54	30	40	1	.249	.445	34	6	OF-82
1957 STL N	22	35	11	0	0	0	0.0	1	2	4	2	0	.314	.314	16	4	OF-8
1958 SF N	34	56	12	2	1	2	3.6	8	8	10	8	0	.214	.393	14	3	OF-15
1961 WAS A	110	263	71	12	1	11	4.2	43	46	38	45	4	.270	.449	17	1	OF-91, C-1
1962	132	333	81	15	0	11	3.3	39	35	55	37	4	.243	.387	31	8	OF-101
1963	136	459	106	16	5	24	5.2	61	62	45	43	3	.231	.444	22	2	OF-123
1964	134	415	100	15	1	18	4.3	46	56	55	65	3	.241	.412	22	7	OF-121
1965	120	258	55	10	2	14	5.4	46	49	44	50	1	.213	.430	37	8	OF-88
1966	117	310	77	14	2	10	3.2	41	30	38	41	4	.248	.403	34	7	OF-85
1967 3 teams		WAS A (47G – .210)				CHI A (23G – .120)				CLE A (19G – .143)							
" total	89	171	30	3	2	1	0.6	14	14	20	31	1	.175	.234	42	11	OF-44, C-1
11 yrs.	1125	2918	699	112	19	117	4.0	374	401	363	401	23	.240	.411	287	63	OF-851, C-2
1 yr.	23	50	6	1	0	0	0.0	2	2	4	16	0	.120	.140	12	3	OF-12

Joe Kirrene

KIRRENE, JOSEPH JOHN
B. Oct. 4, 1931, San Francisco, Calif.

BR TR 6'2" 195 lbs.

1950 CHI A	1	4	1	0	0	0	0.0	0	0	0	1	0	.250	.250	0	0	3B-1
1954	9	23	7	1	0	0	0.0	4	4	5	2	1	.304	.348	1	0	3B-9
2 yrs.	10	27	8	1	0	0	0.0	4	4	5	3	1	.296	.333	1	0	3B-10
2 yrs.	10	27	8	1	0	0	0.0	4	4	5	3	1	.296	.333	1	0	3B-10

Ron Kittle

KITTLE, RONALD DALE
B. Jan. 5, 1958, Gary, Ind.

BR TR 6'3" 195 lbs.

1982 CHI A	20	29	7	2	0	1	3.4	3	7	3	12	0	.241	.414	13	2	OF-5, DH-3
1983	145	520	132	19	3	35	6.7	75	100	39	150	8	.254	.504	6	0	OF-139, DH-2
2 yrs.	165	549	139	21	3	36	6.6	78	107	42	162	8	.253	.499	19	2	OF-144, DH-5
2 yrs.	165	549	139	21	3	36	6.6	78	107	42	162	8	.253	.499	19	2	OF-144, DH-5

LEAGUE CHAMPIONSHIP SERIES
| 1983 CHI A | 3 | 7 | 2 | 1 | 0 | 0 | 0.0 | 1 | 0 | 1 | 2 | 0 | .286 | .429 | 0 | 0 | OF-3 |

Player Register

	G	AB	H	2B	3B	HR	HR %	R	RBI	BB	SO	SB	BA	SA	Pinch Hit AB H	G by POS

Joe Klinger
KLINGER, JOSEPH JOHN   BR TR 6'   190 lbs.
B. Aug. 2, 1902, Canonsburg, Pa.   D. July 31, 1960, Little Rock, Ark.

	G	AB	H	2B	3B	HR	HR%	R	RBI	BB	SO	SB	BA	SA	PH AB	PH H	G by POS
1927 NY N	3	5	2	0	0	0	0.0	0	0	0	2	0	.400	.400	2	0	OF-1
1930 CHI A	4	8	3	0	0	0	0.0	0	1	0	0	0	.375	.375	0	0	1B-2, C-2
2 yrs.	7	13	5	0	0	0	0.0	0	1	0	2	0	.385	.385	2	0	1B-2, C-2, OF-1
1 yr.	4	8	3	0	0	0	0.0	0	1	0	0	0	.375	.375	0	0	1B-2, C-2

Ted Kluszewski
KLUSZEWSKI, THEODORE BERNARD (Klu)   BL TL 6'2"   225 lbs.
B. Sept. 10, 1924, Argo, Ill.

	G	AB	H	2B	3B	HR	HR%	R	RBI	BB	SO	SB	BA	SA	PH AB	PH H	G by POS
1947 CIN N	9	10	1	0	0	0	0.0	1	2	1	2	0	.100	.100	5	0	1B-2
1948	113	379	104	23	4	12	3.2	49	57	18	32	1	.274	.451	15	5	1B-98
1949	136	531	164	26	2	8	1.5	63	68	19	24	3	.309	.411	2	1	1B-134
1950	134	538	165	37	0	25	4.6	76	111	33	28	3	.307	.515	2	0	1B-131
1951	154	607	157	35	2	13	2.1	74	77	35	33	6	.259	.387	1	0	1B-154
1952	135	497	159	24	11	16	3.2	62	86	47	28	3	.320	.509	3	1	1B-133
1953	149	570	180	25	0	40	7.0	97	108	55	34	2	.316	.570	1	0	1B-147
1954	149	573	187	28	3	49	8.6	104	141	78	35	0	.326	.642	0	0	1B-149
1955	153	612	192	25	0	47	7.7	116	113	66	40	1	.314	.585	0	0	1B-153
1956	138	517	156	14	1	35	6.8	91	102	49	31	1	.302	.536	7	1	1B-131
1957	69	127	34	7	0	6	4.7	12	21	5	5	0	.268	.465	47	12	1B-23
1958 PIT N	100	301	88	13	4	4	1.3	29	37	26	16	0	.292	.402	24	9	1B-72
1959 2 teams	PIT N (60G – .262)					CHI A (31G – .297)											
" total	91	223	62	12	2	4	1.8	22	27	14	24	0	.278	.404	39	7	1B-49
1960 CHI A	81	181	53	9	0	5	2.8	20	39	22	10	0	.293	.425	34	8	1B-39
1961 LA A	107	263	64	12	0	15	5.7	32	39	24	23	0	.243	.460	43	9	1B-66
15 yrs.	1718	5929	1766	290	29	279	4.7	848	1028	492	365	20	.298	.498	223	53	1B-1481
2 yrs.	112	282	83	11	1	7	2.5	31	49	31	20	0	.294	.415	36	8	1B-68

WORLD SERIES
| 1959 CHI A | 6 | 23 | 9 | 1 | 0 | 3 | 13.0 | 5 | 10 | 2 | 0 | 0 | .391 | .826 | 0 | 0 | 1B-6 |

Bill Knickerbocker
KNICKERBOCKER, WILLIAM HART   BR TR 5'11"   170 lbs.
B. Dec. 29, 1911, Los Angeles, Calif.

	G	AB	H	2B	3B	HR	HR%	R	RBI	BB	SO	SB	BA	SA	PH AB	PH H	G by POS
1933 CLE A	80	279	63	16	3	2	0.7	20	32	11	30	1	.226	.326	1	0	SS-80
1934	146	593	188	32	5	4	0.7	82	67	25	40	6	.317	.408	0	0	SS-146
1935	132	540	161	34	5	0	0.0	77	55	27	31	2	.298	.380	3	0	SS-128
1936	155	618	182	35	3	8	1.3	81	73	56	30	5	.294	.400	0	0	SS-155
1937 STL A	121	491	128	29	5	4	0.8	53	61	30	32	3	.261	.365	0	0	SS-115, 2B-6
1938 NY A	46	128	32	8	3	1	0.8	15	21	11	10	0	.250	.383	9	1	2B-34, SS-3
1939	6	13	2	1	0	0	0.0	2	1	0	0	0	.154	.231	2	0	SS-2, 2B-2
1940	45	124	30	8	1	1	0.8	17	10	14	8	1	.242	.347	7	2	SS-19, 3B-17
1941 CHI A	89	343	84	23	2	7	2.0	51	29	41	27	6	.245	.385	1	0	2B-88
1942 PHI A	87	289	73	12	0	1	0.3	25	19	29	30	1	.253	.304	6	0	2B-81, SS-1
10 yrs.	907	3418	943	198	27	28	0.8	423	368	244	238	25	.276	.374	29	3	SS-649, 2B-211, 3B-17
1 yr.	89	343	84	23	2	7	2.0	51	29	41	27	6	.245	.385	1	0	2B-88

Bobby Knoop
KNOOP, ROBERT FRANK   BR TR 6'1"   170 lbs.
B. Oct. 18, 1938, Sioux City, Iowa

	G	AB	H	2B	3B	HR	HR%	R	RBI	BB	SO	SB	BA	SA	PH AB	PH H	G by POS
1964 LA A	162	486	105	8	1	7	1.4	42	38	46	109	3	.216	.280	1	0	2B-161
1965 CAL A	142	465	125	24	4	7	1.5	47	43	31	101	3	.269	.383	0	0	2B-142
1966	161	590	137	18	11	17	2.9	54	72	43	144	1	.232	.386	0	0	2B-161
1967	159	511	125	18	5	9	1.8	51	38	44	136	2	.245	.352	0	0	2B-159
1968	152	494	123	20	4	3	0.6	48	39	35	128	3	.249	.324	1	1	2B-151
1969 2 teams	CAL A (27G – .197)					CHI A (104G – .229)											
" total	131	416	93	15	1	7	1.7	39	47	48	84	3	.224	.315	1	0	2B-131
1970 CHI A	130	402	92	13	2	5	1.2	34	36	34	79	0	.229	.308	3	1	2B-126
1971 KC A	72	161	33	8	1	1	0.6	14	11	15	36	1	.205	.286	16	3	2B-52, 3B-1
1972	44	97	23	5	0	0	0.0	8	7	9	16	0	.237	.289	9	2	2B-33, 3B-4
9 yrs.	1153	3622	856	129	29	56	1.5	337	331	305	833	16	.236	.334	31	7	2B-1116, 3B-5
2 yrs.	234	747	171	27	3	11	1.5	68	77	69	147	2	.229	.317	4	1	2B-230

Don Kolloway
KOLLOWAY, DONALD MARTIN (Butch, Cab)   BR TR 6'3"   200 lbs.
B. Aug. 4, 1918, Posen, Ill.

	G	AB	H	2B	3B	HR	HR%	R	RBI	BB	SO	SB	BA	SA	PH AB	PH H	G by POS
1940 CHI A	10	40	9	1	0	0	0.0	5	3	0	3	1	.225	.250	0	0	2B-10
1941	71	280	76	8	3	3	1.1	33	24	6	12	11	.271	.354	3	1	2B-62, 1B-4
1942	147	601	164	40	4	3	0.5	72	60	30	39	16	.273	.368	0	0	2B-126, 1B-33
1943	85	348	75	14	4	1	0.3	29	33	9	30	11	.216	.287	0	0	2B-85
1946	123	482	135	23	4	3	0.6	45	53	9	29	14	.280	.363	1	0	2B-90, 3B-31
1947	124	485	135	25	4	2	0.4	49	35	17	34	11	.278	.359	7	2	2B-99, 1B-11, 3B-8
1948	119	417	114	14	4	6	1.4	60	38	18	18	2	.273	.369	12	3	2B-83, 3B-18
1949 2 teams	CHI A (4G – .000)					DET A (126G – .294)											
" total	130	487	142	19	2	2	0.4	71	47	49	26	7	.292	.355	12	2	2B-62, 1B-57, 3B-9
1950 DET A	125	467	135	20	4	6	1.3	55	62	29	28	1	.289	.388	5	1	1B-118, 2B-1
1951	78	212	54	7	0	1	0.5	28	17	15	12	2	.255	.302	17	4	1B-59
1952	65	173	42	9	0	2	1.2	19	21	7	19	0	.243	.329	25	5	1B-32, 2B-8
1953 PHI A	2	1	0	0	0	0	0.0	0	0	1	0	0	.000	.000	1	0	3B-1
12 yrs.	1079	3993	1081	180	30	29	0.7	466	393	189	251	76	.271	.353	83	18	2B-616, 1B-314, 3B-67
8 yrs.	683	2657	708	125	23	18	0.7	293	246	89	166	68	.266	.351	26	6	2B-545, 3B-59, 1B-48

Fabian Kowalik
KOWALIK, FABIAN LORENZ   BR TR 5'11"   185 lbs.
B. Apr. 22, 1908, Falls City, Tex.   BL 1932, BB 1935
D. Aug. 14, 1954, Karnes City, Tex.

	G	AB	H	2B	3B	HR	HR%	R	RBI	BB	SO	SB	BA	SA	PH AB	PH H	G by POS
1932 CHI A	6	13	5	2	0	0	0.0	2	2	1	0	0	.385	.538	1	0	3B-2, P-2
1935 CHI N	20	15	3	0	0	0	0.0	1	1	0	2	0	.200	.200	0	0	P-20
1936 3 teams	CHI N (6G – .000)					PHI N (42G – .228)					BOS N (2G – .400)						
" total	50	67	15	1	0	0	0.0	3	8	2	9	0	.224	.239	17	2	P-29, OF-4
3 yrs.	76	95	23	3	0	0	0.0	6	11	3	11	0	.242	.274	18	2	P-51, OF-4, 3B-2
1 yr.	6	13	5	2	0	0	0.0	2	2	1	0	0	.385	.538	1	0	3B-2, P-2

WORLD SERIES
| 1935 CHI N | 1 | 2 | 1 | 0 | 0 | 0 | 0.0 | 1 | 0 | 0 | 0 | 0 | .500 | .500 | 0 | 0 | P-1 |

	G	AB	H	2B	3B	HR	HR%	R	RBI	BB	SO	SB	BA	SA	Pinch Hit AB H	G by POS

Al Kozar
KOZAR, ALBERT KENNETH
B. July 5, 1922, McKees Rocks, Pa. BR TR 5'9½" 173 lbs.

	G	AB	H	2B	3B	HR	HR%	R	RBI	BB	SO	SB	BA	SA	PH AB	PH H	G by POS
1948 WAS A	150	577	144	25	8	1	0.2	61	58	66	52	4	.250	.326	0	0	2B-149
1949	105	350	94	15	2	4	1.1	46	31	25	23	2	.269	.357	4	0	2B-102
1950 2 teams	WAS A (20G – .200)			CHI A (10G – .300)													
" total	30	65	14	1	0	1	1.5	11	5	5	11	0	.215	.277	6	1	2B-19, 3B-1
3 yrs.	285	992	252	41	10	6	0.6	118	94	96	86	6	.254	.334	10	1	2B-270, 3B-1
1 yr.	10	10	3	0	0	1	10.0	4	2	0	3	0	.300	.600	2	0	2B-4, 3B-1

Mike Kreevich
KREEVICH, MICHAEL ANDREAS
B. June 10, 1908, Mount Olive, Ill. BR TR 5'7½" 168 lbs.

	G	AB	H	2B	3B	HR	HR%	R	RBI	BB	SO	SB	BA	SA	PH AB	PH H	G by POS
1931 CHI N	5	12	2	0	0	0	0.0	0	0	0	6	1	.167	.167	1	0	OF-4
1935 CHI A	6	23	10	2	0	0	0.0	3	2	1	0	1	.435	.522	0	0	3B-6
1936	137	550	169	32	11	5	0.9	99	69	61	46	10	.307	.433	3	2	OF-133
1937	144	583	176	29	16	12	2.1	94	73	43	45	10	.302	.468	3	1	OF-138
1938	129	489	145	26	12	6	1.2	73	73	55	23	13	.297	.436	3	0	OF-127
1939	145	541	175	30	8	5	0.9	85	77	59	40	23	.323	.436	3	0	OF-139, 3B-4
1940	144	582	154	27	10	8	1.4	86	55	34	49	15	.265	.387	0	0	OF-144
1941	121	436	101	16	8	0	0.0	44	37	35	26	17	.232	.305	7	4	OF-113
1942 PHI A	116	444	113	19	1	1	0.2	57	30	47	31	7	.255	.309	6	2	OF-107
1943 STL A	60	161	41	6	0	0	0.0	24	10	26	13	4	.255	.292	7	1	OF-51
1944	105	402	121	15	6	5	1.2	55	44	27	24	3	.301	.405	5	0	OF-100
1945 2 teams	STL A (81G – .237)			WAS A (45G – .278)													
" total	126	453	114	19	3	0.7		56	44	58	38	11	.252	.327	7	2	OF-118
12 yrs.	1238	4676	1321	221	75	45	1.0	676	514	446	341	115	.283	.391	45	12	OF-1174, 3B-10
7 yrs.	826	3204	930	162	65	36	1.1	484	386	288	229	89	.290	.415	19	7	OF-794, 3B-10
				10th													

WORLD SERIES

| 1944 STL A | 6 | 26 | 6 | 3 | 0 | 0 | 0.0 | 0 | 0 | | 5 | 0 | .231 | .346 | 0 | 0 | OF-6 |

Ralph Kreitz
KREITZ, RALPH WESLEY (Red)
B. Nov. 13, 1886, Plum Creek, Neb. D. July 20, 1941, Portland, Ore. BR TR 5'9½" 175 lbs.

| 1911 CHI A | 7 | 17 | 4 | 1 | 0 | 0 | 0.0 | 0 | 0 | 2 | | 0 | .235 | .294 | 0 | 0 | C-7 |

Charlie Kress
KRESS, CHARLES STEVEN (Chuck)
B. Dec. 9, 1921, Philadelphia, Pa. BL TL 6' 190 lbs.

	G	AB	H	2B	3B	HR	HR%	R	RBI	BB	SO	SB	BA	SA	PH AB	PH H	G by POS
1947 CIN N	11	27	4	0	0	0	0.0	4	0	6	4	0	.148	.148	2	1	1B-8
1949 2 teams	CIN N (27G – .207)			CHI A (97G – .278)													
" total	124	382	104	20	6	1	0.3	48	47	42	49	6	.272	.364	11	3	1B-111
1950 CHI A	3	8	0	0	0	0	0.0	0	0	0	2	0	.000	.000	1	0	1B-2
1954 2 teams	DET A (24G – .189)			BKN N (13G – .083)													
" total	37	49	8	0	1	0	0.0	5	5	1	4	0	.163	.204	27	3	1B-8, OF-1
4 yrs.	175	466	116	20	7	1	0.2	57	52	49	59	6	.249	.328	41	7	1B-129, OF-1
2 yrs.	100	361	98	17	6	1	0.3	45	44	39	46	6	.271	.360	2	1	1B-97

Red Kress
KRESS, RALPH
B. Jan. 2, 1907, Columbia, Calif. D. Nov. 29, 1962, Los Angeles, Calif. BR TR 5'11½" 165 lbs.

	G	AB	H	2B	3B	HR	HR%	R	RBI	BB	SO	SB	BA	SA	PH AB	PH H	G by POS
1927 STL A	7	23	7	2	1	1	4.3	3	3	3	3	0	.304	.609	0	0	SS-7
1928	150	560	153	26	10	3	0.5	78	81	48	70	5	.273	.371	0	0	SS-150
1929	147	557	170	38	4	9	1.6	82	107	52	54	5	.305	.436	1	0	SS-146
1930	154	614	192	43	8	16	2.6	94	112	50	56	3	.313	.487	0	0	SS-123, 3B-31
1931	150	605	188	46	8	16	2.6	87	114	46	48	3	.311	.493	1	0	3B-84, OF-40, SS-38, 1B-10
1932 2 teams	STL A (14G – .173)			CHI A (135G – .285)													
" total	149	567	156	42	5	11	1.9	85	66	51	42	7	.275	.425	0	0	OF-64, SS-53, 3B-33
1933 CHI A	129	467	116	20	5	10	2.1	47	78	37	40	4	.248	.377	12	6	1B-111, OF-8
1934 2 teams	CHI A (8G – .286)			WAS A (56G – .228)													
" total	64	185	43	4	3	4	2.2	21	25	20	22	3	.232	.351	9	2	1B-30, OF-10, 2B-9, SS-1, 3B-1
1935 WAS A	84	252	75	13	4	2	0.8	32	42	25	16	3	.298	.405	18	4	SS-53, 1B-5, P-3, OF-2, 2B-1
1936	109	391	111	20	6	8	2.0	51	51	39	25	6	.284	.427	5	0	SS-64, 2B-33, 1B-5
1938 STL A	150	566	171	33	3	7	1.2	74	79	69	47	5	.302	.408	1	1	SS-150
1939 2 teams	STL A (13G – .279)			DET A (51G – .242)													
" total	64	200	50	8	1	1	0.5	24	30	23	18	3	.250	.305	6	4	SS-38, 2B-16, 3B-4
1940 DET A	33	99	22	3	1	1	1.0	13	11	10	12	0	.222	.303	5	3	3B-17, SS-12
1946 NY N	1	1	0	0	0	0	0.0	0	0	1	0	0	.000	.000	0	0	P-1
14 yrs.	1391	5087	1454	298	58	89	1.7	691	799	474	453	47	.286	.420	58	20	SS-835, 3B-170, 1B-161, OF-124, 2B-59, P-4
3 yrs.	272	996	267	62	3	19	1.9	133	136	87	79	10	.268	.406	16	7	1B-111, OF-72, SS-53, 3B-19, 2B-3

Rocky Krsnich
KRSNICH, ROCCO PETER
Brother of Mike Krsnich.
B. Aug. 5, 1927, West Allis, Wis. BR TR 6'1" 174 lbs.

	G	AB	H	2B	3B	HR	HR%	R	RBI	BB	SO	SB	BA	SA	PH AB	PH H	G by POS
1949 CHI A	16	55	12	3	1	1	1.8	7	9	6	4	0	.218	.364	0	0	2B-16
1952	40	91	21	7	2	1	1.1	11	15	12	9	0	.231	.385	2	0	3B-37
1953	64	129	26	8	0	1	0.8	9	14	12	11	0	.202	.287	6	1	3B-57
3 yrs.	120	275	59	18	3	3	1.1	27	38	30	24	0	.215	.335	8	1	3B-94, 2B-16
3 yrs.	120	275	59	18	3	3	1.1	27	38	30	24	0	.215	.335	8	1	3B-94, 2B-16

Joe Kuhel
KUHEL, JOSEPH ANTHONY
B. June 25, 1906, Cleveland, Ohio
Manager 1948-49. BL TL 6' 180 lbs.

	G	AB	H	2B	3B	HR	HR%	R	RBI	BB	SO	SB	BA	SA	PH AB	PH H	G by POS
1930 WAS A	18	63	18	3	3	0	0.0	9	17	5	6	1	.286	.429	1	0	1B-16
1931	139	524	141	34	8	8	1.5	70	85	47	45	7	.269	.410	0	0	1B-139
1932	101	347	101	21	5	4	1.2	52	52	32	19	5	.291	.415	9	1	1B-85
1933	153	602	194	34	10	11	1.8	89	107	59	48	17	.322	.467	0	0	1B-153

Player Register

	G	AB	H	2B	3B	HR	HR%	R	RBI	BB	SO	SB	BA	SA	Pinch Hit AB	H	G by POS

Joe Kuhel continued

1934	63	263	76	12	3	3	1.1	49	25	30	14	2	.289	.392	0	0	1B-63
1935	151	633	165	25	9	2	0.3	99	74	78	44	5	.261	.338	0	0	1B-151
1936	149	588	189	42	8	16	2.7	107	118	64	30	15	.321	.502	0	0	1B-149, 3B-1
1937	136	547	155	24	11	6	1.1	73	61	63	39	6	.283	.400	0	0	1B-136
1938 CHI A	117	412	110	27	4	8	1.9	67	51	72	35	9	.267	.410	6	0	1B-111
1939	139	546	164	24	9	15	2.7	107	56	64	51	18	.300	.460	3	0	1B-136
1940	155	603	169	28	8	27	4.5	111	94	87	59	12	.280	.488	0	0	1B-155
1941	153	600	150	39	5	12	2.0	99	63	70	55	20	.250	.392	1	0	1B-151
1942	115	413	103	14	4	4	1.0	60	52	60	22	22	.249	.332	3	0	1B-112
1943	153	531	113	21	1	5	0.9	55	46	76	45	14	.213	.284	0	0	1B-153
1944 WAS A	139	518	144	26	7	4	0.8	90	51	68	40	11	.278	.378	1	1	1B-138
1945	142	533	152	29	13	2	0.4	73	75	79	31	10	.285	.400	1	0	1B-141
1946 2 teams		WAS A	(14G –	.150)		CHI A	(64G –	.273)									
" total	78	258	68	9	3	4	1.6	26	22	26	26	4	.264	.368	8	2	1B-68
1947 CHI A	4	4	0	0	0	0	0.0	0	0	0	3	0	.000	.000	4	0	
18 yrs.	2105	7985	2212	412	111	131	1.6	1236	1049	980	612	178	.277	.406	37	4	1B-2057, 3B-1
8 yrs.	900	3347	874	162	34	75	2.2	523	382	450	294	99	.261	.397	18	0	1B-880

WORLD SERIES

1933 WAS A	5	20	3	0	0	0	0.0	1	1	1	4	0	.150	.150	0	0	1B-5

Walt Kuhn

KUHN, WALTER CHARLES (Red) BR TR
B. Feb. 2, 1884, Fresno, Calif. D. June 14, 1935, Fresno, Calif.

1912 CHI A	75	178	36	7	0	0	0.0	16	10	20		5	.202	.242	0	0	C-75
1913	26	50	8	1	0	0	0.0	5	5	13	8	1	.160	.180	2	0	C-24
1914	17	40	11	1	0	0	0.0	4	0	8	11	2	.275	.300	0	0	C-16
3 yrs.	118	268	55	9	0	0	0.0	25	15	41	19	8	.205	.239	2	0	C-115
3 yrs.	118	268	55	9	0	0	0.0	25	15	41	19	8	.205	.239	2	0	C-115

Rusty Kuntz

KUNTZ, RUSSELL JAY BR TR 6'3" 190 lbs.
B. Feb. 4, 1955, Orange, Calif.

1979 CHI A	5	11	1	0	0	0	0.0	0	0	2	6	0	.091	.091	0	0	OF-5
1980	36	62	14	4	0	0	0.0	5	3	5	13	1	.226	.290	3	2	OF-34
1981	67	55	14	2	0	0	0.0	15	4	6	8	1	.255	.291	3	0	OF-51, DH-5
1982	21	26	5	1	0	0	0.0	4	3	2	8	0	.192	.231	0	0	OF-21, P-1
1983 2 teams		CHI A	(28G –	.262)		MIN A	(31G –	.190)									
" total	59	142	30	4	0	3	2.1	19	6	18	41	1	.211	.303	4	1	OF-57, DH-1
5 yrs.	188	296	64	11	0	3	1.0	43	16	33	76	3	.216	.284	10	3	OF-168, DH-6, P-1
5 yrs.	157	196	45	8	0	0	0.0	30	11	21	48	3	.230	.270	10	3	OF-138, DH-6, P-1

Art Kusnyer

KUSNYER, ARTHUR WILLIAM BR TR 6'2" 197 lbs.
B. Dec. 19, 1945, Akron, Ohio

1970 CHI A	4	10	1	0	0	0	0.0	0	0	0	4	0	.100	.100	1	0	C-3
1971 CAL A	6	13	2	0	0	0	0.0	0	0	0	3	0	.154	.154	0	0	C-6
1972	64	179	37	2	1	2	1.1	13	13	16	33	0	.207	.263	2	0	C-63
1973	41	64	8	2	0	0	0.0	5	3	2	12	0	.125	.156	0	0	C-41
1976 MIL A	15	34	4	1	0	0	0.0	2	3	1	5	1	.118	.147	0	0	C-15
1978 KC A	9	13	3	1	0	1	7.7	1	2	2	4	0	.231	.538	0	0	C-9
6 yrs.	139	313	55	6	1	3	1.0	21	21	21	61	1	.176	.230	3	0	C-136
1 yr.	4	10	1	0	0	0	0.0	0	0	0	4	0	.100	.100	1	0	C-3

Cass Kwietniewski

Playing record listed under Cass Michaels

Ken Landenberger

LANDENBERGER, KENNETH HENRY (Red) BL TL 6'3" 200 lbs.
B. July 29, 1928, Lyndhurst, Ohio D. July 28, 1960, Cleveland, Ohio

1952 CHI A	2	5	1	0	0	0	0.0	0	0	0	2	0	.200	.200	1	0	1B-1

Jim Landis

LANDIS, JAMES HENRY BR TR 6'1" 180 lbs.
B. Mar. 9, 1934, Fresno, Calif.

1957 CHI A	96	274	58	11	3	2	0.7	38	16	45	61	14	.212	.296	4	1	OF-90
1958	142	523	145	23	7	15	2.9	72	64	52	80	19	.277	.434	1	0	OF-142
1959	149	515	140	26	7	5	1.0	78	60	78	68	20	.272	.379	0	0	OF-148
1960	148	494	125	25	6	10	2.0	89	49	80	84	23	.253	.389	0	0	OF-147
1961	140	534	151	18	8	22	4.1	87	85	65	71	19	.283	.470	2	0	OF-139
1962	149	534	122	21	6	15	2.8	82	61	80	105	19	.228	.375	4	1	OF-144
1963	133	396	89	6	6	13	3.3	56	45	47	75	8	.225	.369	11	3	OF-124
1964	106	298	62	8	4	1	0.3	30	18	36	64	5	.208	.272	7	1	OF-101
1965 KC A	118	364	87	15	1	3	0.8	46	36	57	84	8	.239	.310	13	3	OF-108
1966 CLE A	85	158	35	5	1	3	1.9	23	14	20	25	2	.222	.323	22	4	OF-61
1967 3 teams		HOU N	(50G –	.252)		DET A	(25G –	.208)		BOS A	(5G –	.143)					
" total	80	198	47	11	1	4	2.0	24	19	28	50	2	.237	.364	16	1	OF-61
11 yrs.	1346	4288	1061	169	50	93	2.2	625	467	588	767	139	.247	.375	80	14	OF-1265
8 yrs.	1063	3568	892	138	47	83	2.3	532	398	483	608	127	.250	.385	29	6	OF-1035
					8th				9th	1st							

WORLD SERIES

1959 CHI A	6	24	7	0	0	0	0.0	6	1	7	1	0	.292	.292	0	0	OF-6

Jesse Landrum

LANDRUM, JESSE GLENN BR TR 5'11½" 175 lbs.
B. July 31, 1912, Crockett, Tex.

1938 CHI A	4	6	0	0	0	0	0.0	0	1	0	2	0	.000	.000	1	0	2B-3

Player Register

	G	AB	H	2B	3B	HR	HR%	R	RBI	BB	SO	SB	BA	SA	Pinch Hit AB	H	G by POS

Dick Lane
LANE, RICHARD HARRISON
B. June 28, 1927, Highland Park, Mich.   BR TR 5'11" 178 lbs.

	G	AB	H	2B	3B	HR	HR%	R	RBI	BB	SO	SB	BA	SA	PH AB	PH H	G by POS
1949 CHI A	12	42	5	0	0	0	0.0	4	4	5	3	0	.119	.119	1	0	OF-11

Frank Lange
LANGE, FRANK HERMAN
B. Oct. 28, 1883, Columbus, Wis.   D. Dec. 26, 1945, Madison, Wis.   BR TR 5'11" 180 lbs.

	G	AB	H	2B	3B	HR	HR%	R	RBI	BB	SO	SB	BA	SA	PH AB	PH H	G by POS
1910 CHI A	23	51	13	4	0	0	0.0	3	8	2		0	.255	.333	0	0	P-23
1911	54	76	22	6	2	0	0.0	7	16	7		0	.289	.421	19	8	P-29
1912	40	65	14	4	1	0	0.0	4	7	4		0	.215	.308	9	2	P-31
1913	17	18	3	1	0	0	0.0	1	1	3	5	0	.167	.222	5	1	P-12
4 yrs.	134	210	52	15	3	0	0.0	15	32	16	5	0	.248	.348	33	11	P-95
4 yrs.	134	210	52	15	3	0	0.0	15	32	16	5	0	.248	.348	33	11	P-95

Jack Lapp
LAPP, JOHN WALKER
B. Sept. 10, 1884, Frazer, Pa.   D. Feb. 6, 1920, Philadelphia, Pa.   BL TR 5'8"

	G	AB	H	2B	3B	HR	HR%	R	RBI	BB	SO	SB	BA	SA	PH AB	PH H	G by POS
1908 PHI A	13	35	5	0	1	0	0.0	4	1	5		0	.143	.200	2	0	C-13
1909	21	56	19	3	1	0	0.0	8	10	3		1	.339	.429	2	0	C-19
1910	71	192	45	4	3	0	0.0	18	17	20		0	.234	.286	7	3	C-63
1911	68	167	59	10	3	1	0.6	35	26	24		4	.353	.467	6	3	C-57, 1B-4
1912	90	281	82	15	6	1	0.4	26	35	19		3	.292	.399	8	4	C-82
1913	81	238	54	4	4	1	0.4	23	20	37	26	1	.227	.290	2	0	C-77, 1B-1
1914	69	199	46	7	2	0	0.0	22	19	31	14	1	.231	.286	3	1	C-67
1915	112	312	85	16	5	2	0.6	26	31	30	29	5	.272	.375	10	4	C-89, 1B-12
1916 CHI A	40	101	21	0	1	0	0.0	6	7	8	10	1	.208	.228	4	0	C-34
9 yrs.	565	1581	416	59	26	5	0.3	168	166	177	79	16	.263	.343	42	15	C-501, 1B-17
1 yr.	40	101	21	0	1	0	0.0	6	7	8	10	1	.208	.228	4	0	C-34

WORLD SERIES
	G	AB	H	2B	3B	HR	HR%	R	RBI	BB	SO	SB	BA	SA	PH AB	PH H	G by POS
1910 PHI A	1	4	1	0	0	0	0.0	0	1	0	2	0	.250	.250	0	0	C-1
1911	2	8	2	0	0	0	0.0	1	0	0	1	0	.250	.250	0	0	C-2
1913	1	4	1	0	0	0	0.0	0	0	0	1	0	.250	.250	0	0	C-1
1914	1	1	0	0	0	0	0.0	0	0	0	0	0	.000	.000	0	0	C-1
4 yrs.	5	17	4	0	0	0	0.0	1	1	0	4	0	.235	.235	0	0	C-5

Don Larsen
LARSEN, DONALD JAMES
B. Aug. 7, 1929, Michigan City, Ind.   BR TR 6'4" 215 lbs.

	G	AB	H	2B	3B	HR	HR%	R	RBI	BB	SO	SB	BA	SA	PH AB	PH H	G by POS
1953 STL A	50	81	23	3	1	3	3.7	11	10	4	14	0	.284	.457	10	1	P-38, OF-1
1954 BAL A	44	88	22	5	3	1	1.1	6	4	5	15	0	.250	.409	15	0	P-29
1955 NY A	21	41	6	1	0	2	4.9	4	7	4	13	0	.146	.317	3	1	P-19
1956	45	79	19	5	0	2	2.5	10	12	6	17	0	.241	.380	7	2	P-38
1957	31	56	14	5	0	0	0.0	6	5	6	11	0	.250	.339	1	0	P-27
1958	28	49	15	1	0	4	8.2	9	13	5	9	0	.306	.571	7	2	P-19
1959	29	47	12	2	0	0	0.0	8	8	7	15	0	.255	.298	3	1	P-25
1960 KC A	23	29	6	1	0	0	0.0	3	3	0	11	0	.207	.241	1	0	P-22
1961 2 teams	KC A (18G – .300)				CHI A (25G – .320)												
" total	43	45	14	0	2	2	4.4	4	8	1	10	0	.311	.444	12	5	P-33, OF-1
1962 SF N	52	25	5	0	1	0	0.0	3	1	0	7	0	.200	.280	4	0	P-49
1963	46	11	2	0	0	0	0.0	1	0	1	1	0	.182	.182	0	0	P-46
1964 2 teams	SF N (6G – .000)				HOU N (31G – .097)												
" total	37	32	3	1	0	0	0.0	0		4	10	0	.094	.125	3	0	P-36
1965 2 teams	HOU N (1G – .000)				BAL A (27G – .273)												
" total	28	13	3	1	0	0	0.0	0	1	0	5	0	.231	.308	0	0	P-28
1967 CHI N	3	0	0	0	0	0	–	0	0	0	0	0	–	–	0	0	P-3
14 yrs.	480	596	144	25	5	14	2.3	65	72	43	138	0	.242	.371	66	12	P-412, OF-2
1 yr.	25	25	8	0	0	1	4.0	2	4	0	5	0	.320	.440	0	0	P-25

WORLD SERIES
	G	AB	H	2B	3B	HR	HR%	R	RBI	BB	SO	SB	BA	SA	PH AB	PH H	G by POS
1955 NY A	1	2	0	0	0	0	0.0	0	0	0	0	0	.000	.000	0	0	P-1
1956	2	3	1	0	0	0	0.0	1	0	1	0	1	.333	.333	0	0	P-2
1957	2	2	0	0	0	0	0.0	0	0	0	2	0	.000	.000	0	0	P-2
1958	2	2	0	0	0	0	0.0	–	0	0	0	0	.000	.000	0	0	P-1
1962 SF N	3	0	0	0	0	0	–	0	0	0	0	0	–	–	0	0	P-3
5 yrs.	10	9	1	0	0	0	0.0	2	1	3	2	0	.111	.111	0	0	P-9

Tony LaRussa
LaRUSSA, ANTHONY
B. Oct. 4, 1944, Tampa, Fla.
Manager 1979-83.   BR TR 6' 175 lbs.

	G	AB	H	2B	3B	HR	HR%	R	RBI	BB	SO	SB	BA	SA	PH AB	PH H	G by POS
1963 KC A	34	44	11	1	0	0	0.0	4	7	12	0	.250	.318	1	1	SS-14, 2B-3	
1968 OAK A	5	3	1	0	0	0	0.0	0	0	0	0	0	.333	.333	3	1	
1969	8	8	0	0	0	0	0.0	0	0	0	1	0	.000	.000	8	0	
1970	52	106	21	4	1	0	0.0	6	6	15	19	0	.198	.255	11	2	2B-44
1971 2 teams	OAK A (23G – .000)				ATL N (9G – .286)												
" total	32	15	2	0	0	0	0.0	4	0	1	5	0	.133	.133	6	0	2B-16, SS-4, 3B-2
1973 CHI N	1	0	0	0	0	0	–	1	0	0	0	0	–	–	0	0	
6 yrs.	132	176	35	5	2	0	0.0	15	7	23	37	0	.199	.250	29	4	2B-63, SS-18, 3B-2

Rudy Law
LAW, RUDY KARL
B. Oct. 7, 1956, Waco, Tex.   BL TL 6'1" 165 lbs.

	G	AB	H	2B	3B	HR	HR%	R	RBI	BB	SO	SB	BA	SA	PH AB	PH H	G by POS
1978 LA N	11	12	3	0	0	0	0.0	9	2	1	2	3	.250	.250	1	0	OF-6
1980	128	388	101	5	4	1	0.3	55	23	23	27	40	.260	.302	16	4	OF-106
1982 CHI A	121	336	107	15	8	3	0.9	55	32	23	41	36	.318	.438	17	3	OF-94, DH-3
1983	141	501	142	20	7	3	0.6	95	34	42	36	77	.283	.369	13	4	OF-132, DH-3
4 yrs.	401	1237	353	40	19	7	0.6	207	90	89	106	156	.285	.365	47	11	OF-338, DH-6
2 yrs.	262	837	249	35	15	6	0.7	150	66	65	77	113	.297	.397	30	7	OF-226, DH-6

LEAGUE CHAMPIONSHIP SERIES
	G	AB	H	2B	3B	HR	HR%	R	RBI	BB	SO	SB	BA	SA	PH AB	PH H	G by POS
1983 CHI A	4	18	7	1	0	0	0.0	1	0	0	1	2	.389	.444	0	0	OF-4

	G	AB	H	2B	3B	HR	HR%	R	RBI	BB	SO	SB	BA	SA	Pinch Hit AB	H	G by POS

Vance Law
LAW, VANCE AARON
Son of Vern Law.
B. Oct. 1, 1956, Boise, Ida.
BR TR 6'2" 185 lbs.

1980 PIT N	25	74	17	2	2	0	0.0	11	3	3	7	2	.230	.311	3	1	2B-11, SS-8, 3B-1
1981	30	67	9	0	1	0	0.0	1	3	2	15	1	.134	.164	2	0	2B-19, SS-7, 3B-2
1982 CHI A	114	359	101	20	1	5	1.4	40	54	26	46	4	.281	.384	1	1	SS-85, 3B-39, 2B-10, OF-1
1983	145	408	99	21	5	4	1.0	55	42	51	56	3	.243	.348	0	0	3B-139, 2B-3, SS-2, DH-1, OF-1
4 yrs.	314	908	226	43	9	9	1.0	107	102	82	124	10	.249	.346	6	2	3B-181, SS-102, 2B-43, OF-2, DH-1
2 yrs.	259	767	200	41	6	9	1.2	95	96	77	102	7	.261	.365	1	1	3B-178, SS-87, 2B-13, OF-2, DH-1

LEAGUE CHAMPIONSHIP SERIES
| 1983 CHI A | 4 | 11 | 2 | 0 | 0 | 0 | 0.0 | 0 | 1 | 1 | 3 | 0 | .182 | .182 | 0 | 0 | 3B-4 |

George Lees
LEES, GEORGE EDWARD
B. Feb. 2, 1895, Bethlehem, Pa.
BR TR 5'9" 150 lbs.

| 1921 CHI A | 20 | 42 | 9 | 2 | 0 | 0 | 0.0 | 3 | 4 | 0 | 3 | 0 | .214 | .262 | 4 | 0 | C-16 |

Ron LeFlore
LeFLORE, RONALD
B. June 16, 1948, Detroit, Mich.
BR TR 6' 200 lbs.

1974 DET A	59	254	66	8	1	2	0.8	37	13	13	58	23	.260	.323	0	0	OF-59
1975	136	550	142	13	6	8	1.5	66	37	33	139	28	.258	.347	0	0	OF-134
1976	135	544	172	23	8	4	0.7	93	39	51	111	58	.316	.410	1	0	OF-132, DH-1
1977	154	652	212	30	10	16	2.5	100	57	37	121	39	.325	.475	3	2	OF-154
1978	155	666	198	30	3	12	1.8	126	62	65	104	68	.297	.405	0	0	OF-155
1979	148	600	180	22	10	9	1.5	110	57	52	95	78	.300	.415	1	1	OF-113, DH-34
1980 MON N	139	521	134	21	11	4	0.8	95	39	62	99	97	.257	.363	1	1	OF-130
1981 CHI A	82	337	83	10	4	0	0.0	46	24	28	70	36	.246	.300	0	0	OF-82
1982	91	334	96	15	4	4	1.2	58	25	22	91	28	.287	.392	5	1	OF-83, DH-2
9 yrs.	1099	4458	1283	172	57	59	1.3	731	353	363	888	455	.288	.392	11	5	OF-1042, DH-37
2 yrs.	173	671	179	25	8	4	0.6	104	49	50	161	64	.267	.346	5	1	OF-165, DH-2

Paul Lehner
LEHNER, PAUL EUGENE (Gulliver)
B. July 1, 1920, Dolomite, Ala. D. Dec. 27, 1967, Birmingham, Ala.
BL TL 5'9" 160 lbs.

1946 STL A	16	45	10	1	2	0	0.0	6	5	1	5	0	.222	.333	4	1	OF-12
1947	135	483	120	25	9	7	1.4	59	48	28	29	5	.248	.381	6	2	OF-127
1948	103	333	92	15	4	2	0.6	23	46	30	19	0	.276	.363	13	6	OF-89, 1B-2
1949	104	297	68	13	0	3	1.0	25	37	16	20	0	.229	.303	26	7	OF-55, 1B-18
1950 PHI A	114	427	132	17	5	9	2.1	48	52	31	33	1	.309	.436	8	3	OF-101
1951 4 teams	PHI	A (9G – .143)		CHI	A (23G – .208)			STL	A (21G – .134)			CLE	A (12G – .231)				
" total	65	180	31	9	1	1	0.6	14	7	18	12	0	.172	.250	19	4	OF-45
1952 BOS A	3	3	2	0	0	0	0.0	0	2	2	0	0	.667	.667	1	1	OF-2
7 yrs.	540	1768	455	80	21	22	1.2	175	197	126	118	6	.257	.364	77	24	OF-431, 1B-20
1 yr.	23	72	15	3	1	0	0.0	9	3	10	4	0	.208	.278	3	1	OF-20

Nemo Leibold
LEIBOLD, HARRY LORAN
B. Feb. 17, 1892, Butler, Ind. D. Feb. 4, 1977, Detroit, Mich.
BL TR 5'6½" 157 lbs.

1913 CLE A	84	286	74	11	6	0	0.0	37	12	21	43	16	.259	.339	10	1	OF-72
1914	114	402	106	13	3	0	0.0	46	32	54	56	12	.264	.311	6	1	OF-107
1915 2 teams	CLE	A (57G – .256)		CHI	A (36G – .230)												
" total	93	281	70	6	4	0	0.0	38	15	39	27	6	.249	.299	14	5	OF-75
1916 CHI A	45	82	20	1	2	0	0.0	5	13	7	7	7	.244	.305	20	4	OF-24
1917	125	428	101	12	6	0	0.0	59	29	74	34	27	.236	.292	3	0	OF-122
1918	116	440	110	14	6	1	0.2	57	31	63	32	13	.250	.316	1	0	OF-114
1919	122	434	131	18	2	0	0.0	81	26	72	30	17	.302	.353	0	0	OF-122
1920	108	413	91	16	3	1	0.2	61	28	55	30	7	.220	.281	3	1	OF-108
1921 BOS A	123	467	143	26	6	0	0.0	88	30	41	27	13	.306	.388	5	0	OF-117
1922	81	271	70	8	1	1	0.4	42	18	41	14	1	.258	.306	9	3	OF-71
1923 2 teams	BOS	A (12G – .111)		WAS	A (95G – .305)												
" total	107	333	98	13	4	1	0.3	69	22	54	18	7	.294	.366	9	2	OF-94
1924 WAS A	84	246	72	6	4	0	0.0	41	20	42	10	6	.293	.350	11	1	OF-70
1925	56	84	23	1	1	0	0.0	14	7	8	7	1	.274	.310	19	3	OF-26, 3B-1
13 yrs.	1258	4167	1109	145	48	4	0.1	638	283	571	335	133	.266	.327	110	21	OF-1122, 3B-1
6 yrs.	552	1871	470	62	19	2	0.1	273	138	286	144	72	.251	.308	39	9	OF-512

WORLD SERIES
1917 CHI A	2	5	2	0	0	0	0.0	1	2	1	1	0	.400	.400	2	0	OF-2
1919	5	18	1	0	0	0	0.0	0	2	3	1	0	.056	.056	1	0	OF-5
1924 WAS A	3	6	1	1	0	0	0.0	1	0	1	0	0	.167	.333	2	1	OF-1
1925	3	2	1	0	0	0	0.0	1	0	1	0	0	.500	1.000	2	1	
4 yrs.	13	31	5	2	0	0	0.0	3	2	5	4	1	.161	.226	7 6th	2	OF-8

Elmer Leifer
LEIFER, ELMER EDWIN
B. May 23, 1893, Clarington, Ohio D. Sept. 26, 1948, Everett, Wash.
BL TR 5'9½" 170 lbs.

| 1921 CHI A | 9 | 10 | 3 | 0 | 0 | 0 | 0.0 | 1 | 1 | 4 | 0 | 0 | .300 | .300 | 7 | 2 | OF-1, 3B-1 |

Bob Lemon
LEMON, ROBERT GRANVILLE
B. Sept. 22, 1920, San Bernardino, Calif.
Manager 1970-72, 1977-79, 1981-82.
Hall of Fame 1976.
BL TR 6' 180 lbs.

1941 CLE A	5	4	1	0	0	0	0.0	0	0	0	1	0	.250	.250	3	1	3B-1
1942	5	5	0	0	0	0	0.0	0	0	0	3	0	.000	.000	3	0	3B-1
1946	55	89	16	3	0	1	1.1	9	4	7	18	0	.180	.247	7	1	P-32, OF-12
1947	47	56	18	4	3	2	3.6	11	5	6	9	0	.321	.607	3	1	P-37, OF-2
1948	52	119	34	9	0	5	4.2	20	21	8	23	0	.286	.487	4	1	P-43
1949	46	108	29	6	2	7	6.5	17	19	10	20	0	.269	.556	8	4	P-37

Player Register

	G	AB	H	2B	3B	HR	HR %	R	RBI	BB	SO	SB	BA	SA	Pinch Hit AB	Pinch Hit H	G by POS

Bob Lemon continued

Year	G	AB	H	2B	3B	HR	HR%	R	RBI	BB	SO	SB	BA	SA	PH AB	PH H	G by POS
1950	72	136	37	9	1	6	4.4	21	26	13	25	0	.272	.485	26	6	P-44
1951	56	102	21	4	1	3	2.9	11	13	9	22	0	.206	.353	14	4	P-42
1952	54	124	28	5	0	2	1.6	14	9	4	21	0	.226	.315	8	1	P-42
1953	51	112	26	9	1	2	1.8	12	17	7	20	2	.232	.384	6	1	P-41
1954	40	98	21	4	1	2	2.0	11	10	6	24	0	.214	.337	3	1	P-36
1955	49	78	19	0	0	1	1.3	11	9	13	16	0	.244	.282	9	4	P-35
1956	43	93	18	0	0	5	5.4	8	12	9	21	0	.194	.355	5	3	P-39
1957	25	46	3	1	0	1	2.2	2	1	0	14	0	.065	.152	4	0	P-21
1958	15	13	3	0	0	0	0.0	1	1	1	4	0	.231	.231	6	3	P-11
15 yrs.	615	1183	274	54	9	37	3.1	148	147	93	241	2	.232	.386	109	31	P-460, OF-14, 3B-2

WORLD SERIES

Year	G	AB	H	2B	3B	HR	HR%	R	RBI	BB	SO	SB	BA	SA	PH AB	PH H	G by POS
1948 CLE A	2	7	0	0	0	0	0.0	0	0	0	0	0	.000	.000	0	0	P-2
1954	3	6	0	0	0	0	0.0	0	0	1	1	0	.000	.000	1	0	P-2
2 yrs.	5	13	0	0	0	0	0.0	0	0	1	1	0	.000	.000	1	0	P-4

Chet Lemon

LEMON, CHESTER EARL
B. Feb. 12, 1955, Jackson, Miss.
BR TR 6' 190 lbs.

Year	G	AB	H	2B	3B	HR	HR%	R	RBI	BB	SO	SB	BA	SA	PH AB	PH H	G by POS
1975 CHI A	9	35	9	2	0	0	0.0	2	1	2	6	1	.257	.314	1	0	3B-6, DH-2, OF-1
1976	132	451	111	15	5	4	0.9	46	38	28	65	13	.246	.328	1	0	OF-131
1977	150	553	151	38	4	19	3.4	99	67	52	88	8	.273	.459	0	0	OF-149
1978	105	357	107	24	6	13	3.6	51	55	39	46	5	.300	.510	1	0	OF-95, DH-10
1979	148	556	177	44	2	17	3.1	79	86	56	68	7	.318	.496	0	0	OF-147, DH-1
1980	147	514	150	32	6	11	2.1	76	51	71	56	6	.292	.442	1	0	OF-139, DH-6, 2B-1
1981	94	328	99	23	6	9	2.7	50	50	33	48	5	.302	.491	0	0	OF-94
1982 DET A	125	436	116	20	1	19	4.4	75	52	56	69	1	.266	.447	2	1	OF-121, DH-1
1983	145	491	125	21	5	24	4.9	78	69	54	70	0	.255	.464	2	1	OF-145
9 yrs.	1055	3721	1045	219	35	116	3.1	556	469	391	516	46	.281	.452	8	2	OF-1022, DH-20, 3B-6, 2B-1
7 yrs.	785	2794	804	178	29	73	2.6	403	348	281	377	45	.288	.451 7th	4	0	OF-756, DH-19, 3B-6, 2B-1

Jim Lemon

LEMON, JAMES ROBERT
B. Mar. 23, 1928, Covington, Va.
Manager 1968.
BR TR 6'4" 200 lbs.

Year	G	AB	H	2B	3B	HR	HR%	R	RBI	BB	SO	SB	BA	SA	PH AB	PH H	G by POS
1950 CLE A	12	34	6	1	0	1	2.9	4	3	3	12	0	.176	.294	3	1	OF-10
1953	16	46	8	1	0	1	2.2	5	5	3	15	0	.174	.261	3	0	OF-11, 1B-2
1954 WAS A	37	128	30	2	3	2	1.6	12	13	9	34	0	.234	.344	4	1	OF-33
1955	10	25	5	2	0	1	4.0	3	3	3	4	0	.200	.400	3	2	OF-6
1956	146	538	146	21	11	27	5.0	77	96	65	138	2	.271	.502	4	1	OF-141
1957	137	518	147	22	6	17	3.3	58	64	49	94	1	.284	.448	6	1	OF-131, 1B-3
1958	142	501	123	15	9	26	5.2	65	75	50	120	1	.246	.467	8	3	OF-137
1959	147	531	148	18	3	33	6.2	73	100	46	99	5	.279	.510	5	1	OF-142
1960	148	528	142	10	1	38	7.2	81	100	67	114	0	.269	.508	5	1	OF-145
1961 MIN A	129	423	109	26	1	14	3.3	57	52	44	98	1	.258	.423	10	2	OF-120
1962	12	17	3	0	0	1	5.9	1	5	3	4	0	.176	.353	8	3	OF-3
1963 3 teams		MIN A (7G – .118)			PHI N (31G – .271)				CHI A (36G – .200)								
" total	74	156	34	2	1	3	1.9	10	15	21	55	0	.218	.301	26	6	1B-25, OF-22
12 yrs.	1010	3445	901	120	35	164	4.8	446	529	363	787	13	.262	.460	83	22	OF-901, 1B-30
1 yr.	36	80	16	0	1	1	1.3	4	8	12	32	0	.200	.263	9	1	1B-25

Don Lenhardt

LENHARDT, DONALD EUGENE (Footsie)
B. Oct. 4, 1922, Alton, Ill.
BR TR 6'3" 190 lbs.

Year	G	AB	H	2B	3B	HR	HR%	R	RBI	BB	SO	SB	BA	SA	PH AB	PH H	G by POS
1950 STL A	139	480	131	22	6	22	4.6	75	81	90	94	3	.273	.481	10	3	1B-86, OF-39, 3B-10
1951 2 teams		STL A (31G – .262)			CHI A (64G – .266)												
" total	95	302	80	12	1	15	5.0	32	63	30	38	2	.265	.460	13	3	OF-80, 1B-3
1952 3 teams		BOS A (30G – .295)			DET A (45G – .188)				STL A (18G – .271)								
" total	93	297	71	10	2	11	3.7	41	42	47	44	0	.239	.397	10	2	OF-81, 1B-2
1953 STL A	97	303	96	15	0	10	3.3	37	35	41	41	1	.317	.465	17	4	OF-77, 3B-6
1954 2 teams		BAL A (13G – .152)			BOS A (44G – .273)												
" total	57	99	23	5	0	3	3.0	7	18	6	18	0	.232	.374	35	6	OF-20, 1B-2, 3B-1
5 yrs.	481	1481	401	64	9	61	4.1	192	239	214	235	6	.271	.450	85	18	OF-297, 1B-93, 3B-17
1 yr.	64	199	53	9	4	10	5.0	23	45	24	25	1	.266	.472	8	3	OF-53, 1B-2

Eddie Leon

LEON, EDUARDO ANTONIO
B. Aug. 11, 1946, Tucson, Ariz.
BR TR 6' 170 lbs.

Year	G	AB	H	2B	3B	HR	HR%	R	RBI	BB	SO	SB	BA	SA	PH AB	PH H	G by POS
1968 CLE A	6	1	0	0	0	0	0.0	0	1	0	0	0	.000	.000	0	0	SS-6
1969	64	213	51	6	0	3	1.4	20	19	19	37	2	.239	.310	0	0	SS-64
1970	152	549	136	20	4	10	1.8	58	56	47	89	1	.248	.353	0	0	2B-141, SS-23, 3B-1
1971	131	429	112	12	2	4	0.9	35	35	34	69	3	.261	.326	4	1	2B-107, SS-24
1972	89	225	45	2	1	4	1.8	14	16	20	47	0	.200	.271	23	5	2B-36, SS-35
1973 CHI A	127	399	91	10	3	3	0.8	37	30	34	103	1	.228	.291	2	0	SS-122, 2B-3
1974	31	46	5	1	0	0	0.0	1	3	2	12	0	.109	.130	5	0	SS-21, 2B-7, 3B-2, DH-1
1975 NY A	1	0	0	0	0	0	–	0	0	0	0	0	–	–	0	0	SS-1
8 yrs.	601	1862	440	51	10	24	1.3	165	159	156	358	7	.236	.313	29	6	SS-296, 2B-294, 3B-3, DH-1
2 yrs.	158	445	96	11	3	3	0.7	38	33	36	115	1	.216	.274	2	0	SS-143, 2B-10, 3B-2, DH-1

Ted Lepcio

LEPCIO, THADDEUS STANLEY
B. July 28, 1930, Utica, N.Y.
BR TR 5'10" 177 lbs.

Year	G	AB	H	2B	3B	HR	HR%	R	RBI	BB	SO	SB	BA	SA	PH AB	PH H	G by POS
1952 BOS A	84	274	72	17	2	5	1.8	34	26	24	41	3	.263	.394	0	0	2B-57, 3B-25, SS-1
1953	66	161	38	4	2	2.5	17	11	17	24	0	.236	.360	4	1	2B-34, SS-20, 3B-11
1954	116	398	102	19	4	8	2.0	42	45	42	62	3	.256	.384	2	0	2B-80, 3B-24, SS-14
1955	51	134	31	9	0	6	4.5	19	15	13	36	1	.231	.433	4	0	3B-45
1956	83	284	74	10	3	15	5.3	34	51	30	77	1	.261	.454	9	3	2B-57, 3B-22

Player Register

	G	AB	H	2B	3B	HR	HR%	R	RBI	BB	SO	SB	BA	SA	Pinch Hit AB	Pinch Hit H	G by POS

Ted Lepcio continued

1957	79	232	56	10	2	9	3.9	24	37	29	61	0	.241	.418	10	2	2B-68
1958	50	136	27	3	0	6	4.4	10	14	12	47	0	.199	.353	10	3	2B-40
1959 2 teams	BOS A (3G – .333)				DET A (76G – .279)												
" total	79	218	61	9	0	7	3.2	26	25	17	51	2	.280	.417	16	5	SS-35, 2B-25, 3B-11
1960 PHI N	69	141	32	7	0	2	1.4	16	8	17	41	0	.227	.319	9	1	3B-50, SS-14, 2B-5
1961 2 teams	CHI A (5G – .000)				MIN A (47G – .170)												
" total	52	114	19	3	1	7	6.1	11	19	9	31	1	.167	.395	5	0	3B-36, 2B-22, SS-6
10 yrs.	729	2092	512	91	11	69	3.3	233	251	210	471	11	.245	.398	69	15	2B-388, 3B-224, SS-90
1 yr.	5	2	0	0	0	0	0.0	0	0	1	0	0	.000	.000	2	0	3B-1

Charlie Lindstrom

LINDSTROM, CHARLES WILLIAM (Chuck)
Son of Freddie Lindstrom.
B. Sept. 7, 1936, Chicago, Ill.

BR TR 5'11" 175 lbs.

| 1958 CHI A | 1 | 1 | 1 | 0 | 1 | 0 | 0.0 | 1 | 1 | 1 | 0 | 0 | 1.000 | 3.000 | 0 | 0 | C-1 |

Dario Lodigiani

LODIGIANI, DARIO JOSEPH (Lodi)
B. June 6, 1916, San Francisco, Calif.

BR TR 5'8" 150 lbs.

1938 PHI A	93	325	91	15	1	6	1.8	36	44	34	25	3	.280	.388	0	0	2B-80, 3B-13
1939	121	393	102	22	4	6	1.5	46	44	42	18	2	.260	.382	4	1	3B-89, 2B-28
1940	1	1	0	0	0	0	0.0	0	0	0	0	0	.000	.000	1	0	
1941 CHI A	87	322	77	19	2	4	1.2	39	40	31	19	0	.239	.348	0	0	3B-86
1942	59	168	47	7	0	0	0.0	9	15	18	10	3	.280	.321	5	1	3B-43, 2B-7
1946	44	155	38	8	0	0	0.0	12	13	16	14	4	.245	.297	0	0	3B-44
6 yrs.	405	1364	355	71	7	16	1.2	142	156	141	86	12	.260	.358	10	2	3B-275, 2B-115
3 yrs.	190	645	162	34	2	4	0.6	60	68	65	43	7	.251	.329	5	1	3B-173, 2B-7

Ron Lolich

LOLICH, RONALD
B. Sept. 19, 1946, Portland, Ore.

BR TR 6'1" 185 lbs.

1971 CHI A	2	8	1	1	0	0	0.0	0	0	0	2	0	.125	.250	0	0	OF-2
1972 CLE A	24	80	15	1	0	2	2.5	4	8	4	20	0	.188	.275	3	0	OF-22
1973	61	140	32	7	0	2	1.4	16	15	7	27	0	.229	.321	19	4	OF-32, DH-12
3 yrs.	87	228	48	9	0	4	1.8	20	23	11	49	0	.211	.303	22	4	OF-56, DH-12
1 yr.	2	8	1	1	0	0	0.0	0	0	0	2	0	.125	.250	0	0	OF-2

Sherm Lollar

LOLLAR, JOHN SHERMAN
B. Aug. 23, 1924, Durham, Ark.   D. Sept. 24, 1977, Springfield, Mo.

BR TR 6' 185 lbs.

1946 CLE A	28	62	15	6	0	1	1.6	7	9	5	9	0	.242	.387	4	1	C-24
1947 NY A	11	32	7	0	1	3	3.1	4	6	1	5	0	.219	.375	2	0	C-9
1948	22	38	8	0	0	0	0.0	0	4	1	6	0	.211	.211	12	4	C-10
1949 STL A	109	284	74	9	1	8	2.8	28	49	32	20	0	.261	.384	15	4	C-93
1950	126	396	111	22	3	13	3.3	55	65	64	25	2	.280	.449	13	4	C-109
1951	98	310	78	21	0	8	2.6	44	44	43	26	1	.252	.397	10	2	C-85, 3B-1
1952 CHI A	132	375	90	15	0	13	3.5	35	50	54	34	1	.240	.384	11	2	C-120
1953	113	334	96	19	0	8	2.4	46	54	47	29	1	.287	.416	5	1	C-107, 1B-1
1954	107	316	77	13	0	7	2.2	31	34	37	28	0	.244	.351	15	3	C-93
1955	138	426	111	13	1	16	3.8	67	61	68	34	2	.261	.408	4	1	C-136
1956	136	450	132	28	2	11	2.4	55	75	53	34	2	.293	.438	5	2	C-132
1957	101	351	90	11	2	11	3.1	33	70	35	24	2	.256	.393	9	3	C-96
1958	127	421	115	16	0	20	4.8	53	84	57	37	2	.273	.454	13	5	C-116
1959	140	505	134	22	3	22	4.4	63	84	55	49	4	.265	.451	5	3	C-122, 1B-24
1960	129	421	106	23	0	7	1.7	43	46	42	39	2	.252	.356	7	2	C-123
1961	116	337	95	10	1	7	2.1	38	41	37	22	0	.282	.380	10	4	C-107
1962	84	220	59	12	0	2	0.9	17	26	32	23	1	.268	.350	19	2	C-66
1963	35	73	17	4	0	0	0.0	4	6	8	7	0	.233	.288	11	2	C-23, 1B-2
18 yrs.	1752	5351	1415	244	14	155	2.9	623	808	671	453	20	.264	.402	170	43	C-1571, 1B-27, 3B-1
12 yrs.	1358	4229	1122	186	9	124	2.9	485	631	525	360	17	.265	.402	114	30	C-1241, 1B-27
		7th	10th			3rd		8th		5th	8th				6th	6th	

WORLD SERIES

1947 NY A	2	4	3	2	0	0	0.0	3	1	0	0	0	.750	1.250	0	0	C-2
1959 CHI A	6	22	5	0	0	1	4.5	3	5	1	3	0	.227	.364	0	0	C-6
2 yrs.	8	26	8	2	0	1	3.8	6	6	1	3	0	.308	.500	0	0	C-8

Jeoff Long

LONG, JEOFFREY KEITH
B. Oct. 9, 1941, Covington, Ky.

BR TR 6'1" 200 lbs.

1963 STL N	5	5	1	0	0	0	0.0	0	0	0	1	0	.200	.200	5	1	
1964 2 teams	STL N (28G – .233)				CHI A (23G – .143)												
" total	51	78	15	1	0	1	1.3	5	9	10	33	0	.192	.244	28	4	OF-9, 1B-8
2 yrs.	56	83	16	1	0	1	1.2	5	9	10	34	0	.193	.241	33	5	OF-9, 1B-8
1 yr.	23	35	5	0	0	0	0.0	0	5	4	15	0	.143	.143	12	1	OF-5, 1B-5

Jim Long

LONG, JAMES ALBERT
B. June 29, 1898, Fort Dodge, Iowa   D. Sept. 14, 1970, Fort Dodge, Iowa

BR TR 5'11" 160 lbs.

| 1922 CHI A | 3 | 3 | 0 | 0 | 0 | 0 | 0.0 | 0 | 2 | 0 | 0 | 0 | .000 | .000 | 1 | 0 | C-2 |

Dean Look

LOOK, DEAN ZACHARY
Brother of Bruce Look.
B. July 23, 1937, Lansing, Mich.

BR TR 5'11" 185 lbs.

| 1961 CHI A | 3 | 6 | 0 | 0 | 0 | 0 | 0.0 | 0 | 0 | 1 | 0 | 0 | .000 | .000 | 2 | 0 | OF-1 |

Al Lopez

LOPEZ, ALFONSO RAYMOND
B. Aug. 20, 1908, Tampa, Fla.
Manager 1951-65, 1968-69.
Hall of Fame 1977.

BR TR 5'11" 165 lbs.

| 1928 BKN N | 3 | 12 | 0 | 0 | 0 | 0 | 0.0 | 0 | 0 | 0 | 0 | 0 | .000 | .000 | 0 | 0 | C-3 |
| 1930 | 128 | 421 | 130 | 20 | 4 | 6 | 1.4 | 60 | 57 | 33 | 35 | 3 | .309 | .418 | 1 | 1 | C-126 |

Player Register

	G	AB	H	2B	3B	HR	HR%	R	RBI	BB	SO	SB	BA	SA	Pinch Hit AB	Pinch Hit H	G by POS

Al Lopez continued
1931	111	360	97	13	4	0	0.0	38	40	28	33	1	.269	.328	5	1	C-105
1932	126	404	111	18	6	1	0.2	44	43	34	35	3	.275	.356	1	0	C-125
1933	126	372	112	11	4	3	0.8	39	41	21	39	10	.301	.376	1	1	C-124, 2B-1
1934	140	439	120	23	2	7	1.6	58	54	49	44	2	.273	.383	1	0	C-137, 3B-2, 2B-2
1935	128	379	95	12	4	3	0.8	50	39	35	36	2	.251	.327	1	0	C-126
1936 BOS N	128	426	103	12	4	8	1.9	46	50	41	41	1	.242	.345	1	0	C-127, 1B-1
1937	105	334	68	11	1	3	0.9	31	38	35	57	3	.204	.269	1	1	C-102
1938	71	236	63	6	1	1	0.4	19	14	11	24	5	.267	.314	0	0	C-71
1939	131	412	104	22	1	8	1.9	32	49	40	45	1	.252	.369	0	0	C-129
1940 2 teams	BOS N (36G – .294)					PIT N (59G – .259)											
" total	95	293	80	9	3	3	1.0	35	41	19	21	6	.273	.355	0	0	C-95
1941 PIT N	114	317	84	9	1	5	1.6	33	43	31	23	0	.265	.347	0	0	C-114
1942	103	289	74	8	2	1	0.3	17	26	34	17	0	.256	.308	2	2	C-99
1943	118	372	98	9	4	1	0.3	40	39	49	25	2	.263	.317	1	0	C-116, 3B-1
1944	115	331	76	12	1	1	0.3	27	34	34	24	4	.230	.281	0	0	C-115
1945	91	243	53	8	0	0	0.0	22	18	35	12	1	.218	.251	0	0	C-91
1946	56	150	46	2	0	1	0.7	13	12	23	14	1	.307	.340	0	0	C-56
1947 CLE A	61	126	33	1	0	0	0.0	9	14	9	13	1	.262	.270	4	0	C-57
19 yrs.	1950	5916	1547	206	42	52	0.9	613	652	561	538	46	.261	.337	19	6	C-1918, 3B-3, 2B-3, 1B-1

Harry Lord
LORD, HARRY DONALD   BL TR 5'10½" 165 lbs.
B. Mar. 8, 1882, Porter, Me.   D. Aug. 9, 1948, Westbrook, Me.
Manager 1915.

1907 BOS A	10	38	6	1	0	0	0.0	4	3	1		1	.158	.184	0	0	3B-10
1908	145	558	145	15	6	2	0.4	61	37	22		23	.260	.319	1	0	3B-143
1909	136	534	166	12	7	0	0.0	85	31	20		36	.311	.360	1	0	3B-134
1910 2 teams	BOS A (77G – .250)					CHI A (44G – .297)											
" total	121	453	121	11	8	1	0.2	51	42	28		34	.267	.333	3	1	3B-114, SS-1
1911 CHI A	141	561	180	18	18	3	0.5	103	61	32		43	.321	.433	2	0	3B-138
1912	151	570	152	19	12	5	0.9	81	54	52		28	.267	.368	0	0	3B-106, OF-45
1913	150	547	144	18	12	1	0.2	62	42	45	39	24	.263	.346	0	0	3B-150
1914	21	69	13	1	1	1	1.4	8	3	5	3	2	.188	.275	0	0	3B-19, OF-1
1915 BUF F	97	359	97	12	6	1	0.3	50	21	21		15	.270	.345	3	1	3B-92, OF-1
9 yrs.	972	3689	1024	107	70	14	0.4	505	294	226	42	206	.278	.356	10	2	3B-906, OF-47, SS-1
5 yrs.	507	1912	538	62	46	10	0.5	280	170	148	42	114	.281	.378	2	0	3B-457, OF-46

Mem Lovett
LOVETT, MERRITT MARWOOD   BR TR 5'9½" 165 lbs.
B. June 15, 1912, Chicago, Ill.

1933 CHI A	1	1	0	0	0	0	0.0	0	0	0	0	0	.000	.000	1	0	

Jay Loviglio
LOVIGLIO, JOHN PAUL   BR TR 5'9" 160 lbs.
B. May 30, 1956, Freeport, N.Y.

1980 PHI N	16	5	0	0	0	0	0.0	7	0	1	0	1	.000	.000	0	0	2B-1
1981 CHI A	14	15	4	0	0	0	0.0	5	2	1	1	2	.267	.267	0	0	3B-4, 2B-3, DH-2
1982	15	31	6	0	0	0	0.0	5	2	1	4	2	.194	.194	0	0	2B-13, DH-2
1983 CHI N	1	1	0	0	0	0	0.0	0	0	1	0	0	.000	.000	1	0	
4 yrs.	46	52	10	0	0	0	0.0	17	4	3	6	5	.192	.192	1	0	2B-17, DH-4, 3B-4
2 yrs.	29	46	10	0	0	0	0.0	10	4	2	5	4	.217	.217	0	0	2B-16, DH-4, 3B-4

Tony Lupien
LUPIEN, ULYSSES JOHN   BL TL 5'10½" 185 lbs.
B. Apr. 23, 1917, Chelmsford, Mass.

1940 BOS A	10	19	9	3	2	0	0.0	5	4	1	0	0	.474	.842	2	1	1B-8
1942	128	463	130	25	7	3	0.6	63	70	50	20	10	.281	.384	6	0	1B-121
1943	154	608	155	21	9	4	0.7	65	47	54	23	16	.255	.339	1	0	1B-153
1944 PHI N	153	597	169	23	9	5	0.8	82	52	56	29	18	.283	.377	1	1	1B-151
1945	15	54	17	1	0	0	0.0	1	3	6	0	2	.315	.333	0	0	1B-15
1948 CHI A	154	617	152	19	3	6	1.0	69	54	74	38	11	.246	.316	0	0	1B-154
6 yrs.	614	2358	632	92	30	18	0.8	285	230	241	111	57	.268	.355	10	2	1B-602
1 yr.	154	617	152	19	3	6	1.0	69	54	74	38	11	.246	.316	0	0	1B-154

Greg Luzinski
LUZINSKI, GREGORY MICHAEL   BR TR 6'1" 220 lbs.
B. Nov. 22, 1950, Chicago, Ill.

1970 PHI N	8	12	2	0	0	0	0.0	0	0	3	5	0	.167	.167	5	1	1B-3
1971	28	100	30	8	0	3	3.0	13	15	12	32	2	.300	.470	0	0	1B-28
1972	150	563	158	33	5	18	3.2	66	68	42	114	0	.281	.453	4	1	OF-145, 1B-2
1973	161	610	174	26	4	29	4.8	76	97	51	135	3	.285	.484	4	2	OF-159
1974	85	302	82	14	1	7	2.3	29	48	29	76	3	.272	.394	4	0	OF-82
1975	161	596	179	35	3	34	5.7	85	120	89	151	3	.300	.540	2	0	OF-159
1976	149	533	162	28	1	21	3.9	74	95	50	107	1	.304	.478	5	0	OF-144
1977	149	554	171	35	3	39	7.0	99	130	80	140	0	.309	.594	1	0	OF-148
1978	155	540	143	32	2	35	6.5	85	101	100	135	8	.265	.526	1	0	OF-154
1979	137	452	114	23	1	18	4.0	47	81	56	103	3	.252	.427	9	1	OF-125
1980	106	368	84	19	1	19	5.2	44	56	60	100	3	.228	.440	1	0	OF-105
1981 CHI A	104	378	100	15	1	21	5.6	55	62	58	80	0	.265	.476	0	0	DH-103
1982	159	583	170	37	1	18	3.1	87	102	89	120	1	.292	.451	2	1	DH-156
1983	144	502	128	26	1	32	6.4	73	95	70	117	2	.255	.502	2	0	OF-139, 1B-2
14 yrs.	1696	6093	1697	331	24	294	4.8	833	1070	789	1415	32	.279	.485	40	6	OF-1221, DH-398, 1B-35
3 yrs.	407	1463	398	78	3	71	4.9	215	259	217	317	3	.272	.475	4	1	DH-398, 1B-2

LEAGUE CHAMPIONSHIP SERIES

1976 PHI N	3	11	3	2	0	1	9.1	2	3	1	4	0	.273	.727	0	0	OF-3
1977	4	14	4	1	0	1	7.1	2	2	3	3	1	.286	.571	0	0	OF-4
1978	4	16	6	0	1	2	12.5	3	3	1	2	0	.375	.875	0	0	OF-4
1980	5	17	5	2	0	1	5.9	3	4	0	6	0	.294	.588	1	1	OF-4

Player Register

	G	AB	H	2B	3B	HR	HR %	R	RBI	BB	SO	SB	BA	SA	Pinch Hit AB	H	G by POS

Greg Luzinski continued

		G	AB	H	2B	3B	HR	HR%	R	RBI	BB	SO	SB	BA	SA	PH AB	PH H	G by POS
1983	CHI A	4	15	2	1	0	0	0.0	0	0	1	5	0	.133	.200	0	0	DH-4
5 yrs.		20	73	20	6	1	5	6.8	10	12	6	20	1	.274	.589	1	1	OF-15, DH-4
WORLD SERIES																		
1980	PHI N	3	9	0	0	0	0	0.0	0	0	1	5	0	.000	.000	0	0	OF-1

Byrd Lynn

LYNN, BYRD
B. Mar. 13, 1889, Unionville, Ill. D. Feb. 5, 1940, Napa, Calif.
BR TR 5'11" 165 lbs.

		G	AB	H	2B	3B	HR	HR%	R	RBI	BB	SO	SB	BA	SA	PH AB	PH H	G by POS
1916	CHI A	31	40	9	1	0	0	0.0	4	3	4	7	2	.225	.250	15	3	C-13
1917		35	72	16	2	0	0	0.0	7	5	7	11	1	.222	.250	6	1	C-29
1918		5	8	2	0	0	0	0.0	0	0	2	1	0	.250	.250	1	1	C-4
1919		29	66	15	4	0	0	0.0	4	4	4	9	0	.227	.288	1	1	C-28
1920		16	25	8	2	1	0	0.0	0	3	1	3	0	.320	.480	2	2	C-14
5 yrs.		116	211	50	9	1	0	0.0	15	15	18	31	3	.237	.289	25	8	C-88
5 yrs.		116	211	50	9	1	0	0.0	15	15	18	31	3	.237	.289	25	8	C-88
WORLD SERIES																		
1917	CHI A	1	1	0	0	0	0	0.0	0	0	0	1	0	.000	.000	1	0	
1919		1	1	0	0	0	0	0.0	0	0	0	0	0	.000	.000	0	0	C-1
2 yrs.		2	2	0	0	0	0	0.0	0	0	0	1	0	.000	.000	1	0	C-1

Ted Lyons

LYONS, THEODORE AMAR
B. Dec. 28, 1900, Lake Charles, La.
Manager 1946-48.
Hall of Fame 1955.
BB TR 5'11" 200 lbs.
BR 1925-27

		G	AB	H	2B	3B	HR	HR%	R	RBI	BB	SO	SB	BA	SA	PH AB	PH H	G by POS
1923	CHI A	9	5	1	0	0	0	0.0	0	1	1	3	0	.200	.200	0	0	P-9
1924		41	77	17	0	1	0	0.0	10	6	5	13	0	.221	.247	0	0	P-41
1925		43	97	18	3	0	0	0.0	6	7	3	13	0	.186	.216	0	0	P-43
1926		41	104	22	1	1	0	0.0	7	3	1	10	0	.212	.240	1	0	P-39
1927		41	110	28	6	2	1	0.9	16	9	6	17	0	.255	.373	0	0	P-39
1928		49	91	23	2	0	0	0.0	10	8	1	9	0	.253	.275	0	0	P-39
1929		40	91	20	4	0	0	0.0	7	11	9	13	0	.220	.264	0	0	P-37, OF-1
1930		57	122	38	6	3	1	0.8	20	15	2	18	0	.311	.434	9	3	P-42
1931		42	33	5	0	0	0	0.0	6	3	2	1	0	.152	.152	2	1	P-22
1932		49	73	19	2	1	1	1.4	11	10	4	10	0	.260	.356	1	0	P-33
1933		51	91	26	2	1	1	1.1	11	11	4	6	0	.286	.363	7	1	P-36
1934		50	97	20	4	0	1	1.0	9	16	3	19	0	.206	.278	17	3	P-30
1935		29	82	18	4	0	0	0.0	5	6	3	4	0	.220	.268	6	1	P-23
1936		26	70	11	0	0	0	0.0	2	5	5	12	0	.157	.157	0	0	P-26
1937		23	57	12	0	0	0	0.0	6	3	9	14	0	.211	.211	0	0	P-22
1938		24	72	14	2	0	0	0.0	9	4	2	9	0	.194	.222	1	0	P-23
1939		21	61	18	3	0	0	0.0	5	8	5	7	0	.295	.344	0	0	P-21
1940		22	75	18	4	0	0	0.0	4	7	2	7	0	.240	.293	0	0	P-22
1941		22	74	20	2	0	0	0.0	8	6	2	6	0	.270	.297	0	0	P-22
1942		20	67	16	4	0	0	0.0	10	10	3	7	0	.239	.299	0	0	P-20
1946		5	14	0	0	0	0	0.0	0	0	1	3	0	.000	.000	0	0	P-5
21 yrs.		705	1563	364	49	9	5	0.3	162	149	73	201	0	.233	.285	44	9	P-594, OF-1
21 yrs.		705	1563	364	49	9	5	0.3	162	149	73	201	0	.233	.285	44	9	P-594, OF-1

Jim Lyttle

LYTTLE, JAMES LAWRENCE
B. May 20, 1946, Hamilton, Ohio
BL TR 6' 180 lbs.

		G	AB	H	2B	3B	HR	HR%	R	RBI	BB	SO	SB	BA	SA	PH AB	PH H	G by POS
1969	NY A	28	83	15	4	0	0	0.0	7	4	4	19	1	.181	.229	1	0	OF-28
1970		87	126	39	7	1	3	2.4	20	14	10	26	3	.310	.452	7	3	OF-70
1971		49	86	17	5	0	1	1.2	7	7	8	18	0	.198	.291	15	1	OF-29
1972	CHI A	44	82	19	5	2	0	0.0	8	5	1	28	0	.232	.341	21	6	OF-21
1973	MON N	49	116	30	5	1	4	3.4	12	19	9	14	0	.259	.422	11	2	OF-36
1974		25	9	3	0	0	0	0.0	1	2	1	3	0	.333	.333	6	2	OF-18
1975		44	55	15	4	0	0	0.0	7	6	13	6	0	.273	.345	19	4	OF-16
1976	2 teams	MON N (42G – .271)	LA N (23G – .221)															
"	total	65	153	38	7	1	1	0.7	9	13	15	25	0	.248	.327	20	5	OF-47
8 yrs.		391	710	176	37	5	9	1.3	71	70	61	139	4	.248	.352	100	23	OF-265
1 yr.		44	82	19	5	2	0	0.0	8	5	1	28	0	.232	.341	21	6	OF-21

Ed Madjeski

MADJESKI, EDWARD WILLIAM
Born Edward William Majewski.
B. July 24, 1909, Far Rockaway, N. Y.
BR TR 5'11" 178 lbs.

		G	AB	H	2B	3B	HR	HR%	R	RBI	BB	SO	SB	BA	SA	PH AB	PH H	G by POS
1932	PHI A	17	35	8	0	0	0	0.0	4	3	3	6	0	.229	.229	8	2	C-8
1933		51	142	40	4	0	0	0.0	17	17	4	21	0	.282	.310	12	4	C-41
1934	2 teams	PHI A (8G – .375)	CHI A (85G – .221)															
"	total	93	289	65	15	2	5	1.7	37	34	14	32	2	.225	.343	11	3	C-80
1937	NY N	5	15	3	0	0	0	0.0	0	2	0	2	0	.200	.200	0	0	C-5
4 yrs.		166	481	116	19	2	5	1.0	58	56	21	61	2	.241	.320	31	9	C-134
1 yr.		85	281	62	14	2	5	1.8	36	32	14	31	2	.221	.338	4	1	C-79

George Magoon

MAGOON, GEORGE HENRY (Topsy)
B. May 27, 1875, St. Albans, Me. D. Dec. 6, 1943, Rochester, N. H.
BR TR 5'10" 160 lbs.

		G	AB	H	2B	3B	HR	HR%	R	RBI	BB	SO	SB	BA	SA	PH AB	PH H	G by POS
1898	BKN N	93	343	77	7	1	1	0.3	35	39	30		7	.224	.254	0	0	SS-93
1899	2 teams	BAL N (62G – .256)	CHI N (59G – .228)															
"	total	121	396	96	13	4	0	0.0	50	52	50		12	.242	.295	0	0	SS-121
1901	CIN N	127	460	116	16	7	1	0.2	47	53	52		15	.252	.324	0	0	SS-112, 2B-15
1902		45	162	44	9	2	0	0.0	29	23	13		7	.272	.352	1	0	2B-41, SS-3
1903	2 teams	CIN N (42G – .216)	CHI A (94G – .228)															
"	total	136	473	106	17	3	0	0.0	38	34	49		6	.224	.273	1	0	2B-126, 3B-9
5 yrs.		522	1834	439	62	16	2	0.1	199	201	194		47	.239	.294	2	0	SS-329, 2B-182, 3B-9
1 yr.		94	334	76	11	3	0	0.0	32	25	30		4	.228	.278	0	0	2B-94

285 Player Register

	G	AB	H	2B	3B	HR	HR%	R	RBI	BB	SO	SB	BA	SA	Pinch Hit AB	H	G by POS

Hank Majeski
MAJESKI, HENRY (Heeney)
B. Dec. 13, 1916, Staten Island, N. Y.   BR TR 5'9" 174 lbs.

	G	AB	H	2B	3B	HR	HR%	R	RBI	BB	SO	SB	BA	SA	PH AB	H	G by POS
1939 BOS N	106	367	100	16	1	7	1.9	35	54	18	30	2	.272	.379	7	2	3B-99
1940	3	3	0	0	0	0	0.0	0	0	0	0	0	.000	.000	3	0	
1941	19	55	8	5	0	0	0.0	5	3	1	13	0	.145	.236	8	1	3B-11
1946 2 teams		NY A (8G – .083)			PHI A (78G – .250)												
" total	86	276	67	14	4	1	0.4	26	25	26	16	3	.243	.333	11	0	3B-74
1947 PHI A	141	479	134	26	5	8	1.7	54	72	53	31	1	.280	.405	2	0	3B-134, SS-4, 2B-1
1948	148	590	183	41	4	12	2.0	88	120	48	43	2	.310	.454	0	0	3B-142, SS-8
1949	114	448	124	26	5	9	2.0	62	67	29	23	0	.277	.417	1	0	3B-113
1950 CHI A	122	414	128	18	2	6	1.4	47	46	42	34	1	.309	.406	9	1	3B-112
1951 2 teams		CHI A (12G – .257)			PHI A (89G – .285)												
" total	101	358	101	23	4	5	1.4	45	48	36	24	1	.282	.411	5	2	3B-97
1952 2 teams		PHI A (34G – .256)			CLE A (36G – .296)												
" total	70	171	46	4	2	2	1.2	21	29	26	17	0	.269	.351	23	6	3B-45, 2B-3
1953 CLE A	50	50	15	1	0	2	4.0	6	12	3	8	0	.300	.440	31	11	2B-10, 3B-7, OF-1
1954	57	121	34	4	0	3	2.5	10	17	7	14	0	.281	.388	26	8	2B-25, 3B-10
1955 2 teams		CLE A (36G – .188)			BAL A (16G – .171)												
" total	52	89	16	3	0	2	2.2	5	8	10	7	0	.180	.281	23	1	3B-17, 2B-9
13 yrs.	1069	3421	956	181	27	57	1.7	404	501	299	260	10	.279	.398	149	32	3B-861, 2B-48, SS-12, OF-1
2 yrs.	134	449	137	22	2	6	1.3	51	52	43	34	1	.305	.403	12	2	3B-121
WORLD SERIES																	
1954 CLE A	4	6	1	0	0	1	16.7	1	3	0	1	0	.167	.667	2	1	3B-1

Jule Mallonee
MALLONEE, JULIUS NORRIS
B. Apr. 4, 1900, Charlotte, N. C.   D. Dec. 26, 1934, Charlotte, N. C.   BL TR 6'2" 180 lbs.

	G	AB	H	2B	3B	HR	HR%	R	RBI	BB	SO	SB	BA	SA	PH AB	H	G by POS
1925 CHI A	2	3	0	0	0	0	0.0	1	0	1	0	0	.000	.000	1	0	OF-1

Eddie Malone
MALONE, EDWARD RUSSELL
B. June 16, 1920, Chicago, Ill.   BR TR 5'10" 175 lbs.

	G	AB	H	2B	3B	HR	HR%	R	RBI	BB	SO	SB	BA	SA	PH AB	H	G by POS
1949 CHI A	55	170	46	7	2	1	0.6	17	16	29	19	2	.271	.353	3	1	C-51
1950	31	71	16	2	0	0	0.0	2	10	10	8	0	.225	.254	10	2	C-21
2 yrs.	86	241	62	9	2	1	0.4	19	26	39	27	2	.257	.324	13	3	C-72
2 yrs.	86	241	62	9	2	1	0.4	19	26	39	27	2	.257	.324	13	3	C-72

Carl Manda
MANDA, CARL ALAN
B. Nov. 16, 1888, Little River, Kans.   BR TR 5'10" 170 lbs.

	G	AB	H	2B	3B	HR	HR%	R	RBI	BB	SO	SB	BA	SA	PH AB	H	G by POS
1914 CHI A	9	15	4	0	0	0	0.0	2	1	3	3	1	.267	.267	0	0	2B-7

Johnny Mann
MANN, JOHN LEO
B. Feb. 4, 1898, Fontanet, Ind.   D. Mar. 31, 1977, Terre Haute, Ind.   BR TR 5'11" 160 lbs.

	G	AB	H	2B	3B	HR	HR%	R	RBI	BB	SO	SB	BA	SA	PH AB	H	G by POS
1928 CHI A	6	6	2	0	0	0	0.0	1	1	0	0	0	.333	.333	6	2	3B-2

Johnny Marcum
MARCUM, JOHN ALFRED (Footsie)
B. Sept. 9, 1908, Campbellsburg, Ky.   BL TR 5'11" 197 lbs.

	G	AB	H	2B	3B	HR	HR%	R	RBI	BB	SO	SB	BA	SA	PH AB	H	G by POS
1933 PHI A	5	12	2	0	0	0	0.0	2	2	2	1	0	.167	.167	0	0	P-4
1934	58	112	30	4	0	1	0.9	10	13	3	5	0	.268	.330	20	3	P-37
1935	64	119	37	2	1	2	1.7	13	17	9	5	0	.311	.395	23	7	P-39
1936 BOS A	48	88	18	3	0	2	2.3	6	7	3	5	0	.205	.307	18	0	P-31
1937	51	86	23	8	0	0	0.0	12	13	7	4	0	.267	.360	13	2	P-37
1938	19	37	5	0	0	0	0.0	3	3	6	9	0	.135	.135	3	0	P-15
1939 2 teams		STL A (16G – .455)			CHI A (38G – .281)												
" total	54	79	26	1	0	0	0.0	10	17	6	3	0	.329	.342	22	5	P-31
7 yrs.	299	533	141	18	1	5	0.9	56	70	36	32	0	.265	.330	99	17	P-194
1 yr.	38	57	16	0	0	0	0.0	7	12	5	1	0	.281	.281	17	3	P-19

Marty Marion
MARION, MARTIN WHITFORD (Slats, The Octopus)
Brother of Red Marion.
B. Dec. 1, 1917, Richburg, S. C.
Manager 1951-56.   BR TR 6'2" 170 lbs.

	G	AB	H	2B	3B	HR	HR%	R	RBI	BB	SO	SB	BA	SA	PH AB	H	G by POS
1940 STL N	125	435	121	18	1	3	0.7	44	46	21	34	9	.278	.345	0	0	SS-125
1941	155	547	138	22	3	3	0.5	50	58	42	48	8	.252	.320	0	0	SS-155
1942	147	485	134	38	5	0	0.0	66	54	48	50	8	.276	.375	0	0	SS-147
1943	129	418	117	15	3	1	0.2	38	52	32	37	1	.280	.337	1	0	SS-128
1944	144	506	135	26	2	6	1.2	50	63	43	50	1	.267	.362	0	0	SS-144
1945	123	430	119	27	5	1	0.2	63	59	39	39	2	.277	.370	0	0	SS-122
1946	146	498	116	29	4	3	0.6	51	46	59	53	1	.233	.325	1	0	SS-145
1947	149	540	147	19	6	4	0.7	57	74	49	58	3	.272	.352	0	0	SS-149
1948	144	567	143	26	4	4	0.7	70	43	37	54	1	.252	.333	2	0	SS-142
1949	134	515	140	31	2	5	1.0	61	70	37	42	0	.272	.369	0	0	SS-134
1950	106	372	92	10	2	4	1.1	36	40	44	55	1	.247	.317	5	1	SS-101
1952 STL A	67	186	46	11	0	2	1.1	16	19	19	17	0	.247	.339	4	2	SS-63
1953	3	7	0	0	0	0	0.0	0	0	0	0	0	.000	.000	1	0	3B-2
13 yrs.	1572	5506	1448	272	37	36	0.7	602	624	470	537	35	.263	.345	14	3	SS-1555, 3B-2
WORLD SERIES																	
1942 STL N	5	18	2	0	1	0	0.0	2	3	1	2	0	.111	.222	0	0	SS-5
1943	5	14	5	2	0	1	7.1	1	2	3	1	0	.357	.714	0	0	SS-5
1944	6	22	5	3	0	0	0.0	1	2	2	3	0	.227	.364	0	0	SS-6
1946	7	24	6	2	0	0	0.0	1	4	1	1	0	.250	.333	0	0	SS-7
4 yrs.	23	78	18	7	1	1	1.3	5	11	7	7	1	.231	.385	0	0	SS-23
				8th													

Freddie Marsh
MARSH, FRED FRANCIS
B. Jan. 5, 1924, Valley Falls, Kans.   BR TR 5'10" 180 lbs.

	G	AB	H	2B	3B	HR	HR%	R	RBI	BB	SO	SB	BA	SA	PH AB	H	G by POS
1949 CLE A	1	0	0	0	0	0	–	0	0	0	0	0	–	–	0	0	
1951 STL A	130	445	108	21	4	4	0.9	44	43	36	56	4	.243	.335	10	2	3B-117, SS-3, 2B-2

Player Register

	G	AB	H	2B	3B	HR	HR%	R	RBI	BB	SO	SB	BA	SA	Pinch Hit AB	H	G by POS

Freddie Marsh continued

1952 3 teams	STL A (11G – .217)					WAS A (9G – .042)			STL A (76G – .286)								
" total	96	271	70	9	1	2	0.7	29	28	28	37	3	.258	.321	3	2	SS-60, 3B-21, 2B-14, OF-2
1953 CHI A	67	95	19	1	0	2	2.1	22	2	13	26	0	.200	.274	11	2	3B-32, SS-17, 1B-5, 2B-2
1954	62	98	30	5	2	0	0.0	21	4	9	16	4	.306	.398	2	0	3B-36, SS-3, 1B-2, OF-1
1955 BAL A	89	303	66	7	1	2	0.7	30	19	35	33	1	.218	.267	1	0	2B-76, 3B-18, SS-16
1956	20	24	3	0	0	0	0.0	2	0	4	3	1	.125	.125	0	0	SS-8, 3B-8, 2B-5
7 yrs.	465	1236	296	43	8	10	0.8	148	96	125	171	13	.239	.311	27	6	3B-232, SS-107, 2B-99, 1B-7, OF-3
2 yrs.	129	193	49	6	2	2	1.0	43	6	22	42	4	.254	.337	13	2	3B-68, SS-20, 1B-7, 2B-2, OF-1

Willard Marshall

MARSHALL, WILLARD WARREN
B. Feb. 8, 1921, Richmond, Va.
BL TR 6'1" 205 lbs.

1942 NY N	116	401	103	9	2	11	2.7	41	59	26	20	1	.257	.372	8	2	OF-107
1946	131	510	144	18	3	13	2.5	63	48	33	29	3	.282	.406	7	2	OF-125
1947	155	587	171	19	6	36	6.1	102	107	67	30	3	.291	.528	0	0	OF-155
1948	143	537	146	21	8	14	2.6	72	86	64	34	2	.272	.419	0	0	OF-142
1949	141	499	153	19	3	12	2.4	81	70	78	20	4	.307	.429	3	1	OF-138
1950 BOS N	105	298	70	10	2	5	1.7	38	40	36	5	1	.235	.332	20	4	OF-85
1951	136	469	132	24	7	11	2.3	65	62	48	18	0	.281	.433	7	1	OF-127
1952 2 teams	BOS N (21G – .227)					CIN N (107G – .267)											
" total	128	463	121	27	2	10	2.2	57	57	41	25	0	.261	.393	9	0	OF-121
1953 CIN N	122	357	95	14	6	17	4.8	51	62	41	28	0	.266	.482	33	4	OF-95
1954 CHI A	47	71	18	2	0	1	1.4	7	7	11	9	0	.254	.324	19	4	OF-29
1955	22	41	7	0	0	0	0.0	6	6	13	1	0	.171	.171	7	0	OF-12
11 yrs.	1246	4233	1160	163	39	130	3.1	583	604	458	219	14	.274	.423	113	18	OF-1136
2 yrs.	69	112	25	2	0	1	0.9	13	13	24	10	0	.223	.268	26	4	OF-41

J. C. Martin

MARTIN, JOSEPH CLIFTON
B. Dec. 13, 1936, Axton, Va.
BL TR 6'2" 188 lbs.

1959 CHI A	3	4	1	0	0	0	0.0	0	1	0	1	0	.250	.250	1	0	3B-2
1960	4	20	2	1	0	0	0.0	0	2	0	6	0	.100	.150	0	0	3B-5, 1B-1
1961	110	274	63	8	3	5	1.8	26	32	21	31	1	.230	.336	11	2	1B-60, 3B-36
1962	18	26	2	0	0	0	0.0	0	2	0	3	0	.077	.077	11	0	C-6, 3B-1, 1B-1
1963	105	259	53	11	1	5	1.9	25	28	26	35	0	.205	.313	12	3	C-98, 1B-3, 3B-1
1964	122	294	58	10	1	4	1.4	23	22	16	30	0	.197	.279	6	0	C-120
1965	119	230	60	12	0	2	0.9	21	21	24	29	2	.261	.339	15	3	C-112, 1B-4, 3B-2
1966	67	157	40	5	3	2	1.3	13	20	14	24	0	.255	.363	4	1	C-63
1967	101	252	59	12	1	4	1.6	22	22	30	41	4	.234	.337	6	1	C-96, 1B-1
1968 NY N	78	244	55	9	2	3	1.2	20	31	21	31	0	.225	.316	8	1	C-53, 1B-14
1969	66	177	37	5	1	4	2.3	12	21	12	32	0	.209	.316	18	3	C-48, 1B-2
1970 CHI N	40	77	12	1	0	1	1.3	11	4	20	11	0	.156	.208	3	0	C-36, 1B-3
1971	47	125	33	5	0	2	1.6	13	17	12	16	1	.264	.352	5	0	C-43, OF-1
1972	25	50	12	3	0	0	0.0	3	7	5	9	1	.240	.300	9	2	C-17
14 yrs.	905	2189	487	82	12	32	1.5	189	230	201	299	9	.222	.315	109	16	C-692, 1B-89, 3B-47, OF-1
9 yrs.	649	1516	338	59	9	22	1.5	130	150	131	200	7	.223	.317	66	10	C-495, 1B-70, 3B-47

LEAGUE CHAMPIONSHIP SERIES

| 1969 NY N | 2 | 2 | 1 | 0 | 0 | 0 | 0.0 | 0 | 2 | 0 | 0 | 0 | .500 | .500 | 2 | 1 | |

WORLD SERIES

| 1969 NY N | 1 | 0 | 0 | 0 | 0 | 0 | – | 0 | 0 | 0 | 0 | 0 | – | – | 0 | 0 | |

Joe Martin

MARTIN, WILLIAM JOSEPH (Smokey Joe)
B. Aug. 28, 1911, Seymour, Mo. D. Sept. 28, 1960, Buffalo, N. Y.
BR TR 5'11½" 181 lbs.

1936 NY N	7	15	4	1	0	0	0.0	2	2	4	0	0	.267	.333	0	0	3B-7
1938 CHI A	1	0	0	0	0	0	–	0	0	0	0	0	–	–	0	0	
2 yrs.	8	15	4	1	0	0	0.0	2	2	4	0	0	.267	.333	0	0	3B-7
1 yr.	1	0	0	0	0	0	–	0	0	0	0	0	–	–	0	0	

Phil Masi

MASI, PHILIP SAMUEL
B. Jan. 6, 1917, Chicago, Ill.
BR TR 5'10" 177 lbs.

1939 BOS N	46	114	29	7	2	1	0.9	14	14	9	15	0	.254	.377	3	0	C-42
1940	63	138	27	4	1	1	0.7	11	14	14	14	0	.196	.261	9	3	C-52
1941	87	180	40	8	2	3	1.7	17	18	16	13	4	.222	.339	3	1	C-83
1942	57	87	19	3	1	0	0.0	14	9	12	4	2	.218	.276	1	0	C-39, OF-4
1943	80	238	65	9	1	2	0.8	27	28	27	20	7	.273	.345	1	1	C-73
1944	89	251	69	13	5	3	1.2	33	23	31	20	4	.275	.402	8	1	C-63, 1B-12, 3B-2
1945	111	371	101	25	4	7	1.9	55	46	42	32	9	.272	.418	9	1	C-95, 1B-7
1946	133	397	106	17	5	3	0.8	52	62	55	41	5	.267	.358	5	2	C-124
1947	126	411	125	22	4	9	2.2	54	50	47	27	7	.304	.443	3	1	C-123
1948	113	376	95	19	0	5	1.3	43	44	35	26	2	.253	.343	1	0	C-109
1949 2 teams	BOS N (37G – .210)					PIT N (48G – .274)											
" total	85	240	59	8	1	2	0.8	29	19	31	26	2	.246	.313	3	0	C-81, 1B-2
1950 CHI A	122	377	105	17	2	7	1.9	38	55	49	36	2	.279	.390	9	1	C-114
1951	84	225	61	11	2	4	1.8	24	28	32	27	1	.271	.391	3	0	C-78
1952	30	63	16	1	0	0	0.0	9	7	10	10	0	.254	.302	3	1	C-25
14 yrs.	1226	3468	917	164	31	47	1.4	420	417	410	311	45	.264	.370	61	12	C-1101, 1B-21, OF-4, 3B-2
3 yrs.	236	665	182	29	5	11	1.7	71	90	91	73	3	.274	.382	15	2	C-217

WORLD SERIES

| 1948 BOS N | 5 | 8 | 1 | 1 | 0 | 0 | 0.0 | 1 | 1 | 0 | 0 | 0 | .125 | .250 | 1 | 1 | C-5 |

Player Register

	G	AB	H	2B	3B	HR	HR%	R	RBI	BB	SO	SB	BA	SA	Pinch Hit AB H	G by POS

John Matias
MATIAS, JOHN ROY BL TL 5'11" 170 lbs.
B. Aug. 15, 1944, Honolulu, Hawaii

| 1970 CHI A | 58 | 117 | 22 | 2 | 0 | 2 | 1.7 | 7 | 6 | 3 | 22 | 1 | .188 | .256 | 27 5 | OF-22, 1B-18 |

Wally Mattick
MATTICK, WALTER JOSEPH (Chick) BR TR 5'10" 180 lbs.
Father of Bobby Mattick.
B. Mar. 12, 1887, St. Louis, Mo.   D. Nov. 5, 1968, Los Altos, Calif.

1912 CHI A	88	285	74	7	9	1	0.4	45	35	27		15	.260	.358	8 3	OF-78
1913	68	207	39	8	1	0	0.0	15	11	18	16	3	.188	.237	3 1	OF-63
1918 STL N	8	14	2	0	0	0	0.0	0	1	2	3	0	.143	.143	5 1	OF-3
3 yrs.	164	506	115	15	10	1	0.2	60	47	47	19	18	.227	.302	16 5	OF-144
2 yrs.	156	492	113	15	10	1	0.2	60	46	45	16	18	.230	.307	11 4	OF-141

Mark Mauldin
MAULDIN, MARSHALL REESE BR TR 5'11" 170 lbs.
B. Nov. 5, 1914, Atlanta, Ga.

| 1934 CHI A | 10 | 38 | 10 | 2 | 0 | 1 | 2.6 | 3 | 3 | 3 | | 0 | .263 | .395 | 0 0 | 3B-10 |

Charlie Maxwell
MAXWELL, CHARLES RICHARD (Smokey) BL TL 5'11" 185 lbs.
B. Apr. 28, 1927, Lawton, Mich.

1950 BOS A	3	8	0	0	0	0	0.0	1	0	1	3	0	.000	.000	1 0	OF-2
1951	49	80	15	1	0	3	3.8	8	12	9	18	0	.188	.313	31 7	OF-13
1952	8	15	1	1	0	0	0.0	0	3	11	0	.067	.133	3 0	OF-3, 1B-3
1954	74	104	26	4	1	0	0.0	9	5	12	21	3	.250	.308	45 12	OF-27
1955 2 teams	BAL A (4G – .000)					DET A (55G – .266)										
" total	59	113	29	7	1	7	6.2	19	18	8	21	0	.257	.522	30 7	OF-26, 1B-2
1956 DET A	141	500	163	14	3	28	5.6	96	87	79	74	1	.326	.534	7 4	OF-136
1957	138	492	136	23	4	24	4.9	75	82	76	84	3	.276	.482	3 3	OF-137
1958	131	397	108	14	4	13	3.3	56	65	64	54	6	.272	.426	8 1	OF-114, 1B-14
1959	145	518	130	12	2	31	6.0	81	95	81	91	0	.251	.461	8 3	OF-136
1960	134	482	114	16	5	24	5.0	70	81	58	75	5	.237	.440	14 1	OF-120
1961	79	131	30	4	2	5	3.8	11	18	20	24	0	.229	.405	45 12	OF-25
1962 2 teams	DET A (30G – .194)					CHI A (69G – .296)										
" total	99	273	74	10	3	10	3.7	35	52	42	42	0	.271	.440	20 3	OF-71, 1B-7
1963 CHI A	71	130	30	4	2	3	2.3	17	17	31	27	0	.231	.362	21 3	OF-24, 1B-17
1964	2	2	0	0	0	0	0.0	0	0	0	0	0	.000	.000	2 0	
14 yrs.	1133	3245	856	110	26	148	4.6	478	532	484	545	18	.264	.451	238 56	OF-834, 1B-43
3 yrs.	142	338	91	8	2	12	3.6	47	60	65	59	0	.269	.441	32 4	OF-80, 1B-23

Carlos May
MAY, CARLOS BL TR 5'11" 200 lbs.
Brother of Lee May.
B. May 17, 1948, Birmingham, Ala.

1968 CHI A	17	67	12	1	0	0	0.0	4	1	3	15	0	.179	.194	0 0	OF-17
1969	100	367	103	18	2	18	4.9	62	62	58	66	1	.281	.488	2 1	OF-100
1970	150	555	158	28	4	12	2.2	83	68	79	96	12	.285	.414	2 0	OF-141, 1B-7
1971	141	500	147	21	7	7	1.4	64	70	62	61	16	.294	.406	5 2	1B-130, OF-9
1972	148	523	161	26	3	12	2.3	83	68	79	70	23	.308	.438	0 0	OF-145, 1B-5
1973	149	553	148	20	0	20	3.6	61	96	53	73	8	.268	.412	2 0	DH-75, OF-70, 1B-2
1974	149	551	137	19	2	8	1.5	66	76	8	76	8	.249	.334	10 0	OF-129, DH-13
1975	128	454	123	19	2	8	1.8	55	53	67	46	12	.271	.374	1 0	1B-63, OF-46, DH-19
1976 2 teams	CHI A (20G – .175)					NY A (87G – .278)										
" total	107	351	91	13	2	3	0.9	45	43	43	37	5	.259	.333	15 5	DH-81, OF-16, 1B-1
1977 2 teams	NY A (65G – .227)					CAL A (11G – .333)										
" total	76	199	47	7	1	2	1.0	21	17	22	25	0	.236	.312	14 6	DH-54, OF-4, 1B-3
10 yrs.	1165	4120	1127	172	23	90	2.2	544	536	512	565	85	.274	.392	51 14	OF-677, DH-242, 1B-211
9 yrs.	1002	3633	1000	154	20	85	2.3	485	479	456	508	84	.275	.399	28 3	OF-666, 1B-207, DH-114
								5th		10th	5th					

LEAGUE CHAMPIONSHIP SERIES
| 1976 NY A | 3 | 10 | 2 | 1 | 0 | 0 | 0.0 | 1 | 0 | 1 | 4 | 0 | .200 | .300 | 1 0 | DH-3 |

WORLD SERIES
| 1976 NY A | 4 | 9 | 0 | 0 | 0 | 0 | 0.0 | 0 | 0 | 0 | 1 | 0 | .000 | .000 | 2 0 | DH-4 |

Milt May
MAY, MILTON SCOTT BL TR 6' 190 lbs.
Son of Pinky May.
B. Aug. 1, 1950, Gary, Ind.

1970 PIT N	5	4	2	1	0	0	0.0	1	2	0	0	0	.500	.750	6 3	C-31
1971	49	126	35	1	0	6	4.8	15	25	9	16	0	.278	.429	17 3	C-33
1972	57	139	39	10	0	0	0.0	12	14	10	13	0	.281	.353	18 2	C-79
1973	101	283	76	8	1	7	2.5	29	31	34	26	0	.269	.378	18 2	C-116
1974 HOU N	127	405	117	17	4	7	1.7	47	54	39	33	0	.289	.402	9 2	C-116
1975	111	386	93	15	1	4	1.0	29	52	26	41	1	.241	.316	8 3	C-102
1976 DET A	6	25	7	1	0	0	0.0	2	1	0	1	0	.280	.320	0 0	C-6
1977	115	397	99	9	3	12	3.0	32	46	26	31	0	.249	.378	5 2	C-111
1978	105	352	88	9	0	10	2.8	24	37	27	26	0	.250	.361	12 1	C-94
1979 2 teams	DET A (6G – .273)					CHI A (65G – .252)										
" total	71	213	54	15	0	7	3.3	24	31	15	28	0	.254	.423	2 0	C-70
1980 SF N	111	358	93	16	2	6	1.7	27	50	25	40	0	.260	.366	15 6	C-103
1981	97	316	98	17	0	2	0.6	20	33	34	29	1	.310	.383	9 5	C-93
1982	114	395	104	19	0	9	2.3	29	39	28	38	0	.263	.380	13 6	C-110
1983 2 teams	SF N (66G – .247)					PIT N (7G – .250)										
" total	73	198	49	6	0	6	3.0	18	20	22	24	2	.247	.369	13 3	C-60
14 yrs.	1142	3597	954	144	11	76	2.1	309	435	295	346	4	.265	.375	145 40	C-1008
1 yr.	65	202	51	13	0	7	3.5	23	28	14	20	0	.252	.421	1 0	C-65

LEAGUE CHAMPIONSHIP SERIES
| 1971 PIT N | 1 | 1 | 0 | 0 | 0 | 0 | 0.0 | 0 | 0 | 0 | 0 | 0 | .000 | .000 | 1 0 | |

Player Register

	G	AB	H	2B	3B	HR	HR%	R	RBI	BB	SO	SB	BA	SA	Pinch Hit AB	H	G by POS

Milt May continued

| 1972 | 1 | 2 | 1 | 0 | 0 | 0 | 0.0 | 0 | 1 | 0 | 0 | 0 | .500 | .500 | 0 | 0 | C-1 |
| 2 yrs. | 2 | 3 | 1 | 0 | 0 | 0 | 0.0 | 0 | 1 | 0 | 0 | 0 | .333 | .333 | 1 | 0 | C-1 |

WORLD SERIES
| 1971 PIT N | 2 | 2 | 1 | 0 | 0 | 0 | 0.0 | 0 | 1 | 0 | 0 | 0 | .500 | .500 | 2 | 1 | |

Lee Maye
MAYE, ARTHUR LEE
B. Dec. 11, 1934, Tuscaloosa, Ala. BL TR 6'2" 190 lbs.

1959 MIL N	51	140	42	5	1	4	2.9	17	16	7	26	2	.300	.436	7	4	OF-44
1960	41	83	25	6	0	0	0.0	14	2	7	21	5	.301	.373	17	2	OF-19
1961	110	373	101	11	5	14	3.8	68	41	36	50	10	.271	.440	17	5	OF-96
1962	99	349	85	10	0	10	2.9	40	41	25	58	9	.244	.358	8	1	OF-94
1963	124	442	120	22	7	11	2.5	67	34	36	52	14	.271	.428	18	3	OF-111
1964	153	588	179	44	5	10	1.7	96	74	34	54	5	.304	.447	13	2	OF-135, 3B-5
1965 2 teams	MIL	N (15G – .302)				HOU	N (108G – .251)										
" total	123	468	120	19	7	5	1.1	46	43	22	43	1	.256	.359	8	1	OF-116
1966 HOU N	115	358	103	12	4	9	2.5	38	36	20	26	4	.288	.419	20	4	OF-97
1967 CLE A	115	297	77	20	4	9	3.0	43	27	26	47	3	.259	.444	42	10	OF-77, 2B-1
1968	109	299	84	13	2	4	1.3	20	26	15	24	0	.281	.378	30	9	OF-80, 1B-1
1969 2 teams	CLE	A (43G – .250)				WAS	A (71G – .290)										
" total	114	346	96	14	3	10	2.9	50	41	28	40	2	.277	.422	24	4	OF-93, 3B-1
1970 2 teams	WAS	A (6G – .263)				CHI	A (96G – .167)										
" total	102	261	68	12	1	7	2.7	28	31	21	33	4	.261	.395	39	7	OF-68, 3B-1
1971 CHI A	32	44	9	2	0	1	2.3	6	7	5	7	0	.205	.318	17	5	OF-10
13 yrs.	1288	4048	1109	190	39	94	2.3	533	419	282	481	59	.274	.410	260	57	OF-1040, 3B-7, 2B-1, 1B-1
2 yrs.	38	50	10	2	0	1	2.0	6	8	5	8	0	.200	.300	23	6	OF-10

Wally Mayer
MAYER, WALTER A.
B. Aug. 3, 1889, Cincinnati, Ohio D. Nov. 18, 1951, Minneapolis, Minn. BR TR 5'11" 168 lbs.

1911 CHI A	1	3	0	0	0	0	0.0	0	2	0		0	.000	.000	0	0	C-1
1912	7	9	0	0	0	0	0.0	1	0	1		0	.000	.000	1	0	C-6
1914	39	85	14	3	1	0	0.0	7	5	14	23	1	.165	.224	5	0	C-33, 3B-1
1915	22	54	12	3	1	0	0.0	5	5	8		0	.222	.315	2	0	C-20
1917 BOS A	4	12	2	0	0	0	0.0	2	0	5		0	.167	.167	0	0	C-4
1918	26	49	11	4	0	0	0.0	7	5	7		0	.224	.306	3	0	C-23
1919 STL A	30	62	14	4	1	0	0.0	2	5	8	11	0	.226	.323	5	1	C-25
7 yrs.	129	274	53	14	3	0	0.0	22	20	42	51	1	.193	.266	16	1	C-112, 3B-1
4 yrs.	69	151	26	6	2	0	0.0	11	10	22	31	1	.172	.238	8	0	C-60, 3B-1

John McAleese
McALEESE, JOHN JAMES
B. Aug. 22, 1879, Sharon, Pa. D. Nov. 14, 1950, New York, N.Y. BR TR

1901 CHI A	1	1	0	0	0	0	0.0	0	0	0		0	.000	.000	1	0	P-1
1909 STL A	85	267	57	7	0	0	0.0	33	12	32		18	.213	.240	2	0	OF-79, 3B-2
2 yrs.	86	268	57	7	0	0	0.0	33	12	32		18	.213	.239	2	0	OF-79, 3B-2, P-1
1 yr.	1	1	0	0	0	0	0.0	0	0	0		0	.000	.000	0	0	P-1

Jim McAnany
McANANY, JAMES
B. Sept. 4, 1936, Los Angeles, Calif. BR TR 5'10" 196 lbs.

1958 CHI A	5	13	0	0	0	0	0.0	0	0	0	5	0	.000	.000	1	0	OF-3
1959	67	210	58	9	3	0	0.0	22	27	19	26	2	.276	.348	0	0	OF-67
1960	3	2	0	0	0	0	0.0	0	0	2	0	0	.000	.000	2	0	
1961 CHI N	11	10	3	1	0	0	0.0	1	0	1	3	0	.300	.400	10	3	OF-1
1962	7	6	0	0	0	0	0.0	0	0	1	2	0	.000	.000	6	0	
5 yrs.	93	241	61	10	3	0	0.0	23	27	21	38	2	.253	.320	19	3	OF-71
3 yrs.	75	225	58	9	3	0	0.0	22	27	19	33	2	.258	.324	3	0	OF-70

WORLD SERIES
| 1959 CHI A | 3 | 5 | 0 | 0 | 0 | 0 | 0.0 | 0 | 0 | 1 | 0 | 0 | .000 | .000 | 0 | 0 | OF-3 |

Brian McCall
McCALL, BRIAN ALLEN (Bam)
B. Jan. 25, 1943, Kentfield, Calif. BL TL 5'10" 170 lbs.

1962 CHI A	4	8	3	0	0	2	25.0	2	3	0	2	0	.375	1.125	3	1	OF-1
1963	3	7	0	0	0	0	0.0	1	0	1	2	0	.000	.000	0	0	OF-2
2 yrs.	7	15	3	0	0	2	13.3	3	3	1	4	0	.200	.600	3	1	OF-3
2 yrs.	7	15	3	0	0	2	13.3	3	3	1	4	0	.200	.600	3	1	OF-3

Harvey McClellan
McCLELLAN, HARVEY McDOWELL
B. Dec. 22, 1896, Maysville, Ky. D. Nov. 6, 1925, Cynthiana, Ky. BR TR 5'9½" 143 lbs.

1919 CHI A	7	12	4	0	0	0	0.0	2	1	1	1	0	.333	.333	1	0	3B-3, SS-2
1920	10	18	6	1	1	0	0.0	4	5	4	1	2	.333	.500	2	1	SS-4, 3B-2
1921	63	196	35	4	1	1	0.5	20	14	14	18	2	.179	.224	3	0	2B-20, OF-15, SS-15, 3B-5
1922	91	301	68	17	3	2	0.7	28	28	16	32	3	.226	.322	5	4	3B-71, SS-8, 2B-2, OF-1
1923	141	550	129	29	3	1	0.2	67	41	27	44	14	.235	.304	1	1	SS-138, 2B-5
1924	32	85	15	3	0	0	0.0	9	9	6	7	2	.176	.212	1	0	SS-21, 2B-7, OF-1, 3B-1
6 yrs.	344	1162	257	54	8	4	0.3	130	98	68	103	23	.221	.292	13	5	SS-188, 3B-82, 2B-31, OF-17
6 yrs.	344	1162	257	54	8	4	0.3	130	98	68	103	23	.221	.292	13	5	SS-188, 3B-82, 2B-31, OF-17

Amby McConnell
McCONNELL, AMBROSE MOSES
B. Apr. 29, 1883, N. Pownal, Vt. D. May 20, 1942, Utica, N.Y. BL TR

1908 BOS A	140	502	140	10	8	2	0.4	77	43	38		31	.279	.335	10	5	2B-126, SS-3
1909	121	453	108	7	8	0	0.0	59	36	34		26	.238	.289	0	0	2B-121
1910 2 teams	BOS	A (12G – .167)				CHI	A (32G – .277)										
" total	44	155	39	2	3	0	0.0	19	6	12		8	.252	.303	2	0	2B-42

Player Register

	G	AB	H	2B	3B	HR	HR%	R	RBI	BB	SO	SB	BA	SA	Pinch Hit AB	H	G by POS

Amby McConnell continued

1911 CHI A	104	396	111	11	5	0	0.3	45	34	23		7	.280	.341	1	0	2B-103
4 yrs.	409	1506	398	30	22	3	0.2	200	119	107		72	.264	.319	13	5	2B-392, SS-3
2 yrs.	136	515	144	13	8	1	0.2	58	39	30		11	.280	.342	2	0	2B-135

Mike McCormick
McCORMICK, MYRON WINTHROP BR TR 6' 195 lbs.
B. May 6, 1917, Angels Camp, Calif. D. Apr. 14, 1976, Los Angeles, Calif.

1940 CIN N	110	417	125	20	0	1	0.2	48	30	13	36	8	.300	.355	2	0	OF-107
1941	110	369	106	17	3	4	1.1	52	31	30	24	4	.287	.382	4	0	OF-101
1942	40	135	32	2	3	1	0.7	18	11	13	7	0	.237	.319	1	0	OF-38
1943	4	15	2	0	0	0	0.0	0	0	2	0	0	.133	.133	0	0	OF-4
1946 2 teams		CIN N (23G – .216)			BOS N (59G – .262)					19	12	0	.248	.311	10	2	OF-69
" total	82	238	59	8	2	1	0.4	33	24						12	4	OF-79
1947 BOS N	92	284	81	13	7	3	1.1	42	36	20	21	1	.285	.412	14	6	OF-100
1948	115	343	104	22	7	1	0.3	45	39	32	34	1	.303	.417	6	2	OF-49
1949 BKN N	55	139	29	5	1	2	1.4	17	14	14	12	1	.209	.302			
1950 2 teams		NY N (4G – .000)			CHI A (55G – .232)					16	8	0	.225	.296	11	1	OF-44
" total	59	142	32	4	3	0	0.0	16	10						15	7	OF-62
1951 WAS A	81	243	70	9	3	1	0.4	31	23	29	20	1	.288	.362			
10 yrs.	748	2325	640	100	29	14	0.6	302	215	188	174	16	.275	.361	75	22	OF-653
1 yr.	55	138	32	4	3	0	0.0	16	10	16	6	0	.232	.304	7	1	OF-44

WORLD SERIES

1940 CIN N	7	29	9	3	0	0	0.0	1	2	1	6	0	.310	.414	0	0	OF-7
1948 BOS N	6	23	6	0	0	0	0.0	1	2	0	4	0	.261	.261	0	0	OF-6
1949 BKN N	1	0	0	0	0	0	–	0	0	0	0	0	–	–	0	0	OF-1
3 yrs.	14	52	15	3	0	0	0.0	2	4	1	10	0	.288	.346	0	0	OF-14

Tom McCraw
McCRAW, THOMAS LEE BL TL 6' 183 lbs.
B. Nov. 21, 1941, Malvern, Ark.

1963 CHI A	102	280	71	11	3	6	2.1	38	33	21	46	15	.254	.379	3	1	1B-97
1964	125	368	96	11	5	6	1.6	47	36	32	65	15	.261	.367	20	2	1B-84, OF-36
1965	133	273	65	12	1	5	1.8	38	21	25	48	12	.238	.344	22	5	1B-72, OF-64
1966	151	389	89	16	4	5	1.3	49	48	29	40	20	.229	.329	7	1	1B-121, OF-41
1967	125	453	107	18	3	11	2.4	55	45	33	55	24	.236	.362	6	2	1B-123, OF-6
1968	136	477	112	16	12	9	1.9	51	44	36	58	20	.235	.375	3	0	1B-135
1969	93	240	62	12	2	8	0.8	21	25	21	24	1	.258	.350	17	4	1B-64, OF-41
1970	129	332	73	11	2	6	1.8	39	31	21	50	12	.220	.319	32	8	1B-59, OF-49
1971 WAS A	122	207	44	6	4	7	3.4	33	25	19	38	3	.213	.382	40	9	OF-60, 1B-30
1972 CLE A	129	391	101	13	5	7	1.8	43	33	41	47	12	.258	.371	2	0	OF-84, 1B-38
1973 CAL A	99	264	70	7	0	3	1.1	25	24	30	42	3	.265	.326	23	5	OF-34, 1B-25, DH-8
1974 2 teams		CAL A (56G – .286)			CLE A (45G – .304)					17	24	2	.294	.442	23	6	1B-67, OF-13, DH-2
" total	101	231	68	16	0	6	2.6	38	34						4	2	1B-16, OF-3
1975 CLE A	23	51	14	1	1	2	3.9	7	5	7	7	4	.275	.451			
13 yrs.	1468	3956	972	150	42	75	1.9	484	404	332	544	143	.246	.362	208	47	1B-911, OF-431, DH-10
8 yrs.	994	2812	675	107	32	50	1.8	338	283	218	386	119	.240	.354	106	23	1B-735, OF-237
														8th			

Harry McCurdy
McCURDY, HARRY HENRY BL TR 5'11" 187 lbs.
B. Sept. 15, 1900, Stevens Point, Wis. D. July 21, 1972, Houston, Tex.

1922 STL N	13	27	8	2	0	0	0.0	3	5	1	1	0	.296	.519	3	0	C-9, 1B-2
1923	67	185	49	11	2	0	0.0	17	15	11	11	3	.265	.346	2	0	C-58
1926 CHI N	44	86	28	7	2	1	1.2	16	11	6	10	0	.326	.488	11	2	C-25, 1B-8
1927	86	262	75	19	3	1	0.4	34	27	32	24	6	.286	.393	3	0	C-82
1928	49	103	27	10	0	2	1.9	12	13	8	15	1	.262	.417	14	3	C-34
1930 PHI N	80	148	49	6	2	1	0.7	23	25	15	12	0	.331	.419	32	8	C-41
1931	66	150	43	9	0	1	0.7	21	25	23	16	2	.287	.367	17	7	C-45
1932	62	136	32	6	1	1	0.7	13	14	17	13	0	.235	.316	15	2	C-42
1933	73	54	15	1	0	2	3.7	9	12	16	6	0	.278	.407	52	15	C-2
1934 CIN N	3	6	0	0	0	0	0.0	0	1	0	0	0	.000	.000	2	0	1B-3
10 yrs.	543	1157	326	71	12	9	0.8	148	148	129	108	12	.282	.387	158	37	C-338, 1B-13
3 yrs.	179	451	130	36	5	4	0.9	62	51	46	49	7	.288	.417	28	5	C-141, 1B-8

Ed McFarland
McFARLAND, EDWARD WILLIAM BR TR 5'10" 180 lbs.
B. Aug. 3, 1874, Cleveland, Ohio D. Nov. 28, 1959, Cleveland, Ohio

1893 CLE N	8	22	9	2	1	0	0.0	5	6	1	2	0	.409	.591	0	0	OF-5, 3B-2, C-1
1896 STL N	83	290	70	13	4	3	1.0	48	36	15	17	7	.241	.345	1	0	C-80, OF-2
1897 2 teams		STL N (31G – .327)			PHI N (38G – .223)					22		4	.270	.388	2	0	C-60, OF-3, 1B-3, 2B-1
" total	69	237	64	8	7	2	0.8	32	33						0	0	C-121
1898 PHI N	121	429	121	21	5	3	0.7	65	71	44		9	.282	.375	2	0	C-94
1899	96	324	108	22	10	1	0.3	59	57	36		9	.333	.472	1	0	C-93, 3B-1
1900	94	344	105	14	8	0	0.0	50	38	29		9	.305	.392	0	0	C-74
1901	74	295	84	14	2	1	0.3	33	32	18		11	.285	.356			
1902 CHI A	73	244	56	9	2	1	0.4	29	25	19		8	.230	.295	2	0	C-69, 1B-2
1903	61	201	42	7	2	1	0.5	15	19	14		3	.209	.279	4	1	C-56, 1B-1
1904	50	160	44	11	3	0	0.0	22	20	17		2	.275	.381	1	0	C-49
1905	80	250	70	13	4	0	0.0	24	31	23		5	.280	.364	9	4	C-70
1906	7	22	3	1	0	0	0.0	5	3	3		0	.136	.182	3	0	C-3
1907	52	138	39	9	1	0	0.0	11	8	12		3	.283	.362	7	2	C-43
1908 BOS A	19	48	10	2	1	0	0.0	1	0	0		0	.208	.292	6	2	C-13
14 yrs.	887	3004	825	146	50	12	0.4	398	383	254		19	65	.275	.369	38	11	C-826, OF-10, 1B-5, 3B-3, 2B-1
6 yrs.	323	1015	254	50	12	2	0.2	101	106	88		21	.250	.329	26	9	C-290, 1B-2

WORLD SERIES

| 1906 CHI A | 1 | 1 | 0 | 0 | 0 | 0 | 0.0 | 0 | 0 | 0 | 0 | 0 | .000 | .000 | 1 | 0 | |

Player Register

	G	AB	H	2B	3B	HR	HR%	R	RBI	BB	SO	SB	BA	SA	Pinch Hit AB H	G by POS

Herm McFarland
McFARLAND, HERMUS W.
B. Mar. 11, 1870, Des Moines, Iowa D. Sept. 21, 1935, Richmond, Va. BL TR

	G	AB	H	2B	3B	HR	HR%	R	RBI	BB	SO	SB	BA	SA	PH AB	PH H	G by POS
1896 LOU N	30	110	21	4	1	1	0.9	11	12	9		14	4	.191	.273	1	0	OF-28, C-1
1898 CIN N	19	64	18	1	3	0	0.0	10	11	7			3	.281	.391	1	0	OF-17
1901 CHI A	132	473	130	21	9	4	0.8	83	59	75			33	.275	.383	0	0	OF-132
1902 2 teams		CHI A (9G – .172)				BAL A (61G – .322)												
" total	70	271	83	19	6	3	1.1	59	40	38			11	.306	.454	2	0	OF-68
1903 NY A	103	362	88	16	9	5	1.4	41	45	46			13	.243	.378	0	0	OF-103
5 yrs.	354	1280	340	61	28	13	1.0	204	167	175		14	64	.266	.388	4	0	OF-348, C-1
2 yrs.	141	502	135	21	9	4	0.8	88	63	77			34	.269	.371	2	0	OF-139

Ed McGhee
McGHEE, WARREN EDWARD
B. Sept. 29, 1924, Perry, Ark. BR TR 5'11" 170 lbs.

	G	AB	H	2B	3B	HR	HR%	R	RBI	BB	SO	SB	BA	SA	PH AB	PH H	G by POS
1950 CHI A	3	6	1	0	1	0	0.0	0	0	0	1	0	.167	.500	1	0	OF-1
1953 PHI A	104	358	94	11	4	1	0.3	36	29	32	43	4	.263	.324	7	2	OF-99
1954 2 teams		PHI A (21G – .208)				CHI A (42G – .227)												
" total	63	128	28	3	0	2	1.6	17	14	16	16	5	.219	.289	11	1	OF-47
1955 CHI A	26	13	1	0	0	0	0.0	6	0	6	1	2	.077	.077	2	1	OF-17
4 yrs.	196	505	124	14	5	3	0.6	59	43	54	61	11	.246	.311	21	4	OF-164
3 yrs.	71	94	19	1	1	0	0.0	18	5	18	10	7	.202	.234	7	1	OF-52

Matty McIntyre
McINTYRE, MATTHEW W.
B. June 12, 1880, Stonington, Conn. D. Apr. 2, 1920, Detroit, Mich. BL TL

	G	AB	H	2B	3B	HR	HR%	R	RBI	BB	SO	SB	BA	SA	PH AB	PH H	G by POS
1901 PHI A	82	308	85	12	4	0	0.0	38	46	30		11	.276	.341	0	0	OF-82
1904 DET A	152	578	146	11	10	2	0.3	74	46	44		11	.253	.317	0	0	OF-152
1905	131	495	130	21	5	0	0.0	59	30	48		9	.263	.325	0	0	OF-131
1906	133	493	128	19	11	0	0.0	63	39	56		29	.260	.343	0	0	OF-133
1907	20	81	23	1	1	0	0.0	6	9	7		3	.284	.321	0	0	OF-20
1908	151	569	168	24	13	0	0.0	105	28	83		20	.295	.383	0	0	OF-151
1909	125	476	116	18	9	1	0.2	65	34	54		13	.244	.326	2	0	OF-122
1910	83	305	72	15	5	0	0.0	40	25	39		4	.236	.318	6	1	OF-77
1911 CHI A	146	569	184	19	11	1	0.2	102	52	64		17	.323	.401	0	0	OF-146
1912	45	84	14	0	0	0	0.0	10	10	14		3	.167	.167	0	0	OF-45
10 yrs.	1068	3958	1066	140	69	4	0.1	562	319	439		120	.269	.343	8	1	OF-1059
2 yrs.	191	653	198	19	11	1	0.2	112	62	78		20	.303	.371	0	0	OF-191

WORLD SERIES

	G	AB	H	2B	3B	HR	HR%	R	RBI	BB	SO	SB	BA	SA	PH AB	PH H	G by POS
1908 DET A	5	18	4	1	0	0	0.0	2	0	3	2	1	.222	.278	0	0	OF-5
1909	4	3	0	0	0	0	0.0	0	0	0	1	0	.000	.000	3	0	OF-1
2 yrs.	9	21	4	1	0	0	0.0	2	0	3	3	1	.190	.238	3	0	OF-6

Rich McKinney
McKINNEY, CHARLES RICHARD
B. Nov. 22, 1946, Piqua, Ohio BR TR 5'11" 185 lbs.

	G	AB	H	2B	3B	HR	HR%	R	RBI	BB	SO	SB	BA	SA	PH AB	PH H	G by POS
1970 CHI A	43	119	20	5	0	4	3.4	12	17	11	25	3	.168	.311	8	1	3B-23, SS-11
1971	114	369	100	11	2	8	2.2	35	46	35	37	0	.271	.377	19	11	2B-67, OF-25, 3B-5
1972 NY A	37	121	26	2	0	1	0.8	10	7	7	13	1	.215	.256	4	0	3B-33
1973 OAK A	48	65	16	3	0	1	1.5	9	7	7	4	0	.246	.338	19	2	3B-17, 2B-7, DH-6, OF-3
1974	5	7	1	0	0	0	0.0	0	0	0	0	0	.143	.143	3	0	2B-3
1975	8	7	1	0	0	0	0.0	0	2	1	2	0	.143	.143	4	0	DH-2, 1B-1
1977	86	198	35	7	0	6	3.0	13	21	16	43	0	.177	.303	31	6	1B-32, DH-18, 3B-7, OF-5, 2B-3
7 yrs.	341	886	199	28	2	20	2.3	79	100	77	124	4	.225	.328	88	20	3B-85, 2B-80, OF-33, 1B-33, DH-26, SS-11
2 yrs.	157	488	120	16	2	12	2.5	47	63	46	62	3	.246	.361	27	12	2B-67, 3B-28, OF-25, SS-11

Polly McLarry
McLARRY, HOWARD BELL
B. Mar. 25, 1891, Leonard, Tex. D. Nov. 4, 1971, Bonham, Tex. BL TR 6' 185 lbs.

	G	AB	H	2B	3B	HR	HR%	R	RBI	BB	SO	SB	BA	SA	PH AB	PH H	G by POS
1912 CHI A	2	2	0	0	0	0	0.0	0	0			0	.000	.000	2	0	
1915 CHI N	68	127	25	3	0	1	0.8	16	12	14	20	2	.197	.244	21	2	1B-25, 2B-20
2 yrs.	70	129	25	3	0	1	0.8	16	12	14	20	2	.194	.240	23	2	1B-25, 2B-20
1 yr.	2	2	0	0	0	0	0.0	0	0			0	.000	.000	2	0	

Fred McMullin
McMULLIN, FREDERICK WILLIAM
B. Oct. 13, 1891, Scammon, Kans. D. Nov. 21, 1952, Los Angeles, Calif. BR TR 5'11" 170 lbs.

	G	AB	H	2B	3B	HR	HR%	R	RBI	BB	SO	SB	BA	SA	PH AB	PH H	G by POS
1914 DET A	1	1	0	0	0	0	0.0	0	0	0	1	0	.000	.000	0	0	SS-1
1916 CHI A	68	187	48	3	0	0	0.0	8	10	19	30	9	.257	.273	2	1	3B-63, SS-2, 2B-1
1917	59	194	46	2	1	0	0.0	35	12	27	17	9	.237	.258	5	1	3B-52, SS-2
1918	70	235	65	7	0	1	0.4	32	16	25	26	7	.277	.319	0	0	3B-69, 2B-1
1919	60	170	50	8	4	0	0.0	31	19	11	18	4	.294	.388	8	4	3B-46, 2B-5
1920	46	127	25	1	4	0	0.0	14	13	9	13	1	.197	.268	11	1	3B-29, 2B-3, SS-1
6 yrs.	304	914	234	21	9	1	0.1	120	70	91	105	30	.256	.302	26	7	3B-259, 2B-10, SS-6
5 yrs.	303	913	234	21	9	1	0.1	120	70	91	104	30	.256	.302	26	7	3B-259, 2B-10, SS-5

WORLD SERIES

	G	AB	H	2B	3B	HR	HR%	R	RBI	BB	SO	SB	BA	SA	PH AB	PH H	G by POS
1917 CHI A	6	24	3	1	0	0	0.0	2	1		6	0	.125	.167	0	0	3B-6
1919	2	2	1	0	0	0	0.0	0	0		0	0	.500	.500	2	1	
2 yrs.	8	26	4	1	0	0	0.0	2	1		6	0	.154	.192	2	1	3B-6

Eric McNair
McNAIR, DONALD ERIC (Boob)
B. Apr. 12, 1909, Meridian, Miss. D. Mar. 11, 1949, Meridian, Miss. BR TR 5'8" 160 lbs.

	G	AB	H	2B	3B	HR	HR%	R	RBI	BB	SO	SB	BA	SA	PH AB	PH H	G by POS
1929 PHI A	4	8	4	0	0	0	0.0	2	3	0	1		.500	.625	0	0	SS-4
1930	78	237	63	12	2	0	0.0	27	34	9	19	5	.266	.333	7	1	SS-31, 3B-29, 2B-5, OF-1
1931	79	280	76	10	1	5	1.8	41	33	11	19	1	.271	.368	3	1	3B-47, 2B-16, SS-13
1932	135	554	158	47	3	18	3.2	87	95	28	29	8	.285	.478	2	0	SS-133
1933	89	310	81	15	4	7	2.3	57	48	15	32	2	.261	.403	16	5	SS-46, 2B-28
1934	151	599	168	20	4	17	2.8	80	82	35	42	7	.280	.412	0	0	SS-151
1935	137	526	142	22	4	4	0.8	55	57	35	33	3	.270	.342	3	0	SS-121, 3B-11, 1B-2
1936 BOS A	128	494	141	36	2	4	0.8	68	74	27	34	3	.285	.391	0	0	SS-84, 2B-35, 3B-11

Player Register

	G	AB	H	2B	3B	HR	HR%	R	RBI	BB	SO	SB	BA	SA	Pinch Hit AB	H	G by POS

Eric McNair continued
1937	126	455	133	29	4	12	2.6	60	76	30	33	10	.292	.453	9	2	2B-106, SS-9, 3B-4, 1B-1
1938	46	96	15	1	1	0	0.0	9	7	3	6	0	.156	.188	14	2	SS-15, 2B-14, 3B-3
1939 CHI A	129	479	155	18	5	7	1.5	62	82	38	41	17	.324	.426	1	0	3B-103, 2B-19, SS-9
1940	66	251	57	13	1	7	2.8	26	31	12	26	1	.227	.371	0	0	2B-65, 3B-1
1941 DET A	23	59	11	1	0	0	0.0	5	3	4	4	0	.186	.203	9	3	3B-11, SS-3
1942 2 teams		DET A (26G – .162)				PHI A (34G – .243)											
" total	60	171	36	4	0	1	0.6	13	8	14	10	1	.211	.251	8	1	SS-50, 2B-1
14 yrs.	1251	4519	1240	229	29	82	1.8	592	633	261	328	59	.274	.392	72	15	SS-669, 2B-289, 3B-220, 1B-3, OF-1
2 yrs.	195	730	212	31	6	14	1.9	88	113	50	67	18	.290	.407	1	0	3B-104, 2B-84, SS-9
WORLD SERIES																	
1930 PHI A	1	1	0	0	0	0	0.0	0	0	0	0	0	.000	.000	1	0	
1931	2	2	0	0	0	0	0.0	1	0	0	1	0	.000	.000	1	0	2B-1
2 yrs.	3	3	0	0	0	0	0.0	1	0	0	1	0	.000	.000	2	0	2B-1

Jerry McNertney
McNERTNEY, GERALD EDWARD   BR TR 6' 180 lbs.
B. Aug. 7, 1936, Boone, Iowa

	G	AB	H	2B	3B	HR	HR%	R	RBI	BB	SO	SB	BA	SA	PH AB	H	G by POS
1964 CHI A	73	186	40	5	0	3	1.6	16	23	19	24	0	.215	.290	6	0	C-69
1966	44	59	13	0	0	0	0.0	3	1	7	6	1	.220	.220	5	0	C-37
1967	56	123	28	6	0	3	2.4	8	13	6	14	0	.228	.350	1	1	C-52
1968	74	169	37	4	1	3	1.8	18	18	18	29	0	.219	.308	11	3	C-64, 1B-1
1969 SEA A	128	410	99	18	1	8	2.0	39	55	29	63	1	.241	.349	7	3	C-122
1970 MIL A	111	296	72	11	0	6	2.0	27	22	22	33	1	.243	.348	18	4	C-94, 1B-13
1971 STL N	56	128	37	4	2	4	3.1	15	22	12	14	0	.289	.445	16	5	C-36
1972	39	48	10	3	1	0	0.0	3	9	6	16	0	.208	.313	28	4	C-10
1973 PIT N	9	4	1	0	0	0	0.0	0	0	0	0	0	.250	.250	0	0	C-9
9 yrs.	590	1423	337	51	6	27	1.9	129	163	119	199	3	.237	.338	92	20	C-493, 1B-14
4 yrs.	247	537	118	15	1	9	1.7	45	55	50	73	1	.220	.302	23	4	C-222, 1B-1

Sam Mele
MELE, SABATH ANTHONY   BR TR 6'1" 183 lbs.
B. Jan. 21, 1923, Astoria, N. Y.
Manager 1961-67.

	G	AB	H	2B	3B	HR	HR%	R	RBI	BB	SO	SB	BA	SA	PH AB	H	G by POS
1947 BOS A	123	453	137	14	8	12	2.6	71	73	37	35	0	.302	.448	6	3	OF-115, 1B-1
1948	66	180	42	12	1	2	1.1	25	25	13	21	1	.233	.344	9	1	OF-55
1949 2 teams		BOS A (18G – .196)				WAS A (78G – .242)											
" total	96	310	73	13	3	3	1.0	22	32	24	48	4	.235	.326	15	2	OF-74, 1B-11
1950 WAS A	126	435	119	21	6	12	2.8	57	86	51	40	2	.274	.432	10	4	OF-99, 1B-16
1951	143	558	153	36	7	5	0.9	58	94	32	31	2	.274	.391	6	1	OF-124, 1B-15
1952 2 teams		WAS A (9G – .429)				CHI A (123G – .248)											
" total	132	451	117	21	2	16	3.5	49	69	49	42	1	.259	.421	12	2	OF-119, 1B-3
1953 CHI A	140	481	132	26	8	12	2.5	64	82	58	47	3	.274	.437	6	3	OF-138, 1B-2
1954 2 teams		BAL A (72G – .239)				BOS A (42G – .318)											
" total	114	362	97	15	4	12	3.3	39	55	30	38	1	.268	.431	19	7	OF-75, 1B-22
1955 2 teams		BOS A (14G – .129)				CIN N (35G – .210)											
" total	49	93	17	3	0	2	2.2	5	8	5	20	1	.183	.280	25	1	OF-20, 1B-1
1956 CLE A	57	114	29	7	0	4	3.5	17	20	12	20	0	.254	.421	28	8	OF-20, 1B-8
10 yrs.	1046	3437	916	168	39	80	2.3	406	544	311	342	15	.267	.408	136	32	OF-839, 1B-79
2 yrs.	263	904	237	44	10	26	2.9	110	141	106	87	4	.262	.419	16	4	OF-250, 1B-5

Paul Meloan
MELOAN, PAUL (Molly)   BL TR 5'10½" 175 lbs.
B. Aug. 23, 1888, Paynesville, Mo.   D. Feb. 11, 1950, Taft, Calif.

	G	AB	H	2B	3B	HR	HR%	R	RBI	BB	SO	SB	BA	SA	PH AB	H	G by POS
1910 CHI A	65	222	54	6	6	0	0.0	23	23	17		4	.243	.324	0	0	OF-65
1911 2 teams		CHI A (1G – .333)				STL A (64G – .262)											
" total	65	209	55	11	2	3	1.4	30	15	15		7	.263	.378	9	0	OF-55
2 yrs.	130	431	109	17	8	3	0.7	53	38	32		11	.253	.350	9	0	OF-120
2 yrs.	66	225	55	6	6	0	0.0	23	24	17		4	.244	.324	0	0	OF-66

Bill Melton
MELTON, WILLIAM   BR TR 6'2" 200 lbs.
B. July 7, 1945, Gulfport, Miss.

	G	AB	H	2B	3B	HR	HR%	R	RBI	BB	SO	SB	BA	SA	PH AB	H	G by POS
1968 CHI A	34	109	29	8	0	2	1.8	5	16	10	32	1	.266	.394	1	0	3B-33
1969	157	556	142	26	2	23	4.1	67	87	56	106	1	.255	.433	4	1	3B-148, OF-11
1970	141	514	135	15	0	33	6.4	74	96	56	107	2	.263	.488	0	0	OF-71, 3B-70
1971	150	543	146	18	2	33	6.1	72	86	61	87	3	.269	.492	0	0	3B-148
1972	57	208	51	5	0	7	3.4	22	30	23	31	1	.245	.370	1	0	3B-56
1973	152	561	155	29	1	20	3.6	85	87	75	66	4	.276	.439	0	0	3B-151, DH-1
1974	136	495	120	17	0	21	4.2	63	63	59	60	3	.242	.404	0	0	3B-123, DH-11
1975	149	512	123	16	0	15	2.9	62	70	78	106	5	.240	.359	0	0	3B-138, DH-11
1976 CAL A	118	341	71	17	3	6	1.8	31	42	44	53	2	.208	.328	26	7	DH-51, 1B-30, 3B-21
1977 CLE A	50	133	32	11	0	0	0.0	17	14	17	21	1	.241	.323	10	3	1B-15, DH-14, 3B-13
10 yrs.	1144	3972	1004	162	9	160	4.0	498	591	479	669	23	.253	.419	43	11	3B-901, DH-88, OF-82, 1B-45
8 yrs.	976	3498	901	134	6	154	4.4	450	535	418	595	20	.258	.431	7	1	3B-867, OF-82, DH-23
					1st	2nd					2nd						

Lloyd Merriman
MERRIMAN, LLOYD ARCHER (Citation)   BL TL 6' 190 lbs.
B. Aug. 2, 1924, Clovis, Calif.

	G	AB	H	2B	3B	HR	HR%	R	RBI	BB	SO	SB	BA	SA	PH AB	H	G by POS
1949 CIN N	103	287	66	12	5	4	1.4	35	26	21	36	2	.230	.348	11	0	OF-86
1950	92	298	77	15	3	2	0.7	44	31	30	23	6	.258	.349	4	1	OF-84
1951	114	359	87	23	2	5	1.4	34	36	31	34	8	.242	.359	14	4	OF-102
1954	73	112	30	8	1	0	0.0	12	16	23	10	3	.268	.357	38	11	OF-25
1955 2 teams		CHI A (1G – .000)				CHI N (72G – .214)											
" total	73	146	31	6	1	1	0.7	15	8	21	21	1	.212	.288	20	4	OF-49
5 yrs.	455	1202	291	64	12	12	1.0	140	117	126	124	20	.242	.345	87	21	OF-346
1 yr.	1	1	0	0	0	0	0.0	0	0	0	0	0	.000	.000	1	0	

Player Register

	G	AB	H	2B	3B	HR	HR%	R	RBI	BB	SO	SB	BA	SA	Pinch Hit AB	H	G by POS

Sam Mertes
MERTES, SAMUEL BLAIR (Sandow)
B. Aug. 6, 1872, San Francisco, Calif. D. Mar. 11, 1945, San Francisco, Calif. BR TR 5'10" 185 lbs.

Year	Team	Lg	G	AB	H	2B	3B	HR	HR%	R	RBI	BB	SO	SB	BA	SA	PH-AB	PH-H	G by POS
1896	PHI	N	37	143	34	4	4	0	0.0	20	14	8	10	19	.238	.322	1	0	OF-35, SS-1, 2B-1
1898	CHI	N	83	269	80	4	8	1	0.4	45	47	34		27	.297	.383	5	0	OF-60, SS-14, 2B-4, 1B-2
1899			117	426	127	13	16	9	2.1	83	81	33		45	.298	.467	5	1	OF-108, 1B-3, SS-1
1900			127	481	142	25	4	7	1.5	72	60	42		38	.295	.407	0	0	OF-88, 1B-33, SS-7
1901	CHI	A	137	545	151	16	17	5	0.9	94	98	52		46	.277	.396	0	0	2B-132, OF-5
1902			129	497	140	23	7	1	0.2	60	79	37		46	.282	.362	0	0	OF-120, SS-5, C-2, 3B-1, 2B-1, 1B-1, P-1
1903	NY	N	138	517	145	32	14	7	1.4	100	104	61		45	.280	.437	0	0	OF-137, 1B-1, C-1
1904			148	532	147	28	11	4	0.8	83	78	54		47	.276	.393	0	0	OF-147, SS-1
1905			150	551	154	27	17	5	0.9	81	108	56		52	.279	.417	0	0	OF-150
1906	2 teams		NY	N (71G – .237)			STL	N (53G – .246)											
"	total		124	444	107	16	10	1	0.2	57	52	45		31	.241	.329	0	0	OF-124
10 yrs.			1190	4405	1227	188	108	40	0.9	695	721	422	10	396	.279	.398	11	1	OF-974, 2B-138, 1B-40, SS-29, C-3, 3B-1, P-1
2 yrs.			266	1042	291	39	24	6	0.6	154	177	89		92	.279	.380	0	0	2B-133, OF-125, SS-5, C-2, 3B-1, 1B-1, P-1

WORLD SERIES

1905	NY	N	5	17	3	1	0	0	0.0	2	3	2	5	0	.176	.235	0	0	OF-5

Bobby Messenger
MESSENGER, CHARLES WALTER
B. Mar. 19, 1884, Bangor, Me. D. July 10, 1951, Bath, Me. BL TR 5'10½" 165 lbs.

Year	Team	Lg	G	AB	H	2B	3B	HR	HR%	R	RBI	BB	SO	SB	BA	SA	PH-AB	PH-H	G by POS
1909	CHI	A	31	112	19	1	1	0	0.0	18	0	13		7	.170	.196	0	0	OF-31
1910			9	26	6	0	0	0	0.0	7	4	4		3	.231	.308	1	0	OF-9
1911			13	17	2	0	1	0	0.0	4	0	3		0	.118	.235	9	2	OF-4
1914	STL	A	1	2	0	0	0	0	0.0	0	0	0		0	.000	.000	0	0	OF-1
4 yrs.			54	157	27	1	3	0	0.0	29	4	20	0	10	.172	.217	10	2	OF-45
3 yrs.			53	155	27	1	3	0	0.0	29	4	20		10	.174	.219	10	2	OF-44

Catfish Metkovich
METKOVICH, GEORGE MICHAEL
B. Oct. 8, 1921, Angel's Camp, Calif. BL TL 6'1" 185 lbs.

Year	Team	Lg	G	AB	H	2B	3B	HR	HR%	R	RBI	BB	SO	SB	BA	SA	PH-AB	PH-H	G by POS
1943	BOS	A	78	321	79	14	4	5	1.6	34	27	19	38	1	.246	.361	0	0	OF-76, 1B-2
1944			134	549	152	28	8	9	1.6	94	59	31	57	13	.277	.406	2	1	OF-82, 1B-50
1945			138	539	140	26	3	5	0.9	65	62	51	70	19	.260	.347	3	0	1B-97, OF-42
1946			86	281	69	15	2	4	1.4	42	25	36	39	8	.246	.356	3	0	OF-81
1947	CLE	A	126	473	120	22	7	5	1.1	68	40	32	51	5	.254	.362	6	2	OF-119, 1B-1
1949	CHI	A	93	338	80	9	4	5	1.5	50	45	41	24	5	.237	.331	5	1	OF-87
1951	PIT	N	120	423	124	21	3	3	0.7	51	40	28	23	3	.293	.378	13	6	OF-69, 1B-37
1952			125	373	101	18	3	7	1.9	41	41	32	29	5	.271	.391	20	4	1B-72, OF-33
1953	2 teams		PIT	N (26G – .146)			CHI	N (61G – .234)											
"	total		87	165	35	9	1	3	1.8	24	19	22	19	2	.212	.333	33	8	OF-42, 1B-12
1954	MIL	N	68	123	34	5	1	1	0.8	7	15	15	15	0	.276	.358	31	9	1B-18, OF-13
10 yrs.			1055	3585	934	167	36	47	1.3	476	373	307	359	61	.261	.367	116	31	OF-644, 1B-289
1 yr.			93	338	80	9	4	5	1.5	50	45	41	24	5	.237	.331	5	1	OF-87

WORLD SERIES

1946	BOS	A	2	2	1	1	0	0	0.0	1	0	0	0	0	.500	1.000	2	1	

Bill Metzig
METZIG, WILLIAM ANDREW
B. Dec. 4, 1920, Fort Dodge, Iowa BR TR 6'1" 180 lbs.

1944	CHI	A	5	16	2	0	0	0	0.0	1	1	1	4	0	.125	.125	0	0	2B-5

Alex Metzler
METZLER, ALEXANDER
B. Jan. 4, 1903, Fresno, Calif. D. Nov. 30, 1973, Fresno, Calif. BL TR 5'9" 167 lbs.

Year	Team	Lg	G	AB	H	2B	3B	HR	HR%	R	RBI	BB	SO	SB	BA	SA	PH-AB	PH-H	G by POS
1925	CHI	N	9	38	7	2	0	0	0.0	2	2	3	7	0	.184	.237	0	0	OF-9
1926	PHI	A	20	67	16	3	0	0	0.0	8	12	7	5	1	.239	.284	3	1	OF-17
1927	CHI	A	134	543	173	29	11	3	0.6	87	61	61	39	15	.319	.429	0	0	OF-134
1928			139	464	141	18	14	3	0.6	71	55	77	30	16	.304	.422	6	2	OF-134
1929			146	568	156	23	13	2	0.4	80	49	80	45	11	.275	.371	4	0	OF-141
1930	2 teams		CHI	A (56G – .184)			STL	A (56G – .258)											
"	total		112	285	68	10	3	1	0.4	42	28	32	18	5	.239	.305	24	4	OF-83
6 yrs.			560	1965	561	85	41	9	0.5	290	207	260	144	48	.285	.384	37	7	OF-518
4 yrs.			475	1651	484	74	38	8	0.5	250	170	229	120	42	.293	.399	34	6	OF-436

Billy Meyer
MEYER, WILLIAM ADAM
B. Jan. 14, 1892, Knoxville, Tenn. D. Mar. 31, 1957, Knoxville, Tenn. BR TR 5'9½" 170 lbs.
Manager 1948-52.

Year	Team	Lg	G	AB	H	2B	3B	HR	HR%	R	RBI	BB	SO	SB	BA	SA	PH-AB	PH-H	G by POS
1913	CHI	A	1	1	1	0	0	0	0.0	0	0	0	0	0	1.000	1.000	0	0	C-1
1916	PHI	A	50	138	32	2	2	1	0.7	6	12	8	11	3	.232	.297	2	0	C-48
1917			62	162	38	5	1	0	0.0	9	9	7	14	0	.235	.278	7	0	C-55
3 yrs.			113	301	71	7	3	1	0.3	15	21	15	25	3	.236	.289	9	0	C-104
1 yr.			1	1	1	0	0	0	0.0	0	0	0	0	0	1.000	1.000	0	0	C-1

George Meyer
MEYER, GEORGE FRANCIS
B. Aug. 22, 1912, Chicago, Ill. BR TR 5'11" 165 lbs.

1938	CHI	A	24	81	24	2	2	0	0.0	10	9	11	17	3	.296	.370	0	0	2B-24

Cass Michaels
MICHAELS, CASIMIR EUGENE
Born Casimir Eugene Kwietniewski.
B. Mar. 4, 1926, Detroit, Mich. D. Nov. 12, 1982, Grosse Point, Mich. BR TR 5'11" 175 lbs.

Year	Team	Lg	G	AB	H	2B	3B	HR	HR%	R	RBI	BB	SO	SB	BA	SA	PH-AB	PH-H	G by POS
1943	CHI	A	2	7	0	0	0	0	0.0	0	0	0	0	0	.000	.000	0	0	3B-2
1944			27	68	12	4	1	0	0.0	4	5	2	5	0	.176	.265	1	0	SS-21, 3B-3
1945			129	445	109	8	5	2	0.4	47	54	37	28	8	.245	.299	2	0	SS-126, 2B-1
1946			91	291	75	8	0	1	0.3	37	22	29	36	9	.258	.296	3	0	2B-66, 3B-13, SS-6
1947			110	355	97	15	4	3	0.8	31	34	39	28	10	.273	.363	3	0	2B-60, 3B-44, SS-2
1948			145	484	120	12	6	5	1.0	47	56	69	42	8	.248	.329	4	2	SS-85, 2B-55, OF-1
1949			154	561	173	27	9	6	1.1	73	83	101	50	5	.308	.421	0	0	2B-154

	G	AB	H	2B	3B	HR	HR%	R	RBI	BB	SO	SB	BA	SA	Pinch Hit AB	H	G by POS

Cass Michaels continued

	G	AB	H	2B	3B	HR	HR%	R	RBI	BB	SO	SB	BA	SA	PH AB	PH H	G by POS
1950 2 teams	CHI A (36G – .312)					WAS A (106G – .250)											
" total	142	526	140	14	7	8	1.5	69	66	68	47	2	.266	.365	3	2	2B-139
1951 WAS A	138	485	125	20	4	4	0.8	59	45	61	41	1	.258	.340	7	2	2B-128
1952 3 teams	WAS A (22G – .233)					STL A (55G – .265)					PHI A (55G – .250)							
" total	132	452	114	16	8	5	1.1	53	50	53	42	4	.252	.356	6	2	2B-85, 3B-42
1953 PHI A	117	411	103	10	0	12	2.9	53	42	51	56	7	.251	.363	6	2	2B-110
1954 CHI A	101	282	74	13	2	7	2.5	35	44	56	31	10	.262	.397	7	0	3B-91, 2B-2
12 yrs.	1288	4367	1142	147	46	53	1.2	508	501	566	406	64	.262	.353	42	10	2B-800, SS-240, 3B-195, OF-1
9 yrs.	795	2631	703	93	30	28	1.1	295	317	346	228	50	.267	.357	21	3	2B-373, SS-240, 3B-153, OF-1

Minnie Minoso
MINOSO, SATURNINO ORESTES ARRIETA ARMAS
B. Nov. 29, 1922, Havana, Cuba
BR TR 5'10" 175 lbs.

	G	AB	H	2B	3B	HR	HR%	R	RBI	BB	SO	SB	BA	SA	PH AB	PH H	G by POS
1949 CLE A	9	16	3	0	0	1	6.3	2	1	2	2	0	.188	.375	1	0	OF-7
1951 2 teams	CLE A (8G – .429)					CHI A (138G – .324)											
" total	146	530	173	34	14	10	1.9	112	76	72	42	31	.326	.500	2	0	OF-82, 3B-68, 1B-7, SS-1
1952 CHI A	147	569	160	24	9	13	2.3	96	61	71	46	22	.281	.424	0	0	OF-143, 3B-9, SS-1
1953	157	556	174	24	8	15	2.7	104	104	74	43	25	.313	.466	0	0	OF-147, 3B-10
1954	153	568	182	29	18	19	3.3	119	116	77	46	18	.320	.535	0	0	OF-146, 3B-9
1955	139	517	149	26	7	10	1.9	79	70	76	43	19	.288	.424	1	0	OF-138, 3B-2
1956	151	545	172	29	11	21	3.9	106	88	86	40	12	.316	.525	3	1	OF-148, 3B-8, 1B-1
1957	153	568	176	36	5	12	2.1	96	103	79	54	18	.310	.454	0	0	OF-152, 3B-1
1958 CLE A	149	556	168	25	2	24	4.3	94	80	59	53	14	.302	.484	3	1	OF-147, 3B-1
1959	148	570	172	32	0	21	3.7	92	92	54	46	8	.302	.468	0	0	OF-148
1960 CHI A	154	591	184	32	4	20	3.4	89	105	52	63	17	.311	.481	0	0	OF-154
1961	152	540	151	28	3	14	2.6	91	82	67	46	9	.280	.420	1	1	OF-147
1962 STL N	39	97	19	5	0	1	1.0	14	10	7	17	4	.196	.278	6	0	OF-27
1963 WAS A	109	315	72	12	2	4	1.3	38	30	33	38	8	.229	.317	26	4	OF-74, 3B-8
1964 CHI A	30	31	7	0	0	1	3.2	4	5	5	3	0	.226	.323	22	4	OF-5
1976	3	8	1	0	0	0	0.0	0	0	0	2	0	.125	.125	0	0	DH-3
1980	2	2	0	0	0	0	0.0	0	0	0	0	0	.000	.000	2	0	
17 yrs.	1841	6579	1963	336	83	186	2.8	1136	1023	814	584	205	.298	.459	67	11	OF-1665, 3B-116, 1B-8, DH-3, SS-2
12 yrs.	1379	5011	1523	260	79	135	2.7	893	808	658	427	171	.304	.468	30	6	OF-1262, 3B-107, DH-3, SS-2, 1B-1
	6th	6th	5th	4th	6th	2nd	10th	4th	2nd	3rd	9th	10th		6th			

Willie Miranda
MIRANDA, GUILLERMO PEREZ
B. May 24, 1926, Velasco, Cuba
BB TR 5'9½" 150 lbs.

	G	AB	H	2B	3B	HR	HR%	R	RBI	BB	SO	SB	BA	SA	PH AB	PH H	G by POS
1951 WAS A	7	9	4	0	0	0	0.0	2	0	0	0	0	.444	.444	2	2	SS-2, 1B-1
1952 3 teams	CHI A (12G – .250)					STL A (7G – .091)					CHI A (58G – .218)							
" total	77	161	34	4	2	0	0.0	16	8	16	15	1	.211	.261	1	0	SS-61, 3B-5, 2B-2
1953 2 teams	STL A (17G – .167)					NY A (48G – .224)											
" total	65	64	14	0	0	1	1.6	14	5	6	11	2	.219	.266	0	0	SS-53, 3B-6
1954 NY A	92	116	29	4	2	1	0.9	12	12	10	10	0	.250	.345	1	0	SS-88, 2B-4, 3B-1
1955 BAL A	153	487	124	12	6	1	0.2	42	38	42	58	4	.255	.310	0	0	SS-153, 2B-1
1956	148	461	100	16	4	2	0.4	38	34	46	73	3	.217	.282	0	0	SS-147
1957	115	314	61	3	0	0	0.0	29	20	24	42	2	.194	.204	0	0	SS-115
1958	102	214	43	6	0	1	0.5	15	8	14	25	1	.201	.243	0	0	SS-102
1959	65	88	14	5	0	0	0.0	8	7	7	16	0	.159	.216	0	0	SS-47, 3B-11, 2B-5
9 yrs.	824	1914	423	50	14	6	0.3	176	132	165	250	13	.221	.271	4	2	SS-768, 3B-23, 2B-12, 1B-1
2 yrs.	70	150	33	4	1	0	0.0	14	7	13	14	1	.220	.260	1	0	SS-54, 3B-5, 2B-2

Bob Molinaro
MOLINARO, ROBERT JOSEPH
B. May 21, 1950, Newark, N. J.
BL TR 6' 190 lbs.

	G	AB	H	2B	3B	HR	HR%	R	RBI	BB	SO	SB	BA	SA	PH AB	PH H	G by POS
1975 DET A	6	19	5	0	1	0	0.0	2	1	1	0	0	.263	.368	0	0	OF-6
1977 2 teams	DET A (4G – .250)					CHI A (1G – .500)											
" total	5	6	2	1	0	0	0.0	0	0	0	3	1	.333	.500	4	1	OF-1
1978 CHI A	105	286	75	5	5	6	2.1	39	27	19	12	22	.262	.378	12	4	OF-62, DH-32
1979 BAL A	8	6	0	0	0	0	0.0	0	0	1	3	1	.000	.000	1	0	OF-5
1980 CHI A	119	344	100	16	4	5	1.5	48	36	26	29	18	.291	.404	21	7	OF-49, DH-47
1981	47	42	11	1	1	1	2.4	7	9	8	1	1	.262	.405	35	9	DH-4, OF-2
1982 2 teams	CHI N (65G – .197)					PHI N (19G – .286)											
" total	84	80	17	1	0	1	1.3	6	14	9	6	2	.213	.263	67	14	OF-4
1983 2 teams	PHI N (19G – .111)					DET A (8G – .000)											
" total	27	20	2	1	0	0	5.0	4	3	1	3	1	.100	.300	20	2	DH-1
8 yrs.	401	803	212	25	11	14	1.7	106	90	65	57	46	.264	.375	160	37	OF-129, DH-84
4 yrs.	272	674	187	22	10	12	1.8	94	72	53	43	42	.277	.393	68	20	OF-114, DH-83

Jim Moore
MOORE, JAMES WILLIAM
B. Apr. 24, 1903, Paris, Tenn.
BR TR 6'½" 187 lbs.

	G	AB	H	2B	3B	HR	HR%	R	RBI	BB	SO	SB	BA	SA	PH AB	PH H	G by POS
1930 2 teams	CHI A (16G – .205)					PHI A (15G – .380)											
" total	31	89	27	5	0	2	2.2	14	14	8	7	1	.303	.427	9	4	OF-22
1931 PHI A	49	143	32	5	1	2	1.4	18	21	11	13	0	.224	.315	11	0	OF-36
2 yrs.	80	232	59	10	1	4	1.7	32	35	19	20	1	.254	.358	20	4	OF-58
1 yr.	16	39	8	2	0	0	0.0	4	2	6	3	0	.205	.256	5	2	OF-9
WORLD SERIES																	
1930 PHI A	3	3	1	0	0	0	0.0	0	0	1	1	0	.333	.333	1	1	OF-1

Player Register

	G	AB	H	2B	3B	HR	HR%	R	RBI	BB	SO	SB	BA	SA	Pinch Hit AB	H	G by POS

Jim Moore continued
| 1931 | 2 | 3 | 1 | 0 | 0 | 0 | 0.0 | 0 | 0 | 0 | 1 | 0 | .333 | .333 | 1 | 0 | OF-1 |
| 2 yrs. | 5 | 6 | 2 | 0 | 0 | 0 | 0.0 | 0 | 0 | 1 | 2 | 0 | .333 | .333 | 2 | 1 | OF-2 |

Junior Moore
MOORE, ALVIN EARL
B. Jan. 25, 1953, Waskom, Tex.   BR TR 5'11" 185 lbs.

1976 ATL N	20	26	7	1	0	0	0.0	1	2	4	4	0	.269	.308	12	4	3B-6, OF-1, 2B-1
1977	112	361	94	9	3	5	1.4	41	34	33	29	4	.260	.343	10	3	3B-104, 2B-1
1978 CHI A	24	65	19	0	1	0	0.0	8	4	6	7	1	.292	.323	5	2	DH-12, 3B-6, OF-5
1979	88	201	53	6	2	1	0.5	24	23	12	20	0	.264	.328	25	6	OF-61, DH-10, 2B-2
1980	45	121	31	4	1	1	0.8	9	10	7	11	0	.256	.331	4	2	3B-34, OF-3, DH-2, 1B-1
5 yrs.	289	774	204	20	7	7	0.9	83	73	62	71	5	.264	.335	56	17	3B-150, OF-70, DH-24, 2B-4, 1B-1
3 yrs.	157	387	103	10	4	2	0.5	41	37	25	38	1	.266	.328	34	10	OF-69, 3B-40, DH-24, 2B-2, 1B-1

Randy Moore
MOORE, RANDOLPH EDWARD
B. June 21, 1905, Naples, Tex.   BL TR 6' 185 lbs.

1927 CHI A	6	15	0	0	0	0	0.0	0	0	0	2	0	.000	.000	2	0	OF-4
1928	24	61	13	4	1	0	0.0	6	5	3	5	0	.213	.311	6	2	OF-16
1930 BOS N	83	191	55	9	0	2	1.0	24	34	10	13	3	.288	.366	30	6	OF-34, 3B-13
1931	83	192	50	8	1	3	1.6	19	34	13	3	1	.260	.359	32	6	OF-29, 3B-22, 2B-1
1932	107	351	103	21	2	3	0.9	41	43	15	11	1	.293	.390	14	4	OF-41, 3B-31, 1B-22, C-1
1933	135	497	150	23	7	8	1.6	64	70	40	16	3	.302	.425	6	1	OF-122, 1B-10
1934	123	422	120	21	2	7	1.7	55	64	40	16	2	.284	.393	13	5	OF-72, 1B-37
1935	125	407	112	20	4	4	1.0	42	42	26	16	1	.275	.373	23	5	OF-78, 1B-21
1936 BKN N	42	88	21	3	0	0	0.0	4	14	8	1	0	.239	.273	18	7	OF-21
1937 2 teams	BKN N (13G – .136)					STL N (8G – .000)											
" total	21	29	3	1	0	0	0.0	3	2	3	2	0	.103	.138	9	0	C-10, OF-1
10 yrs.	749	2253	627	110	17	27	1.2	258	308	158	85	11	.278	.378	153	36	OF-418, 1B-90, 3B-66, C-11, 2B-1
2 yrs.	30	76	13	4	1	0	0.0	6	5	3	7	0	.171	.250	8	2	OF-20

Rich Morales
MORALES, RICHARD ANGELO
B. Sept. 20, 1943, San Francisco, Calif.   BR TR 5'11" 170 lbs.

1967 CHI A	8	10	0	0	0	0	0.0	0	0	0	2	0	.000	.000	0	0	SS-7
1968	10	29	5	0	0	0	0.0	2	0	2	5	0	.172	.172	0	0	SS-7, 2B-5
1969	55	121	26	0	1	0	0.0	12	6	7	18	1	.215	.231	3	1	2B-38, SS-13, 3B-1
1970	62	112	18	2	0	1	0.9	6	2	9	16	1	.161	.205	9	1	SS-24, 3B-20, 2B-12
1971	84	185	45	8	0	2	1.1	19	14	22	26	2	.243	.319	12	3	SS-57, 3B-18, 2B-3, OF-1
1972	110	287	59	7	1	2	0.7	24	20	19	49	2	.206	.258	5	1	SS-86, 2B-16, 3B-14
1973 2 teams	CHI A (7G – .000)				SD N (90G – .164)												
" total	97	248	40	6	1	0	0.0	10	17	28	37	0	.161	.194	2	0	2B-81, SS-10, 3B-5
1974 SD N	54	61	12	3	0	1	1.6	8	5	8	6	1	.197	.295	2	1	SS-29, 2B-18, 3B-6, 1B-1
8 yrs.	480	1053	205	26	3	6	0.6	81	64	95	159	7	.195	.242	33	7	SS-233, 2B-173, 3B-64, OF-1, 1B-1
7 yrs.	336	748	153	17	2	5	0.7	64	43	60	117	6	.205	.253	29	6	SS-194, 2B-76, 3B-58, OF-1

Ray Morehart
MOREHART, RAYMOND ANDERSON
B. Dec. 2, 1899, Abner, Tex.   BL TR 5'9" 157 lbs.

1924 CHI A	31	100	20	4	2	0	0.0	10	8	17	7	3	.200	.280	2	0	SS-27, 2B-2
1926	73	192	61	10	3	0	0.0	27	21	11	15	3	.318	.401	17	6	2B-48
1927 NY A	73	195	50	7	2	1	0.5	45	20	29	18	4	.256	.328	14	2	2B-53
3 yrs.	177	487	131	21	7	1	0.2	82	49	57	40	10	.269	.347	33	8	2B-103, SS-27
2 yrs.	104	292	81	14	5	0	0.0	37	29	28	22	6	.277	.360	19	6	2B-50, SS-27

George Moriarty
MORIARTY, GEORGE JOSEPH
Brother of Bill Moriarty.
B. July 7, 1884, Chicago, Ill.   D. Apr. 8, 1964, Miami, Fla.
Manager 1927-28.   BR TR 6' 185 lbs.

1903 CHI N	1	5	0	0	0	0	0.0	1	0	0		0	.000	.000	0	0	3B-1
1904	4	13	0	0	0	0	0.0	0	0	1		0	.000	.000	0	0	OF-2, 3B-2
1906 NY A	65	197	46	7	7	0	0.0	22	23	17		8	.234	.340	4	1	3B-39, OF-15, 1B-5, 2B-1
1907	126	437	121	16	5	0	0.0	51	43	25		28	.277	.336	1	0	3B-75, 1B-22, OF-9, 2B-8, SS-1
1908	101	348	82	12	1	0	0.0	25	27	11		22	.236	.276	8	2	1B-52, 3B-28, OF-10, 2B-4
1909 DET A	133	473	129	20	4	1	0.2	43	39	24		34	.273	.338	3	1	3B-106, 1B-24
1910	136	490	123	24	3	2	0.4	53	60	33		33	.251	.324	1	0	3B-134
1911	130	478	116	20	4	1	0.2	51	60	27		28	.243	.308	0	0	3B-129, 1B-1
1912	105	375	93	23	1	0	0.0	38	54	26		27	.248	.315	1	1	1B-71, 3B-33
1913	102	347	83	5	2	0	0.0	29	30	24	25	23	.239	.265	0	0	3B-93, OF-7
1914	130	465	118	19	5	1	0.2	56	40	39	27	34	.254	.323	0	0	3B-126, 1B-3
1915	31	38	8	1	0	0	0.0	2	0	5	7	1	.211	.237	10	2	3B-12, OF-1, 2B-1, 1B-1
1916 CHI A	7	5	1	0	0	0	0.0	1	0	2	0	0	.200	.200	3	1	3B-1, 1B-1
13 yrs.	1071	3671	920	147	32	5	0.1	372	376	234	59	248	.251	.312	31	8	3B-779, 1B-180, OF-44, 2B-14, SS-1
1 yr.	7	5	1	0	0	0	0.0	1	0	2	0	0	.200	.200	3	1	3B-1, 1B-1

WORLD SERIES
| 1909 DET A | 7 | 22 | 6 | 1 | 0 | 0 | 0.0 | 4 | 1 | 3 | 1 | 0 | .273 | .318 | 0 | 0 | 3B-7 |

Bugs Morris
Playing record listed under Bugs Bennett

295 Player Register

	G	AB	H	2B	3B	HR	HR %	R	RBI	BB	SO	SB	BA	SA	Pinch Hit AB	Pinch Hit H	G by POS

Jim Morrison
MORRISON, JAMES FORREST
B. Sept. 23, 1952, Pensacola, Fla.   BR TR 5'11" 175 lbs.

	G	AB	H	2B	3B	HR	HR%	R	RBI	BB	SO	SB	BA	SA	PH AB	PH H	G by POS
1977 PHI N	5	7	3	0	0	0	0.0	3	1	1	1	0	.429	.429	0	0	3B-5
1978	53	108	17	1	1	3	2.8	12	10	10	21	1	.157	.269	12	0	2B-31, 3B-3, OF-1
1979 CHI A	67	240	66	14	0	14	5.8	38	35	15	48	11	.275	.508	4	0	2B-48, 3B-29
1980	162	604	171	40	0	15	2.5	66	57	36	74	9	.283	.424	0	0	2B-161, DH-1, SS-1
1981	90	290	68	8	1	10	3.4	27	34	10	29	3	.234	.372	2	0	3B-87, DH-1, 2B-1
1982 2 teams	CHI A (51G – .223)			PIT N (44G – .279)													
" total	95	252	61	11	4	11	4.4	27	34	18	29	2	.242	.448	16	3	3B-76, OF-2, DH-1, SS-1, 2B-1
1983 PIT N	66	158	48	7	2	6	3.8	16	25	9	25	2	.304	.487	15	4	2B-28, 3B-25, SS-7
7 yrs.	538	1659	434	81	8	59	3.6	189	196	99	227	28	.262	.427	49	7	2B-270, 3B-225, SS-9, DH-3, OF-3
4 yrs.	370	1300	342	69	4	46	3.5	148	145	74	166	23	.263	.428	6	0	2B-210, 3B-166, DH-3, SS-1

LEAGUE CHAMPIONSHIP SERIES
| 1978 PHI N | 1 | 1 | 0 | 0 | 0 | 0 | 0.0 | 0 | 0 | 0 | 1 | 0 | .000 | .000 | 1 | 0 | |

Jo-Jo Morrissey
MORRISSEY, JOSEPH ANSELM
B. Jan. 16, 1904, Warren, R.I.   D. May 2, 1950, Worcester, Mass.   BR TR 6'1½" 178 lbs.

	G	AB	H	2B	3B	HR	HR%	R	RBI	BB	SO	SB	BA	SA	PH AB	PH H	G by POS
1932 CIN N	89	269	65	10	1	0	0.0	15	13	14	15	2	.242	.286	1	0	SS-45, 2B-42, 3B-12, OF-1
1933	148	534	123	20	0	0	0.0	43	26	20	22	5	.230	.268	1	1	2B-88, SS-63, 3B-15
1936 CHI A	17	38	7	1	0	0	0.0	3	6	2	3	0	.184	.211	4	2	3B-9, SS-4, 2B-1
3 yrs.	254	841	195	31	1	0	0.0	61	45	36	40	7	.232	.271	6	3	2B-131, SS-112, 3B-36, OF-1
1 yr.	17	38	7	1	0	0	0.0	3	6	2	3	0	.184	.211	4	2	3B-9, SS-4, 2B-1

Gerry Moses
MOSES, GERALD BRAHEEN
B. Aug. 9, 1946, Yazoo City, Miss.   BR TR 6'3" 210 lbs.

	G	AB	H	2B	3B	HR	HR%	R	RBI	BB	SO	SB	BA	SA	PH AB	PH H	G by POS
1965 BOS A	4	4	1	0	0	1	25.0	1	1	0	2	0	.250	1.000	4	1	
1968	6	18	6	0	0	2	11.1	2	4	1	4	0	.333	.667	0	0	C-6
1969	53	135	41	9	1	4	3.0	13	17	5	23	0	.304	.474	17	2	C-36
1970	92	315	83	18	1	6	1.9	26	35	21	45	1	.263	.384	5	2	C-88, OF-1
1971 CAL A	69	181	41	8	2	4	2.2	12	15	10	34	0	.227	.359	8	0	C-63, OF-1
1972 CLE A	52	141	31	3	0	4	2.8	9	14	11	29	0	.220	.326	10	2	C-39, 1B-3
1973 NY A	20	59	15	2	0	0	0.0	5	3	2	6	0	.254	.288	3	1	C-17, DH-1
1974 DET A	74	198	47	6	3	4	2.0	19	19	11	38	0	.237	.359	1	0	C-74
1975 2 teams	CHI A (2G – .500)			SD N (13G – .158)													
" total	15	21	4	2	1	0	0.0	2	1	2	3	0	.190	.381	6	1	C-5, DH-1, 1B-1
9 yrs.	385	1072	269	48	8	25	2.3	89	109	63	184	1	.251	.381	54	9	C-328, 1B-4, DH-2, OF-2
1 yr.	2	2	1	0	1	0	0.0	0	0	0	0	0	.500	1.500	0	0	DH-1, 1B-1

Wally Moses
MOSES, WALLACE
B. Oct. 8, 1910, Uvalda, Ga.   BL TL 5'10" 160 lbs.

	G	AB	H	2B	3B	HR	HR%	R	RBI	BB	SO	SB	BA	SA	PH AB	PH H	G by POS
1935 PHI A	85	345	112	21	3	5	1.4	60	35	25	18	3	.325	.446	6	4	OF-80
1936	146	585	202	35	11	7	1.2	98	66	62	32	12	.345	.479	2	0	OF-144
1937	154	649	208	48	13	25	3.9	113	86	54	38	9	.320	.550	0	0	OF-154
1938	142	589	181	29	8	8	1.4	86	49	58	31	15	.307	.424	3	1	OF-139
1939	115	437	134	28	7	3	0.7	68	33	44	23	7	.307	.423	11	2	OF-103
1940	142	537	166	41	9	9	1.7	90	51	75	44	6	.309	.469	8	1	OF-133
1941	116	438	132	31	4	4	0.9	78	35	62	27	3	.301	.418	6	1	OF-109
1942 CHI A	146	577	156	28	4	7	1.2	73	49	74	27	16	.270	.369	1	0	OF-145
1943	150	599	147	22	12	3	0.5	82	48	55	47	56	.245	.337	2	0	OF-148
1944	136	535	150	26	9	3	0.6	82	34	52	22	21	.280	.379	1	0	OF-134
1945	140	569	168	35	15	2	0.4	79	50	69	33	11	.295	.420	1	0	OF-139
1946 2 teams	CHI A (56G – .274)			BOS A (48G – .206)													
" total	104	343	82	20	4	6	1.7	33	33	31	35	4	.239	.373	24	4	OF-80
1947 BOS A	90	255	70	18	2	2	0.8	32	27	27	16	3	.275	.384	29	5	OF-58
1948	78	189	49	12	1	2	1.1	26	29	21	19	5	.259	.365	27	6	OF-45
1949 PHI A	110	308	85	19	3	1	0.3	49	25	51	19	1	.276	.367	17	5	OF-92
1950	88	265	70	16	5	2	0.8	47	21	40	17	0	.264	.385	21	4	OF-62
1951	70	136	26	6	0	0	0.0	17	9	21	9	2	.191	.235	34	4	OF-27
17 yrs.	2012	7356	2138	435	110	89	1.2	1114	679	821	457	174	.291	.416	193	37	OF-1792
5 yrs.	628	2448	667	120	41	19	0.8	336	197	267	149	106	.272	.378	25	4	OF-602

WORLD SERIES
| 1946 BOS A | 4 | 12 | 5 | 0 | 0 | 0 | 0.0 | 1 | 0 | 1 | 2 | 0 | .417 | .417 | 0 | 0 | OF-4 |

Les Moss
MOSS, JOHN LESTER
B. May 14, 1925, Tulsa, Okla.   BR TR 5'11" 205 lbs.
Manager 1968, 1979

	G	AB	H	2B	3B	HR	HR%	R	RBI	BB	SO	SB	BA	SA	PH AB	PH H	G by POS
1946 STL A	12	35	13	3	0	0	0.0	4	5	3	5	1	.371	.457	0	0	C-12
1947	96	274	43	5	2	6	2.2	17	27	35	48	0	.157	.255	1	0	C-96
1948	107	335	86	12	1	14	4.2	35	46	39	50	0	.257	.424	5	0	C-103
1949	97	278	81	11	0	10	3.6	28	39	49	32	0	.291	.439	2	0	C-83
1950	84	222	59	6	0	8	3.6	24	34	26	32	0	.266	.401	19	5	C-60
1951 2 teams	STL A (16G – .170)			BOS A (71G – .198)													
" total	87	249	48	8	0	4	1.6	23	33	31	42	1	.193	.273	6	0	C-81
1952 STL A	52	118	29	3	0	3	2.5	11	12	15	13	0	.246	.347	13	4	C-39
1953	78	239	66	14	1	2	0.8	21	28	18	31	0	.276	.368	6	0	C-71
1954 BAL A	50	126	31	3	0	0	0.0	7	5	14	16	0	.246	.270	12	2	C-38
1955 2 teams	BAL A (29G – .339)			CHI A (32G – .254)													
" total	61	115	34	3	0	4	3.5	10	13	13	14	0	.296	.426	12	2	C-49
1956 CHI A	56	127	31	4	0	10	7.9	20	22	18	15	0	.244	.512	8	1	C-49
1957	42	115	31	3	0	2	1.7	10	20	18	10	0	.270	.348	4	2	C-39

Player Register   296

	G	AB	H	2B	3B	HR	HR%	R	RBI	BB	SO	SB	BA	SA	Pinch Hit AB H	G by POS

Les Moss continued
1958	2	1	0	0	0	0	0.0	0	0	1	0	0	.000	.000	1 0	
13 yrs.	824	2234	552	75	4	63	2.8	210	276	282	316	2	.247	.369	99 18	C-720
4 yrs.	132	302	77	9	0	14	4.6	35	41	45	43	0	.255	.424	14 3	C-121

Johnny Mostil
MOSTIL, JOHN ANTHONY   BR TR 5'8½" 168 lbs.
B. June 1, 1896, Chicago, Ill.   D. Dec. 10, 1970, Midlothian, Ill.

1918 CHI A	10	33	9	2	0	0	0.0	4	4	1	6	1	.273	.455	0 0	2B-9
1921	100	326	98	21	7	3	0.9	43	42	28	35	10	.301	.436	5 2	OF-91, 2B-1
1922	132	458	139	28	14	7	1.5	74	70	38	39	14	.303	.472	9 4	OF-132
1923	153	546	159	37	15	3	0.5	91	64	62	51	41	.291	.430	4 0	OF-143, 3B-6, SS-1
1924	118	385	125	22	5	4	1.0	75	49	45	41	7	.325	.439	14 5	OF-102
1925	153	605	181	36	16	2	0.3	135	50	90	52	43	.299	.421	0 0	OF-153
1926	148	600	197	41	15	4	0.7	120	42	79	55	35	.328	.467	0 0	OF-147
1927	13	16	2	0	0	0	0.0	3	1	0	1	1	.125	.125	1 0	OF-6
1928	133	503	136	19	8	0	0.0	69	51	66	54	23	.270	.340	2 0	OF-131
1929	12	35	8	3	0	0	0.0	4	3	6	2	1	.229	.314	0 0	OF-11
10 yrs.	972	3507	1054	209	82	23	0.7	618	376	415	336	176	.301	.427	35 11	OF-916, 2B-10, 3B-6, SS-1
10 yrs.	972	3507	1054	209	82	23	0.7	618	376	415	336	176	.301	.427	35 11	OF-916, 2B-10, 3B-6, SS-1
				9th	5th			8th				7th				

Bill Mueller
MUELLER, WILLIAM LAWRENCE (Hawk)   BR TR 6'1½" 180 lbs.
B. Nov. 9, 1920, Bay City, Mich.

1942 CHI A	26	85	14	1	0	0	0.0	5	5	12	9	2	.165	.176	1 0	OF-26
1945	13	9	0	0	0	0	0.0	3	0	2	1	1	.000	.000	1 0	OF-7
2 yrs.	39	94	14	1	0	0	0.0	8	5	14	10	3	.149	.160	2 0	OF-33
2 yrs.	39	94	14	1	0	0	0.0	8	5	14	10	3	.149	.160	2 0	OF-33

Don Mueller
MUELLER, DONALD FREDERICK (Mandrake the Magician)   BL TR 6' 185 lbs.
Son of Walter Mueller.
B. Apr. 14, 1927, St. Louis, Mo.

1948 NY N	36	81	29	4	1	1	1.2	12	9	0	3	0	.358	.469	14 6	OF-22
1949	51	56	13	4	0	0	0.0	5	1	5	6	0	.232	.304	42 7	OF-6
1950	132	525	153	15	6	7	1.3	60	84	10	26	1	.291	.383	6 2	OF-125
1951	122	469	130	10	7	16	3.4	58	69	19	13	1	.277	.431	7 1	OF-115
1952	126	456	128	14	7	12	2.6	61	49	34	24	2	.281	.421	4 0	OF-120
1953	131	480	160	12	2	6	1.3	56	60	19	13	2	.333	.404	8 4	OF-122
1954	153	619	212	35	8	4	0.6	90	71	22	17	2	.342	.444	1 1	OF-153
1955	147	605	185	21	4	8	1.3	67	83	19	12	1	.306	.393	1 1	OF-146
1956	138	453	122	12	1	5	1.1	38	41	15	7	0	.269	.333	21 5	OF-117
1957	135	450	116	7	1	6	1.3	45	37	13	16	2	.258	.318	23 6	OF-115
1958 CHI A	70	166	42	5	0	0	0.0	7	16	11	9	0	.253	.283	26 9	OF-43
1959	4	4	2	0	0	0	0.0	0	0	0	0	0	.500	.500	4 2	
12 yrs.	1245	4364	1292	139	37	65	1.5	499	520	167	146	11	.296	.390	157 44	OF-1084
2 yrs.	74	170	44	5	0	0	0.0	7	16	11	9	0	.259	.288	30 11	OF-43

WORLD SERIES
| 1954 NY N | 4 | 18 | 7 | 0 | 0 | 0 | 0.0 | 4 | 1 | 0 | 1 | 0 | .389 | .389 | 0 0 | OF-4 |

Greg Mulleavy
MULLEAVY, GREGORY THOMAS (Moe)   BR TR 5'9" 167 lbs.
B. Sept. 25, 1905, Detroit, Mich.   D. Feb. 1, 1980, Arcadia, Calif.

1930 CHI A	77	289	76	14	5	0	0.0	27	28	20	23	5	.263	.346	4 1	SS-73
1932	1	3	0	0	0	0	0.0	0	0	0	0	0	.000	.000	0 0	2B-1
1933 BOS A	1	0	0	0	0	0	—	1	0	0	0	0	—	—	0 0	
3 yrs.	79	292	76	14	5	0	0.0	28	28	20	23	5	.260	.342	4 1	SS-73, 2B-1
2 yrs.	78	292	76	14	5	0	0.0	27	28	20	23	5	.260	.342	4 1	SS-73, 2B-1

Charlie Mullen
MULLEN, CHARLES GEORGE   BR TR 5'10½" 155 lbs.
B. Mar. 15, 1889, Seattle, Wash.   D. June 6, 1963, Seattle, Wash.

1910 CHI A	41	123	24	2	1	0	0.0	15	13	4		4	.195	.228	1 1	1B-37, OF-2
1911	20	59	12	2	1	0	0.0	7	5	5		1	.203	.271	0 0	1B-20
1914 NY A	93	323	84	8	0	0	0.0	33	44	33	55	11	.260	.285	0 0	1B-93
1915	40	90	24	1	0	0	0.0	11	7	10	12	5	.267	.278	10 3	1B-27
1916	59	146	39	9	1	0	0.0	11	18	9	13	7	.267	.342	14 5	2B-20, 1B-17, OF-6
5 yrs.	253	741	183	22	3	0	0.0	77	87	61	80	28	.247	.285	25 9	1B-194, 2B-20, OF-8
2 yrs.	61	182	36	4	2	0	0.0	22	18	9		5	.198	.242	1 1	1B-57, OF-2

Eddie Mulligan
MULLIGAN, EDWARD JOSEPH   BR TR 5'9" 152 lbs.
B. Aug. 27, 1894, St. Louis, Mo.   D. Mar. 15, 1982, San Rafael, Calif.

1915 CHI N	11	22	8	1	0	0	0.0	5	2	5	1	2	.364	.409	0 0	SS-10, 3B-1
1916	58	189	29	3	4	0	0.0	13	9	8	30	1	.153	.212	0 0	SS-58
1921 CHI A	152	609	153	21	12	1	0.2	82	45	32	53	13	.251	.330	0 0	3B-152, SS-1
1922	103	372	87	14	8	0	0.0	39	31	22	32	7	.234	.315	10 2	3B-86, SS-7
1928 PIT N	27	43	10	2	0	0	0.0	4	1	3	4	0	.233	.279	9 5	3B-6, 2B-4
5 yrs.	351	1235	287	41	24	1	0.1	143	88	70	120	23	.232	.307	19 7	3B-245, SS-76, 2B-4
2 yrs.	255	981	240	35	20	1	0.1	121	76	54	85	20	.245	.324	10 2	3B-238, SS-8

Fran Mullins
MULLINS, FRANCIS JOSEPH   BR TR 6' 180 lbs.
B. May 14, 1957, Oakland, Calif.

| 1980 CHI A | 21 | 62 | 12 | 4 | 0 | 0 | 0.0 | 3 | 9 | 8 | 0 | 0 | .194 | .258 | 0 0 | 3B-21 |

Danny Murphy
MURPHY, DANIEL FRANCIS   BL TR 5'11" 185 lbs.
B. Aug. 23, 1942, Beverly, Mass.

1960 CHI N	31	75	9	2	0	1	1.3	7	6	4	13	0	.120	.187	7 0	OF-21
1961	4	13	5	0	0	2	15.4	3	3	1	5	0	.385	.846	0 0	OF-4
1962	14	35	7	3	1	0	0.0	5	3	2	9	0	.200	.343	6 0	OF-9

	G	AB	H	2B	3B	HR	HR%	R	RBI	BB	SO	SB	BA	SA	Pinch Hit AB	Pinch Hit H	G by POS

Danny Murphy continued

		G	AB	H	2B	3B	HR	HR%	R	RBI	BB	SO	SB	BA	SA	PH AB	PH H	G by POS
1969	CHI A	17	1	0	0	0	0	0.0	0	0	2	0	0	.000	.000	0	0	P-17
1970		51	6	2	0	0	1	16.7	3	1	2	2	0	.333	.833	0	0	P-51
5 yrs.		117	130	23	5	1	4	3.1	18	13	11	29	0	.177	.323	13	0	P-68, OF-34
2 yrs.		68	7	2	0	0	1	14.3	3	1	4	2	0	.286	.714	0	0	P-68

Eddie Murphy

MURPHY, JOHN EDWARD (Honest Eddie)
B. Oct. 2, 1891, Hancock, N. Y. D. Feb. 20, 1969, Dunmore, Pa.
BL TR 5'9" 155 lbs.

		G	AB	H	2B	3B	HR	HR%	R	RBI	BB	SO	SB	BA	SA	PH AB	PH H	G by POS
1912	PHI A	33	142	45	4	1	0	0.0	24	6	11		7	.317	.359	0	0	OF-33
1913		136	508	150	14	7	1	0.2	105	30	70	44	21	.295	.356	1	0	OF-135
1914		148	573	156	12	9	3	0.5	101	43	87	46	36	.272	.340	0	0	OF-148
1915	2 teams		PHI A (68G – .231)			CHI A (70G – .315)												
"	total	138	533	146	14	9	0	0.0	88	43	68	27	33	.274	.334	4	0	OF-128, 3B-8
1916	CHI A	51	105	22	5	1	0	0.0	14	9	9	5	3	.210	.276	20	4	OF-24, 3B-1
1917		53	51	16	2	1	0	0.0	9	16	5	1	4	.314	.392	32	12	OF-9
1918		91	286	85	9	3	0	0.0	36	23	22	18	6	.297	.350	18	4	OF-63, 2B-8
1919		30	35	17	4	0	0	0.0	8	5	7	0	0	.486	.600	21	8	OF-6
1920		58	118	40	2	1	0	0.0	22	19	12	4	1	.339	.373	33	13	OF-19, 3B-3
1921		6	5	1	0	0	0	0.0	1	0	0	0	0	.200	.200	5	1	
1926	PIT N	16	17	2	0	0	0	0.0	3	6	3	0	0	.118	.118	11	1	OF-3
11 yrs.		760	2373	680	66	32	4	0.2	411	195	294	145	111	.287	.346	145	43	OF-568, 3B-10, 2B-8
7 yrs.		359	873	267	33	11	0	0.0	141	93	94	40	34	.306	.369	129 4th	42 2nd	OF-191, 2B-8, 3B-4

WORLD SERIES

		G	AB	H	2B	3B	HR	HR%	R	RBI	BB	SO	SB	BA	SA	PH AB	PH H	G by POS
1913	PHI A	5	22	5	0	0	0	0.0	2	0	2	0	0	.227	.227	0	0	OF-5
1914		4	16	3	2	0	0	0.0	2	0	2	2	0	.188	.313	0	0	OF-4
1919	CHI A	3	2	0	0	0	0	0.0	0	0	0	1	0	.000	.000	2	0	
3 yrs.		12	40	8	2	0	0	0.0	4	0	4	3	0	.200	.250	2	0	OF-9

Tony Muser

MUSER, ANTHONY JOSEPH
B. Aug. 1, 1947, Van Nuys, Calif.
BL TL 6'2" 180 lbs.

		G	AB	H	2B	3B	HR	HR%	R	RBI	BB	SO	SB	BA	SA	PH AB	PH H	G by POS
1969	BOS A	2	9	1	0	0	0	0.0	0	0	1	1	0	.111	.111	0	0	1B-2
1971	CHI A	11	16	5	0	1	0	0.0	2	0	1	1	0	.313	.438	7	2	1B-4
1972		44	61	17	2	2	1	1.6	6	9	2	6	1	.279	.426	12	4	1B-29, OF-1
1973		109	309	88	14	3	4	1.3	38	30	33	36	8	.285	.388	9	4	1B-89, OF-2
1974		103	206	60	5	1	1	0.5	16	18	6	22	1	.291	.340	13	3	1B-80, DH-13
1975	2 teams		CHI A (43G – .243)			BAL A (80G – .317)												
"	total	123	193	53	6	0	0	0.0	22	17	15	17	2	.275	.306	18	6	1B-103
1976	BAL A	136	326	74	7	1	1	0.3	25	30	21	34	1	.227	.264	16	4	1B-109, OF-12, DH-10
1977		120	118	27	6	0	0	0.0	14	7	13	16	1	.229	.280	31	6	1B-77, OF-11, DH-1
1978	MIL A	15	30	4	1	0	0	0.0	0	5	3	5	0	.133	.233	3	0	1B-12
9 yrs.		663	1268	329	41	9	7	0.6	123	117	95	138	14	.259	.323	109	29	1B-505, OF-26, DH-24
5 yrs.		310	703	197	24	7	6	0.9	73	63	49	73	12	.280	.360	44	13	1B-243, DH-13, OF-3

Bill Nagel

NAGEL, WILLIAM TAYLOR
B. Aug. 19, 1915, Memphis, Tenn.
BR TR 6' 190 lbs.

		G	AB	H	2B	3B	HR	HR%	R	RBI	BB	SO	SB	BA	SA	PH AB	PH H	G by POS
1939	PHI A	105	341	86	19	4	12	3.5	39	39	25	86	2	.252	.437	4	0	2B-56, 3B-43, P-1
1941	PHI N	17	56	8	1	1	0	0.0	2	6	3	14	0	.143	.196	2	0	2B-12, OF-2, 3B-1
1945	CHI A	67	220	46	10	3	3	1.4	21	27	15	41	3	.209	.323	9	0	1B-57, 3B-1
3 yrs.		189	617	140	30	8	15	2.4	62	72	43	141	5	.227	.374	15	0	2B-68, 1B-57, 3B-45, OF-2, P-1
1 yr.		67	220	46	10	3	3	1.4	21	27	15	41	3	.209	.323	9	0	1B-57, 3B-1

Bill Nahorodny

NAHORODNY, WILLIAM GERARD
B. Aug. 31, 1953, Hamtramck, Mich.
BR TR 6'2" 200 lbs.

		G	AB	H	2B	3B	HR	HR%	R	RBI	BB	SO	SB	BA	SA	PH AB	PH H	G by POS
1976	PHI N	3	5	1	1	0	0	0.0	0	0	0	0	0	.200	.400	2	0	C-2
1977	CHI A	7	23	6	1	0	1	4.3	3	4	2	3	0	.261	.435	0	0	C-7
1978		107	347	82	11	2	8	2.3	29	35	23	52	1	.236	.349	1	0	C-104, 1B-4, DH-1
1979		65	179	46	10	0	6	3.4	20	29	18	23	0	.257	.413	11	6	C-60, DH-3
1980	ATL N	59	157	38	12	0	5	3.2	14	18	8	21	0	.242	.414	6	1	C-54, 1B-1
1981		14	13	3	1	0	0	0.0	0	2	1	3	0	.231	.308	9	2	C-3, 1B-1
1982	CLE A	39	94	21	5	1	4	4.3	6	18	2	9	0	.223	.426	7	2	C-35
1983	DET A	2	1	0	0	0	0	0.0	0	0	1	0	0	.000	.000	1	0	
8 yrs.		296	819	197	41	3	24	2.9	72	106	55	111	1	.241	.386	37	12	C-265, 1B-6, DH-4
3 yrs.		179	549	134	22	3	15	2.7	52	68	43	78	1	.244	.373	12	6	C-171, DH-4, 1B-1

Frank Naleway

NALEWAY, FRANK (Chick)
B. July 4, 1901, Chicago, Ill. D. Jan. 28, 1949, Chicago, Ill.
BR TR 5'9½" 165 lbs.

		G	AB	H	2B	3B	HR	HR%	R	RBI	BB	SO	SB	BA	SA	PH AB	PH H	G by POS
1924	CHI A	1	2	0	0	0	0	0.0	1	0	0	1	0	.000	.000	0	0	SS-1

Cotton Nash

NASH, CHARLES FRANCIS
B. July 24, 1942, Jersey City, N. J.
BR TR 6'6" 220 lbs.

		G	AB	H	2B	3B	HR	HR%	R	RBI	BB	SO	SB	BA	SA	PH AB	PH H	G by POS
1967	CHI A	3	3	0	0	0	0	0.0	0	0	1	0	0	.000	.000	3	0	1B-3
1969	MIN A	6	9	2	0	0	0	0.0	0	0	1	2	0	.222	.222	0	0	1B-6, OF-1
1970		4	4	1	0	0	0	0.0	1	2	1	0	0	.250	.250	2	0	1B-2
3 yrs.		13	16	3	0	0	0	0.0	1	2	3	2	0	.188	.188	5	0	1B-11, OF-1
1 yr.		3	3	0	0	0	0	0.0	0	0	1	0	0	.000	.000	3	0	1B-3

Bernie Neis

NEIS, BERNARD EDMUND
B. Sept. 26, 1895, Bloomington, Ill.
D. Nov. 29, 1972, Inverness, Fla.
BB TR 5'7" 160 lbs.
BR 1920-21, 1926

		G	AB	H	2B	3B	HR	HR%	R	RBI	BB	SO	SB	BA	SA	PH AB	PH H	G by POS
1920	BKN N	95	249	63	11	2	2	0.8	38	22	26	35	9	.253	.337	4	0	OF-83
1921		102	230	59	5	4	4	1.7	34	34	25	41	9	.257	.365	16	6	OF-77, 2B-1
1922		61	70	16	4	1	0	0.0	15	9	13	8	3	.229	.357	9	1	OF-27
1923		126	445	122	17	6	5	1.1	78	37	36	38	8	.274	.364	8	1	OF-111
1924		80	211	64	8	3	4	1.9	43	26	27	17	4	.303	.427	11	2	OF-62
1925	BOS N	106	355	101	20	2	5	1.4	47	45	38	19	8	.285	.394	14	6	OF-87

Player Register

	G	AB	H	2B	3B	HR	HR%	R	RBI	BB	SO	SB	BA	SA	Pinch Hit AB	H	G by POS

Bernie Neis continued

1926		30	93	20	5	2	0	0.0	16	8	8	10	4	.215	.312	2	0	OF-23
1927 2 teams	CLE A (32G – .302)					CHI A (45G – .289)												
" total		77	172	51	14	0	4	2.3	26	29	28	18	1	.297	.448	20	5	OF-50
8 yrs.		677	1825	496	84	18	25	1.4	297	210	201	186	46	.272	.379	84	21	OF-520, 2B-1
1 yr.		45	76	22	5	0	0	0.0	9	11	10	9	1	.289	.355	18	4	OF-21

WORLD SERIES
| 1920 BKN N | 4 | 5 | 0 | 0 | 0 | 0 | 0.0 | 0 | 0 | 1 | 0 | 0 | .000 | .000 | 1 | 0 | OF-2 |

Rocky Nelson
NELSON, GLENN RICHARD BL TL 5'10½" 175 lbs.
B. Nov. 18, 1924, Portsmouth, Ohio

1949 STL N	82	244	54	8	4	4	1.6	28	32	11	12	1	.221	.336	8	2	1B-70
1950	76	235	58	10	4	1	0.4	27	20	26	9	4	.247	.336	4	1	1B-70
1951 3 teams	STL N (9G – .222)			PIT N (71G – .267)			CHI A (6G – .000)										
" total	86	218	56	8	4	1	0.5	32	15	12	7	0	.257	.344	31	6	1B-36, OF-13
1952 BKN N	37	39	10	1	0	0	0.0	6	3	7	4	0	.256	.282	27	7	1B-5
1954 CLE A	4	4	0	0	0	0	0.0	0	0	0	1	0	.000	.000	3	0	1B-2
1956 2 teams	BKN N (31G – .208)			STL N (38G – .232)													
" total	69	152	33	7	0	7	4.6	13	23	10	16	0	.217	.401	26	3	1B-39, OF-8
1959 PIT N	98	175	51	11	0	6	3.4	31	32	23	19	0	.291	.457	33	13	1B-56, OF-2
1960	93	200	60	11	1	7	3.5	34	35	24	15	1	.300	.470	18	4	1B-73
1961	75	127	25	5	1	5	3.9	15	13	17	11	0	.197	.370	37	5	1B-35
9 yrs.	620	1394	347	61	14	31	2.2	186	173	130	94	6	.249	.379	187	41	1B-386, OF-23
1 yr.	6	5	0	0	0	0	0.0	0	0	1	0	0	.000	.000	5	0	

WORLD SERIES
1952 BKN N	4	3	0	0	0	0	0.0	0	0	1	2	0	.000	.000	3	0	
1960 PIT N	4	9	3	0	0	1	11.1	2	2	1	1	0	.333	.667	1	0	1B-3
2 yrs.	8	12	3	0	0	1	8.3	2	2	2	3	0	.250	.500	4	0	1B-3

Jack Ness
NESS, JOHN CHARLES BR TR 6'2" 165 lbs.
B. Nov. 11, 1885, Chicago, Ill.   D. Dec. 3, 1957, DeLand, Fla.

1911 DET A	12	39	6	0	0	0	0.0	6	2	2		0	.154	.154	0	0	1B-12
1916 CHI A	75	258	69	7	5	1	0.4	32	34	9	32	4	.267	.345	6	3	1B-69
2 yrs.	87	297	75	7	5	1	0.3	38	36	11	32	4	.253	.320	6	3	1B-81
1 yr.	75	258	69	7	5	1	0.4	32	34	9	32	4	.267	.345	6	3	1B-69

Gus Niarhos
NIARHOS, CONSTANTINE GREGORY BR TR 6' 160 lbs.
B. Dec. 6, 1920, Birmingham, Ala.

1946 NY A	37	40	9	1	1	0	0.0	11	2	11	2	1	.225	.300	2	0	C-29
1948	83	228	61	12	2	0	0.0	41	19	52	15	1	.268	.338	0	0	C-82
1949	32	43	12	2	1	0	0.0	7	6	13	8	0	.279	.372	2	1	C-30
1950 2 teams	NY A (1G – .000)			CHI A (41G – .324)													
" total	42	105	34	4	0	0	0.0	17	16	14	6	0	.324	.362	2	0	C-36
1951 CHI A	66	168	43	6	0	1	0.6	27	10	47	9	4	.256	.310	4	2	C-59
1952 BOS A	29	58	6	0	0	0	0.0	4	4	12	9	0	.103	.103	3	0	C-25
1953	16	35	7	1	1	0	0.0	6	2	4	4	0	.200	.286	0	0	C-16
1954 PHI N	3	5	1	0	0	0	0.0	0	1	0	1	0	.200	.200	0	0	C-3
1955	7	9	1	0	0	0	0.0	1	0	0	2	0	.111	.111	0	0	C-7
9 yrs.	315	691	174	26	5	1	0.1	114	59	153	56	6	.252	.308	13	3	C-287
2 yrs.	107	273	77	10	0	1	0.4	44	26	61	15	4	.282	.330	6	2	C-95

WORLD SERIES
| 1949 NY A | 1 | 0 | 0 | 0 | 0 | 0 | 0.0 | 0 | 0 | 0 | 0 | – | – | 0 | 0 | C-1 |

Don Nicholas
NICHOLAS, DONALD LEIGH BL TR 5'7" 150 lbs.
B. Oct. 30, 1930, Phoenix, Ariz.

1952 CHI A	3	2	0	0	0	0	0.0	0	0	0	0	0	.000	.000	2	0	OF-3
1954	7	0	0	0	0	0	–	3	0	1	0	0	–	–	0	0	OF-7
2 yrs.	10	2	0	0	0	0	0.0	3	0	1	0	0	.000	.000	2	0	OF-10
2 yrs.	10	2	0	0	0	0	0.0	3	0	1	0	0	.000	.000	2	0	OF-10

Dave Nicholson
NICHOLSON, DAVID LAWRENCE BR TR 6'2" 215 lbs.
B. Aug. 29, 1939, St. Louis, Mo.

1960 BAL A	54	113	21	1	1	5	4.4	17	11	20	55	0	.186	.345	9	0	OF-44
1962	97	173	30	4	1	9	5.2	25	15	27	76	3	.173	.364	4	0	OF-80
1963 CHI A	126	449	103	11	4	22	4.9	53	70	63	175	2	.229	.419	3	1	OF-123
1964	97	294	60	6	1	13	4.4	40	39	52	126	0	.204	.354	7	1	OF-92
1965	54	85	13	2	1	2	2.4	11	12	9	40	0	.153	.271	12	0	OF-36
1966 HOU N	100	280	69	8	4	10	3.6	36	31	46	92	1	.246	.411	16	2	OF-90
1967 ATL N	10	25	5	0	0	0	0.0	2	1	2	9	0	.200	.200	1	0	OF-7
7 yrs.	538	1419	301	32	12	61	4.3	184	179	219	573	6	.212	.381	52	4	OF-472
3 yrs.	277	828	176	19	6	37	4.5	104	121	124	341	2	.213	.384	22	2	OF-251

Bob Nieman
NIEMAN, ROBERT CHARLES BR TR 5'11" 195 lbs.
B. Jan. 26, 1927, Cincinnati, Ohio

1951 STL A	12	43	16	3	1	2	4.7	8	8	3	5	0	.372	.628	1	1	OF-11
1952	131	478	138	22	2	18	3.8	66	74	46	73	0	.289	.456	9	1	OF-125
1953 DET A	142	508	143	25	5	15	3.0	72	69	57	57	0	.281	.453	7	1	OF-135
1954	91	251	66	14	1	8	3.2	24	35	22	32	0	.263	.422	26	8	OF-62
1955 CHI A	99	272	77	11	2	11	4.0	36	53	36	37	1	.283	.460	24	7	OF-78
1956 2 teams	CHI A (14G – .300)			BAL A (114G – .322)													
" total	128	428	137	21	6	14	3.3	63	68	90	63	1	.320	.495	1	1	OF-124
1957 BAL A	129	445	123	17	6	13	2.9	61	70	63	86	4	.276	.429	9	0	OF-120
1958	105	366	119	20	2	16	4.4	56	60	44	57	0	.325	.522	6	1	OF-100
1959	118	360	105	18	2	21	5.8	49	60	42	55	0	.292	.528	17	4	OF-97
1960 STL N	81	188	54	13	5	4	2.1	19	31	24	31	0	.287	.473	26	4	OF-55

299   Player Register

	G	AB	H	2B	3B	HR	HR%	R	RBI	BB	SO	SB	BA	SA	Pinch Hit AB	Pinch Hit H	G by POS

Bob Nieman continued

1961 2 teams	STL N (6G – .471)			CLE A (39G – .354)													
" total	45	82	31	7	0	2	2.4	2	12	7	6	1	.378	.537	27	9	OF-16
1962 2 teams	CLE A (2G – .000)			SF N (30G – .300)													
" total	32	31	9	2	0	1	3.2	1	4	1	10	0	.290	.452	30	8	OF-3
12 yrs.	1113	3452	1018	180	32	125	3.6	455	544	435	512	10	.295	.474	183	45	OF-926
2 yrs.	113	312	89	12	2	13	4.2	39	57	40	41	1	.285	.462	25	8	OF-88

WORLD SERIES
| 1962 SF N | 1 | 0 | 0 | 0 | 0 | 0 | – | 0 | 0 | 1 | 0 | 0 | – | – | 0 | 0 | |

Tim Nordbrook

NORDBROOK, TIMOTHY CHARLES   BR TR 6'1"   180 lbs.
B. July 4, 1949, Baltimore, Md.

1974 BAL A	6	15	4	0	0	0	0.0	4	1	2	2	1	.267	.267	0	0	SS-5, 2B-1
1975	40	34	4	1	0	0	0.0	6	0	7	7	0	.118	.147	0	0	SS-36, 2B-3
1976 2 teams	BAL A (27G – .227)			CAL A (5G – .000)													
" total	32	30	5	0	0	0	0.0	5	0	4	8	1	.167	.167	0	0	SS-16, 2B-15, DH-1
1977 2 teams	CHI A (15G – .000)			TOR A (24G – .175)													
" total	39	83	16	0	1	0	0.0	11	2	11	15	2	.193	.217	12	3	SS-35, DH-2, 3B-1
1978 2 teams	TOR A (7G – .000)			MIL A (2G – .000)													
" total	9	5	0	0	0	0	0.0	1	0	1	1	0	.000	.000	0	0	SS-9
1979 MIL A	2	2	1	0	0	0	0.0	0	0	0	0	0	.500	.500	0	0	SS-2
6 yrs.	128	169	30	1	1	0	0.0	27	3	25	33	4	.178	.195	12	3	SS-103, 2B-19, DH-3, 3B-1
1 yr.	15	20	5	0	0	0	0.0	2	1	7	4	1	.250	.250	12	3	SS-11, DH-2, 3B-1

Wayne Nordhagen

NORDHAGEN, WAYNE OREN   BR TR 6'2"   205 lbs.
B. July 4, 1948, Three River Falls, Minn.

1976 CHI A	22	53	10	2	0	0	0.0	6	5	4	12	0	.189	.226	2	0	OF-10, DH-6, C-5
1977	52	124	39	7	3	4	3.2	16	22	2	12	1	.315	.516	7	2	OF-46, C-3, DH-2
1978	68	206	62	16	0	5	2.4	29	35	5	18	0	.301	.451	15	6	OF-36, DH-16, C-12
1979	78	193	54	15	0	7	3.6	20	25	13	22	0	.280	.466	21	7	DH-47, OF-12, C-5, P-2
1980	123	415	115	22	4	15	3.6	45	59	10	45	0	.277	.458	21	5	OF-74, DH-32
1981	65	208	64	8	1	6	2.9	19	33	10	25	0	.308	.442	7	1	OF-60
1982 2 teams	TOR A (72G – .270)			PIT N (1G – .500)													
" total	73	189	52	6	0	1	0.5	12	22	10	23	0	.275	.323	26	11	DH-60, 1B-10, OF-1
1983 CHI N	21	35	5	1	0	1	2.9	1	4	0	5	0	.143	.257	15	2	OF-7
8 yrs.	502	1423	401	77	8	39	2.7	147	205	54	162	1	.282	.429	114	34	OF-246, DH-163, C-25, 1B-10, P-2
6 yrs.	408	1199	344	70	8	37	3.1	134	179	44	134	1	.287	.451	73	21	OF-238, DH-103, C-25, P-2

Bill Norman

NORMAN, HENRY WILLIS PATRICK   BR TR 6'2"   190 lbs.
B. July 16, 1910, St. Louis, Mo.   D. Apr. 21, 1962, Milwaukee, Wis.
Manager 1958-59.

1931 CHI A	24	55	10	2	0	0	0.0	7	6	4	10	0	.182	.218	4	0	OF-17
1932	13	48	11	3	1	0	0.0	6	2	2	3	0	.229	.333	0	0	OF-13
2 yrs.	37	103	21	5	1	0	0.0	13	8	6	13	0	.204	.272	4	0	OF-30
2 yrs.	37	103	21	5	1	0	0.0	13	8	6	13	0	.204	.272	4	0	OF-30

Ron Northey

NORTHEY, RONALD JAMES (The Round Man)   BL TR 5'10"   195 lbs.
Father of Scott Northey.
B. Apr. 26, 1920, Mahanoy City, Pa.   D. Apr. 16, 1971, Pittsburgh, Pa.

1942 PHI N	127	402	101	13	2	5	1.2	31	31	28	33	2	.251	.331	17	4	OF-109
1943	147	586	163	31	5	16	2.7	72	68	51	52	2	.278	.430	2	0	OF-145
1944	152	570	164	35	9	22	3.9	72	104	67	51	1	.288	.496	1	0	OF-151
1946	128	438	109	24	6	16	3.7	55	62	39	59	1	.249	.441	14	5	OF-111
1947 2 teams	PHI N (13G – .255)			STL N (110G – .293)													
" total	123	358	103	22	3	15	4.2	59	66	54	32	1	.288	.492	13	3	OF-107, 3B-2
1948 STL N	96	246	79	10	1	13	5.3	40	64	38	25	0	.321	.528	25	11	OF-67
1949	90	265	69	18	2	7	2.6	28	50	31	15	0	.260	.423	12	0	OF-73
1950 2 teams	CIN N (27G – .260)			CHI N (53G – .281)													
" total	80	191	52	14	0	9	4.7	22	29	25	15	0	.272	.487	27	5	OF-51
1952 CHI N	1	1	0	0	0	0	0.0	0	0	0	0	0	.000	.000	1	0	
1955 CHI A	14	14	5	2	0	1	7.1	1	4	3	3	0	.357	.714	10	4	OF-2
1956	53	48	17	2	0	3	6.3	4	23	8	1	0	.354	.583	39	15	OF-4
1957 2 teams	CHI A (40G – .185)			PHI N (33G – .269)													
" total	73	53	12	1	0	1	1.9	1	12	17	11	0	.226	.302	53	12	
12 yrs.	1084	3172	874	172	28	108	3.4	385	513	361	297	7	.276	.450	214	59	OF-820, 3B-2
3 yrs.	107	89	27	5	0	4	4.5	5	34	22	9	0	.303	.494	76	24	OF-6
																9th	

Chris Nyman

NYMAN, CHRISTOPHER CURTIS   BR TR 6'4"   200 lbs.
Brother of Nyls Nyman.
B. June 6, 1955, Pomona, Calif.

1982 CHI A	28	65	16	1	0	0	0.0	6	2	3	9	3	.246	.262	5	0	1B-24, OF-2
1983	21	28	8	0	0	2	7.1	12	4	4	7	2	.286	.500	0	0	DH-10, 1B-10
2 yrs.	49	93	24	1	0	2	2.2	18	6	7	16	5	.258	.333	5	0	1B-34, DH-10, OF-2
2 yrs.	49	93	24	1	0	2	2.2	18	6	7	16	5	.258	.333	5	0	1B-34, DH-10, OF-2

Nyls Nyman

NYMAN, NYLS WALLACE   BL TL 6'   170 lbs.
Also known as Rex Nyman.   Brother of Chris Nyman.
B. Mar. 7, 1954, Detroit, Mich.

1974 CHI A	5	14	9	2	1	0	0.0	5	4	0	1	1	.643	.929	1	1	OF-3
1975	106	327	74	6	3	2	0.6	36	28	11	34	10	.226	.281	3	1	OF-94, DH-4
1976	8	15	2	1	0	0	0.0	2	1	0	3	1	.133	.200	0	0	OF-7

Player Register

	G	AB	H	2B	3B	HR	HR%	R	RBI	BB	SO	SB	BA	SA	Pinch Hit AB	H	G by POS

Nyls Nyman continued

1977	1	1	0	0	0	0	0.0	0	0	0	0	0	.000	.000	0	0	
4 yrs.	120	357	85	9	4	2	0.6	43	33	11	38	12	.238	.303	4	2	OF-104, DH-4
4 yrs.	120	357	85	9	4	2	0.6	43	33	11	38	12	.238	.303	4	2	OF-104, DH-4

Syd O'Brien
O'BRIEN, SYDNEY LLOYD
B. Dec. 18, 1944, Compton, Calif.   BR TR 6'1" 185 lbs.

1969 BOS A	100	263	64	10	5	9	3.4	47	29	15	37	2	.243	.422	18	5	3B-53, SS-15, 2B-12
1970 CHI A	121	441	109	13	2	8	1.8	48	44	22	62	3	.247	.340	8	2	3B-68, 2B-43, SS-5
1971 CAL A	90	251	50	8	1	5	2.0	25	21	15	33	0	.199	.299	20	6	SS-52, 2B-7, 3B-6, OF-1, 1B-1
1972 2 teams	CAL A (36G – .179)				MIL A (31G – .207)												
" total	67	97	19	4	0	2	2.1	15	6	8	23	0	.196	.299	22	4	3B-17, 2B-10, SS-4, 1B-1
4 yrs.	378	1052	242	35	8	24	2.3	135	100	60	155	5	.230	.347	68	17	3B-144, SS-76, 2B-72, 1B-2, OF-1
1 yr.	121	441	109	13	2	8	1.8	48	44	22	62	3	.247	.340	8	2	3B-68, 2B-43, SS-5

Bill O'Neill
O'NEILL, WILLIAM JOHN   BB
B. Jan. 22, 1880, St. John, N. B., Canada   D. July 27, 1920, St. John, N. B., Canada

1904 2 teams	BOS A (17G – .196)				WAS A (95G – .244)												
" total	112	416	99	11	1	1	0.2	40	21	24		22	.238	.276	6	2	OF-102, 2B-3, SS-2
1906 CHI A	94	330	82	4	1	1	0.3	37	21	22		19	.248	.276	1	0	OF-93
2 yrs.	206	746	181	15	2	2	0.3	77	42	46		41	.243	.276	7	2	OF-195, 2B-3, SS-2
1 yr.	94	330	82	4	1	1	0.3	37	21	22		19	.248	.276	1	0	OF-93

WORLD SERIES

| 1906 CHI A | 1 | 1 | 0 | 0 | 0 | 0 | 0.0 | 1 | 0 | 0 | 0 | 0 | .000 | .000 | 0 | 0 | OF-1 |

Jack Onslow
ONSLOW, JOHN JAMES   BR TR 5'11" 180 lbs.
Brother of Eddie Onslow.
B. Oct. 13, 1888, Scottdale, Pa.   D. Dec. 22, 1960, Concord, Mass.
Manager 1949-50.

1912 DET A	31	69	11	1	0	0	0.0	7	4	10		1	.159	.174	0	0	C-31
1917 NY N	9	8	2	1	0	0	0.0	1	0	0	1	0	.250	.375	0	0	C-9
2 yrs.	40	77	13	2	0	0	0.0	8	4	10	1	1	.169	.195	0	0	C-40

Joe Orengo
ORENGO, JOSEPH CHARLES   BR TR 6' 185 lbs.
B. Nov. 29, 1914, San Francisco, Calif.

1939 STL N	7	3	0	0	0	0	0.0	0	0	0	1	0	.000	.000	0	0	SS-7
1940	129	415	119	23	4	7	1.7	58	56	65	90	9	.287	.412	0	0	2B-77, 3B-34, SS-19
1941 NY N	77	252	54	11	2	4	1.6	23	25	28	49	1	.214	.321	3	1	3B-59, SS-9, 2B-6
1943 2 teams	NY N (83G – .218)				BKN N (7G – .200)												
" total	90	281	61	10	2	6	2.1	29	30	40	48	1	.217	.331	2	2	1B-82, 3B-6
1944 DET A	46	154	31	10	0	0	0.0	14	10	20	29	1	.201	.266	1	0	SS-29, 3B-11, 1B-5, 2B-2
1945 CHI A	17	15	1	0	0	0	0.0	5	1	3	2	0	.067	.067	5	0	3B-7, 2B-1
6 yrs.	366	1120	266	54	8	17	1.5	129	122	156	219	12	.238	.346	11	3	3B-117, 1B-87, 2B-86, SS-64
1 yr.	17	15	1	0	0	0	0.0	5	1	3	2	0	.067	.067	5	0	3B-7, 2B-1

Jorge Orta
ORTA, JORGE NUNEZ   BL TR 5'10" 170 lbs.
B. Dec. 26, 1950, Mazatlan, Mexico

1972 CHI A	51	124	25	3	1	3	2.4	20	11	6	37	3	.202	.315	11	1	SS-18, 2B-14, 3B-9
1973	128	425	113	9	10	6	1.4	46	40	37	87	8	.266	.376	5	2	2B-122, SS-1
1974	139	525	166	31	2	10	1.9	73	67	40	88	9	.316	.440	7	1	2B-123, DH-10, SS-3
1975	140	542	165	26	10	11	2.0	64	83	48	67	16	.304	.450	3	2	2B-135, DH-2
1976	158	636	174	29	8	14	2.2	74	72	38	77	24	.274	.410	3	0	OF-77, 3B-49, DH-31
1977	144	564	159	27	8	11	2.0	71	84	46	49	4	.282	.417	7	1	2B-139
1978	117	420	115	19	2	13	3.1	45	53	42	39	1	.274	.421	3	1	2B-114, DH-2
1979	113	325	85	18	3	11	3.4	49	46	44	33	1	.262	.437	22	4	DH-62, 2B-41
1980 CLE A	129	481	140	18	3	10	2.1	78	64	71	44	6	.291	.403	2	0	OF-120, DH-7
1981	88	338	92	14	3	5	1.5	50	34	21	43	4	.272	.376	5	2	OF-86
1982 LA N	86	115	25	5	0	2	1.7	13	8	12	13	0	.217	.313	60	9	OF-17
1983 TOR A	103	245	58	6	3	10	4.1	30	38	19	29	1	.237	.408	26	5	DH-69, OF-17
12 yrs.	1396	4740	1317	205	53	106	2.2	613	600	424	606	77	.278	.411	154	28	2B-688, OF-317, DH-183, 3B-58, SS-22
8 yrs.	990	3561	1002	162	44	79	2.2	442	456	301	477	66	.281	.418	61	12	2B-688, DH-107, OF-77, 3B-58, SS-22
							9th				6th						

Jose Ortiz
ORTIZ, JOSE LUIS   BR TR 5'9½" 155 lbs.
B. June 25, 1947, Ponce, Puerto Rico

1969 CHI A	16	11	3	1	0	0	0.0	0	2	1	0	0	.273	.364	1	0	OF-8
1970	15	24	8	1	0	0	0.0	4	1	2	2	1	.333	.375	1	0	OF-8
1971 CHI N	36	88	26	7	1	0	0.0	10	3	4	10	2	.295	.398	1	0	OF-20
3 yrs.	67	123	37	9	1	0	0.0	14	6	7	12	3	.301	.390	3	0	OF-36
2 yrs.	31	35	11	2	0	0	0.0	4	3	3	2	1	.314	.371	2	0	OF-16

Red Ostergard
OSTERGARD, ROBERT LUND   BL TR 5'10½" 175 lbs.
B. May 11, 1898, Galveston, Tex.

| 1921 CHI A | 12 | 11 | 4 | 0 | 0 | 0 | 0.0 | 2 | 0 | 2 | | 0 | .364 | .364 | 11 | 4 | |

John Ostrowski
OSTROWSKI, JOHN THADDEUS   BR TR 5'10½" 170 lbs.
B. Oct. 17, 1917, Chicago, Ill.

1943 CHI N	10	29	6	0	1	0	0.0	2	3	3	8	0	.207	.276	0	0	OF-5, 3B-4
1944	8	13	2	1	0	0	0.0	2	2	1	4	0	.154	.231	5	2	OF-2
1945	7	10	3	2	0	0	0.0	4	0	0	0	0	.300	.500	0	0	3B-4
1946	64	160	34	4	2	3	1.9	20	12	20	31	1	.213	.319	10	0	3B-50, 2B-1
1948 BOS A	1	1	0	0	0	0	0.0	0	1	0	0	0	.000	.000	1	0	

Player Register

	G	AB	H	2B	3B	HR	HR %	R	RBI	BB	SO	SB	BA	SA	Pinch Hit AB H	G by POS

John Ostrowski continued
1949 CHI A	49	158	42	9	4	5	3.2	19	31	15	41	4	.266	.468	6 1	OF-41, 3B-8
1950 2 teams	CHI A (22G – .245)				WAS A (55G – .227)											
" total	77	190	44	4	2	6	3.2	26	25	29	40	2	.232	.368	16 0	OF-61
7 yrs.	216	561	131	20	9	14	2.5	73	74	68	125	7	.234	.376	40 3	OF-109, 3B-66, 2B-1
2 yrs.	71	207	54	11	5	7	3.4	29	33	24	50	4	.261	.464	13 1	OF-57, 3B-8

Marv Owen
OWEN, MARVIN JAMES BR TR 6'1" 175 lbs.
B. Mar. 22, 1906, Agnew, Calif.

1931 DET A	105	377	84	11	6	3	0.8	35	39	29	38	2	.223	.308	3 1	SS-37, 3B-37, 1B-27, 2B-4
1933	138	550	144	24	9	2	0.4	77	65	44	56	2	.262	.349	1 0	3B-136
1934	154	565	179	34	9	8	1.4	79	96	59	37	3	.317	.451	0 0	3B-154
1935	134	483	127	24	5	2	0.4	52	71	43	37	1	.263	.346	2 1	3B-131
1936	154	583	172	20	4	9	1.5	72	105	53	41	9	.295	.389	0 0	3B-153, 1B-2
1937	107	396	114	22	5	1	0.3	48	45	41	24	3	.288	.376	1 0	3B-106
1938 CHI A	141	577	162	23	6	6	1.0	84	55	45	31	6	.281	.373	1 0	3B-140
1939	58	194	46	9	0	0	0.0	22	15	16	15	4	.237	.284	2 0	3B-55
1940 BOS A	20	57	12	0	0	0	0.0	4	6	8	4	0	.211	.211	3 0	3B-9, 1B-8
9 yrs.	1011	3782	1040	167	44	31	0.8	473	497	338	283	30	.275	.367	13 2	3B-921, SS-37, 1B-37, 2B-4
2 yrs.	199	771	208	32	6	6	0.8	106	70	61	46	10	.270	.350	3 0	3B-195

WORLD SERIES
1934 DET A	7	29	2	0	0	0	0.0	0	1	0	5	1	.069	.069	0 0	3B-7
1935	6	20	1	0	0	0	0.0	2	1	2	3	0	.050	.050	0 0	3B-2
2 yrs.	13	49	3	0	0	0	0.0	2	2	2	8	1	.061	.061	0 0	3B-9

Frank Owens
OWENS, FRANK WALTER BR TR
B. Jan. 25, 1884, Toronto, Ont., Canada   D. July 2, 1958, Minneapolis, Minn.

1905 BOS A	1	2	0	0	0	0	0.0	0		0		0	.000	.000	0 0	C-1
1909 CHI A	64	174	35	4	1	0	0.0	12	17	8		3	.201	.236	6 1	C-57
1914 BKN F	58	184	51	7	3	2	1.1	15	20	9		2	.277	.380	0 0	C-58
1915 BAL F	99	334	84	14	7	3	0.9	32	28	17		4	.251	.362	0 0	C-99
4 yrs.	222	694	170	25	11	5	0.7	59	65	34		9	.245	.334	6 1	C-215
1 yr.	64	174	35	4	1	0	0.0	12	17	8		3	.201	.236	6 1	C-57

Tom Paciorek
PACIOREK, THOMAS MARIAN BR TR 6'4" 215 lbs.
Brother of John Paciorek.
B. Nov. 2, 1946, Detroit, Mich.

1970 LA N	8	9	2	1	0	0	0.0	2	0	0	3	0	.222	.333	5 1	OF-3
1971	2	2	1	0	0	0	0.0	0	0	0	0	0	.500	.500	2 1	OF-1
1972	11	47	12	4	0	1	2.1	4	6	1	7	1	.255	.404	0 0	OF-6, 1B-6
1973	96	195	51	8	0	5	2.6	26	18	11	35	3	.262	.379	17 4	OF-77, 1B-4
1974	85	175	42	8	6	1	0.6	23	24	10	32	1	.240	.371	18 6	OF-77, 1B-1
1975	62	145	28	8	0	1	0.7	14	5	11	29	4	.193	.269	10 2	OF-54
1976 ATL N	111	324	94	10	4	4	1.2	39	36	19	57	2	.290	.383	20 8	OF-84, 1B-12, 3B-1
1977	72	155	37	8	0	3	1.9	20	15	6	46	1	.239	.348	32 6	1B-32, OF-9, 3B-1
1978 2 teams	ATL N (5G – .333)				SEA A (70G – .299)											
" total	75	260	78	20	3	4	1.5	34	30	15	40	2	.300	.446	7 2	OF-54, DH-12, 1B-5
1979 SEA A	103	310	89	23	4	6	1.9	38	42	28	62	6	.287	.445	17 4	OF-75, 1B-15
1980	126	418	114	19	1	15	3.6	44	59	17	67	3	.273	.431	14 2	OF-60, 1B-36, DH-23
1981	104	405	132	28	2	14	3.5	50	66	35	50	13	.326	.509	1 1	OF-103
1982 CHI A	104	382	119	27	4	11	2.9	49	55	24	53	3	.312	.490	0 0	1B-102, OF-6
1983	115	420	129	32	3	9	2.1	65	63	25	58	6	.307	.462	9 3	1B-67, OF-55, DH-2
14 yrs.	1074	3247	928	196	27	74	2.3	408	420	202	539	45	.286	.431	152 40	OF-664, 1B-280, DH-37, 3B-2
2 yrs.	219	802	248	59	7	20	2.5	114	118	49	111	9	.309	.475	9 3	1B-169, OF-61, DH-2

LEAGUE CHAMPIONSHIP SERIES
1974 LA N	1	1	1	0	0	0	0.0	0	0	0	0	0	1.000	1.000	1 1	OF-1
1983 CHI A	4	16	4	0	0	0	0.0	1	1	1	2	0	.250	.250	0 0	1B-3
2 yrs.	5	17	5	0	0	0	0.0	1	1	1	2	0	.294	.294	1 1	1B-3, OF-1

WORLD SERIES
1974 LA N	3	2	1	1	0	0	0.0	1	0	0	0	0	.500	1.000	2 1	

Del Paddock
PADDOCK, DELMAR HAROLD BL TR 5'9" 165 lbs.
B. June 6, 1887, Volga, S. D.   D. Feb. 6, 1952, Rice Lake, Minn.

1912 2 teams	CHI A (1G – .000)				NY A (45G – .288)											
" total	46	157	45	5	3	1	0.6	26	14	23		9	.287	.376	2 0	3B-41, 2B-2, OF-1

Freddy Parent
PARENT, FREDERICK ALFRED BR TR 5'5½" 148 lbs.
B. Nov. 25, 1875, Biddeford, Me.   D. Nov. 2, 1972, Sanford, Me.

1899 STL N	2	8	1	0	0	0	0.0	0	1	0		0	.125	.125	0 0	2B-2
1901 BOS A	138	517	158	23	9	4	0.8	87	59	41		16	.306	.408	0 0	SS-138
1902	138	567	156	31	8	3	0.5	91	62	24		16	.275	.374	0 0	SS-138
1903	139	560	170	31	17	4	0.7	83	80	13		24	.304	.441	0 0	SS-139
1904	155	591	172	22	9	6	1.0	85	77	28		20	.291	.389	0 0	SS-155
1905	153	602	141	16	5	0	0.0	55	33	47		25	.234	.277	0 0	SS-153
1906	149	600	141	14	10	1	0.2	67	49	31		16	.235	.297	0 0	SS-143, 2B-6
1907	114	409	113	19	5	1	0.2	51	26	22		12	.276	.355	12 3	OF-47, SS-43, 3B-7, 2B-5
1908 CHI A	119	391	81	7	5	0	0.0	28	35	50		9	.207	.251	0 0	SS-118
1909	136	472	123	10	5	1	0.2	61	30	46		32	.261	.303	0 0	SS-98, OF-37, 2B-1
1910	81	258	46	6	1	1	0.4	23	16	29		14	.178	.221	0 0	OF-62, 2B-11, SS-4, 3B-1
1911	3	9	4	1	0	0	0.0	2	3	2		0	.444	.556	0 0	2B-3
12 yrs.	1327	4984	1306	180	74	20	0.4	633	471	333		184	.262	.340	12 2	SS-1129, OF-146, 2B-28, 3B-8
4 yrs.	339	1130	254	24	11	1	0.1	114	84	127		55	.225	.268	0 0	SS-220, OF-99, 2B-15, 3B-1

	G	AB	H	2B	3B	HR	HR%	R	RBI	BB	SO	SB	BA	SA	Pinch Hit AB H	G by POS

Freddy Parent continued
WORLD SERIES
| 1903 BOS A | 8 | 32 | 9 | 0 | 3 4th | 0 | 0.0 | 8 | 3 | 1 | 1 | 0 | .281 | .469 | 0 0 | SS-8 |

Casey Parsons
PARSONS, CASEY   BL TR 6'1" 180 lbs.
B. Apr. 14, 1954, Wenatchee, Wash.

1981 SEA A	36	22	5	1	0	1	4.5	6	5	1	4	0	.227	.409	8 1	OF-24, 1B-1
1983 CHI A	8	5	1	0	0	0	0.0	1	0	2	1	0	.200	.200	4 0	OF-3, DH-2
2 yrs.	44	27	6	1	0	1	3.7	7	5	3	5	0	.222	.370	12 1	OF-27, DH-2, 1B-1
1 yr.	8	5	1	0	0	0	0.0	1	0	2	1	0	.200	.200	4 0	OF-3, DH-2

Johnny Pasek
PASEK, JOHN PAUL   BR TR 5'10" 175 lbs.
B. June 25, 1905, Niagara Falls, N.Y.   D. Mar. 13, 1976, St. Petersburg, Fla.

1933 DET A	28	61	15	4	0	0	0.0	6	4	7	7	2	.246	.311	0 0	C-28
1934 CHI A	4	9	3	0	0	0	0.0	1	0	1	1	0	.333	.333	0 0	C-4
2 yrs.	32	70	18	4	0	0	0.0	7	4	8	8	2	.257	.314	0 0	C-32
1 yr.	4	9	3	0	0	0	0.0	1	0	1	1	0	.333	.333	0 0	C-4

Ham Patterson
PATTERSON, HAMILTON   TR
Brother of Pat Patterson.
B. Oct. 13, 1877, Belleville, Ill.   D. Nov. 25, 1945, E. St. Louis, Ill.

| 1909 2 teams | STL A (17G – .204) | | | | CHI A (1G – .000) | | | | | | | | | | | |
| " total | 18 | 52 | 10 | 1 | 0 | 0 | 0.0 | 4 | 5 | 1 | | 1 | .192 | .212 | 5 0 | 1B-7, OF-6 |

Don Pavletich
PAVLETICH, DONALD STEPHEN   BR TR 5'11" 190 lbs.
B. July 13, 1938, Milwaukee, Wis.

1957 CIN N	1	1	0	0	0	0	0.0	0	0	0	0	0	.000	.000	1 0	
1959	1	0	0	0	0	0	–	1	0	0	0	0	–	–	0 0	
1962	34	63	14	3	0	1	1.6	7	7	8	18	0	.222	.317	11 3	1B-25, C-2
1963	71	183	38	11	0	5	2.7	18	18	17	12	0	.208	.350	16 0	1B-57, C-13
1964	34	91	22	4	0	5	5.5	12	11	10	17	0	.242	.451	7 1	C-27, 1B-1
1965	68	191	61	11	1	8	4.2	25	32	23	27	1	.319	.513	11 4	C-54, 1B-9
1966	83	235	69	13	2	12	5.1	29	38	18	37	1	.294	.519	23 6	C-55, 1B-10
1967	74	231	55	14	3	6	2.6	25	34	21	38	2	.238	.403	8 1	C-66, 1B-6, 3B-1
1968	46	98	28	3	1	2	2.0	11	11	8	23	0	.286	.398	20 4	1B-22, C-5
1969 CHI A	78	188	46	12	0	6	3.2	26	33	28	45	0	.245	.404	19 4	C-51, 1B-13
1970 BOS A	32	65	9	1	1	0	0.0	4	6	10	15	1	.138	.185	7 1	1B-16, C-10
1971	14	27	7	1	0	1	3.7	5	3	5	5	0	.259	.407	5 1	C-8
12 yrs.	536	1373	349	73	8	46	3.4	163	193	148	237	5	.254	.420	128 25	C-291, 1B-159, 3B-1
1 yr.	78	188	46	12	0	6	3.2	26	33	28	45	0	.245	.404	19 4	C-51, 1B-13

Fred Payne
PAYNE, FREDERICK THOMAS   BR TR
B. Sept. 2, 1880, Camden, N.Y.   D. Jan. 16, 1954, Camden, N.Y.

1906 DET A	72	222	60	5	5	0	0.0	23	20	13		4	.270	.338	7 3	C-47, OF-17
1907	53	169	28	2	2	0	0.0	17	14	7		4	.166	.201	1 0	C-46, OF-5
1908	20	45	3	0	0	0	0.0	3	2	3		1	.067	.067	2 0	C-16, OF-2
1909 CHI A	32	82	20	2	0	0	0.0	8	12	5		0	.244	.268	2 1	C-27, OF-3
1910	91	257	56	5	4	0	0.0	17	19	11		6	.218	.268	9 2	C-78, OF-2
1911	66	133	27	2	1	1	0.8	14	19	8		6	.203	.256	9 3	C-56
6 yrs.	334	908	194	16	12	1	0.1	82	86	47		21	.214	.261	30 9	C-270, OF-29
3 yrs.	189	472	103	9	5	1	0.2	39	50	24		12	.218	.265	20 6	C-161, OF-5

WORLD SERIES
| 1907 DET A | 2 | 4 | 1 | 0 | 0 | 0 | 0.0 | 0 | 1 | 0 | 0 | 0 | .250 | .250 | 0 0 | C-1 |

Roger Peckinpaugh
PECKINPAUGH, ROGER THORPE   BR TR 5'10½" 165 lbs.
B. Feb. 5, 1891, Wooster, Ohio   D. Nov. 17, 1977, Cleveland, Ohio
Manager 1914, 1928-33, 1941.

1910 CLE A	15	45	9	0	0	0	0.0	1	6	1		3	.200	.200	1 0	SS-14
1912	69	236	50	4	1	1	0.4	18	22	16		11	.212	.250	2 0	SS-67
1913 2 teams	CLE A (1G – .000)				NY A (95G – .268)											
" total	96	340	91	10	7	1	0.3	36	32	24	47	19	.268	.347	1 0	SS-94
1914 NY A	157	570	127	14	6	3	0.5	55	51	51	73	38	.223	.284	0 0	SS-157
1915	142	540	119	18	7	5	0.9	67	44	49	72	19	.220	.307	0 0	SS-142
1916	146	552	141	22	8	4	0.7	65	58	62	50	18	.255	.346	0 0	SS-146
1917	148	543	141	24	7	0	0.0	63	41	64	46	17	.260	.330	0 0	SS-148
1918	122	446	103	15	3	0	0.0	59	43	43	41	12	.231	.278	0 0	SS-122
1919	122	453	138	20	2	7	1.5	89	33	59	37	10	.305	.404	1 0	SS-121
1920	139	534	144	26	6	8	1.5	109	54	72	47	8	.270	.386	1 0	SS-137
1921	149	577	166	25	7	8	1.4	128	71	84	44	2	.288	.397	0 0	SS-149
1922 WAS A	147	520	132	14	4	2	0.4	62	48	55	36	11	.254	.308	0 0	SS-147
1923	154	568	150	18	4	2	0.4	73	62	64	30	10	.264	.320	0 0	SS-154
1924	155	523	142	20	5	2	0.4	72	73	72	45	11	.272	.340	0 0	SS-155
1925	126	422	124	16	4	4	0.9	67	64	49	23	13	.294	.379	0 0	SS-124, 1B-1
1926	57	147	35	4	1	1	0.7	19	14	28	12	3	.238	.299	9 2	SS-46, 1B-1
1927 CHI A	68	217	64	10	0	0	0.0	23	27	21	6	2	.295	.350	7 2	SS-60
17 yrs.	2012	7233	1876	256	75	48	0.7	1006	739	814	609	207	.259	.335	22 4	SS-1983, 1B-2
1 yr.	68	217	64	10	0	0	0.0	23	27	21	6	2	.295	.350	7 2	SS-60

WORLD SERIES
1921 NY A	8	28	5	1	0	0	0.0	2	5	4	3	0	.179	.214	0 0	SS-8
1924 WAS A	4	12	5	2	0	0	0.0	1	2	1	0	1	.417	.583	0 0	SS-4
1925	7	24	6	1	0	1	4.2	1	4	2	1	5	.250	.417	0 0	SS-7
3 yrs.	19	64	16	4	0	1	1.6	4	4	6	5	2	.250	.359	0 0	SS-19

	G	AB	H	2B	3B	HR	HR%	R	RBI	BB	SO	SB	BA	SA	Pinch Hit AB H	G by POS

Elmer Pence
PENCE, ELMER CLAIR BR TR 6' 185 lbs.
B. Aug. 17, 1900, Valley Springs, Calif. D. Sept. 17, 1968, San Francisco, Calif.

1922 CHI A	1	0	0	0	0	0	–	0	0	0	0	0	–	–	0 0	OF-1

Gary Peters
PETERS, GARY CHARLES BL TL 6'2" 200 lbs.
B. Apr. 21, 1937, Grove City, Pa.

1959 CHI A	2	0	0	0	0	0	–	0	0	0	0	0	–	–	0 0	P-2
1960	2	0	0	0	0	0	–	0	0	0	0	0	–	–	0 0	P-2
1961	3	3	1	0	0	0	0.0	1	0	0	1	0	.333	.333	0 0	P-3
1962	5	0	0	0	0	0	–	0	0	0	0	0	–	–	0 0	P-5
1963	50	81	21	4	1	3	3.7	12	12	3	19	0	.259	.444	1 0	P-41
1964	54	120	25	7	0	4	3.3	9	19	2	29	0	.208	.367	15 4	P-37
1965	42	72	13	1	0	1	1.4	2	6	2	15	0	.181	.236	7 3	P-33
1966	38	81	19	3	2	1	1.2	12	9	0	19	0	.235	.358	5 1	P-30
1967	48	99	21	0	2	2	2.0	10	13	2	23	0	.212	.313	6 1	P-38
1968	46	72	15	3	1	2	2.8	10	8	6	13	0	.208	.361	14 2	P-31
1969	37	71	12	4	0	2	2.8	9	4	2	15	0	.169	.310	0 0	P-36
1970 BOS A	37	82	20	3	1	1	1.2	12	11	8	11	0	.244	.341	0 0	P-34
1971	53	96	26	4	0	3	3.1	7	19	3	20	0	.271	.406	18 5	P-34
1972	33	30	6	2	0	0	0.0	2	1	1	7	0	.200	.267	0 0	P-33
14 yrs.	450	807	179	31	7	19	2.4	86	102	29	172	0	.222	.348	66 16	P-359
11 yrs.	327	599	127	22	6	15	2.5	65	71	17	134	0	.212	.344	48 11	P-258

Buddy Peterson
PETERSON, CARL FRANCIS BR TR 5'9½" 170 lbs.
B. Apr. 23, 1925, Portland, Ore.

1955 CHI A	6	21	6	1	0	0	0.0	7	2	3	2	0	.286	.333	1 1	SS-6
1957 BAL A	7	17	3	2	0	0	0.0	1	0	2	2	0	.176	.294	1 0	SS-7
2 yrs.	13	38	9	3	0	0	0.0	8	2	5	4	0	.237	.316	2 1	SS-13
1 yr.	6	21	6	1	0	0	0.0	7	2	3	2	0	.286	.333	1 1	SS-6

Dave Philley
PHILLEY, DAVID EARL BB TR 6' 188 lbs.
B. May 16, 1920, Paris, Tex.

1941 CHI A	7	9	2	1	0	0	0.0	4	0	3	3	0	.222	.333	4 0	OF-2
1946	17	68	24	2	3	0	0.0	10	17	4	4	5	.353	.471	0 0	OF-17
1947	143	551	142	25	11	2	0.4	55	45	35	39	21	.258	.354	6 2	OF-133, 3B-4
1948	137	488	140	28	3	5	1.0	51	42	50	33	8	.287	.387	8 1	OF-128
1949	146	598	171	20	8	0	0.0	84	44	54	51	13	.286	.346	1 0	OF-145
1950	156	619	150	21	5	14	2.3	69	80	52	57	6	.242	.360	1 0	OF-154
1951 2 teams	CHI A (7G – .240)				PHI A (125G – .263)											
" total	132	493	129	20	7	7	1.4	71	61	65	41	10	.262	.373	5 1	OF-126
1952 PHI A	151	586	154	25	4	7	1.2	80	71	59	35	11	.263	.355	0 0	OF-149, 3B-2
1953	157	620	188	30	9	9	1.5	80	59	51	35	13	.303	.424	1 0	OF-157, 3B-1
1954 CLE A	133	452	102	13	3	12	2.7	48	60	57	48	2	.226	.347	4 1	OF-129
1955 2 teams	CLE A (43G – .298)				BAL A (83G – .299)											
" total	126	415	124	17	5	8	1.9	65	50	46	48	1	.299	.422	10 4	OF-116, 3B-2
1956 2 teams	BAL A (32G – .205)				CHI A (86G – .265)											
" total	118	396	98	18	4	5	1.3	57	64	48	40	4	.247	.351	12 0	OF-61, 1B-51, 3B-5
1957 2 teams	CHI A (22G – .324)				DET A (65G – .283)											
" total	87	244	72	12	1	2	0.8	24	25	11	26	4	.295	.377	29 12	OF-29, 1B-29, 3B-1
1958 PHI N	91	207	64	11	4	3	1.4	30	31	15	20	1	.309	.444	44 18	OF-24, 1B-18
1959	99	254	74	18	2	7	2.8	32	37	18	27	0	.291	.461	38 15	OF-34, 1B-24
1960 3 teams	PHI N (14G – .333)				SF N (39G – .164)				BAL A (14G – .265)							
" total	67	110	24	4	1	2	1.8	13	16	13	21	0	.218	.327	48 11	OF-21, 3B-4, 1B-2
1961 BAL A	99	144	36	9	2	1	0.7	13	23	10	20	2	.250	.361	72 24	OF-25, 1B-1
1962 BOS A	38	42	6	2	0	0	0.0	3	4	5	3	0	.143	.190	28 4	OF-4
18 yrs.	1904	6296	1700	276	72	84	1.3	789	729	596	551	102	.270	.377	311 93	OF-1454, 1B-125, 3B-19
9 yrs.	721	2708	732	117	32	25	0.9	326	286	232	227	55	.270	.365	37 5	OF-632, 1B-53, 3B-4

WORLD SERIES

| 1954 CLE A | 4 | 8 | 1 | 0 | 0 | 0 | 0.0 | 0 | 0 | 1 | 3 | 0 | .125 | .125 | 2 0 | OF-2 |

Bubba Phillips
PHILLIPS, JOHN MELVIN BR TR 5'9" 180 lbs.
B. Feb. 24, 1930, West Point, Miss.

1955 DET A	95	184	43	4	0	3	1.6	18	23	14	20	2	.234	.304	17 1	OF-65, 3B-4
1956 CHI A	67	99	27	6	0	2	2.0	16	11	6	12	1	.273	.394	13 4	OF-35, 3B-2
1957	121	393	106	13	3	7	1.8	38	42	28	32	5	.270	.372	3 0	3B-97, OF-20
1958	84	260	71	10	0	5	1.9	26	30	15	14	3	.273	.369	4 0	3B-47, OF-37
1959	117	379	100	27	1	5	1.3	43	40	27	28	1	.264	.380	1 0	3B-100, OF-23
1960 CLE A	113	304	63	14	1	4	1.3	34	33	14	37	0	.207	.299	5 0	3B-85, OF-25, SS-1
1961	143	546	144	23	1	18	3.3	64	72	29	61	1	.264	.408	0 0	3B-143
1962	148	562	145	26	0	10	1.8	53	54	20	55	0	.258	.358	1 0	3B-145, OF-3, 2B-1
1963 DET A	128	464	114	11	2	5	1.1	42	45	19	42	6	.246	.310	6 2	3B-117, OF-5
1964	46	87	22	1	0	3	3.4	14	6	10	13	1	.253	.368	17 4	3B-22, OF-1
10 yrs.	1062	3278	835	135	8	62	1.9	348	356	182	314	25	.255	.358	67 11	3B-762, OF-214, SS-1, 2B-1
4 yrs.	389	1131	304	56	4	19	1.7	123	123	76	86	10	.269	.376	21 4	3B-246, OF-115

WORLD SERIES

| 1959 CHI A | 3 | 10 | 3 | 1 | 0 | 0 | 0.0 | 0 | 0 | 0 | 0 | 0 | .300 | .400 | 0 0 | 3B-3 |

Tony Piet
PIET, ANTHONY FRANCIS BR TR 6' 175 lbs.
Also known as Anthony Francis Pietruszka.
B. Dec. 7, 1906, Berwick, Pa. D. Dec. 1, 1981, Hinsdale, Ill.

1931 PIT N	44	167	50	12	4	0	0.0	22	24	13	24	10	.299	.419	0 0	2B-44, SS-1
1932	154	574	162	25	8	7	1.2	66	85	46	56	19	.282	.390	0 0	2B-154
1933	107	362	117	21	5	1	0.3	45	42	19	28	12	.323	.417	9 2	2B-97
1934 CIN N	106	421	109	20	5	1	0.2	58	38	23	44	6	.259	.337	4 2	3B-51, 2B-49

Player Register

	G	AB	H	2B	3B	HR	HR%	R	RBI	BB	SO	SB	BA	SA	Pinch Hit AB	H	G by POS

Tony Piet continued

1935 2 teams	CIN N (6G – .200)					CHI A (77G – .298)											
" total	83	297	88	18	5	3	1.0	49	29	33	27	2	.296	.421	1	0	2B-59, 3B-17, OF-1
1936 CHI A	109	352	96	15	2	7	2.0	69	42	66	48	15	.273	.386	7	1	2B-68, 3B-32
1937	100	332	78	15	1	4	1.2	34	38	32	36	14	.235	.322	1	1	3B-86, 2B-13
1938 DET A	41	80	17	6	0	0	0.0	9	14	15	11	2	.213	.288	17	5	3B-18, 2B-1
8 yrs.	744	2585	717	132	30	23	0.9	352	312	247	274	80	.277	.378	39	11	2B-485, 3B-204, OF-1, SS-1
3 yrs.	286	976	261	47	8	14	1.4	150	107	131	111	31	.267	.375	8	2	2B-140, 3B-135

Al Pilarcik
PILARCIK, ALFRED JAMES
B. July 3, 1930, Whiting, Ind. BL TL 5'10" 180 lbs.

1956 KC A	69	239	60	10	1	4	1.7	28	22	30	32	9	.251	.351	4	1	OF-67
1957 BAL A	142	407	113	16	3	9	2.2	52	49	53	28	14	.278	.398	15	3	OF-126
1958	141	379	92	21	0	1	0.3	40	24	42	37	7	.243	.306	24	7	OF-118
1959	130	273	77	12	1	3	1.1	37	16	30	25	9	.282	.366	21	7	OF-106
1960	104	194	48	5	1	4	2.1	30	17	15	16	0	.247	.345	23	6	OF-75
1961 2 teams	KC A (35G – .200)					CHI A (47G – .177)											
" total	82	122	23	2	1	1	0.8	18	15	15	12	2	.189	.246	28	6	OF-38
6 yrs.	668	1614	413	66	7	22	1.4	205	143	185	150	41	.256	.346	115	30	OF-530
1 yr.	47	62	11	1	0	1	1.6	9	6	9	5	1	.177	.242	17	4	OF-17

Babe Pinelli
PINELLI, RALPH ARTHUR
Born Rinaldo Angelo Paolinelli.
B. Oct. 18, 1895, San Francisco, Calif. BR TR 5'9" 165 lbs.

1918 CHI A	24	78	18	1	1	1	1.3	7	7	7	8	3	.231	.308	0	0	3B-24
1920 DET A	102	284	65	9	3	0	0.0	33	21	25	16	6	.229	.282	4	0	3B-74, SS-18, 2B-1
1922 CIN N	156	547	167	19	7	1	0.2	77	72	48	37	17	.305	.371	0	0	3B-156
1923	117	423	117	14	5	0	0.0	44	51	27	29	10	.277	.333	0	0	3B-116
1924	144	510	156	16	7	0	0.0	61	70	32	32	23	.306	.365	1	1	3B-143
1925	130	492	139	33	6	2	0.4	68	49	22	28	8	.283	.386	6	2	3B-109, SS-17
1926	71	207	46	7	4	0	0.0	26	24	15	5	2	.222	.295	3	1	3B-40, SS-27, 2B-3
1927	30	76	15	2	0	1	1.3	11	4	6	7	2	.197	.263	0	0	3B-15, SS-9, 2B-5
8 yrs.	774	2617	723	101	33	5	0.2	327	298	182	162	71	.276	.346	14	4	3B-677, SS-71, 2B-9
1 yr.	24	78	18	1	1	1	1.3	7	7	7	8	3	.231	.308	0	0	3B-24

Whitey Platt
PLATT, MIZELL GEORGE
B. Aug. 21, 1920, West Palm Beach, Fla. D. July 27, 1970, West Palm Beach, Fla. BR TR 6'1½" 190 lbs.

1942 CHI N	4	16	1	0	0	0	0.0	1	2	0	3	0	.063	.063	0	0	OF-4
1943	20	41	7	3	0	0	0.0	2	2	1	7	0	.171	.244	4	1	OF-14
1946 CHI A	84	247	62	8	5	3	1.2	28	32	17	34	1	.251	.360	24	6	OF-61
1948 STL A	123	454	123	22	10	7	1.5	57	82	39	51	1	.271	.410	8	2	OF-114
1949	102	244	63	8	2	3	1.2	29	29	24	27	0	.258	.344	34	7	OF-59, 1B-2
5 yrs.	333	1002	256	41	17	13	1.3	117	147	81	122	2	.255	.369	70	16	OF-252, 1B-2
1 yr.	84	247	62	8	5	3	1.2	28	32	17	34	1	.251	.360	24	6	OF-61

Irv Porter
PORTER, IRVING MARBLE
B. May 17, 1888, Lynn, Mass. D. Feb. 20, 1971, Lynn, Mass. BB TR 5'9" 155 lbs.

1914 CHI A	1	4	1	0	0	0	0.0	1		1	0		.250	.250	0	0	OF-1

Bob Powell
POWELL, ROBERT LEROY
B. Oct. 17, 1933, Flint, Mich. BR TR 6'1" 190 lbs.

1955 CHI A	1	0	0	0	0	0	–	0	0	0	0		–	–	0	0	
1957	1	0	0	0	0	0	–	1	0	0	0		–	–	0	0	
2 yrs.	2	0	0	0	0	0	–	1	0	0	0		–	–	0	0	
2 yrs.	2	0	0	0	0	0	–	1	0	0	0		–	–	0	0	

Frank Pratt
PRATT, FRANCIS BRUCE (Truckhorse)
B. Aug. 24, 1897, Blocton, Ala. D. Apr. 8, 1974, Centreville, Ala. BL TR 5'9½" 155 lbs.

1921 CHI A	1	1	0	0	0	0	0.0	0	0	0	0	0	.000	.000	1	0	

Ron Pruitt
PRUITT, RONALD RALPH
B. Oct. 21, 1951, Flint, Mich. BR TR 6' 185 lbs.

1975 TEX A	14	17	3	0	0	0	0.0	2	0	1	3	0	.176	.176	0	0	C-13, OF-1
1976 CLE A	47	86	23	1	1	0	0.0	7	5	16	8	2	.267	.302	7	3	OF-26, 3B-6, C-6, DH-4, 1B-1
1977	78	219	63	10	2	2	0.9	29	32	28	22	2	.288	.379	8	1	OF-69, DH-4, C-4, 3B-1
1978	71	187	44	6	1	6	3.2	17	17	16	20	2	.235	.374	10	3	C-48, OF-16, DH-5, 3B-2
1979	64	166	47	7	0	2	1.2	23	21	19	21	2	.283	.361	18	6	OF-29, DH-14, C-11, 3B-3
1980 2 teams	CLE A (23G – .306)					CHI A (33G – .300)											
" total	56	106	32	3	0	2	1.9	9	15	12	13	0	.302	.387	20	5	OF-17, DH-9, 3B-5, C-5, 1B-1
1981 CLE N	5	9	0	0	0	0	0.0	0	0	1	2	0	.000	.000	2	0	OF-3, DH-1, C-1
1982 SF N	5	4	2	1	0	0	0.0	1	2	1	1	0	.500	.750	2	1	OF-1, C-1
1983	1	1	0	0	0	0	0.0	0	0	0	0	0	.000	.000	1	0	
9 yrs.	341	795	214	28	4	12	1.5	88	92	94	90	8	.269	.360	68	19	OF-162, C-89, DH-37, 3B-17, 1B-2
1 yr.	33	70	21	2	0	2	2.9	8	11	8	7	0	.300	.414	11	2	OF-11, DH-7, C-5, 3B-3, 1B-1

Greg Pryor
PRYOR, GREGORY RUSSELL
B. Oct. 2, 1949, Marietta, Ohio BR TR 6' 180 lbs.

1976 TEX A	5	8	3	0	0	0	0.0	2	1	0	1	0	.375	.375	0	0	2B-3, SS-1, 3B-1
1978 CHI A	82	222	58	11	0	2	0.9	27	15	11	18	3	.261	.338	0	0	2B-35, SS-28, 3B-20
1979	143	476	131	23	3	3	0.6	60	34	35	41	3	.275	.355	1	0	SS-119, 2B-25, 3B-22
1980	122	338	81	18	4	1	0.3	32	29	12	35	2	.240	.325	5	1	SS-76, 3B-41, 2B-5, DH-1
1981	47	76	17	1	0	0	0.0	4	6	6	8	0	.224	.237	1	0	3B-27, SS-13, 2B-5

	G	AB	H	2B	3B	HR	HR%	R	RBI	BB	SO	SB	BA	SA	Pinch Hit AB	H	G by POS

Greg Pryor continued
	G	AB	H	2B	3B	HR	HR%	R	RBI	BB	SO	SB	BA	SA	PH AB	PH H	G by POS
1982 KC A	73	152	41	10	1	2	1.3	23	12	10	20	2	.270	.388	3	0	3B-40, 2B-15, 1B-14, SS-7
1983	68	115	25	4	0	1	0.9	9	14	7	8	0	.217	.278	1	0	3B-60, 1B-6, 2B-3
7 yrs.	540	1387	356	67	8	9	0.6	157	111	81	131	10	.257	.336	11	1	SS-244, 3B-211, 2B-91, 1B-20, DH-1
4 yrs.	394	1112	287	53	7	6	0.5	123	84	64	102	8	.258	.335	7	1	SS-236, 3B-110, 2B-70, DH-1

Pid Purdy
PURDY, EVERETT VIRGIL BL TR 5'6" 150 lbs.
B. June 15, 1904, Beatrice, Neb. D. Jan. 16, 1951, Beatrice, Neb.

	G	AB	H	2B	3B	HR	HR%	R	RBI	BB	SO	SB	BA	SA	PH AB	PH H	G by POS
1926 CHI A	11	33	6	2	1	0	0.0	5	6	2	1	0	.182	.303	2	0	OF-9
1927 CIN N	18	62	22	2	4	1	1.6	15	12	4	3	0	.355	.565	2	1	OF-16
1928	70	223	69	11	1	0	0.0	32	25	23	13	1	.309	.368	8	6	OF-61
1929	82	181	49	7	5	1	0.6	22	16	19	8	2	.271	.381	33	8	OF-42
4 yrs.	181	499	146	22	11	2	0.4	74	59	48	25	3	.293	.393	45	15	OF-128
1 yr.	11	33	6	2	1	0	0.0	5	6	2	1	0	.182	.303	2	0	OF-9

Billy Purtell
PURTELL, WILLIAM PATRICK BR TR 5'9" 170 lbs.
B. Jan. 6, 1886, Columbus, Ohio D. Mar. 17, 1962, Bradenton, Fla.

	G	AB	H	2B	3B	HR	HR%	R	RBI	BB	SO	SB	BA	SA	PH AB	PH H	G by POS
1908 CHI A	26	69	9	2	0	0	0.0	3	3	2		2	.130	.159	1	0	3B-25
1909	103	361	93	3	0	0	0.0	34	40	19		14	.258	.299	0	0	3B-71, 2B-32
1910 2 teams	CHI A (102G – .234)				BOS A (49G – .208)												
" total	151	536	121	6	5	2	0.4	36	51	39		7	.226	.267	0	0	3B-143, SS-8
1911 BOS A	27	82	23	5	3	0	0.0	5	7	1		1	.280	.415	5	1	3B-16, SS-3, 2B-3, OF-1
1914 DET A	26	76	13	4	0	0	0.0	4	3	2	7	0	.171	.224	1	0	3B-16, SS-1, 2B-1
5 yrs.	333	1124	259	26	11	2	0.2	82	104	63	7	24	.230	.278	14	2	3B-271, 2B-36, SS-12, OF-1
3 yrs.	231	798	188	16	6	1	0.1	58	79	42		21	.236	.274	1	0	3B-198, 2B-32

Jim Qualls
QUALLS, JAMES ROBERT BB TR 5'10" 158 lbs.
B. Oct. 9, 1946, Exeter, Calif.

	G	AB	H	2B	3B	HR	HR%	R	RBI	BB	SO	SB	BA	SA	PH AB	PH H	G by POS
1969 CHI N	43	120	30	5	3	0	0.0	12	9	2	14	2	.250	.342	4	2	OF-35, 2B-4
1970 MON N	9	9	1	0	0	0	0.0	1	1	0	0	0	.111	.111	5	1	OF-2, 2B-2
1972 CHI A	11	10	0	0	0	0	0.0	0	0	0	2	0	.000	.000	7	0	OF-1
3 yrs.	63	139	31	5	3	0	0.0	13	10	2	16	2	.223	.302	16	3	OF-38, 2B-6
1 yr.	11	10	0	0	0	0	0.0	0	0	0	2	0	.000	.000	7	0	OF-1

Lee Quillin
QUILLIN, LEE ABNER TR
B. May 5, 1882, North Branch, Minn. D. Dec. 14, 1965, White Bear Lake, Minn.

	G	AB	H	2B	3B	HR	HR%	R	RBI	BB	SO	SB	BA	SA	PH AB	PH H	G by POS
1906 CHI A	4	9	3	0	0	0	0.0	1	0	0		1	.333	.333	1	0	SS-3
1907	49	151	29	5	0	0	0.0	17	14	10		8	.192	.225	0	0	3B-48
2 yrs.	53	160	32	5	0	0	0.0	18	14	10		9	.200	.231	1	0	3B-48, SS-3
2 yrs.	53	160	32	5	0	0	0.0	18	14	10		9	.200	.231	1	0	3B-48, SS-3

Finners Quinlan
QUINLAN, THOMAS ALOYSIUS BL TL 5'8" 154 lbs.
B. Oct. 21, 1887, Scranton, Pa. D. Feb. 17, 1966, Scranton, Pa.

	G	AB	H	2B	3B	HR	HR%	R	RBI	BB	SO	SB	BA	SA	PH AB	PH H	G by POS
1913 STL N	13	50	8	0	0	0	0.0	1	1	1	9	0	.160	.160	1	0	OF-12
1915 CHI A	42	114	22	3	0	0	0.0	11	7	4	11	3	.193	.219	4	0	OF-32
2 yrs.	55	164	30	3	0	0	0.0	12	8	5	20	3	.183	.201	5	0	OF-44
1 yr.	42	114	22	3	0	0	0.0	11	7	4	11	3	.193	.219	4	0	OF-32

Rip Radcliff
RADCLIFF, RAYMOND ALLEN BL TL 5'10" 170 lbs.
B. Jan. 19, 1906, Kiowa, Okla. D. May 23, 1962, Enid, Okla.

	G	AB	H	2B	3B	HR	HR%	R	RBI	BB	SO	SB	BA	SA	PH AB	PH H	G by POS
1934 CHI A	14	56	15	2	1	0	0.0	7	5	0	2	1	.268	.339	0	0	OF-14
1935	146	623	178	28	8	10	1.6	95	68	53	21	4	.286	.404	2	0	OF-142
1936	138	618	207	31	7	8	1.3	120	82	44	12	6	.335	.447	6	3	OF-132
1937	144	584	190	38	10	4	0.7	105	79	53	25	6	.325	.445	3	0	OF-139
1938	129	503	166	23	6	5	1.0	64	81	36	17	5	.330	.429	7	2	OF-99, 1B-23
1939	113	397	105	25	2	2	0.5	49	53	26	21	6	.264	.353	13	1	OF-78, 1B-20
1940 STL A	150	584	200	33	9	7	1.2	83	81	47	20	6	.342	.466	5	1	OF-139, 1B-4
1941 2 teams	STL A (19G – .282)				DET A (96G – .317)												
" total	115	450	140	16	7	5	1.1	59	53	29	14	5	.311	.411	8	0	OF-101, 1B-3
1942 DET A	62	144	36	5	0	1	0.7	13	20	9	6	0	.250	.306	29	3	OF-24, 1B-4
1943	70	115	30	4	0	0	0.0	3	10	3	3	1	.261	.296	44	11	OF-19, 1B-1
10 yrs.	1081	4074	1267	205	50	42	1.0	598	532	310	141	40	.311	.417	119	24	OF-887, 1B-55
6 yrs.	684	2781	861	147	34	29	1.0	440	368	212	98	28	.310	.418	33	9	OF-604, 1B-43
												9th					

Don Rader
RADER, DONALD RUSSELL BL TR 5'10" 164 lbs.
B. Sept. 5, 1893, Wolcott, Ind.

	G	AB	H	2B	3B	HR	HR%	R	RBI	BB	SO	SB	BA	SA	PH AB	PH H	G by POS
1913 CHI A	2	3	1	1	0	0	0.0	1	0	0	0	0	.333	.667	0	0	OF-1, 3B-1
1921 PHI N	9	32	9	2	0	0	0.0	4	3	3	5	0	.281	.344	0	0	SS-9
2 yrs.	11	35	10	3	0	0	0.0	5	3	3	5	0	.286	.371	0	0	SS-9, OF-1, 3B-1
1 yr.	2	3	1	1	0	0	0.0	1	0	0	0	0	.333	.667	0	0	OF-1, 3B-1

Earl Rapp
RAPP, EARL WELLINGTON BL TR 6'2" 185 lbs.
B. May 20, 1921, Corunna, Mich.

	G	AB	H	2B	3B	HR	HR%	R	RBI	BB	SO	SB	BA	SA	PH AB	PH H	G by POS
1949 2 teams	DET A (1G – .000)				CHI A (19G – .259)												
" total	20	54	14	1	0	0	0.0	3	11	6	6	1	.259	.315	5	1	OF-13
1951 2 teams	NY N (13G – .091)				STL A (26G – .327)												
" total	39	109	33	5	3	2	1.8	14	15	13	14	1	.303	.459	12	1	OF-25
1952 2 teams	STL A (30G – .143)				WAS A (46G – .284)												
" total	76	116	26	10	0	0	0.0	10	13	6	21	0	.224	.310	54	10	OF-17
3 yrs.	135	279	73	16	4	2	0.7	27	39	25	41	2	.262	.369	71	12	OF-55
1 yr.	19	54	14	1	0	0	0.0	3	11	5	6	1	.259	.315	5	1	OF-13

Player Register

	G	AB	H	2B	3B	HR	HR%	R	RBI	BB	SO	SB	BA	SA	Pinch Hit AB H	G by POS

Morrie Rath
RATH, MAURICE CHARLES
B. Dec. 25, 1887, Mobeetie, Tex. D. Nov. 18, 1945, Upper Darby, Pa.
BL TR 5'8½" 160 lbs.

Year	Team	G	AB	H	2B	3B	HR	HR%	R	RBI	BB	SO	SB	BA	SA	PH AB	PH H	G by POS
1909	PHI A	7	26	7	1	0	0	0.0	4	3	2		1	.269	.308	0	0	SS-4, 3B-2
1910	2 teams		PHI A (18G – .154)						CLE A (24G – .194)									
"	total	42	93	17	3	0	0	0.0	8	1	15		2	.183	.215	3	0	3B-33, 2B-3, SS-1
1912	CHI A	157	591	161	10	2	1	0.2	104	19	95		30	.272	.301	0	0	2B-157
1913		90	295	59	2	0	0	0.0	37	12	46	22	22	.200	.207	2	1	2B-86
1919	CIN N	138	537	142	13	1	1	0.2	77	29	64	24	17	.264	.298	0	0	2B-138
1920		129	506	135	7	4	2	0.4	61	28	36	24	10	.267	.308	1	0	2B-126, OF-1, 3B-1
	6 yrs.	563	2048	521	36	7	4	0.2	291	92	258	70	82	.254	.285	6	1	2B-510, 3B-36, SS-5, OF-1
	2 yrs.	247	886	220	12	2	1	0.1	141	31	141	22	52	.248	.270	2	1	2B-243

WORLD SERIES
| 1919 | CIN N | 8 | 31 | 7 | 1 | 0 | 0 | 0.0 | 5 | 2 | 4 | 1 | 2 | .226 | .258 | 0 | 0 | 2B-8 |

Buck Redfern
REDFERN, GEORGE HOWARD
B. Apr. 7, 1902, Asheville, N.C. D. Sept. 8, 1964, Asheville, N.C.
BR TR 5'11" 165 lbs.

1928	CHI A	86	261	61	6	3	0	0.0	22	35	12	19	8	.234	.280	1	0	2B-45, SS-33, 3B-1
1929		21	44	6	0	0	0	0.0	0	3	3	3	1	.136	.136	1	0	2B-11, 3B-5, SS-4
	2 yrs.	107	305	67	6	3	0	0.0	22	38	15	22	9	.220	.259	2	0	2B-56, SS-37, 3B-5
	2 yrs.	107	305	67	6	3	0	0.0	22	38	15	22	9	.220	.259	2	0	2B-56, SS-37, 3B-6

Rick Reichardt
REICHARDT, FREDERIC CARL
B. Mar. 16, 1943, Madison, Wis.
BR TR 6'3" 210 lbs.

1964	LA A	11	37	6	0	0	0	0.0	0	0	1	12	1	.162	.162	0	0	OF-11
1965	CAL A	20	75	20	4	0	1	1.3	8	6	5	12	4	.267	.360	2	1	OF-20
1966		89	319	92	5	4	16	5.0	48	44	27	61	8	.288	.480	2	1	OF-87
1967		146	498	132	14	2	17	3.4	56	69	35	90	5	.265	.404	9	2	OF-138
1968		151	534	136	20	3	21	3.9	62	73	42	118	8	.255	.421	5	1	OF-148
1969		137	493	125	11	4	13	2.6	60	68	43	100	3	.254	.371	0	0	OF-136, 1B-3
1970	2 teams		CAL A (9G – .167)						WAS A (107G – .253)									
"	total	116	283	71	14	2	15	5.3	43	47	26	69	2	.251	.473	41	8	OF-80, 3B-1
1971	CHI A	138	496	138	14	2	19	3.8	53	62	37	90	5	.278	.429	7	2	OF-128, 1B-9
1972		101	291	73	14	4	8	2.7	31	43	28	63	2	.251	.409	10	1	OF-90
1973	2 teams		CHI A (41G – .275)						KC A (46G – .220)									
"	total	87	280	70	13	3	6	2.1	30	33	19	57	2	.250	.382	9	3	OF-44, DH-37
1974	KC A	1	1	1	0	0	0	0.0	0	0	0	0	0	1.000	1.000	1	1	
	11 yrs.	997	3307	864	109	24	116	3.5	391	445	263	672	40	.261	.414	84	19	OF-882, DH-37, 1B-12, 3B-1
	3 yrs.	285	940	253	36	7	30	3.2	99	121	73	182	9	.269	.418	23	5	OF-255, 1B-9, DH-6

Barney Reilly
REILLY, BERNARD EUGENE
B. Feb. 7, 1884, Brockton, Mass. D. Nov. 15, 1934, St. Joseph, Mo.
BR TR 6' 175 lbs.

| 1909 | CHI A | 12 | 25 | 5 | 0 | 0 | 0 | 0.0 | 3 | 3 | 3 | | 2 | .200 | .200 | 0 | 0 | 2B-11, OF-1 |

Tony Rensa
RENSA, TONY GEORGE (Pug)
B. Sept. 29, 1901, Parsons, Pa.
BR TR 5'10" 180 lbs.

1930	2 teams		DET A (20G – .270)						PHI N (54G – .285)									
"	total	74	209	59	13	3	4	1.9	37	34	16	25	1	.282	.431	6	1	C-67
1931	PHI N	19	29	3	1	0	0	0.0	2	2	6	2	0	.103	.138	2	0	C-17
1933	NY A	8	29	9	2	1	0	0.0	4	3	1	3	0	.310	.448	0	0	C-8
1937	CHI A	26	57	17	5	1	0	0.0	10	5	8	6	3	.298	.421	2	1	C-23
1938		59	165	41	5	0	3	1.8	15	19	25	16	1	.248	.333	2	1	C-57
1939		14	25	5	0	0	0	0.0	3	2	1	2	0	.200	.200	1	1	C-13
	6 yrs.	200	514	134	26	5	7	1.4	71	65	57	54	5	.261	.372	13	3	C-185
	3 yrs.	99	247	63	10	1	3	1.2	28	26	34	24	4	.255	.340	5	2	C-93

Carl Reynolds
REYNOLDS, CARL NETTLES
B. Feb. 1, 1903, LaRue, Tex. D. Dec. 29, 1978, Houston, Tex.
BR TR 6' 194 lbs.

1927	CHI A	14	42	9	3	0	1	2.4	5	7	5	7	1	.214	.357	0	0	OF-13
1928		84	291	94	21	11	2	0.7	51	36	17	13	15	.323	.491	10	6	OF-74
1929		131	517	164	24	12	11	2.1	81	67	20	37	19	.317	.474	0	0	OF-131
1930		138	563	202	25	18	22	3.9	103	100	20	39	16	.359	.584	5	0	OF-132
1931		118	462	134	24	14	6	1.3	71	77	24	26	17	.290	.442	9	5	OF-109
1932	WAS A	102	406	124	28	7	9	2.2	53	63	14	19	8	.305	.475	5	1	OF-95
1933	STL A	135	475	136	26	14	8	1.7	81	71	50	25	5	.286	.451	13	3	OF-124
1934	BOS A	113	413	125	26	9	4	1.0	61	86	27	28	5	.303	.438	14	3	OF-100
1935		78	244	66	13	4	6	2.5	33	35	24	20	4	.270	.430	11	2	OF-64
1936	WAS A	89	293	81	18	2	4	1.4	41	41	21	22	8	.276	.392	15	3	OF-72
1937	CHI N	7	11	3	1	0	0	0.0	0	1	2	2	0	.273	.364	4	0	OF-2
1938		125	497	150	28	10	3	0.6	59	67	22	32	9	.302	.416	0	0	OF-125
1939		88	281	69	10	6	4	1.4	33	44	16	38	5	.246	.367	14	3	OF-72
	13 yrs.	1222	4495	1357	247	107	80	1.8	672	695	262	308	112	.302	.458	100	25	OF-1113
	5 yrs.	485	1875	603	97	55	42	2.2	311	287	86	122	68	.322	.499	24	9	OF-459
														3rd	2nd			

WORLD SERIES
| 1938 | CHI N | 4 | 12 | 0 | 0 | 0 | 0 | 0.0 | 0 | 0 | 1 | 3 | 0 | .000 | .000 | 1 | 0 | OF-3 |

Danny Reynolds
REYNOLDS, DANIEL VANCE (Squirrel)
B. Nov. 27, 1919, Stony Point, N.C.
BR TR 5'11" 158 lbs.

| 1945 | CHI A | 29 | 72 | 12 | 2 | 1 | 0 | 0.0 | 6 | 4 | 3 | 8 | 1 | .167 | .222 | 4 | 0 | SS-14, 2B-11 |

Bobby Rhawn
RHAWN, ROBERT JOHN (Rocky)
B. Feb. 13, 1919, Catawissa, Pa.
BR TR 5'8" 180 lbs.

| 1947 | NY N | 13 | 45 | 14 | 3 | 0 | 1 | 2.2 | 7 | 3 | 8 | 1 | 0 | .311 | .444 | 0 | 0 | 2B-8, 3B-5 |
| 1948 | | 36 | 44 | 12 | 2 | 1 | 1 | 2.3 | 11 | 8 | 6 | 3 | 0 | .273 | .432 | 4 | 2 | SS-14, 3B-7 |

307

	G	AB	H	2B	3B	HR	HR%	R	RBI	BB	SO	SB	BA	SA	Pinch Hit AB	H	G by POS

Bobby Rhawn continued
1949 3 teams	NY	N (14G – .172)		PIT	N (3G – .143)			CHI	A (24G – .205)								
" total	41	109	21	4	1	0	0.0	20	7	19	10	1	.193	.248	3	1	3B-21, 2B-8, SS-3
3 yrs.	90	198	47	9	2	2	1.0	38	18	35	17	4	.237	.333	7	3	3B-33, SS-17, 2B-16
1 yr.	24	73	15	4	1	0	0.0	12	5	12	8	0	.205	.288	2	1	3B-19, SS-3

Hal Rhyne
RHYNE, HAROLD J.
B. Mar. 30, 1899, Paso Robles, Calif.   D. Jan. 7, 1971, Orangevale, Calif.
BR TR 5'8½" 163 lbs.

1926 PIT N	109	366	92	14	3	2	0.5	46	39	35	21	1	.251	.322	0	0	2B-66, SS-44, 3B-1
1927	62	168	46	5	0	0	0.0	21	17	14	9	0	.274	.304	1	0	2B-45, 3B-10, SS-7
1929 BOS A	120	346	87	24	5	0	0.0	41	38	25	14	4	.251	.350	1	0	SS-114, OF-1, 3B-1
1930	107	296	60	8	5	0	0.0	34	23	25	19	1	.203	.264	0	0	SS-107
1931	147	565	154	34	3	0	0.0	75	51	57	41	3	.273	.343	0	0	SS-147
1932	71	207	47	12	5	0	0.0	26	14	23	14	3	.227	.333	10	3	SS-55, 3B-4, 2B-1
1933 CHI A	39	83	22	1	1	0	0.0	9	10	5	9	1	.265	.301	6	1	2B-19, 3B-13, SS-2
7 yrs.	655	2031	508	98	22	2	0.1	252	192	184	127	13	.250	.323	18	4	SS-476, 2B-131, 3B-29, OF-1
1 yr.	39	83	22	1	1	0	0.0	9	10	5	9	1	.265	.301	6	1	2B-19, 3B-13, SS-2

WORLD SERIES
| 1927 PIT N | 1 | 4 | 0 | 0 | 0 | 0 | 0.0 | 0 | 0 | 0 | 0 | 0 | .000 | .000 | 0 | 0 | 2B-1 |

Lee Richard
RICHARD, LEE EDWARD (Bee Bee)
B. Sept. 18, 1948, Lafayette, La.
BR TR 5'11" 165 lbs.

1971 CHI A	87	260	60	7	3	2	0.8	38	17	20	46	8	.231	.304	6	0	SS-68, OF-16
1972	11	29	7	0	0	0	0.0	5	1	0	7	1	.241	.241	1	1	OF-6, SS-1
1974	32	67	11	1	0	0	0.0	5	1	5	8	0	.164	.179	0	0	3B-12, SS-6, DH-5, 2B-3, OF-1
1975	43	45	9	0	1	0	0.0	11	5	4	7	2	.200	.244	0	0	3B-12, SS-9, DH-5, 2B-5
1976 STL N	66	91	16	4	2	0	0.0	12	5	4	9	1	.176	.264	3	0	2B-26, SS-12, 3B-1
5 yrs.	239	492	103	12	6	2	0.4	71	29	33	77	12	.209	.270	10	1	SS-96, 2B-34, 3B-25, OF-23, DH-10
4 yrs.	173	401	87	8	4	2	0.5	59	24	29	68	11	.217	.272	7	1	SS-84, 3B-24, OF-23, DH-10, 2B-8

Paul Richards
RICHARDS, PAUL RAPIER
B. Nov. 21, 1908, Waxahachie, Tex.
Manager 1951-61, 1976
BR TR 6'1½" 180 lbs.

1932 BKN N	3	8	0	0	0	0	0.0	0	0	0	2	0	.000	.000	0	0	C-3
1933 NY N	51	87	17	3	0	0	0.0	4	10	3	12	0	.195	.230	14	2	C-36
1934	42	75	12	1	0	0	0.0	9	10	3	13	8	0	.160	.173	3	2	C-37
1935 2 teams	NY	N (7G – .250)		PHI	A (85G – .245)												
" total	92	261	64	10	1	4	1.5	31	29	26	13	0	.245	.337	6	2	C-83
1943 DET A	100	313	69	7	1	5	1.6	32	33	38	35	1	.220	.297	0	0	C-100
1944	95	300	71	13	0	3	1.0	24	37	35	30	8	.237	.310	3	0	C-90
1945	83	234	60	12	1	3	1.3	26	32	19	31	4	.256	.355	0	0	C-83
1946	57	139	28	5	2	0	0.0	13	11	23	18	2	.201	.266	3	2	C-54
8 yrs.	523	1417	321	51	5	15	1.1	140	155	157	149	15	.227	.301	29	8	C-486

WORLD SERIES
| 1945 DET A | 7 | 19 | 4 | 2 | 0 | 0 | 0.0 | 0 | 6 | 4 | 3 | 0 | .211 | .316 | 0 | 0 | C-7 |

Marv Rickert
RICKERT, MARVIN AUGUST (Twitch)
B. Jan. 8, 1921, Long Branch, Wash.   D. June 3, 1978, Oakville, Wash.
BL TR 6'2" 195 lbs.

1942 CHI N	8	26	7	0	0	0	0.0	5	1	1	5	0	.269	.269	1	0	OF-6
1946	111	392	103	18	3	7	1.8	44	47	28	54	3	.263	.378	6	0	OF-104
1947	71	137	20	0	2	2	1.5	7	15	15	17	0	.146	.190	27	6	OF-30, 1B-7
1948 2 teams	CIN	N (8G – .167)		BOS	N (3G – .231)												
" total	11	19	4	0	1	0	0.0	1	2	0	1	0	.211	.316	6	1	OF-3
1949 BOS N	100	277	81	18	3	6	2.2	44	49	23	38	1	.292	.444	12	3	OF-75, 1B-12
1950 2 teams	PIT	N (17G – .150)		CHI	A (84G – .237)												
" total	101	298	69	9	2	4	1.3	38	31	21	46	0	.232	.315	20	1	OF-81, 1B-1
6 yrs.	402	1149	284	45	9	19	1.7	139	145	88	161	4	.247	.352	72	11	OF-299, 1B-20
1 yr.	84	278	66	9	2	4	1.4	38	27	21	42	0	.237	.327	6	0	OF-78, 1B-1

WORLD SERIES
| 1948 BOS N | 5 | 19 | 4 | 0 | 0 | 1 | 5.3 | 2 | 2 | 0 | 4 | 0 | .211 | .368 | 0 | 0 | OF-5 |

Johnny Riddle
RIDDLE, JOHN LUDY (Mutt)
Brother of Elmer Riddle.
B. Oct. 3, 1905, Clinton, S. C.
BR TR 5'11" 190 lbs.

1930 CHI A	25	58	14	3	1	0	0.0	7	4	3	6	0	.241	.328	0	0	C-25
1937 2 teams	WAS	A (8G – .269)		BOS	N (2G – .000)												
" total	10	29	7	0	0	0	0.0	2	3	1	2	0	.241	.241	0	0	C-10
1938 BOS N	19	57	16	1	0	0	0.0	6	2	4	2	0	.281	.298	0	0	C-19
1941 CIN N	10	10	3	0	0	0	0.0	2	0	0	1	0	.300	.300	0	0	C-10
1944	1	0	0	0	0	0	–	0	0	0	0	0	–	–	0	0	C-1
1945	23	45	8	0	0	0	0.0	0	2	4	6	0	.178	.178	0	0	C-23
1948 PIT N	10	15	3	0	0	0	0.0	0	1	2	0	0	.200	.200	0	0	C-10
7 yrs.	98	214	51	4	1	0	0.0	18	11	13	19	0	.238	.266	1	0	C-98
1 yr.	25	58	14	3	1	0	0.0	7	4	3	6	0	.241	.328	0	0	C-25

Swede Risberg
RISBERG, CHARLES AUGUST
B. Oct. 13, 1894, San Francisco, Calif.   D. Oct. 13, 1975, Red Bluff, Calif.
BR TR 6' 175 lbs.

1917 CHI A	149	474	96	20	8	1	0.2	59	45	59	65	16	.203	.285	2	1	SS-146
1918	82	273	70	12	3	1	0.4	36	27	29	32	5	.256	.333	4	1	SS-30, 3B-24, 2B-12, 1B-7, OF-3
1919	119	414	106	19	6	2	0.5	48	38	35	38	19	.256	.345	0	0	SS-97, 1B-22

Player Register

Player Register 308

	G	AB	H	2B	3B	HR	HR%	R	RBI	BB	SO	SB	BA	SA	Pinch Hit AB	H	G by POS

Swede Risberg continued

1920		126	458	122	21	10	2	0.4	53	65	31	45	12	.266	.369	2	0	SS-124
4 yrs.		476	1619	394	72	27	6	0.4	196	175	148	180	52	.243	.332	8	2	SS-397, 1B-29, 3B-24, 2B-12, OF-3
4 yrs.		476	1619	394	72	27	6	0.4	196	175	148	180	52	.243	.332	8	2	SS-397, 1B-29, 3B-24, 2B-12, OF-3

WORLD SERIES
1917 CHI A	2	2	1	0	0	0	0.0	0	1	0	0	0	.500	.500	2	1	
1919	8	25	2	0	1	0	0.0	3	0	5	3	1	.080	.160	0	0	SS-8
2 yrs.	10	27	3	0	1	0	0.0	3	1	5	3	1	.111	.185	2	1	SS-8

Jim Rivera

RIVERA, MANUEL JOSEPH (Jungle Jim)   BL TL 6'   196 lbs.
B. July 22, 1922, New York, N. Y.

1952 2 teams	STL A (97G – .256)	CHI A (53G – .249)																
" total		150	537	136	20	9	7	1.3	72	48	50	86	21	.253	.363	6	2	OF-141
1953 CHI A		156	567	147	26	16	11	1.9	79	78	53	70	22	.259	.420	0	0	OF-156
1954		145	490	140	16	8	13	2.7	62	61	49	68	18	.286	.431	3	0	OF-143
1955		147	454	120	24	4	10	2.2	71	52	62	59	25	.264	.401	7	2	OF-143
1956		139	491	125	23	5	12	2.4	76	66	49	75	20	.255	.395	9	2	OF-134
1957		125	402	103	21	6	14	3.5	51	52	40	80	18	.256	.443	11	3	OF-82, 1B-31
1958		116	276	62	8	4	9	3.3	37	35	24	49	21	.225	.380	9	0	OF-99
1959		80	177	39	9	4	4	2.3	18	19	11	19	5	.220	.384	4	0	OF-69
1960		48	17	5	0	0	1	5.9	17	1	3	3	4	.294	.471	2	0	OF-24
1961 2 teams	CHI A (1G – .000)	KC A (64G – .241)																
" total		65	141	34	8	0	2	1.4	20	10	24	14	6	.241	.340	23	4	OF-43
10 yrs.		1171	3552	911	155	56	83	2.3	503	422	365	523	160	.256	.402	74	13	OF-1034, 1B-31
10 yrs.		1010	3075	791	134	50	77	2.5	438	382	312	450	146	.257	.408	45	7	OF-903, 1B-31
												8th						

WORLD SERIES
| 1959 CHI A | 5 | 11 | 0 | 0 | 0 | 0 | 0.0 | 1 | 0 | 3 | 1 | 0 | .000 | .000 | 0 | 1 | OF-5 |

Aaron Robinson

ROBINSON, AARON ANDREW   BL TR 6'2"   205 lbs.
B. June 23, 1915, Lancaster, S. C.   D. Mar. 9, 1966, Lancaster, S. C.

1943 NY A		1	1	0	0	0	0	0.0	0	0	0	1	0	.000	.000	1	0	
1945		50	160	45	6	1	8	5.0	19	24	21	23	0	.281	.481	4	3	C-45
1946		100	330	98	17	2	16	4.8	32	64	48	39	0	.297	.506	4	1	C-95
1947		82	252	68	11	5	5	2.0	23	36	40	26	0	.270	.413	7	1	C-74
1948 CHI A		98	326	82	14	2	8	2.5	47	39	46	30	0	.252	.380	6	1	C-92
1949 DET A		110	331	89	12	0	13	3.9	38	56	73	21	0	.269	.423	2	0	C-108
1950		107	283	64	7	0	9	3.2	37	37	75	35	0	.226	.346	3	3	C-103
1951 2 teams	DET A (36G – .207)	BOS A (26G – .203)																
" total		62	156	32	7	1	2	1.3	12	16	34	19	0	.205	.301	2	1	C-60
8 yrs.		610	1839	478	74	11	61	3.3	208	272	337	194	0	.260	.412	29	10	C-577
1 yr.		98	326	82	14	2	8	2.5	47	39	46	30	0	.252	.380	6	1	C-92

WORLD SERIES
| 1947 NY A | 3 | 10 | 2 | 0 | 0 | 0 | 0.0 | 2 | 1 | 2 | 1 | 0 | .200 | .200 | 0 | 0 | C-3 |

Eddie Robinson

ROBINSON, WILLIAM EDWARD   BL TR 6'2½"   210 lbs.
B. Dec. 15, 1920, Paris, Tex.

1942 CLE A		8	8	1	0	0	0	0.0	1	2	1	0	0	.125	.125	6	1	1B-1
1946		7	27	11	0	0	3	11.1	5	4	1	4	0	.407	.741	0	0	1B-7
1947		95	318	78	10	1	14	4.4	52	52	30	18	1	.245	.415	5	1	1B-87
1948		134	493	125	18	5	16	3.2	53	83	36	42	1	.254	.408	4	1	1B-131
1949 WAS A		143	527	155	27	3	18	3.4	66	78	67	30	3	.294	.459	0	0	1B-143
1950 2 teams	WAS A (36G – .240)	CHI A (119G – .311)																
" total		155	553	163	15	4	21	3.8	83	86	85	32	0	.295	.450	0	0	1B-155
1951 CHI A		151	564	159	23	5	29	5.1	85	117	77	54	2	.282	.495	2	0	1B-147
1952		155	594	176	33	1	22	3.7	79	104	70	49	2	.296	.466	0	0	1B-155
1953 PHI A		156	615	152	28	4	22	3.6	64	102	63	56	1	.247	.413	1	0	1B-155
1954 NY A		85	142	37	9	0	3	2.1	11	27	19	21	0	.261	.387	49	15	1B-29
1955		88	173	36	1	0	16	9.2	25	42	36	26	0	.208	.491	34	5	1B-46
1956 2 teams	NY A (26G – .222)	KC A (75G – .198)																
" total		101	226	46	6	1	7	3.1	20	23	31	23	0	.204	.332	34	6	1B-61
1957 3 teams	DET A (13G – .000)	CLE A (19G – .222)	BAL A (4G – .000)															
" total		36	39	6	1	0	2	2.6	1	3	4	4	0	.154	.256	21	1	1B-8
13 yrs.		1314	4279	1145	171	24	172	4.0	545	723	520	359	10	.268	.439	156	30	1B-1125
3 yrs.		425	1586	468	67	8	71	4.5	226	294	207	131	4	.295	.482	2	0	1B-421
								1st						4th				

WORLD SERIES
1948 CLE A	6	20	6	0	0	0	0.0	1	1	0	0	0	.300	.300	0	0	1B-6
1955 NY A	4	3	2	0	0	0	0.0	0	1	2	1	0	.667	.667	1	1	1B-1
2 yrs.	10	23	8	0	0	0	0.0	1	2	2	1	0	.348	.348	1	1	1B-7

Floyd Robinson

ROBINSON, FLOYD ANDREW   BL TR 5'9"   175 lbs.
B. May 9, 1936, Prescott, Ark.

1960 CHI A		22	46	13	0	0	0	0.0	7	1	11	8	2	.283	.283	4	0	OF-17
1961		132	432	134	20	7	11	2.5	69	59	52	32	7	.310	.465	23	6	OF-106
1962		156	600	187	45	10	11	1.8	89	109	72	47	4	.312	.475	1	0	OF-155
1963		146	527	149	21	6	13	2.5	71	71	62	43	9	.283	.419	9	2	OF-137
1964		141	525	158	17	3	11	2.1	83	59	70	41	9	.301	.408	6	2	OF-138
1965		156	577	153	15	6	14	2.4	70	66	76	51	4	.265	.385	9	2	OF-153
1966		127	342	81	11	2	5	1.5	44	35	44	32	8	.237	.325	17	0	OF-113
1967 CIN N		55	130	31	6	2	1	0.8	19	10	14	14	3	.238	.338	15	2	OF-39
1968 2 teams	OAK A (53G – .247)	BOS A (24G – .125)																
" total		77	105	23	5	0	1	1.0	6	16	7	14	1	.219	.295	42	9	OF-29
9 yrs.		1012	3284	929	140	36	67	2.0	458	426	408	282	42	.283	.409	126	23	OF-887
7 yrs.		880	3049	875	129	34	65	2.1	433	400	387	254	38	.287	.416	69	12	OF-819

Player Register

	G	AB	H	2B	3B	HR	HR%	R	RBI	BB	SO	SB	BA	SA	Pinch Hit AB H	G by POS

Les Rock
ROCK, LESTER HENRY BL TR 6'2" 184 lbs.
Born Lester Henry Schwarzrock.
B. Aug. 19, 1912, Springfield, Minn.

| 1936 CHI A | 2 | 1 | 0 | 0 | 0 | 0 | 0.0 | 0 | 1 | 0 | 0 | 0 | .000 | .000 | 0 0 | 1B-2 |

Aurelio Rodriguez
RODRIGUEZ, AURELIO ITUARTE (Leo) BR TR 5'10" 180 lbs.
B. Dec. 28, 1947, Cananea Sonora, Mexico

1967 CAL A	29	130	31	3	1	1	0.8	14	8	2	21	1	.238	.300	0 0	3B-29
1968	76	223	54	10	1	1	0.4	14	16	17	35	0	.242	.309	3 2	3B-70, 2B-2
1969	159	561	130	17	2	7	1.2	47	49	32	88	5	.232	.307	0 0	3B-159
1970 2 teams	CAL A (17G – .270)				WAS A (142G – .247)											
" total	159	610	152	33	7	19	3.1	70	83	40	87	15	.249	.420	0 0	3B-153, SS-7
1971 DET A	154	604	153	30	7	15	2.5	68	39	27	93	4	.253	.401	3 1	3B-153, SS-1
1972	153	601	142	23	5	13	2.2	65	56	28	104	2	.236	.356	0 0	3B-153, SS-1
1973	160	555	123	27	3	9	1.6	46	58	31	85	3	.222	.330	0 0	3B-160, SS-1
1974	159	571	127	23	5	5	0.9	54	49	26	70	2	.222	.306	0 0	3B-159
1975	151	507	124	20	6	13	2.6	47	60	30	63	1	.245	.385	0 0	3B-151
1976	128	480	115	13	2	8	1.7	40	50	19	61	0	.240	.325	0 0	3B-128
1977	96	306	67	14	1	10	3.3	30	32	16	36	1	.219	.369	10 1	3B-95, SS-1
1978	134	385	102	25	2	7	1.8	40	43	19	37	0	.265	.395	20 7	3B-131
1979	106	343	87	18	0	5	1.5	27	36	11	40	0	.254	.350	3 0	3B-106, 1B-1
1980 2 teams	SD N (89G – .200)				NY A (52G – .220)											
" total	141	339	71	13	3	5	1.5	21	27	13	61	1	.209	.310	6 0	3B-137, 2B-6, SS-2
1981 NY A	27	52	18	2	0	2	3.8	4	8	2	10	0	.346	.500	1 1	3B-20, 2B-3, DH-2, 1B-1
1982 CHI A	118	257	62	15	1	3	1.2	24	31	11	35	0	.241	.342	1 0	3B-112, 2B-3, SS-2
1983 2 teams	BAL A (45G – .119)				CHI A (22G – .200)											
" total	67	87	12	1	0	1	1.1	3	0	16	0	0	.138	.184	0 0	3B-67
17 yrs.	2017	6611	1570	287	46	124	1.9	612	648	324	942	35	.237	.351	48 12	3B-1983, SS-16, 2B-14, DH-2, 1B-2
2 yrs.	140	277	66	16	1	4	1.4	25	32	11	38	0	.238	.347	1 0	3B-134, 2B-3, SS-2

LEAGUE CHAMPIONSHIP SERIES

1972 DET A	5	16	0	0	0	0	0.0	0	0	2	2	0	.000	.000	0 0	3B-5
1980 NY A	2	6	2	1	0	0	0.0	0	0	0	0	0	.333	.500	0 0	3B-2
1981	1	0	0	0	0	0	–	0	0	0	0	0	–	–	0 0	3B-1
1983 CHI A	2	0	0	0	0	0	–	0	0	0	0	0	–	–	0 0	3B-2
4 yrs.	10	22	2	1	0	0	0.0	0	0	2	2	0	.091	.136	0 0	3B-10

WORLD SERIES

| 1981 NY A | 4 | 12 | 5 | 0 | 0 | 0 | 0.0 | 1 | 0 | 1 | 2 | 0 | .417 | .417 | 0 0 | 3B-3 |

Hec Rodriguez
RODRIGUEZ, ANTONIO HECTOR BR TR 5'8" 165 lbs.
B. June 13, 1920, Villa Alquizar, Cuba

| 1952 CHI A | 124 | 407 | 108 | 14 | 0 | 2 | 0.5 | 55 | 40 | 47 | 22 | 7 | .265 | .307 | 8 2 | 3B-113 |

George Rohe
ROHE, GEORGE ANTHONY BR TR
B. Sept. 15, 1875, Cincinnati, Ohio D. June 10, 1957, Cincinnati, Ohio

1901 BAL A	14	36	10	2	0	0	0.0	7	4	5		1	.278	.333	1 0	1B-8, 3B-6
1905 CHI A	34	113	24	1	0	1	0.9	14	12	12		2	.212	.248	1 0	3B-17, 2B-16
1906	75	225	58	5	1	0	0.0	14	25	16		8	.258	.289	12 2	3B-57, 2B-5, OF-1
1907	144	494	105	11	2	2	0.4	46	51	39		16	.213	.255	2 0	3B-76, 2B-39, SS-30
4 yrs.	267	868	197	19	3	3	0.3	81	92	72		27	.227	.266	16 2	3B-156, 2B-60, SS-30, 1B-8, OF-1
3 yrs.	253	832	187	17	3	3	0.4	74	88	67		26	.225	.263	15 2	3B-150, 2B-60, SS-30, OF-1

WORLD SERIES

| 1906 CHI A | 6 | 21 | 7 | 1 | 2 | 0 | 0.0 | 2 | 4 | 3 | | 2 | .333 | .571 | 0 0 | 3B-6 |

Johnny Romano
ROMANO, JOHN ANTHONY (Honey) BR TR 5'11" 205 lbs.
B. Aug. 23, 1934, Hoboken, N. J.

1958 CHI A	4	7	2	0	0	0	0.0	1	1	1	1	0	.286	.286	2 0	C-2
1959	53	126	37	5	1	5	4.0	20	25	23	18	0	.294	.468	13 8	C-38
1960 CLE A	108	316	86	12	2	16	5.1	40	52	37	50	0	.272	.475	11 0	C-99
1961	142	509	152	29	1	21	4.1	76	80	61	60	0	.299	.483	2 0	C-141
1962	135	459	120	19	3	25	5.4	71	81	73	64	0	.261	.479	4 3	C-130
1963	89	255	55	5	2	10	3.9	28	34	38	49	4	.216	.369	16 4	C-71, OF-4
1964	106	352	85	18	1	19	5.4	46	47	51	83	2	.241	.460	10 2	C-96, 1B-1
1965 CHI A	122	356	86	11	0	18	5.1	39	48	59	74	0	.242	.424	8 1	C-111, OF-4, 1B-2
1966	122	329	76	12	0	15	4.6	33	47	58	72	0	.231	.404	6 1	C-102
1967 STL N	24	58	7	1	0	0	0.0	1	2	13	15	1	.121	.138	4 0	C-20
10 yrs.	905	2767	706	112	10	129	4.7	355	417	414	485	7	.255	.443	86 22	C-810, OF-8, 1B-3
4 yrs.	301	818	201	28	1	38	4.6	93	121	141	164	0	.246	.422	39 13	C-253, OF-4, 1B-2

WORLD SERIES

| 1959 CHI A | 2 | 1 | 0 | 0 | 0 | 0 | 0.0 | 0 | 0 | 0 | 0 | 0 | .000 | .000 | 1 0 | |

Phil Roof
ROOF, PHILLIP ANTHONY BR TR 6'2" 190 lbs.
Brother of Gene Roof.
B. Mar. 5, 1941, Paducah, Ky.

1961 MIL N	1	0	0	0	0	0	–	0	0	0	0	0	–	–	0 0	C-1
1964	1	2	0	0	0	0	0.0	0	0	0	1	0	.000	.000	0 0	C-1
1965 2 teams	CAL A (9G – .136)				CLE A (43G – .173)											
" total	52	74	12	1	0	0	0.0	4	3	5	19	0	.162	.176	4 0	C-50
1966 KC A	127	369	77	14	3	7	1.9	33	44	37	95	2	.209	.320	4 0	C-123, 1B-2
1967	114	327	67	14	5	6	1.8	23	24	23	85	4	.205	.333	1 0	C-113
1968 OAK A	34	64	12	0	0	1	1.6	5	2	9	15	1	.188	.234	2 0	C-32
1969	106	247	58	6	1	2	0.8	19	19	33	55	1	.235	.291	1 0	C-106
1970 MIL A	110	321	73	7	1	13	4.0	39	37	32	72	3	.227	.377	3 1	C-107, 1B-1

	G	AB	H	2B	3B	HR	HR %	R	RBI	BB	SO	SB	BA	SA	Pinch Hit AB H	G by POS

Phil Roof continued

1971 2 teams	MIL A (41G – .193)					MIN A (31G – .241)										
" total	72	201	43	6	1	1	0.5	12	16	16	46	0	.214	.269	5 0	C-68
1972 MIN A	61	146	30	11	1	3	2.1	16	12	6	27	0	.205	.356	0 0	C-61
1973	47	117	23	4	1	1	0.9	10	15	13	27	0	.197	.274	0 0	C-47
1974	44	97	19	1	0	2	2.1	10	13	6	24	0	.196	.268	0 0	C-44
1975	63	126	38	2	0	7	5.6	18	21	9	28	0	.302	.484	0 0	C-63
1976 2 teams	MIN A (18G – .217)					CHI A (4G – .111)										
" total	22	55	11	3	0	0		1	4	2	9	0	.200	.255	5 1	C-16, DH-1
1977 TOR A	3	5	0	0	0	0	0.0	0	0	1	1	0	.000	.000	0 0	C-3
15 yrs.	857	2151	463	69	13	43	2.0	190	210	184	504	11	.215	.319	25 2	C-835, 1B-3, DH-1
1 yr.	4	9	1	0	0	0	0.0	0	0	0	3	0	.111	.111	0 0	C-4

Bob Roselli

ROSELLI, ROBERT EDWARD
B. Dec. 10, 1931, San Francisco, Calif.
BR TR 5'11" 185 lbs.

1955 MIL N	6	9	2	1	0	0	0.0	1	0	1	4	0	.222	.333	3 0	C-2
1956	4	2	1	0	0	1	50.0	1	1	0	1	0	.500	2.000	1 1	C-3
1958	1	1	0	0	0	0	0.0	0	0	0	0	0	.000	.000	1 0	
1961 CHI A	22	38	10	3	0	0	0.0	2	4	0	11	0	.263	.342	12 4	C-10
1962	35	64	12	3	1	1	1.6	4	5	11	15	1	.188	.313	15 2	C-20
5 yrs.	68	114	25	7	1	2	1.8	8	10	12	31	1	.219	.351	32 7	C-35
2 yrs.	57	102	22	6	1	1	1.0	6	9	11	26	1	.216	.324	27 6	C-30

Lou Rosenberg

ROSENBERG, LOUIS C.
Brother of Harry Rosenberg.
B. Mar. 5, 1903, San Francisco, Calif.
BR TR 5'7" 155 lbs.

1923 CHI A	3	4	1	0	0	0	0.0	0	0	0	1	0	.250	.250	1 0	2B-2

Larry Rosenthal

ROSENTHAL, LAWRENCE JOHN
B. May 21, 1912, St. Paul, Minn.
BL TL 6'½" 190 lbs.

1936 CHI A	85	317	89	15	8	3	0.9	71	46	59	37	2	.281	.407	4 3	OF-80
1937	58	97	28	5	3	0	0.0	20	9	9	20	1	.289	.402	29 9	OF-25
1938	61	105	30	5	1	1	1.0	14	12	12	13	0	.286	.381	30 6	OF-22
1939	107	324	86	21	5	10	3.1	50	51	53	46	6	.265	.454	12 1	OF-93
1940	107	276	83	14	5	6	2.2	46	42	64	32	2	.301	.453	11 2	OF-91
1941 2 teams	CHI A (20G – .237)					CLE A (45G – .187)										
" total	65	134	28	7	1	1	0.7	19	9	21	15	1	.209	.299	30 6	OF-32, 1B-1
1944 2 teams	NY A (36G – .198)					PHI A (32G – .204)										
" total	68	155	31	5	0	1	0.6	14	15	24	24	1	.200	.252	19 4	OF-45
1945 PHI A	28	75	15	3	2	0	0.0	6	5	9	8	0	.200	.293	4 0	OF-8
8 yrs.	579	1483	390	75	25	22	1.5	240	189	251	195	13	.263	.392	139 31	OF-409, 1B-1
6 yrs.	438	1178	330	64	22	20	1.7	210	161	209	153	11	.280	.423	88 21	OF-329
														10th		

Braggo Roth

ROTH, ROBERT FRANK
Brother of Frank Roth.
B. Aug. 28, 1892, Burlington, Wis. D. Sept. 11, 1936, Chicago, Ill.
BR TR 5'7½" 170 lbs.

1914 CHI A	34	126	37	4	6	1	0.8	14	10	8	25	3	.294	.444	0 0	OF-34
1915 2 teams	CHI A (70G – .250)					CLE A (39G – .299)										
" total	109	384	103	10	17	7	1.8	67	55	51	72	26	.268	.438	4 0	OF-69, 3B-35
1916 CLE A	125	409	117	19	7	4	1.0	50	72	38	48	29	.286	.396	12 6	OF-112
1917	145	495	141	30	9	1	0.2	69	72	52	73	51	.285	.388	10 3	OF-135
1918	106	375	106	21	12	1	0.3	53	59	53	41	35	.283	.411	0 0	OF-106
1919 2 teams	PHI A (48G – .323)					BOS A (63G – .256)										
" total	111	422	121	22	12	5	1.2	65	52	39	53	20	.287	.431	5 1	OF-103
1920 WAS A	138	468	136	23	8	9	1.9	80	92	75	57	24	.291	.432	8 3	OF-128
1921 NY A	43	152	43	9	2	2	1.3	29	10	19	20	1	.283	.408	6 2	OF-37
8 yrs.	811	2831	804	138	73	30	1.1	427	422	335	389	189	.284	.416	45 15	OF-724, 3B-35
2 yrs.	104	366	97	10	16	4	1.1	58	45	37	75	15	.265	.413	4 0	OF-64, 3B-35

Frank Roth

ROTH, FRANCIS CHARLES
Brother of Braggo Roth.
B. Oct. 11, 1878, Chicago, Ill. D. Mar. 27, 1955, Burlington, Wis.
BR TR 5'10" 160 lbs.

1903 PHI N	68	220	60	11	4	0	0.0	27	22	9		3	.273	.359	7 3	C-60, 3B-1
1904	81	229	59	8	1	1	0.4	28	20	12		8	.258	.314	12 4	C-67, 2B-1, 1B-1
1905 STL A	35	107	25	3	0	0	0.0	9	7	6		1	.234	.262	5 0	C-29
1906 CHI A	16	51	10	1	1	0	0.0	4	7	3		1	.196	.255	1 0	C-15
1909 CIN N	56	147	35	7	2	0	0.0	12	16	6		5	.238	.313	2 0	C-54
1910	26	29	7	2	0	0	0.0	3	3	0		2	.241	.310	19 4	C-4, OF-1
6 yrs.	282	783	196	32	8	1	0.1	83	75	36		19	.250	.315	46 11	C-229, OF-1, 3B-1, 2B-1, 1B-1
1 yr.	16	51	10	1	1	0	0.0	4	7	3		1	.196	.255	1 0	C-15

Jack Rothrock

ROTHROCK, JOHN HOUSTON
B. Mar. 14, 1905, Long Beach, Calif.
D. Feb. 2, 1980, San Bernardino, Calif.
BB TR 5'11½" 165 lbs.
BR 1925-27

1925 BOS A	22	55	19	3	0	0	0.0	6	7	3	7	0	.345	.509	0 0	SS-22
1926	15	17	5	1	0	0	0.0	3	2	3	1	0	.294	.353	10 4	SS-2
1927	117	428	111	24	8	0	0.2	61	36	24	46	5	.259	.360	6 1	SS-40, 2B-36, 3B-20, 1B-13
1928	117	344	92	9	4	3	0.9	52	22	33	40	12	.267	.343	9 2	OF-53, 3B-17, 1B-16, SS-13, 2B-2, C-1, P-1
1929	143	473	142	19	7	6	1.3	70	59	43	47	23	.300	.408	10 5	OF-128
1930	45	65	18	3	1	0	0.0	4	4	2	9	0	.277	.354	32 9	OF-9, 3B-1
1931	133	475	132	32	3	4	0.8	81	42	47	48	13	.278	.383	20 5	OF-79, 2B-23, 1B-8, SS-1
1932 2 teams	BOS A (12G – .208)					CHI A (39G – .188)										
" total	51	112	22	3	1	0	0.0	11	6	10	7	4	.196	.241	7 1	OF-31, 3B-8, 1B-1
1934 STL N	154	647	184	35	3	11	1.7	106	72	49	56	10	.284	.399	0 0	OF-154, 2B-1

Player Register

	G	AB	H	2B	3B	HR	HR%	R	RBI	BB	SO	SB	BA	SA	Pinch Hit AB	H	G by POS

Jack Rothrock continued

1935	129	502	137	18	5	3	0.6	76	56	57	29	7	.273	.347	1	0	OF-127
1937 PHI A	88	232	62	15	0	0	0.0	28	21	28	15	1	.267	.332	29	8	OF-58, 2B-1
11 yrs.	1014	3350	924	162	35	28	0.8	498	327	299	312	75	.276	.370	124	36	OF-639, SS-78, 2B-63, 3B-48, 1B-38, C-1, P-1
1 yr.	39	64	12	2	1	0	0.0	8	6	5	9	1	.188	.250	7	1	OF-19, 3B-8, 1B-1

WORLD SERIES

1934 STL N	7	30	7	3	1	0	0.0	3	6	1	2	0	.233	.400	0	0	OF-7

Edd Roush

ROUSH, EDD J (Eddie) BL TL 5'11" 170 lbs.
B. May 8, 1893, Oakland City, Ind.
Hall of Fame 1962.

1913 CHI A	9	10	1	0	0	0	0.0	2	0	0	2	0	.100	.100	4	1	OF-2
1914 IND F	74	166	54	8	4	1	0.6	26	30	6		12	.325	.440	27	7	OF-43, 1B-2
1915 NWK F	145	551	164	20	11	3	0.5	73	60	38		28	.298	.390	1	1	OF-144
1916 2 teams	NY	N (39G –	.188)		CIN	N (69G –	.287)										
" total	108	341	91	7	15	0	0.0	38	20	14	23	19	.267	.375	23	2	OF-84
1917 CIN N	136	522	178	19	14	4	0.8	82	67	27	24	21	.341	.454	1	0	OF-134
1918	113	435	145	18	10	5	1.1	61	62	22	10	24	.333	.455	0	0	OF-113
1919	133	504	162	19	13	3	0.6	73	71	42	19	20	.321	.429	0	0	OF-133
1920	149	579	196	22	16	4	0.7	81	90	42	22	36	.339	.453	0	0	OF-139, 1B-11, 2B-1
1921	112	418	147	27	12	4	1.0	68	71	31	8	19	.352	.502	2	1	OF-108
1922	49	165	58	7	4	1	0.6	29	24	19	5	5	.352	.461	6	1	OF-43
1923	138	527	185	41	18	6	1.1	88	88	46	16	10	.351	.531	1	0	OF-137
1924	121	483	168	23	21	3	0.6	67	72	22	11	17	.348	.501	2	2	OF-119
1925	134	540	183	28	16	8	1.5	91	83	35	14	22	.339	.494	0	0	OF-134
1926	144	563	182	37	10	7	1.2	95	79	38	17	8	.323	.462	0	0	OF-144, 1B-1
1927 NY N	140	570	173	27	4	7	1.2	83	58	26	15	18	.304	.402	2	0	OF-138
1928	46	163	41	5	3	2	1.2	20	13	14	8	1	.252	.356	6	3	OF-39
1929	115	450	146	19	7	8	1.8	76	52	45	16	6	.324	.451	6	3	OF-107
1931 CIN N	101	376	102	12	5	1	0.3	46	41	17	5	2	.271	.338	13	3	OF-88
18 yrs.	1967	7363	2376	339	183	67	0.9	1099	981	484	215	268	.323	.446	94	24	OF-1849, 1B-14, 2B-1
1 yr.	9	10	1	0	0	0	0.0	2	0	0	2	0	.100	.100	4	1	OF-2

WORLD SERIES

1919 CIN N	8	28	6	2	1	0	0.0	6	7	3	0	2	.214	.357	0	0	OF-8

Muddy Ruel

RUEL, HEROLD DOMINIC BR TR 5'9" 150 lbs.
B. Feb. 20, 1896, St. Louis, Mo. D. Nov. 13, 1963, Palo Alto, Calif.
Manager 1947.

1915 STL A	10	14	0	0	0	0	0.0	0	1	5	5	0	.000	.000	2	0	C-6
1917 NY A	6	17	2	0	0	0	0.0	1	1	2	2	1	.118	.118	0	0	C-6
1918	3	6	2	0	0	0	0.0	0	0	2	1	1	.333	.333	0	0	C-2
1919	81	233	56	6	0	0	0.0	18	31	34	26	4	.240	.266	0	0	C-81
1920	82	261	70	14	1	1	0.4	30	15	15	18	4	.268	.341	1	0	C-80
1921 BOS A	113	358	99	21	1	1	0.3	41	43	41	15	2	.277	.349	2	0	C-109
1922	116	361	92	15	1	0	0.0	34	28	41	26	4	.255	.302	4	1	C-112
1923 WAS A	136	449	142	24	3	0	0.0	63	54	55	21	4	.316	.383	3	2	C-133
1924	149	501	142	20	2	0	0.0	50	57	62	20	7	.283	.331	2	1	C-147
1925	127	393	122	9	2	0	0.0	55	54	63	16	4	.310	.344	0	0	C-126, 1B-1
1926	117	368	110	22	4	1	0.3	42	53	61	14	7	.299	.389	0	0	C-117
1927	131	428	132	16	5	1	0.2	61	52	63	18	9	.308	.376	2	0	C-128
1928	108	350	90	18	2	0	0.0	31	55	44	14	12	.257	.320	4	2	C-101, 1B-2
1929	69	188	46	4	2	0	0.0	16	20	31	7	0	.245	.287	6	0	C-63
1930	66	198	50	3	4	0	0.0	18	26	24	13	1	.253	.308	4	2	C-60
1931 2 teams	BOS	A (33G –	.301)		DET	A (14G –	.120)										
" total	47	133	31	6	0	0	0.0	7	9	14	7	0	.233	.278	2	0	C-44
1932 DET A	50	136	32	4	2	0	0.0	10	18	17	6	1	.235	.294	3	1	C-49
1933 STL A	28	63	12	2	0	0	0.0	13	8	24	4	0	.190	.222	5	0	C-28
1934 CHI A	22	57	12	3	0	0	0.0	4	7	8	5	0	.211	.263	4	0	C-21
19 yrs.	1461	4514	1242	187	29	4	0.1	494	532	606	238	61	.275	.332	41	9	C-1413, 1B-3
1 yr.	22	57	12	3	0	0	0.0	4	7	8	5	0	.211	.263	1	0	C-21

WORLD SERIES

1924 WAS A	7	21	2	1	0	0	0.0	2	6	6	1	0	.095	.143	0	0	C-7
1925	7	19	6	1	0	0	0.0	0	1	3	2	0	.316	.368	0	0	C-7
2 yrs.	14	40	8	2	0	0	0.0	2	7	9	3	0	.200	.250	0	0	C-14

Red Ruffing

RUFFING, CHARLES HERBERT BR TR 6'1½" 205 lbs.
B. May 3, 1904, Granville, Ill.
Hall of Fame 1967.

1924 BOS A	8	7	1	0	1	0	0.0	0	0	1	0	0	.143	.429	0	0	P-8
1925	37	79	17	4	2	0	0.0	6	11	1	22	0	.215	.316	0	0	P-37
1926	37	51	10	1	0	1	2.0	8	5	2	12	0	.196	.275	0	0	P-37
1927	29	55	14	3	1	0	0.0	5	4	0	6	0	.255	.345	2	0	P-26
1928	60	121	38	13	1	2	1.7	12	19	3	12	0	.314	.488	17	5	P-42
1929	60	114	35	9	2	1.8	9	17	2	13	0	.307	.439	22	6	P-35, OF-2
1930 2 teams	BOS	A (6G –	.273)		NY	A (52G –	.374)										
" total	58	110	40	8	2	4	3.6	17	22	7	8	0	.364	.582	17	6	P-38
1931 NY A	48	109	36	8	1	3	2.8	14	12	1	13	0	.330	.505	10	3	P-37, OF-1
1932	55	124	38	6	1	3	2.4	20	19	6	10	0	.306	.444	18	4	P-35
1933	55	115	29	3	1	2	1.7	10	13	7	15	0	.252	.348	19	2	P-35
1934	45	113	28	3	0	2	1.8	11	13	3	17	0	.248	.327	8	0	P-36
1935	50	109	37	10	0	2	1.8	13	18	3	9	0	.339	.486	18	6	P-30
1936	53	127	37	5	0	5	3.9	14	22	11	12	0	.291	.449	17	6	P-33
1937	54	129	26	3	0	1	0.8	11	10	13	24	0	.202	.248	21	2	P-31
1938	45	107	24	4	1	3	2.8	12	17	17	21	0	.224	.364	12	2	P-31
1939	44	114	35	1	0	1	0.9	12	20	7	18	1	.307	.342	11	1	P-28

Player Register 312

	G	AB	H	2B	3B	HR	HR%	R	RBI	BB	SO	SB	BA	SA	Pinch Hit AB	H	G by POS

Red Ruffing continued

	G	AB	H	2B	3B	HR	HR%	R	RBI	BB	SO	SB	BA	SA	PH AB	PH H	G by POS
1940	33	89	11	4	0	1	1.1	8	7	3	9	0	.124	.202	1	0	P-30
1941	38	89	27	8	1	2	2.2	10	22	4	12	0	.303	.483	15	6	P-23
1942	30	80	20	4	0	1	1.3	8	13	5	13	0	.250	.338	6	1	P-24
1945	21	46	10	0	1	1	2.2	4	5	0	8	0	.217	.326	10	1	P-11
1946	8	25	3	1	0	0	0.0	1	1	1	8	0	.120	.160	0	0	P-8
1947 CHI A	14	24	5	0	0	0	0.0	2	3	1	3	0	.208	.208	4	1	P-9
22 yrs.	882	1937	521	98	13	36	1.9	207	273	97	266	1	.269	.389	228	58	P-624, OF-3
1 yr.	14	24	5	0	0	0	0.0	2	3	1	3	0	.208	.208	4	1	P-9

WORLD SERIES

	G	AB	H	2B	3B	HR	HR%	R	RBI	BB	SO	SB	BA	SA	PH AB	PH H	G by POS
1932 NY A	2	4	0	0	0	0	0.0	0	0	1	1	0	.000	.000	0	0	P-1
1936	3	5	0	0	0	0	0.0	0	0	1	2	0	.000	.000	1	0	P-2
1937	1	4	2	1	0	0	0.0	0	3	0	0	0	.500	.750	0	0	P-1
1938	2	6	1	0	0	0	0.0	1	1	1	0	0	.167	.167	0	0	P-2
1939	1	3	1	0	0	0	0.0	0	0	0	1	0	.333	.333	0	0	P-1
1941	1	3	0	0	0	0	0.0	0	0	0	0	0	.000	.000	0	0	P-1
1942	4	9	2	0	0	0	0.0	0	0	0	2	0	.222	.222	2	0	P-2
7 yrs.	14	34	6	1	0	0	0.0	1	4	3	6	0	.176	.206	3	0	P-10

Reb Russell
RUSSELL, EWELL ALBERT BL TL 5'11" 185 lbs.
B. Apr. 12, 1889, Jackson, Miss. D. Sept. 30, 1973, Indianapolis, Ind.

	G	AB	H	2B	3B	HR	HR%	R	RBI	BB	SO	SB	BA	SA	PH AB	PH H	G by POS
1913 CHI A	52	106	20	5	3	0	0.0	9	7	1	29	0	.189	.292	1	1	P-51
1914	43	64	17	1	1	0	0.0	6	7	1	14	0	.266	.313	5	2	P-38
1915	45	86	21	2	3	0	0.0	11	7	4	14	1	.244	.337	3	0	P-41
1916	56	91	13	2	0	0	0.0	9	6	0	18	1	.143	.165	0	0	P-56
1917	39	68	19	3	3	0	0.0	5	9	2	10	0	.279	.412	3	0	P-35, OF-1
1918	27	50	7	3	0	0	0.0	2	3	0	6	0	.140	.200	6	0	P-19, OF-1
1919	1	0	0	0	0	0	–	0	0	0	0	0	–	–	0	0	P-1
1922 PIT N	60	220	81	14	8	12	5.5	51	75	14	18	4	.368	.668	0	0	OF-60
1923	94	291	84	18	7	9	3.1	49	58	20	21	3	.289	.491	17	5	OF-76
9 yrs.	417	976	262	48	25	21	2.2	142	172	42	130	9	.268	.433	35	8	P-241, OF-138
7 yrs.	263	465	97	16	10	0	0.0	42	39	8	91	2	.209	.286	18	3	P-241, OF-2

WORLD SERIES

	G	AB	H	2B	3B	HR	HR%	R	RBI	BB	SO	SB	BA	SA	PH AB	PH H	G by POS
1917 CHI A	1	0	0	0	0	0	–	0	0	0	0	0	–	–	0	0	P-1

Blondy Ryan
RYAN, JOHN COLLINS BR TR 6'1" 178 lbs.
B. Jan. 4, 1906, Lynn, Mass. D. Nov. 28, 1959, Swampscott, Mass.

	G	AB	H	2B	3B	HR	HR%	R	RBI	BB	SO	SB	BA	SA	PH AB	PH H	G by POS
1930 CHI A	28	87	18	0	4	1	1.1	9	10	6	13	2	.207	.333	0	0	3B-23, SS-2, 2B-1
1933 NY N	146	525	125	10	5	3	0.6	47	48	15	62	0	.238	.293	0	0	SS-146
1934	110	385	93	19	0	2	0.5	35	41	19	68	3	.242	.306	1	0	3B-65, SS-30, 2B-25
1935 2 teams	PHI N (39G – .264)							NY A (30G – .238)									
" total	69	234	59	4	3	1	0.4	25	21	10	30	1	.252	.308	2	1	SS-65, 3B-1, 2B-1
1937 NY N	21	75	18	3	1	1	1.3	10	13	6	8	0	.240	.347	1	1	SS-19, 3B-1, 2B-1
1938	12	24	5	0	0	0	0.0	1	0	1	3	0	.208	.208	2	1	2B-5, 3B-3, SS-2
6 yrs.	386	1330	318	36	13	8	0.6	127	133	57	184	6	.239	.304	6	3	SS-264, 3B-93, 2B-33
1 yr.	28	87	18	0	4	1	1.1	9	10	6	13	2	.207	.333	0	0	3B-23, SS-2, 2B-1

WORLD SERIES

	G	AB	H	2B	3B	HR	HR%	R	RBI	BB	SO	SB	BA	SA	PH AB	PH H	G by POS
1933 NY N	5	18	5	0	0	0	0.0	0	1	1	5	0	.278	.278	0	0	SS-5
1937	1	1	0	0	0	0	0.0	0	0	0	1	0	.000	.000	1	0	
2 yrs.	6	19	5	0	0	0	0.0	0	1	1	6	0	.263	.263	1	0	SS-5

Connie Ryan
RYAN, CORNELIUS JOSEPH BR TR 5'11" 175 lbs.
B. Feb. 27, 1920, New Orleans, La.
Manager 1975, 1977.

	G	AB	H	2B	3B	HR	HR%	R	RBI	BB	SO	SB	BA	SA	PH AB	PH H	G by POS
1942 NY N	11	27	5	0	0	0	0.0	4	2	4	3	1	.185	.185	0	0	2B-11
1943 BOS N	132	457	97	10	2	1	0.2	52	24	58	56	7	.212	.249	1	0	2B-100, 3B-30
1944	88	332	98	18	5	4	1.2	56	25	36	40	13	.295	.416	0	0	2B-80, 3B-14
1946	143	502	121	28	8	1	0.2	55	48	55	63	7	.241	.335	1	0	2B-120, 3B-24
1947	150	544	144	33	5	5	0.9	60	69	71	60	5	.265	.371	0	0	2B-150, SS-1
1948	51	122	26	3	0	0	0.0	14	10	21	16	0	.213	.238	7	1	2B-40, 3B-4
1949	85	208	52	13	1	6	2.9	28	20	21	30	1	.250	.409	23	5	3B-25, SS-18, 2B-16, 1B-3
1950 2 teams	BOS N (20G – .194)							CIN N (106G – .259)									
" total	126	439	109	20	5	6	1.4	57	49	64	55	4	.248	.358	1	0	2B-123
1951 CIN N	136	473	112	17	4	16	3.4	75	53	79	72	11	.237	.391	7	3	2B-121, 3B-3, 1B-2, OF-1
1952 PHI N	154	577	139	24	6	12	2.1	81	49	69	72	13	.241	.366	0	0	2B-154
1953 2 teams	PHI N (90G – .296)							CHI A (17G – .222)									
" total	107	301	85	15	6	5	1.7	53	32	39	47	7	.282	.422	22	8	2B-65, 3B-16, 1B-2
1954 CIN N	1	0	0	0	0	0	–	0	0	1	0	0	–	–	0	0	
12 yrs.	1184	3982	988	181	42	56	1.4	535	381	518	514	69	.248	.357	62	17	2B-980, 3B-116, SS-19, 1B-7, OF-1
1 yr.	17	54	12	1	0	0	0.0	6	6	9	12	2	.222	.241	1	1	3B-16

WORLD SERIES

	G	AB	H	2B	3B	HR	HR%	R	RBI	BB	SO	SB	BA	SA	PH AB	PH H	G by POS
1948 BOS N	2	1	0	0	0	0	0.0	0	0	1	0	0	.000	.000	1	0	

Bob Sadowski
SADOWSKI, ROBERT FRANK (Sid) BL TR 6' 175 lbs.
B. Jan. 15, 1937, St. Louis, Mo.

	G	AB	H	2B	3B	HR	HR%	R	RBI	BB	SO	SB	BA	SA	PH AB	PH H	G by POS
1960 STL N	1	1	0	0	0	0	0.0	1	0	0	0	0	.000	.000	0	0	2B-1
1961 PHI N	16	54	7	0	0	0	0.0	4	0	4	7	1	.130	.130	3	0	3B-14
1962 CHI A	79	130	30	3	3	6	4.6	22	24	13	22	0	.231	.438	44	10	3B-16, 2B-12
1963 LA A	88	144	36	6	0	1	0.7	12	22	15	34	2	.250	.313	50	12	OF-25, 3B-6, 2B-4
4 yrs.	184	329	73	9	3	7	2.1	38	46	33	63	3	.222	.331	97	22	3B-36, OF-25, 2B-17
1 yr.	79	130	30	3	3	6	4.6	22	24	13	22	0	.231	.438	44	10	3B-16, 2B-12

Player Register

	G	AB	H	2B	3B	HR	HR%	R	RBI	BB	SO	SB	BA	SA	Pinch Hit AB	H	G by POS

Bill Salkeld
SALKELD, WILLIAM FRANKLIN BL TR 5'10" 190 lbs.
B. Mar. 8, 1917, Pocatello, Ida. D. Apr. 22, 1967, Los Angeles, Calif.

	G	AB	H	2B	3B	HR	HR%	R	RBI	BB	SO	SB	BA	SA	AB	H	G by POS
1945 PIT N	95	267	83	16	1	15	5.6	45	52	50	16	2	.311	.547	8	2	C-86
1946	69	160	47	8	0	3	1.9	18	19	39	16	2	.294	.400	17	3	C-51
1947	47	61	13	2	0	0	0.0	5	8	6	8	0	.213	.246	29	9	C-15
1948 BOS N	78	198	48	8	1	8	4.0	26	28	42	37	1	.242	.414	12	1	C-59
1949	66	161	41	5	0	5	3.1	17	25	44	24	1	.255	.379	4	0	C-63
1950 CHI A	1	3	0	0	0	0	0.0	0	0	1	0	0	.000	.000	0	0	C-1
6 yrs.	356	850	232	39	2	31	3.6	111	132	182	101	6	.273	.433	70	15	C-275
1 yr.	1	3	0	0	0	0	0.0	0	0	1	0	0	.000	.000	0	0	C-1
WORLD SERIES																	
1948 BOS N	5	9	2	0	0	1	11.1	2	1	5	1	0	.222	.556	1	0	C-5

Ron Santo
SANTO, RONALD EDWARD BR TR 6' 190 lbs.
B. Feb. 25, 1940, Seattle, Wash.

	G	AB	H	2B	3B	HR	HR%	R	RBI	BB	SO	SB	BA	SA	AB	H	G by POS
1960 CHI N	95	347	87	24	2	9	2.6	44	44	31	44	0	.251	.409	1	0	3B-94
1961	154	578	164	32	6	23	4.0	84	83	73	77	2	.284	.479	1	1	3B-153
1962	162	604	137	20	4	17	2.8	44	83	65	94	4	.227	.358	2	0	3B-157, SS-8
1963	162	630	187	29	6	25	4.0	79	99	42	92	6	.297	.481	0	0	3B-162
1964	161	592	185	33	13	30	5.1	94	114	86	96	3	.313	.564	0	0	3B-161
1965	164	608	173	30	4	33	5.4	88	101	88	109	3	.285	.510	0	0	3B-164
1966	155	561	175	21	8	30	5.3	93	94	95	78	4	.312	.538	0	0	3B-152, SS-8
1967	161	586	176	23	4	31	5.3	107	98	96	103	1	.300	.512	0	0	3B-161
1968	162	577	142	17	3	26	4.5	86	98	96	106	2	.246	.421	0	0	3B-162
1969	160	575	166	18	4	29	5.0	97	123	96	97	1	.289	.485	1	0	3B-160
1970	154	555	148	30	4	26	4.7	83	114	92	108	2	.267	.476	2	1	3B-152, OF-1
1971	154	555	148	22	1	21	3.8	77	88	79	95	4	.267	.423	1	0	3B-149, OF-6
1972	133	464	140	25	5	17	3.7	68	74	69	75	1	.302	.487	1	1	3B-129, 2B-3, OF-1, SS-1
1973	149	536	143	29	2	20	3.7	65	77	63	97	1	.267	.440	2	0	3B-146
1974 CHI A	117	375	83	12	1	5	1.3	29	41	37	72	0	.221	.299	5	1	DH-47, 2B-39, 3B-28, 1B-3, SS-1
15 yrs.	2243	8143	2254	365	67	342	4.2	1138	1331	1108	1343	35	.277	.464	16	6	3B-2130, DH-47, 2B-42, SS-18, OF-8, 1B-3
1 yr.	117	375	83	12	1	5	1.3	29	41	37	72	0	.221	.299	5	1	DH-47, 2B-39, 3B-28, 1B-3, SS-1

Carl Sawatski
SAWATSKI, CARL ERNEST (Swats) BL TR 5'10" 210 lbs.
B. Nov. 4, 1927, Shickshinny, Pa.

	G	AB	H	2B	3B	HR	HR%	R	RBI	BB	SO	SB	BA	SA	AB	H	G by POS
1948 CHI N	2	2	0	0	0	0	0.0	0	0	0	0	0	.000	.000	2	0	
1950	38	103	18	1	0	1	1.0	4	7	11	19	0	.175	.214	7	0	C-32
1953	43	59	13	3	0	1	1.7	5	5	7	7	0	.220	.322	29	6	C-15
1954 CHI A	43	109	20	3	3	1	0.9	6	12	15	20	0	.183	.294	8	1	C-33
1957 MIL N	38	105	25	4	0	6	5.7	13	17	10	15	0	.238	.448	31	6	C-28
1958 2 teams	MIL N (10G – .100)				PHI N (60G – .230)												
" total	70	193	43	4	1	5	2.6	13	13	18	47	0	.223	.332	13	4	C-56
1959 PHI N	74	198	58	10	0	9	4.5	15	43	32	36	0	.293	.480	7	1	C-69
1960 STL N	78	179	41	4	0	6	3.4	16	27	22	24	0	.229	.352	27	7	C-67
1961	86	174	52	8	0	10	5.7	23	33	25	17	0	.299	.517	39	10	C-60, OF-1
1962	85	222	56	9	1	13	5.9	26	42	36	38	0	.252	.477	15	2	C-70
1963	56	105	25	0	0	6	5.7	12	14	15	28	2	.238	.410	31	4	C-27
11 yrs.	633	1449	351	46	5	58	4.0	133	213	191	251	2	.242	.401	209	41	C-457, OF-1
1 yr.	43	109	20	3	3	1	0.9	6	12	15	20	0	.183	.294	8	1	C-33
WORLD SERIES																	
1957 MIL N	2	2	0	0	0	0	0.0	0	0	0	2	0	.000	.000	2	0	

Jerry Scala
SCALA, GERARD MICHAEL BL TR 5'11" 178 lbs.
B. Sept. 27, 1926, Bayonne, N. J.

	G	AB	H	2B	3B	HR	HR%	R	RBI	BB	SO	SB	BA	SA	AB	H	G by POS
1948 CHI A	3	6	0	0	0	0	0.0	1	0	3	0	0	.000	.000	0	0	OF-2
1949	37	120	30	7	1	1	0.8	17	13	17	19	3	.250	.350	5	1	OF-37
1950	40	67	13	2	1	0	0.0	8	6	10	10	0	.194	.254	5	3	OF-23
3 yrs.	80	193	43	9	2	1	0.5	26	19	27	32	3	.223	.306	10	4	OF-62
3 yrs.	80	193	43	9	2	1	0.5	26	19	27	32	3	.223	.306	10	4	OF-62

Jimmie Schaffer
SCHAFFER, JIMMIE RONALD BR TR 5'9" 170 lbs.
B. Apr. 5, 1936, Limeport, Pa.

	G	AB	H	2B	3B	HR	HR%	R	RBI	BB	SO	SB	BA	SA	AB	H	G by POS
1961 STL N	68	153	39	7	0	1	0.7	15	16	9	29	0	.255	.320	1	1	C-68
1962	70	66	16	2	1	0	0.0	7	6	6	16	1	.242	.303	1	0	C-69
1963 CHI N	57	142	34	7	0	7	4.9	17	19	11	35	0	.239	.437	1	0	C-54
1964	54	122	25	7	0	2	1.6	9	9	17	17	2	.205	.320	9	3	C-43
1965 2 teams	CHI A (17G – .194)				NY N (24G – .135)												
" total	41	68	11	5	1	0	0.0	2	1	4	19	0	.162	.265	7	0	C-35
1966 PHI N	18	15	2	1	0	1	6.7	2	4	1	7	0	.133	.400	2	0	C-6
1967	2	2	0	0	0	0	0.0	1	0	1	1	0	.000	.000	0	0	C-1
1968 CIN N	4	6	1	0	0	0	0.0	0	1	0	3	0	.167	.167	2	0	C-2
8 yrs.	314	574	128	28	3	11	1.9	53	56	49	127	3	.223	.340	23	4	C-278
1 yr.	17	31	6	3	1	0	0.0	2	1	1	5	0	.194	.355	3	0	C-14

Ray Schalk
SCHALK, RAYMOND WILLIAM (Cracker) BR TR 5'9" 165 lbs.
B. Aug. 12, 1892, Harvel, Ill. D. May 19, 1970, Chicago, Ill.
Manager 1927-28.
Hall of Fame 1955.

	G	AB	H	2B	3B	HR	HR%	R	RBI	BB	SO	SB	BA	SA	AB	H	G by POS
1912 CHI A	23	63	18	2	0	0	0.0	7	8	3		2	.286	.317	0	0	C-23
1913	128	401	98	15	5	1	0.2	38	38	27	36	14	.244	.314	3	0	C-125
1914	135	392	106	13	2	0	0.0	30	36	38	24	24	.270	.314	9	3	C-124
1915	135	413	110	14	4	1	0.2	46	54	62	21	15	.266	.327	1	0	C-134
1916	129	410	95	12	9	0	0.0	36	41	41	31	30	.232	.305	3	0	C-124
1917	140	424	96	12	4	3	0.7	48	51	59	27	19	.226	.295	1	0	C-139
1918	108	333	73	6	3	0	0.0	35	22	36	22	12	.219	.255	1	1	C-106

Player Register 314

	G	AB	H	2B	3B	HR	HR%	R	RBI	BB	SO	SB	BA	SA	Pinch Hit AB	H	G by POS

Ray Schalk continued

	G	AB	H	2B	3B	HR	HR%	R	RBI	BB	SO	SB	BA	SA	PH-AB	PH-H	G by POS
1919	131	394	111	9	3	0	0.0	57	34	51	25	11	.282	.320	2	0	C-129
1920	151	485	131	25	5	1	0.2	64	61	68	19	10	.270	.348	0	0	C-151
1921	128	416	105	24	4	0	0.0	32	47	40	36	3	.252	.329	2	0	C-126
1922	142	442	124	22	3	4	0.9	57	60	67	36	12	.281	.371	0	0	C-142
1923	123	382	87	12	2	1	0.3	42	44	39	28	6	.228	.277	2	0	C-121
1924	57	153	30	4	2	1	0.7	15	11	21	10	1	.196	.268	1	0	C-56
1925	125	343	94	18	1	0	0.0	44	52	57	27	11	.274	.332	0	0	C-125
1926	82	226	60	9	1	0	0.0	26	32	27	11	5	.265	.314	1	0	C-80
1927	16	26	6	2	0	0	0.0	2	2	2	1	0	.231	.308	1	0	C-15
1928	2	1	1	0	0	0	0.0	0	1	0	0	1	1.000	1.000	0	0	C-1
1929 NY N	5	2	0	0	0	0	0.0	0	0	0	1	0	.000	.000	0	0	C-5
18 yrs.	1760	5306	1345	199	48	12	0.2	579	594	638	355	176	.253	.316	28	5	C-1726
17 yrs.	1755	5304	1345	199	48	12	0.2	579	594	638	354	176	.254	.316	28	5	C-1721
	3rd	5th	6th					9th	7th	5th		7th					

WORLD SERIES
1917 CHI A	6	19	5	0	0	0	0.0	1	0	2	1	1	.263	.263	0	0	C-6
1919	8	23	7	0	0	0	0.0	1	2	4	2	1	.304	.304	0	0	C-8
2 yrs.	14	42	12	0	0	0	0.0	2	2	6	3	2	.286	.286	0	0	C-14

Roy Schalk
SCHALK, LeROY JOHN BR TR 5'10" 168 lbs.
B. Nov. 9, 1908, Chicago, Ill.

1932 NY A	3	12	3	1	0	0	0.0	3	0	2	2	0	.250	.333	0	0	2B-3
1944 CHI A	146	587	129	14	4	1	0.2	47	44	45	52	5	.220	.262	0	0	2B-142, SS-5
1945	133	513	127	23	1	1	0.2	50	65	32	41	3	.248	.302	0	0	2B-133
3 yrs.	282	1112	259	38	5	2	0.2	100	109	79	95	8	.233	.281	0	0	2B-278, SS-5
2 yrs.	279	1100	256	37	5	2	0.2	97	109	77	93	8	.233	.281	0	0	2B-275, SS-5

Biff Schaller
SCHALLER, WALTER BL TR
B. Sept. 23, 1889, Chicago, Ill. D. Oct. 9, 1939, Emeryville, Calif.

1911 DET A	40	60	8	0	1	1	1.7	8	7	4		1	.133	.217	17	6	OF-16, 1B-1
1913 CHI A	34	96	21	3	0	0	0.0	12	4	20	16	5	.219	.250	2	0	OF-32
2 yrs.	74	156	29	3	1	1	0.6	20	11	24	16	6	.186	.237	19	6	OF-48, 1B-1
1 yr.	34	96	21	3	0	0	0.0	12	4	20	16	5	.219	.250	2	0	OF-32

Norm Schlueter
SCHLUETER, NORMAN JOHN BR TR 5'10" 175 lbs.
B. Sept. 25, 1916, Belleville, Ill.

1938 CHI A	35	118	27	5	0	0	0.0	11	7	4	15	1	.229	.288	1	0	C-34
1939	34	56	13	2	1	0	0.0	5	8	1	11	2	.232	.304	2	0	C-32
1944 CLE A	49	122	15	4	0	0	0.0	2	11	12	22	0	.123	.156	6	0	C-43
3 yrs.	118	296	55	11	2	0	0.0	18	26	17	48	3	.186	.236	9	0	C-109
2 yrs.	69	174	40	7	2	0	0.0	16	15	5	26	3	.230	.293	3	0	C-66

Ossee Schreckengost
SCHRECKENGOST, OSSEE FREEMAN BR TR
Also appeared in box score as Schreck
B. Apr. 11, 1875, New Bethlehem, Pa. D. July 9, 1914, Philadelphia, Pa.

1897 LOU N	1	3	0	0	0	0	0.0	0	0	0		0	.000	.000	0	0	C-1
1898 CLE N	10	35	11	2	3	0	0.0	5	10	0		1	.314	.543	1	0	C-9
1899 2 teams			STL N (72G – .278)				CLE N (43G – .313)										
" total	115	427	124	20	5	2	0.5	57	47	21		18	.290	.375	6	0	C-64, 1B-43, OF-2, SS-1, 2B-1
1901 BOS A	86	280	85	13	5	0	0.0	37	38	19		6	.304	.386	9	3	C-72, 1B-4
1902 2 teams			CLE A (18G – .338)				PHI A (79G – .324)										
" total	97	358	117	17	2	2	0.6	50	52	9		5	.327	.402	2	0	C-71, 1B-24, OF-1
1903 PHI A	92	306	78	13	4	3	1.0	26	30	11		0	.255	.353	5	1	C-77, 1B-10
1904	95	311	58	9	1	1	0.3	23	21	5		3	.186	.232	3	1	C-84, 1B-9
1905	121	416	113	19	6	0	0.0	30	45	3		9	.272	.346	7	1	C-112, 1B-2
1906	98	338	96	20	1	1	0.3	29	41	10		5	.284	.358	5	0	C-89, 1B-4
1907	101	356	97	16	3	0	0.0	30	38	17		4	.272	.334	2	0	C-99, 1B-2
1908 2 teams			PHI A (71G – .222)				CHI A (6G – .188)										
" total	77	223	49	7	1	0	0.0	17	16	7		1	.220	.260	5	3	C-72, 1B-1
11 yrs.	893	3053	828	136	31	9	0.3	304	338	102		52	.271	.345	45	9	C-750, 1B-99, OF-3, SS-1, 2B-1
1 yr.	6	16	3	0	0	0	0.0	1	0	1		0	.188	.188	0	0	C-6

WORLD SERIES
| 1905 PHI A | 3 | 9 | 2 | 1 | 0 | 0 | 0.0 | 2 | 0 | 0 | 0 | | .222 | .333 | 0 | 0 | C-3 |

Hank Schreiber
SCHREIBER, HENRY WALTER BR TR 5'11" 165 lbs.
B. July 12, 1891, Cleveland, Ohio D. Feb. 21, 1968, Indianapolis, Ind.

1914 CHI A	1	2	0	0	0	0	0.0	0	0	0	1	0	.000	.000	0	0	OF-1
1917 BOS N	2	7	2	0	0	0	0.0	1	0	0	1	0	.286	.286	0	0	SS-1, 3B-1
1919 CIN N	19	58	13	4	0	0	0.0	5	4	0	12	0	.224	.293	0	0	3B-17, SS-2
1921 NY N	4	6	2	0	0	0	0.0	2	2	1	1	0	.333	.333	0	0	SS-2, 2B-2, 3B-1
1926 CHI N	10	18	1	1	0	0	0.0	2	0	0	1	0	.056	.111	0	0	SS-3, 3B-3, 2B-1
5 yrs.	36	91	18	5	0	0	0.0	10	6	1	16	0	.198	.253	0	0	3B-22, SS-8, 2B-3, OF-1
1 yr.	1	2	0	0	0	0	0.0	0	0	0	1	0	.000	.000	0	0	OF-1

Everett Scott
SCOTT, LEWIS EVERETT (Deacon) BR TR 5'8" 148 lbs.
B. Nov. 19, 1892, Bluffton, Ind. D. Nov. 2, 1960, Fort Wayne, Ind.

1914 BOS A	144	539	129	15	6	2	0.4	66	37	32	43	9	.239	.301	1	1	SS-143
1915	100	359	72	15	0	0	0.0	25	28	17	21	4	.201	.231	0	0	SS-100
1916	123	366	85	19	2	0	0.0	37	27	23	24	8	.232	.295	0	0	SS-121, 3B-1, 2B-1
1917	157	528	127	24	7	0	0.0	40	50	20	46	12	.241	.313	0	0	SS-157
1918	126	443	98	11	5	0	0.0	40	43	12	16	11	.221	.269	0	0	SS-126
1919	138	507	141	19	0	0	0.0	41	38	19	26	6	.278	.316	0	0	SS-138
1920	154	569	153	21	12	4	0.7	41	61	21	15	4	.269	.369	0	0	SS-154

Player Register

	G	AB	H	2B	3B	HR	HR%	R	RBI	BB	SO	SB	BA	SA	Pinch Hit AB	H	G by POS

Everett Scott continued

1921		154	576	151	21	9	1	0.2	65	60	27	21	5	.262	.335	0	0	SS-154
1922	NY A	154	557	150	23	5	3	0.5	64	45	23	22	2	.269	.345	0	0	SS-154
1923		152	533	131	16	4	6	1.1	48	60	13	19	1	.246	.325	0	0	SS-152
1924		153	548	137	12	6	4	0.7	56	64	21	15	3	.250	.316	0	0	SS-153
1925	2 teams	NY	A (22G –	.217)	WAS	A (33G –	.272)										
"	total	55	163	41	6	1	0	0.0	13	22	6	6	1	.252	.301	4	2	SS-48, 3B-2
1926	2 teams	CHI	A (40G –	.252)	CIN	N (4G –	.667)										
"	total	44	149	40	10	1	0	0.0	16	14	9	8	1	.268	.349	1	0	SS-43
13 yrs.		1654	5837	1455	208	58	20	0.3	552	549	243	282	69	.249	.315	6	3	SS-1643, 3B-3, 2B-1
1 yr.		40	143	36	10	1	0	0.0	15	13	9	8	1	.252	.336	1	0	SS-39
WORLD SERIES																		
1915	BOS A	5	18	1	0	0	0	0.0	0	0	0	3	0	.056	.056	0	0	SS-5
1916		5	16	2	0	1	0	0.0	1	1	1	1	0	.125	.250	0	0	SS-5
1918		6	20	2	0	0	0	0.0	1	0	1	1	0	.100	.100	0	0	SS-6
1922	NY A	5	14	2	0	0	0	0.0	0	1	1	0	0	.143	.143	0	0	SS-5
1923		6	22	7	0	0	0	0.0	2	3	0	1	0	.318	.318	0	0	SS-6
5 yrs.		27	90	14	0	1	0	0.0	3	5	3	6	0	.156	.178	0	0	SS-27

Bob Seeds

SEEDS, ROBERT IRA (Suitcase Bob)
B. Feb. 24, 1907, Ringgold, Tex.
BR TR 6' 180 lbs.

1930	CLE A	85	277	79	11	3	3	1.1	37	32	12	22	1	.285	.379	15	4	OF-70
1931		48	134	41	4	1	1	0.7	26	10	11	11	1	.306	.373	9	1	OF-33, 1B-2
1932	2 teams	CLE	A (2G –	.000)	CHI	A (116G –	.290)										
"	total	118	438	126	18	6	2	0.5	53	45	31	37	5	.288	.370	4	0	OF-113
1933	BOS A	82	230	56	13	4	0	0.0	26	23	21	20	1	.243	.335	7	2	1B-41, OF-32
1934	2 teams	BOS	A (8G –	.167)	CLE	A (61G –	.247)										
"	total	69	192	47	8	1	0	0.0	28	19	21	14	2	.245	.297	15	3	OF-49
1936	NY A	13	42	11	1	0	4	9.5	12	10	5	3	3	.262	.571	1	0	OF-9, 3B-3
1938	NY N	81	296	86	12	3	9	3.0	35	52	20	33	0	.291	.443	2	0	OF-76
1939		63	173	46	5	1	5	2.9	33	26	22	31	1	.266	.393	12	2	OF-50
1940		56	155	45	5	2	4	2.6	18	16	17	19	0	.290	.426	15	4	OF-40
9 yrs.		615	1937	537	77	21	28	1.4	268	233	160	190	14	.277	.382	80	16	OF-472, 1B-43, 3B-3
1 yr.		116	434	126	18	6	2	0.5	53	45	31	37	5	.290	.373	4	0	OF-112
WORLD SERIES																		
1936	NY A	1	0	0	0	0	0	–	0	0	0	0	0	–	–	0	0	

Pat Seerey

SEEREY, JAMES PATRICK
B. Mar. 17, 1923, Wilburton, Okla.
BR TR 5'10" 200 lbs.

1943	CLE A	26	72	16	3	0	1	1.4	8	5	4	19	0	.222	.306	9	2	OF-16
1944		101	342	80	16	0	15	4.4	39	39	19	99	0	.234	.412	18	3	OF-86
1945		126	414	98	22	2	14	3.4	56	56	66	97	1	.237	.401	8	0	OF-117
1946		117	404	91	17	2	26	6.4	57	62	65	101	2	.225	.470	2	0	OF-115
1947		82	216	37	4	1	11	5.1	24	29	34	66	0	.171	.352	12	1	OF-68
1948	2 teams	CLE	A (10G –	.261)	CHI	A (95G –	.229)										
"	total	105	363	84	11	0	19	5.2	51	70	90	102	0	.231	.419	3	0	OF-100
1949	CHI A	4	4	0	0	0	0	0.0	0	0	3	1	0	.000	.000	2	0	OF-2
7 yrs.		561	1815	406	73	5	86	4.7	236	261	281	485	3	.224	.412	54	6	OF-504
2 yrs.		99	344	78	11	0	18	5.2	45	64	86	95	0	.227	.416	4	0	OF-95

Rick Seilheimer

SEILHEIMER, RICKY ALLEN
B. Aug. 30, 1960, Brenham, Tex.
BL TR 5'11" 185 lbs.

| 1980 | CHI A | 21 | 52 | 11 | 3 | 1 | 1 | 1.9 | 4 | 3 | 4 | 15 | 1 | .212 | .365 | 0 | 0 | C-21 |

Carey Selph

SELPH, CAREY ISUM
B. Dec. 5, 1901, Donaldson, Ark. D. Feb. 24, 1976, Houston, Tex.
BR TR 5'9½" 175 lbs.

1929	STL N	25	51	12	1	1	0	0.0	8	7	6	4	1	.235	.294	5	1	2B-16
1932	CHI A	116	396	112	19	8	0	0.0	50	51	31	9	7	.283	.371	18	2	3B-71, 2B-26
2 yrs.		141	447	124	20	9	0	0.0	58	58	37	13	8	.277	.362	23	3	3B-71, 2B-42
1 yr.		116	396	112	19	8	0	0.0	50	51	31	9	7	.283	.371	18	2	3B-71, 2B-26

Luke Sewell

SEWELL, JAMES LUTHER
Brother of Tommy Sewell. Brother of Joe Sewell.
B. Jan. 5, 1901, Titus, Ala.
Manager 1941-46, 1949-52.
BR TR 5'9" 160 lbs.

1921	CLE A	3	6	0	0	0	0	0.0	0	1	0	3	0	.000	.000	0	0	C-3
1922		41	87	23	5	0	0	0.0	14	10	5	8	1	.264	.322	1	0	C-38
1923		10	10	2	0	1	0	0.0	2	1	1	0	0	.200	.400	2	0	C-7
1924		63	165	48	9	1	0	0.0	27	17	22	13	1	.291	.358	3	1	C-56
1925		74	220	51	10	2	0	0.0	30	18	33	18	6	.232	.295	4	1	C-66, OF-2
1926		126	433	103	16	4	0	0.0	41	46	36	27	9	.238	.293	1	0	C-125
1927		128	470	138	27	6	0	0.0	52	53	20	23	4	.294	.377	2	0	C-126
1928		122	411	111	16	9	3	0.7	52	52	26	27	3	.270	.375	4	1	C-118
1929		124	406	96	17	3	1	0.2	41	39	29	26	6	.236	.300	0	0	C-124
1930		76	292	75	21	2	1	0.3	40	43	14	9	5	.257	.353	0	0	C-76
1931		108	375	103	30	4	1	0.3	45	53	36	17	1	.275	.384	3	1	C-105
1932		87	300	76	20	2	2	0.7	36	52	38	24	4	.253	.353	2	0	C-84
1933	WAS A	141	474	125	30	4	2	0.4	65	61	48	24	7	.264	.357	0	0	C-141
1934		72	207	49	7	3	2	1.0	27	21	22	10	0	.237	.329	7	2	C-50, OF-7, 1B-6, 3B-1, 2B-1
1935	CHI A	118	421	120	19	3	2	0.5	52	67	32	18	3	.285	.359	5	0	C-112
1936		128	451	113	20	5	5	1.1	59	73	54	16	11	.251	.350	2	0	C-126
1937		122	412	111	21	6	1	0.2	51	61	46	18	4	.269	.357	3	0	C-118
1938		65	211	45	4	1	0	0.0	23	27	20	20	0	.213	.242	0	0	C-65
1939	CLE A	16	20	3	1	0	0	0.0	1	1	3	1	0	.150	.200	0	0	C-15, 1B-1

Player Register

	G	AB	H	2B	3B	HR	HR%	R	RBI	BB	SO	SB	BA	SA	Pinch Hit AB	H	G by POS

Luke Sewell continued
1942 STL A	6	12	1	0	0	0	0.0	1	0	1	5	0	.083	.083	0	0	C-6
20 yrs.	1630	5383	1393	273	56	20	0.4	653	696	486	307	65	.259	.341	39	8	C-1561, OF-9, 1B-7, 3B-1, 2B-1
4 yrs.	433	1495	389	64	15	8	0.5	185	228	152	72	18	.260	.339	10	2	C-421

WORLD SERIES
| 1933 WAS A | 5 | 17 | 3 | 0 | 0 | 0 | 0.0 | 1 | 1 | 2 | 0 | 1 | .176 | .176 | 0 | 0 | C-5 |

Bill Sharp
SHARP, WILLIAM HOWARD BL TL 5'10" 178 lbs.
B. Jan. 18, 1950, Lima, Ohio

1973 CHI A	76	196	54	8	3	4	2.0	23	22	19	28	2	.276	.408	5	2	OF-70, DH-1
1974	100	320	81	13	2	4	1.3	45	24	25	37	0	.253	.344	3	1	OF-99
1975 2 teams	CHI A (18G – .200)					MIL A (125G – .255)											
" total	143	408	102	27	3	1	0.2	38	38	21	29	0	.250	.338	10	1	OF-138
1976 MIL A	78	180	44	4	0	0	0.0	16	11	10	15	1	.244	.267	17	5	OF-56, DH-7
4 yrs.	397	1104	281	52	8	9	0.8	122	95	75	109	3	.255	.341	35	9	OF-363, DH-8
3 yrs.	194	551	142	21	5	8	1.5	69	50	46	68	2	.258	.358	15	4	OF-183, DH-1

Al Shaw
SHAW, ALFRED BR TR 5'8" 170 lbs.
B. Oct. 3, 1874, Burslem, England D. Mar. 25, 1958, Uhrichsville, Ohio

1901 DET A	55	171	46	7	0	1	0.6	20	23	10		2	.269	.327	4	0	C-42, 1B-9, 3B-2, SS-1
1907 BOS A	76	198	38	1	3	0	0.0	10	7	18		4	.192	.227	1	0	C-73, 1B-1
1908 CHI A	32	49	4	1	0	0	0.0	0	2	2		0	.082	.102	3	0	C-29
1909 BOS N	17	41	4	0	0	0	0.0	1	0	5		0	.098	.098	2	0	C-13
4 yrs.	180	459	92	9	3	1	0.2	31	32	35		6	.200	.240	10	0	C-157, 1B-10, 3B-2, SS-1
1 yr.	32	49	4	1	0	0	0.0	0	2	2		0	.082	.102	3	0	C-29

Merv Shea
SHEA, MERVIN DAVID JOHN BR TR 5'11" 175 lbs.
B. Sept. 5, 1900, San Francisco, Calif. D. Jan. 27, 1953, Sacramento, Calif.

1927 DET A	34	85	15	6	3	0	0.0	5	9	7	15	0	.176	.318	3	0	C-31
1928	39	85	20	2	3	0	0.0	8	9	9	11	2	.235	.329	7	0	C-30
1929	50	162	47	6	0	3	1.9	23	24	19	18	2	.290	.383	3	0	C-50
1933 2 teams	BOS A (16G – .143)					STL A (94G – .262)											
" total	110	335	81	14	1	1	0.3	27	35	47	33	2	.242	.299	8	2	C-101
1934 CHI A	62	176	28	3	0	0	0.0	8	5	24	19	0	.159	.176	2	0	C-60
1935	46	122	28	2	0	0	0.0	8	13	30	9	0	.230	.246	2	0	C-43
1936	14	24	3	0	0	0	0.0	3	2	6	5	0	.125	.125	0	0	C-14
1937	25	71	15	1	0	0	0.0	7	5	15	10	1	.211	.225	0	0	C-25
1938 BKN N	48	120	22	5	0	0	0.0	14	12	28	20	1	.183	.225	0	0	C-47
1939 DET A	4	2	0	0	0	0	0.0	0	0	1	0	0	.000	.000	0	0	C-4
1944 PHI N	7	15	4	0	0	1	6.7	2	1	4	4	0	.267	.467	1	0	C-6
11 yrs.	439	1197	263	39	7	5	0.4	105	115	189	145	8	.220	.277	26	2	C-411
4 yrs.	147	393	74	6	0	0	0.0	26	25	75	43	1	.188	.204	4	0	C-142

Bud Sheely
SHEELY, HOLLIS KIMBALL BL TR 6'1" 200 lbs.
Son of Earl Sheely.
B. Nov. 26, 1920, Spokane, Wash.

1951 CHI A	34	89	16	2	0	0	0.0	2	7	6	7	0	.180	.202	1	0	C-33
1952	36	75	18	2	0	0	0.0	1	3	12	7	0	.240	.267	6	2	C-31
1953	31	46	10	1	0	0	0.0	4	2	9	8	0	.217	.239	10	4	C-17
3 yrs.	101	210	44	5	0	0	0.0	7	12	27	22	0	.210	.233	17	6	C-81
3 yrs.	101	210	44	5	0	0	0.0	7	12	27	22	0	.210	.233	17	6	C-81

Earl Sheely
SHEELY, EARL HOMER (Whitey) BR TR 6'3½" 195 lbs.
Father of Bud Sheely.
B. Feb. 12, 1893, Bushnell, Ill. D. Sept. 16, 1952, Seattle, Wash.

1921 CHI A	154	563	171	25	6	11	2.0	68	95	57	34	4	.304	.428	0	0	1B-154
1922	149	526	167	37	4	6	1.1	72	80	60	27	4	.317	.437	0	0	1B-149
1923	156	570	169	25	3	4	0.7	74	88	79	30	5	.296	.372	0	0	1B-156
1924	146	535	171	34	3	3	0.6	84	103	95	28	7	.320	.411	0	0	1B-146
1925	153	600	189	43	3	9	1.5	93	111	68	23	3	.315	.442	0	0	1B-153
1926	145	525	157	40	2	6	1.1	77	89	75	13	3	.299	.417	0	0	1B-144
1927	45	129	27	3	0	2	1.6	11	16	20	5	1	.209	.279	8	1	1B-36
1929 PIT N	139	485	142	22	4	6	1.2	63	88	75	24	6	.293	.392	0	0	1B-139
1931 BOS N	147	538	147	15	2	1	0.2	30	77	34	21	0	.273	.314	3	0	1B-143
9 yrs.	1234	4471	1340	244	27	48	1.1	572	747	563	205	33	.300	.399	11	1	1B-1220
7 yrs.	948	3448	1051	207	21	41	1.2	479	582	454	160	27	.305	.413	8	1	1B-938
				10th					9th					10th			

Art Shires
SHIRES, CHARLES ARTHUR (Art the Great) BL TR 6'1" 195 lbs.
B. Aug. 13, 1907, Milford, Tex. D. July 13, 1967, Italy, Tex.

1928 CHI A	33	123	42	6	1	1	0.8	20	11	13	10	0	.341	.431	1	1	1B-32
1929	100	353	110	20	7	3	0.8	41	41	32	20	4	.312	.433	9	1	1B-88, 2B-2
1930 2 teams	CHI A (37G – .258)					WAS A (38G – .369)											
" total	75	212	64	10	1	2	0.9	25	37	11	11	3	.302	.387	19	6	1B-54
1932 BOS N	82	298	71	9	3	5	1.7	32	30	25	21	1	.238	.339	2	0	1B-82
4 yrs.	290	986	287	45	12	11	1.1	118	119	81	62	8	.291	.395	31	8	1B-256, 2B-2
3 yrs.	170	604	185	31	9	5	0.8	75	70	51	36	6	.306	.412	14	4	1B-153, 2B-2

Ray Shook
SHOOK, RAYMOND CURTIS BR TR 5'7½" 155 lbs.
B. Nov. 18, 1890, Perry, Ohio D. Sept. 16, 1970, South Bend, Ind.

| 1916 CHI A | 1 | 0 | 0 | 0 | 0 | 0 | – | 0 | 0 | 0 | 0 | 0 | – | – | 0 | 0 | |

316

	G	AB	H	2B	3B	HR	HR%	R	RBI	BB	SO	SB	BA	SA	Pinch Hit AB H	G by POS

Dave Short
SHORT, DAVID ORVIS
B. May 11, 1917, Magnolia, Ark.
BL TR 5'11½" 162 lbs.

	G	AB	H	2B	3B	HR	HR%	R	RBI	BB	SO	SB	BA	SA	PH AB	PH H	G by POS
1940 CHI A	4	3	1	0	0	0	0.0	1	0	1	2	0	.333	.333	3	1	
1941	3	8	0	0	0	0	0.0	0	0	2	1	0	.000	.000	1	0	OF-2
2 yrs.	7	11	1	0	0	0	0.0	1	0	3	3	0	.091	.091	4	1	OF-2
2 yrs.	7	11	1	0	0	0	0.0	1	0	3	3	0	.091	.091	4	1	OF-2

Frank Shugart
SHUGART, WILLIAM FRANK
B. 1867, Chicago, Ill. Deceased.
BL TR

	G	AB	H	2B	3B	HR	HR%	R	RBI	BB	SO	SB	BA	SA	PH AB	PH H	G by POS
1890 CHI P	29	106	20	5	5	0	0.0	8	15	5	13	5	.189	.330	0	0	SS-25, OF-5
1891 PIT N	75	320	88	19	8	2	0.6	57	33	20	26	21	.275	.403	0	0	SS-75
1892	137	554	148	19	14	0	0.0	94	62	47	48	28	.267	.352	0	0	SS-134, C-2, OF-1
1893 2 teams	PIT N (52G – .262)			STL N (59G – .280)													
" total	111	456	124	17	7	1	0.2	78	60	41	25	25	.272	.346	0	0	SS-74, OF-29, 3B-9
1894 STL N	133	527	154	19	18	7	1.3	103	72	38	37	21	.292	.436	0	0	OF-122, SS-7, 3B-7
1895 LOU N	113	473	125	14	13	4	0.8	61	70	31	25	14	.264	.374	0	0	SS-88, OF-27
1897 PHI N	40	163	41	8	2	5	3.1	20	25	8		5	.252	.417	0	0	SS-40
1901 CHI N	107	415	104	9	12	2	0.5	62	47	28		12	.251	.345	0	0	SS-107
8 yrs.	745	3014	804	110	79	21	0.7	483	384	218	174	131	.267	.377	0	0	SS-550, OF-184, 3B-16, C-2
1 yr.	107	415	104	9	12	2	0.5	62	47	28		12	.251	.345	0	0	SS-107

Roy Sievers
SIEVERS, ROY EDWARD (Squirrel)
B. Nov. 18, 1926, St. Louis, Mo.
BR TR 6'1" 195 lbs.

	G	AB	H	2B	3B	HR	HR%	R	RBI	BB	SO	SB	BA	SA	PH AB	PH H	G by POS
1949 STL A	140	471	144	28	1	16	3.4	84	91	70	75	1	.306	.471	7	2	OF-125, 3B-7
1950	113	370	88	20	4	10	2.7	46	57	34	42	1	.238	.395	15	2	OF-78, 3B-21
1951	31	89	20	2	1	1	1.1	10	11	9	21	0	.225	.303	8	1	OF-25
1952	11	30	6	3	0	0	0.0	3	5	1	4	0	.200	.300	5	0	1B-7
1953	92	285	77	15	0	8	2.8	37	35	32	47	0	.270	.407	17	3	1B-76
1954 WAS A	145	514	119	26	6	24	4.7	75	102	80	77	2	.232	.446	5	0	OF-133, 1B-8
1955	144	509	138	20	8	25	4.9	74	106	73	66	1	.271	.489	2	0	OF-129, 1B-17, 3B-2
1956	152	550	139	27	2	29	5.3	92	95	100	88	0	.253	.467	0	0	OF-78, 1B-76
1957	152	572	172	23	5	42	7.3	99	114	76	55	1	.301	.579	2	2	OF-130, 1B-21
1958	148	550	162	18	1	39	7.1	85	108	53	63	3	.295	.544	4	1	OF-114, 1B-33
1959	115	385	93	19	0	21	5.5	55	49	53	62	1	.242	.455	7	1	1B-93, OF-13
1960 CHI A	127	444	131	22	0	28	6.3	87	93	74	69	1	.295	.534	9	1	1B-114, OF-6
1961	141	492	145	26	6	27	5.5	76	92	61	62	1	.295	.537	10	4	1B-132
1962 PHI N	144	477	125	19	5	21	4.4	61	80	56	80	2	.262	.455	12	1	1B-130, OF-7
1963	138	450	108	19	2	19	4.2	46	82	43	72	0	.240	.418	18	6	1B-126
1964 2 teams	PHI N (49G – .183)			WAS A (33G – .172)													
" total	82	178	32	4	1	8	4.5	12	27	22	34	0	.180	.348	29	6	1B-48
1965 WAS A	12	21	4	1	0	0	0.0	3	0	4	3	0	.190	.238	4	1	1B-7
17 yrs.	1887	6387	1703	292	42	318	5.0	945	1147	841	920	14	.267	.475	154	31	1B-888, OF-838, 3B-30
2 yrs.	268	936	276	48	6	55	5.9	163	185	135	131	2	.295	.535	19	5	1B-246, OF-6

Frank Sigafoos
SIGAFOOS, FRANCIS LEONARD
B. Mar. 21, 1904, Easton, Pa. D. Apr. 12, 1968, Indianapolis, Ind.
BR TR 5'9" 170 lbs.

	G	AB	H	2B	3B	HR	HR%	R	RBI	BB	SO	SB	BA	SA	PH AB	PH H	G by POS
1926 PHI A	13	43	11	0	0	0	0.0	4	2	0	3	0	.256	.256	1	0	SS-12
1929 2 teams	DET A (14G – .174)			CHI A (7G – .333)													
" total	21	26	5	1	0	0	0.0	4	3	7	5	0	.192	.231	1	0	3B-6, 2B-6, SS-5
1931 CIN N	21	65	11	2	0	0	0.0	6	8	0	6	0	.169	.200	4	1	3B-15, SS-2
3 yrs.	55	134	27	3	0	0	0.0	14	13	7	14	0	.201	.224	6	1	3B-21, SS-19, 2B-6
1 yr.	7	3	1	0	0	0	0.0	1	1	2	1	0	.333	.333	0	0	2B-6

Ken Silvestri
SILVESTRI, KENNETH JOSEPH (Hawk)
B. May 3, 1916, Chicago, Ill.
Manager 1967.
BB TR 6'1" 200 lbs.

	G	AB	H	2B	3B	HR	HR%	R	RBI	BB	SO	SB	BA	SA	PH AB	PH H	G by POS
1939 CHI A	22	75	13	3	0	2	2.7	6	5	6	13	0	.173	.293	2	1	C-20
1940	28	24	6	2	0	2	8.3	5	10	4	7	0	.250	.583	24	6	C-1
1941 NY A	17	40	10	5	0	1	2.5	6	4	7	6	0	.250	.450	3	0	C-13
1946	13	21	6	1	0	0	0.0	4	1	3	7	0	.286	.333	1	0	C-12
1947	3	10	2	0	0	0	0.0	2	0	2	2	0	.200	.200	0	0	C-3
1949 PHI N	4	4	0	0	0	0	0.0	0	0	2	1	0	.000	.000	2	0	SS-1, 2B-1, C-1
1950	11	20	5	0	1	0	0.0	2	4	4	3	0	.250	.350	2	1	C-9
1951	4	9	2	0	0	0	0.0	2	1	3	2	0	.222	.222	0	0	C-3
8 yrs.	102	203	44	11	1	5	2.5	26	25	31	41	0	.217	.355	34	8	C-62, SS-1, 2B-1
2 yrs.	50	99	19	5	0	4	4.0	11	15	10	20	0	.192	.364	26	7	C-21

WORLD SERIES
| 1950 PHI N | 1 | 0 | 0 | 0 | 0 | 0 | – | 0 | 0 | 0 | 0 | 0 | – | – | 0 | 0 | C-1 |

Al Simmons
SIMMONS, ALOYSIUS HARRY (Bucketfoot Al)
Born Aloysius Harry Szymanski.
B. May 22, 1902, Milwaukee, Wis. D. May 26, 1956, Milwaukee, Wis.
Hall of Fame 1953.
BR TR 5'11" 190 lbs.

	G	AB	H	2B	3B	HR	HR%	R	RBI	BB	SO	SB	BA	SA	PH AB	PH H	G by POS
1924 PHI A	152	594	183	31	9	8	1.3	69	102	30	60	16	.308	.431	0	0	OF-152
1925	153	658	253	43	12	24	3.6	122	129	35	41	7	.384	.596	0	0	OF-153
1926	147	581	199	53	10	19	3.3	90	109	48	49	10	.343	.566	0	0	OF-147
1927	106	406	159	36	11	15	3.7	86	108	31	30	10	.392	.645	0	0	OF-105
1928	119	464	163	33	9	15	3.2	78	107	31	30	1	.351	.558	3	2	OF-114
1929	143	581	212	41	9	34	5.9	114	157	31	38	4	.365	.642	0	0	OF-142
1930	138	554	211	41	16	36	6.5	152	165	39	34	9	.381	.708	2	1	OF-136
1931	128	513	200	37	13	22	4.3	105	128	47	45	3	.390	.641	0	0	OF-128
1932	154	670	216	28	9	35	5.2	144	151	47	76	4	.322	.548	0	0	OF-154
1933 CHI A	146	605	200	29	10	14	2.3	85	119	39	49	5	.331	.481	1	0	OF-145
1934	138	558	192	36	7	18	3.2	102	104	53	58	3	.344	.530	0	0	OF-138
1935	128	525	140	22	7	16	3.0	68	79	33	43	4	.267	.427	3	0	OF-126
1936 DET A	143	568	186	38	6	13	2.3	96	112	49	35	7	.327	.484	4	1	OF-138, 1B-8

	G	AB	H	2B	3B	HR	HR%	R	RBI	BB	SO	SB	BA	SA	Pinch Hit AB	H	G by POS

Al Simmons continued

	G	AB	H	2B	3B	HR	HR%	R	RBI	BB	SO	SB	BA	SA	PH AB	PH H	G by POS
1937 WAS A	103	419	117	21	10	8	1.9	60	84	27	35	3	.279	.434	1	0	OF-102
1938	125	470	142	23	6	21	4.5	79	95	38	40	2	.302	.511	9	2	OF-117
1939 2 teams	BOS N (93G – .282)					CIN N (9G – .143)											
" total	102	351	96	17	5	7	2.0	39	44	24	43	0	.274	.410	14	2	OF-87
1940 PHI A	37	81	25	4	0	1	1.2	7	19	4	8	0	.309	.395	16	8	OF-18
1941	9	24	3	1	0	0	0.0	1	1	1	2	0	.125	.167	4	0	OF-5
1943 BOS A	40	133	27	5	0	1	0.8	9	12	8	21	0	.203	.263	7	0	OF-33
1944 PHI A	4	6	3	0	0	0	0.0	1	2	0	0	0	.500	.500	2	1	OF-2
20 yrs.	2215	8761	2927	539	149	307	3.5	1507	1827	615	737	87	.334	.535	66	17	OF-2142, 1B-1
3 yrs.	412	1688	532	87	24	48	2.8	255	302	125	150	12	.315	.480	4	0	OF-409
													9th		5th	5th	

WORLD SERIES

	G	AB	H	2B	3B	HR	HR%	R	RBI	BB	SO	SB	BA	SA	PH AB	PH H	G by POS
1929 PHI A	5	20	6	1	0	2	10.0	6	5	1	4	0	.300	.650	0	0	OF-5
1930	6	22	8	2	0	2	9.1	4	4	2	2	0	.364	.727	0	0	OF-6
1931	7	27	9	2	0	2	7.4	4	8	3	3	0	.333	.630	0	0	OF-7
1939 CIN N	1	4	1	1	0	0	0.0	1	0	0	0	0	.250	.500	0	0	OF-1
4 yrs.	19	73	24	6	0	6	8.2	15	17	6	9	0	.329	.658	0	0	OF-19
														6th		4th	

Mel Simons

SIMONS, MELBERN ELLIS (Butch) BL TR 5'10" 175 lbs.
B. July 1, 1900, Carlyle, Ill. D. Nov. 10, 1974, Paducah, Ky.

	G	AB	H	2B	3B	HR	HR%	R	RBI	BB	SO	SB	BA	SA	PH AB	PH H	G by POS
1931 CHI A	68	189	52	9	0	0	0.0	24	12	12	17	1	.275	.323	6	1	OF-59
1932	7	5	0	0	0	0	0.0	0	0	0	1	0	.000	.000	1	0	OF-6
2 yrs.	75	194	52	9	0	0	0.0	24	12	12	18	1	.268	.314	7	1	OF-65
2 yrs.	75	194	52	9	0	0	0.0	24	12	12	18	1	.268	.314	7	1	OF-65

Harry Simpson

SIMPSON, HARRY LEON (Suitcase) BL TR 6'1" 180 lbs.
B. Dec. 3, 1925, Atlanta, Ga. D. Apr. 3, 1979, Akron, Ohio

	G	AB	H	2B	3B	HR	HR%	R	RBI	BB	SO	SB	BA	SA	PH AB	PH H	G by POS
1951 CLE A	122	332	76	7	0	7	2.1	51	24	45	48	6	.229	.313	10	2	OF-68, 1B-50
1952	146	545	145	21	10	10	1.8	66	65	56	82	5	.266	.396	1	1	OF-127, 1B-28
1953	82	242	55	3	1	7	2.9	25	22	18	27	0	.227	.335	10	1	OF-69, 1B-2
1955 2 teams	CLE A (3G – .000)					KC A (112G – .301)											
" total	115	397	119	16	7	5	1.3	43	52	36	61	3	.300	.413	11	4	OF-100, 1B-3
1956 KC A	141	543	159	22	11	21	3.9	76	105	47	82	2	.293	.490	3	0	OF-111, 1B-32
1957 2 teams	KC A (50G – .296)					NY A (75G – .250)											
" total	125	403	109	16	9	13	3.2	51	63	31	64	1	.270	.452	20	4	OF-63, 1B-48
1958 2 teams	NY A (24G – .216)					KC A (78G – .264)											
" total	102	263	67	9	2	7	2.7	22	33	32	45	0	.255	.384	30	5	1B-43, OF-26
1959 3 teams	KC A (8G – .286)					CHI A (38G – .187)			PIT N (9G – .267)								
" total	55	104	22	7	1	3	2.9	9	17	6	20	0	.212	.385	34	6	OF-15, 1B-5
8 yrs.	888	2829	752	101	41	73	2.6	343	381	271	429	17	.266	.408	119	23	OF-579, 1B-211
1 yr.	38	75	14	5	1	2	2.7	5	13	4	14	0	.187	.360	24	4	OF-12, 1B-1

WORLD SERIES

	G	AB	H	2B	3B	HR	HR%	R	RBI	BB	SO	SB	BA	SA	PH AB	PH H	G by POS
1957 NY A	5	12	1	0	0	0	0.0	0	1	0	4	0	.083	.083	1	0	1B-4

Bud Sketchley

SKETCHLEY, HARRY CLEMENT BL TL 5'10½" 180 lbs.
B. Mar. 30, 1919, Virden, Man., Canada

	G	AB	H	2B	3B	HR	HR%	R	RBI	BB	SO	SB	BA	SA	PH AB	PH H	G by POS
1942 CHI A	13	36	7	1	0	0	0.0	3	7	4	0	0	.194	.222	1	0	OF-12

Joel Skinner

SKINNER, JOEL PATRICK BR TR 6'4" 195 lbs.
Son of Bob Skinner.
B. Feb. 27, 1961, San Diego, Calif.

	G	AB	H	2B	3B	HR	HR%	R	RBI	BB	SO	SB	BA	SA	PH AB	PH H	G by POS
1983 CHI A	6	11	3	0	0	0	0.0	2	1	0	1	0	.273	.273	0	0	C-6

Lou Skizas

SKIZAS, LOUIS PETER (The Nervous Greek) BR TR 5'11" 175 lbs.
B. June 2, 1932, Chicago, Ill.

	G	AB	H	2B	3B	HR	HR%	R	RBI	BB	SO	SB	BA	SA	PH AB	PH H	G by POS
1956 2 teams	NY A (6G – .167)					KC A (83G – .316)											
" total	89	303	95	11	3	11	3.6	39	40	15	19	3	.314	.479	15	3	OF-74
1957 KC A	119	376	92	14	1	18	4.8	34	44	27	15	5	.245	.431	24	2	OF-76, 3B-32
1958 DET A	23	33	8	2	0	1	3.0	4	2	5	1	0	.242	.394	13	2	OF-5, 3B-4
1959 CHI A	8	13	1	0	0	0	0.0	3	0	3	2	0	.077	.077	2	0	OF-6
4 yrs.	239	725	196	27	4	30	4.1	80	86	50	37	8	.270	.443	54	7	OF-161, 3B-36
1 yr.	8	13	1	0	0	0	0.0	3	0	3	2	0	.077	.077	2	0	OF-6

Bill Skowron

SKOWRON, WILLIAM JOSEPH (Moose) BR TR 5'11" 195 lbs.
B. Dec. 18, 1930, Chicago, Ill.

	G	AB	H	2B	3B	HR	HR%	R	RBI	BB	SO	SB	BA	SA	PH AB	PH H	G by POS
1954 NY A	87	215	73	12	9	7	3.3	37	41	19	18	2	.340	.577	22	7	1B-61, 3B-5, 2B-2
1955	108	288	92	17	3	12	4.2	46	61	21	32	1	.319	.524	35	6	1B-74, 3B-3
1956	134	464	143	21	6	23	5.0	78	90	50	60	4	.308	.528	12	2	1B-120, 3B-2
1957	122	457	139	15	5	17	3.7	54	88	31	60	3	.304	.470	9	3	1B-115
1958	126	465	127	22	3	14	3.0	61	73	28	69	1	.273	.424	7	3	1B-118, 3B-2
1959	74	282	84	13	5	15	5.3	39	59	20	47	1	.298	.539	3	1	1B-72
1960	146	538	166	34	3	26	4.8	63	91	38	95	2	.309	.528	6	3	1B-142
1961	150	561	150	23	4	28	5.0	76	89	35	108	0	.267	.472	1	0	1B-149
1962	140	478	129	16	6	23	4.8	63	80	36	99	0	.270	.473	12	4	1B-135
1963 LA N	89	237	48	9	0	4	1.7	19	19	13	49	0	.203	.287	24	2	1B-66, 3B-1
1964 2 teams	WAS A (73G – .271)					CHI A (73G – .293)											
" total	146	535	151	21	3	17	3.2	47	79	30	92	0	.282	.428	13	5	1B-136
1965 CHI A	146	559	153	24	3	18	3.2	63	78	32	77	1	.274	.424	1	1	1B-145
1966	120	337	84	15	2	6	1.8	27	29	26	45	1	.249	.359	23	3	1B-98
1967 2 teams	CHI A (8G – .000)					CAL A (62G – .220)											
" total	70	131	27	2	1	1	0.8	8	11	4	19	0	.206	.260	37	7	1B-32
14 yrs.	1658	5547	1566	243	53	211	3.8	681	888	383	870	16	.282	.459	205	47	1B-1463, 3B-13, 2B-2
4 yrs.	347	1177	317	50	8	28	2.4	109	146	77	159	2	.269	.397	35	4	1B-313

WORLD SERIES

	G	AB	H	2B	3B	HR	HR%	R	RBI	BB	SO	SB	BA	SA	PH AB	PH H	G by POS
1955 NY A	5	12	4	2	0	1	8.3	2	3	1	0	0	.333	.750	2	0	1B-3

318

319　　　*Player Register*

	G	AB	H	2B	3B	HR	HR %	R	RBI	BB	SO	SB	BA	SA	Pinch Hit AB H	G by POS

Bill Skowron continued

1956	3	10	1	0	0	1	10.0	1	4	0	3	0	.100	.400	1　0	1B-2
1957	2	4	0	0	0	0	0.0	0	0	0	0	0	.000	.000	1　0	1B-2
1958	7	27	7	0	0	2	7.4	3	7	1	4	0	.259	.481	0　0	1B-7
1960	7	32	12	2	0	2	6.3	7	6	0	6	0	.375	.625	0　0	1B-7
1961	5	17	6	0	0	1	5.9	3	5	3	4	0	.353	.529	0　0	1B-5
1962	6	18	4	0	1	0	0.0	1	1	1	5	0	.222	.333	0　0	1B-6
1963 LA N	4	13	5	0	0	1	7.7	2	3	1	3	0	.385	.615	0　0	1B-4
8 yrs.	39	133	39	4	1	8	6.0	19	29	6	26	0	.293	.519	4　0	1B-36
							7th		6th		6th					

Jack Slattery

SLATTERY, JOHN TERRENCE　　　　　　　　　　　　　　　BR　TR　6'2"　　191 lbs.
B. Jan. 6, 1877, Boston, Mass.　D. July 17, 1949, Boston, Mass.
Manager 1928.

1901 BOS A	1	3	1	0	0	0	0.0	1	1		0		.333	.333	0　0	C-1
1903 2 teams		CLE A (4G – .000)				CHI A (63G – .218)										
" total	67	222	46	3	2	0	0.0	9	20	2		2	.207	.239	4　0	C-56, 1B-7
1906 STL N	3	7	2	0	0	0	0.0	0	0	1		0	.286	.286	1　0	C-2
1909 WAS A	32	56	12	2	0	0	0.0	4	6	2		1	.214	.250	15　4	1B-11, C-5
4 yrs.	103	288	61	5	2	0	0.0	14	27	6		3	.212	.243	20　4	C-64, 1B-18
1 yr.	63	211	46	3	2	0	0.0	8	20	2		2	.218	.251	2　0	C-56, 1B-5

Joe Smaza

SMAZA, JOSEPH PAUL　　　　　　　　　　　　　　　　BL　TL　5'11"　　175 lbs.
B. July 7, 1923, Detroit, Mich.

1946 CHI A	2	5	1	0	0	0	0.0	0	0	0	0	0	.200	.200	0　0	OF-1

Al Smith

SMITH, ALPHONSE EUGENE (Fuzzy)　　　　　　　　　BR　TR　6'½"　　189 lbs.
B. Feb. 7, 1928, Kirkwood, Mo.

1953 CLE A	47	150	36	9	0	3	2.0	28	14	20	25	2	.240	.360	2　1	OF-39, 3B-2
1954	131	481	135	29	6	11	2.3	101	50	88	65	2	.281	.435	2　0	OF-109, 3B-21, SS-4
1955	154	607	186	27	4	22	3.6	**123**	77	93	77	11	.306	.473	0　0	OF-120, 3B-45, SS-5, 2B-1
1956	141	526	144	26	5	16	3.0	87	71	84	72	6	.274	.433	1　0	OF-122, 3B-28, 2B-1
1957	135	507	125	23	5	11	2.2	78	49	79	70	12	.247	.377	1　1	3B-84, OF-50
1958 CHI A	139	480	121	23	5	12	2.5	61	58	48	77	3	.252	.396	3　1	OF-138, 3B-1
1959	129	472	112	16	4	17	3.6	65	55	46	74	7	.237	.396	1　0	OF-128, 3B-1
1960	142	536	169	31	3	12	2.2	80	72	50	65	8	.315	.451	1　0	OF-141
1961	147	532	148	29	4	28	5.3	88	93	56	67	4	.278	.506	5　2	3B-80, OF-71
1962	142	511	149	23	8	16	3.1	62	82	57	60	3	.292	.462	4　2	3B-105, OF-39
1963 BAL A	120	368	100	17	1	10	2.7	45	39	32	74	9	.272	.405	21　5	OF-97
1964 2 teams		CLE A (61G – .162)				BOS A (29G – .216)										
" total	90	187	33	5	1	6	3.2	25	21	42	0		.176	.310	30　4	OF-56, 3B-12
12 yrs.	1517	5357	1458	258	46	164	3.1	843	676	674	768	67	.272	.429	71　15	OF-1110, 3B-379, SS-9, 2B-2
5 yrs.	699	2531	699	122	24	85	3.4	356	360	257	343	25	.276	.444	14　5	OF-517, 3B-187
							5th		6th					9th		

WORLD SERIES

1954 CLE A	4	14	3	0	0	1	7.1	2	2	2	2	0	.214	.429	0　0	OF-4
1959 CHI A	6	20	5	3	0	0	0.0	1	1	4	4	0	.250	.400	0　0	OF-6
2 yrs.	10	34	8	3	0	1	2.9	3	3	6	6	0	.235	.412	0　0	OF-10

Charley Smith

SMITH, CHARLES WILLIAM　　　　　　　　　　　　　　BR　TR　6'1"　　170 lbs.
B. Sept. 15, 1937, Charleston, S. C.

1960 LA N	18	60	10	1	1	0	0.0	2	5	1	15	0	.167	.217	0　0	3B-18
1961 2 teams		LA N (9G – .250)				PHI N (112G – .248)										
" total	121	435	108	14	4	11	2.5	47	50	24	82	3	.248	.375	5　1	3B-98, SS-17
1962 CHI A	65	145	30	4	0	2	1.4	11	17	9	32	0	.207	.276	13　2	3B-54
1963	4	7	2	0	1	0	0.0	0	1	0	2	0	.286	.571	3　1	SS-1
1964 2 teams		CHI A (2G – .143)				NY N (127G – .239)										
" total	129	450	107	12	1	20	4.4	45	58	20	102	2	.238	.402	7　2	3B-87, SS-36, OF-13
1965 NY N	135	499	122	20	3	16	3.2	49	62	17	123	2	.244	.393	3　0	3B-131, SS-6, 2B-1
1966 STL N	116	391	104	13	4	10	2.6	34	43	22	81	0	.266	.396	8　3	3B-115, SS-1
1967 NY N	135	425	95	15	3	9	2.1	38	38	32	110	0	.224	.336	20　6	3B-115
1968	46	70	16	4	1	1	1.4	2	7	5	18	0	.229	.357	31　10	3B-13
1969 CHI N	2	2	0	0	0	0	0.0	0	0	0	0	0	.000	.000	2　0	
10 yrs.	771	2484	594	83	18	69	2.8	228	281	130	565	7	.239	.370	92　25	3B-623, SS-61, OF-13, 2B-1
3 yrs.	71	159	33	4	2	2	1.3	12	18	10	35	0	.208	.296	16　3	3B-56, SS-1

Ernie Smith

SMITH, ERNEST HENRY　　　　　　　　　　　　　　　　BR　TR　5'8"　　155 lbs.
B. Oct. 11, 1901, Paterson, N. J.　D. Apr. 6, 1973, Brooklyn, N. Y.

1930 CHI A	24	79	19	3	0	0	0.0	5	3	5	6	2	.241	.278	3　1	SS-21

Roxy Snipes

SNIPES, WYATT EURE (Rock)　　　　　　　　　　　　BL　TR　6'　　185 lbs.
B. Oct. 28, 1896, Marion, S. C.　D. May 1, 1941, Fayetteville, N. C.

1923 CHI A	1	1	0	0	0	0	0.0	0	0	0	0	0	.000	.000	1　0	

Russ Snyder

SNYDER, RUSSELL HENRY　　　　　　　　　　　　　　BL　TR　6'1"　　190 lbs.
B. June 22, 1934, Oak, Neb.

1959 KC A	73	243	76	13	2	3	1.2	41	21	19	29	6	.313	.420	8　2	OF-64
1960	125	304	79	10	5	4	1.3	45	26	20	28	7	.260	.365	32　5	OF-91
1961 BAL A	115	312	91	13	5	1	0.3	46	13	20	32	5	.292	.375	8　0	OF-108
1962	139	416	127	19	4	9	2.2	47	40	17	46	7	.305	.435	21　6	OF-121
1963	148	429	110	21	2	7	1.6	51	36	40	48	18	.256	.364	22　4	OF-130
1964	56	93	27	3	0	1	1.1	11	7	11	22	0	.290	.355	18　3	OF-40
1965	132	345	93	11	2	1	0.3	49	29	27	38	6	.270	.322	23　4	OF-106

Player Register

	G	AB	H	2B	3B	HR	HR%	R	RBI	BB	SO	SB	BA	SA	Pinch Hit AB	H	G by POS

Russ Snyder continued

1966	117	373	114	21	5	3	0.8	66	41	38	37	2	.306	.413	15	2	OF-104
1967	108	275	65	8	2	4	1.5	40	23	32	48	5	.236	.324	33	4	OF-69
1968 2 teams		CHI	A (38G – .134)					CLE	A (68G – .281)								
" total	106	299	72	10	2	3	1.0	32	28	29	37	1	.241	.318	29	6	OF-76, 1B-1
1969 CLE A	122	266	66	10	0	2	0.8	26	24	25	33	3	.248	.308	41	7	OF-84
1970 MIL A	124	276	64	11	0	4	1.4	34	31	16	40	1	.232	.315	28	6	OF-106
12 yrs.	1365	3631	984	150	29	42	1.2	488	319	294	438	58	.271	.363	278	49	OF-1099, 1B-1
1 yr.	38	82	11	2	0	1	1.2	2	5	4	16	0	.134	.195	17	3	OF-22

WORLD SERIES

| 1966 BAL A | 3 | 6 | 1 | 0 | 0 | 0 | 0.0 | 1 | 1 | 2 | 0 | 0 | .167 | .167 | 0 | 0 | OF-3 |

Eric Soderholm

SODERHOLM, ERIC THANE
B. Sept. 24, 1948, Cortland, N.Y.
BR TR 5'11" 187 lbs.

1971 MIN A	21	64	10	4	0	1	1.6	9	4	10	17	0	.156	.266	0	0	3B-20
1972	93	287	54	10	0	13	4.5	28	39	19	48	3	.188	.359	11	3	3B-79
1973	35	111	33	7	2	1	0.9	22	9	21	16	1	.297	.423	3	1	3B-33, SS-1
1974	141	464	128	18	3	10	2.2	63	51	48	68	7	.276	.392	6	0	3B-130, SS-1
1975	117	419	120	17	2	11	2.6	62	58	53	66	3	.286	.415	1	0	3B-113, DH-3
1977 CHI A	130	460	129	20	3	25	5.4	77	67	47	47	2	.280	.500	0	0	3B-126, DH-3
1978	143	457	118	17	1	20	4.4	57	67	39	44	2	.258	.431	7	4	3B-128, DH-11, 2B-1
1979 2 teams		CHI	A (56G – .252)					TEX	A (63G – .272)								
" total	119	357	93	14	2	10	2.8	46	53	31	28	0	.261	.395	14	3	3B-93, DH-14, 1B-2
1980 NY A	95	275	79	13	1	11	4.0	38	35	27	25	0	.287	.462	11	3	DH-51, 3B-37
9 yrs.	894	2894	764	120	14	102	3.5	402	383	295	359	18	.264	.421	53	14	3B-759, DH-82, SS-2, 1B-2, 2B-1
3 yrs.	329	1127	300	45	6	51	4.5	165	168	105	110	4	.266	.453	8	5	3B-310, DH-14, 2B-1

LEAGUE CHAMPIONSHIP SERIES

| 1980 NY A | 2 | 6 | 1 | 0 | 0 | 0 | 0.0 | 0 | 0 | 0 | 0 | 0 | .167 | .167 | 0 | 0 | DH-2 |

Moose Solters

SOLTERS, JULIUS JOSEPH
Born Julius Joseph Soltesz.
B. Mar. 22, 1906, Pittsburgh, Pa. D. Sept. 28, 1975, Pittsburgh, Pa.
BR TR 6' 190 lbs.

1934 BOS A	101	365	109	25	4	7	1.9	61	58	18	50	9	.299	.447	13	4	OF-89
1935 2 teams		BOS	A (24G – .241)					STL	A (127G – .330)								
" total	151	631	201	45	7	18	2.9	94	112	36	42	11	.319	.498	3	1	OF-148
1936 STL A	152	628	183	45	7	17	2.7	100	134	41	76	3	.291	.467	3	0	OF-147
1937 CLE A	152	589	190	42	11	20	3.4	90	109	42	56	6	.323	.533	3	0	OF-149
1938	67	199	40	6	3	2	1.0	30	22	13	28	4	.201	.291	23	4	OF-46
1939 2 teams		CLE	A (41G – .275)					STL	A (40G – .206)								
" total	81	233	55	13	3	2	0.9	33	33	19	35	3	.236	.343	27	7	OF-55
1940 CHI A	116	428	132	28	3	12	2.8	65	80	27	54	3	.308	.472	9	1	OF-107
1941	76	251	65	9	4	4	1.6	24	43	18	31	3	.259	.375	12	3	OF-63
1943	42	97	15	0	0	1	1.0	6	8	7	5	0	.155	.186	19	2	OF-21
9 yrs.	938	3421	990	213	42	83	2.4	503	599	221	377	42	.289	.449	112	22	OF-825
3 yrs.	234	776	212	37	7	17	2.2	95	131	52	90	6	.273	.405	40	6	OF-191

Steve Souchock

SOUCHOCK, STEPHEN (Bud)
B. Mar. 3, 1919, Yatesboro, Pa.
BR TR 6'2½" 203 lbs.

1946 NY A	47	86	26	3	3	2	2.3	15	10	7	13	0	.302	.477	17	5	1B-20
1948	44	118	24	3	1	3	2.5	11	11	7	13	3	.203	.322	11	2	1B-32
1949 CHI A	84	252	59	13	5	7	2.8	29	37	25	38	5	.234	.409	17	4	OF-39, 1B-30
1951 DET A	91	188	46	10	3	11	5.9	33	28	18	27	0	.245	.505	34	7	OF-59, 2B-1, 1B-1
1952	92	265	66	16	4	13	4.9	40	45	21	28	1	.249	.487	17	4	OF-56, 3B-13, 1B-9
1953	89	278	84	13	3	11	4.0	29	46	8	35	5	.302	.489	10	3	OF-80, 1B-1
1954	25	39	7	0	1	3	7.7	6	8	2	10	1	.179	.462	14	2	OF-9, 3B-2
1955	1	1	1	0	0	0	0.0	0	0	0	0	0	1.000	1.000	1	1	
8 yrs.	473	1227	313	58	20	50	4.1	163	186	88	164	15	.255	.457	121	28	OF-243, 1B-93, 3B-15, 2B-1
1 yr.	84	252	59	13	5	7	2.8	29	37	25	38	5	.234	.409	17	4	OF-39, 1B-30

Bob Spence

SPENCE, JOHN ROBERT
B. Feb. 10, 1946, San Diego, Calif.
BL TR 6'4" 215 lbs.

1969 CHI A	12	26	4	1	0	0	0.0	0	3	0	9	0	.154	.192	7	0	1B-6
1970	46	130	29	4	1	4	3.1	11	15	11	32	0	.223	.362	9	1	1B-37
1971	14	27	4	0	0	0	0.0	2	1	5	6	0	.148	.148	5	0	1B-7
3 yrs.	72	183	37	5	1	4	2.2	13	19	16	47	0	.202	.306	21	1	1B-50
3 yrs.	72	183	37	5	1	4	2.2	13	19	16	47	0	.202	.306	21	1	1B-50

Jim Spencer

SPENCER, JAMES LLOYD
B. July 30, 1947, Hanover, Pa.
BL TL 6'2" 195 lbs.

1968 CAL A	19	68	13	1	0	0	0.0	2	5	3	10	0	.191	.206	0	0	1B-19
1969	113	386	98	14	3	10	2.6	39	31	26	53	1	.254	.383	8	2	1B-107
1970	146	511	140	20	4	12	2.3	61	68	28	61	0	.274	.399	6	2	1B-142
1971	148	510	121	21	2	18	3.5	50	59	48	63	0	.237	.392	7	1	1B-145
1972	82	212	47	5	0	1	0.5	13	14	12	25	0	.222	.259	22	4	1B-35, OF-24
1973 2 teams		CAL	A (29G – .241)					TEX	A (102G – .267)								
" total	131	439	115	16	5	6	1.4	45	54	43	50	0	.262	.362	8	0	1B-125, DH-3
1974 TEX A	118	352	98	11	4	7	2.0	36	44	22	27	1	.278	.392	8	3	1B-60, DH-54
1975	132	403	107	18	1	11	2.7	50	47	35	43	0	.266	.397	8	1	1B-99, DH-25
1976 CHI A	150	518	131	13	2	14	2.7	53	70	42	57	6	.253	.367	4	0	1B-143, DH-2
1977	128	470	116	16	1	18	3.8	56	69	36	50	1	.247	.400	2	1	1B-125
1978 NY A	71	150	34	9	1	7	4.7	12	24	15	32	0	.227	.440	24	7	DH-35, 1B-15
1979	106	295	85	15	3	23	7.8	60	53	38	25	0	.288	.593	16	3	DH-71, 1B-26
1980	97	259	61	9	0	13	5.0	38	43	30	44	1	.236	.421	22	8	1B-75, DH-15

320

321 Player Register

	G	AB	H	2B	3B	HR	HR%	R	RBI	BB	SO	SB	BA	SA	Pinch Hit AB	Pinch Hit H	G by POS

Jim Spencer continued

1981 2 teams	NY	A (25G – .143)		OAK	A (54G – .205)												
" total	79	234	44	8	0	4	1.7	20	13	19	27	1	.188	.274	13	4	1B-73
1982 OAK A	33	101	17	3	1	2	2.0	6	5	3	20	0	.168	.277	3	2	1B-32
15 yrs.	1553	4908	1227	179	27	146	3.0	541	599	407	582	11	.250	.387	151	40	1B-1221, DH-205, OF-24
2 yrs.	278	988	247	29	3	32	3.2	109	139	85	102	7	.250	.383	6	1	1B-268, DH-2

DIVISIONAL PLAYOFF SERIES
1981 OAK A	1	4	1	1	0	0	0.0	0	0	0	0	0	.250	.500	0	0	1B-1

LEAGUE CHAMPIONSHIP SERIES
1980 NY A	1	1	0	0	0	0	0.0	0	0	0	0	0	.000	.000	1	0	
1981 OAK A	2	2	0	0	0	0	0.0	0	0	0	0	0	.000	.000	2	0	1B-2
2 yrs.	3	3	0	0	0	0	0.0	0	0	0	0	0	.000	.000	3	0	1B-2

WORLD SERIES
1978 NY A	4	12	2	0	0	0	0.0	3	0	2	4	0	.167	.167	1	0	1B-3

Tom Spencer
SPENCER, HUBERT THOMAS
B. Feb. 28, 1951, Gallipolis, Ohio
BR TR 6' 170 lbs.

1978 CHI A	29	65	12	1	0	0	0.0	3	4	2	9	0	.185	.200	7	0	OF-27, DH-2

Ed Spiezio
SPIEZIO, EDWARD WAYNE
B. Oct. 31, 1941, Joliet, Ill.
BR TR 5'11" 180 lbs.

1964 STL N	12	12	4	0	0	0	0.0	0	0	0	1	0	.333	.333	12	4	
1965	10	18	3	0	0	0	0.0	0	5	1	4	0	.167	.167	7	2	3B-3
1966	26	73	16	5	1	2	2.7	4	10	5	11	1	.219	.397	6	0	3B-19
1967	55	105	22	2	0	3	2.9	9	10	7	18	2	.210	.314	27	8	3B-19, OF-7
1968	29	51	8	0	0	0	0.0	1	2	5	6	1	.157	.157	14	4	OF-11, 3B-2
1969 SD N	121	355	83	9	0	13	3.7	29	43	38	64	1	.234	.369	23	5	3B-98, OF-1
1970	110	316	90	18	1	12	3.8	45	42	43	42	4	.285	.462	21	7	3B-93
1971	97	308	71	10	1	7	2.3	16	36	22	50	6	.231	.338	7	2	3B-91, OF-1
1972 2 teams	SD	N (20G – .138)		CHI	A (74G – .238)												
" total	94	306	70	12	1	2	0.7	22	26	14	49	1	.229	.294	17	1	3B-79
9 yrs.	554	1544	367	56	4	39	2.5	126	174	135	245	16	.238	.355	134	33	3B-404, OF-20
1 yr.	74	277	66	10	1	2	0.7	20	22	13	43	0	.238	.303	0	0	3B-74

WORLD SERIES
1967 STL N	1	1	0	0	0	0	0.0	0	0	0	0	0	.000	.000	1	0	
1968	1	1	1	0	0	0	0.0	0	0	0	0	0	1.000	1.000	1	1	
2 yrs.	2	2	1	0	0	0	0.0	0	0	0	0	0	.500	.500	2	1	

Mike Squires
SQUIRES, MICHAEL LYNN
B. Mar. 5, 1952, Kalamazoo, Ill.
BL TL 5'11" 185 lbs.

1975 CHI A	20	65	15	0	0	0	0.0	5	4	8	5	3	.231	.231	0	0	1B-20
1977	3	3	0	0	0	0	0.0	0	0	0	1	0	.000	.000	2	0	1B-1
1978	46	150	42	9	2	0	0.0	25	19	16	21	4	.280	.367	1	1	1B-45
1979	122	295	78	10	1	2	0.7	44	22	22	9	15	.264	.325	6	1	1B-110, OF-1
1980	131	343	97	11	3	2	0.6	38	33	33	24	8	.283	.350	14	4	1B-114, C-2
1981	92	294	78	9	0	0	0.0	35	25	22	17	7	.265	.296	6	2	1B-88, OF-1
1982	116	195	52	9	3	1	0.5	33	21	14	13	3	.267	.359	14	3	1B-109
1983	143	153	34	4	1	1	0.7	21	11	22	11	3	.222	.281	23	4	1B-124, DH-5, 3B-1
8 yrs.	673	1498	396	52	10	6	0.4	201	135	137	101	43	.264	.324	66	15	1B-611, DH-5, OF-2, C-2, 3B-1
8 yrs.	673	1498	396	52	10	6	0.4	201	135	137	101	43	.264	.324	66	15	1B-611, DH-5, OF-2, C-2, 3B-1

LEAGUE CHAMPIONSHIP SERIES
1983 CHI A	4	4	0	0	0	0	0.0	0	0	0	0	0	.000	.000	2	0	1B-3

Marv Staehle
STAEHLE, MARVIN GUSTAVE
B. Mar. 13, 1942, Oak Park, Ill.
BL TR 5'10" 165 lbs.

1964 CHI A	6	5	2	0	0	0	0.0	0	2	0	0	1	.400	.400	5	2	
1965	7	7	3	0	0	0	0.0	0	2	0	0	0	.429	.429	7	3	
1966	8	15	2	0	0	0	0.0	2	0	4	2	1	.133	.133	2	0	2B-6
1967	32	54	6	1	0	0	0.0	1	1	4	8	1	.111	.130	8	0	2B-17, SS-5
1969 MON N	6	17	7	2	0	1	5.9	4	1	2	0	0	.412	.706	2	1	2B-4
1970	104	321	70	9	1	0	0.0	41	26	39	21	7	.218	.252	13	2	2B-91, SS-1
1971 ATL N	22	36	4	0	0	0	0.0	5	1	5	4	0	.111	.111	11	0	2B-7, 3B-1
7 yrs.	185	455	94	12	1	1	0.2	53	33	54	35	4	.207	.244	48	8	2B-125, SS-6, 3B-1
4 yrs.	53	81	13	1	0	0	0.0	3	5	8	10	3	.160	.173	22	5	2B-23, SS-5

Eddie Stanky
STANKY, EDWARD RAYMOND (The Brat, Muggsy)
B. Sept. 3, 1916, Philadelphia, Pa.
Manager 1952-55, 1966-68, 1977
BR TR 5'8" 170 lbs.

1943 CHI N	142	510	125	15	1	0	0.0	92	47	92	42	4	.245	.278	0	0	2B-131, SS-12, 3B-2
1944 2 teams	CHI	N (13G – .240)		BKN	N (89G – .276)												
" total	102	286	78	9	3	0	0.0	36	16	46	15	4	.273	.325	5	0	2B-61, SS-38, 3B-4
1945 BKN N	153	555	143	29	5	1	0.2	128	39	148	42	6	.258	.333	0	0	2B-153, SS-1
1946	144	483	132	24	7	0	0.0	98	36	137	56	8	.273	.352	2	0	2B-141
1947	146	559	141	24	5	3	0.5	97	53	103	39	3	.252	.329	1	0	2B-146
1948 BOS N	67	247	79	14	2	2	0.8	49	29	61	13	3	.320	.417	1	1	2B-66
1949	138	506	144	24	5	1	0.2	90	42	113	41	3	.285	.358	3	0	2B-135
1950 NY N	152	527	158	25	5	8	1.5	115	51	144	50	9	.300	.412	0	0	2B-151
1951	145	515	127	17	2	14	2.7	88	43	127	63	8	.247	.369	4	0	2B-140
1952 STL N	53	83	19	4	0	0	0.0	13	7	19	9	0	.229	.277	26	9	2B-20
1953	17	30	8	0	0	0	0.0	5	1	6	4	0	.267	.267	5	0	2B-8
11 yrs.	1259	4301	1154	185	35	29	0.7	811	364	996	374	48	.268	.348	46	10	2B-1152, SS-51, 3B-6

WORLD SERIES
1947 BKN N	7	25	6	1	0	0	0.0	4	2	3	2	0	.240	.280	0	0	2B-7

Player Register

	G	AB	H	2B	3B	HR	HR%	R	RBI	BB	SO	SB	BA	SA	Pinch Hit AB	Pinch Hit H	G by POS

Eddie Stanky continued

	G	AB	H	2B	3B	HR	HR%	R	RBI	BB	SO	SB	BA	SA	PH AB	PH H	G by POS
1948 BOS N	6	14	4	1	0	0	0.0	0	1	7	1	0	.286	.357	0	0	2B-6
1951 NY N	6	22	3	0	0	0	0.0	3	1	3	2	0	.136	.136	0	0	2B-6
3 yrs.	19	61	13	2	0	0	0.0	7	4	13	5	0	.213	.246	0	0	2B-19

Dave Stegman
STEGMAN, DAVID WILLIAM
B. Jan. 30, 1954, Inglewood, Calif.   BR TR 5'11" 190 lbs.

	G	AB	H	2B	3B	HR	HR%	R	RBI	BB	SO	SB	BA	SA	PH AB	PH H	G by POS
1978 DET A	8	14	4	2	0	1	7.1	3	3	1	2	0	.286	.643	0	0	OF-7
1979	12	31	6	0	0	3	9.7	6	5	2	3	1	.194	.484	1	0	OF-12
1980	65	130	23	5	0	2	1.5	12	9	14	23	1	.177	.262	6	1	OF-57, DH-2
1982 NY A	2	0	0	0	0	0	—	0	0	0	0	0	—	—	0	0	
1983 CHI A	29	53	9	2	0	0	0.0	5	4	10	9	0	.170	.208	3	0	OF-28
5 yrs.	116	228	42	9	0	6	2.6	26	21	27	37	2	.184	.303	10	1	OF-104, DH-2
1 yr.	29	53	9	2	0	0	0.0	5	4	10	9	0	.170	.208	3	0	OF-28

Bill Stein
STEIN, WILLIAM ALLEN
B. Jan. 21, 1947, Battle Creek, Mich.   BR TR 5'10" 170 lbs.

	G	AB	H	2B	3B	HR	HR%	R	RBI	BB	SO	SB	BA	SA	PH AB	PH H	G by POS
1972 STL N	14	35	11	0	0	2	5.7	2	3	0	7	1	.314	.543	6	3	OF-4, 3B-4
1973	32	55	12	2	0	0	0.0	4	2	7	18	0	.218	.255	18	3	OF-10, 1B-2, 3B-1
1974 CHI A	13	43	12	1	0	0	0.0	5	5	7	8	0	.279	.302	6	0	3B-11, DH-2
1975	76	226	61	7	1	3	1.3	23	21	18	32	2	.270	.350	6	0	2B-28, 3B-24, DH-18, OF-1
1976	117	392	105	15	2	4	1.0	32	36	22	67	4	.268	.347	8	2	3B-58, 2B-58, DH-1, OF-1, SS-1, 1B-1
1977 SEA A	151	556	144	26	5	13	2.3	53	67	29	79	3	.259	.394	1	0	3B-147, DH-3, SS-2
1978	114	403	105	24	4	4	1.0	41	37	37	56	1	.261	.370	2	0	3B-111, DH-1
1979	88	250	62	9	2	7	2.8	28	27	17	28	1	.248	.384	8	0	3B-67, 2B-17, SS-3
1980	67	198	53	5	1	5	2.5	16	27	16	25	1	.268	.379	11	1	3B-34, 2B-14, 1B-8, DH-5
1981 TEX A	53	115	38	6	0	2	1.7	21	22	7	15	1	.330	.435	20	9	1B-20, OF-8, 3B-7, 2B-3, SS-1
1982	85	184	44	8	0	1	0.5	14	16	12	23	0	.239	.299	34	10	2B-34, 3B-28, SS-6, DH-3, 1B-2, OF-1
1983	78	232	72	15	2	2	0.9	21	33	8	31	2	.310	.409	18	6	2B-32, 1B-23, 3B-10, DH-6
12 yrs.	888	2689	719	118	17	43	1.6	260	296	180	389	16	.267	.372	138	34	3B-502, 2B-186, 1B-56, DH-39, OF-25, SS-13
3 yrs.	206	661	178	23	3	7	1.1	60	62	47	107	6	.269	.345	20	2	3B-93, 2B-86, DH-21, OF-2, SS-1, 1B-1

Hank Steinbacher
STEINBACHER, HENRY JOHN
B. Mar. 22, 1913, Sacramento, Calif.   D. Apr. 3, 1977, Sacramento, Calif.   BL TR 5'11" 180 lbs.

	G	AB	H	2B	3B	HR	HR%	R	RBI	BB	SO	SB	BA	SA	PH AB	PH H	G by POS
1937 CHI A	26	73	19	4	1	1	1.4	13	9	4	7	2	.260	.384	11	1	OF-15
1938	106	399	132	23	8	4	1.0	59	61	41	19	1	.331	.459	4	1	OF-101
1939	71	111	19	2	1	1	0.9	16	15	21	8	0	.171	.234	39	8	OF-22
3 yrs.	203	583	170	29	10	6	1.0	88	85	66	34	3	.292	.407	54	10	OF-138
3 yrs.	203	583	170	29	10	6	1.0	88	85	66	34	3	.292	.407	54	10	OF-138

Gene Stephens
STEPHENS, GLEN EUGENE
B. Jan. 20, 1933, Gravette, Ark.   BL TR 6'3½" 175 lbs.

	G	AB	H	2B	3B	HR	HR%	R	RBI	BB	SO	SB	BA	SA	PH AB	PH H	G by POS
1952 BOS A	21	53	12	5	0	0	0.0	10	5	3	8	4	.226	.321	4	1	OF-13
1953	78	221	45	6	2	3	1.4	30	18	29	56	3	.204	.290	1	0	OF-72
1955	109	157	46	9	4	3	1.9	25	18	20	34	0	.293	.459	23	4	OF-75
1956	104	63	17	2	0	1	1.6	22	7	12	12	0	.270	.349	24	7	OF-71
1957	120	173	46	6	4	3	1.7	25	26	26	20	0	.266	.399	29	5	OF-90
1958	134	270	59	10	1	9	3.3	38	25	22	46	1	.219	.363	22	3	OF-110
1959	92	270	75	13	1	3	1.1	34	39	29	33	5	.278	.367	7	3	OF-85
1960 2 teams			BOS A (35G – .229)			BAL A (84G – .238)											
" total	119	302	71	15	0	7	2.3	47	22	39	47	9	.235	.354	11	2	OF-108
1961 2 teams			BAL A (32G – .190)			KC A (62G – .208)											
" total	94	241	49	8	1	4	1.7	26	28	30	34	4	.203	.295	11	2	OF-84
1962 KC A	5	4	0	0	0	0	0.0	0	0	1	0	0	.000	.000	4	0	
1963 CHI A	6	18	7	0	0	1	5.6	5	2	1	3	0	.389	.556	0	0	OF-5
1964	82	141	33	4	2	3	2.1	21	17	21	28	1	.234	.355	19	7	OF-59
12 yrs.	964	1913	460	78	15	37	1.9	283	207	233	322	27	.240	.355	155	34	OF-772
2 yrs.	88	159	40	4	2	4	2.5	26	19	22	31	1	.252	.377	19	7	OF-64

Vern Stephens
STEPHENS, VERNON DECATUR (Junior, Buster)
B. Oct. 23, 1920, McAlister, N. M.   D. Nov. 3, 1968, Long Beach, Calif.   BR TR 5'10" 185 lbs.

	G	AB	H	2B	3B	HR	HR%	R	RBI	BB	SO	SB	BA	SA	PH AB	PH H	G by POS
1941 STL A	3	2	1	0	0	0	0.0	0	0	0	0	0	.500	.500	1	0	SS-1
1942	145	575	169	26	6	14	2.4	84	92	41	53	1	.294	.433	1	1	SS-144
1943	137	512	148	27	3	22	4.3	75	91	54	73	3	.289	.482	3	1	SS-123, OF-11
1944	145	559	164	32	1	20	3.6	91	109	62	54	0	.293	.462	1	0	SS-143
1945	149	571	165	27	3	24	4.2	90	89	55	70	2	.289	.473	1	1	SS-144, 3B-4
1946	115	450	138	19	4	14	3.1	67	64	35	49	0	.307	.460	3	0	SS-112
1947	150	562	157	18	4	15	2.7	74	83	70	61	8	.279	.406	0	0	SS-149
1948 BOS A	155	635	171	25	8	29	4.6	114	137	77	56	1	.269	.471	0	0	SS-155
1949	155	610	177	31	2	39	6.4	113	159	101	73	2	.290	.539	0	0	SS-155
1950	149	628	185	34	6	30	4.8	125	144	65	43	1	.295	.511	3	0	SS-146
1951	109	377	113	21	2	17	4.5	62	78	38	33	1	.300	.501	17	4	3B-89, SS-2
1952 2 teams	92	295	75	13	2	7	2.4	35	44	39	31	2	.254	.383	9	2	SS-53, 3B-29
1953 2 teams			CHI A (44G – .186)			STL A (46G – .321)											
" total	90	294	77	14	0	5	1.7	30	31	31	42	0	.262	.361	4	0	3B-84, SS-3
1954 BAL A	101	365	104	18	1	8	2.2	31	46	17	36	0	.285	.403	5	0	3B-96
1955 2 teams			BAL A (3G – .167)			CHI A (22G – .250)											
" total	25	62	15	3	0	3	4.8	10	7	7	11	0	.242	.435	6	1	3B-20
15 yrs.	1720	6497	1859	307	42	247	3.8	1001	1174	692	685	25	.286	.460	54	10	SS-1330, 3B-322, OF-11
2 yrs.	66	185	38	9	0	4	2.2	24	21	20	29	2	.205	.319	9	1	3B-56, SS-3

WORLD SERIES
	G	AB	H	2B	3B	HR	HR%	R	RBI	BB	SO	SB	BA	SA	PH AB	PH H	G by POS
1944 STL A	6	22	5	1	0	0	0.0	2	0	3	3	0	.227	.273	0	0	SS-6

	G	AB	H	2B	3B	HR	HR%	R	RBI	BB	SO	SB	BA	SA	Pinch Hit AB	H	G by POS

Joe Stephenson
STEPHENSON, JOSEPH CHESTER
Father of Jerry Stephenson.
B. June 30, 1921, Detroit, Mich.
BR TR 6'2" 185 lbs.

	G	AB	H	2B	3B	HR	HR%	R	RBI	BB	SO	SB	BA	SA	PH AB	H	G by POS
1943 NY N	9	24	6	1	0	0	0.0	4	1	0	5	0	.250	.292	1	0	C-6
1944 CHI N	4	8	1	0	0	0	0.0	1	0	1	3	0	.125	.125	1	0	C-3
1947 CHI A	16	35	5	0	0	0	0.0	3	3	1	7	0	.143	.143	1	0	C-13
3 yrs.	29	67	12	1	0	0	0.0	8	4	2	15	0	.179	.194	3	0	C-22
1 yr.	16	35	5	0	0	0	0.0	3	3	1	7	0	.143	.143	1	0	C-13

Bud Stewart
STEWART, EDWARD PERRY
B. June 15, 1916, Sacramento, Calif.
BL TR 5'11" 160 lbs.

	G	AB	H	2B	3B	HR	HR%	R	RBI	BB	SO	SB	BA	SA	PH AB	H	G by POS
1941 PIT N	73	172	46	7	0	0	0.0	27	10	12	17	3	.267	.308	25	10	OF-41
1942	82	183	40	8	4	0	0.0	21	20	22	16	2	.219	.306	28	6	OF-34, 3B-10, 2B-6
1948 2 teams	NY A (6G – .200)			WAS A (118G – .279)													
" total	124	406	113	18	13	7	1.7	57	69	49	27	8	.278	.438	9	1	OF-114
1949 WAS A	118	388	110	23	4	8	2.1	58	43	49	33	6	.284	.425	11	4	OF-105
1950	118	378	101	15	6	4	1.1	46	35	46	33	5	.267	.370	18	2	OF-100
1951 CHI A	95	217	60	13	5	6	2.8	40	40	29	9	1	.276	.465	31	9	OF-63
1952	92	225	60	10	0	5	2.2	23	30	28	17	3	.267	.378	34	6	OF-60
1953	53	59	16	2	0	2	3.4	16	13	14	3	1	.271	.407	34	10	OF-16
1954	18	13	1	0	0	0	0.0	0	0	3	2	0	.077	.077	12	1	OF-2
9 yrs.	773	2041	547	96	32	32	1.6	288	260	252	157	29	.268	.393	202	49	OF-535, 3B-10, 2B-6
4 yrs.	258	514	137	25	5	13	2.5	79	83	74	31	5	.267	.411	111 7th	26 8th	OF-141

Jimmy Stewart
STEWART, JAMES FRANKLIN
B. June 11, 1939, Opelika, Ala.
BB TR 6' 165 lbs.

	G	AB	H	2B	3B	HR	HR%	R	RBI	BB	SO	SB	BA	SA	PH AB	H	G by POS
1963 CHI N	13	37	11	2	0	0	0.0	1	1	1	7	1	.297	.351	5	1	SS-9, 2B-1
1964	132	415	105	17	0	3	0.7	59	33	49	61	10	.253	.316	31	9	2B-61, SS-45, OF-4, 3B-1
1965	116	282	63	9	4	0	0.0	26	19	30	53	13	.223	.284	41	6	OF-55, SS-48
1966	57	90	16	4	1	0	0.0	4	4	7	12	1	.178	.244	31	6	OF-15, 2B-4, SS-2, 3B-2
1967 2 teams	CHI N (6G – .167)			CHI A (24G – .167)													
" total	30	24	4	0	0	0	0.0	6	2	1	6	1	.167	.167	13	1	OF-6, 2B-5, SS-2
1969 CIN N	119	221	56	3	4	4	1.8	26	24	19	33	4	.253	.357	38	9	OF-66, 2B-18, 3B-6, SS-1
1970	101	105	28	3	1	1	1.0	15	8	8	13	5	.267	.343	39	13	OF-48, 2B-18, 3B-9, 1B-1, C-1
1971	80	82	19	2	2	0	0.0	7	9	9	12	3	.232	.305	48	11	OF-19, 3B-9, 2B-8
1972 HOU N	68	96	21	5	2	0	0.0	14	9	6	9	0	.219	.313	40	7	OF-11, 1B-9, 2B-8, 3B-2
1973	61	68	13	0	0	0	0.0	6	3	9	12	0	.191	.191	44	8	3B-8, OF-3, 1B-1
10 yrs.	777	1420	336	45	14	8	0.6	164	112	139	218	38	.237	.305	330	71	OF-227, 2B-122, SS-107, 3B-37, 1B-10, C-1
1 yr.	24	18	3	0	0	0	0.0	5	1	1	6	1	.167	.167	7	0	OF-6, 2B-5, SS-2

LEAGUE CHAMPIONSHIP SERIES

| 1970 CIN N | 1 | 2 | 0 | 0 | 0 | 0 | 0.0 | 0 | 0 | 0 | 0 | 0 | .000 | .000 | 0 | 0 | OF-1 |

WORLD SERIES

| 1970 CIN N | 2 | 2 | 0 | 0 | 0 | 0 | 0.0 | 0 | 0 | 0 | 1 | 0 | .000 | .000 | 2 | 0 | |

Royle Stillman
STILLMAN, ROYLE ELDON
B. Jan. 2, 1951, Santa Monica, Calif.
BL TL 5'11" 180 lbs.

	G	AB	H	2B	3B	HR	HR%	R	RBI	BB	SO	SB	BA	SA	PH AB	H	G by POS
1975 BAL A	13	14	6	0	0	0	0.0	1	1	1	3	0	.429	.429	4	1	SS-6, OF-2
1976	20	22	2	0	0	0	0.0	0	1	3	4	0	.091	.091	15	1	DH-5, 1B-2
1977 CHI A	56	119	25	7	1	3	2.5	18	13	17	21	2	.210	.361	17	3	OF-26, DH-13, 1B-1
3 yrs.	89	155	33	7	1	3	1.9	19	15	21	28	2	.213	.329	36	5	OF-28, DH-18, SS-6, 1B-3
1 yr.	56	119	25	7	1	3	2.5	18	13	17	21	2	.210	.361	17	3	OF-26, DH-13, 1B-1

John Stoneham
STONEHAM, JOHN ANDREW
B. Nov. 8, 1908, Wood River, Ill.
BL TR 5'9½" 168 lbs.

| 1933 CHI A | 10 | 25 | 3 | 0 | 0 | 1 | 4.0 | 4 | 3 | 2 | 2 | 0 | .120 | .240 | 0 | 0 | OF-9 |

Sammy Strang
STRANG, SAMUEL NICKLIN (The Dixie Thrush)
Born Samuel Strang Nicklin.
B. Dec. 16, 1876, Chattanooga, Tenn. D. Mar. 13, 1932, Chattanooga, Tenn.
BB TR

	G	AB	H	2B	3B	HR	HR%	R	RBI	BB	SO	SB	BA	SA	PH AB	H	G by POS
1896 LOU N	14	46	12	0	0	0	0.0	6	7	6	6	4	.261	.261	0	0	SS-14
1900 CHI N	27	102	29	3	0	0	0.0	15	9	8		1	.284	.314	0	0	3B-16, SS-9, 2B-2
1901 NY N	135	493	139	14	6	1	0.2	55	34	59		40	.282	.341	0	0	3B-91, 2B-37, OF-5, SS-4
1902 2 teams	CHI A (137G – .295)			CHI N (3G – .364)													
" total	140	547	162	18	5	3	0.5	109	46	76		39	.296	.364	0	0	3B-139, 2B-2
1903 BKN N	135	508	138	21	5	0	0.0	101	38	75		46	.272	.333	0	0	3B-124, OF-8, 2B-3
1904	77	271	52	11	0	1	0.4	28	9	45		16	.192	.244	0	0	2B-63, 3B-12, SS-1
1905 NY N	111	294	76	9	4	3	1.0	51	29	58		23	.259	.347	14	8	2B-47, OF-38, SS-9, 3B-1, 1B-1
1906	113	313	100	16	4	4	1.3	50	49	54		21	.319	.435	9	1	2B-57, OF-39, SS-4, 3B-3, 1B-1
1907	123	306	77	20	4	4	1.3	56	30	60		21	.252	.382	19	4	OF-70, 2B-13, 3B-7, 1B-5, SS-1
1908	28	53	5	0	0	0	0.0	8	2	23		5	.094	.094	4	2	2B-14, OF-5, SS-3
10 yrs.	903	2933	790	112	28	16	0.5	479	253	464	6	216	.269	.343	46	15	3B-393, 2B-238, OF-165, SS-45, 1B-7
1 yr.	137	536	158	18	5	3	0.6	108	46	76		38	.295	.364	0	0	3B-137

WORLD SERIES

| 1905 NY N | 1 | 1 | 0 | 0 | 0 | 0 | 0.0 | 0 | 0 | 0 | 1 | 0 | .000 | .000 | 1 | 0 | |

Ed Stroud
STROUD, EDWIN MARVIN (The Creeper)
B. Oct. 31, 1939, Lapine, Ala.
BL TR 5'11" 180 lbs.

	G	AB	H	2B	3B	HR	HR%	R	RBI	BB	SO	SB	BA	SA	PH AB	H	G by POS
1966 CHI A	12	36	6	2	0	0	0.0	3	1	2	8	3	.167	.222	0	0	OF-11
1967 2 teams	CHI A (20G – .296)			WAS A (87G – .201)													
" total	107	231	49	5	4	1	0.4	42	13	26	34	15	.212	.281	6	0	OF-91
1968 WAS A	105	306	73	10	10	4	1.3	41	23	20	50	9	.239	.376	22	2	OF-84

Player Register

	G	AB	H	2B	3B	HR	HR%	R	RBI	BB	SO	SB	BA	SA	Pinch Hit AB H	G by POS

Ed Stroud continued
1969	123	206	52	5	6	4	1.9	35	29	30	33	12	.252	.393	44 14	OF-85
1970	129	433	115	11	5	5	1.2	69	32	40	79	29	.266	.349	19 6	OF-118
1971 CHI A	53	141	25	4	3	0	0.0	19	2	11	20	4	.177	.248	14 2	OF-44
6 yrs.	529	1353	320	37	28	14	1.0	209	100	129	224	72	.237	.336	105 24	OF-433
3 yrs.	85	204	39	6	4	0	0.0	28	6	14	33	14	.191	.260	16 2	OF-67

Amos Strunk
STRUNK, AMOS AARON   BL TL 5'11½" 175 lbs.
B. Nov. 22, 1889, Philadelphia, Pa.   D. July 22, 1979, Llanerch, Pa.

1908 PHI A	12	34	8	1	0	0	0.0	4	0	4		0	.235	.265	1 1	OF-11
1909	11	35	4	0	0	0	0.0	1	2	1		2	.114	.114	2 0	OF-9
1910	16	48	16	0	1	0	0.0	9	2	3		4	.333	.375	0 0	OF-14
1911	74	215	55	7	2	1	0.5	42	21	35		13	.256	.321	7 2	OF-62, 1B-2
1912	120	412	119	13	12	3	0.7	58	63	47		29	.289	.400	3 2	OF-118
1913	93	292	89	11	12	0	0.0	30	46	29	23	14	.305	.425	11 4	OF-80
1914	122	404	111	15	3	2	0.5	58	45	57	38	25	.275	.342	2 0	OF-120
1915	132	485	144	28	16	1	0.2	76	45	56	45	17	.297	.427	2 0	OF-111, 1B-19
1916	150	544	172	30	9	3	0.6	71	49	66	59	21	.316	.421	0 0	OF-143, 1B-7
1917	148	540	152	26	7	1	0.2	83	45	68	37	16	.281	.361	0 0	OF-146
1918 BOS A	114	413	106	18	9	0	0.0	50	35	36	13	20	.257	.344	1 0	OF-113
1919 2 teams		BOS	A (48G –	.272)		PHI	A (60G –	.211)								
" total	108	378	91	17	7	0	0.0	42	30	36	28	6	.241	.323	5 2	OF-100
1920 2 teams		PHI	A (58G –	.297)		CHI	A (51G –	.230)								
" total	109	385	102	16	4	1	0.3	55	34	49	24	1	.265	.335	7 1	OF-103
1921 CHI A	121	401	133	15	10	3	0.7	68	69	38	27	7	.332	.451	8 3	OF-111
1922	92	311	90	11	4	0	0.0	36	33	33	28	9	.289	.350	10 3	OF-75, 1B-9
1923	54	54	17	0	0	0	0.0	7	8	8	5	1	.315	.315	39 12	OF-4, 1B-3
1924 2 teams		CHI	A (1G –	.000)		PHI	A (30G –	.143)								
" total	31	43	6	0	0	0	0.0	5	1	7	4	0	.140	.140	20 3	OF-8
17 yrs.	1507	4994	1415	212	96	15	0.3	695	528	573	331	185	.283	.373	118 33	OF-1328, 1B-40
5 yrs.	319	950	282	37	15	4	0.4	143	124	107	75	18	.297	.380	61 18	OF-239, 1B-12

WORLD SERIES
1910 PHI A	4	18	5	1	1	0	0.0	2	2	2	5	0	.278	.444	0 0	OF-4
1911	1	0	0	0	0	0	–	0	0	0	0	0	–	–	0 0	
1913	5	17	2	0	0	0	0.0	3	0	2	2	0	.118	.118	0 0	OF-5
1914	2	7	2	0	0	0	0.0	0	0	0	2	0	.286	.286	0 0	OF-2
1918 BOS A	6	23	4	1	1	0	0.0	1	0	0	5	0	.174	.304	0 0	OF-6
5 yrs.	18	65	13	2	2	0	0.0	6	2	4	14	0	.200	.292	0 0	OF-17

George Stumpf
STUMPF, GEORGE FREDERICK   BL TL 5'8" 155 lbs.
B. Dec. 15, 1910, New Orleans, La.

1931 BOS A	7	28	7	1	1	0	0.0	2	4	1	2	0	.250	.357	0 0	OF-7
1932	79	169	34	2	2	1	0.6	18	18	18	21	1	.201	.254	25 4	OF-51
1933	22	41	14	3	0	0	0.0	8	5	4	2	4	.341	.415	5 1	OF-15
1936 CHI A	10	22	6	1	0	0	0.0	3	5	2	1	0	.273	.318	5 3	OF-4
4 yrs.	118	260	61	7	3	1	0.4	31	32	25	26	5	.235	.296	35 8	OF-77
1 yr.	10	22	6	1	0	0	0.0	3	5	2	1	0	.273	.318	5 3	OF-4

Joe Sugden
SUGDEN, JOSEPH   BB TR 5'10" 180 lbs.
B. July 31, 1870, Philadelphia, Pa.   D. June 28, 1959, Philadelphia, Pa.

1893 PIT N	27	92	24	4	3	0	0.0	20	12	10	11	1	.261	.370	0 0	C-27
1894	39	139	46	13	2	2	1.4	23	23	14	2	1	.331	.496	0 0	C-31, 3B-4, SS-3, OF-1
1895	49	155	48	4	1	1	0.6	28	17	16	12	4	.310	.368	0 0	C-49
1896	80	301	89	5	7	0	0.0	42	36	19	9	5	.296	.359	0 0	C-70, 1B-7, OF-4
1897	84	288	64	6	4	0	0.0	31	38	18		9	.222	.271	0 0	C-81, 1B-3
1898 STL N	89	289	73	7	1	0	0.0	29	34	23		5	.253	.284	7 2	C-60, OF-15, 1B-8
1899 CLE N	76	250	69	5	1	0	0.0	19	14	11		2	.276	.304	2 1	C-66, OF-4, 1B-3, 3B-1
1901 CHI A	48	153	42	7	1	0	0.0	21	19	13		4	.275	.333	2 0	C-42, 1B-5
1902 STL A	68	200	50	7	2	0	0.0	25	15	20		2	.250	.305	3 1	C-61, 1B-4, P-1
1903	79	241	51	4	0	0	0.0	18	22	25		4	.212	.228	5 0	C-66, 1B-8
1904	105	348	93	6	3	0	0.0	25	30	28		6	.267	.302	1 0	C-79, 1B-28
1905	85	266	46	4	0	0	0.0	21	23	23		3	.173	.188	4 0	C-71, 1B-9
1912 DET A	1	4	1	0	0	0	0.0	1	0	0		0	.250	.250	0 0	1B-1
13 yrs.	830	2726	696	72	25	3	0.1	303	283	220	34	48	.255	.303	24 4	C-703, 1B-76, OF-24, 3B-5, SS-3, P-1
1 yr.	48	153	42	7	1	0	0.0	21	19	13		4	.275	.333	2 0	C-42, 1B-5

Billy Sullivan
SULLIVAN, WILLIAM JOSEPH, SR.   BR TR 5'9" 155 lbs.
Father of Billy Sullivan.
B. Feb. 1, 1875, Oakland, Wis.   D. Jan. 28, 1965, Newberg, Ore.
Manager 1909.

1899 BOS N	22	74	20	2	0	2	2.7	10	12	1		2	.270	.378	0 0	C-22
1900	72	238	65	6	0	8	3.4	36	41	9		4	.273	.399	3 2	C-66, SS-1, 2B-1
1901 CHI A	98	367	90	15	4	4	1.1	54	56	10		12	.245	.351	0 0	C-97, 3B-1
1902	76	263	64	12	3	1	0.4	36	26	6		11	.243	.323	2 0	C-70, OF-2, 1B-2
1903	32	111	21	4	0	1	0.9	10	7	5		3	.189	.252	1 0	C-31
1904	108	371	85	18	4	1	0.3	29	44	12		11	.229	.307	1 0	C-107
1905	99	323	65	10	3	2	0.6	25	26	13		14	.201	.269	3 0	C-93, 1B-2, 3B-1
1906	118	387	83	18	4	1	0.3	37	33	22		10	.214	.289	0 0	C-118
1907	112	339	59	8	4	0	0.0	30	36	21		6	.174	.221	3 0	C-108, 2B-1
1908	137	430	82	8	4	0	0.0	40	29	22		15	.191	.228	1 0	C-137
1909	97	265	43	3	0	0	0.0	11	16	17		9	.162	.174	0 0	C-97
1910	45	142	26	4	1	0	0.0	10	6	7		0	.183	.225	0 0	C-45
1911	89	256	55	9	3	0	0.0	26	31	16		1	.215	.273	0 0	C-89
1912	39	91	19	2	1	0	0.0	9	15	9		0	.209	.253	0 0	C-39
1914	1	0	0	0	0	0	–	0	0	0	2	0	–	–	0 0	C-1

Player Register

	G	AB	H	2B	3B	HR	HR%	R	RBI	BB	SO	SB	BA	SA	Pinch Hit AB	H	G by POS

Billy Sullivan continued
1916 DET A	1	0	0	0	0	0	–	0	0	0	0	–	–	0	0	C-1
16 yrs.	1146	3657	777	119	33	20	0.5	363	378	170	0	98	.212	.279	14	2	C-1121, 1B-4, OF-2, 3B-2, 2B-2, SS-1
13 yrs.	1051	3345	692	111	33	10	0.3	317	325	160	0	92	.207	.269	11	0	C-1032, 1B-4, OF-4, 3B-2, 2B-1

WORLD SERIES
| 1906 CHI A | 6 | 21 | 0 | 0 | 0 | 0 | 0.0 | 0 | 0 | 0 | 9 | 0 | .000 | .000 | 0 | 0 | C-6 |

Billy Sullivan
SULLIVAN, WILLIAM JOSEPH, JR.
Son of Billy Sullivan.
B. Oct. 23, 1910, Chicago, Ill.
BL TR 6' 170 lbs.

1931 CHI A	92	363	100	16	5	2	0.6	48	33	20	14	4	.275	.364	7	4	3B-83, OF-2, 1B-1
1932	93	307	97	16	1	1	0.3	31	45	20	9	1	.316	.384	19	3	1B-52, 3B-17, C-5
1933	54	125	24	0	1	0	0.0	9	13	10	5	0	.192	.208	22	5	1B-22, C-8
1935 CIN N	85	241	64	9	4	2	0.8	29	36	19	16	4	.266	.361	21	7	1B-40, 3B-15, 2B-6
1936 CLE A	93	319	112	32	6	2	0.6	39	48	16	9	5	.351	.508	11	5	C-72, 3B-5, 1B-3, OF-1
1937	72	168	48	12	3	3	1.8	26	22	17	7	1	.286	.446	24	5	C-38, 1B-5, 3B-1
1938 STL A	111	375	104	16	1	7	1.9	35	49	20	10	8	.277	.381	8	1	C-99, 1B-6
1939	118	332	96	17	5	5	1.5	53	50	34	18	3	.289	.416	33	9	OF-59, C-19, 1B-4
1940 DET A	78	220	68	14	4	3	1.4	36	41	31	11	2	.309	.450	15	5	C-57, 3B-6
1941	85	234	66	15	1	3	1.3	29	29	35	11	0	.282	.393	21	6	C-63
1942 BKN N	43	101	27	2	1	1	1.0	11	14	12	6	1	.267	.337	1	0	C-41
1947 PIT N	38	55	14	3	0	0	0.0	1	8	6	3	1	.255	.309	25	5	C-12
12 yrs.	962	2840	820	152	32	29	1.0	347	388	240	119	30	.289	.395	207	55	C-414, 1B-133, 3B-127, OF-62, 2B-6
3 yrs.	239	795	221	32	7	3	0.4	88	91	50	28	5	.278	.347	48	12	3B-100, 1B-75, C-13, OF-2

WORLD SERIES
| 1940 DET A | 5 | 13 | 2 | 0 | 0 | 0 | 0.0 | 3 | 0 | 5 | 2 | 0 | .154 | .154 | 1 | 0 | C-4 |

Eddie Sullivan
Playing record listed under Eddie Collins

Leo Sutherland
SUTHERLAND, LEONARDO C.
B. Apr. 6, 1958, Santiago, Cuba
BL TL 5'10" 165 lbs.

1980 CHI A	34	89	23	3	0	0	0.0	9	5	1	11	4	.258	.292	10	4	OF-23
1981	11	12	2	0	0	0	0.0	6	0	3	1	2	.167	.167	1	0	OF-7
2 yrs.	45	101	25	3	0	0	0.0	15	5	4	12	6	.248	.277	11	4	OF-30
2 yrs.	45	101	25	3	0	0	0.0	15	5	4	12	6	.248	.277	11	4	OF-30

Evar Swanson
SWANSON, ERNEST EVAR
B. Oct. 15, 1902, DeKalb, Ill. D. July 17, 1973, Galesburg, Ill.
BR TR 5'9" 170 lbs.

1929 CIN N	145	574	172	35	12	4	0.7	100	43	41	47	33	.300	.423	2	1	OF-142
1930	95	301	93	15	3	2	0.7	43	22	11	17	4	.309	.399	15	1	OF-71
1932 CHI A	14	52	16	3	1	0	0.0	9	8	8	3	3	.308	.404	0	0	OF-14
1933	144	539	165	25	7	1	0.2	102	63	93	35	19	.306	.384	6	2	OF-139
1934	117	426	127	9	5	0	0.0	71	34	59	31	10	.298	.343	9	2	OF-105
5 yrs.	515	1892	573	87	28	7	0.4	325	170	212	133	69	.303	.390	32	6	OF-471
3 yrs.	275	1017	308	52	13	1	0.1	182	105	160	69	32	.303	.368	15	4	OF-258

Karl Swanson
SWANSON, KARL EDWARD
B. Dec. 17, 1903, North Henderson, Ill.
BL TR 5'10" 155 lbs.

1928 CHI A	22	64	9	1	0	0	0.0	2	6	4	7	3	.141	.156	0	0	2B-21
1929	2	1	0	0	0	0	0.0	0	0	0	0	0	.000	.000	1	0	
2 yrs.	24	65	9	1	0	0	0.0	2	6	4	7	3	.138	.154	1	0	2B-21
2 yrs.	24	65	9	1	0	0	0.0	2	6	4	7	3	.138	.154	1	0	2B-21

Augie Swentor
SWENTOR, AUGUST WILLIAM
B. Nov. 21, 1899, Seymour, Conn. D. Nov. 10, 1969, Waterbury, Conn.
BR TR 6' 185 lbs.

| 1922 CHI A | 1 | 1 | 0 | 0 | 0 | 0 | 0.0 | 0 | 0 | 0 | 1 | 0 | .000 | .000 | 0 | 0 | C-1 |

Doug Taitt
TAITT, DOUGLAS JOHN (Poco)
B. Aug. 3, 1902, Bay City, Mich. D. Dec. 12, 1970, Portland, Ore.
BL TR 6' 176 lbs.

1928 BOS A	143	482	144	28	14	3	0.6	51	61	36	32	13	.299	.434	3	0	OF-139, P-1
1929 2 teams		BOS A (26G – .277)				CHI A (47G – .169)											
" total	73	189	39	11	0	0	0.0	17	18	16	18	0	.206	.265	21	6	OF-51
1931 PHI N	38	151	34	4	2	1	0.7	13	15	4	14	0	.225	.298	0	0	OF-38
1932	4	2	0	0	0	0	0.0	0	1	2	0	0	.000	.000	2	0	
4 yrs.	258	824	217	43	16	4	0.5	81	95	58	64	13	.263	.369	26	6	OF-228, P-1
1 yr.	47	124	21	7	0	0	0.0	11	12	8	13	0	.169	.226	16	5	OF-30

Leo Tankersley
TANKERSLEY, LAWRENCE WILLIAM
B. June 8, 1901, Terrell, Tex.
BR TR 6' 176 lbs.

| 1925 CHI A | 1 | 3 | 0 | 0 | 0 | 0 | 0.0 | 0 | 0 | 0 | 1 | 0 | .000 | .000 | 0 | 0 | C-1 |

Lee Tannehill
TANNEHILL, LEE FORD
Brother of Jesse Tannehill.
B. Oct. 26, 1880, Dayton, Ky. D. Feb. 16, 1938, Live Oak, Fla.
BR TR 5'11" 170 lbs.

1903 CHI A	138	503	113	14	3	2	0.4	48	50	25		10	.225	.276	0	0	SS-138
1904	153	547	125	31	5	0	0.0	50	61	20		14	.229	.303	0	0	3B-153
1905	142	480	96	17	2	0	0.0	38	39	45		8	.200	.244	0	0	3B-142
1906	116	378	69	8	3	0	0.0	26	33	31		9	.183	.220	0	0	3B-99, SS-17
1907	33	108	26	2	0	0	0.0	9	11	8		3	.241	.259	0	0	3B-31, SS-2
1908	141	482	104	15	3	0	0.0	44	35	25		6	.216	.259	0	0	3B-136, SS-5

Player Register

Lee Tannehill continued

	G	AB	H	2B	3B	HR	HR%	R	RBI	BB	SO	SB	BA	SA	Pinch Hit AB	H	G by POS
1909	155	531	118	21	5	0	0.0	39	47	31		12	.222	.281	0	0	3B-91, SS-64
1910	67	230	51	10	0	1	0.4	17	21	11		3	.222	.278	0	0	SS-38, 1B-23, 3B-6
1911	141	516	131	17	6	0	0.0	60	49	32		0	.254	.310	0	0	SS-102, 2B-27, 3B-8, 1B-5
1912	3	3	0	0	0	0	0.0	0	0	1		0	.000	.000	0	0	3B-3
10 yrs.	1089	3778	833	135	27	3	0.1	331	346	229		63	.220	.273	0	0	3B-669, SS-366, 1B-28, 2B-27
10 yrs.	1089	3778	833	135	27	3	0.1	331	346	229		63	.220	.273	0	0	3B-669, SS-366, 1B-28, 2B-27

WORLD SERIES

	G	AB	H	2B	3B	HR	HR%	R	RBI	BB	SO	SB	BA	SA	AB	H	G by POS
1906 CHI A	3	9	1	0	0	0	0.0	1	0	0	2	0	.111	.111	0	0	SS-3

Chuck Tanner

TANNER, CHARLES WILLIAM BL TL 6' 185 lbs.
B. July 4, 1929, New Castle, Pa.
Manager 1970-83.

	G	AB	H	2B	3B	HR	HR%	R	RBI	BB	SO	SB	BA	SA	AB	H	G by POS
1955 MIL N	97	243	60	9	3	6	2.5	27	27	27	32	0	.247	.383	32	7	OF-62
1956	60	63	15	2	0	1	1.6	6	4	10	10	0	.238	.317	44	10	OF-8
1957 2 teams		MIL N (22G – .246)				CHI N (95G – .286)											
" total	117	387	108	19	2	9	2.3	47	48	28	24	0	.279	.408	16	4	OF-100
1958 CHI N	73	103	27	6	0	4	3.9	10	17	9	10	1	.262	.437	53	12	OF-15
1959 CLE A	14	48	12	2	0	1	2.1	6	5	2	9	0	.250	.354	4	0	OF-10
1960	21	25	7	1	0	0	0.0	2	4	4	6	1	.280	.320	15	3	OF-4
1961 LA A	7	8	1	0	0	0	0.0	0	0	2	2	0	.125	.125	4	1	OF-1
1962	7	8	1	0	0	0	0.0	0	0	0	0	0	.125	.125	6	1	OF-2
8 yrs.	396	885	231	39	5	21	2.4	98	105	82	93	2	.261	.388	174	38	OF-202

Bennie Tate

TATE, HENRY BENNETT BL TR 5'8" 165 lbs.
B. Dec. 3, 1901, Whitwell, Tenn. D. Oct. 27, 1973, W. Frankfort, Ill.

	G	AB	H	2B	3B	HR	HR%	R	RBI	BB	SO	SB	BA	SA	AB	H	G by POS
1924 WAS A	21	43	13	2	0	0	0.0	2	7	1	2	0	.302	.349	6	3	C-14
1925	16	27	13	3	0	0	0.0	0	7	2	2	0	.481	.593	2	1	C-14
1926	59	142	38	5	2	1	0.7	17	13	15	1	0	.268	.352	9	2	C-45
1927	61	131	41	5	1	1	0.8	12	24	8	4	0	.313	.389	16	5	C-39
1928	57	122	30	6	0	0	0.0	10	15	10	4	0	.246	.295	25	9	C-30
1929	81	265	78	12	3	0	0.0	26	30	16	8	2	.294	.362	6	3	C-74
1930 2 teams		WAS A (14G – .250)				CHI A (72G – .317)											
" total	86	250	78	11	2	0	0.0	27	29	18	11	2	.312	.372	5	2	C-79
1931 CHI A	89	273	73	12	3	0	0.0	27	22	26	10	1	.267	.333	4	1	C-85
1932 2 teams		CHI A (4G – .100)				BOS A (81G – .245)											
" total	85	283	68	12	5	2	0.7	22	26	21	6	0	.240	.339	5	3	C-80
1934 CHI N	11	24	3	0	0	0	0.0	1	0	1	3	0	.125	.125	2	0	C-8
10 yrs.	566	1560	435	68	16	4	0.3	144	173	118	51	5	.279	.351	81	29	C-468
3 yrs.	165	513	147	23	5	0	0.0	54	49	45	20	3	.287	.351	5	1	C-159

WORLD SERIES

| 1924 WAS A | 3 | 0 | 0 | 0 | 0 | 0 | – | 0 | 1 | 3 | 0 | 0 | – | – | 0 | 0 | |

Fred Tauby

TAUBY, FRED JOSEPH BR TR 5'9½" 168 lbs.
Born Fred Joseph Taubensee.
B. Mar. 27, 1906, Canton, Ohio D. Nov. 23, 1955, Concordia, Calif.

	G	AB	H	2B	3B	HR	HR%	R	RBI	BB	SO	SB	BA	SA	AB	H	G by POS
1935 CHI A	13	32	4	1	0	0	0.0	5	2	2	3	0	.125	.156	4	0	OF-7
1937 PHI N	11	20	0	0	0	0	0.0	2	3	0	5	1	.000	.000	3	0	OF-7
2 yrs.	24	52	4	1	0	0	0.0	7	5	2	8	1	.077	.096	7	0	OF-14
1 yr.	13	32	4	1	0	0	0.0	5	2	2	3	0	.125	.156	4	0	OF-7

Leo Taylor

TAYLOR, LEO THOMAS (Chink) BR TR 5'10½" 150 lbs.
B. May 13, 1901, Walla Walla, Wash.

| 1923 CHI A | 2 | 0 | 0 | 0 | 0 | 0 | – | 0 | 0 | 0 | 0 | 0 | – | – | 0 | 0 | |

Zeb Terry

TERRY, ZEBULON ALEXANDER BR TR 5'8" 129 lbs.
B. June 17, 1891, Denison, Tex.

	G	AB	H	2B	3B	HR	HR%	R	RBI	BB	SO	SB	BA	SA	AB	H	G by POS
1916 CHI A	94	269	51	8	4	0	0.0	20	17	33	36	4	.190	.249	1	1	SS-93
1917	2	1	0	0	0	0	0.0	0	0	2	0	0	.000	.000	0	0	SS-1
1918 BOS N	28	105	32	2	2	0	0.0	17	8	8	14	1	.305	.362	0	0	SS-27
1919 PIT N	129	472	107	12	6	0	0.0	46	27	31	26	9	.227	.278	2	1	SS-127
1920 CHI N	133	496	139	26	9	0	0.0	56	52	44	22	12	.280	.369	0	0	SS-70, 2B-63
1921	123	488	134	18	1	2	0.4	59	45	27	19	1	.275	.328	1	0	2B-123
1922	131	496	142	24	2	0	0.0	56	67	34	16	2	.286	.343	0	0	2B-125, SS-4, 3B-3
7 yrs.	640	2327	605	90	24	2	0.1	254	216	179	133	32	.260	.322	4	2	SS-322, 2B-311, 3B-3
2 yrs.	96	270	51	8	4	0	0.0	20	17	35	36	4	.189	.248	1	1	SS-94

Leo Thomas

THOMAS, LEO RAYMOND (Tommy) BR TR 5'11½" 178 lbs.
B. July 26, 1924, Turlock, Calif.

	G	AB	H	2B	3B	HR	HR%	R	RBI	BB	SO	SB	BA	SA	AB	H	G by POS
1950 STL A	35	121	24	6	0	1	0.8	19	9	20	14	0	.198	.273	0	0	3B-35
1952 2 teams		STL A (41G – .234)				CHI A (19G – .167)											
" total	60	148	33	5	1	0	0.0	13	18	23	11	2	.223	.270	6	1	3B-46, SS-3, 2B-1
2 yrs.	95	269	57	11	1	1	0.4	32	27	43	25	2	.212	.271	6	1	3B-81, SS-3, 2B-1
1 yr.	19	24	4	0	0	0	0.0	1	6	6	7	0	.167	.167	5	1	3B-9

Tommy Thompson

THOMPSON, RUPERT LUCKHART BL TR 5'9½" 155 lbs.
B. May 19, 1910, Elkhart, Ind. D. May 24, 1971, Auburn, Calif.

	G	AB	H	2B	3B	HR	HR%	R	RBI	BB	SO	SB	BA	SA	AB	H	G by POS
1933 BOS N	24	97	18	1	0	0	0.0	6	6	4	6	0	.186	.196	0	0	OF-24
1934	105	343	91	12	3	0	0.0	40	37	13	19	2	.265	.318	23	8	OF-82
1935	112	297	81	7	1	4	1.3	34	30	36	17	2	.273	.343	24	3	OF-85
1936	106	266	76	9	0	4	1.5	37	36	31	12	3	.286	.365	37	10	OF-39, 1B-25
1938 CHI A	19	18	2	0	0	0	0.0	2	2	1	2	0	.111	.111	17	2	1B-1

Tommy Thompson continued

	G	AB	H	2B	3B	HR	HR%	R	RBI	BB	SO	SB	BA	SA	Pinch Hit AB	H	G by POS
1939 2 teams	CHI A (1G – .000)			STL A (30G – .302)													
" total	31	86	26	5	0	1	1.2	23	8	23	7	0	.302	.395	5	1	OF-23
6 yrs.	397	1107	294	34	4	9	0.8	142	119	108	63	7	.266	.328	106	24	OF-253, 1B-26
2 yrs.	20	18	2	0	0	0	0.0	2	3	1	2	0	.111	.111	17	2	1B-1

Sloppy Thurston
THURSTON, HOLLIS JOHN BR TR 5'11" 165 lbs.
B. June 2, 1899, Fremont, Neb. D. Sept. 14, 1973, Los Angeles, Calif.

	G	AB	H	2B	3B	HR	HR%	R	RBI	BB	SO	SB	BA	SA	PH AB	H	G by POS
1923 2 teams	STL A (2G – .000)			CHI A (45G – .316)													
" total	47	79	25	5	1	0	0.0	10	4	2	6	0	.316	.405	1	0	P-46
1924 CHI A	51	122	31	6	3	1	0.8	15	9	5	14	0	.254	.377	10	3	P-38, OF-1
1925	44	84	24	7	2	0	0.0	2	13	5	13	0	.286	.417	6	2	P-36
1926	38	61	19	4	0	0	0.0	5	5	3	6	0	.311	.377	5	0	P-31
1927 WAS A	42	92	29	4	2	2	2.2	11	17	5	10	1	.315	.467	9	1	P-29
1930 BKN N	36	50	10	3	0	1	2.0	3	11	0	16	0	.200	.320	10	2	P-24
1931	24	60	13	2	1	1	1.7	8	8	2	10	0	.217	.333	0	0	P-24
1932	29	56	17	5	1	0	0.0	7	5	2	9	0	.304	.429	1	0	P-28
1933	32	44	7	2	0	0	0.0	4	7	0	7	0	.159	.205	0	0	P-32
9 yrs.	343	648	175	38	10	5	0.8	65	79	24	91	1	.270	.383	42	8	P-288, OF-1
4 yrs.	178	346	99	22	6	1	0.3	32	31	15	39	0	.286	.393	22	5	P-149, OF-1

Joe Tipton
TIPTON, JOE HICKS BR TR 5'11" 185 lbs.
B. Feb. 18, 1923, McCaysville, Ga.

	G	AB	H	2B	3B	HR	HR%	R	RBI	BB	SO	SB	BA	SA	PH AB	H	G by POS
1948 CLE A	47	90	26	3	0	1	1.1	11	13	4	10	0	.289	.356	6	0	C-40
1949 CHI A	67	191	39	5	3	3	1.6	20	19	27	17	1	.204	.309	14	1	C-53
1950 PHI A	64	184	49	5	1	6	3.3	15	20	19	16	0	.266	.402	5	1	C-59
1951	72	213	51	9	0	3	1.4	23	20	51	25	1	.239	.324	0	0	C-72
1952 2 teams	PHI A (23G – .191)			CLE A (43G – .248)													
" total	66	173	39	6	0	9	5.2	21	30	36	31	1	.225	.416	5	2	C-58
1953 CLE A	47	109	25	2	0	6	5.5	17	13	19	13	0	.229	.413	5	0	C-46
1954 WAS A	54	157	35	6	1	1	0.6	9	10	30	30	0	.223	.293	2	0	C-52
7 yrs.	417	1117	264	36	5	29	2.6	116	125	186	142	3	.236	.355	37	4	C-380
1 yr.	67	191	39	5	3	3	1.6	20	19	27	17	1	.204	.309	14	1	C-53
WORLD SERIES																	
1948 CLE A	1	1	0	0	0	0	0.0	0	0	0	1	0	.000	.000	1	0	

Earl Torgeson
TORGESON, CLIFFORD EARL (The Earl of Snohomish) BL TL 6'3" 180 lbs.
B. Jan. 1, 1924, Snohomish, Wash.

	G	AB	H	2B	3B	HR	HR%	R	RBI	BB	SO	SB	BA	SA	PH AB	H	G by POS
1947 BOS N	128	399	112	20	6	16	4.0	73	78	82	59	11	.281	.481	11	1	1B-117
1948	134	438	111	23	5	10	2.3	70	67	81	54	19	.253	.397	4	2	1B-129
1949	25	100	26	5	1	4	4.0	17	19	13	4	4	.260	.450	0	0	1B-25
1950	156	576	167	30	3	23	4.0	120	87	119	69	15	.290	.472	0	0	1B-156
1951	155	581	153	21	4	24	4.1	99	92	102	70	20	.263	.437	0	0	1B-155
1952	122	382	88	17	0	5	1.3	49	34	81	38	11	.230	.314	12	2	1B-105, OF-5
1953 PHI N	111	379	104	25	8	11	2.9	58	64	53	57	7	.274	.470	6	1	1B-105
1954	135	490	133	22	6	5	1.0	63	54	75	52	7	.271	.371	1	0	1B-133
1955 2 teams	PHI N (47G – .267)			DET A (89G – .283)													
" total	136	450	125	15	4	10	2.2	87	67	93	49	11	.278	.396	9	3	1B-126
1956 DET A	117	318	84	9	3	12	3.8	61	42	78	47	6	.264	.425	27	10	1B-83
1957 2 teams	DET A (30G – .240)			CHI A (86G – .295)													
" total	116	301	86	13	3	8	2.7	58	51	61	54	7	.286	.429	28	8	1B-87, OF-1
1958 CHI A	96	188	50	8	0	10	5.3	37	30	48	29	7	.266	.468	24	9	1B-73
1959	127	277	61	5	3	9	3.2	40	45	62	55	7	.220	.357	24	5	1B-103
1960	68	57	15	2	0	2	3.5	12	9	21	8	1	.263	.404	41	12	1B-10
1961 2 teams	CHI A (20G – .067)			NY A (22G – .111)													
" total	42	33	3	0	0	0	0.0	4	1	11	8	0	.091	.091	23	2	1B-9
15 yrs.	1668	4969	1318	215	46	149	3.0	848	740	980	653	133	.265	.417	210	55	1B-1416, OF-6
5 yrs.	397	788	201	26	5	28	3.6	143	131	183	141	22	.255	.407	120	32	1B-257, OF-1
															5th	4th	
WORLD SERIES																	
1948 BOS N	5	18	7	3	0	0	0.0	2	1	2	1	1	.389	.556	0	0	1B-5
1959 CHI A	3	1	0	0	0	0	0.0	1	0	1	0	0	.000	.000	1	0	1B-1
2 yrs.	8	19	7	3	0	0	0.0	3	1	3	1	1	.368	.526	1	0	1B-6

Rusty Torres
TORRES, ROSENDO JR. BB TR 5'10" 175 lbs.
B. Sept. 30, 1948, Aguadilla, Puerto Rico

	G	AB	H	2B	3B	HR	HR%	R	RBI	BB	SO	SB	BA	SA	PH AB	H	G by POS
1971 NY A	9	26	10	3	0	2	7.7	5	3	0	8	0	.385	.731	4	0	OF-5
1972	80	199	42	9	0	3	1.5	15	13	18	44	0	.211	.291	22	7	OF-62
1973 CLE A	122	312	64	8	1	7	2.2	31	28	50	62	6	.205	.304	7	3	OF-113
1974	108	150	28	2	0	3	2.0	19	12	13	24	2	.187	.260	12	1	OF-94, DH-1
1976 CAL A	120	264	54	16	3	6	2.3	37	27	36	39	4	.205	.356	3	0	OF-105, DH-6, 3B-1
1977	58	77	12	1	1	3	3.9	9	10	10	18	0	.156	.312	2	1	OF-54
1978 CHI A	16	44	14	3	0	3	6.8	7	6	6	7	0	.318	.591	1	0	OF-14
1979	90	170	43	5	0	8	4.7	26	24	23	37	0	.253	.424	12	1	OF-85
1980 KC A	51	72	12	0	0	0	0.0	10	3	8	7	1	.167	.167	9	1	OF-40, DH-1
9 yrs.	654	1314	279	45	5	35	2.7	159	126	164	246	13	.212	.334	64	14	OF-572, DH-8, 3B-1
2 yrs.	106	214	57	8	0	11	5.1	33	30	29	44	0	.266	.458	13	1	OF-99

Babe Towne
TOWNE, JAY KING BL TR
B. Mar. 12, 1880, Coon Rapids, Iowa   D. Oct. 29, 1938, Des Moines, Iowa

	G	AB	H	2B	3B	HR	HR%	R	RBI	BB	SO	SB	BA	SA	PH AB	H	G by POS
1906 CHI A	13	36	10	0	0	0	0.0	3	6	7		0	.278	.278	1	0	C-12
WORLD SERIES																	
1906 CHI A	1	1	0	0	0	0	0.0	0	0	0	0	0	.000	.000	1	0	

Player Register

	G	AB	H	2B	3B	HR	HR%	R	RBI	BB	SO	SB	BA	SA	Pinch Hit AB H	G by POS

Mike Tresh
TRESH, MICHAEL BR TR 5'11" 170 lbs.
Father of Tom Tresh.
B. Feb. 23, 1914, Hazleton, Pa. D. Oct. 4, 1966, Detroit, Mich.

Year	Team	Lg	G	AB	H	2B	3B	HR	HR%	R	RBI	BB	SO	SB	BA	SA	PH AB	PH H	G by POS
1938	CHI	A	10	29	7	2	0	0	0.0	3	2	8	4	0	.241	.310	0	0	C-10
1939			119	352	91	5	2	0	0.0	49	38	64	30	3	.259	.284	0	0	C-119
1940			135	480	135	15	5	1	0.2	62	64	49	40	3	.281	.340	0	0	C-135
1941			115	390	98	10	1	0	0.0	38	33	38	27	1	.251	.282	0	0	C-115
1942			72	233	54	8	1	0	0.0	21	15	28	24	2	.232	.275	0	0	C-72
1943			86	279	60	3	0	0	0.0	20	20	37	20	2	.215	.226	0	0	C-85
1944			93	312	81	8	1	0	0.0	22	25	37	15	0	.260	.292	0	0	C-93
1945			150	458	114	11	0	0	0.0	50	47	65	37	6	.249	.273	0	0	C-150
1946			80	217	47	5	2	0	0.0	28	21	36	24	0	.217	.258	1	0	C-79
1947			90	274	66	6	2	0	0.0	19	20	26	26	2	.241	.277	1	0	C-89
1948			39	108	27	1	0	1	0.9	10	11	9	9	0	.250	.287	5	2	C-34
1949	CLE		38	37	8	0	0	0	0.0	4	1	5	7	0	.216	.216	0	0	C-38
12 yrs.			1027	3169	788	74	14	2	0.1	326	297	402	263	19	.249	.283	7	2	C-1019
11 yrs.			989	3132	780	74	14	2	0.1	322	296	397	256	19	.249	.284	7	2	C-981

Hal Trosky
TROSKY, HAROLD ARTHUR, SR. BL TR 6'2" 207 lbs.
Born Harold Arthurà Sr. Troyavesky. Father of Hal Trosky. BB 1946
B. Nov. 11, 1912, Norway, Iowa D. June 18, 1979, Cedar Rapids, Iowa

Year	Team	Lg	G	AB	H	2B	3B	HR	HR%	R	RBI	BB	SO	SB	BA	SA	PH AB	PH H	G by POS
1933	CLE	A	11	44	13	1	2	1	2.3	6	8	2	12	0	.295	.477	0	0	1B-11
1934			154	625	206	45	9	35	5.6	117	142	58	49	2	.330	.598	0	0	1B-154
1935			154	632	171	33	7	26	4.1	84	113	46	60	1	.271	.468	1	1	1B-153
1936			151	629	216	45	9	42	6.7	124	**162**	36	58	6	.343	.644	0	0	1B-151, 2B-1
1937			153	601	179	36	9	32	5.3	104	128	65	60	3	.298	.547	1	0	1B-152
1938			150	554	185	40	9	19	3.4	106	110	67	40	5	.334	.542	1	1	1B-148
1939			122	448	150	31	4	25	5.6	89	104	52	28	2	.335	.589	4	0	1B-118
1940			140	522	154	39	4	25	4.8	85	93	79	45	0	.295	.529	0	0	1B-139
1941			89	310	91	17	0	11	3.5	43	51	44	21	1	.294	.455	4	2	1B-85
1944	CHI	A	135	497	120	32	2	10	2.0	55	70	62	30	3	.241	.374	4	1	1B-130
1946			88	299	76	12	3	2	0.7	22	31	34	37	4	.254	.334	6	1	1B-80
11 yrs.			1347	5161	1561	331	58	228	4.4	835	1012	545	440	28	.302	.522	21	6	1B-1321, 2B-1
2 yrs.			223	796	196	44	5	12	1.5	77	101	96	67	7	.246	.359	10	2	1B-210

Thurman Tucker
TUCKER, THURMAN LOWELL (Joe E.) BL TR 5'10½" 165 lbs.
B. Sept. 26, 1917, Gordon, Tex.

Year	Team	Lg	G	AB	H	2B	3B	HR	HR%	R	RBI	BB	SO	SB	BA	SA	PH AB	PH H	G by POS
1942	CHI	A	7	24	3	0	1	0	0.0	2	1	0	4	0	.125	.208	2	0	OF-5
1943			139	528	124	15	6	3	0.6	81	39	79	72	29	.235	.303	6	1	OF-132
1944			124	446	128	15	6	2	0.4	59	46	57	40	13	.287	.361	1	0	OF-120
1946			121	438	126	20	3	1	0.2	62	36	54	45	9	.288	.354	8	3	OF-110
1947			89	254	60	9	4	1	0.4	28	17	38	25	10	.236	.315	19	4	OF-65
1948	CLE	A	83	242	63	13	2	1	0.4	52	19	31	17	11	.260	.343	10	3	OF-66
1949			80	197	48	5	2	0	0.0	28	14	18	19	4	.244	.289	22	2	OF-52
1950			57	101	18	2	0	1	1.0	13	7	14	14	1	.178	.228	18	3	OF-34
1951			1	1	0	0	0	0	0.0	0	0	1	0	0	.000	.000	1	0	
9 yrs.			701	2231	570	79	24	9	0.4	325	179	291	237	77	.255	.325	87	16	OF-584
5 yrs.			480	1690	441	59	20	7	0.4	232	139	228	186	61	.261	.332	36	8	OF-432

WORLD SERIES

Year	Team	Lg	G	AB	H	2B	3B	HR	HR%	R	RBI	BB	SO	SB	BA	SA	PH AB	PH H	G by POS
1948	CLE	A	1	3	1	0	0	0	0.0	1	0	1	0	0	.333	.333	0	0	OF-1

Jerry Turner
TURNER, JOHN WEBBER BL TL 5'9" 180 lbs.
B. Jan. 17, 1954, Texarkana, Ark.

Year	Team	Lg	G	AB	H	2B	3B	HR	HR%	R	RBI	BB	SO	SB	BA	SA	PH AB	PH H	G by POS
1974	SD	N	17	48	14	1	0	0	0.0	4	2	3	5	2	.292	.313	6	3	OF-13
1975			11	22	6	0	0	0	0.0	1	0	2	1	0	.273	.273	6	3	OF-4
1976			105	281	75	16	5	5	1.8	41	37	32	38	12	.267	.413	25	5	OF-74
1977			118	289	71	16	1	10	3.5	43	48	31	43	12	.246	.412	45	12	OF-69
1978			106	225	63	9	1	8	3.6	28	37	21	32	6	.280	.436	49	**20**	OF-58
1979			138	448	111	23	2	9	2.0	55	61	34	58	4	.248	.368	5	0	OF-115
1980			85	153	44	5	0	3	2.0	22	18	10	18	8	.288	.379	47	13	OF-34
1981	2 teams		SD	N (33G — .226)	CHI	A (10G — .167)													
"	total		43	43	9	0	2	4.7	6	8	5	5	0	.209	.349	29	5	OF-5
1982	DET	A	85	210	52	8	3	8	3.8	21	27	20	37	1	.248	.376	24	4	DH-50, OF-13
1983	SD	N	25	23	3	0	0	0	0.0	1	0	1	8	0	.130	.130	23	3	OF-1
10 yrs.			733	1742	448	73	9	45	2.6	222	238	159	245	45	.257	.387	282	73	OF-386, DH-50
1 yr.			10	12	2	0	0	0	0.0	1	0	1	2	0	.167	.167	8	1	OF-1

Tom Turner
TURNER, THOMAS RICHARD BR TR 6'2" 195 lbs.
B. Sept. 8, 1916, Custer, Okla.

Year	Team	Lg	G	AB	H	2B	3B	HR	HR%	R	RBI	BB	SO	SB	BA	SA	PH AB	PH H	G by POS
1940	CHI	A	37	96	20	1	2	0	0.0	11	6	3	12	1	.208	.260	7	1	C-29
1941			38	126	30	5	0	0	0.0	7	8	9	15	2	.238	.278	3	1	C-35
1942			56	182	44	9	1	3	1.6	18	21	19	15	0	.242	.352	2	1	C-54
1943			51	154	37	7	1	2	1.3	16	11	13	21	1	.240	.338	2	0	C-49
1944	2 teams		CHI	A (36G — .230)	STL	A (15G — .320)													
"	total		51	138	34	7	0	2	1.4	11	17	7	21	0	.246	.341	4	0	C-47
5 yrs.			233	696	165	29	4	7	1.0	63	63	51	84	4	.237	.320	18	3	C-214
5 yrs.			218	671	157	28	4	7	1.0	61	59	49	79	4	.234	.319	14	3	C-203

WORLD SERIES

Year	Team	Lg	G	AB	H	2B	3B	HR	HR%	R	RBI	BB	SO	SB	BA	SA	PH AB	PH H	G by POS
1944	STL	A	1	1	0	0	0	0	0.0	0	0	0	0	0	.000	.000	1	0	

Frenchy Uhalt
UHALT, BERNARD BARTHOLOMEW BL TR 5'10" 180 lbs.
B. Apr. 27, 1910, Bakersville, Calif.

Year	Team	Lg	G	AB	H	2B	3B	HR	HR%	R	RBI	BB	SO	SB	BA	SA	PH AB	PH H	G by POS
1934	CHI	A	57	165	40	5	1	0	0.0	28	16	29	12	6	.242	.285	13	4	OF-40

Player Register

	G	AB	H	2B	3B	HR	HR %	R	RBI	BB	SO	SB	BA	SA	Pinch Hit AB H	G by POS

Charlie Uhlir
UHLIR, CHARLES
B. July 30, 1912, Chicago, Ill.
BL TL 5'7½" 150 lbs.

	G	AB	H	2B	3B	HR	HR%	R	RBI	BB	SO	SB	BA	SA	PH AB	PH H	G by POS
1934 CHI A	14	27	4	0	0	0	0.0	3	3	2	6	0	.148	.148	5	1	OF-6

Pete Varney
VARNEY, RICHARD FRED
B. Apr. 10, 1949, North Quincy, Mass.
BR TR 6'3" 235 lbs.

	G	AB	H	2B	3B	HR	HR%	R	RBI	BB	SO	SB	BA	SA	PH AB	PH H	G by POS
1973 CHI A	5	4	0	0	0	0	0.0	0	0	1	0	0	.000	.000	0	0	C-5
1974	9	28	7	0	0	0	0.0	1	2	1	8	0	.250	.250	0	0	C-9
1975	36	107	29	5	1	2	1.9	12	8	6	28	2	.271	.393	3	0	C-34, DH-2
1976 2 teams	ATL N (5G – .100)					CHI A (14G – .244)											
" total	19	51	11	2	0	3	5.9	6	5	2	11	0	.216	.431	0	0	C-19
4 yrs.	69	190	47	7	1	5	2.6	19	15	10	47	2	.247	.374	3	0	C-67, DH-2
4 yrs.	64	180	46	7	1	5	2.8	18	15	10	45	2	.256	.389	3	0	C-62, DH-2

Art Veltman
VELTMAN, ARTHUR PATRICK
B. Mar. 24, 1906, Mobile, Ala. D. Oct. 1, 1980, San Antonio, Tex.
BR TR 6' 175 lbs.

	G	AB	H	2B	3B	HR	HR%	R	RBI	BB	SO	SB	BA	SA	PH AB	PH H	G by POS
1926 CHI A	5	4	1	0	0	0	0.0	1	0	1	0	0	.250	.250	3	1	SS-1
1928 NY N	1	3	1	0	1	0	0.0	0	1	0	0	0	.333	1.000	0	0	OF-1
1929	2	1	0	0	0	0	0.0	1	0	2	0	0	.000	.000	0	0	C-1
1931 BOS N	1	1	0	0	0	0	0.0	0	0	0	0	0	.000	.000	1	0	
1932 NY N	2	1	0	0	0	0	0.0	0	0	0	1	0	.000	.000	1	0	
1934 PIT N	12	28	3	0	0	0	0.0	1	2	0	2	0	.107	.107	1	0	C-11
6 yrs.	23	38	5	0	1	0	0.0	4	2	4	3	0	.132	.184	6	1	C-12, OF-1, SS-1
1 yr.	5	4	1	0	1	0	0.0	1	0	1	0	0	.250	.250	3	1	SS-1

Rube Vinson
VINSON, ERNEST AUGUSTUS
B. Mar. 20, 1879, Dover, Del. D. Oct. 12, 1951, Chester, Pa.
5'9" 168 lbs.

	G	AB	H	2B	3B	HR	HR%	R	RBI	BB	SO	SB	BA	SA	PH AB	PH H	G by POS
1904 CLE A	15	49	15	1	0	0	0.0	12	2	10		2	.306	.327	0	0	OF-15
1905	38	133	26	3	1	0	0.0	12	9	7		4	.195	.233	2	0	OF-36
1906 CHI A	7	24	6	0	0	0	0.0	2	3	2		1	.250	.250	1	1	OF-4
3 yrs.	60	206	47	4	1	0	0.0	26	14	19		7	.228	.257	3	1	OF-55
1 yr.	7	24	6	0	0	0	0.0	2	3	2		1	.250	.250	1	1	OF-4

Fritz Von Kolnitz
VON KOLNITZ, ALFRED HOLMES
B. May 20, 1893, Charleston, S. C. D. Mar. 18, 1948, Mount Pleasant, S. C.
BR TR 5'10½" 175 lbs.

	G	AB	H	2B	3B	HR	HR%	R	RBI	BB	SO	SB	BA	SA	PH AB	PH H	G by POS
1914 CIN N	41	104	23	2	0	0	0.0	8	6	6	16	4	.221	.240	7	0	3B-20, OF-11, C-2, 1B-1
1915	50	78	15	4	1	0	0.0	6	6	7	11	1	.192	.269	20	6	3B-18, SS-6, 1B-3, C-2, OF-1
1916 CHI A	24	44	10	3	0	0	0.0	1	7	2	6	0	.227	.295	10	3	3B-13
3 yrs.	115	226	48	9	1	0	0.0	15	19	15	33	5	.212	.261	37	9	3B-51, OF-12, SS-6, 1B-4, C-4
1 yr.	24	44	10	3	0	0	0.0	1	7	2	6	0	.227	.295	10	3	3B-13

Bill Voss
VOSS, WILLIAM EDWARD
B. Oct. 31, 1945, Glendale, Calif.
BL TL 6'2" 160 lbs.

	G	AB	H	2B	3B	HR	HR%	R	RBI	BB	SO	SB	BA	SA	PH AB	PH H	G by POS
1965 CHI A	11	33	6	0	1	1	3.0	4	3	3	5	0	.182	.333	0	0	OF-10
1966	2	2	0	0	0	0	0.0	0	0	0	2	0	.000	.000	1	0	OF-1
1967	13	22	2	0	0	0	0.0	4	0	0	1	1	.091	.091	0	0	OF-11
1968	61	167	26	2	1	2	1.2	14	15	16	34	5	.156	.216	7	2	OF-55
1969 CAL A	133	349	91	11	4	2	0.6	33	40	35	40	5	.261	.332	16	6	OF-111, 1B-2
1970	80	181	44	4	3	3	1.7	21	30	23	18	2	.243	.348	26	6	OF-55
1971 MIL A	97	275	69	4	0	10	3.6	31	30	24	45	2	.251	.375	20	5	OF-79
1972 3 teams	MIL A (27G – .083)					OAK A (40G – .227)					STL N (11G – .267)						
" total	78	148	29	8	1	1	0.7	12	9	16	22	0	.196	.284	30	5	OF-47
8 yrs.	475	1177	267	29	10	19	1.6	119	127	117	167	15	.227	.317	100	24	OF-369, 1B-2
4 yrs.	87	224	34	2	2	3	1.3	22	18	19	42	6	.152	.219	8	2	OF-77

Leon Wagner
WAGNER, LEON LAMAR (Daddy Wags)
B. May 13, 1934, Chattanooga, Tenn.
BL TR 6'1" 195 lbs.

	G	AB	H	2B	3B	HR	HR%	R	RBI	BB	SO	SB	BA	SA	PH AB	PH H	G by POS
1958 SF N	74	221	70	9	0	13	5.9	31	35	18	34	1	.317	.534	18	4	OF-57
1959	87	129	29	4	3	5	3.9	20	22	25	24	0	.225	.419	52	10	OF-28
1960 STL N	39	98	21	2	0	4	4.1	12	11	17	17	0	.214	.357	7	1	OF-32
1961 LA A	133	453	127	19	2	28	6.2	74	79	48	65	5	.280	.517	16	3	OF-116
1962	160	612	164	21	5	37	6.0	96	107	50	87	7	.268	.500	3	1	OF-156
1963	149	550	160	11	1	26	4.7	73	90	49	73	5	.291	.456	9	2	OF-141
1964 CLE A	163	641	162	19	2	31	4.8	94	100	56	121	14	.253	.434	2	1	OF-163
1965	144	517	152	18	1	28	5.4	91	79	60	52	12	.294	.495	11	3	OF-134
1966	150	549	153	20	0	23	4.2	70	66	46	69	5	.279	.441	10	3	OF-139
1967	135	433	105	15	1	15	3.5	56	54	37	76	3	.242	.386	15	4	OF-117
1968 2 teams	CLE A (38G – .184)					CHI A (69G – .284)											
" total	107	211	55	0	1	0.5	19	24	27	37	2	.261	.332	46	11	OF-56		
1969 SF N	11	12	4	0	0	0	0.0	0	2	2	1	0	.333	.333	7	3	OF-1
12 yrs.	1352	4426	1202	150	15	211	4.8	636	669	435	656	54	.272	.455	196	46	OF-1140
1 yr.	69	162	46	8	0	1	0.6	14	18	21	31	2	.284	.352	22	5	OF-46

Dixie Walker
WALKER, FRED (The People's Cherce)
Son of Dixie Walker. Brother of Harry Walker.
B. Sept. 24, 1910, Villa Rica, Ga. D. May 17, 1982, Birmingham, Ala.
BL TR 6'1" 175 lbs.

	G	AB	H	2B	3B	HR	HR%	R	RBI	BB	SO	SB	BA	SA	PH AB	PH H	G by POS
1931 NY A	2	10	3	2	0	0	0.0	1	1	0	4	0	.300	.500	0	0	OF-2
1933	98	328	90	15	7	15	4.6	68	51	26	28	2	.274	.500	18	4	OF-77
1934	17	17	2	0	0	0	0.0	2	0	1	3	0	.118	.118	12	2	OF-1
1935	8	13	2	1	0	0	0.0	1	0	1	0	0	.154	.231	5	1	OF-2
1936 2 teams	NY A (6G – .350)					CHI A (26G – .271)											
" total	32	90	26	2	1	1	1.1	15	16	15	9	2	.289	.389	10	2	OF-22
1937 CHI A	154	593	179	28	16	9	1.5	105	95	78	26	1	.302	.449	0	0	OF-154
1938 DET A	127	454	140	27	6	6	1.3	84	43	65	32	5	.308	.434	10	3	OF-114

Player Register 330

	G	AB	H	2B	3B	HR	HR %	R	RBI	BB	SO	SB	BA	SA	Pinch Hit AB	H	G by POS

Dixie Walker continued

1939 2 teams	DET A (43G – .305)					BKN N (61G – .280)											
" total	104	379	110	10	9	6	1.6	57	57	35	18	5	.290	.412	6	2	OF-96
1940 BKN N	143	556	171	37	8	6	1.1	75	66	42	21	3	.308	.435	6	4	OF-136
1941	148	531	165	32	8	9	1.7	88	71	70	18	4	.311	.452	2	0	OF-146
1942	118	393	114	28	1	6	1.5	57	54	47	15	1	.290	.412	6	2	OF-110
1943	138	540	163	32	6	5	0.9	83	71	49	24	3	.302	.411	2	1	OF-136
1944	147	535	191	37	8	13	2.4	77	91	72	27	6	.357	.529	7	2	OF-140
1945	154	607	182	42	9	8	1.3	102	124	75	16	6	.300	.438	1	0	OF-153
1946	150	576	184	29	9	9	1.6	80	116	67	28	14	.319	.448	1	0	OF-149
1947	148	529	162	31	3	9	1.7	77	94	97	26	6	.306	.427	1	0	OF-147
1948 PIT N	129	408	129	19	3	2	0.5	39	54	52	18	1	.316	.392	16	3	OF-112
1949	88	181	51	4	1	0	0.6	26	18	26	11	0	.282	.331	40	13	OF-39, 1B-3
18 yrs.	1905	6740	2064	376	96	105	1.6	1037	1023	817	325	59	.306	.437	143	39	OF-1736, 1B-3
2 yrs.	180	663	198	30	16	9	1.4	117	106	92	32	2	.299	.433	9	2	OF-171

WORLD SERIES

1941 BKN N	5	18	4	2	0	0	0.0	3	0	2	1	0	.222	.333	0	0	OF-5
1947	7	27	6	1	0	1	3.7	1	4	3	1	1	.222	.370	0	0	OF-7
2 yrs.	12	45	10	3	0	1	2.2	4	4	5	2	1	.222	.356	0	0	OF-12

Gee Walker

WALKER, GERALD HOLMES
Brother of Hub Walker.
B. Mar. 19, 1908, Gulfport, Miss.   D. Mar. 20, 1981, Whitfield, Miss.   BR TR 5'11" 188 lbs.

	G	AB	H	2B	3B	HR	HR%	R	RBI	BB	SO	SB	BA	SA	PH AB	H	G by POS
1931 DET A	59	189	56	17	2	1	0.5	20	28	14	21	10	.296	.423	9	4	OF-44
1932	126	480	155	32	6	8	1.7	71	78	13	38	30	.323	.465	8	1	OF-116
1933	127	483	135	29	7	9	1.9	68	64	15	49	26	.280	.424	12	2	OF-113
1934	98	347	104	19	2	6	1.7	54	39	19	20	20	.300	.418	17	5	OF-80
1935	98	362	109	22	6	7	1.9	52	53	15	21	6	.301	.453	14	7	OF-85
1936	134	550	194	55	5	12	2.2	105	93	23	30	17	.353	.536	9	1	OF-125
1937	151	635	213	42	4	18	2.8	105	113	41	74	23	.335	.499	0	0	OF-151
1938 CHI A	120	442	135	23	6	16	3.6	69	87	38	32	9	.305	.493	12	4	OF-107
1939	149	598	174	30	11	13	2.2	95	111	28	43	17	.291	.443	2	0	OF-147
1940 WAS A	140	595	175	29	7	13	2.2	87	96	24	58	21	.294	.432	0	0	OF-140
1941 CLE A	121	445	126	26	11	6	1.3	56	48	18	46	12	.283	.431	13	5	OF-105
1942 CIN N	119	422	97	20	2	5	1.2	40	50	31	44	11	.230	.322	8	1	OF-110
1943	114	429	105	23	2	3	0.7	48	54	12	38	6	.245	.329	6	1	OF-106
1944	121	478	133	21	3	5	1.0	56	62	23	48	7	.278	.366	3	1	OF-117
1945	106	316	80	11	2	2	0.6	28	21	16	38	8	.253	.320	35	9	OF-67, 3B-3
15 yrs.	1783	6771	1991	399	76	124	1.8	954	997	330	600	223	.294	.430	148	41	OF-1613, 3B-3
2 yrs.	269	1040	309	53	17	29	2.8	164	198	66	75	26	.297	.464	14	4	OF-254

WORLD SERIES

1934 DET A	3	3	1	0	0	0	0.0	0	1	0	0	1	.333	.333	3	1	
1935	3	4	1	0	0	0	0.0	1	0	1	1	0	.250	.250	2	0	OF-1
2 yrs.	6	7	2	0	0	0	0.0	1	1	1	1	1	.286	.286	5	1	OF-1

Greg Walker

WALKER, GREGORY LEE
B. Oct. 6, 1959, Douglas, Ga.   BL TR 6'3" 205 lbs.

	G	AB	H	2B	3B	HR	HR%	R	RBI	BB	SO	SB	BA	SA	PH AB	H	G by POS
1982 CHI A	11	17	7	2	1	2	11.8	3	7	2	3	0	.412	1.000	4	2	DH-4
1983	118	307	83	16	3	10	3.3	32	55	28	57	2	.270	.440	35	13	1B-59, DH-21
2 yrs.	129	324	90	18	4	12	3.7	35	62	30	60	2	.278	.469	39	15	1B-59, DH-25
2 yrs.	129	324	90	18	4	12	3.7	35	62	30	60	2	.278	.469	39	15	1B-59, DH-25

LEAGUE CHAMPIONSHIP SERIES

1983 CHI A	2	3	1	0	0	0	0.0	0	0	1	2	0	.333	.333	1	0	1B-1

Jack Wallaesa

WALLAESA, JOHN
B. Aug. 31, 1919, Easton, Pa.   BR TR 6'3" 191 lbs.
BB 1948

	G	AB	H	2B	3B	HR	HR%	R	RBI	BB	SO	SB	BA	SA	PH AB	H	G by POS
1940 PHI A	6	20	3	0	0	0	0.0	0	2	0	2	0	.150	.150	0	0	SS-6
1942	36	117	30	4	1	2	1.7	13	13	1	26	0	.256	.359	0	0	SS-36
1946	63	194	38	4	2	5	2.6	16	11	14	47	1	.196	.314	3	1	SS-59
1947 CHI A	81	205	40	9	1	7	3.4	25	32	23	51	2	.195	.351	27	4	SS-27, OF-22, 3B-1
1948	33	48	9	0	0	1	2.1	2	3	1	12	0	.188	.250	27	6	SS-5, OF-1
5 yrs.	219	584	120	17	4	15	2.6	56	61	39	138	3	.205	.325	57	11	SS-133, OF-23, 3B-1
2 yrs.	114	253	49	9	1	8	3.2	27	35	24	63	2	.194	.332	54	10	SS-32, OF-23, 3B-1

Ed Walsh

WALSH, EDWARD AUGUSTINE (Big Ed)
Father of Ed Walsh.
B. May 14, 1881, Plains, Pa.   D. May 26, 1959, Pompano Beach, Fla.   BR TR 6'1" 193 lbs.
Hall of Fame 1946.

	G	AB	H	2B	3B	HR	HR%	R	RBI	BB	SO	SB	BA	SA	PH AB	H	G by POS
1904 CHI A	18	41	9	1	1	1	2.4	5	4	3		1	.220	.366	0	0	P-18
1905	29	58	9	2	0	0	0.0	5	2	4		0	.155	.190	2	0	P-22, OF-5
1906	42	99	14	3	2	0	0.0	12	4	3		0	.141	.212	1	0	P-41
1907	57	154	25	6	3	1	0.6	7	10	0		2	.162	.260	1	0	P-56
1908	66	157	27	7	1	1	0.6	10	10	7		2	.172	.248	0	0	P-66
1909	32	84	18	5	0	0	0.0	5	11	6	4		.214	.274	0	0	P-31, OF-1
1910	52	138	30	3	3	0	0.0	12	4	5		5	.217	.283	7	1	P-45
1911	62	155	32	3	0	0	0.0	22	9	1		0	.206	.226	7	2	P-56
1912	64	136	33	4	1	0	0.0	12	12	14		0	.243	.287	2	1	P-62
1913	17	32	5	1	0	0	0.0	1	2	1	7	0	.156	.188	1	0	P-16
1914	10	16	1	1	0	0	0.0	0	0	1	4	0	.063	.125	2	0	P-8
1915	5	11	4	0	0	0	0.0	0	1	0	1	0	.364	.364	2	1	P-3
1916	2	0	0	0	0	0	–	0	0	0	0	0	–	–	0	0	P-2
1917 BOS N	4	4	1	0	0	0	0.0	0	1	0	1	0	.250	.250	0	0	P-4
14 yrs.	460	1085	208	36	11	3	0.3	92	69	46	14	14	.192	.253	25	5	P-430, OF-6
13 yrs.	456	1081	207	36	11	3	0.3	91	69	45	12	14	.191	.253	25	5	P-426, OF-6

WORLD SERIES

1906 CHI A	2	4	0	0	0	0	0.0	1	0	3	3	0	.000	.000	0	0	P-2

Player Register

	G	AB	H	2B	3B	HR	HR%	R	RBI	BB	SO	SB	BA	SA	Pinch Hit AB H	G by POS

Aaron Ward
WARD, AARON LEE BR TR 5'10½" 160 lbs.
B. Aug. 28, 1896, Booneville, Ark.   D. Jan. 30, 1961, New Orleans, La.

Year	Tm	Lg	G	AB	H	2B	3B	HR	HR%	R	RBI	BB	SO	SB	BA	SA	PH AB	PH H	G by POS
1917	NY	A	8	26	3	0	0	0	0.0	0	1	1	5	0	.115	.115	1	0	SS-7
1918			20	32	4	1	0	0	0.0	2	1	2	7	1	.125	.156	1	0	SS-11, OF-4, 2B-4
1919			27	34	7	2	0	0	0.0	5	2	5	6	0	.206	.265	14	4	1B-5, 3B-3, SS-2, 2B-1
1920			127	496	127	18	7	11	2.2	62	54	33	84	7	.256	.387	1	0	3B-114, SS-12
1921			153	556	170	30	10	5	0.9	77	75	42	68	6	.306	.423	0	0	2B-123, 3B-33
1922			154	558	149	19	5	7	1.3	69	68	45	64	7	.267	.357	0	0	2B-152, 3B-2
1923			152	567	161	26	11	10	1.8	79	82	56	65	8	.284	.422	0	0	2B-152
1924			120	400	101	13	10	8	2.0	42	66	40	45	1	.253	.395	0	0	2B-120, SS-1
1925			125	439	108	22	3	4	0.9	41	38	49	49	1	.246	.337	2	0	2B-113, 3B-10
1926			22	31	10	2	0	0	0.0	5	3	2	6	0	.323	.387	15	5	2B-4, 3B-1
1927	CHI		145	463	125	25	8	5	1.1	75	56	63	56	6	.270	.391	1	0	2B-138, 3B-6
1928	CLE		6	9	1	0	0	0	0.0	0	0	1	2	0	.111	.111	0	0	3B-3, SS-2, 2B-1
12 yrs.			1059	3611	966	158	54	50	1.4	457	446	339	457	37	.268	.383	35	9	2B-808, 3B-172, SS-35, 1B-5, OF-4
1 yr.			145	463	125	25	8	5	1.1	75	56	63	56	6	.270	.391	1	0	2B-138, 3B-6

WORLD SERIES

Year	Tm	Lg	G	AB	H	2B	3B	HR	HR%	R	RBI	BB	SO	SB	BA	SA	PH AB	PH H	G by POS
1921	NY	A	8	26	6	0	0	0	0.0	1	4	2	6	0	.231	.231	0	0	2B-8
1922			5	13	2	0	0	2	15.4	3	3	3	3	0	.154	.615	0	0	2B-5
1923			6	24	10	0	0	1	4.2	4	2	1	3	1	.417	.542	0	0	2B-6
3 yrs.			19	63	18	0	0	3	4.8	8	9	6	12	1	.286	.429	0	0	2B-19

Pete Ward
WARD, PETER THOMAS BL TR 6'1" 185 lbs.
B. July 26, 1939, Montreal, Que., Canada

Year	Tm	Lg	G	AB	H	2B	3B	HR	HR%	R	RBI	BB	SO	SB	BA	SA	PH AB	PH H	G by POS
1962	BAL	A	8	21	3	2	0	0	0.0	1	2	4	5	0	.143	.238	1	1	OF-6
1963	CHI	A	157	600	177	34	6	22	3.7	80	84	52	77	7	.295	.482	3	1	3B-154, SS-1, 2B-1
1964			144	539	152	28	3	23	4.3	61	94	56	76	1	.282	.473	5	1	3B-138
1965			138	507	125	25	3	10	2.0	62	57	56	83	2	.247	.367	5	1	3B-134, 2B-1
1966			84	251	55	7	1	3	1.2	22	28	24	49	3	.219	.291	9	0	OF-59, 3B-16, 1B-5
1967			146	467	109	16	2	18	3.9	49	62	61	109	3	.233	.392	6	3	OF-89, 1B-39, 3B-22
1968			125	399	86	15	0	15	3.8	43	50	76	85	4	.216	.366	6	1	3B-77, 1B-31, OF-22
1969			105	199	49	7	0	6	3.0	22	32	33	38	0	.246	.372	46	17	1B-25, 3B-21, OF-9
1970	NY	A	66	77	20	2	0	2	2.6	5	18	9	17	0	.260	.377	44	10	1B-13
9 yrs.			973	3060	776	136	15	98	3.2	345	427	371	539	20	.254	.405	125	35	3B-562, OF-185, 1B-113, 2B-2, SS-1
7 yrs.			899	2962	753	132	15	97	3.3	339	407	358	517	20	.254	.407	80	24	3B-562, OF-179, 1B-100, 2B-2, SS-1
						4th	7th						4th					9th	

Claudell Washington
WASHINGTON, CLAUDELL BL TL 6' 190 lbs.
B. Aug. 31, 1954, Los Angeles, Calif.

Year	Tm	Lg	G	AB	H	2B	3B	HR	HR%	R	RBI	BB	SO	SB	BA	SA	PH AB	PH H	G by POS
1974	OAK	A	73	221	63	10	5	0	0.0	16	19	13	44	7	.285	.376	8	3	DH-38, OF-32
1975			148	590	182	24	7	10	1.7	86	77	32	80	40	.308	.424	2	1	OF-148
1976			134	490	126	20	6	5	1.0	65	53	30	90	37	.257	.353	3	2	OF-126, DH-6
1977	TEX	A	129	521	148	31	2	12	2.3	63	68	25	112	21	.284	.420	2	0	OF-127
1978	2 teams		TEX	A	(12G – .167)			CHI	A	(86G – .264)									
"	total		98	356	90	16	5	6	1.7	34	33	13	69	5	.253	.376	6	2	OF-89, DH-5
1979	CHI	A	131	471	132	33	5	13	2.8	79	66	28	93	19	.280	.454	13	4	OF-122, DH-3
1980	2 teams		CHI	A	(32G – .289)			NY	N	(79G – .275)									
"	total		111	374	104	20	6	11	2.9	53	54	25	82	21	.278	.452	17	1	OF-93, DH-2
1981	ATL	N	85	320	93	22	3	5	1.6	37	37	15	47	12	.291	.425	5	3	OF-79
1982			150	563	150	24	6	16	2.8	94	80	50	107	33	.266	.416	7	0	OF-139
1983			134	496	138	24	8	9	1.8	75	44	35	103	31	.278	.413	7	2	OF-128
10 yrs.			1193	4402	1226	224	53	87	2.0	602	531	266	827	226	.279	.413	70	18	OF-1083, DH-54
3 yrs.			249	875	241	53	12	20	2.3	127	109	45	169	28	.275	.432	26	6	OF-227, DH-6

LEAGUE CHAMPIONSHIP SERIES

Year	Tm	Lg	G	AB	H	2B	3B	HR	HR%	R	RBI	BB	SO	SB	BA	SA	PH AB	PH H	G by POS
1974	OAK	A	4	11	3	1	0	0	0.0	1	0	0	0	0	.273	.364	1	1	OF-3
1975			3	12	3	1	0	0	0.0	1	1	0	2	0	.250	.333	0	0	OF-2
1982	ATL	N	3	9	3	0	0	0	0.0	0	0	2	2	0	.333	.333	0	0	OF-3
3 yrs.			10	32	9	2	0	0	0.0	2	1	2	4	0	.281	.344	1	1	OF-8

WORLD SERIES

Year	Tm	Lg	G	AB	H	2B	3B	HR	HR%	R	RBI	BB	SO	SB	BA	SA	PH AB	PH H	G by POS
1974	OAK	A	5	7	4	0	0	0	0.0	1	0	1	1	0	.571	.571	1	1	OF-5

George Washington
WASHINGTON, SLOANE VERNON BL TR 5'11½" 190 lbs.
B. June 7, 1907, Linden, Tex.

Year	Tm	Lg	G	AB	H	2B	3B	HR	HR%	R	RBI	BB	SO	SB	BA	SA	PH AB	PH H	G by POS
1935	CHI	A	108	339	96	22	3	8	2.4	40	47	10	18	1	.283	.437	29	9	OF-79
1936			20	49	8	2	0	1	2.0	6	5	1	4	0	.163	.265	6	1	OF-12
2 yrs.			128	388	104	24	3	9	2.3	46	52	11	22	1	.268	.415	35	10	OF-91
2 yrs.			128	388	104	24	3	9	2.3	46	52	11	22	1	.268	.415	35	10	OF-91

Cliff Watwood
WATWOOD, JOHN CLIFFORD BL TL 6'1" 186 lbs.
B. Aug. 17, 1906, Alexander City, Ala.   D. Mar. 1, 1980, Goodwater, Ala.

Year	Tm	Lg	G	AB	H	2B	3B	HR	HR%	R	RBI	BB	SO	SB	BA	SA	PH AB	PH H	G by POS
1929	CHI	A	85	278	84	12	6	2	0.7	33	18	22	21	6	.302	.410	7	2	OF-77
1930			133	427	129	25	4	2	0.5	75	51	52	35	5	.302	.393	19	4	1B-62, OF-43
1931			128	367	104	16	6	1	0.3	51	47	56	30	9	.283	.368	17	5	OF-102, 1B-4
1932	2 teams		CHI	A	(13G – .306)			BOS	A	(95G – .248)									
"	total		108	315	81	13	0	0	0.0	31	30	21	14	7	.257	.298	27	9	OF-59, 1B-18
1933	BOS	A	13	30	4	0	0	0	0.0	2	2	3	3	0	.133	.133	5	0	OF-9
1939	PHI	N	6	1	0	0	0	0	0.0	0	0	0	0	0	.167	.167	0	0	1B-2
6 yrs.			469	1423	403	66	16	5	0.4	192	148	154	103	27	.283	.363	73	20	OF-290, 1B-86
4 yrs.			359	1121	332	55	16	5	0.4	164	116	131	89	20	.296	.387	43	11	OF-235, 1B-66

Bob Way
WAY, ROBERT CLINTON BR TR 5'10½" 168 lbs.
B. Apr. 2, 1906, Emlenton, Pa.   D. June 20, 1974, Pittsburgh, Pa.

Year	Tm	Lg	G	AB	H	2B	3B	HR	HR%	R	RBI	BB	SO	SB	BA	SA	PH AB	PH H	G by POS
1927	CHI	A	5	3	1	0	0	0	0.0	3	1	0	1	0	.333	.333	3	1	2B-1

Player Register 332

	G	AB	H	2B	3B	HR	HR%	R	RBI	BB	SO	SB	BA	SA	Pinch Hit AB H	G by POS

Art Weaver
WEAVER, ARTHUR COGGSHALL TR
B. Apr. 7, 1879, Wichita, Kans. D. Mar. 23, 1917, Denver, Colo.

1902 STL N	11	33	6	2	0	0	0.0	2	3	1		0	.182	.242	0 0	C-11
1903 2 teams	STL	N (16G – .245)				PIT	N (16G – .229)									
" total	32	97	23	0	1	0	0.0	12	8	6		1	.237	.258	0 0	C-27, 1B-5
1905 STL A	28	92	11	2	1	0	0.0	5	3	1		0	.120	.163	0 0	C-28
1908 CHI A	15	35	7	1	0	0	0.0	1	1	1		0	.200	.229	0 0	C-15
4 yrs.	86	257	47	5	2	0	0.0	20	15	9		1	.183	.218	0 0	C-81, 1B-5
1 yr.	15	35	7	1	0	0	0.0	1	1	1		0	.200	.229	0 0	C-15

Buck Weaver
WEAVER, GEORGE DAVIS BB TR 5'11" 170 lbs.
B. Aug. 18, 1890, Stowe, Pa. D. Jan. 31, 1956, Chicago, Ill.

1912 CHI A	147	523	117	21	8	1	0.2	55	43	9		12	.224	.300	0 0	SS-147
1913	151	533	145	17	8	4	0.8	51	52	15	60	20	.272	.356	0 0	SS-151
1914	136	541	133	20	9	2	0.4	64	28	20	40	14	.246	.327	2 0	SS-134
1915	148	563	151	18	11	3	0.5	83	49	32	58	24	.268	.355	0 0	SS-148
1916	151	582	132	27	6	3	0.5	78	38	30	48	22	.227	.309	0 0	3B-85, SS-66
1917	118	447	127	16	5	3	0.7	64	32	27	29	19	.284	.362	1 0	3B-107, SS-10
1918	112	420	126	12	5	0	0.0	37	29	11	24	20	.300	.352	2 1	SS-98, 3B-11, 2B-1
1919	140	571	169	33	9	3	0.5	89	75	11	21	22	.296	.401	0 0	3B-97, SS-43
1920	151	630	210	35	8	2	0.3	104	75	28	23	19	.333	.424	0 0	3B-126, SS-25
9 yrs.	1254	4810	1310	199	69	21	0.4	625	421	183	303	172	.272	.356	5 1	SS-822, 3B-426, 2B-1
9 yrs. 2 teams	1254	4810	1310	199	69	21	0.4	625	421	183	303	172	.272	.356	5 1	SS-822, 3B-426, 2B-1
	9th	7th	7th		8th		0.4	7th				9th				

WORLD SERIES

1917 CHI A	6	21	7	1	0	0	0.0	3	1	0	2	0	.333	.381	0 0	SS-6
1919	8	34	11	4	1	0	0.0	4	0	0	2	0	.324	.500	0 0	3B-8
2 yrs.	14	55	18	5	1	0	0.0	7	1	0	4	0	.327	.455	0 0	3B-8, SS-6

Earl Webb
WEBB, WILLIAM EARL BL TR 6'1" 185 lbs.
B. Sept. 17, 1898, Bon Air, Tenn. D. May 23, 1965, Jamestown, Tenn.

1925 NY N	4	3	0	0	0	0	0.0	0	0	1	1	0	.000	.000	3 0	
1927 CHI N	102	332	100	18	4	14	4.2	58	52	48	31	3	.301	.506	15 3	OF-86
1928	62	140	35	7	3	3	2.1	22	23	14	17	0	.250	.407	24 8	OF-31
1930 BOS A	127	449	145	30	6	16	3.6	61	66	44	56	2	.323	.523	8 2	OF-116
1931	151	589	196	67¹	3	14	2.4	96	103	70	51	2	.333	.528	0 0	OF-151
1932 2 teams	BOS	A (52G – .281)				DET	A (87G – .287)									
" total	139	530	151	28	9	8	1.5	72	78	64	33	1	.285	.417	1 0	OF-134, 1B-2
1933 2 teams	DET	A (6G – .273)				CHI	A (58G – .290)									
" total	64	118	34	5	0	1	0.8	17	11	19	13	0	.288	.356	30 8	OF-18, 1B-10
7 yrs.	649	2161	661	155	25	56	2.6	326	333	260	202	8	.306	.478	81 21	OF-536, 1B-12
1 yr.	58	107	31	5	0	1	0.9	16	8	16	13	0	.290	.364	28 8	OF-16, 1B-10

Skeeter Webb
WEBB, JAMES LAVERNE BR TR 5'9½" 150 lbs.
B. Nov. 4, 1909, Meridian, Miss.

1932 STL N	1	0	0	0	0	0	–	0	0	0	0	0	–	–	0 0	SS-1
1938 CLE A	20	58	16	2	0	0	0.0	11	2	8	7	1	.276	.310	0 0	SS-13, 3B-3, 2B-2
1939	81	269	71	14	1	2	0.7	28	26	15	24	1	.264	.346	0 0	SS-81
1940 CHI A	84	334	79	11	2	1	0.3	33	29	30	33	3	.237	.290	2 0	2B-74, SS-7, 3B-1
1941	29	84	16	2	0	0	0.0	7	6	3	9	1	.190	.214	3 1	2B-18, SS-5, 3B-3
1942	32	94	16	2	1	0	0.0	5	4	4	13	1	.170	.213	0 0	2B-29
1943	58	213	50	5	2	0	0.0	15	22	6	19	5	.235	.277	3 0	2B-54
1944	139	513	108	19	6	0	0.0	44	30	20	39	7	.211	.271	0 0	SS-135, 2B-5
1945 DET A	118	407	81	12	2	0	0.0	43	21	30	35	8	.199	.238	0 0	SS-104, 2B-11
1946	64	169	37	1	1	0	0.0	12	17	9	18	3	.219	.237	1 0	2B-50, SS-8
1947	50	79	16	3	0	0	0.0	13	6	7	9	3	.203	.241	2 0	2B-30, SS-6
1948 PHI A	23	54	8	2	0	0	0.0	5	3	0	9	0	.148	.185	0 0	2B-9, SS-8
12 yrs.	699	2274	498	73	15	3	0.1	216	166	132	215	33	.219	.268	11 1	SS-368, 2B-282, 3B-7
5 yrs.	342	1238	269	39	11	1	0.1	104	91	63	113	17	.217	.269	8 1	2B-180, SS-147, 3B-4

WORLD SERIES

1945 DET A	7	27	5	0	0	0	0.0	4	1	3	1	0	.185	.185	0 0	SS-7

Ralph Weigel
WEIGEL, RALPH RICHARD (Wig) BR TR 6'1" 180 lbs.
B. Oct. 2, 1921, Coldwater, Ohio

1946 CLE A	6	12	2	0	0	0	0.0	0	0	0	2	1	.167	.167	0 0	C-6
1948 CHI A	66	163	38	7	3	0	0.0	8	26	13	18	1	.233	.313	24 6	C-39, OF-2
1949 WAS A	34	60	14	2	0	0	0.0	4	4	8	6	0	.233	.267	12 2	C-21
3 yrs.	106	235	54	9	3	0	0.0	12	30	21	26	2	.230	.294	36 8	C-66, OF-2
1 yr.	66	163	38	7	3	0	0.0	8	26	13	18	1	.233	.313	24 6	C-39, OF-2

Al Weis
WEIS, ALBERT JOHN BB TR 6' 160 lbs.
B. Apr. 2, 1938, Franklin Square, N. Y. BR 1969

1962 CHI A	7	12	1	0	0	0	0.0	2	0	2	3	1	.083	.083	0 0	SS-4, 3B-1, 2B-1
1963	99	210	57	9	0	0	0.0	41	18	18	37	15	.271	.314	9 2	2B-48, SS-27, 3B-1
1964	133	328	81	4	4	2	0.6	36	23	22	41	22	.247	.302	6 1	2B-116, SS-9, OF-2
1965	103	135	40	4	3	1	0.7	29	12	12	22	4	.296	.393	6 2	2B-74, SS-7, OF-2, 3B-2
1966	129	187	29	4	1	0	0.0	20	9	17	50	3	.155	.187	0 0	2B-96, SS-18
1967	50	53	13	2	0	0	0.0	9	2	1	7	3	.245	.283	0 0	2B-32, SS-13
1968 NY N	90	274	47	9	0	1	0.4	15	14	21	63	3	.172	.204	3 0	SS-59, 2B-29, 3B-2
1969	103	247	53	9	2	2	0.8	20	23	15	51	2	.215	.291	3 0	SS-52, 2B-43, 3B-1
1970	75	121	25	7	1	1	0.8	20	11	7	21	1	.207	.306	2 0	2B-44, SS-15
1971	11	11	0	0	0	0	0.0	3	1	2	4	0	.000	.000	4 0	2B-5, 3B-2
10 yrs.	800	1578	346	45	11	7	0.4	195	115	117	299	55	.219	.275	33 5	2B-488, SS-204, 3B-9, OF-4
6 yrs.	521	925	221	23	8	3	0.3	137	66	72	160	48	.239	.291	21 5	2B-367, SS-78, OF-4, 3B-4

LEAGUE CHAMPIONSHIP SERIES

1969 NY N	3	1	0	0	0	0	0.0	0	0	0	0	0	.000	.000	0 0	2B-3

	G	AB	H	2B	3B	HR	HR%	R	RBI	BB	SO	SB	BA	SA	Pinch Hit AB	Pinch Hit H	G by POS

Al Weis continued
WORLD SERIES
| 1969 NY N | 5 | 11 | 5 | 0 | 0 | 1 | 9.1 | 1 | 3 | 4 | 2 | 0 | .455 | .727 | 0 | 0 | 2B-5 |

Mike Welday
WELDAY, LYNDON EARL
B. Dec. 19, 1879, Conway, Iowa   D. May 28, 1942, Leavenworth, Kans.   BL TL

1907 CHI A	24	35	8	1	1	0	0.0	2	0	6		0	.229	.314	6	1	OF-15
1909	29	74	14	0	0	0	0.0	3	5	4		2	.189	.189	8	2	OF-20
2 yrs.	53	109	22	1	1	0	0.0	5	5	10		2	.202	.229	14	3	OF-35
2 yrs.	53	109	22	1	1	0	0.0	5	5	10		2	.202	.229	14	3	OF-35

Leo Wells
WELLS, LEO DONALD
B. July 18, 1917, Kansas City, Kans.   BR TR 5'9" 170 lbs.

1942 CHI A	35	62	12	2	0	1	1.6	8	4	5	1	.194	.274	13	5	SS-12, 3B-6
1946	45	127	24	4	1	1	0.8	11	11	12	34	3	.189	.260	2	0	3B-38, SS-2
2 yrs.	80	189	36	6	1	2	1.1	19	15	16	39	4	.190	.265	15	5	3B-44, SS-14
2 yrs.	80	189	36	6	1	2	1.1	19	15	16	39	4	.190	.265	15	5	3B-44, SS-14

Sammy West
WEST, SAMUEL FILMORE
B. Oct. 5, 1904, Longview, Tex.   BL TL 5'11" 165 lbs.

1927 WAS A	38	67	16	4	1	0	0.0	9	6	8	8	1	.239	.328	19	4	OF-18
1928	125	378	114	30	7	3	0.8	59	40	20	23	5	.302	.442	7	0	OF-116
1929	142	510	136	16	8	3	0.6	60	75	45	41	9	.267	.347	3	1	OF-139
1930	120	411	135	22	10	6	1.5	75	67	37	34	5	.328	.474	0	0	OF-118
1931	132	526	175	43	13	3	0.6	77	91	30	37	6	.333	.481	0	0	OF-127
1932	146	554	159	27	12	6	1.1	88	83	48	57	4	.287	.412	3	0	OF-143
1933 STL A	133	517	155	25	12	11	2.1	93	48	59	49	10	.300	.458	6	1	OF-127
1934	122	482	157	22	10	9	1.9	90	55	62	55	3	.326	.469	2	0	OF-120
1935	138	527	158	37	4	10	1.9	93	70	75	46	1	.300	.442	3	0	OF-135
1936	152	533	148	26	4	7	1.3	78	70	94	70	2	.278	.381	3	0	OF-148
1937	122	457	150	37	4	7	1.5	68	58	46	28	1	.328	.473	14	3	OF-105
1938 2 teams	STL A (44G – .309)				WAS A (92G – .302)												
" total	136	509	155	27	7	6	1.2	68	74	47	30	2	.305	.420	9	2	OF-126
1939 WAS A	115	390	110	20	8	3	0.8	52	52	67	29	1	.282	.397	6	0	OF-89, 1B-17
1940	57	99	25	6	1	1	1.0	7	18	16	13	0	.253	.364	26	8	1B-12, OF-9
1941	26	37	10	0	0	0	0.0	3	6	11	2	1	.270	.270	12	4	OF-8
1942 CHI A	49	151	35	5	0	0	0.0	14	25	31	18	2	.232	.265	2	0	OF-45
16 yrs.	1753	6148	1838	347	101	75	1.2	934	838	696	540	53	.299	.425	115	26	OF-1573, 1B-29
1 yr.	49	151	35	5	0	0	0.0	14	25	31	18	2	.232	.265	2	0	OF-45

Don Wheeler
WHEELER, DONALD WESLEY (Scotty)
B. Sept. 29, 1922, Minneapolis, Miss.   BR TR 5'10" 175 lbs.

| 1949 CHI A | 67 | 192 | 46 | 9 | 2 | 1 | 0.5 | 17 | 22 | 27 | 19 | 2 | .240 | .323 | 8 | 1 | C-58 |

Doc White
WHITE, GUY HARRIS
B. Apr. 9, 1879, Washington, D. C.   D. Feb. 17, 1969, Silver Spring, Md.   BL TL 6'1" 150 lbs.

1901 PHI N	31	98	27	3	2	0	0.0	15	10	2		1	.276	.347	0	0	P-31, OF-1
1902	61	179	47	3	1	1	0.6	17	15	11		5	.263	.307	5	1	P-36, OF-19
1903 CHI A	38	99	20	3	0	0	0.0	10	5	19		1	.202	.232	0	0	P-37, OF-1
1904	33	76	12	2	0	0	0.0	7	2	10		3	.158	.184	0	0	P-30, OF-2
1905	37	86	14	4	1	0	0.0	7	7	4		1	.163	.233	0	0	P-36, OF-1
1906	28	65	12	1	1	0	0.0	11	3	13		3	.185	.231	0	0	P-28, OF-1
1907	48	90	20	1	0	0	0.0	12	2	12		2	.222	.233	0	0	P-46, OF-2
1908	51	109	25	1	0	0	0.0	12	10	12		4	.229	.239	6	1	P-41, OF-3
1909	72	192	45	1	5	0	0.0	24	7	33		7	.234	.292	8	1	OF-40, P-24
1910	56	126	25	1	2	0	0.0	14	8	14		2	.198	.238	8	0	P-33, OF-14
1911	39	78	20	1	1	0	0.0	12	6	7		1	.256	.295	0	0	P-34, 1B-2, OF-1
1912	33	56	7	1	0	0	0.0	5	0	7		0	.125	.179	1	0	P-32
1913	20	25	3	0	0	0	0.0	1	0	3	1	0	.120	.120	0	0	P-19, 1B-1
13 yrs.	547	1279	277	22	14	1	0.1	147	75	147	1	32	.217	.258	28	3	P-427, OF-85, 1B-3
11 yrs.	455	1002	203	16	11	0	0.0	115	50	134	1	26	.203	.241	23	2	P-360, OF-65, 1B-3

WORLD SERIES
| 1906 CHI A | 3 | 3 | 0 | 0 | 0 | 0 | 0.0 | 0 | 0 | 1 | 0 | 0 | .000 | .000 | 0 | 0 | P-3 |

Ed White
WHITE, EDWARD PERRY
B. Apr. 6, 1926, Anniston, Ala.   BR TR 6'2" 200 lbs.

| 1955 CHI A | 3 | 4 | 2 | 0 | 0 | 0 | 0.0 | 1 | 0 | 1 | 0 | .500 | .500 | 1 | 0 | OF-2 |

Frank Whitman
WHITMAN, WALTER FRANKLIN (Hooker)
B. Aug. 15, 1924, Marengo, Ind.   BR TR 6'2" 175 lbs.

1946 CHI A	17	16	1	0	0	0	0.0	7	1	2	6	0	.063	.063	0	0	SS-6, 2B-1, 1B-1
1948	3	6	0	0	0	0	0.0	0	0	3	0	.000	.000	2	0	SS-1
2 yrs.	20	22	1	0	0	0	0.0	7	1	2	9	0	.045	.045	2	0	SS-7, 2B-1, 1B-1
2 yrs.	20	22	1	0	0	0	0.0	7	1	2	9	0	.045	.045	2	0	SS-7, 2B-1, 1B-1

Walt Williams
WILLIAMS, WALTER ALLEN (No-Neck)
B. Dec. 19, 1943, Brownwood, Tex.   BR TR 5'6" 165 lbs.

1964 HOU N	10	9	0	0	0	0	0.0	0	2	1	.000	.000	2	0	OF-5
1967 CHI A	104	275	66	16	3	3	1.1	35	15	17	20	3	.240	.353	30	4	OF-73
1968	63	133	32	6	0	1	0.8	6	8	4	17	0	.241	.308	28	5	OF-34
1969	135	471	143	22	9	3	0.6	59	32	26	33	6	.304	.374	24	7	OF-111
1970	110	315	79	18	1	3	1.0	43	15	19	30	3	.251	.343	29	8	OF-79
1971	114	361	106	17	3	8	2.2	43	35	24	27	5	.294	.424	27	9	OF-90, 3B-1
1972	77	221	55	7	2	2	0.9	22	11	13	20	6	.249	.317	23	4	OF-57, 3B-1
1973 CLE A	104	350	101	15	1	8	2.3	43	38	14	29	9	.289	.406	17	4	OF-61, DH-26

	G	AB	H	2B	3B	HR	HR%	R	RBI	BB	SO	SB	BA	SA	Pinch Hit AB H	G by POS

Walt Williams continued
1974 NY A	43	53	6	0	0	0	0.0	5	3	1	10	1	.113	.113	15 1	OF-24, DH-3
1975	82	185	52	5	1	5	2.7	27	16	8	23	0	.281	.400	31 10	OF-31, DH-17, 2B-6
10 yrs.	842	2373	640	106	11	33	1.4	284	173	126	211	34	.270	.365	226 52	OF-565, DH-46, 2B-6, 3B-2
6 yrs.	603	1776	481	86	9	20	1.1	208	116	103	147	23	.271	.363	161 37 2nd 3rd	OF-444, 3B-2

Hugh Willingham
WILLINGHAM, THOMAS HUGH
B. May 30, 1908, Dalhart, Tex.
BR TR 6' 180 lbs.

1930 CHI A	3	4	1	0	0	0	0.0	2	0	2	1	0	.250	.250	2 1	2B-1
1931 PHI N	23	35	9	2	1	1	2.9	5	3	2	9	0	.257	.457	5 1	SS-8, 3B-2, OF-1
1932	4	2	0	0	0	0	0.0	0	0	0	0	0	.000	.000	2 0	
1933	1	1	0	0	0	0	0.0	0	0	0	0	0	.000	.000	1 0	
4 yrs.	31	42	10	2	1	1	2.4	7	3	4	10	0	.238	.405	10 2	SS-8, 3B-2, OF-1, 2B-1
1 yr.	3	4	1	0	0	0	0.0	2	0	2	1	0	.250	.250	2 1	2B-1

Kid Willson
WILLSON, FRANK HOXIE
B. Nov. 3, 1895, Bloomington, Neb. D. Apr. 17, 1964, Union Gap, Wash.
BL TR 6'1" 190 lbs.

1918 CHI A	4	1	0	0	0	0	0.0	2	0	1	1	0	.000	.000	1 0	
1927	7	10	1	0	0	0	0.0	1	1	0	2	0	.100	.100	4 0	OF-2
2 yrs.	11	11	1	0	0	0	0.0	3	1	1	3	0	.091	.091	5 0	OF-2
2 yrs.	11	11	1	0	0	0	0.0	3	1	1	3	0	.091	.091	5 0	OF-2

Bill Wilson
WILSON, WILLIAM DONALD
B. Nov. 6, 1928, Central City, Neb.
BR TR 6'2" 200 lbs.

1950 CHI A	3	6	0	0	0	0	0.0	0	0	2	2	0	.000	.000	0 0	OF-2
1953	9	17	1	0	0	0	0.0	1	1	0	7	0	.059	.059	4 0	OF-3
1954 2 teams	CHI A (20G – .171)			PHI A (94G – .238)												
" total	114	358	83	11	1	17	4.7	47	38	46	64	1	.232	.411	5 0	OF-110
1955 KC A	98	273	61	12	0	15	5.5	39	38	24	63	1	.223	.432	14 3	OF-82, P-1
4 yrs.	224	654	145	23	1	32	4.9	87	77	72	136	2	.222	.407	23 3	OF-197, P-1
3 yrs.	32	58	7	1	0	2	3.4	5	6	9	14	0	.121	.241	6 0	OF-24

Red Wilson
WILSON, ROBERT JAMES
B. Mar. 7, 1929, Milwaukee, Wis.
BR TR 5'10" 160 lbs.

1951 CHI A	4	11	3	1	0	0	0.0	1	0	1	2	0	.273	.364	0 0	C-4
1952	2	3	0	0	0	0	0.0	0	0	0	1	0	.000	.000	0 0	C-2
1953	71	164	41	6	1	0	0.0	21	10	26	12	2	.250	.299	7 1	C-63
1954 2 teams	CHI A (8G – .200)			DET A (54G – .282)												
" total	62	190	52	11	1	3	1.6	24	23	28	14	3	.274	.389	1 0	C-61
1955 DET A	78	241	53	9	0	2	0.8	26	17	26	23	1	.220	.282	8 1	C-72
1956	78	228	66	12	2	7	3.1	32	38	42	18	2	.289	.452	1 0	C-78
1957	59	178	43	8	1	3	1.7	21	13	24	19	2	.242	.348	0 0	C-59
1958	103	298	89	13	0	3	1.0	31	29	35	30	10	.299	.379	3 0	C-101
1959	67	228	60	17	2	4	1.8	28	35	10	23	2	.263	.408	3 0	C-64
1960 2 teams	DET A (45G – .216)			CLE A (32G – .216)												
" total	77	222	48	7	0	2	0.9	22	24	22	21	3	.216	.275	2 1	C-75
10 yrs.	601	1763	455	84	8	24	1.4	206	189	214	163	25	.258	.356	25 3	C-579
4 yrs.	85	198	48	7	1	1	0.5	24	11	28	17	2	.242	.303	7 1	C-77

Ted Wilson
WILSON, GEORGE WASHINGTON (Teddy)
B. Aug. 30, 1925, Cherryville, N. C. D. Oct. 29, 1974, Gastonia, N. C.
BL TR 6'1½" 185 lbs.

1952 2 teams	CHI A (8G – .111)			NY N (62G – .241)												
" total	70	121	28	7	0	2	1.7	9	17	4	16	0	.231	.339	48 12	OF-22, 1B-2
1953 NY N	11	8	1	0	0	0	0.0	0	0	2	2	0	.125	.125	8 1	
1956 2 teams	NY N (53G – .132)			NY A (11G – .167)												
" total	64	80	11	1	0	1	1.3	6	2	8	14	0	.138	.188	48 8	OF-14
3 yrs.	145	209	40	8	0	3	1.4	15	19	14	32	0	.191	.273	104 21	OF-36, 1B-2
1 yr.	8	9	1	0	0	0	0.0	0	1	1	2	0	.111	.111	7 1	OF-1

WORLD SERIES
1956 NY A	1	1	0	0	0	0	0.0	0	0	0	1	0	.000	.000	1 0	

Kettle Wirtz
WIRTZ, ELWOOD VERNON
B. Oct. 30, 1897, Edge Hill, Pa. D. July 12, 1968, Sacramento, Calif.
BR TR 5'11" 170 lbs.

1921 CHI N	7	11	2	0	0	0	0.0	0	1	0	3	0	.182	.182	2 2	C-5
1922	31	58	10	2	0	1	1.7	6	12	15	9	1	.172	.259	3 0	C-27
1923	5	5	1	0	0	0	0.0	2	1	2	0	0	.200	.200	0 0	C-3
1924 CHI A	6	12	1	0	0	0	0.0	0	2	2	1	0	.083	.083	0 0	C-5
4 yrs.	49	86	14	2	0	1	1.2	9	8	16	20	1	.163	.221	5 2	C-40
1 yr.	6	12	1	0	0	0	0.0	0	2	2	1	0	.083	.083	0 0	C-5

Polly Wolfe
WOLFE, ROY CHAMBERLAIN
B. Sept. 1, 1888, Knoxville, Ill. D. Nov. 21, 1938, Morris, Ill.
BL TR 5'10" 170 lbs.

1912 CHI A	1	1	0	0	0	0	0.0	0	0	0	0		.000	.000	1 0	
1914	9	28	6	0	0	0	0.0	0	3	6	0	1	.214	.214	1 0	OF-8
2 yrs.	10	29	6	0	0	0	0.0	0	3	6	1		.207	.207	2 0	OF-8
2 yrs.	10	29	6	0	0	0	0.0	0	3	6	1		.207	.207	2 0	OF-8

Ceylon Wright
WRIGHT, EDWARD YATMAN
B. Chicago, Ill.
BL TR 5'9" 150 lbs.

1916 CHI A	8	18	0	0	0	0	0.0	0	0	1	7	0	.000	.000	0 0	SS-8

Player Register

	G	AB	H	2B	3B	HR	HR%	R	RBI	BB	SO	SB	BA	SA	Pinch Hit AB	H	G by POS

Glenn Wright
WRIGHT, FORREST GLENN (Buckshot)
B. Feb. 6, 1901, Archie, Mo.
BR TR 5'11" 170 lbs.

Year	Team	G	AB	H	2B	3B	HR	HR%	R	RBI	BB	SO	SB	BA	SA	PH AB	H	G by POS
1924	PIT N	153	616	177	28	18	7	1.1	80	111	27	52	14	.287	.425	0	0	SS-153
1925		153	614	189	32	10	18	2.9	97	121	31	32	3	.308	.480	0	0	SS-153, 3B-1
1926		119	458	141	15	15	8	1.7	73	77	19	26	6	.308	.459	3	0	SS-116
1927		143	570	160	26	4	9	1.6	78	105	39	46	4	.281	.388	0	0	SS-143
1928		108	407	126	20	8	8	2.0	63	66	21	53	3	.310	.457	6	1	SS-101, OF-1, 1B-1
1929	BKN N	24	25	5	0	0	1	4.0	4	6	3	6	0	.200	.320	17	2	SS-3
1930		135	532	171	2b	12	22	4.1	83	126	32	70	2	.321	.543	1	0	SS-134
1931		77	268	76	9	4	9	3.4	36	32	14	35	1	.284	.448	2	0	SS-75
1932		127	446	122	31	5	10	2.2	50	60	12	57	4	.274	.433	4	0	SS-122, 1B-2
1933		71	192	49	13	0	1	0.5	19	18	11	24	1	.255	.339	9	2	SS-51, 1B-9, 3B-2
1935	CHI A	9	25	3	1	0	0	0.0	1	1	0	6	0	.120	.160	2	0	2B-7
11 yrs.		1119	4153	1219	203	76	93	2.2	584	723	209	407	38	.294	.446	44	5	SS-1051, 1B-12, 2B-7, 3B-3, OF-1
1 yr.		9	25	3	1	0	0	0.0	1	1	0	6	0	.120	.160	2	0	2B-7

WORLD SERIES

Year	Team	G	AB	H	2B	3B	HR	HR%	R	RBI	BB	SO	SB	BA	SA	PH AB	H	G by POS
1925	PIT N	7	27	5	1	0	1	3.7	3	3	1	4	0	.'85	.333	0	0	SS-7
1927		4	13	2	0	0	0	0.0	1	2	0	0	0	.154	.154	0	0	SS-4
2 yrs.		11	40	7	1	0	1	2.5	4	5	1	4	0	.175	.275	0	0	SS-11

Taffy Wright
WRIGHT, TAFT SHEDRON
B. Aug. 10, 1911, Tabor City, N. C. D. Oct. 22, 1981, Orlando, Fla.
BL TR 5'10" 180 lbs.

Year	Team	G	AB	H	2B	3B	HR	HR%	R	RBI	BB	SO	SB	BA	SA	PH AB	H	G by POS
1938	WAS A	100	263	92	18	10	2	0.8	37	36	13	17	1	.350	.517	39	13	OF-60
1939		129	499	154	29	11	4	0.8	77	93	38	19	1	.309	.435	6	3	OF-123
1940	CHI A	147	581	196	31	9	5	0.9	79	88	43	25	4	.337	.448	2	1	OF-144
1941		136	513	165	35	5	10	1.9	71	97	60	27	5	.322	.468	1	0	OF-134
1942		85	300	100	13	5	0	0.0	43	47	48	9	1	.333	.410	4	1	OF-81
1946		115	422	116	19	4	7	1.7	46	52	42	17	10	.275	.389	7	2	OF-107
1947		124	401	130	13	0	4	1.0	48	54	48	17	8	.324	.387	18	3	OF-100
1948		134	455	127	15	6	4	0.9	50	61	39	18	2	.279	.365	19	6	OF-114
1949	PHI A	59	149	35	2	5	2	1.3	14	25	16	6	0	.235	.356	19	3	OF-35
9 yrs.		1029	3583	1115	175	55	38	1.1	465	553	347	155	32	.311	.423	115	32	OF-898
6 yrs.		741	2672	834	126	29	30	1.1	337	399	280	113	30	.312	.415	51	13	OF-680
															7th			

Tom Wright
WRIGHT, THOMAS EVERETTE
B. Sept. 22, 1923, Shelby, N. C.
BL TR 5'11½" 180 lbs.

Year	Team	G	AB	H	2B	3B	HR	HR%	R	RBI	BB	SO	SB	BA	SA	PH AB	H	G by POS
1948	BOS A	3	2	1	0	1	0	0.0	1	0	0	0	0	.500	1.500	2	1	
1949		5	4	1	0	0	0	0.0	0	1	1	1	0	.250	.500	4	1	
1950		54	107	34	7	0	0	0.0	17	20	6	18	0	.318	.383	28	7	OF-24
1951		28	63	14	1	1	1	1.6	8	9	11	8	0	.222	.317	10	1	OF-18
1952	2 teams	STL A (29G – .242)							CHI A (60G – .258)									
"	total	89	198	50	10	2	2	1.0	21	27	28	36	2	.253	.354	34	10	OF-52
1953	CHI A	77	132	33	5	3	2	1.5	14	25	12	21	0	.250	.379	42	13	OF-33
1954	WAS A	76	171	42	4	4	1	0.6	13	17	18	38	0	.246	.333	32	8	OF-43
1955		7	7	0	0	0	0	0.0	1	0	1	0	0	.000	.000	7	0	
1956		2	1	0	0	0	0	0.0	0	0	0	1	0	.000	.000	1	0	
9 yrs.		341	685	175	28	11	6	0.9	75	99	76	123	2	.255	.355	160	41	OF-170
2 yrs.		137	264	67	15	5	3	1.1	29	46	28	37	1	.254	.383	65	21	OF-67

Early Wynn
WYNN, EARLY (Gus)
B. Jan. 6, 1920, Hartford, Ala.
Hall of Fame 1971.
BB TR 6' 190 lbs.
BR 1939-44

Year	Team	G	AB	H	2B	3B	HR	HR%	R	RBI	BB	SO	SB	BA	SA	PH AB	H	G by POS
1939	WAS A	3	6	1	0	0	0	0.0	0	1	1	1	0	.167	.167	0	0	P-3
1941		5	15	2	1	0	0	0.0	1	0	0	5	0	.133	.200	0	0	P-5
1942		30	69	15	2	0	0	0.0	4	7	3	13	0	.217	.246	0	0	P-30
1943		38	98	29	3	1	0	1.0	6	11	1	11	0	.296	.378	1	0	P-37
1944		43	92	19	2	0	1	1.1	4	6	3	21	0	.207	.261	11	1	P-33
1946		25	47	15	2	0	1	2.1	4	9	5	7	0	.319	.426	6	3	P-17
1947		54	120	33	6	0	2	1.7	6	13	1	19	0	.275	.375	20	6	P-33
1948		73	106	23	3	1	0	0.0	9	16	14	22	0	.217	.264	32	3	P-33
1949	CLE A	35	70	10	1	0	1	1.4	3	7	4	10	0	.143	.200	7	0	P-26
1950		39	77	18	5	1	2	2.6	12	10	10	12	0	.234	.403	5	1	P-32
1951		41	108	20	8	1	1	0.9	8	13	7	9	0	.185	.306	3	0	P-37
1952		44	99	22	2	0	0	0.0	5	10	9	15	0	.222	.242	2	1	P-42
1953		37	91	25	2	0	3	3.3	11	10	7	17	0	.275	.396	1	0	P-36
1954		40	93	17	3	0	0	0.0	10	4	7	13	0	.183	.215	0	0	P-40
1955		34	84	15	3	0	1	1.2	8	7	6	17	0	.179	.250	2	0	P-32
1956		38	101	23	5	0	1	1.0	5	15	7	22	1	.228	.307	0	0	P-38
1957		40	86	10	0	0	0	0.0	4	4	11	23	0	.116	.116	0	0	P-40
1958	CHI A	40	75	15	1	0	0	0.0	7	11	10	25	0	.200	.213	0	0	P-40
1959		37	90	22	7	0	2	2.2	11	8	9	18	0	.244	.389	0	0	P-37
1960		36	75	15	2	0	1	1.3	8	7	14	17	0	.200	.293	0	0	P-36
1961		17	37	6	0	0	0	0.0	4	2	3	11	0	.162	.162	0	0	P-17
1962		27	54	7	1	0	0	0.0	5	2	7	17	0	.130	.148	0	0	P-27
1963	CLE A	20	11	3	0	0	0	0.0	1	0	2	5	0	.273	.273	0	0	P-20
23 yrs.		796	1704	365	59	5	17	1.0	136	173	141	330	1	.214	.285	90	15	P-691
5 yrs.		157	331	65	11	1	3	0.9	35	30	43	88	0	.196	.263	0	0	P-157

WORLD SERIES

Year	Team	G	AB	H	2B	3B	HR	HR%	R	RBI	BB	SO	SB	BA	SA	PH AB	H	G by POS
1954	CLE A	1	2	1	1	0	0	0.0	0	0	0	1	0	.500	1.000	0	0	P-1
1959	CHI A	3	5	1	1	0	0	0.0	0	1	0	2	0	.200	.400	0	0	P-3
2 yrs.		4	7	2	2	0	0	0.0	0	1	0	3	0	.286	.571	0	0	P-4

Player Register

	G	AB	H	2B	3B	HR	HR%	R	RBI	BB	SO	SB	BA	SA	Pinch Hit AB	H	G by POS

Hugh Yancy
YANCY, HUGH JR
B. Oct. 16, 1949, Sarasota, Fla.   BR TR 5'11" 170 lbs.

	G	AB	H	2B	3B	HR	HR%	R	RBI	BB	SO	SB	BA	SA	PH-AB	PH-H	G by POS
1972 CHI A	3	9	1	0	0	0	0.0	0	0	0	0	0	.111	.111	0	0	3B-3
1974	1	0	0	0	0	0	–	0	0	0	0	0	–	–	0	0	DH-1
1976	3	10	1	1	0	0	0.0	0	0	0	3	0	.100	.200	0	0	2B-3
3 yrs.	7	19	2	1	0	0	0.0	0	0	0	3	0	.105	.158	0	0	3B-3, 2B-3, DH-1
3 yrs.	7	19	2	1	0	0	0.0	0	0	0	3	0	.105	.158	0	0	3B-3, 2B-3, DH-1

George Yankowski
YANKOWSKI, GEORGE EDWARD
B. Nov. 19, 1922, Cambridge, Mass.   BR TR 6' 180 lbs.

	G	AB	H	2B	3B	HR	HR%	R	RBI	BB	SO	SB	BA	SA	PH-AB	PH-H	G by POS
1942 PHI A	6	13	2	1	0	0	0.0	0	2	0	2	0	.154	.231	0	0	C-6
1949 CHI A	12	18	3	1	0	0	0.0	0	2	0	2	0	.167	.222	6	0	C-6
2 yrs.	18	31	5	2	0	0	0.0	0	4	0	4	0	.161	.226	6	0	C-12
1 yr.	12	18	3	1	0	0	0.0	0	2	0	2	0	.167	.222	6	0	C-6

Yam Yaryan
YARYAN, CLARENCE EVERETT
B. Nov. 5, 1893, Knowlton, Iowa   D. Nov. 16, 1964, Birmingham, Ala.   BR TR 5'10½" 180 lbs.

	G	AB	H	2B	3B	HR	HR%	R	RBI	BB	SO	SB	BA	SA	PH-AB	PH-H	G by POS
1921 CHI A	45	102	31	8	2	0	0.0	11	15	9	16	0	.304	.422	10	1	C-34
1922	36	71	14	2	0	2	2.8	9	9	6	10	1	.197	.310	8	0	C-25
2 yrs.	81	173	45	10	2	2	1.2	20	24	15	26	1	.260	.376	18	1	C-59
2 yrs.	81	173	45	10	2	2	1.2	20	24	15	26	1	.260	.376	18	1	C-59

Rudy York
YORK, RUDOLPH PRESTON
B. Aug. 17, 1913, Ragland, Ala.   D. Feb. 2, 1970, Rome, Ga.   BR TR 6'1" 209 lbs.
Manager 1959.

	G	AB	H	2B	3B	HR	HR%	R	RBI	BB	SO	SB	BA	SA	PH-AB	PH-H	G by POS
1934 DET A	3	6	1	0	0	0	0.0	0	0	1	3	0	.167	.167	2	1	C-2
1937	104	375	115	18	3	35	9.3	72	103	41	52	3	.307	.651	7	1	C-54, 3B-41
1938	135	463	138	27	2	33	7.1	85	127	92	74	1	.298	.579	3	0	C-116, OF-14, 1B-1
1939	102	329	101	16	1	20	6.1	66	68	41	50	5	.307	.544	16	2	C-67, 1B-19
1940	155	588	186	46	6	33	5.6	105	134	89	88	3	.316	.583	0	0	1B-155
1941	155	590	153	29	3	27	4.6	91	111	92	88	3	.259	.456	0	0	1B-155
1942	153	577	150	26	4	21	3.6	81	90	73	71	3	.260	.428	1	1	1B-152
1943	155	571	155	22	11	34	6.0	90	118	84	88	5	.271	.527	0	0	1B-155
1944	151	583	161	27	7	18	3.1	77	98	68	73	5	.276	.439	0	0	1B-151
1945	155	595	157	25	5	18	3.0	71	87	59	85	6	.264	.413	0	0	1B-155
1946 BOS A	154	579	160	30	6	17	2.9	78	119	86	93	3	.276	.437	0	0	1B-154
1947 2 teams	BOS A (48G – .212)						CHI A (102G – .243)											
" total	150	584	136	25	4	21	3.6	56	91	58	87	1	.233	.397	0	0	1B-150
1948 PHI A	31	51	8	0	0	0	0.0	4	6	7	15	0	.157	.157	18	2	1B-14
13 yrs.	1603	5891	1621	291	52	277	4.7	876	1152	791	867	38	.275	.483	47	7	1B-1261, C-239, 3B-41, OF-14
1 yr.	102	400	97	18	4	15	3.8	40	64	36	55	1	.243	.420	0	0	1B-102

WORLD SERIES

	G	AB	H	2B	3B	HR	HR%	R	RBI	BB	SO	SB	BA	SA	PH-AB	PH-H	G by POS
1940 DET A	7	26	6	0	1	1	3.8	3	2	4	7	0	.231	.423	0	0	1B-7
1945	7	28	5	1	0	0	0.0	1	3	3	4	0	.179	.214	0	0	1B-7
1946 BOS A	7	23	6	1	1	2	8.7	6	5	6	4	0	.261	.652	0	0	1B-7
3 yrs.	21	77	17	2	2	3	3.9	10	10	13	15	0	.221	.416	0	0	1B-21

Al Zarilla
ZARILLA, ALLEN LEE (Zeke)
B. May 1, 1919, Los Angeles, Calif.   BL TR 5'11" 180 lbs.

	G	AB	H	2B	3B	HR	HR%	R	RBI	BB	SO	SB	BA	SA	PH-AB	PH-H	G by POS
1943 STL A	70	228	58	7	1	2	0.9	27	17	17	20	1	.254	.320	11	4	OF-60
1944	100	288	86	13	6	6	2.1	43	45	29	33	1	.299	.448	15	2	OF-79
1946	125	371	96	14	9	4	1.1	46	43	27	37	3	.259	.377	15	5	OF-107
1947	127	380	85	15	6	3	0.8	34	38	40	45	3	.224	.318	16	0	OF-110
1948	144	529	174	39	3	12	2.3	77	74	48	48	11	.329	.482	9	3	OF-136
1949 2 teams	STL A (15G – .250)						BOS A (124G – .281)											
" total	139	530	147	33	4	10	1.9	78	77	56	53	5	.277	.411	2	0	OF-137
1950 BOS A	130	471	153	32	10	9	1.9	92	74	76	47	2	.325	.493	1	0	OF-128
1951 CHI A	120	382	98	21	0	10	2.6	56	60	57	52	2	.257	.401	3	0	OF-117
1952 3 teams	CHI A (39G – .232)						STL A (48G – .238)						BOS A (21G – .183)					
" total	108	289	65	10	2	5	1.7	43	24	48	29	5	.225	.325	18	1	OF-86
1953 BOS A	57	67	13	2	0	0	0.0	11	4	14	13	0	.194	.224	30	4	OF-18
10 yrs.	1120	3535	975	186	43	61	1.7	507	456	415	382	33	.276	.405	120	15	OF-978
2 yrs.	159	481	121	25	3	12	2.5	70	67	74	63	3	.252	.391	9	0	OF-149

WORLD SERIES

	G	AB	H	2B	3B	HR	HR%	R	RBI	BB	SO	SB	BA	SA	PH-AB	PH-H	G by POS
1944 STL A	4	10	1	0	0	0	0.0	1	1	0	4	0	.100	.100	2	0	OF-3

Rollie Zeider
ZEIDER, ROLLIE HUBERT (Bunions)
B. Nov. 16, 1883, Auburn, Ind.   D. Sept. 12, 1967, Garrett, Ind.   BR TR 5'10" 162 lbs.

	G	AB	H	2B	3B	HR	HR%	R	RBI	BB	SO	SB	BA	SA	PH-AB	PH-H	G by POS
1910 CHI A	136	498	108	9	2	0	0.0	57	31	62		49	.217	.243	0	0	2B-87, SS-45, 3B-4
1911	73	217	55	3	0	2	0.9	39	21	29		28	.253	.295	8	4	1B-29, SS-17, 3B-10, 2B-9
1912	129	420	103	12	10	1	0.2	57	42	50		47	.245	.329	3	1	1B-66, 3B-56, SS-1
1913 2 teams	CHI A (13G – .350)						NY A (49G – .233)											
" total	62	179	44	2	0	0	0.0	19	14	29	10	6	.246	.257	2	0	SS-23, 2B-20, 3B-8, 1B-7
1914 CHI F	119	452	124	13	2	1	0.2	60	36	44		35	.274	.319	1	0	3B-117, SS-1
1915	129	494	112	22	2	0	0.0	65	34	43		16	.227	.279	0	0	2B-83, 3B-30, SS-21
1916 CHI N	98	345	81	11	2	1	0.3	29	22	26	26	9	.235	.287	1	0	3B-55, 3B-26, 2B-33, OF-7, SS-5, 1B-2
1917	108	354	86	14	2	0	0.0	36	27	28	30	17	.243	.294	15	2	SS-48, 3B-26, 2B-24, OF-1, 1B-1
1918	82	251	56	3	2	0	0.0	31	26	23	20	16	.223	.251	7	1	2B-79, 3B-1, 1B-1
9 yrs.	936	3210	769	89	22	5	0.2	393	253	334	86	223	.240	.286	37	8	2B-335, 3B-307, SS-161, 1B-106, OF-8
4 yrs.	351	1155	273	24	12	3	0.3	157	96	145	1	127	.236	.286	12	5	1B-98, 2B-97, 3B-76, SS-63

WORLD SERIES

	G	AB	H	2B	3B	HR	HR%	R	RBI	BB	SO	SB	BA	SA	PH-AB	PH-H	G by POS
1918 CHI N	2	0	0	0	0	0	–	0	0	2	0	0	–	–	0	0	3B-2

	G	AB	H	2B	3B	HR	HR%	R	RBI	BB	SO	SB	BA	SA	Pinch Hit AB	H	G by POS

Gus Zernial

ZERNIAL, GUS EDWARD (Ozark Ike) BR TR 6'2½" 210 lbs.
B. June 27, 1923, Beaumont, Tex.

Year	Team	Lg	G	AB	H	2B	3B	HR	HR%	R	RBI	BB	SO	SB	BA	SA	PH AB	PH H	G by POS
1949	CHI	A	73	198	63	17	2	5	2.5	29	38	15	26	0	.318	.500	25	8	OF-46
1950			143	543	152	16	4	29	5.3	75	93	38	110	0	.280	.484	5	1	OF-137
1951	2 teams		CHI	A (4G – .105)			PHI	A (139G – .274)											
"	total		143	571	153	30	5	33	5.8	92	129	63	101	2	.268	.511	1	1	OF-142
1952	PHI	A	145	549	144	15	1	29	5.3	76	100	70	87	5	.262	.452	3	1	OF-141
1953			147	556	158	21	3	42	7.6	85	108	57	79	4	.284	.559	4	3	OF-141
1954			97	336	84	8	2	14	4.2	42	62	30	60	0	.250	.411	6	2	OF-90, 1B-2
1955	KC	A	120	413	105	9	3	30	7.3	62	84	30	90	1	.254	.508	17	2	OF-103
1956			109	272	61	12	0	16	5.9	36	44	33	66	2	.224	.445	35	4	OF-69
1957			131	437	103	20	1	27	6.2	56	69	34	84	1	.236	.471	17	4	OF-113, 1B-1
1958	DET	A	66	124	40	7	1	5	4.0	8	23	6	25	0	.323	.516	38	15	OF-24
1959			60	132	30	4	0	7	5.3	11	26	7	27	0	.227	.417	27	6	1B-32, OF-1
11 yrs.			1234	4131	1093	159	22	237	5.7	572	776	383	755	15	.265	.486	178	47	OF-1007, 1B-35
3 yrs.			220	760	217	33	6	34	4.5	106	135	55	138	0	.286	.479	30	9	OF-187

Richie Zisk

ZISK, RICHARD WALTER BR TR 6'1" 200 lbs.
B. Feb. 6, 1949, Brooklyn, N.Y.

Year	Team	Lg	G	AB	H	2B	3B	HR	HR%	R	RBI	BB	SO	SB	BA	SA	PH AB	PH H	G by POS
1971	PIT	N	7	15	3	1	0	1	6.7	2	2	4	7	0	.200	.467	1	0	OF-6
1972			17	37	7	3	0	0	0.0	4	4	7	10	0	.189	.270	5	1	OF-12
1973			103	333	108	23	7	10	3.0	44	54	21	63	0	.324	.526	19	4	OF-84
1974			149	536	168	30	3	17	3.2	75	100	65	91	1	.313	.476	9	4	OF-141
1975			147	504	146	27	3	20	4.0	69	75	68	109	0	.290	.474	6	0	OF-140
1976			155	581	168	35	2	21	3.6	91	89	52	96	1	.289	.465	3	2	OF-152
1977	CHI	A	141	531	154	17	6	30	5.6	78	101	55	98	0	.290	.514	3	0	OF-109, DH-28
1978	TEX	A	140	511	134	19	1	22	4.3	68	85	58	76	3	.262	.432	1	0	OF-90, DH-49
1979			144	503	132	21	1	18	3.6	69	64	57	75	1	.262	.416	7	2	OF-134, DH-3
1980			135	448	130	17	1	19	4.2	48	77	39	72	0	.290	.460	19	3	DH-86, OF-37
1981	SEA	A	94	357	111	12	1	16	4.5	42	43	28	63	0	.311	.485	1	0	DH-93
1982			131	503	147	28	1	21	4.2	61	62	49	89	2	.292	.477	0	0	DH-130
1983			90	285	69	12	0	12	4.2	30	36	30	61	0	.242	.411	10	2	DH-84
13 yrs.			1453	5144	1477	245	26	207	4.0	681	792	533	910	8	.287	.466	84	18	OF-905, DH-473
1 yr.			141	531	154	17	6	30	5.6	78	101	55	98	0	.290	.514	3	0	OF-109, DH-28

LEAGUE CHAMPIONSHIP SERIES

Year	Team	Lg	G	AB	H	2B	3B	HR	HR%	R	RBI	BB	SO	SB	BA	SA	PH AB	PH H	G by POS
1974	PIT	N	3	10	3	0	0	0	0.0	1	0	0	3	0	.300	.300	1	1	OF-2
1975			3	10	5	1	0	0	0.0	0	0	2	2	0	.500	.600	0	0	OF-3
2 yrs.			6	20	8	1	0	0	0.0	1	0	2	5	0	.400	.450	1	1	OF-5

Dutch Zwilling

ZWILLING, EDWARD HARRISON BL TL 5'6½" 160 lbs.
B. Nov. 2, 1888, St. Louis, Mo. D. Mar. 27, 1978, La Crescenta, Calif.

Year	Team	Lg	G	AB	H	2B	3B	HR	HR%	R	RBI	BB	SO	SB	BA	SA	PH AB	PH H	G by POS
1910	CHI	A	27	87	16	5	0	0	0.0	7	5	11		1	.184	.241	0	0	OF-27
1914	CHI	F	154	592	185	38	8	15	2.5	91	95	46		21	.313	.480	0	0	OF-154
1915			150	548	157	32	7	13	2.4	65	94	67		24	.286	.442	1	0	OF-148, 1B-3
1916	CHI	N	35	53	6	1	0	1	1.9	4	8	4	6	0	.113	.189	23	4	OF-10
4 yrs.			366	1280	364	76	15	29	2.3	167	202	128	6	46	.284	.435	24	4	OF-339, 1B-3
1 yr.			27	87	16	5	0	0	0.0	7	5	11		1	.184	.241	0	0	OF-27

Pitcher Register

The Pitcher Register is an alphabetical list of every man who pitched in the major leagues and played or managed for the Chicago White Sox from 1901 through today. Included are lifetime totals of League Championship Series and World Series.

The player and team information for the Pitcher Register is the same as that for the Player Register explained on page 211.

	W	L	PCT	ERA	G	GS	CG	IP	H	BB	SO	ShO	Relief Pitching W	L	SV	BATTING AB	H	HR	BA

John Doe

DOE, JOHN LEE (Slim) TR 6'2" 165 lbs.
Played as John Cherry part of 1900.
Born John Lee Doughnut. Brother of Bill Doe.
B. Jan. 1, 1850, New York, N.Y. D. July 1, 1955, New York, N.Y.
Hall of Fame 1946.

Year	Team	Lg	W	L	PCT	ERA	G	GS	CG	IP	H	BB	SO	ShO	RP W	RP L	SV	AB	H	HR	BA
1884	STL	U	4	2	.667	3.40	26	0	0	54.2	41	38	40	0	1	0	0	4	0	0	.000
1885	LOU	AA	14	10	.583	4.12	40	19	10	207.2	193	76	70	0	1	0	1	16	2	0	.111
1886	CLE	N	10	5	.667	4.08	40	8	4	117	110	55	77	0	0	1	0	10	0	0	.000
1887	BOS	N	9	3	.750	3.38	27	5	2	88	90	36	34	0	2	2	5	44	3	0	.214
1888	NY	N	13	4	.765	4.17	39	4	0	110	121	50	**236**	0	0	0	0	3	0	0	—
1889	3 teams				DET N (10G 4–2)			PIT N (2G 0–0)			PHI N (10G 4–0)										
"	total		8	2	.800	4.25	22	2	2	91.1	90	41	43	0	2	1	10	37	1	0	.036
1890	NY	P	13	6	.684	4.43	38	0	0	61.1	57	28	30	0	4	4	8	45	0	0	.000
1900	CHI	N	18	4	.818	3.71	35	1	0	63.1	58	15	23	0	4	2	3	42	2	0	.027
1901	BAL	A	18	4	.818	1.98	35	0	0	77.1	68	40	29	0	0	2	0	38	10	0	.132
1906	CHI	A	14	10	.583	2.78	31	0	0	58	66	23	24	0	0	0	1	32	3	0	.057
1907			13	4	.765	2.51	37	0	0	68	44	30	31	0	0	1	0	31	1	0	.500
1908			0	0	—	3.38	1	1	0	8	8	1	14	0	1	2	3	25	0	0	.000
1914	CHI	F	3	1	.750	2.78	6	0	0	54.2	41	28	9	0	1	0	1	41	2	0	.400
13 yrs.			137	55	.714	3.50	377	40	18	1059.1	987	461	647	0	16	18	32 8th	*			
3 yrs.			27	14	.659	2.96	69	1	0	134	118	54	56	0	5	5	3	79	25	1	.316

LEAGUE CHAMPIONSHIP SERIES

Year	Team	Lg	W	L	PCT	ERA	G	GS	CG	IP	H	BB	SO	ShO	RP W	RP L	SV	AB	H	HR	BA
1901	BAL	A	1	1	.500	4.76	4	0	0	22.2	26	8	16	8	0	0	0	0	0	0	—

WORLD SERIES

Year	Team	Lg	W	L	PCT	ERA	G	GS	CG	IP	H	BB	SO	ShO	RP W	RP L	SV	AB	H	HR	BA
1901	BAL	A	2	0	1.000	1.00	2	2	2	18	14	7	31	0	0	0	1	7	1	0	.143
1908	STL	N	2	0	.500	2.30	4	4	3	30	20	3	24	0	0	0	0	4	1	0	.250
2 yrs.			4	0	1.000	1.15	6	6	5	48	34	10	55 9th	0	0	0	1	11	2	0	.182

COLUMN HEADINGS INFORMATION

	W	L	PCT	ERA	G	GS	CG	IP	H	BB	SO	ShO	Relief Pitching W	L	SV	BATTING AB	H	HR	BA

Total Pitching (including all starting and relief appearances)

W	Wins		*Relief Pitching*
L	Losses		
PCT	Winning Percentage	W	Wins
ERA	Earned Run Average	L	Losses
G	Games Pitched	SV	Saves
GS	Games Started		
CG	Complete Games		*Batting*
IP	Innings Pitched		
H	Hits Allowed	AB	At Bats
BB	Bases on Balls Allowed	H	Hits
SO	Strikeouts	HR	Home Runs
ShO	Shutouts	BA	Batting Average

Partial Innings Pitched. These are shown in the Innings Pitched column, and are indicated by a ".1" or ".2" after the total. Doe, for example, pitched 54²/₃ innings in 1884.

All-Time Single Season Leaders. (Starts with 1893, the first year that the pitcher's box was moved to its present distance of 60 feet 6 inches.) Indicated by the small number that appears next to the statistic. Doe, for example, is shown by a small number "1" next to his earned run average in 1901. This means he is first on the all-time major league list for having the lowest earned run average in a single season. All pitchers who tied for first are also shown by the same number.

Meaningless Averages. Indicated by the use of a dash (—). In the case of Doe, a dash is shown for his 1908 winning percentage. This means that although he pitched in one game he never had a decision. A percentage of .000 would mean that he had at least one loss.

Estimated Earned Run Averages. Any time an earned run average appears in italics, it indicates that not all the earned runs allowed by the pitcher are known, and the information had to be estimated. Doe's 1885 earned run average, for example, appears in italics. It is known that Doe's team, Louisville, allowed 560 runs in 112 games. Of these games, it is known that in 90 of them Louisville allowed 420 runs of which 315 or 75% were earned. Doe pitched 207²/₃ innings in 40 games and allowed 134 runs. In 35 of these games, it is known that he allowed 118 runs of which 83 were earned. By multiplying the team's known ratio of earned runs to total runs (75%), by Doe's 16 (134 minus 118) remaining runs allowed, a figure of 12 additional estimated earned runs is calculated. This means that Doe allowed an estimated total of 95 earned runs in 207²/₃ innings, for an estimated earned run average of 4.12. In all cases at least 50% of the runs allowed by the team were "known" as a basis for estimating earned run averages. (Any time the symbol "infinity" (∞) is shown for a pitcher's earned run average, it means that the pitcher allowed one or more earned runs during a season without retiring a batter.)

Batting Statistics. Because a pitcher's batting statistics are of relatively minor importance—and the Designated Hitter rule may eliminate pitchers' batting entirely—only the most significant statistics are given; number of hits, home runs, and batting average.

An asterisk (*) shown in the lifetime batting totals means that the pitcher's complete year-by-year and lifetime batting record is listed in the Player Register.

Pitcher Register

	W	L	PCT	ERA	G	GS	CG	IP	H	BB	SO	ShO	Relief Pitching W L SV	BATTING AB H HR	BA

Fritz Ackley
ACKLEY, FLORIAN FREDERICK BL TR 6'1½" 202 lbs.
B. Apr. 10, 1937, Hayward, Wis.

	W	L	PCT	ERA	G	GS	CG	IP	H	BB	SO	ShO	W	L	SV	AB	H	HR	BA
1963 CHI A	1	0	1.000	2.08	2	2	0	13	7	7	11	0	0	0	0	5	1	0	.200
1964	0	0	—	8.53	3	2	0	6.1	10	4	6	0	0	0	0	1	1	0	1.000
2 yrs.	1	0	1.000	4.19	5	4	0	19.1	17	11	17	0	0	0	0	6	2	0	.333
2 yrs.	1	0	1.000	4.19	5	4	0	19.1	17	11	17	0	0	0	0	6	2	0	.333

Cecilio Acosta
ACOSTA, CECILIO (Cy) BR TR 5'10" 165 lbs.
B. Nov. 22, 1946, El Sabino, Mexico

	W	L	PCT	ERA	G	GS	CG	IP	H	BB	SO	ShO	W	L	SV	AB	H	HR	BA
1972 CHI A	3	0	1.000	1.56	26	0	0	34.2	25	17	28	0	3	0	5	4	0	0	.000
1973	10	6	.625	2.23	48	0	0	97	66	39	60	0	10	6	18	1	0	0	.000
1974	0	3	.000	3.72	27	0	0	46	43	18	19	0	0	3	3	2	0	0	.000
1975 PHI N	0	0	—	6.00	6	0	0	9	9	3	2	0	0	0	1	0	0	0	—
4 yrs.	13	9	.591	2.65	107	0	0	186.2	143	77	109	0	13	9	27	7	0	0	.000
3 yrs.	13	9	.591	2.48	101	0	0	177.2	134	74	107	0	13	9	26	7	0	0	.000

Jose Acosta
ACOSTA, JOSE BR TR 5'7" 140 lbs.
B. Mar. 4, 1894, Havana, Cuba

	W	L	PCT	ERA	G	GS	CG	IP	H	BB	SO	ShO	W	L	SV	AB	H	HR	BA
1920 WAS A	5	4	.556	4.03	17	5	4	82.2	92	26	9	1	2	2	1	25	6	0	.240
1921	5	4	.556	4.36	33	7	2	115.2	148	36	30	0	3	1	3	30	2	0	.067
1922 CHI A	0	2	.000	8.40	5	1	0	15	25	6	6	0	0	1	0	5	1	0	.200
3 yrs.	10	10	.500	4.51	55	13	6	213.1	265	68	45	1	5	4	4	60	9	0	.150
1 yr.	0	2	.000	8.40	5	1	0	15	25	6	6	0	0	1	0	5	1	0	.200

Grady Adkins
ADKINS, GRADY EMMETT (Butcher Boy) BR TR 5'11" 175 lbs.
B. June 29, 1897, Jacksonville, Ark. D. Mar. 31, 1966, Little Rock, Ark.

	W	L	PCT	ERA	G	GS	CG	IP	H	BB	SO	ShO	W	L	SV	AB	H	HR	BA
1928 CHI A	10	16	.385	3.73	36	27	14	224.2	233	89	54	0	3	1	1	70	10	0	.143
1929	2	11	.154	5.33	31	15	5	138.1	168	67	24	0	0	1	0	46	11	0	.239
2 yrs.	12	27	.308	4.34	67	42	19	363	401	156	78	0	3	2	1	116	21	0	.181
2 yrs.	12	27	.308	4.34	67	42	19	363	401	156	78	0	3	2	1	116	21	0	.181

Juan Agosto
AGOSTO, JUAN ROBERTO BL TL 6' 175 lbs.
B. Feb. 23, 1958, Rio Piedras, Puerto Rico

	W	L	PCT	ERA	G	GS	CG	IP	H	BB	SO	ShO	W	L	SV	AB	H	HR	BA
1981 CHI A	0	0	—	4.50	2	0	0	6	5	0	3	0	0	0	0	0	0	0	—
1982	0	0	—	18.00	1	0	0	2	7	0	1	0	0	0	0	0	0	0	—
1983	2	2	.500	4.10	39	0	0	41.2	41	11	29	0	2	2	7	0	0	0	—
3 yrs.	2	2	.500	4.71	42	0	0	49.2	53	11	33	0	2	2	7	0	0	0	—
3 yrs.	2	2	.500	4.71	42	0	0	49.2	53	11	33	0	2	2	7	0	0	0	—

LEAGUE CHAMPIONSHIP SERIES
| 1983 CHI A | 0 | 0 | — | 0.00 | 1 | 0 | 0 | .1 | 0 | 0 | 0 | 0 | 0 | 0 | 0 | 0 | 0 | 0 | — |

Lloyd Allen
ALLEN, LLOYD CECIL BR TR 6'1" 185 lbs.
B. May 8, 1950, Merced, Calif.

	W	L	PCT	ERA	G	GS	CG	IP	H	BB	SO	ShO	W	L	SV	AB	H	HR	BA
1969 CAL A	0	1	.000	5.40	4	1	0	10	5	10	5	0	0	0	0	2	1	0	.500
1970	1	1	.500	2.63	8	2	0	24	23	11	12	0	0	0	0	4	0	0	.000
1971	4	6	.400	2.49	54	1	0	94	75	40	72	0	4	6	15	17	5	1	.294
1972	3	7	.300	3.49	42	0	0	85	76	55	53	0	3	3	5	17	2	0	.118
1973 2 teams	CAL A (5G 0-0)					TEX A (23G 0-6)													
" total	0	6	.000	9.42	28	5	0	49.2	73	44	29	0	0	2	0	0	0	0	—
1974 2 teams	TEX A (14G 0-1)					CHI A (6G 0-1)													
" total	0	2	.000	7.45	20	2	0	29	31	30	21	0	0	2	0	0	0	0	—
1975 CHI A	0	2	.000	11.81	3	2	0	5.1	8	6	2	0	0	0	0	0	0	0	—
7 yrs.	8	25	.242	4.70	159	19	0	297	291	196	194	0	7	13	22	40	8	1	.200
2 yrs.	0	3	.000	10.95	9	4	0	12.1	15	18	5	0	0	1	0	0	0	0	—

Luis Aloma
ALOMA, LUIS BARBA (Witto) BR TR 6'2" 195 lbs.
B. June 19, 1923, Havana, Cuba

	W	L	PCT	ERA	G	GS	CG	IP	H	BB	SO	ShO	W	L	SV	AB	H	HR	BA
1950 CHI A	7	2	.778	3.80	42	0	0	87.2	77	53	49	0	7	2	4	15	1	0	.067
1951	6	0	1.000	1.82	25	1	1	69.1	52	24	25	1	5	0	3	20	7	0	.350
1952	3	1	.750	4.28	25	0	0	40	42	11	18	0	3	1	6	7	0	0	.000
1953	2	0	1.000	4.70	24	0	0	38.1	41	23	23	0	2	0	2	6	0	0	.000
4 yrs.	18	3	.857	3.44	116	1	1	235.1	212	111	115	1	17	3	15	48	8	0	.167
4 yrs.	18	3	.857	3.44	116	1	1	235.1	212	111	115	1	17	3	15	48	8	0	.167

Nick Altrock
ALTROCK, NICHOLAS BB TL 5'10" 197 lbs.
B. Sept. 15, 1876, Cincinnati, Ohio D. Jan. 20, 1965, Washington, D. C.

	W	L	PCT	ERA	G	GS	CG	IP	H	BB	SO	ShO	W	L	SV	AB	H	HR	BA
1898 LOU N	3	3	.500	4.50	11	7	6	70	89	21	13	0	0	0	0	29	7	0	.241
1902 BOS A	0	2	.000	2.00	3	2	1	18	19	7	5	0	0	0	0	8	0	0	.000
1903 2 teams	BOS A (1G 0-1)					CHI A (12G 5-3)													
" total	5	4	.556	2.85	13	9	7	79	72	23	22	1	1	0	0	33	11	0	.333
1904 CHI A	20	15	.571	2.96	38	36	31	307	274	48	87	6	1	1	0	111	22	1	.198
1905	22	12	.647	1.88	38	34	31	315.2	274	63	97	3	1	1	1	114	14	0	.123
1906	21	12	.636	2.06	38	30	25	287.2	269	42	99	4	7	0	0	100	16	0	.160
1907	8	12	.400	2.57	30	21	15	213.2	210	31	61	1	2	1	1	72	13	0	.181
1908	3	7	.300	2.71	23	13	8	136	127	18	21	1	3	0	1	49	10	0	.204
1909 2 teams	CHI A (1G 0-0)					WAS A (9G 1-3)													
" total	1	4	.200	5.36	10	6	3	47	71	6	11	0	0	0	0	22	1	0	.045
1912 WAS A	0	1	.000	13.50	1	0	0	1.1	2	0	0	0	0	1	0	1	0	0	.000
1913	0	0	—	4.82	4	0	0	9.1	7	4	2	0	0	0	0	1	0	0	.000
1914	0	0	—	0.00	1	0	0	1	3	0	0	0	0	0	0	0	0	0	—
1915	0	0	—	9.00	1	0	0	2	7	2	0	0	0	0	0	1	0	0	.000
1918	1	2	.333	2.96	5	3	1	24.1	24	6	5	0	0	0	0	8	1	1	.125
1919	0	0	—	∞	1	0	0	0	4	0	0	0	0	0	0	0	0	0	—
1924	0	0	—	0.00	1	0	0	2	0	0	0	0	0	0	0	1	1	0	1.000
1929	0	0	—	0.00	1	0	0	0	0	0	0	0	0	0	0	1	1	0	1.000
1931	0	0	—	0.00	1	0	0	0	0	0	0	0	0	0	0	0	0	0	—

Pitcher Register

	W	L	PCT	ERA	G	GS	CG	IP	H	BB	SO	ShO	Relief Pitching W L SV	BATTING AB H HR	BA

Nick Altrock continued

1933	0	0	–	0.00	0	0	0	0	0	0	0	0	0 0 0	1 0 0	.000
19 yrs.	84	74	.532	2.67	218	161	128	1515	1455	272	425	16	15 4 6	552 97 2	.176
7 yrs.	79	62	.560	2.40	180	143	117	1340	1229	222	386	16	15 3 4	479 84 1	.175

WORLD SERIES
| 1906 CHI A | 1 | 1 | .500 | 1.00 | 2 | 2 | 2 | 18 | 11 | 2 | 5 | 0 | 0 0 0 | 4 1 0 | .250 |

Larry Anderson

ANDERSON, LAWRENCE DENNIS BR TR 6'3" 190 lbs.
B. Dec. 3, 1952, Pico Rivera, Calif.

1974 MIL A	0	0	–	0.00	2	0	0	2	2	1	3	0	0 0 0	0 0 0	–
1975	1	0	1.000	5.04	8	1	1	30.1	36	6	13	1	0 0 0	0 0 0	–
1977 CHI A	1	3	.250	9.00	6	0	0	9	10	15	7	0	1 3 0	0 0 0	–
3 yrs.	2	3	.400	5.66	16	1	1	41.1	48	22	23	1	1 3 0	0 0 0	–
1 yr.	1	3	.250	9.00	6	0	0	9	10	15	7	0	1 3 0	0 0 0	–

Pete Appleton

APPLETON, PETER WILLIAM BR TR 5'11" 180 lbs.
Played as Pete Jablonowski 1927-33. Also known as Peter William Jablonowski.
B. May 20, 1904, Terryville, Conn. D. Jan. 18, 1974, Trenton, N. J.

1927 CIN N	2	1	.667	1.82	6	2	2	29.2	29	17	3	1	0 0 0	11 6 0	.545
1928	3	4	.429	4.68	31	1	0	82.2	101	22	20	0	3 4 0	31 10 0	.323
1930 CLE A	8	7	.533	4.02	39	7	2	118.2	122	53	45	0	6 5 1	40 8 0	.200
1931	4	4	.500	4.63	29	4	3	79.2	100	29	25	0	1 3 0	24 5 0	.208
1932 2 teams			CLE A (4G 0-0)		BOS A (11G 0-3)										
" total	0	3	.000	5.29	15	3	0	51	60	29	16	0	0 0 0	17 3 0	.176
1933 NY A	0	0	–	0.00	1	0	0	2	3	1	0	0	0 0 0	0 0 0	–
1936 WAS A	14	9	.609	3.53	38	20	12	201.2	199	77	77	1	4 1 3	76 19 0	.250
1937	8	15	.348	4.39	35	18	7	168	167	72	62	0	3 4 2	59 11 0	.186
1938	7	9	.438	4.60	43	10	5	164.1	175	61	62	0	3 4 5	59 15 0	.254
1939	5	10	.333	4.56	40	4	2	102.2	104	48	50	0	4 7 6	25 4 0	.160
1940 CHI A	4	0	1.000	5.62	25	0	0	57.2	54	28	21	0	4 0 5	17 3 0	.176
1941	0	3	.000	5.27	13	0	0	27.1	27	17	12	0	0 3 1	4 1 0	.250
1942 2 teams			CHI A (4G 0-0)		STL A (14G 1-1)										
" total	1	1	.500	3.09	18	0	0	32	27	14	14	0	1 1 2	6 1 0	.167
1945 2 teams			STL A (2G 0-0)		WAS A (6G 1-0)										
" total	1	0	1.000	4.56	8	2	1	23.2	19	18	13	0	0 0 1	5 1 0	.200
14 yrs.	57	66	.463	4.30	341	71	34	1141	1187	486	420	6	29 32 26	374 87 0	.233
3 yrs.	4	3	.571	5.42	42	0	0	89.2	83	48	35	0	4 3 6	21 4 0	.190

Rudy Arias

ARIAS, RODOLFO MARTINEZ BL TL 5'10" 165 lbs.
B. June 6, 1931, Mordoza Las Villas, Cuba

| 1959 CHI A | 2 | 0 | 1.000 | 4.09 | 34 | 0 | 0 | 44 | 49 | 20 | 28 | 0 | 2 0 2 | 4 0 0 | .000 |

Jerry Arrigo

ARRIGO, GERALD WILLIAM BL TL 6'1" 185 lbs.
B. June 12, 1941, Chicago, Ill.

1961 MIN A	0	1	.000	10.24	7	2	0	9.2	9	10	6	0	0 0 0	2 1 0	.500
1962	0	0	–	18.00	1	0	0	1	3	1	1	0	0 0 0	0 0 0	–
1963	1	2	.333	2.87	5	1	0	15.2	12	4	13	0	1 1 0	4 0 0	.000
1964	7	4	.636	3.84	41	12	2	105.1	97	45	96	1	3 2 1	29 5 0	.172
1965 CIN N	2	4	.333	6.17	27	5	0	54	75	30	43	0	1 2 2	12 2 1	.167
1966 2 teams			CIN N (3G 0-0)		NY N (17G 3-3)										
" total	3	3	.500	3.91	20	5	0	50.2	54	19	31	0	2 0 0	11 5 0	.455
1967 CIN N	6	6	.500	3.16	32	5	1	74	61	35	56	1	4 3 1	19 4 0	.211
1968	12	10	.545	3.33	36	31	5	205.1	181	77	140	1	1 0 0	67 5 0	.075
1969	4	7	.364	4.14	20	16	1	91.1	89	61	35	0	0 0 0	31 5 0	.161
1970 CHI A	0	3	.000	13.15	5	3	0	13	24	9	12	0	0 0 0	4 0 0	.000
10 yrs.	35	40	.467	4.14	194	80	9	620	605	291	433	3	12 8 4	179 27 1	.151
1 yr.	0	3	.000	13.15	5	3	0	13	24	9	12	0	0 0 0	4 0 0	.000

Ken Ash

ASH, KENNETH LOWTHER BR TR 5'11" 165 lbs.
B. Sept. 16, 1901, Anmoore, W. Va. D. Nov. 15, 1979, Clarksburg, W. Va.

1925 CHI A	0	0	–	9.00	2	0	0	4	7	0	0	0	0 0 0	0 0 0	–
1928 CIN N	3	3	.500	6.50	8	5	2	36	43	13	6	0	1 0 0	14 1 0	.071
1929	1	5	.167	4.83	29	7	2	82	91	30	26	0	1 1 2	21 3 0	.143
1930	2	0	1.000	3.43	16	1	1	39.1	37	16	15	0	1 0 0	11 2 0	.182
4 yrs.	6	8	.429	4.96	55	13	5	161.1	178	59	47	0	3 1 2	46 6 0	.130
1 yr.	0	0	–	9.00	2	0	0	4	7	0	0	0	0 0 0	0 0 0	–

Stan Bahnsen

BAHNSEN, STANLEY RAYMOND BR TR 6'2" 185 lbs.
B. Dec. 15, 1944, Council Bluffs, Iowa

1966 NY A	1	1	.500	3.52	4	3	1	23	15	7	16	0	0 0 1	7 1 0	.143
1968	17	12	.586	2.05	37	34	10	267.1	216	68	162	1	0 0 0	81 4 0	.049
1969	9	16	.360	3.83	40	33	5	220.2	222	90	130	2	1 2 1	60 5 0	.083
1970	14	11	.560	3.32	36	35	6	233	227	75	116	2	0 0 0	74 11 0	.149
1971	14	12	.538	3.35	36	34	14	242	221	72	110	3	0 0 0	79 12 0	.152
1972 CHI A	21	16	.568	3.60	43	41	5	252.1	263	73	157	1	0 0 0	92 14 0	.152
1973	18	21	.462	3.57	42	42	14	282.1	290	117	120	4	0 0 0	0 0 0	–
1974	12	15	.444	4.71	38	35	10	216	230	110	102	1	1 1 0	0 0 0	–
1975 2 teams			CHI A (12G 4-6)		OAK A (21G 6-7)										
" total	10	13	.435	4.36	33	28	4	167.1	166	77	80	0	1 0 0	1 0 0	.000
1976 OAK A	8	7	.533	3.34	35	14	1	143	124	43	82	1	3 2 0	0 0 0	–
1977 2 teams			OAK A (11G 1-2)		MON N (23G 8-9)										
" total	9	11	.450	5.01	34	24	3	149	166	51	79	1	0 1 1	42 5 0	.119
1978 MON N	1	5	.167	3.84	44	1	0	75	74	31	44	0	1 5 7	11 1 0	.091
1979	3	1	.750	3.16	55	0	0	94	80	42	71	0	3 1 5	14 1 1	.071
1980	7	6	.538	3.07	57	0	0	91	80	33	48	0	7 6 4	9 1 0	.111
1981	2	1	.667	4.96	25	3	0	49	45	24	28	0	2 0 1	9 1 0	.111

Pitcher Register

	W	L	PCT	ERA	G	GS	CG	IP	H	BB	SO	ShO	Relief Pitching W L SV	BATTING AB H HR	BA

Stan Bahnsen continued

	W	L	PCT	ERA	G	GS	CG	IP	H	BB	SO	ShO	W	L	SV	AB	H	HR	BA
1982 2 teams	CAL A (7G 0–1)			PHI N (8G 0–0)															
" total	0	1	.000	2.74	15	0	0	23	21	11	14	0	0	1	0	0	0	0	—
16 yrs.	146	149	.495	3.61	574	327	73	2528	2440	924	1359	16	18	20	20	479	56	1	.117
4 yrs.	55	58	.487	4.08	135	130	31	818	861	340	410	6	1	1	0	92	14	0	.152

DIVISIONAL PLAYOFF SERIES
| 1981 MON N | 0 | 0 | — | 0.00 | 1 | 0 | 0 | 1.1 | 1 | 1 | 1 | 0 | 0 | 0 | 0 | 0 | 0 | 0 | — |

Jesse Baker

BAKER, JESSE ORMOND   BL TL 5'11" 188 lbs.
Also known as Jesse Ormond Silverman.
B. June 3, 1888, Steilacoom, Wash. D. Sept. 26, 1972, Tacoma, Wash.

| 1911 CHI A | 2 | 7 | .222 | 3.93 | 22 | 8 | 3 | 94 | 101 | 30 | 51 | 0 | 1 | 0 | 1 | 29 | 3 | 0 | .103 |

Dave Baldwin

BALDWIN, DAVID GEORGE   BR TR 6'2" 200 lbs.
B. Mar. 30, 1938, Tucson, Ariz.

1966 WAS A	0	0	—	3.86	4	0	0	7	8	1	4	0	0	0	0	0	0	0	—
1967	2	4	.333	1.70	58	0	0	68.2	53	20	52	0	2	4	12	4	0	0	.000
1968	0	2	.000	4.07	40	0	0	42	40	12	30	0	0	2	5	2	0	0	.000
1969	2	4	.333	4.05	43	0	0	66.2	57	34	51	0	2	4	4	7	0	0	.000
1970 MIL A	2	1	.667	2.57	28	0	0	35	25	18	26	0	2	1	1	2	1	0	.500
1973 CHI A	0	0	—	3.60	3	0	0	5	7	4	1	0	0	0	0	0	0	0	—
6 yrs.	6	11	.353	3.09	176	0	0	224.1	190	89	164	0	6	11	22	15	1	0	.067
1 yr.	0	0	—	3.60	3	0	0	5	7	4	1	0	0	0	0	0	0	0	—

Floyd Bannister

BANNISTER, FLOYD FRANKLIN   BL TL 6'1" 190 lbs.
B. June 10, 1955, Pierre, S. D.

1977 HOU N	8	9	.471	4.03	24	23	4	143	138	68	112	1	0	0	0	48	9	0	.188
1978	3	9	.250	4.83	28	16	2	110	120	63	94	2	0	0	0	31	5	0	.161
1979 SEA A	10	15	.400	4.05	30	30	6	182	185	68	115	2	0	0	0	0	0	0	—
1980	9	13	.409	3.47	32	32	8	218	200	66	155	0	0	0	0	0	0	0	—
1981	9	9	.500	4.46	21	20	5	121	128	39	85	2	0	0	0	0	0	0	—
1982	12	13	.480	3.43	35	35	5	247	225	77	209	3	0	0	0	0	0	0	—
1983 CHI A	16	10	.615	3.35	34	34	5	217.1	191	71	193	2	0	0	0	0	0	0	—
7 yrs.	67	78	.462	3.81	204	190	35	1238.1	1187	452	963	12	0	0	0	79	14	0	.177
1 yr.	16	10	.615	3.35	34	34	5	217.1	191	71	193	2	0	0	0	0	0	0	—

LEAGUE CHAMPIONSHIP SERIES
| 1983 CHI A | 0 | 1 | .000 | 4.50 | 1 | 1 | 0 | 6 | 5 | 1 | 5 | 0 | 0 | 0 | 0 | 0 | 0 | 0 | — |

Charlie Barnabe

BARNABE, CHARLES EDWARD   BL TL 5'11½" 164 lbs.
B. June 12, 1900, Russell Gulch, Colo. D. Aug. 16, 1977, Waco, Tex.

1927 CHI A	0	5	.000	5.31	17	5	1	61	86	20	5	0	0	2	0	19	3	0	.158
1928	0	2	.000	6.52	7	2	0	9.2	17	0	3	0	0	0	0	8	4	1	.500
2 yrs.	0	7	.000	5.48	24	7	1	70.2	103	20	8	0	0	2	0	27	7	1	.259
2 yrs.	0	7	.000	5.48	24	7	1	70.2	103	20	8	0	0	2	0	27	7	1	.259

Bob Barnes

BARNES, ROBERT AVERY (Lefty)   BL TL 5'11½" 150 lbs.
B. Jan. 6, 1902, Washburn, Ill.

| 1924 CHI A | 0 | 0 | — | 19.29 | 2 | 0 | 0 | 4.2 | 14 | 0 | 1 | 0 | 0 | 0 | 0 | 2 | 0 | 0 | .000 |

Rich Barnes

BARNES, RICHARD MONROE   BB TL 6'4" 180 lbs.
B. July 21, 1959, Palm Beach, Fla.

1982 CHI A	0	2	.000	4.76	6	2	0	17	21	4	6	0	0	0	1	0	0	0	—
1983 CLE A	1	1	.500	6.94	4	2	0	11.2	18	10	2	0	1	0	0	0	0	0	—
2 yrs.	1	3	.250	5.65	10	4	0	28.2	39	14	8	0	1	0	1	0	0	0	—
1 yr.	0	2	.000	4.76	6	2	0	17	21	4	6	0	0	0	1	0	0	0	—

Salome Barojas

BAROJAS, SALOME   BR TR 5'9" 160 lbs.
B. June 16, 1957, Corova Vera Cruz, Mexico

1982 CHI A	6	6	.500	3.54	61	0	0	106.2	96	46	56	0	6	6	21	0	0	0	—
1983	3	3	.500	2.47	52	0	0	87.1	70	32	38	0	3	3	12	0	0	0	—
2 yrs.	9	9	.500	3.06	113	0	0	194	166	78	94	0	9	9	33	0	0	0	—
2 yrs.	9	9	.500	3.06	113	0	0	194	166	78	94	0	9	9	33	0	0	0	—

LEAGUE CHAMPIONSHIP SERIES
| 1983 CHI A | 0 | 0 | — | 18.00 | 2 | 0 | 0 | 1 | 4 | 0 | 0 | 0 | 0 | 0 | 0 | 0 | 0 | 0 | — |

Bill Barrett

BARRETT, WILLIAM JOSEPH (Whispering Bill)   BR TR 6' 175 lbs.
B. May 28, 1900, Cambridge, Mass. D. Jan. 26, 1951, Cambridge, Mass.

| 1921 PHI A | 1 | 0 | 1.000 | 7.20 | 4 | 0 | 0 | 5 | 2 | 9 | 2 | 0 | 1 | 0 | 0 | * | | | |

Francisco Barrios

BARRIOS, FRANCISCO JAVIER   BR TR 5'11" 155 lbs.
Also known as Francisco Javier Jimenez.
B. June 10, 1953, Hermosillo, Mexico D. Apr. 9, 1982, Hermosillo, Mexico

1974 CHI A	0	0	—	27.00	2	0	0	2	7	2	2	0	0	0	0	0	0	0	—
1976	5	9	.357	4.31	35	14	6	142	136	46	81	0	1	3	3	0	0	0	—
1977	14	7	.667	4.13	33	31	9	231	241	58	119	0	1	0	0	0	0	0	—
1978	9	15	.375	4.05	33	32	9	195.2	180	85	79	2	0	0	0	0	0	0	—
1979	8	3	.727	3.60	15	15	2	95	88	33	28	0	0	0	0	0	0	0	—
1980	1	1	.500	5.06	3	3	0	16	21	8	2	0	0	0	0	0	0	0	—
1981	1	3	.250	4.00	8	7	1	36	45	14	12	0	0	0	0	0	0	0	—
7 yrs.	38	38	.500	4.15	129	102	27	717.2	718	246	323	2	2	3	3	0	0	0	—
7 yrs.	38	38	.500	4.15	129	102	27	717.2	718	246	323	2	2	3	3	0	0	0	—

Pitcher Register 344

	W	L	PCT	ERA	G	GS	CG	IP	H	BB	SO	ShO	Relief Pitching W	L	SV	BATTING AB	H	HR	BA

Les Bartholomew
BARTHOLOMEW, LESTER JUSTIN   BR TL 5'11½" 195 lbs.
B. Apr. 4, 1903, Madison, Wis.   D. Sept. 19, 1972, Madison, Wis.

1928 PIT N	0	0	—	7.15	6	0	0	22.2	29	9	6	0	0	0	0	7	1	0	.143
1932 CHI A	0	0	—	5.06	3	0	0	5.1	5	6	1	0	0	0	0	1	0	0	.000
2 yrs.	0	0	—	6.75	9	0	0	28	36	15	7	0	0	0	0	8	1	0	.125
1 yr.	0	0	—	5.06	3	0	0	5.1	5	6	1	0	0	0	0	1	0	0	.000

Frank Baumann
BAUMANN, FRANK MATT (The Beau)   BL TL 6'   205 lbs.
B. July 1, 1933, St. Louis, Mo.

1955 BOS A	2	1	.667	5.82	7	5	0	34	38	17	27	0	1	0	0	13	3	0	.231
1956	2	1	.667	3.28	7	1	0	24.2	22	14	18	0	1	1	0	9	3	0	.333
1957	1	0	1.000	3.75	4	1	0	12	13	3	7	0	0	0	0	2	1	0	.500
1958	2	2	.500	4.47	10	7	2	52.1	56	27	31	0	0	0	0	14	3	0	.214
1959	6	4	.600	4.05	26	10	2	95.2	96	55	48	0	2	0	1	29	6	0	.207
1960 CHI A	13	6	.684	2.67	47	20	7	185.1	169	53	71	2	6	2	3	52	8	0	.154
1961	10	13	.435	5.61	53	23	5	187.2	249	59	75	1	4	4	3	61	16	2	.262
1962	7	6	.538	3.38	40	10	3	119.2	117	36	55	1	4	2	4	30	8	0	.267
1963	2	1	.667	3.04	24	1	0	50.1	52	17	31	0	2	0	1	11	1	0	.091
1964	0	3	.000	6.19	22	0	0	32	40	16	19	0	0	3	1	4	0	0	.000
1965 CHI N	0	1	.000	7.36	4	0	0	3.2	4	3	2	0	0	1	0	0	0	0	—
11 yrs.	45	38	.542	4.11	244	78	19	797.1	856	300	384	4	20	13	13	225	49	2	.218
5 yrs.	32	29	.525	4.01	186	54	15	575	627	181	251	4	16	11	12	158	33	2	.209

Ross Baumgarten
BAUMGARTEN, ROSS   BL TL 6'1" 180 lbs.
Also known as Antonio Baumgarten.
B. May 27, 1955, Highland Park, Ill.

1978 CHI A	2	2	.500	5.87	7	4	1	23	29	9	15	0	0	0	0	0	0	0	—
1979	13	8	.619	3.53	28	28	4	191	175	83	72	3	0	0	0	0	0	0	—
1980	2	12	.143	3.44	24	23	3	136	127	52	66	1	0	0	0	0	0	0	—
1981	5	9	.357	4.06	19	19	2	102	101	40	52	1	0	0	0	0	0	0	—
1982 PIT N	0	5	.000	6.55	12	10	0	44	60	27	17	0	0	0	0	12	1	0	.083
5 yrs.	22	36	.379	3.99	90	84	10	496	492	211	222	6	0	0	0	12	1	0	.083
4 yrs.	22	31	.415	3.74	78	74	10	452	432	184	205	6	0	0	0	0	0	0	—

Gene Bearden
BEARDEN, HENRY EUGENE   BL TL 6'3" 198 lbs.
B. Sept. 5, 1920, Lexa, Ark.

1947 CLE A	0	0	—	81.00	1	0	0	.1	2	1	0	0	0	0	0	0	0	0	—
1948	20	7	.741	2.43	37	29	15	229.2	187	106	80	6	0	2	1	90	23	2	.256
1949	8	8	.500	5.10	32	19	5	127	140	92	41	0	1	1	0	45	5	0	.111
1950 2 teams	CLE A (14G 1-3)				WAS A (12G 3-5)														
" total	4	8	.333	4.99	26	12	4	113.2	138	65	30	0	1	2	0	35	7	0	.200
1951 2 teams	WAS A (1G 0-0)				DET A (37G 3-4)														
" total	3	4	.429	4.64	38	5	2	108.2	118	60	39	1	1	2	0	32	6	2	.188
1952 STL A	7	8	.467	4.30	34	16	3	150.2	158	78	45	0	1	2	0	65	23	0	.354
1953 CHI A	3	3	.500	2.93	25	3	0	58.1	48	33	24	0	3	1	0	21	4	0	.190
7 yrs.	45	38	.542	3.96	193	84	29	788.1	791	435	259	7	7	10	1	288	68	4	.236
1 yr.	3	3	.500	2.93	25	3	0	58.1	48	33	24	0	3	1	0	21	4	0	.190

WORLD SERIES
1948 CLE A	1	0	1.000	0.00	2	1	1	10.2	6	1	4	1	0	0	1	4	2	0	.500

Gary Bell
BELL, GARY   BR TR 6'1" 196 lbs.
B. Nov. 17, 1936, San Antonio, Tex.

1958 CLE A	12	10	.545	3.31	33	23	10	182	141	73	110	0	1	2	1	56	11	0	.196
1959	16	11	.593	4.04	44	28	12	234	208	105	136	1	3	1	5	75	18	0	.240
1960	9	10	.474	4.13	28	23	6	154.2	139	82	109	2	0	0	1	47	7	0	.149
1961	12	16	.429	4.10	34	34	11	228.1	214	100	163	2	0	0	0	81	16	0	.198
1962	10	9	.526	4.26	57	6	1	107.2	104	52	80	0	9	6	12	24	5	0	.208
1963	8	5	.615	2.95	58	7	0	119	91	52	98	0	7	1	5	26	3	0	.115
1964	8	6	.571	4.33	56	2	0	106	106	53	89	0	7	5	4	16	6	0	.375
1965	6	5	.545	3.04	60	0	0	103.2	86	50	86	0	6	5	17	16	1	1	.063
1966	14	15	.483	3.22	40	37	12	254.1	211	79	194	0	1	0	0	76	10	0	.132
1967 2 teams	CLE A (9G 1-5)				BOS A (29G 12-8)														
" total	13	13	.500	3.31	38	33	9	226	193	71	154	0	0	0	3	74	12	0	.162
1968 BOS A	11	11	.500	3.12	35	27	9	199.1	177	68	103	3	1	1	1	59	13	0	.220
1969 2 teams	SEA A (13G 2-6)				CHI A (23G 0-0)														
" total	2	6	.250	5.31	36	13	1	100	124	57	56	1	0	0	2	19	3	0	.158
12 yrs.	121	117	.508	3.68	519	233	71	2015	1794	842	1378	9	35	21	51	569	105	1	.185
1 yr.	0	0	—	6.28	23	2	0	38.2	48	23	26	0	0	0	0	5	0	0	.000

WORLD SERIES
1967 BOS A	0	1	.000	5.06	3	1	0	5.1	8	1	1	0	0	0	1	0	0	0	—

Ralph Bell
BELL, RALPH A.   BL TL 5'11½" 170 lbs.
B. Nov. 16, 1891, Kohoka, Mo.   D. Oct. 18, 1959, Burlington, Iowa

1912 CHI A	0	0	—	9.00	3	0	0	6	8	8	5	0	0	0	0	2	0	0	.000

Chief Bender
BENDER, CHARLES ALBERT   BR TR 6'2" 185 lbs.
B. May 5, 1883, Brainerd, Minn.   D. May 22, 1954, Philadelphia, Pa.
Hall of Fame 1953.

1903 PHI A	17	15	.531	3.07	36	33	30	270	239	65	127	2	1	0	0	120	22	0	.183
1904	10	11	.476	2.87	29	20	18	203.2	167	59	149	4	2	1	0	79	18	0	.228
1905	16	11	.593	2.70	35	23	19	240	193	90	142	4	3	0	3	92	20	0	.217
1906	15	10	.600	2.53	36	27	24	238.1	208	48	159	0	1	1	3	99	25	3	.253
1907	16	8	.667	2.05	33	24	20	219.1	185	34	112	4	0	1	3	100	23	0	.230
1908	8	9	.471	1.75	18	17	15	138.2	121	21	85	2	0	0	0	50	11	0	.220
1909	18	8	.692	1.66	34	29	24	250	196	45	161	5	0	0	1	93	20	0	.215
1910	23	5	**.821**	1.58	30	28	25	250	182	47	155	3	0	0	1	93	25	0	.269

Pitcher Register

	W	L	PCT	ERA	G	GS	CG	IP	H	BB	SO	ShO	Relief Pitching W	L	SV	BATTING AB	H	HR	BA

Chief Bender continued

1911	17	5	.773	2.16	31	24	16	216.1	198	58	114	3	1	1	4	79	13	0	.165
1912	13	8	.619	2.74	27	19	12	171	169	33	90	1	2	3	2	60	9	0	.150
1913	21	10	.677	2.21	48	22	13	236.2	208	59	135	2	6	4	12	78	12	0	.154
1914	17	3	.850	2.26	28	23	15	179	159	55	107	7	2	1	0	62	9	1	.145
1915 BAL F	4	16	.200	3.99	26	23	15	178.1	198	37	89	0	0	1	1	60	16	1	.267
1916 PHI N	7	7	.500	3.74	27	13	8	122.2	137	34	43	0	2	1	3	43	12	0	.279
1917	8	2	.800	1.67	20	10	8	113	84	26	43	4	0	0	2	39	8	1	.205
1925 CHI	0	0	–	18.00	1	0	0	1	1	1	0	0	0	0	0	0	0	0	–
16 yrs.	210	128	.621	2.45	459	335	261	3028	2645	712	1711	41	20	14	36	*			
1 yr.	0	0	–	18.00	1	0	0	1	1	1	0	0	0	0	0	0	0	0	–

WORLD SERIES

1905 PHI A	1	1	.500	1.06	2	2	2	17	9	6	13	1	0	0	0	5	0	0	.000
1910	1	1	.500	1.93	2	2	2	18.2	12	4	14	0	0	0	0	6	2	0	.333
1911	2	1	.667	1.04	3	3	3	26	16	8	20	0	0	0	0	11	1	0	.091
1913	2	0	1.000	4.00	2	2	2	18	19	1	9	0	0	0	0	8	0	0	.000
1914	0	1	.000	10.13	1	1	0	5.1	8	2	3	0	0	0	0	2	0	0	.000
5 yrs.	6	4	.600	2.44	10	10	9	85	64	21	59	1	0	0	0	32	3	0	.094
	5th	7th				4th	2nd	4th		4th	5th					6th			

Bugs Bennett

BENNETT, JOSEPH HARLEY   BR TR 5'9½" 163 lbs.
Played as Bugs Morris 1921. Also known as Joseph Harley Morris.
B. Apr. 19, 1892, Kansas City, Mo.   D. Nov. 21, 1957, Noel, Mo.

1918 STL A	0	2	.000	3.48	4	2	0	10.1	12	7	0	0	0	2	0	4	1	0	.250
1921 2 teams			CHI A (3G 0–3)				STL A (3G 0–0)												
" total	0	3	.000	8.10	6	3	1	23.1	30	22	5	0	0	1	0	7	3	0	.429
2 yrs.	0	5	.000	6.68	10	5	1	33.2	42	29	5	0	0	3	0	11	4	0	.364
1 yr.	0	3	.000	6.11	3	2	1	17.2	19	16	2	0	0	1	0	6	2	0	.333

Joe Benz

BENZ, JOSEPH LOUIS (Blitzen)   BR TR 6'1½" 196 lbs.
B. Jan. 21, 1886, New Alsace, Ind.   D. Apr. 23, 1957, Chicago, Ill.

1911 CHI A	3	2	.600	2.26	12	6	2	55.2	52	13	28	0	1	0	0	17	1	0	.059
1912	12	18	.400	2.92	41	31	11	237.2	230	70	96	3	2	2	0	76	10	0	.132
1913	6	10	.375	2.74	33	17	7	151	146	59	79	1	2	1	2	50	9	0	.180
1914	15	19	.441	2.26	48	35	16	283.1	245	66	142	4	3	0	2	92	12	0	.130
1915	15	11	.577	2.11	39	28	17	238.1	209	43	81	2	0	0	0	79	10	0	.127
1916	9	5	.643	2.03	28	16	6	142	108	32	57	4	1	1	0	46	3	0	.065
1917	6	3	.667	2.47	19	13	7	94.2	76	23	25	2	1	1	0	30	5	0	.167
1918	7	8	.467	2.51	29	17	10	154	156	28	30	1	1	1	0	51	11	0	.216
1919	0	0	–	0.00	1	0	0	2	2	0	0	0	0	0	0	0	0	0	–
9 yrs.	73	76	.490	2.42	250	163	76	1358.2	1224	334	538	17	10	8	4	441	61	0	.138
9 yrs.	73	76	.490	2.42	250	163	76	1358.2	1224	334	538	17	10	8	4	441	61	0	.138
							8th												

Charlie Biggs

BIGGS, CHARLES ORVAL   BR TR 6'1" 185 lbs.
B. Sept. 15, 1906, French Lick, Ind.   D. May 24, 1954, French Lick, Ind.

1932 CHI A	1	1	.500	6.93	6	4	0	24.2	32	12	1	0	0	0	0	9	1	0	.111

Hi Bithorn

BITHORN, HIRAM GABRIEL   BR TR 6'1" 200 lbs.
B. Mar. 18, 1916, Santurce, Puerto Rico   D. Jan. 1, 1952, El Mante, Mexico

1942 CHI N	9	14	.391	3.68	38	16	9	171.1	191	81	65	0	3	5	2	57	7	0	.123
1943	18	12	.600	2.60	39	30	19	249.2	226	65	86	7	1	1	2	92	16	0	.174
1946	6	5	.545	3.84	26	7	2	86.2	97	25	34	1	4	2	1	28	5	0	.179
1947 CHI A	1	0	1.000	0.00	2	0	0	2	2	0	0	0	1	0	0	0	0	0	–
4 yrs.	34	31	.523	3.16	105	53	30	509.2	516	171	185	8	9	8	5	177	28	0	.158
1 yr.	1	0	1.000	0.00	2	0	0	2	2	0	0	0	1	0	0	0	0	0	–

Babe Blackburn

BLACKBURN, FOSTER EDWIN   BR TR 6' 200 lbs.
B. Jan. 6, 1895, Chicago, Ill.

1915 KC F	0	1	.000	8.62	7	2	0	15.2	19	13	7	0	0	0	0	4	0	0	.000
1921 CHI A	0	0	–	0.00	1	0	0	1	0	1	0	0	0	0	0	0	0	0	–
2 yrs.	0	1	.000	8.10	8	2	0	16.2	19	14	7	0	0	0	0	4	0	0	.000
1 yr.	0	0	–	0.00	1	0	0	1	0	1	0	0	0	0	0	0	0	0	–

Lena Blackburne

BLACKBURNE, RUSSELL AUBREY (Slats)   BR TR 5'11" 160 lbs.
B. Oct. 23, 1886, Clifton Heights, Pa.   D. Feb. 29, 1968, Riverside, N. J.
Manager 1928-29.

1929 CHI A	0	0	–	0.00	1	0	0	.1	1	0	0	0	0	0	0	*			

Homer Blankenship

BLANKENSHIP, HOMER (Si)   BR TR 6' 185 lbs.
Brother of Ted Blankenship.
B. Aug. 4, 1902, Bonham, Tex.   D. June 22, 1974, Longview, Tex.

1922 CHI A	0	0	–	4.85	4	0	0	13	21	5	3	0	0	0	0	4	0	0	.000
1923	1	1	.500	3.60	4	0	0	5	9	1	1	0	1	1	1	0	0	0	–
1928 PIT N	0	2	.000	5.82	5	2	1	21.2	27	9	6	0	0	0	0	8	3	0	.375
3 yrs.	1	3	.250	5.22	13	2	1	39.2	57	15	10	0	1	1	1	12	3	0	.250
2 yrs.	1	1	.500	4.50	8	0	0	18	30	6	4	0	1	1	1	4	0	0	.000

Ted Blankenship

BLANKENSHIP, THEODORE   BR TR 6'1" 170 lbs.
Brother of Homer Blankenship.
B. May 10, 1901, Bonham, Tex.   D. Jan. 14, 1945, Atoko, Okla.

1922 CHI A	8	10	.444	3.81	24	15	7	127.2	124	47	42	0	3	3	1	41	7	0	.171
1923	9	14	.391	4.27	44	23	9	208.2	219	100	57	1	3	3	0	76	16	3	.211
1924	7	6	.538	5.17	25	11	7	125.1	167	38	36	0	1	1	1	46	15	1	.326
1925	17	8	.680	3.16	40	23	16	222	218	69	81	3	3	3	1	88	18	2	.205
1926	13	10	.565	3.61	29	26	15	209.1	217	65	66	1	1	0	1	76	10	0	.132

Pitcher Register

	W	L	PCT	ERA	G	GS	CG	IP	H	BB	SO	ShO	Relief Pitching W	L	SV	BATTING AB	H	HR	BA

Ted Blankenship continued

	W	L	PCT	ERA	G	GS	CG	IP	H	BB	SO	ShO	RW	RL	SV	AB	H	HR	BA
1927	12	17	.414	5.06	37	34	11	236.2	280	74	51	3	0	0	0	80	15	3	.188
1928	9	11	.450	4.61	27	22	8	158	186	80	36	0	0	0	0	59	10	0	.169
1929	0	2	.000	8.84	8	1	0	18.1	28	9	7	0	0	1	0	4	1	0	.250
1930	2	1	.667	9.20	7	1	0	14.2	23	7	2	0	2	0	0	5	1	0	.200
9 yrs.	77	79	.494	4.32	241	156	73	1320.2	1462	489	378	8	13	11	4	475	93	9	.196
9 yrs.	77	79	.494	4.32	241	156	73	1320.2	1462	489	378	8	13	11	4	475	93	9	.196

Greg Bollo

BOLLO, GREGORY GENE BR TR 6'4" 183 lbs.
B. Nov. 16, 1943, Detroit, Mich.

	W	L	PCT	ERA	G	GS	CG	IP	H	BB	SO	ShO	RW	RL	SV	AB	H	HR	BA
1965 CHI A	0	0	—	3.57	15	0	0	22.2	12	9	16	0	0	0	0	0	0	0	—
1966	0	1	.000	2.57	3	1	0	7	7	3	4	0	0	0	0	1	0	0	.000
2 yrs.	0	1	.000	3.34	18	1	0	29.2	19	12	20	0	0	0	0	1	0	0	.000
2 yrs.	0	1	.000	3.34	18	1	0	29.2	19	12	20	0	0	0	0	1	0	0	.000

Grant Bowler

BOWLER, GRANT TIERNEY (Moose) BR TR 6' 190 lbs.
B. Oct. 24, 1907, Denver, Colo. D. June 25, 1968, Denver, Colo.

	W	L	PCT	ERA	G	GS	CG	IP	H	BB	SO	ShO	RW	RL	SV	AB	H	HR	BA
1931 CHI A	0	1	.000	5.35	13	3	1	35.1	40	24	15	0	0	0	0	10	1	0	.100
1932	0	0	—	15.63	4	0	0	6.1	15	3	2	0	0	0	0	2	0	0	.000
2 yrs.	0	1	.000	6.91	17	3	1	41.2	55	27	17	0	0	0	0	12	1	0	.083
2 yrs.	0	1	.000	6.91	17	3	1	41.2	55	27	17	0	0	0	0	12	1	0	.083

Emmett Bowles

BOWLES, EMMETT JEROME (Chief) BR TR 6' 180 lbs.
B. Aug. 2, 1898, Wanette, Okla. D. Sept. 3, 1959, Flagstaff, Ariz.

	W	L	PCT	ERA	G	GS	CG	IP	H	BB	SO	ShO	RW	RL	SV	AB	H	HR	BA
1922 CHI A	0	0	—	27.00	1	0	0	1	2	1	0	0	0	0	0	0	0	0	—

Harry Boyles

BOYLES, HARRY (Stretch) BR TR 6'5" 185 lbs.
B. Nov. 29, 1911, Granite City, Ill.

	W	L	PCT	ERA	G	GS	CG	IP	H	BB	SO	ShO	RW	RL	SV	AB	H	HR	BA
1938 CHI A	0	4	.000	5.22	9	2	1	29.1	31	25	18	0	0	2	1	8	1	0	.125
1939	0	0	—	10.80	2	0	0	3.1	4	6	1	0	0	0	0	1	0	0	.000
2 yrs.	0	4	.000	5.79	11	2	1	32.2	35	31	19	0	0	2	1	9	1	0	.111
2 yrs.	0	4	.000	5.79	11	2	1	32.2	35	31	19	0	0	2	1	9	1	0	.111

Fred Bradley

BRADLEY, FRED LANGDON BR TR 6'1" 180 lbs.
B. July 31, 1920, Parsons, Kans.

	W	L	PCT	ERA	G	GS	CG	IP	H	BB	SO	ShO	RW	RL	SV	AB	H	HR	BA
1948 CHI A	0	0	—	4.60	8	0	0	15.2	11	4	2	0	0	0	0	1	0	0	.000
1949	0	0	—	13.50	1	1	0	2	4	3	0	0	0	0	0	1	0	0	.000
2 yrs.	0	0	—	5.60	9	1	0	17.2	15	7	2	0	0	0	0	2	0	0	.000
2 yrs.	0	0	—	5.60	9	1	0	17.2	15	7	2	0	0	0	0	2	0	0	.000

Tom Bradley

BRADLEY, THOMAS WILLIAM BR TR 6'2½" 180 lbs.
B. Mar. 16, 1947, Asheville, N. C.

	W	L	PCT	ERA	G	GS	CG	IP	H	BB	SO	ShO	RW	RL	SV	AB	H	HR	BA
1969 CAL A	0	1	.000	27.00	3	0	0	2	9	0	2	0	0	1	0	0	0	0	—
1970	2	5	.286	4.11	17	11	1	70	71	33	53	1	0	0	0	18	3	0	.167
1971 CHI A	15	15	.500	2.96	45	39	7	286	273	74	206	6	0	1	2	96	15	1	.156
1972	15	14	.517	2.98	40	40	11	260	225	65	209	2	0	0	0	91	12	0	.132
1973 SF N	13	12	.520	3.90	35	34	6	223.2	212	69	136	1	0	0	0	77	15	0	.195
1974	8	11	.421	5.17	30	21	2	134	152	52	72	0	0	1	0	40	3	0	.075
1975	2	3	.400	6.21	13	6	0	42	57	18	13	0	0	0	0	10	0	0	.000
7 yrs.	55	61	.474	3.72	183	151	27	1017.2	999	311	691	10	0	3	2	332	48	1	.145
2 yrs.	30	29	.508	2.97	85	79	18	546	498	139	415	8	0	1	2	187	27	1	.144

Garland Braxton

BRAXTON, EDGAR GARLAND BL TL 5'11" 152 lbs.
B. June 10, 1900, Snow Camp, N. C. BR 1921-22, BB 1925-26,
D. Feb. 25, 1966, Norfolk, Va. 1933

	W	L	PCT	ERA	G	GS	CG	IP	H	BB	SO	ShO	RW	RL	SV	AB	H	HR	BA
1921 BOS N	1	3	.250	4.82	17	2	0	37.1	44	17	16	0	1	0	0	7	0	0	.000
1922	1	2	.333	3.38	25	4	2	66.2	75	24	15	0	0	1	0	16	1	0	.063
1925 NY A	1	1	.500	6.52	3	2	0	19.1	26	5	11	0	0	0	0	6	2	0	.333
1926	5	1	.833	2.67	37	1	0	67.1	71	19	30	0	5	1	2	20	6	0	.300
1927 WAS A	10	9	.526	2.95	58	2	0	155.1	143	33	95	0	10	7	13	39	9	0	.231
1928	13	11	.542	2.51	38	24	15	218.1	177	44	94	2	1	3	6	72	9	0	.125
1929	12	10	.545	4.85	37	20	9	182	219	51	59	0	4	1	4	54	8	0	.148
1930 2 teams	WAS A (15G 3-2)				CHI A (19G 4-10)														
" total	7	12	.368	5.72	34	10	2	118	149	42	51	0	5	4	6	28	2	0	.071
1931 2 teams	CHI A (17G 0-3)				STL A (11G 0-0)														
" total	0	3	.000	7.85	28	4	0	65.1	98	33	35	0	0	1	1	14	3	0	.214
1933 STL A	0	1	.000	9.72	5	1	0	8.1	11	8	5	0	0	0	0	1	0	0	.000
10 yrs.	50	53	.485	4.13	282	70	28	938	1013	276	411	2	26	19	32	257	40	0	.156
2 yrs.	4	13	.235	6.59	36	13	2	138	198	56	72	0	3	2	1	34	3	0	.088

Ken Brett

BRETT, KENNETH ALVIN BL TL 6' 190 lbs.
Brother of George Brett.
B. Sept. 18, 1948, Brooklyn, N. Y.

	W	L	PCT	ERA	G	GS	CG	IP	H	BB	SO	ShO	RW	RL	SV	AB	H	HR	BA
1967 BOS A	0	0	—	4.50	1	0	0	2	3	0	2	0	0	0	0	0	0	0	—
1969	2	3	.400	5.26	8	8	0	39.1	41	22	23	0	0	0	0	10	3	1	.300
1970	8	9	.471	4.08	40	14	1	139	118	79	155	0	3	5	2	41	13	2	.317
1971	0	3	.000	5.34	29	2	0	59	57	35	57	0	0	2	1	10	2	0	.200
1972 MIL A	7	12	.368	4.53	26	22	2	133	121	49	74	1	0	0	0	44	10	0	.227
1973 PHI N	13	9	.591	3.44	31	25	10	211.2	206	74	111	1	0	0	0	80	20	4	.250
1974 PIT N	13	9	.591	3.30	27	27	10	191	192	52	96	3	0	0	0	87	27	2	.310
1975	9	5	.643	3.36	23	16	4	118	110	43	47	0	1	1	0	52	12	1	.231
1976 2 teams	NY A (2G 0-0)				CHI A (27G 10-12)														
" total	10	12	.455	3.28	29	26	16	203	173	76	92	1	0	0	2	12	1	0	.083

Pitcher Register

	W	L	PCT	ERA	G	GS	CG	IP	H	BB	SO	ShO	Relief Pitching W L SV	BATTING AB H HR	BA

Ken Brett continued

1977 2 teams	CHI	A (13G 6–4)			CAL	A (21G 7–10)									
" total	13	14	.481	4.52	34	34	7	225	258	53	80	0	0 0 0	0 0 0	—
1978 CAL A	3	5	.375	4.95	31	10	1	100	100	42	43	1	1 0 1	0 0 0	—
1979 2 teams	MIN	A (9G 0–0)			LA	N (30G 4–3)									
" total	4	3	.571	3.75	39	0	0	60	68	18	16	0	4 3 2	11 3 0	.273
1980 KC A	0	0	—	0.00	8	0	0	13	8	5	4	0	0 0 1	0 0 0	—
1981	1	1	.500	4.22	22	0	0	32	35	14	7	0	1 1 2	0 0 0	—
14 yrs.	83	85	.494	3.93	349	184	51	1526	1490	562	807	9	11 13 11	*	—
2 yrs.	16	16	.500	3.81	40	39	18	283.2	272	91	130	1	0 0 1	12 1 0	.083

LEAGUE CHAMPIONSHIP SERIES

1974 PIT N	0	0	—	7.71	1	0	0	2.1	3	2	1	0	0 0 0	1 0 0	.000
1975	0	0	—	0.00	2	0	0	2.1	1	0	1	0	0 0 0	0 0 0	—
2 yrs.	0	0	—	3.86	3	0	0	4.2	4	2	2	0	0 0 0	1 0 0	.000

WORLD SERIES

1967 BOS A	0	0	—	0.00	2	0	0	1.1	0	1	1	0	0 0 0	0 0 0	—

Alan Brice

BRICE, ALAN HEALEY BR TR 6'5" 215 lbs.
B. Oct. 1, 1937, New York, N. Y.

1961 CHI A	0	1	.000	0.00	3	0	0	3.1	4	3	3	0	0 1 0	0 0 0	—

Jim Brosnan

BROSNAN, JAMES PATRICK (Professor) BR TR 6'4" 197 lbs.
B. Oct. 24, 1929, Cincinnati, Ohio

1954 CHI N	1	0	1.000	9.45	18	0	0	33.1	44	18	17	0	1 0 0	8 1 0	.125
1956	5	9	.357	3.79	30	10	1	95	95	45	51	1	3 4 1	22 4 0	.182
1957	5	5	.500	3.38	41	5	1	98.2	79	46	73	0	4 4 0	20 5 0	.250
1958 2 teams	CHI	N (8G 3–4)			STL	N (33G 8–4)									
" total	11	8	.579	3.35	41	20	4	166.2	148	79	89	0	4 1 7	50 5 0	.100
1959 2 teams	STL	N (20G 1–3)			CIN	N (26G 8–3)									
" total	9	6	.600	3.79	46	10	1	116.1	113	41	74	1	5 3 4	30 3 0	.100
1960 CIN N	7	2	.778	2.36	57	2	0	99	79	22	62	0	7 2 12	15 3 1	.200
1961	10	4	.714	3.04	53	0	0	80	77	18	40	0	10 4 16	13 2 0	.154
1962	4	4	.500	3.34	48	0	0	64.2	76	18	51	0	4 4 13	6 0 0	.000
1963 2 teams	CIN	N (6G 0–1)			CHI	A (45G 3–8)									
" total	3	9	.250	3.13	51	0	0	77.2	79	25	50	0	3 9 14	13 4 0	.308
9 yrs.	55	47	.539	3.54	385	47	7	831.1	790	312	507	2	41 31 67	177 27 1	.153
1 yr.	3	8	.273	2.84	45	0	0	73	71	22	46	0	3 8 14	13 4 0	.308

WORLD SERIES

1961 CIN N	0	0	—	7.50	3	0	0	6	9	4	5	0	0 0 0	0 0 0	—

Clint Brown

BROWN, CLINTON HAROLD BL TR 6'1" 190 lbs.
B. July 8, 1903, Blackash, Pa. D. Dec. 31, 1955, Rocky River, Ohio

1928 CLE A	0	1	.000	4.91	2	1	1	11	14	2	2	0	0 0 0	5 1 0	.200
1929	0	2	.000	3.31	3	1	1	16.1	18	6	1	0	0 1 0	7 0 0	.000
1930	11	12	.478	4.97	35	31	16	213.2	271	51	54	2	0 0 1	73 18 0	.247
1931	11	15	.423	4.71	39	33	12	233.1	284	55	50	2	0 0 0	87 15 0	.172
1932	15	12	.556	4.08	37	32	21	262.2	298	50	59	1	0 0 1	100 25 2	.250
1933	11	12	.478	3.41	33	23	10	185	202	34	47	2	1 1 1	62 9 0	.145
1934	4	3	.571	5.90	17	2	0	50.1	83	14	15	0	4 2 1	17 5 0	.294
1935	4	3	.571	5.14	23	5	1	49	61	14	20	0	3 0 2	10 2 0	.200
1936 CHI A	6	2	.750	4.99	38	2	0	83	106	24	19	0	6 1 5	25 4 0	.160
1937	7	7	.500	3.42	53	0	0	100	92	36	51	0	7 7 18	18 4 0	.222
1938	1	3	.250	4.61	8	0	0	13.2	16	9	2	0	1 3 2	2 1 0	.500
1939	11	10	.524	3.88	61	0	0	118.1	127	27	41	0	11 10 18	19 4 0	.211
1940	4	6	.400	3.68	37	0	0	66	75	16	23	0	4 6 10	14 1 0	.071
1941 CLE A	3	3	.500	3.27	41	0	0	74.1	77	28	22	0	3 3 5	17 2 0	.118
1942	1	1	.500	6.00	7	0	0	9	16	2	4	0	1 1 0	1 0 0	.000
15 yrs.	89	92	.492	4.26	434	130	62	1485.2	1740	368	410	7	41 35 64	457 91 2	.199
5 yrs.	29	28	.509	3.99	197	2	0	381	416	112	136	0	29 27 53	78 14 0	.179
													4th 5th		

Hal Brown

BROWN, HECTOR HAROLD (Skinny) BR TR 6'2" 180 lbs.
B. Dec. 11, 1924, Greensboro, N. C.

1951 CHI A	0	0	—	9.35	3	0	0	8.2	15	4	4	0	0 0 1	2 2 0	1.000
1952	2	3	.400	4.23	24	8	1	72.1	82	21	31	0	0 0 0	19 3 1	.158
1953 BOS A	11	6	.647	4.65	30	25	6	166.1	177	57	62	0	0 1 0	58 17 1	.293
1954	1	8	.111	4.12	40	5	1	118	126	41	66	0	1 4 0	24 3 0	.125
1955 2 teams	BOS	A (2G 1–0)			BAL	A (15G 0–4)									
" total	1	4	.200	3.98	17	5	1	61	53	28	20	0	1 1 0	17 1 0	.059
1956 BAL A	9	7	.563	4.04	35	14	4	151.2	142	37	57	1	3 2 2	42 8 0	.190
1957	7	8	.467	3.90	25	20	7	150	132	37	62	2	0 0 1	48 10 0	.208
1958	7	5	.583	3.07	19	17	4	96.2	96	20	44	2	0 0 1	27 4 0	.148
1959	11	9	.550	3.79	31	21	2	164	158	32	81	0	1 0 3	42 2 0	.048
1960	12	5	.706	3.06	30	20	6	159	155	22	66	1	4 1 0	44 8 0	.182
1961	10	6	.625	3.19	27	23	6	166.2	153	33	61	3	0 1 1	50 7 0	.140
1962 2 teams	BAL	A (22G 6–4)			NY	A (2G 0–1)									
" total	6	5	.545	4.29	24	12	0	92.1	97	23	27	0	2 2 1	29 8 0	.276
1963 HOU N	5	11	.313	3.31	26	20	2	141.1	137	8	68	3	1 0 0	43 4 0	.093
1964	3	15	.167	3.95	27	21	3	132	126	26	53	0	1 0 1	39 5 0	.128
14 yrs.	85	92	.480	3.81	358	211	47	1680	1677	389	710	13	14 12 11	484 82 2	.169
2 yrs.	2	3	.400	4.78	27	8	1	81	97	25	35	0	0 0 1	21 5 1	.238

Joe Brown

BROWN, JOSEPH HENRY BR TR 6' 176 lbs.
B. July 3, 1901, Little Rock, Ark. D. 1949, Little Rock, Ark.

1927 CHI A	0	0	—	∞	1	0	0		2	1	0	0	0 0 0	0 0 0	—

Pitcher Register

	W	L	PCT	ERA	G	GS	CG	IP	H	BB	SO	ShO	Relief Pitching W	L	SV	BATTING AB	H	HR	BA

Jack Bruner
BRUNER, JACK RAYMOND (Pappy) BL TL 6'1" 185 lbs.
B. July 1, 1924, Waterloo, Iowa

1949 CHI A	1	2	.333	8.22	4	2	0	7.2	10	8	4	0	1	0	0	1	0	0	.000
1950 2 teams					CHI A (9G 0-0)			STL A (13G 1-2)											
" total	1	2	.333	4.37	22	1	0	47.1	43	37	24	0	1	1	1	10	0	0	.000
2 yrs.	2	4	.333	4.91	26	3	0	55	53	45	28	0	2	1	1	11	0	0	.000
2 yrs.	1	2	.333	5.40	13	2	0	20	17	22	12	0	1	0	0	1	0	0	.000

Warren Brusstar
BRUSSTAR, WARREN SCOTT BR TR 6'3" 200 lbs.
B. Feb. 2, 1952, Oakland, Calif.

1977 PHI N	7	2	.778	2.66	46	0	0	71	64	24	46	0	7	2	3	6	0	0	.000
1978	6	3	.667	2.33	58	0	0	89	74	30	60	0	6	3	0	7	1	0	.143
1979	1	0	1.000	7.07	13	0	0	14	23	4	3	0	1	0	1	0	0	0	—
1980	2	2	.500	3.69	26	0	0	39	42	13	21	0	2	2	0	1	0	0	.000
1981	0	1	.000	4.50	14	0	0	12	12	10	8	0	0	1	0	0	0	0	—
1982 2 teams					PHI N (22G 2-3)			CHI A (10G 2-0)											
" total	4	3	.571	4.17	32	0	0	41	50	8	19	0	4	3	2	2	0	0	.000
1983 CHI N	3	1	.750	2.35	59	0	0	80.1	67	37	46	0	3	1	1	4	0	0	.000
7 yrs.	23	12	.657	3.04	248	0	0	346.1	332	126	203	0	23	12	7	20	1	0	.050
1 yr.	2	0	1.000	3.44	10	0	0	18.1	19	3	8	0	2	0	0	0	0	0	—

DIVISIONAL PLAYOFF SERIES
| 1981 PHI N | 0 | 0 | — | 4.91 | 2 | 0 | 0 | 3.2 | 5 | 1 | 3 | 0 | 0 | 0 | 0 | 0 | 0 | 0 | — |

LEAGUE CHAMPIONSHIP SERIES
1977 PHI N	0	0	—	3.38	2	0	0	2.2	2	1	2	0	0	0	0	0	0	0	—
1978	0	0	—	0.00	3	0	0	2.2	2	1	0	0	0	0	0	0	0	0	—
1980	1	0	1.000	3.38	2	0	0	2.2	1	1	0	0	1	0	0	1	0	0	.000
3 yrs.	1	0	1.000	2.25	7	0	0	8	5	3	2	0	1	0	0	1	0	0	.000

WORLD SERIES
| 1980 PHI N | 0 | 0 | — | 0.00 | 1 | 0 | 0 | 2.1 | 0 | 1 | 0 | 0 | 0 | 0 | 0 | 0 | 0 | 0 | — |

Bill Burns
BURNS, WILLIAM THOMAS (Sleepy Bill) BB TL 6'2" 195 lbs.
B. Jan. 29, 1880, San Saba, Tex.   D. June 6, 1953, Ramona, Calif.

1908 WAS A	6	11	.353	1.69	23	19	11	165	135	18	55	2	0	1	0	54	8	0	.148
1909 2 teams					WAS A (6G 1-0)			CHI A (22G 7-13)											
" total	8	13	.381	1.86	28	23	9	203.2	194	42	65	3	1	1	0	69	12	0	.174
1910 2 teams					CHI A (1G 0-0)			CIN N (31G 8-13)											
" total	8	13	.381	3.47	32	21	13	179	183	50	57	2	0	3	0	61	16	0	.262
1911 2 teams					CIN N (6G 1-0)			PHI N (21G 6-10)											
" total	7	10	.412	3.38	27	17	8	138.2	149	29	52	3	1	2	1	47	9	0	.191
1912 DET A	1	4	.200	5.35	6	5	2	38.2	52	9	6	0	0	0	0	13	3	0	.231
5 yrs.	30	51	.370	2.69	116	85	43	725	713	148	235	10	2	7	1	244	48	0	.197
2 yrs.	7	13	.350	1.96	23	19	8	174.2	169	36	52	3	1	1	0	58	10	0	.172

Britt Burns
BURNS, ROBERT BRITT BR TL 6'5" 215 lbs.
B. June 8, 1959, Houston, Tex.

1978 CHI A	0	2	.000	12.91	2	2	0	7.2	14	3	3	0	0	0	0	0	0	0	—
1979	0	0	—	5.40	6	0	0	5	10	1	2	0	0	0	0	0	0	0	—
1980	15	13	.536	2.84	34	32	11	238	213	63	133	1	1	0	0	0	0	0	—
1981	10	6	.625	2.64	24	23	5	157	139	49	108	1	0	0	0	0	0	0	—
1982	13	5	.722	4.04	28	28	5	169.1	168	67	116	1	0	0	0	0	0	0	—
1983	10	11	.476	3.58	29	26	8	173.2	165	55	115	4	0	0	0	0	0	0	—
6 yrs.	48	37	.565	3.36	123	111	29	750.2	709	238	477	7	2	0	0	0	0	0	—
6 yrs.	48	37	.565	3.36	123	111	29	750.2	709	238	477	7	2	0	0	0	0	0	—
				10th															

LEAGUE CHAMPIONSHIP SERIES
| 1983 CHI A | 0 | 1 | .000 | 0.96 | 1 | 1 | 0 | 9.1 | 6 | 5 | 8 | 0 | 0 | 0 | 0 | 0 | 0 | 0 | — |

John Buzhardt
BUZHARDT, JOHN WILLIAM BR TR 6'2½" 195 lbs.
B. Aug. 15, 1936, Prosperity, S. C.

1958 CHI N	3	0	1.000	1.85	6	2	1	24.1	16	7	9	0	1	0	0	8	1	0	.125
1959	4	5	.444	4.97	28	10	1	101.1	107	29	33	1	1	2	0	29	2	0	.069
1960 PHI N	5	16	.238	3.86	30	29	5	200.1	198	68	73	0	0	0	0	62	10	0	.161
1961	6	18	.250	4.49	41	27	6	202.1	200	65	92	1	0	2	0	57	6	0	.105
1962 CHI A	8	12	.400	4.19	28	25	8	152.1	156	59	64	2	1	0	0	51	6	0	.118
1963	9	4	.692	2.42	19	18	6	126.1	100	31	59	3	0	0	0	48	4	0	.083
1964	10	8	.556	2.98	31	25	8	160	150	35	97	3	0	0	0	54	11	0	.204
1965	13	8	.619	3.01	32	30	4	188.2	167	56	108	1	0	1	1	56	7	0	.125
1966	6	11	.353	3.83	33	22	5	150.1	144	30	66	4	1	2	0	43	5	0	.116
1967 3 teams					CHI A (28G 3-9)			BAL A (7G 0-1)			HOU N (1G 0-0)								
" total	3	10	.231	4.01	36	8	0	101	114	42	40	0	1	5	0	21	4	0	.190
1968 HOU N	4	4	.500	3.12	39	4	0	83.2	73	35	37	0	3	3	5	16	4	0	.250
11 yrs.	71	96	.425	3.66	326	200	44	1490.2	1425	457	678	15	8	15	7	445	60	0	.135
6 yrs.	49	52	.485	3.37	171	127	31	866.1	817	248	427	13	3	8	2	272	37	0	.136

Harry Byrd
BYRD, HARRY GLADWIN BR TR 6'1" 188 lbs.
B. Feb. 3, 1925, Darlington, S. C.   BB 1955

1950 PHI A	0	0	—	16.88	6	0	0	10.2	25	9	2	0	0	0	0	2	0	0	.000
1952	15	15	.500	3.31	37	28	15	228.1	244	98	116	3	0	2	2	75	10	0	.133
1953	11	20	.355	5.51	40	37	11	236.2	279	115	122	2	0	1	0	81	18	0	.222
1954 NY A	9	7	.563	2.99	25	21	5	132.1	131	43	52	1	0	0	0	46	9	0	.196
1955 2 teams					BAL A (14G 3-2)			CHI A (25G 4-6)											
" total	7	8	.467	4.61	39	20	2	156.1	149	58	69	2	1	1	2	49	5	0	.102
1956 CHI A	0	1	.000	10.38	3	1	0	4.1	9	4	0	0	0	0	0	- 1	0	0	.000
1957 DET A	4	3	.571	3.36	37	1	0	59	53	28	20	0	4	3	5	8	0	0	.000
7 yrs.	46	54	.460	4.35	187	108	33	827.2	890	355	381	8	5	7	9	262	42	0	.160
2 yrs.	4	7	.364	4.91	28	13	1	95.1	94	34	44	1	1	1	1	31	2	0	.065

Pitcher Register

	W	L	PCT	ERA	G	GS	CG	IP	H	BB	SO	ShO	Relief Pitching W	L	SV	AB	BATTING H	HR	BA

Jerry Byrne
BYRNE, GERALD WILFORD BR TR 6' 170 lbs.
B. Feb. 2, 1907, Parnell, Mich. D. Aug. 11, 1955, Lansing, Mich.

| 1929 CHI A | 0 | 1 | .000 | 7.36 | 3 | 1 | 0 | 7.1 | 11 | 6 | 1 | 0 | 0 | 0 | 0 | 2 | 0 | 0 | .000 |

Tommy Byrne
BYRNE, THOMAS JOSEPH BL TL 6'1" 182 lbs.
B. Dec. 31, 1919, Baltimore, Md.

1943 NY A	2	1	.667	6.54	11	2	0	31.2	28	35	22	0	2	0	0	11	1	0	.091
1946	0	1	.000	5.79	4	1	0	9.1	7	8	5	0	0	0	0	9	2	0	.222
1947	0	0	–	4.15	4	1	0	4.1	5	6	2	0	0	0	0	0	0	0	–
1948	8	5	.615	3.30	31	11	5	133.2	79	101	93	1	2	1	2	46	15	1	.326
1949	15	7	.682	3.72	32	30	12	196	125	179	129	3	0	1	0	83	16	0	.193
1950	15	9	.625	4.74	31	31	10	203.1	188	160	118	2	0	0	0	81	22	2	.272
1951 2 teams			NY A (9G 2–1)				STL A (19G 4–10)												
" total	6	11	.353	4.26	28	20	7	143.2	120	150	71	2	2	0	0	66	18	2	.273
1952 STL A	7	14	.333	4.68	29	24	14	196	182	112	91	0	1	0	0	84	21	1	.250
1953 2 teams			CHI A (6G 2–0)				WAS A (6G 0–5)												
" total	2	5	.286	6.16	12	11	2	49.2	53	48	26	0	0	1	0	35	4	1	.114
1954 NY A	3	2	.600	2.70	5	5	4	40	36	19	24	1	0	0	0	19	7	0	.368
1955	16	5	**.762**	3.15	27	22	9	160	137	87	76	3	1	0	2	78	16	1	.205
1956	7	3	.700	3.36	37	8	1	109.2	108	72	52	0	6	2	6	52	14	3	.269
1957	4	6	.400	4.36	30	4	1	84.2	70	60	57	0	4	4	2	37	7	3	.189
13 yrs.	85	69	.552	4.11	281	170	65	1362	1138	1037	766	12	18	9	12	*			
1 yr.	2	0	1.000	10.13	6	6	0	16	18	26	4	0	0	0	0	18	3	1	.167

WORLD SERIES

1949 NY A	0	0	–	2.70	1	1	0	3.1	2	2	1	0	0	0	0	1	1	0	1.000
1955	1	1	.500	1.88	2	2	1	14.1	8	8	8	0	0	0	0	6	1	0	.167
1956	0	0	–	0.00	1	0	0	.1	1	0	1	0	0	0	0	1	0	0	.000
1957	0	0	–	5.40	2	0	0	3.1	1	2	1	0	0	0	0	2	1	0	.500
4 yrs.	1	1	.500	2.53	6	3	1	21.1	12	12	11	0	0	0	0	10	3	0	.300

Leon Cadore
CADORE, LEON JOSEPH BR TR 6'1" 190 lbs.
B. Nov. 20, 1891, Chicago, Ill. D. Mar. 16, 1958, Spokane, Wash.

1915 BKN N	0	2	.000	5.57	7	2	1	21	28	8	12	0	0	0	0	6	0	0	.000
1916	0	0	–	4.50	1	0	0	6	10	0	2	0	0	0	0	3	0	0	.000
1917	13	13	.500	2.45	37	30	21	264	231	63	115	1	0	0	3	92	24	0	.261
1918	1	0	1.000	0.53	2	2	1	17	6	2	5	1	0	0	0	4	0	0	.000
1919	14	12	.538	2.37	35	27	16	250.2	228	39	94	3	2	0	0	87	14	0	.161
1920	15	14	.517	2.62	35	30	16	254.1	256	56	79	4	1	1	0	91	20	2	.220
1921	13	14	.481	4.17	35	30	12	211.2	243	46	79	1	1	2	0	75	14	1	.187
1922	8	15	.348	4.35	34	27	13	190.1	224	57	49	0	4	0	0	71	19	2	.268
1923 2 teams			BKN N (8G 4–1)				CHI A (1G 0–1)												
" total	4	2	.667	4.46	9	5	3	38.1	45	15	11	0	1	0	0	13	1	0	.077
1924 NY N	0	0	–	0.00	2	0	0	4	2	3	2	0	0	0	0	0	0	0	–
10 yrs.	68	72	.486	3.14	192	147	83	1257.1	1273	289	445	10	9	3	3	442	92	5	.208
1 yr.	0	1	.000	23.14	1	1	0	2.1	6	2	3	0	0	0	0	0	0	0	–

WORLD SERIES

| 1920 BKN N | 0 | 1 | .000 | 9.00 | 2 | 1 | 0 | 2 | 4 | 1 | 1 | 0 | 0 | 0 | 0 | 0 | 0 | 0 | – |

Bob Cain
CAIN, ROBERT MAX (Sugar) BL TL 6' 165 lbs.
B. Oct. 16, 1924, Longford, Kans.

1949 CHI A	0	0	–	2.45	6	0	0	11	7	5	5	0	0	0	1	3	0	0	.000
1950	9	12	.429	3.93	34	23	11	171.2	153	109	77	1	1	1	2	61	12	0	.197
1951 2 teams			CHI A (4G 1–2)				DET A (35G 11–10)												
" total	12	12	.500	4.56	39	26	7	175.2	160	95	61	1	2	2	2	62	16	0	.258
1952 STL A	12	10	.545	4.13	29	27	8	170	169	62	70	1	0	0	1	58	8	0	.138
1953	4	10	.286	6.23	32	13	1	99.2	129	45	36	0	0	4	1	30	6	0	.200
1954 CHI A	0	0	–	0.00	0	0	0	0	0	0	0	0	0	0	0	0	0	0	–
6 yrs.	37	44	.457	4.50	140	89	27	628	618	316	249	3	3	7	8	214	42	0	.196
3 yrs.	10	14	.417	3.83	44	27	12	209	185	127	85	1	1	1	3	73	15	0	.205

Sugar Cain
CAIN, MERRITT PATRICK BL TR 5'11" 190 lbs.
B. Apr. 5, 1907, Macon, Ga. BR 1932, BB 1933
D. May 10, 1975, Carrollton, Ga.

1932 PHI A	3	4	.429	5.00	10	6	3	45	42	28	24	0	1	0	0	12	3	0	.250
1933	13	12	.520	4.25	38	32	16	218	244	137	43	1	0	1	1	80	16	0	.200
1934	9	17	.346	4.41	36	32	15	230.2	235	128	66	0	1	1	0	82	13	0	.159
1935 2 teams			PHI A (6G 0–5)				STL A (31G 9–8)												
" total	9	13	.409	5.44	37	29	8	193.2	236	**123**	73	0	1	0	0	65	11	0	.169
1936 2 teams			STL A (4G 1–1)				CHI A (30G 14–10)												
" total	15	11	.577	4.89	34	29	15	211.2	248	84	50	1	1	0	0	75	9	0	.120
1937 CHI A	4	2	.667	6.16	18	6	.1	68.2	88	51	17	0	3	0	0	22	4	0	.182
1938	0	1	.000	4.58	5	3	0	19.2	26	18	6	0	0	0	0	8	0	0	.000
7 yrs.	53	60	.469	4.83	178	137	58	987.1	1119	569	279	2	6	4	1	344	56	0	.163
3 yrs.	18	13	.581	5.08	53	35	15	283.2	342	144	65	1	4	1	0	98	11	0	.112

Earl Caldwell
CALDWELL, EARL WELTON (Teach) BR TR 6'1" 178 lbs.
B. Apr. 9, 1905, Sparks, Tex.

1928 PHI N	1	4	.200	5.71	5	5	1	34.2	46	17	6	1	0	0	0	9	1	0	.111
1935 STL A	3	2	.600	3.68	6	5	3	36.2	34	17	5	1	0	0	0	11	2	0	.182
1936	7	16	.304	6.00	41	25	10	189	252	83	59	2	0	2	2	58	11	1	.190
1937	0	0	–	6.83	9	0	0	29	39	13	8	0	0	0	0	9	2	0	.222
1945 CHI A	6	7	.462	3.59	27	11	5	105.1	108	37	45	1	1	3	4	37	8	0	.216
1946	13	4	.765	2.08	39	0	0	90.2	60	29	42	0	**13**	4	8	18	3	0	.167
1947	1	4	.200	3.64	40	0	0	54.1	53	30	22	0	1	4	8	7	0	0	.000
1948 2 teams			CHI A (25G 1–5)				BOS A (8G 1–1)												
" total	2	6	.250	6.75	33	1	0	48	64	33	15	0	2	5	3	8	1	0	.125
8 yrs.	33	43	.434	4.69	200	49	18	587.2	656	259	202	5	17	18	25	157	28	1	.178
4 yrs.	21	20	.512	3.36	131	12	5	289.1	274	118	119	1	16	15	23	67	11	0	.164

Pitcher Register

	W	L	PCT	ERA	G	GS	CG	IP	H	BB	SO	ShO	Relief Pitching W L SV	BATTING AB H HR	BA

Nixey Callahan
CALLAHAN, JAMES JOSEPH BR TR 5'10½" 180 lbs.
B. Mar. 18, 1874, Fitchburg, Mass.   D. Oct. 4, 1934, Boston, Mass.
Manager 1903-04, 1912-14, 1916-17.

Year	Team		W	L	PCT	ERA	G	GS	CG	IP	H	BB	SO	ShO	W	L	SV	AB	H	HR	BA
1894	PHI	N	1	2	.333	9.89	9	2	1	33.2	64	17	9	0	1	0	2	21	5	0	.238
1897	CHI	N	12	9	.571	4.03	23	22	21	189.2	221	55	52	1	0	1	0	360	105	3	.292
1898			20	10	.667	2.46	31	31	30	274.1	267	71	73	2	0	0	0	164	43	0	.262
1899			21	12	.636	3.06	35	34	33	294.1	327	76	77	3	1	0	0	150	39	0	.260
1900			13	16	.448	3.82	32	32	32	285.1	347	74	77	2	0	0	0	115	27	0	.235
1901	CHI	A	15	8	.652	2.42	27	22	20	215.1	195	50	70	1	1	2	0	118	39	1	.331
1902			16	14	.533	3.60	35	31	29	282.1	287	89	75	2	1	0	0	218	51	0	.234
1903			1	2	.333	4.50	3	3	3	28	40	5	12	0	0	0	0	439	128	2	.292
8 yrs.			99	73	.576	3.39	195	177	169	1603	1748	437	445	11	4	3	2	*			
3 yrs.			32	24	.571	3.17	65	56	52	525.2	522	144	157	3	2	2	0	2485	682	8	.274

Pat Caraway
CARAWAY, CECIL BRADFORD BL TL 6'4" 175 lbs.
B. Sept. 26, 1906, Gordon, Tex.   D. June 9, 1974, El Paso, Tex.

Year	Team		W	L	PCT	ERA	G	GS	CG	IP	H	BB	SO	ShO	W	L	SV	AB	H	HR	BA
1930	CHI	A	10	10	.500	3.86	38	21	9	193.1	194	57	83	1	2	1	1	64	11	0	.172
1931			10	24	.294	6.22	51	32	11	220	268	101	55	1	1	3	2	72	14	0	.194
1932			2	6	.250	6.82	19	9	1	64.2	80	37	13	0	0	1	0	21	3	0	.143
3 yrs.			22	40	.355	5.35	108	62	21	478	542	195	151	2	3	5	3	157	28	0	.178
3 yrs.			22	40	.355	5.35	108	62	21	478	542	195	151	2	3	5	3	157	28	0	.178

Cisco Carlos
CARLOS, FRANCISCO MANUEL BR TR 6'3" 205 lbs.
B. Sept. 17, 1940, Monrovia, Calif.

Year	Team		W	L	PCT	ERA	G	GS	CG	IP	H	BB	SO	ShO	W	L	SV	AB	H	HR	BA
1967	CHI	A	2	0	1.000	0.86	8	7	1	41.2	23	9	27	1	0	0	0	16	1	0	.063
1968			4	14	.222	3.90	29	21	0	122.1	121	37	57	0	0	0	0	31	2	0	.065
1969	2 teams				CHI	A (25G 4-3)			WAS	A (6G 1-1)											
"	total		5	4	.556	5.37	31	8	0	67	75	29	33	0	3	2	0	15	1	0	.067
1970	WAS	A	0	0	—	1.50	5	0	0	6	3	4	2	0	0	0	0	0	0	0	—
4 yrs.			11	18	.379	3.72	73	36	1	237	222	79	119	1	3	2	0	62	4	0	.065
3 yrs.			10	17	.370	3.71	62	32	1	213.1	196	69	112	1	3	2	0	57	3	0	.053

Eddie Carnett
CARNETT, EDWIN ELLIOTT (Lefty) BL TL 6' 185 lbs.
B. Oct. 21, 1916, Springfield, Mo.

Year	Team		W	L	PCT	ERA	G	GS	CG	IP	H	BB	SO	ShO	W	L	SV	AB	H	HR	BA
1941	BOS	N	0	0	—	20.25	2	0	0	1.1	4	3	2	0	0	0	0	0	0	0	—
1944	CHI	A	0	0	—	9.00	2	0	0	2	3	0	1	0	0	0	0	457	126	1	.276
1945	CLE	A	0	0	—	0.00	2	0	0	2	0	0	1	0	0	0	0	73	16	0	.219
3 yrs.			0	0	—	8.44	6	0	0	5.1	7	3	4	0	0	0	0	*			
1 yr.			0	0	—	9.00	2	0	0	2	3	0	1	0	0	0	0	457	126	1	.276

Alex Carrasquel
CARRASQUEL, ALEJANDRO ALEXANDER APARICIO ELROY BR TR 6'1" 182 lbs.
B. July 24, 1912, Caracas, Venezuela   D. Aug. 19, 1969, Caracas, Venezuela

Year	Team		W	L	PCT	ERA	G	GS	CG	IP	H	BB	SO	ShO	W	L	SV	AB	H	HR	BA
1939	WAS	A	5	9	.357	4.69	40	17	7	159.1	165	68	41	0	1	1	2	42	7	1	.167
1940			6	2	.750	4.88	28	0	0	48	42	29	19	0	6	2	0	7	0	0	.000
1941			6	2	.750	3.44	35	5	4	96.2	103	49	30	0	4	1	2	21	2	0	.095
1942			7	7	.500	3.43	35	15	7	152.1	161	53	40	1	1	2	4	44	6	0	.136
1943			11	7	.611	3.68	39	13	4	144.1	160	54	48	1	5	3	5	43	8	0	.186
1944			8	7	.533	3.43	43	7	3	134	143	50	35	0	5	3	2	36	7	0	.194
1945			7	5	.583	2.71	35	7	5	122.2	105	40	38	2	4	3	1	36	3	0	.083
1949	CHI	A	0	0	—	14.73	3	0	0	3.2	8	4	1	0	0	0	0	0	0	0	—
8 yrs.			50	39	.562	3.73	258	64	30	861	887	347	252	4	26	15	16	229	33	1	.144
1 yr.			0	0	—	14.73	3	0	0	3.2	8	4	1	0	0	0	0	0	0	0	—

Clay Carroll
CARROLL, CLAY PALMER (Hawk) BR TR 6'1" 178 lbs.
B. May 2, 1941, Clanton, Ala.

Year	Team		W	L	PCT	ERA	G	GS	CG	IP	H	BB	SO	ShO	W	L	SV	AB	H	HR	BA
1964	MIL	N	2	0	1.000	1.77	11	1	0	20.1	15	3	17	0	2	0	1	2	0	0	.000
1965			0	1	.000	4.41	19	1	0	34.2	35	13	16	0	0	1	1	5	0	0	.000
1966	ATL	N	8	7	.533	2.37	73	3	0	144.1	127	29	67	0	8	7	11	30	3	0	.100
1967			6	12	.333	5.52	42	7	1	93	111	29	35	0	3	8	0	16	1	0	.063
1968	2 teams				ATL	N (10G 0-1)			CIN	N (58G 7-7)											
"	total		7	8	.467	2.69	68	1	0	144	128	38	71	0	7	8	17	29	6	0	.207
1969	CIN	N	12	6	.667	3.52	71	4	0	151	149	78	90	0	11	6	7	29	6	1	.207
1970			9	4	.692	2.60	65	0	0	104	104	27	63	0	9	4	16	14	1	0	.071
1971			10	4	.714	2.49	61	0	0	94	78	42	64	0	10	4	15	10	1	0	.100
1972			6	4	.600	2.25	65	0	0	96	89	32	51	0	6	4	37	11	2	0	.182
1973			8	8	.500	3.69	53	5	0	92.2	111	34	41	0	6	8	14	14	3	0	.214
1974			12	5	.706	2.14	57	3	0	101	96	30	46	0	10	4	6	18	3	0	.167
1975			7	5	.583	2.63	56	2	0	96	93	32	44	0	7	5	7	19	0	0	.000
1976	CHI	A	4	4	.500	2.57	29	0	0	77	67	24	38	0	4	4	6	0	0	0	—
1977	2 teams				CHI	A (8G 1-3)			STL	N (51G 4-2)											
"	total		5	5	.500	2.76	59	1	0	101	91	28	38	0	5	5	5	11	1	0	.091
1978	PIT	N	0	0	—	2.25	2	0	0	4	2	3	0	0	0	0	0	0	0	0	—
15 yrs.			96	73	.568	2.94	731	28	1	1353	1296	442	681	0	88 8th	68	143	208	27	1	.130
2 yrs.			5	7	.417	2.86	37	0	0	88	81	28	42	0	5	7	7	0	0	0	—

LEAGUE CHAMPIONSHIP SERIES

Year	Team		W	L	PCT	ERA	G	GS	CG	IP	H	BB	SO	ShO	W	L	SV	AB	H	HR	BA
1970	CIN	N	0	0	—	0.00	2	0	0	1.1	2	0	2	0	0	0	1	0	0	0	—
1972			1	1	.500	3.38	2	0	0	2.2	2	3	0	0	1	1	0	0	0	0	—
1973			1	0	1.000	1.29	3	0	0	7	5	1	2	0	1	0	0	0	0	0	—
1975			0	0	—	0.00	1	0	0	1	0	1	0	0	0	0	0	0	0	0	—
4 yrs.			2	1	.667	1.50	8	0	0	12	9	5	5	0	2	1	1	0	0	0	—

WORLD SERIES

Year	Team		W	L	PCT	ERA	G	GS	CG	IP	H	BB	SO	ShO	W	L	SV	AB	H	HR	BA
1970	CIN	N	1	0	1.000	0.00	4	0	0	9	5	2	11	0	1	0	0	1	0	0	.000
1972			0	1	.000	1.59	5	0	0	5.2	6	4	3	0	0	1	1	0	0	0	—

Pitcher Register

	W	L	PCT	ERA	G	GS	CG	IP	H	BB	SO	ShO	Relief Pitching W L SV	BATTING AB H HR	BA

Clay Carroll continued
1975	1	0	1.000	3.18	5	0	0	5.2	4	2	3	0	1 0 0	0 0 0	–
3 yrs.	2	1	.667	1.33	14	0	0	20.1	15	8	17	0	2 1 1	1 0 0	.000
					5th										

Paul Castner
CASTNER, PAUL HENRY (Lefty) BL TL 5'11" 187 lbs.
B. Feb. 16, 1897, St. Paul, Minn.

| 1923 CHI A | 0 | 0 | – | 6.30 | 6 | 0 | 0 | 10 | 14 | 5 | 0 | 0 | 0 0 0 | 3 0 0 | .000 |

Bob Chakales
CHAKALES, ROBERT EDWARD (Chick) BR TR 6'1" 185 lbs.
B. Aug. 10, 1927, Asheville, N. C.

1951 CLE A	3	4	.429	4.74	17	10	2	68.1	80	43	32	1	0 0 0	20 7 1	.350
1952	1	2	.333	9.75	5	1	0	12	19	8	7	0	0 2 0	4 2 0	.500
1953	0	2	.000	2.67	7	3	1	27	28	10	6	0	0 0 0	7 2 0	.286
1954 2 teams			CLE A (3G 2-0)			BAL A (38G 3-7)									
" total	5	7	.417	3.43	41	6	0	99.2	85	55	47	0	5 4 3	25 9 0	.360
1955 2 teams			CHI A (7G 0-0)			WAS A (29G 2-3)									
" total	2	3	.400	4.57	36	0	0	67	66	31	34	0	2 3 0	10 0 0	.000
1956 WAS A	4	4	.500	4.03	43	1	0	96	94	57	33	0	4 4 4	20 3 0	.150
1957 2 teams			WAS A (4G 0-1)			BOS A (18G 0-2)									
" total	0	3	.000	7.15	22	2	0	50.1	73	21	28	0	0 3 3	10 3 0	.300
7 yrs.	15	25	.375	4.54	171	23	3	420.1	445	225	187	1	11 16 10	96 26 1	.271
1 yr.	0	0	–	1.46	7	0	0	12.1	11	6	6	0	0 0 0	2 0 0	.000

Bill Chamberlain
CHAMBERLAIN, WILLIAM VINCENT BR TL 5'10½" 173 lbs.
B. Apr. 21, 1909, Stoughton, Mass.

| 1932 CHI A | 0 | 5 | .000 | 4.57 | 12 | 5 | 0 | 41.1 | 39 | 25 | 11 | 0 | 0 0 0 | 10 1 0 | .100 |

Ben Chapman
CHAPMAN, WILLIAM BENJAMIN BR TR 6' 190 lbs.
B. Dec. 25, 1908, Nashville, Tenn.
Manager 1945-48.

1944 BKN N	5	3	.625	3.40	11	9	6	79.1	75	33	37	0	0 1 0	38 14 0	.368
1945 2 teams			BKN N (10G 3-3)			PHI N (3G 0-0)									
" total	3	3	.500	5.79	13	7	2	60.2	71	38	27	0	1 0 0	73 19 0	.260
1946 PHI N	0	0	–	0.00	1	0	0	1.1	1	0	1	0	0 0 0	1 0 0	.000
3 yrs.	8	6	.571	4.39	25	16	8	141.1	147	71	65	0	1 1 0	*	

Italo Chelini
CHELINI, ITALO VINCENT (Lefty) BL TL 5'10½" 175 lbs.
B. Oct. 10, 1914, San Francisco, Calif.   D. Aug. 25, 1972, San Francisco, Calif.

1935 CHI A	0	0	–	12.60	2	0	0	5	7	4	1	0	0 0 0	2 1 0	.500
1936	4	3	.571	4.95	18	6	5	83.2	100	30	16	0	1 0 0	32 5 0	.156
1937	0	1	.000	10.38	4	0	0	8.2	15	0	3	0	0 1 0	1 0 0	.000
3 yrs.	4	4	.500	5.83	24	6	5	97.1	122	34	20	0	1 1 0	35 6 0	.171
3 yrs.	4	4	.500	5.83	24	6	5	97.1	122	34	20	0	1 1 0	35 6 0	.171

Chief Chouneau
CHOUNEAU, WILLIAM BR TR 5'9" 150 lbs.
Born William Cadreau.
B. Sept. 2, 1889, Cloquet, Minn.   D. Sept. 17, 1948, Cloquet, Minn.

| 1910 CHI A | 0 | 1 | .000 | 3.38 | 1 | 1 | 0 | 5.1 | 7 | 0 | 1 | 0 | 0 0 0 | 1 0 0 | .000 |

Eddie Cicotte
CICOTTE, EDWARD VICTOR BB TR 5'9" 175 lbs.
B. June 19, 1884, Detroit, Mich.   D. May 5, 1969, Detroit, Mich.

1905 DET A	1	1	.500	3.50	3			18	25	5	6	0	0 1 0	7 3 0	.429
1908 BOS A	11	12	.478	2.43	39	24	17	207.1	198	59	95	2	1 2 2	72 17 0	.236
1909	13	5	.722	1.97	27	15	10	159.2	117	56	82	1	4 0 2	49 11 0	.224
1910	15	11	.577	2.74	36	30	20	250	213	86	104	4	1 0 0	85 12 0	.141
1911	11	15	.423	2.81	35	25	16	221	236	73	106	1	2 2 0	71 10 0	.141
1912 2 teams			BOS A (9G 1-3)			CHI A (20G 9-7)									
" total	10	10	.500	3.50	29	24	19	198	217	52	90	1	0 1 0	69 15 0	.217
1913 CHI A	18	12	.600	1.58	41	30	18	268	224	73	121	3	3 1 0	91 13 0	.143
1914	13	16	.448	2.04	45	29	19	269.1	220	72	122	4	1 0 3	86 14 0	.163
1915	13	12	.520	3.02	39	26	15	223.1	216	48	106	1	0 1 3	67 14 0	.209
1916	15	7	**.682**	1.78	44	20	11	187	138	70	91	2	3 2 4	57 12 0	.211
1917	**28**	12	**.700**	**1.53**	49	35	29	**346.2**	246	70	**150**	7	5 1 4	112 20 0	.179
1918	12	19	.387	2.64	38	30	24	266	275	40	104	1	3 1 2	86 14 0	.163
1919	**29**	7	**.806**	1.82	40	35	**29**	**306.2**	256	49	110	5	2 1 1	99 20 0	.202
1920	21	10	.677	3.26	37	35	28	303.1	316	74	87	4	0 0 2	112 22 0	.196
14 yrs.	210	149	.585	2.37	502	359	248	3224.1	2897	827	1374	36	25 13 23	1063 197 0	.185
9 yrs.	158	102	.608	2.24	353	258	182	2322.1	2050	533	961	28	17 7 19	766 142 0	.185
	7th	10th	5th	3rd		8th		6th	7th		9th	5th			

WORLD SERIES
1917 CHI A	1	1	.500	1.96	3	2	2	23	23	2	13	0	0 0 0	7 1 0	.143
1919	1	2	.333	2.91	3	3	2	21.2	19	5	7	0	0 0 0	8 0 0	.000
2 yrs.	2	3	.400	2.42	6	5	4	44.2	42	7	20	0	0 0 0	15 1 0	.067

Rocky Colavito
COLAVITO, ROCCO DOMENICO BR TR 6'3" 190 lbs.
B. Aug. 10, 1933, New York, N. Y.

1958 CLE A	0	0	–	0.00	1	0	0	3	0	3	1	0	0 0 0	489 148 41	.303
1968 NY A	1	0	1.000	0.00	1	0	0	2.2	1	2	1	0	1 0 0	204 43 8	.211
2 yrs.	1	0	1.000	0.00	2	0	0	5.2	1	5	2	0	1 0 0	*	

Bert Cole
COLE, ALBERT GEORGE BL TL 6'1" 180 lbs.
B. July 1, 1898, San Francisco, Calif.   D. May 30, 1975, San Mateo, Calif.

1921 DET A	7	4	.636	4.27	20	11	7	109.2	134	36	22	1	1 0 1	46 13 0	.283
1922	1	6	.143	4.88	23	5	2	79.1	105	39	21	1	0 3 0	25 4 0	.160
1923	13	5	.722	4.14	52	13	5	163	183	61	32	1	5 2 5	55 14 1	.255

Pitcher Register

	W	L	PCT	ERA	G	GS	CG	IP	H	BB	SO	ShO	Relief Pitching W	L	SV	BATTING AB	H	HR	BA

Bert Cole continued

1924	3	9	.250	4.69	28	11	2	109.1	135	35	16	1	1	2	2	37	10	0	.270
1925 2 teams	DET A (14G 2-3)					CLE A (13G 1-1)													
" total	3	4	.429	6.03	27	4	1	77.2	99	40	16	0	2	2	2	24	5	0	.208
1927 CHI A	1	4	.200	4.73	27	2	0	66.2	79	19	12	0	1	3	0	18	3	0	.167
6 yrs.	28	32	.467	4.67	177	46	17	605.2	735	230	119	4	10	12	10	205	49	1	.239
1 yr.	1	4	.200	4.73	27	2	0	66.2	79	19	12	0	1	3	0	18	3	0	.167

Sarge Connally

CONNALLY, GEORGE WALTER
B. Aug. 31, 1898, McGregor, Tex. D. Jan. 27, 1978, Temple, Tex. BR TR 5'11" 170 lbs.

1921 CHI A	0	1	.000	6.45	5	2	0	22.1	29	10	6	0	0	0	0	8	4	0	.500
1923	0	0	-	6.23	3	0	0	8.2	7	12	3	0	0	0	0	3	1	0	.333
1924	7	13	.350	4.05	44	13	6	160	177	68	55	0	5	5	6	50	11	0	.220
1925	6	7	.462	4.64	40	2	0	104.2	122	58	45	0	5	6	8	28	7	0	.250
1926	6	5	.545	3.16	31	8	5	108.1	128	35	47	0	2	4	3	32	5	0	.156
1927	10	15	.400	4.08	43	18	11	198.1	217	83	58	1	5	3	5	67	22	0	.328
1928	2	5	.286	4.84	28	5	1	74.1	89	29	28	0	1	4	2	19	2	0	.105
1929	0	0	-	4.76	11	0	0	11.1	13	8	3	0	0	0	1	0	0	0	-
1931 CLE A	5	5	.500	4.20	17	9	5	85.2	87	50	37	0	2	0	1	27	5	0	.185
1932	8	6	.571	4.33	35	7	4	112.1	119	42	32	1	4	4	3	40	7	1	.175
1933	5	3	.625	4.89	41	3	1	103	112	49	30	0	4	2	1	26	6	0	.231
1934	0	0	-	5.06	5	0	0	5.1	4	5	1	0	0	0	1	1	0	0	.000
12 yrs.	49	60	.450	4.30	303	67	33	994.1	1104	449	345	2	28	28	31	301	70	1	.233
8 yrs.	31	46	.403	4.21	205	48	23	688	782	303	245	1	18	22	25	207	52	0	.251

Bill Connelly

CONNELLY, WILLIAM WIRT (Wild Bill)
B. June 29, 1925, Alberta, Va. BL TR 6' 175 lbs.

1945 PHI A	1	1	.500	4.50	2	1	0	8	7	8	0	0	1	0	0	1	0	0	.000
1950 2 teams	CHI N (2G 0-0)					DET A (2G 0-0)													
" total	0	0	-	8.53	4	0	0	6.1	9	3	1	0	0	0	0	1	0	0	.000
1952 NY N	5	0	1.000	4.55	11	4	0	31.2	22	25	22	0	2	0	0	11	4	0	.364
1953	0	1	.000	11.07	8	2	0	20.1	33	17	11	0	0	0	0	6	0	0	.000
4 yrs.	6	2	.750	6.92	25	7	0	66.1	71	53	34	0	3	0	0	19	4	0	.211
1 yr.	0	0	-	11.57	2	0	0	2.1	5	1	0	0	0	0	0	0	0	0	-

Sandy Consuegra

CONSUEGRA, SANDALIO SIMEON CASTELLON
B. Sept. 3, 1920, Potrerillo, Cuba BR TR 5'11" 165 lbs.

1950 WAS A	7	8	.467	4.40	21	18	8	124.2	132	57	38	2	0	0	2	40	7	0	.175
1951	7	8	.467	4.01	40	12	5	146	140	63	31	0	2	5	3	43	10	0	.233
1952	6	0	1.000	3.05	30	2	0	73.2	80	27	19	0	5	0	5	17	3	0	.176
1953 2 teams	WAS A (4G 0-0)					CHI A (29G 7-5)													
" total	7	5	.583	2.86	33	13	5	129	131	32	30	1	3	0	3	35	2	0	.057
1954 CHI A	16	3	.842	2.69	39	17	3	154	142	35	31	2	8	0	3	48	11	0	.229
1955	6	5	.545	2.64	44	7	3	126.1	120	18	35	0	3	3	7	29	3	0	.103
1956 2 teams	CHI A (28G 1-2)					BAL A (4G 1-1)													
" total	2	3	.400	4.98	32	2	0	47	55	13	8	0	1	0	3	6	1	0	.167
1957 2 teams	BAL A (5G 0-0)					NY N (4G 0-0)													
" total	0	0	-	2.08	9	0	0	8.2	11	1	1	0	0	0	0	0	0	0	-
8 yrs.	51	32	.614	3.37	248	71	24	809.1	811	246	193	5	22	9	26	218	37	0	.170
4 yrs.	30	15	.667	2.85	140	38	11	442.2	429	92	103	3	15	4	16	116	16	0	.138

Nardi Contreras

CONTRERAS, ARNALDO JUAN
B. Sept. 19, 1951, Tampa, Fla. BB TR 6'2" 193 lbs.

| 1980 CHI A | 0 | 0 | - | 5.79 | 8 | 0 | 0 | 14 | 18 | 7 | 8 | 0 | 0 | 0 | 0 | 0 | 0 | 0 | - |

Ed Corey

COREY, EDWARD N.
B. Apr. 10, 1900, Chicago, Ill. BR TR

| 1918 CHI A | 0 | 0 | - | 4.50 | 1 | 0 | 0 | 2 | 2 | 1 | 0 | 0 | 0 | 0 | 0 | 1 | 0 | 0 | .000 |

Henry Courtney

COURTNEY, HARRY SEYMOUR
B. Nov. 19, 1898, Asheville, N.C. BL TL 6'4" 185 lbs.

1919 WAS A	3	0	1.000	2.73	4	3	3	26.1	25	19	6	1	0	0	0	10	2	0	.200
1920	8	11	.421	4.74	37	24	10	188	223	77	48	1	0	2	0	69	16	1	.232
1921	6	9	.400	5.63	30	15	3	132.2	159	71	26	0	1	1	1	47	14	0	.298
1922 2 teams	WAS A (5G 0-0)					CHI A (18G 5-6)													
" total	5	6	.455	4.81	23	11	5	97.1	111	46	32	0	1	0	0	37	9	0	.243
4 yrs.	22	26	.458	4.90	94	53	21	444.1	518	213	112	2	2	3	1	163	41	1	.252
1 yr.	5	6	.455	4.93	18	11	5	87.2	100	37	28	0	1	0	0	33	9	0	.273

Bill Cox

COX, WILLIAM DONALD
B. June 23, 1913, Ashmore, Ill. BR TR 6'1" 185 lbs.

1936 STL N	0	0	-	6.75	2	0	0	2.2	4	1	1	0	0	0	0	0	0	0	-
1937 CHI A	1	0	1.000	0.71	3	2	1	12.2	9	5	8	0	0	0	0	4	1	0	.250
1938 2 teams	CHI A (7G 0-2)					STL A (22G 1-4)													
" total	1	6	.143	6.99	29	8	1	74.2	92	48	21	0	0	1	0	19	1	0	.053
1939 STL A	0	2	.000	9.64	4	2	1	9.1	10	8	8	0	0	0	0	1	0	0	.000
1940	0	1	.000	7.27	12	0	0	17.1	23	12	7	0	0	1	0	1	0	0	.000
5 yrs.	2	9	.182	6.56	50	12	3	116.2	138	74	45	0	0	2	0	25	2	0	.080
2 yrs.	1	2	.333	3.70	10	3	1	24.1	20	18	13	0	0	1	0	6	1	0	.167

Ernie Cox

COX, ERNEST THOMPSON (Elmer)
B. Feb. 19, 1894, Birmingham, Ala. BL TR 6'1" 180 lbs.

| 1922 CHI A | 0 | 0 | - | 18.00 | 1 | 0 | 0 | 1 | 2 | 0 | 0 | 0 | 0 | 0 | 0 | 0 | 0 | 0 | - |

Pitcher Register

	W	L	PCT	ERA	G	GS	CG	IP	H	BB	SO	ShO	Relief Pitching W	L	SV	AB	BATTING H	HR	BA

George Cox
COX, GEORGE MELVIN BR TR 6'1" 170 lbs.
B. Nov. 15, 1904, Sherman, Tex.
| 1928 CHI A | 1 | 2 | .333 | 5.26 | 26 | 2 | 0 | 89 | 110 | 39 | 22 | 0 | 1 | 1 | 0 | 26 | 2 | 0 | .077 |

Les Cox
COX, LESLIE WARREN BR TR 6' 164 lbs.
B. Aug. 14, 1905, Junction, Tex. D. Oct. 12, 1934, Brownwood, Tex.
| 1926 CHI A | 0 | 1 | .000 | 5.40 | 2 | 0 | 0 | 5 | 6 | 5 | 3 | 0 | 0 | 1 | 0 | 2 | 1 | 0 | .500 |

Jim Crabb
CRABB, JAMES ROY BR TR 5'11" 160 lbs.
B. Aug. 23, 1890, Monticello, Iowa D. Mar. 30, 1940, Lewistown, Mont.
| 1912 2 teams | CHI A (2G 0–1) | PHI A (7G 2–4) | | | | | | | | | | | | | | | | | |
| " total | 2 | 5 | .286 | 3.29 | 9 | 8 | 3 | 52 | 54 | 21 | 15 | 0 | 0 | 0 | 0 | 19 | 0 | 0 | .000 |

Jerry Crider
CRIDER, JERRY STEPHEN BR TR 6'2" 200 lbs.
B. Sept. 2, 1941, Sioux Falls, S. D.
1969 MIN A	1	0	1.000	4.71	21	1	0	28.2	31	15	16	0	1	0	1	9	4	0	.444
1970 CHI A	4	7	.364	4.45	32	8	0	91	101	34	40	0	2	2	4	24	2	0	.083
2 yrs.	5	7	.417	4.51	53	9	0	119.2	132	49	56	0	3	2	5	33	6	0	.182
1 yr.	4	7	.364	4.45	32	8	0	91	101	34	40	0	2	2	4	24	2	0	.083

Charlie Cuellar
CUELLAR, JESUS PATRACIS BR TR 5'11" 183 lbs.
B. Sept. 24, 1917, Ybor City, Fla.
| 1950 CHI A | 0 | 0 | – | 33.75 | 2 | 0 | 0 | 1.1 | 6 | 3 | 1 | 0 | 0 | 0 | 0 | 0 | 0 | 0 | – |

Mike Cvengros
CVENGROS, MICHAEL JOHN BL TL 5'8" 159 lbs.
B. Dec. 1, 1901, Pana, Ill. D. Aug. 2, 1970, Hotsprings, Ark.
1922 NY N	0	1	.000	4.00	1	1	1	9	6	3	3	0	0	0	0	3	0	0	.000
1923 CHI A	12	13	.480	4.39	41	26	14	215.1	216	107	86	0	2	1	3	74	15	0	.203
1924	3	12	.200	5.88	26	15	2	105.2	119	67	36	0	1	3	0	30	6	0	.200
1925	3	9	.250	4.30	22	11	4	104.2	109	55	32	0	1	2	0	33	5	0	.152
1927 PIT N	2	1	.667	3.35	23	4	0	53.2	55	24	21	0	2	0	1	19	3	0	.158
1929 CHI N	5	4	.556	4.64	32	2	0	64	82	29	23	0	5	4	2	15	6	0	.400
6 yrs.	25	40	.385	4.58	145	59	21	552.1	587	285	201	0	11	10	6	174	35	0	.201
3 yrs.	18	34	.346	4.74	89	52	20	425.2	444	229	154	0	4	6	3	137	26	0	.190

WORLD SERIES
| 1927 PIT N | 0 | 0 | – | 3.86 | 2 | 0 | 0 | 2.1 | 3 | 0 | 2 | 0 | 0 | 0 | 0 | 0 | 0 | 0 | – |

Pete Daglia
DAGLIA, PETER GEORGE BR TR 6'1" 200 lbs.
B. Feb. 28, 1906, Napa, Calif. D. Mar. 11, 1952, Willits, Calif.
| 1932 CHI A | 2 | 4 | .333 | 5.76 | 12 | 5 | 2 | 50 | 67 | 20 | 16 | 0 | 1 | 0 | 0 | 13 | 1 | 0 | .077 |

Jerry Dahlke
DAHLKE, JEROME ALEX (Joe) BR TR 6' 180 lbs.
B. June 8, 1930, Marathon, Wis.
| 1956 CHI A | 0 | 0 | – | 19.29 | 5 | 0 | 0 | 2.1 | 5 | 6 | 1 | 0 | 0 | 0 | 0 | 0 | 0 | 0 | – |

Bruce Dal Canton
Dal CANTON, JOHN BRUCE BR TR 6'2" 205 lbs.
B. June 15, 1942, California, Pa.
1967 PIT N	2	1	.667	1.88	8	2	1	24	19	10	13	0	2	0	0	6	2	0	.333
1968	1	1	.500	2.12	7	0	0	17	7	6	8	0	1	1	2	3	0	0	.000
1969	8	2	.800	3.35	57	0	0	86	79	49	56	0	8	2	5	10	3	0	.300
1970	9	4	.692	4.55	41	6	1	85	94	39	53	0	6	3	1	16	0	0	.000
1971 KC A	8	6	.571	3.45	25	22	2	141	144	44	58	0	0	0	0	46	4	0	.087
1972	6	6	.500	3.40	35	16	1	132.1	135	29	75	0	2	2	2	41	4	0	.098
1973	4	3	.571	4.82	32	3	1	97	108	46	39	0	3	1	3	0	0	0	–
1974	8	10	.444	3.14	31	22	9	175	135	82	96	2	2	2	0	0	0	0	–
1975 2 teams	KC A (4G 0–2)	ATL N (26G 2–7)																	
" total	2	9	.182	4.76	30	11	0	75.2	86	31	43	0	2	2	3	19	2	0	.105
1976 ATL N	3	5	.375	3.58	42	1	0	73	67	42	36	0	3	4	1	9	2	0	.222
1977 CHI A	0	2	.000	3.75	8	0	0	24	20	13	9	0	0	2	0	0	0	0	–
11 yrs.	51	49	.510	3.68	316	83	15	930	894	391	486	2	29	19	19	150	17	0	.113
1 yr.	0	2	.000	3.75	8	0	0	24	20	13	9	0	0	2	2	0	0	0	–

Dave Danforth
DANFORTH, DAVID CHARLES (Dauntless Dave) BL TL 6' 167 lbs.
B. Mar. 7, 1890, Granger, Tex. D. Sept. 19, 1970, Baltimore, Md.
1911 PHI A	4	2	.667	3.74	14	2	1	33.2	29	17	21	0	3	0	0	6	1	0	.167
1912	0	0	–	3.98	3	0	0	20.1	26	12	8	0	0	0	0	8	2	0	.250
1916 CHI A	5	5	.500	3.27	28	8	1	93.2	87	37	49	0	0	0	2	23	2	0	.087
1917	15	6	.714	2.65	50	9	1	173	155	74	79	1	9	3	7	46	6	0	.130
1918	6	15	.286	3.43	39	13	5	139	148	40	48	0	6	5	2	42	6	0	.143
1919	1	2	.333	7.78	15	1	0	41.2	58	20	17	0	1	1	1	9	1	0	.111
1922 STL A	5	2	.714	3.28	20	10	3	79.2	93	38	48	0	0	0	1	23	2	0	.087
1923	16	14	.533	3.94	38	29	16	226.1	221	87	96	1	1	2	1	71	15	0	.211
1924	15	12	.556	4.51	41	27	12	219.2	246	69	65	1	3	2	4	76	13	0	.171
1925	7	9	.438	4.36	38	15	5	159	172	61	53	0	3	2	2	46	8	0	.174
10 yrs.	74	67	.525	3.89	286	114	44	1186	1235	455	484	3	26	15	20	350	56	0	.160
4 yrs.	27	28	.491	3.50	132	31	7	447.1	448	171	193	1	16	9	12	120	15	0	.125

WORLD SERIES
| 1917 CHI A | 0 | 0 | – | 18.00 | 1 | 0 | 0 | 3 | 3 | 2 | 0 | 0 | 0 | 0 | 0 | 0 | 0 | 0 | – |

Lum Davenport
DAVENPORT, JOUBERT LUM BL TL 6'1" 165 lbs.
B. June 27, 1900, Tucson, Ariz. D. Apr. 21, 1961, Dallas, Tex.
1921 CHI A	0	3	.000	6.88	13	2	0	35.1	47	32	9	0	0	2	0	17	7	0	.412
1922	1	1	.500	10.80	9	1	0	16.2	14	13	9	0	0	1	0	3	0	0	.000
1923	0	0	–	6.23	2	0	0	4.1	7	4	1	0	0	0	0	1	1	0	1.000

Pitcher Register

	W	L	PCT	ERA	G	GS	CG	IP	H	BB	SO	ShO	Relief Pitching W	L	SV	BATTING AB	H	HR	BA

Lum Davenport continued

1924	0	0	–	0.00	1	0	0	2	1	2	1	0	0	0	0	0	0	0	–
4 yrs.	1	4	.200	7.71	25	3	0	58.1	63	51	20	0	0	3	0	21	8	0	.381
4 yrs.	1	4	.200	7.71	25	3	0	58.1	63	51	20	0	0	3	0	21	8	0	.381

Dixie Davis
DAVIS, FRANK TALMADGE   BR TR 5'11" 155 lbs.
B. Oct. 12, 1890, Wilson Mills, N. C.   D. Feb. 4, 1944, Raleigh, N. C.

1912 CIN N	0	1	.000	2.70	7	0	0	26.2	25	16	12	0	0	1	0	10	2	0	.200
1915 CHI A	0	0	–	0.00	2	0	0	3	2	2	2	0	0	0	0	0	0	0	–
1918 PHI N	0	2	.000	3.06	17	2	1	47	43	30	18	0	0	0	0	9	0	0	.000
1920 STL A	18	12	.600	3.17	38	31	22	269.1	270	149	85	0	1	0	0	94	25	0	.266
1921	16	16	.500	4.44	40	36	20	265.1	279	123	100	2	0	0	0	95	20	0	.211
1922	11	6	.647	4.08	25	25	7	174.1	162	87	65	2	0	0	0	59	8	0	.136
1923	4	6	.400	3.62	19	17	5	109.1	106	63	36	1	0	0	0	40	10	0	.250
1924	11	13	.458	4.10	29	24	11	160.1	159	72	45	5	1	0	0	46	7	0	.152
1925	12	7	.632	4.59	35	23	9	180.1	192	106	58	0	2	1	1	64	11	0	.172
1926	3	8	.273	4.66	27	7	2	83	93	40	39	0	3	3	1	24	4	0	.167
10 yrs.	75	71	.514	3.97	239	165	77	1318.2	1311	688	460	10	7	5	2	441	87	0	.197
1 yr.	0	0	–	0.00	2	0	0	3	2	2	2	0	0	0	0	0	0	0	–

George Davis
DAVIS, GEORGE STACEY   BB TR 5'9" 180 lbs.
B. Aug. 23, 1870, Cohoes, N. Y.   D. Oct. 17, 1940, Philadelphia, Pa.
Manager 1895, 1900-01.

| 1891 CLE N | 0 | 1 | .000 | 15.75 | 3 | 0 | 0 | 4 | 8 | 3 | 4 | 0 | 0 | 1 | 1 | * | | | |

Dave DeBusschere
DeBUSSCHERE, DAVID ALBERT   BR TR 6'6" 225 lbs.
B. Oct. 16, 1940, Detroit, Mich.

1962 CHI A	0	0	–	2.00	12	0	0	18	5	23	8	0	0	0	0	0	0	0	–
1963	3	4	.429	3.09	24	10	1	84.1	80	34	53	1	0	0	0	22	1	0	.045
2 yrs.	3	4	.429	2.90	36	10	1	102.1	85	57	61	1	0	0	0	22	1	0	.045
2 yrs.	3	4	.429	2.90	36	10	1	102.1	85	57	61	1	0	0	0	22	1	0	.045

Mike DeGerick
DeGERICK, MICHAEL ARTHUR   BR TR 6'2" 178 lbs.
B. Apr. 1, 1943, New York, N. Y.

1961 CHI A	0	0	–	5.40	1	0	0	1.2	2	1	0	0	0	0	0	0	0	0	–
1962	0	0	–	0.00	1	0	0	1	1	1	0	0	0	0	0	0	0	0	–
2 yrs.	0	0	–	3.38	2	0	0	2.2	3	2	0	0	0	0	0	0	0	0	–
2 yrs.	0	0	–	3.38	2	0	0	2.2	3	2	0	0	0	0	0	0	0	0	–

Flame Delhi
DELHI, LEE WILLIAM   BR TR 6'2½" 198 lbs.
B. Nov. 2, 1890, Harqua Hala, Ariz.   D. May 9, 1966, San Rafael, Calif.

| 1912 CHI A | 0 | 0 | – | 9.00 | 1 | 0 | 0 | 3 | 7 | 3 | 2 | 0 | 0 | 0 | 0 | 0 | 0 | 0 | – |

Jim Derrington
DERRINGTON, CHARLES JAMES (Blackie)   BL TL 6'3" 190 lbs.
B. Nov. 29, 1939, Compton, Calif.

1956 CHI A	0	1	.000	7.50	1	1	0	6	9	6	3	0	0	0	0	2	1	0	.500
1957	0	1	.000	4.86	20	5	0	37	29	29	14	0	0	0	0	4	0	0	.000
2 yrs.	0	2	.000	5.23	21	6	0	43	38	35	17	0	0	0	0	6	1	0	.167
2 yrs.	0	2	.000	5.23	21	6	0	43	38	35	17	0	0	0	0	6	1	0	.167

Bill Dietrich
DIETRICH, WILLIAM JOHN (Bullfrog)   BR TR 6' 185 lbs.
B. Mar. 29, 1910, Philadelphia, Pa.   D. June 20, 1978, Philadelphia, Pa.

1933 PHI A	0	1	.000	5.82	8	1	0	17	13	19	4	0	0	0	0	3	1	0	.333
1934	11	12	.478	4.68	39	23	14	207.2	201	114	88	4	0	2	3	72	15	1	.208
1935	7	13	.350	5.39	43	15	8	185.1	203	101	59	1	4	3	3	60	5	0	.083
1936 3 teams			PHI A (21G 4-6)					WAS A (5G 0-1)			CHI A (14G 4-4)								
" total	8	11	.421	5.75	40	15	6	162.2	197	82	77	1	4	3	3	57	11	0	.193
1937 CHI A	8	10	.444	4.90	29	20	7	143.1	162	72	62	1	0	3	0	44	8	0	.182
1938	2	4	.333	5.44	8	7	1	48	49	31	11	0	0	0	0	16	1	0	.063
1939	7	8	.467	5.22	25	19	2	127.2	134	56	43	0	1	0	0	37	8	1	.216
1940	10	6	.625	4.03	23	17	6	149.2	154	65	43	1	1	0	0	50	12	1	.240
1941	5	8	.385	5.35	19	15	4	109.1	114	50	26	1	0	1	1	34	3	0	.088
1942	6	11	.353	4.89	26	23	6	160	173	70	39	0	0	0	1	48	5	0	.104
1943	12	10	.545	2.80	28	26	12	186.2	180	53	52	2	0	0	0	56	8	1	.143
1944	16	17	.485	3.62	36	36	15	246	269	68	70	2	0	0	0	77	9	1	.117
1945	7	10	.412	4.19	18	16	6	122.1	136	36	43	4	0	2	0	36	6	0	.167
1946	3	3	.500	2.61	11	9	3	62	63	24	20	0	0	0	1	19	1	0	.053
1947 PHI A	5	2	.714	3.12	11	9	2	60.2	48	40	18	1	1	0	0	16	1	0	.063
1948	1	2	.333	5.87	4	2	0	15.1	21	9	5	0	1	0	0	2	0	0	.000
16 yrs.	108	128	.458	4.48	366	253	92	2003.2	2117	890	660	18	13	11	11	627	94	5	.150
11 yrs.	80	91	.468	4.23	235	199	68	1437.2	1527	561	448	12	3	3	2	447	69	4	.154
								8th											

John Dobb
DOBB, JOHN KENNETH (Lefty)   BR TL 6'2" 180 lbs.
B. Nov. 15, 1901, Muskegon, Mich.

| 1924 CHI A | 0 | 0 | – | 9.00 | 2 | 0 | 0 | 2 | 4 | 1 | 2 | 0 | 0 | 0 | 0 | 0 | 0 | 0 | – |

Jess Dobernic
DOBERNIC, ANDREW JOSEPH   BR TR 5'10" 170 lbs.
B. Nov. 20, 1917, Mt. Olive, Ill.

1939 CHI A	0	1	.000	13.50	4	0	0	3.1	5	6	1	0	0	1	0	1	0	0	.000
1948 CHI N	7	2	.778	3.15	54	0	0	85.2	67	40	48	0	7	2	1	10	2	0	.200
1949 2 teams			CHI N (4G 0-0)					CIN N (14G 0-0)											
" total	0	0	–	11.57	18	0	0	23.1	37	20	6	0	0	0	0	2	0	0	.000
3 yrs.	7	3	.700	5.21	76	0	0	112.1	107	66	55	0	7	3	1	13	2	0	.154
1 yr.	0	1	.000	13.50	4	0	0	3.1	5	6	1	0	0	1	0	1	0	0	.000

Pitcher Register

	W	L	PCT	ERA	G	GS	CG	IP	H	BB	SO	ShO	Relief Pitching W	L	SV	BATTING AB	H	HR	BA

Joe Dobson
DOBSON, JOSEPH GORDON (Burrhead)   BR TR 6'2"   197 lbs.
B. Jan. 20, 1917, Durant, Okla.

1939 CLE A	2	3	.400	5.88	35	3	0	78	87	51	27	0	2	1	1	18	1	0	.056
1940	3	7	.300	4.95	40	7	2	100	101	48	57	1	2	2	3	24	3	0	.125
1941 BOS A	12	5	.706	4.49	27	18	7	134.1	136	67	69	1	2	1	0	47	7	1	.149
1942	11	9	.550	3.30	30	23	10	182.2	155	68	72	3	1	1	0	69	10	0	.145
1943	7	11	.389	3.12	25	20	9	164.1	144	57	63	3	0	1	0	52	5	0	.096
1946	13	7	.650	3.24	32	24	9	166.2	148	68	91	1	2	0	0	50	5	0	.100
1947	18	8	.692	2.95	33	31	15	228.2	203	73	110	1	0	0	1	77	16	0	.208
1948	16	10	.615	3.56	38	32	16	245.1	237	92	116	5	0	2	2	84	17	1	.202
1949	14	12	.538	3.85	33	27	12	212.2	219	97	87	2	2	1	2	68	10	0	.147
1950	15	10	.600	4.18	39	27	12	206.2	217	81	81	1	2	0	4	70	15	0	.214
1951 CHI A	7	6	.538	3.62	28	21	6	146.2	136	51	67	0	0	0	3	46	3	0	.065
1952	14	10	.583	2.51	29	25	11	200.2	164	60	101	3	1	1	1	63	12	0	.190
1953	5	5	.500	3.67	23	15	3	100.2	96	37	50	1	0	0	1	29	2	0	.069
1954 BOS A	0	0	–	6.75	2	0	0	2.2	5	1	1	0	0	0	0	0	0	0	–
14 yrs.	137	103	.571	3.62	414	273	112	2170	2048	851	992	22	14	10	18	697	106	2	.152
3 yrs.	26	21	.553	3.13	80	61	20	448	396	148	218	4	1	1	5	138	17	0	.123

WORLD SERIES
| 1946 BOS A | 1 | 0 | 1.000 | 0.00 | 3 | 1 | 1 | 12.2 | 4 | 3 | 10 | 0 | 0 | 0 | 0 | 3 | 0 | 0 | .000 |

Cozy Dolan
DOLAN, PATRICK HENRY   BL TL 5'10"   160 lbs.
B. Dec. 3, 1872, Cambridge, Mass.   D. Mar. 29, 1907, Louisville, Ky.

1895 BOS N	11	7	.611	4.27	25	21	18	198.1	215	67	47	3	0	0	1	83	20	0	.241
1896	1	4	.200	4.83	6	5	3	41	55	27	14	0	0	0	0	14	2	0	.143
1905	0	1	.000	9.00	2	0	0	4	7	1	0	0	0	1	0	510	137	3	.269
1906	0	1	.000	4.50	2	0	0	12	12	6	7	0	0	1	0	549	136	0	.248
4 yrs.	12	13	.480	4.44	35	26	21	255.1	289	101	69	3	0	2	1	*			

Dick Donovan
DONOVAN, RICHARD EDWARD   BL TR 6'3"   190 lbs.
B. Dec. 7, 1927, Boston, Mass.

1950 BOS N	0	2	.000	8.19	10	3	0	29.2	28	34	9	0	0	0	0	6	1	0	.167
1951	0	0	–	5.27	8	2	0	13.2	17	11	4	0	0	0	0	3	1	0	.333
1952	0	2	.000	5.54	7	2	0	13	18	12	6	0	0	0	1	3	0	0	.000
1954 DET A	0	0	–	10.50	2	0	0	6	9	5	2	0	0	0	0	1	0	0	.000
1955 CHI A	15	9	.625	3.32	29	24	11	187	186	48	88	5	2	1	0	76	17	1	.224
1956	12	10	.545	3.64	34	31	14	234.2	212	59	120	3	0	0	0	90	20	3	.222
1957	16	6	.727	2.77	28	28	16	220.2	203	45	88	2	0	0	0	83	12	3	.145
1958	15	14	.517	3.01	34	34	16	248	240	53	127	4	0	0	0	80	9	0	.113
1959	9	10	.474	3.66	31	29	5	179.2	171	58	71	1	0	0	0	61	8	1	.131
1960	6	1	.857	5.38	33	8	0	78.2	87	25	30	0	5	0	3	23	3	0	.130
1961 WAS A	10	10	.500	2.40	23	22	11	168.2	138	35	62	2	0	0	0	56	10	1	.179
1962 CLE A	20	10	.667	3.59	34	34	16	250.2	255	47	94	5	0	0	0	89	16	4	.180
1963	11	13	.458	4.24	30	30	7	206	211	28	84	3	0	0	0	69	9	1	.130
1964	7	9	.438	4.55	30	23	5	158.1	181	29	83	0	0	0	1	48	7	1	.146
1965	1	3	.250	5.96	12	3	0	22.2	32	6	12	0	0	1	0	6	0	0	.000
15 yrs.	122	99	.552	3.67	345	273	101	2017.1	1988	495	880	25	7	2	5	694	113	15	.163
6 yrs.	73	50	.593	3.41	189	154	62	1148.2	1099	288	524	15	7	1	3	413	69	8	.167
				6th															

WORLD SERIES
| 1959 CHI A | 0 | 1 | .000 | 5.40 | 3 | 1 | 0 | 8.1 | 4 | 3 | 5 | 0 | 0 | 0 | 1 | 3 | 1 | 0 | .333 |

Harry Dorish
DORISH, HARRY (Fritz)   BR TR 5'11"   204 lbs.
B. July 13, 1921, Swoyersville, Pa.

1947 BOS A	7	8	.467	4.70	41	9	2	136	149	54	50	0	4	3	2	35	5	0	.143
1948	0	1	.000	5.65	9	0	0	14.1	18	6	5	0	0	1	0	4	1	0	.250
1949	0	0	–	2.35	5	0	0	7.2	7	1	5	0	0	0	0	0	0	0	–
1950 STL A	2	9	.308	6.44	29	13	4	109	162	36	36	0	1	2	0	31	5	0	.161
1951 CHI A	5	6	.455	3.54	32	4	2	96.2	101	31	29	1	3	5	0	31	8	0	.258
1952	8	4	.667	2.47	39	1	1	91	66	42	47	0	7	4	11	22	2	0	.091
1953	10	6	.625	3.40	55	6	2	145.2	140	52	69	0	7	4	18	41	7	0	.171
1954	6	4	.600	2.72	37	6	2	109	88	29	48	1	2	2	6	27	3	0	.111
1955 2 teams	CHI	A	(13G 2–0)		BAL	A	(35G 3–3)												
" total	5	3	.625	2.83	48	1	0	82.2	74	37	28	0	5	2	7	13	1	0	.077
1956 2 teams	BAL	A	(13G 0–0)		BOS	A	(15G 0–2)												
" total	0	2	.000	3.83	28	0	0	42.1	45	13	15	0	0	2	0	0	0	0	–
10 yrs.	45	43	.511	3.83	323	40	13	834.1	850	301	332	2	29	25	44	204	32	0	.157
5 yrs.	31	20	.608	3.02	176	17	7	459.1	411	163	199	2	21	15	36	124	21	0	.169
												9th							

Rich Dotson
DOTSON, RICHARD ELLIOTT   BR TR 6'1"   190 lbs.
B. Jan. 10, 1959, Cincinnati, Ohio

1979 CHI A	2	0	1.000	3.75	5	5	1	24	28	6	13	1	0	0	0	0	0	0	–
1980	12	10	.545	4.27	33	32	8	198	185	87	109	0	0	0	0	0	0	0	–
1981	9	8	.529	3.77	24	24	5	141	145	49	73	4	0	0	0	0	0	0	–
1982	11	15	.423	3.84	34	31	3	196.2	219	73	109	1	0	0	0	0	0	0	–
1983	22	7	.759	3.23	35	35	8	240	209	106	137	1	0	0	0	0	0	0	–
5 yrs.	56	40	.583	3.75	131	127	25	799.2	786	321	441	7	0	0	0	0	0	0	–
5 yrs.	56	40	.583	3.75	131	127	25	799.2	786	321	441	7	0	0	0	0	0	0	–
				7th															

LEAGUE CHAMPIONSHIP SERIES
| 1983 CHI A | 0 | 1 | .000 | 10.80 | 1 | 1 | 0 | 5 | 6 | 3 | 3 | 0 | 0 | 0 | 0 | 0 | 0 | 0 | – |

Pitcher Register 356

	W	L	PCT	ERA	G	GS	CG	IP	H	BB	SO	ShO	Relief Pitching W L SV	BATTING AB H HR	BA

Tom Dougherty
DOUGHERTY, THOMAS JAMES (Sugar Boy)   BL TR
B. May 30, 1881, Chicago, Ill.   D. Nov. 6, 1953, Milwaukee, Wis.

| 1904 CHI A | 1 | 0 | 1.000 | 0.00 | 1 | 0 | 0 | 2 | 0 | 0 | 0 | 0 | 1 | 0 | 0 | 1 | 0 | 0 | .000 |

Phil Douglas
DOUGLAS, PHILIPS BROOKS (Shufflin' Phil)   BR TR 6'3"   190 lbs.
B. June 17, 1890, Cedartown, Ga.   D. Aug. 1, 1952, Sequatchie Valley, Tenn.

1912 CHI N	0	1	.000	7.30	3	1	0	12.1	21	6	7	0	0	0	0	2	0	0	.000
1914 CIN N	11	18	.379	2.56	45	25	13	239.1	186	92	121	0	4	4	1	73	10	0	.137
1915 3 teams			CIN N (8G 1–5)			BKN N (20G 5–5)			CHI N (4G 1–1)										
" total	7	11	.389	3.25	32	24	7	188.1	174	47	110	2	0	0	0	64	8	0	.125
1917 CHI N	14	20	.412	2.55	51	37	20	293.1	269	50	151	5	3	0	1	89	11	0	.124
1918	9	9	.500	2.13	25	19	11	156.2	145	31	51	2	1	1	2	55	14	0	.255
1919 2 teams			CHI N (25G 10–6)			NY N (8G 2–4)														
" total	12	10	.545	2.03	33	25	12	213	186	40	84	4	2	0	0	66	8	0	.121
1920 NY N	14	10	.583	2.71	46	21	10	226	225	55	71	3	4	5	2	73	11	0	.151
1921	15	10	.600	4.22	40	27	13	221.2	266	55	55	3	2	1	2	81	16	1	.198
1922	11	4	.733	2.63	24	21	9	157.2	154	35	33	1	1	0	0	58	12	1	.207
9 yrs.	93	93	.500	2.80	299	200	95	1708.1	1626	411	683	20	17	11	8	561	90	2	.160
1 yr.	0	1	.000	7.30	3	1	0	12.1	21	6	7	0	0	0	0	2	0	0	.000

WORLD SERIES

1918 CHI N	0	1	.000	0.00	1	0	0	1	1	0	1	0	0	1	0	0	0	0	—
1921 NY N	2	1	.667	2.08	3	3	2	26	24	5	17	0	0	0	0	7	0	0	.000
2 yrs.	2	2	.500	2.00	4	3	2	27	25	5	17	0	0	1	0	7	0	0	.000

Moe Drabowsky
DRABOWSKY, MYRON WALTER   BR TR 6'3"   190 lbs.
B. July 21, 1935, Ozanna, Poland

1956 CHI N	2	4	.333	2.47	9	7	3	51	37	39	36	0	0	0	0	16	4	0	.250
1957	13	15	.464	3.53	36	33	12	239.2	214	94	170	2	0	0	0	82	15	1	.183
1958	9	11	.450	4.51	22	20	4	125.2	118	73	77	1	1	0	0	45	7	0	.156
1959	5	10	.333	4.13	31	23	3	141.2	138	75	70	1	0	0	0	45	5	0	.111
1960	3	1	.750	6.44	32	7	0	50.1	71	23	26	0	2	0	1	6	0	0	.000
1961 MIL N	0	2	.000	4.62	16	0	0	25.1	26	18	5	0	0	2	2	4	1	0	.250
1962 2 teams			CIN N (23G 2–6)			KC A (10G 1–1)														
" total	3	7	.300	5.03	33	13	1	111	113	41	75	0	1	1	1	23	1	0	.043
1963 KC A	7	13	.350	3.05	26	22	9	174.1	135	64	109	2	0	1	0	62	10	2	.161
1964	5	13	.278	5.29	53	21	1	168.1	176	72	119	0	1	2	1	43	1	0	.023
1965	1	5	.167	4.42	14	5	0	38.2	44	18	25	0	1	2	0	11	1	0	.091
1966 BAL A	6	0	1.000	2.81	44	3	0	96	62	29	98	0	5	0	7	22	8	0	.364
1967	7	5	.583	1.60	43	0	0	95.1	66	25	96	0	7	5	12	20	7	0	.350
1968	4	4	.500	1.91	45	0	0	61.1	35	25	46	0	4	4	7	7	2	0	.286
1969 KC A	11	9	.550	2.94	52	0	0	98	68	30	76	0	11	9	11	17	4	0	.235
1970 2 teams			KC A (24G 1–2)			BAL A (21G 4–2)														
" total	5	4	.556	3.52	45	0	0	69	58	27	59	0	5	4	3	9	1	0	.111
1971 STL N	6	1	.857	3.45	51	0	0	60	45	33	49	0	6	1	8	6	1	0	.167
1972 2 teams			STL N (30G 1–1)			CHI A (7G 0–0)														
" total	1	1	.500	2.57	37	0	0	35	35	16	26	0	1	1	2	2	0	0	.000
17 yrs.	88	105	.456	3.71	589	154	33	1640.2	1441	702	1162	6	45	32	55	420	68	3	.162
1 yr.	0	0	—	2.45	7	0	0	7.1	6	2	4	0	0	0	0	1	0	0	.000

WORLD SERIES

1966 BAL A	1	0	1.000	0.00	1	0	0	6.2	1	2	11	0	1	0	0	2	0	0	.000
1970	0	0	—	2.70	2	0	0	3.1	2	1	1	0	0	0	0	1	0	0	.000
2 yrs.	1	0	1.000	0.90	3	0	0	10	3	3	12	0	1	0	0	3	0	0	.000

Larry Duff
DUFF, CECIL ELBA   BL TR 6'1"   175 lbs.
B. Nov. 30, 1896, Radersburg, Mont.   D. Nov. 10, 1969, Bend, Ore.

| 1922 CHI A | 1 | 1 | .500 | 4.97 | 3 | 1 | 0 | 12.2 | 16 | 3 | 7 | 0 | 1 | 0 | 0 | 5 | 2 | 0 | .400 |

Dan Dugan
DUGAN, DANIEL PHILLIP   BL TL 6'1½"   187 lbs.
B. Feb. 22, 1907, Plainfield, N. J.   D. June 25, 1968, Greenbrook, N. J.

1928 CHI A	0	0	—	0.00	1	0	0	.1	0	0	0	0	0	0	0	0	0	0	—
1929	1	4	.200	6.65	19	2	0	65	77	19	15	0	1	2	1	20	3	0	.150
2 yrs.	1	4	.200	6.61	20	2	0	65.1	77	19	15	0	1	2	1	20	3	0	.150
2 yrs.	1	4	.200	6.61	20	2	0	65.1	77	19	15	0	1	2	1	20	3	0	.150

Davey Dunkle
DUNKLE, EDWARD PERKS   BB TR 6'2"   220 lbs.
B. Aug. 19, 1872, Philipsburg, Pa.   D. Nov. 19, 1941, Lock Haven, Pa.

1897 PHI N	5	2	.714	3.48	7	7	7	62	72	23	9	0	0	0	0	23	4	0	.174
1898	1	4	.200	6.98	12	7	4	68.1	83	38	21	0	0	0	0	28	6	0	.214
1899 WAS N	0	2	.000	10.04	4	2	2	26	46	14	9	0	0	0	0	11	3	0	.273
1903 2 teams			CHI A (12G 4–4)			WAS A (14G 5–8)														
" total	9	12	.429	4.16	26	20	16	190.1	207	64	77	0	2	0	1	74	14	0	.189
1904 WAS A	1	9	.100	4.96	12	11	7	74.1	95	23	23	0	0	0	0	28	4	0	.143
5 yrs.	16	29	.356	5.02	61	47	36	421	503	162	139	0	2	0	1	164	31	0	.189
1 yr.	4	4	.500	4.06	12	7	6	82	96	31	26	0	1	0	1	33	10	0	.303

Frank Dupee
DUPEE, FRANK OLIVER
B. Apr. 29, 1877, Monkton, Vt.   D. Aug. 14, 1956, West Falmouth, Me.

| 1901 CHI A | 0 | 1 | .000 | ∞ | 1 | 1 | 0 | 0 | 3 | 0 | 0 | 0 | 0 | 0 | 0 | 0 | 0 | 0 | — |

Ed Durham
DURHAM, EDWARD FANT (Bull)   BL TR 5'11"   170 lbs.
B. Aug. 17, 1907, Chester, S. C.   D. Apr. 27, 1976, Chester, S. C.

1929 BOS A	1	0	1.000	9.27	14	1	0	22.1	34	14	6	0	0	0	0	4	0	0	.000
1930	4	15	.211	4.69	33	12	6	140	144	43	28	1	2	5	1	41	4	0	.098
1931	8	10	.444	4.25	38	15	7	165.1	175	50	53	2	2	3	0	54	3	0	.056
1932	6	13	.316	3.80	34	22	4	175.1	187	49	52	0	2	1	0	57	7	0	.123

Pitcher Register

	W	L	PCT	ERA	G	GS	CG	IP	H	BB	SO	ShO	Relief Pitching W L SV	BATTING AB H HR	BA

Ed Durham continued
	W	L	PCT	ERA	G	GS	CG	IP	H	BB	SO	ShO	W	L	SV	AB	H	HR	BA
1933 CHI A	10	6	.625	4.48	24	21	6	138.2	137	46	65	0	1	0	0	46	10	0	.217
5 yrs.	29	44	.397	4.45	143	71	23	641.2	677	202	204	3	7	9	1	202	24	0	.119
1 yr.	10	6	.625	4.48	24	21	6	138.2	137	46	65	0	1	0	0	46	10	0	.217

Jimmy Durham
DURHAM, JAMES GARFIELD BR TR 6' 175 lbs.
Brother of Bull Durham.
B. Oct. 7, 1881, Douglass, Kans. D. May 7, 1949, Coffeyville, Kans.

	W	L	PCT	ERA	G	GS	CG	IP	H	BB	SO	ShO	W	L	SV	AB	H	HR	BA
1902 CHI A	1	1	.500	5.85	3	3	3	20	21	16	3	0	0	0	0	15	1	0	.067

Jimmy Dykes
DYKES, JAMES JOSEPH BR TR 5'9" 185 lbs.
B. Nov. 10, 1896, Philadelphia, Pa. D. June 15, 1976, Philadelphia, Pa.
Manager 1934-46, 1951-54, 1958-61.

	W	L	PCT	ERA	G	GS	CG	IP	H	BB	SO	ShO	W	L	SV	AB	H	HR	BA
1927 PHI A	0	0	—	4.50	2	0	0	2	2	1	0	0	0	0	0	*			

George Earnshaw
EARNSHAW, GEORGE LIVINGSTON (Moose) BR TR 6'4" 210 lbs.
B. Feb. 15, 1900, New York, N. Y. D. Dec. 1, 1976, Little Rock, Ark.

	W	L	PCT	ERA	G	GS	CG	IP	H	BB	SO	ShO	W	L	SV	AB	H	HR	BA
1928 PHI A	7	7	.500	3.81	26	22	7	158.1	143	100	117	3	0	0	1	57	14	0	.246
1929	24	8	.750	3.29	44	33	13	254.2	233	125	149	3	3	0	1	87	15	1	.172
1930	22	13	.629	4.44	49	39	20	296	299	139	193	3	2	2	2	114	26	0	.228
1931	21	7	.750	3.67	43	30	23	281.2	255	75	152	0	1	0	6	114	30	2	.263
1932	19	13	.594	4.77	36	33	21	245.1	262	94	109	1	1	1	0	91	26	0	.286
1933	5	10	.333	5.97	21	18	4	117.2	153	58	37	0	1	0	0	44	8	0	.182
1934 CHI A	14	11	.560	4.52	33	30	16	227	242	104	97	2	0	1	0	79	16	0	.203
1935 2 teams	CHI A (3G 1–2)				BKN N (25G 8–12)														
" total	9	14	.391	4.60	28	25	6	184	201	64	80	2	1	1	0	67	15	0	.224
1936 2 teams	BKN N (19G 4–9)				STL N (20G 2–1)														
" total	6	10	.375	5.73	39	19	5	150.2	193	50	71	1	3	0	2	51	12	0	.235
9 yrs.	127	93	.577	4.38	319	249	115	1915.1	1981	809	1005	18	12	5	12	704	162	3	.230
2 yrs.	15	13	.536	4.85	36	33	16	245	268	115	105	2	0	1	0	86	18	0	.209

WORLD SERIES
	W	L	PCT	ERA	G	GS	CG	IP	H	BB	SO	ShO	W	L	SV	AB	H	HR	BA
1929 PHI A	1	1	.500	2.63	2	2	1	13.2	14	6	17	0	0	0	0	5	0	0	.000
1930	2	0	1.000	0.72	3	3	2	25	13	7	19	0	0	0	0	9	0	0	.000
1931	1	2	.333	1.88	3	3	2	24	12	4	20	1	0	0	0	8	0	0	.000
3 yrs.	4	3	.571	1.58	8	8	5	62.2	39	17	56	1	0	0	0	22	0	0	.000
								10th	10th		7th								

Vallie Eaves
EAVES, VALLIE ENNIS (Chief) BR TR 6'2½" 180 lbs.
B. Sept. 6, 1911, Allen, Okla. D. Apr. 19, 1960, Norman, Okla.

	W	L	PCT	ERA	G	GS	CG	IP	H	BB	SO	ShO	W	L	SV	AB	H	HR	BA
1935 PHI A	1	2	.333	5.14	3	3	1	14	12	15	6	0	0	0	0	4	0	0	.000
1939 CHI A	0	1	.000	4.63	2	1	1	11.2	11	8	5	0	0	0	0	6	2	0	.333
1940	0	2	.000	6.75	5	3	0	18.2	22	24	11	0	0	0	0	5	0	0	.000
1941 CHI N	3	3	.500	3.53	12	7	4	58.2	56	21	24	0	1	0	0	20	2	0	.100
1942	0	0		9.00	2	0	0	3	4	2	0	0	0	0	0	0	0	0	—
5 yrs.	4	8	.333	4.58	24	14	6	106	105	70	46	0	1	0	0	35	4	0	.114
2 yrs.	0	3	.000	5.93	7	4	1	30.1	33	32	16	0	0	0	0	11	2	0	.182

Don Eddy
EDDY, DONALD EUGENE BR TL 5'11" 170 lbs.
B. Oct. 25, 1946, Mason City, Iowa

	W	L	PCT	ERA	G	GS	CG	IP	H	BB	SO	ShO	W	L	SV	AB	H	HR	BA
1970 CHI A	0	0	—	2.25	7	0	0	12	10	6	9	0	0	0	0	0	0	0	—
1971	0	2	.000	2.35	22	0	0	23	19	19	14	0	0	2	0	1	1	0	1.000
2 yrs.	0	2	.000	2.31	29	0	0	35	29	25	23	0	0	2	0	1	1	0	1.000
2 yrs.	0	2	.000	2.31	29	0	0	35	29	25	23	0	0	2	0	1	1	0	1.000

Paul Edmondson
EDMONDSON, PAUL MICHAEL BR TR 6'5" 195 lbs.
B. Feb. 12, 1943, Kansas City, Kans. D. Feb. 13, 1970, Santa Barbara, Calif.

	W	L	PCT	ERA	G	GS	CG	IP	H	BB	SO	ShO	W	L	SV	AB	H	HR	BA
1969 CHI A	1	6	.143	3.70	14	13	1	87.2	72	39	46	0	0	1	0	29	5	0	.172

Jim Joe Edwards
EDWARDS, JAMES CORBETTE BR TL 6'2" 185 lbs.
B. Dec. 14, 1894, Banner, Miss. D. Jan. 19, 1965, Pontotoc, Miss.

	W	L	PCT	ERA	G	GS	CG	IP	H	BB	SO	ShO	W	L	SV	AB	H	HR	BA
1922 CLE A	3	8	.273	4.70	25	7	0	88	113	40	44	0	2	3	0	23	2	0	.087
1923	10	10	.500	3.71	38	21	7	179.1	200	75	68	1	0	3	1	59	7	0	.119
1924	4	3	.571	2.84	10	7	5	57	64	34	15	1	0	0	0	20	3	0	.150
1925 2 teams	CLE A (13G 0–3)				CHI A (9G 1–2)														
" total	1	5	.167	5.86	22	7	2	81.1	106	46	32	1	0	2	0	26	4	0	.154
1926 CHI A	6	9	.400	4.18	32	16	8	142	140	63	41	3	2	3	1	46	5	0	.109
1928 CIN N	2	2	.500	7.59	18	1	0	32	43	20	11	0	1	2	2	10	3	0	.300
6 yrs.	26	37	.413	4.41	145	59	22	579.2	666	278	211	6	5	13	4	184	24	0	.130
2 yrs.	7	11	.389	4.13	41	20	9	187.1	186	86	61	4	2	4	1	63	8	0	.127

Sammy Ellis
ELLIS, SAMUEL JOSEPH BL TR 6'1" 175 lbs.
B. Feb. 11, 1941, Youngstown, Ohio

	W	L	PCT	ERA	G	GS	CG	IP	H	BB	SO	ShO	W	L	SV	AB	H	HR	BA
1962 CIN N	2	2	.500	6.75	8	4	0	28	29	29	27	0	0	0	0	10	2	0	.200
1964	10	3	.769	2.57	52	5	2	122.1	101	28	125	0	7	2	14	24	2	0	.083
1965	22	10	.688	3.79	44	39	15	263.2	222	104	183	2	0	0	2	96	12	0	.125
1966	12	19	.387	5.29	41	36	7	221	226	78	154	0	1	0	0	70	8	0	.114
1967	8	11	.421	3.84	32	27	8	175.2	197	67	80	1	0	0	0	49	4	0	.082
1968 CAL A	9	10	.474	3.95	42	24	3	164	150	56	93	0	1	1	2	44	2	0	.045
1969 CHI A	0	3	.000	5.83	10	5	0	29.1	42	16	15	0	0	1	0	6	1	0	.167
7 yrs.	63	58	.521	4.15	229	140	35	1004	967	378	677	3	11	4	18	299	31	0	.104
1 yr.	0	3	.000	5.83	10	5	0	29.1	42	16	15	0	0	1	0	6	1	0	.167

Slim Embry
EMBRY, CHARLES AKIN BR TR 6'2" 184 lbs.
B. Aug. 17, 1901, Columbia, Tenn. D. Oct. 10, 1947, Nashville, Tenn.

	W	L	PCT	ERA	G	GS	CG	IP	H	BB	SO	ShO	W	L	SV	AB	H	HR	BA
1923 CHI A	0	0	—	10.13	1	0	0	2.2	7	2	1	0	0	0	0	0	0	0	—

Pitcher Register 358

	W	L	PCT	ERA	G	GS	CG	IP	H	BB	SO	ShO	Relief Pitching W	L	SV	BATTING AB	H	HR	BA

Ernesto Escarrega
ESCARREGA, CHICO ERNESTO
B. Dec. 27, 1949, Los Mochis, Mexico
BR TR 5'10" 196 lbs.

| 1982 CHI A | 1 | 3 | .250 | 3.67 | 38 | 2 | 0 | 73.2 | 73 | 16 | 33 | 0 | 1 | 1 | 1 | 0 | 0 | 0 | — |

Mark Esser
ESSER, MARK GERALD
B. Apr. 1, 1956, Erie, Pa.
BR TL 6'1" 190 lbs.

| 1979 CHI A | 0 | 0 | — | 13.50 | 2 | 0 | 0 | 2 | 2 | 4 | 1 | 0 | 0 | 0 | 0 | 0 | 0 | 0 | — |

Art Evans
EVANS, WILLIAM ARTHUR
B. Aug. 3, 1911, Elvins, Mo.   D. Jan. 8, 1952, Wichita, Kans.
BB TL 6'1½" 181 lbs.

| 1932 CHI A | 0 | 0 | — | 3.00 | 7 | 0 | 0 | 18 | 19 | 10 | 6 | 0 | 0 | 0 | 0 | 5 | 0 | 0 | .000 |

Bill Evans
EVANS, WILLIAM LAWRENCE
B. Mar. 25, 1919, Childress, Tex.
BR TR 6'2" 180 lbs.

1949 CHI A	0	1	.000	7.11	4	0	0	6.1	6	8	1	0	0	1	0	1	0	0	.000
1951 BOS A	0	0	—	4.11	9	0	0	15.1	15	8	3	0	0	0	0	4	0	0	.000
2 yrs.	0	1	.000	4.98	13	0	0	21.2	21	16	4	0	0	1	0	5	0	0	.000
1 yr.	0	1	.000	7.11	4	0	0	6.1	6	8	1	0	0	1	0	1	0	0	.000

Red Evans
EVANS, RUSSELL EARL
B. Nov. 12, 1906, Chicago, Ill.   D. July, 1982, Lakeview, Ark.
BR TR 5'11" 168 lbs.

1936 CHI A	0	3	.000	7.61	17	0	0	47.1	70	22	19	0	0	3	1	15	2	0	.133
1939 BKN N	1	8	.111	5.18	24	6	0	64.1	74	26	28	0	1	2	1	13	4	0	.308
2 yrs.	1	11	.083	6.21	41	6	0	111.2	144	48	47	0	1	5	2	28	6	0	.214
1 yr.	0	3	.000	7.61	17	0	0	47.1	70	22	19	0	0	3	1	15	2	0	.133

Red Faber
FABER, URBAN CLARENCE
B. Sept. 6, 1888, Cascade, Iowa
D. Sept. 25, 1976, Chicago, Ill.
Hall of Fame 1964.
BB TR 6'2" 180 lbs.
BR 1925

1914 CHI A	10	9	.526	2.68	40	20	11	181.1	154	64	88	2	2	2	4	55	8	0	.145
1915	24	14	.632	2.55	50	32	22	299.2	264	99	182	3	5	4	2	84	11	0	.131
1916	17	9	.654	2.02	35	25	15	205.1	167	61	87	3	1	1	2	63	6	0	.095
1917	16	13	.552	1.92	41	29	17	248	224	85	84	3	2	4	3	69	4	0	.058
1918	4	1	.800	1.23	11	9	5	80.2	70	23	26	1	1	0	0	24	1	0	.042
1919	11	9	.550	3.83	25	20	9	162.1	185	45	45	0	3	0	0	54	10	0	.185
1920	23	13	.639	2.99	40	39	28	319	332	88	108	2	0	0	1	104	11	0	.106
1921	25	15	.625	2.48	43	39	32	330.2	293	87	124	4	1	1	1	108	16	0	.148
1922	21	17	.553	2.80	43	38	31	353	334	83	148	4	1	1	2	125	25	0	.200
1923	14	11	.560	3.41	32	31	15	232.1	233	62	91	2	0	1	0	69	15	1	.217
1924	9	11	.450	3.85	21	20	9	161.1	173	58	47	0	0	1	0	54	8	0	.148
1925	12	11	.522	3.78	34	32	16	238	266	59	71	1	1	1	0	77	8	0	.104
1926	15	8	.652	3.56	27	25	13	184.2	203	57	65	1	0	2	0	60	9	0	.150
1927	4	7	.364	4.55	18	15	6	110.2	131	41	39	0	0	0	0	37	10	0	.270
1928	13	9	.591	3.75	27	27	16	201.1	223	68	43	2	0	0	0	70	8	1	.114
1929	13	13	.500	3.88	31	31	15	234	241	61	68	1	0	0	0	78	10	1	.128
1930	8	13	.381	4.21	29	26	10	169	188	49	62	0	0	0	1	49	2	0	.041
1931	10	14	.417	3.82	44	19	5	184	210	57	49	1	5	2	1	53	4	0	.075
1932	2	11	.154	3.74	42	5	0	106	123	38	26	0	2	6	6	18	4	0	.222
1933	3	4	.429	3.44	36	2	0	86.1	92	28	18	0	3	2	5	18	0	0	.000
20 yrs.	254	212	.545	3.15	669	484	275	4087.2	4106	1213	1471	30	27	28	28	1269	170	3	.134
20 yrs.	254	212	.545	3.15	669	484	275	4087.2	4106	1213	1471	30	27	28	28	1269	170	3	.134
	2nd	2nd			1st		2nd	2nd		1st	3rd	4th		6th					

WORLD SERIES
| 1917 CHI A | 3 | 1 | .750 | 2.33 | 4 | 3 | 2 | 27 | 21 | 3 | 9 | 0 | 1 | 0 | 0 | 7 | 1 | 0 | .143 |

Ed Farmer
FARMER, EDWARD JOSEPH
B. Oct. 18, 1949, Auburn, Calif.
BR TR 6'5" 200 lbs.

1971 CLE A	5	4	.556	4.33	43	4	0	79	77	41	48	0	5	2	4	14	1	0	.071
1972	2	5	.286	4.43	46	1	0	61	51	27	33	0	2	4	7	7	1	0	.143
1973 2 teams			CLE A (16G 0–2)				DET A (24G 3–0)												
" total	3	2	.600	4.91	40	0	0	62.1	77	32	38	0	3	2	3	9	0	0	—
1974 PHI N	2	1	.667	8.42	14	3	0	31	41	27	20	0	1	0	0	9	1	0	.111
1977 BAL A	0	0	—	∞	1	0	0	1	1	0	0	0	0	0	0	0	0	0	—
1978 MIL A	1	0	1.000	0.82	3	0	0	11	7	4	6	0	0	0	1	0	0	0	—
1979 2 teams			TEX A (11G 2–0)				CHI A (42G 3–7)												
" total	5	7	.417	3.00	53	5	0	114	96	53	73	0	5	7	14	0	0	0	—
1980 CHI A	7	9	.438	3.33	64	0	0	100	92	56	54	0	7	9	30	0	0	0	—
1981	3	3	.500	4.58	42	0	0	53	53	34	42	0	3	3	10	0	0	0	—
1982 PHI N	2	6	.250	4.86	47	4	0	76	66	50	58	0	1	3	6	11	0	0	.000
1983 2 teams			PHI N (12G 0–6)				OAK A (5G 0–0)												
" total	0	6	.000	5.35	17	4	0	37	50	20	23	0	0	3	0	6	1	0	.167
11 yrs.	30	43	.411	4.30	370	21	0	624.1	611	345	395	0	28	33	75	47	4	0	.085
3 yrs.	13	19	.406	3.31	148	3	0	234	211	124	144	0	13	19	54	0	0	0	—
														4th					

Kerby Farrell
FARRELL, KERBY
B. Sept. 3, 1913, Leapwood, Tenn.   D. Dec. 17, 1975, Nashville, Tenn.
Manager 1957.
BL TL 5'11" 172 lbs.

| 1943 BOS N | 0 | 1 | .000 | 4.30 | 5 | 0 | 0 | 23 | 24 | 9 | 4 | 0 | 0 | 1 | 0 | * | | | |

Hod Fenner
FENNER, HORACE ALFRED
B. July 12, 1897, Martin, Mich.   D. Nov. 20, 1954, Detroit, Mich.
BR TR 5'10½" 165 lbs.

| 1921 CHI A | 0 | 0 | — | 7.71 | 2 | 1 | 0 | 7 | 14 | 3 | 1 | 0 | 0 | 0 | 0 | 2 | 0 | 0 | .000 |

Pitcher Register

	W	L	PCT	ERA	G	GS	CG	IP	H	BB	SO	ShO	Relief Pitching W	L	SV	BATTING AB	H	HR	BA

Don Ferrarese
FERRARESE, DONALD HUGH (Midget)   BR TL 5'9"   170 lbs.
B. June 19, 1929, Oakland, Calif.

1955 BAL A	0	0	–	3.00	6	0	0	9	8	11	5	0	0	0	0	1	0	0	.000
1956	4	10	.286	5.03	36	14	3	102	86	64	81	1	2	2	2	28	1	0	.036
1957	1	1	.500	4.74	8	2	0	19	14	12	13	0	1	0	0	3	0	0	.000
1958 CLE A	3	4	.429	3.71	28	10	2	94.2	91	46	62	0	2	1	1	26	3	0	.115
1959	5	3	.625	3.20	15	10	4	76	58	51	45	0	0	0	0	27	7	0	.259
1960 CHI A	0	1	.000	18.00	5	0	0	4	8	9	4	0	0	1	0	2	1	0	.500
1961 PHI N	5	12	.294	3.76	42	14	3	138.2	120	68	89	1	2	3	1	35	6	0	.171
1962 2 teams			PHI	N (5G 0–1)	STL	N (38G 1–4)													
" total	1	5	.167	3.27	43	0	0	63.1	64	34	51	0	1	5	1	6	2	1	.333
8 yrs.	19	36	.345	4.00	183	50	12	506.2	449	295	350	2	8	12	5	128	20	1	.156
1 yr.	0	1	.000	18.00	5	0	0	4	8	9	4	0	0	1	0	2	1	0	.500

Clarence Fieber
FIEBER, CLARENCE THOMAS (Lefty)   BL TL 6'4"   187 lbs.
B. Sept. 4, 1913, San Francisco, Calif.

1932 CHI A	1	0	1.000	1.69	3	0	0	5.1	6	3	1	0	1	0	0	0	0	0	–

Lou Fiene
FIENE, LOUIS HENRY (Big Finn)   BR TR 6'   175 lbs.
B. Dec. 29, 1884, Fort Dodge, Iowa   D. Dec. 22, 1964, Chicago, Ill.

1906 CHI A	1	1	.500	2.90	6	2	1	31	35	9	12	0	0	0	0	10	2	0	.200
1907	0	1	.000	4.15	6	1	1	26	30	7	15	0	0	0	1	11	2	0	.182
1908	0	1	.000	4.00	1	1	1	9	9	1	3	0	0	0	0	3	0	0	.000
1909	2	5	.286	4.13	13	6	4	72	75	18	24	0	1	0	0	29	2	0	.069
4 yrs.	3	8	.273	3.85	26	10	7	138	149	35	54	0	1	0	1	53	6	0	.113
4 yrs.	3	8	.273	3.85	26	10	7	138	149	35	54	0	1	0	1	53	6	0	.113

Bill Fischer
FISCHER, WILLIAM CHARLES   BR TR 6'   190 lbs.
B. Oct. 11, 1930, Wausau, Wis.

1956 CHI A	0	0	–	21.60	3	0	0	1.2	6	1	2	0	0	0	0	0	0	0	–
1957	7	8	.467	3.48	33	11	3	124	139	35	48	1	3	4	1	40	6	0	.150
1958 3 teams			CHI	A (17G 2–3)	DET	A (22G 2–4)	WAS	A (3G 0–3)											
" total	4	10	.286	6.34	42	6	0	88	113	31	42	0	2	6	2	13	2	0	.154
1959 WAS A	9	11	.450	4.28	34	29	6	187.1	211	43	62	1	0	0	0	54	7	0	.130
1960 2 teams			WAS	A (20G 3–5)	DET	A (20G 5–3)													
" total	8	8	.500	4.30	40	13	2	132	135	35	55	0	2	1	0	30	7	1	.233
1961 2 teams			DET	A (26G 3–2)	KC	A (15G 1–0)													
" total	4	2	.667	4.66	41	1	0	67.2	80	23	30	0	4	1	5	9	0	0	.000
1962 KC A	4	12	.250	3.95	34	16	5	127.2	150	8	38	0	1	0	2	38	4	0	.105
1963	9	6	.600	3.57	45	2	0	95.2	86	29	34	0	9	6	3	15	1	0	.067
1964 MIN A	0	1	.000	7.36	9	0	0	7.1	16	5	2	0	0	1	0	0	0	0	–
9 yrs.	45	58	.437	4.34	281	78	16	831.1	936	210	313	2	21	19	13	199	27	1	.136
3 yrs.	9	11	.450	4.39	53	14	3	162	188	49	66	1	3	6	1	47	7	0	.149

Carl Fischer
FISCHER, CHARLES WILLIAM   BR TL 6'   180 lbs.
B. Nov. 5, 1905, Medina, N. Y.   D. Dec. 10, 1963, Medina, N. Y.

1930 WAS A	1	1	.500	4.86	8	4	1	33.1	37	18	21	0	0	0	1	9	0	0	.000
1931	13	9	.591	4.38	46	23	7	191	207	80	96	0	2	0	3	66	8	0	.121
1932 2 teams			WAS	A (12G 3–2)	STL	A (24G 3–7)													
" total	6	9	.400	5.36	36	18	5	147.2	179	76	58	1	1	0	1	49	12	0	.245
1933 DET A	11	15	.423	3.55	35	22	9	182.2	176	84	93	0	5	1	3	62	9	0	.145
1934	6	4	.600	4.37	20	15	4	94.2	107	38	39	1	1	1	1	31	2	0	.065
1935 2 teams			DET	A (3G 0–1)	CHI	A (24G 5–5)													
" total	5	6	.455	6.17	27	12	3	100.2	118	44	38	1	2	1	0	23	4	0	.174
1937 2 teams			CLE	A (2G 0–1)	WAS	A (17G 4–5)													
" total	4	6	.400	4.58	19	11	2	72.2	76	32	31	0	0	2	2	22	3	0	.136
7 yrs.	46	50	.479	4.63	191	105	31	822.2	900	372	376	3	11	5	11	262	38	0	.145
1 yr.	5	5	.500	6.19	24	11	3	88.2	102	39	31	1	2	0	0	21	4	0	.190

Eddie Fisher
FISHER, EDDIE GENE   BR TR 6'2½"   200 lbs.
B. July 16, 1936, Shreveport, La.

1959 SF N	2	6	.250	7.88	17	5	0	40	57	8	15	0	0	4	1	8	0	0	.000
1960	1	0	1.000	3.55	3	1	1	12.2	11	2	7	0	0	0	0	5	3	0	.600
1961	0	2	.000	5.35	15	1	0	33.2	36	9	16	0	0	2	1	7	1	0	.143
1962 CHI A	9	5	.643	3.10	57	12	2	182.2	169	45	88	1	4	3	5	46	6	0	.130
1963	9	8	.529	3.95	33	15	2	120.2	114	28	67	1	2	3	0	36	5	0	.139
1964	6	3	.667	3.02	59	2	0	125	86	32	74	0	0	0	9	18	3	0	.167
1965	15	7	.682	2.40	82	0	0	165.1	118	43	90	0	15	7	24	29	4	0	.138
1966 2 teams			CHI	A (23G 1–3)	BAL	A (44G 5–3)													
" total	6	6	.500	2.52	67	0	0	107	87	36	57	0	6	6	19	15	2	0	.133
1967 BAL A	4	3	.571	3.61	46	0	0	89.2	82	26	53	0	4	3	1	5	1	0	.200
1968 CLE A	4	2	.667	2.85	54	0	0	94.2	87	17	42	0	4	2	4	12	0	0	.000
1969 CAL A	3	2	.600	3.63	52	1	0	96.2	100	28	47	0	2	2	2	13	0	0	.000
1970	4	4	.500	3.05	67	2	0	130	117	35	74	0	4	4	8	11	1	0	.091
1971	10	8	.556	2.72	57	3	0	119	92	50	82	0	9	6	3	16	1	0	.063
1972 2 teams			CAL	A (43G 4–5)	CHI	A (6G 0–1)													
" total	4	6	.400	3.91	49	5	0	103.2	104	40	42	0	4	3	4	24	2	0	.083
1973 2 teams			CHI	A (26G 6–7)	STL	N (6G 2–1)													
" total	8	8	.500	4.67	32	16	2	117.2	138	39	58	0	2	1	0	1	1	0	1.000
15 yrs.	85	70	.548	3.41	690	63	7	1538.1	1398	438	812	2	56	46	81	246	30	0	.122
7 yrs.	46	34	.575	3.33	286	49	6	762	680	212	404	2	22	16	44	138	18	0	.130
				8th									8th		8th				

Jack Fisher
FISHER, JOHN HOWARD (Fat Jack)   BR TR 6'2"   215 lbs.
B. Mar. 4, 1939, Frostburg, Md.

1959 BAL A	1	6	.143	3.05	27	7	1	88.2	76	38	52	1	0	2	2	23	3	0	.130
1960	12	11	.522	3.41	40	20	8	197.2	174	78	99	3	6	3	2	60	11	1	.183
1961	10	13	.435	3.90	36	25	10	196	205	75	118	1	0	4	1	56	5	0	.089

Pitcher Register

Jack Fisher continued

	W	L	PCT	ERA	G	GS	CG	IP	H	BB	SO	ShO	Relief W	Relief L	Relief SV	AB	H	HR	BA
1962	7	9	.438	5.09	32	25	4	152	173	56	81	0	0	1	1	49	5	0	.102
1963 SF N	6	10	.375	4.58	36	12	2	116	132	38	57	0	3	2	1	29	3	0	.103
1964 NY N	10	17	.370	4.23	40	34	8	227.2	256	56	115	1	0	2	0	76	12	0	.158
1965	8	24	.250	3.94	43	36	10	253.2	252	68	116	0	0	2	1	78	12	0	.154
1966	11	14	.440	3.68	38	33	10	230	229	54	127	2	1	0	0	67	6	0	.090
1967	9	18	.333	4.70	39	30	7	220.1	251	64	117	1	1	1	0	70	7	0	.100
1968 CHI A	8	13	.381	2.99	35	28	2	180.2	176	48	80	0	0	1	0	53	6	0	.113
1969 CIN N	4	4	.500	5.50	32	15	0	113	137	30	55	0	1	0	1	33	4	0	.121
11 yrs.	86	139	.382	4.06	400	265	62	1975.2	2061	605	1017	9	12	18	9	594	74	1	.125
1 yr.	8	13	.381	2.99	35	28	2	180.2	176	48	80	0	0	1	0	53	6	0	.113

Patsy Flaherty
FLAHERTY, PATRICK JOSEPH BL TL
B. June 29, 1876, Carnegie, Pa.   D. Jan. 23, 1968, Alexandria, La.

	W	L	PCT	ERA	G	GS	CG	IP	H	BB	SO	ShO	RW	RL	SV	AB	H	HR	BA
1899 LOU N	2	3	.400	2.31	5	4	4	39	41	5	5	0	1	0	0	24	5	0	.208
1900 PIT N	0	0	—	6.14	4	1	0	22	30	9	5	0	0	0	0	9	1	0	.111
1903 CHI A	11	25	.306	3.74	40	34	29	293.2	338	50	65	2	3	1	0	102	14	0	.137
1904 2 teams			CHI A (5G 1–2)					PIT N (29G 19–9)											
" total	20	11	.645	2.05	34	33	32	285	246	69	68	5	0	0	0	116	26	2	.224
1905 PIT N	9	9	.500	3.49	27	20	15	188	197	49	44	0	0	1	1	76	15	0	.197
1907 BOS N	12	15	.444	2.70	27	25	23	217	197	59	34	0	1	1	0	115	22	2	.191
1908	12	18	.400	3.25	31	31	21	244	221	81	50	0	0	0	0	86	12	0	.140
1910 PHI N	0	0	—	0.00	1	0	0	.1	1	1	0	0	0	0	0	2	1	0	.500
1911 BOS N	0	2	.000	7.07	4	2	1	14	21	8	0	0	0	0	0	94	27	2	.287
9 yrs.	66	83	.443	3.10	173	150	125	1303	1292	331	271	7	5	3	1	*			
2 yrs.	12	27	.308	3.53	45	39	33	336.2	374	60	79	2	3	1	0	114	18	0	.158

Tom Flanigan
FLANIGAN, THOMAS ANTHONY BR TL 6'3" 175 lbs.
B. Sept. 6, 1934, Cincinnati, Ohio

	W	L	PCT	ERA	G	GS	CG	IP	H	BB	SO	ShO	RW	RL	SV	AB	H	HR	BA
1954 CHI A	0	0	—	0.00	2	0	0	1.2	1	1	0	0	0	0	0	0	0	0	—
1958 STL N	0	0	—	9.00	1	0	0	1	2	1	0	0	0	0	0	0	0	0	—
2 yrs.	0	0	—	3.38	3	0	0	2.2	3	2	0	0	0	0	0	0	0	0	—
1 yr.	0	0	—	0.00	2	0	0	1.2	1	1	0	0	0	0	0	0	0	0	—

Lew Fonseca
FONSECA, LEWIS ALBERT BR TR 5'10½" 180 lbs.
B. Jan. 21, 1899, Oakland, Calif.
Manager 1932–34.

	W	L	PCT	ERA	G	GS	CG	IP	H	BB	SO	ShO	RW	RL	SV	AB	H	HR	BA
1932 CHI A	0	0	—	0.00	1	0	0	1	0	0	0	0	0	0	0	*			

Gene Ford
FORD, EUGENE MATTHEW BR TR 6'2" 195 lbs.
B. June 23, 1912, Fort Dodge, Iowa   D. Sept. 7, 1970, Emmetsburg, Iowa

	W	L	PCT	ERA	G	GS	CG	IP	H	BB	SO	ShO	RW	RL	SV	AB	H	HR	BA
1936 BOS N	0	0	—	13.50	2	1	0	2	2	3	0	0	0	0	0	0	0	0	—
1938 CHI A	0	0	—	10.29	4	0	0	14	21	12	2	0	0	0	0	6	1	0	.167
2 yrs.	0	0	—	10.69	6	1	0	16	23	15	2	0	0	0	0	6	1	0	.167
1 yr.	0	0	—	10.29	4	0	0	14	21	12	2	0	0	0	0	6	1	0	.167

Happy Foreman
FOREMAN, AUGUST BL TL 5'7" 160 lbs.
B. July 20, 1897, Memphis, Tenn.   D. Feb. 13, 1953, New York, N. Y.

	W	L	PCT	ERA	G	GS	CG	IP	H	BB	SO	ShO	RW	RL	SV	AB	H	HR	BA
1924 CHI A	0	0	—	2.25	3	0	0	4	7	4	1	0	0	0	0	2	0	0	.000
1926 BOS A	0	0	—	3.68	3	0	0	7.1	3	5	3	0	0	0	0	2	0	0	.000
2 yrs.	0	0	—	3.18	6	0	0	11.1	10	9	4	0	0	0	0	4	0	0	.000
1 yr.	0	0	—	2.25	3	0	0	4	7	4	1	0	0	0	0	2	0	0	.000

Mike Fornieles
FORNIELES, JOSE MIGUEL TORRES BR TR 5'11" 155 lbs.
B. Jan. 18, 1932, Havana, Cuba

	W	L	PCT	ERA	G	GS	CG	IP	H	BB	SO	ShO	RW	RL	SV	AB	H	HR	BA
1952 WAS A	2	2	.500	1.37	4	2	2	26.1	13	11	12	1	1	0	0	10	0	0	.000
1953 CHI A	8	7	.533	3.59	39	16	5	153	160	61	72	0	4	1	3	41	4	0	.098
1954	1	2	.333	4.29	15	6	0	42	41	14	18	0	1	1	1	11	3	0	.273
1955	6	3	.667	3.86	26	9	2	86.1	84	29	23	0	3	1	2	29	3	0	.103
1956 2 teams			CHI A (6G 0–1)					BAL A (30G 4–7)											
" total	4	8	.333	4.05	36	11	1	126.2	131	31	59	1	3	2	1	35	6	0	.171
1957 2 teams			BAL A (15G 2–6)					BOS A (25G 8–7)											
" total	10	13	.435	3.75	40	22	8	182.1	193	55	107	2	3	3	2	62	11	0	.177
1958 BOS A	4	6	.400	4.96	37	7	1	110.2	123	33	49	0	3	3	1	29	6	0	.207
1959	5	3	.625	3.23	46	0	0	82	77	29	54	0	5	3	11	19	3	0	.158
1960	10	5	.667	2.64	70	0	0	109	86	49	64	0	10	5	14	15	6	0	.400
1961	9	8	.529	4.68	57	2	1	119.1	121	54	70	0	8	7	15	32	5	1	.156
1962	3	6	.333	5.36	42	1	0	82.1	96	37	36	0	3	5	5	16	3	0	.188
1963 2 teams			BOS A (9G 0–0)					MIN A (11G 1–1)											
" total	1	1	.500	5.40	20	0	0	36.2	40	18	12	0	1	1	0	9	2	0	.222
12 yrs.	63	64	.496	3.96	432	76	20	1156.2	1165	421	576	4	45	33	55	308	52	1	.169
4 yrs.	15	13	.536	3.82	86	31	7	297	307	110	119	0	8	4	6	86	11	0	.128

Terry Forster
FORSTER, TERRY JAY BL TL 6'3" 200 lbs.
B. Jan. 14, 1952, Sioux City, S. D.

	W	L	PCT	ERA	G	GS	CG	IP	H	BB	SO	ShO	RW	RL	SV	AB	H	HR	BA
1971 CHI A	2	3	.400	3.96	45	3	0	50	46	23	48	0	2	2	1	5	2	0	.400
1972	6	5	.545	2.25	62	0	0	100	75	44	104	0	6	5	29	19	10	0	.526
1973	6	11	.353	3.23	15	12	4	172.2	174	78	120	0	3	4	16	1	0	0	.000
1974	7	8	.467	3.63	59	1	0	134	120	48	105	0	7	7	24	0	0	0	—
1975	3	3	.500	2.19	17	1	0	37	30	24	32	0	3	3	4	0	0	0	—
1976	2	12	.143	4.38	29	16	1	111	126	41	70	0	0	5	1	0	0	0	—
1977 PIT N	6	4	.600	4.45	33	6	0	87	90	32	58	0	4	1	1	26	9	0	.346
1978 LA N	5	4	.556	1.94	47	0	0	65	56	23	46	0	5	4	22	8	4	0	.500
1979	1	2	.333	5.63	17	0	0	16	18	11	8	0	1	2	2	0	0	0	—
1980	0	0	—	3.00	9	0	0	12	10	4	2	0	0	0	0	0	0	0	—
1981	0	1	.000	4.06	21	0	0	31	37	15	17	0	0	1	0	2	0	0	.000

Pitcher Register

	W	L	PCT	ERA	G	GS	CG	IP	H	BB	SO	ShO	Relief Pitching W L SV	BATTING AB H HR	BA

Terry Forster continued

1982	5	6	.455	3.04	56	0	0	83	66	31	52	0	5 6 3	2 0 0	.000
1983 ATL N	3	2	.600	2.16	56	0	0	79.1	60	31	54	0	3 2 13	8 4 0	.500
13 yrs.	46	61	.430	3.29	502	39	5	978	908	405	716	0	39 42 116	71 29 0	.408
6 yrs.	26	42	.382	3.36	263	33	5	604.2	571	258	479	0	21 26 75 9th 2nd	25 12 0	.480

DIVISIONAL PLAYOFF SERIES
| 1981 LA N | 0 | 0 | — | 0.00 | 1 | 0 | 0 | .1 | 0 | 0 | 0 | 0 | 0 0 0 | 0 0 0 | — |

LEAGUE CHAMPIONSHIP SERIES
1978 LA N	1	0	1.000	0.00	1	0	0	1	1	0	2	0	1 0 0	0 0 0	—
1981	0	0	—	0.00	1	0	0	.1	0	0	1	0	0 0 0	0 0 0	—
2 yrs.	1	0	1.000	0.00	2	0	0	1.1	1	0	3	0	1 0 0	0 0 0	—

WORLD SERIES
1978 LA N	0	0	—	0.00	3	0	0	4	5	1	6	0	0 0 0	0 0 0	—
1981	0	0	—	0.00	2	0	0	2	1	3	0	0	0 0 0	0 0 0	—
2 yrs.	0	0	—	0.00	5	0	0	6	6	4	6	0	0 0 0	0 0 0	—

Jack Fournier

FOURNIER, JOHN FRANK (Jacques)
B. Sept. 28, 1892, Au Sable, Mich. D. Sept. 5, 1973, Tacoma, Wash.
BL TR 6' 195 lbs.

| 1922 STL N | 0 | 0 | — | 0.00 | 1 | 0 | 0 | 1 | 0 | 0 | 0 | 0 | 0 0 0 | * | |

Ken Frailing

FRAILING, KENNETH DOUGLAS
B. Jan. 19, 1948, Marion, Wis.
BL TL 6' 190 lbs.

1972 CHI A	1	0	1.000	3.00	4	0	0	3	3	1	1	0	1 0 0	0 0 0	—
1973	0	0	—	1.96	10	0	0	18.1	18	7	15	0	0 0 0	0 0 0	—
1974 CHI N	6	9	.400	3.89	55	16	1	125	150	43	71	0	1 2 1	31 8 0	.258
1975	2	5	.286	5.43	41	0	0	53	61	26	39	0	2 5 1	7 1 0	.143
1976	1	2	.333	2.37	6	3	0	19	20	5	10	0	1 0 0	3 0 0	.000
5 yrs.	10	16	.385	3.96	116	19	1	218.1	252	82	136	0	5 7 2	41 9 0	.220
2 yrs.	1	0	1.000	2.11	14	0	0	21.1	21	8	16	0	1 0 0	0 0 0	—

Vic Frazier

FRAZIER, VICTOR PATRICK
B. Aug. 5, 1904, Ruston, La. D. Jan. 10, 1977, Jacksonville, Tex.
BR TR 6' 182 lbs.

1931 CHI A	13	15	.464	4.46	46	29	13	254	258	127	87	2	1 1 0	86 18 0	.209
1932	3	13	.188	6.23	29	21	4	146	180	70	33	0	0 1 0	44 4 0	.091
1933 2 teams	CHI A (10G 1–1)				DET A (20G 5–5)										
" total	6	6	.500	7.00	30	15	4	124.2	161	70	30	0	0 2 0	41 7 0	.171
1934 DET A	1	3	.250	5.96	8	2	0	22.2	30	12	11	0	1 2 0	7 2 0	.286
1937 BOS N	0	0	—	5.63	3	0	0	8	12	1	2	0	0 0 0	1 0 0	.000
1939 CHI A	0	1	.000	10.27	10	1	0	23.2	45	11	7	0	0 0 0	7 2 0	.286
6 yrs.	23	38	.377	5.77	126	68	21	579	686	291	170	2	2 6 4	186 33 0	.177
4 yrs.	17	30	.362	5.55	95	52	17	444	515	219	131	2	1 3 4	141 24 0	.170

Jake Freeze

FREEZE, CARL ALEXANDER
B. Apr. 25, 1900, Huntington, Ark.
BR TR 5'8" 105 lbs.

| 1925 CHI A | 0 | 0 | — | 2.45 | 2 | 0 | 0 | 3.2 | 5 | 3 | 1 | 0 | 0 0 0 | 1 0 0 | .000 |

Dave Frost

FROST, CARL DAVID
B. Nov. 17, 1952, Long Beach, Calif.
BR TR 6'6" 235 lbs.

1977 CHI A	1	1	.500	3.00	4	3	0	24	30	3	15	0	0 0 0	0 0 0	—
1978 CAL A	5	4	.556	2.58	11	10	2	80.1	71	24	30	1	0 0 0	0 0 0	—
1979	16	10	.615	3.58	36	33	12	239	226	77	107	2	0 1 1	0 0 0	—
1980	4	8	.333	5.31	15	15	2	78	97	21	28	0	0 0 0	0 0 0	—
1981	1	8	.111	5.55	12	9	0	47	44	19	16	0	0 1 0	0 0 0	—
1982 KC A	6	6	.500	5.51	21	14	0	81.2	103	30	26	0	3 0 0	0 0 0	—
6 yrs.	33	37	.471	4.11	99	84	16	550	571	174	222	3	3 2 1	0 0 0	—
1 yr.	1	1	.500	3.00	4	3	0	24	30	3	15	0	0 0 0	0 0 0	—

LEAGUE CHAMPIONSHIP SERIES
| 1979 CAL A | 0 | 1 | .000 | 18.69 | 2 | 1 | 0 | 4.1 | 8 | 5 | 1 | 0 | 0 0 0 | 0 0 0 | — |

Frank Gabler

GABLER, FRANK HAROLD (The Great Gabbo)
B. Nov. 6, 1911, East Highlands, Calif. D. Nov. 1, 1967, Long Beach, Calif.
BR TR 6'1" 175 lbs.

1935 NY N	2	1	.667	5.70	26	1	0	60	79	20	24	0	2 0 0	16 2 0	.125
1936	9	8	.529	3.12	43	14	5	161.2	170	34	46	0	3 2 6	48 10 0	.208
1937 2 teams	NY N (6G 0–0)				BOS N (19G 4–7)										
" total	4	7	.364	5.61	25	9	2	85	104	18	22	1	2 2 2	22 4 0	.182
1938 2 teams	BOS N (1G 0–0)				CHI A (18G 1–7)										
" total	1	7	.125	9.43	19	7	3	69.2	104	35	17	0	0 3 0	21 5 0	.238
4 yrs.	16	23	.410	5.26	113	31	10	376.1	457	107	109	1	7 7 8	107 21 0	.196
1 yr.	1	7	.125	9.09	18	7	3	69.1	101	34	17	0	0 3 0	21 5 0	.238

WORLD SERIES
| 1936 NY N | 0 | 0 | — | 7.20 | 2 | 0 | 0 | 5 | 7 | 4 | 0 | 0 | 0 0 0 | 0 0 0 | — |

Phil Gallivan

GALLIVAN, PHILIP JOSEPH
B. May 29, 1907, Seattle, Wash. D. Nov. 24, 1969, St. Paul, Minn.
BR TR 6' 180 lbs.

1931 BKN N	0	1	.000	5.28	6	1	0	15.1	23	7	1	0	0 0 0	3 0 0	.000
1932 CHI A	1	3	.250	7.56	13	3	1	33.1	49	24	12	0	1 0 0	8 3 0	.375
1934	4	7	.364	5.61	35	7	3	126.2	155	64	55	0	4 4 1	40 9 0	.225
3 yrs.	5	11	.313	5.95	54	11	4	175.1	227	95	68	0	5 4 1	51 12 0	.235
2 yrs.	5	10	.333	6.02	48	10	4	160	204	88	67	0	5 4 1	48 12 0	.250

Mike Garcia

GARCIA, EDWARD MIGUEL (The Big Bear)
B. Nov. 17, 1923, San Gabriel, Calif.
BR TR 6'1" 195 lbs.

| 1948 CLE A | 0 | 0 | — | 0.00 | 1 | 0 | 0 | 2 | 3 | 0 | 1 | 0 | 0 0 0 | 0 0 0 | — |
| 1949 | 14 | 5 | .737 | 2.36 | 41 | 20 | 8 | 175.2 | 154 | 60 | 94 | 5 | 3 1 2 | 51 12 0 | .235 |

Pitcher Register

	W	L	PCT	ERA	G	GS	CG	IP	H	BB	SO	ShO	Relief Pitching W L SV	Batting AB H HR	BA

Mike Garcia continued

1950	11	11	.500	3.86	33	29	11	184	191	74	76	0	0 0 0	65 13 0	.200
1951	20	13	.606	3.15	47	30	15	254	239	82	118	1	3 2 6	85 18 1	.212
1952	22	11	.667	2.37	46	36	19	292.1	284	87	143	6	1 2 4	95 13 0	.137
1953	18	9	.667	3.25	38	35	21	271.2	260	81	134	3	0 1 0	96 24 0	.250
1954	19	8	.704	**2.64**	45	34	13	258.2	220	71	129	5	0 0 5	81 11 0	.136
1955	11	13	.458	4.02	38	31	6	210.2	230	56	120	2	0 2 3	69 15 0	.217
1956	11	12	.478	3.78	35	30	8	197.2	213	74	119	4	0 1 0	61 7 0	.115
1957	12	8	.600	3.75	38	27	9	211.1	221	73	110	1	1 0 0	75 12 0	.160
1958	1	0	1.000	9.00	6	1	0	8	15	7	2	0	1 0 0	1 0 0	.000
1959	3	6	.333	4.00	29	8	1	72	72	31	49	0	3 3 1	14 1 0	.071
1960 CHI A	0	0	—	4.58	15	0	0	17.2	23	10	8	0	0 0 2	3 1 0	.333
1961 WAS A	0	1	.000	4.74	16	0	0	19	23	13	14	0	0 1 0	0 0 0	—
14 yrs.	142	97	.594	3.27	428	281	111	2174.2	2148	719	1117	27	12 13 23	696 127 2	.182
1 yr.	0	0	—	4.58	15	0	0	17.2	23	10	8	0	0 0 2	3 1 0	.333

WORLD SERIES

| 1954 CLE A | 0 | 1 | .000 | 5.40 | 2 | 1 | 0 | 5 | 6 | 4 | 4 | 0 | 0 0 0 | 0 0 0 | — |

Lou Garland
GARLAND, LOUIS LYMAN
B. July 16, 1905, Archie, Mo.
BR TR 6'2½" 200 lbs.

| 1931 CHI A | 0 | 2 | .000 | 10.26 | 7 | 2 | 0 | 16.2 | 30 | 14 | 4 | 0 | 0 2 0 | 3 0 0 | .000 |

Ned Garvin
GARVIN, VIRGIL LEE
B. Jan. 1, 1874, Navasota, Tex. D. June 16, 1908, Fresno, Calif.
TR 6'3½" 160 lbs.

1896 PHI N	0	1	.000	7.62	2	1	1	13	19	7	4	0	0 0 0	6 0 0	.000
1899 CHI N	9	13	.409	2.85	24	23	22	199	202	42	69	4	0 0 0	71 11 0	.155
1900	10	18	.357	2.41	30	28	25	246.1	225	63	107	1	0 1 0	91 14 0	.154
1901 MIL A	7	20	.259	3.46	37	27	22	257.1	258	90	122	1	0 0 2	93 10 0	.108
1902 2 teams			CHI	A (23G 10–11)			BKN	N (2G 1–1)							
" total	11	12	.478	2.09	25	21	18	193.1	184	47	62	3	1 1 0	66 10 0	.152
1903 BKN N	15	18	.455	3.08	38	34	30	298	277	84	154	2	0 1 2	106 8 0	.075
1904 2 teams			BKN	N (23G 5–15)			NY	A (2G 0–1)							
" total	5	16	.238	1.72	25	24	16	193.2	155	80	94	2	0 0 0	67 8 0	.119
7 yrs.	57	98	.368	2.72	181	158	134	1400.2	1320	413	612	13	1 3 4	500 61 0	.122
1 yr.	10	11	.476	2.21	23	19	16	175.1	169	43	55	2	1 1 0	59 9 0	.153

Milt Gaston
GASTON, NATHANIEL MILTON
Brother of Alex Gaston.
B. Jan. 27, 1896, Ridgefield Park, N. J.
BR TR 6'1" 185 lbs.
BB 1933

1924 NY A	5	3	.625	4.50	29	2	0	86	92	44	24	0	5 1 1	27 6 0	.222
1925 STL A	15	14	.517	4.41	42	30	16	238.2	284	101	84	0	3 3 1	80 21 1	.263
1926	10	**18**	.357	4.33	32	28	14	214.1	227	101	39	1	0 2 0	78 13 1	.167
1927	13	17	.433	5.00	37	30	21	254	275	100	77	0	0 2 1	96 25 3	.260
1928 WAS A	6	12	.333	5.51	28	22	8	148.2	179	53	45	3	0 1 0	49 7 0	.143
1929 BOS A	12	19	.387	3.73	39	29	20	243.2	265	81	83	1	2 3 2	78 15 1	.192
1930	13	**20**	.394	3.92	38	34	20	273	272	98	99	2	0 1 2	98 20 0	.204
1931	2	13	.133	4.46	23	18	4	119	137	41	33	0	0 0 0	38 6 0	.158
1932 CHI A	7	17	.292	4.00	28	25	7	166.2	183	73	44	1	0 1 1	60 14 0	.233
1933	8	12	.400	4.85	30	25	7	167	177	60	39	1	0 0 0	52 8 0	.154
1934	6	19	.240	5.85	29	28	10	194	247	84	48	1	0 0 0	68 10 0	.147
11 yrs.	97	164	.372	4.55	355	271	127	2105	2338	836	615	10	10 14 8	724 145 6	.200
3 yrs.	21	48	.304	4.95	87	78	24	527.2	607	217	131	3	0 1 1	180 32 0	.178

Pete Gebrian
GEBRIAN, PETER (Gabe)
B. Aug. 10, 1923, Bayonne, N. J.
BR TR 6' 170 lbs.

| 1947 CHI A | 2 | 3 | .400 | 4.48 | 27 | 4 | 0 | 66.1 | 61 | 33 | 17 | 0 | 2 0 5 | 13 0 0 | .000 |

Jim Geddes
GEDDES, JAMES LEE
B. Mar. 23, 1949, Columbus, Ohio
BR TR 6'2" 200 lbs.

1972 CHI A	0	0	—	6.97	5	1	0	10.1	12	10	3	0	0 0 0	1 0 0	.000
1973	0	0	—	2.87	6	1	0	15.2	13	14	7	0	0 0 0	0 0 0	—
2 yrs.	0	0	—	4.50	11	2	0	26	25	24	10	0	0 0 0	1 0 0	.000
2 yrs.	0	0	—	4.50	11	2	0	26	25	24	10	0	0 0 0	1 0 0	.000

Al Gettel
GETTEL, ALLEN JONES
B. Sept. 17, 1917, Norfolk, Va.
BR TR 6'3½" 200 lbs.

1945 NY A	9	8	.529	3.90	27	17	9	154.2	141	53	67	0	0 0 3	57 16 0	.281
1946	6	7	.462	2.97	26	11	5	103	89	40	54	2	3 0 0	32 4 0	.125
1947 CLE A	11	10	.524	3.20	31	21	9	149	122	62	64	2	1 2 0	51 15 0	.294
1948 2 teams			CLE	A (5G 0–1)	CHI	A (22G 8–10)									
" total	8	11	.421	4.68	27	21	7	155.2	169	70	53	0	0 2 1	57 13 0	.228
1949 2 teams			CHI	A (19G 2–5)	WAS	A (16G 0–2)									
" total	2	7	.222	6.08	35	8	1	97.2	112	50	29	1	1 4 2	26 3 0	.115
1951 NY N	1	2	.333	4.87	30	1	0	57.1	52	25	36	0	1 2 0	12 1 0	.083
1955 STL N	1	0	1.000	9.00	8	0	0	17	26	10	7	0	1 0 0	6 3 0	.500
7 yrs.	38	45	.458	4.28	184	79	31	734.1	711	310	310	5	7 10 6	241 55 0	.228
2 yrs.	10	15	.400	4.73	41	26	8	211	223	86	71	0	1 3 2	72 16 0	.222

George Gick
GICK, GEORGE EDWARD
B. Oct. 18, 1915, Dunnington, Ind.
BB TR 6' 190 lbs.

1937 CHI A	0	0	—	0.00	1	0	0	2	0	0	1	0	0 0 1	0 0 0	—
1938	0	0	—	0.00	1	0	0	1	0	0	1	0	0 0 0	0 0 0	—
2 yrs.	0	0	—	0.00	2	0	0	3	0	0	2	0	0 0 1	0 0 0	—
2 yrs.	0	0	—	0.00	2	0	0	3	0	0	2	0	0 0 1	0 0 0	—

Pitcher Register

	W	L	PCT	ERA	G	GS	CG	IP	H	BB	SO	ShO	Relief Pitching W L SV	BATTING AB H HR	BA

Claral Gillenwater
GILLENWATER, CLARAL LEWIS   BR TR 6'   187 lbs.
B. May 20, 1900, Simes, Ind.   D. Feb. 26, 1978, Pensacola, Fla.

| 1923 CHI A | 1 | 3 | .250 | 5.48 | 5 | 3 | 1 | 21.1 | 28 | 6 | 2 | 1 | 1 | 1 | 0 | 6 | 0 | 0 | .000 |

Bob Gillespie
GILLESPIE, ROBERT WILLIAM (Bunch)   BR TR 6'4"   187 lbs.
B. Oct. 8, 1918, Columbus, Ohio

1944 DET A	0	1	.000	6.55	7	0	0	11	7	12	4	0	0	1	0	2	0	0	.000
1947 CHI A	5	8	.385	4.73	25	17	1	118	133	53	36	0	0	0	0	33	2	0	.061
1948	0	4	.000	5.13	25	6	1	72	81	33	19	0	0	0	0	16	0	0	.000
1950 BOS A	0	0	–	20.25	1	0	0	1.1	2	4	0	0	0	0	0	0	0	0	–
4 yrs.	5	13	.278	5.07	58	23	2	202.1	223	102	59	0	0	1	0	51	2	0	.039
2 yrs.	5	12	.294	4.88	50	23	2	190	214	86	55	0	0	0	0	49	2	0	.041

Kid Gleason
GLEASON, WILLIAM J.   BL TR 5'7"   158 lbs.
Brother of Harry Gleason.
B. Oct. 26, 1866, Camden, N.J.   D. Jan. 2, 1933, Philadelphia, Pa.
Manager 1919-23.

1888 PHI N	7	16	.304	2.84	24	23	23	199.2	199	53	89	1	0	0	0	83	17	0	.205
1889	9	15	.375	5.58	29	21	15	205	242	97	64	0	2	2	1	99	25	0	.253
1890	38	17	.691	2.63	60	55	54	506	479	167	222	6	1	0	2	224	47	0	.210
1891	24	22	.522	3.51	53	44	40	418	431	165	100	1	1	2	1	214	53	0	.248
1892 STL N	16	24	.400	3.33	47	45	43	400	389	151	133	2	0	0	0	233	50	3	.215
1893	21	25	.457	4.61	48	45	37	380.1	436	187	86	1	1	1	1	199	51	0	.256
1894 2 teams		STL	N (8G 2-6)		BAL	N (21G 15-5)													
" total	17	11	.607	4.85	29	28	25	230	299	65	44	0	0	0	0	114	37	0	.325
1895 BAL N	2	4	.333	6.97	9	5	3	50.1	77	21	6	0	1	2	1	421	130	0	.309
8 yrs.	134	134	.500	3.79	299	266	240	2389.1	2552	906	744	11	6	7	6	*			

Bill Gogolewski
GOGOLEWSKI, WILLIAM JOSEPH   BL TR 6'4"   190 lbs.
B. Oct. 26, 1947, Oshkosh, Wis.

1970 WAS A	2	2	.500	4.76	8	5	0	34	33	25	19	0	0	0	0	7	0	0	.000
1971	6	5	.545	2.76	27	17	4	124	112	39	70	1	0	0	0	32	5	0	.156
1972 TEX A	4	11	.267	4.23	36	21	2	151	136	58	95	1	0	1	2	40	5	0	.125
1973	3	6	.333	4.21	49	1	0	124	139	48	77	0	3	6	6	0	0	0	–
1974 CLE A	0	0	–	4.50	5	0	0	14	15	2	3	0	0	0	0	0	0	0	–
1975 CHI A	0	0	–	5.24	19	0	0	55	61	28	37	0	0	0	2	0	0	0	–
6 yrs.	15	24	.385	4.02	144	44	6	502	496	200	301	2	3	7	10	79	10	0	.127
1 yr.	0	0	–	5.24	19	0	0	55	61	28	37	0	0	0	2	0	0	0	–

Wilbur Good
GOOD, WILBUR DAVID (Lefty)   BL TL 5'6"   165 lbs.
B. Sept. 28, 1885, Punxsutawney, Pa.   D. Dec. 30, 1963, Brooksville, Fla.

| 1905 NY A | 0 | 2 | .000 | 4.74 | 5 | 2 | 0 | 19 | 18 | 14 | 13 | 0 | 0 | 0 | 0 | * | | | |

John Goodell
GOODELL, JOHN HENRY WILLIAM (Lefty)   BR TL 5'10"   165 lbs.
B. Apr. 5, 1907, Muskogee, Okla.

| 1928 CHI A | 0 | 0 | – | 18.00 | 2 | 0 | 0 | 3 | 6 | 2 | 0 | 0 | 0 | 0 | 0 | 0 | 0 | 0 | – |

Jim Goodwin
GOODWIN, JAMES PATRICK   BL TL 6'1"   170 lbs.
B. Aug. 15, 1926, St. Louis, Mo.

| 1948 CHI A | 0 | 0 | – | 8.71 | 8 | 1 | 0 | 10.1 | 9 | 12 | 3 | 0 | 0 | 0 | 1 | 2 | 1 | 0 | .500 |

Goose Gossage
GOSSAGE, RICHARD MICHAEL (Goose)   BR TR 6'3"   180 lbs.
B. June 5, 1951, Colorado Springs, Colo.

1972 CHI A	7	1	.875	4.28	36	1	0	80	72	44	57	0	7	0	2	16	0	0	.000
1973	0	4	.000	7.43	20	4	1	49.2	57	37	33	0	0	0	0	0	0	0	–
1974	4	6	.400	4.15	39	3	0	89	92	47	64	0	4	5	1	0	0	0	–
1975	9	8	.529	1.84	62	0	0	141.2	99	70	130	0	9	8	26	0	0	0	–
1976	9	17	.346	3.94	31	29	15	224	214	90	135	0	0	1	1	0	0	0	–
1977 PIT N	11	9	.550	1.62	72	0	0	133	78	49	151	0	11	9	26	23	5	0	.217
1978 NY A	10	11	.476	2.01	63	0	0	134.1	87	59	122	0	10	11	27	0	0	0	–
1979	5	3	.625	2.64	36	0	0	58	48	19	41	0	5	3	18	0	0	0	–
1980	6	2	.750	2.27	64	0	0	99	74	37	103	0	6	2	33	0	0	0	–
1981	3	2	.600	0.77	32	0	0	47	22	14	48	0	3	2	20	0	0	0	–
1982	4	5	.444	2.23	56	0	0	93	63	28	102	0	4	5	30	0	0	0	–
1983	13	5	.722	2.27	57	0	0	87.1	82	25	90	0	13	5	22	0	0	0	–
12 yrs.	81	73	.526	2.85	568	37	16	1236	988	519	1076	0	72	51	206 5th	39	5	0	.128
5 yrs.	29	36	.446	3.80	188	37	16	584.1	534	288	419	0	20	14	30 10th	16	0	0	.000

DIVISIONAL PLAYOFF SERIES
| 1981 NY A | 0 | 0 | – | 0.00 | 3 | 0 | 0 | 6.2 | 3 | 2 | 8 | 0 | 0 | 0 | 3 | 0 | 0 | 0 | – |

LEAGUE CHAMPIONSHIP SERIES
1978 NY A	1	0	1.000	4.50	2	0	0	4	3	0	3	0	1	0	1	0	0	0	–
1980	0	1	.000	54.00	1	0	0	.1	3	0	0	0	0	1	0	0	0	0	–
1981	0	0	–	0.00	2	0	0	2.2	1	0	2	0	0	0	1	0	0	0	–
3 yrs.	1	1	.500	5.14	5	0	0	7	7	0	5	0	1	1	2	0	0	0	–

WORLD SERIES
1978 NY A	0	0	1.000	0.00	3	0	0	6	1	1	4	0	1	0	0	1	0	0	.000
1981	0	0	–	0.00	3	0	0	5	2	2	5	0	0	0	2	0	0	0	–
2 yrs.	1	0	1.000	0.00	6	0	0	11	3	3	9	0	1	0	2	1	0	0	.000

Wayne Granger
GRANGER, WAYNE ALLAN   BR TR 6'2"   165 lbs.
B. Mar. 15, 1944, Springfield, Mass.

1968 STL N	4	2	.667	2.25	34	0	0	44	40	12	27	0	4	2	4	5	1	0	.200
1969 CIN N	9	6	.600	2.79	90	0	0	145	143	40	68	0	9	6	27	21	2	0	.095
1970	6	5	.545	2.65	67	0	0	85	79	27	38	0	6	5	35	10	1	0	.100

Pitcher Register

364

	W	L	PCT	ERA	G	GS	CG	IP	H	BB	SO	ShO	Relief Pitching W	L	SV	BATTING AB	H	HR	BA

Wayne Granger continued

1971	7	6	.538	3.33	70	0	0	100	94	28	51	0	7	6	11	7	1	1	.143
1972 MIN A	4	6	.400	3.00	63	0	0	90	83	28	45	0	4	6	19	10	2	0	.200
1973 2 teams		STL	N (33G 2–4)		NY	A (7G 0–1)													
" total	2	5	.286	3.63	40	0	0	62	69	24	24	0	2	5	5	3	0	0	.000
1974 CHI A	0	0	–	7.88	5	0	0	8	16	3	4	0	0	0	0	0	0	0	–
1975 HOU N	2	5	.286	3.65	55	0	0	74	76	23	30	0	2	5	5	9	0	0	.000
1976 MON N	1	0	1.000	3.66	27	0	0	32	32	16	16	0	1	0	2	3	0	0	.000
9 yrs.	35	35	.500	3.14	451	0	0	640	632	201	303	0	35	35	108	68	7	1	.103
1 yr.	0	0	–	7.88	5	0	0	8	16	3	4	0	0	0	0	0	0	0	–

LEAGUE CHAMPIONSHIP SERIES
| 1970 CIN N | 0 | 0 | – | 0.00 | 1 | 0 | 0 | .2 | 1 | 0 | 0 | 0 | 0 | 0 | 0 | 0 | 0 | 0 | – |

WORLD SERIES
1968 STL N	0	0	–	0.00	1	0	0	2	0	1	1	0	0	0	0	0	0	0	–
1970 CIN N	0	0	–	33.75	2	0	0	1.1	7	1	1	0	0	0	0	0	0	0	–
2 yrs.	0	0	–	13.50	3	0	0	3.1	7	2	2	0	0	0	0	0	0	0	–

Ted Gray

GRAY, TED GLENN   BB TL 5'11" 175 lbs.
B. Dec. 31, 1924, Detroit, Mich.

1946 DET A	0	2	.000	8.49	3	2	0	11.2	17	5	5	0	0	0	1	3	0	0	.000
1948	6	2	.750	4.22	26	11	3	85.1	73	72	60	1	0	0	0	29	7	0	.241
1949	10	10	.500	3.51	34	27	8	195	163	103	96	3	0	0	1	63	8	0	.127
1950	10	7	.588	4.40	27	21	7	149.1	139	72	102	0	1	0	1	50	7	0	.140
1951	7	14	.333	4.06	34	28	9	197.1	194	95	131	1	0	1	1	63	9	0	.143
1952	12	17	.414	4.14	35	32	13	224	212	101	138	2	0	0	0	76	13	0	.171
1953	10	15	.400	4.60	30	28	8	176	166	76	115	0	0	0	0	61	14	0	.230
1954	3	5	.375	5.38	19	10	2	72	70	56	29	0	0	0	0	22	1	0	.045
1955 4 teams		CHI	A (2G 0–0)		CLE	A (2G 0–0)		NY	A (1G 0–0)			BAL	A (9G 1–2)						
" total	1	2	.333	9.64	14	3	0	23.1	38	15	11	0	1	1	0	3	0	0	.000
9 yrs.	59	74	.444	4.37	222	162	50	1134	1072	595	687	7	2	2	4	370	59	0	.159
1 yr.	0	0	–	18.00	2	1	0	3	9	2	1	0	0	0	0	0	0	0	–

Paul Gregory

GREGORY, PAUL EDWIN (Pop)   BR TR 6'2" 180 lbs.
B. July 9, 1908, Tomnolen, Miss.

1932 CHI A	5	3	.625	4.51	33	9	3	117.2	125	51	39	0	2	0	0	38	3	0	.079
1933	4	11	.267	4.95	23	17	5	103.2	124	47	18	0	0	0	0	35	5	0	.143
2 yrs.	9	14	.391	4.72	56	26	8	221.1	249	98	57	0	2	0	0	73	8	0	.110
2 yrs.	9	14	.391	4.72	56	26	8	221.1	249	98	57	0	2	0	0	73	8	0	.110

Clark Griffith

GRIFFITH, CLARK CALVIN (The Old Fox)   BR TR 5'6½" 156 lbs.
B. Nov. 20, 1869, Stringtown, Mo.   D. Oct. 27, 1955, Washington, D. C.
Manager 1901-20.
Hall of Fame 1946.

1891 2 teams		STL	AA (27G 14–6)		BOS	AA (7G 3–1)													
" total	17	7	.708	3.74	34	21	15	226.1	242	73	88	0	7	0	0	100	16	2	.160
1893 CHI N	1	1	.500	5.03	4	2	2	19.2	24	5	9	0	0	1	0	11	2	0	.182
1894	21	11	.656	4.92	36	30	28	261.3	328	85	71	0	3	3	0	142	33	0	.232
1895	25	13	.658	3.93	42	41	39	353	434	91	79	0	1	0	0	144	46	1	.319
1896	22	13	.629	3.54	36	35	35	317.2	370	70	81	0	0	0	0	135	36	1	.267
1897	21	19	.525	3.72	41	38	38	343.2	410	86	102	1	1	0	1	162	38	0	.235
1898	26	10	.722	1.88	38	38	36	325.2	305	64	97	4	0	0	0	122	20	0	.164
1899	22	13	.629	2.79	38	38	35	319.2	329	65	73	0	0	0	0	120	31	0	.258
1900	14	13	.519	3.05	30	30	27	248	245	51	61	4	0	0	0	95	24	1	.253
1901 CHI A	24	7	.774	2.67	35	30	26	266.2	275	50	67	5	3	0	1	89	27	2	.303
1902	15	9	.625	4.19	28	24	20	212.2	247	47	51	3	2	0	0	92	20	0	.217
1903 NY A	14	10	.583	2.70	25	24	22	213	201	33	69	3	1	0	0	69	11	1	.159
1904	7	5	.583	2.87	16	11	8	100.1	91	16	36	1	1	0	1	42	6	0	.143
1905	9	6	.600	1.67	25	7	4	102.2	82	15	46	2	4	3	3	32	7	0	.219
1906	2	2	.500	3.02	17	2	1	59.2	58	15	16	0	1	3	2	18	2	0	.111
1907	0	0	–	8.64	4	0	0	8.1	15	6	5	0	0	0	0	2	0	0	.000
1909 CIN N	0	1	.000	6.00	1	1	1	6	11	2	3	0	0	0	0	2	0	0	.000
1910	0	0	–	0.00	0	0	0	0	0	0	0	0	0	0	0	0	0	0	–
1912 WAS A	0	0	–	∞	1	0	0	0	1	0	0	0	0	0	0	1	0	0	.000
1913	0	0	–	0.00	1	0	0	1	1	1	0	0	0	0	0	1	1	0	1.000
1914	0	0	–	0.00	1	0	0	1	1	0	1	0	0	0	0	1	1	0	1.000
21 yrs.	240	140	.632	3.31	453	372	337	3386.1	3670	774	955	23	24	10	9	*			
2 yrs.	39	16	.709	3.34	63	54	46	479.1	522	97	118	8	5	0	1	181	47	2	.260

Ross Grimsley

GRIMSLEY, ROSS ALBERT (Lefty)   BL TL 6' 175 lbs.
Father of Ross Grimsley.
B. June 4, 1922, Americus, Kans.

| 1951 CHI A | 0 | 0 | – | 3.86 | 7 | 0 | 0 | 14 | 12 | 10 | 8 | 0 | 0 | 0 | 0 | 2 | 0 | 0 | .000 |

Marv Grissom

GRISSOM, MARVIN EDWARD   BR TR 6'3" 190 lbs.
Brother of Lee Grissom.
B. Mar. 31, 1918, Los Molinos, Calif.

1946 NY N	0	2	.000	4.34	4	3	0	18.2	17	13	9	0	0	0	0	5	1	0	.200
1949 DET A	2	4	.333	6.41	27	2	0	39.1	56	34	17	0	2	3	0	9	2	0	.222
1952 CHI A	12	10	.545	3.74	28	24	7	166	156	79	97	1	0	1	0	53	8	0	.151
1953 2 teams		BOS	A (13G 2–6)		NY	N (21G 4–2)													
" total	6	8	.429	4.26	34	18	4	143.2	144	61	77	1	0	1	0	45	2	0	.044
1954 NY N	10	7	.588	2.35	56	3	1	122.1	100	50	64	1	9	7	19	32	5	0	.156
1955	5	4	.556	2.92	55	0	0	89.1	76	41	49	0	5	4	8	13	2	0	.154
1956	1	1	.500	1.56	43	0	0	80.2	71	16	49	0	1	1	7	11	1	0	.091
1957	4	4	.500	2.61	55	0	0	82.2	74	23	51	0	4	4	14	12	2	0	.167
1958 SF N	7	5	.583	3.99	51	0	0	65.1	71	26	46	0	7	5	10	9	0	0	.000

	W	L	PCT	ERA	G	GS	CG	IP	H	BB	SO	ShO	Relief Pitching W L SV	BATTING AB H HR	BA

Marv Grissom continued
1959 STL N	0	0	–	22.50	3	0	0	2	6	0	0	0	0 0 0	0 0 0	–
10 yrs.	47	45	.511	3.41	356	52	12	810	771	343	459	3	28 26 58	189 23 0	.122
1 yr.	12	10	.545	3.74	28	24	7	166	156	79	97	1	0 1 0	53 8 0	.151

WORLD SERIES
| 1954 NY N | 1 | 0 | 1.000 | 0.00 | 1 | 0 | 0 | 2.2 | 1 | 3 | 2 | 0 | 1 0 0 | 1 0 0 | .000 |

Ernie Groth
GROTH, ERNEST WILLIAM
B. May 3, 1922, Beaver Falls, Pa.   BR TR 5'9" 185 lbs.

1947 CLE A	0	0	–	0.00	2	0	0	1.1	0	1	1	0	0 0 0	0 0 0	–
1948	0	0	–	9.00	1	0	0	1	1	2	0	0	0 0 0	0 0 0	–
1949 CHI A	0	1	.000	5.40	3	0	0	5	2	3	1	0	0 1 0	0 0 0	–
3 yrs.	0	1	.000	4.91	6	0	0	7.1	3	6	2	0	0 1 0	0 0 0	–
1 yr.	0	1	.000	5.40	3	0	0	5	2	3	1	0	0 1 0	0 0 0	–

Orval Grove
GROVE, LeROY ORVAL
B. Aug. 29, 1919, Mineral, Kans.   BR TR 6'3" 196 lbs.

1940 CHI A	0	0	–	3.00	3	0	0	6	4	4	1	0	0 0 0	1 0 0	.000
1941	0	0	–	10.29	2	0	0	7	9	5	5	0	0 0 0	2 0 0	.000
1942	4	6	.400	5.16	12	8	4	66.1	77	33	21	0	1 1 0	22 5 1	.227
1943	15	9	.625	2.75	32	25	18	216.1	192	72	76	3	1 0 2	66 12 0	.182
1944	14	15	.483	3.72	34	33	11	234.2	237	71	105	2	1 0 0	77 8 0	.104
1945	14	12	.538	3.44	33	30	16	217	233	68	54	4	0 0 1	71 7 0	.099
1946	8	13	.381	3.02	33	26	10	205.1	213	78	60	1	0 0 0	65 7 0	.108
1947	6	8	.429	4.44	25	19	6	135.2	158	70	33	1	0 0 0	48 7 0	.146
1948	2	10	.167	6.16	32	11	1	87.2	110	42	18	0	1 2 1	21 2 0	.095
1949	0	0	–	54.00	1	0	0	.2	4	1	1	0	0 0 0	0 0 0	–
10 yrs.	63	73	.463	3.78	207	152	66	1176.2	1237	444	374	11	4 3 4	373 48 1	.129
10 yrs.	63	73	.463	3.78	207	152	66	1176.2	1237	444	374	11	4 3 4	373 48 1	.129

Randy Gumpert
GUMPERT, RANDALL PENNINGTON
B. Jan. 23, 1918, Monocacy, Pa.   BR TR 6'3" 185 lbs.

1936 PHI A	1	2	.333	4.76	22	3	2	62.1	74	32	9	0	0 0 2	22 6 0	.273
1937	0	0	–	12.00	10	1	0	12	16	15	5	0	0 0 0	3 1 0	.333
1938	0	2	.000	10.95	4	2	0	12.1	24	10	1	0	0 0 0	4 1 0	.250
1946 NY A	11	3	.786	2.31	33	12	4	132.2	113	32	63	0	3 0 1	47 6 0	.128
1947	4	1	.800	5.43	24	6	2	56.1	71	28	25	0	1 0 0	14 1 0	.071
1948 2 teams			NY	A (15G 1–0)			CHI	A (16G 2–6)							
" total	3	6	.333	3.60	31	11	6	122.1	130	19	43	1	1 3 0	29 4 0	.138
1949 CHI A	13	16	.448	3.81	34	32	18	234	223	83	78	3	0 0 1	84 16 0	.190
1950	5	12	.294	4.75	40	17	6	155.1	165	58	48	1	2 2 0	42 3 0	.071
1951	9	8	.529	4.32	33	16	7	141.2	156	34	45	1	2 3 2	45 15 0	.333
1952 2 teams			BOS	A (10G 1–0)			WAS	A (20G 4–9)							
" total	5	9	.357	4.22	30	13	2	123.2	127	35	35	0	2 2 1	39 7 0	.179
10 yrs.	51	59	.464	4.17	261	113	47	1052.2	1099	346	352	6	11 10 7	329 60 0	.182
4 yrs.	29	42	.408	4.15	123	76	37	628.1	647	188	202	6	4 8 3	200 38 0	.190

Warren Hacker
HACKER, WARREN LOUIS
B. Nov. 21, 1924, Marissa, Ill.   BR TR 6'1" 185 lbs.

1948 CHI N	0	1	.000	21.00	3	1	0	3	7	3	0	0	0 0 0	0 0 0	–
1949	5	8	.385	4.23	30	12	3	125.2	141	53	40	0	3 1 0	38 7 0	.184
1950	0	1	.000	5.28	5	3	1	15.1	20	8	5	0	0 0 0	5 0 0	.000
1951	0	0	–	13.50	2	0	0	1.1	3	0	2	0	0 0 0	0 0 0	–
1952	15	9	.625	2.58	33	20	12	185	144	31	84	5	2 2 1	58 7 0	.121
1953	12	19	.387	4.38	39	32	9	221.2	225	54	106	0	1 2 2	78 17 0	.218
1954	6	13	.316	4.25	39	18	4	158.2	157	37	80	1	1 6 2	55 13 0	.236
1955	11	15	.423	4.27	35	30	13	213	202	43	80	0	1 0 3	72 18 0	.250
1956	3	13	.188	4.66	34	24	4	168	190	44	65	0	0 0 0	54 8 0	.148
1957 2 teams			CIN	N (15G 3–2)			PHI	N (20G 4–4)							
" total	7	6	.538	4.76	35	16	1	117.1	122	31	51	0	1 0 0	31 7 0	.226
1958 PHI N	0	1	.000	7.41	9	1	0	17	24	8	4	0	0 0 0	1 0 0	.000
1961 CHI A	3	3	.500	3.77	42	0	0	57.1	62	8	40	0	3 3 8	9 1 0	.111
12 yrs.	62	89	.411	4.21	306	157	47	1283.1	1297	320	557	6	12 14 17	401 78 0	.195
1 yr.	3	3	.500	3.77	42	0	0	57.1	62	8	40	0	3 3 8	9 1 0	.111

Bump Hadley
HADLEY, IRVING DARIUS
B. July 5, 1904, Lynn, Mass.   D. Feb. 15, 1963, Lynn, Mass.   BR TR 5'11" 190 lbs.

1926 WAS A	0	0	–	12.00	1	0	0	3	6	2	0	0	0 0 0	0 0 0	–
1927	14	6	.700	2.85	30	27	13	198.2	177	86	60	0	0 0 0	70 19 0	.271
1928	12	13	.480	3.54	33	31	16	231.2	236	100	80	3	0 0 0	81 17 0	.210
1929	6	16	.273	5.65	37	27	6	194.1	196	85	98	1	0 4 0	62 6 0	.097
1930	15	11	.577	3.73	42	34	15	260.1	242	105	162	1	1 1 2	93 21 0	.226
1931	11	10	.524	3.06	55	11	2	179.2	145	92	124	1	8 5 8	54 9 0	.167
1932 2 teams			CHI	A (3G 1–1)			STL	A (40G 13–20)							
" total	14	21	.400	5.40	43	35	13	248.1	261	171	145	1	0 3 2	84 23 0	.274
1933 STL A	15	20	.429	3.92	45	36	19	316.2	309	141	149	2	2 1 3	109 17 0	.156
1934	10	16	.385	4.35	39	32	7	213	212	127	79	2	0 2 1	64 13 0	.203
1935 WAS A	10	15	.400	4.92	45	32	13	230.1	268	102	77	0	0 0 0	77 15 0	.195
1936 NY A	14	4	.778	4.35	31	17	8	173.2	194	89	74	1	3 1 1	68 16 0	.235
1937	11	8	.579	5.30	29	25	6	178.1	199	83	70	0	1 0 0	65 11 0	.169
1938	9	8	.529	3.60	29	17	8	167.1	165	66	61	1	1 1 1	54 5 0	.093
1939	12	6	.667	2.98	26	18	7	154	132	85	65	1	2 0 2	62 11 0	.177
1940	3	5	.375	5.74	25	2	0	80	88	52	39	0	3 3 2	27 3 0	.111
1941 2 teams			NY	N (3G 1–0)			PHI	A (25G 4–6)							
" total	5	6	.455	5.15	28	11	1	115.1	150	56	35	0	1 1 3	34 4 0	.118
16 yrs.	161	165	.494	4.25	528	355	134	2944.2	2980	1442 10th	1318	14	21 23 25	1004 190 0	.189
1 yr.	1	1	.500	3.86	3	2	1	18.2	17	8	13	0	0 0 1	6 1 0	.167

Pitcher Register

	W	L	PCT	ERA	G	GS	CG	IP	H	BB	SO	ShO	Relief Pitching W	L	SV	BATTING AB	H	HR	BA

Bump Hadley continued
WORLD SERIES
1936 NY A	1	0	1.000	1.13	1	1	0	8	10	1	2	0	0	0	0	2	0	0	.000
1937	0	1	.000	33.75	1	1	0	1.1	6	0	0	0	0	0	0	0	0	0	—
1939	1	0	1.000	2.25	1	0	0	8	7	3	2	0	1	0	0	3	0	0	.000
3 yrs.	2	1	.667	4.15	3	2	0	17.1	23	4	4	0	1	0	0	5	0	0	.000

Mickey Haefner
HAEFNER, MILTON ARNOLD BL TL 5'8" 160 lbs.
B. Oct. 9, 1912, Lenzburg, Ill.

1943 WAS A	11	5	.688	2.29	36	13	8	165.1	126	60	65	1	3	1	6	45	6	0	.133
1944	12	15	.444	3.04	31	28	18	228	221	71	86	3	0	1	1	70	11	0	.157
1945	16	14	.533	3.47	37	28	19	238.1	226	69	83	1	2	0	3	82	20	0	.244
1946	14	11	.560	2.85	33	27	17	227.2	220	80	85	2	0	1	1	74	15	0	.203
1947	10	14	.417	3.64	31	28	14	193	195	85	77	4	0	0	1	59	8	0	.136
1948	5	13	.278	4.02	28	20	4	147.2	151	61	45	0	1	1	0	43	7	0	.163
1949 2 teams			WAS A (19G 5–5)			CHI A (14G 4–6)													
" total	9	11	.450	4.40	33	24	8	172	169	94	40	2	0	1	1	48	11	0	.229
1950 2 teams			CHI A (24G 1–6)			BOS N (8G 0–2)													
" total	1	8	.111	5.70	32	11	3	94.2	106	57	27	0	0	0	0	27	6	0	.222
8 yrs.	78	91	.462	3.50	261	179	91	1466.2	1414	577	508	13	6	5	13	448	84	0	.188
2 yrs.	5	12	.294	5.01	38	21	6	151	167	86	34	1	0	0	1	43	10	0	.233

Bud Hafey
HAFEY, DANIEL ALBERT BR TR 6' 185 lbs.
Brother of Tom Hafey.
B. Aug. 6, 1912, Berkeley, Calif.

| 1939 CIN N | 0 | 0 | — | 33.75 | 2 | 0 | 0 | 1.1 | 7 | 1 | 1 | 0 | 0 | 0 | 0 | * | | | |

Hal Haid
HAID, HAROLD AUGUSTINE BR TR 5'10½" 150 lbs.
B. Dec. 21, 1897, Barberton, Ohio D. Aug. 13, 1952, Beverly Hills, Calif.

1919 STL A	0	0	—	18.00	1	0	0	2	5	3	1	0	0	0	0	0	0	0	—
1928 STL N	2	2	.500	2.30	27	0	0	47	39	11	21	0	2	2	5	8	3	0	.375
1929	9	9	.500	4.07	38	12	8	154.2	171	66	41	0	4	3	4	49	4	0	.082
1930	3	2	.600	4.09	20	0	0	33	38	14	13	0	3	2	2	3	0	0	.000
1931 BOS N	0	2	.000	4.50	27	0	0	56	59	16	20	0	0	2	1	8	1	0	.125
1933 CHI A	0	0	—	7.98	6	0	0	14.2	18	13	7	0	0	0	0	4	1	0	.250
6 yrs.	14	15	.483	4.16	119	12	8	307.1	330	123	103	0	9	9	12	72	9	0	.125
1 yr.	0	0	—	7.98	6	0	0	14.2	18	13	7	0	0	0	0	4	1	0	.250

Jack Hallett
HALLETT, JACK PRICE BR TR 6'4" 215 lbs.
B. Nov. 13, 1913, Toledo, Ohio

1940 CHI A	1	1	.500	6.43	2	2	1	14	15	6	9	0	0	0	0	5	2	0	.400
1941	5	5	.500	6.03	22	6	3	74.2	96	38	25	0	3	1	0	26	4	0	.154
1942 PIT N	0	1	.000	4.84	3	3	2	22.1	23	8	16	0	0	0	0	8	3	1	.375
1943	1	2	.333	1.70	9	4	2	47.2	36	11	11	1	0	1	0	14	4	0	.286
1946	5	7	.417	3.29	35	9	3	115	107	39	64	1	3	2	0	26	6	0	.231
1948 NY N	0	0	—	4.50	2	0	0	4	3	4	3	0	0	0	0	1	0	0	.000
6 yrs.	12	16	.429	4.05	73	24	11	277.2	280	106	128	2	6	4	0	80	19	1	.238
2 yrs.	6	6	.500	6.09	24	8	4	88.2	111	44	34	0	3	1	0	31	6	0	.194

Dave Hamilton
HAMILTON, DAVID EDWARD BL TL 6' 180 lbs.
B. Dec. 14, 1947, Seattle, Wash.

1972 OAK A	6	6	.500	2.93	25	14	1	101.1	94	31	55	0	0	1	0	26	4	0	.154
1973	6	4	.600	4.39	16	11	1	69.2	74	24	34	0	1	0	0	0	0	0	—
1974	7	4	.636	3.15	29	18	1	117	104	48	69	1	1	0	0	0	0	0	—
1975 2 teams			OAK A (11G 1–2)			CHI A (30G 6–5)													
" total	7	7	.500	3.25	41	5	0	105.1	105	47	71	0	7	4	6	0	0	0	—
1976 CHI A	6	6	.500	3.60	45	1	0	90	81	45	62	0	5	6	10	0	0	0	—
1977	4	5	.444	3.63	55	0	0	67	71	33	45	0	4	5	9	0	0	0	—
1978 2 teams			STL N (13G 0–0)			PIT N (16G 0–2)													
" total	0	2	.000	4.46	29	0	0	40.1	39	18	23	0	0	2	1	7	0	0	.000
1979 OAK A	3	4	.429	3.29	40	7	1	83	80	43	52	0	2	0	5	0	0	0	—
1980	0	3	.000	11.40	21	1	0	30	44	28	23	0	0	3	0	0	0	0	—
9 yrs.	39	41	.488	3.85	301	57	4	703.2	692	317	434	1	20	21	31	33	4	0	.121
3 yrs.	16	16	.500	3.38	130	2	0	226.2	215	107	158	0	16	15	25	0	0	0	—

LEAGUE CHAMPIONSHIP SERIES
| 1972 OAK A | 0 | 0 | — | 0.00 | 1 | 0 | 0 | 1 | 1 | 0 | 0 | 0 | 0 | 0 | 0 | 0 | 0 | 0 | — |

WORLD SERIES
| 1972 OAK A | 0 | 0 | — | 27.00 | 2 | 0 | 0 | 1.1 | 3 | 1 | 1 | 0 | 0 | 0 | 0 | 0 | 0 | 0 | — |

Jack Hamilton
HAMILTON, JACK EDWIN (Hairbreadth Harry) BR TR 6' 200 lbs.
B. Dec. 25, 1938, Burlington, Iowa

1962 PHI N	9	12	.429	5.09	41	26	4	182	185	107	101	1	2	0	2	54	3	0	.056
1963	2	1	.667	5.40	19	3	0	30	22	17	23	0	2	0	1	3	0	0	.000
1964 DET A	0	1	.000	8.40	5	1	0	15	24	8	5	0	0	0	0	3	0	0	.000
1965	1	1	.500	14.54	4	1	0	4.1	6	4	3	0	1	0	0	0	0	0	—
1966 NY N	6	13	.316	3.93	57	13	3	148.2	138	88	93	1	2	6	13	38	5	0	.132
1967 2 teams			NY N (17G 2–0)			CAL A (26G 9–6)													
" total	11	6	.647	3.35	43	21	0	150.2	128	79	96	0	3	0	1	43	7	1	.163
1968 CAL A	3	1	.750	3.32	21	2	1	38	34	15	18	0	2	0	2	7	1	0	.143
1969 2 teams			CLE A (20G 0–2)			CHI A (8G 0–3)													
" total	0	5	.000	6.49	28	0	0	43	60	30	18	0	0	5	1	2	0	0	.000
8 yrs.	32	40	.444	4.53	218	65	8	611.2	597	348	357	2	12	11	20	150	16	1	.107
1 yr.	0	3	.000	11.68	8	0	0	12.1	23	7	5	0	0	3	0	0	0	0	—

Pitcher Register

	W	L	PCT	ERA	G	GS	CG	IP	H	BB	SO	ShO	Relief Pitching W L SV	BATTING AB H HR	BA

Steve Hamilton
HAMILTON, STEVE ABSHER BL TL 6'6" 190 lbs.
B. Nov. 30, 1935, Columbia, Ky.

	W	L	PCT	ERA	G	GS	CG	IP	H	BB	SO	ShO	W	L	SV	AB	H	HR	BA
1961 CLE A	0	0	–	2.70	2	0	0	3.1	2	3	4	0	0	0	0	1	1	0	1.000
1962 WAS A	3	8	.273	3.77	41	10	1	107.1	103	39	83	0	2	4	2	26	2	0	.077
1963 2 teams		WAS	A (3G 0–1)		NY	A (34G 5–1)													
" total	5	2	.714	2.94	37	0	0	64.1	54	26	64	0	5	2	5	14	4	0	.286
1964 NY A	7	2	.778	3.28	30	3	1	60.1	55	15	49	0	5	2	3	20	4	0	.200
1965	3	1	.750	1.39	46	1	0	58.1	47	16	51	0	3	1	5	6	1	0	.167
1966	8	3	.727	3.00	44	0	0	90	69	22	57	1	7	2	3	19	1	0	.053
1967	2	4	.333	3.48	44	0	0	62	57	23	55	0	2	4	4	9	1	0	.111
1968	2	2	.500	2.13	40	0	0	50.2	37	13	42	0	2	2	11	3	0	0	.000
1969	3	4	.429	3.32	38	0	0	57	39	21	39	0	3	4	2	5	0	0	.000
1970 2 teams		NY	A (35G 4–3)		CHI	A (3G 0–0)													
" total	4	3	.571	2.98	38	0	0	48.1	40	17	36	0	4	3	3	6	0	0	.000
1971 SF N	2	2	.500	3.00	39	0	0	45	29	11	38	0	2	2	4	2	0	0	.000
1972 CHI N	1	0	1.000	4.76	22	0	0	17	24	8	13	0	1	0	0	1	0	0	.000
12 yrs.	40	31	.563	3.05	421	17	3	663.2	556	214	531	1	36	26	42	112	14	0	.125
1 yr.	0	0	–	6.00	3	0	0	3	4	1	3	0	0	0	0	0	0	0	–

LEAGUE CHAMPIONSHIP SERIES

| 1971 SF N | 0 | 0 | – | 9.00 | 1 | 0 | 0 | 1 | 1 | 0 | 3 | 0 | 0 | 0 | 0 | 0 | 0 | 0 | – |

WORLD SERIES

1963 NY A	0	0	–	0.00	1	0	0	1	0	0	1	0	0	0	0	0	0	0	–
1964	0	0	–	4.50	2	0	0	2	3	0	2	0	0	0	1	0	0	0	–
2 yrs.	0	0	–	3.00	3	0	0	3	3	0	3	0	0	0	1	0	0	0	–

Ralph Hamner
HAMNER, RALPH CONANT (Bruz) BR TR 6'3" 165 lbs.
B. Sept. 12, 1916, Gibsland, La.

	W	L	PCT	ERA	G	GS	CG	IP	H	BB	SO	ShO	W	L	SV	AB	H	HR	BA
1946 CHI A	2	7	.222	4.42	25	7	1	71.1	80	39	29	0	0	0	1	18	3	0	.167
1947 CHI N	1	2	.333	2.52	3	3	2	25	24	16	14	0	0	0	0	8	1	0	.125
1948	5	9	.357	4.69	27	17	5	111.1	110	69	53	0	0	1	0	33	6	1	.182
1949	0	2	.000	8.76	6	1	0	12.1	22	8	3	0	0	1	0	2	0	0	.000
4 yrs.	8	20	.286	4.58	61	28	8	220	236	132	99	0	0	2	1	61	10	1	.164
1 yr.	2	7	.222	4.42	25	7	1	71.1	80	39	29	0	0	0	1	18	3	0	.167

Don Hanski
HANSKI, DONALD THOMAS BL TL 5'11" 180 lbs.
Born Donald Thomas Hanyzewski.
B. Feb. 27, 1916, LaPorte, Ind. D. Sept. 2, 1957, Worth, Ill.

	W	L	PCT	ERA	G	GS	CG	IP	H	BB	SO	ShO	W	L	SV	AB	H	HR	BA
1943 CHI A	0	0	–	0.00	1	0	0	1	1	1	0	0	0	0	0	21	5	0	.238
1944	0	0	–	12.00	2	0	0	3	5	2	0	0	0	0	0	1	0	0	.000
2 yrs.	0	0	–	9.00	3	0	0	4	6	3	0	0	0	0	0	*			
2 yrs.	0	0	–	9.00	3	0	0	4	6	3	0	0	0	0	0	22	5	0	.227

Earl Harrist
HARRIST, EARL (Irish) BR TR 6' 175 lbs.
B. Aug. 20, 1919, Dubach, La.

	W	L	PCT	ERA	G	GS	CG	IP	H	BB	SO	ShO	W	L	SV	AB	H	HR	BA
1945 CIN N	2	4	.333	3.61	14	5	1	62.1	60	27	15	0	1	0	0	15	0	0	.000
1947 CHI A	3	8	.273	3.56	33	4	0	93.2	85	49	55	0	3	5	5	24	5	0	.208
1948 2 teams		CHI	A (11G 1–3)		WAS	A (23G 3–3)													
" total	4	6	.400	4.93	34	5	0	84	93	50	35	0	4	3	0	22	3	0	.136
1952 STL A	2	8	.200	4.01	36	9	1	116.2	119	47	49	0	2	2	5	31	3	0	.097
1953 2 teams		CHI	A (7G 1–0)		DET	A (8G 0–2)													
" total	1	2	.333	8.33	15	1	0	27	34	20	8	0	1	1	0	4	0	0	.000
5 yrs.	12	28	.300	4.34	132	24	2	383.2	391	193	162	0	11	11	10	96	11	0	.115
3 yrs.	5	11	.313	4.24	51	5	0	125.1	117	67	70	0	5	7	5	29	5	0	.172

Jack Harshman
HARSHMAN, JOHN ELVIN BL TL 6'2" 178 lbs.
B. July 12, 1927, San Diego, Calif.

	W	L	PCT	ERA	G	GS	CG	IP	H	BB	SO	ShO	W	L	SV	AB	H	HR	BA
1948 NY N	0	0	–	0.00	0	0	0		0	0	0	0	0	0	0	8	2	0	.250
1950	0	0	–		0	0	0		0	0	0	0	0	0	0	32	4	2	.125
1952	0	2	.000	14.21	2	2	0	6.1	12	6	6	0	0	0	0	2	0	0	.000
1954 CHI A	14	8	.636	2.95	35	21	9	177	157	96	134	4	1	3	1	56	8	2	.143
1955	11	7	.611	3.36	32	23	9	179.1	144	97	116	0	0	0	0	60	11	2	.183
1956	15	11	.577	3.10	34	30	15	226.2	183	102	143	4	0	0	0	71	12	6	.169
1957	8	8	.500	4.10	30	26	6	151.1	142	82	83	0	0	2	1	45	10	2	.222
1958 BAL A	12	15	.444	2.89	34	29	17	236.1	204	75	161	3	1	0	4	82	16	6	.195
1959 3 teams		BAL	A (14G 0–6)		BOS	A (8G 2–3)		CLE	A (13G 5–1)										
" total	7	10	.412	4.76	35	16	5	138	133	51	73	1	2	4	1	51	10	1	.196
1960 CLE A	2	4	.333	3.98	15	8	0	54.1	50	30	25	0	0	0	0	17	3	0	.176
10 yrs.	69	65	.515	3.50	217	155	61	1169.1	1025	539	741	12	4	9	7	*			
4 yrs.	48	34	.585	3.33	131	100	39	734.1	626	377	476	8	1	5	2	232	41	12	.177

Erwin Harvey
HARVEY, ERWIN KING (Zaza) TL
B. Jan. 5, 1879, Saratoga, Calif. D. June 3, 1954, Santa Monica, Calif.

	W	L	PCT	ERA	G	GS	CG	IP	H	BB	SO	ShO	W	L	SV	AB	H	HR	BA
1900 CHI N	0	0	–	0.00	1	0	0	4	3	1	0	0	0	0	0	3	0	0	.000
1901 CHI A	3	6	.333	3.62	16	9	5	92	91	34	27	0	2	0	1	210	70	1	.333
2 yrs.	3	6	.333	3.47	17	9	5	96	94	35	27	0	2	0	1	*			
1 yr.	3	6	.333	3.62	16	9	5	92	91	34	27	0	2	0	1	40	10	0	.250

Joe Haynes
HAYNES, JOSEPH WALTER BR TR 6'2½" 190 lbs.
B. Sept. 21, 1917, Lincolnton, Ga. D. Jan. 7, 1967, Hopkins, Minn.

	W	L	PCT	ERA	G	GS	CG	IP	H	BB	SO	ShO	W	L	SV	AB	H	HR	BA
1939 WAS A	8	12	.400	5.36	27	20	10	173	186	78	64	1	2	0	0	67	14	0	.209
1940	3	6	.333	6.54	22	7	1	63.1	85	34	23	0	2	3	0	19	2	0	.105
1941 CHI A	0	0	–	3.86	8	0	0	28	30	11	18	0	0	0	0	11	3	0	.273
1942	8	5	.615	2.62	40	1	1	103	88	47	35	0	8	4	6	28	5	0	.179
1943	7	2	.778	2.96	35	2	1	109.1	114	32	37	0	5	2	3	34	9	0	.265
1944	5	6	.455	2.57	33	12	8	154.1	148	43	44	0	2	0	2	50	10	0	.200
1945	5	5	.500	3.55	14	13	8	104	92	29	34	1	0	0	1	40	7	0	.175
1946	7	9	.438	3.76	32	23	9	177.1	203	60	60	0	0	0	0	57	14	0	.246

Pitcher Register

	W	L	PCT	ERA	G	GS	CG	IP	H	BB	SO	ShO	Relief Pitching W L SV	AB	BATTING H HR	BA

Joe Haynes continued

1947		14	6	.700	2.42	29	22	7	182	174	61	50	2	3	0	0	65	17	0	.262
1948		9	10	.474	3.97	27	22	6	149.2	167	52	40	0	1	0	0	50	8	0	.160
1949 WAS A		2	9	.182	6.26	37	10	0	96.1	106	55	19	0	0	5	2	25	6	0	.240
1950		7	5	.583	5.84	27	10	1	101.2	124	46	15	1	3	1	0	35	7	0	.200
1951		1	4	.200	4.56	26	3	1	73	85	37	18	0	1	3	2	21	7	1	.333
1952		0	3	.000	4.50	22	2	0	66	70	35	18	0	0	1	3	19	2	0	.105
14 yrs.		76	82	.481	4.01	379	147	53	1581	1672	620	475	5	27	19	21	521	111	1	.213
8 yrs.		55	43	.561	3.14	218	95	40	1007.2	1016	335	318	3	19	6	14	335	73	0	.218

Spencer Heath

HEATH, SPENCER PAUL BB TR 6' 170 lbs.
B. Nov. 5, 1895, Chicago, Ill.   D. Jan. 25, 1930, Chicago, Ill.

| 1920 CHI A | 0 | 0 | – | 15.43 | 4 | 0 | 0 | 7 | 19 | 2 | 0 | 0 | 0 | 0 | 0 | 3 | 0 | 0 | .000 |

Joe Henderson

HENDERSON, JOSEPH LEE BR TR 6'2" 195 lbs.
B. July 4, 1946, Lake Cormorant, Miss.

1974 CHI A	1	0	1.000	8.40	5	3	0	15	21	11	12	0	1	0	0	1	0	0	.000
1976 CIN N	2	0	1.000	0.00	4	0	0	11	9	8	7	0	2	0	0	0	0	0	–
1977	0	2	.000	12.00	7	0	0	9	17	6	8	0	0	2	0	1	0	0	.000
3 yrs.	3	2	.600	6.69	16	3	0	35	47	25	27	0	3	2	0	2	0	0	.000
1 yr.	1	0	1.000	8.40	5	3	0	15	21	11	12	0	1	0	0	1	0	0	.000

Dutch Henry

HENRY, FRANK JOHN BL TL 6'1" 173 lbs.
B. May 12, 1902, Cleveland, Ohio   D. Aug. 23, 1968, Cleveland, Ohio

1921 STL A	0	0	–	4.50	1	0	0	2	2	0	1	0	0	0	0	1	1	0	1.000
1922	0	0	–	5.40	4	0	0	5	7	5	3	0	0	0	0	0	0	0	–
1923 BKN N	4	6	.400	3.91	17	9	5	94.1	105	28	28	2	1	1	0	35	8	0	.229
1924	1	2	.333	5.67	16	4	0	46	69	15	11	0	1	1	0	20	5	0	.250
1927 NY N	11	6	.647	4.23	45	15	7	163.2	184	31	40	1	6	2	4	55	13	0	.236
1928	3	6	.333	3.80	17	8	4	64	82	25	23	0	0	1	1	19	3	0	.158
1929 2 teams			NY	N (27G 5–6)		CHI	A (2G 1–0)												
" total	6	6	.500	4.10	29	10	5	116.1	149	38	29	0	1	3	1	35	8	0	.229
1930 CHI A	2	17	.105	4.88	35	16	4	155	211	48	35	0	2	2	0	51	12	0	.235
8 yrs.	27	43	.386	4.39	164	62	25	646.1	809	190	170	3	11	10	6	216	50	0	.231
2 yrs.	3	17	.150	4.98	37	17	5	170	231	55	37	0	2	2	0	58	13	0	.224

Ray Herbert

HERBERT, RAYMOND ERNEST BR TR 5'11" 185 lbs.
B. Dec. 15, 1929, Detroit, Mich.

1950 DET A	1	2	.333	3.63	8	3	1	22.1	20	12	5	0	1	0	1	7	2	0	.286
1951	4	0	1.000	1.42	5	0	0	12.2	8	9	9	0	4	0	0	4	0	0	.000
1953	4	6	.400	5.24	43	3	0	87.2	109	46	37	0	4	4	6	19	3	0	.158
1954	3	6	.333	5.87	42	4	0	84.1	114	50	44	0	3	3	0	17	3	1	.176
1955 KC A	1	8	.111	6.26	23	11	2	87.2	99	40	30	0	0	1	0	21	4	0	.190
1958	8	8	.500	3.50	42	16	5	175	161	55	108	0	1	3	3	52	10	0	.192
1959	11	11	.500	4.85	37	26	10	183.2	196	62	99	2	0	1	1	57	12	1	.211
1960	14	15	.483	3.28	37	33	14	252.2	256	72	122	0	0	1	1	76	13	0	.171
1961 2 teams			KC	A (13G 3–6)		CHI	A (21G 9–6)												
" total	12	12	.500	4.55	34	32	5	221.1	245	66	84	0	1	0	0	81	15	2	.185
1962 CHI A	20	9	.690	3.27	35	35	12	236.2	228	74	115	2	0	0	0	82	16	2	.195
1963	13	10	.565	3.24	33	33	14	224.2	230	35	105	7	0	0	0	63	14	1	.222
1964	6	7	.462	3.47	20	19	1	111.2	117	17	40	1	0	0	0	36	5	0	.139
1965 PHI N	5	8	.385	3.86	25	19	4	130.2	162	19	51	1	0	0	1	41	11	0	.268
1966	2	5	.286	4.29	23	2	0	50.1	55	14	15	0	2	4	2	13	1	0	.077
14 yrs.	104	107	.493	4.01	407	236	68	1881.1	2000	571	864	13	16	17	15	569	109	7	.192
4 yrs.	48	32	.600	3.44	109	107	31	710.2	717	162	310	10	1	0	0	234	47	5	.201

Art Herring

HERRING, ARTHUR L (Sandy) BR TR 5'7" 168 lbs.
B. Mar. 10, 1907, Altus, Okla.

1929 DET A	2	1	.667	4.78	4	4	2	32	38	19	15	0	0	0	0	14	3	0	.214
1930	3	3	.500	5.33	23	6	1	77.2	97	36	16	0	1	0	0	23	3	0	.130
1931	7	13	.350	4.31	35	16	9	165	186	67	64	0	1	4	1	55	11	0	.200
1932	1	2	.333	5.24	12	0	0	22.1	25	15	12	0	1	2	2	4	0	0	.000
1933	1	2	.333	3.84	24	3	1	61	61	20	20	0	0	2	0	13	1	0	.077
1934 BKN N	2	4	.333	6.20	14	4	2	49.1	63	29	15	0	1	3	0	14	2	0	.143
1939 CHI A	0	0	–	5.65	7	0	0	14.1	13	5	8	0	0	0	0	4	0	0	.000
1944 BKN N	3	4	.429	3.42	12	6	3	55.1	59	17	19	1	1	0	1	15	3	0	.200
1945	7	4	.636	3.48	22	15	7	124	103	43	34	2	1	0	2	42	4	0	.095
1946	7	2	.778	3.35	35	2	0	86	91	29	34	0	5	2	5	22	4	0	.182
1947 PIT N	1	3	.250	8.44	11	0	0	10.2	18	4	6	0	1	3	2	2	0	0	.000
11 yrs.	34	38	.472	4.32	199	56	25	697.2	754	284	243	3	12	16	13	208	31	0	.149
1 yr.	0	0	–	5.65	7	0	0	14.1	13	5	8	0	0	0	0	4	0	0	.000

Joe Heving

HEVING, JOSEPH WILLIAM BR TR 6'1" 185 lbs.
Brother of Johnnie Heving.
B. Sept. 2, 1900, Covington, Ky.   D. Apr. 11, 1970, Covington, Ky.

1930 NY N	7	5	.583	5.22	41	2	0	89.2	109	27	37	0	7	5	6	22	5	0	.227
1931	1	6	.143	4.89	22	0	0	42.1	48	11	26	0	1	6	3	8	1	0	.125
1933 CHI A	7	5	.583	2.67	40	6	3	118	113	27	47	1	5	1	6	38	8	0	.211
1934	1	7	.125	7.26	33	2	0	88	133	48	40	0	1	5	4	27	5	0	.185
1937 CLE A	8	4	.667	4.83	40	0	0	72.2	92	30	35	0	8	4	5	19	5	0	.263
1938 2 teams			CLE	A (3G 1–1)		BOS	A (16G 8–1)												
" total	9	2	.818	4.09	19	11	7	88	104	27	34	1	1	1	2	31	4	0	.129
1939 BOS A	11	3	.786	3.70	46	5	1	107	124	34	43	0	11	2	7	32	6	0	.188
1940	12	7	.632	4.01	39	7	4	119	129	42	55	0	8	4	3	40	8	0	.200
1941 CLE A	5	2	.714	2.29	27	3	2	70.2	63	31	18	1	3	2	5	15	0	0	.000
1942	5	3	.625	4.86	27	2	0	46.1	52	25	13	0	5	2	3	7	0	0	.000

Pitcher Register

	W	L	PCT	ERA	G	GS	CG	IP	H	BB	SO	ShO	Relief Pitching W L SV	BATTING AB H HR	BA

Joe Heving continued

1943	1	1	.500	2.75	30	1	0	72	58	34	34	0	1 1 9	14 1 0	.071
1944	8	3	.727	1.96	63	1	0	119.1	106	41	46	0	8 2 10	22 4 0	.182
1945 BOS N	1	0	1.000	3.38	3	0	0	5.1	5	3	1	0	1 0 0	1 0 0	.000
13 yrs.	76	48	.613	3.90	430	40	17	1038.1	1136	380	429	3	60 35 63	276 47 0	.170
2 yrs.	8	12	.400	4.63	73	8	3	206	246	75	87	1	6 6 10	65 13 0	.200

Kevin Hickey

HICKEY, KEVIN JOHN
B. Feb. 25, 1957, Chicago, Ill.
BL TL 6'1" 170 lbs.

1981 CHI A	0	2	.000	3.68	41	0	0	44	38	18	17	0	0 2 3	0 0 0	—
1982	4	4	.500	3.00	60	0	0	78	73	30	38	0	4 4 6	0 0 0	—
1983	1	2	.333	5.23	23	0	0	20.2	23	11	8	0	1 2 5	0 0 0	—
3 yrs.	5	8	.385	3.53	124	0	0	142.2	134	59	63	0	5 8 14	0 0 0	—
3 yrs.	5	8	.385	3.53	124	0	0	142.2	134	59	63	0	5 8 14	0 0 0	—

Piano Legs Hickman

HICKMAN, CHARLES TAYLOR
B. Mar. 4, 1876, Dunkirk, N.Y. D. Apr. 19, 1934, Morgantown, W. Va.
BR TR 5'11½" 215 lbs.

1897 BOS N	0	0	—	5.87	2	0	0	7.2	10	5	0	0	0 0 1	3 2 1	.667
1898	1	1	.500	2.18	6	3	3	33	22	13	9	1	0 0 2	58 15 0	.259
1899	7	0	1.000	4.48	11	9	5	66.1	52	40	14	2	0 0 1	63 25 0	.397
1901 NY N	3	5	.375	4.57	9	9	6	65	76	26	11	0	0 0 0	406 113 4	.278
1902 BOS N	0	1	.000	7.88	1	1	1	8	11	5	1	0	0 0 0	534 193 11	.361
1907 CHI A	0	—	—	3.60	1	0	0	5	4	5	2	0	0 0 0	216 61 1	.282
6 yrs.	11	7	.611	4.28	30	22	15	185	175	94	37	3	0 0 4	*	

Dennis Higgins

HIGGINS, DENNIS DEAN
B. Aug. 4, 1939, Jefferson City, Mo.
BR TR 6'3" 180 lbs.

1966 CHI A	1	0	1.000	2.52	42	1	0	93	66	33	86	0	0 0 5	17 3 0	.176
1967	1	2	.333	5.84	9	0	0	12.1	13	10	8	0	1 2 0	1 0 0	.000
1968 WAS A	4	4	.500	3.25	59	0	0	99.2	81	46	66	0	4 4 13	15 2 0	.133
1969	10	9	.526	3.48	55	0	0	85.1	79	56	71	0	10 9 16	11 1 0	.091
1970 CLE A	4	6	.400	4.00	58	0	0	90	82	54	82	0	4 6 11	12 3 0	.250
1971 STL N	1	0	1.000	3.86	3	0	0	7	6	2	6	0	1 0 0	1 0 0	.000
1972	1	2	.333	3.97	15	1	0	22.2	19	22	20	0	1 1 1	1 0 0	.000
7 yrs.	22	23	.489	3.42	241	2	0	410	346	223	339	0	21 22 46	58 9 0	.155
2 yrs.	2	2	.500	2.91	51	1	0	105.1	79	43	94	0	1 2 5	18 3 0	.167

Rich Hinton

HINTON, RICHARD MICHAEL
B. May 22, 1947, Tucson, Ariz.
BL TL 6'2" 185 lbs.

1971 CHI A	2	4	.333	4.50	18	2	0	24	27	6	15	0	2 2 0	1 0 0	.000
1972 2 teams	NY A (7G 1-0)				TEX A (5G 0-1)										
" total	1	1	.500	3.86	12	3	0	28	27	18	17	0	0 1 0	5 1 0	.200
1975 CHI A	1	0	1.000	4.82	15	0	0	37.1	41	15	30	0	1 0 0	0 0 0	—
1976 CIN N	1	2	.333	7.50	12	1	0	18	30	11	8	0	1 2 0	1 0 0	.000
1978 CHI A	2	6	.250	4.02	29	4	2	80.2	78	28	48	0	1 2 1	0 0 0	—
1979 2 teams	CHI A (16G 1-2)				SEA A (14G 0-2)										
" total	1	4	.200	5.81	30	3	0	62	80	13	34	0	1 1 2	0 0 0	—
6 yrs.	8	17	.320	4.86	116	13	2	250	283	91	152	0	6 8 3	7 1 0	.143
4 yrs.	6	12	.333	4.70	78	8	2	184	203	57	120	0	5 4 3	0 0 0	—

Myril Hoag

HOAG, MYRIL OLIVER
B. Mar. 9, 1908, Davis, Calif. D. July 28, 1971, High Springs, Fla.
BR TR 5'11" 180 lbs.

1939 STL A	0	0	—	0.00	1	0	0	1	0	0	0	0	0 0 0	482 142 10	.295
1945 CLE A	0	0	—	0.00	2	0	0	3	3	1	0	0	0 0 0	128 27 0	.211
2 yrs.	0	0	—	0.00	3	0	0	4	3	1	0	0	0 0 0	*	

Shovel Hodge

HODGE, CLARENCE CLEMENT
B. July 6, 1893, Mount Andrew, Ala. D. Dec. 31, 1967, Ft. Walton Beach, Fla.
BL TR 6'4" 190 lbs.

1920 CHI A	1	1	.500	2.29	4	2	1	19.2	15	12	5	0	0 0 0	6 0 0	.000
1921	6	8	.429	6.56	36	11	6	142.2	191	54	25	0	4 1 2	52 17 0	.327
1922	7	6	.538	4.14	35	8	2	139	154	65	37	0	5 2 1	58 12 0	.207
3 yrs.	14	15	.483	5.17	75	21	9	301.1	360	131	67	0	9 3 3	116 29 0	.250
3 yrs.	14	15	.483	5.17	75	21	9	301.1	360	131	67	0	9 3 3	116 29 0	.250

Guy Hoffman

HOFFMAN, GUY ALAN
B. July 9, 1956, Ottawa, Ill.
BL TL 5'9" 175 lbs.

1979 CHI A	0	5	.000	5.40	24	0	0	30	30	23	18	0	0 5 2	0 0 0	—
1980	1	0	1.000	2.61	23	1	0	38	38	17	24	0	1 0 1	0 0 0	—
1983	1	0	1.000	7.50	11	0	0	6	14	2	2	0	1 0 0	0 0 0	—
3 yrs.	2	5	.286	4.14	58	1	0	74	82	42	44	0	2 5 3	0 0 0	—
3 yrs.	2	5	.286	4.14	58	1	0	74	82	42	44	0	2 5 3	0 0 0	—

Ken Holcombe

HOLCOMBE, KENNETH EDWARD
B. Aug. 23, 1918, Burnsville, N.C.
BR TR 5'11½" 169 lbs.

1945 NY A	3	3	.500	1.79	23	2	0	55.1	43	27	20	0	3 2 0	15 2 0	.133
1948 CIN N	0	0	—	7.71	2	0	0	2.1	3	0	2	0	0 0 0	1 0 0	.000
1950 CHI A	3	10	.231	4.59	24	15	5	96	122	45	37	0	0 1 1	32 5 0	.156
1951	11	12	.478	3.78	28	23	12	159.1	142	68	39	2	1 0 0	44 11 0	.250
1952 2 teams	CHI A (7G 0-5)				STL A (12G 0-2)										
" total	0	7	.000	5.30	19	8	1	56	58	27	19	0	0 1 1	13 1 0	.077
1953 BOS A	1	0	1.000	6.00	3	0	0	6	9	3	1	0	1 0 1	2 0 0	.000
6 yrs.	18	32	.360	3.98	99	48	18	375	377	170	118	2	5 4 2	106 19 0	.179
3 yrs.	14	27	.341	4.34	59	45	18	290.1	302	131	88	2	1 1 1	86 16 0	.186

Pitcher Register

	W	L	PCT	ERA	G	GS	CG	IP	H	BB	SO	ShO	Relief Pitching W L SV	BATTING AB H HR BA

Al Hollingsworth
HOLLINGSWORTH, ALBERT WAYNE (Boots) BL TL 6' 174 lbs.
B. Feb. 25, 1908, St. Louis, Mo.

Year	Team	W	L	PCT	ERA	G	GS	CG	IP	H	BB	SO	ShO	RW	RL	SV	AB	H	HR	BA
1935	CIN N	6	13	.316	3.89	38	22	8	173.1	165	76	89	0	1	1	0	54	8	0	.148
1936		9	10	.474	4.16	29	25	9	184	204	66	76	0	1	1	0	73	23	1	.315
1937		9	15	.375	3.91	43	24	11	202.1	229	73	74	1	2	3	5	76	19	0	.250
1938	2 teams			CIN N	(9G 2–2)		PHI N	(24G 5–16)												
"	total	7	18	.280	4.36	33	25	12	208.1	220	89	93	1	2	1	0	79	18	0	.228
1939	2 teams			PHI N	(15G 1–9)		BKN N	(8G 1–2)												
"	total	2	11	.154	5.67	23	15	4	87.1	111	38	35	0	1	1	0	28	3	0	.107
1940	WAS A	1	0	1.000	5.50	3	2	0	18	18	11	7	0	0	0	0	6	1	0	.167
1942	STL A	10	6	.625	2.96	33	18	7	161	173	52	60	1	1	2	4	56	10	0	.179
1943		6	13	.316	4.21	35	20	9	154	169	51	63	1	1	2	3	50	7	0	.140
1944		5	7	.417	4.47	26	10	3	92.2	108	37	22	2	2	1	1	28	2	0	.071
1945		12	9	.571	2.70	26	22	15	173.1	164	68	64	1	1	1	1	61	12	1	.197
1946	2 teams			STL A	(5G 0–0)		CHI A	(21G 3–2)												
"	total	3	2	.600	4.91	26	2	0	66	86	26	25	0	3	1	1	14	0	0	.000
11 yrs.		70	104	.402	3.99	315	185	78	1520.1	1647	587	608	7	15	14	15	525	103	2	.196
1 yr.		3	2	.600	4.58	21	2	0	55	63	22	22	0	3	1	1	12	0	0	.000

WORLD SERIES
| 1944 | STL A | 0 | 0 | – | 2.25 | 1 | 0 | 0 | 4 | 5 | 2 | 1 | 0 | 0 | 0 | 0 | 1 | 0 | 0 | .000 |

Ducky Holmes
HOLMES, JAMES WILLIAM BL TR 5'6" 170 lbs.
B. Jan. 28, 1869, Des Moines, Iowa D. Aug. 6, 1932, Truro, Iowa

1895	LOU N	1	0	1.000	5.79	2	1	1	14	16	4	0	0	0	0	0	161	60	3	.373
1896		0	1	.000	7.50	2	1	0	12	26	8	3	0	0	0	0	141	38	0	.270
2 yrs.		1	1	.500	6.58	4	2	1	26	42	12	3	0	0	0	0	*			

Harry Hooper
HOOPER, HARRY BARTHOLOMEW BL TR 5'10" 168 lbs.
B. Aug. 24, 1887, Bell Station, Calif. D. Dec. 18, 1974, Santa Cruz, Calif.
Hall of Fame 1971.

| 1913 | BOS A | 0 | 0 | – | 0.00 | 1 | 0 | 0 | 1 | 0 | 1 | 0 | 0 | 0 | 0 | 0 | * | | | |

Joe Horlen
HORLEN, JOEL EDWARD BR TR 6' 170 lbs.
B. Aug. 14, 1937, San Antonio, Tex.

1961	CHI A	1	3	.250	6.62	5	4	0	17.2	25	13	11	0	1	0	0	7	0	0	.000
1962		7	6	.538	4.89	20	19	5	108.2	108	43	63	1	0	0	0	38	2	0	.053
1963		11	7	.611	3.27	33	21	3	124	122	55	61	0	0	2	0	40	9	0	.225
1964		13	9	.591	1.88	32	28	9	210.2	142	55	138	2	1	0	0	69	11	0	.159
1965		13	13	.500	2.88	34	34	7	219	203	39	125	4	0	0	0	68	9	0	.132
1966		10	13	.435	2.43	37	29	4	211	185	53	124	2	1	0	1	60	4	0	.067
1967		19	7	.731	2.06	35	35	13	258	188	58	103	6	0	0	0	83	14	0	.169
1968		12	14	.462	2.37	35	35	4	223.2	197	70	102	1	0	0	0	67	7	0	.104
1969		13	16	.448	3.78	36	35	7	235.2	237	77	121	2	0	0	0	77	14	0	.182
1970		6	16	.273	4.87	28	26	4	172	198	41	77	0	0	0	0	52	6	0	.115
1971		8	9	.471	4.27	34	18	3	137	150	30	82	0	1	2	2	40	4	0	.100
1972	OAK A	3	4	.429	3.00	32	6	0	84	74	20	58	0	2	0	1	17	3	0	.176
12 yrs.		116	117	.498	3.11	361	290	59	2001.1	1829	554	1065	18	6	4	4	618	83	0	.134
11 yrs.		113	113	.500	3.11	329	284	59	1917.1	1755	534	1007	18	4	4	3	601	80	0	.133
		8th	7th		9th				8th			8th								

LEAGUE CHAMPIONSHIP SERIES
| 1972 | OAK A | 0 | 1 | .000 | ∞ | 1 | 0 | 0 | | 0 | 1 | 0 | 0 | 0 | 1 | 0 | 0 | 0 | 0 | – |

WORLD SERIES
| 1972 | OAK A | 0 | 0 | – | 6.75 | 1 | 0 | 0 | 1.1 | 2 | 2 | 1 | 0 | 0 | 0 | 0 | 0 | 0 | 0 | – |

Joe Hovlik
HOVLIK, JOSEPH BR TR 5'10½" 194 lbs.
Brother of Ed Hovlik.
B. Aug. 16, 1884, Czechoslovakia D. Nov. 3, 1951, Oxford Junction, Iowa

1909	WAS A	0	0	–	4.50	3	0	0	6	13	3	1	0	0	0	0	2	0	0	.000
1910		0	0	–	16.20	1	0	0	1.2	6	0	0	0	0	0	0	0	0	0	–
1911	CHI A	3	0	1.000	3.06	12	3	1	47	47	20	24	1	1	0	0	13	1	0	.077
3 yrs.		3	0	1.000	3.62	16	3	1	54.2	66	23	25	1	1	0	0	15	1	0	.067
1 yr.		3	0	1.000	3.06	12	3	1	47	47	20	24	1	1	0	0	13	1	0	.077

Bruce Howard
HOWARD, BRUCE ERNEST BB TR 6'2" 180 lbs.
B. Mar. 23, 1943, Salisbury, Md.

1963	CHI A	2	1	.667	2.65	7	0	0	17	12	14	9	0	2	1	1	4	1	0	.250
1964		2	1	.667	0.81	3	3	1	22.1	10	8	17	1	0	0	0	8	0	0	.000
1965		9	8	.529	3.47	30	22	1	148	123	72	120	1	2	1	0	41	6	0	.146
1966		9	5	.643	2.30	27	21	4	149	110	44	85	2	1	0	0	43	3	0	.070
1967		3	10	.231	3.43	30	17	1	112.2	102	52	76	0	1	1	0	28	5	0	.179
1968	2 teams			BAL A	(10G 0–2)		WAS A	(13G 1–4)												
"	total	1	6	.143	4.74	23	12	0	79.2	92	49	42	0	0	0	0	23	2	1	.087
6 yrs.		26	31	.456	3.18	120	75	7	528.2	449	239	349	4	6	3	1	147	17	1	.116
5 yrs.		25	25	.500	2.91	97	63	7	449	357	190	307	4	6	3	1	124	15	0	.121

Fred Howard
HOWARD, FRED IRVING III BR TR 6'3" 190 lbs.
B. Sept. 2, 1956, Portland, Me.

| 1979 | CHI A | 1 | 5 | .167 | 3.57 | 28 | 6 | 0 | 68 | 73 | 32 | 36 | 0 | 0 | 0 | 1 | 0 | 0 | 0 | – |

Dixie Howell
HOWELL, MILLARD FILLMORE BL TR 6'2" 210 lbs.
B. Jan. 7, 1920, Herald, Ky. D. Mar. 18, 1960, Hollywood, Fla.

1940	CLE A	0	0	–	1.80	3	0	0	5	2	4	2	0	0	0	0	0	0	0	–
1949	CIN N	0	1	.000	8.10	5	1	0	13.1	21	8	7	0	0	0	0	9	1	0	.111
1955	CHI A	8	3	.727	2.93	35	0	0	73.2	70	25	25	0	8	3	9	21	8	0	.381
1956		5	6	.455	4.62	34	1	0	64.1	79	36	28	0	4	6	4	17	4	2	.235
1957		6	5	.545	3.29	37	0	0	68.1	64	30	37	0	6	5	6	27	5	3	.185

Pitcher Register

	W	L	PCT	ERA	G	GS	CG	IP	H	BB	SO	ShO	Relief Pitching W	L	SV	BATTING AB	H	HR	BA

Dixie Howell continued
1958	0	0	–	0.00	1	0	0	1.2	0	0	0	0	0	0	0	0	0	0	–
6 yrs.	19	15	.559	3.78	115	2	0	226.1	236	103	99	0	18	14	19	74	18	5	.243
4 yrs.	19	14	.576	3.55	107	1	0	208	213	91	90	0	18	14	19	65	17	5	.262

LaMarr Hoyt
HOYT, DEWEY LaMARR B. Jan. 1, 1955, Columbia, S. C. BR TR 6'3" 195 lbs.

1979 CHI A	0	0	–	0.00	2	0	0	3	2	0	0	0	0	0	0	0	0	0	–
1980	9	3	.750	4.58	24	13	3	112	123	41	55	1	2	0	0	0	0	0	–
1981	9	3	.750	3.56	43	1	0	91	80	28	60	0	9	3	10	0	0	0	–
1982	19	15	.559	3.53	39	32	14	239.2	248	48	124	2	4	0	0	0	0	0	–
1983	24	10	.706	3.66	36	36	11	260.2	236	31	148	1	0	0	0	0	0	0	–
5 yrs.	61	31	.663	3.73	144	82	28	706.1	689	148	387	4	15	3	10	0	0	0	–
5 yrs.	61	31	.663	3.73	144	82	28	706.1	689	148	387	4	15	3	10	0	0	0	–

LEAGUE CHAMPIONSHIP SERIES
| 1983 CHI A | 1 | 0 | 1.000 | 1.00 | 1 | 1 | 1 | 9 | 5 | 0 | 4 | 0 | 0 | 0 | 0 | 0 | 0 | 0 | – |

Hal Hudson
HUDSON, HAL CAMPBELL (Lefty) B. May 4, 1927, Grosse Point, Mich. BL TL 5'10" 175 lbs.

1952 2 teams	STL A (3G 0–0)	CHI A (2G 0–0)
" total	0	0	–	8.38	5	0	0	9.2	16	7	4	0	0	0	0	1	0	0	.000
1953 CHI A	0	0	–	0.00	1	0	0	.2	0	0	0	0	0	0	0	0	0	0	–
2 yrs.	0	0	–	7.84	6	0	0	10.1	16	7	4	0	0	0	0	1	0	0	.000
2 yrs.	0	0	–	1.93	3	0	0	4.2	7	1	4	0	0	0	0	0	0	0	–

Jim Hughes
HUGHES, JAMES ROBERT B. Mar. 21, 1923, Chicago, Ill. BR TR 6'1" 200 lbs.

1952 BKN N	2	1	.667	1.45	6	0	0	18.2	16	11	8	0	2	1	0	4	0	0	.000
1953	4	3	.571	3.47	48	0	0	85.2	80	41	49	0	4	3	9	14	4	0	.286
1954	8	4	.667	3.22	60	0	0	86.2	76	44	58	0	8	4	24	16	3	0	.188
1955	0	2	.000	4.22	24	0	0	42.2	41	19	20	0	0	2	6	10	0	0	.000
1956 2 teams	BKN N (5G 0–0)	CHI N (25G 1–3)
" total	1	3	.250	5.18	30	0	0	57.1	53	34	28	0	1	2	0	9	2	0	.222
1957 CHI A	0	0	–	10.80	4	0	0	5	12	3	2	0	0	0	0	0	0	0	–
6 yrs.	15	13	.536	3.83	172	1	0	296	278	152	165	0	15	12	39	53	9	0	.170
1 yr.	0	0	–	10.80	4	0	0	5	12	3	2	0	0	0	0	0	0	0	–

WORLD SERIES
| 1953 BKN N | 0 | 0 | – | 2.25 | 1 | 0 | 0 | 4 | 3 | 1 | 3 | 0 | 0 | 0 | 0 | 1 | 0 | 0 | .000 |

John Humphries
HUMPHRIES, JOHN WILLIAM B. June 23, 1915, Clifton Forge, Va. D. June 24, 1965, New Orleans, La. BR TR 6'1" 185 lbs.

1938 CLE A	9	8	.529	5.23	45	6	1	103.1	105	63	56	0	8	3	6	29	3	0	.103
1939	2	4	.333	8.26	15	1	0	28.1	30	32	12	0	2	3	2	7	0	0	.000
1940	0	2	.000	8.29	19	1	1	33.2	35	29	17	0	0	1	1	6	0	0	.000
1941 CHI A	4	2	.667	1.84	14	6	4	73.1	63	22	25	4	0	0	1	23	2	0	.087
1942	12	12	.500	2.68	28	28	17	228.1	227	59	71	2	0	0	0	80	18	0	.225
1943	11	11	.500	3.30	28	27	8	188.1	198	54	51	2	0	0	0	69	20	0	.290
1944	8	10	.444	3.67	30	20	8	169	170	57	42	0	2	1	1	53	10	0	.189
1945	6	14	.300	4.24	22	21	10	153	172	48	33	1	0	1	0	54	8	0	.148
1946 PHI N	0	0	–	4.01	10	1	0	24.2	24	9	10	0	0	0	0	8	2	0	.250
9 yrs.	52	63	.452	3.78	211	111	49	1002	1024	373	317	9	12	8	12	329	63	0	.191
5 yrs.	41	49	.456	3.25	122	102	47	812	830	240	222	9	2	1	3	279	58	0	.208

Ira Hutchinson
HUTCHINSON, IRA KENDALL B. Aug. 31, 1910, Chicago, Ill. D. Aug. 21, 1973, Chicago, Ill. BR TR 5'10½" 180 lbs.

1933 CHI A	0	0	–	13.50	1	0	0	4	7	3	2	0	0	0	0	2	1	0	.500
1937 BOS N	4	6	.400	3.73	31	8	1	91.2	99	35	29	1	4	0	0	26	3	0	.115
1938	9	8	.529	2.74	36	12	4	151	150	61	38	1	5	3	4	52	9	0	.173
1939 BKN N	5	2	.714	4.34	41	1	0	105.2	103	51	46	0	5	2	1	27	1	0	.037
1940 STL N	4	2	.667	3.13	20	2	1	63.1	68	19	19	0	2	2	1	18	4	0	.222
1941	1	5	.167	3.86	29	0	0	46.2	32	19	19	0	1	5	5	8	2	0	.250
1944 BOS N	9	7	.563	4.21	40	8	1	119.2	136	53	22	1	6	4	1	29	4	0	.138
1945	2	3	.400	5.02	11	0	0	28.2	33	8	4	0	2	3	1	9	0	0	.000
8 yrs.	34	33	.507	3.76	209	32	7	610.2	628	249	179	2	25	19	13	171	24	0	.140
1 yr.	0	0	–	13.50	1	0	0	4	7	3	2	0	0	0	0	2	1	0	.500

Frank Isbell
ISBELL, WILLIAM FRANK (Bald Eagle) B. Aug. 21, 1875, Delavan, N. Y. D. July 15, 1941, Wichita, Kans. BL TR 5'11" 190 lbs.

1898 CHI N	4	7	.364	3.56	13	9	7	81	86	42	16	0	1	1	0	159	37	0	.233
1901 CHI A	0	0	–	9.00	1	0	0	1	2	0	1	0	0	0	0	556	143	3	.257
1902	0	0	–	9.00	1	0	0	1	1	1	0	0	0	0	0	520	133	4	.256
1906	0	0	–	0.00	1	0	0	2	1	0	2	0	0	0	0	549	153	0	.279
1907	0	0	–	0.00	1	0	0	.1	0	0	0	0	0	0	0	486	118	0	.243
5 yrs.	4	7	.364	3.59	17	10	7	85.1	92	43	19	0	1	1	1	* 4065	1029	13	.253
4 yrs.	0	0	–	4.15	4	1	0	4.1	6	1	3	0	0	0	0				

Elmer Jacobs
JACOBS, WILLIAM ELMER B. Aug. 10, 1892, Salem, Mo. D. Feb. 10, 1958, Salem, Mo. BR TR 6' 165 lbs.

1914 PHI N	1	3	.250	4.80	14	7	1	50.2	65	20	17	0	0	0	0	14	0	0	.000
1916 PIT N	6	10	.375	2.94	34	17	8	153	151	38	46	0	2	1	0	40	3	0	.075
1917	6	19	.240	2.81	38	25	10	227.1	214	76	58	1	1	3	2	67	12	0	.179
1918 2 teams	PIT N (8G 0–1)	PHI N (18G 9–5)
" total	9	6	.600	2.95	26	18	12	146.1	122	56	35	4	0	0	1	45	8	0	.178
1919 2 teams	PHI N (17G 6–10)	STL N (17G 2–6)
" total	8	16	.333	3.32	34	23	17	214	231	69	68	0	1	1	1	68	16	0	.235
1920 STL N	4	8	.333	5.21	23	9	1	77.2	91	33	21	0	2	2	1	26	5	0	.192

Pitcher Register

	W	L	PCT	ERA	G	GS	CG	IP	H	BB	SO	ShO	Relief Pitching W L SV	BATTING AB H HR	BA

Elmer Jacobs continued

1924 CHI N	11	12	.478	3.74	38	22	13	190.1	181	72	50	1	2 2 1	54 6 0	.111
1925	2	3	.400	5.17	18	4	1	55.2	63	22	19	1	1 2 1	13 3 0	.231
1927 CHI A	2	4	.333	4.60	25	8	2	74.1	105	37	22	1	0 0 0	20 3 0	.150
9 yrs.	49	81	.377	3.55	250	133	65	1189.1	1223	423	336	9	9 12 7	347 56 0	.161
1 yr.	2	4	.333	4.60	25	8	2	74.1	105	37	22	1	0 0 0	20 3 0	.150

Pat Jacquez

JACQUEZ, PAT THOMAS
B. Apr. 23, 1947, Stockton, Calif. BR TR 6' 200 lbs.

| 1971 CHI A | 0 | 0 | — | 4.50 | 2 | 0 | 0 | 2 | 4 | 2 | 1 | 0 | 0 0 0 | 1 0 0 | .000 |

Bill James

JAMES, WILLIAM HENRY (Big Bill)
B. Jan. 20, 1888, Ann Arbor, Mich. D. May 24, 1942, Venice, Calif. BB TR 6'4" 195 lbs.

1911 CLE A	2	4	.333	4.88	8	6	4	51.2	58	32	21	0	0 0 0	17 1 0	.059
1912	0	0	—	4.61	3	0	0	13.2	15	9	5	0	0 0 0	3 0 0	.000
1914 STL A	16	14	.533	2.85	44	35	19	284	269	109	109	3	0 1 0	89 10 0	.112
1915 2 teams	STL A (34G 6-10)	DET A (11G 7-3)
" total	13	13	.500	3.26	45	32	11	237.1	212	125	82	1	2 0 1	63 14 0	.222
1916 DET A	8	12	.400	3.68	30	20	8	151.2	141	79	61	0	3 0 1	44 3 0	.068
1917	13	10	.565	2.09	34	23	10	198	163	96	62	2	2 1 1	57 12 0	.211
1918	6	11	.353	3.76	19	18	8	122	127	68	42	1	1 0 0	46 5 0	.109
1919 3 teams	DET A (2G 1-0)	BOS A (13G 3-5)	CHI A (5G 3-2)
" total	7	7	.500	3.71	20	13	7	121.1	129	58	26	2	0 2 0	39 6 0	.154
8 yrs.	65	71	.478	3.20	203	147	67	1179.2	1114	576	408	9	8 4 3	358 51 0	.142
1 yr.	3	2	.600	2.52	5	5	3	39.1	39	14	11	2	0 0 0	14 2 0	.143

WORLD SERIES
| 1919 CHI A | 0 | 0 | — | 5.79 | 1 | 0 | 0 | 4.2 | 8 | 3 | 2 | 0 | 0 0 0 | 2 0 0 | .000 |

Gerry Janeski

JANESKI, GERALD JOSEPH
B. Apr. 18, 1946, Pasadena, Calif. BR TR 6'4" 205 lbs.

1970 CHI A	10	17	.370	4.76	35	35	4	206	247	63	79	1	0 0 0	66 5 0	.076
1971 WAS A	1	5	.167	4.94	23	10	0	62	72	34	19	0	1 0 1	14 3 0	.214
1972 TEX A	0	1	.000	2.77	4	1	0	13	11	7	7	0	0 0 0	2 0 0	.000
3 yrs.	11	23	.324	4.71	62	46	4	281	330	104	105	1	1 0 1	82 8 0	.098
1 yr.	10	17	.370	4.76	35	35	4	206	247	63	79	1	0 0 0	66 5 0	.076

Hi Jasper

JASPER, HARRY W.
B. May 24, 1887, St. Louis, Mo. D. May 22, 1937, St. Louis, Mo. BR TR 5'11" 180 lbs.

1914 CHI A	1	0	1.000	3.34	16	0	0	32.1	22	20	19	0	1 0 0	5 0 0	.000
1915	0	1	.000	4.60	3	2	1	15.2	8	9	15	0	0 0 0	7 2 0	.286
1916 STL N	5	6	.455	3.28	21	9	2	107	97	42	37	0	3 1 1	33 7 1	.212
1919 CLE A	4	5	.444	3.59	12	10	5	82.2	83	28	25	0	1 0 0	29 3 0	.103
4 yrs.	10	12	.455	3.48	52	21	8	237.2	210	99	96	0	5 1 1	74 12 1	.162
2 yrs.	1	1	.500	3.75	19	2	1	48	30	29	34	0	1 0 0	12 2 0	.167

Jesse Jefferson

JEFFERSON, JESSE HARRISON
B. Mar. 3, 1950, Midlothian, Va. BR TR 6'3" 188 lbs.

1973 BAL A	6	5	.545	4.10	18	15	3	101	104	46	52	0	1 0 0	0 0 0	—
1974	1	0	1.000	4.42	20	2	0	57	55	38	31	0	0 0 0	0 0 0	—
1975 2 teams	BAL A (4G 0-2)	CHI A (22G 5-9)
" total	5	11	.313	4.92	26	21	1	115.1	105	102	71	0	0 2 0	0 0 0	—
1976 CHI A	2	5	.286	8.56	19	9	0	62	86	42	30	0	0 1 0	0 0 0	—
1977 TOR A	9	17	.346	4.31	33	33	8	217	224	83	114	0	0 0 0	0 0 0	—
1978	7	16	.304	4.38	31	30	9	211.2	214	86	97	2	0 0 0	0 0 0	—
1979	2	10	.167	5.51	34	10	2	116	150	45	43	0	0 3 1	0 0 0	—
1980 2 teams	TOR A (29G 4-13)	PIT N (1G 1-0)
" total	5	13	.278	5.23	30	19	2	129	133	54	57	2	1 1 0	1 0 0	.000
1981 CAL A	2	4	.333	3.62	26	5	0	77	80	24	27	0	1 0 0	0 0 0	—
9 yrs.	39	81	.325	4.81	237	144	25	1086	1151	520	522	4	3 7 1	1 0 0	.000
2 yrs.	7	14	.333	6.37	41	30	1	169.2	186	136	97	0	0 1 0	0 0 0	—

Tommy John

JOHN, THOMAS EDWARD
B. May 22, 1943, Terre Haute, Ind. BR TL 6'3" ·180 lbs.

1963 CLE A	0	2	.000	2.21	6	3	0	20.1	23	6	9	0	0 0 0	6 0 0	.000
1964	2	9	.182	3.91	25	14	2	94.1	97	35	65	1	0 0 0	24 5 0	.208
1965 CHI A	14	7	.667	3.09	39	27	6	183.2	162	58	126	1	1 1 3	59 10 1	.169
1966	14	11	.560	2.62	34	33	10	223	195	57	138	5	0 0 0	69 10 2	.145
1967	10	13	.435	2.47	31	29	9	178.1	143	47	110	6	0 1 0	51 8 0	.157
1968	10	5	.667	1.98	25	25	5	177.1	135	49	117	1	0 0 0	62 12 1	.194
1969	9	11	.450	3.25	33	33	6	232.1	230	90	128	2	0 0 0	79 9 0	.114
1970	12	17	.414	3.28	37	37	10	269	253	101	138	3	0 0 0	84 17 0	.202
1971	13	16	.448	3.62	38	35	10	229	244	58	131	3	0 0 0	69 10 0	.145
1972 LA N	11	5	.688	2.89	29	29	4	186.2	172	40	117	1	0 0 0	63 10 0	.159
1973	16	7	.696	3.10	36	31	4	218	202	50	116	2	0 0 0	74 15 0	.203
1974	13	3	.813	2.59	22	22	5	153	133	42	78	3	0 0 0	51 6 0	.118
1976	10	10	.500	3.09	31	31	6	207	207	61	91	2	0 0 0	64 7 0	.109
1977	20	7	.741	2.78	31	31	11	220	225	50	123	4	0 0 0	79 14 1	.177
1978	17	10	.630	3.30	33	30	7	213	230	53	124	0	1 0 1	66 8 0	.121
1979 NY A	21	9	.700	2.97	37	36	17	276	268	65	111	3	1 0 0	0 0 0	—
1980	22	9	.710	3.43	36	36	16	265	270	56	78	6	0 0 0	0 0 0	—
1981	9	8	.529	2.64	20	20	7	140	135	39	50	0	0 0 0	0 0 0	—
1982 2 teams	NY A (30G 10-10)	CAL A (7G 4-2)
" total	14	12	.538	3.69	37	33	10	221.2	239	39	68	2	0 0 0	0 0 0	—
1983 CAL A	11	13	.458	4.33	34	34	9	234.2	287	49	65	0	0 0 0	0 0 0	—
20 yrs.	248	184	.574	3.13	614	569	154	3942.1	3850	1045	1983	44	3 2 4	900 141 5	.157
7 yrs.	82	80	.506	2.95	237	219	56	1492.2	1362	460	888	21	1 2 3	473 76 4	.161

DIVISIONAL PLAYOFF SERIES
| 1981 NY A | 0 | 1 | .000 | 6.43 | 1 | 1 | 0 | 7 | 8 | 2 | 0 | 0 | 0 0 0 | 0 0 0 | — |

	W	L	PCT	ERA	G	GS	CG	IP	H	BB	SO	ShO	Relief Pitching W	L	SV	BATTING AB	H	HR	BA

Tommy John continued
LEAGUE CHAMPIONSHIP SERIES
1977 LA N	1	0	1.000	0.66	2	2	1	13.2	11	5	11	0	0	0	0	5	1	0	.200
1978	1	0	1.000	0.00	1	1	1	9	4	2	4	1	0	0	0	3	0	0	.000
1980 NY A	0	0	—	2.70	1	1	0	6.2	8	1	3	0	0	0	0	0	0	0	—
1981	1	0	1.000	1.50	1	1	0	6	6	1	3	0	0	0	0	0	0	0	—
1982 CAL A	1	1	.500	5.11	2	2	1	12.1	11	6	6	0	0	0	0	0	0	0	—
5 yrs.	4	1	.800	2.08	7	7	3	47.2	40	15	27	1	0	0	0	8	1	0	.125

WORLD SERIES
1977 LA N	0	1	.000	6.00	1	1	0	6	9	3	7	0	0	0	0	2	0	0	.000
1978	1	0	1.000	3.07	2	2	0	14.2	14	4	6	0	0	0	0	0	0	0	—
1981 NY A	1	0	1.000	0.69	3	2	0	13	11	0	8	0	0	0	0	2	0	0	.000
3 yrs.	2	1	.667	2.67	6	5	0	33.2	34	7	21	0	0	0	0	4	0	0	.000

Bart Johnson
JOHNSON, CLAIR BARTH   BR TR 6'5"   190 lbs.
B. Jan. 3, 1950, Torrance, Calif.

1969 CHI A	1	3	.250	3.22	4	3	0	22.1	22	6	18	0	0	1	0	6	1	0	.167
1970	4	7	.364	4.80	18	15	2	90	92	46	71	1	0	0	0	29	8	0	.276
1971	12	10	.545	2.93	53	16	4	178	148	111	153	0	4	4	14	57	11	0	.193
1972	0	3	.000	9.22	9	0	0	13.2	18	13	9	0	0	3	1	1	0	0	.000
1973	3	3	.500	4.13	22	9	0	80.2	76	40	56	0	1	0	0	0	0	0	—
1974	10	4	.714	2.73	18	18	8	122	105	32	76	2	0	0	0	0	0	0	—
1976	9	16	.360	4.73	32	32	8	211	231	62	91	3	0	0	0	0	0	0	—
1977	4	5	.444	4.01	29	4	0	92	114	38	46	0	3	2	2	0	0	0	—
8 yrs.	43	51	.457	3.93	185	97	22	809.2	806	348	520	6	8	10	17	93	20	0	.215
8 yrs.	43	51	.457	3.93	185	97	22	809.2	806	348	520	6	8	10	17	93	20	0	.215

Connie Johnson
JOHNSON, CLIFFORD   BR TR 6'4"   200 lbs.
B. Dec. 27, 1922, Stone Mountain, Ga.

1953 CHI A	4	4	.500	3.56	14	10	2	60.2	55	38	44	1	0	0	0	20	1	0	.050
1955	7	4	.636	3.45	17	16	5	99	95	52	72	2	0	0	0	33	5	0	.152
1956 2 teams	CHI A (5G 0–1)				BAL A (26G 9–10)														
" total	9	11	.450	3.44	31	27	9	196	176	69	136	2	0	0	0	61	15	0	.246
1957 BAL A	14	11	.560	3.20	35	30	14	242	221	66	177	3	0	1	0	89	12	0	.135
1958	6	9	.400	3.88	26	17	4	118.1	116	32	68	0	1	1	1	34	7	0	.206
5 yrs.	40	39	.506	3.44	123	100	34	716	654	257	497	8	1	2	1	237	40	0	.169
3 yrs.	11	9	.550	3.51	36	28	7	172	161	97	122	3	0	0	0	56	6	0	.107

Don Johnson
JOHNSON, DONALD ROY   BR TR 6'3"   200 lbs.
B. Nov. 12, 1926, Portland, Ore.

1947 NY A	4	3	.571	3.64	15	8	2	54.1	57	23	16	0	1	1	0	13	0	0	.000
1950 2 teams	NY A (8G 1–0)				STL A (25G 5–6)														
" total	6	6	.500	6.71	33	12	4	114	161	67	40	0	2	0	1	32	2	0	.063
1951 2 teams	STL A (6G 0–1)				WAS A (21G 7–11)														
" total	7	12	.368	4.76	27	23	8	158.2	165	76	60	1	0	0	0	50	5	0	.100
1952 WAS A	0	5	.000	4.43	29	6	0	69	80	33	37	0	0	2	2	13	1	0	.077
1954 CHI A	8	7	.533	3.13	46	16	3	144	129	43	68	3	2	3	7	35	1	0	.029
1955 BAL A	2	4	.333	5.82	31	5	0	68	89	35	27	0	2	1	1	10	0	0	.000
1958 SF N	0	1	.000	6.26	17	0	0	23	31	8	14	0	0	1	1	2	0	0	.000
7 yrs.	27	38	.415	4.78	198	70	17	631	712	285	262	4	7	8	12	155	9	0	.058
1 yr.	8	7	.533	3.13	46	16	3	144	129	43	68	3	2	3	7	35	1	0	.029

Ellis Johnson
JOHNSON, ELLIS WATT   BR TR 6'½"   180 lbs.
B. Dec. 8, 1892, Minneapolis, Minn.   D. Jan. 14, 1965, Minneapolis, Minn.

1912 CHI A	0	0	—	3.29	4	0	0	13.2	11	10	8	0	0	0	0	3	0	0	.000
1915	0	0	—	9.00	1	0	0	2	3	0	3	0	0	0	0	0	0	0	—
1917 PHI A	0	2	.000	7.24	4	2	0	13.2	15	5	8	0	0	0	0	1	0	0	.000
3 yrs.	0	2	.000	5.52	9	2	0	29.1	29	15	19	0	0	0	0	4	0	0	.000
2 yrs.	0	0	—	4.02	5	0	0	15.2	14	10	11	0	0	0	0	3	0	0	.000

Johnny Johnson
JOHNSON, JOHN CLIFFORD (Swede)   BL TL 6'   182 lbs.
B. Sept. 29, 1914, Belmore, Ohio

1944 NY A	0	2	.000	4.05	22	1	0	26.2	25	24	11	0	0	1	3	6	3	0	.500
1945 CHI A	3	0	1.000	4.26	29	0	0	69.2	85	35	38	0	3	0	4	14	4	0	.286
2 yrs.	3	2	.600	4.20	51	1	0	96.1	110	59	49	0	3	1	7	20	7	0	.350
1 yr.	3	0	1.000	4.26	29	0	0	69.2	85	35	38	0	3	0	4	14	4	0	.286

Al Jones
JONES, ALFORNIA   BR TR 6'4"   210 lbs.
B. Feb. 10, 1959, Charleston, Miss.

| 1983 CHI A | 0 | 0 | — | 3.86 | 2 | 0 | 0 | 2.1 | 3 | 2 | 2 | 0 | 0 | 0 | 0 | 0 | 0 | 0 | — |

Sad Sam Jones
JONES, SAMUEL POND   BR TR 6'   170 lbs.
B. July 26, 1892, Woodsfield, Ohio   D. July 6, 1966, Barnesville, Ohio

1914 CLE A	0	0	—	2.70	1	0	0	3.1	2	2	0	0	0	0	0	2	1	0	.500
1915	4	9	.308	3.65	48	9	2	145.2	131	63	42	0	2	3	4	32	5	0	.156
1916 BOS A	0	1	.000	3.67	12	0	0	27	25	10	7	0	0	1	1	6	2	0	.333
1917	0	1	.000	4.41	9	0	0	16.1	15	6	5	0	0	0	0	4	0	0	.000
1918	16	5	.762	2.25	24	21	16	184	151	70	44	5	0	0	0	57	10	0	.175
1919	12	20	.375	3.75	35	31	21	245	258	95	67	5	0	3	1	81	11	0	.136
1920	13	16	.448	3.94	37	33	20	274	302	79	86	3	0	2	0	92	20	0	.217
1921	23	16	.590	3.22	40	38	25	298.2	318	78	98	5	1	0	1	100	24	2	.240
1922 NY A	13	13	.500	3.67	45	28	21	260	270	76	81	0	1	0	8	87	23	1	.264
1923	21	8	.724	3.63	39	27	18	243	239	69	68	3	2	2	4	85	19	0	.224
1924	9	6	.600	3.63	36	21	8	178.2	187	76	53	3	2	1	3	51	9	1	.176
1925	15	21	.417	4.63	43	31	14	246.2	267	104	92	1	4	3	2	80	13	0	.163
1926	9	8	.529	4.98	39	23	6	161	186	80	69	1	2	1	0	49	10	0	.204

Pitcher Register

	W	L	PCT	ERA	G	GS	CG	IP	H	BB	SO	ShO	Relief Pitching W	L	SV	AB	H	HR	BA

Sad Sam Jones continued

	W	L	PCT	ERA	G	GS	CG	IP	H	BB	SO	ShO	W	L	SV	AB	H	HR	BA
1927 STL A	8	14	.364	4.32	30	26	11	189.2	211	102	72	0	0	0	0	55	6	0	.109
1928 WAS A	17	7	.708	2.84	30	27	19	224.2	209	78	63	4	0	0	0	79	20	2	.253
1929	9	9	.500	3.92	24	24	8	153.2	156	49	36	1	0	0	0	51	8	0	.157
1930	15	7	.682	4.07	25	25	14	183.1	195	61	60	1	0	0	0	61	9	0	.148
1931	9	10	.474	4.32	25	24	8	148	185	47	58	1	0	0	1	48	15	0	.313
1932 CHI A	10	15	.400	4.22	30	28	10	200.1	217	75	64	0	2	0	0	57	11	0	.193
1933	10	12	.455	3.36	27	25	11	176.2	181	65	60	2	0	1	0	58	9	0	.155
1934	8	12	.400	5.11	27	26	11	183.1	217	60	60	1	0	0	0	60	12	0	.200
1935	8	7	.533	4.05	21	19	7	140	162	51	38	0	0	0	0	48	8	0	.167
22 yrs.	229	217	.513	3.84	647	487	250	3883	4084	1396	1223	36	16	17	31	1243	245	6	.197
4 yrs.	36	46	.439	4.20	105	98	39	700.1	777	251	222	3	2	1	0	223	40	0	.179

WORLD SERIES

	W	L	PCT	ERA	G	GS	CG	IP	H	BB	SO	ShO	W	L	SV	AB	H	HR	BA
1918 BOS A	0	1	.000	3.00	1	1	1	9	7	5	5	1	0	0	0	1	0	0	.000
1922 NY A	0	0	–	0.00	2	0	0	2	1	1	0	0	0	0	0	0	0	0	–
1923	0	1	.000	0.90	2	1	0	10	5	2	3	0	0	0	1	2	0	0	.000
1926	0	0	–	9.00	1	0	0	1	2	2	1	0	0	0	0	0	0	0	–
4 yrs.	0	2	.000	2.05	6	2	1	22	15	10	9	1	0	0	1	3	0	0	.000

Steve Jones

JONES, STEVEN HOWELL
Brother of Gary Jones.
B. Apr. 22, 1941, Huntington Park, Calif.

BL TL 5'10" 175 lbs.

	W	L	PCT	ERA	G	GS	CG	IP	H	BB	SO	ShO	W	L	SV	AB	H	HR	BA
1967 CHI A	2	2	.500	4.21	11	3	0	25.2	21	12	17	0	1	0	0	4	1	0	.250
1968 WAS A	1	2	.333	5.91	7	0	0	10.2	8	7	11	0	1	2	0	1	0	0	.000
1969 KC A	2	3	.400	4.23	20	4	0	44.2	45	24	31	0	0	1	0	8	1	0	.125
3 yrs.	5	7	.417	4.44	38	7	0	81	74	43	59	0	2	3	0	13	2	0	.154
1 yr.	2	2	.500	4.21	11	3	0	25.2	21	12	17	0	1	0	0	4	1	0	.250

Rip Jordan

JORDAN, RAYMOND WILLIS (Lanky)
B. Sept. 28, 1889, Portland, Me. D. June 5, 1960, Meriden, Conn.

BL TR 6' 172 lbs.

	W	L	PCT	ERA	G	GS	CG	IP	H	BB	SO	ShO	W	L	SV	AB	H	HR	BA
1912 CHI A	0	0	–	6.10	3	0	0	10.1	13	0	0	0	0	0	0	4	0	0	.000
1919 WAS A	0	0	–	11.25	1	1	0	4	6	2	2	0	0	0	0	1	0	0	.000
2 yrs.	0	0	–	7.53	4	1	0	14.1	19	2	2	0	0	0	0	5	0	0	.000
1 yr.	0	0	–	6.10	3	0	0	10.1	13	0	0	0	0	0	0	4	0	0	.000

Mike Joyce

JOYCE, MICHAEL LEWIS
B. Feb. 12, 1941, Detroit, Mich.

BR TR 6'2" 193 lbs.

	W	L	PCT	ERA	G	GS	CG	IP	H	BB	SO	ShO	W	L	SV	AB	H	HR	BA
1962 CHI A	2	1	.667	3.32	25	1	0	43.1	40	14	9	0	2	1	2	7	3	0	.429
1963	0	0	–	8.44	6	0	0	10.2	13	8	7	0	0	0	0	0	0	0	–
2 yrs.	2	1	.667	4.33	31	1	0	54	53	22	16	0	2	1	2	7	3	0	.429
2 yrs.	2	1	.667	4.33	31	1	0	54	53	22	16	0	2	1	2	7	3	0	.429

Howie Judson

JUDSON, HOWARD KOLLS
B. Feb. 16, 1926, Hebron, Ill.

BR TR 6'1" 195 lbs.

	W	L	PCT	ERA	G	GS	CG	IP	H	BB	SO	ShO	W	L	SV	AB	H	HR	BA
1948 CHI A	4	5	.444	4.78	40	5	1	107.1	102	56	38	0	4	2	8	29	3	0	.103
1949	1	14	.067	4.58	26	12	3	108	114	70	36	0	0	4	1	31	2	0	.065
1950	2	3	.400	3.94	46	3	1	112	105	63	34	0	2	2	0	20	2	0	.100
1951	5	6	.455	3.77	27	14	3	121.2	124	55	43	0	0	1	1	33	4	0	.121
1952	0	1	.000	4.24	21	0	0	34	30	22	15	0	0	1	1	4	0	0	.000
1953 CIN N	0	1	.000	5.59	10	6	0	38.2	58	11	11	0	0	0	0	9	1	0	.111
1954	5	7	.417	3.95	37	8	0	93.1	86	42	27	0	1	3	3	24	2	0	.083
7 yrs.	17	37	.315	4.29	207	48	8	615	619	319	204	0	7	13	14	150	14	0	.093
5 yrs.	12	29	.293	4.25	160	34	8	483	475	266	166	0	6	10	11	117	11	0	.094

Jim Kaat

KAAT, JAMES LEE
B. Nov. 7, 1938, Zeeland, Mich.

BL TL 6'4½" 205 lbs.

	W	L	PCT	ERA	G	GS	CG	IP	H	BB	SO	ShO	W	L	SV	AB	H	HR	BA
1959 WAS A	0	2	.000	12.60	3	2	0	5	7	4	2	0	0	0	0	1	0	0	.000
1960	1	5	.167	5.58	13	9	0	50	48	31	25	0	0	0	0	14	2	0	.143
1961 MIN A	9	17	.346	3.90	36	29	8	200.2	188	82	122	1	0	1	0	63	15	0	.238
1962	18	14	.563	3.14	39	35	16	269	243	75	173	5	1	0	1	100	18	1	.180
1963	10	10	.500	4.19	31	27	7	178.1	195	38	105	1	0	1	1	61	8	1	.131
1964	17	11	.607	3.22	36	34	13	243	231	60	171	0	0	1	1	83	14	3	.169
1965	18	11	.621	2.83	45	42	7	264.1	267	63	154	2	0	0	2	93	23	1	.247
1966	25	13	.658	2.75	41	41	19	304.2	271	55	205	3	0	0	0	118	23	2	.195
1967	16	13	.552	3.04	42	38	13	263.1	269	42	211	2	0	0	0	99	17	1	.172
1968	14	12	.538	2.94	30	29	9	208	192	40	130	2	0	0	0	77	12	0	.156
1969	14	13	.519	3.49	40	32	10	242.1	252	75	139	0	3	1	1	87	18	2	.207
1970	14	10	.583	3.56	45	34	4	230	244	58	120	1	1	0	0	76	15	1	.197
1971	13	14	.481	3.32	39	38	15	260	275	47	137	4	0	0	0	93	15	0	.161
1972	10	2	.833	2.07	15	15	5	113	94	20	64	2	0	0	0	45	13	2	.289
1973 2 teams			MIN A (29G 11–12)			CHI A (7G 4–1)													
" total	15	13	.536	4.37	36	35	10	224.1	250	43	109	3	1	0	0	0	0	0	–
1974 CHI A	21	13	.618	2.92	42	39	15	277	263	63	142	3	1	0	0	1	0	0	.000
1975	20	14	.588	3.11	43	41	12	303.2	321	77	142	1	0	0	0	0	0	0	–
1976 PHI N	12	14	.462	3.48	38	35	7	227.2	241	32	83	1	0	1	0	79	14	1	.177
1977	6	11	.353	5.40	35	27	2	160	211	40	55	0	0	0	0	53	10	0	.189
1978	8	5	.615	4.11	26	24	2	140	150	32	48	1	0	0	0	48	7	0	.146
1979 2 teams			PHI N (3G 1–0)			NY A (40G 2–3)													
" total	3	3	.500	3.95	43	2	0	66	73	19	25	0	3	3	2	1	0	0	.000
1980 2 teams			NY A (4G 0–1)			STL N (49G 8–7)													
" total	8	8	.500	3.93	53	14	5	135	148	37	37	1	3	3	4	35	5	1	.143
1981 STL N	6	6	.500	3.40	41	1	0	53	60	17	8	0	6	5	4	8	3	0	.375
1982	5	3	.625	4.08	62	2	0	75	79	23	35	0	5	3	2	12	0	0	.000

Pitcher Register

	W	L	PCT	ERA	G	GS	CG	IP	H	BB	SO	ShO	Relief Pitching W	L	SV	BATTING AB	H	HR	BA

Jim Kaat continued

	W	L	PCT	ERA	G	GS	CG	IP	H	BB	SO	ShO	W	L	SV	AB	H	HR	BA
1983	0	0	–	3.89	24	0	0	34.2	48	10	19	0	0	0	0	4	0	0	.000
25 yrs.	283	237	.544	3.45	898	625	180	4528	4620	1083	2461	31	24	19	18	1251	232	16	.185
		10th				5th													
3 yrs.	45	28	.616	3.10	92	87	30	623.1	628	144	300	5	2	0	0	1	0	0	.000

LEAGUE CHAMPIONSHIP SERIES

1970 MIN A	0	1	.000	9.00	1	1	0	2	6	2	1	0	0	0	0	1	0	0	.000
1976 PHI N	0	0	–	3.00	1	1	0	6	2	2	1	0	0	0	0	2	1	0	.500
2 yrs.	0	1	.000	4.50	2	2	0	8	8	4	2	0	0	0	0	3	1	0	.333

WORLD SERIES

1965 MIN A	1	2	.333	3.77	3	3	1	14.1	18	2	6	0	0	0	0	6	1	0	.167
1982 STL N	0	0	–	3.86	4	0	0	2.1	4	2	2	0	0	0	0	0	0	0	–
2 yrs.	1	2	.333	3.78	7	3	1	16.2	22	4	8	0	0	0	0	6	1	0	.167

John Katoll
KATOLL, JOHN BR TR 5'11" 195 lbs.
B. June 24, 1875, Etnon, Ohio D. June 18, 1955, Hartland, Ill.

1898 CHI N	0	1	.000	0.82	2	1	1	11	8	1	3	0	0	0	0	4	0	0	.000
1899	1	1	.500	6.00	2	2	2	18	17	4	1	0	0	0	0	7	0	0	.000
1901 CHI A	11	10	.524	2.81	27	25	19	208	231	53	59	0	0	0	0	80	10	1	.125
1902 2 teams			CHI	A (1G 0–0)		BAL	A (15G 5–10)												
" total	5	10	.333	3.99	16	13	13	124	176	32	27	0	2	0	0	58	10	0	.172
4 yrs.	17	22	.436	3.32	47	41	35	361	432	90	90	0	2	0	0	149	20	1	.134
2 yrs.	11	10	.524	2.80	28	25	19	209	232	53	61	0	0	0	0	81	10	1	.123

Steve Kealey
KEALEY, STEVEN WILLIAM BR TR 6' 185 lbs.
B. May 13, 1947, Torrance, Calif.

1968 CAL A	0	1	.000	2.70	6	0	0	10	10	5	4	0	0	1	0	0	0	0	–
1969	2	0	1.000	3.93	15	3	1	36.2	48	13	17	1	1	0	0	9	0	0	.000
1970	1	0	1.000	4.09	17	0	0	22	19	6	14	0	1	0	1	4	1	0	.250
1971 CHI A	2	2	.500	3.86	54	1	0	77	69	26	50	0	2	2	6	10	2	1	.200
1972	3	2	.600	3.30	40	0	0	57.1	50	12	37	0	3	2	4	3	0	0	.000
1973	0	0	–	15.09	7	0	0	11.1	23	7	4	0	0	0	0	0	0	0	–
6 yrs.	8	5	.615	4.28	139	4	1	214.1	219	69	126	1	7	5	11	26	3	1	.115
3 yrs.	5	4	.556	4.51	101	1	0	145.2	142	45	91	0	5	4	10	13	2	1	.154

Bob Keegan
KEEGAN, ROBERT CHARLES (Smiley) BR TR 6'2½" 207 lbs.
B. Aug. 4, 1920, Rochester, N. Y.

1953 CHI A	7	5	.583	2.74	22	11	4	98.2	80	33	32	2	2	0	1	28	9	0	.321
1954	16	9	.640	3.09	31	27	14	209.2	211	82	61	2	0	0	2	75	9	0	.120
1955	2	5	.286	5.83	18	11	1	58.2	83	28	29	0	0	1	0	18	6	0	.333
1956	5	7	.417	3.93	20	16	4	105.1	119	35	32	0	1	0	0	32	4	0	.125
1957	10	8	.556	3.53	30	20	6	142.2	131	37	36	2	2	2	2	39	4	0	.103
1958	0	2	.000	6.07	14	2	0	29.2	44	18	8	0	0	2	0	4	0	0	.000
6 yrs.	40	36	.526	3.66	135	87	29	644.2	668	233	198	6	5	5	5	196	32	0	.163
6 yrs.	40	36	.526	3.66	135	87	29	644.2	668	233	198	6	5	5	5	196	32	0	.163

Russ Kemmerer
KEMMERER, RUSSELL PAUL (Rusty, Dutch) BR TR 6'2" 198 lbs.
B. Nov. 1, 1931, Pittsburgh, Pa.

1954 BOS A	5	3	.625	3.82	19	9	2	75.1	71	41	37	1	2	0	0	21	3	0	.143
1955	1	1	.500	7.27	7	2	0	17.1	18	15	13	0	1	0	0	3	0	0	.000
1957 2 teams			BOS	A (1G 0–0)		WAS	A (39G 7–11)												
" total	7	11	.389	4.95	40	26	6	176.1	219	73	82	0	1	0	0	46	3	2	.065
1958 WAS A	6	15	.286	4.61	40	30	6	224.1	234	74	111	0	0	0	0	69	11	0	.159
1959	8	17	.320	4.50	37	28	8	206	221	71	89	0	0	0	0	60	8	0	.133
1960 2 teams			WAS	A (3G 0–2)		CHI	A (36G 6–3)												
" total	6	5	.545	3.59	39	10	2	138	129	55	86	1	4	2	2	33	0	0	.000
1961 CHI A	3	3	.500	4.38	47	2	0	96.2	102	26	35	0	3	3	2	15	3	0	.200
1962 2 teams			CHI	A (20G 2–1)		HOU	N (36G 5–3)												
" total	7	4	.636	4.03	56	2	0	96	102	26	40	0	7	2	3	11	4	0	.364
1963 HOU N	0	0	–	5.65	17	0	0	36.2	48	8	12	0	0	0	1	7	2	0	.286
9 yrs.	43	59	.422	4.46	302	109	24	1066.2	1144	389	505	2	18	7	8	265	34	2	.128
3 yrs.	11	7	.611	3.63	103	9	2	245.1	243	82	128	1	9	6	4	46	4	0	.087

Bill Kennedy
KENNEDY, WILLIAM AULTON (Lefty) BL TL 6'2½" 200 lbs.
B. Mar. 14, 1921, Carnesville, Ga.

1948 2 teams			CLE	A (6G 1–0)		STL	A (26G 7–8)												
" total	8	8	.500	5.21	32	23	3	143.1	148	117	89	0	0	0	0	47	13	0	.277
1949 STL A	4	11	.267	4.69	48	16	2	153.2	172	73	69	0	2	1	1	40	6	0	.150
1950	0	0	–	0.00	1	0	0	2	1	2	1	0	0	0	0	0	0	0	–
1951	1	5	.167	5.63	19	5	1	56	76	37	29	0	1	2	0	16	2	0	.125
1952 CHI A	2	2	.500	2.80	47	1	0	70.2	54	38	46	0	2	1	5	13	3	0	.231
1953 BOS A	0	0	–	3.70	16	0	0	24.1	24	17	14	0	0	0	2	2	1	0	.500
1956 CIN N	0	0	–	18.00	1	0	0	2	6	0	0	0	0	0	0	0	0	0	–
1957	0	2	.000	6.39	8	0	0	12.2	16	5	8	0	0	2	3	2	0	0	.000
8 yrs.	15	28	.349	4.71	172	45	6	464.2	497	289	256	0	4	6	11	120	25	0	.208
1 yr.	2	2	.500	2.80	47	1	0	70.2	54	38	46	0	2	1	5	13	3	0	.231

Vern Kennedy
KENNEDY, LLOYD VERNON BL TR 6' 175 lbs.
B. Mar. 20, 1907, Kansas City, Mo.

1934 CHI A	0	2	.000	3.72	3	3	1	19.1	21	9	7	0	0	0	0	7	2	0	.286
1935	11	11	.500	3.91	31	25	16	211.2	211	95	65	2	0	1	1	73	18	0	.247
1936	21	9	.700	4.63	35	34	20	274.1	282	147	99	1	0	0	0	113	32	0	.283
1937	14	13	.519	5.09	32	30	15	221	238	124	114	1	0	0	0	87	20	2	.230
1938 DET A	12	9	.571	5.06	33	26	11	190.1	215	113	53	0	1	0	2	79	23	0	.291
1939 2 teams			DET	A (4G 0–3)		STL	A (33G 9–17)												
" total	9	20	.310	5.80	37	31	13	212.2	254	124	64	1	0	0	1	74	12	0	.162
1940 STL A	12	17	.414	5.59	34	32	18	222.1	263	122	70	0	1	0	0	84	25	2	.298

Pitcher Register

	W	L	PCT	ERA	G	GS	CG	IP	H	BB	SO	ShO	Relief Pitching W L SV	AB	H	HR	BA

Vern Kennedy continued

	W	L	PCT	ERA	G	GS	CG	IP	H	BB	SO	ShO	RW	RL	SV	AB	H	HR	BA
1941 2 teams	STL	A (6G 2-4)			WAS	A (17G 1-7)													
" total	3	11	.214	5.17	23	13	4	111.1	121	66	28	0	1	1	0	36	9	0	.250
1942 CLE A	4	8	.333	4.08	28	12	4	108	99	50	37	0	0	2	1	30	6	0	.200
1943	10	7	.588	2.45	28	17	8	146.2	130	59	63	1	3	1	0	52	12	0	.231
1944 2 teams	CLE	A (12G 2-5)			PHI	N (12G 1-5)													
" total	3	10	.231	4.64	24	17	5	114.1	126	57	40	0	1	0	0	44	8	0	.182
1945 2 teams	PHI	N (12G 0-3)			CIN	N (24G 5-12)													
" total	5	15	.250	4.28	36	23	11	193.2	213	83	51	1	0	2	1	64	14	0	.219
12 yrs.	104	132	.441	4.67	344	263	126	2025.2	2173	1049	691	7	8	9	5	743	181	4	.244
4 yrs.	46	35	.568	4.54	101	92	52	726.1	752	375	285	4	1	2	1	280	72	2	.257

Gus Keriazakos

KERIAZAKOS, CONSTANTINE NICHOLAS BR TR 6'3" 187 lbs.
B. July 28, 1931, West Orange, N. J.

	W	L	PCT	ERA	G	GS	CG	IP	H	BB	SO	ShO	RW	RL	SV	AB	H	HR	BA
1950 CHI A	0	1	.000	19.29	1	1	0	2.1	7	5	1	0	0	0	0	1	1	0	1.000
1954 WAS A	2	3	.400	3.77	22	3	2	59.2	59	30	33	0	1	1	0	15	1	0	.067
1955 KC A	0	1	.000	12.34	5	1	0	11.2	15	7	8	0	0	1	0	3	0	0	.000
3 yrs.	2	5	.286	5.62	28	5	2	73.2	81	42	42	0	1	2	0	19	2	0	.105
1 yr.	0	1	.000	19.29	1	1	0	2.1	7	5	1	0	0	0	0	1	1	0	1.000

Jim Kern

KERN, JAMES LESTER BR TR 6'5" 185 lbs.
B. Mar. 15, 1949, Gladwin County, Mich.

	W	L	PCT	ERA	G	GS	CG	IP	H	BB	SO	ShO	RW	RL	SV	AB	H	HR	BA
1974 CLE A	0	1	.000	4.70	4	3	1	15.1	16	14	11	0	0	0	0	0	0	0	—
1975	1	2	.333	3.77	13	7	0	71.2	60	45	55	0	0	0	0	0	0	0	—
1976	10	7	.588	2.36	50	2	0	118	91	50	111	0	9	6	15	0	0	0	—
1977	8	10	.444	3.42	60	0	0	92	85	47	91	0	8	10	18	0	0	0	—
1978	10	10	.500	3.08	58	0	0	99.1	77	58	95	0	10	10	13	1	0	0	.000
1979 TEX A	13	5	.722	1.57	71	0	0	143	99	62	136	0	13	5	29	0	0	0	—
1980	3	11	.214	4.86	38	1	0	63	65	45	40	0	3	11	2	0	0	0	—
1981	1	2	.333	2.70	23	0	0	30	21	22	20	0	1	2	6	0	0	0	—
1982 2 teams	CIN	N (50G 3-5)			CHI	A (13G 2-1)													
" total	5	6	.455	3.46	63	0	0	104	81	60	66	0	4	6	5	7	0	0	.000
1983 CHI N	0	0	—	0.00	1	0	0	.2	1	0	0	0	0	0	0	0	0	0	—
10 yrs.	51	54	.486	3.00	381	14	1	737	596	403	625	0	48	50	88	8	0	0	.000
2 yrs.	2	1	.667	5.02	14	1	0	28.2	21	12	23	0	1	1	3	0	0	0	—

Dickie Kerr

KERR, RICHARD HENRY BL TL 5'7" 155 lbs.
B. July 3, 1893, St. Louis, Mo. D. May 4, 1963, Houston, Tex.

	W	L	PCT	ERA	G	GS	CG	IP	H	BB	SO	ShO	RW	RL	SV	AB	H	HR	BA
1919 CHI A	13	7	.650	2.88	39	17	10	212.1	208	64	79	1	5	1	0	68	17	0	.250
1920	21	9	.700	3.37	45	28	20	253.2	266	72	72	3	3	1	5	90	14	0	.156
1921	19	17	.528	4.72	44	37	25	308.2	357	96	80	3	3	0	1	105	25	0	.238
1925	0	1	.000	5.15	12	2	0	36.2	45	18	4	0	0	0	0	12	4	0	.333
4 yrs.	53	34	.609	3.84	140	84	55	811.1	876	250	235	7	11	2	6	275	60	0	.218
4 yrs.	53	34	.609	3.84	140	84	55	811.1	876	250	235	7	11	2	6	275	60	0	.218
				4th															

WORLD SERIES
| 1919 CHI A | 2 | 0 | 1.000 | 1.42 | 2 | 2 | 2 | 19 | 14 | 3 | 6 | 1 | 0 | 0 | 0 | 6 | 1 | 0 | .167 |

Joe Kiefer

KIEFER, JOSEPH WILLIAM (Smoke, Harlem Joe) BR TR 5'11" 190 lbs.
B. July 19, 1899, West Leyden, N. Y.

	W	L	PCT	ERA	G	GS	CG	IP	H	BB	SO	ShO	RW	RL	SV	AB	H	HR	BA
1920 CHI A	0	1	.000	15.43	2	1	0	4.2	7	5	1	0	0	0	0	2	0	0	.000
1925 BOS A	0	2	.000	6.00	2	2	0	15	20	9	4	0	0	0	0	4	0	0	.000
1926	0	2	.000	4.80	11	2	0	30	29	16	4	0	0	1	0	7	1	0	.143
3 yrs.	0	5	.000	6.16	15	4	0	49.2	56	30	9	0	0	1	0	13	1	0	.077
1 yr.	0	1	.000	15.43	2	1	0	4.2	7	5	1	0	0	0	0	2	0	0	.000

Chad Kimsey

KIMSEY, CLYDE ELIAS BL TR 6'2" 200 lbs.
B. Aug. 6, 1905, Copperhill, Tenn. D. Dec. 3, 1942, Pryor, Okla.

	W	L	PCT	ERA	G	GS	CG	IP	H	BB	SO	ShO	RW	RL	SV	AB	H	HR	BA
1929 STL A	3	6	.333	5.04	24	3	1	64.1	88	19	13	0	1	5	1	30	8	2	.267
1930	6	10	.375	6.35	42	4	1	113.1	139	45	32	0	6	7	1	70	24	3	.343
1931	4	6	.400	4.39	42	1	0	94.1	121	27	27	0	4	5	7	37	10	2	.270
1932 2 teams	STL	A (33G 4-2)			CHI	A (7G 1-1)													
" total	5	3	.625	3.83	40	0	0	89.1	93	38	19	0	5	3	5	20	6	0	.300
1933 CHI A	4	1	.800	5.53	28	2	0	96	124	36	19	0	4	0	0	33	5	0	.152
1936 DET A	2	3	.400	4.85	22	0	0	52	58	29	11	0	2	3	3	16	5	0	.313
6 yrs.	24	29	.453	5.07	198	10	2	509.1	623	194	121	0	22	23	17	*			
2 yrs.	5	5	.714	5.21	35	2	0	107	132	41	25	0	5	1	2	35	5	0	.143

Ellis Kinder

KINDER, ELLIS RAYMOND (Old Folks) BR TR 6' 195 lbs.
B. July 26, 1914, Atkins, Ark. D. Oct. 16, 1968, Jackson, Tenn.

	W	L	PCT	ERA	G	GS	CG	IP	H	BB	SO	ShO	RW	RL	SV	AB	H	HR	BA
1946 STL A	3	3	.500	3.32	33	7	1	86.2	78	36	59	0	0	0	1	19	1	0	.053
1947	8	15	.348	4.49	34	26	10	194.1	201	82	110	2	0	0	0	62	8	0	.129
1948 BOS A	10	7	.588	3.74	28	22	10	178	183	63	53	1	1	2	0	62	6	0	.097
1949	23	6	.793	3.36	43	30	19	252	251	99	138	6	2	1	4	92	12	0	.130
1950	14	12	.538	4.26	48	23	11	207	212	78	95	1	3	4	9	71	13	1	.183
1951	11	2	.846	2.55	63	2	1	127	108	46	84	0	10	1	14	34	4	0	.118
1952	5	6	.455	2.58	23	10	4	97.2	85	28	50	0	1	2	4	32	0	0	.000
1953	10	6	.625	1.85	69	0	0	107	84	38	39	0	10	6	27	29	11	0	.379
1954	8	8	.500	3.62	48	2	0	104	106	36	67	0	7	8	15	27	5	0	.185
1955	5	5	.500	2.84	43	0	0	66.2	57	15	31	0	5	5	18	12	3	0	.250
1956 2 teams	STL	N (22G 2-0)			CHI	A (29G 3-1)													
" total	5	1	.833	3.09	51	0	0	55.1	56	17	23	0	5	1	9	4	0	0	.000
1957 CHI A	0	0	—	0.00	2	0	0	2	0	1	0	0	0	0	0	0	0	0	—
12 yrs.	102	71	.590	3.43	484	122	56	1479.2	1421	539	749	10	44	30	102	444	63	1	.142
2 yrs.	3	1	.750	2.64	30	0	0	30.2	33	9	19	0	3	1	3	2	0	0	.000

376

Pitcher Register

	W	L	PCT	ERA	G	GS	CG	IP	H	BB	SO	ShO	Relief Pitching W L SV	BATTING AB H HR	BA

Harry Kinzy
KINZY, HENRY HERSEL (Slim)
B. July 19, 1910, Hallsville, Tex.   BR TR 6'4"   185 lbs.

| 1934 CHI A | 0 | 1 | .000 | 4.98 | 13 | 2 | 1 | 34.1 | 38 | 31 | 12 | 0 | 0 0 0 | 10 3 0 | .300 |

Don Kirkwood
KIRKWOOD, DONALD PAUL
B. Sept. 24, 1950, Pontiac, Mich.   BR TR 6'3"   175 lbs.

1974 CAL A	0	0	–	9.00	3	0	0	7	12	6	4	0	0 0 0	0 0 0	–
1975	6	5	.545	3.11	44	2	0	84	85	28	49	0	6 4 7	0 0 0	–
1976	6	12	.333	4.61	28	26	4	158	167	57	78	0	0 1 0	0 0 0	–
1977 2 teams			CAL	A (13G 1-0)			CHI	A (16G 1-1)							
" total	2	1	.667	5.15	29	0	0	57.2	69	19	34	0	2 1 1	0 0 0	–
1978 TOR A	4	5	.444	4.24	16	9	3	68	76	25	29	0	1 1 0	0 0 0	–
5 yrs.	18	23	.439	4.37	120	37	7	374.2	409	135	194	0	9 7 8	0 0 0	–
1 yr.	1	1	.500	5.18	16	0	0	40	49	10	24	0	1 1 0	0 0 0	–

Hugo Klaerner
KLAERNER, HUGO EMIL (Dutch)
B. Oct. 15, 1908, Fredericksburg, Tex.   BR TR 5'11"   190 lbs.

| 1934 CHI A | 0 | 2 | .000 | 10.90 | 3 | 3 | 1 | 17.1 | 24 | 16 | 9 | 0 | 0 0 0 | 6 2 0 | .333 |

Fred Klages
KLAGES, FREDERICK ANTHONY
B. Oct. 31, 1943, Ambridge, Pa.   BR TR 6'2"   185 lbs.

1966 CHI A	1	0	1.000	1.72	3	3	0	15.2	9	7	6	0	0 0 0	6 3 0	.500
1967	4	4	.500	3.83	11	9	0	44.2	43	16	17	0	1 0 0	12 0 0	.000
2 yrs.	5	4	.556	3.28	14	12	0	60.1	52	23	23	0	1 0 0	18 3 0	.167
2 yrs.	5	4	.556	3.28	14	12	0	60.1	52	23	23	0	1 0 0	18 3 0	.167

Ed Klepfer
KLEPFER, EDWARD LLOYD (Big Ed)
B. Mar. 17, 1888, Summerville, Pa.   D. Aug. 9, 1950, Tulsa, Okla.   BR TR 6'   185 lbs.

1911 NY A	0	0	–	6.75	2	0	0	4	5	2	4	0	0 0 0	1 0 0	.000
1913	0	0	–	7.66	8	1	0	24.2	38	12	10	0	0 0 0	6 1 0	.167
1915 2 teams			CHI	A (3G 1-0)			CLE	A (8G 1-6)							
" total	2	6	.250	2.26	11	9	3	55.2	58	16	16	0	0 1 0	15 2 0	.133
1916 CLE A	6	7	.462	2.52	31	13	4	143	136	46	62	1	0 3 2	40 1 0	.025
1917	13	4	.765	2.37	41	27	9	213	208	55	66	1	2 1 1	62 2 0	.032
1919	0	0	–	7.36	5	0	0	7.1	12	6	7	0	0 0 0	1 0 0	.000
6 yrs.	21	18	.538	2.81	98	50	16	447.2	457	137	165	2	2 5 3	125 6 0	.048
1 yr.	1	0	1.000	2.84	3	2	1	12.2	11	5	3	0	0 0 0	3 0 0	.000

Eddie Klieman
KLIEMAN, EDWARD FREDERICK (Babe)
B. Mar. 21, 1918, Norwood, Ohio   D. Nov. 15, 1979, Homosassa, Fla.   BR TR 6'1"   190 lbs.

1943 CLE A	0	1	.000	1.00	1	1	1	9	8	5	2	0	0 0 0	3 0 0	.000
1944	11	13	.458	3.38	47	19	5	178.1	185	70	44	1	5 3 5	57 6 0	.105
1945	5	8	.385	3.85	38	12	4	126.1	123	49	33	1	1 2 4	40 8 1	.200
1946	0	0	–	6.60	9	0	0	15	18	10	2	0	0 0 0	1 0 0	.000
1947	5	4	.556	3.03	58	0	0	92	78	39	21	0	5 4 17	19 2 0	.105
1948	3	2	.600	2.60	44	0	0	79.2	62	46	18	0	3 2 4	14 2 0	.143
1949 2 teams			WAS	A (2G 0-0)			CHI	A (18G 2-0)							
" total	2	0	1.000	4.25	20	0	0	36	41	18	10	0	2 0 3	9 3 0	.333
1950 PHI A	0	0	–	9.53	5	0	0	5.2	10	2	0	0	0 0 0	1 0 0	.000
8 yrs.	26	28	.481	3.49	222	32	10	542	525	239	130	2	16 11 33	144 21 1	.146
1 yr.	2	0	1.000	3.00	18	0	0	33	33	15	9	0	2 0 3	8 2 0	.250

WORLD SERIES
| 1948 CLE A | 0 | 0 | – | ∞ | 1 | 0 | 0 | | 1 | 2 | 0 | 0 | 0 0 0 | 0 0 0 | – |

Chris Knapp
KNAPP, ROBERT CHRISTIAN
B. Sept. 16, 1953, Cherry Point, N. C.   BR TR 6'5"   195 lbs.

1975 CHI A	0	0	–	4.50	2	0	0	2	2	4	3	0	0 0 0	0 0 0	–
1976	3	1	.750	4.85	11	6	1	52	54	32	41	0	0 1 0	0 0 0	–
1977	12	7	.632	4.81	27	26	4	146	166	61	103	0	0 0 0	0 0 0	–
1978 CAL A	14	8	.636	4.21	30	29	6	188.1	178	67	126	0	0 0 0	0 0 0	–
1979	5	5	.500	5.51	20	18	3	98	109	35	36	0	0 0 0	0 0 0	–
1980	2	11	.154	6.15	32	20	1	117	133	51	46	0	1 1 0	0 0 0	–
6 yrs.	36	32	.529	5.00	122	99	15	603.1	642	250	355	0	1 2 1	0 0 0	–
3 yrs.	15	8	.652	4.82	40	32	5	200	222	97	147	0	0 1 0	0 0 0	–

LEAGUE CHAMPIONSHIP SERIES
| 1979 CAL A | 0 | 1 | .000 | 7.71 | 1 | 1 | 0 | 2.1 | 5 | 1 | 0 | 0 | 0 0 0 | 0 0 0 | – |

Jack Knott
KNOTT, JOHN HENRY
B. Mar. 2, 1907, Dallas, Tex.   BR TR 6'2½"   200 lbs.

1933 STL A	1	8	.111	5.01	20	9	0	82.2	88	33	19	0	0 2 0	23 7 0	.304
1934	10	3	.769	4.96	45	10	2	138	149	67	56	0	7 0 4	30 4 0	.133
1935	11	8	.579	4.60	48	19	7	187.2	219	78	45	2	5 4 7	61 7 0	.115
1936	9	17	.346	7.29	47	23	9	192.2	272	93	60	0	3 3 6	57 4 0	.070
1937	8	18	.308	4.89	38	22	8	191.1	220	91	74	0	2 5 2	57 8 0	.140
1938 2 teams			STL	A (7G 1-2)			CHI	A (20G 5-10)							
" total	6	12	.333	4.19	27	22	9	161	170	69	43	0	0 1 0	50 6 0	.120
1939 CHI A	11	6	.647	4.15	25	23	8	149.2	157	41	56	0	0 0 0	53 8 0	.151
1940	11	9	.550	4.56	25	23	4	158	166	52	44	2	0 0 0	57 5 0	.088
1941 PHI A	13	11	.542	4.40	27	26	11	194.1	212	81	54	0	0 0 0	65 5 0	.077
1942	2	10	.167	5.57	20	14	4	95.1	127	36	31	0	1 0 0	29 4 0	.138
1946	0	1	–	5.68	3	1	0	6.1	7	1	2	0	0 0 0	0 0 0	–
11 yrs.	82	103	.443	4.97	325	192	62	1557	1787	642	484	4	18 16 19	482 58 0	.120
3 yrs.	27	25	.519	4.27	70	64	21	438.2	458	147	135	2	0 0 0	150 18 0	.120

Pitcher Register

	W	L	PCT	ERA	G	GS	CG	IP	H	BB	SO	ShO	Relief Pitching W	L	SV	BATTING AB	H	HR	BA

Jerry Koosman
KOOSMAN, JEROME MARTIN
B. Dec. 23, 1943, Appleton, Minn.
BR TL 6'2" 205 lbs.

Year/Team	W	L	PCT	ERA	G	GS	CG	IP	H	BB	SO	ShO	RW	RL	SV	AB	H	HR	BA
1967 NY N	0	2	.000	6.04	9	3	0	22.1	22	19	11	0	0	0	0	2	0	0	.000
1968	19	12	.613	2.08	35	34	17	263.2	221	69	178	7	0	0	0	91	7	1	.077
1969	17	9	.654	2.28	32	32	16	241	187	68	180	6	0	0	0	84	4	0	.048
1970	12	7	.632	3.14	30	29	5	212	189	71	118	1	1	0	0	70	6	0	.086
1971	6	11	.353	3.04	26	24	4	166	160	51	96	0	0	0	0	50	8	0	.160
1972	11	12	.478	4.14	34	24	4	163	155	52	147	1	2	0	1	47	4	0	.085
1973	14	15	.483	2.84	35	35	12	263	234	76	156	3	0	0	0	78	8	0	.103
1974	15	11	.577	3.36	35	35	13	265	258	85	188	0	0	0	0	86	16	0	.186
1975	14	13	.519	3.41	36	34	11	240	234	98	173	4	0	0	2	78	14	0	.179
1976	21	10	.677	2.70	34	32	17	247	205	66	200	3	0	0	0	79	17	0	.215
1977	8	20	.286	3.49	32	32	6	227	195	81	192	1	0	0	0	72	8	1	.111
1978	3	15	.167	3.75	38	32	3	235	221	84	160	0	0	0	2	70	6	0	.086
1979 MIN A	20	13	.606	3.38	37	36	10	264	268	83	157	2	0	0	0	0	0	0	—
1980	16	13	.552	4.04	38	34	8	243	252	69	149	0	1	1	2	0	0	0	—
1981 2 teams MIN A (19G 3-9) CHI A (8G 1-4)																			
" total	4	13	.235	4.02	27	16	3	121	125	41	76	1	0	2	5	0	0	0	—
1982 CHI A	11	7	.611	3.84	42	19	3	173.1	194	38	88	1	2	3	3	0	0	0	—
1983	11	7	.611	4.77	37	24	2	169.2	176	53	90	1	1	0	2	0	0	0	—
17 yrs.	202	190	.515	3.33	557	475	134	3516	3296	1104	2359	31	7	6	17	807	98	2	.121
3 yrs.	23	18	.561	4.23	87	46	6	370	397	98	199	2	3	5	5	0	0	0	—

LEAGUE CHAMPIONSHIP SERIES

Year/Team	W	L	PCT	ERA	G	GS	CG	IP	H	BB	SO	ShO	RW	RL	SV	AB	H	HR	BA
1969 NY N	0	0	—	11.57	1	1	0	4.2	7	4	5	0	0	0	0	2	0	0	.000
1973	1	0	1.000	2.00	1	1	1	9	8	0	9	0	0	0	0	4	2	0	.500
1983 CHI A	0	0	—	54.00	1	0	0	.1	1	2	0	0	0	0	0	0	0	0	—
3 yrs.	1	0	1.000	6.43	3	2	1	14	16	6	14	0	0	0	0	6	2	0	.333

WORLD SERIES

Year/Team	W	L	PCT	ERA	G	GS	CG	IP	H	BB	SO	ShO	RW	RL	SV	AB	H	HR	BA
1969 NY N	2	0	1.000	2.04	2	2	1	17.2	7	4	9	0	0	0	0	7	1	0	.143
1973	1	0	1.000	3.12	2	2	0	8.2	9	7	8	0	0	0	0	4	0	0	.000
2 yrs.	3	0	1.000	2.39	4	4	1	26.1	16	11	17	0	0	0	0	11	1	0	.091

1st

Fabian Kowalik
KOWALIK, FABIAN LORENZ
B. Apr. 22, 1908, Falls City, Tex.
D. Aug. 14, 1954, Karnes City, Tex.
BR TR 5'11" 185 lbs.
BL 1932, BB 1935

Year/Team	W	L	PCT	ERA	G	GS	CG	IP	H	BB	SO	ShO	RW	RL	SV	AB	H	HR	BA
1932 CHI A	0	1	.000	6.97	2	1	0	10.1	16	4	2	0	0	0	0	13	5	0	.385
1935 CHI N	2	2	.500	4.42	20	2	1	55	60	19	20	0	2	0	1	15	3	0	.200
1936 3 teams CHI N (6G 0-2) PHI N (22G 1-5) BOS N (1G 0-1)																			
" total	1	8	.111	5.82	29	9	3	102	142	40	20	0	0	2	1	67	15	0	.224
3 yrs.	3	11	.214	5.43	51	12	4	167.1	218	63	42	0	2	2	2	*			
1 yr.	0	1	.000	6.97	2	1	0	10.1	16	4	2	0	0	0	0	13	5	0	.385

WORLD SERIES

Year/Team	W	L	PCT	ERA	G	GS	CG	IP	H	BB	SO	ShO	RW	RL	SV	AB	H	HR	BA
1935 CHI N	0	0	—	2.08	1	0	0	4.1	3	1	1	0	0	0	0	2	1	0	.500

Ken Kravec
KRAVEC, KENNETH PETER
B. July 29, 1951, Cleveland, Ohio
BL TL 6'2" 185 lbs.

Year/Team	W	L	PCT	ERA	G	GS	CG	IP	H	BB	SO	ShO	RW	RL	SV	AB	H	HR	BA
1975 CHI A	0	1	.000	6.23	2	1	0	4.1	1	8	1	0	0	0	0	0	0	0	—
1976	1	5	.167	4.86	9	8	1	50	49	32	38	0	0	0	0	0	0	0	—
1977	11	8	.579	4.10	26	25	6	167	161	57	125	1	0	0	0	0	0	0	—
1978	11	16	.407	4.08	30	30	7	203	188	95	154	2	0	0	0	0	0	0	—
1979	15	13	.536	3.74	36	35	10	250	208	111	132	3	0	0	1	0	0	0	—
1980	3	6	.333	6.91	20	15	0	82	100	44	37	0	0	0	0	0	0	0	—
1981 CHI N	1	6	.143	5.08	24	12	0	78	80	39	50	0	0	1	0	15	0	0	.000
1982	1	1	.500	6.12	13	2	0	25	27	18	20	0	1	1	0	3	0	0	.000
8 yrs.	43	56	.434	4.46	160	128	24	859.1	814	404	557	6	1	2	1	18	0	0	.000
6 yrs.	41	49	.456	4.34	123	114	24	756.1	707	347	487	6	0	0	1	0	0	0	—

Red Kress
KRESS, RALPH
B. Jan. 2, 1907, Columbia, Calif. D. Nov. 29, 1962, Los Angeles, Calif.
BR TR 5'11½" 165 lbs.

Year/Team	W	L	PCT	ERA	G	GS	CG	IP	H	BB	SO	ShO	RW	RL	SV	AB	H	HR	BA
1935 WAS A	0	0	—	12.71	3	0	0	5.2	8	5	5	0	0	0	0	252	75	2	.298
1946 NY N	0	0	—	12.27	1	0	0	3.2	5	1	1	0	0	0	0	1	0	0	.000
2 yrs.	0	0	—	12.54	4	0	0	9.1	13	6	6	0	0	0	0	*			

Lou Kretlow
KRETLOW, LOUIS HENRY
B. June 27, 1923, Apache, Okla.
BR TR 6'2" 185 lbs.

Year/Team	W	L	PCT	ERA	G	GS	CG	IP	H	BB	SO	ShO	RW	RL	SV	AB	H	HR	BA
1946 DET A	1	0	1.000	3.00	1	1	1	9	7	2	4	0	0	0	0	4	2	0	.500
1948	2	1	.667	4.63	5	2	1	23.1	21	11	9	0	1	0	0	8	4	0	.500
1949	3	2	.600	6.16	25	10	1	76	85	69	40	0	2	1	0	26	0	0	.000
1950 2 teams STL A (9G 0-2) CHI A (11G 0-0)																			
" total	0	2	.000	7.07	20	3	0	35.2	42	45	24	0	0	1	0	7	0	0	.000
1951 CHI A	6	9	.400	4.20	26	18	7	137	129	74	89	1	0	1	0	48	4	0	.083
1952	4	4	.500	2.96	19	11	4	79	52	56	63	2	0	0	1	20	1	0	.050
1953 2 teams CHI A (9G 0-0) STL A (22G 1-5)																			
" total	1	5	.167	4.78	31	14	0	101.2	105	82	52	0	0	0	0	29	5	0	.172
1954 BAL A	6	11	.353	4.37	32	20	5	166.2	169	82	82	0	0	1	0	51	8	0	.157
1955	0	4	.000	8.22	15	5	0	38.1	50	27	26	0	0	0	0	11	1	0	.091
1956 KC A	4	9	.308	5.31	25	20	3	118.2	121	74	61	0	0	0	0	33	2	0	.061
10 yrs.	27	47	.365	4.87	199	104	22	785.1	781	522	450	3	3	4	1	237	27	0	.114
4 yrs.	10	13	.435	3.73	65	33	11	250	287	210	187	181	3	0	1	1	76	5	0	.066

Frank Kreutzer
KREUTZER, FRANK JAMES
B. Feb. 7, 1939, Buffalo, N.Y.
BR TL 6'1" 175 lbs.

Year/Team	W	L	PCT	ERA	G	GS	CG	IP	H	BB	SO	ShO	RW	RL	SV	AB	H	HR	BA
1962 CHI A	0	0	—	0.00	1	0	0	1.1	0	1	1	0	0	0	0	0	0	0	—
1963	1	0	1.000	1.80	1	1	0	5	3	1	0	0	0	0	0	2	0	0	.000

379   *Pitcher Register*

	W	L	PCT	ERA	G	GS	CG	IP	H	BB	SO	ShO	Relief Pitching W	L	SV	BATTING AB	H	HR	BA

Frank Kreutzer continued

1964 2 teams	CHI	A (17G 3-1)		WAS	A (13G 2-6)														
" total	5	7	.417	4.10	30	11	0	85.2	85	41	59	0	2	2	1	19	1	0	.053
1965 WAS A	2	6	.250	4.32	33	14	2	85.1	73	54	65	1	0	1	0	22	1	1	.045
1966	0	5	.000	6.03	9	6	0	31.1	30	10	24	0	0	0	0	8	2	0	.250
1969	0	0	—	4.50	4	0	0	2	3	2	2	0	0	0	0	0	0	0	—
6 yrs.	8	18	.308	4.40	78	32	2	210.2	194	109	151	1	2	3	1	51	4	1	.078
3 yrs.	4	1	.800	3.09	19	3	0	46.2	40	20	33	0	2	1	1	10	1	0	.100

Jack Kucek   KUCEK, JOHN ANDREW   BR TR 6'2"   200 lbs.
B. June 8, 1953, Newton Falls, Ohio

1974 CHI A	1	4	.200	5.21	9	7	0	38	48	21	25	0	0	0	0	0	0	0	—
1975	0	0	—	4.91	2	0	0	3.2	9	4	2	0	0	0	0	0	0	0	—
1976	0	0	—	9.00	2	0	0	5	9	4	2	0	0	0	0	0	0	0	—
1977	0	1	.000	3.60	8	3	0	35	35	10	25	0	0	0	0	0	0	0	—
1978	2	3	.400	3.29	10	5	3	52	42	27	30	0	0	0	1	0	0	0	—
1979 2 teams	CHI	A (1G 0-0)		PHI	N (4G 1-0)														
" total	1	0	1.000	7.20	5	0	0	5	6	4	2	0	1	0	0	0	0	0	—
1980 TOR A	3	8	.273	6.75	23	12	0	68	83	41	35	0	1	2	1	0	0	0	—
7 yrs.	7	16	.304	5.10	59	27	3	206.2	232	111	121	0	2	2	2	0	0	0	—
6 yrs.	3	8	.273	4.14	32	15	3	134.2	143	69	84	0	0	0	1	0	0	0	—

Bob Kuzava   KUZAVA, ROBERT LeROY (Sarge)   BB TL 6'2"   202 lbs.
B. May 28, 1923, Wyandotte, Mich.   BR 1946

1946 CLE A	1	0	1.000	3.00	2	2	0	12	9	11	4	0	0	0	0	5	1	0	.200
1947	1	1	.500	4.15	4	4	1	21.2	22	9	9	1	0	0	0	9	1	0	.111
1949 CHI A	10	6	.625	4.02	29	18	9	156.2	139	91	83	1	2	0	0	56	2	0	.036
1950 2 teams	CHI	A (10G 1-3)		WAS	A (22G 8-7)														
" total	9	10	.474	4.33	32	29	9	199.1	199	102	105	1	0	0	0	62	6	1	.097
1951 2 teams	WAS	A (8G 3-3)		NY	A (23G 8-4)														
" total	11	7	.611	3.61	31	16	7	134.2	133	55	72	1	5	1	5	39	6	0	.154
1952 NY A	8	8	.500	3.45	28	12	6	133	115	63	67	0	3	2	3	43	4	0	.093
1953	6	5	.545	3.31	33	6	2	92.1	92	34	48	2	4	1	4	21	1	0	.048
1954 2 teams	NY	A (20G 1-3)		BAL	A (4G 1-3)														
" total	2	6	.250	4.97	24	7	0	63.1	76	29	37	0	1	1	1	13	0	0	.000
1955 2 teams	BAL	A (6G 0-1)		PHI	N (17G 1-0)														
" total	1	1	.500	6.25	23	5	0	44.2	57	16	18	0	0	0	0	8	1	0	.125
1957 2 teams	PIT	N (4G 0-0)		STL	N (3G 0-0)														
" total	0	0	—	6.23	7	0	0	4.1	7	5	3	0	0	0	0	0	0	0	—
10 yrs.	49	44	.527	4.05	213	99	34	862	849	415	446	7	15	5	13	256	22	1	.086
2 yrs.	11	9	.550	4.39	39	25	10	201	182	118	104	1	2	0	0	68	3	0	.044

WORLD SERIES
1951 NY A	0	0	—	0.00	1	0	0	1	0	0	0	0	0	0	1	0	0	0	—
1952	0	0	—	0.00	1	0	0	2.2	0	0	2	0	0	0	1	1	0	0	.000
1953	0	0	—	13.50	1	0	0	.2	2	0	1	0	0	0	0	1	0	0	.000
3 yrs.	0	0	—	2.08	3	0	0	4.1	2	0	3	0	0	0	2	2	0	0	.000

Lerrin LaGrow   LaGROW, LERRIN HARRIS   BR TR 6'5"   220 lbs.
B. July 8, 1948, Phoenix, Ariz.

1970 DET A	0	1	.000	7.50	10	0	0	12	16	6	7	0	0	1	0	0	0	0	.000
1972	0	1	.000	1.33	16	0	0	27	22	6	9	0	0	1	2	0	0	0	—
1973	1	5	.167	4.33	21	3	0	54	54	23	33	0	0	3	3	0	0	0	—
1974	8	19	.296	4.67	37	34	11	216	245	80	85	0	0	0	0	0	0	0	—
1975	7	14	.333	4.38	32	26	7	164.1	183	66	75	2	0	0	0	0	0	0	—
1976 STL N	0	1	.000	1.48	8	2	1	24.1	21	7	10	0	0	0	0	5	0	0	.000
1977 CHI A	7	3	.700	2.45	66	0	0	99	81	35	63	0	7	3	25	0	0	0	—
1978	6	5	.545	4.40	52	0	0	88	85	38	41	0	6	5	16	0	0	0	—
1979 2 teams	CHI	A (11G 0-3)		LA	N (31G 5-1)														
" total	5	4	.556	5.24	42	2	0	55	65	34	31	0	5	2	5	3	1	0	.333
1980 PHI N	0	2	.000	4.15	25	0	0	39	42	17	21	0	0	2	3	4	1	0	.250
10 yrs.	34	55	.382	4.11	309	67	19	778.2	814	312	375	2	18	17	54	13	2	0	.154
3 yrs.	13	11	.542	3.86	129	2	0	205	193	89	113	0	13	9	42 9th	0	0	0	—

LEAGUE CHAMPIONSHIP SERIES
1972 DET A	0	0	—	0.00	1	0	0	1	0	0	1	0	0	0	0	0	0	0	—

Jack Lamabe   LAMABE, JOHN ALEXANDER   BR TR 6'1"   198 lbs.
B. Oct. 3, 1936, Farmingdale, N.Y.

1962 PIT N	3	1	.750	2.88	46	0	0	78	70	40	56	0	3	1	2	9	0	0	.000
1963 BOS A	7	4	.636	3.15	65	2	0	151.1	139	46	93	0	7	3	6	32	3	1	.094
1964	9	13	.409	5.89	39	25	3	177.1	235	57	109	0	1	2	1	52	6	0	.115
1965 2 teams	BOS	A (14G 0-3)		HOU	N (3G 0-2)														
" total	0	5	.000	6.87	17	2	0	38	51	17	23	0	0	3	0	8	1	0	.125
1966 CHI A	7	9	.438	3.93	34	17	3	121.1	116	35	67	2	2	0	0	35	2	0	.057
1967 3 teams	CHI	A (3G 1-0)		NY	N (16G 0-3)		STL	N (23G 3-4)											
" total	4	7	.364	3.20	42	3	1	84.1	74	19	56	1	3	5	5	15	2	0	.133
1968 CHI N	3	2	.600	4.30	42	0	0	60.2	68	24	30	0	3	2	1	5	1	0	.200
7 yrs.	33	41	.446	4.24	285	49	7	711	753	238	434	3	19	16	15	156	15	1	.096
2 yrs.	8	9	.471	3.85	37	17	3	126.1	123	36	70	2	3	0	0	35	2	0	.057

WORLD SERIES
1967 STL N	0	1	.000	6.75	3	0	0	2.2	5	0	4	0	0	1	0	0	0	0	—

Fred Lamline   LAMLINE, FREDERICK ARTHUR (Dutch)   BR TR 5'11"   171 lbs.
B. Aug. 14, 1891, Port Huron, Mich.   D. Sept. 20, 1970, Port Huron, Mich.

1912 CHI A	0	0	—	31.50	1	0	0	2	7	2	1	0	0	0	0	0	0	0	—

Pitcher Register

	W	L	PCT	ERA	G	GS	CG	IP	H	BB	SO	ShO	Relief Pitching W	L	SV	BATTING AB	H	HR	BA

Fred Lamline continued

1915 STL N	0	0	—	2.84	4	0	0	19	21	3	11	0	0	0	0	8	1	0	.125
2 yrs.	0	0	—	5.57	5	0	0	21	28	5	12	0	0	0	0	8	1	0	.125
1 yr.	0	0	—	31.50	1	0	0	2	7	2	1	0	0	0	0	0	0	0	—

Dennis Lamp

LAMP, DENNIS PATRICK
B. Sept. 23, 1952, Los Angeles, Calif.
BR TR 6'4" 200 lbs.

1977 CHI N	0	2	.000	6.30	11	3	0	30	43	8	12	0	0	0	0	8	3	0	.375
1978	7	15	.318	3.29	37	36	6	224	221	56	73	3	0	0	0	73	15	0	.205
1979	11	10	.524	3.51	38	32	6	200	223	46	86	1	0	0	0	58	9	0	.155
1980	10	14	.417	5.19	41	37	2	203	259	82	83	1	1	2	0	61	6	0	.098
1981 CHI A	7	6	.538	2.41	27	10	3	127	103	43	71	0	3	1	0	0	0	0	—
1982	11	8	.579	3.99	44	27	3	189.2	206	59	78	2	1	1	5	0	0	0	—
1983	7	7	.500	3.71	49	5	1	116.1	123	29	44	0	4	5	15	0	0	0	—
7 yrs.	53	62	.461	3.83	247	150	21	1090	1178	323	447	7	9	9	20	200	33	0	.165
3 yrs.	25	21	.543	3.45	120	42	7	433	432	131	193	2	8	7	20	0	0	0	—

LEAGUE CHAMPIONSHIP SERIES

| 1983 CHI A | 0 | 0 | — | 0.00 | 3 | 0 | 0 | 2 | 0 | 2 | 1 | 0 | 0 | 0 | 0 | 0 | 0 | 0 | — |

Frank Lange

LANGE, FRANK HERMAN
B. Oct. 28, 1883, Columbus, Wis. D. Dec. 26, 1945, Madison, Wis.
BR TR 5'11" 180 lbs.

1910 CHI A	9	4	.692	1.65	23	15	6	130.2	93	54	98	1	1	0	0	51	13	0	.255
1911	8	8	.500	3.23	29	22	8	161.2	151	77	104	1	0	1	0	76	22	0	.289
1912	10	10	.500	3.27	31	21	11	165.1	165	68	96	2	3	1	3	65	14	0	.215
1913	1	2	.333	4.87	12	3	0	40.2	46	20	20	0	0	0	0	18	3	0	.167
4 yrs.	28	24	.538	2.96	95	61	25	498.1	455	219	318	4	4	2	3	*			
4 yrs.	28	24	.538	2.96	95	61	25	498.1	455	219	318	4	4	2	3	210	52	0	.248

Paul LaPalme

LaPALME, PAUL EDMORE (Lefty)
B. Dec. 14, 1923, Springfield, Mass.
BL TL 5'10" 175 lbs.

1951 PIT N	1	5	.167	6.29	22	8	1	54.1	79	31	24	1	0	2	0	10	1	0	.100
1952	1	2	.333	3.92	31	2	0	59.2	56	37	25	0	1	2	0	10	1	0	.100
1953	8	16	.333	4.59	35	24	7	176.1	191	64	86	1	1	1	2	59	5	0	.085
1954	4	10	.286	5.52	33	15	2	120.2	147	54	57	0	1	1	0	35	5	0	.143
1955 STL N	4	3	.571	2.75	56	0	0	91.2	76	34	39	0	4	3	3	19	4	0	.211
1956 3 teams		STL	N (1G 0-0)		CIN	N (11G 2-4)		CHI	A (29G 3-1)										
" total	5	5	.500	3.93	41	2	0	73.1	61	33	27	0	4	4	2	10	2	0	.200
1957 CHI A	1	4	.200	3.35	30	0	0	40.1	35	19	19	0	1	4	7	4	2	0	.500
7 yrs.	24	45	.348	4.42	253	51	10	616.1	645	272	277	2	12	17	14	147	20	0	.136
2 yrs.	4	5	.444	2.83	64	0	0	86	66	46	42	0	4	5	9	10	2	0	.200

Don Larsen

LARSEN, DONALD JAMES
B. Aug. 7, 1929, Michigan City, Ind.
BR TR 6'4" 215 lbs.

1953 STL A	7	12	.368	4.16	38	22	7	192.2	201	64	96	2	1	2	2	81	23	3	.284
1954 BAL A	3	21	.125	4.37	29	28	12	201.2	213	89	80	1	0	1	0	88	22	1	.250
1955 NY A	9	2	.818	3.06	19	13	5	97	81	51	44	1	1	1	2	41	6	2	.146
1956	11	5	.688	3.26	38	20	6	179.2	133	96	107	1	2	1	1	79	19	2	.241
1957	10	4	.714	3.74	27	20	4	139.2	113	87	81	1	2	0	0	56	14	0	.250
1958	9	6	.600	3.07	19	19	3	114.1	100	52	55	3	0	0	0	49	15	4	.306
1959	6	7	.462	4.33	25	18	3	124.2	122	76	69	1	0	0	0	47	12	0	.255
1960 KC A	1	10	.091	5.38	22	9	0	83.2	97	42	43	0	0	1	0	29	6	0	.207
1961 2 teams		KC	A (8G 1-0)		CHI	A (25G 7-2)													
" total	8	2	.800	4.13	33	4	0	89.1	85	40	66	0	6	1	2	45	14	2	.311
1962 SF N	5	4	.556	4.38	49	0	0	86.1	83	47	58	0	5	4	11	25	5	0	.200
1963	7	7	.500	3.05	46	0	0	62	46	30	44	0	7	7	3	11	2	0	.182
1964 2 teams		SF	N (6G 0-1)		HOU	N (30G 4-8)													
" total	4	9	.308	2.45	36	10	2	113.2	102	26	64	1	1	4	1	32	3	0	.094
1965 2 teams		HOU	N (1G 0-0)		BAL	A (27G 1-2)													
" total	1	2	.333	2.88	28	2	0	59.1	61	23	41	0	1	1	1	13	3	0	.231
1967 CHI N	0	0	—	9.00	3	0	0	5	2	1	2	0	0	0	0	0	0	0	—
14 yrs.	81	91	.471	3.78	412	171	44	1548	1442	725	849	11	26	23	23	*			
1 yr.	7	2	.778	4.12	25	3	0	74.1	64	29	53	0	5	1	2	25	8	1	.320

WORLD SERIES

1955 NY A	0	1	.000	11.25	1	1	0	4	5	2	2	0	0	0	0	2	0	0	.000
1956	1	0	1.000	0.00	2	2	1	10.2	1	4	7	1	0	0	0	3	1	0	.333
1957	1	1	.500	3.72	2	1	0	9.2	8	5	6	0	1	0	0	2	0	0	.000
1958	1	0	1.000	0.96	2	2	0	9.1	9	6	9	0	0	0	0	2	0	0	.000
1962 SF N	1	0	1.000	3.86	3	0	0	2.1	1	2	0	0	1	0	0	0	0	0	—
5 yrs.	4	2	.667	2.75	10	6	1	36	24	19	24	1	2	0	0	9	1	0	.111

Frank Lary

LARY, FRANK STRONG (Mule, The Yankee Killer)
Brother of Al Lary.
B. Apr. 10, 1930, Northport, Ala.
BR TR 5'11" 175 lbs.

1954 DET A	0	0	—	2.45	3	0	0	3.2	4	3	5	0	0	0	0	0	0	0	—
1955	14	15	.483	3.10	36	31	16	235	232	89	98	2	1	1	0	82	16	0	.195
1956	21	13	.618	3.15	41	38	20	294	289	116	165	3	0	0	0	103	19	1	.184
1957	11	16	.407	3.98	40	35	12	237.2	250	72	107	2	0	1	3	73	9	0	.123
1958	16	15	.516	2.90	39	34	19	260.1	249	68	131	3	0	2	1	88	15	1	.170
1959	17	10	.630	3.55	32	32	11	223	225	46	137	3	0	0	0	80	10	1	.125
1960	15	15	.500	3.51	38	36	15	274.1	262	62	149	2	0	0	1	93	17	2	.183
1961	23	9	.719	3.24	36	36	22	275.1	252	66	146	4	0	0	0	108	25	0	.231
1962	2	6	.250	5.74	17	14	2	80	98	21	41	1	0	1	0	24	4	0	.167
1963	4	9	.308	3.27	16	14	6	107.1	90	26	46	0	0	0	0	35	8	0	.229
1964 3 teams		DET	A (6G 0-2)		NY	N (13G 2-3)		MIL	N (5G 1-0)										
" total	3	5	.375	5.03	24	14	3	87.2	101	24	37	1	0	0	1	27	2	0	.074

	W	L	PCT	ERA	G	GS	CG	IP	H	BB	SO	ShO	Relief Pitching W L SV	BATTING AB H HR	BA

Frank Lary continued

1965 2 teams	NY	N (14G 1–3)		CHI	A (14G 1–0)										
" total	2	3	.400	3.32	28	8	0	84	71	23	37	0	0 0 3	21 5 0	.238
12 yrs.	128	116	.525	3.49	350	292	126	2162.1	2123	616	1099	21	1 5 11	734 130 6	.177
1 yr.	1	0	1.000	4.05	14	1	0	26.2	23	7	14	0	0 0 2	2 1 0	.500

Bill Lathrop

LATHROP, WILLIAM GEORGE BR TR 6'2½" 184 lbs.
B. Aug. 12, 1891, Hanover, Wis. D. Nov. 20, 1958, Janesville, Wis.

1913 CHI A	0	0	–	4.24	6	0	0	17	16	12	9	0	0 0 0	4 0 0	.000
1914	1	2	.333	2.64	19	1	0	47.2	41	19	7	0	1 1 0	12 0 0	.000
2 yrs.	1	2	.333	3.06	25	1	0	64.2	57	31	16	0	1 1 0	16 0 0	.000
2 yrs.	1	2	.333	3.06	25	1	0	64.2	57	31	16	0	1 1 0	16 0 0	.000

Barry Latman

LATMAN, ARNOLD BARRY BR TR 6'3" 210 lbs.
B. May 21, 1936, Los Angeles, Calif.

1957 CHI A	1	2	.333	8.03	7	2	0	12.1	12	13	9	0	1 1 1	1 0 0	.000
1958	3	0	1.000	0.76	13	3	1	47.2	27	17	28	1	1 0 0	12 1 0	.083
1959	8	5	.615	3.75	37	21	5	156	138	72	97	2	0 0 0	47 6 0	.128
1960 CLE A	7	7	.500	4.03	31	20	4	147.1	146	72	94	0	1 1 0	41 9 0	.220
1961	13	5	.722	4.02	45	18	4	176.2	163	54	108	2	6 0 5	55 4 0	.073
1962	8	13	.381	4.17	45	21	7	179.1	179	72	117	1	2 2 5	53 10 1	.189
1963	7	12	.368	4.94	38	21	4	149.1	146	52	133	2	1 1 2	44 8 1	.182
1964 LA A	6	10	.375	3.85	40	18	2	138	128	52	81	1	3 2 2	40 5 0	.125
1965 CAL A	1	1	.500	2.84	18	0	0	31.2	30	16	18	0	1 1 0	2 0 0	.000
1966 HOU N	4	7	.222	2.71	39	9	1	103	88	35	74	1	1 2 1	26 4 0	.154
1967	3	6	.333	4.52	39	1	0	77.2	73	34	70	0	3 6 0	11 1 0	.091
11 yrs.	59	68	.465	3.91	344	134	28	1219	1130	489	829	10	20 16 16	332 48 2	.145
3 yrs.	12	7	.632	3.33	57	26	6	216	177	102	134	3	2 1 1	60 7 0	.117

Bob Lawrence

LAWRENCE, ROBERT ANDREW (Larry) BR TR 5'11" 180 lbs.
B. Dec. 14, 1899, Brooklyn, N.Y.

| 1924 CHI A | 0 | 0 | – | 9.00 | 1 | 0 | 0 | 1 | 1 | 1 | 1 | 0 | 0 0 0 | 0 0 0 | – |

Danny Lazar

LAZAR, JOHN DAN BL TL 6'1" 190 lbs.
B. Nov. 14, 1943, East Chicago, Ind.

1968 CHI A	0	1	.000	4.05	8	1	0	13.1	14	4	11	0	0 0 0	2 0 0	.000
1969	0	0	–	6.53	9	3	0	20.2	21	11	9	0	0 0 0	4 0 0	.000
2 yrs.	0	1	.000	5.56	17	4	0	34	35	15	20	0	0 0 0	6 0 0	.000
2 yrs.	0	1	.000	5.56	17	4	0	34	35	15	20	0	0 0 0	6 0 0	.000

Thornton Lee

LEE, THORNTON STARR (Lefty) BL TL 6'3" 205 lbs.
Father of Don Lee.
B. Sept. 13, 1906, Sonoma, Calif.

1933 CLE A	1	1	.500	4.15	3	2	2	17.1	13	11	7	0	0 0 0	8 3 0	.375
1934	1	1	.500	5.04	24	6	0	85.2	105	44	41	0	0 0 0	21 2 0	.095
1935	7	10	.412	4.04	32	20	8	180.2	179	71	81	1	2 1 1	61 12 0	.197
1936	3	5	.375	4.89	43	8	2	127	138	67	49	0	1 2 3	41 5 0	.122
1937 CHI A	12	10	.545	3.52	30	25	13	204.2	209	60	80	2	0 0 0	71 15 0	.211
1938	13	12	.520	3.49	33	30	18	245.1	252	94	77	0	0 1 1	97 25 0	.258
1939	15	11	.577	4.21	33	29	15	235	260	70	81	2	0 1 3	91 15 0	.165
1940	12	13	.480	3.47	28	27	24	228	223	56	87	1	0 0 0	84 23 0	.274
1941	22	11	.667	2.37	35	34	30	300.1	258	92	130	3	0 0 1	114 29 0	.254
1942	2	6	.250	3.32	11	8	6	76	82	31	25	1	0 0 0	30 6 0	.200
1943	5	9	.357	4.18	19	19	7	127	129	50	35	1	0 0 0	42 3 0	.071
1944	3	9	.250	3.02	15	14	6	113.1	105	25	39	0	0 0 0	42 4 0	.095
1945	15	12	.556	2.44	29	28	19	228.1	208	76	108	1	1 0 0	78 14 0	.179
1946	2	4	.333	3.53	7	7	2	43.1	39	23	23	0	0 0 0	15 4 0	.267
1947	3	7	.300	4.47	21	11	2	86.2	86	56	57	1	0 3 1	29 6 0	.207
1948 NY N	1	3	.250	4.41	11	4	1	32.2	41	12	17	0	1 0 0	11 1 0	.091
16 yrs.	117	124	.485	3.56	374	272	155	2331.1	2327	838	937	14	4 9 10	835 167 0	.200
11 yrs.	104	104	.500	3.33	261	232	142	1888	1851	633	742	13	1 5 6	693 144 0	.208
			9th				8th	9th			5th				

Dummy Leitner

LEITNER, GEORGE MICHAEL BL TR 5'7" 120 lbs.
B. June 19, 1871, Parkton, Md. D. Feb. 20, 1960, Baltimore, Md.

1901 2 teams	PHI	A (1G 0–0)		NY	N (2G 0–2)										
" total	0	2	.000	4.05	3	2	2	20	28	5	4	0	0 0 0	8 1 0	.125
1902 2 teams	CLE	A (1G 0–0)		CHI	A (1G 0–0)										
" total	0	0	–	7.50	2	1	0	12	20	3	0	0	0 0 0	7 1 0	.143
2 yrs.	0	2	.000	5.34	5	3	2	32	48	8	4	0	0 0 0	15 2 0	.133
1 yr.	0	2	.000	13.50	1	0	0	4	9	2	0	0	0 0 0	3 0 0	.000

Bob Lemon

LEMON, ROBERT GRANVILLE BL TR 6' 180 lbs.
B. Sept. 22, 1920, San Bernardino, Calif.
Manager 1970–72, 1977–79, 1981–82.
Hall of Fame 1976.

1941 CLE A	0	0	–	0.00	0	0	0	0	0	0	0	0	0 0 0	4 1 0	.250
1942	0	0	–	0.00	0	0	0	0	0	0	0	0	0 0 0	5 0 0	.000
1946	4	5	.444	2.49	32	5	1	94	77	68	39	0	3 2 1	89 16 1	.180
1947	11	5	.688	3.44	37	15	6	167.1	150	97	65	1	1 2 3	56 18 2	.321
1948	20	14	.588	2.82	43	37	20	293.2	231	129	147	10	1 1 2	119 34 5	.286
1949	22	10	.688	2.99	37	33	22	279.2	211	137	138	2	0 0 0	108 29 7	.269
1950	23	11	.676	3.84	44	37	22	288	281	146	170	3	1 0 3	136 37 6	.272
1951	17	14	.548	3.52	42	34	17	263.1	244	124	132	1	0 0 0	102 21 3	.206
1952	22	11	.667	2.50	42	36	28	309.2	236	105	131	5	0 1 4	124 28 2	.226
1953	21	15	.583	3.36	41	36	23	286.2	283	110	98	5	1 1 1	112 26 0	.232

Pitcher Register

	W	L	PCT	ERA	G	GS	CG	IP	H	BB	SO	ShO	Relief Pitching W L SV	BATTING AB H HR	BA

Bob Lemon continued

1954	23	7	.767	2.72	36	33	21	258.1	228	92	110	2	1 0 0	98 21 2	.214
1955	18	10	.643	3.88	35	31	5	211.1	218	74	100	0	1 0 2	78 19 1	.244
1956	20	14	.588	3.03	39	35	21	255.1	230	89	94	2	0 0 3	93 18 5	.194
1957	6	11	.353	4.60	21	17	2	117.1	129	64	45	0	1 2 0	46 3 1	.065
1958	0	1	.000	5.33	11	1	0	25.1	41	16	8	0	0 0 0	13 3 0	.231
15 yrs.	207	128	.618	3.23	460	350	188	2850	2559	1251	1277	31	12 10 22	*	

WORLD SERIES
1948 CLE A	2	0	1.000	1.65	2	2	1	16.1	16	7	6	0	0 0 0	7 0 0	.000
1954	0	2	.000	6.75	2	2	1	13.1	16	8	11	0	0 0 0	6 0 0	.000
2 yrs.	2	2	.500	3.94	4	4	2	29.2	32	15	17	0	0 0 0	13 0 0	.000

Dave Lemonds
LEMONDS, DAVID LEE
B. July 5, 1948, Charlotte, N. C.
BL TL 6'1½" 180 lbs.

1969 CHI N	0	1	.000	3.60	2	1	0	5	5	5	0	0	0 0 0	1 0 0	.000
1972 CHI A	4	7	.364	2.95	31	18	0	94.2	87	38	69	0	1 1 0	25 3 0	.120
2 yrs.	4	8	.333	2.98	33	19	0	99.2	92	43	69	0	1 1 0	26 3 0	.115
1 yr.	4	7	.364	2.95	31	18	0	94.2	87	38	69	0	1 1 0	25 3 0	.120

Rudy Leopold
LEOPOLD, RUDOLPH MATAS
B. July 27, 1905, Grand Cane, La. D. Sept. 3, 1965, Baton Rouge, La.
BL TL 6' 160 lbs.

| 1928 CHI A | 0 | 0 | — | 3.86 | 2 | 0 | 0 | 2.1 | 3 | 0 | 0 | 0 | 0 0 0 | 1 0 0 | .000 |

Dixie Leverett
LEVERETT, GORHAM VANCE
B. Mar. 29, 1894, Georgetown, Tex. D. Feb. 20, 1957, Beaverton, Ore.
BR TR 5'11" 190 lbs.

1922 CHI A	13	10	.565	3.32	33	27	16	224.2	224	79	60	4	0 0 2	83 21 0	.253
1923	10	13	.435	4.06	38	24	9	192.2	212	64	64	0	1 3 3	60 16 0	.267
1924	2	3	.400	5.82	21	11	4	99	123	41	29	0	0 0 0	32 6 0	.188
1926	1	1	.500	6.00	6	3	1	24	31	7	12	0	0 0 0	7 1 0	.143
1929 BOS N	3	7	.300	6.36	24	12	3	97.2	135	30	28	0	0 1 1	32 6 0	.188
5 yrs.	29	34	.460	4.50	122	77	33	638	725	221	193	4	1 4 6	214 50 0	.234
4 yrs.	26	27	.491	4.16	98	65	30	540.1	590	191	165	4	1 3 5	182 44 0	.242

Dick Littlefield
LITTLEFIELD, RICHARD BERNARD
B. Mar. 18, 1926, Detroit, Mich.
BL TL 6' 180 lbs.

1950 BOS A	2	2	.500	9.26	15	2	0	23.1	27	24	13	0	2 0 1	4 0 0	.000
1951 CHI A	1	1	.500	8.38	4	2	0	9.2	9	17	7	0	1 0 0	1 0 0	.000
1952 2 teams	DET A (28G 0-3)	STL A (7G 2-3)
" total	2	6	.250	3.54	35	6	3	94	81	42	66	0	1 3 1	23 2 0	.087
1953 STL A	7	12	.368	5.08	36	22	2	152.1	153	84	104	0	2 1 0	42 8 0	.190
1954 2 teams	BAL A (3G 0-0)	PIT N (23G 10-11)
" total	10	11	.476	3.86	26	21	7	161	148	91	97	1	1 0 0	50 8 0	.160
1955 PIT N	5	12	.294	5.12	35	17	4	130	148	68	70	1	1 3 0	34 6 0	.176
1956 3 teams	PIT N (6G 0-0)	STL N (3G 0-2)	NY N (31G 4-4)
" total	4	6	.400	4.37	40	11	0	119.1	101	49	80	0	1 2 2	28 2 0	.071
1957 NY N	2	3	.400	5.35	48	2	0	65.2	76	37	51	0	2 1 4	11 2 0	.182
1958 MIL N	0	1	.000	4.26	4	0	0	6.1	7	1	7	0	0 0 0	0 0 0	—
9 yrs.	33	54	.379	4.71	243	83	16	761.2	750	413	495	2	11 11 9	193 28 0	.145
1 yr.	1	1	.500	8.38	4	2	0	9.2	9	17	7	0	1 0 0	1 0 0	.000

Bob Locker
LOCKER, ROBERT AWTRY
B. Mar. 15, 1938, Hull, Iowa
BR TR 6'3" 200 lbs.
BB 1968

1965 CHI A	5	2	.714	3.15	51	0	0	91.1	71	30	69	0	5 2 2	14 0 0	.000
1966	9	8	.529	2.46	56	0	0	95	73	23	70	0	9 8 12	16 4 0	.250
1967	7	5	.583	2.09	77	0	0	124.2	102	23	80	0	7 5 20	10 0 0	.000
1968	5	4	.556	2.29	70	0	0	90.1	78	27	62	0	5 4 10	8 0 0	.000
1969 2 teams	CHI A (17G 2-3)	SEA A (51G 3-3)
" total	5	6	.455	3.14	68	0	0	100.1	95	32	61	0	5 6 10	13 1 0	.077
1970 2 teams	MIL A (28G 0-1)	OAK A (38G 3-3)
" total	3	4	.429	3.07	66	0	0	88	86	29	52	0	3 4 7	7 1 0	.143
1971 OAK A	7	2	.778	2.88	47	0	0	72	68	19	46	0	7 2 6	6 0 0	.000
1972	6	1	.857	2.65	56	0	0	78	69	16	47	0	6 1 10	6 0 0	.000
1973 CHI N	10	6	.625	2.55	63	0	0	106	96	42	76	0	10 6 18	15 1 0	.067
1975	0	1	.000	4.91	22	0	0	33	38	16	14	0	0 1 0	0 0 0	—
10 yrs.	57	39	.594	2.76	576	0	0	878.2	776	257	577	0	57 39 95	95 7 0	.074
5 yrs.	28	22	.560	2.68	271	0	0	423.1	350	109	296	0	28 22 48 5th	49 4 0 6th	.082

LEAGUE CHAMPIONSHIP SERIES
1971 OAK A	0	0	—	0.00	1	0	0	.2	0	2	0	0	0 0 0	0 0 0	—
1972	0	0	—	13.50	2	0	0	2	4	0	1	0	0 0 0	0 0 0	—
2 yrs.	0	0	—	10.13	3	0	0	2.2	4	2	1	0	0 0 0	0 0 0	—

WORLD SERIES
| 1972 OAK A | 0 | 0 | — | 0.00 | 1 | 0 | 0 | .1 | 1 | 0 | 0 | 0 | 0 0 0 | 0 0 0 | — |

Ed Lopat
LOPAT, EDMUND WALTER (Steady Eddie)
Born Edmund Walter Lopatynski.
B. June 21, 1918, New York, N. Y.
Manager 1963-64.
BL TL 5'10" 185 lbs.

1944 CHI A	11	10	.524	3.26	27	25	13	210	217	59	75	1	0 0 0	81 25 0	.309
1945	10	13	.435	4.11	26	24	17	199.1	226	56	74	1	0 0 1	82 24 1	.293
1946	13	13	.500	2.73	29	29	20	231	216	48	89	2	0 0 0	87 22 0	.253
1947	16	13	.552	2.81	31	31	22	252.2	241	73	109	3	0 0 0	96 19 0	.198
1948 NY A	17	11	.607	3.65	33	31	13	226.2	246	66	83	3	1 0 0	81 14 0	.173
1949	15	10	.600	3.26	31	30	14	215.1	222	69	70	4	0 0 1	76 20 1	.263
1950	18	8	.692	3.47	35	32	15	236.1	244	65	72	3	1 0 1	82 19 0	.232
1951	21	9	.700	2.91	31	31	20	234.2	209	71	93	5	0 0 0	84 15 3	.179
1952	10	5	.667	2.53	20	19	10	149.1	127	53	56	2	0 0 0	52 9 0	.173

Pitcher Register

	W	L	PCT	ERA	G	GS	CG	IP	H	BB	SO	ShO	Relief Pitching W L SV	BATTING AB H HR	BA

Ed Lopat continued

1953	16	4	.800	2.42	25	24	9	178.1	169	32	50	3	0 0 0	63 12 0	.190
1954	12	4	.750	3.55	26	23	7	170	189	33	54	0	0 0 0	57 1 0	.018
1955 2 teams			NY	A (16G 4–8)		BAL	A (10G 3–4)								
" total	7	12	.368	3.91	26	19	4	135.2	158	25	34	1	0 3 0	46 7 0	.152
12 yrs.	166	112	.597	3.21	340	318	164	2439.1	2464	650	859	28	2 3 3	887 187 5	.211
4 yrs.	50	49	.505	3.18	113	109	72	893	900	236	347	7	0 0 1	346 90 1	.260

WORLD SERIES
1949 NY A	1	0	1.000	6.35	1	1	0	5.2	9	1	4	0	0 0 0	3 1 0	.333
1950	0	0	–	2.25	1	1	0	8	9	0	5	0	0 0 0	2 1 0	.500
1951	2	0	1.000	0.50	2	2	2	18	10	3	4	0	0 0 0	8 1 0	.125
1952	0	1	.000	4.76	2	2	0	11.1	14	4	3	0	0 0 0	3 1 0	.333
1953	1	0	1.000	2.00	1	1	1	9	9	4	3	0	0 0 0	3 0 0	.000
5 yrs.	4	1	.800	2.60	7	7	3	52	51	12	19	0	0 0 0	19 4 0	.211

Grover Lowdermilk

LOWDERMILK, GROVER CLEVELAND (Slim)   BR TR 6'4"   190 lbs.
Brother of Lou Lowdermilk.
B. Jan. 15, 1885, Sandborn, Ind.   D. Mar. 31, 1968, Odin, Ill.

1909 STL N	0	2	.000	6.21	7	3	1	29	28	30	14	0	0 0 0	10 1 0	.100
1911	0	1	.000	7.29	11	2	1	33.1	37	33	15	0	0 0 0	9 1 0	.111
1912 CHI N	0	1	.000	9.69	2	1	1	13	17	14	8	0	0 0 0	4 0 0	.000
1915 2 teams			STL	A (38G 9–17)		DET	A (7G 4–1)								
" total	13	18	.419	3.24	45	34	14	250.1	200	157	148	1	3 2 0	80 10 0	.125
1916 2 teams			DET	A (1G 0–0)		CLE	A (10G 1–5)								
" total	1	5	.167	5.75	11	9	2	51.2	52	48	28	0	0 0 0	18 3 0	.167
1917 STL A	2	1	.667	1.42	3	2	2	19	16	4	9	1	0 1 0	7 0 0	.000
1918	2	6	.250	3.15	13	11	4	80	74	38	25	0	0 0 0	28 7 0	.250
1919 2 teams			STL	A (7G 0–0)		CHI	A (20G 5–5)								
" total	5	5	.500	2.57	27	11	3	108.2	101	47	49	0	0 2 0	35 3 0	.086
1920 CHI A	0	0	–	6.75	3	0	0	5.1	9	5	0	0	0 0 0	0 0 0	–
9 yrs.	23	39	.371	3.81	122	73	30	590.1	534	376	296	2	3 5 0	191 25 0	.131
2 yrs.	5	5	.500	3.00	23	11	5	102	104	48	43	0	0 2 0	34 3 0	.088

WORLD SERIES
| 1919 CHI A | 0 | 0 | – | 9.00 | 1 | 0 | 0 | 1 | 2 | 1 | 0 | 0 | 0 0 0 | 0 0 0 | – |

Turk Lown

LOWN, OMAR JOSEPH   BR TR 6'   180 lbs.
B. May 30, 1924, Brooklyn, N. Y.

1951 CHI N	4	9	.308	5.46	31	18	3	127	80	90	39	1	1 2 0	39 8 0	.205
1952	4	11	.267	4.37	33	19	5	156.2	154	93	73	0	1 2 0	50 7 0	.140
1953	8	7	.533	5.16	49	12	2	148.1	166	84	76	0	7 3 3	48 6 0	.125
1954	0	2	.000	6.14	15	0	0	22	23	15	16	0	0 2 0	0 0 0	–
1956	9	8	.529	3.58	61	0	0	110.2	95	78	74	0	9 8 13	23 5 1	.217
1957	5	7	.417	3.77	67	0	0	93	74	51	51	0	5 7 12	10 2 0	.200
1958 3 teams			CHI	N (4G 0–0)		CIN	N (11G 0–2)		CHI	A (27G 3–3)					
" total	3	5	.375	4.31	42	0	0	56.1	63	43	53	0	3 5 8	10 3 0	.300
1959 CHI A	9	2	.818	2.89	60	0	0	93.1	73	42	63	0	9 2 15	12 3 0	.250
1960	2	3	.400	3.88	45	0	0	67.1	60	34	39	0	2 3 5	5 1 0	.200
1961	7	5	.583	3.43	59	0	0	101	87	35	50	0	7 5 11	14 0 0	.000
1962	4	2	.667	3.04	42	0	0	56.1	58	25	40	0	4 2 6	3 0 0	.000
11 yrs.	55	61	.474	4.12	504	49	10	1032	933	590	574	1	48 41 73	214 35 1	.164
5 yrs.	25	15	.625	3.19	233	0	0	358.2	327	164	232	0	25 15 45	43 7 0	.163
													7th 7th		

WORLD SERIES
| 1959 CHI A | 0 | 0 | – | 0.00 | 3 | 0 | 0 | 3.1 | 2 | 1 | 3 | 0 | 0 0 0 | 0 0 0 | – |

Sparky Lyle

LYLE, ALBERT WALTER   BL TL 6'1"   182 lbs.
B. July 22, 1944, DuBois, Pa.

1967 BOS A	1	2	.333	2.28	27	0	0	43.1	33	14	42	0	1 2 5	8 2 0	.250
1968	6	1	.857	2.74	49	0	0	65.2	67	14	52	0	6 1 11	8 1 0	.125
1969	8	3	.727	2.54	71	0	0	102.2	91	48	93	0	8 3 17	17 2 0	.118
1970	1	7	.125	3.90	63	0	0	67	62	34	51	0	1 7 20	13 0 0	.000
1971	6	4	.600	2.77	50	0	0	52	41	23	37	0	6 4 16	3 3 0	1.000
1972 NY A	9	5	.643	1.91	59	0	0	108.1	84	29	75	0	9 5 35	21 4 0	.190
1973	5	9	.357	2.51	51	0	0	82.1	66	18	63	0	5 9 27	0 0 0	–
1974	9	3	.750	1.66	66	0	0	114	93	43	89	0	9 3 15	1 0 0	.000
1975	5	7	.417	3.12	49	0	0	89.1	94	36	65	0	5 7 6	0 0 0	–
1976	7	8	.467	2.26	64	0	0	103.2	82	42	61	0	7 8 23	0 0 0	–
1977	13	5	.722	2.17	72	0	0	137	131	33	68	0	13 5 26	0 0 0	–
1978	9	3	.750	3.47	59	0	0	111.2	116	33	33	0	9 3 9	0 0 0	–
1979 TEX A	5	8	.385	3.13	67	0	0	95	78	28	48	0	5 8 13	0 0 0	–
1980 2 teams			TEX	A (49G 3–2)		PHI	N (10G 0–0)								
" total	3	2	.600	4.26	59	0	0	95	108	34	49	0	3 2 10	0 0 0	–
1981 PHI N	9	6	.600	4.44	48	0	0	75	85	33	29	0	9 6 2	5 2 0	.400
1982 2 teams			PHI	N (34G 3–3)		CHI	A (11G 0–0)								
" total	3	3	.500	4.62	45	0	0	48.2	61	19	18	0	3 3 3	2 1 0	.500
16 yrs.	99	76	.566	2.88	899	0	0	1390.2	1292	481	873	0	99 76 238	78 15 0	.192
					4th								4th 2nd		
1 yr.	0	0	–	3.00	11	0	0	12	11	7	6	0	0 0 1	0 0 0	–

DIVISIONAL PLAYOFF SERIES
| 1981 PHI N | 0 | 0 | – | 0.00 | 3 | 0 | 0 | 2.1 | 4 | 2 | 1 | 0 | 0 0 0 | 0 0 0 | – |

LEAGUE CHAMPIONSHIP SERIES
| 1976 NY A | 0 | 0 | – | 0.00 | 1 | 0 | 0 | 1 | 0 | 1 | 0 | 0 | 0 0 1 | 0 0 0 | – |
| 1977 | 2 | 0 | 1.000 | 0.96 | 4 | 0 | 0 | 9.1 | 7 | 0 | 3 | 0 | 2 0 0 | 0 0 0 | – |

Pitcher Register

	W	L	PCT	ERA	G	GS	CG	IP	H	BB	SO	ShO	Relief Pitching W	L	SV	BATTING AB	H	HR	BA

Sparky Lyle continued

| 1978 | 0 | 0 | – | 13.50 | 1 | 0 | 0 | 1.1 | 3 | 0 | 0 | 0 | 0 | 0 | 0 | 0 | 0 | 0 | – |
| 3 yrs. | 2 | 0 | 1.000 | 2.31 | 6 | 0 | 0 | 11.2 | 10 | 1 | 3 | 0 | 2 | 0 | 1 | 0 | 0 | 0 | – |

WORLD SERIES
1976 NY A	0	0	–	0.00	2	0	0	2.2	1	0	3	0	0	0	0	0	0	0	–
1977	1	0	1.000	1.93	2	0	0	4.2	2	0	2	0	1	0	0	2	0	0	.000
2 yrs.	1	0	1.000	1.23	4	0	0	7.1	3	0	5	0	1	0	0	2	0	0	.000

Ted Lyons

LYONS, THEODORE AMAR
B. Dec. 28, 1900, Lake Charles, La.
Manager 1946-48.
Hall of Fame 1955.

BB TR 5'11" 200 lbs.
BR 1925-27

1923 CHI A	2	1	.667	6.35	9	1	0	22.2	30	15	6	0	2	0	0	5	1	0	.200
1924	12	11	.522	4.87	41	22	12	216.1	279	72	52	0	1	1	3	77	17	0	.221
1925	21	11	.656	3.26	43	32	19	262.2	274	83	45	5	2	2	3	97	18	0	.186
1926	18	16	.529	3.01	39	31	24	283.2	268	106	51	3	1	3	2	104	22	0	.212
1927	22	14	.611	2.84	39	34	30	307.2	291	67	71	2	0	2	2	110	28	1	.255
1928	15	14	.517	3.98	39	27	21	240	276	68	60	0	3	1	6	91	23	0	.253
1929	14	20	.412	4.10	37	31	21	259.1	276	76	57	1	1	3	2	91	20	0	.220
1930	22	15	.595	3.78	42	36	29	297.2	331	57	69	1	2	1	1	122	38	1	.311
1931	4	6	.400	4.01	22	12	7	101	117	33	16	0	1	1	0	33	5	0	.152
1932	10	15	.400	3.28	33	26	19	230.2	243	71	58	1	0	1	2	73	19	1	.260
1933	10	21	.323	4.38	36	27	14	228	260	74	74	2	4	3	1	91	26	1	.286
1934	11	13	.458	4.87	30	24	21	205.1	249	66	53	0	0	1	1	97	20	1	.206
1935	15	8	.652	3.02	23	22	19	190.2	194	56	54	3	0	1	0	82	18	0	.220
1936	10	13	.435	5.14	26	24	15	182	227	45	48	1	0	1	0	70	11	0	.157
1937	12	7	.632	4.15	22	22	11	169.1	182	45	45	0	0	0	0	57	12	0	.211
1938	9	11	.450	3.70	23	23	17	194.2	238	52	54	1	0	0	0	72	14	0	.194
1939	14	6	.700	2.76	21	21	16	172.2	162	26	65	0	0	0	0	61	18	0	.295
1940	12	8	.600	3.24	22	22	17	186.1	188	37	72	4	0	0	0	75	18	0	.240
1941	12	10	.545	3.70	22	22	19	187.1	199	37	63	2	0	0	0	74	20	0	.270
1942	14	6	.700	2.10	20	20	20	180.1	167	26	50	1	0	0	0	67	16	0	.239
1946	1	4	.200	2.32	5	5	5	42.2	38	9	10	0	0	0	0	14	0	0	.000
21 yrs.	260	230	.531	3.67	594	484	356	4161	4489	1121	1073	27	17	21	23	*			
21 yrs.	260	230	.531	3.67	594	484	356	4161	4489	1121	1073	27	17	21	23	1563	364	5	.233
	1st	1st			2nd		1st	1st		2nd	7th	6th							

Frank Mack

MACK, FRANK GEORGE (Stubby)
B. Feb. 2, 1900, Oklahoma City, Okla.

BR TR 6'1½" 180 lbs.

1922 CHI A	2	2	.500	3.67	8	4	1	34.1	36	16	11	1	0	0	0	12	3	0	.250
1923	0	1	.000	4.24	11	0	0	23.1	23	11	6	0	0	1	0	6	0	0	.000
1925	0	0	–	9.45	8	0	0	13.1	24	13	6	0	0	0	0	3	1	0	.333
3 yrs.	2	3	.400	4.94	27	4	1	71	83	40	23	1	0	1	0	21	4	0	.190
3 yrs.	2	3	.400	4.94	27	4	1	71	83	40	23	1	0	1	0	21	4	0	.190

Jim Magnuson

MAGNUSON, JAMES ROBERT
B. Aug. 18, 1946, Marinette, Wis.

BR TL 6'2" 190 lbs.

1970 CHI A	1	5	.167	4.80	13	6	0	45	45	16	20	0	0	0	0	11	0	0	.000
1971	2	1	.667	4.50	15	4	0	30	30	16	11	0	0	0	0	4	0	0	.000
1973 NY A	0	1	.000	4.28	8	0	0	27.1	38	9	9	0	0	1	0	0	0	0	–
3 yrs.	3	7	.300	4.57	36	10	0	102.1	113	41	40	0	0	1	0	15	0	0	.000
2 yrs.	3	6	.333	4.68	28	10	0	75	75	32	31	0	0	0	0	15	0	0	.000

Bob Mahoney

MAHONEY, ROBERT PAUL
B. June 20, 1928, LeRoy, Minn.

BR TR 6'1" 185 lbs.

1951 2 teams			CHI	A	(3G 0–0)	STL	A	(30G 2–5)											
" total	2	5	.286	4.52	33	4	0	87.2	91	46	33	0	2	2	0	18	4	0	.222
1952 STL A	0	0	–	18.00	3	0	0	3	8	4	1	0	0	0	0	0	0	0	–
2 yrs.	2	5	.286	4.96	36	4	0	90.2	99	50	34	0	2	2	0	18	4	0	.222
1 yr.	0	0	–	5.40	3	0	0	6.2	5	5	3	0	0	0	0	0	0	0	–

Gordon Maltzberger

MALTZBERGER, GORDON RALPH (Maltzy)
B. Sept. 4, 1912, Utopia, Tex. D. Dec. 11, 1974, Rialto, Calif.

BR TR 6' 170 lbs.

1943 CHI A	7	4	.636	2.46	37	0	0	98.2	86	24	48	0	7	4	14	25	3	0	.120
1944	10	5	.667	2.96	46	0	0	91.1	81	19	49	0	10	5	12	22	3	0	.136
1946	2	0	1.000	1.59	19	0	0	39.2	30	6	17	0	2	0	2	6	0	0	.000
1947	1	4	.200	3.39	33	0	0	63.2	61	25	22	0	1	4	5	7	1	0	.143
4 yrs.	20	13	.606	2.70	135	0	0	293.1	258	74	136	0	20	13	33	60	7	0	.117
4 yrs.	20	13	.606	2.70	135	0	0	293.1	258	74	136	0	20	13	33	60	7	0	.117
															10th				

Leo Mangum

MANGUM, LEON ALLEN (Blackie)
B. May 24, 1898, Durham, N. C. D. July 9, 1974, Lima, Ohio

BR TR 6'1" 187 lbs.

1924 CHI A	1	4	.200	7.09	13	7	1	47	69	25	12	0	1	0	0	14	1	0	.071
1925	1	0	1.000	7.80	7	0	0	15	25	6	6	0	1	0	0	4	2	0	.500
1928 NY N	0	0	–	15.00	1	1	0	3	6	5	1	0	0	0	0	1	1	0	1.000
1932 BOS N	0	0	–	5.23	7	0	0	10.1	17	0	3	0	0	0	0	2	0	0	.000
1933	4	3	.571	3.32	25	5	2	84	93	11	28	1	2	1	0	22	2	0	.091
1934	5	3	.625	5.72	29	3	1	94.1	127	23	28	0	4	2	1	32	9	0	.281
1935	0	0	–	3.86	3	0	0	4.2	6	2	0	0	0	0	0	0	0	0	–
7 yrs.	11	10	.524	5.37	85	16	4	258.1	343	72	78	1	8	3	1	75	15	0	.200
2 yrs.	2	4	.333	7.26	20	7	1	62	94	31	18	0	2	0	0	18	3	0	.167

Pitcher Register

	W	L	PCT	ERA	G	GS	CG	IP	H	BB	SO	ShO	Relief Pitching W L SV	BATTING AB H HR	BA

Moxie Manuel
MANUEL, MARK GARFIELD
D. Apr. 26, 1924, Memphis, Tenn.

Year	Team	W	L	PCT	ERA	G	GS	CG	IP	H	BB	SO	ShO	RW	RL	SV	AB	H	HR	BA
1905	WAS A	0	1	.000	5.40	3	1	1	10	9	3	3	0	0	1	0	4	1	0	.250
1908	CHI A	3	3	.500	3.28	18	6	3	60.1	52	25	25	0	1	0	1	16	1	0	.063
2 yrs.		3	4	.429	3.58	21	7	4	70.1	61	28	28	0	1	1	1	20	2	0	.100
1 yr.		3	3	.500	3.28	18	6	3	60.1	52	25	25	0	1	0	1	16	1	0	.063

Johnny Marcum
MARCUM, JOHN ALFRED (Footsie)
B. Sept. 9, 1908, Campbellsburg, Ky.
BL TR 5'11" 197 lbs.

Year	Team	W	L	PCT	ERA	G	GS	CG	IP	H	BB	SO	ShO	RW	RL	SV	AB	H	HR	BA
1933	PHI A	3	2	.600	1.95	5	5	4	37	28	20	14	2	0	0	0	12	2	0	.167
1934		14	11	.560	4.50	37	31	17	232	257	88	92	2	1	2	0	112	30	1	.268
1935		17	12	.586	4.08	39	27	19	242.2	256	83	99	2	2	0	3	119	37	2	.311
1936	BOS A	8	13	.381	4.81	31	23	9	174	194	52	57	1	1	2	1	88	18	2	.205
1937		13	11	.542	4.85	37	23	9	183.2	230	47	59	1	5	1	3	86	23	0	.267
1938		5	6	.455	4.09	15	11	7	92.1	113	25	25	0	1	0	0	37	5	0	.135
1939	2 teams	STL A (12G 2–5)				CHI A (19G 3–3)														
"	total	5	8	.385	6.60	31	12	4	137.2	191	29	46	0	0	3	0	79	26	0	.329
7 yrs.		65	63	.508	4.66	195	132	69	1099.1	1269	344	392	8	10	8	7	*			
1 yr.		3	3	.500	6.00	19	6	2	90	125	19	32	0	0	2	0	57	16	0	.281

Dick Marlowe
MARLOWE, RICHARD BURTON
B. June 27, 1927, Hickory, N. C. D. Dec. 30, 1968, Toledo, Ohio
BR TR 6'2" 165 lbs.

Year	Team	W	L	PCT	ERA	G	GS	CG	IP	H	BB	SO	ShO	RW	RL	SV	AB	H	HR	BA
1951	DET A	0	1	.000	32.40	2	1	0	1.2	5	2	1	0	0	0	0	0	0	0	—
1952		0	2	.000	7.36	4	1	0	11	21	3	3	0	0	1	0	2	0	0	.000
1953		6	7	.462	5.26	42	11	3	119.2	152	42	52	0	3	1	0	32	7	0	.219
1954		5	4	.556	4.18	38	2	0	84	76	40	39	0	5	2	2	18	3	0	.167
1955		1	0	1.000	1.80	4	1	1	15	12	4	9	0	0	0	1	4	0	0	.000
1956	2 teams	DET A (7G 1–1)				CHI A (1G 0–0)														
"	total	1	1	.500	6.00	8	1	0	12	14	10	4	0	1	0	0	1	0	0	.000
6 yrs.		13	15	.464	4.99	98	17	3	243.1	280	101	108	0	9	4	3	57	10	0	.175
1 yr.		0	0	—	9.00	1	0	0	1	2	1	0	0	0	0	0	0	0	0	—

Morrie Martin
MARTIN, MORRIS WEBSTER
B. Sept. 3, 1922, Dixon, Mo.
BL TL 6' 173 lbs.

Year	Team	W	L	PCT	ERA	G	GS	CG	IP	H	BB	SO	ShO	RW	RL	SV	AB	H	HR	BA
1949	BKN N	1	3	.250	7.04	10	4	0	30.2	39	15	15	0	1	0	0	10	2	0	.200
1951	PHI A	11	4	.733	3.78	35	13	3	138	139	63	35	1	5	0	0	50	11	0	.220
1952		0	2	.000	6.39	5	5	0	25.1	32	15	13	0	0	0	0	9	1	0	.111
1953		10	12	.455	4.43	58	11	2	156.1	158	59	64	0	8	5	7	42	4	0	.095
1954	2 teams	PHI A (13G 2–4)				CHI A (35G 5–4)														
"	total	7	8	.467	3.52	48	8	3	122.2	109	43	55	0	4	5	5	32	6	0	.188
1955	CHI A	2	3	.400	3.63	37	0	0	52	50	22	22	0	2	3	2	10	3	0	.300
1956	2 teams	CHI A (10G 1–0)				BAL A (9G 1–1)														
"	total	2	1	.667	6.17	19	0	0	23.1	31	9	12	0	2	1	0	5	1	0	.200
1957	STL N	0	0	—	2.53	4	1	0	10.2	5	4	7	0	0	0	0	2	0	0	.000
1958	2 teams	STL N (17G 3–1)				CLE A (14G 2–0)														
"	total	5	1	.833	3.74	31	0	0	43.1	39	20	21	0	5	1	1	5	0	0	.000
1959	CHI N	0	0	—	19.29	3	0	0	2.1	5	1	1	0	0	0	0	0	0	0	—
10 yrs.		38	34	.528	4.29	250	42	8	604.2	607	251	245	1	27	15	15	165	28	0	.170
3 yrs.		8	7	.533	3.01	82	2	0	140.1	123	53	62	0	6	7	7	30	6	0	.200

Silvio Martinez
MARTINEZ, SILVIO RAMON
B. Aug. 31, 1955, Santiago, Dominican Republic
BR TR 5'10" 170 lbs.

Year	Team	W	L	PCT	ERA	G	GS	CG	IP	H	BB	SO	ShO	RW	RL	SV	AB	H	HR	BA
1977	CHI A	0	1	.000	5.57	10	0	0	21	28	12	10	0	0	1	1	0	0	0	—
1978	STL N	9	8	.529	3.65	22	22	5	138	114	71	45	2	0	0	0	47	8	0	.170
1979		15	8	.652	3.26	32	29	7	207	204	67	102	2	0	0	0	62	8	0	.129
1980		5	10	.333	4.80	25	20	2	120	127	48	39	0	1	0	0	35	3	0	.086
1981		2	5	.286	3.99	18	16	0	97	95	39	34	0	0	0	0	35	7	0	.200
5 yrs.		31	32	.492	3.87	107	87	14	583	568	237	230	4	1	1	1	179	26	0	.145
1 yr.		0	1	.000	5.57	10	0	0	21	28	12	10	0	0	1	1	0	0	0	—

Randy Martz
MARTZ, RANDY CARL
B. May 28, 1956, Harrisburg, Pa.
BL TR 6'4" 210 lbs.

Year	Team	W	L	PCT	ERA	G	GS	CG	IP	H	BB	SO	ShO	RW	RL	SV	AB	H	HR	BA
1980	CHI N	1	2	.333	2.10	6	6	0	30	28	11	5	0	0	0	0	9	1	0	.111
1981		5	7	.417	3.67	33	14	1	108	103	49	32	0	2	0	6	28	6	0	.214
1982		11	10	.524	4.21	28	24	1	147.2	157	36	40	0	1	1	1	42	6	0	.143
1983	CHI A	0	0	—	3.60	1	1	0	5	4	4	1	0	0	0	0	0	0	0	—
4 yrs.		17	19	.472	3.78	68	45	2	290.2	292	100	78	0	3	1	7	79	13	0	.165
1 yr.		0	0	—	3.60	1	1	0	5	4	4	1	0	0	0	0	0	0	0	—

Erskine Mayer
MAYER, JAMES ERSKINE
Born James Erskine. Brother of Sam Mayer.
B. Jan. 16, 1891, Atlanta, Ga. D. Mar. 10, 1957, Los Angeles, Calif.
BR TR 6' 168 lbs.

Year	Team	W	L	PCT	ERA	G	GS	CG	IP	H	BB	SO	ShO	RW	RL	SV	AB	H	HR	BA
1912	PHI N	0	1	.000	6.33	7	1	0	21.1	27	7	5	0	0	0	0	3	0	0	.000
1913		9	9	.500	3.11	39	20	7	170.2	172	46	51	2	3	1	1	50	6	0	.120
1914		21	19	.525	2.58	48	39	24	321	308	91	116	4	3	1	2	108	21	1	.194
1915		21	15	.583	2.36	43	33	20	274.2	240	59	114	2	4	1	2	88	21	1	.239
1916		7	7	.500	3.15	28	16	9	140	148	33	62	2	1	0	0	38	5	0	.132
1917		11	6	.647	2.76	28	18	11	160	160	33	64	1	1	0	0	51	10	0	.196
1918	2 teams	PHI N (13G 7–4)				PIT N (15G 9–3)														
"	total	16	7	.696	2.65	28	27	18	227.1	230	53	41	1	0	0	0	79	15	0	.190
1919	2 teams	PIT N (18G 5–3)				CHI N (6G 1–3)														
"	total	6	6	.500	5.30	24	12	6	112	130	23	29	0	2	1	1	36	6	0	.167
8 yrs.		91	70	.565	2.96	245	166	93	1427	1415	345	482	12	14	5	6	453	84	2	.185
1 yr.		1	3	.250	8.37	6	2	0	23.2	30	11	9	0	1	1	0	7	0	0	.000

WORLD SERIES

Year	Team	W	L	PCT	ERA	G	GS	CG	IP	H	BB	SO	ShO	RW	RL	SV	AB	H	HR	BA
1915	PHI N	0	1	.000	2.38	2	2	1	11.1	16	2	7	0	0	0	0	4	0	0	.000

Pitcher Register

	W	L	PCT	ERA	G	GS	CG	IP	H	BB	SO	ShO	Relief Pitching W	L	SV	BATTING AB	H	HR	BA

Erskine Mayer continued
| 1919 CHI A | 0 | 0 | — | 0.00 | 1 | 0 | 0 | 1 | 0 | 1 | 0 | 0 | 0 | 0 | 0 | 0 | 0 | 0 | — |
| 2 yrs. | 0 | 1 | .000 | 2.19 | 3 | 2 | 1 | 12.1 | 16 | 3 | 7 | 0 | 0 | 0 | 0 | 4 | 0 | 0 | .000 |

John McAleese
McALEESE, JOHN JAMES BR TR
B. Aug. 22, 1879, Sharon, Pa. D. Nov. 14, 1950, New York, N.Y.

| 1901 CHI A | 0 | 0 | — | 9.00 | 1 | 0 | 0 | 3 | 7 | 1 | 1 | 0 | 0 | 0 | 0 | * | | | |

Pryor McBee
McBEE, PRYOR EDWARD (Lefty) BR TL 6'1" 190 lbs.
B. June 20, 1901, Blanco, Okla. D. Apr. 19, 1963, Roseville, Calif.

| 1926 CHI A | 0 | 0 | — | 6.75 | 1 | 0 | 0 | 1.1 | 1 | 3 | 1 | 0 | 0 | 0 | 0 | 0 | 0 | 0 | — |

Ken McBride
McBRIDE, KENNETH FAYE BR TR 6'1" 190 lbs.
B. Aug. 12, 1935, Huntsville, Ala.

1959 CHI A	0	1	.000	3.18	11	2	0	22.2	20	17	12	0	0	0	1	6	1	0	.167
1960	0	1	.000	3.86	5	0	0	4.2	6	3	4	0	0	1	0	0	0	0	—
1961 LA A	12	15	.444	3.65	38	36	11	241.2	229	102	180	1	0	1	1	83	7	0	.084
1962	11	5	.688	3.50	24	23	6	149.1	136	70	83	4	0	0	0	55	9	1	.164
1963	13	12	.520	3.26	36	36	11	251	198	82	147	2	0	0	0	87	15	0	.172
1964	4	13	.235	5.26	29	21	0	116.1	104	75	66	0	1	0	1	28	6	0	.214
1965 CAL A	0	3	.000	6.14	8	4	0	22	24	14	11	0	0	0	0	5	0	0	.000
7 yrs.	40	50	.444	3.79	151	122	28	807.2	717	363	503	7	1	2	3	264	38	1	.144
2 yrs.	0	2	.000	3.29	16	2	0	27.1	26	20	16	0	0	1	1	6	1	0	.167

Dick McCabe
McCABE, RICHARD JAMES BR TR 5'10½" 159 lbs.
B. Feb. 21, 1896, Mamaroneck, N.Y. D. Apr. 11, 1950, Buffalo, N.Y.

1918 BOS A	0	1	.000	2.79	3	1	0	9.2	13	2	3	0	0	0	0	2	0	0	.000
1922 CHI A	1	0	1.000	5.40	3	0	0	3.1	4	0	1	0	1	0	0	0	0	0	—
2 yrs.	1	1	.500	3.46	6	1	0	13	17	2	4	0	1	0	0	2	0	0	.000
1 yr.	1	0	1.000	5.40	3	0	0	3.1	4	0	1	0	1	0	0	0	0	0	—

Jim McDonald
McDONALD, JAMES LeROY (Hot Rod) BR TR 5'10½" 185 lbs.
B. May 17, 1927, Grants Pass, Ore. BB 1950-51

1950 BOS A	1	0	1.000	3.79	9	0	0	19	23	10	5	0	1	0	0	3	1	0	.333
1951 STL A	4	7	.364	4.07	16	11	5	84	84	46	28	0	0	0	1	29	6	0	.207
1952 NY A	3	4	.429	3.50	26	5	1	69.2	71	40	20	0	2	3	0	19	6	0	.316
1953	9	7	.563	3.82	27	18	6	129.2	128	39	43	2	1	1	0	41	4	0	.098
1954	4	1	.800	3.17	16	10	3	71	54	45	20	1	0	0	0	19	4	0	.211
1955 BAL A	3	5	.375	7.14	21	8	0	51.2	76	30	20	0	1	0	0	11	2	0	.182
1956 CHI A	0	2	.000	8.68	8	3	0	18.2	29	7	10	0	0	0	0	5	0	0	.000
1957	0	1	.000	2.01	10	0	0	22.1	18	10	12	0	0	1	0	1	0	0	.000
1958	0	0	—	19.29	3	0	0	2.1	6	4	0	0	0	0	0	0	0	0	—
9 yrs.	24	27	.471	4.27	136	55	15	468	489	231	158	3	5	5	1	128	23	0	.180
3 yrs.	0	3	.000	5.82	21	3	0	43.1	53	21	22	0	0	1	0	6	0	0	.000

WORLD SERIES
| 1953 NY A | 1 | 0 | 1.000 | 5.87 | 1 | 1 | 0 | 7.2 | 12 | 0 | 3 | 0 | 0 | 0 | 0 | 2 | 1 | 0 | .500 |

Lynn McGlothen
McGLOTHEN, LYNN EVERATT BL TR 6'2" 185 lbs.
B. Mar. 27, 1950, Monroe, La.

1972 BOS A	8	7	.533	3.41	22	22	4	145.1	135	59	112	1	0	0	0	53	10	0	.189
1973	1	2	.333	8.22	6	3	0	23	39	8	16	0	0	0	0	0	0	0	—
1974 STL N	16	12	.571	2.70	31	31	8	237	212	89	142	3	0	0	0	83	15	0	.181
1975	15	13	.536	3.92	35	34	9	239	231	97	146	2	0	0	0	80	7	0	.088
1976	13	15	.464	3.91	33	32	10	205	209	68	106	4	0	0	0	71	15	0	.211
1977 SF N	2	9	.182	5.63	21	15	2	80	94	52	42	0	0	1	0	19	2	0	.105
1978 2 teams	SF N (5G 0–0)				CHI N (49G 5–3)														
" total	5	3	.625	3.30	54	2	0	92.2	92	43	69	0	5	2	0	16	3	0	.188
1979 CHI N	13	14	.481	4.12	42	29	6	212	236	55	147	1	3	1	2	71	16	0	.225
1980	12	14	.462	4.80	39	27	2	182	211	64	119	0	0	1	0	51	10	0	.196
1981 2 teams	CHI N (20G 1–4)				CHI A (11G 0–0)														
" total	1	4	.200	4.56	31	9	0	77	85	35	38	0	1	1	0	12	1	0	.083
1982 NY A	0	0	—	10.80	4	0	0	5	9	2	2	0	0	0	0	0	0	0	—
11 yrs.	86	93	.480	3.98	318	201	41	1498	1553	572	939	13	9	6	2	456	79	0	.173
1 yr.	0	0	—	4.09	11	0	0	22	14	7	12	0	0	0	0	0	0	0	—

Jim McGlothlin
McGLOTHLIN, JAMES MILTON (Red) BR TR 6'1" 185 lbs.
B. Oct. 6, 1943, Los Angeles, Calif. D. Dec. 23, 1975, Union, Ky.

1965 CAL A	0	3	.000	3.50	3	3	1	18	18	7	9	0	0	0	0	6	0	0	.000
1966	3	1	.750	4.52	19	11	0	67.2	79	19	41	0	0	0	0	17	1	0	.059
1967	12	8	.600	2.96	32	29	9	197.1	163	56	137	6	1	0	0	57	8	0	.140
1968	10	15	.400	3.54	40	32	8	208.1	187	60	135	0	0	0	3	63	7	0	.111
1969	8	16	.333	3.18	37	35	4	201	188	58	96	1	0	0	0	58	7	0	.121
1970 CIN N	14	10	.583	3.58	35	34	5	211	192	86	97	3	0	0	0	66	8	1	.121
1971	8	12	.400	3.21	30	26	6	171	151	47	93	0	0	0	0	51	7	1	.137
1972	9	8	.529	3.91	31	21	3	145	165	49	69	1	1	3	0	46	8	1	.174
1973 2 teams	CIN N (24G 3–3)				CHI A (5G 0–1)														
" total	3	4	.429	6.06	29	10	0	81.2	104	36	32	0	0	0	0	16	2	0	.125
9 yrs.	67	77	.465	3.61	256	201	36	1301	1247	418	709	11	2	3	3	380	48	3	.126
1 yr.	0	0	.000	3.93	5	1	0	18.1	13	13	14	0	0	0	0	0	0	0	—

LEAGUE CHAMPIONSHIP SERIES
| 1972 CIN N | 0 | 0 | — | 0.00 | 1 | 0 | 0 | 1 | 0 | 0 | 1 | 0 | 0 | 0 | 0 | 0 | 0 | 0 | — |

WORLD SERIES
| 1970 CIN N | 0 | 0 | — | 8.31 | 1 | 1 | 0 | 4.1 | 6 | 2 | 2 | 0 | 0 | 0 | 0 | 2 | 0 | 0 | .000 |

Pitcher Register

	W	L	PCT	ERA	G	GS	CG	IP	H	BB	SO	ShO	Relief Pitching W L SV	BATTING AB H HR	BA

Jim McGlothlin continued

| 1972 | 0 | 0 | – | 12.00 | 1 | 1 | 0 | 3 | 2 | 2 | 3 | 0 | 0 0 0 | 1 0 0 | .000 |
| 2 yrs. | 0 | 0 | – | 9.82 | 2 | 2 | 0 | 7.1 | 8 | 4 | 5 | 0 | 0 0 0 | 3 0 0 | .000 |

Tom McGuire

McGUIRE, THOMAS PATRICK (Elmer) BR TR 6' 175 lbs.
B. Feb. 1, 1892, Chicago, Ill. D. Dec. 7, 1959, Phoenix, Ariz.

1914 CHI F	5	7	.417	3.70	24	12	7	131.1	143	57	37	0	0 3 0	70 19 1	.271
1919 CHI A	0	0	–	9.00	1	0	0	3	5	3	0	0	0 0 0	1 0 0	.000
2 yrs.	5	7	.417	3.82	25	12	7	134.1	148	60	37	0	0 3 0	71 19 1	.268
1 yr.	0	0	–	9.00	1	0	0	3	5	3	0	0	0 0 0	1 0 0	.000

Stover McIlwain

McILWAIN, WILLIAM STOVER (Smokey) BR TR 6'2" 195 lbs.
B. Sept. 22, 1939, Savannah, Ga. D. Jan. 15, 1966, Buffalo, N. Y.

1957 CHI A	0	0	–	0.00	1	0	0	1	2	1	0	0	0 0 0	0 0 0	–
1958	0	0	–	2.25	1	1	0	4	4	0	4	0	0 0 0	1 0 0	.000
2 yrs.	0	0	–	1.80	2	1	0	5	6	1	4	0	0 0 0	1 0 0	.000
2 yrs.	0	0	–	1.80	2	1	0	5	6	1	4	0	0 0 0	1 0 0	.000

Hal McKain

McKAIN, HAROLD LEROY BL TR 5'11" 185 lbs.
B. July 10, 1906, Logan, Iowa D. Jan. 24, 1970, Sacramento, Calif.

1927 CLE A	0	1	.000	4.09	2	1	0	11	18	4	5	0	0 0 0	4 0 0	.000
1929 CHI A	6	9	.400	3.65	34	10	4	158	158	85	33	1	3 4 1	44 10 0	.227
1930	6	4	.600	5.56	32	5	0	89	108	42	52	0	0 3 5	31 13 0	.419
1931	6	9	.400	5.71	27	8	3	112	134	57	39	0	0 6 0	42 5 0	.119
1932	0	0	–	11.12	8	0	0	11.1	17	5	7	0	0 0 0	1 0 0	.000
5 yrs.	18	23	.439	4.93	103	24	7	381.1	435	193	136	1	3 13 6	122 28 0	.230
4 yrs.	18	22	.450	4.96	101	23	7	370.1	417	189	131	1	3 13 6	118 28 0	.237

Cal McLish

McLISH, CALVIN COOLIDGE JULIUS CAESAR TUSKAHOMA (Buster) BR TR 6' 179 lbs.
B. Dec. 1, 1925, Anadarko, Okla. BR 1944

1944 BKN N	3	10	.231	7.82	23	13	3	84	110	48	20	0	0 2 0	32 7 0	.219
1946	0	0	–	∞	1	0	0	0	1	0	0	0	0 0 0	0 0 0	–
1947 PIT N	0	0	–	18.00	1	0	0	1	2	2	0	0	0 0 0	1 0 0	.000
1948	0	0	–	9.00	2	1	0	5	8	2	1	0	0 0 0	1 0 0	.000
1949 CHI N	1	1	.500	5.87	8	2	0	23	31	12	6	0	0 0 0	9 3 0	.333
1951	4	10	.286	4.45	30	17	5	145.2	159	52	46	1	0 1 0	42 5 0	.119
1956 CLE A	2	4	.333	4.96	37	2	0	61.2	67	32	27	0	1 3 1	9 1 0	.111
1957	9	7	.563	2.74	42	7	2	144.1	117	67	88	0	7 5 1	43 8 2	.186
1958	16	8	.667	2.99	39	30	13	225.2	214	70	97	0	0 0 1	64 6 0	.094
1959	19	8	.704	3.63	35	32	13	235.1	253	72	113	0	0 0 1	74 14 0	.189
1960 CIN N	4	14	.222	4.16	37	21	2	151.1	170	48	56	1	0 3 0	41 2 0	.049
1961 CHI A	10	13	.435	4.38	31	27	4	162.1	178	47	80	0	0 0 1	54 9 0	.167
1962 PHI N	11	5	.688	4.25	32	24	5	154.2	184	45	71	1	1 0 1	51 4 0	.078
1963	13	11	.542	3.26	32	32	10	209.2	184	56	98	1	0 0 0	69 14 0	.203
1964	0	1	.000	3.38	2	1	0	5.1	6	1	6	0	0 0 0	1 0 0	.000
15 yrs.	92	92	.500	4.01	352	209	57	1609	1684	552	713	5	9 14 6	490 73 3	.149
1 yr.	10	13	.435	4.38	31	27	4	162.1	178	47	80	0	0 0 1	54 9 0	.167

Sam McMackin

McMACKIN, SAMUEL
B. Cleveland, Ohio D. Feb. 11, 1903, Columbus, Ohio

| 1902 2 teams | CHI A (1G 0-0) | DET A (1G 0-1) |
| " total | 0 | 1 | .000 | 2.38 | 2 | 1 | 1 | 11.1 | 10 | 4 | 4 | 0 | 0 0 0 | 5 2 0 | .400 |

Don McMahon

McMAHON, DONALD JOHN BR TR 6'2" 215 lbs.
B. Jan. 4, 1930, Brooklyn, N. Y.

1957 MIL N	2	3	.400	1.54	32	0	0	46.2	33	29	46	0	2 3 9	8 2 0	.250
1958	7	2	.778	3.68	38	0	0	58.2	50	29	37	0	7 2 8	9 1 0	.111
1959	5	3	.625	2.57	60	0	0	80.2	81	37	55	0	5 3 15	9 2 0	.222
1960	3	6	.333	5.94	48	0	0	63.2	66	32	50	0	3 6 10	11 0 0	.000
1961	6	4	.600	2.84	53	0	0	92	84	51	55	0	6 4 8	16 3 0	.188
1962 2 teams	MIL N (2G 0-1)	HOU N (51G 5-5)
" total	5	6	.455	1.69	53	0	0	79.2	56	33	72	0	5 6 8	12 1 0	.083
1963 HOU N	1	5	.167	4.05	49	2	0	80	83	26	51	0	1 3 5	12 1 0	.083
1964 CLE A	6	4	.600	2.41	70	0	0	101	67	52	92	0	6 4 16	14 2 0	.143
1965	3	3	.500	3.28	58	0	0	85	79	37	60	0	3 3 11	9 2 0	.222
1966 2 teams	CLE A (12G 1-1)	BOS A (49G 8-7)
" total	9	8	.529	2.69	61	0	0	90.1	73	44	62	0	9 8 10	13 1 0	.077
1967 2 teams	BOS A (11G 1-2)	CHI A (52G 5-0)
" total	6	2	.750	1.98	63	0	0	109.1	68	40	84	0	6 2 5	13 2 0	.154
1968 2 teams	CHI A (25G 2-1)	DET A (20G 3-1)
" total	5	2	.714	1.98	45	0	0	81.2	53	30	65	0	5 2 13	7 1 0	.143
1969 2 teams	DET A (34G 3-5)	SF N (13G 3-1)
" total	6	6	.500	3.54	47	0	0	61	38	27	59	0	6 6 13	9 1 0	.111
1970 SF N	9	5	.643	2.97	61	0	0	94	70	45	74	0	9 5 19	14 2 0	.143
1971	10	6	.625	4.06	61	0	0	82	73	37	71	0	10 6 4	7 0 0	.000
1972	3	3	.500	3.71	44	0	0	63	46	21	45	0	3 3 5	4 1 0	.250
1973	4	0	1.000	1.50	22	0	0	30	21	7	20	0	4 0 0	1 1 0	1.000
1974	0	0	–	3.00	9	0	0	12	13	2	5	0	0 0 0	0 0 0	–
18 yrs.	90	68	.570	2.96	874 6th	2	0	1310.2	1054	579	1003	0	90 66 153 7th	168 23 0	.137
2 yrs.	7	1	.875	1.77	77	0	0	137.2	85	47	106	0	7 1 3	14 3 0	.214

LEAGUE CHAMPIONSHIP SERIES
| 1971 SF N | 0 | 0 | – | 0.00 | 2 | 0 | 0 | 3 | 0 | 0 | 3 | 0 | 0 0 0 | 0 0 0 | – |

WORLD SERIES
| 1957 MIL N | 0 | 0 | – | 0.00 | 3 | 0 | 0 | 5 | 3 | 3 | 5 | 0 | 0 0 0 | 0 0 0 | – |
| 1958 | 0 | 0 | – | 5.40 | 3 | 0 | 0 | 3.1 | 3 | 3 | 5 | 0 | 0 0 0 | 0 0 0 | – |

Pitcher Register

	W	L	PCT	ERA	G	GS	CG	IP	H	BB	SO	ShO	Relief Pitching W	L	SV	AB	BATTING H	HR	BA

Don McMahon continued
1968 DET A	0	0	—	13.50	2	0	0	2	4	0	1	0	0	0	0	0	0	0	—
3 yrs.	0	0	—	4.35	8	0	0	10.1	10	6	11	0	0	0	0	0	0	0	—

Doug McWeeny
McWEENY, DOUGLAS LAWRENCE (Buzz) BR TR 6'2" 180 lbs.
B. Aug. 17, 1896, Chicago, Ill. D. Jan. 1, 1953, Chicago, Ill.

	W	L	PCT	ERA	G	GS	CG	IP	H	BB	SO	ShO	W	L	SV	AB	H	HR	BA
1921 CHI A	3	6	.333	6.08	27	9	4	97.2	127	45	46	0	1	0	2	31	1	0	.032
1922	0	1	.000	5.91	4	1	0	10.2	13	7	5	0	0	0	0	1	0	0	.000
1924	1	3	.250	4.57	13	5	2	43.1	47	17	18	0	1	0	0	9	0	0	.000
1926 BKN N	11	13	.458	3.04	42	25	10	216.1	213	84	96	1	2	0	1	64	7	0	.109
1927	4	8	.333	3.56	34	22	6	164.1	167	70	73	0	0	1	1	47	2	0	.043
1928	14	14	.500	3.17	42	32	12	244	218	114	79	4	0	2	1	81	14	0	.173
1929	4	10	.286	6.10	36	24	4	146	167	93	59	0	0	2	1	48	5	0	.104
1930 CIN N	0	2	.000	7.36	8	2	0	25.2	28	20	10	0	0	1	0	7	1	0	.143
8 yrs.	37	57	.394	4.17	206	120	38	948	980	450	386	5	4	6	6	288	30	0	.104
3 yrs.	4	10	.286	5.64	44	15	6	151.2	187	69	69	0	2	0	2	41	1	0	.024

Sam Mertes
MERTES, SAMUEL BLAIR (Sandow) BR TR 5'10" 185 lbs.
B. Aug. 6, 1872, San Francisco, Calif. D. Mar. 11, 1945, San Francisco, Calif.

	W	L	PCT	ERA	G	GS	CG	IP	H	BB	SO	ShO	W	L	SV	AB	H	HR	BA
1902 CHI A	1	0	1.000	1.17	1	0	0	7.2	6	0	0	0	1	0	0	*			

John Michaelson
MICHAELSON, JOHN AUGUST (Mike) BR TR 5'9" 165 lbs.
B. Aug. 12, 1893, Tivalkoski, Finland D. Apr. 16, 1968, Woodruff, Wis.

	W	L	PCT	ERA	G	GS	CG	IP	H	BB	SO	ShO	W	L	SV	AB	H	HR	BA
1921 CHI A	0	0	—	10.13	2	0	0	2.2	4	1	1	0	0	0	0	0	0	0	—

Bob Miller
MILLER, ROBERT LANE BR TR 6'1" 180 lbs.
B. Feb. 18, 1939, St. Louis, Mo.

	W	L	PCT	ERA	G	GS	CG	IP	H	BB	SO	ShO	W	L	SV	AB	H	HR	BA
1957 STL N	0	0	—	7.00	5	0	0	9	13	5	7	0	0	0	0	0	0	0	—
1959	4	3	.571	3.31	11	10	3	70.2	66	21	43	0	0	0	0	24	5	0	.208
1960	4	3	.571	3.42	15	7	0	52.2	53	17	33	0	1	0	0	14	2	0	.143
1961	1	3	.250	4.24	34	5	0	74.1	82	46	39	0	1	1	3	14	5	0	.357
1962 NY N	1	12	.077	4.89	33	21	1	143.2	146	62	91	0	0	1	1	41	5	0	.122
1963 LA N	10	8	.556	2.89	42	23	2	187	171	65	125	0	4	2	1	57	4	0	.070
1964	7	7	.500	2.62	74	2	0	137.2	115	63	94	0	6	7	9	19	3	0	.158
1965	6	7	.462	2.97	61	1	0	103	82	26	77	0	6	6	9	16	0	0	.000
1966	4	2	.667	2.77	46	0	0	84.1	70	29	58	0	4	2	5	13	1	0	.077
1967	2	9	.182	4.31	52	4	0	85.2	88	27	32	0	2	6	0	8	1	0	.125
1968 MIN A	0	3	.000	2.74	45	0	0	72.1	65	24	41	0	0	3	2	7	1	0	.143
1969	5	5	.500	3.02	48	11	1	119.1	118	32	57	0	0	4	3	31	0	0	.000
1970 3 teams					CLE A (15G 2-2)			CHI N (7G 0-0)			CHI A (15G 4-6)								
" total	6	8	.429	4.79	37	15	0	107	129	54	55	0	2	0	3	28	5	0	.179
1971 3 teams					CHI N (2G 0-0)			SD N (38G 7-3)			PIT N (16G 1-2)								
" total	8	5	.615	1.64	56	0	0	98.2	83	40	51	0	8	5	10	12	0	0	.000
1972 PIT N	5	2	.714	2.65	36	0	0	54.1	54	24	18	0	5	2	3	4	0	0	.000
1973 3 teams					DET A (22G 4-2)			SD N (18G 0-0)			NY N (1G 0-0)								
" total	4	2	.667	3.67	41	0	0	73.2	63	34	39	0	4	2	1	2	0	0	.000
1974 NY N	2	2	.500	3.58	58	0	0	78	89	39	35	0	2	2	2	9	1	0	.111
17 yrs.	69	81	.460	3.37	694	99	7	1551.1	1487	608	895	0	45	43	52	299	33	0	.110
1 yr.	4	6	.400	5.01	15	12	0	70	88	33	36	0	0	0	0	23	4	0	.174

LEAGUE CHAMPIONSHIP SERIES
	W	L	PCT	ERA	G	GS	CG	IP	H	BB	SO	ShO	W	L	SV	AB	H	HR	BA
1969 MIN A	0	1	.000	5.40	1	1	0	1.2	5	0	0	0	0	0	0	0	0	0	—
1971 PIT N	0	0	—	6.00	1	0	0	3	3	3	3	0	0	0	0	1	0	0	.000
1972	0	0	—	0.00	1	0	0	0.1	0	1	0	0	0	0	0	0	0	0	—
3 yrs.	0	1	.000	4.76	3	1	0	5.2	8	3	4	0	0	0	0	1	0	0	.000

WORLD SERIES
	W	L	PCT	ERA	G	GS	CG	IP	H	BB	SO	ShO	W	L	SV	AB	H	HR	BA
1965 LA N	0	0	—	0.00	2	0	0	1.1	0	0	0	0	0	0	0	0	0	0	—
1966	0	0	—	0.00	1	0	0	3	2	2	1	0	0	0	0	0	0	0	—
1971 PIT N	0	1	.000	3.86	3	0	0	4.2	7	1	2	0	0	0	0	0	0	0	—
3 yrs.	0	1	.000	2.00	6	0	0	9	9	3	3	0	0	0	0	0	0	0	—

Frank Miller
MILLER, FRANK LEE (Bullet) BR TR 6' 188 lbs.
B. Mar. 13, 1886, Salem, Mich. D. Feb. 19, 1974, Allegan, Mich.

	W	L	PCT	ERA	G	GS	CG	IP	H	BB	SO	ShO	W	L	SV	AB	H	HR	BA
1913 CHI A	0	1	.000	27.00	1	1	0	1.2	4	3	2	0	0	0	0	0	0	0	—
1916 PIT N	7	10	.412	2.29	30	20	10	173	135	49	88	2	0	2	1	51	7	0	.137
1917	10	19	.345	3.13	38	28	14	224	216	60	92	5	1	2	1	76	9	0	.118
1918	11	8	.579	2.38	23	23	14	170.1	152	37	47	2	0	0	0	57	6	0	.105
1919	13	12	.520	3.03	32	26	16	201.2	170	34	59	3	0	0	0	66	7	0	.106
1922 BOS N	11	13	.458	3.51	31	23	14	200	213	60	65	2	2	1	1	68	8	0	.118
1923	0	3	.000	4.58	8	6	0	39.1	54	11	6	0	0	0	1	7	1	0	.143
7 yrs.	52	66	.441	3.01	163	127	68	1010	944	254	359	14	3	5	4	325	38	0	.117
1 yr.	0	1	.000	27.00	1	1	0	1.2	4	3	2	0	0	0	0	0	0	0	—

Jake Miller
MILLER, WALTER JACOB BL TL 6'1" 185 lbs.
Brother of Russ Miller.
B. Feb. 28, 1898, Wagram, Ohio D. Aug. 20, 1975, Venice, Fla.

	W	L	PCT	ERA	G	GS	CG	IP	H	BB	SO	ShO	W	L	SV	AB	H	HR	BA
1924 CLE A	0	1	.000	3.00	2	2	0	12	13	5	4	0	0	0	0	5	0	0	.000
1925	10	13	.435	3.31	32	22	13	190.1	207	62	51	0	2	2	2	71	13	0	.183
1926	7	4	.636	3.27	18	11	5	82.2	99	18	24	3	2	0	1	24	2	0	.083
1927	10	8	.556	3.21	34	23	11	185.1	189	48	53	0	0	1	0	58	8	0	.138
1928	8	9	.471	4.44	25	23	8	158	203	43	37	0	0	0	0	52	7	0	.135
1929	14	12	.538	3.58	29	29	16	206	227	60	58	2	0	0	0	75	15	0	.200
1930	4	5	.444	7.13	24	9	1	88.1	147	38	31	0	2	0	0	33	10	0	.303
1931	2	1	.667	4.35	10	5	1	41.1	45	19	17	1	1	0	0	13	1	0	.077

Pitcher Register

	W	L	PCT	ERA	G	GS	CG	IP	H	BB	SO	ShO	Relief Pitching W	L	SV	BATTING AB	H	HR	BA

Jake Miller continued
1933 CHI A	5	6	.455	5.62	26	14	4	105.2	130	47	30	2	0	1	0	37	7	0	.189
9 yrs.	60	59	.504	4.09	200	138	58	1069.2	1260	340	305	8	7	4	3	368	63	0	.171
1 yr.	5	6	.455	5.62	26	14	4	105.2	130	47	30	2	0	1	0	37	7	0	.189

Roy Mitchell
MITCHELL, ALBERT ROY BR TR 5'9½" 170 lbs.
B. Apr. 19, 1885, Belton, Tex.   D. Sept. 8, 1959, Temple, Tex.

1910 STL A	4	2	.667	2.60	6	6	6	52	43	12	23	0	0	0	0	19	4	0	.211
1911	4	8	.333	3.84	28	12	8	133.2	134	45	40	1	1	1	0	49	11	0	.224
1912	3	4	.429	4.65	13	8	5	62	81	17	22	0	0	0	0	19	6	0	.316
1913	13	16	.448	3.01	33	27	21	245.1	265	47	59	4	0	2	1	88	13	0	.148
1914	4	5	.444	4.35	28	9	4	103.1	134	38	38	0	2	1	4	34	7	0	.206
1918 2 teams			CHI A (2G 0-1)		CIN N (5G 4-0)														
" total	4	1	.800	2.42	7	5	3	48.1	45	9	12	2	1	0	0	16	3	0	.188
1919 CIN N	0	1	.000	2.32	7	1	0	31	32	9	10	0	0	0	0	10	0	0	.000
7 yrs.	32	37	.464	3.42	122	68	47	675.2	734	177	204	7	4	4	5	235	44	0	.187
1 yr.	0	1	.000	7.50	2	2	0	12	18	4	3	0	0	0	0	2	0	0	.000

George Mogridge
MOGRIDGE, GEORGE ANTHONY BL TL 6'2" 165 lbs.
B. Feb. 18, 1889, Rochester, N. Y.   D. Mar. 4, 1962, Rochester, N. Y.

1911 CHI A	0	1	.000	4.97	4	1	0	12.2	12	1	5	0	0	1	0	5	2	0	.400
1912	3	4	.429	4.04	17	7	2	64.2	69	15	31	0	1	1	2	16	2	0	.125
1915 NY A	2	3	.400	1.76	6	6	3	41	33	11	11	1	0	0	0	12	1	0	.083
1916	6	12	.333	2.31	30	21	9	194.2	174	45	66	1	1	0	0	66	14	0	.212
1917	9	11	.450	2.98	29	25	15	196.1	185	39	46	1	1	0	0	69	11	0	.159
1918	17	13	.567	2.27	45	19	13	230.1	232	43	62	1	6	7	5	79	15	0	.190
1919	10	7	.588	2.50	35	18	13	187	159	46	58	3	1	1	0	48	6	0	.125
1920	5	9	.357	4.31	26	15	7	125.1	146	36	35	0	0	1	1	42	7	0	.167
1921 WAS A	18	14	.563	3.00	38	26	21	288	301	66	101	4	1	0	0	98	15	0	.153
1922	18	13	.581	3.58	34	32	18	251.2	300	72	61	3	0	2	0	86	21	1	.244
1923	13	13	.500	3.11	33	28	17	211	228	56	62	3	0	1	1	75	17	0	.227
1924	16	11	.593	3.76	30	30	13	213	217	61	48	2	0	0	0	74	13	0	.176
1925 2 teams			WAS A (10G 4-3)		STL A (2G 1-1)														
" total	5	4	.556	3.95	12	10	4	68.1	73	23	21	0	0	1	0	23	2	0	.087
1926 BOS N	6	10	.375	4.50	39	10	2	142	173	36	46	0	5	3	3	46	8	0	.174
1927	6	4	.600	3.70	20	1	0	48.2	48	15	26	0	6	3	5	15	3	0	.200
15 yrs.	134	129	.510	3.20	398	259	137	2274.2	2350	565	679	19	22	21	17	754	137	1	.182
2 yrs.	3	5	.375	4.19	21	8	2	77.1	81	16	36	0	1	2	2	21	4	0	.190

WORLD SERIES
| 1924 WAS A | 1 | 0 | 1.000 | 2.25 | 2 | 1 | 0 | 12 | 7 | 6 | 5 | 0 | 0 | 0 | 0 | 5 | 0 | 0 | .000 |

Rich Moloney
MOLONEY, RICHARD HENRY BR TR 6'3" 185 lbs.
B. June 7, 1950, Brookline, Mass.

| 1970 CHI A | 0 | 0 | – | 0.00 | 1 | 0 | 0 | 1 | 2 | 1 | 0 | 1 | 0 | 0 | 0 | 0 | 0 | 0 | – |

Larry Monroe
MONROE, LAWRENCE JAMES BR TR 6'4" 200 lbs.
B. June 20, 1956, Detroit, Mich.

| 1976 CHI A | 0 | 1 | .000 | 4.09 | 8 | 2 | 0 | 22 | 23 | 13 | 9 | 0 | 0 | 0 | 0 | 0 | 0 | 0 | – |

Aurelio Monteagudo
MONTEAGUDO, AURELIO FAUTINO CINTRA BR TR 5'11" 180 lbs.
B. Nov. 28, 1943, Caibarien, Cuba

1963 KC A	0	0	–	2.57	4	0	0	7	4	3	3	0	0	0	0	0	0	0	–
1964	0	4	.000	8.90	11	6	0	31.1	40	10	14	0	0	0	0	7	2	0	.286
1965	0	0	–	3.86	4	0	0	7	5	4	5	0	0	0	0	0	0	0	–
1966 2 teams			KC A (6G 0-0)		HOU N (10G 0-0)														
" total	0	0	–	3.86	16	0	0	28	26	18	10	0	0	0	1	0	0	0	.000
1967 CHI A	0	1	.000	20.25	1	1	0	1.1	4	2	0	0	0	0	0	0	0	0	–
1970 KC A	1	1	.500	3.00	21	0	0	27	20	9	18	0	1	1	0	2	0	0	.000
1973 CAL A	2	1	.667	4.20	15	0	0	30	23	16	8	0	2	1	3	0	0	0	–
7 yrs.	3	7	.300	5.06	72	7	0	131.2	122	62	58	0	3	2	4	10	2	0	.200
1 yr.	0	1	.000	20.25	1	1	0	1.1	4	2	0	0	0	0	0	0	0	0	–

Barry Moore
MOORE, ROBERT BARRY BL TL 6'1" 190 lbs.
B. Apr. 3, 1943, Statesville, N. C.

1965 WAS A	0	0	–	0.00	1	0	0	1	1	1	0	0	0	0	0	0	0	0	–
1966	3	3	.500	3.75	12	11	1	62.1	55	39	28	0	0	0	0	19	2	0	.105
1967	7	11	.389	3.76	27	26	3	143.2	127	71	74	1	0	0	0	46	6	0	.130
1968	4	6	.400	3.37	32	18	0	117.2	116	66	42	0	1	0	3	31	3	0	.097
1969	9	8	.529	4.30	39	25	4	134	123	67	51	0	0	2	0	43	9	0	.209
1970 2 teams			CLE A (13G 3-5)		CHI A (24G 0-4)														
" total	3	9	.250	5.30	37	19	0	141	155	80	69	0	0	2	3	40	7	0	.175
6 yrs.	26	37	.413	4.16	140	99	8	599.2	577	300	278	1	0	2	3	179	27	0	.151
1 yr.	0	4	.000	6.37	24	9	0	70.2	85	34	34	0	0	1	0	19	5	0	.263

Jim Moore
MOORE, JAMES STANFORD BR TR 6' 165 lbs.
B. Dec. 14, 1904, Prescott, Ark.

1928 CLE A	0	1	.000	2.00	1	1	1	9	5	5	1	0	0	0	0	3	0	0	.000
1929	0	0	–	9.53	2	0	0	5.2	6	4	0	0	0	0	0	2	0	0	.000
1930 CHI A	2	1	.667	3.60	9	5	2	40	42	12	11	0	0	0	1	13	3	0	.231
1931	0	2	.000	4.95	33	4	0	83.2	93	27	15	0	0	0	0	16	1	0	.063
1932	0	0	–	0.00	1	0	0	1	1	1	2	0	0	0	0	1	0	0	.000
5 yrs.	2	4	.333	4.52	46	10	3	139.1	147	49	29	0	0	0	1	35	4	0	.114
3 yrs.	2	3	.400	4.48	43	9	2	124.2	136	40	28	0	0	0	1	30	4	0	.133

Pitcher Register

	W	L	PCT	ERA	G	GS	CG	IP	H	BB	SO	ShO	Relief Pitching W	L	SV	BATTING AB	H	HR	BA

Ray Moore
MOORE, RAYMOND LEROY (Farmer)
B. June 1, 1926, Meadows, Md. BR TR 6' 195 lbs.

Year	Team	W	L	PCT	ERA	G	GS	CG	IP	H	BB	SO	ShO	RW	RL	SV	AB	H	HR	BA
1952	BKN N	1	2	.333	4.76	14	2	0	28.1	29	26	11	0	1	0	0	3	0	0	.000
1953		0	1	.000	3.38	1	1	1	8	6	4	4	0	0	0	0	3	0	0	.000
1955	BAL A	10	10	.500	3.92	46	14	3	151.2	128	80	80	1	3	7	6	44	6	0	.136
1956		12	7	.632	4.18	32	27	9	185	161	99	105	1	1	1	0	70	19	2	.271
1957		11	13	.458	3.72	34	32	7	227.1	196	112	117	1	0	1	0	84	18	3	.214
1958	CHI A	9	7	.563	3.82	32	20	4	136.2	107	70	73	2	2	3	2	44	9	1	.205
1959		3	6	.333	4.12	29	8	0	89.2	86	46	49	0	2	1	0	23	2	0	.087
1960	2 teams			CHI A (14G 1–1)	WAS A (37G 3–2)															
"	total	4	3	.571	3.54	51	0	0	86.1	68	38	32	0	4	3	13	16	1	0	.063
1961	MIN A	4	4	.500	3.67	46	0	0	56.1	49	38	45	0	4	4	14	4	0	0	.000
1962		8	3	.727	4.73	49	0	0	64.2	55	30	58	0	8	3	9	5	0	0	.000
1963		1	3	.250	6.98	31	1	0	38.2	50	17	38	0	1	2	2	3	1	0	.333
11 yrs.		63	59	.516	4.06	365	105	24	1072.2	935	560	612	5	26	25	46	299	56	6	.187
3 yrs.		13	14	.481	4.08	75	28	4	247	212	127	125	2	5	5	2	69	11	1	.159

WORLD SERIES

| 1959 | CHI A | 0 | 0 | — | 9.00 | 1 | 0 | 0 | 1 | 1 | 0 | 1 | 0 | 0 | 0 | 0 | 0 | 0 | 0 | 0 |

Carl Moran
MORAN, CARL WILLIAM (Bugs)
B. Sept. 26, 1950, Portsmouth, Va. BR TR 6'4" 210 lbs.

| 1974 | CHI A | 1 | 3 | .250 | 4.70 | 15 | 5 | 0 | 46 | 57 | 23 | 17 | 0 | 0 | 1 | 0 | 0 | 0 | 0 | — |

Don Mossi
MOSSI, DONALD LOUIS (The Sphinx)
B. Jan. 11, 1929, St. Helena, Calif. BL TL 6'1" 195 lbs.

Year	Team	W	L	PCT	ERA	G	GS	CG	IP	H	BB	SO	ShO	RW	RL	SV	AB	H	HR	BA
1954	CLE A	6	1	.857	1.94	40	5	2	93	56	39	55	0	4	0	7	19	3	0	.158
1955		4	3	.571	2.42	57	1	0	81.2	81	18	69	0	4	3	9	9	1	0	.111
1956		6	5	.545	3.59	48	3	0	87.2	79	33	59	0	0	4	11	20	3	0	.150
1957		11	10	.524	4.13	36	22	6	159	166	57	97	1	1	1	2	55	12	0	.218
1958		7	8	.467	3.90	43	5	0	101.2	106	30	55	0	7	4	3	26	3	0	.115
1959	DET A	17	9	.654	3.36	34	30	15	228	210	49	125	3	0	1	0	77	13	1	.169
1960		9	8	.529	3.47	23	22	9	158.1	158	32	69	2	1	0	0	43	5	0	.116
1961		15	7	.682	2.96	35	34	12	240.1	237	47	137	1	0	0	1	79	13	1	.165
1962		11	13	.458	4.19	35	27	8	180.1	195	36	121	1	0	2	1	55	9	0	.164
1963		7	7	.500	3.74	24	16	3	122.2	110	17	68	0	2	0	2	39	8	0	.205
1964	CHI A	3	1	.750	2.93	34	0	0	40	37	7	36	0	3	1	7	6	1	0	.167
1965	KC A	5	8	.385	3.74	51	0	0	55.1	59	20	41	0	5	8	7	8	0	0	.000
12 yrs.		101	80	.558	3.43	460	165	55	1548	1494	385	932	8	27	24	50	436	71	2	.163
1 yr.		3	1	.750	2.93	34	0	0	40	37	7	36	0	3	1	7	6	1	0	.167

WORLD SERIES

| 1954 | CLE A | 0 | 0 | — | 0.00 | 3 | 0 | 0 | 4 | 3 | 0 | 1 | 0 | 0 | 0 | 0 | 0 | 0 | 0 | — |

Glen Moulder
MOULDER, GLEN HUBERT
B. Sept. 28, 1917, Cleveland, Okla. BR TR 6' 180 lbs.

1946	BKN N	0	0	—	4.50	1	0	0	2	2	1	1	0	0	0	0	0	0	0	—
1947	STL A	4	2	.667	3.82	32	2	0	73	78	43	23	0	3	1	2	17	4	0	.235
1948	CHI A	3	6	.333	6.41	33	9	0	85.2	108	54	26	0	1	2	2	20	6	0	.300
3 yrs.		7	8	.467	5.21	66	11	0	160.2	188	98	50	0	4	3	4	37	10	0	.270
1 yr.		3	6	.333	6.41	33	9	0	85.2	108	54	26	0	1	2	2	20	6	0	.300

Dominic Mulrenan
MULRENAN, DOMINIC JOSEPH
B. Dec. 18, 1893, Woburn, Mass. D. July 27, 1964, Melrose, Mass. BR TR 5'11" 170 lbs.

| 1921 | CHI A | 2 | 8 | .200 | 7.23 | 12 | 10 | 3 | 56 | 84 | 36 | 10 | 0 | 0 | 1 | 0 | 20 | 3 | 0 | .150 |

Steve Mura
MURA, STEPHEN ANDREW
B. Dec. 2, 1955, New Orleans, La. BR TR 6'2" 188 lbs.

1978	SD N	0	2	.000	11.25	5	2	0	8	15	5	5	0	0	0	0	1	0	0	.000
1979		4	4	.500	3.08	38	5	0	73	57	37	59	0	3	2	2	10	0	0	.000
1980		8	7	.533	3.67	37	23	3	169	149	86	109	1	0	0	0	51	7	0	.137
1981		5	14	.263	4.27	23	22	2	139	156	50	70	0	0	1	0	44	6	0	.136
1982	STL N	12	11	.522	4.05	35	30	7	184.1	196	80	84	1	0	0	0	53	3	0	.057
1983	CHI A	0	0	—	4.38	6	0	0	12.1	13	6	4	0	0	0	0	0	0	0	—
6 yrs.		29	38	.433	3.98	144	82	12	585.2	586	264	331	2	3	3	4	159	16	0	.101
1 yr.		0	0	—	4.38	6	0	0	12.1	13	6	4	0	0	0	0	0	0	0	—

Danny Murphy
MURPHY, DANIEL FRANCIS
B. Aug. 23, 1942, Beverly, Mass. BL TR 5'11" 185 lbs.

1960	CHI N	0	0	—	0.00	0	0	0	0	0	0	0	0	0	0	0	75	9	1	.120
1961		0	0	—	0.00	0	0	0	0	0	0	0	0	0	0	0	13	5	2	.385
1962		0	0	—	—	0	0	0	0	0	0	0	0	0	0	0	35	7	0	.200
1969	CHI A	2	1	.667	2.01	17	0	0	31.1	28	10	16	0	2	1	4	1	0	0	.000
1970		2	3	.400	5.67	51	0	0	81	82	49	42	0	2	3	5	6	2	1	.333
5 yrs.		4	4	.500	4.65	68	0	0	112.1	110	59	58	0	4	4	9	*			
2 yrs.		4	4	.500	4.65	68	0	0	112.1	110	59	58	0	4	4	9	7	2	1	.286

George Murray
MURRAY, GEORGE KING (Smiler)
B. Sept. 23, 1898, Charlotte, N.C. D. Oct. 18, 1955, Memphis, Tenn. BR TR 6'2" 200 lbs.

1922	NY A	4	2	.667	3.97	22	3	0	56.2	53	26	14	0	4	1	0	18	5	1	.278
1923	BOS A	7	11	.389	4.91	39	18	5	177.2	190	87	40	0	3	1	0	55	9	0	.164
1924		2	9	.182	6.72	28	7	0	80.1	97	32	27	0	1	3	0	22	4	0	.182
1926	WAS A	6	3	.667	5.64	12	12	5	81.1	89	37	28	0	0	0	0	36	5	0	.139
1927		1	1	.500	7.00	7	3	0	18	18	15	5	0	0	1	0	6	1	0	.167
1933	CHI A	0	0	—	7.71	2	0	0	2.1	3	2	0	0	0	0	0	0	0	0	—
6 yrs.		20	26	.435	5.38	110	43	10	416.1	450	199	114	0	8	6	0	137	24	1	.175
1 yr.		0	0	—	7.71	2	0	0	2.1	3	2	0	0	0	0	0	0	0	0	—

390

Pitcher Register

	W	L	PCT	ERA	G	GS	CG	IP	H	BB	SO	ShO	Relief Pitching W L SV	BATTING AB H HR	BA

Bill Nagel
NAGEL, WILLIAM TAYLOR
B. Aug. 19, 1915, Memphis, Tenn. BR TR 6' 190 lbs.

| 1939 PHI A | 0 | 0 | — | 12.00 | 1 | 0 | 0 | 3 | 7 | 1 | 0 | 0 | 0 0 0 | * | |

Andy Nelson
NELSON, ANDREW (Peaches)
B. Unknown.

| 1908 CHI A | 0 | 0 | — | 2.00 | 2 | 1 | 0 | 9 | 11 | 4 | 1 | 0 | 0 0 0 | 2 0 0 | .000 |

Roger Nelson
NELSON, ROGER EUGENE (Spider) BR TR 6'3" 200 lbs.
B. June 7, 1944, Altadena, Calif.

1967 CHI A	0	1	.000	1.29	5	0	0	7	4	0	4	0	0 1 0	0 0 0	—
1968 BAL A	4	3	.571	2.41	19	6	0	71	49	26	70	0	2 1 1	16 1 0	.063
1969 KC A	7	13	.350	3.31	29	29	8	193.1	170	65	82	1	0 0 0	58 8 0	.138
1970	0	2	.000	10.00	4	2	0	9	18	0	3	0	0 0 0	0 0 0	—
1971	0	1	.000	5.29	13	1	0	34	35	5	29	0	0 1 0	6 2 0	.333
1972	11	6	.647	2.08	34	19	0	173.1	120	31	120	6	1 1 2	54 5 0	.093
1973 CIN N	3	2	.600	3.46	14	8	1	54.2	49	24	17	0	0 0 0	18 2 0	.111
1974	4	4	.500	3.39	14	12	1	85	67	35	42	0	0 0 1	28 5 0	.179
1976 KC A	0	0	—	2.00	3	0	0	9	4	4	4	0	0 0 0	0 0 0	—
9 yrs.	29	32	.475	3.06	135	77	20	636.1	516	190	371	7	3 4 4	180 23 0	.128
1 yr.	0	1	—	1.29	5	0	0	7	4	0	4	0	0 1 0	0 0 0	—

LEAGUE CHAMPIONSHIP SERIES
| 1973 CIN N | 0 | 0 | — | 0.00 | 1 | 0 | 0 | 2.1 | 0 | 1 | 0 | 0 | 0 0 0 | 1 0 0 | .000 |

Dan Neumeier
NEUMEIER, DANIEL GEORGE BR TR 6'5" 205 lbs.
B. Mar. 9, 1948, Shawano, Wis.

| 1972 CHI A | 0 | 0 | — | 7.36 | 3 | 0 | 0 | 3.2 | 2 | 3 | 0 | 0 | 0 0 0 | 1 0 0 | .000 |

Wayne Nordhagen
NORDHAGEN, WAYNE OREN BR TR 6'2" 205 lbs.
B. July 4, 1948, Three River Falls, Minn.

| 1979 CHI A | 0 | 0 | — | 9.00 | 2 | 0 | 0 | 2 | 2 | 1 | 2 | 0 | 0 0 0 | * | |

Wynn Noyes
NOYES, WINFIELD CHARLES BR TR 6' 180 lbs.
B. June 16, 1889, Pleasanton, Neb. D. Apr. 8, 1969, Cashmere, Wash.

1913 BOS N	0	0	—	4.79	11	0	0	20.2	22	6	5	0	0 0 0	4 1 0	.250
1917 PHI A	10	10	.500	2.95	27	22	11	171	156	77	64	1	1 1 1	52 6 0	.115
1919 2 teams	PHI A (10G 1–5)	CHI A (1G 0–0)													
" total	1	5	.167	5.89	11	7	3	55	76	15	24	0	1 1 1	18 3 0	.167
3 yrs.	11	15	.423	3.76	49	29	14	246.2	254	98	93	1	1 1 1	74 10 0	.135
1 yr.	0	0	—	7.50	1	0	0	4	6	0	4	0	0 0 0	2 1 0	.500

Jerry Nyman
NYMAN, GERALD SMITH BL TL 5'10" 165 lbs.
B. Nov. 23, 1942, Logan, Utah

1968 CHI A	2	1	.667	2.01	8	7	1	40.1	38	16	27	1	0 0 0	13 2 0	.154
1969	4	4	.500	5.29	20	10	2	64.2	58	39	40	1	0 0 0	20 1 0	.050
1970 SD N	0	2	.000	16.20	2	2	0	5	8	2	2	0	0 0 0	0 0 0	—
3 yrs.	6	7	.462	4.58	30	19	3	110	104	57	69	2	0 0 0	33 3 0	.091
2 yrs.	6	5	.545	4.03	28	17	3	105	96	55	67	2	0 0 0	33 3 0	.091

Buck O'Brien
O'BRIEN, THOMAS JOSEPH BR TR 5'10" 188 lbs.
B. May 10, 1882, Brockton, Mass. D. July 25, 1959, Dorchester, Mass.

1911 BOS A	5	1	.833	0.38	6	5	5	47.2	30	21	31	2	1 0 0	16 2 0	.125
1912	20	13	.606	2.58	37	34	26	275.2	237	90	115	2	2 0 0	94 13 0	.138
1913 2 teams	BOS A (15G 4–9)	CHI A (6G 0–2)													
" total	4	11	.267	3.73	21	15	6	108.2	124	48	58	0	0 2 0	33 5 0	.152
3 yrs.	29	25	.537	2.63	64	54	37	432	391	159	204	4	3 2 0	143 20 0	.140
1 yr.	0	2	.000	3.93	6	3	0	18.1	21	13	4	0	0 0 0	3 0 0	.000

WORLD SERIES
| 1912 BOS A | 0 | 2 | .000 | 7.00 | 2 | 2 | 0 | 9 | 12 | 3 | 4 | 0 | 0 0 0 | 2 0 0 | .000 |

Blue Moon Odom
ODOM, JOHNNY LEE BR TR 6' 178 lbs.
B. May 29, 1945, Macon, Ga.

1964 KC A	1	2	.333	10.06	5	5	1	17	29	11	10	1	0 0 0	5 0 0	.000
1965	0	0	—	9.00	1	0	0	1	2	2	0	0	0 0 0	0 0 0	—
1966	5	5	.500	2.49	14	14	4	90.1	70	53	47	2	0 0 0	31 3 0	.097
1967	3	8	.273	5.04	29	17	0	103.2	94	68	67	0	0 0 0	28 8 0	.286
1968 OAK A	16	10	.615	2.45	32	31	9	231.1	179	98	143	4	0 0 0	78 17 1	.218
1969	15	6	.714	2.92	32	32	10	231.1	179	112	150	3	0 0 0	79 21 5	.266
1970	9	8	.529	3.81	29	29	4	156	128	100	88	1	0 0 0	54 13 3	.241
1971	10	12	.455	4.28	25	25	3	141	147	71	69	1	0 0 0	50 8 1	.160
1972	15	6	.714	2.50	31	30	4	194.1	164	87	86	2	0 0 0	66 8 2	.121
1973	5	12	.294	4.49	30	24	3	150.1	153	67	83	0	1 0 0	1 0 0	.000
1974	1	5	.167	3.83	34	5	1	87	85	52	52	0	1 0 1	0 0 0	—
1975 3 teams	OAK A (7G 0–2)	CLE A (3G 1–0)	ATL N (15G 1–7)												
" total	2	9	.182	7.22	25	13	1	77.1	101	47	44	0	0 1 0	13 1 0	.077
1976 CHI A	2	2	.500	5.79	8	4	0	28	31	20	18	0	0 0 0	0 0 0	—
13 yrs.	84	85	.497	3.70	295	229	40	1508.2	1362	788	857	15	2 1 1	405 79 12	.195
1 yr.	2	2	.500	5.79	8	4	0	28	31	20	18	0	0 0 0	0 0 0	—

LEAGUE CHAMPIONSHIP SERIES
1972 OAK A	2	0	1.000	0.00	2	2	1	14	5	2	5	1	0 0 0	4 1 0	.250
1973	0	0	—	1.80	1	0	0	5	6	2	4	0	0 0 0	0 0 0	—
1974	0	0	—	0.00	1	0	0	3.1	1	0	1	0	0 0 0	0 0 0	—
3 yrs.	2	0	1.000	0.40	4	2	1	22.1	12	4	10	1	0 0 0	4 1 0	.250

WORLD SERIES
| 1972 OAK A | 0 | 1 | .000 | 1.59 | 2 | 2 | 0 | 11.1 | 5 | 6 | 13 | 0 | 0 0 0 | 4 0 0 | .000 |

Pitcher Register

	W	L	PCT	ERA	G	GS	CG	IP	H	BB	SO	ShO	Relief Pitching W L SV	BATTING AB H HR	BA

Blue Moon Odom continued

1973	0	0	–	3.86	2	0	0	4.2	5	2	2	0	0 0 0	1 0 0	.000
1974	1	0	1.000	0.00	2	0	0	1.1	0	1	2	0	1 0 0	0 0 0	–
3 yrs.	1	1	.500	2.08	6	2	0	17.1	10	9	17	0	1 0 0	5 0 0	.000

Fred Olmstead

OLMSTEAD, FREDERICK D.
B. Nov. 21, 1881, Garden, Mich. D. June 16, 1972, Escanaba, Mich.

1908 CHI A	0	0	–	13.50	1	0	0	2	6	1	1	0	0 0 0	1 0 0	.000
1909	3	2	.600	1.81	8	6	5	54.2	52	12	21	0	0 0 0	21 2 0	.095
1910	11	12	.478	1.95	32	20	14	184.1	174	50	68	4	3 1 0	65 10 0	.154
1911	7	6	.538	4.21	25	11	7	117.2	146	30	45	1	2 0 2	37 7 0	.189
4 yrs.	21	20	.512	2.74	66	37	26	358.2	378	93	135	5	5 1 2	124 19 0	.153
4 yrs.	21	20	.512	2.74	66	37	26	358.2	378	93	135	5	5 1 2	124 19 0	.153

Emmett O'Neill

O'NEILL, ROBERT EMMETT (Pinky) BR TR 6'3" 185 lbs.
B. Jan. 13, 1918, San Mateo, Calif.

1943 BOS A	1	4	.200	4.53	11	5	1	57.2	56	46	20	0	1 0 0	16 3 0	.188
1944	6	11	.353	4.63	28	22	8	151.2	154	89	68	1	0 0 0	55 10 0	.182
1945	8	11	.421	5.15	24	22	10	141.2	134	117	55	1	0 0 0	50 9 1	.180
1946 2 teams		CHI N (1G 0-0)			CHI A (2G 0-0)										
" total	0	0	–	0.00	3	0	0	4.2	4	8	1	0	0 0 0	1 0 0	.000
4 yrs.	15	26	.366	4.76	66	49	19	355.2	348	260	144	2	1 0 0	122 22 1	.180
1 yr.	0	0	–	0.00	2	0	0	3.2	4	5	0	0	0 0 0	1 0 0	.000

Danny Osborn

OSBORN, DANIEL LEON BR TR 6'2" 195 lbs.
B. June 19, 1946, Springfield, Ohio

| 1975 CHI A | 3 | 0 | 1.000 | 4.50 | 24 | 0 | 0 | 58 | 57 | 37 | 38 | 0 | 3 0 0 | 0 0 0 | – |

Dan Osinski

OSINSKI, DANIEL BR TR 6'1½" 190 lbs.
B. Nov. 17, 1933, Chicago, Ill.

1962 2 teams		KC A (4G 0-0)			LA A (33G 6-4)										
" total	6	4	.600	3.97	37	0	0	59	53	38	48	0	6 4 4	11 0 0	.000
1963 LA A	8	8	.500	3.28	47	16	4	159.1	145	80	100	1	4 2 0	45 5 0	.111
1964	3	3	.500	3.48	47	4	1	93	87	39	88	1	2 2 2	18 1 0	.056
1965 MIL N	0	3	.000	2.82	61	0	0	83	81	40	54	0	0 3 6	6 1 0	.167
1966 BOS A	4	3	.571	3.61	44	1	0	67.1	68	28	44	0	3 3 2	6 2 0	.333
1967	3	1	.750	2.54	34	0	0	63.2	61	14	38	0	3 1 2	9 3 0	.333
1969 CHI A	5	5	.500	3.56	51	0	0	60.2	56	23	27	0	5 5 2	3 0 0	.000
1970 HOU N	0	1	.000	9.00	3	0	0	4	5	2	1	0	0 1 0	0 0 0	–
8 yrs.	29	28	.509	3.34	324	21	5	590	556	264	400	2	23 21 18	98 12 0	.122
1 yr.	5	5	.500	3.56	51	0	0	60.2	56	23	27	0	5 5 2	3 0 0	.000

WORLD SERIES

| 1967 BOS A | 0 | 0 | – | 6.75 | 2 | 0 | 0 | 1.1 | 2 | 0 | 0 | 0 | 0 0 0 | 0 0 0 | – |

Claude Osteen

OSTEEN, CLAUDE WILSON BL TL 5'11" 160 lbs.
B. Aug. 9, 1939, Caney Springs, Tenn.

1957 CIN N	0	0	–	2.25	3	0	0	4	4	3	3	0	0 0 0	1 0 0	.000
1959	0	0	–	7.04	2	0	0	7.2	11	9	3	0	0 0 0	2 0 0	.000
1960	0	1	.000	5.03	20	3	0	48.1	53	30	15	0	0 0 0	12 1 0	.083
1961 2 teams		CIN N (1G 0-0)			WAS A (3G 1-1)										
" total	1	1	.500	4.82	4	3	0	18.2	14	9	14	0	0 0 0	7 1 0	.143
1962 WAS A	8	13	.381	3.65	28	22	7	150.1	140	47	59	2	0 0 1	48 10 0	.208
1963	9	14	.391	3.35	40	29	8	212.1	222	60	109	2	1 1 0	70 12 1	.171
1964	15	13	.536	3.33	37	36	13	257	256	64	133	0	0 0 0	90 14 1	.156
1965 LA N	15	15	.500	2.79	40	40	9	287	253	78	162	1	0 0 0	99 12 0	.121
1966	17	14	.548	2.85	39	38	8	240.1	238	65	137	3	0 0 0	76 16 1	.211
1967	17	17	.500	3.22	39	39	14	288.1	298	52	152	5	0 0 0	101 18 2	.178
1968	12	18	.400	3.08	39	36	5	254	267	54	119	3	0 0 0	84 15 0	.179
1969	20	15	.571	2.66	41	41	16	321	293	74	183	7	0 0 0	111 24 1	.216
1970	16	14	.533	3.82	37	37	11	259	280	52	114	4	0 0 0	93 19 1	.204
1971	14	11	.560	3.51	38	38	11	259	262	63	109	4	0 0 0	86 16 0	.186
1972	20	11	.645	2.64	33	33	14	252	232	69	100	4	0 0 0	88 24 1	.273
1973	16	11	.593	3.31	33	33	12	236.2	227	61	86	3	0 0 0	78 12 0	.154
1974 2 teams		HOU N (23G 9-9)			STL N (8G 0-2)										
" total	9	11	.450	3.80	31	23	7	161	184	58	51	2	0 1 0	53 13 0	.245
1975 CHI A	7	16	.304	4.36	37	37	5	204.1	237	92	63	0	0 0 0	0 0 0	–
18 yrs.	196	195	.501	3.30	541	488	140	3461	3471	940	1612	40	1 2 1	1099 207 8	.188
1 yr.	7	16	.304	4.36	37	37	5	204.1	237	92	63	0	0 0 0	0 0 0	–

WORLD SERIES

1965 LA N	1	1	.500	0.64	2	2	1	14	9	5	4	1	0 0 0	3 1 0	.333
1966	0	1	.000	1.29	1	1	0	7	3	1	3	0	0 0 0	2 0 0	.000
2 yrs.	1	2	.333	0.86	3	3	1	21	12	6	7	1	0 0 0	5 1 0	.200

Denny O'Toole

O'TOOLE, DENNIS JOSEPH BR TR 6'3" 195 lbs.
Brother of Jim O'Toole.
B. Mar. 13, 1949, Chicago, Ill.

1969 CHI A	0	0	–	6.75	2	0	0	4	5	2	4	0	0 0 0	0 0 0	–
1970	0	0	–	3.00	3	0	0	3	5	2	3	0	0 0 0	0 0 0	–
1971	0	0	–	0.00	1	0	0	2	0	1	2	0	0 0 0	0 0 0	–
1972	0	0	–	5.40	3	0	0	5	10	2	5	0	0 0 0	0 0 0	–
1973	0	0	–	5.29	6	0	0	17	23	3	8	0	0 0 0	0 0 0	–
5 yrs.	0	0	–	4.94	15	0	0	31	43	10	22	0	0 0 0	0 0 0	–
5 yrs.	0	0	–	4.94	15	0	0	31	43	10	22	0	0 0 0	0 0 0	–

Pitcher Register

	W	L	PCT	ERA	G	GS	CG	IP	H	BB	SO	ShO	Relief Pitching W L SV	BATTING AB H HR	BA

Jim O'Toole
O'TOOLE, JAMES JEROME
Brother of Denny O'Toole.
B. Jan. 10, 1937, Chicago, Ill.   BB TL 6'   190 lbs.

	W	L	PCT	ERA	G	GS	CG	IP	H	BB	SO	ShO	W	L	SV	AB	H	HR	BA
1958 CIN N	0	1	.000	1.29	1	1	0	7	4	5	4	0	0	0	0	2	0	0	.000
1959	5	8	.385	5.15	28	19	3	129.1	144	73	68	1	0	0	0	37	5	0	.135
1960	12	12	.500	3.80	34	31	7	196.1	198	66	124	2	0	0	1	66	7	0	.106
1961	19	9	.679	3.10	39	35	11	252.2	229	93	178	3	1	0	2	93	16	0	.172
1962	16	13	.552	3.50	36	34	11	251.2	222	87	170	3	2	0	0	91	10	0	.110
1963	17	14	.548	2.88	33	32	12	234.1	208	57	146	5	0	0	0	74	11	0	.149
1964	17	7	.708	2.66	30	30	9	220	194	51	145	3	0	0	0	70	7	0	.100
1965	3	10	.231	5.92	29	22	2	127.2	154	47	71	0	0	0	1	45	4	0	.089
1966	5	7	.417	3.55	25	24	2	142	139	49	96	0	0	0	0	47	6	0	.128
1967 CHI A	4	3	.571	2.82	15	10	1	54.1	53	18	37	1	0	0	0	13	1	0	.077
10 yrs.	98	84	.538	3.57	270	238	58	1615.1	1545	546	1039	18	3	0	4	538	67	0	.125
1 yr.	4	3	.571	2.82	15	10	1	54.1	53	18	37	1	0	0	0	13	1	0	.077

WORLD SERIES
| 1961 CIN N | 0 | 2 | .000 | 3.00 | 2 | 2 | 0 | 12 | 11 | 7 | 4 | 0 | 0 | 0 | 0 | 3 | 0 | 0 | .000 |

Jim Otten
OTTEN, JAMES EDWARD
B. July 1, 1951, Lewiston, Mont.   BR TR 6'2"   195 lbs.

	W	L	PCT	ERA	G	GS	CG	IP	H	BB	SO	ShO	W	L	SV	AB	H	HR	BA
1974 CHI A	0	1	.000	5.63	5	1	0	16	22	12	11	0	0	0	0	0	0	0	—
1975	0	0	—	6.75	2	0	0	5.1	4	7	3	0	0	0	0	0	0	0	—
1976	0	0	—	4.50	2	0	0	6	9	2	3	0	0	0	0	0	0	0	—
1980 STL N	0	5	.000	5.56	31	4	0	55	71	26	38	0	0	1	0	5	1	0	.200
1981	1	0	1.000	5.25	24	0	0	36	44	20	20	0	1	0	0	2	0	0	.000
5 yrs.	1	6	.143	5.48	64	5	0	118.1	150	67	75	0	1	1	0	7	1	0	.143
3 yrs.	0	1	.000	5.60	9	1	0	27.1	35	21	17	0	0	0	0	0	0	0	—

Frank Owen
OWEN, FRANK MALCOLM (Yip)
B. Dec. 23, 1879, Ypsilanti, Mich.   D. Nov. 27, 1942, Detroit, Mich.   TR

	W	L	PCT	ERA	G	GS	CG	IP	H	BB	SO	ShO	W	L	SV	AB	H	HR	BA
1901 DET A	1	3	.250	4.34	8	5	3	56	70	30	17	0	0	0	0	20	1	0	.050
1903 CHI A	8	12	.400	3.50	26	20	15	167.1	167	44	66	1	1	2	1	57	7	0	.123
1904	21	15	.583	1.94	37	36	34	315	243	61	103	4	0	0	1	107	23	2	.215
1905	21	13	.618	2.10	42	38	32	334	276	56	125	3	0	1	0	124	18	0	.145
1906	19	12	.613	2.33	42	36	27	293	289	54	66	7	1	0	2	103	14	0	.136
1907	2	3	.400	2.49	11	4	2	47	43	13	15	0	0	1	0	16	4	0	.250
1908	6	9	.400	3.41	25	14	5	140	142	37	48	1	2	1	0	50	9	0	.180
1909	1	1	.500	4.50	3	2	1	16	19	3	3	0	0	0	0	6	1	0	.167
8 yrs.	79	68	.537	2.55	194	155	119	1368.1	1249	298	443	16	4	5	4	483	77	2	.159
7 yrs.	78	65	.545	2.48	186	150	116	1312.1	1179	268	426	16	4	5	4	463	76	2	.164
								9th											

WORLD SERIES
| 1906 CHI A | 0 | 0 | — | 3.00 | 1 | 0 | 0 | 6 | 6 | 3 | 2 | 0 | 0 | 0 | 0 | 2 | 0 | 0 | .000 |

Al Papai
PAPAI, ALFRED THOMAS
B. May 7, 1919, Divernon, Ill.   BR TR 6'3"   185 lbs.

	W	L	PCT	ERA	G	GS	CG	IP	H	BB	SO	ShO	W	L	SV	AB	H	HR	BA
1948 STL N	0	1	.000	5.06	10	0	0	16	14	7	8	0	0	1	0	2	0	0	.000
1949 STL N	4	11	.267	5.06	42	15	6	142.1	175	81	31	0	2	3	2	38	3	0	.079
1950 2 teams	BOS A (16G 4-2)						STL N (13G 1-0)												
" total	5	2	.714	6.33	29	3	2	69.2	82	42	26	0	4	0	2	20	3	0	.150
1955 CHI N	0	0	—	3.86	7	0	0	11.2	10	8	5	0	0	0	0	2	0	0	.000
4 yrs.	9	14	.391	5.37	88	18	8	239.2	281	138	70	0	6	4	4	62	6	0	.097
1 yr.	0	0	—	3.86	7	0	0	11.2	10	8	5	0	0	0	0	2	0	0	.000

Frank Papish
PAPISH, FRANK RICHARD (Pap)
B. Oct. 21, 1917, Pueblo, Colo.   D. Aug. 30, 1965, Pueblo, Colo.   BR TL 6'2"   192 lbs.

	W	L	PCT	ERA	G	GS	CG	IP	H	BB	SO	ShO	W	L	SV	AB	H	HR	BA
1945 CHI A	4	4	.500	3.74	19	5	3	84.1	75	40	45	0	4	4	1	26	6	0	.231
1946	7	5	.583	2.74	31	15	6	138	122	63	66	2	0	1	0	43	8	0	.186
1947	12	12	.500	3.26	38	26	6	199	185	98	79	1	2	0	3	58	5	0	.086
1948	2	8	.200	5.00	32	14	2	95.1	97	75	41	0	0	1	4	27	5	0	.185
1949 CLE A	1	0	1.000	3.19	25	3	1	62	54	39	23	0	1	0	1	8	1	0	.125
1950 PIT N	0	0	—	27.00	4	1	0	2.1	8	4	1	0	0	0	0	0	0	0	—
6 yrs.	26	29	.473	3.58	149	64	18	581	541	319	255	3	7	6	9	162	25	0	.154
4 yrs.	25	29	.463	3.52	120	60	17	516.2	479	276	231	3	6	6	8	154	24	0	.156

Reggie Patterson
PATTERSON, REGINALD ALLEN
B. Nov. 7, 1958, Birmingham, Ala.   BR TR 6'4"   180 lbs.

	W	L	PCT	ERA	G	GS	CG	IP	H	BB	SO	ShO	W	L	SV	AB	H	HR	BA
1981 CHI A	0	1	.000	14.14	6	1	0	7	14	6	2	0	0	0	0	0	0	0	—
1983 CHI N	1	2	.333	4.82	5	2	0	18.2	17	6	10	0	0	1	0	6	0	0	.000
2 yrs.	1	3	.250	7.36	11	3	0	25.2	31	12	12	0	0	1	0	6	0	0	.000
1 yr.	0	1	.000	14.14	6	1	0	7	14	6	2	0	0	0	0	0	0	0	—

Roy Patterson
PATTERSON, ROY LEWIS (Boy Wonder)
B. Dec. 17, 1876, Stoddard, Wis.   D. Apr. 14, 1953, St. Croix Falls, Wis.   BR TR 6'   185 lbs.

	W	L	PCT	ERA	G	GS	CG	IP	H	BB	SO	ShO	W	L	SV	AB	H	HR	BA
1901 CHI A	20	16	.556	3.37	41	35	30	312.1	345	62	127	4	2	0	0	117	26	1	.222
1902	19	14	.576	3.06	34	30	26	268	262	67	61	2	2	2	0	105	20	0	.190
1903	16	15	.516	2.70	34	30	26	293	275	69	89	2	2	0	0	105	11	0	.105
1904	9	8	.529	2.29	22	17	14	165	148	24	64	4	1	0	0	58	6	0	.103
1905	4	5	.444	1.83	15	9	7	88.2	73	16	29	1	0	0	0	30	8	0	.267
1906	10	6	.625	2.09	21	18	12	142	119	17	45	3	0	0	0	49	3	0	.061
1907	4	6	.400	2.63	19	13	4	96	105	18	27	1	0	0	0	31	3	0	.097
7 yrs.	82	70	.539	2.75	184	152	119	1365	1327	273	442	17	7	4	1	495	77	1	.156
7 yrs.	82	70	.539	2.75	184	152	119	1365	1327	273	442	17	7	4	1	495	77	1	.156
					10th			10th											

Pitcher Register

	W	L	PCT	ERA	G	GS	CG	IP	H	BB	SO	ShO	Relief Pitching W L SV	BATTING AB H HR	BA

George Payne
PAYNE, GEORGE WASHINGTON BR TR 5'11" 172 lbs.
B. May 23, 1894, Mt. Vernon, Ky. D. Jan. 24, 1959, Long Beach, Calif.

| 1920 CHI A | 1 | 1 | .500 | 5.46 | 12 | 0 | 0 | 29.2 | 39 | 9 | 9 | 0 | 1 1 0 | 8 1 0 | .125 |

Ike Pearson
PEARSON, ISSAC OVERTON BR TR 6'1" 180 lbs.
B. Mar. 1, 1917, Grenada, Miss.

1939 PHI N	2	13	.133	5.76	26	13	4	125	144	56	29	0	0 2 0	37 2 0	.054
1940	3	14	.176	5.45	29	20	5	145.1	160	57	43	1	0 1 1	44 9 0	.205
1941	4	14	.222	3.57	46	10	0	136	139	70	38	0	4 4 6	40 5 0	.125
1942	1	6	.143	4.54	35	7	0	85.1	87	50	21	0	1 1 0	23 1 0	.043
1946	1	0	1.000	3.77	5	2	1	14.1	19	8	6	1	0 0 0	5 1 1	.200
1948 CHI A	2	3	.400	4.92	23	2	0	53	62	27	12	0	1 2 1	10 2 0	.200
6 yrs.	13	50	.206	4.83	164	54	10	559	611	268	149	2	6 10 8	159 20 1	.126
1 yr.	2	3	.400	4.92	23	2	0	53	62	27	12	0	1 2 1	10 2 0	.200

Russ Pence
PENCE, RUSSELL WILLIAM BR TR 6' 185 lbs.
B. Mar. 11, 1900, Marine, Ill. D. Aug. 11, 1971, Hot Springs, Ark.

| 1921 CHI A | 0 | 0 | – | 8.44 | 4 | 0 | 0 | 5.1 | 6 | 7 | 2 | 0 | 0 0 0 | 1 0 0 | .000 |

John Perkovich
PERKOVICH, JOHN JOSEPH BR TR 5'11" 175 lbs.
B. Mar. 10, 1924, Chicago, Ill.

| 1950 CHI A | 0 | 0 | – | 7.20 | 1 | 0 | 0 | 5 | 7 | 1 | 3 | 0 | 0 0 0 | 1 0 0 | .000 |

Len Perme
PERME, LEONARD JOHN BL TL 6' 170 lbs.
B. Nov. 25, 1917, Cleveland, Ohio

1942 CHI A	0	1	.000	1.38	4	1	1	13	5	4	4	0	0 0 0	3 1 0	.333
1946	0	0	–	8.31	4	0	0	4.1	6	7	2	0	0 0 0	0 0 0	–
2 yrs.	0	1	.000	3.12	8	1	1	17.1	11	11	6	0	0 0 0	3 1 0	.333
2 yrs.	0	1	.000	3.12	8	1	1	17.1	11	11	6	0	0 0 0	3 1 0	.333

Stan Perzanowski
PERZANOWSKI, STANLEY BR TR 6'2" 170 lbs.
B. Aug. 25, 1950, East Chicago, Ind.

1971 CHI A	0	1	.000	12.00	5	0	0	6	14	3	5	0	0 1 0	0 0 0	.000
1974	0	0	–	22.50	2	1	0	2	8	2	2	0	0 0 0	0 0 0	–
1975 TEX A	3	3	.500	3.00	12	8	1	66	59	25	26	0	0 0 0	0 0 0	–
1976	0	0	–	9.75	5	0	0	12	20	4	6	0	0 0 0	0 0 0	–
1978 MIN A	2	7	.222	5.24	13	7	1	56.2	59	26	31	0	0 3 1	0 0 0	–
5 yrs.	5	11	.313	5.11	37	16	2	142.2	160	60	70	0	0 4 2	2 0 0	.000
2 yrs.	0	1	.000	14.63	7	1	0	8	22	5	7	0	0 1 0	2 0 0	.000

Gary Peters
PETERS, GARY CHARLES BL TL 6'2" 200 lbs.
B. Apr. 21, 1937, Grove City, Pa.

1959 CHI A	0	0	–	0.00	2	0	0	1	2	1	0	0	0 0 0	0 0 0	–
1960	0	0	–	2.70	2	0	0	3.1	4	1	4	0	0 0 0	0 0 0	–
1961	0	0	–	1.74	3	0	0	10.1	10	2	6	0	0 0 1	3 1 0	.333
1962	0	1	.000	5.00	5	0	0	6.1	8	1	4	0	0 1 0	0 0 0	–
1963	19	8	.704	2.33	41	30	13	243	192	68	189	4	0 2 1	81 21 3	.259
1964	20	8	.714	2.50	37	36	11	273.2	217	104	205	3	0 0 0	120 25 4	.208
1965	10	12	.455	3.62	33	30	1	176.1	181	63	95	0	0 0 0	72 13 1	.181
1966	12	10	.545	1.98	30	27	11	204.2	156	45	129	4	0 1 0	81 19 1	.235
1967	16	11	.593	2.28	38	36	11	260	187	91	215	3	0 0 0	99 21 2	.212
1968	4	13	.235	3.76	31	25	6	162.2	146	60	110	1	0 0 1	72 15 2	.208
1969	10	15	.400	4.53	36	32	7	218.2	238	78	140	3	0 0 0	71 12 2	.169
1970 BOS A	16	11	.593	4.05	34	34	10	222	221	83	155	4	0 0 0	82 20 1	.244
1971	14	11	.560	4.37	34	32	9	214	241	70	100	1	0 0 1	96 26 3	.271
1972	3	3	.500	4.34	33	4	0	85	91	38	67	0	2 1 1	30 6 0	.200
14 yrs.	124	103	.546	3.25	359	286	79	2081	1894	706	1420	23	2 5 5	*	
11 yrs.	91	78	.538	2.92	258	216	60	1560	1341	515	1098	18	0 4 3	599 127 15	.212

5th

Rube Peters
PETERS, OSCAR C. BR TR 6' 185 lbs.
B. Mar. 15, 1886, Grand Fork, Ill.

1912 CHI A	5	6	.455	4.14	28	11	4	108.2	134	33	39	0	1 1 0	31 6 0	.194
1914 BKN F	2	2	.500	3.82	11	3	1	37.2	52	16	13	0	1 0 0	11 1 0	.091
2 yrs.	7	8	.467	4.06	39	14	5	146.1	186	49	52	0	2 1 0	42 7 0	.167
1 yr.	5	6	.455	4.14	28	11	4	108.2	134	33	39	0	1 1 0	31 6 0	.194

Ray Phelps
PHELPS, RAYMOND CLIFFORD BR TR 6'2" 200 lbs.
B. Dec. 11, 1903, Dunlap, Tenn. D. July 7, 1971, Fort Pierce, Fla.

1930 BKN N	14	7	.667	4.11	36	24	11	179.2	198	52	64	2	2 1 0	68 10 1	.147
1931	7	9	.438	5.00	28	26	3	149.1	184	44	50	2	0 0 0	51 8 0	.157
1932	4	5	.444	5.90	20	8	4	79.1	101	27	21	1	1 3 0	23 2 0	.087
1935 CHI A	4	8	.333	4.82	27	17	4	125	126	55	38	0	0 1 0	41 5 0	.122
1936	4	6	.400	6.03	15	4	2	68.2	91	42	17	0	3 3 0	26 6 0	.231
5 yrs.	33	35	.485	4.93	126	79	24	602	700	220	190	5	6 8 1	209 31 1	.148
2 yrs.	8	14	.364	5.25	42	21	6	193.2	217	97	55	0	3 4 0	67 11 0	.164

Taylor Phillips
PHILLIPS, WILLIAM TAYLOR (Tay) BL TL 5'11" 185 lbs.
B. June 18, 1933, Atlanta, Ga.

1956 MIL N	5	3	.625	2.26	23	6	3	87.2	69	33	36	0	2 1 2	21 0 0	.000
1957	3	2	.600	5.55	27	6	0	73	82	40	36	0	2 1 0	20 2 0	.100
1958 CHI N	7	10	.412	4.76	39	27	5	170.1	178	79	102	1	1 0 0	54 3 0	.056
1959 2 teams	CHI N (7G 0–2)				PHI N (32G 1–4)										
" total	1	6	.143	5.54	39	5	1	79.2	94	42	40	0	0 3 0	15 1 0	.067
1960 PHI N	0	1	.000	8.36	10	1	0	14	21	4	6	0	0 0 0	1 0 0	.000

394

Pitcher Register

	W	L	PCT	ERA	G	GS	CG	IP	H	BB	SO	ShO	Relief Pitching W L SV	BATTING AB H HR	BA

Taylor Phillips continued

1963 CHI A	0	0	–	10.29	9	0	0	14	16	13	13	0	0 0 0	2 0 0	.000
6 yrs.	16	22	.421	4.82	147	45	9	438.2	460	211	233	1	5 5 6	113 6 0	.053
1 yr.	0	0	–	10.29	9	0	0	14	16	13	13	0	0 0 0	2 0 0	.000

Wiley Piatt

PIATT, WILEY HAROLD (Iron Man)   BL TL 5'10" 175 lbs.
B. July 13, 1874, Blue Creek, Ohio   D. Sept. 20, 1946, Cincinnati, Ohio

1898 PHI N	24	14	.632	3.18	39	37	33	306	285	97	121	6	1 0 0	122 32 0	.262
1899	23	15	.605	3.45	39	38	31	305	323	86	89	2	1 0 0	122 33 0	.270
1900	9	10	.474	4.65	22	20	16	160.2	194	71	47	1	0 1 0	68 17 0	.250
1901 2 teams			PHI	A (18G 5–12)	CHI	A (7G 4–2)									
" total	9	14	.391	4.13	25	22	19	191.2	218	74	64	1	1 1 1	75 15 0	.200
1902 CHI A	12	12	.500	3.51	32	30	22	246	263	66	96	2	0 0 0	85 17 0	.200
1903 BOS N	8	13	.381	3.18	25	23	18	181	198	61	100	0	0 1 0	71 16 0	.225
6 yrs.	85	78	.521	3.60	182	170	139	1390.1	1481	455	517	12	3 3 1	543 130 0	.239
2 yrs.	16	14	.533	3.39	39	36	26	297.2	305	80	115	3	1 0 0	102 19 0	.186

Billy Pierce

PIERCE, WALTER WILLIAM   BL TL 5'10" 160 lbs.
B. Apr. 2, 1927, Detroit, Mich.

1945 DET A	0	0	–	1.80	5	0	0	10	6	10	10	0	0 0 0	2 0 0	.000
1948	3	0	1.000	6.34	22	5	0	55.1	47	51	36	0	1 0 0	17 5 0	.294
1949 CHI A	7	15	.318	3.88	32	26	8	171.2	145	112	95	0	1 0 0	51 9 0	.176
1950	12	16	.429	3.98	33	29	15	219.1	189	137	118	1	1 0 1	77 20 0	.260
1951	15	14	.517	3.03	37	28	18	240.1	237	73	113	1	0 3 2	79 16 0	.203
1952	15	12	.556	2.57	33	32	14	255.1	214	79	144	4	0 0 1	91 17 0	.187
1953	18	12	.600	2.72	40	33	19	271.1	216	102	186	7	3 0 3	87 11 0	.126
1954	9	10	.474	3.48	36	26	12	188.2	179	86	148	4	0 0 3	57 11 0	.193
1955	15	10	.600	1.97	33	26	16	205.2	162	64	157	6	2 0 1	70 12 0	.171
1956	20	9	.690	3.32	35	33	21	276.1	261	100	192	1	0 1 1	102 16 0	.157
1957	20	12	.625	3.26	37	34	16	257	228	71	171	4	0 1 2	99 17 0	.172
1958	17	11	.607	2.68	35	32	19	245	204	66	144	3	0 0 0	83 17 0	.205
1959	14	15	.483	3.62	34	33	12	224	217	62	114	2	0 0 0	68 13 0	.191
1960	14	7	.667	3.62	32	30	8	196.1	201	46	108	1	1 0 0	67 12 0	.179
1961	10	9	.526	3.80	39	28	5	180	190	54	106	1	3 0 3	56 8 0	.143
1962 SF N	16	6	.727	3.49	30	23	7	162.1	147	35	76	2	0 0 1	56 12 0	.214
1963	3	11	.214	4.27	38	13	3	99	106	20	52	1	0 5 8	31 4 0	.129
1964	3	0	1.000	2.20	34	1	0	49	40	10	29	0	2 0 4	9 3 0	.333
18 yrs.	211	169	.555	3.27	585	432	193	3306.2	2989	1178	1999	38	14 10 32	1102 203 0	.184
13 yrs.	186	152	.550	3.19	456	390	183	2931	2643	1052	1796	35	11 5 19	987 179 0	.181
				4th	3rd			4th			5th	4th		3rd 1st 3rd	

WORLD SERIES

1959 CHI A	0	0	–	0.00	3	0	0	4	2	2	3	0	0 0 0	0 0 0	–
1962 SF N	1	1	.500	2.40	2	2	1	15	8	2	5	0	0 0 0	5 0 0	.000
2 yrs.	1	1	.500	1.89	5	2	1	19	10	4	8	0	0 0 0	5 0 0	.000

Marino Pieretti

PIERETTI, MARINO PAUL (Chick)   BR TR 5'7" 153 lbs.
B. Sept. 23, 1920, Lucca, Italy   D. Jan. 30, 1981, San Francisco, Calif.

1945 WAS A	14	13	.519	3.32	44	27	14	233.1	235	91	66	3	1 1 2	81 18 0	.222
1946	3	2	.600	5.95	30	2	1	62	70	40	20	0	1 1 0	14 3 0	.214
1947	2	4	.333	4.21	23	10	2	83.1	97	47	32	1	0 1 0	26 6 0	.231
1948 2 teams			WAS	A (8G 0–2)	CHI	A (21G 8–10)									
" total	8	12	.400	5.47	29	19	4	131.2	135	59	34	0	1 1 1	41 7 0	.171
1949 CHI A	4	6	.400	5.51	39	9	0	116	131	54	25	0	2 1 4	38 9 0	.237
1950 CLE A	0	1	.000	4.18	29	1	0	47.1	45	30	11	0	0 1 1	7 2 0	.286
6 yrs.	30	38	.441	4.53	194	68	21	673.2	713	321	188	4	5 6 8	207 45 0	.217
2 yrs.	12	16	.429	5.22	60	27	4	236	248	106	53	0	3 1 5	77 16 0	.208

Skip Pitlock

PITLOCK, LEE PATRICK (Skip)   BL TL 6'2" 180 lbs.
B. Nov. 6, 1947, Hillside, Ill.

1970 SF N	5	5	.500	4.66	18	15	1	87	92	48	56	0	0 0 0	25 2 1	.080
1974 CHI A	3	3	.500	4.42	40	5	0	106	103	55	68	0	2 2 1	0 0 0	–
1975	0	0	–	0.00	1	0	0	0	1	0	0	0	0 0 0	0 0 0	–
3 yrs.	8	8	.500	4.52	59	20	1	193	196	103	124	0	2 2 1	25 2 1	.080
2 yrs.	3	3	.500	4.42	41	5	0	106	104	55	68	0	2 2 1	0 0 0	–

Juan Pizarro

PIZARRO, JUAN CORDOVA   BL TL 5'11" 170 lbs.
B. Feb. 7, 1938, Santurce, Puerto Rico

1957 MIL N	5	6	.455	4.62	24	10	3	99.1	99	51	68	0	3 1 0	36 9 1	.250
1958	6	4	.600	2.70	16	10	7	96.2	75	47	84	1	1 1 1	32 8 0	.250
1959	6	2	.750	3.77	29	14	6	133.2	117	70	126	2	0 0 0	41 5 0	.122
1960	6	7	.462	4.55	21	17	3	114.2	105	72	88	0	1 1 0	40 11 0	.275
1961 CHI A	14	7	.667	3.05	39	25	12	194.2	164	89	188	1	0 0 2	69 17 0	.246
1962	12	14	.462	3.81	36	32	9	203.1	182	97	173	1	3 0 1	69 11 0	.159
1963	16	8	.667	2.39	32	28	10	214.2	177	63	163	3	2 0 1	73 13 2	.178
1964	19	9	.679	2.56	33	33	11	239	193	55	162	4	0 0 0	90 19 3	.211
1965	6	3	.667	3.43	18	18	2	97	96	37	65	1	0 0 0	34 8 1	.235
1966	8	6	.571	3.76	34	9	1	88.2	91	39	42	0	4 2 3	26 4 0	.154
1967 PIT N	8	10	.444	3.95	50	9	1	107	99	52	96	1	7 5 9	27 7 0	.259
1968 2 teams			PIT	N (12G 1–1)	BOS	A (19G 6–8)									
" total	7	9	.438	3.29	31	12	6	118.2	111	54	90	0	2 3 2	33 5 0	.152
1969 3 teams			BOS	A (6G 0–1)	CLE	A (48G 3–3)	OAK	A (3G 1–1)							
" total	4	5	.444	3.35	57	4	1	99.1	84	58	52	0	3 5 7	20 5 0	.250
1970 CHI N	0	0	–	4.50	10	0	0	16	16	9	14	0	0 0 0	3 0 0	.000
1971	7	6	.538	3.48	16	14	6	101	78	40	67	3	0 0 0	34 6 1	.176
1972	4	5	.444	3.97	16	7	1	59	66	32	24	0	3 0 1	21 3 0	.143

Pitcher Register

	W	L	PCT	ERA	G	GS	CG	IP	H	BB	SO	ShO	Relief Pitching W L SV	BATTING AB H HR	BA

Juan Pizarro continued

1973 2 teams	CHI N (2G 0-1)				HOU N (15G 2-2)										
" total	2	3	.400	7.24	17	1	0	27.1	34	12	13	0	2 2 0	4 0 0	.000
1974 PIT N	1	1	.500	1.88	7	2	0	24	20	11	7	0	0 0 0	6 2 0	.333
18 yrs.	131	105	.555	3.43	488	245	79	2034	1807	888	1522	17	31 20 28	658 133 8	.202
6 yrs.	75	47	.615	3.05 2nd	192	145	45	1037.1	903	380	793	10	9 2 7	361 72 6	.199

LEAGUE CHAMPIONSHIP SERIES

| 1974 PIT N | 0 | 0 | — | 0.00 | 1 | 0 | 0 | .2 | 0 | 1 | 0 | 0 | 0 0 0 | 0 0 0 | — |

WORLD SERIES

1957 MIL N	0	0	—	10.80	1	0	0	1.2	3	2	1	0	0 0 0	1 0 0	.000
1958	0	0	—	5.40	1	0	0	1.2	2	1	3	0	0 0 0	0 0 0	—
2 yrs.	0	0	—	8.10	2	0	0	3.1	5	3	4	0	0 0 0	1 0 0	.000

Howie Pollet

POLLET, HOWARD JOSEPH   BL TL 6'1½" 175 lbs.
B. June 26, 1921, New Orleans, La.   D. Aug. 8, 1974, Houston, Tex.

1941 STL N	5	2	.714	1.93	9	8	6	70	55	27	37	2	0 0 0	28 5 0	.179
1942	7	5	.583	2.88	27	13	5	109.1	102	39	42	2	0 1 0	31 7 0	.226
1943	8	4	.667	1.75	16	14	12	118.1	83	32	61	5	0 0 0	43 7 0	.163
1946	21	10	.677	2.10	40	32	22	266	228	86	107	4	0 0 5	87 14 0	.161
1947	9	11	.450	4.34	37	24	9	176.1	195	87	73	0	1 0 2	65 15 0	.231
1948	13	8	.619	4.54	36	26	11	186.1	216	67	80	0	2 0 0	68 8 0	.118
1949	20	9	.690	2.77	39	28	17	230.2	228	59	108	5	3 1 1	82 16 0	.195
1950	14	13	.519	3.29	37	30	14	232.1	228	68	117	2	1 1 2	84 12 0	.143
1951 2 teams	STL N (6G 0-3)				PIT N (21G 6-10)										
" total	6	13	.316	4.98	27	23	4	141	151	59	57	1	0 2 1	37 5 0	.135
1952 PIT N	7	16	.304	4.12	31	30	9	214	217	71	90	1	0 0 0	68 13 0	.191
1953 2 teams	PIT N (5G 1-1)				CHI N (25G 5-6)										
" total	6	7	.462	4.79	30	18	2	124	147	50	53	0	0 1 1	34 5 0	.147
1954 CHI N	8	10	.444	3.58	20	20	4	128.1	131	54	58	2	0 0 0	47 13 0	.277
1955	4	3	.571	5.61	24	7	1	61	62	27	27	1	3 0 5	15 6 0	.400
1956 2 teams	CHI A (11G 3-1)				PIT N (19G 0-4)										
" total	3	5	.375	3.62	30	4	0	49.2	45	19	24	0	3 4 3	9 3 0	.333
14 yrs.	131	116	.530	3.51	403	277	116	2107.1	2088	745	934	25	13 10 20	698 129 0	.185
1 yr.	3	1	.750	4.10	11	4	0	26.1	27	11	14	0	3 0 0	8 3 0	.375

WORLD SERIES

1942 STL N	0	0	—	0.00	1	0	0	.1	0	0	0	0	0 0 0	0 0 0	—
1946	0	1	.000	3.48	2	2	1	10.1	12	4	3	0	0 0 0	4 0 0	.000
2 yrs.	0	1	.000	3.38	3	2	1	10.2	12	4	3	0	0 0 0	4 0 0	.000

John Pomorski

POMORSKI, JOHN LEON   BR TR 6' 178 lbs.
B. Dec. 30, 1905, Brooklyn, N. Y.

| 1934 CHI A | 0 | 0 | — | 5.40 | 3 | 0 | 0 | 1.2 | 1 | 2 | 0 | 0 | 0 0 0 | 0 0 0 | — |

Bob Poser

POSER, JOHN FALK   BL TR 6' 173 lbs.
B. Mar. 16, 1910, Columbus, Wis.

1932 CHI A	0	0	—	27.00	1	0	0	.2	3	2	1	0	0 0 0	3 0 0	.000
1935 STL A	1	1	.500	9.22	4	1	0	13.2	26	4	1	0	1 0 0	4 1 0	.250
2 yrs.	1	1	.500	10.05	5	1	0	14.1	29	6	2	0	1 0 0	7 1 0	.143
1 yr.	0	0	—	27.00	1	0	0	.2	3	2	1	0	0 0 0	3 0 0	.000

Bob Priddy

PRIDDY, ROBERT SIMPSON   BR TR 6'1" 200 lbs.
B. Dec. 10, 1939, Pittsburgh, Pa.

1962 PIT N	1	0	1.000	3.00	2	0	0	3	4	1	1	0	1 0 0	0 0 0	—
1964	1	2	.333	3.93	19	0	0	34.1	35	15	23	0	1 2 1	3 0 0	.000
1965 SF N	1	0	1.000	1.74	8	0	0	10.1	6	2	7	0	1 0 0	1 0 0	.000
1966	6	3	.667	3.96	38	3	0	91	88	28	51	0	6 0 1	17 3 0	.176
1967 WAS A	3	7	.300	3.44	46	8	1	110	98	33	57	0	0 3 4	22 4 0	.182
1968 CHI A	3	11	.214	3.63	35	18	2	114	106	41	66	0	0 2 0	24 1 1	.042
1969 3 teams	CHI A (4G 0-0)				CAL A (15G 0-1)				ATL N (1G 0-0)						
" total	0	1	.000	4.46	20	0	0	36.1	35	10	21	0	0 1 0	2 0 0	.000
1970 ATL N	5	5	.500	5.42	41	0	0	73	75	24	32	0	5 5 8	15 3 0	.200
1971	4	9	.308	4.22	40	0	0	64	71	44	36	0	4 9 4	11 2 0	.182
9 yrs.	24	38	.387	4.00	249	29	3	536	518	198	294	0	18 22 18	95 13 1	.137
2 yrs.	3	11	.214	3.69	39	18	2	122	116	43	71	0	0 0 0	24 1 1	.042

Red Proctor

PROCTOR, NOAH RICHARD   BR TR 6'1" 165 lbs.
B. Oct. 27, 1900, Williamsburg, Va.   D. Feb. 24, 1967, Columbus, Miss.

| 1923 CHI A | 0 | 0 | — | 13.50 | 2 | 0 | 0 | 4 | 11 | 2 | 0 | 0 | 0 0 0 | 0 0 0 | — |

Mike Proly

PROLY, MICHAEL JAMES   BR TR 6' 185 lbs.
B. Dec. 15, 1950, Jamaica, N. Y.

1976 STL N	1	0	1.000	3.71	14	0	0	17	21	6	4	0	1 0 0	0 0 0	—
1978 CHI A	5	2	.714	2.74	14	6	2	65.2	63	12	19	0	0 0 1	0 0 0	—
1979	3	8	.273	3.89	38	6	0	88	89	40	32	0	3 4 9	0 0 0	—
1980	5	10	.333	3.06	62	3	0	147	136	58	56	0	4 4 8	0 0 0	—
1981 PHI N	2	1	.667	3.86	35	2	0	63	66	19	19	0	2 1 2	7 0 0	.000
1982 CHI N	5	3	.625	2.30	44	1	0	82	77	22	24	0	5 3 1	14 4 0	.286
1983	1	5	.167	4.04	58	0	0	83	79	38	31	0	1 5 1	11 1 0	.091
7 yrs.	22	29	.431	3.23	267	18	2	545.2	531	195	185	0	16 17 22	32 5 0	.156
3 yrs.	13	20	.394	3.23	114	15	2	300.2	288	110	107	0	7 8 18	0 0 0	—

Pitcher Register

	W	L	PCT	ERA	G	GS	CG	IP	H	BB	SO	ShO	Relief Pitching W L SV	AB	BATTING H HR	BA

Tom Qualters
QUALTERS, THOMAS FRANCIS (Money Bags)
B. Apr. 1, 1935, McKeesport, Pa.
BR TR 6'½" 190 lbs.

1953 PHI N	0	0	–	162.00	1	0	0	.1	4	1	0	0	0	0	0	0	0	0	–
1957	0	0	–	8.10	6	0	0	6.2	12	4	6	0	0	0	0	0	0	0	–
1958 2 teams		PHI N (1G 0–0)			CHI A (26G 0–0)														
" total	0	0	–	4.20	27	0	0	45	47	21	14	0	0	0	0	2	0	0	.000
3 yrs.	0	0	–	5.71	34	0	0	52	63	26	20	0	0	0	0	2	0	0	.000
1 yr.	0	0	–	4.19	26	0	0	43	45	20	14	0	0	0	0	2	0	0	.000

Jack Quinn
QUINN, JOHN PICUS
Born John Quinn Picus.
B. July 5, 1884, Jeanesville, Pa.   D. Apr. 17, 1946, Pottsville, Pa.
BR TR 6' 196 lbs.

1909 NY A	9	5	.643	1.97	23	11	8	118.2	110	24	36	0	3	0	2	45	7	0	.156
1910	18	12	.600	2.36	35	31	20	236.2	214	58	82	0	3	0	0	82	19	0	.232
1911	8	9	.471	3.76	40	16	7	174.2	203	41	71	0	2	2	3	61	10	1	.164
1912	5	7	.417	5.79	18	11	7	102.2	139	23	47	0	2	0	0	39	8	0	.205
1913 BOS N	4	3	.571	2.40	8	7	6	56.1	55	7	33	1	0	0	0	20	4	0	.200
1914 BAL F	26	14	.650	2.60	46	42	27	342.2	**335**	65	164	4	2	1	1	121	33	2	.273
1915	9	**22**	.290	3.45	44	31	21	273.2	289	63	118	0	2	2	1	110	29	0	.264
1918 CHI A	5	1	.833	2.29	6	5	5	51	38	7	22	0	1	0	0	18	4	0	.222
1919 NY A	15	14	.517	2.63	38	31	18	264	242	65	97	4	3	1	0	91	19	0	.209
1920	18	10	.643	3.20	41	31	16	253.1	271	48	101	2	1	0	3	88	8	2	.091
1921	8	7	.533	3.48	33	13	6	129.1	158	32	44	0	3	2	0	41	9	1	.220
1922 BOS A	13	15	.464	3.48	40	32	16	256	263	59	67	4	1	3	0	91	9	1	.099
1923	13	17	.433	3.89	42	28	16	243	302	53	71	1	2	2	7	80	18	0	.225
1924	12	13	.480	3.20	43	25	13	227.2	237	51	64	2	3	0	7	77	14	0	.182
1925 2 teams		BOS A (19G 7–8)			PHI A (18G 6–3)														
" total	13	11	.542	4.13	37	29	12	204.2	259	42	43	0	1	2	0	63	6	0	.095
1926 PHI A	10	11	.476	3.41	31	21	8	163.2	191	36	58	3	1	2	1	46	8	0	.174
1927	15	10	.600	3.17	34	25	11	207.1	211	37	43	3	1	2	1	66	6	0	.091
1928	18	7	.720	2.90	31	28	18	211.1	239	34	43	4	0	0	1	79	13	0	.165
1929	11	9	.550	3.97	35	18	7	161	182	39	41	0	4	2	2	60	8	0	.133
1930	9	7	.563	4.42	35	7	0	89.2	109	22	28	0	8	3	6	34	9	1	.265
1931 BKN N	5	4	.556	2.66	39	1	0	64.1	65	24	25	0	5	3	**15**	15	3	0	.200
1932	3	7	.300	3.30	42	0	0	87.1	102	24	28	0	3	7	**8**	20	4	0	.200
1933 CIN N	0	1	.000	4.02	14	0	0	15.2	20	5	3	0	0	1	1	1	0	0	.000
23 yrs.	247	216	.533	3.27	755	443	242	3934.2	4234	859	1329	28	51	35	59	1348	248	8	.184
1 yr.	5	1	.833	2.29	6	5	5	51	38	7	22	0	1	0	0	18	4	0	.222

WORLD SERIES

1921 NY A	0	1	.000	9.82	1	0	0	3.2	8	2	2	0	0	1	0	2	0	0	.000
1929 PHI A	0	0	–	9.00	1	1	0	5	7	2	2	0	0	0	0	2	0	0	.000
1930			–	4.50	1	0	0	2	3	0	1	0	0	0	0	0	0	0	–
3 yrs.	0	1	.000	8.44	3	1	0	10.2	18	4	5	0	0	1	0	4	0	0	.000

Pat Ragan
RAGAN, DON CARLOS PATRICK
B. Nov. 15, 1888, Blanchard, Iowa   D. Sept. 4, 1956, Los Angeles, Calif.
BR TR 5'10½" 185 lbs.

1909 2 teams		CIN N (2G 0–1)			CHI N (2G 0–0)														
" total	0	1	.000	3.09	4	0	0	11.2	11	5	4	0	0	1	0	4	1	0	.250
1911 BKN N	4	3	.571	2.11	22	7	5	93.2	81	31	39	2	0	0	1	29	4	0	.138
1912	6	18	.250	3.63	36	26	12	208	211	65	101	1	1	2	1	67	4	0	.060
1913	15	18	.455	3.77	44	32	14	264.2	284	64	109	0	3	3	0	91	15	0	.165
1914	10	15	.400	2.98	38	26	14	208.1	214	85	106	1	1	2	3	75	10	0	.133
1915 2 teams		BKN N (5G 1–0)			BOS N (33G 14–12)														
" total	15	12	.556	2.34	38	26	13	246.2	219	67	88	3	4	1	0	86	13	0	.151
1916 BOS N	9	9	.500	2.08	28	23	14	182	143	47	94	3	0	0	0	60	13	0	.217
1917	7	9	.438	2.93	30	13	5	147.2	138	35	61	1	3	2	0	48	6	1	.125
1918	8	17	.320	3.23	30	25	15	206.1	212	54	68	2	0	2	0	71	13	0	.183
1919 3 teams		BOS N (4G 0–2)			NY N (7G 1–0)			CHI A (1G 0–0)											
" total	1	2	.333	3.44	12	4	1	36.2	36	17	10	0	0	0	0	11	4	0	.364
1923 PHI N	0	0	–	6.00	3	0	0	3	6	0	0	0	0	0	0	2	1	0	.500
11 yrs.	75	104	.419	2.99	283	182	93	1608.2	1555	470	680	13	12	13	5	544	84	1	.154
1 yr.	0	0	–	0.00	1	0	0	1	1	0	0	0	0	0	0	0	0	0	–

Fred Rath
RATH, FREDERICK HELSHER
B. Sept. 1, 1943, Little Rock, Ark.
BR TR 6'3" 200 lbs.

1968 CHI A	0	0	–	1.59	5	0	0	11.1	8	3	3	0	0	0	0	0	0	0	–
1969	0	2	.000	7.71	3	2	0	11.2	11	8	4	0	0	0	0	3	0	0	.000
2 yrs.	0	2	.000	4.70	8	2	0	23	19	11	7	0	0	0	0	3	0	0	.000
2 yrs.	0	2	.000	4.70	8	2	0	23	19	11	7	0	0	0	0	3	0	0	.000

Claude Raymond
RAYMOND, JOSEPH CLAUDE MARC (Frenchy)
B. May 7, 1937, St. Jean, Que., Canada
BR TR 5'10" 175 lbs.

1959 CHI A	0	0	–	9.00	3	0	0	4	5	2	1	0	0	0	0	0	0	0	–
1961 MIL N	1	0	1.000	3.98	13	0	0	20.1	22	9	13	0	1	0	2	3	0	0	.000
1962	5	5	.500	2.74	26	0	0	42.2	37	15	40	0	5	5	10	8	0	0	.000
1963	4	6	.400	5.40	45	0	0	53.1	57	27	44	0	4	6	5	4	2	0	.500
1964 HOU N	5	5	.500	2.82	38	0	0	79.2	64	22	56	0	5	5	0	14	1	0	.071
1965	7	4	.636	2.90	33	7	2	96.1	87	16	79	0	3	2	5	26	3	0	.115
1966	7	5	.583	3.13	62	0	0	92	85	25	73	0	7	5	16	9	1	0	.111
1967 2 teams		HOU N (21G 0–4)			ATL N (28G 4–1)														
" total	4	5	.444	2.89	49	0	0	65.1	64	18	31	0	4	5	10	7	1	0	.143
1968 ATL N	3	5	.375	2.83	36	0	0	60.1	56	18	37	0	3	5	10	7	1	0	.143
1969 2 teams		ATL N (33G 2–2)			MON N (15G 1–2)														
" total	3	4	.429	4.89	48	0	0	70	77	21	26	0	3	4	2	11	2	0	.182
1970 MON N	6	7	.462	4.45	59	0	0	83	76	27	68	0	6	7	23	11	0	0	.000

Pitcher Register 398

	W	L	PCT	ERA	G	GS	CG	IP	H	BB	SO	ShO	Relief Pitching W L SV	BATTING AB H HR	BA

Claude Raymond continued
1971	1	7	.125	4.67	37	0	0	54	81	25	29	0	1	7	0	1	0	0	.000
12 yrs.	46	53	.465	3.66	449	7	2	721	711	225	497	0	42	51	83	101	11	0	.109
1 yr.	0	0	—	9.00	3	0	0	4	5	2	1	0	0	0	0	0	0	0	—

Phil Regan
REGAN, PHILIP RAYMOND (The Vulture) BR TR 6'3" 200 lbs.
B. Apr. 6, 1937, Otsego, Mich.

1960 DET A	0	4	.000	4.50	17	7	0	68	70	25	38	0	0	0	1	17	1	0	.059
1961	10	7	.588	5.25	32	16	6	120	134	41	46	0	2	2	2	40	3	0	.075
1962	11	9	.550	4.04	35	23	6	171.1	169	64	87	0	1	2	0	63	13	0	.206
1963	15	9	.625	3.86	38	27	5	189	179	59	115	1	2	1	1	63	9	1	.143
1964	5	10	.333	5.03	32	21	2	146.2	162	49	91	0	1	0	1	41	13	0	.317
1965	1	5	.167	5.05	16	7	1	51.2	57	20	37	0	0	0	0	12	1	0	.083
1966 LA N	14	1	.933	1.62	65	0	0	116.2	85	24	88	0	14	1	21	21	3	0	.143
1967	6	9	.400	2.99	55	3	0	96.1	108	32	53	0	5	7	6	10	1	0	.100
1968 2 teams	LA	N (5G 2-0)			CHI	N (68G 10-5)													
" total	12	5	.706	2.27	73	0	0	134.2	119	25	67	0	12	5	25	21	3	0	.143
1969 CHI N	12	6	.667	3.70	71	0	0	112	120	35	56	0	12	6	17	15	1	0	.067
1970	5	9	.357	4.74	54	0	0	76	81	32	31	0	5	9	12	9	0	0	.000
1971	5	5	.500	3.95	48	1	0	73	84	33	28	0	4	5	6	8	0	0	.000
1972 2 teams	CHI	N (5G 0-1)			CHI	A (10G 0-1)													
" total	0	2	.000	3.63	15	0	0	17.1	24	8	6	0	0	2	0	1	1	0	1.000
13 yrs.	96	81	.542	3.84	551	105	20	1372.2	1392	447	743	1	58	40	92	321	49	1	.153
1 yr.	0	1	.000	4.05	10	0	0	13.1	18	6	4	0	0	1	0	1	1	0	1.000

WORLD SERIES
| 1966 LA N | 0 | 0 | — | 0.00 | 2 | 0 | 0 | 1.2 | 0 | 1 | 2 | 0 | 0 | 0 | 0 | 0 | 0 | 0 | — |

Steve Renko
RENKO, STEVEN BR TR 6'5" 230 lbs.
B. Dec. 10, 1944, Kansas City, Kans.

1969 MON N	6	7	.462	4.02	18	15	4	103	94	50	68	0	0	0	0	36	6	1	.167
1970	13	11	.542	4.32	41	33	7	223	203	104	142	1	0	0	1	80	16	1	.200
1971	15	14	.517	3.75	40	37	9	276	256	135	129	3	0	0	0	100	21	2	.210
1972	1	10	.091	5.20	30	12	0	97	96	67	66	0	0	0	0	24	7	0	.292
1973	15	11	.577	2.81	36	34	9	249.2	201	108	164	0	0	0	1	88	24	0	.273
1974	12	16	.429	4.03	37	35	8	228	222	81	138	1	0	0	0	81	17	1	.210
1975	6	12	.333	4.08	31	25	3	170	175	76	99	1	0	0	1	54	15	1	.278
1976 2 teams	MON	N (5G 0-1)			CHI	N (28G 8-11)													
" total	8	12	.400	3.98	33	28	4	176.1	179	46	116	0	0	0	0	56	6	0	.107
1977 2 teams	CHI	N (13G 2-2)			CHI	A (8G 5-0)													
" total	7	2	.778	4.07	21	16	0	104	106	38	70	0	0	0	1	12	2	0	.167
1978 OAK A	6	12	.333	4.29	27	25	3	151	152	67	89	1	0	0	0	0	0	0	—
1979 BOS A	11	9	.550	4.11	27	27	4	171	174	53	99	1	0	0	0	0	0	0	—
1980	9	9	.500	4.20	32	23	1	165	180	56	90	0	2	0	0	0	0	0	—
1981 CAL A	8	4	.667	3.44	22	15	0	102	93	42	50	0	1	0	1	0	0	0	—
1982	11	6	.647	4.44	31	23	4	156	163	51	81	0	3	1	0	0	0	0	—
1983 KC A	6	11	.353	4.30	25	17	1	121.1	144	56	54	0	0	3	1	0	0	0	—
15 yrs.	134	146	.479	4.00	451	365	57	2493.1	2438	1010	1455	8	6	4	6	531	114	6	.215
1 yr.	5	0	1.000	3.57	8	8	0	53	55	17	36	0	0	0	0	0	0	0	—

Dennis Ribant
RIBANT, DENNIS JOSEPH BR TR 5'11" 165 lbs.
B. Sept. 20, 1941, Detroit, Mich.

1964 NY N	1	5	.167	5.15	14	7	1	57.2	65	9	35	1	0	0	1	20	2	0	.100
1965	1	3	.250	3.82	19	1	0	35.1	29	6	13	0	1	3	3	6	0	0	.000
1966	11	9	.550	3.20	39	26	10	188.1	184	40	84	1	0	0	3	61	12	0	.197
1967 PIT N	9	8	.529	4.08	38	22	2	172	186	40	75	0	3	2	0	60	16	0	.267
1968 2 teams	DET	A (14G 2-2)			CHI	A (17G 0-2)													
" total	2	4	.333	4.37	31	0	0	55.2	62	27	27	0	2	4	2	12	1	0	.083
1969 2 teams	STL	N (1G 0-0)			CIN	N (7G 0-0)													
" total	0	0	—	2.79	8	0	0	9.2	10	4	7	0	0	0	0	0	0	0	—
6 yrs.	24	29	.453	3.87	149	56	13	518.2	536	126	241	2	6	9	9	159	31	0	.195
1 yr.	0	2	.000	6.03	17	0	0	31.1	42	17	20	0	0	2	1	7	0	0	.000

Johnny Rigney
RIGNEY, JOHN DUNCAN BR TR 6'2" 190 lbs.
B. Oct. 28, 1914, Oak Park, Ill.

1937 CHI A	2	5	.286	4.96	22	4	3	90.2	107	46	38	1	2	2	1	30	5	0	.167
1938	9	9	.500	3.56	38	12	7	167	164	72	84	1	5	3	1	55	8	0	.145
1939	15	8	.652	3.70	35	29	11	218.2	208	84	119	2	0	0	0	80	16	0	.200
1940	14	18	.438	3.11	39	33	19	280.2	240	90	141	2	2	1	3	93	20	0	.215
1941	13	13	.500	3.84	30	29	18	237	224	92	119	3	0	0	0	84	17	0	.202
1942	3	3	.500	3.20	7	7	6	59	40	16	34	0	0	0	0	19	1	0	.053
1946	5	5	.500	4.03	15	11	3	82.2	76	35	51	2	0	1	0	26	4	0	.154
1947	2	3	.400	1.95	11	7	2	50.2	42	15	19	0	0	0	0	14	0	0	.000
8 yrs.	63	64	.496	3.59	197	132	67	1186.1	1101	450	605	11	9	7	5	401	71	0	.177
8 yrs.	63	64	.496	3.59	197	132	67	1186.1	1101	450	605	11	9	7	5	401	71	0	.177

Tink Riviere
RIVIERE, ARTHUR BERNARD BR TR 5'10" 167 lbs.
B. Aug. 2, 1899, Liberty, Tex. D. Sept. 27, 1965, Liberty, Tex.

1921 STL N	1	0	1.000	6.10	18	2	0	38.1	45	20	15	0	1	0	0	8	3	0	.375
1925 CHI A	0	0	—	13.50	3	0	0	4.2	6	7	1	0	0	0	0	1	0	0	.000
2 yrs.	1	0	1.000	6.91	21	2	0	43	51	27	16	0	1	0	0	9	3	0	.333
1 yr.	0	0	—	13.50	3	0	0	4.2	6	7	1	0	0	0	0	1	0	0	.000

Charlie Robertson
ROBERTSON, CHARLES CULBERTSON BL TR 6' 175 lbs.
B. Jan. 31, 1897, Sherman, Tex.

| 1919 CHI A | 0 | 1 | .000 | 9.00 | 1 | 1 | 0 | 2 | 5 | 0 | 1 | 0 | 0 | 0 | 0 | 0 | 0 | 0 | — |
| 1922 | 14 | 15 | .483 | 3.64 | 37 | 34 | 21 | 272 | 294 | 89 | 83 | 3 | 1 | 1 | 0 | 87 | 16 | 0 | .184 |

Pitcher Register

	W	L	PCT	ERA	G	GS	CG	IP	H	BB	SO	ShO	Relief Pitching W L SV	BATTING AB H HR	BA

Charlie Robertson continued

	W	L	PCT	ERA	G	GS	CG	IP	H	BB	SO	ShO	W	L	SV	AB	H	HR	BA
1923	13	18	.419	3.81	38	34	18	255	262	104	91	1	0	3	0	85	21	0	.247
1924	4	10	.286	4.99	17	14	5	97.1	108	54	29	0	2	0	0	33	6	0	.182
1925	8	12	.400	5.26	24	23	6	137	181	47	27	2	0	0	0	45	10	0	.222
1926 STL A	1	2	.333	8.36	8	7	1	28	38	21	13	0	0	0	0	10	3	0	.300
1927 BOS N	7	17	.292	4.72	28	22	6	154.1	188	46	49	0	1	1	0	50	12	0	.240
1928	2	5	.286	5.31	13	7	3	59.1	73	16	17	0	0	1	1	17	0	0	.000
8 yrs.	49	80	.380	4.44	166	142	60	1005	1149	377	310	6	4	6	1	327	68	0	.208
5 yrs.	39	56	.411	4.17	117	106	50	763.1	850	294	231	6	3	4	0	250	53	0	.212

Dewey Robinson

ROBINSON, DEWEY EVERETT BR TR 6' 180 lbs.
B. Apr. 28, 1955, Evanston, Ill.

	W	L	PCT	ERA	G	GS	CG	IP	H	BB	SO	ShO	W	L	SV	AB	H	HR	BA
1979 CHI A	0	1	.000	6.43	11	0	0	14	11	9	5	0	0	1	0	0	0	0	—
1980	1	1	.500	3.09	15	0	0	35	26	16	28	0	1	1	0	0	0	0	—
1981	1	0	1.000	4.50	4	0	0	4	5	3	2	0	1	0	0	0	0	0	—
3 yrs.	2	2	.500	4.08	30	0	0	53	42	28	35	0	2	2	0	0	0	0	—
3 yrs.	2	2	.500	4.08	30	0	0	53	42	28	35	0	2	2	0	0	0	0	—

Saul Rogovin

ROGOVIN, SAUL WALTER BR TR 6'2" 205 lbs.
B. Oct. 10, 1922, Brooklyn, N. Y.

	W	L	PCT	ERA	G	GS	CG	IP	H	BB	SO	ShO	W	L	SV	AB	H	HR	BA
1949 DET A	0	1	.000	14.29	5	0	0	5.2	13	7	2	0	0	1	0	0	0	0	—
1950	2	1	.667	4.50	11	5	1	40	39	26	11	0	1	0	0	16	3	1	.188
1951 2 teams	DET A (5G 1–1)				CHI A (22G 11–7)														
" total	12	8	.600	2.78	27	26	17	216.2	189	74	82	3	1	0	0	81	17	0	.210
1952 CHI A	14	9	.609	3.85	33	30	12	231.2	224	79	121	3	0	0	1	84	17	1	.202
1953	7	12	.368	5.22	22	19	4	131	151	48	62	1	1	0	0	37	5	0	.135
1955 2 teams	BAL A (14G 1–8)				PHI N (12G 5–3)														
" total	6	11	.353	3.81	26	23	6	144	139	44	62	2	0	0	0	46	8	1	.174
1956 PHI N	7	6	.538	4.98	22	18	3	106.2	122	27	48	0	0	0	0	36	4	0	.111
1957	0	0	—	9.00	4	0	0	8	11	3	0	0	0	0	0	0	0	0	—
8 yrs.	48	48	.500	4.06	150	121	43	883.2	888	308	388	9	3	1	2	300	54	3	.180
3 yrs.	32	28	.533	3.70	77	71	33	555.1	541	194	260	7	1	0	2	195	37	1	.190

Vicente Romo

ROMO, VICENTE NAVARRO (Huevo) BR TR 6'1" 180 lbs.
B. Apr. 12, 1943, Santa Rosalia, Mexico

	W	L	PCT	ERA	G	GS	CG	IP	H	BB	SO	ShO	W	L	SV	AB	H	HR	BA
1968 2 teams	LA N (1G 0–0)				CLE A (40G 5–3)														
" total	5	3	.625	1.60	41	1	0	84.1	44	33	54	0	5	2	12	14	2	0	.143
1969 2 teams	CLE A (3G 1–1)				BOS A (52G 7–9)														
" total	8	10	.444	3.13	55	11	4	135.1	123	53	96	1	3	8	11	33	5	0	.152
1970 BOS A	7	3	.700	4.08	48	10	0	108	115	43	71	0	6	0	6	27	4	1	.148
1971 CHI A	1	7	.125	3.38	45	2	0	72	52	37	48	0	1	5	5	11	4	0	.364
1972	3	0	1.000	3.31	28	0	0	51.2	47	18	46	0	3	0	1	9	0	0	.000
1973 SD N	2	3	.400	3.70	49	1	0	87.2	85	46	51	0	2	2	7	16	2	0	.125
1974	5	5	.500	4.56	54	1	0	71	78	37	26	0	5	5	9	6	0	0	.000
1982 LA N	1	2	.333	3.03	15	6	0	35.2	25	14	24	0	0	1	1	5	1	0	.200
8 yrs.	32	33	.492	3.36	335	32	4	645.2	569	281	416	1	25	23	52	121	18	1	.149
2 yrs.	4	7	.364	3.35	73	2	0	123.2	99	55	94	0	4	5	6	20	4	0	.200

Gil Rondon

RONDON, GILBERT BR TR 6'2" 200 lbs.
B. Nov. 18, 1953, Bronx, N. Y.

	W	L	PCT	ERA	G	GS	CG	IP	H	BB	SO	ShO	W	L	SV	AB	H	HR	BA
1976 HOU N	2	2	.500	5.67	19	7	0	54	70	39	21	0	0	0	0	14	4	0	.286
1979 CHI A	0	0	—	3.60	4	0	0	10	11	6	3	0	0	0	0	0	0	0	—
2 yrs.	2	2	.500	5.34	23	7	0	64	81	45	24	0	0	0	0	14	4	0	.286
1 yr.	0	0	—	3.60	4	0	0	10	11	6	3	0	0	0	0	0	0	0	—

Buck Ross

ROSS, LEE RAVON BR TR 6'2" 170 lbs.
B. Feb. 3, 1915, Norwood, N. C.

	W	L	PCT	ERA	G	GS	CG	IP	H	BB	SO	ShO	W	L	SV	AB	H	HR	BA
1936 PHI A	9	14	.391	5.83	30	27	12	200.2	253	83	47	1	0	0	0	71	12	0	.169
1937	5	10	.333	4.89	28	22	7	147.1	183	63	37	1	0	0	0	49	5	0	.102
1938	9	16	.360	5.32	29	28	10	184.1	218	80	54	0	0	0	0	63	12	1	.190
1939	6	14	.300	6.00	29	28	6	174	226	95	43	1	0	0	0	58	12	0	.207
1940	5	10	.333	4.38	24	19	10	156.1	160	60	43	0	0	0	1	53	7	1	.132
1941 2 teams	PHI A (1G 0–1)				CHI A (20G 3–8)														
" total	3	9	.250	3.69	21	12	7	112.1	109	45	30	0	1	0	0	33	7	0	.212
1942 CHI A	5	7	.417	5.00	22	14	4	113.1	118	39	37	2	0	1	0	38	6	0	.158
1943	11	7	.611	3.19	21	21	7	149.1	140	56	41	1	0	0	0	46	4	0	.087
1944	2	7	.222	5.18	20	9	2	90.1	97	35	20	0	1	3	0	26	2	0	.077
1945	1	1	.500	5.79	13	2	0	37.1	51	17	8	0	1	0	0	11	2	0	.182
10 yrs.	56	95	.371	4.94	237	182	65	1365.1	1545	573	360	6	3	4	2	448	69	3	.154
5 yrs.	22	30	.423	4.15	96	57	20	498.2	505	190	136	3	3	4	1	153	21	1	.137

Marv Rotblatt

ROTBLATT, MARVIN JOSEPH BB TL 5'8" 165 lbs.
B. Oct. 18, 1927, Chicago, Ill.

	W	L	PCT	ERA	G	GS	CG	IP	H	BB	SO	ShO	W	L	SV	AB	H	HR	BA
1948 CHI A	0	1	.000	7.85	7	2	0	18.1	19	23	4	0	0	0	0	5	0	0	.000
1950	0	0	—	6.23	2	0	0	8.2	11	5	6	0	0	0	0	2	0	0	.000
1951	4	2	.667	3.40	26	2	0	47.2	44	23	20	0	3	2	2	9	0	0	.000
3 yrs.	4	3	.571	4.82	35	4	0	74.2	74	51	30	0	3	2	2	15	0	0	.000
3 yrs.	4	3	.571	4.82	35	4	0	74.2	74	51	30	0	3	2	2	15	0	0	.000

Jack Rothrock

ROTHROCK, JOHN HOUSTON BB TR 5'11½" 165 lbs.
B. Mar. 14, 1905, Long Beach, Calif. BR 1925-27
D. Feb. 2, 1980, San Bernardino, Calif.

	W	L	PCT	ERA	G	GS	CG	IP	H	BB	SO	ShO	W	L	SV	AB	H	HR	BA
1928 BOS A	0	0	—	0.00	1	0	0	1	0	0	0	0	0	0	0	*			

Pitcher Register

	W	L	PCT	ERA	G	GS	CG	IP	H	BB	SO	ShO	Relief Pitching W L SV	BATTING AB H HR	BA

Virle Rounsaville
ROUNSAVILLE, VIRLE GENE (Gene)
B. Sept. 27, 1944, Konawa, Okla. BR TR 6'3" 205 lbs.

| 1970 CHI A | 0 | 1 | .000 | 10.50 | 8 | 0 | 0 | 6 | 10 | 2 | 3 | 0 | 0 1 0 | 0 0 0 | — |

Don Rudolph
RUDOLPH, FREDERICK DONALD
B. Aug. 16, 1931, Baltimore, Md. D. Sept. 12, 1968, Granada Hills, Calif. BL TL 5'11" 195 lbs.

1957 CHI A	1	0	1.000	2.25	5	0	0	12	6	2	2	0	1 0 0	2 1 0	.500
1958	1	0	1.000	2.57	7	0	0	7	4	5	2	0	1 0 1	0 0 0	—
1959 2 teams			CHI A (4G 0–0)			CIN N (5G 0–0)									
" total	0	0	—	3.48	9	0	0	10.1	17	5	8	0	0 0 1	1 0 0	.000
1962 2 teams			CLE A (1G 0–0)			WAS A (37G 8–10)									
" total	8	10	.444	3.62	38	23	6	176.2	188	42	68	2	0 2 0	57 10 0	.175
1963 WAS A	7	19	.269	4.55	37	26	4	174	189	36	70	0	0 2 1	45 8 1	.178
1964	1	3	.250	4.09	28	8	0	70.1	81	12	32	0	0 0 0	15 1 0	.067
6 yrs.	18	32	.360	4.00	124	57	10	450.1	485	102	182	2	2 4 3	120 20 1	.167
3 yrs.	2	0	1.000	2.05	16	0	0	22	14	9	4	0	2 0 2	2 1 0	.500

Red Ruffing
RUFFING, CHARLES HERBERT
B. May 3, 1904, Granville, Ill.
Hall of Fame 1967. BR TR 6'1½" 205 lbs.

1924 BOS A	0	0	—	6.65	8	2	0	23	29	9	10	0	0 0 0	7 1 0	.143
1925	9	18	.333	5.01	37	27	13	217.1	253	75	64	3	1 1 1	79 17 0	.215
1926	6	15	.286	4.39	37	22	6	166	169	68	58	0	1 2 2	51 10 1	.196
1927	5	13	.278	4.66	26	18	10	158.1	160	87	77	0	1 1 0	55 14 0	.255
1928	10	25	.286	3.89	42	34	25	289.1	303	96	118	1	0 2 2	121 38 2	.314
1929	9	22	.290	4.86	35	30	18	244.1	280	118	109	2	0 3 1	114 35 2	.307
1930 2 teams			BOS A (4G 0–3)			NY A (34G 15–5)									
" total	15	8	.652	4.38	38	28	13	221.2	242	68	131	2	2 1 1	110 40 4	.364
1931 NY A	16	14	.533	4.41	37	30	19	237	240	87	132	1	1 2 2	109 36 3	.330
1932	18	7	.720	3.09	35	29	22	259	219	115	190	3	1 1 2	124 38 3	.306
1933	9	14	.391	3.91	35	28	18	235	230	93	122	0	1 0 3	115 29 2	.252
1934	19	11	.633	3.93	36	31	19	256.1	232	104	149	5	1 1 0	113 28 2	.248
1935	16	11	.593	3.12	30	29	19	222	201	76	81	2	0 1 0	109 37 2	.339
1936	20	12	.625	3.85	33	33	25	271	274	90	102	3	0 0 0	127 37 5	.291
1937	20	7	.741	2.98	31	31	22	256.1	242	68	131	5	0 0 0	129 26 1	.202
1938	21	7	.750	3.31	31	31	22	247.1	246	82	127	4	0 0 0	107 24 3	.224
1939	21	7	.750	2.93	28	28	22	233.1	211	75	95	5	0 0 0	114 35 1	.307
1940	15	12	.556	3.38	30	30	20	226	218	76	97	3	0 0 0	89 11 1	.124
1941	15	6	.714	3.54	23	23	13	185.2	177	54	60	2	0 0 0	89 27 2	.303
1942	14	7	.667	3.21	24	24	16	193.2	183	41	80	4	0 0 0	80 20 1	.250
1945	7	3	.700	2.89	11	11	8	87.1	85	20	24	1	0 0 0	46 10 1	.217
1946	5	1	.833	1.77	8	8	4	61	37	23	19	2	0 0 0	25 3 0	.120
1947 CHI A	3	5	.375	6.11	9	9	1	53	63	16	11	0	0 0 0	24 5 0	.208
22 yrs.	273	225	.548	3.80	624	536	335	4344	4294	1541	1987	48	9 15 16	*	
										7th					
1 yr.	3	5	.375	6.11	9	9	1	53	63	16	11	0	0 0 0	24 5 0	.208

WORLD SERIES

1932 NY A	1	0	1.000	4.00	1	1	1	9	10	6	10	0	0 0 0	4 0 0	.000
1936	0	1	.000	4.50	2	2	0	14	16	5	12	0	0 0 0	5 0 0	.000
1937	1	0	1.000	1.00	1	1	1	9	7	3	8	0	0 0 0	4 2 0	.500
1938	2	0	1.000	1.50	2	2	2	18	17	2	11	0	0 0 0	6 1 0	.167
1939	1	0	1.000	1.00	1	1	1	9	4	1	4	0	0 0 0	3 1 0	.333
1941	1	0	1.000	1.00	1	1	1	9	6	3	5	0	0 0 0	3 0 0	.000
1942	1	1	.500	4.08	2	2	1	17.2	14	7	11	0	0 0 0	9 2 0	.222
7 yrs.	7	2	.778	2.63	10	10	7	85.2	74	27	61	0	0 0 0	34 6 0	.176
	2nd					4th	4th	3rd	4th	6th	4th				

Bob Rush
RUSH, ROBERT RANSOM
B. Dec. 21, 1925, Battle Creek, Mich. BR TR 6'4" 205 lbs.

1948 CHI N	5	11	.313	3.92	36	16	4	133.1	153	37	72	0	2 0 0	39 5 0	.128
1949	10	18	.357	4.07	35	27	9	201	197	79	80	1	2 0 4	63 2 0	.032
1950	13	20	.394	3.71	39	34	19	254.2	261	93	93	1	0 2 1	90 15 1	.167
1951	11	12	.478	3.83	37	29	12	211.1	219	68	129	2	2 0 2	68 13 0	.191
1952	17	13	.567	2.70	34	32	17	250.1	205	81	157	4	0 2 0	96 28 0	.292
1953	9	14	.391	4.54	29	28	8	166.2	177	66	84	1	0 0 0	54 6 0	.111
1954	13	15	.464	3.77	33	32	11	236.2	213	103	124	0	0 0 0	83 23 2	.277
1955	13	11	.542	3.50	33	33	14	234	204	73	130	3	0 0 0	82 9 1	.110
1956	13	10	.565	3.19	32	32	13	239.2	210	59	104	1	0 0 0	82 8 0	.098
1957	6	16	.273	4.38	31	29	5	205.1	211	66	103	0	0 0 0	69 14 0	.203
1958 MIL N	10	6	.625	3.42	28	20	5	147.1	142	31	84	2	3 1 0	45 9 0	.200
1959	5	6	.455	2.40	31	9	1	101.1	102	23	64	1	3 2 0	32 6 0	.188
1960 2 teams			MIL N (10G 2–0)			CHI A (9G 0–0)									
" total	2	0	1.000	4.91	19	0	0	29.1	40	10	20	0	2 0 1	4 2 0	.500
13 yrs.	127	152	.455	3.65	417	321	118	2410.2	2334	789	1244	16	14 7 8	807 140 4	.173
1 yr.	0	0	—	5.65	9	0	0	14.1	16	5	12	0	0 0 0	1 1 0	1.000

WORLD SERIES

| 1958 MIL N | 0 | 1 | .000 | 3.00 | 1 | 1 | 0 | 6 | 3 | 5 | 2 | 0 | 0 0 0 | 2 0 0 | .000 |

John Russell
RUSSELL, JOHN ALBERT
B. Oct. 20, 1895, San Mateo, Calif. D. Nov. 20, 1930, Ely, Nev. BL TL 6'2" 195 lbs.

1917 BKN N	0	1	.000	4.50	5	1	1	16	12	6	1	0	0 0 0	4 1 0	.250
1918	0	0	—	18.00	1	0	0	1	2	1	0	0	0 0 0	0 0 0	—
1921 CHI N	2	5	.286	5.29	11	8	4	66.1	82	35	15	0	0 0 1	25 10 0	.400
1922	0	1	.000	6.75	4	1	0	6.2	7	4	3	0	0 0 0	1 0 0	.000
4 yrs.	2	7	.222	5.40	21	10	5	90	103	46	19	0	0 0 1	30 11 0	.367
2 yrs.	2	6	.250	5.42	15	9	4	73	89	39	18	0	0 0 1	26 10 0	.385

Pitcher Register 401

	W	L	PCT	ERA	G	GS	CG	IP	H	BB	SO	ShO	Relief Pitching W L SV	BATTING AB H HR	BA

Reb Russell
RUSSELL, EWELL ALBERT   BL TL 5'11" 185 lbs.
B. Apr. 12, 1889, Jackson, Miss.   D. Sept. 30, 1973, Indianapolis, Ind.

Year	Team	W	L	PCT	ERA	G	GS	CG	IP	H	BB	SO	ShO	W	L	SV	AB	H	HR	BA
1913	CHI A	21	17	.553	1.91	51	36	25	316	249	79	122	8	4	3	4	106	20	0	.189
1914		7	12	.368	2.90	38	23	8	167.1	168	33	79	1	1	0	1	64	17	0	.266
1915		11	10	.524	2.59	41	25	10	229.1	215	47	90	3	1	2	2	86	21	0	.244
1916		17	11	.607	2.42	56	26	16	264.1	207	42	112	5	3	1	4	91	13	0	.143
1917		12	5	.706	1.95	35	24	11	189.1	170	32	54	5	0	1	4	68	19	0	.279
1918		6	5	.545	2.60	19	14	10	124.2	117	33	38	2	1	0	0	50	7	0	.140
1919		0	0	–	0.00	1	0	0		1	1	0	0	0	0	0	0	0	0	–
1922	PIT N	0	0	–	0.00	0	0	0		0	0	0	0	0	0	0	220	81	12	.368
1923		0	0	–	0.00	0	0	0		0	0	0	0	0	0	0	291	84	9	.289
9 yrs.		74	60	.552	2.34	241	148	80	1291	1127	267	495	24	10	7	15	*			
7 yrs.		74	60	.552	2.34	241	148	80	1291	1127	267	495	24	10	7	15	465	97	0	.209
					6th								9th							

WORLD SERIES
| 1917 | CHI A | 0 | 0 | – | ∞ | 1 | 1 | 0 | | 2 | 1 | 0 | 0 | 0 | 0 | 0 | 0 | 0 | 0 | – |

Jack Salveson
SALVESON, JOHN THEODORE   BR TR 6'½" 180 lbs.
B. Jan. 5, 1914, Fullerton, Calif.   D. Dec. 28, 1974, Norwalk, Calif.

1933	NY N	0	2	.000	3.82	8	2	2	30.2	30	14	8	0	0	0	0	9	1	0	.111
1934		3	1	.750	3.52	12	4	0	38.1	43	13	18	0	2	0	0	10	3	0	.300
1935 2 teams	PIT N (5G 0–1)								CHI A (20G 1–2)											
" total		1	3	.250	5.25	25	2	2	73.2	90	28	24	0	1	3	1	22	6	1	.273
1943	CLE A	5	3	.625	3.35	23	11	4	86	87	26	24	3	1	1	3	26	6	1	.231
1945		0	0	–	3.68	19	0	0	44	52	6	11	0	0	0	0	10	4	1	.400
5 yrs.		9	9	.500	3.99	87	19	8	272.2	302	87	85	3	4	4	4	77	20	3	.260
1 yr.		1	2	.333	4.86	20	2	2	66.2	79	23	22	0	1	2	1	20	6	1	.300

Rick Sawyer
SAWYER, RICHARD CLYDE   BR TR 6'2" 205 lbs.
B. Apr. 7, 1948, Bakersfield, Calif.

1974	NY A	0	0	–	9.00	1	0	0	2	2	1	1	0	0	0	0	0	0	0	–
1975 2 teams	NY A (4G 0–0)								CHI A (4G 0–0)											
" total		0	0	–	3.00	8	0	0	12	14	4	6	0	0	0	0	0	0	0	–
1976	SD N	5	3	.625	2.53	13	11	4	81.2	84	38	33	2	0	1	0	24	5	0	.208
1977		7	6	.538	5.84	56	9	0	111	136	55	45	0	6	1	0	20	3	0	.150
4 yrs.		12	9	.571	4.40	78	20	4	206.2	236	98	85	2	6	2	0	44	8	0	.182
1 yr.		0	0	–	3.00	4	0	0	6	7	2	3	0	0	0	0	0	0	0	–

Randy Scarbery
SCARBERY, RANDY JAMES   BB TR 6'1" 185 lbs.
B. June 22, 1952, Fresno, Calif.

1979	CHI A	2	8	.200	4.63	45	5	0	101	102	34	45	0	2	3	4	0	0	0	–
1980		1	2	.333	4.03	15	0	0	29	24	7	18	0	1	2	2	0	0	0	–
2 yrs.		3	10	.231	4.50	60	5	0	130	126	41	63	0	3	5	6	0	0	0	–
2 yrs.		3	10	.231	4.50	60	5	0	130	126	41	63	0	3	5	6	0	0	0	–

Ray Scarborough
SCARBOROUGH, RAY WILSON   BR TR 6' 185 lbs.
B. July 23, 1917, Mt. Gilead, N. C.   D. July 1, 1982, Mt. Olive, N. C.

1942	WAS A	2	1	.667	4.12	17	5	1	63.1	68	32	16	1	0	0	0	21	4	0	.190
1943		4	4	.500	2.83	24	6	2	86	93	46	43	0	2	2	3	24	8	0	.333
1946		7	11	.389	4.05	32	20	6	155.2	176	74	46	1	3	1	1	50	7	0	.140
1947		6	13	.316	3.41	33	18	8	161	165	67	63	2	1	2	0	50	6	0	.120
1948		15	8	.652	2.82	31	26	9	185.1	166	72	76	0	1	1	1	64	14	0	.219
1949		13	11	.542	4.60	34	27	11	199.2	204	88	81	1	3	0	0	67	13	0	.194
1950 2 teams	WAS A (8G 3–5)								CHI A (27G 10–13)											
" total		13	18	.419	4.94	35	31	12	207.2	222	84	94	3	1	1	1	66	10	0	.152
1951	BOS A	12	9	.571	5.09	37	22	8	184	201	61	71	0	2	2	0	68	13	0	.191
1952 2 teams	BOS A (28G 1–5)								NY A (9G 5–1)											
" total		6	6	.500	4.23	37	12	2	110.2	106	50	42	1	2	1	2	32	9	0	.281
1953 2 teams	NY A (25G 2–2)								DET A (13G 0–2)											
" total		2	4	.333	4.66	38	1	0	75.1	86	37	32	0	1	4	4	14	1	1	.071
10 yrs.		80	85	.485	4.13	318	168	59	1428.2	1487	611	564	9	16	14	14	456	85	1	.186
1 yr.		10	13	.435	5.30	27	23	8	149.1	160	62	70	1	1	1	1	46	8	0	.174

WORLD SERIES
| 1952 | NY A | 0 | 0 | – | 9.00 | 1 | 0 | 0 | 1 | 1 | 0 | 1 | 0 | 0 | 0 | 0 | 0 | 0 | 0 | – |

Ron Schueler
SCHUELER, RONALD RICHARD   BR TR 6'4" 205 lbs.
B. Apr. 18, 1948, Hays, Kans.

1972	ATL N	5	8	.385	3.66	37	18	3	145	122	60	96	0	3	0	2	42	8	0	.190
1973		8	7	.533	3.86	39	20	4	186.1	179	66	124	2	2	3	2	62	11	0	.177
1974	PHI N	11	16	.407	3.72	44	27	5	203	202	98	109	0	2	2	1	51	6	0	.118
1975		4	4	.500	5.23	46	6	1	93	88	40	69	0	2	1	0	13	2	0	.154
1976		1	0	1.000	2.90	35	0	0	49.2	44	16	43	0	1	0	3	2	0	0	.000
1977	MIN A	8	7	.533	4.40	52	7	0	135	131	61	77	0	7	6	3	0	0	0	–
1978	CHI A	3	5	.375	4.30	30	7	0	81.2	76	39	39	0	1	1	0	0	0	0	–
1979		0	1	.000	7.20	8	1	0	20	19	13	6	0	0	0	0	0	0	0	–
8 yrs.		40	48	.455	4.08	291	86	13	913.2	861	393	563	2	18	13	11	170	27	0	.159
2 yrs.		3	6	.333	4.87	38	8	0	101.2	95	52	45	0	1	1	0	0	0	0	–

Webb Schultz
SCHULTZ, WEBB CARL   BR TR 5'11" 172 lbs.
B. Jan. 31, 1898, Wautoma, Wis.

| 1924 | CHI A | 0 | 0 | – | 9.00 | 1 | 0 | 0 | 1 | 1 | 0 | 0 | 0 | 0 | 0 | 0 | 0 | 0 | 0 | – |

Ferdie Schupp
SCHUPP, FERDINAND MAURICE   BR TL 5'10" 150 lbs.
B. Jan. 16, 1891, Louisville, Ky.   D. Dec. 16, 1971, Los Angeles, Calif.

1913	NY N	0	0	–	0.75	5	1	0	12	10	3	2	0	0	0	0	3	1	0	.333
1914		0	0	–	5.82	8	0	0	17	19	9	9	0	0	0	1	2	0	0	.000
1915		1	0	1.000	5.10	23	1	0	54.2	57	29	28	0	1	0	0	10	2	0	.200

Pitcher Register 402

	W	L	PCT	ERA	G	GS	CG	IP	H	BB	SO	ShO	Relief Pitching W L SV	BATTING AB H HR	BA

Ferdie Schupp continued

		W	L	PCT	ERA	G	GS	CG	IP	H	BB	SO	ShO	W	L	SV	AB	H	HR	BA
1916		10	3	.769	0.90	30	11	8	140.1	79	37	86	4	2	1	0	41	4	0	.098
1917		21	7	**.750**	1.95	36	32	25	272	202	70	147	6	0	1	0	93	15	0	.161
1918		0	1	.000	7.56	10	2	1	33.1	42	27	22	0	0	0	0	9	1	0	.111
1919 2 teams	NY N (9G 1–3)					STL N (10G 4–4)														
" total		5	7	.417	4.34	19	13	6	101.2	87	48	54	0	1	0	1	26	3	1	.115
1920 STL N		16	13	.552	3.52	38	37	17	250.2	246	**127**	119	0	0	0	0	86	22	0	.256
1921 2 teams	STL N (9G 2–0)					BKN N (20G 3–4)														
" total		5	4	.556	4.39	29	11	2	98.1	117	48	48	0	3	0	3	26	5	0	.192
1922 CHI A		4	4	.500	6.08	18	12	3	74	79	66	38	1	1	0	0	25	5	0	.200
10 yrs.		62	39	.614	3.32	216	120	62	1054	938	464	553	11	8	2	5	321	58	1	.181
1 yr.		4	4	.500	6.08	18	12	3	74	79	66	38	1	1	0	0	25	5	0	.200

WORLD SERIES

1917 NY N	1	0	1.000	1.74	2	2	1	10.1	11	2	9	1	0	0	0	4	1	0	.250

Jim Scoggins
SCOGGINS, JESSE LEONARD (Lefty) BL TL 5'11" 165 lbs.
B. July 19, 1891, Killeen, Tex. D. Aug. 16, 1923, Columbia, S. C.

1913 CHI A	0	0	–	0.00	1	1	0		0	1	0	0	0	0	0	0	0	0	–

Herb Score
SCORE, HERBERT JUDE BL TL 6'2" 185 lbs.
B. June 7, 1933, Rosedale, N. Y.

	W	L	PCT	ERA	G	GS	CG	IP	H	BB	SO	ShO	W	L	SV	AB	H	HR	BA
1955 CLE A	16	10	.615	2.85	33	32	11	227.1	158	154	**245**	2	0	0	0	84	10	0	.119
1956	20	9	.690	2.53	35	33	16	249.1	162	129	**263**	5	0	0	0	87	16	1	.184
1957	2	1	.667	2.00	5	5	3	36	18	26	39	1	0	0	0	11	1	0	.091
1958	2	3	.400	3.95	12	5	2	41	29	34	48	1	1	1	3	11	1	0	.091
1959	9	11	.450	4.71	30	25	9	160.2	123	115	147	1	0	0	0	52	5	0	.096
1960 CHI A	5	10	.333	3.72	23	22	5	•113.2	91	87	78	1	0	0	0	30	3	0	.100
1961	1	2	.333	6.66	8	5	1	24.1	22	24	14	0	0	0	0	6	0	0	.000
1962	0	0	–	4.50	4	0	0	6	6	4	3	0	0	0	0	0	0	0	–
8 yrs.	55	46	.545	3.36	150	127	47	858.1	609	573	837	11	1	1	3	281	36	1	.128
3 yrs.	6	12	.333	4.25	35	27	6	144	119	115	95	1	0	0	0	36	3	0	.083

Jim Scott
SCOTT, JAMES (Death Valley Jim) BR TR 6'1" 235 lbs.
B. Apr. 23, 1888, Deadwood, S. D. D. Apr. 7, 1957, Palm Springs, Calif.

	W	L	PCT	ERA	G	GS	CG	IP	H	BB	SO	ShO	W	L	SV	AB	H	HR	BA
1909 CHI A	13	12	.520	2.30	36	29	19	250.1	194	93	135	4	1	0	0	85	9	0	.106
1910	9	17	.346	2.43	41	23	14	229.2	182	86	135	2	2	4	1	74	15	0	.203
1911	12	11	.522	2.63	39	26	14	202	195	81	128	3	2	2	2	71	11	0	.155
1912	2	2	.500	2.15	6	4	2	37.2	36	15	23	1	1	0	0	12	0	0	.000
1913	20	21	.488	1.90	48	**38**	27	312.1	252	86	158	4	1	4	1	97	7	1	.072
1914	16	18	.471	2.84	43	33	12	253.1	228	75	138	2	3	3	0	86	14	0	.163
1915	24	11	.686	2.03	48	35	23	296.1	256	78	120	**7**	4	1	2	95	12	0	.126
1916	9	14	.391	2.72	32	20	8	165.1	155	53	71	1	1	**5**	2	52	6	0	.115
1917	6	7	.462	1.87	24	17	6	125	126	42	37	2	2	2	0	42	5	0	.119
9 yrs.	111	113	.496	2.32	317	225	125	1872	1624	609	945	26	17	21	8	614	79	1	.129
9 yrs.	111	113	.496	2.32	317	225	125	1872	1624	609	945	26	17	21	8	614	79	1	.129
	9th	7th		5th	10th		9th		10th		6th	10th	7th						

Don Secrist
SECRIST, DONALD LAVERN BL TL 6'2" 195 lbs.
B. Feb. 26, 1945, Seattle, Wash.

1969 CHI A	0	1	.000	6.08	19	0	0	40	35	14	23	0	0	1	0	7	1	0	.143
1970	0	0	–	5.40	9	0	0	15	19	12	9	0	0	0	0	0	0	0	–
2 yrs.	0	1	.000	5.89	28	0	0	55	54	26	32	0	0	1	0	7	1	0	.143
2 yrs.	0	1	.000	5.89	28	0	0	55	54	26	32	0	0	1	0	7	1	0	.143

Bob Shaw
SHAW, ROBERT JOHN BR TR 6'2" 195 lbs.
B. June 29, 1933, New York, N. Y.

	W	L	PCT	ERA	G	GS	CG	IP	H	BB	SO	ShO	W	L	SV	AB	H	HR	BA
1957 DET A	0	1	.000	7.45	7	0	0	9.2	11	7	4	0	0	1	0	2	0	0	.000
1958 2 teams	DET A (11G 1–2)					CHI A (29G 4–2)														
" total	5	4	.556	4.76	40	5	0	90.2	99	41	35	0	5	1	1	22	3	0	.136
1959 CHI A	18	6	**.750**	2.69	47	26	8	230.2	217	54	89	3	2	0	3	73	9	0	.123
1960	13	13	.500	4.06	36	32	7	192.2	221	62	46	1	1	1	0	58	8	0	.138
1961 2 teams	CHI A (14G 3–4)					KC A (26G 9–10)														
" total	12	14	.462	4.14	40	34	9	221.2	250	78	91	0	1	0	0	73	11	0	.151
1962 MIL N	15	9	.625	2.80	38	29	12	225	223	44	124	3	1	0	2	73	10	0	.137
1963	7	11	.389	2.66	48	16	3	159	144	55	105	3	3	5	13	41	5	0	.122
1964 SF N	7	6	.538	3.76	61	1	0	93.1	105	31	57	0	7	5	11	13	0	0	.000
1965	16	9	.640	2.64	42	33	6	235	213	53	148	1	1	1	2	79	8	0	.101
1966 2 teams	SF N (13G 1–4)					NY N (26G 11–10)														
" total	12	14	.462	4.29	39	31	7	199.1	216	49	125	2	0	1	0	56	13	0	.232
1967 2 teams	NY N (23G 3–9)					CHI N (9G 0–2)														
" total	3	11	.214	4.61	32	16	3	121	138	37	56	1	2	0	0	29	2	0	.069
11 yrs.	108	98	.524	3.52	430	223	55	1778	1837	511	880	14	22	17	32	519	69	0	.133
4 yrs.	38	25	.603	3.53	126	71	18	558.2	590	164	184	7	4	2	4	163	17	0	.104

WORLD SERIES

1959 CHI A	1	1	.500	2.57	2	2	0	14	17	2	2	0	0	0	0	4	1	0	.250

Frank Shellenback
SHELLENBACK, FRANK VICTOR BR TR 6'2" 192 lbs.
B. Dec. 16, 1898, Joplin, Mo. D. Aug. 17, 1969, Newton, Mass.

1918 CHI A	10	12	.455	2.66	28	20	10	182.2	180	74	47	3	0	1	1	54	7	0	.130
1919	1	3	.250	5.14	8	4	2	35	40	16	10	0	0	1	0	11	1	0	.091
2 yrs.	11	15	.423	3.06	36	24	12	217.2	220	90	57	3	0	2	1	65	8	0	.123
2 yrs.	11	15	.423	3.06	36	24	12	217.2	220	90	57	3	0	2	1	65	8	0	.123

Pitcher Register

	W	L	PCT	ERA	G	GS	CG	IP	H	BB	SO	ShO	Relief Pitching W	L	SV	BATTING AB	H	HR	BA

Joe Shipley
SHIPLEY, JOSEPH CLARK (Moses)
B. May 9, 1935, Morristown, Tenn.
BR TR 6'4" 210 lbs.

	W	L	PCT	ERA	G	GS	CG	IP	H	BB	SO	ShO	W	L	SV	AB	H	HR	BA
1958 SF N	0	0	–	33.75	1	0	0	1.1	3	3	0	0	0	0	0	0	0	0	–
1959	0	0	–	4.50	10	1	0	18	16	17	11	0	0	0	0	3	0	0	.000
1960	0	0	–	5.40	15	0	0	20	20	9	9	0	0	0	0	0	0	0	–
1963 CHI A	0	1	.000	5.79	3	0	0	4.2	9	6	3	0	0	1	0	2	0	0	.000
4 yrs.	0	1	.000	5.93	29	1	0	44	48	35	23	0	0	1	0	5	0	0	.000
1 yr.	0	1	.000	5.79	3	0	0	4.2	9	6	3	0	0	1	0	2	0	0	.000

Bill Shores
SHORES, WILLIAM DAVID
B. May 26, 1904, Abilene, Tex.
BR TR 6' 185 lbs.

	W	L	PCT	ERA	G	GS	CG	IP	H	BB	SO	ShO	W	L	SV	AB	H	HR	BA
1928 PHI A	1	1	.500	3.21	3	2	1	14	13	7	5	0	0	0	0	5	0	0	.000
1929	11	6	.647	3.60	39	13	5	152.2	150	59	49	1	6	2	7	40	5	0	.125
1930	12	4	.750	4.19	31	19	7	159	169	70	48	1	2	0	0	57	11	0	.193
1931	0	3	.000	5.06	6	2	0	16	26	10	2	0	0	2	0	3	1	0	.333
1933 NY N	2	1	.667	3.93	8	3	1	36.2	41	14	20	0	1	0	0	11	3	0	.273
1936 CHI N	0	0	–	9.53	9	0	0	17	26	8	5	0	0	0	0	5	1	0	.200
6 yrs.	26	15	.634	4.17	96	39	14	395.1	425	168	129	2	9	4	7	121	21	0	.174
1 yr.	0	0	–	9.53	9	0	0	17	26	8	5	0	0	0	0	5	1	0	.200

WORLD SERIES
| 1930 PHI A | 0 | 0 | – | 13.50 | 1 | 0 | 0 | 1.1 | 3 | 0 | 0 | 0 | 0 | 0 | 0 | 0 | 0 | 0 | – |

Clyde Shoun
SHOUN, CLYDE MITCHELL (Hardrock)
B. Mar. 20, 1912, Mountain City, Tenn. D. Mar. 20, 1968, Mountain Home, Tenn.
BL TL 6'1" 188 lbs.

	W	L	PCT	ERA	G	GS	CG	IP	H	BB	SO	ShO	W	L	SV	AB	H	HR	BA
1935 CHI N	1	0	1.000	2.84	5	1	0	12.2	14	5	5	0	0	0	0	3	0	0	.000
1936	0	0	–	12.46	4	0	0	4.1	3	6	1	0	0	0	0	0	0	0	–
1937	7	7	.500	5.61	37	9	2	93	118	45	43	0	3	3	0	29	4	0	.138
1938 STL N	6	6	.500	4.14	40	12	3	117.1	130	43	37	0	2	2	1	31	8	0	.258
1939	3	1	.750	3.76	53	2	0	103	98	42	50	0	3	1	9	26	3	0	.115
1940	13	11	.542	3.92	54	19	13	197.1	193	46	82	1	3	4	5	63	12	0	.190
1941	3	5	.375	5.66	26	6	0	70	98	20	34	0	3	1	0	22	4	0	.182
1942 2 teams STL N (2G 0–0) CIN N (34G 1–3)																			
" total	1	3	.250	2.18	36	0	0	74.1	56	24	32	0	1	3	0	13	4	0	.308
1943 CIN N	14	5	.737	3.06	45	5	2	147	131	46	61	0	13	3	7	42	13	0	.310
1944	13	10	.565	3.02	38	21	12	202.2	193	42	55	1	3	2	2	67	15	0	.224
1946	1	6	.143	4.10	27	5	0	79	87	26	20	0	1	3	0	21	2	0	.095
1947 2 teams CIN N (10G 0–0) BOS N (26G 5–3)																			
" total	5	3	.625	4.50	36	3	1	88	89	26	30	1	4	1	1	19	3	0	.158
1948 BOS N	5	1	.833	4.01	36	2	1	74	77	20	25	0	4	1	4	21	4	0	.190
1949 2 teams BOS N (1G 0–0) CHI A (16G 1–1)																			
" total	1	1	.500	5.55	17	0	0	24.1	38	13	8	0	1	1	0	5	1	0	.200
14 yrs.	73	59	.553	3.91	454	85	34	1287	1325	404	483	3	41	25	29	362	73	0	.202
1 yr.	1	1	.500	5.79	16	0	0	23.1	37	13	8	0	1	1	0	5	1	0	.200

Al Sima
SIMA, ALBERT
B. Oct. 7, 1921, Mahwah, N. J.
BL TL 6' 190 lbs.

	W	L	PCT	ERA	G	GS	CG	IP	H	BB	SO	ShO	W	L	SV	AB	H	HR	BA
1950 WAS A	4	5	.444	4.79	17	9	1	77	89	26	23	0	1	0	0	26	3	0	.115
1951	3	7	.300	4.79	18	8	1	77	79	41	26	0	1	2	0	17	3	1	.176
1953	2	3	.400	3.42	31	5	1	68.1	63	31	25	0	2	0	1	17	2	0	.118
1954 2 teams CHI A (5G 0–1) PHI A (29G 2–5)																			
" total	2	6	.250	5.21	34	8	1	86.1	112	34	37	0	1	1	3	22	1	0	.045
4 yrs.	11	21	.344	4.61	100	30	4	308.2	343	132	111	0	5	3	4	82	9	1	.110
1 yr.	0	1	.000	5.14	5	1	0	7	11	2	1	0	0	0	1	2	0	0	.000

Tommie Sisk
SISK, TOMMIE WAYNE
B. Apr. 12, 1942, Ardmore, Okla.
BR TR 6'3" 195 lbs.

	W	L	PCT	ERA	G	GS	CG	IP	H	BB	SO	ShO	W	L	SV	AB	H	HR	BA
1962 PIT N	0	2	.000	4.08	5	3	1	17.2	18	8	6	0	0	0	0	5	1	0	.200
1963	1	3	.250	2.92	57	4	1	108	85	45	73	0	1	1	1	16	1	0	.063
1964	1	4	.200	6.16	42	1	0	61.1	91	29	35	0	1	4	0	8	0	0	.000
1965	7	3	.700	3.40	38	12	1	111.1	103	50	66	1	3	0	0	33	2	0	.061
1966	10	5	.667	4.14	34	23	4	150	146	52	60	1	2	0	1	51	5	0	.098
1967	13	13	.500	3.34	37	31	11	207.2	196	78	85	2	0	0	1	69	7	0	.101
1968	5	5	.500	3.28	33	11	0	96	101	35	41	0	3	1	1	24	2	0	.083
1969 SD N	2	13	.133	4.78	53	13	1	143	160	48	59	0	0	0	6	25	3	0	.120
1970 CHI A	1	1	.500	5.45	17	1	0	33	37	13	16	0	1	1	0	4	1	0	.250
9 yrs.	40	49	.449	3.92	316	99	19	928	937	358	441	4	11	7	10	235	22	0	.094
1 yr.	1	1	.500	5.45	17	1	0	33	37	13	16	0	1	1	0	4	1	0	.250

Jim Siwy
SIWY, JAMES GERARD
B. Sept. 20, 1959, Central Falls, R. I.
BR TR 6'4" 200 lbs.

	W	L	PCT	ERA	G	GS	CG	IP	H	BB	SO	ShO	W	L	SV	AB	H	HR	BA
1982 CHI A	0	0	–	10.29	2	1	0	7	10	5	3	0	0	0	0	0	0	0	–

John Skopec
SKOPEC, JOHN S. (Buckshot)
B. May 8, 1880, Chicago, Ill. D. Oct. 20, 1912, Chicago, Ill.
BL TL 5'10" 190 lbs.

	W	L	PCT	ERA	G	GS	CG	IP	H	BB	SO	ShO	W	L	SV	AB	H	HR	BA
1901 CHI A	6	3	.667	3.16	9	9	6	68.1	62	45	24	0	0	0	0	30	10	1	.333
1903 DET A	3	2	.600	3.43	6	5	3	39.1	46	13	14	0	0	0	0	13	2	0	.154
2 yrs.	9	5	.643	3.26	15	14	9	107.2	108	58	38	0	0	0	0	43	12	1	.279
1 yr.	6	3	.667	3.16	9	9	6	68.1	62	45	24	0	0	0	0	30	10	1	.333

Art Smith
SMITH, ARTHUR LAIRD
B. June 21, 1906, Boston, Mass.
BR TR 6' 175 lbs.

	W	L	PCT	ERA	G	GS	CG	IP	H	BB	SO	ShO	W	L	SV	AB	H	HR	BA
1932 CHI A	0	1	.000	11.57	3	2	0	7	17	4	1	0	0	0	0	1	0	0	.000

Bob Smith
SMITH, ROBERT ASHLEY
B. July 19, 1891, Hardwick, Vt.
BR TR 5'11" 160 lbs.

	W	L	PCT	ERA	G	GS	CG	IP	H	BB	SO	ShO	W	L	SV	AB	H	HR	BA
1913 CHI A	0	0	–	13.50	1	0	0	2	3	3	1	0	0	0	0	0	0	0	–

Pitcher Register

	W	L	PCT	ERA	G	GS	CG	IP	H	BB	SO	ShO	Relief Pitching W L SV	BATTING AB H HR	BA

Bob Smith continued
1915 BUF F	0	0	–	18.00	1	0	0	1	1	2	0	0	0 0 0	0 0 0	–
2 yrs.	0	0	–	15.00	2	0	0	3	4	5	1	0	0 0 0	0 0 0	–
1 yr.	0	0	–	13.50	1	0	0	2	3	3	1	0	0 0 0	0 0 0	–

Eddie Smith
SMITH, EDGAR B. Dec. 14, 1913, Columbus, N. J.   BB TL 5'10" 174 lbs.

1936 PHI A	1	1	.500	1.89	2	2	2	19	22	8	7	0	0 0 0	8 1 0	.125
1937	4	17	.190	3.94	38	23	14	196.2	178	90	79	1	0 1 5	73 17 0	.233
1938	3	10	.231	5.92	43	7	0	130.2	151	76	78	0	0 5 4	42 12 0	.286
1939 2 teams	PHI	A (3G 1–0)			CHI	A (29G 9–11)									
" total	10	11	.476	3.79	32	22	7	180.1	168	92	70	1	2 0 0	52 6 0	.115
1940 CHI A	14	9	.609	3.21	32	28	12	207.1	179	95	119	0	0 1 0	69 15 0	.217
1941	13	17	.433	3.18	34	33	21	263.1	243	114	111	1	0 0 1	88 19 0	.216
1942	7	20	.259	3.98	29	28	18	215	223	86	78	2	0 0 1	73 9 0	.123
1943	11	11	.500	3.69	25	25	14	187.2	197	76	66	2	0 0 0	69 11 1	.159
1946	8	11	.421	2.85	24	21	3	145.1	135	60	59	1	1 0 1	45 8 0	.178
1947 2 teams	CHI	A (15G 1–3)			BOS	A (8G 1–3)									
" total	2	6	.250	7.33	23	8	0	50.1	58	42	27	0	0 1 0	12 2 0	.167
10 yrs.	73	113	.392	3.82	282	197	91	1595.2	1554	739	694	8	3 8 12	531 100 1	.188
7 yrs.	63	82	.434	3.55	188	162	75	1228.2	1178	545	512	7	2 1 3	402 69 1	.172
											9th				

Frank Smith
SMITH, FRANK ELMER (Nig) Born Frank Elmer Schmidt. B. Oct. 28, 1879, Pittsburgh, Pa. D. Nov. 3, 1952, Pittsburgh, Pa.   BR TR 5'10½" 194 lbs.

1904 CHI A	16	9	.640	2.09	26	23	22	202.1	157	58	107	4	2 0 0	72 18 0	.250
1905	19	13	.594	2.13	39	31	27	291.2	215	107	171	4	2 1 0	106 24 1	.226
1906	5	6	.455	3.39	20	13	8	122	124	37	53	1	0 0 2	41 12 0	.293
1907	22	11	.667	2.47	41	37	29	310	280	111	139	3	0 0 0	92 18 0	.196
1908	17	16	.515	2.03	41	35	24	297.2	213	73	129	3	1 1 1	106 20 0	.189
1909	24	17	.585	1.80	51	41	37	365	278	70	177	7	2 2 1	127 22 0	.173
1910 2 teams	CHI	A (19G 4–9)			BOS	A (4G 1–2)									
" total	5	11	.313	2.53	23	18	11	156.2	113	51	58	3	0 0 0	52 9 0	.173
1911 2 teams	BOS	A (1G 0–0)			CIN	N (34G 9–14)									
" total	9	14	.391	4.13	35	19	10	178.2	204	58	68	0	4 5 1	56 12 0	.214
1912 CIN N	1	1	.500	6.35	7	3	1	22.2	34	15	5	0	1 0 0	6 0 0	.000
1914 BAL F	9	8	.529	2.99	39	22	9	174.2	180	47	83	1	1 2 2	59 12 0	.203
1915 2 teams	BAL	F (17G 4–4)			BKN	F (15G 5–2)									
" total	9	6	.600	4.04	32	14	6	151.2	177	49	61	1	3 0 0	49 9 1	.184
11 yrs.	136	112	.548	2.59	354	256	184	2273	1975	676	1051	27	16 11 7	766 156 2	.204
7 yrs.	107	81	.569	2.18	237	195	156	1717.1	1358	496	826	25	7 4 4	587 122 1	.208
	10th		9th	2nd			7th					8th			

Harry Smith
SMITH, HARRISON M. B. Aug. 15, 1889, Avoca, Neb. D. July 26, 1964, Dunbar, Neb.   BR TR 5'9" 160 lbs.

| 1912 CHI A | 1 | 0 | 1.000 | 1.80 | 1 | 1 | 0 | 5 | 6 | 0 | 1 | 0 | 0 0 0 | 1 0 0 | .000 |

Pop Boy Smith
SMITH, CLARENCE OSSIE B. May 23, 1892, Newport, Tenn. D. Feb. 16, 1924, Sweetwater, Tex.   BR TR 6'1" 176 lbs.

1913 CHI A	0	2	.000	3.38	15	2	0	32	31	11	13	0	0 0 0	5 0 0	.000
1916 CLE A	1	2	.333	3.86	5	3	0	25.2	25	11	4	0	1 1 0	7 2 0	.286
1917	0	1	.000	8.31	6	0	0	8.2	14	4	3	0	0 1 0	1 0 0	.000
3 yrs.	1	5	.167	4.21	26	5	0	66.1	70	26	20	0	1 2 0	13 2 0	.154
1 yr.	0	2	.000	3.38	15	2	0	32	31	11	13	0	0 0 0	5 0 0	.000

Eddie Solomon
SOLOMON, EDDIE JR. B. Feb. 9, 1952, Houston County, Ga.   BR TR 6'2" 185 lbs.

1973 LA N	0	0	–	7.11	4	0	0	6.1	10	4	6	0	0 0 0	1 0 0	.000
1974	0	0	–	1.35	4	0	0	6.2	5	2	2	0	0 0 1	0 0 0	–
1975 CHI N	0	0	–	1.29	6	0	0	7	7	6	3	0	0 0 0	0 0 0	–
1976 STL N	1	1	.500	4.86	26	2	0	37	45	16	19	0	0 1 0	5 2 0	.400
1977 ATL N	6	6	.500	4.55	18	16	0	89	110	34	54	0	0 0 0	31 4 0	.129
1978	4	6	.400	4.08	37	8	0	106	98	50	64	0	1 3 2	29 4 0	.138
1979	7	14	.333	4.21	31	30	4	186	184	51	96	0	0 0 0	64 13 0	.203
1980 PIT N	7	3	.700	2.70	26	12	2	100	96	37	35	0	2 0 0	32 7 0	.219
1981	8	6	.571	3.12	22	17	2	127	133	27	38	0	1 1 1	43 7 0	.163
1982 2 teams	PIT	N (11G 2–6)			CHI	A (6G 1–0)									
" total	3	6	.333	6.33	17	10	0	54	76	20	20	0	2 0 0	15 2 0	.133
10 yrs.	36	42	.462	3.99	191	95	8	719	764	247	337	0	6 5 4	220 39 0	.177
1 yr.	1	0	1.000	3.68	6	0	0	7.1	7	2	2	0	1 0 0	0 0 0	–

LEAGUE CHAMPIONSHIP SERIES
| 1974 LA N | 0 | 0 | – | 0.00 | 1 | 0 | 0 | 2 | 2 | 1 | 1 | 0 | 0 0 0 | 0 0 0 | – |

Floyd Speer
SPEER, VERNIE FLOYD B. Jan. 27, 1913, Booneville, Ark. D. Mar. 22, 1969, Little Rock, Ark.   BR TR 6' 180 lbs.

1943 CHI A	0	0	–	9.00	1	0	0	1	1	2	1	0	0 0 0	0 0 0	–
1944	0	0	–	9.00	2	0	0	2	4	0	1	0	0 0 0	0 0 0	–
2 yrs.	0	0	–	9.00	3	0	0	3	5	2	2	0	0 0 0	0 0 0	–
2 yrs.	0	0	–	9.00	3	0	0	3	5	2	2	0	0 0 0	0 0 0	–

Gerry Staley
STALEY, GERALD LEE B. Aug. 21, 1920, Brush Prairie, Wash.   BR TR 6' 195 lbs.

1947 STL N	1	0	1.000	2.76	18	1	1	29.1	33	8	14	0	0 0 0	6 0 0	.000
1948	4	4	.500	6.92	31	3	0	52	61	21	23	0	4 3 0	9 2 1	.222
1949	10	10	.500	2.73	45	17	5	171.1	154	41	55	2	4 2 6	41 5 0	.122

Pitcher Register

	W	L	PCT	ERA	G	GS	CG	IP	H	BB	SO	ShO	Relief Pitching W	L	SV	BATTING AB	H	HR	BA

Gerry Staley continued

	W	L	PCT	ERA	G	GS	CG	IP	H	BB	SO	ShO	W	L	SV	AB	H	HR	BA
1950	13	13	.500	4.99	42	22	7	169.2	201	61	62	1	6	1	3	55	8	0	.145
1951	19	13	.594	3.81	42	30	10	227	244	74	67	4	6	1	3	81	13	0	.160
1952	17	14	.548	3.27	35	33	15	239.2	238	52	93	0	0	2	0	85	13	0	.153
1953	18	9	.667	3.99	40	32	10	230	243	54	88	1	0	0	4	78	8	0	.103
1954	7	13	.350	5.26	48	20	3	155.2	198	47	50	1	3	6	2	36	5	0	.139
1955 2 teams			CIN	N (30G 5–8)		NY	A (2G 0–0)												
" total	5	8	.385	4.81	32	18	2	121.2	151	29	40	0	0	1	0	36	2	0	.056
1956 2 teams			NY	A (1G 0–0)		CHI	A (26G 8–3)												
" total	8	3	.727	3.26	27	10	5	102	102	20	26	0	1	1	0	33	3	0	.091
1957 CHI A	5	1	.833	2.06	47	0	0	105	95	27	44	0	5	1	2	22	1	0	.045
1958	4	5	.444	3.16	50	0	0	85.1	81	24	27	0	4	5	8	11	0	0	.000
1959	8	5	.615	2.24	67	0	0	116.1	111	25	54	0	8	5	14	13	2	0	.154
1960	13	8	.619	2.42	64	0	0	115.1	94	25	52	0	13	8	10	17	4	0	.235
1961 3 teams			CHI	A (16G 0–3)		KC	A (23G 1–1)		DET	A (13G 1–1)									
" total	2	5	.286	3.96	52	0	0	61.1	64	21	32	0	2	5	4	2	0	0	.000
15 yrs.	134	111	.547	3.70	640	186	58	1981.2	2070	529	727	9	56	41	61	525	66	1	.126
6 yrs.	38	25	.603	2.61	270	10	5	541.2	496	126	210	0	31	23	39	95	10	0	.105
													3rd						

WORLD SERIES
| 1959 CHI A | 0 | 1 | .000 | 2.16 | 4 | 0 | 0 | 8.1 | 8 | 0 | 3 | 0 | 0 | 1 | 1 | 1 | 0 | 0 | .000 |

Lee Stange
STANGE, ALBERT LEE
B. Oct. 27, 1936, Chicago, Ill.
BR TR 5'10" 165 lbs.

	W	L	PCT	ERA	G	GS	CG	IP	H	BB	SO	ShO	W	L	SV	AB	H	HR	BA
1961 MIN A	1	0	1.000	2.92	7	0	0	12.1	15	10	10	0	1	0	0	1	0	0	.000
1962	4	3	.571	4.45	44	6	1	95	98	39	70	0	2	3	3	17	1	0	.059
1963	12	5	.706	2.62	32	20	7	164.2	145	43	100	2	0	0	0	52	5	0	.096
1964 2 teams			MIN	A (14G 3–6)		CLE	A (23G 4–8)												
" total	7	14	.333	4.41	37	25	2	171.1	176	50	132	0	0	3	0	50	3	0	.060
1965 CLE A	8	4	.667	3.34	41	12	4	132	122	26	80	2	2	1	0	28	3	0	.107
1966 2 teams			CLE	A (8G 1–0)		BOS	A (28G 7–9)												
" total	8	9	.471	3.30	36	21	9	169.1	157	46	85	2	0	2	0	52	4	0	.077
1967 BOS A	8	10	.444	2.77	35	24	6	181.2	171	32	101	2	0	2	1	49	3	0	.061
1968	5	5	.500	3.93	50	2	1	103	89	25	53	0	5	3	12	15	2	0	.133
1969	6	9	.400	3.68	41	15	2	137	137	56	59	0	2	1	3	35	3	0	.086
1970 2 teams			BOS	A (20G 2–2)		CHI	A (16G 1–0)												
" total	3	2	.600	5.44	36	0	0	49.2	62	17	28	0	3	2	2	6	0	0	.000
10 yrs.	62	61	.504	3.56	359	125	32	1216	1172	344	718	8	15	17	21	305	24	0	.079
1 yr.	1	0	1.000	5.24	16	0	0	22.1	28	5	14	0	1	0	0	1	0	0	.000

WORLD SERIES
| 1967 BOS A | 0 | 0 | – | 0.00 | 1 | 0 | 0 | 2 | 3 | 0 | 0 | 0 | 0 | 0 | 0 | 0 | 0 | 0 | – |

Joe Stanka
STANKA, JOE DONALD
B. July 23, 1931, Hammon, Okla.
BR TR 6'5" 201 lbs.

| 1959 CHI A | 1 | 0 | 1.000 | 3.38 | 2 | 0 | 0 | 5.1 | 2 | 4 | 3 | 0 | 1 | 0 | 0 | 3 | 1 | 0 | .333 |

Milt Steengrafe
STEENGRAFE, MILTON HENRY
B. May 26, 1900, San Francisco, Calif. D. June 2, 1977, Oklahoma City, Okla.
BR TR 6' 170 lbs.

1924 CHI A	0	0	–	12.71	3	0	0	5.2	15	4	3	0	0	0	0	1	0	0	.000
1926	1	1	.500	3.99	13	1	0	38.1	43	19	10	0	1	1	0	14	0	0	.000
2 yrs.	1	1	.500	5.11	16	1	0	44	58	23	13	0	1	1	0	15	0	0	.000
2 yrs.	1	1	.500	5.11	16	1	0	44	58	23	13	0	1	1	0	15	0	0	.000

Frank Stewart
STEWART, FRANK
B. Sept. 8, 1906, Minneapolis, Minn.
BR TR 6'½" 178 lbs.

| 1927 CHI A | 0 | 1 | .000 | 9.00 | 1 | 1 | 0 | 4 | 5 | 4 | 0 | 0 | 0 | 0 | 0 | 1 | 0 | 0 | .000 |

Lee Stine
STINE, LEE ELBERT
B. Nov. 17, 1913, Stillwater, Okla.
BR TR 5'11" 185 lbs.

1934 CHI A	0	0	–	8.18	4	0	0	11	11	10	8	0	0	0	0	1	0	0	.000
1935	0	0	–	9.00	1	0	0	2	2	3	1	0	0	0	0	0	0	0	–
1936 CIN N	3	8	.273	5.03	40	13	5	121.2	157	41	26	1	0	1	2	27	8	0	.296
1938 NY A	0	0	–	1.04	4	0	0	8.2	9	1	4	0	0	0	0	2	1	0	.500
4 yrs.	3	8	.273	5.09	49	13	5	143.1	179	55	39	1	0	1	2	30	9	0	.300
2 yrs.	0	0	–	8.31	5	0	0	13	13	13	9	0	0	0	0	1	0	0	.000

Chuck Stobbs
STOBBS, CHARLES KLEIN
B. July 2, 1929, Wheeling, W. Va.
BL TL 6'1" 185 lbs.

1947 BOS A	0	1	.000	6.00	4	1	0	9	10	10	5	0	0	0	0	1	0	0	.000
1948	0	0	–	6.43	6	0	0	7	9	7	4	0	0	0	0	1	0	0	.000
1949	11	6	.647	4.03	26	19	10	152	145	75	70	0	0	0	2	53	11	0	.208
1950	12	7	.632	5.10	32	21	6	169.1	158	88	78	0	1	1	1	57	14	0	.246
1951	10	9	.526	4.76	34	25	6	170	180	74	75	0	0	0	0	61	11	0	.180
1952 CHI A	7	12	.368	3.13	38	17	2	135	118	72	73	0	3	1	1	38	3	0	.079
1953 WAS A	11	8	.579	3.29	27	20	8	153	146	44	67	0	0	0	0	44	10	0	.227
1954	11	11	.500	4.10	31	24	10	182	189	67	67	3	1	0	0	51	7	0	.137
1955	4	14	.222	5.00	41	16	2	140.1	169	57	60	0	3	3	3	35	6	0	.171
1956	15	15	.500	3.60	37	33	15	240	264	54	97	1	1	0	1	84	15	0	.179
1957	8	20	.286	5.36	42	31	5	211.2	235	80	114	2	1	2	1	76	16	0	.211
1958 2 teams			WAS	A (19G 2–6)		STL	N (17G 1–3)												
" total	3	9	.250	5.04	36	8	0	96.1	127	30	48	0	2	3	1	16	1	0	.063
1959 WAS A	1	8	.111	2.98	41	7	0	90.2	82	24	50	0	0	3	7	19	2	0	.105
1960	12	7	.632	3.32	40	13	1	119.1	115	38	72	1	6	2	2	34	3	0	.088
1961 MIN A	2	3	.400	7.46	24	3	0	44.2	56	15	17	0	2	1	2	8	3	0	.375
15 yrs.	107	130	.451	4.29	459	238	65	1920.1	2003	735	897	7	20	18	19	578	102	0	.176
1 yr.	7	12	.368	3.13	38	17	2	135	118	72	73	0	3	1	1	38	3	0	.079

Pitcher Register

	W	L	PCT	ERA	G	GS	CG	IP	H	BB	SO	ShO	Relief Pitching W	L	SV	BATTING AB	H	HR	BA

Tim Stoddard
STODDARD, TIMOTHY PAUL
B. Jan. 24, 1953, East Chicago, Ind.
BR TR 6'7" 230 lbs.

1975 CHI A	0	0	—	9.00	1	0	0	1	2	0	0	0	0	0	0	0	0	0	—
1978 BAL A	0	1	.000	6.00	8	0	0	18	22	8	14	0	0	1	0	0	0	0	—
1979	3	1	.750	1.71	29	0	0	58	44	19	47	0	3	1	3	0	0	0	—
1980	5	3	.625	2.51	64	0	0	86	72	38	64	0	5	3	26	0	0	0	—
1981	4	2	.667	3.89	31	0	0	37	38	18	32	0	4	2	7	0	0	0	—
1982	3	4	.429	4.02	50	0	0	56	53	29	42	0	3	4	12	0	0	0	—
1983	4	3	.571	6.09	47	0	0	57.2	65	29	50	0	4	3	9	0	0	0	—
7 yrs.	19	14	.576	3.67	230	0	0	313.2	296	141	249	0	19	14	57	0	0	0	—
1 yr.	0	0	—	9.00	1	0	0	1	2	0	0	0	0	0	0	0	0	0	—

WORLD SERIES
| 1979 BAL A | 1 | 0 | 1.000 | 5.40 | 4 | 0 | 0 | 5 | 6 | 1 | 3 | 0 | 1 | 0 | 0 | 1 | 1 | 0 | 1.000 |

Dean Stone
STONE, DARRAH DEAN
B. Sept. 1, 1930, Moline, Ill.
BL TL 6'4" 205 lbs.

1953 WAS A	0	1	.000	8.31	3	1	0	8.2	13	5	5	0	0	0	0	2	0	0	.000
1954	12	10	.545	3.22	31	23	10	178.2	161	69	87	2	1	0	0	52	5	1	.096
1955	6	13	.316	4.15	43	24	5	180	180	114	84	1	0	2	1	46	2	0	.043
1956	5	7	.417	6.27	41	21	2	132	148	93	86	0	0	1	3	34	3	0	.088
1957 2 teams			WAS A (3G 0-0)				BOS A (17G 1-3)												
" total	1	3	.250	5.27	20	8	0	54.2	61	37	35	0	0	0	1	14	0	0	.000
1959 STL N	0	1	.000	4.20	18	1	0	30	30	16	17	0	0	0	1	4	0	0	.000
1962 2 teams			HOU N (15G 3-2)				CHI A (27G 1-0)												
" total	4	2	.667	4.03	42	7	2	82.2	89	29	54	2	2	0	5	18	5	0	.278
1963 BAL A	1	2	.333	5.12	17	0	0	19.1	23	10	12	0	1	2	1	0	0	0	—
8 yrs.	29	39	.426	4.47	215	85	19	686	705	373	380	5	4	5	12	170	15	1	.088
1 yr.	1	0	1.000	3.26	27	0	0	30.1	28	9	23	0	1	0	5	2	1	0	.500

Steve Stone
STONE, STEVEN MICHAEL
B. July 14, 1947, Cleveland, Ohio
BR TR 5'10" 175 lbs.

1971 SF N	5	9	.357	4.14	24	19	2	111	110	55	63	2	0	0	0	34	0	0	.000
1972	6	8	.429	2.98	27	16	4	124	97	49	85	1	1	0	0	34	4	0	.118
1973 CHI A	6	11	.353	4.29	36	22	3	176.1	163	82	138	0	0	1	1	0	0	0	—
1974 CHI N	8	6	.571	4.13	38	23	1	170	185	64	90	0	1	1	0	58	7	0	.121
1975	12	8	.600	3.95	33	32	6	214	198	80	139	1	0	0	0	72	8	0	.111
1976	3	6	.333	4.08	17	15	1	75	70	21	33	1	0	0	0	21	3	0	.143
1977 CHI A	15	12	.556	4.52	31	31	8	207	228	80	124	1	0	0	0	0	0	0	—
1978	12	12	.500	4.37	30	30	6	212	196	84	118	1	0	0	0	0	0	0	—
1979 BAL A	11	7	.611	3.77	32	32	3	186	173	73	96	0	0	0	0	0	0	0	—
1980	25	7	.781	3.23	37	37	9	251	224	101	149	1	0	0	0	0	0	0	—
1981	4	7	.364	4.57	15	12	0	63	63	27	30	0	0	1	0	0	0	0	—
11 yrs.	107	93	.535	3.97	320	269	43	1789.1	1707	716	1065	7	2	3	1	219	22	0	.100
3 yrs.	33	35	.485	4.40	97	83	17	595.1	587	246	380	1	0	1	1	0	0	0	—

WORLD SERIES
| 1979 BAL A | 0 | 0 | — | 9.00 | 1 | 0 | 0 | 2 | 4 | 2 | 2 | 0 | 0 | 0 | 0 | 0 | 0 | 0 | — |

Dick Strahs
STRAHS, RICHARD BERNARD
B. Dec. 4, 1924, Evanston, Ill.
BL TR 6' 192 lbs.

| 1954 CHI A | 0 | 0 | — | 5.65 | 9 | 0 | 0 | 14.1 | 16 | 8 | 8 | 0 | 0 | 0 | 1 | 1 | 0 | 0 | .000 |

Monty Stratton
STRATTON, MONTY FRANKLIN PIERCE (Gander)
B. May 21, 1912, Celeste, Tex. D. Sept. 28, 1982, Greenville, Tex.
BR TR 6'5" 180 lbs.

1934 CHI A	0	0	—	5.40	1	0	0	3.1	4	1	0	0	0	0	0	2	0	0	.000
1935	1	2	.333	4.03	5	5	2	38	40	9	8	0	0	0	0	14	2	0	.143
1936	5	7	.417	5.21	16	14	3	95	117	46	37	0	0	1	0	37	8	1	.216
1937	15	5	.750	2.40	22	21	14	164.2	142	37	69	5	0	0	0	60	12	1	.200
1938	15	9	.625	4.01	26	22	17	186.1	186	56	82	0	1	1	2	79	21	2	.266
5 yrs.	36	23	.610	3.71	70	62	36	487.1	489	149	196	5	1	2	2	192	43	4	.224
5 yrs.	36	23	.610	3.71	70	62	36	487.1	489	149	196	5	1	2	2	192	43	4	.224

Elmer Stricklett
STRICKLETT, ELMER GRIFFIN
B. Aug. 29, 1876, Glasco, Kans. D. June 7, 1964, Santa Cruz, Calif.
BR TR 5'6" 140 lbs.

1904 CHI A	0	1	.000	10.29	1	1	0	7	12	2	3	0	0	0	0	3	0	0	.000
1905 BKN N	9	18	.333	3.34	33	28	25	237	259	71	77	1	0	0	1	88	13	0	.148
1906	14	18	.438	2.72	41	35	28	291.2	273	77	88	5	0	1	5	97	20	0	.206
1907	12	14	.462	2.27	29	26	25	229.2	211	65	69	4	1	1	0	81	12	0	.148
4 yrs.	35	51	.407	2.85	104	90	78	765.1	755	215	237	10	1	2	6	269	45	0	.167
1 yr.	0	1	.000	10.29	1	1	0	7	12	2	3	0	0	0	0	3	0	0	.000

Jake Striker
STRIKER, WILBUR SCOTT
B. Oct. 23, 1933, New Washington, Ohio
BL TL 6'2" 200 lbs.

1959 CLE A	1	0	1.000	2.70	1	1	0	6.2	8	4	5	0	0	0	0	1	0	0	.000
1960 CHI A	0	0	—	4.91	2	0	0	3.2	5	1	1	0	0	0	0	0	0	0	—
2 yrs.	1	0	1.000	3.48	3	1	0	10.1	13	5	6	0	0	0	0	1	0	0	1.000
1 yr.	0	0	—	4.91	2	0	0	3.2	5	1	1	0	0	0	0	0	0	0	—

Joe Sugden
SUGDEN, JOSEPH
B. July 31, 1870, Philadelphia, Pa. D. June 28, 1959, Philadelphia, Pa.
BB TR 5'10" 180 lbs.

| 1902 STL A | 0 | 0 | — | 0.00 | 1 | 0 | 0 | 1 | 1 | 0 | 0 | 0 | 0 | 0 | 0 | * | | | |

John Sullivan
SULLIVAN, JOHN JEREMIAH
B. May 31, 1894, Chicago, Ill. D. July 7, 1958, Chicago, Ill.
BL TL 5'11" 165 lbs.

| 1919 CHI A | 0 | 1 | .000 | 4.20 | 4 | 2 | 1 | 15 | 24 | 8 | 9 | 0 | 0 | 0 | 0 | 3 | 0 | 0 | .000 |

Pitcher Register

	W	L	PCT	ERA	G	GS	CG	IP	H	BB	SO	ShO	Relief Pitching W	L	SV	BATTING AB	H	HR	BA

Max Surkont
SURKONT, MATTHEW CONSTANTINE BR TR 6'1" 195 lbs.
B. June 16, 1922, Central Falls, R. I.

	W	L	PCT	ERA	G	GS	CG	IP	H	BB	SO	ShO	W	L	SV	AB	H	HR	BA
1949 CHI A	3	5	.375	4.78	44	2	0	96	92	60	38	0	3	4	4	22	1	0	.045
1950 BOS N	5	2	.714	3.23	9	6	2	55.2	63	20	21	0	2	0	0	23	10	1	.435
1951	12	16	.429	3.99	37	33	11	237	230	89	110	2	1	0	1	73	11	0	.151
1952	12	13	.480	3.77	31	29	12	215	201	76	125	3	0	0	0	63	7	0	.111
1953 MIL N	11	5	.688	4.18	28	24	11	170	168	64	83	2	0	0	0	56	16	0	.286
1954 PIT N	9	18	.333	4.41	33	29	11	208.1	216	78	78	0	1	0	0	60	10	0	.167
1955	7	14	.333	5.57	35	22	5	166.1	194	78	84	0	1	1	2	50	7	0	.140
1956 3 teams	PIT N (1G 0-0)				STL N (5G 0-0)			NY N (8G 2-2)											
" total	2	2	.500	5.45	14	4	1	39.2	36	14	24	0	0	0	1	10	1	0	.100
1957 NY N	0	1	.000	9.95	5	0	0	6.1	9	2	8	0	0	1	0	—	—	—	—
9 yrs.	61	76	.445	4.38	236	149	53	1194.1	1209	481	571	7	8	6	8	357	63	1	.176
1 yr.	3	5	.375	4.78	44	2	0	96	92	60	38	0	3	4	4	22	1	0	.045

Rube Suter
SUTER, HARRY RICHARD TL
B. Portland, Ore. D. July 24, 1971, Topeka, Kans.

	W	L	PCT	ERA	G	GS	CG	IP	H	BB	SO	ShO	W	L	SV	AB	H	HR	BA
1909 CHI A	2	3	.400	2.47	18	6	3	87.1	72	28	53	1	1	0	1	32	3	0	.094

Bill Swift
SWIFT, WILLIAM VINCENT BR TR 6'1½" 192 lbs.
B. Jan. 10, 1908, Elmira, N. Y. D. Feb. 23, 1969, Bartow, Fla.

	W	L	PCT	ERA	G	GS	CG	IP	H	BB	SO	ShO	W	L	SV	AB	H	HR	BA
1932 PIT N	14	10	.583	3.61	39	23	11	214.1	205	26	64	0	6	1	4	78	15	0	.192
1933	14	10	.583	3.13	37	29	13	218.1	214	36	64	2	2	0	0	82	20	0	.244
1934	11	13	.458	3.98	37	24	13	212.2	244	46	81	1	1	2	0	84	18	0	.214
1935	15	8	.652	2.70	39	21	11	203.2	193	37	74	3	3	4	1	78	19	0	.244
1936	16	16	.500	4.01	45	31	17	262.1	275	63	92	0	4	1	2	105	31	2	.295
1937	9	10	.474	3.95	36	17	9	164	160	34	84	0	2	2	3	54	9	0	.167
1938	7	5	.583	3.24	36	9	2	150	155	40	77	0	5	2	4	50	10	1	.200
1939	5	7	.417	3.89	36	8	2	129.2	150	28	56	1	2	4	4	42	10	0	.238
1940 BOS N	1	1	.500	2.89	4	0	0	9.1	12	7	7	0	1	1	1	3	0	0	.000
1941 BKN N	3	0	1.000	3.27	9	0	0	22	26	7	9	0	3	0	1	5	1	0	.200
1943 CHI A	0	2	.000	4.21	18	1	0	51.1	48	27	28	0	0	1	0	10	1	0	.100
11 yrs.	95	82	.537	3.58	336	163	78	1637.2	1682	351	636	7	29	18	20	591	134	3	.227
1 yr.	0	2	.000	4.21	18	1	0	51.1	48	27	28	0	0	1	0	10	1	0	.100

Doug Taitt
TAITT, DOUGLAS JOHN (Poco) BL TR 6' 176 lbs.
B. Aug. 3, 1902, Bay City, Mich. D. Dec. 12, 1970, Portland, Ore.

	W	L	PCT	ERA	G	GS	CG	IP	H	BB	SO	ShO	W	L	SV	AB	H	HR	BA
1928 BOS A	0	0	—	27.00	1	0	0	1	2	2	1	0	0	0	0	*			

Fred Talbot
TALBOT, FRED LEALAND (Bubby) BR TR 6'2" 195 lbs.
B. June 28, 1941, Washington, D. C.

	W	L	PCT	ERA	G	GS	CG	IP	H	BB	SO	ShO	W	L	SV	AB	H	HR	BA
1963 CHI A	0	0	—	3.00	1	0	0	3	2	4	2	0	0	0	0	1	0	0	.000
1964	4	5	.444	3.70	17	12	3	75.1	83	20	34	2	1	1	0	19	5	0	.263
1965 KC A	10	12	.455	4.14	39	33	2	198	188	86	117	1	0	1	0	70	14	0	.200
1966 2 teams	KC A (11G 4-4)				NY A (23G 7-7)														
" total	11	11	.500	4.36	34	30	3	192	188	73	85	0	0	0	0	55	8	0	.145
1967 NY A	6	8	.429	4.22	29	22	2	138.2	132	54	61	0	1	1	0	38	6	1	.158
1968	1	9	.100	3.36	29	11	1	99	89	42	67	0	1	0	0	17	2	1	.118
1969 3 teams	NY A (8G 0-0)				SEA A (25G 5-8)			OAK A (12G 1-2)											
" total	6	10	.375	4.38	45	18	1	146	160	54	83	1	2	2	1	41	7	2	.171
1970 OAK A	0	1	.000	9.00	1	0	0	2	2	1	0	0	0	0	0	0	0	0	—
8 yrs.	38	56	.404	4.12	195	126	12	854	844	334	449	4	5	7	1	241	42	4	.174
2 yrs.	4	5	.444	3.68	18	12	3	78.1	85	24	36	2	1	1	0	20	5	0	.250

Ken Tatum
TATUM, KENNETH RAY BR TR 6'2" 205 lbs.
B. Apr. 25, 1944, Alexandria, La.

	W	L	PCT	ERA	G	GS	CG	IP	H	BB	SO	ShO	W	L	SV	AB	H	HR	BA
1969 CAL A	7	2	.778	1.36	45	0	0	86.1	51	39	65	0	7	2	22	21	6	2	.286
1970	7	4	.636	2.93	62	0	0	89	68	26	50	0	7	4	17	11	2	1	.182
1971 BOS A	2	4	.333	4.17	36	1	0	54	50	25	21	0	2	3	9	10	3	0	.300
1972	0	2	.000	3.10	22	0	0	29	32	15	15	0	0	2	4	2	0	0	.000
1973	0	0	—	9.00	1	0	0	4	6	3	0	0	0	0	0	0	0	0	—
1974 CHI A	0	0	—	4.71	10	1	0	21	23	9	5	0	0	0	0	1	0	0	.000
6 yrs.	16	12	.571	2.92	176	2	0	283.1	230	117	156	0	16	11	52	45	11	4	.244
1 yr.	0	0	—	4.71	10	1	0	21	23	9	5	0	0	0	0	1	0	0	.000

Wiley Taylor
TAYLOR, PHILIP WILEY BR TR 6'1" 175 lbs.
B. Mar. 18, 1888, Wamego, Kans. D. July 8, 1954, Westmoreland, Kans.

	W	L	PCT	ERA	G	GS	CG	IP	H	BB	SO	ShO	W	L	SV	AB	H	HR	BA
1911 DET A	0	2	.000	3.79	3	2	1	19	18	10	9	0	0	0	0	6	0	0	.000
1912 CHI A	1	1	.500	4.95	3	3	0	20	21	14	4	0	0	0	0	5	0	0	.000
1913 STL A	0	2	.000	4.83	5	4	1	31.2	33	16	12	0	0	0	0	10	0	0	.000
1914	2	5	.286	3.42	16	8	2	50	41	25	20	1	0	1	0	12	2	0	.167
4 yrs.	3	10	.231	4.10	27	17	4	120.2	113	65	45	1	0	1	0	33	2	0	.061
1 yr.	1	1	.500	4.95	3	3	0	20	21	14	4	0	0	0	0	5	0	0	.000

Tommy Thomas
THOMAS, ALPHONSE BR TR 5'10" 175 lbs.
B. Dec. 23, 1899, Baltimore, Md.

	W	L	PCT	ERA	G	GS	CG	IP	H	BB	SO	ShO	W	L	SV	AB	H	HR	BA
1926 CHI A	15	12	.556	3.80	44	32	13	249	225	110	127	2	3	2	2	86	16	0	.186
1927	19	16	.543	2.98	40	36	24	307.2	271	94	107	3	1	0	1	95	14	1	.147
1928	17	16	.515	3.08	36	32	24	283	277	76	129	3	1	0	0	96	21	0	.219
1929	14	18	.438	3.19	36	31	24	259.2	270	60	62	2	0	0	1	98	25	0	.255
1930	5	13	.278	5.22	34	27	7	169	229	44	58	0	0	0	0	56	7	0	.125
1931	10	14	.417	4.80	42	36	11	242	296	69	71	2	0	0	0	87	21	0	.241
1932 2 teams	CHI A (12G 3-3)				WAS A (18G 8-7)														
" total	11	10	.524	4.26	30	17	8	160.2	169	61	47	0	4	1	0	55	11	0	.200
1933 WAS A	7	7	.500	4.80	35	14	2	135	149	49	35	0	4	4	3	42	10	0	.238
1934	8	9	.471	5.47	33	18	7	133.1	154	58	42	1	2	2	1	38	7	0	.184

Pitcher Register

Tommy Thomas continued

	W	L	PCT	ERA	G	GS	CG	IP	H	BB	SO	ShO	Relief W	Pitching L	SV	AB	H	HR	BA
1935 2 teams	WAS	A (1G 0–0)			PHI	N (4G 0–1)													
" total	0	1	.000	6.57	5	1	0	12.1	18	5	3	0	0	1	0	3	0	0	.000
1936 STL A	11	9	.550	5.26	36	21	8	179.2	219	72	40	1	2	0	0	58	8	0	.138
1937 2 teams	STL	A (17G 0–1)			BOS	A (9G 0–2)													
" total	0	3	.000	6.26	26	2	0	41.2	62	14	14	0	0	2	0	8	1	0	.125
12 yrs.	117	128	.478	4.12	397	267	128	2173	2339	712	735	15	18	12	12	722	141	3	.195
7 yrs.	83	92	.474	3.78	244	197	104	1554	1623	468	565	12	8	3	8	531	105	3	.198

WORLD SERIES

| 1933 WAS A | 0 | 0 | – | 0.00 | 2 | 0 | 0 | 1.1 | 1 | 0 | 2 | 0 | 0 | 0 | 0 | 0 | 0 | 0 | |

Lee Thompson

THOMPSON, JOHN DUDLEY (Lefty)   BL TL 6'1"   185 lbs.
B. Feb. 26, 1898, Smithfield, Utah   D. Feb. 17, 1963, Santa Barbara, Calif.

| 1921 CHI A | 0 | 3 | .000 | 8.27 | 4 | 4 | 0 | 20.2 | 32 | 6 | 4 | 0 | 0 | 0 | 0 | 7 | 2 | 0 | .286 |

Sloppy Thurston

THURSTON, HOLLIS JOHN   BR TR 5'11"   165 lbs.
B. June 2, 1899, Fremont, Neb.   D. Sept. 14, 1973, Los Angeles, Calif.

	W	L	PCT	ERA	G	GS	CG	IP	H	BB	SO	ShO	W	L	SV	AB	H	HR	BA
1923 2 teams	STL	A (2G 0–0)			CHI	A (44G 7–8)													
" total	7	8	.467	3.13	46	13	8	195.2	231	38	55	0	4	3	4	79	25	0	.316
1924 CHI A	20	14	.588	3.80	38	36	28	291	330	60	37	1	0	1	1	122	31	1	.254
1925	10	14	.417	6.17	36	25	9	175	250	47	35	0	1	4	1	84	24	0	.286
1926	6	8	.429	5.02	31	13	6	134.1	164	36	35	1	2	3	3	61	19	0	.311
1927 WAS A	13	13	.500	4.47	29	28	13	205.1	254	60	38	2	0	1	0	92	29	2	.315
1930 BKN N	6	4	.600	3.40	24	11	5	106	110	17	26	2	1	0	1	50	10	1	.200
1931	9	9	.500	3.97	24	17	11	143	175	39	23	0	1	3	0	60	13	1	.217
1932	12	8	.600	4.06	28	20	10	153	174	38	35	2	1	1	0	56	17	0	.304
1933	6	8	.429	4.52	32	15	5	131.1	171	34	22	0	3	1	3	44	7	0	.159
9 yrs.	89	86	.509	4.26	288	178	95	1534.2	1859	369	306	8	13	17	13	*			
4 yrs.	43	44	.494	4.35	149	86	51	792	967	179	162	2	7	11	9	346	99	1	.286

Dick Tidrow

TIDROW, RICHARD WILLIAM   BR TR 6'4"   210 lbs.
B. May 14, 1947, San Francisco, Calif.

	W	L	PCT	ERA	G	GS	CG	IP	H	BB	SO	ShO	W	L	SV	AB	H	HR	BA
1972 CLE A	14	15	.483	2.77	39	34	10	237	200	70	123	3	1	0	0	70	7	0	.100
1973	14	16	.467	4.42	42	40	13	274.2	289	95	138	2	0	0	0	0	0	0	–
1974 2 teams	CLE	A (4G 1–3)			NY	A (33G 11–9)													
" total	12	12	.500	4.16	37	29	5	210	226	66	108	0	2	0	1	0	0	0	–
1975 NY A	6	3	.667	3.13	37	0	0	69	65	31	38	0	6	3	5	0	0	0	–
1976	4	5	.444	2.63	47	2	0	92.1	80	24	65	0	4	5	10	0	0	0	–
1977	11	4	.733	3.16	49	7	0	151	143	41	83	0	6	4	5	0	0	0	–
1978	7	11	.389	3.84	31	25	4	185.1	191	53	73	0	0	1	0	0	0	0	–
1979 2 teams	NY	A (14G 2–1)			CHI	N (63G 11–5)													
" total	13	6	.684	3.64	77	0	0	126	124	46	75	0	13	6	6	10	2	0	.200
1980 CHI N	6	5	.545	2.79	84	0	0	116	97	53	97	0	6	5	6	4	0	0	.000
1981	3	10	.231	5.04	51	0	0	75	73	30	39	0	3	10	9	5	0	0	.000
1982	8	3	.727	3.39	65	0	0	103.2	106	29	62	0	8	3	6	6	0	0	.000
1983 CHI A	2	4	.333	4.22	50	1	0	91.2	86	34	66	0	2	4	7	0	0	0	–
12 yrs.	100	94	.515	3.63	609	138	32	1731.2	1680	572	967	5	51	41	55	95	9	0	.095
1 yr.	2	4	.333	4.22	50	1	0	91.2	86	34	66	0	2	4	7	0	0	0	–

LEAGUE CHAMPIONSHIP SERIES

1976 NY A	1	0	1.000	3.68	3	0	0	7.1	6	4	0	0	1	0	0	0	0	0	–
1977	0	0	–	3.86	2	0	0	7	6	3	3	0	0	0	0	0	0	0	–
1978	0	0	–	4.76	1	0	0	5.2	8	2	1	0	0	0	0	0	0	0	–
1983 CHI A	0	0	–	3.00	1	0	0	3	1	3	3	0	0	0	0	0	0	0	–
4 yrs.	1	0	1.000	3.91	7	0	0	23	21	12	7	0	1	0	0	0	0	0	–

WORLD SERIES

1976 NY A	0	0	–	7.71	2	0	0	2.1	5	1	1	0	0	0	0	0	0	0	–
1977	0	0	–	4.91	2	0	0	3.2	5	0	1	0	0	0	0	1	0	0	.000
1978	0	0	–	1.93	2	0	0	4.2	4	0	5	0	0	0	0	0	0	0	–
3 yrs.	0	0	–	4.22	6	0	0	10.2	14	1	7	0	0	0	0	1	0	0	.000

Verle Tiefenthaler

TIEFENTHALER, VERLE MATTHEW   BL TR 6'1"   190 lbs.
B. July 11, 1937, Breda, Iowa

| 1962 CHI A | 0 | 0 | – | 9.82 | 3 | 0 | 0 | 3.2 | 6 | 7 | 1 | 0 | 0 | 0 | 0 | 0 | 0 | 0 | – |

Les Tietje

TIETJE, LESLIE WILLIAM (Toots)   BR TR 6'1½"   178 lbs.
B. Sept. 11, 1911, Summer, Iowa

	W	L	PCT	ERA	G	GS	CG	IP	H	BB	SO	ShO	W	L	SV	AB	H	HR	BA
1933 CHI A	2	0	1.000	2.42	3	3	1	22.1	16	15	9	0	0	0	0	8	1	0	.125
1934	5	14	.263	4.81	34	22	6	176	174	96	81	1	1	0	0	59	1	0	.017
1935	9	15	.375	4.30	30	21	9	169.2	184	81	64	1	1	5	0	61	12	0	.197
1936 2 teams	CHI	A (2G 0–0)			STL	A (14G 3–5)													
" total	3	5	.375	7.52	16	7	2	52.2	71	35	19	0	1	0	0	15	1	0	.067
1937 STL A	1	2	.333	4.20	5	4	2	30	32	17	5	0	0	0	0	10	0	0	.000
1938	2	5	.286	7.55	17	8	2	62	83	38	15	1	0	1	0	18	2	0	.111
6 yrs.	22	41	.349	5.11	105	65	22	512.2	560	282	193	3	3	6	0	171	17	0	.099
4 yrs.	16	29	.356	4.57	69	46	16	370.1	380	197	157	2	2	5	0	128	14	0	.109

Pablo Torrealba

TORREALBA, PABLO ARNOLDO   BL TL 5'10"   173 lbs.
B. Apr. 28, 1949, Barouisimento, Venezuela

1975 ATL N	0	1	.000	1.29	6	0	0	7	7	3	5	0	0	0	0	1	1	0	1.000
1976	0	2	.000	3.57	36	0	0	53	67	22	33	0	0	2	2	4	0	0	.000
1977 OAK A	4	6	.400	2.62	41	10	3	117	127	38	51	0	3	1	2	0	0	0	–
1978 CHI A	2	4	.333	4.71	25	3	1	57.1	69	39	23	1	1	3	1	0	0	0	–
1979	0	0	–	1.50	3	0	0	6	5	2	1	0	0	0	0	0	0	0	–
5 yrs.	6	13	.316	3.26	111	13	4	240.1	275	104	113	1	4	7	5	5	1	0	.200
2 yrs.	2	4	.333	4.41	28	3	1	63.1	74	41	24	1	1	3	1	0	0	0	–

Pitcher Register

	W	L	PCT	ERA	G	GS	CG	IP	H	BB	SO	ShO	Relief Pitching W	L	SV	BATTING AB	H	HR	BA

Clay Touchstone
TOUCHSTONE, CLAYTON MAFFITT   BR TR 5'9"   175 lbs.
B. Jan. 24, 1904, Moore, Pa.   D. Apr. 28, 1949, Beaumont, Tex.

1928 BOS N	0	0	–	4.50	5	0	0	8	15	2	1	0	0	0	0	2	0	0	.000
1929	0	0	–	16.88	1	0	0	2.2	6	0	1	0	0	0	0	1	1	0	1.000
1945 CHI A	0	0	–	5.40	6	0	0	10	14	6	4	0	0	0	0	1	0	0	.000
3 yrs.	0	0	–	6.53	12	0	0	20.2	35	8	6	0	0	0	0	4	1	0	.250
1 yr.	0	0	–	5.40	6	0	0	10	14	6	4	0	0	0	0	1	0	0	.000

Hal Trosky
TROSKY, HAROLD ARTHUR, JR. (Hoot)   BR TR 6'3"   205 lbs.
Born Harold Arthur Troyavesky, Jr.   Son of Hal Trosky.
B. Sept. 29, 1936, Cleveland, Ohio

| 1958 CHI A | 1 | 0 | 1.000 | 6.00 | 2 | 0 | 0 | 3 | 5 | 2 | 1 | 0 | 1 | 0 | 0 | 0 | 0 | 0 | – |

Steve Trout
TROUT, STEVEN RUSSELL (Rainbow)   BL TL 6'4"   195 lbs.
Son of Dizzy Trout.
B. July 30, 1957, Detroit, Mich.

1978 CHI A	3	0	1.000	4.03	4	3	1	22.1	19	11	11	0	0	0	0	0	0	0	–
1979	11	8	.579	3.89	34	18	6	155	165	59	76	2	1	2	4	0	0	0	–
1980	9	16	.360	3.69	32	30	7	200	229	49	89	2	0	0	0	0	0	0	–
1981	8	7	.533	3.46	20	18	3	125	122	38	54	0	1	0	0	0	0	0	–
1982	6	9	.400	4.26	25	19	2	120.1	130	50	62	0	0	0	0	0	0	0	–
1983 CHI N	10	14	.417	4.65	34	32	1	180	217	59	80	0	1	0	0	62	12	0	.194
6 yrs.	47	54	.465	4.00	149	120	20	802.2	882	266	372	4	3	2	4	62	12	0	.194
5 yrs.	37	40	.481	3.82	115	88	19	622.2	665	207	292	4	2	2	4	0	0	0	–

Virgil Trucks
TRUCKS, VIRGIL OLIVER (Fire)   BR TR 5'11"   198 lbs.
B. Apr. 26, 1919, Birmingham, Ala.

1941 DET A	0	0	–	9.00	1	0	0	2	4	0	3	0	0	0	0	0	0	0	–
1942	14	8	.636	2.74	28	20	8	167.2	147	74	91	2	4	1	0	65	8	0	.123
1943	16	10	.615	2.84	33	25	10	202.2	170	52	118	3	2	1	2	72	13	0	.181
1945	0	0	–	1.69	1	1	0	5.1	3	2	3	0	0	0	0	2	0	0	.000
1946	14	9	.609	3.23	32	29	15	236.2	217	75	161	3	1	1	0	95	17	0	.179
1947	10	12	.455	4.53	36	26	8	180.2	186	79	108	2	0	2	2	70	19	0	.271
1948	14	13	.519	3.78	43	26	7	211.2	190	85	123	0	4	2	2	79	13	0	.165
1949	19	11	.633	2.81	41	32	17	275	209	124	153	6	2	0	4	100	12	0	.120
1950	3	1	.750	3.54	7	7	2	48.1	45	21	25	1	0	0	0	20	3	0	.150
1951	13	8	.619	4.33	37	18	6	153.2	153	75	89	1	4	2	1	55	13	0	.236
1952	5	19	.208	3.97	35	29	8	197	190	82	129	3	0	1	1	64	12	1	.188
1953 2 teams		STL A (16G 5–4)				CHI A (24G 15–6)													
" total	20	10	.667	2.93	40	33	17	264.1	234	99	149	5	0	1	3	88	19	1	.216
1954 CHI A	19	12	.613	2.79	40	33	16	264.2	224	95	152	5	3	1	3	93	17	0	.183
1955	13	8	.619	3.96	32	26	7	175	176	61	91	3	1	0	0	64	8	0	.125
1956 DET A	6	5	.545	3.83	22	16	3	120	104	63	43	1	0	1	1	45	11	0	.244
1957 KC A	9	7	.563	3.03	48	7	0	116	106	62	55	0	8	3	7	28	4	0	.143
1958 2 teams		KC A (16G 0–1)				NY A (25G 2–1)													
" total	2	2	.500	3.65	41	0	0	61.2	58	39	41	0	2	2	4	9	2	0	.222
17 yrs.	177	135	.567	3.39	517	328	124	2682.1	2416	1088	1534	35	31	18	30	949	171	2	.180
3 yrs.	47	26	.644	3.14	96	80	36	616	551	223	345	11	4	2	4	220	40	1	.182

WORLD SERIES

| 1945 DET A | 1 | 0 | 1.000 | 3.38 | 2 | 2 | 1 | 13.1 | 14 | 5 | 7 | 0 | 0 | 0 | 0 | 4 | 0 | 0 | .000 |

Cy Twombly
TWOMBLY, EDWIN PARKER   BR TR 5'10½" 170 lbs.
B. June 15, 1897, Groveland, Mass.   D. Dec. 3, 1974, Savannah, Ga.

| 1921 CHI A | 1 | 2 | .333 | 5.86 | 7 | 4 | 0 | 27.2 | 26 | 25 | 7 | 0 | 0 | 0 | 0 | 10 | 0 | 0 | .000 |

Bob Uhle
UHLE, ROBERT ELLWOOD (Lefty)   BB TL 5'11"   175 lbs.
B. Sept. 17, 1913, San Francisco, Calif.

1938 CHI A	0	0	–	0.00	1	0	0	2	1	0	0	0	0	0	0	0	0	0	–
1940 DET A	0	0	–	∞	1	0	0	0	4	2	0	0	0	0	0	0	0	0	–
2 yrs.	0	0	–	18.00	2	0	0	2	5	2	0	0	0	0	0	0	0	0	–
1 yr.	0	0	–	0.00	1	0	0	2	1	0	0	0	0	0	0	0	0	0	–

Cecil Upshaw
UPSHAW, CECIL LEE   BR TR 6'6"   205 lbs.
B. Oct. 22, 1942, Spearsville, La.

1966 ATL N	0	0	–	0.00	1	0	0	3	0	3	2	0	0	0	0	1	1	0	1.000
1967	2	3	.400	2.58	30	0	0	45.1	42	8	31	0	2	3	8	6	1	0	.167
1968	8	7	.533	2.47	52	0	0	116.2	98	24	74	0	8	7	13	23	4	0	.174
1969	6	4	.600	2.91	62	0	0	105	102	29	57	0	6	4	27	21	5	1	.238
1971	11	6	.647	3.51	49	0	0	82	95	28	56	0	11	6	17	15	0	0	.000
1972	3	5	.375	3.67	42	0	0	54	50	19	23	0	3	5	13	7	1	0	.143
1973 2 teams		ATL N (5G 0–1)				HOU N (35G 2–3)													
" total	2	4	.333	4.93	40	0	0	42	46	17	24	0	2	4	1	2	0	0	.000
1974 2 teams		CLE A (7G 0–1)				NY A (36G 1–5)													
" total	1	6	.143	3.04	43	0	0	68	63	28	34	0	1	6	6	0	0	0	–
1975 CHI A	1	1	.500	3.23	29	0	0	47.1	49	21	22	0	1	1	1	0	0	0	–
9 yrs.	34	36	.486	3.13	348	0	0	563.1	545	177	323	0	34	36	86	75	12	1	.160
1 yr.	1	1	.500	3.23	29	0	0	47.1	49	21	22	0	1	1	1	0	0	0	–

LEAGUE CHAMPIONSHIP SERIES

| 1969 ATL N | 0 | 0 | – | 2.84 | 3 | 0 | 0 | 6.1 | 5 | 1 | 4 | 0 | 0 | 0 | 0 | 1 | 0 | 0 | .000 |

Vito Valentinetti
VALENTINETTI, VITO JOHN   BR TR 6'   195 lbs.
B. Sept. 16, 1928, West New York, N. J.

1954 CHI A	0	0	–	54.00	1	0	0	0	4	2	1	0	0	0	0	0	0	0	–
1956 CHI N	6	4	.600	3.78	42	2	0	95.1	84	36	26	0	6	3	1	20	2	0	.100
1957 2 teams		CHI N (9G 0–2)				CLE A (11G 2–2)													
" total	2	2	.500	4.04	20	2	0	35.2	38	20	17	0	1	2	0	7	1	0	.143

Pitcher Register 410

	W	L	PCT	ERA	G	GS	CG	IP	H	BB	SO	ShO	Relief Pitching W	L	SV	BATTING AB	H	HR	BA

Vito Valentinetti continued

1958 2 teams	DET A (15G 1–0)				WAS A (23G 4–6)														
" total	5	6	.455	4.80	38	10	2	114.1	124	54	43	0	1	1	2	28	9	0	.321
1959 WAS A	0	2	.000	10.13	7	1	0	10.2	16	10	7	0	0	1	0	0	0	0	—
5 yrs.	13	14	.481	4.73	108	15	3	257	266	122	94	0	8	7	3	55	12	0	.218
1 yr.	0	0	—	54.00	1	0	0	4	2	1	0	0	0	0	0	0	0	0	—

Joe Vance

VANCE, JOSEPH ALBERT (Sandy) BR TR 6'1½" 190 lbs.
B. Sept. 16, 1905, Devine, Tex. D. July 4, 1978, Devine, Tex.

1935 CHI A	2	2	.500	6.68	10	0	0	31	36	21	12	0	2	0	0	11	2	0	.182
1937 NY A	1	0	1.000	3.00	2	2	0	15	11	9	3	0	0	0	0	5	0	0	.000
1938	0	0	—	7.15	3	1	0	11.1	20	4	2	0	0	0	0	4	3	0	.750
3 yrs.	3	2	.600	5.81	15	3	0	57.1	67	34	17	0	2	2	0	20	5	0	.250
1 yr.	2	2	.500	6.68	10	0	0	31	36	21	12	0	2	0	0	11	2	0	.182

John Verhoeven

VERHOEVEN, JOHN C. BR TR 6'5" 200 lbs.
B. July 3, 1953, Long Beach, Calif.

1976 CAL A	0	2	.000	3.41	21	0	0	37	35	14	23	0	0	2	4	0	0	0	—
1977 2 teams	CAL A (3G 0–2)				CHI A (6G 0–0)														
" total	0	2	.000	2.40	9	0	0	15	13	6	9	0	0	2	0	0	0	0	—
1980 MIN A	3	4	.429	3.96	44	0	0	100	109	29	42	0	3	4	0	0	0	0	—
1981	0	0	—	3.98	25	0	0	52	57	14	16	0	0	0	0	0	0	0	—
4 yrs.	3	8	.273	3.75	99	0	0	204	214	63	90	0	3	8	4	0	0	0	—
1 yr.	0	0	—	1.74	6	0	0	10.1	9	2	6	0	0	0	0	0	0	0	—

Pete Vuckovich

VUCKOVICH, PETER DENNIS BR TR 6'4" 215 lbs.
B. Oct. 27, 1952, Johnstown, Pa.

1975 CHI A	0	1	.000	13.06	4	2	0	10.1	17	7	5	0	0	0	0	0	0	0	—
1976	7	4	.636	4.66	33	7	1	110	122	60	62	0	2	2	0	0	0	0	—
1977 TOR A	7	7	.500	3.47	53	8	3	148	143	59	123	1	4	3	8	0	0	0	—
1978 STL N	12	12	.500	2.55	45	23	6	198	187	59	149	2	1	4	1	58	8	0	.138
1979	15	10	.600	3.59	34	32	9	233	229	64	145	0	0	1	0	79	12	0	.152
1980	12	9	.571	3.41	32	30	7	222	203	68	132	3	0	0	1	71	13	0	.183
1981 MIL A	14	4	.778	3.54	24	23	2	150	137	57	84	1	0	0	0	0	0	0	—
1982	18	6	.750	3.34	30	30	9	223.2	234	102	105	1	0	0	0	0	0	0	—
1983	0	2	.000	4.91	3	3	0	14.2	15	10	10	0	0	0	0	0	0	0	—
9 yrs.	85	55	.607	3.52	258	158	37	1309.2	1287	486	815	8	7	10	10	208	33	0	.159
2 yrs.	7	5	.583	5.39	37	9	1	120.1	139	67	67	0	2	2	0	0	0	0	—

DIVISIONAL PLAYOFF SERIES
| 1981 MIL A | 1 | 0 | 1.000 | 0.00 | 2 | 1 | 0 | 5.1 | 2 | 3 | 4 | 0 | 0 | 0 | 0 | 0 | 0 | 0 | — |

LEAGUE CHAMPIONSHIP SERIES
| 1982 MIL A | 0 | 1 | .000 | 4.40 | 2 | 2 | 1 | 14.1 | 15 | 7 | 8 | 0 | 0 | 0 | 0 | 0 | 0 | 0 | — |

WORLD SERIES
| 1982 MIL A | 0 | 1 | .000 | 4.50 | 2 | 2 | 0 | 14 | 16 | 5 | 4 | 0 | 0 | 0 | 0 | 0 | 0 | 0 | — |

Jake Wade

WADE, JACOB FIELDS (Whistlin' Jake) BL TL 6'2" 175 lbs.
Brother of Ben Wade.
B. Apr. 1, 1912, Morehead City, N. C.

1936 DET A	4	5	.444	5.29	13	11	4	78.1	93	52	30	0	0	0	0	29	5	0	.172
1937	7	10	.412	5.39	33	25	7	165.1	160	107	69	1	0	1	0	59	11	0	.186
1938	3	2	.600	6.56	27	2	0	70	73	48	23	0	3	0	0	21	1	0	.048
1939 2 teams	BOS A (20G 1–4)				STL A (4G 0–2)														
" total	1	6	.143	7.45	24	8	2	64	94	56	30	0	1	1	0	17	0	0	.000
1942 CHI A	5	5	.500	4.10	15	10	3	85.2	84	56	32	0	1	0	0	29	7	0	.241
1943	3	7	.300	3.01	21	9	3	83.2	66	54	41	1	0	1	0	27	4	0	.148
1944	2	4	.333	4.82	19	5	1	74.2	75	41	35	0	1	1	2	24	7	0	.292
1946 2 teams	NY A (13G 2–1)				WAS A (6G 0–0)														
" total	2	1	.667	2.89	19	1	0	46.2	45	26	31	0	2	0	1	10	1	0	.100
8 yrs.	27	40	.403	5.00	171	71	20	668.1	690	440	291	3	8	4	3	216	36	0	.167
3 yrs.	10	16	.385	3.95	55	24	7	244	225	151	108	1	2	2	2	80	18	0	.225

Ed Walsh

WALSH, EDWARD ARTHUR BR TR 6'1" 180 lbs.
Son of Ed Walsh.
B. Feb. 11, 1905, Meriden, Conn. D. Oct. 31, 1937, Meriden, Conn.

1928 CHI A	4	7	.364	4.96	14	10	3	78	86	42	32	0	1	0	0	27	3	0	.111
1929	6	11	.353	5.65	24	20	7	129	156	64	31	0	0	1	0	43	10	0	.233
1930	1	4	.200	5.38	37	4	4	103.2	131	30	37	0	1	3	0	34	9	0	.265
1932	0	2	.000	8.41	4	4	1	20.1	26	13	7	0	0	0	0	7	2	0	.286
4 yrs.	11	24	.314	5.57	79	38	15	331	399	149	107	0	2	4	0	111	24	0	.216
4 yrs.	11	24	.314	5.57	79	38	15	331	399	149	107	0	2	4	0	111	24	0	.216

Ed Walsh

WALSH, EDWARD AUGUSTINE (Big Ed) BR TR 6'1" 193 lbs.
Father of Ed Walsh.
B. May 14, 1881, Plains, Pa. D. May 26, 1959, Pompano Beach, Fla.
Hall of Fame 1946.

1904 CHI A	6	3	.667	2.60	18	8	6	110.2	90	32	57	1	2	1	1	41	9	1	.220
1905	8	3	.727	2.17	22	13	9	136.2	121	29	71	1	1	0	1	58	9	0	.155
1906	17	13	.567	1.88	41	31	24	278.1	215	58	171	10	2	3	3	99	14	0	.141
1907	24	18	.571	1.60	56	46	37	422.1	341	87	206	5	1	1	2	154	25	1	.162
1908	40	15	.727	1.42	66	49	42	464	343	56	269	12	4	1	7	157	27	1	.172
1909	15	11	.577	1.41	31	28	20	230.1	166	50	127	8	0	1	2	84	18	0	.214
1910	18	20	.474	1.27	45	36	33	369.2	242	61	258	7	0	2	6	138	30	0	.217
1911	27	18	.600	2.22	56	37	33	368.2	327	72	255	5	3	4	7	155	32	0	.206
1912	27	17	.614	2.15	62	41	32	393	332	94	254	6	3	2	10	136	33	0	.243
1913	8	3	.727	2.58	16	14	7	97.2	91	39	34	1	0	0	1	32	5	0	.156
1914	2	3	.400	2.82	8	5	3	44.2	33	20	15	1	0	0	0	16	1	0	.063

Pitcher Register

	W	L	PCT	ERA	G	GS	CG	IP	H	BB	SO	ShO	Relief Pitching W L SV	BATTING AB H HR	BA

Ed Walsh continued

1915	3	0	1.000	1.33	3	3	3	27	19	7	12	1	0 0 0	11 4 0	.364
1916	0	1	.000	2.70	2	1	0	3.1	4	3	3	0	0 0 0	0 0 0	–
1917 BOS N	0	1	.000	3.50	4	3	1	18	22	9	4	0	0 0 0	4 1 0	.250
14 yrs.	195	126	.607	1.82 1st	430	315	250	2964.1	2346	617	1736	58 8th	16 15 40	*	
13 yrs.	195	125	.609 3rd	1.81 5th 1st	426 5th	312	249 3rd	2946.1 3rd	2324	608 7th	1732 2nd	58 1st	16 15 40 10th	1081 207 3	.191

WORLD SERIES
| 1906 CHI A | 2 | 0 | 1.000 | 1.80 | 2 | 2 | 1 | 15 | 7 | 6 | 17 | 1 | 0 0 0 | 4 0 0 | .000 |

Floyd Weaver
WEAVER, DAVID FLOYD　　　　BR TR 6'4" 195 lbs.
B. May 12, 1941, Ben Franklin, Tex.

1962 CLE A	1	0	1.000	1.80	1	1	0	5	3	0	8	0	0 0 0	2 1 0	.500
1965	2	2	.500	5.43	32	1	0	61.1	61	24	37	0	2 2 1	11 1 0	.091
1970 CHI A	1	2	.333	4.35	31	3	0	62	52	31	51	0	1 2 0	7 0 0	.000
1971 MIL A	0	1	.000	7.33	21	0	0	27	33	18	12	0	0 1 0	0 0 0	–
4 yrs.	4	5	.444	5.21	85	5	0	155.1	149	73	108	0	3 5 1	20 2 0	.100
1 yr.	1	2	.333	4.35	31	3	0	62	52	31	51	0	1 2 0	7 0 0	.000

Biggs Wehde
WEHDE, WILBUR　　　　BR TR 5'10½" 180 lbs.
B. Nov. 23, 1906, Holstein, Iowa　　D. Sept. 21, 1970, Sioux Falls, S. D.

1930 CHI A	0	0	–	9.95	4	0	0	6.1	7	7	3	0	0 0 0	1 0 0	.000
1931	1	0	1.000	6.75	8	0	0	16	19	10	3	0	1 0 0	3 0 0	.000
2 yrs.	1	0	1.000	7.66	12	0	0	22.1	26	17	6	0	1 0 0	4 0 0	.000
2 yrs.	1	0	1.000	7.66	12	0	0	22.1	26	17	6	0	1 0 0	4 0 0	.000

Bob Weiland
WEILAND, ROBERT GEORGE (Lefty)　　　　BL TL 6'4" 215 lbs.
Brother of Ed Weiland.
B. Dec. 14, 1905, Chicago, Ill.

1928 CHI A	1	0	1.000	0.00	1	1	1	9	7	5	9	1	0 0 0	3 1 0	.333
1929	0	4	.333	5.81	15	9	1	62	62	43	25	0	0 0 1	18 2 0	.111
1930	0	4	.000	6.61	14	3	0	32.2	38	21	15	0	0 0 0	8 0 0	.000
1931	2	7	.222	5.16	15	8	3	75	75	46	38	0	0 1 0	22 4 0	.182
1932 BOS A	6	16	.273	4.51	43	27	7	195.2	231	97	63	0	0 1 1	61 9 0	.148
1933	8	14	.364	3.87	39	27	12	216.1	197	100	97	0	0 0 3	65 7 0	.108
1934 2 teams	BOS A (11G 1–5)				CLE A (16G 1–5)										
" total	2	10	.167	4.73	27	14	4	125.2	134	57	71	0	0 1 0	43 5 1	.116
1935 STL A	0	2	.000	9.56	14	4	0	32	39	31	11	0	0 0 0	8 0 0	.000
1937 STL N	15	14	.517	3.54	41	34	21	264.1	283	94	105	2	0 0 2	89 15 2	.169
1938	16	11	.593	3.59	35	29	11	228.1	248	67	117	1	0 0 1	80 11 0	.138
1939	10	12	.455	3.57	32	23	6	146.1	146	50	63	3	2 1 1	46 3 0	.065
1940	0	0	–	40.50	1	0	0	.2	3	4	0	0	0 0 0	0 0 0	–
12 yrs.	62	94	.397	4.24	277	179	66	1388	1463	611	614	7	2 6 7	443 57 3	.129
4 yrs.	5	15	.250	5.39	45	21	5	178.2	182	115	87	1	0 1 1	51 7 0	.137

Ed Weiland
WEILAND, EDWIN NICHOLAS　　　　BL TR 5'11" 180 lbs.
Brother of Bob Weiland.
B. Nov. 26, 1914, Evanston, Ill.　　D. July 12, 1971, Chicago, Ill.

1940 CHI A	0	0	–	8.79	5	0	0	14.1	15	7	3	0	0 0 0	5 1 0	.200
1942	0	0	–	7.45	5	0	0	9.2	18	3	4	0	0 0 0	2 0 0	.000
2 yrs.	0	0	–	8.25	10	0	0	24	33	10	7	0	0 0 0	7 1 0	.143
2 yrs.	0	0	–	8.25	10	0	0	24	33	10	7	0	0 0 0	7 1 0	.143

Doc White
WHITE, GUY HARRIS　　　　BL TL 6'1" 150 lbs.
B. Apr. 9, 1879, Washington, D. C.　　D. Feb. 17, 1969, Silver Spring, Md.

1901 PHI N	14	13	.519	3.19	31	27	22	236.2	241	56	132	0	1 1 0	98 27 0	.276
1902	16	20	.444	2.53	36	35	34	306	277	72	185	3	0 0 1	179 47 1	.263
1903 CHI A	16	15	.516	2.13	37	36	29	300	258	69	135	3	0 0 0	99 20 0	.202
1904	16	12	.571	1.71	30	30	23	237	201	68	115	7	0 0 0	76 12 0	.158
1905	18	14	.563	1.76	36	33	25	260.1	204	58	120	4	1 0 0	86 14 0	.163
1906	18	6	.750	1.52	28	24	20	219.1	160	38	102	7	2 1 0	65 12 0	.185
1907	27	13	.675	2.26	47	35	24	291	270	38	141	7	3 1 2	90 20 0	.222
1908	19	13	.594	2.55	41	37	24	296	267	69	126	5	0 0 0	109 25 0	.229
1909	10	9	.526	1.72	24	21	14	177.2	149	31	77	3	1 0 0	192 45 0	.234
1910	15	13	.536	2.56	33	29	20	245.2	219	50	111	2	1 0 1	126 25 0	.198
1911	10	14	.417	2.98	34	29	16	214.1	219	35	72	4	1 1 2	78 20 0	.256
1912	8	10	.444	3.24	32	19	9	172	172	47	57	1	2 2 0	56 7 0	.125
1913	2	4	.333	3.50	19	8	2	103	106	39	39	0	0 1 0	25 3 0	.120
13 yrs.	189	156	.548	2.38 4th	428	363	262 4th	3059	2743	670	1412 10th	46	12 7 6	*	
11 yrs.	159	123	.564 6th	2.28 6th	361	301	206	2516.1	2225	542 6th	1095 2nd	43	11 6 5	1002 203 0	.203

WORLD SERIES
| 1906 CHI A | 1 | 1 | .500 | 1.80 | 3 | 2 | 1 | 15 | 12 | 7 | 3 | 0 | 0 0 1 | 3 0 0 | .000 |

John Whitehead
WHITEHEAD, JOHN HENDERSON (Silent John)　　　　BR TR 6'2" 195 lbs.
B. Apr. 27, 1909, Coleman, Tex.　　D. Oct. 20, 1964, Bonham, Tex.

1935 CHI A	13	13	.500	3.72	28	27	18	222.1	209	101	72	1	0 0 0	82 12 0	.146
1936	13	13	.500	4.64	34	32	15	230.2	254	98	70	1	0 0 1	87 21 0	.241
1937	11	8	.579	4.07	26	24	8	165.2	191	56	45	4	0 0 0	58 13 0	.224
1938	10	11	.476	4.76	32	24	10	183.1	218	80	38	2	1 0 2	60 6 0	.100
1939 2 teams	CHI A (7G 0–3)				STL A (26G 1–3)										
" total	1	6	.143	6.61	33	8	0	98	148	22	18	0	1 1 0	26 1 0	.038
1940 STL A	1	3	.250	5.40	15	4	1	40	46	14	11	1	0 2 0	12 2 0	.167

Pitcher Register   412

	W	L	PCT	ERA	G	GS	CG	IP	H	BB	SO	ShO	Relief Pitching W	L	SV	BATTING AB	H	HR	BA

John Whitehead continued

1942	0	0	–	6.75	4	0	0	4	8	1	0	0	0	0	0	0	0	0	–
7 yrs.	49	54	.476	4.60	172	119	52	944	1074	372	254	9	2	3	4	325	55	0	.169
5 yrs.	47	48	.495	4.45	127	111	51	834	932	340	234	8	1	0	3	296	52	0	.176

Al Widmar

WIDMAR, ALBERT JOSEPH
B. Mar. 20, 1925, Cleveland, Ohio
BR TR 6'3" 185 lbs.

1947 BOS A	0	0	–	13.50	2	0	0	1.1	1	2	1	0	0	0	0	0	0	0	–
1948 STL A	2	6	.250	4.46	49	0	0	82.2	88	48	34	0	2	6	1	10	3	0	.300
1950	7	15	.318	4.76	36	26	8	194.2	211	74	78	1	0	1	4	67	10	0	.149
1951	4	9	.308	6.52	26	16	4	107.2	157	52	28	0	1	1	0	30	5	0	.167
1952 CHI A	0	0	–	4.50	1	0	0	2	4	0	2	0	0	0	0	0	0	0	–
5 yrs.	13	30	.302	5.21	114	42	12	388.1	461	176	143	1	3	8	5	107	18	0	.168
1 yr.	0	0	–	4.50	1	0	0	2	4	0	2	0	0	0	0	0	0	0	–

Jack Wieneke

WIENEKE, JOHN
B. Mar. 10, 1894, Saltsburg, Pa.   D. Mar. 16, 1933, Pleasant Ridge, Mich.
BR TL 6' 182 lbs.

| 1921 CHI A | 0 | 1 | .000 | 8.17 | 10 | 3 | 0 | 25.1 | 39 | 17 | 10 | 0 | 0 | 0 | 0 | 9 | 1 | 0 | .111 |

Bill Wight

WIGHT, WILLIAM ROBERT (Lefty)
B. Apr. 12, 1922, Rio Vista, Calif.
BL TL 6'1" 180 lbs.

1946 NY A	2	2	.500	4.46	14	4	1	40.1	44	30	11	0	0	0	0	9	0	0	.000
1947	1	0	1.000	1.00	1	1	1	9	8	2	3	0	0	0	0	2	0	0	.000
1948 CHI A	9	20	.310	4.80	34	32	7	223.1	238	135	68	1	0	0	1	73	6	0	.082
1949	15	13	.536	3.31	35	33	14	245	254	96	78	3	0	0	1	85	14	0	.165
1950	10	16	.385	3.58	30	28	13	206	213	79	62	3	0	1	0	61	0	0	.000
1951 BOS A	7	7	.500	5.10	34	17	4	118.1	128	63	38	2	2	0	0	41	3	0	.073
1952 2 teams	BOS A (10G 2–1)				DET A (23G 5–9)														
" total	7	10	.412	3.75	33	21	8	168	181	69	70	3	1	0	0	57	12	0	.211
1953 2 teams	DET A (13G 0–3)				CLE A (20G 2–1)														
" total	2	4	.333	6.23	33	4	0	52	64	30	24	0	2	2	1	12	3	0	.250
1955 2 teams	CLE A (17G 0–0)				BAL A (19G 6–8)														
" total	6	8	.429	2.48	36	14	8	141.1	135	48	63	2	0	1	3	36	3	0	.083
1956 BAL A	9	12	.429	4.02	35	26	7	174.2	198	72	84	1	1	0	0	60	12	0	.200
1957	6	6	.500	3.64	27	17	2	121	122	54	50	0	0	0	0	34	1	0	.029
1958 2 teams	CIN N (7G 0–1)				STL N (28G 3–0)														
" total	3	1	.750	4.92	35	1	1	64	71	36	23	0	2	1	2	10	1	0	.100
12 yrs.	77	99	.438	3.95	347	198	66	1563	1656	714	574	15	8	5	8	480	55	0	.115
3 yrs.	34	49	.410	3.88	99	93	34	674.1	705	310	208	7	0	1	2	219	20	0	.091

Randy Wiles

WILES, RANDALL E.
B. Sept. 10, 1951, Conroe, Tex.
BL TL 6'1" 185 lbs.

| 1977 CHI A | 1 | 1 | .500 | 9.00 | 5 | 0 | 0 | 3 | 5 | 3 | 0 | 0 | 1 | 1 | 0 | 0 | 0 | 0 | – |

Hoyt Wilhelm

WILHELM, JAMES HOYT
B. July 26, 1923, Huntersville, N. C.
BR TR 6' 190 lbs.

1952 NY N	15	3	.833	2.43	71	0	0	159.1	127	57	108	0	15	3	11	38	6	1	.158
1953	7	8	.467	3.04	68	0	0	145	127	77	71	0	7	8	15	33	5	0	.152
1954	12	4	.750	2.10	57	0	0	111.1	77	52	64	0	12	4	7	21	1	0	.048
1955	4	1	.800	3.93	59	0	0	103	104	40	71	0	4	1	0	19	3	0	.158
1956	4	9	.308	3.83	64	0	0	89.1	97	43	71	0	4	9	8	9	2	0	.222
1957 2 teams	STL N (40G 1–4)				CLE A (2G 1–0)														
" total	2	4	.333	4.14	42	0	0	58.2	54	22	29	0	2	4	12	6	0	0	.000
1958 2 teams	CLE A (30G 2–7)				BAL A (9G 1–3)														
" total	3	10	.231	2.34	39	10	4	131	95	45	92	1	2	4	5	32	3	0	.094
1959 BAL A	15	11	.577	2.19	32	27	13	226	178	77	139	3	0	1	0	76	4	0	.053
1960	11	8	.579	3.31	41	11	3	147	125	39	107	1	7	5	7	42	3	0	.071
1961	9	7	.563	2.30	51	1	0	109.2	89	41	87	0	9	7	18	20	1	0	.050
1962	7	10	.412	1.94	52	0	0	93	64	34	90	0	7	10	15	16	2	0	.125
1963 CHI A	5	8	.385	2.64	55	3	0	136.1	106	30	111	0	5	7	21	29	2	0	.069
1964	12	9	.571	1.99	73	0	0	131.1	94	30	95	0	12	9	27	21	3	0	.143
1965	7	7	.500	1.81	66	0	0	144	88	32	106	0	7	7	20	22	0	0	.000
1966	5	2	.714	1.66	46	0	0	81.1	50	17	61	0	5	2	6	8	1	0	.125
1967	8	3	.727	1.31	49	0	0	89	58	34	76	0	8	3	12	13	1	0	.077
1968	4	4	.500	1.73	72	0	0	93.2	69	24	72	0	4	4	12	3	0	0	.000
1969 2 teams	CAL A (44G 5–7)				ATL N (8G 2–0)														
" total	7	7	.500	2.20	52	0	0	77.2	50	22	67	0	7	7	14	9	0	0	.000
1970 2 teams	ATL N (50G 6–4)				CHI N (3G 0–1)														
" total	6	5	.545	3.40	53	0	0	82	73	42	68	0	6	5	13	11	1	0	.091
1971 2 teams	ATL N (3G 0–0)				LA N (9G 0–1)														
" total	0	1	.000	2.70	12	0	0	20	12	5	16	0	0	1	3	3	0	0	.000
1972 LA N	0	1	.000	4.62	16	0	2	25.1	20	15	9	0	0	1	1	1	0	0	.000
21 yrs.	143	122	.540	2.52	1070	52	20	2254	1757	778	1610	5	123	102	227	432	38	1	.088
					1st								1st		3rd				
6 yrs.	41	33	.554	1.92	361	3	0	675.2	465	167	521	0	41	32	98	96	7	0	.073
					6th								1st		1st				

WORLD SERIES

| 1954 NY N | 0 | 0 | – | 0.00 | 2 | 0 | 0 | 2.1 | 1 | 0 | 3 | 0 | 0 | 0 | 1 | 1 | 0 | 0 | .000 |

Roy Wilkinson

WILKINSON, ROY HAMILTON
B. May 8, 1894, Canandaigua, N. Y.
BR TR 6'1" 170 lbs.

1918 CLE A	0	0	–	0.00	1	0	0	0	0	0	0	0	0	0	0	0	0	0	–
1919 CHI A	1	1	.500	2.05	4	1	1	22	21	10	5	1	0	1	0	8	3	0	.375
1920	7	9	.438	4.03	34	11	9	145	162	48	30	0	5	0	2	48	7	0	.146
1921	4	20	.167	5.13	36	22	11	198.1	259	78	50	0	0	3	3	65	8	0	.123

Pitcher Register

	W	L	PCT	ERA	G	GS	CG	IP	H	BB	SO	ShO	Relief Pitching W	L	SV	AB	H	HR	BA

Roy Wilkinson continued

	W	L	PCT	ERA	G	GS	CG	IP	H	BB	SO	ShO	W	L	SV	AB	H	HR	BA
1922	0	1	.000	8.79	4	1	0	14.1	24	6	3	0	0	0	1	3	0	0	.000
5 yrs.	12	31	.279	4.66	79	35	21	380.2	466	142	88	1	5	4	6	124	18	0	.145
4 yrs.	12	31	.279	4.67	78	35	21	379.2	466	142	88	1	5	4	6	124	18	0	.145

WORLD SERIES
| 1919 CHI A | 0 | 0 | — | 3.68 | 2 | 0 | 0 | 7.1 | 9 | 4 | 3 | 0 | 0 | 0 | 0 | 2 | 0 | 0 | .000 |

Lefty Williams

WILLIAMS, CLAUD PRESTON BR TL 5'9" 160 lbs.
B. Mar. 9, 1893, Aurora, Mo. D. Nov. 4, 1959, Laguna Beach, Calif.

	W	L	PCT	ERA	G	GS	CG	IP	H	BB	SO	ShO	W	L	SV	AB	H	HR	BA
1913 DET A	1	3	.250	4.97	5	4	3	29	34	4	9	0	0	0	1	10	1	0	.100
1914	0	1	.000	0.00	1	1	0	1	3	2	0	0	0	0	0	0	0	0	—
1916 CHI A	13	7	.650	2.89	43	25	10	224.1	220	65	138	2	1	2	1	74	10	0	.135
1917	17	8	.680	2.97	45	29	8	230	221	81	85	1	4	2	1	67	6	0	.090
1918	6	4	.600	2.73	15	14	7	105.2	76	47	30	2	0	0	1	38	5	0	.132
1919	23	11	.676	2.64	41	40	27	297	265	58	125	5	0	0	0	94	17	0	.181
1920	22	14	.611	3.91	39	38	26	299	302	90	128	0	1	0	0	101	22	0	.218
7 yrs.	82	48	.631	3.13	189	151	81	1186	1121	347	515	10	6	4	4	384	61	0	.159
5 yrs.	81	44	.648	3.09 1st	183	146	78	1156	1084	341	506	10	6	4	3	374	60	0	.160

WORLD SERIES
1917 CHI A	0	0	—	9.00	1	0	0	1	2	0	3	0	0	0	0	0	0	0	—
1919	0	3	.000	6.61	3	3	1	16.1	12	8	4	0	0	0	0	5	1	0	.200
2 yrs.	0	3	.000	6.75	4	3	1	17.1	14	8	7	0	0	0	0	5	1	0	.200

Al Williamson

WILLIAMSON, SILAS ALBERT BR TR 5'11" 160 lbs.
B. Feb. 20, 1900, Buckville, Ark.

| 1928 CHI A | 0 | 0 | — | 0.00 | 1 | 0 | 0 | 2 | 1 | 0 | 0 | 0 | 0 | 0 | 0 | 0 | 0 | 0 | — |

Jim Willoughby

WILLOUGHBY, JAMES ARTHUR BR TR 6'2" 185 lbs.
B. Jan. 31, 1949, Salinas, Calif.

	W	L	PCT	ERA	G	GS	CG	IP	H	BB	SO	ShO	W	L	SV	AB	H	HR	BA
1971 SF N	0	1	.000	9.00	2	1	0	4	8	1	3	0	0	0	0	1	0	0	.000
1972	6	4	.600	2.35	11	11	7	88	72	14	40	0	0	0	0	27	5	0	.185
1973	4	5	.444	4.70	39	12	1	122.2	138	37	60	1	1	2	1	28	4	1	.143
1974	1	4	.200	4.61	18	4	0	41	51	9	12	0	0	1	0	10	1	0	.100
1975 BOS A	5	2	.714	3.54	24	0	0	48.1	46	16	29	0	5	2	8	0	0	0	—
1976	3	12	.200	2.82	54	0	0	99	94	31	37	0	3	12	10	1	0	0	.000
1977	6	2	.750	4.94	31	0	0	54.2	54	18	33	0	6	2	2	0	0	0	—
1978 CHI A	1	6	.143	3.86	59	0	0	93.1	95	19	36	0	1	6	13	0	0	0	—
8 yrs.	26	36	.419	3.79	238	28	8	551	558	145	250	1	16	25	34	67	10	1	.149
1 yr.	1	6	.143	3.86	59	0	0	93.1	95	19	36	0	1	6	13	0	0	0	—

WORLD SERIES
| 1975 BOS A | 0 | 1 | .000 | 0.00 | 3 | 0 | 0 | 6.1 | 3 | 0 | 2 | 0 | 0 | 1 | 0 | 0 | 0 | 0 | — |

Ted Wills

WILLS, THEODORE CARL BL TL 6'2" 200 lbs.
B. Feb. 9, 1934, Fresno, Calif.

	W	L	PCT	ERA	G	GS	CG	IP	H	BB	SO	ShO	W	L	SV	AB	H	HR	BA
1959 BOS A	2	6	.250	5.27	9	8	2	56.1	68	24	24	0	0	0	0	16	4	0	.250
1960	1	1	.500	7.42	15	0	0	30.1	38	16	28	0	1	1	1	8	2	0	.250
1961	3	2	.600	5.95	17	0	0	19.2	24	19	11	0	3	2	0	2	0	0	.000
1962 2 teams			BOS A (1G 0–0)			CIN N (26G 0–2)													
" total	0	2	.000	5.46	27	5	0	61	63	24	58	0	0	1	3	16	5	0	.313
1965 CHI A	2	0	1.000	2.84	15	0	0	19	17	14	12	0	2	0	1	2	0	0	.000
5 yrs.	8	11	.421	5.51	83	13	2	186.1	210	97	133	0	6	4	5	44	11	0	.250
1 yr.	2	0	1.000	2.84	15	0	0	19	17	14	12	0	2	0	1	2	0	0	.000

Bill Wilson

WILSON, WILLIAM DONALD BR TR 6'2" 200 lbs.
B. Nov. 6, 1928, Central City, Neb.

| 1955 KC A | 0 | 0 | — | 0.00 | 1 | 0 | 0 | 1 | 1 | 1 | 1 | 0 | 0 | 0 | 0 | * | | | |

Jim Wilson

WILSON, JAMES ALGER BR TR 6'1½" 200 lbs.
B. Feb. 20, 1922, San Diego, Calif.

	W	L	PCT	ERA	G	GS	CG	IP	H	BB	SO	ShO	W	L	SV	AB	H	HR	BA
1945 BOS A	6	8	.429	3.30	23	21	8	144.1	121	88	50	2	0	0	0	53	13	0	.245
1946	0	0	—	27.00	1	0	0	.2	2	0	0	0	0	0	0	0	0	0	—
1948 STL A	0	0	—	13.50	4	0	0	2.2	5	5	1	0	0	0	0	0	0	0	—
1949 PHI A	0	0	—	14.40	2	0	0	5	7	5	2	0	0	0	0	3	0	0	.000
1951 BOS N	7	7	.500	5.40	20	15	5	110	131	40	33	0	1	0	1	39	7	0	.179
1952	12	14	.462	4.23	33	33	14	234	234	90	104	0	0	0	0	86	14	0	.163
1953 MIL N	4	9	.308	4.34	20	18	5	114	107	43	71	0	0	0	0	36	6	1	.167
1954	8	2	.800	3.52	27	19	6	127.2	129	36	52	4	0	0	0	44	7	0	.159
1955 BAL A	12	18	.400	3.44	34	31	14	235.1	200	87	96	4	0	0	0	89	15	0	.169
1956 2 teams			BAL A (7G 4–2)			CHI A (28G 9–12)													
" total	13	14	.481	4.28	35	28	7	208	198	86	113	3	2	1	0	77	23	1	.299
1957 CHI A	15	8	.652	3.48	30	29	12	201.2	189	65	100	5	0	1	0	68	10	0	.147
1958	9	9	.500	4.10	28	23	4	155.2	156	63	70	1	1	2	1	51	4	0	.078
12 yrs.	86	89	.491	4.01	257	217	75	1539	1479	608	692	19	4	5	2	546	99	2	.181
3 yrs.	33	29	.532	3.85	86	73	22	517	494	198	252	7	3	4	1	181	33	1	.182

Roy Wilson

WILSON, ROY EDWARD (Lefty) BL TL 6' 175 lbs.
B. Sept. 13, 1896, Foster, Iowa D. Dec. 3, 1969, Clarion, Iowa

| 1928 CHI A | 0 | 0 | — | 0.00 | 1 | 0 | 0 | 3.1 | 2 | 3 | 2 | 0 | 0 | 0 | 0 | 1 | 0 | 0 | .000 |

Archie Wise

WISE, ARCHIBALD EDWIN BR TR 6' 165 lbs.
B. July 31, 1912, Waxahachie, Tex. D. Feb. 2, 1978, Dallas, Tex.

| 1932 CHI A | 0 | 0 | — | 4.91 | 2 | 0 | 0 | 7.1 | 8 | 5 | 2 | 0 | 0 | 0 | 0 | 4 | 0 | 0 | .000 |

Pitcher Register 414

	W	L	PCT	ERA	G	GS	CG	IP	H	BB	SO	ShO	Relief Pitching W L SV	BATTING AB H HR	BA

Mellie Wolfgang
WOLFGANG, MELDON JOHN — BR TR 5'9" 160 lbs.
B. Mar. 20, 1890, Albany, N.Y. D. June 30, 1947, Albany, N.Y.

	W	L	PCT	ERA	G	GS	CG	IP	H	BB	SO	ShO	W	L	SV	AB	H	HR	BA
1914 CHI A	7	5	.583	1.89	24	11	9	119.1	96	32	50	2	2	0	2	40	7	0	.175
1915	2	2	.500	1.84	17	2	0	53.2	39	12	21	0	2	1	0	17	2	0	.118
1916	5	6	.455	1.98	27	14	6	127	103	42	36	1	1	2	0	40	9	0	.225
1917	0	0	—	5.09	5	0	0	17.2	18	6	3	0	0	0	0	4	0	0	.000
1918	0	1	.000	5.40	4	0	0	8.1	12	3	1	0	0	1	0	2	1	0	.500
5 yrs.	14	14	.500	2.18	77	27	15	326	268	95	111	3	5	4	2	103	19	0	.184
5 yrs.	14	14	.500	2.18	77	27	15	326	268	95	111	3	5	4	2	103	19	0	.184

Wilbur Wood
WOOD, WILBUR FORRESTER — BR TL 6' 180 lbs.
B. Oct. 22, 1941, Cambridge, Mass.

	W	L	PCT	ERA	G	GS	CG	IP	H	BB	SO	ShO	W	L	SV	AB	H	HR	BA
1961 BOS A	0	0	—	5.54	6	1	0	13	14	7	7	0	0	0	0	3	0	0	.000
1962	0	1	.000	3.52	1	1	0	7.2	6	3	3	0	0	0	0	3	0	0	.000
1963	0	5	.000	3.76	25	6	0	64.2	67	13	28	0	0	1	0	12	0	0	.000
1964 2 teams			BOS A (4G 0-0)			PIT N (3G 0-2)													
" total	0	2	.000	7.04	7	2	1	23	29	14	12	0	0	0	0	6	0	0	.000
1965 PIT N	1	1	.500	3.16	34	1	0	51.1	44	16	29	0	1	0	0	6	0	0	.000
1967 CHI A	4	2	.667	2.45	51	8	0	95.1	95	28	47	0	0	0	4	16	1	0	.063
1968	13	12	.520	1.87	88	2	0	159	127	33	74	0	12	11	16	22	2	0	.091
1969	10	11	.476	3.01	76	0	0	119.2	113	40	73	0	10	11	15	15	0	0	.000
1970	9	13	.409	2.80	77	0	0	122	118	36	85	0	9	13	21	18	2	0	.111
1971	22	13	.629	1.91	44	42	22	334	272	62	210	7	0	0	1	96	5	0	.052
1972	24	17	.585	2.51	49	49	20	376.2	325	74	193	8	0	0	0	125	17	0	.136
1973	24	20	.545	3.46	49	48	21	359.1	381	91	199	4	1	0	0	0	0	0	—
1974	20	19	.513	3.60	42	42	22	320	305	80	169	1	0	0	0	0	0	0	—
1975	16	20	.444	4.11	43	43	14	291.1	309	92	140	2	0	0	0	0	0	0	—
1976	4	3	.571	2.25	7	7	5	56	51	11	31	1	0	0	0	0	0	0	—
1977	7	8	.467	4.98	24	18	5	123	139	50	42	1	0	0	0	0	0	0	—
1978	10	10	.500	5.20	28	27	4	168	187	74	69	0	0	0	0	0	0	0	—
17 yrs.	164	156	.513	3.24	651	297	114	2684	2582	724	1411	24	33	36	57	322	27	0	.084
12 yrs.	163	148	.524	3.18	578	286	113	2524.1	2422	671	1332	24	32	35	57	292	27	0	.092
	5th	4th			3rd			5th		4th	4th	9th	2nd		3rd				

Frank Woodward
WOODWARD, FRANK RUSSELL — BR TR 5'10" 175 lbs.
B. May 17, 1894, New Haven, Conn. D. June 11, 1961, New Haven, Conn.

	W	L	PCT	ERA	G	GS	CG	IP	H	BB	SO	ShO	W	L	SV	AB	H	HR	BA
1918 PHI N	0	0	—	6.00	2	0	0	6	6	4	4	0	0	0	0	3	1	0	.333
1919 2 teams			PHI N (17G 6-9)			STL N (17G 4-5)													
" total	10	14	.417	3.86	34	19	8	172.2	174	63	45	0	4	2	0	50	7	0	.140
1921 WAS A	0	0	—	5.91	3	1	0	10.2	11	3	4	0	0	0	0	3	1	0	.333
1922	0	0	—	11.57	1	0	0	2.1	3	3	2	0	0	0	0	1	0	0	.000
1923 CHI A	0	1	.000	13.50	2	1	0	2	5	1	0	0	0	0	0	0	0	0	—
5 yrs.	10	15	.400	4.23	42	21	8	193.2	199	74	55	0	4	2	0	57	9	0	.158
1 yr.	0	1	.000	13.50	2	1	0	2	5	1	0	0	0	0	0	0	0	0	—

Rich Wortham
WORTHAM, RICHARD COOPER — BR TL 6' 185 lbs.
B. Oct. 22, 1953, Odessa, Tex.

	W	L	PCT	ERA	G	GS	CG	IP	H	BB	SO	ShO	W	L	SV	AB	H	HR	BA
1978 CHI A	3	2	.600	3.05	8	8	2	59	59	23	25	0	0	0	0	0	0	0	—
1979	14	14	.500	4.90	34	33	5	204	195	100	119	0	0	0	0	0	0	0	—
1980	4	7	.364	5.97	41	10	0	92	102	58	45	0	2	0	1	0	0	0	—
1983 OAK A	0	0	—	∞	1	0	0	0	3	1	0	0	0	0	0	0	0	0	—
4 yrs.	21	23	.477	4.89	84	51	7	355	359	182	189	0	2	2	1	0	0	0	—
3 yrs.	21	23	.477	4.87	83	51	7	355	356	181	189	0	2	2	1	0	0	0	—

Al Worthington
WORTHINGTON, ALLAN FULTON (Red) — BR TR 6'2" 195 lbs.
B. Feb. 5, 1929, Birmingham, Ala.

	W	L	PCT	ERA	G	GS	CG	IP	H	BB	SO	ShO	W	L	SV	AB	H	HR	BA
1953 NY N	4	8	.333	3.44	20	17	5	102	103	54	52	2	0	1	0	31	2	0	.065
1954	0	2	.000	3.50	10	1	0	18	21	15	8	0	0	0	0	4	0	0	.000
1956	7	14	.333	3.97	28	24	4	165.2	158	74	95	0	0	1	0	51	12	1	.235
1957	8	11	.421	4.22	55	12	1	157.2	140	56	90	1	7	5	4	40	4	0	.100
1958 SF N	11	7	.611	3.63	54	12	1	151.1	152	57	76	0	3	4	6	44	8	0	.182
1959	2	3	.400	3.68	42	3	0	73.1	68	37	45	0	1	2	2	13	1	0	.077
1960 2 teams			BOS A (6G 0-1)			CHI A (4G 1-1)													
" total	1	2	.333	6.35	10	0	0	17	20	15	8	0	1	2	0	3	2	0	.667
1963 CIN N	4	4	.500	2.99	50	0	0	81.1	75	31	55	0	4	4	10	12	1	0	.083
1964 2 teams			CIN N (6G 1-0)			MIN A (41G 5-6)													
" total	6	6	.500	2.16	47	0	0	79.1	61	30	65	0	6	6	14	16	1	0	.063
1965 MIN A	10	7	.588	2.13	62	0	0	80.1	57	41	59	0	10	7	21	10	1	0	.100
1966	6	3	.667	2.46	65	0	0	91.1	66	27	93	0	6	3	16	11	3	0	.273
1967	8	9	.471	2.84	59	0	0	92	77	38	80	0	8	9	16	8	0	0	.000
1968	4	5	.444	2.71	54	0	0	76.1	67	32	57	0	4	5	18	7	0	0	.000
1969	4	1	.800	4.57	46	0	0	61	65	20	51	0	4	1	3	5	0	0	.000
14 yrs.	75	82	.478	3.39	602	69	11	1246.2	1130	527	834	3	54	50	110	255	35	1	.137
1 yr.	1	1	.500	3.38	4	0	0	5.1	3	4	1	0	1	1	0	2	2	0	1.000

LEAGUE CHAMPIONSHIP SERIES

| 1969 MIN A | 0 | 0 | — | 6.75 | 1 | 0 | 0 | 1.1 | 3 | 0 | 1 | 0 | 0 | 0 | 0 | 0 | 0 | 0 | — |

WORLD SERIES

| 1965 MIN A | 0 | 0 | — | 0.00 | 2 | 0 | 0 | 4 | 2 | 2 | 2 | 0 | 0 | 0 | 0 | 0 | 0 | 0 | — |

Whit Wyatt
WYATT, JOHN WHITLOW — BR TR 6'1" 185 lbs.
B. Sept. 27, 1907, Kensington, Ga.

	W	L	PCT	ERA	G	GS	CG	IP	H	BB	SO	ShO	W	L	SV	AB	H	HR	BA
1929 DET A	0	1	.000	6.75	4	4	1	25.1	30	18	14	0	0	0	0	10	1	0	.100
1930	4	5	.444	3.57	21	7	2	85.2	76	35	68	0	3	2	2	34	12	1	.353
1931	0	2	.000	8.44	4	1	1	21.1	30	12	8	0	0	1	0	7	2	0	.286
1932	9	13	.409	5.03	43	22	10	205.2	228	102	82	0	3	1	1	78	15	2	.192
1933 2 teams			DET A (10G 0-1)			CHI A (26G 3-4)													
" total	3	5	.375	4.56	36	7	2	104.2	111	54	40	0	1	2	1	30	6	0	.200
1934 CHI A	4	11	.267	7.18	23	6	2	67.2	83	37	36	0	3	6	2	26	6	0	.231

	W	L	PCT	ERA	G	GS	CG	IP	H	BB	SO	ShO	Relief Pitching W L SV	BATTING AB H HR	BA

Whit Wyatt continued

1935	4	3	.571	6.75	30	1	0	52	65	25	22	0	4 3 5	13 3 0	.231
1936	0	0	–	0.00	3	0	0	3	3	0	0	0	0 0 1	0 0 0	–
1937 CLE A	2	3	.400	4.44	29	4	2	73	67	40	52	0	2 2 0	18 7 0	.389
1939 BKN N	8	3	.727	2.31	16	14	6	109	88	39	52	2	2 0 0	36 6 0	.167
1940	15	14	.517	3.46	37	34	16	239.1	233	62	124	5	1 1 0	80 14 1	.175
1941	22	10	.688	2.34	38	35	23	288.1	223	82	176	7	0 1 1	109 26 3	.239
1942	19	7	.731	2.73	31	30	16	217.1	185	63	104	0	1 0 0	77 14 0	.182
1943	14	5	.737	2.49	26	26	13	180.2	139	43	80	3	0 0 0	60 17 0	.283
1944	2	6	.250	7.17	9	9	1	37.2	51	16	4	0	0 0 0	13 2 0	.154
1945 PHI N	0	7	.000	5.26	10	10	2	51.1	72	14	10	0	0 0 0	16 2 0	.125
16 yrs.	106	95	.527	3.78	360	210	97	1762	1684	642	872	17	20 19 13	607 133 7	.219
4 yrs.	11	18	.379	5.90	82	14	4	210.1	242	107	89	0	8 10 9	67 15 0	.224

WORLD SERIES
| 1941 BKN N | 1 | 1 | .500 | 2.50 | 2 | 2 | 2 | 18 | 15 | 10 | 14 | 0 | 0 0 0 | 6 1 0 | .167 |

Early Wynn

WYNN, EARLY (Gus)
B. Jan. 6, 1920, Hartford, Ala.
Hall of Fame 1971.

BB TR 6' 190 lbs.
BR 1939-44

1939 WAS A	0	2	.000	5.75	3	3	1	20.1	26	10	1	0	0 0 0	6 1 0	.167
1941	3	1	.750	1.58	5	5	4	40	35	10	15	0	0 0 0	15 2 0	.133
1942	10	16	.385	5.12	30	28	10	190	246	73	58	1	0 2 0	69 15 0	.217
1943	18	12	.600	2.91	37	33	12	256.2	232	83	89	3	2 0 0	98 29 1	.296
1944	8	17	.320	3.38	33	25	19	207.2	221	67	65	2	0 2 2	92 19 1	.207
1946	8	5	.615	3.11	17	12	9	107	112	33	36	0	1 0 0	47 15 1	.319
1947	17	15	.531	3.64	33	31	22	247	251	90	73	2	1 0 0	120 33 2	.275
1948	8	19	.296	5.82	33	31	15	198	236	94	49	1	0 0 0	106 23 0	.217
1949 CLE A	11	7	.611	4.15	26	23	6	164.2	186	57	62	0	0 0 0	70 10 1	.143
1950	18	8	.692	3.20	32	28	14	213.2	166	101	143	2	1 2 0	77 18 2	.234
1951	20	13	.606	3.02	37	34	21	274.1	227	107	133	3	1 0 1	108 20 1	.185
1952	23	12	.657	2.90	42	33	19	285.2	239	132	153	4	3 1 3	99 22 0	.222
1953	17	12	.586	3.93	36	34	16	251.2	234	107	138	1	2 0 0	91 25 3	.275
1954	23	11	.676	2.73	40	36	20	270.2	225	83	155	3	0 1 2	93 17 0	.183
1955	17	11	.607	2.82	32	31	16	230	207	80	122	6	0 0 0	84 15 1	.179
1956	20	9	.690	2.72	38	35	18	277.2	233	91	158	4	0 0 0	101 23 1	.228
1957	14	17	.452	4.31	40	37	13	263	270	104	184	1	0 1 1	86 10 0	.116
1958 CHI A	14	16	.467	4.13	40	34	11	239.2	214	104	179	4	0 2 2	75 15 0	.200
1959	22	10	.688	3.17	37	37	14	255.2	202	119	179	5	0 0 0	90 22 2	.244
1960	13	12	.520	3.49	36	35	13	237.1	220	112	158	4	0 0 1	75 15 1	.200
1961	8	2	.800	3.51	17	16	5	110.1	88	47	64	0	0 0 0	37 6 0	.162
1962	7	15	.318	4.46	27	26	11	167.2	171	56	91	3	0 0 0	54 7 0	.130
1963 CLE A	1	2	.333	2.28	20	5	1	55.1	50	15	29	0	0 1 1	11 3 0	.273
23 yrs.	300	244	.551	3.54	691	612	290	4564	4291	1775	2334	49	11 12 15	*	
			9th							2nd					
5 yrs.	64	55	.538	3.72	157	148	54	1010.2	895	438	671	16	0 2 3	331 65 3	.196

WORLD SERIES
1954 CLE A	0	1	.000	3.86	1	1	0	7	4	2	5	0	0 0 0	2 1 0	.500
1959 CHI A	1	1	.500	5.54	3	3	0	13	19	4	10	0	0 0 0	5 1 0	.200
2 yrs.	1	2	.333	4.95	4	4	0	20	23	6	15	0	0 0 0	7 2 0	.286

Billy Wynne

WYNNE, BILLY VERNON
B. July 31, 1943, Williamston, N. C.

BR TR 6'3" 205 lbs.
BB 1967

1967 NY N	0	0	–	3.12	6	1	0	8.2	12	2	4	0	0 0 0	1 0 0	.000
1968 CHI A	0	0	–	4.50	1	0	0	2	2	2	1	0	0 0 0	0 0 0	–
1969	7	7	.500	4.06	20	20	6	128.2	143	50	67	1	0 0 0	41 5 0	.122
1970	1	4	.200	5.32	12	9	0	44	54	22	19	0	0 0 0	13 1 0	.077
1971 CAL A	0	0	–	4.50	3	0	0	4	6	2	6	0	0 0 0	0 0 0	–
5 yrs.	8	11	.421	4.32	42	30	6	187.1	217	78	97	1	0 0 0	55 6 0	.109
3 yrs.	8	11	.421	4.38	33	29	6	174.2	199	74	87	1	0 0 0	54 6 0	.111

Irv Young

YOUNG, IRVING MELROSE (Young Cy, Cy the Second)
B. July 21, 1877, Columbia Falls, Me. D. Jan. 14, 1935, Brewer, Me.

BL TL 5'10" 170 lbs.

1905 BOS N	20	21	.488	2.90	43	42	41	378	337	71	156	7	0 0 0	136 14 0	.103
1906	16	25	.390	2.91	43	41	37	358.1	349	83	151	4	0 1 0	125 12 0	.096
1907	10	23	.303	3.96	40	32	22	245.1	287	58	86	3	2 1 1	80 13 0	.163
1908 2 teams			BOS N (16G 4–7)				PIT N (16G 3–3)								
" total	7	10	.412	2.42	32	18	10	174.2	167	40	63	2	1 1 1	62 11 0	.177
1910 CHI N	4	9	.308	2.72	27	17	7	135.2	122	39	64	4	0 1 0	44 5 0	.114
1911	5	6	.455	4.37	24	11	2	92.2	99	25	40	0	2 0 2	28 5 0	.179
6 yrs.	62	94	.397	3.11	209	161	119	1384.2	1361	316	560	20	5 4 4	475 60 0	.126
2 yrs.	9	15	.375	3.39	51	28	9	228.1	221	64	104	4	2 1 2	72 10 0	.139

Dom Zanni

ZANNI, DOMINICK THOMAS
B. Mar. 1, 1932, Bronx, N. Y.

BR TR 5'11" 180 lbs.

1958 SF N	1	0	1.000	2.25	1	0	0	4	7	1	3	0	1 0 0	2 0 0	.000
1959	0	0	–	6.55	9	0	0	11	12	8	11	0	0 0 0	0 0 0	–
1961	1	0	1.000	3.95	8	0	0	13.2	13	12	11	0	1 0 0	0 0 0	–
1962 CHI A	6	5	.545	3.75	44	2	0	86.1	67	31	66	0	6 3 5	18 5 0	.278
1963 2 teams			CHI A (5G 0–0)				CIN N (31G 1–1)								
" total	1	1	.500	4.56	36	1	0	47.1	44	25	42	0	1 1 5	3 1 0	.333
1965 CIN N	0	0	–	1.35	8	0	0	13.1	7	5	10	0	0 0 0	1 0 0	.000
1966	0	0	–	0.00	5	0	0	7.1	5	3	5	0	0 0 0	1 1 0	1.000
7 yrs.	9	6	.600	3.79	111	3	0	183	155	85	148	0	9 4 10	25 7 0	.280
2 yrs.	6	5	.545	3.97	49	2	0	90.2	72	35	68	0	6 3 5	18 5 0	.278

Manager Register

The Manager Register is an alphabetical listing of every man who has managed the Chicago White Sox. Included are facts about the managers and their year-by-year managerial records for the regular season, League Championship Series, and the World Series.

Most of the information in this section is self-explanatory. That which is not is explained as follows:

Games Managed includes tie games.

Lifetime Total. The first total shown after the regular season's statistics is the manager's total lifetime record in the major leagues.

White Sox Lifetime Total. The second line is the manager's total lifetime record with the White Sox.

Blank space appearing beneath a team and league means that the team and league are the same.

Standing. The figures in this column indicate the standing of the team at the end of the season and when there was a managerial change. The four possible cases are as follows:

> *Only Manager for the Team That Year.* Indicated by a single bold-faced figure that appears in the extreme left-hand column and shows the final standing of the team.
>
> *Manager Started Season, But Did Not Finish.* Indicated by two figures: the first is bold-faced and shows the standing of the team when this manager left; the second shows the final standing of the team.

Manager Finished Season, But Did Not Start. Indicated by two figures: the first shows the standing of the team when this manager started; the second is bold-faced and shows the final standing of the team.

Manager Did Not Start or Finish Season. Indicated by three figures: the first shows the standing of the team when this manager started; the second is bold-faced and shows the standing of the team when this manager left; the third shows the final standing of the team.

1981 Split Season Indicator. The managers' records for the 1981 split season are given separately for each half. "(1st)" or "(2nd)" will appear to the right of the standings to indicate which half.

| | G | W | L | PCT | Standing | | G | W | L | PCT | Standing |

Bill Adair
ADAIR, MARION DANNE
B. Feb. 10, 1916, Mobile, Ala.

| 1970 CHI A | 10 | 4 | 6 | .400 | 6 6 6 |

Lena Blackburne
BLACKBURNE, RUSSELL AUBREY (Slats)
B. Oct. 23, 1886, Clifton Heights, Pa.
D. Feb. 29, 1968, Riverside, N. J.

1928 CHI A	80	40	40	.500	6 5
1929	152	59	93	.388	7
2 yrs.	232	99	133	.427	
2 yrs.	232	99	133	.427	

Donie Bush
BUSH, OWEN JOSEPH
B. Oct. 8, 1887, Indianapolis, Ind.
D. Mar. 28, 1972, Indianapolis, Ind.

1923 WAS A	155	75	78	.490	4
1927 PIT N	156	94	60	.610	1
1928	152	85	67	.559	4
1929	119	67	51	.568	2 2
1930 CHI A	154	62	92	.403	7
1931	156	56	97	.366	8
1933 CIN N	153	58	94	.382	8
7 yrs.	1045	497	539	.480	
2 yrs.	310	118	189	.384	

WORLD SERIES
| 1927 PIT N | 4 | 0 | 4 | .000 |

Nixey Callahan
CALLAHAN, JAMES JOSEPH
B. Mar. 18, 1874, Fitchburg, Mass.
D. Oct. 4, 1934, Boston, Mass.

1903 CHI A	138	60	77	.438	7
1904	41	22	18	.550	4 3
1912	158	78	76	.506	4
1913	153	78	74	.513	5
1914	157	70	84	.455	6
1916 PIT N	157	65	89	.422	6
1917	61	20	40	.333	8 8
7 yrs.	865	393	458	.462	
5 yrs.	647	308	329	.484	

Eddie Collins
COLLINS, EDWARD TROWBRIDGE, SR. (Cocky)
Played as Eddie Sullivan 1906.
Father of Eddie Collins.
B. May 2, 1887, Millerton, N. Y.
D. Mar. 25, 1951, Boston, Mass.
Hall of Fame 1939.

1925 CHI A	154	79	75	.513	5
1926	155	81	72	.529	5
2 yrs.	309	160	147	.521	
2 yrs.	309	160	147	.521	

Red Corriden
CORRIDEN, JOHN MICHAEL, SR.
Father of John Corriden.
B. Sept. 4, 1887, Logansport, Ind.
D. Sept. 28, 1959, Indianapolis, Ind.

| 1950 CHI A | 126 | 52 | 72 | .419 | 8 6 |

Larry Doby
DOBY, LAWRENCE EUGENE
B. Dec. 13, 1923, Camden, S. C.

| 1978 CHI A | 87 | 37 | 50 | .425 | 5 5 |

Hugh Duffy
DUFFY, HUGH
B. Nov. 26, 1866, Cranston, R. I.
D. Oct. 19, 1954, Allston, Mass.
Hall of Fame 1945.

1901 MIL A	139	48	89	.350	8
1904 PHI N	155	52	100	.342	8
1905	155	83	69	.546	4
1906	154	71	82	.464	4
1910 CHI A	156	68	85	.444	6
1911	154	77	74	.510	4
1921 BOS A	154	75	79	.487	5
1922	154	61	93	.396	8
8 yrs.	1221	535	671	.444	
2 yrs.	310	145	159	.477	

Jimmy Dykes
DYKES, JAMES JOSEPH
B. Nov. 10, 1896, Philadelphia, Pa.
D. June 15, 1976, Philadelphia, Pa.

1934 CHI A	136	49	86	.363	8 8
1935	153	74	78	.487	5
1936	153	81	70	.536	3
1937	154	86	68	.558	3
1938	149	65	83	.439	6
1939	155	85	69	.552	4
1940	155	82	72	.532	4
1941	156	77	77	.500	3
1942	148	66	82	.446	6
1943	155	82	72	.532	4
1944	154	71	83	.461	7
1945	150	71	78	.477	6
1946	30	10	20	.333	7 5
1951 PHI A	154	70	84	.455	6
1952	155	79	75	.513	4
1953	157	59	95	.383	7
1954 BAL A	154	54	100	.351	7
1958 CIN N	41	24	17	.585	7 4
1959 DET A	137	74	63	.540	8 4
1960	96	44	52	.458	6 6
1960 CLE A	58	26	32	.448	4 4
1961	160	78	82	.488	5 5
21 yrs.	2960	1407	1538	.478	
				9th	
13 yrs.	1848	899	938	.489	

Johnny Evers
EVERS, JOHN JOSEPH (The Trojan, The Crab)
Brother of Joe Evers.
B. July 21, 1881, Troy, N. Y.
D. Mar. 28, 1947, Albany, N. Y.
Hall of Fame 1946.

1913 CHI N	154	88	65	.575	3
1921	98	42	56	.429	7 7
1924 CHI A	154	66	87	.431	8
3 yrs.	406	196	208	.485	
1 yr.	154	66	87	.431	

Lew Fonseca
FONSECA, LEWIS ALBERT
B. Jan. 21, 1899, Oakland, Calif.

1932 CHI A	152	49	102	.325	7
1933	151	67	83	.447	6
1934	17	4	13	.235	8 8
3 yrs.	320	120	198	.377	
3 yrs.	320	120	198	.377	

Kid Gleason
GLEASON, WILLIAM J.
Brother of Harry Gleason.
B. Oct. 26, 1866, Camden, N. J.
D. Jan. 2, 1933, Philadelphia, Pa.

1919 CHI A	140	88	52	.629	1
1920	154	96	58	.623	2
1921	154	62	92	.403	7
1922	155	77	77	.500	5

Manager Register   420

| | G | W | L | PCT | Standing | | G | W | L | PCT | Standing |

Kid Gleason continued

		G	W	L	PCT	Standing
1923		156	69	85	.448	7
5 yrs.		759	392	364	.519	
5 yrs.		759	392	364	.519	
WORLD SERIES						
1919	CHI A	8	3	5	.375	

Clark Griffith
GRIFFITH, CLARK CALVIN (The Old Fox)
B. Nov. 20, 1869, Stringtown, Mo.
D. Oct. 27, 1955, Washington, D. C.
Hall of Fame 1946.

		G	W	L	PCT	Standing
1901	CHI A	137	83	53	.610	1
1902		138	74	60	.552	4
1903	NY A	136	72	62	.537	4
1904		155	92	59	.609	2
1905		152	71	78	.477	6
1906		155	90	61	.596	2
1907		152	70	78	.473	5
1908		57	24	32	.429	6 8
1909	CIN N	157	77	76	.503	4
1910		156	75	79	.487	5
1911		159	70	83	.458	6
1912	WAS A	154	91	61	.599	2
1913		155	90	64	.584	2
1914		157	81	73	.526	3
1915		155	85	68	.556	4
1916		159	76	77	.497	7
1917		157	74	79	.484	5
1918		130	72	56	.563	3
1919		142	56	84	.400	7
1920		153	68	84	.447	6
20 yrs.		2916	1491	1367	.522	
2 yrs.		275	157	113	.581	

Don Gutteridge
GUTTERIDGE, DONALD JOSEPH
B. June 19, 1912, Pittsburg, Kans.

		G	W	L	PCT	Standing
1969	CHI A	145	60	85	.414	4 5
1970		136	49	87	.360	6 6
2 yrs.		281	109	172	.388	
2 yrs.		281	109	172	.388	

Fielder Jones
JONES, FIELDER ALLISON
B. Aug. 13, 1874, Shinglehouse, Pa.
D. Mar. 13, 1934, Portland, Ore.

		G	W	L	PCT	Standing
1904	CHI A	115	67	47	.588	4 3
1905		157	92	60	.605	2
1906		154	93	58	.616	1
1907		157	87	64	.576	3
1908		156	88	64	.579	3
1914	STL F	40	12	26	.316	7 8
1915		159	87	67	.565	2
1916	STL A	158	79	75	.513	5
1917		155	57	97	.370	7
1918		47	23	24	.489	5 5
10 yrs.		1298	685	582	.541	
5 yrs.		739	427	293	.593	
WORLD SERIES						
1906	CHI A	6	4	2	.667	

Don Kessinger
KESSINGER, DONALD EULON
B. July 17, 1942, Forrest City, Ark.

		G	W	L	PCT	Standing
1979	CHI A	106	46	60	.434	5 5

Tony LaRussa
LaRUSSA, ANTHONY
B. Oct. 4, 1944, Tampa, Fla.

		G	W	L	PCT	Standing
1979	CHI A	54	27	27	.500	5 5

Tony LaRussa continued

		G	W	L	PCT	Standing	
1980		162	70	90	.438	5	
1981		53	31	22	.585	3	(1st)
1981		53	23	30	.434	6	(2nd)
1982		162	87	75	.537	3	
1983		162	99	63	.000	1	
5 yrs.		646	337	307	.523		
5 yrs.		646	337	307	.523		
LEAGUE CHAMPIONSHIP SERIES							
1983	CHI A	4	1	3	.000		

Bob Lemon
LEMON, ROBERT GRANVILLE
B. Sept. 22, 1920, San Bernardino, Calif.
Hall of Fame 1976.

		G	W	L	PCT	Standing	
1970	KC A	108	46	62	.426	6 4	
1971		161	85	76	.528	2	
1972		154	76	78	.494	4	
1977	CHI A	162	90	72	.556	3	
1978		74	34	40	.459	5 5	
1978	NY A	68	48	20	.706	3 1	
1979		64	34	30	.531	4 4	
1981		28	13	15	.464	5 6	(2nd)
1982		14	6	8	.429	4 5	
8 yrs.		833	432	401	.519		
2 yrs.		236	124	112	.525		
DIVISIONAL PLAYOFF SERIES							
1981	NY A	5	3	2	.600		
LEAGUE CHAMPIONSHIP SERIES							
1978	NY A	4	3	1	.750		
1981		3	3	0	1.000		
2 yrs.		7	6	1	.857		
WORLD SERIES							
1978	NY A	6	4	2	.667		
1981		6	2	4	.333		
2 yrs.		12	6	6	.500		

Al Lopez
LOPEZ, ALFONSO RAYMOND
B. Aug. 20, 1908, Tampa, Fla.
Hall of Fame 1977.

		G	W	L	PCT	Standing
1951	CLE A	155	93	61	.604	2
1952		155	93	61	.604	2
1953		155	92	62	.597	2
1954		156	111	43	.721	1
1955		154	93	61	.604	2
1956		155	88	66	.571	2
1957	CHI A	155	90	64	.584	2
1958		155	82	72	.532	2
1959		156	94	60	.610	1
1960		154	87	67	.565	3
1961		163	86	76	.531	4
1962		162	85	77	.525	5
1963		162	94	68	.580	2
1964		162	98	64	.605	2
1965		162	95	67	.586	2
1968		81	33	48	.407	9 9
1969		17	8	9	.471	4 5
17 yrs.		2459	1422	1026	.581	
						9th
11 yrs.		1529	852	672	.559	
WORLD SERIES						
1954	CLE A	4	0	4	.000	
1959	CHI A	6	2	4	.333	
2 yrs.		10	2	8	.200	
1 yr.		6	2	4	.333	

Ted Lyons
LYONS, THEODORE AMAR
B. Dec. 28, 1900, Lake Charles, La.
Hall of Fame 1955.

		G	W	L	PCT	Standing
1946	CHI A	125	64	60	.516	7 5
1947		155	70	84	.455	6
1948		154	51	101	.336	8
3 yrs.		434	185	245	.430	
3 yrs.		434	185	245	.430	

Marty Marion
MARION, MARTIN WHITFORD (Slats, The Octopus)
Brother of Red Marion.
B. Dec. 1, 1917, Richburg, S. C.

		G	W	L	PCT	Standing	
1951	STL N	156	81	73	.526	3	
1952	STL A	105	42	62	.404	7	7
1953		154	54	100	.351	8	
1954	CHI A	9	3	6	.333	3	3
1955		155	91	63	.591	3	
1956		154	85	69	.552	3	
6 yrs.		733	356	373	.488		
3 yrs.		318	179	138	.565		

Les Moss
MOSS, JOHN LESTER
B. May 14, 1925, Tulsa, Okla.

		G	W	L	PCT	Standing	
1968	CHI A	2	0	2	.000	9	9	9
1979	DET A	53	27	26	.509	5	5
2 yrs.		55	27	28	.491		
1 yr.		2	0	2	.000		

Jack Onslow
ONSLOW, JOHN JAMES
Brother of Eddie Onslow.
B. Oct. 13, 1888, Scottdale, Pa.
D. Dec. 22, 1960, Concord, Mass.

		G	W	L	PCT	Standing	
1949	CHI A	154	63	91	.409	6	
1950		30	8	22	.267	8	6
2 yrs.		184	71	113	.386		
2 yrs.		184	71	113	.386		

Paul Richards
RICHARDS, PAUL RAPIER
B. Nov. 21, 1908, Waxahachie, Tex.

		G	W	L	PCT	Standing	
1951	CHI A	155	81	73	.526	4	
1952		156	81	73	.526	3	
1953		156	89	65	.578	3	
1954		146	91	54	.628	3	3
1955	BAL A	156	57	97	.370	7	
1956		154	69	85	.448	6	
1957		154	76	76	.500	5	
1958		154	74	79	.484	6	
1959		155	74	80	.481	6	
1960		154	89	65	.578	2	
1961		135	78	57	.578	3	3
1976	CHI A	161	64	97	.398	6	
12 yrs.		1836	923	901	.506		
5 yrs.		774	406	362	.529		

Pants Rowland
ROWLAND, CLARENCE HENRY
B. Feb. 12, 1879, Platteville, Wis.
D. May 17, 1969, Chicago, Ill.

		G	W	L	PCT	Standing
1915	CHI A	155	93	61	.604	3
1916		155	89	65	.578	2
1917		156	100	54	.649	1
1918		124	57	67	.460	6
4 yrs.		590	339	247	.578	
4 yrs.		590	339	247	.578	

WORLD SERIES
| 1917 | CHI A | 6 | 4 | 2 | .667 |

Ray Schalk
SCHALK, RAYMOND WILLIAM (Cracker)
B. Aug. 12, 1892, Harvel, Ill.
D. May 19, 1970, Chicago, Ill.
Hall of Fame 1955.

		G	W	L	PCT	Standing	
1927	CHI A	153	70	83	.458	5	
1928		75	32	42	.432	6	5
2 yrs.		228	102	125	.449		
2 yrs.		228	102	125	.449		

Eddie Stanky
STANKY, EDWARD RAYMOND (The Brat, Muggsy)
B. Sept. 3, 1916, Philadelphia, Pa.

		G	W	L	PCT	Standing	
1952	STL N	154	88	66	.571	3	
1953		157	83	71	.539	3	
1954		154	72	82	.468	6	
1955		36	17	19	.472	5	7
1966	CHI A	163	83	79	.512	4	
1967		162	89	73	.549	4	
1968		79	34	45	.430	9	9
1977	TEX A	1	1	0	1.000	4	2	2
8 yrs.		906	467	435	.518		
3 yrs.		404	206	197	.511		

Billy Sullivan
SULLIVAN, WILLIAM JOSEPH, SR.
Father of Billy Sullivan.
B. Feb. 1, 1875, Oakland, Wis.
D. Jan. 28, 1965, Newberg, Ore.

		G	W	L	PCT	Standing
1909	CHI A	159	78	74	.513	4

Chuck Tanner
TANNER, CHARLES WILLIAM
B. July 4, 1929, New Castle, Pa.

		G	W	L	PCT	Standing	
1970	CHI A	16	3	13	.188	6	6
1971		162	79	83	.488	3	
1972		154	87	67	.565	2	
1973		162	77	85	.475	5	
1974		160	80	80	.500	4	
1975		161	75	86	.466	5	
1976	OAK A	161	87	74	.540	2	
1977	PIT N	162	96	66	.593	2	
1978		161	88	73	.547	2	
1979		162	98	64	.605	1	
1980		162	83	79	.512	3	
1981		49	25	23	.521	4	(1st)
1981		54	21	33	.389	6	(2nd)
1982		162	84	78	.519	4	
1983		162	84	78	.000	2	
14 yrs.		2050	1067	982	.521		
6 yrs.		815	401	414	.492		

LEAGUE CHAMPIONSHIP SERIES
| 1979 | PIT N | 3 | 3 | 0 | 1.000 |

WORLD SERIES
| 1979 | PIT N | 7 | 4 | 3 | .571 |

White Sox World Series Highlights and Summaries

This section provides information on the four World Series the White Sox have played in through 1983. Included are facts about the individual games; most of the information is self-explanatory. That which may appear unfamiliar is listed below.

INDIVIDUAL GAME INFORMATION

Innings Pitched. Pitchers are listed in the order of appearance. In parentheses, following each pitcher's name, are the number of innings he pitched in the game. For example: Doe (2.1) would mean that he pitched 2⅓ innings.

Winning and Losing Pitchers. Indicated by bold-faced print.

Saves. The pitcher who is credited with a Save is indicated by the abbreviation SV, which appears in bold-faced print after his innings pitched.

Home Runs. Players are listed in the order their home runs were hit.

World Series 1906

		R	H	E	PITCHERS (inn. pit.)	HOME RUNS (men on)	HIGHLIGHTS

Chicago (A.L.) defeats Chicago (N.L.) 4 games to 2

GAME 1 - OCTOBER 9
		R	H	E	Pitchers		Highlights
CHI	A	2	4	1	Altrock (9)		Isbell scores Jones with the tie-breaking run in the sixth on a single in a game played in bitterly cold weather and snow flurries.
CHI	N	1	4	2	Brown (9)		

GAME 2 - OCTOBER 10
CHI	N	7	10	2	Reulbach (9)		Donahue's single in the seventh spoils Reulbach's no-hit bid. The only run for the White Sox comes in the sixth on a wild pitch and an error.
CHI	A	1	1	2	White (3), Owen (6)		

GAME 3 - OCTOBER 11
CHI	A	3	4	1	Walsh (9)		Rohe's three-run triple in the sixth breaks open the game and aids Walsh's record 12-strike-out pitching performance.
CHI	N	0	2	2	Pfiester (9)		

GAME 4 - OCTOBER 12
CHI	N	1	7	1	Brown (9)		Evers singles in Chance in the seventh to tie the Series.
CHI	A	0	2	1	Altrock (9)		

GAME 5 - OCTOBER 13
CHI	A	8	12	6	Walsh (6.1), White (2.2) SV		Isbell hits a record four doubles in pacing the White Sox while Davis drives in three runs.
CHI	N	6	6	0	Reulbach (2), Pfiester (1.1), Overall (5.2)		

GAME 6 - OCTOBER 14
CHI	N	3	7	0	Brown (1.2), Overall (6.1)		The White Sox jump to a 7-1 lead after two innings and win the Series as Hahn contributes four hits and Donahue and Davis each drive in three runs.
CHI	A	8	14	3	White (9)		

Team Totals

		W	AB	H	2B	3B	HR	R	RBI	BA	BB	SO	ERA
CHI	A	4	187	37	10	3	0	22	19	.198	18	35	1.67
CHI	N	2	184	36	9	0	0	18	11	.196	18	27	3.40

Individual Batting

CHICAGO (A.L.)

	AB	H	2B	3B	HR	R	RBI	BA
F. Isbell, 2b	26	8	4	0	0	4	4	.308
E. Hahn, of	22	6	0	0	0	4	0	.273
F. Jones, of	21	2	0	0	0	4	0	.095
G. Rohe, 3b	21	7	1	2	0	2	4	.333
B. Sullivan, c	21	0	0	0	0	0	0	.000
P. Dougherty, of	20	2	0	0	0	1	1	.100
J. Donahue, 1b	18	6	2	1	0	0	4	.333
G. Davis, ss	13	4	3	0	0	4	6	.308
L. Tannehill, ss	9	1	0	0	0	1	0	.111
N. Altrock, p	4	1	0	0	0	0	0	.250
E. Walsh, p	4	0	0	0	0	1	0	.000
D. White, p	3	0	0	0	0	0	0	.000
F. Owen, p	2	0	0	0	0	0	0	.000
E. McFarland	1	0	0	0	0	0	0	.000
B. O'Neill, of	1	0	0	0	0	1	0	.000
B. Towne	1	0	0	0	0	0	0	.000

Errors: F. Isbell (5), G. Rohe (3), G. Davis (2), J. Donahue, P. Dougherty, B. Sullivan, E. Walsh
Stolen bases: P. Dougherty (2), G. Rohe (2), G. Davis, F. Isbell

CHICAGO (N.L.)

	AB	H	2B	3B	HR	R	RBI	BA
W. Schulte, of	26	7	3	0	0	1	3	.269
S. Hofman, of	23	7	1	0	0	3	2	.304
F. Chance, 1b	21	5	1	0	0	3	0	.238
J. Sheckard, of	21	0	0	0	0	0	1	.000
J. Evers, 2b	20	3	1	0	0	2	1	.150
H. Steinfeldt, 3b	20	5	1	0	0	2	2	.250
J. Tinker, ss	18	3	0	0	0	4	1	.167
J. Kling, c	17	3	1	0	0	2	0	.176
T. Brown, p	6	2	0	0	0	0	0	.333
O. Overall, p	4	1	1	0	0	1	0	.250
E. Reulbach, p	3	0	0	0	0	0	1	.000
P. Moran	2	0	0	0	0	0	0	.000
J. Pfiester, p	2	0	0	0	0	0	0	.000
D. Gessler	1	0	0	0	0	0	0	.000

Errors: J. Tinker (2), T. Brown, J. Evers, J. Kling, J. Pfiester, H. Steinfeldt
Stolen bases: F. Chance (2), J. Evers (2), J. Tinker (2), S. Hofman, J. Sheckard

Individual Pitching

CHICAGO (A.L.)

	W	L	ERA	IP	H	BB	SO	SV
N. Altrock	1	1	1.00	18	11	2	5	0
E. Walsh	2	0	1.80	15	7	6	17	0
D. White	1	1	1.80	15	12	7	3	1
F. Owen	0	0	3.00	6	6	3	2	0

CHICAGO (N.L.)

	W	L	ERA	IP	H	BB	SO	SV
T. Brown	1	2	3.66	19.2	14	4	12	0
O. Overall	0	0	1.50	12	10	3	8	0
E. Reulbach	1	0	2.45	11	6	8	4	0
J. Pfiester	0	2	6.10	10.1	7	3	11	0

World Series 1917

		R	H	E	PITCHERS (inn. pit.)	HOME RUNS (men on)	HIGHLIGHTS

Chicago (A.L.) defeats New York (N.L.) 4 games to 2

GAME 1 - OCTOBER 6

		R	H	E	PITCHERS	HR	HIGHLIGHTS
NY	N	1	7	1	Sallee (8)	Felsch	Felsch's homer in the fourth decides the game as Cicotte holds the Giants to seven hits.
CHI	A	2	7	1	Cicotte (9)		

GAME 2 - OCTOBER 7

NY	N	2	8	1	Schupp (1.1), Anderson (2), Perritt (3.2), Tesreau (1)		The White Sox break open the game with a five-run fourth. Jackson and Weaver share the batting honors with three hits each.
CHI	A	7	14	1	Faber (9)		

GAME 3 - OCTOBER 10

CHI	A	0	5	3	Cicotte (8)		Robertson's triple and Holke's double in the fourth sparks the Giants.
NY	N	2	8	2	Benton (9)		

GAME 4 - OCTOBER 11

CHI	A	0	7	0	Faber (7), Danforth (1)	Kauff, Kauff (1 on)	Kauff's two homers pace the Giants attack as Schupp allows seven hits in posting a 5-0 shutout.
NY	N	5	10	1	Schupp (9)		

GAME 5 - OCTOBER 13

NY	N	5	12	3	Sallee (7.1), Perritt (0.2)		Eddie Collins singles in the go-ahead run in a three-run eighth to break open a 5-5 deadlock as both teams account for 26 hits.
CHI	A	8	14	6	Russell (0), Cicotte (6), Williams (1), Faber (2)		

GAME 6 - OCTOBER 15

CHI	A	4	7	1	Faber (9)		The White Sox score all of their runs on errors as Faber holds the Giants to six hits for the Series victory.
NY	N	2	6	3	Benton (5), Perritt (4)		

Team Totals

		W	AB	H	2B	3B	HR	R	RBI	BA	BB	SO	ERA
CHI	A	4	197	54	6	0	1	21	18	.274	11	28	2.77
NY	N	2	199	51	5	4	2	17	16	.256	6	27	2.82

Individual Batting

CHICAGO (A.L.)

	AB	H	2B	3B	HR	R	RBI	BA
F. McMullin, 3b	24	3	1	0	0	1	2	.125
C. Gandil, 1b	23	6	1	0	0	1	5	.261
J. Jackson, of	23	7	0	0	0	4	2	.304
E. Collins, 2b	22	9	1	0	0	4	2	.409
H. Felsch, of	22	6	1	0	1	4	3	.273
S. Collins, of	21	6	1	0	0	2	0	.286
B. Weaver, ss	21	7	1	0	0	3	1	.333
R. Schalk, c	19	5	0	0	0	1	0	.263
E. Cicotte, p	7	1	0	0	0	0	0	.143
R. Faber, p	7	1	0	0	0	0	0	.143
N. Leibold, of	5	2	0	0	0	1	2	.400
S. Risberg	2	1	0	0	0	0	1	.500
B. Lynn	1	0	0	0	0	0	0	.000

Errors: B. Weaver (4), S. Collins (3), R. Schalk (2), E. Cicotte, C. Gandil, L. Williams
Stolen bases: E. Collins (3), C. Gandil, J. Jackson, R. Schalk

NEW YORK (N.L.)

	AB	H	2B	3B	HR	R	RBI	BA
A. Fletcher, ss	25	5	1	0	0	2	0	.200
B. Kauff, of	25	4	1	0	2	2	5	.160
H. Zimmerman, 3b	25	3	0	1	0	1	0	.120
B. Herzog, 2b	24	6	0	1	0	1	2	.250
G. Burns, of	22	5	0	0	0	3	2	.227
D. Robertson, of	22	11	1	1	0	3	1	.500
W. Holke, 1b	21	6	2	0	0	2	1	.286
B. Rariden, c	13	5	0	0	0	2	2	.385
S. Sallee, p	6	1	0	0	0	0	1	.167
L. McCarty, c	5	2	0	1	0	1	1	.400
R. Benton, p	4	0	0	0	0	0	0	.000
F. Schupp, p	4	1	0	0	0	0	1	.250
P. Perritt, p	2	2	0	0	0	0	1	1.000
J. Wilhoit	1	0	0	0	0	0	0	.000
J. Thorpe, of	2	0	0	0	0	0	0	—

Errors: A. Fletcher (3), B. Herzog (2), H. Zimmerman (2), W. Holke, B. Kauff, L. McCarty, D. Robertson
Stolen bases: D. Robertson (2), G. Burns, B. Kauff

Individual Pitching

CHICAGO (A.L.)

	W	L	ERA	IP	H	BB	SO	SV
R. Faber	3	1	2.33	27	21	3	9	0
E. Cicotte	1	1	1.96	23	23	2	13	0
D. Danforth	0	0	18.00	1	3	0	2	0
L. Williams	0	0	9.00	1	2	0	3	0
R. Russell	0	0	∞	0.0	2	1	0	0

NEW YORK (N.L.)

	W	L	ERA	IP	H	BB	SO	SV
S. Sallee	0	2	4.70	15.1	20	4	4	0
R. Benton	1	1	0.00	14	9	1	8	0
F. Schupp	1	0	1.74	10.1	11	2	9	0
P. Perritt	0	0	2.16	8.1	9	3	3	0
F. Anderson	0	1	18.00	2	5	0	3	0
J. Tesreau	0	0	0.00	1	0	1	1	0

World Series 1919

		R	H	E	PITCHERS (inn. pit.)	HOME RUNS (men on)	HIGHLIGHTS

Cincinnati (N.L.) defeats Chicago (A.L.) 5 games to 3

GAME 1 - OCTOBER 1
- CHI A 1 6 1 Cicotte (3.2), Wilkinson (3.1), Lowdermilk (1)
- CIN N 9 14 1 Ruether (9)

The Reds' five runs off Cicotte in the fourth breaks a 1-1 deadlock as Ruether holds Chicago to six hits.

GAME 2 - OCTOBER 2
- CHI A 2 10 1 Williams (8)
- CIN N 4 4 2 Sallee (9)

Kopf's two-run triple in the fourth caps a three-run inning after Williams allows three walks.

GAME 3 - OCTOBER 3
- CIN N 0 3 1 Fisher (7), Luque (1)
- CHI A 3 7 0 Kerr (9)

Kerr allows three hits in shutting out the Reds. Gandil's double drives in Jackson and Felsch in the second.

GAME 4 - OCTOBER 4
- CIN N 2 5 2 Ring (9)
- CHI A 0 3 2 Cicotte (9)

Ring allows three hits and posts a shutout as the Reds score twice in the fifth on Cicotte's two errors.

GAME 5 - OCTOBER 6
- CIN N 5 4 0 Eller (9)
- CHI A 0 3 3 Williams (8), Mayer (1)

Four runs in the sixth capped by Roush's triple broke open a tie game. Eller fanned nine, six in succession, holding the White Sox to 3 hits.

GAME 6 - OCTOBER 7
- CHI A 5 10 3 Kerr (10)
- CIN N 4 11 0 Ruther (5), Ring (5)

Gandil singles home Weaver in the tenth with the deciding run.

GAME 7 - OCTOBER 8
- CHI A 4 10 1 Cicotte (9)
- CIN N 1 7 4 Sallee (4.1), Fisher (0.2), Luque (4)

Shano Collins scores the deciding run on Jackson's single as Cicotte scatters seven hits and holds the Reds to one run in the sixth.

GAME 8 - OCTOBER 9
- CIN N 10 16 2 Eller (9)
- CHI A 5 10 1 Williams (0.1), James (4.2), Wilkinson (4)   Jackson

The Reds score four times in the first and wrap up the series on a 16-hit attack paced by Roush's three hits and four RBI's. (Williams along with Cicotte, Gandil, Felsch, Jackson, McMullin, Risberg and Weaver were later barred for life for their part in what turned out to be a "fixed" Series.)

Team Totals

		W	AB	H	2B	3B	HR	R	RBI	BA	BB	SO	ERA
CIN	N	5	251	64	10	7	0	35	33	.255	25	22	1.63
CHI	A	3	263	59	10	3	1	20	17	.224	15	30	3.68

Individual Batting

CINCINNATI (N.L.)

	AB	H	2B	3B	HR	R	RBI	BA
M. Rath, 2b	31	7	1	0	0	5	2	.226
J. Daubert, 1b	29	7	0	1	0	4	1	.241
H. Groh, 3b	29	5	2	0	0	6	2	.172
G. Neale, of	28	10	1	1	0	3	4	.357
E. Roush, of	28	6	2	1	0	6	7	.214
L. Kopf, ss	27	6	0	2	0	3	2	.222
P. Duncan, of	26	7	2	0	0	3	8	.269
B. Rariden, c	19	4	0	0	0	0	2	.211
H. Eller, p	7	2	1	0	0	2	0	.286
I. Wingo, c	7	4	0	0	0	1	1	.571
D. Ruether, p	6	4	1	2	0	2	4	.667
J. Ring, p	5	0	0	0	0	0	0	.000
S. Sallee, p	4	0	0	0	0	0	0	.000
R. Fisher, p	2	1	0	0	0	0	0	.500
S. Magee	2	1	0	0	0	0	0	.500
D. Luque, p	1	0	0	0	0	0	0	.000
J. Smith	0	0	0	0	0	0	0	–

Errors: J. Daubert (2), H. Groh (2), M. Rath (2), E. Roush (2), R. Fisher, L. Kopf.
Stolen bases: M. Rath (2), E. Roush (2), J. Daubert, G. Neale, B. Rariden

CHICAGO (A.L.)

	AB	H	2B	3B	HR	R	RBI	BA
B. Weaver, 3b	34	11	4	1	0	4	0	.324
J. Jackson, of	32	12	3	0	1	5	6	.375
E. Collins, 2b	31	7	1	0	0	2	1	.226
C. Gandil, 1b	30	7	0	1	0	1	5	.233
H. Felsch, of	26	5	1	0	0	2	3	.192
S. Risberg, ss	25	2	0	1	0	3	0	.080
R. Schalk, c	23	7	0	0	0	1	2	.304
N. Leibold, of	18	1	0	0	0	0	0	.056
S. Collins, of	16	4	1	0	0	2	0	.250
E. Cicotte, p	8	0	0	0	0	0	0	.000
D. Kerr, p	6	1	0	0	0	0	0	.167
L. Williams, p	5	1	0	0	0	0	0	.200
B. James, p	2	0	0	0	0	0	0	.000
F. McMullin	2	1	0	0	0	0	0	.500
E. Murphy	2	0	0	0	0	0	0	.000
R. Wilkinson, p	2	0	0	0	0	0	0	.000
B. Lynn, c	1	0	0	0	0	0	0	.000

Errors: S. Risberg (4), E. Cicotte (2), E. Collins (2), H. Felsch (2), C. Gandil, R. Schalk
Stolen bases: E. Collins, C. Gandil, N. Leibold, S. Risberg, R. Schalk

Individual Pitching

CINCINNATI (N.L.)

	W	L	ERA	IP	H	BB	SO	SV
H. Eller	2	0	2.00	18	13	2	15	0
J. Ring	1	1	0.64	14	7	6	4	0
D. Ruether	1	0	2.57	14	12	4	1	0
S. Sallee	1	1	1.35	13.1	19	1	2	0
R. Fisher	0	1	2.35	7.2	7	2	2	0
D. Luque	0	0	0.00	5	1	0	6	0

CHICAGO (A.L.)

	W	L	ERA	IP	H	BB	SO	SV
E. Cicotte	1	2	2.91	21.2	19	5	7	0
D. Kerr	2	0	1.42	19	14	3	6	0
L. Williams	0	3	6.61	16.1	12	8	4	0
R. Wilkinson	0	0	3.68	7.1	9	4	3	0
B. James	0	0	5.79	4.2	8	3	2	0
G. Lowdermilk	0	0	9.00	1	2	1	0	0
E. Mayer	0	0	0.00	1	0	1	0	0

World Series 1959

Los Angeles (N.L.) defeats Chicago (A.L.) 4 games to 2

		R	H	E	PITCHERS (inn. pit.)	HOME RUNS (men on)	HIGHLIGHTS
					GAME 1 - OCTOBER 1		
LA	N	0	8	3	Craig (2.1), Churn (0.2), Labine (1), Koufax (2), Klippstein (2)	Kluszewski (1 on), Kluszewski (1 on)	Wynn and Staley subdue the Dodgers as Kluszewski's five RBI's pace the 11-run attack.
CHI	A	11	11	0	**Wynn** (7), Staley (2) **SV**		
					GAME 2 - OCTOBER 2		
LA	N	4	9	1	Podres (6), **Sherry** (3) **SV**	Neal, Essegian, Neal (1 on)	A pinch-hit homer by Essegian with two out in the seventh ties the score before Neal homers for the deciding run with Gilliam aboard.
CHI	A	3	8	0	Shaw (6.2), **Lown** (2.1)		
					GAME 3 - OCTOBER 4		
CHI	A	1	12	0	**Donovan** (6.2), Staley (1.1)		Furillo's pinch-hit single in the seventh with the bases full drives in two runs.
LA	N	3	5	0	Drysdale (7), **Sherry** (2) **SV**		
					GAME 4 - OCTOBER 5		
CHI	A	4	10	3	Wynn (2.2), Lown (0.1), Pierce (3), **Staley** (2)	Lollar (2 on)	Hodges' homer in the eighth breaks the deadlock after a four-run seventh inning by the White Sox.
LA	N	5	9	0	Craig (7), **Sherry** (2)	Hodges	
					GAME 5 - OCTOBER 6		
CHI	A	1	5	0	**Shaw** (7.1), Pierce (0), Donovan (1.2) **SV**		Rivera's back-to-the-plate catch of Neal's fly with two men on and two out in the seventh chokes off a Dodger rally as the White Sox set a Series record by using three pitchers in posting a 1-0 shutout. The game is witnessed by a record crowd of 92,706.
LA	N	0	9	0	**Koufax** (7), Williams (2)		
					GAME 6 - OCTOBER 8		
LA	N	9	13	0	Podres (3.1), **Sherry** (5.2)	Snider (1 on), Moon (1 on), Essegian Kluszewski (2 on)	The Dodgers jump to an early 8-0 lead. Kluszewski homers for three runs in the fourth before Sherry relieves and checks the White Sox for a Series victory.
CHI	A	3	6	1	**Wynn** (3.1), Donavan (0), Lown (0.2), Staley (3), Pierce (1), Moore (1)		

Team Totals

		W	AB	H	2B	3B	HR	R	RBI	BA	BB	SO	ERA
LA	N	4	203	53	3	1	7	21	19	.261	12	27	3.23
CHI	A	2	199	52	10	0	4	23	19	.261	20	33	3.46

Individual Batting

LOS ANGELES (N.L.)

	AB	H	2B	3B	HR	R	RBI	BA
C. Neal, 2b	27	10	2	0	2	4	6	.370
J. Gilliam, 3b	25	6	0	0	0	2	0	.240
G. Hodges, 1b	23	9	0	1	1	2	2	.391
W. Moon, of	23	6	0	0	1	3	2	.261
J. Roseboro, c	21	2	0	0	0	0	1	.095
M. Wills, ss	20	5	0	0	0	2	1	.250
N. Larker, of	16	3	0	0	0	2	0	.188
D. Demeter, of	12	3	0	0	0	2	0	.250
D. Snider, of	10	2	0	0	1	1	2	.200
C. Furillo, of	4	1	0	0	0	0	2	.250
J. Podres, p	4	2	1	0	0	1	1	.500
L. Sherry, p	4	2	0	0	0	0	0	.500
R. Craig, p	3	0	0	0	0	0	0	.000
C. Essegian	3	2	0	0	2	2	2	.667
R. Fairly, of	3	0	0	0	0	0	0	.000
D. Drysdale, p	2	0	0	0	0	0	0	.000
S. Koufax, p	2	0	0	0	0	0	0	.000
D. Zimmer, ss	1	0	0	0	0	0	0	.000
J. Pignatano, c	0	0	0	0	0	0	0	–
R. Repulski, of	0	0	0	0	0	0	0	–

Errors: D. Snider (2), C. Neal, M. Wills
Stolen bases: J. Gilliam (2), W. Moon, C. Neal, M. Wills

CHICAGO (A.L.)

	AB	H	2B	3B	HR	R	RBI	BA
L. Aparicio, ss	26	8	1	0	0	1	0	.308
N. Fox, 2b	24	9	3	0	0	4	0	.375
J. Landis, of	24	7	0	0	0	6	1	.292
T. Kluszewski, 1b	23	9	1	0	3	5	10	.391
S. Lollar, c	22	5	0	0	1	3	5	.227
A. Smith, of	20	5	3	0	0	1	1	.250
B. Goodman, 3b	13	3	0	0	0	1	1	.231
J. Rivera, of	11	0	0	0	0	1	0	.000
B. Phillips, 3b, of	10	3	1	0	0	0	0	.300
J. McAnany, of	5	0	0	0	0	0	0	.000
E. Wynn, p	5	1	1	0	0	0	1	.200
N. Cash	4	0	0	0	0	0	0	.000
B. Shaw, p	4	1	0	0	0	0	0	.250
D. Donovan, p	3	1	0	0	0	0	0	.333
S. Esposito, 3b	2	0	0	0	0	0	0	.000
J. Romano	1	0	0	0	0	0	0	.000
G. Staley, p	1	0	0	0	0	0	0	.000
E. Torgeson, 1b	1	0	0	0	0	1	0	.000

Errors: L. Aparicio (2), J. Landis, B. Pierce
Stolen bases: L. Aparicio, J. Landis

Individual Pitching

LOS ANGELES (N.L.)

	W	L	ERA	IP	H	BB	SO	SV
L. Sherry	2	0	0.71	12.2	8	2	5	2
R. Craig	0	1	8.68	9.1	15	5	8	0
S. Koufax	0	1	1.00	9	5	1	7	0
J. Podres	1	0	4.82	9.1	7	6	4	0
D. Drysdale	1	0	1.29	7	11	4	5	0
J. Klippstein	0	0	0.00	2	1	0	2	0
S. Williams	0	0	0.00	2	0	2	1	0
C. Labine	0	0	0.00	1	0	0	1	0
C. Churn	0	0	27.00	0.2	5	0	0	0

CHICAGO (A.L.)

	W	L	ERA	IP	H	BB	SO	SV
B. Shaw	1	1	2.57	14	17	2	2	0
E. Wynn	1	1	5.54	13	19	4	10	0
D. Donovan	0	1	5.40	8.1	4	3	5	1
G. Staley	0	1	2.16	8.1	8	0	3	1
B. Pierce	0	0	0.00	4	2	2	3	0
T. Lown	0	0	0.00	3.1	2	1	3	0
R. Moore	0	0	9.00	1	1	0	1	0

American League Championship Series 1983

Baltimore (East) defeats Chicago (West) 3 games to 1

		R	H	E	PITCHERS (inn. pit.)	HOME RUNS (men on)	HIGHLIGHTS
					GAME 1 - OCTOBER 5		
CHI	W	2	7	0	Hoyt (9)		Five-hit pitching by LaMarr Hoyt carried the White Sox to victory in Game 1. Rudy Law had three hits and scored a run to pace the Chicago attack.
BAL	E	1	5	0	McGregor (6.2), Stewart (0.1), T. Martinez (2)		
					GAME 2 - OCTOBER 6		
CHI	W	0	5	2	Bannister (6), Barojas (1), Lamp (1)		Mike Boddicker struck out 14 batters in his five-hit shutout effort. Gary Roenicke slammed a two-run homer and scored three runs for the Orioles.
BAL	E	4	6	0	Boddicker (9)	Roenicke (1 on)	
					GAME 3 - OCTOBER 7		
BAL	E	11	8	1	Flanagan (5), Stewart (4) SV	Murray (2 on)	Eddie Murray drove in three runs and scored four as Mike Flanagan and Sammy Stewart combined on a six-hitter. Cal Ripken chipped in with two hits and scored three times.
CHI	W	1	6	1	Dotson (5), Tidrow (2), Koosman (0.1), Lamp (0.2)		
					GAME 4 - OCTOBER 8		
BAL	E	3	9	0	Davis (6), T. Martinez (4)	Landrum	Tito Landrum's tenth-inning homer snapped a scoreless tie and ignited a three-run burst that gave Baltimore the American League pennant.
CHI	W	0	10	0	Burns (9.1), Barojas (0), Agosto (0.1), Lamp (0.1)		

Team Totals

		W	AB	H	2B	3B	HR	R	RBI	BA	BB	SO	ERA
BAL	E	3	129	28	9	0	3	19	17	.217	16	24	0.49
CHI	W	1	133	28	4	0	0	3	2	.211	12	26	4.00

Individual Batting

BALTIMORE (EAST)

	AB	H	2B	3B	HR	R	RBI	BA
E. Murray, 1b	15	4	0	0	1	5	3	.267
T. Cruz, 3b	15	2	0	0	0	0	1	.133
C. Ripken, ss	15	6	2	0	0	5	1	.400
R. Dauer, 2b	14	0	0	0	0	0	1	.000
R. Dempsey, c	12	2	0	0	0	1	0	.167
K. Singleton, dh	12	3	2	0	0	0	1	.250
T. Landrum, of	10	2	0	0	1	2	1	.200
J. Shelby, of	9	2	0	0	0	1	0	.222
A. Bumbry, of	8	1	1	0	0	0	1	.125
J. Lowenstein, of, dh	6	1	1	0	0	0	2	.167
D. Ford, of, dh	5	1	1	0	0	0	0	.200
G. Roenicke, of	4	3	0	0	1	4	4	.750
J. Dwyer, of	4	1	1	0	0	1	0	.250
J. Palmer, dh	0	0	0	0	0	0	0	—
B. Ayala, dh	0	0	0	0	0	0	1	—
J. Nolan	0	0	0	0	0	0	1	—

Errors: R. Dempsey, E. Murray
Stolen bases: E. Murray, J. Shelby

CHICAGO (WEST)

	AB	H	2B	3B	HR	R	RBI	BA
R. Law, of	18	7	1	0	0	1	0	.389
C. Fisk, c	17	3	1	0	0	0	0	.176
T. Paciorek, 1b, of	16	4	0	0	0	1	1	.250
H. Baines, of	16	2	0	0	0	0	0	.125
G. Luzinski, dh	15	2	1	0	0	0	0	.133
J. Cruz, 2b	12	4	0	0	0	0	0	.333
V. Law, 3b	11	2	0	0	0	0	1	.182
S. Fletcher, ss	7	0	0	0	0	0	0	.000
R. Kittle, of	7	2	1	0	0	1	0	.286
M. Squires, 1b	4	0	0	0	0	0	0	.000
J. Dybzinski, ss	4	1	0	0	0	0	0	.250
G. Walker, 1b	3	1	0	0	0	0	0	.333
J. Hairston, of	3	0	0	0	0	0	0	.000
A. Rodriguez, 3b	0	0	0	0	0	0	0	—

Errors: A. Rodriguez, V. Law, J. Hairston
Stolen bases: J. Cruz (2), R. Law (2)

Individual Pitching

BALTIMORE (EAST)

	W	L	ERA	IP	H	BB	SO	SV
M. Boddicker	1	0	0.00	9	5	3	14	0
T. Martinez	1	0	0.00	6	5	3	5	0
S. McGregor	0	1	1.35	6.2	6	3	2	0
S. Davis	0	0	0.00	6	5	2	2	0
M. Flanagan	1	0	1.80	5	5	0	1	0
S. Stewart	0	0	0.00	4.1	2	1	2	1

CHICAGO (WEST)

	W	L	ERA	IP	H	BB	SO	SV
B. Burns	0	1	0.96	9.1	6	5	8	0
L. Hoyt	1	0	1.00	9	5	0	4	0
F. Bannister	0	1	4.50	6	5	1	5	0
R. Dotson	0	1	10.80	5	6	3	3	0
D. Tidrow	0	0	3.00	3	1	3	3	0
D. Lamp	0	0	0.00	2	0	2	1	0
S. Barojas	0	0	18.00	1	4	0	0	0
J. Koosman	0	0	54.00	0.1	1	2	0	0
J. Agosto	0	0	0.00	0.1	0	0	0	0